CONTRACTS
A REAL WORLD CASEBOOK

■ ■ ■

Lawrence A. Cunningham
Henry St. George Tucker III Research Professor
The George Washington University Law School
Founding Faculty Director, George Washington in New York (GWNY)

Miriam A. Cherry
Professor of Law
St. Louis University School of Law
Director, William C. Wefel Center for Employment Law

AMERICAN CASEBOOK SERIES®

WEST ACADEMIC PUBLISHING

American Casebook Series is a trademark registered in the U.S. Patent and Trademark Office.

© 2018 LEG, Inc. d/b/a West Academic
    444 Cedar Street, Suite 700
    St. Paul, MN 55101
    1-877-888-1330

West, West Academic Publishing, and West Academic are trademarks of West Publishing Corporation, used under license.

Printed in the United States of America

ISBN: 978-1-64020-622-9

PREFACE AND ACKNOWLEDGMENTS

In 2012, Cambridge University Press released *Contracts in the Real World: Stories of Popular Contracts and Why They Matter*, by Lawrence Cunningham. Miriam Cherry read the book and used some of the stories with her contracts students, who were quite receptive to modern, compelling examples. We soon decided that the inspiration for that short narrative—to engage students with disputes they had heard about—could be adapted into a traditional-length treatment for law school instruction.

You are reading the result, which we believe is uniquely valuable. We have matched canonical cases familiar to law teachers with vibrant topical cases today's law students readily grasp.

Our casebook captivates students and holds their attention, through careful selection of 145 principal cases evenly curated from the best of the classic/vintage opinions professors relish—hairy hands and fertile cows—along with contemporary disputes students enjoy, involving such figures as 50 Cent, Lady Gaga, and Dan Rather.

Opinions are sculpted to ensure robust discussion—there are no "classroom clunkers" here. Cases are animated and students challenged with 65 engaging and fun illustrations, 40 designated as problems—hypotheticals keyed to the materials—and 25 dubbed as examples, based on actual cases better narrated than excerpted.

Our first expression of gratitude is to our students. They cheerfully joined our experiment in pedagogy and helped make this a book of unique promise. We are confident that this textbook will engage the next generation of students with a combination of contemporary and classic cases and materials, along with a trove of intriguing contemporary problems and examples throughout the book.

For their equally indispensable role in developing the book's special content, we thank our fellow professors who commented on either this manuscript or the earlier textbook. These include scholars who published formal reviews of the textbook for a symposium in the *Washington Law Review*: Aditi Bagchi (Fordham), Brian Bix (Minnesota), Larry DiMatteo (Florida State), Erik Gerding (Colorado), Charles Knapp (Hastings), Jake Linford (Florida State), and Jennifer Taub (Vermont). The blog posts from an online symposium were also helpful, and included writing from Ronald Collins (Washington), Susan Heyman (Roger Williams), David Hoffman (University of Pennsylvania), Nancy Kim (California Western), Donald Langevoort (Georgetown), and Tom Lin (Temple).

Other scholars helped identify some of the cases we use: Renee Allen (Florida A&M), Ian Ayres (Yale), Jonathan Barnett (USC), Al Brophy

(North Carolina), Enrique Guerra-Pujol (Florida Central), Gregg Polsky (North Carolina), H. Jefferson Powell (Duke), James Steven Rogers (Boston College), Michael Selmi (George Washington), Jeremy Telman (Valparaiso), Douglas Whaley (Ohio State), John Wladis (Widener), and Jarrod Wong (University of the Pacific-McGeorge).

We are also grateful to the staff members at our schools. At George Washington University, these include Gia Arney, an exceptional researcher in our library, and Lillian White, an enthusiastic faculty assistant. At Saint Louis University, these include David Kullman, librarian, who performed excellent research services, and Sharon "Shari" Baird, administrative assistant, who provided outstanding clerical and administrative support. We appreciate the input and support of a series of terrific research assistants: Umo Ironbar, Cate Aubuchon, Patrick Georgen, Donte Tamprateep, Louie Spinner, and Madhav Bhatt.

We recognize the institutional and financial support of the administrators at our respective law schools. At George Washington, our gratitude to Deans Blake Morant and Roger Fairfax; at Saint Louis University, our gratitude to Dean Bill Johnson, and former Deans Annette Clark and Mike Wolff.

In 2016, Cambridge University Press published a second edition of *Contracts in the Real World*, and generously allowed us to adapt much of the material from it into this book. We are grateful to Cambridge University Press, especially editor John Berger, for permission to do so. We also thank the team at West for support, especially Louis Higgins and Pam Chandler, and acknowledge the deft freelance editing on the penultimate version of this manuscript by Robert L. Rogers.

Five years is a long time to work on a book, and our efforts would not have been fruitful without the support of friends and family. Larry wishes to thank especially his lovely wife Stephanie and incomparable daughters Rebecca and Sarah. Miriam wishes to thank Lucas Amodio for his kindness, patience, and sense of humor. Thanks also to friends Matt Bodie, Marion Crain, Tonie Fitzgibbon, Marcia McCormick, Marianna & Scott Moss, Karen Petroski, and Winnie Poster for their encouragement.

We hope teachers and students alike enjoy this fresh approach to the classical casebook. If you do, please share your reaction with friends in other legal fields and ask them to contact us. We would like to develop a series of books following this approach in other fields from property and torts to admiralty and zoning, offering equally unique, innovative and captivating legal materials for today's busy students.

LAWRENCE A. CUNNINGHAM   MIRIAM A. CHERRY
NEW YORK AND WASHINGTON DC   ST. LOUIS

January 1, 2018

SUMMARY OF CONTENTS

TABLE OF CONTENTS

TABLE OF CASES

The principal cases are in bold type.

CONTRACTS
A REAL WORLD CASEBOOK

INTRODUCTION

■ ■ ■

The Restatement (Second) of Contracts leads off with a definition of the word "contract." The definition may seem obvious or simple, but there are several key terms within the definition (promise, remedy, performance) that in themselves are all separate topics of discussion, and comprise much of what we will learn in this course. The definition of a contract follows:

RESTATEMENT (SECOND) OF CONTRACTS, SECTION 1

§ 1. *Contract Defined.*

A contract is a promise or a set of promises for the breach of which the law gives a remedy, or the performance of which the law in some way recognizes as a duty.

———

Contract law asks the vital question: Of all the promises made in the world, which should be recognized as enforceable in court? Equally important, it asks, among enforceable obligations, what remedy should be awarded upon breach?

There are many promises that contract law views as unenforceable. For example, contract law does not recognize social promises such as meeting for coffee as warranting enforcement, nor does it enforce most promises to make gifts. Instead, contract law concentrates on bargained-for transactions—such as promises to borrow and lend money or rent a car or banquet hall. There are also bargains that are enforceable even though a promise is not made. A customer who drops off suits at a dry cleaner owes the price for the service when performed, whether any promise was made or not. Throughout this course we will repeatedly ask which obligations that the law considers enforceable, and the appropriate remedy for breach of such agreements.

To understand contract law and its place in history, it is useful to recognize legendary figures dating back more than a century. In the 1870s, C. C. Langdell, as dean of Harvard Law School, designed a simple way to organize the vast field of law, still used to this day. He thought that underlying law's complexity were a handful of basic ideas. Examining leading cases organized around these ideas would reveal law's elements and rhythms. Langdell organized the welter of cases on numerous topics according to basic questions: how, what, and why. The question of *how* isolates the procedures private parties follow when resolving disputes

1

using civil litigation. This is the practice of the lawsuit, arranged into the subfield of study called civil procedure. The question of *what* addresses the stakes in a lawsuit, pivoting around entitlement to property. This involves drawing the lines of ownership. Most pertinent, the question of *why* investigates justifications courts give when requiring property to change hands.

The answer to "why" is because of a judgment that one party instead of another is entitled to a sum of money or other property. Dean Langdell identified two sources of these obligations. One arises from behavior required of all people living in a civil society, called the law of torts, epitomized by the idea of negligence. The other comes from self-imposed undertakings, usually by a promise or an agreement, called the law of contracts. These two fields, torts and contracts, define the scope of civil obligation that courts may enforce.

Civil obligation contrasts with criminal law. The substance of criminal law consists of invasions by a person of the rights of another or of the public (like treason) so serious as to require public force (the police and district attorney), not just private remedy, to redress. Such public interests also appear in constitutional law, which sets basic rights of individuals, as against government, plus the powers of the states in relation to each other, and to the federal government. Throughout your first year you will study these fields largely independently, but be on the look out for intersections, especially between tort and contract law.

A. SOURCES OF CONTRACT LAW

Most substantive rules of contract law are based on state law, and they find their roots in common law, such as persuasive authority found in the Restatement (Second) of Contracts. The rules of contract law are also found in binding statutes, such as the Uniform Commercial Code, a codification of the rules governing transactions in goods, sometimes referred to as the law of commercial sales.

1. COMMON LAW AND THE RESTATEMENTS

Common law actions, meaning those that courts resolve one by one, are central to contract law. In the United States, following English traditions, common law is developed by state courts as disputes arise. Originally referring to law "common" to all citizens, today this system yields some variation among states, but general principles tend to prevail. Although the common law evolves as society and the economy change, judges draw on precedents when evaluating new cases, under the principle of *stare decisis*. If a set of facts have been determined to warrant a particular legal outcome, *stare decisis* holds that the previous decision will stand. This leads to stability and predictability within the law.

The state common law of contracts is vast, and even with general principles to guide judges, there is still some variation in contractual doctrines among states. In an attempt to organize, harmonize, and clarify the law, the American Law Institute ("ALI") was established in 1923. The ALI, which is composed of well-respected judges, law professors, and lawyers, issues "Restatements of the Law" to pursue its goals. The ALI Restatements cover a vast array of subjects, including contracts. Drafts of any restatement must be discussed among a specialized committee of subject matter experts. Typically, Restatements undergo many drafts and revisions over a period of years or even decades. After the Restatements are honed by subject matter experts, they are presented to the entire ALI membership for comment and debate, and only after much careful discussion are they finalized and released to the public.

The First Restatement of Contracts was largely the work of Professor Samuel Williston, who was named reporter in 1932. The Second Restatement of Contracts began in the 1960s, bearing a copyright date of 1981, and was strongly influenced by Professor Arthur Corbin. There is no talk at present of a Third Restatement of Contracts, although there has been discussion within the ALI of adding restatements to deal with the issues presented by both consumer contracts and software license contracts.

Williston and Corbin are titans in the development of the common law of contracts, having each produced multi-volume treatises on the subject that continue to be updated and relied upon to this day. Williston, a Harvard colleague of Langdell's, published the first edition of his monumental treatise in 1920 and personally updated it until his death in 1963. In 1950, Arthur Corbin, a professor at Yale, promulgated an equally magisterial and comprehensive treatise based on earlier writings throughout his career. Williston's philosophy, enshrined in the Restatement (First) of Contracts, dovetailed with that of the eminent jurist, Oliver Wendell Holmes, Jr., and Corbin's, which dominates the Restatement (Second) of Contracts, resonated with that of the esteemed judge, Benjamin N. Cardozo. While both Holmes and Cardozo ultimately served on the U.S. Supreme Court, their contributions to the common law of contracts occurred mainly when they served on state high courts, in Massachusetts and New York, respectively.

Williston epitomized a formalist approach to law and reflected what some call the "classical" school of contract. It looks to whether parties in a transaction were giving and getting something, emphasizing a concept called "consideration" as the signal of an enforceable contract. This school of thought held unenforceable not only promises to make gifts or attend dinner, but promises merely inducing another party to take some action. In this view, the remedy for breach of a bargain is to pay the injured party money to put them in the same economic position they would have enjoyed had the other performed. This classical conception of contract law dominated well into the twentieth century and remains a force today.

Corbin took a realist approach to law and offered a more pragmatic conception of contract. Although agreeing with Williston on many points, Corbin recognized, as courts increasingly did in the twentieth century, a wider range of circumstances that create contractual obligations. Williston's bargain model of consideration remained, but loosened so that even some promises to make gifts could be enforced, so long as there was an identifiable return, like naming a college endowment. It recognized reliance on a promise as a basis of contractual liability, in a novel doctrine commonly called "promissory estoppel." Compensation for disappointed expectations remains the primary measure of remedy. But recognizing promissory estoppel gave equal dignity to measuring remedies by out-of-pocket costs incurred relying on a promise.

These twentieth-century developments that Corbin captured and helped shape reflected broader social developments as well, moving law's orientation from a formalist to a realist conception. For example, classical contract's relative strictness, limiting the scope of contractual obligation, was accompanied by an equivalent strictness of enforcement: If a contract was hard to get into, it was also hard to get out of. People could be bound to contracts that were made based on mutually mistaken assumptions, or even where performance became impossible. But as the ambit of contractual obligation expanded, so did grounds for excusing it, like mutual mistake about the terms of a trade, or impossibility of performance, such as a power outage in a rented banquet hall. Similarly, classical contract law venerated written records, limiting the scope of obligation to what was plainly meant within a document's four corners. Corbin and his realist descendants were more willing to consider evidence supplementing these written expressions.

Healthy debate continues about these and many other questions that divided titans like Williston and Corbin, although the range of credible debate is substantially bounded by positions those two staked out, as you will discover throughout your study of contracts. Unbounded is the range of subjects contracts involve, which is as large as life. Contract law addresses all exchange transactions and the universe of promises. Given such a sprawling enterprise, expect to find occasional tensions or contradictions between cases or within doctrines, or variation among states. Despite such findings, however, which tend to be clearest at microscopic levels of inspection, contract law shows a surprising degree of coherence across settings and geography.

Many have tried to provide a grand theory of contract law, but it is unsurprising that contract law's vastness defies tidy explanation using any single account. True, much of contract law is based on promises, but not all promises are recognized as legally binding; much of contract law probes whether people have consented to some exchange, but it is likewise true that not every consented deal is valid, and liability can attach even though consent is not obvious. It is particularly difficult to explain everything about contract law in terms of protecting people when they rely on others or determining which arrangements are the most economically efficient, although both reliance and efficiency are often relevant. If pressed, the best way to account for the vast run of contract law doctrine is pragmatism—a search for what is useful to facilitate exchange transactions people should be free to pursue.

Famous books have been published that consciously demonstrate not contract law's coherence, but its tensions, contradictions, and the dissolution of Langdell's revered categories, including the venerable distinction between torts and contracts. Other approaches include the "law in action" movement, which insists that in contracting, business reality is more important than the law. Proponents joined critics of Langdell's "case method" to debunk the practice of learning contracts from common law opinions, saying that was akin to learning zoology by focusing on unicorns and dodos. Although influential, these tidings did not transform the field, which is still readily learned by the reading of opinions in individual cases and stitching them together into a tapestry of knowledge.

Note that the Restatements are not adopted as the law in any United States jurisdiction. The Restatements are not statutes, and are therefore not binding authority on judges. However, among contemporary courts, most provisions of the Restatement (Second) of Contracts are viewed as highly persuasive, and judges and jurisdictions tend to follow them. Convincing a judge to rule in a way that contradicts the Restatement (Second) of Contracts would usually be difficult for the advocate; most judges on most subjects would balk at doing so absent a compelling reason.

In the modern era, certain types of contracts have become specialized. For example, insurance contracts are highly regulated, and policies within a state will contain similar contractual language that brings the contract into compliance with the state's insurance laws.

2. ARTICLE 2 OF THE UCC

In the 1940s, a joint project between the ALI and the National Conference of Commissioners on Uniform State Laws (NCCUSL) resulted in the drafting of uniform laws on many aspects of commercial transactions. These uniform laws, which came to be known as the Uniform Commercial Code (UCC), have as their purpose the promotion of uniformity, clarity, and modernity in commercial transactions. These uniform laws were promulgated with the intent that they were to be adopted by all the state legislatures. Allen R. Kamp, *Downtown Code: A*

History of the Uniform Commercial Code 1949–1954, 49 BUFF. L. REV. 359, 364 (2001).

Article 2 of the UCC specifically dealt with one type of contract, those that involved *transactions in goods.* Drafted by Professors Soia Mentschikoff and Karl Llewellyn, a married couple, the text of UCC Article 2 went through many intensive revisions. Throughout the drafting process, the committee was guided by the practical details of how businesses actually operated. The drafters were devotees of the realist school of contract, much more aligned with Corbin than with Williston, and may even be seen as being more flexible and focused on context. For instance, they chose to make the default rules of the code incorporate trade usage and those practices that business people used as a matter of custom. *See* Soia Mentschikoff, *Reflections of A Drafter*, 43 OHIO ST. L.J. 537, 540–41 (1982).

Article 2 of the UCC was finalized in 1954, and was adopted by all state legislatures (except Louisiana) in the following years. The UCC is a statute. Unlike the Restatement of Contracts, which are merely persuasive authority, the Uniform Commercial Code is binding legal authority for transactions within its scope. An attempt was made to revise Article 2 in the early 2000s, but no state legislature adopted the proposed changes, and at the writing of this book, there are no active efforts to push forward the revision.

A definitional question arises. As the UCC only applies to "goods," what are "goods"? *See* UCC § 2–105(1), which provides the following statutory definition:

> "Goods" means all things (including specially manufactured goods) which are moveable at the time of identification to the contract for sale other than the money in which the price is to be paid, investment securities (Article 8) and things in action. "Goods" also includes the unborn young of animals and growing crops and other identified things attached to realty as described in the section on goods to be severed from realty.

The statutory definition of "goods" is expansive, including all things moveable. Another way to think about this is that if something is moveable, it is also tangible, so you can touch it or feel it. We are told in this definition that certain sales are *not goods*, including money, securities for investment, and "things in action." Although this phrase is somewhat cryptic, "things in action" is just another way of saying "cause of action" or "lawsuit." Lawsuits, then, are not considered "goods" under this definition. Despite the idea of "all things . . . moveable . . . at the time of . . . the contract for sale" the definition also includes some goods that have yet to come to be, including the unborn young of animals, growing crops, and specially manufactured goods.

Sometimes questions arise because even if part of a transaction is a "good," the other part of the contract is something else. Consider a visit to an optometrist who sells in the same visit both an eye exam (a service, not a good), and a pair of glasses (tangible, moveable, a good). U.S. jurisdictions have formulated two tests to determine the applicable source of law for these so-called "hybrid" transactions.

The first approach, known as the *predominant purpose* test, looks to what aspect of the deal comprised the major part of the transaction. For example, if the eye exam discussed above costs only $45, but the cost of the glasses sold is $850, the predominant purpose of the transaction would be the sale of the glasses. The glasses are a good, so the UCC would apply. The second approach, known as the *gravamen of the complaint test*, looks to the part of the transaction that gave rise to the legal problem. If it was the part of the transaction that involved the good, the UCC will apply. If it was the part that involved the sale of something other than goods, then the common law will apply. To return to the eye exam, if the optometrist misdiagnosed astigmatism, the source of the complaint would be the service component. Thus under the gravamen of the complaint test, common law would apply.

PROBLEMS: WHICH SOURCE OF LAW APPLIES?

In each of the following situations, imagine that a dispute has arisen or may arise between the parties that requires determining whether Article 2 of the UCC applies. Analyze which source of law applies.

1.   Jintong has long had an interest in horses. She contracts with Henry for the purchase of his (recently retired) champion thoroughbred, Musical Chairs.   ✓

2.   Before purchasing Musical Chairs, Jintong pays a local veterinarian to give Musical Chairs a physical. The veterinarian pronounces everything to be in order, but also sells Jintong some inexpensive medications for a minor tooth ailment. The medication turned out to be adulterated and ineffective to combat the toothache.   PP: ✗   GC: ✓

3.   Delighted with her new horse, Jintong buys a large plot adjacent to her current house. Then she hires a contractor to build a new barn and fence in a pasture so that Musical Chairs has room to roam. The general contractor buys a large quantity of lumber from a supply yard in order to build a fence.

4.   Jintong purchases five bushels of her neighbor's ripening carrots for Musical Chairs to munch on.   ✓

5.   Jintong contracts with Gulfstream, special ordering a fancy horse trailer that has more features than most so that Musical Chairs can ride in style.   ✓

6.   A few years later, down on her luck, Jintong makes DVDs of Musical Chairs' adventures with his animal friends in the barn, selling the DVDs online at eBay.

7.   The video is successful, and Jintong signs a Hollywood contract for screen time and rights to the likeness of Musical Chairs.

8.   Jintong hires a fashion designer to draw plans for special "horse clothes" that Musical Chairs will wear. She then hires a tailor to sew the designs.

9.   Jintong buys a special fitness tracker for Musical Chairs to assure the horse is in good shape for all show business performances. The fitness tracker is strapped onto the horse's right flank, and sends signals about fitness performance over the Internet. Based on these signals, the fitness program sends a text message to Jintong with suggestions for improving the horse's exercise routine.

10.   Jintong forms a corporation, MC Inc., in order to develop the career of Musical Chairs. She seeks investors and sells 25% of the company's stock to her cousin, Aimee. Eventually, a show business insider makes them a generous offer to purchase MC Inc., and Jintong, Aimee, and the other investors sell their shares.

Before ending this section introducing the UCC, note one more salient issue. The Uniform Commercial Code applies to anyone buying or selling goods. But certain special rules in the UCC apply to those classified as "merchants." People sometimes are confused and think that the UCC *only* applies to merchants, but this is incorrect. Even a homeowner selling a used coat at a garage sale would be subject to the UCC, because the coat is a good. While the UCC applies, a casual seller at a garage sale would certainly not be a merchant. The parts of the UCC that apply only to merchants would not have any application to the garage-sale seller.

With that distinction noted, let's take a look at the definition of "merchant." According to UCC § 2–104:

> Merchant [means a] person who deals in goods of the kind or otherwise by his occupation holds himself out as having knowledge or skill peculiar to the practices or goods involved in the transaction or to whom such knowledge or skill may be attributed by his employment of an agent or broker or other intermediary who by his occupation holds himself out as having such knowledge or skill.

That is somewhat abstract, and it helps to practice working with the definition. In each of the following situations, goods are being sold, so we know that the UCC is the source of law to be applied. Now, in each of these problems, determine whether the one or both parties to the transaction is a merchant.

PROBLEMS: ARE THEY MERCHANTS?

1. Louie is the owner and chief salesman at "Louie's Used Car Lot." He sells a 2008 truck to Kathleen, an attorney.

2. Kathleen returns to her office, satisfied with her purchase. A year later, however, she wants to get better fuel efficiency, so she decides to sell the truck herself (through some ads in the newspaper and Craigslist). She is able to find a buyer through the paper, actually someone who lives just down the street. They complete the transaction.

3. One of Kathleen's hobbies is jewelry making; she delights in putting together beautiful bracelets. She starts up a company on eBay selling her creations.

4. Kathleen wants additional capital to fund her business. She decides to sell her one major asset, a collection of rare and special books on the law of contracts.

3. CISG

For international transactions in goods, yet another source of law applies. The United Nations Convention on Contracts for the Sale of International Goods (CISG) is a set of contract rules that have been ratified by 85 signatory countries. The purpose of the CISG is to facilitate international trade. The United States is a signatory, as is Canada, historically one of America's largest trading partners.

In the United States, the CISG, as a treaty, is given the same force of law as a federal statute. When a business entity or citizen of a signatory nation enters a contract with a business entity or citizen of another signatory nation, the CISG replaces the national laws that would otherwise govern the transaction.

Note that both citizens or businesses must be located in different signatory nations to the CISG. In addition, the CISG only applies to sales of goods. Services, real estate, and other transactions are not included within its scope. Further, the CISG makes it clear that it only applies to commercial transactions. Normal household or consumer purchases would not be covered by the CISG. Note that this is different than coverage under the UCC, which includes all goods, regardless of business or household use.

At U.S. law schools, the CISG is generally taught not in the basic course in contracts but in an upper level course on international business transactions. We will note in the text the instances in which certain provisions of CISG rules are relevant.

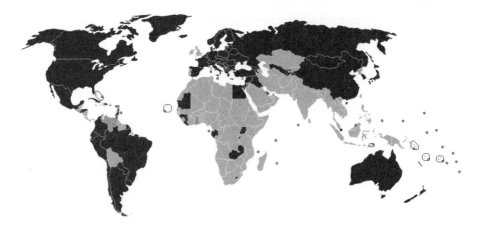

Nations in darker shades have ratified or at least signed the CISG. Those nations in lighter shades are not signatories to the CISG. Source: Wikimedia Commons.

PROBLEMS: CISG

1.   Lucas owns a shoe store in Armstrong, a small town in Missouri. He orders a large number of shoes from a manufacturer of running shoes in Italy.

2.   Sheila is an avid boxing fan who lives in Australia. She orders several boxing-themed T-shirts from a Denmark-based business that sells boxing goods.

3.   Patricia owns a BBQ restaurant located in Portland, Oregon. She contracts with a Canadian-based company to do an accounting of the restaurant's finances.

4.   Madhavi, a clothing store owner in Mexico, orders a large quantity of clothes, bracelets, and bangles from India.

———————

This book contains dozens of statutory excerpts from the UCC and scores of selections from the Restatement (Second) of Contracts. Parsing these materials involves interpretation to determine how the text applies to various fact patterns. For the UCC, judges applying the statute are legally bound to follow it faithfully, out of respect for the legislative branch of government. Judges are not legally bound by the Restatement, and are free to ignore its prescriptions if they wish, though invoking it requires fidelity to its language and rationale. In any event, your engagement with language of both the UCC and the Restatement will differ from your reading of case law, a specialized exercise worth introducing at the outset.

B. READING CASE LAW

This book presents some 150 judicial opinions, written resolutions of legal disputes that share characteristic structures and purposes. These are distinctive texts that you must learn how read, as reading judicial opinions differs greatly from reading other materials. The following excerpt provides an excellent introduction to case analysis.

ORIN S. KERR, *HOW TO READ A LEGAL OPINION: A GUIDE FOR NEW LAW STUDENTS*
11 GREEN BAG 2d 51 (2007)

When two people disagree and that disagreement leads to a lawsuit, the lawsuit will sometimes end with a ruling by a judge in favor of one side. The judge will explain the ruling in a written document referred to as an "opinion." The opinion explains what the case is about, discusses the relevant legal principles, and then applies the law to the facts to reach a ruling in favor of one side and against the other. Modern judicial opinions reflect hundreds of years of history and practice. They usually follow a simple and predictable formula. . . .

I. What's in a Legal Opinion?

The Caption. The first part of the case is the title of the case, known as the "caption." Examples include *Brown v. Board of Education* and *Miranda v. Arizona*. The caption usually tells you the last names of the person who brought the lawsuit and the person who is being sued. These two sides are often referred to as the "parties" or as the "litigants" in the case. For example, if Ms. Smith sues Mr. Jones, the case caption may be *Smith v. Jones* (or, depending on the court, *Jones v. Smith*). . . .

The Case Citation. Below the case name you will find some letters and numbers. These letters and numbers are the legal citation for the case. A citation tells you the name of the court that decided the case, the law book in which the opinion was published, and the year in which the court decided the case. For example, "U.S. Supreme Court, 485 U.S. 759 (1988)" refers to a U.S. Supreme Court case decided in 1988 that appears in Volume 485 of the United States Reports starting at page 759.

The Author of the Opinion. The next information is the name of the judge who wrote the opinion. Most opinions assigned in law school were issued by courts with multiple judges. The name tells you which judge wrote that particular opinion. In older cases, the opinion often simply states a last name followed by the initial "J." No, judges don't all have the first initial "J." The letter stands for "Judge" or "Justice," depending on the court. . . .

The Facts of the Case. . . . The first part of the body of the opinion presents the facts of the case. In other words, what happened? . . . Most discussions of the facts also cover the "procedural history" of the case. The procedural history explains how the legal dispute worked its way through the legal system to the court that is issuing the opinion. It will include various motions, hearings, and trials that occurred after the case was initially filed. . . .

The Law of the Case. After the opinion presents the facts, it will then discuss the law. Many opinions present the law in two stages. The first stage discusses the general principles of law that are relevant to cases such as the one the court is deciding. This section might explore the history of a particular field of law or may include a discussion of past cases (known as "precedents") that are related to the case the court is deciding. . . . The second stage of the legal section applies the general legal principles to the particular facts of the dispute. . . .

Concurring and/or Dissenting Opinions. Most of the opinions you read as a law student are "majority" opinions. When a group of judges get together to decide a case, they vote on which side should win and also try to agree on a legal rationale to explain why that side has won. A majority opinion is an opinion joined by the majority of judges on that court. Although most decisions are unanimous, some cases are not. Some judges may disagree and will write a separate opinion offering a different approach. Those opinions are called "concurring opinions" or "dissenting opinions," and they appear after the majority opinion. A "concurring opinion" (sometimes just called a "concurrence") explains a vote in favor of the winning side but based on a different legal rationale. A "dissenting opinion" (sometimes just called a "dissent") explains a vote in favor of the losing side.

II.   Common Legal Terms Found in Opinions . . .

Terms in Appellate Litigation. Most opinions that you read in law school are appellate opinions, which means that they decide the outcome of appeals. An "appeal" is a legal proceeding that considers whether another court's legal decision was right or wrong. After a court has ruled for one side, the losing side may seek review of that decision by filing an appeal before a higher court. The original court is usually known as the trial court, because that's where the trial occurs if there is one. The higher court is known as the appellate or appeals court, as it is the court that hears the appeal.

A single judge presides over trial court proceedings, but appellate cases are decided by panels of several judges. . . . During the proceedings before the higher court, the party that lost at the original court and is therefore filing the appeal is usually known as the "appellant." The party that won in the lower court and must defend the lower court's decision is known as the "appellee" (accent on the last syllable). Some older opinions may refer to the appellant as the "plaintiff in error" and the appellee as the "defendant in error." . . .

III. What You Need to Learn From Reading a Case . . .

Know the Facts. Law professors love the facts. When they call on students in class, they typically begin by asking students to state the facts of a particular case. Facts are important because law is often highly fact sensitive, which is a fancy way of saying that the proper legal outcome depends on the exact details of what happened. If you don't know the facts, you can't really understand the case and can't understand the law. . . .

Know the Specific Legal Arguments Made by the Parties. Lawsuits are disputes, and judges only issue opinions when two parties to a dispute disagree on a particular legal question. This means that legal opinions focus on resolving the parties' very specific disagreement. The lawyers, not the judges, take the lead role in framing the issues raised by a case. . . .

Know the Disposition. The "disposition" of a case is the action the court took. It is often announced at the very end of the opinion. For example, an appeals court might "affirm" a lower court decision, upholding it, or it might "reverse" the decision, ruling for the other side. . . .

Understand the Reasoning of the Majority Opinion. . . . [I]dentify the method of reasoning that the court used to justify its decision. When a case is governed by a statute, for example, the court usually will simply follow what the statute says. The court's role is narrow in such settings because the legislature has settled the law. Similarly, when past courts have already answered similar questions before, a court may conclude that it is required to reach a particular result because it is bound by the past precedents. This is an application of the judicial practice of "stare decisis," an abbreviation of a Latin phrase meaning "That which has been already decided should remain settled." In other settings, courts may justify their decisions on public policy grounds. That is, they may pick the rule that they think is the best rule, and they may explain in the opinion why they think that rule is best. . . .

Understand the Significance of the Majority Opinion. Some opinions resolve the parties' legal dispute by announcing and applying a clear rule of law that is new to that particular case. That rule is known as the "holding" of the case. Holdings are often contrasted with "dicta" found in an opinion. Dicta refers to legal statements in the opinion not needed to resolve the dispute of the parties; the word is a pluralized abbreviation of the Latin phrase "obiter dictum," which means "a remark by the way."

When a court announces a clear holding, you should take a minute to think about how the court's rule would apply in other situations. During class, professors like to pose "hypotheticals," new sets of facts that are different from those found in the cases you have read. They do this for two reasons. First, it's hard to understand the significance of a legal rule unless you think about how it might apply to lots of different situations. A rule might look good in one setting, but another set of facts might reveal a major problem or ambiguity.

Second, judges often reason by "analogy," which means a new case may be governed by an older case when the facts of the new case are similar to those of the older one. This raises the question, which are the legally relevant facts for this particular rule? The best way to evaluate this is to consider new sets of facts. You'll spend a lot of time doing this in class, and you can get a head start on your class discussions by asking the hypotheticals on your own before class begins.

Finally, you should accept that some opinions are vague. Sometimes a court won't explain its reasoning very well, and that forces us to try to figure out what the opinion means. You'll look for the holding of the case but become frustrated because you can't find one. It's not your fault; some opinions are written in a narrow way so that there is no clear holding, and others are just poorly reasoned or written. Rather than trying to fill in the ambiguity with false certainty, try embracing the ambiguity instead.

One of the skills of topflight lawyers is that they know what they don't know: they know when the law is unclear. Indeed, this skill of identifying when a problem is easy and when it is hard (in the sense of being unsettled or unresolved by the courts) is one of the keys to doing very well in law school. The best law students are the ones who recognize and identify these unsettled issues without pretending that they are easy.

Understand Any Concurring and/or Dissenting Opinions.... Casebook authors edit out any unimportant concurrences and dissents to keep the opinions short. When concurrences and dissents appear in a casebook, it signals that they offer some valuable insights and raise important arguments. Disagreement between the majority opinion and concurring or dissenting opinions often frames the key issue raised by the case; to understand the case, you need to understand the arguments offered in concurring and dissenting opinions.

IV. Why Do Law Professors Use the Case Method?

. . . Every law student quickly realizes that law school classes are very different from college classes. Your college professors probably stood at the podium and droned on while you sat back in your chair, safe in your cocoon. You're now starting law school, and it's very different. You're reading about actual cases, real-life disputes, and you're trying to learn about the law by picking up bits and pieces of it from what the opinions tell you. Even weirder, your professors are asking you questions about those opinions, getting everyone to join in a discussion about them. Why the difference? . . . Why do law schools use the case method at all? . . .

The Historical Reason. The legal system that we have inherited from England is largely judge-focused. The judges have made the law what it is through their written opinions. To understand that law, we need to study the actual decisions that the judges have written. Further, we need to learn to look at law the way that judges look at law. In our system of government, judges can only announce the law when deciding real disputes: they can't just have a press conference and announce a set of legal rules. (This is sometimes referred to as the "case or controversy" requirement; a court has no power to decide an issue unless it is presented by an actual case or controversy before the court.) To look at the law the way that judges do, we need to study actual cases and controversies, just like the judges. . . .

The Practical Reason. A second reason professors use the case method is that it teaches an essential skill for practicing lawyers. Lawyers represent clients, and clients will want to know how laws apply to them. To advise a client, a lawyer needs to understand exactly how an abstract rule of law will apply to the very specific situations a client might encounter. . . . As a result, good lawyers need a vivid imagination; they need to imagine how rules might apply, where they might be unclear, and where they might lead to unexpected outcomes. The case method and the frequent use of hypotheticals will help train your brain to think this way. Learning the law in light of concrete situations will help you deal with particular facts you'll encounter as a practicing lawyer.

Having considered the sources of contract law and some instructions on how to read case law, you are ready to read a judicial opinion about substantive contract doctrine. Here are some questions to think about as you read: How do we determine whether parties have entered into a contract? What markers will signify the presence of a deal? How important is what is in someone's mind when they make a deal compared to their outward signals to others? How do we separate joking and bluffing on the one hand from genuine commitment to making a promise? We will consider these issues in more depth in Chapter One, but for now, as an introduction to contract law, consider the following vintage case that concerns the ownership of a farm.

LUCY V. ZEHMER

84 S.E.2d 516 (Va. 1954)

BUCHANAN, J.

This suit was instituted by W. O. Lucy and J. C. Lucy, complainants, against A. H. Zehmer and Ida S. Zehmer, his wife, defendants, to have specific performance of a contract by which it was alleged the Zehmers had sold to W. O. Lucy a tract of land owned by A. H. Zehmer in Dinwiddie county containing 471.6 acres, more or less, known as the Ferguson farm, for $50,000. J. C. Lucy, the other complainant, is a brother of W. O. Lucy, to whom W. O. Lucy transferred a half interest in his alleged purchase. The instrument sought to be enforced was written by A. H. Zehmer on December 20, 1952, in these words: 'We hereby agree to sell to W. O. Lucy the Ferguson Farm complete for $50,000.00, title satisfactory to buyer,' and signed by the defendants, A. H. Zehmer and Ida S. Zehmer.

The answer of A. H. Zehmer admitted that at the time mentioned W. O. Lucy offered him $50,000 cash for the farm, but that he, Zehmer, considered that the offer was made in jest; that so thinking, and both he and Lucy having had several drinks, he wrote out 'the memorandum' quoted above and induced his wife to sign it; that he did not deliver the memorandum to Lucy, but that Lucy picked it up, read it, put it in his pocket, attempted to offer Zehmer $5 to bind the bargain, which Zehmer refused to accept, and realizing for the first time that Lucy was serious, Zehmer assured him that he had no intention of selling the farm and that the whole matter was a joke. Lucy left the premises insisting that he had purchased the farm. Depositions were taken and the decree appealed from was entered holding that the complainants had failed to establish their right to specific performance, and dismissing their bill. The assignment of error is to this action of the court.

<u>W. O. Lucy, a lumberman and farmer, thus testified in substance:</u>

He had known Zehmer for fifteen or twenty years and had been familiar with the Ferguson farm for ten years. Seven or eight years ago he had offered Zehmer $20,000 for the farm which Zehmer had accepted, but the agreement was verbal and Zehmer backed out. On the night of December 20, 1952, around eight o'clock, he took an employee to McKenney, where Zehmer lived and operated a restaurant, filling station and motor court. While there he decided to see Zehmer and again try to buy the Ferguson farm. He entered the restaurant and talked to Mrs. Zehmer until Zehmer came in. He asked Zehmer if he had sold the Ferguson farm. Zehmer replied that he had not. Lucy said, 'I bet you wouldn't take $50,000.00 for that place.' Zehmer replied, 'Yes, I would too; you wouldn't give fifty.

'Lucy said he would and told Zehmer to write up an agreement to that effect. Zehmer took a restaurant check and wrote on the back of it, 'I do hereby agree to sell to W. O. Lucy the Ferguson Farm for $50,000 complete.' Lucy told him he had better change it to 'We 'because Mrs. Zehmer would have to sign it too. Zehmer then tore up what he had written, wrote the agreement quoted above and asked Mrs. Zehmer, who was at the other end of the counter ten or twelve feet away, to sign it. Mrs. Zehmer said she would for $50,000 and signed it. Zehmer brought it back and gave it to

Lucy, who offered him $5 which Zehmer refused, saying, 'You don't need to give me any money, you got the agreement there signed by both of us.'

The discussion leading to the signing of the agreement, said Lucy, lasted thirty or forty minutes, during which Zehmer seemed to doubt that Lucy could raise $50,000. Lucy suggested the provision for having the title examined and Zehmer made the suggestion that he would sell it 'complete, everything there,' and stated that all he had on the farm was three heifers.

Lucy took a partly filled bottle of whiskey into the restaurant with him for the purpose of giving Zehmer a drink if he wanted it. Zehmer did, and he and Lucy had one or two drinks together. Lucy said that while he felt the drinks he took he was not intoxicated, and from the way Zehmer handled the transaction he did not think he was either.

December 20 was on Saturday. Next day Lucy telephoned to J. C. Lucy and arranged with the latter to take a half interest in the purchase and pay half of the consideration. On Monday he engaged an attorney to examine the title. The attorney reported favorably on December 31 and on January 2 Lucy wrote Zehmer stating that the title was satisfactory, that he was ready to pay the purchase price in cash and asking when Zehmer would be ready to close the deal. Zehmer replied by letter, mailed on January 13, asserting that he had never agreed or intended to sell. . .

Mr. Zehmer testified in substance as follows:

He bought this farm more than ten years ago for $11,000. He had had twenty-five offers, more or less, to buy it, including several from Lucy, who had never offered any specific sum of money. He had given them all the same answer, that he was not interested in selling it. On this Saturday night before Christmas it looked like everybody and his brother came by there to have a drink. He took a good many drinks during the afternoon and had a pint of his own. When he entered the restaurant around eight-thirty Lucy was there and he could see that he was 'pretty high.' He said to Lucy, 'Boy, you got some good liquor, drinking, ain't you?' Lucy then offered him a drink. 'I was already high as a Georgia pine, and didn't have any more better sense than to pour another great big slug out and gulp it down, and he took one too.'

After they had talked a while Lucy asked whether he still had the Ferguson farm. He replied that he had not sold it and Lucy said, 'I bet you wouldn't take $50,000.00 for it.' Zehmer asked him if he would give $50,000 and Lucy said yes. Zehmer replied, 'You haven't got $50,000 in cash.' Lucy said he did and Zehmer replied that he did not believe it. They argued 'pro and con for a long time,' mainly about 'whether he had $50,000 in cash that he could put up right then and buy that farm.'

Finally, said Zehmer, Lucy told him if he didn't believe he had $50,000, 'you sign that piece of paper here and say you will take $50,000.00 for the farm. 'He, Zehmer, 'just grabbed the back off of a guest check there' and wrote on the back of it. At that point in his testimony Zehmer asked to see what he had written to 'see if I recognize my own handwriting.' He examined the paper and exclaimed, 'Great balls of fire, I got 'Firgerson' for Ferguson. I have got satisfactory spelled wrong. I don't recognize that writing if I would see it, wouldn't know it was mine.'

After Zehmer had, as he described it, 'scribbled this thing off,' Lucy said, 'Get your wife to sign it.' Zehmer walked over to where she was and she at first refused to sign but did so after he told her that he 'was just needling him [Lucy], and didn't mean a thing in the world, that I was not selling the farm.' Zehmer then 'took it back over there * * * and I was still looking at the dern thing. I had the drink right there by my hand, and I reached over to get a drink, and he said, 'Let me see it.' He reached and picked it up, and when I looked back again he had it in his pocket and he dropped a five dollar bill over there, and he said, 'Here is five dollars payment on it.' * * * I said, 'Hell no, that is beer and liquor talking. I am not going to sell you the farm. I have told you that too many times before."

<u>Mrs. Zehmer testified</u> that when Lucy came into the restaurant he looked as if he had had a drink. When Zehmer came in he took a drink out of a bottle that Lucy handed him. She went back to help the waitress who was getting things ready for next day. Lucy and Zehmer were talking but she did not pay too much attention to what they were saying. She heard Lucy ask Zehmer if he had sold the Ferguson farm, and Zehmer replied that he had not and did not want to sell it. Lucy said, 'I bet you wouldn't take $50,000 cash for that farm,' and Zehmer replied, 'You haven't got $50,000 cash.' Lucy said, 'I can get it.' Zehmer said he might form a company and get it, 'but you haven't got $50,000.00 cash to pay me tonight.' Lucy asked him if he would put it in writing that he would sell him this farm. Zehmer then wrote on the back of a pad, 'I agree to sell the Ferguson Place to W. O. Lucy for $50,000.00 cash.' Lucy said, 'All right, get your wife to sign it.' Zehmer came back to where she was standing and said, 'You want to put your name to this? 'She said 'No,' but he said in an undertone, 'It is nothing but a joke,' and she signed it.

She said that only one paper was written and it said: 'I hereby agree to sell,' but the 'I' had been changed to 'We'. However, she said she read what she signed and was then asked, 'When you read 'We hereby agree to sell to W. O. Lucy,' what did you interpret that to mean, that particular phrase?' She said she thought that was a cash sale that night; but she also said that when she read that part about 'title satisfactory to buyer' she understood that if the title was good Lucy would pay $50,000 but if the title was bad he would have a right to reject it, and that that was her understanding at the time she signed her name.

[Mrs. Zehmer] said that her husband laid this piece of paper down after it was signed; that Lucy said to let him see it, took it, folded it and put it in his wallet, then said to Zehmer, 'Let me give you $5.00,' but Zehmer said, 'No, this is liquor talking. I don't want to sell the farm, I have told you that I want my son to have it. This is all a joke. 'Lucy then said at least twice, 'Zehmer, you have sold your farm,' wheeled around and started for the door. He paused at the door and said, 'I will bring you $50,000.00 tomorrow. * * * No, tomorrow is Sunday. I will bring it to you Monday.' She said you could tell definitely that he was drinking and she said to her husband, 'You should have taken him home,' but he said, 'Well, I am just about as bad off as he is.'

The waitress referred to by Mrs. Zehmer testified that when Lucy first came in 'He was mouthy.' When Zehmer came in they were laughing and joking and she thought they took a drink or two. She was sweeping and cleaning up for next day. She said she heard Lucy tell Zehmer, 'I will give you so much for the farm,' and Zehmer said, 'You haven't got that much.' Lucy answered, 'Oh, yes, I will give you that much.' Then 'they jotted down something on paper * * * and Mr. Lucy reached over and took it, said let me see it.' He looked at it, put it in his pocket and in about a minute he left. She was asked whether she saw Lucy offer Zehmer any money and replied, 'He had five dollars laying up there, they didn't take it.' She said Zehmer told Lucy he didn't want his money 'because he didn't have enough money to pay for his property, and wasn't going to sell his farm.' Both of them appeared to be drinking right much, she said.

She repeated on cross-examination that she was busy and paying no attention to what was going on. She was some distance away and did not see either of them sign the paper. She was asked whether she saw Zehmer put the agreement down on the table in front of Lucy, and her answer was this: 'Time he got through writing whatever it was on the paper, Mr. Lucy reached over and said, 'Let's see it.' He took it and put it in his pocket,' before showing it to Mrs. Zehmer. Her version was that Lucy kept raising his offer until it got to $50,000.

* * * * *

The defendants insist that the evidence was ample to support their contention that the writing sought to be enforced was prepared as a bluff or dare to force Lucy to admit that he did not have $50,000; that the whole matter was a joke; that the writing was not delivered to Lucy and no binding contract was ever made between the parties.

It is an unusual, if not bizarre, defense. When made to the writing admittedly prepared by one of the defendants and signed by both, clear evidence is required to sustain it.

In his testimony Zehmer claimed that he 'was high as a Georgia pine,' and that the transaction 'was just a bunch of two doggoned drunks bluffing to see who could talk the biggest and say the most.' That claim is inconsistent with his attempt to testify in great detail as to what was said and what was done. It is contradicted by other evidence as to the condition of both parties, and rendered of no weight by the testimony of his wife that when Lucy left the restaurant she suggested that Zehmer drive him home. The record is convincing that Zehmer was not intoxicated to the extent of being unable to comprehend the nature and consequences of the instrument he executed, and hence that instrument is not to be invalidated on that ground. 17 C.J.S., Contracts, § 133 b., p. 483; *Taliaferro v. Emery,* 124 Va. 674, 98 S.E. 627. It was in fact conceded by defendants' counsel in oral argument that under the evidence Zehmer was not too drunk to make a valid contract.

The evidence is convincing also that Zehmer wrote two agreements, the first one beginning 'I hereby agree to sell.' Zehmer first said he could not remember about that, then that 'I don't think I wrote but one out. 'Mrs. Zehmer said that what he wrote was 'I hereby agree,' but that the 'I' was changed to 'We' after that night. The agreement that was written and signed is in the record and indicates no such change. Neither are the mistakes in spelling that Zehmer sought to point out readily apparent.

The appearance of the contract, the fact that it was under discussion for forty minutes or more before it was signed; Lucy's objection to the first draft because it was written in the singular, and he wanted Mrs. Zehmer to sign it also; the rewriting to meet that objection and the signing by Mrs. Zehmer; the discussion of what was to be included in the sale, the provision for the examination of the title, the completeness of the instrument that was executed, the taking possession of it by Lucy with no request or suggestion by either of the defendants that he give it back, are facts which furnish persuasive evidence that the execution of the contract was a serious business transaction rather than a casual, jesting matter as defendants now contend.

On Sunday, the day after the instrument was signed on Saturday night, there was a social gathering in a home in the town of McKenney at which there were general comments that the sale had been made. Mrs. Zehmer testified that on that occasion as she passed by a group of people, including Lucy, who were talking about the transaction, $50,000 was mentioned, whereupon she stepped up and said, 'Well, with the high-price whiskey you were drinking last night you should have paid more. That was cheap.' Lucy testified that at that time Zehmer told him that he did not want to 'stick' Him or hold him to the agreement because he, Lucy, was too tight and didn't know what he was doing, to which Lucy replied that he was not too tight; that he had been stuck before and was going through with it. Zehmer's version was that he said to Lucy: 'I am not trying to claim it wasn't a deal on account of the fact the price was too low. If I had wanted to sell $50,000.00 would be a good price, in fact I think you would get stuck at $50,000.00.' A disinterested witness testified that what Zehmer said to Lucy was that 'He was going to let him up off the deal, because he thought he was too tight, didn't know what he was doing. Lucy said something to the effect that 'I have been stuck before and I will go through with it."

If it be assumed, contrary to what we think the evidence shows, that Zehmer was jesting about selling his farm to Lucy and that the transaction was intended by him to be a joke, nevertheless the evidence shows that Lucy did not so understand it but considered it to be a serious business transaction and the contract to be binding on the Zehmers as well as on himself. The very next day he arranged with his brother to put up half the money and take a half interest in the land. The day after that he employed an attorney to examine the title. The next night, Tuesday, he was back at Zehmer's place and there Zehmer told him for the first time, Lucy said, that he wasn't going to sell and he told Zehmer, 'You know you sold that place fair and square.' After receiving the report from his attorney that the title was good he wrote to Zehmer that he was ready to close the deal.

Not only did Lucy actually believe, but the evidence shows he was warranted in believing, that the contract represented a serious business transaction and a good faith sale and purchase of the farm. In the field of contracts, as generally elsewhere, 'We must look to the outward expression of a person as manifesting his intention rather than to his secret and unexpressed intention. 'The law imputes to a person an intention corresponding to the reasonable meaning of his words and acts." *First Nat. Bank v. Roanoke Oil Co.,* 169 Va. 99, 114, 192 S.E. 764, 770.

At no time prior to the execution of the contract had Zehmer indicated to Lucy by word or act that he was not in earnest about selling the farm. They had argued about it and discussed its terms, as Zehmer admitted, for a long time. Lucy testified that if there was any jesting it was about paying $50,000 that night. The contract and the evidence show that he was not expected to pay the money that night. Zehmer said that after the writing was signed he laid it down on the counter in front of Lucy. Lucy said Zehmer handed it to him. In any event there had been what appeared to be a good faith offer and a good faith acceptance, followed by the execution and apparent delivery of a written contract. Both said that Lucy put the writing in his pocket and then offered Zehmer $5 to seal the bargain. Not until then, even under the defendants' evidence, was anything said or done to indicate that the matter was a joke. Both of the Zehmers testified that when Zehmer asked his wife to sign he whispered that it was a joke so Lucy wouldn't hear and that it was not intended that he should hear.

The mental assent of the parties is not requisite for the formation of a contract. If the words or other acts of one of the parties have but one reasonable meaning, his undisclosed intention is immaterial except when an unreasonable meaning which he attaches to his manifestations is known to the other party. Restatement of the Law of Contracts, Vol. I, § 71, p. 74. * * * The law, therefore, judges of an agreement between two persons exclusively from those expressions of their intentions which are communicated between them. * * * . Clark on Contracts, 4 ed., § 3, p. 4.

An agreement or mutual assent is of course essential to a valid contract but the law imputes to a person an intention corresponding to the reasonable meaning of his words and acts. If his words and acts, judged by a reasonable standard, manifest an intention to agree, it is immaterial what may be the real but unexpressed state of his mind. 17 C.J.S., Contracts, § 32, p. 361; 12 Am. Jur., Contracts, § 19, p. 515. So a person cannot set up that he was merely jesting when his conduct and words would warrant a reasonable person in believing that he intended a real agreement, 17 C.J.S., Contracts, § 47, p. 390; Clark on Contracts, 4 ed., § 27, at p. 54.

Whether the writing signed by the defendants and now sought to be enforced by the complainants was the result of a serious offer by Lucy and a serious acceptance by the defendants, or was a serious offer by Lucy and an acceptance in secret jest by the defendants, in either event it constituted a binding contract of sale between the parties.

Defendants contend further, however, that even though a contract was made, equity should decline to enforce it under the circumstances. These circumstances have been set forth in detail above. They disclose some drinking by the two parties but not to an extent that they were unable to understand fully what they were doing. There was no fraud, no misrepresentation, no sharp practice and no dealing between unequal parties. The farm had been bought for $11,000 and was assessed for taxation at $6,300. The purchase price was $50,000. Zehmer admitted that it was a good price. There is in fact present in this case none of the grounds usually urged against specific performance.

Specific performance, it is true, is not a matter of absolute or arbitrary right, but is addressed to the reasonable and sound discretion of the court. *First Nat. Bank v. Roanoke Oil Co., supra,* 169 Va. at p. 116, 192 S.E. at p. 771. But it is likewise true that the discretion which may be exercised is not an arbitrary or capricious one, but one which is controlled by the established doctrines and settled principles of equity; and, generally, where a contract is in its nature and circumstances unobjectionable, it is as much a matter of course for courts of equity to decree a specific performance of it as it is for a court of law to give damages for a breach of it. *Bond v. Crawford,* 193 Va. 437, 444, 69 S.E.(2d) 470, 475.

The complainants are entitled to have specific performance of the contract sued on. The decree appealed from is therefore reversed and the cause is remanded for the entry of a proper decree requiring the defendants to perform the contract in accordance with the prayer of the bill.

Reversed and Remanded.

NOTES AND QUESTIONS

1.   What happened in this case? Is there just one version of what happened in the bar of Ye Olde Virginnie? Or are there various versions of the facts? It is common for witnesses, at trial, to tell different versions of the same event based on various perspectives. What version of the facts did the trial court adopt? What version of the facts did the Supreme Court of Virginia accept? Here is a copy of the diner check at the center of the case:

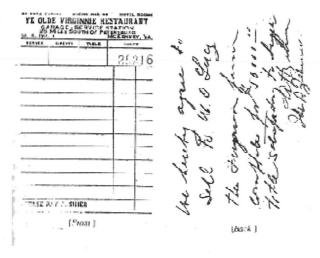

2.   For there to be a contract, there must be mutual assent, or what is sometimes colloquially referred to as the "meeting of the minds." But how do we determine whether there actually was mutual assent among contracting parties? *Lucy v. Zehmer* is often cited for the proposition that in "the field of contracts, as generally elsewhere, 'We must look to the outward expression of a person as manifesting his intention rather than to his secret and unexpressed intention.'" This is commonly known as the *objective theory* and it is the dominant theory used in contract law today. If a disinterested third party were watching (the proverbial "fly on the wall"), would that observer believe a contract had been formed? Under the objective theory, it is the outward manifestations that matter.

3.   In contrast to the objective, or "fly on the wall" approach, is the *subjective theory*. The subjective theory focuses on the party's thoughts and intentions, whether disclosed to anyone else or not. What would be the problem if we allowed Zehmer to escape the contract based on his inward, subjective intentions, upon Zehmer's later claim that the contract was a joke? Would everyone who wanted to escape a contract later claim they lacked subjective intent to go through with the deal? Is this fundamentally a problem of evidence, because some might lie about true intentions just to get out of a deal?

4.   Following up on the last question, would it matter if Zehmer were willing to undergo a lie detector test or swallow truth serum to back up his subjective beliefs? Some have said that not only evidentiary reasons support the objective theory, but also a concern with the other party's reasonable reliance upon the existence of a deal.

5.   When Mr. Zehmer said to Mrs. Zehmer, in effect, "just sign here, it's all a joke," did that make a difference in terms of Lucy's objective belief if there was a deal? Why did Mrs. Zehmer have to sign the paper to make it legally binding?

6.   That is not to say that subjective intent of the parties never matters when probing whether mutual assent existed. Imagine two actors reciting lines in a play making promises to buy and sell a car. There is still no contract in this situation. Why, if the entire audience heard them agree to the sale? The actors lack subjective intent to be bound as neither intended the actual purchase and sale of a car.

7.   Zehmer claimed to have been "high as a Georgia pine." If Zehmer lacked capacity, that would establish a valid defense to the contract. We will study defenses at a later point in the course. In this case, however, the Virginia Supreme Court discounted Zehmer's testimony about drunkenness, finding that he had capacity to enter a contract for the Ferguson Farm.

8.   What if the contract price were $5, not $50,000? Typically, courts do not analyze the amount of money paid in a contract ("consideration"). But if the amount were wildly low, that might bear on whether the parties were serious or not. Here, the court concluded that the $50,000 offered was fair. Interestingly, two researchers delved into the record of the case to explore why Lucy was so persistent in attempting to purchase the Ferguson Farm. They found that timber was in high demand and that Lucy was able to make a large profit from his later sale of timber from the Ferguson Farm. *See* Barak Richman & Dennis Schmelzer, *When Money Grew on Trees: Lucy v. Zehmer and Contracting in a Boom Market*, 61 DUKE L.J. 1511 (2012).

9.   Another point the case illustrates is the idea of the "instant retraction." After Zehmer signed, he immediately tried to "rescind" or take back the deal. However, the common law prefers finality in bargains, and normally as soon as a deal is completed, both parties are bound. The "steel jaws of contract slam shut" at this moment, offering a "bright line" enforcement rule, a basis to know when bargaining ends and contractual liability attaches. This is the default rule, but may be altered by statute in many settings, ranging from certain commercial transactions in goods to consumer protections against improvident impulsive buying. In Missouri, a customer buying a contract to use a health club may cancel the sale within three days, and timeshare purchasers have five days to cancel. See V.A.M.S. 407.330 (three-day grace period for health clubs); V.A.M.S. 407.620 (five-day grace period for timeshare). New York law provides such so-called cooling off periods for real estate purchases (three days) and federal regulations promulgated by the Federal Trade Commission entitle consumers to cancel contracts made in certain

settings (such as door-to-door sales) and receive a full refund until midnight on the third day after the sale.

10.   To return to objective theory, would most people find the contract in *Lucy* to be "funny"? Was the "joke" perhaps more of a bluff or a dare? Who is the "least cost avoider" in this case, meaning the party that could have most cheaply avoided the problem? While humor is a good quality, should people play around or have "fun" with binding legal documents?

PROBLEM: THE PRANKSTER

Suppose that the first letter "A" in A.H. Zehmer's name stood for "Ashton" and that Zehmer had a reputation for pulling pranks and making jokes. In fact, Zehmer even had a variety show called "Pranked" that aired on Virginia broadcast television. In the show, he constantly played ridiculous jokes on his friends, neighbors, and business associates, tricking them into embarrassing situations and even trolling them with fake business deals. Everyone in the area knew that Zehmer was silly and that you couldn't trust him, especially if he had one or two drinks. What if the facts unfolded much as in *Lucy v. Zehmer*, but they transpired on April Fool's Day and a TV camera was visible at the Old Virginnie restaurant? *Same or different legal result?*

PROBLEM: INSTANT RETRACTION

Bob Hopkins, a thirty-five year old journalist, has lived and worked in Richmond, Virginia for five years. Last year, Bob went through many life changes; he married Jenna, an ER doctor, and at about the same time, he found out that his job at the newspaper had been eliminated. Jenna was offered a position with a higher salary at a hospital in Pennsylvania, where they would be closer to their families. Bob and Jenna decided they wanted to make the move in the next few months, and so when they were telephoned by a real estate agent out of the blue who said she had a buyer who was desperate to get into Bob's condominium complex, they were elated. The agent, and her client, Cecilia Wigglesworth, viewed the condominium several times and, after four months of haggling, submitted an offer to Bob for $400,000 along with $5,000 as earnest money.

Bob accepted the offer and he and Cecilia signed a purchase and sale agreement and set a date for the closing of August 1. The agreement stated that the contract was subject to a home inspection and receipt of the condominium documents. By Virginia statute, the purchaser of a condominium unit is given "three days after the receipt of the condominium documents to cancel the contract." According to a discussion from a local government hearing that happened just before the statute was passed, the policy behind the rule was to protect purchasers from being bound to the condominium practices, policies, and terms without the chance to examine them. Thus, the idea was that the purchaser would have three days in which to read the condominium documents and possibly consult an attorney.

In mid-July, Bob and Jenna moved to Pennsylvania. Toward the end of July, Cecilia asked to be let into the condo unit to take another look (she had visited four times previously). With Bob and Jenna's permission, a neighbor let her in. Cecilia saw some ants and became alarmed that there might be an infestation. In addition, the real estate market, which had been doing poorly, dropped as support from the federal government's first-time homebuyer credit dried up and supply once again outstripped demand. Cecilia became concerned that $400,000 was no longer a good deal, despite the condo's great location and spacious interior.

On July 26, the condominium documents were delivered to Cecilia. On the morning of the third day after receipt, July 29, Cecilia, through her agent, notified Bob by e-mail she wished to be released from the contract because of the insect infestation. In this e-mail Cecilia's agent asked for the return of her $5,000 earnest money.

If you were Bob's attorney, how would you proceed? What counter-arguments from Cecilia Wigglesworth would you anticipate? What would be a fair outcome in the case of *Hopkins v. Wigglesworth*?

CHAPTER 1

TRADITIONAL CONTRACT FORMATION

■ ■ ■

No ordinary citizen wants to be involved in a tort case; we can all agree that it would be best if a car accident, for example, never happened. Certainly no one wants to become the victim of a crime, or the defendant in a civil lawsuit. Contracts differs from other subjects of first year study in that people voluntarily, and for the most part, happily, enter into contracts on a daily basis. This notion of consent and choices through exchange is often expressed as "freedom of contract."

Contracts are private agreements that people enter into in order to make themselves—and incidentally others, as well—better off. Just think about all of the contractual transactions that it took in order to get you to a point where you are reading this book. You made a contract with your university to attend law school; you may have paid for a moving truck; rented an apartment or purchased a home near your school; bought new clothes; gone to the bookstore or visited Amazon.com to buy your books; and perhaps paid bus fare or stopped at the gas station on your way to school.

Until now, you might not have given the idea of entering a contract much thought in your everyday life, since the process is routine. But over hundreds of years, the law has developed stylized doctrines for the steps needed in order to "get into" a deal and make it binding, that is, legally enforceable by a court. In this chapter, we discuss the steps necessary to make a contract. We start with the bargain element—in legal terms, we call this "consideration." Thereafter we will turn to the steps of negotiation leading up to the deal—in legal terms, "offer and acceptance."

A. CONSIDERATION

Dating back as far as the Middle Ages, the legal system struggled to find a way to distinguish enforceable promises from those that were not enforceable. Ancient social and moral norms admonish us to keep our word and treat promises as sacred. An important strand of philosophy considers promise keeping an important social or civic duty.

At the same time, the law cannot possibly enforce all promises as contracts; it would be impractical for any legal system to handle, and undesirable to have a judge resolve, every dispute over a broken promise.

For example, can you imagine being dragged into court over a missed coffee date with a friend? While there may be a moral obligation to meet a friend or purchase a gift for a child, these types of social promises are simply beyond the reach of the legal system. So too are the kind of informal alliances or general expressions of goodwill that one often hears in commercial parlance.

Over time, the common law developed doctrines for deciding which promises merited enforcement by the judicial system. One such doctrine is the notion of "consideration." This concept is different from the way the word "consideration" is used in everyday language, where it means to think or to ponder ("I will give your suggestion the utmost *consideration*"), or perhaps even to be kind to someone ("How *considerate* of you."). In the legal context, however, the concept of consideration is not related to these more common uses; it is instead related to the concept of exchange, the idea of having a bargain.

If we are talking about consideration, we mean the motive, the inducement, the *quid-pro-quo*, that is being exchanged between two parties, and that serves to bind one party to another in a way that makes their deal legally enforceable. Section 17 of the Restatement (Second) of Contracts is entitled "Requirement of a Bargain" and notes that consideration, the element of exchange, is a necessary element of a contract.

In most deals that are market commercial transactions, the element of consideration is clear and straightforward to identify. For example, if you hire a plumber to work on your home and pay $150 for a repair of a leaky faucet, the promise of payment and rendering of services constitute consideration for the deal; they induce each other.

Likewise, if you order $300 worth of goods from Amazon.com and pay via your credit card, valid consideration is present. Amazon receives money in exchange for its goods, and the customer receives goods. Under classic economic theory (*e.g.*, the views of the 18th-century philosopher Adam Smith), both parties are made better off by engaging in market exchange. The buyer values their purchase more highly than the money paid in exchange, and the seller wants the money more than the items sold.

More complicated, however, are situations that are not strict market transactions, but instead the murkier domain of gifts or charitable subscriptions; promises or consideration that happened in the past; promises based on morality, social, or religious reasons; or consideration that seems small, lopsided, or otherwise inadequate to one party.

In the materials that follow, we explore these more difficult issues that surround the basic concept of consideration. In each situation, try to think about the policy reasons for why we might want to make certain promises enforceable. On the other hand, you may wish to contemplate why some promises might be better left to the realm of one's inner conscience, rather than being enforceable in a courtroom.

We begin our study of the doctrine of consideration with two cases that the Supreme Judicial Court of Massachusetts decided. Think about the legal reasoning—the why, the explanation—behind the different decisions in these two cases. In both, a significant charitable gift was at stake. In the first case, the court was deciding on the enforceability of a $25,000 pledge that would have helped a congregation add a library to a synagogue. In the second case, the papers of civil rights leader Dr. Martin Luther King Jr. were not only worth millions of dollars, they added a measure of prestige to Boston University.

CONGREGATION KADIMAH TORAS-MOSHE v. DeLEO
540 N.E.2d 691 (Mass. 1989)

LIACOS, C.J.

Congregation Kadimah Toras-Moshe (Congregation), an Orthodox Jewish synagogue, commenced this action in the Superior Court to compel the administrator of an estate (estate) to fulfill the oral promise of the decedent to give the Congregation $25,000. The Superior Court transferred the case to the Boston Municipal Court, which rendered summary judgment for the estate. The case was then transferred back to the Superior Court, which also rendered summary judgment for the estate and dismissed the Congregation's complaint. We granted the Congregation's application for direct appellate review. We now affirm.

The facts are not contested. The decedent suffered a prolonged illness, throughout which he was visited by the Congregation's spiritual leader, Rabbi Abraham Halbfinger. During four or five of these visits, and in the presence of witnesses, the decedent made an oral promise to give the Congregation $25,000. The Congregation planned to use the $25,000 to transform a storage room in the synagogue into a library named after the decedent. The oral promise was never reduced to writing. The decedent died intestate in September, 1985. He had no children, but was survived by his wife.

The Congregation asserts that the decedent's oral promise is an enforceable contract under our case law, because the promise is allegedly supported either by consideration and bargain, or by reliance. See Loranger Constr. Corp. v. E.F. Hauserman Co., 376 Mass. 757, 761, 763, 384 N.E.2d 176 (1978) (distinguishing consideration and bargain from reliance in the absence of consideration). We disagree.

The Superior Court judge determined that "[t]his was an oral gratuitous pledge, with no indication as to how the money should be used, or what [the Congregation] was required to do if anything in return for this promise." There was no legal benefit to the promisor nor detriment to the promisee, and thus no consideration. See Marine Contractors Co. v. Hurley, 365 Mass. 280, 286, 310 N.E.2d 915 (1974); Gishen v. Dura Corp., 362 Mass. 177, 186, 285 N.E.2d 117 (1972) (moral obligation is not legal obligation). Furthermore, there is no evidence in the record that the Congregation's plans to name a library after the decedent induced him to make or to renew his promise. Contrast Allegheny College v. National Chautauqua County Bank, 246 N.Y. 369, 377–379, 159 N.E. 173 (1927) . . .

As to the lack of reliance, the judge stated that the Congregation's "allocation of $25,000 in its budget[,] for the purpose of renovating a storage room, is insufficient to find reliance or an enforceable obligation." We agree. The inclusion of the promised $25,000 in the budget, by itself, merely reduced to writing the Congregation's expectation that it would have additional funds. A hope or expectation, even though well founded, is not equivalent to either legal detriment or reliance. . . Hall v. Horton House Microwave, Inc., 24 Mass.App.Ct. 84, 94, 506 N.E.2d 178 (1987).

The Congregation cites several of our cases in which charitable subscriptions were enforced. These cases are distinguishable because they involved written, as distinguished from oral, promises and also involved substantial consideration or reliance. See, e.g., Trustees of Amherst Academy v. Cowls, 6 Pick. 427, 434 (1828) (subscribers to written agreement could not withdraw "after the execution or during the progress of the work which they themselves set in motion"); Trustees of Farmington Academy v. Allen, 14 Mass. 172, 176 (1817) (trustees justifiably "proceed[ed] to incur expense, on the faith of the defendant's subscription"). Conversely, in the case of Cottage St. Methodist Episcopal Church v. Kendall, 121 Mass. 528(1877), we refused to enforce a promise in favor of a charity where there was no showing of any consideration or reliance. . . .

The Congregation asks us to abandon the requirement of consideration or reliance in the case of charitable subscriptions. The Congregation cites the Restatement (Second) of Contracts § 90 (1981), which provides, in subsection (2): "A charitable subscription . . . is binding under Subsection (1) without proof that the promise induced action or forbearance." Subsection (1), as modified in pertinent part by subsection (2), provides: "A promise which the promisor should reasonably expect to induce action or forbearance on the part of the promisee or a third person . . . is binding if injustice can be avoided only by enforcement of the promise. . . ."

Assuming without deciding that this court would apply § 90, we are of the opinion that in this case there is no injustice in declining to enforce the decedent's promise. Although § 90 dispenses with the absolute requirement of consideration or reliance, the official comments illustrate that these are relevant considerations. Restatement (Second) of Contracts, supra at § 90 comment f. The promise to the Congregation is entirely unsupported by consideration or reliance . . . [Affirmed.]

KING V. TRUSTEES OF BOSTON UNIVERSITY
647 N.E.2d 1196 (Mass. 1995)

ABRAMS, J.

A jury determined that Dr. Martin Luther King, Jr., made a charitable pledge to Boston University (BU) of certain papers he had deposited with BU. The plaintiff, Coretta Scott King, in her capacity as administratrix of the estate of her late husband, and in her individual capacity, appeals from that judgment. The plaintiff sued BU for conversion, alleging that the estate and not BU held title to Dr. King's papers, which have been housed in BU's library's special collection since they were delivered to BU at Dr. King's request in July, 1964.

The case was submitted to the jury on theories of contract [and] charitable pledge . . . In response to special questions the jury determined that Dr. King made a promise to give absolute title to his papers to BU in a letter signed by him and dated July 16, 1964, and that the promise to give the papers was enforceable as a charitable pledge supported by consideration or reliance. . . . The trial judge denied the plaintiff's motion for judgment notwithstanding the verdict or for a new trial. The plaintiff appealed. We granted the plaintiff's application for direct appellate review. We affirm. . . .

will assume jury is right

In reviewing the judge's denial of the plaintiff's motion for directed verdict on the affirmative defense of charitable pledge, we summarize the evidence in a light favorable to the nonmoving party, BU. Young v. Atlantic Richfield Co., 400 Mass. 837, 841, 512 N.E.2d 272 (1987).

In 1963, BU commenced plans to expand its library's special collections. Once plans for construction of a library to house new holdings were firm, the newly appointed director of special collections, Dr. Howard Gotlieb, began his efforts to obtain Dr. King's papers. Dr. King, an alumnus of BU's graduate school program, was one of the first individuals BU officials sought to induce to deposit documents in the archives.

Around the same time, Dr. King was approached regarding his papers by other universities, including his undergraduate alma mater, Morehouse College. Mrs. King testified that, although her late husband thought "Boston seemed to be the only place, the best place, for safety," he was concerned that depositing his papers with BU would evoke criticism that he was "taking them away from a black institution in the South." However, the volatile circumstances during the 1960s in the South led Dr. King to deposit some of his papers with BU pursuant to a letter, which is the centerpiece of this litigation and is set forth herewith . . . :

Dear Sirs:

On this 16th day of July, 1964, I name the Boston University Library the Repository of my correspondence, manuscripts and other papers, along with a few of my awards and other materials which may come to be of interest in historical or other research.

In accordance with this action I have authorized the removal of most of the above-mentioned papers and other objects to Boston University, including most correspondence through 1961, at once. It is my intention that after the end of each calendar year, similar files of materials for an additional year should be sent to Boston University.

All papers and other objects which thus pass into the custody of Boston University remain my legal property until otherwise indicated, according to the statements below. However, if, despite scrupulous care, any such materials are damaged or lost while in custody of Boston University, I absolve Boston University of responsibility to me for such damage or loss.

I intend each year to indicate a portion of the materials deposited with Boston University to become the absolute property of Boston University as an outright gift from me, until all shall have been thus given to the University. In the event of my death, all such materials deposited with the University shall become from that date the absolute property of Boston University.

SINCERELY YOURS,
MARTIN LUTHER KING, JR. /S/

At issue is whether the evidence at trial was sufficient to submit the question of charitable pledge to the jury. BU asserts that the evidence was sufficient to raise a question of fact for the jury as to whether there was a promise by Dr. King to transfer title to his papers to BU and whether any such promise was supported by consideration or reliance by BU. We agree. . . .

A charitable subscription is "an oral or written promise to do certain acts or to give real or personal property to a charity or for a charitable purpose." See generally E.L. Fisch, D.J. Freed, & E.R. Schacter, Charities and Charitable Foundations § 63, at 77 (1974). To enforce a charitable subscription or a charitable pledge in Massachusetts, a party must establish that there was a promise to give some property to a charitable institution and that the promise was supported by consideration or reliance. Congregation Kadimah Toras-Moshe v. DeLeo, 405 Mass. 365, 367 & n. 3, 540 N.E.2d 691 (1989), and cases cited therein.[4] See In re

---

    [4]   In Congregation Kadimah Toras-Moshe v. DeLeo, 405 Mass. 365, 540 N.E.2d 691 (1989), the Congregation sued the estate of a decedent who had made an oral gratuitous promise to give

Morton Shoe Co., 40 B.R. 948 (Bankr.D.Mass.1984) (discussing Massachusetts law of charitable subscriptions).

By requiring that a promise to make a charitable subscription be supported by consideration or reliance, we declined to adopt the standard for enforceable charitable subscriptions set forth in the Restatement (Second) of Contracts § 90 (1981). See id. at 368, 540 N.E.2d 691. Section 90(1), as modified for charitable subscriptions by subsection (2), provides that, "[a] promise which the promisor should reasonably expect to induce action or forbearance on the part of the promisee or a third person. . . is binding if injustice can be avoided only by enforcement of the promise. . . ."

We noted that, although § 90 thus dispenses with a strict requirement of consideration or reasonable reliance for a charitable subscription to be enforceable, the official comments to the Restatement make clear that consideration and reliance remain relevant to whether the promise must be enforced to avoid injustice. Id. See Arrowsmith v. Mercantile-Safe Deposit & Trust Co., supra 313 Md. at 353–354, 545 A.2d 674 (rejecting argument that court should adopt Restatement [Second] of Contracts § 90[2]); Jordan v. Mount Sinai Hosp. of Greater Miami, Inc., supra at 108 ("Courts should act with restraint in respect to the public policy arguments endeavoring to sustain a mere charitable subscription. To ascribe consideration where there is none, or to adopt any other theory which affords charities a different legal rationale than other entities, is to approve fiction").

The jurors were asked two special questions regarding BU's affirmative defense of rightful ownership by way of a charitable pledge: (1) "Does the letter, dated July 16, 1964, from Martin Luther King, Jr., to [BU], set forth a promise by Dr. King to transfer ownership of his papers to [BU]?"; and (2) "Did [BU] take action in reliance on that promise or was that promise supported by consideration?" In determining whether the case properly was submitted to the jury, we consider first, whether the evidence was sufficient to sustain a conclusion that the letter contained a promise to make a gift and second, whether the evidence was sufficient to support a determination that any promise found was supported by consideration or reliance.

. . . "It may be found somewhat difficult to reconcile all the views which have been taken, in the various cases that have arisen upon the validity of promises, where the ground of defence has been that they were gratuitous and without consideration." Ives v. Sterling, 6 Met. 310, 315 (1843). There

---

$25,000 to the synagogue. The Congregation planned to spend the $25,000 on renovation of a storage room in the synagogue into a library. The oral promise was never memorialized in a writing or consummated by delivery before the decedent died intestate. Noting that "[a] hope or expectation, even though well founded, is not equivalent to either legal detriment or reliance," id. at 366–367, 540 N.E.2d 691, we affirmed the judgment of the trial court that the oral charitable subscription was not enforceable because it was oral, not supported by consideration, and without evidence of reliance.

was evidence that BU undertook indexing of the papers, made the papers available to researchers, and provided trained staff to care for the papers and assist researchers. BU held a convocation to commemorate receipt of the papers. Dr. King spoke at the convocation. In a speech at that time, he explained why he chose BU as the repository for his papers.

[T]he letter established that so long as BU, as bailee, attended the papers with "scrupulous care," Dr. King, as bailor, would release them from liability for "any such materials . . . damaged or lost while in [its] custody." The jury could conclude that certain actions of BU, including indexing of the papers, went beyond the obligations BU assumed as a bailee to attend the papers with "scrupulous care" and constituted reliance or consideration for the promises Dr. King included in the letter to transfer ownership of all bailed papers to BU at some future date or at his death. Trustees of Amherst Academy v. Cowls, 6 Pick. 427, 431 (1828) ("It seems that an actual benefit to the promisor, or an actual loss or disadvantage to the promisee, will be a sufficient consideration to uphold a promise deliberately made. Whether the consideration received is equal in value to the sum promised to be paid, seems not to be material to the validity of a note . . ."); Ives, supra at 317–319; Ladies' Collegiate Inst. v. French, 16 Gray 196, 202 (1860).

The issue before us is not whether we agree with the jury's verdict but whether the case was properly submitted to the jury. We conclude that the letter could have been read to contain a promise supported by consideration or reliance; "[t]he issue [of whether transfer of ownership to BU was transferred by way of a charitable pledge by Dr. King] was, therefore, properly submitted to the jury, and their verdicts, unless otherwise untenable, must stand." Carr v. Arthur D Little, Inc., 348 Mass. 469, 474, 204 N.E.2d 466 (1965) (evidence sufficient as matter of contract law to raise question of fact for jury as to existence of common employment). . . . [Affirmed.]

NOTES AND QUESTIONS

1.   Why does the Massachusetts court reach different outcomes in *DeLeo* and *King*? Review the facts of each case. How are the facts of the two cases similar and different? Consider, for example, which side initiated discussions, whether other parties sought to be part of the process, whether any partial performance on either side occurred, and the difference between cash and personal property.

2.   It may be tempting to stress the difference that one promise was oral, while one was written. But while potentially relevant in special circumstances, enforceability of a promise generally does not depend on whether the promise was put in writing. (In a later chapter, we will see that a specialized statute called the Statute of Frauds requires that only a specific subset of promises be

memorialized in a writing to be valid). In reconciling *DeLeo* and *King*, however, the crucial difference is the presence or absence of *consideration*.

3.   Suppose Dr. King had read the letter quoted in the case out loud, rather than writing it down. Would that change the outcome?

4.   What parts of the two opinions deal with elements of consideration, and which with reliance on a promise? Can you articulate the difference between these two different legal theories? We will read additional cases about reliance, typically discussed under the doctrinal heading of "promissory estoppel," in Chapter Two.

5.   The black letter rule is that a straight charitable pledge is just that—a promise to make a gift—lacking the element of exchange that results in an enforceable bargain. But letting a promisor renege on a promise to make a gift seems ironically uncharitable and in some instances, wrong and unfair. Almost a century ago, Justice Benjamin Cardozo struggled to determine whether to enforce as a contract the promise of a cash gift to an educational institution, Allegheny College, motivated by the promisor's love of the school's mission, and on the strength of which the College restructured some of its finances.

Judge Cardozo wrestled with the theories of both consideration and promissory estoppel. At the time, consideration was a venerable legal device judges had long used to sort out which promises to enforce, while promissory estoppel was in its infancy. But while consideration thus provided a strong legal theory, the related facts were weak, given the promisor's emotional, rather than transactional, motive. While promissory estoppel's novelty made it a weaker legal theory, the related facts, of the College's reliance on the promise, were strong. *See Allegheny College v. National Chautauqua County Bank of Jamestown*, 159 N.E. 173 (N.Y. 1927).

6.   Unlike Massachusetts, some U.S. jurisdictions make charitable pledges binding though lacking consideration. Despite having legal grounds, however, most charities hesitate to sue breaching donors, out of obvious concern about alienating other prospects. There are many reasons and circumstances why people holding valid legal claims do not file lawsuits to enforce them or even make legal demands on counterparties. Be alert for possible examples as you begin your legal studies and career.

7.   With the advent of modern technology, will we continue to believe that consideration is lacking in a charitable donation? Professor Hila Keren has argued that those who give money to charity do receive a benefit—albeit a non-financial one—because people receive good feelings when they help others. Hila Keren, *Considering Affective Consideration*, 40 GOLDEN GATE L. REV. 165 (2010). Take a moment to reflect on the last time that you volunteered or helped someone—it is most likely a positive memory. While in the past, the "good feeling" you get from helping someone might have been characterized as intangible, Professor Keren notes that scientists are developing MRIs and other brain scans that could possibly help us quantify the "good feeling" one receives from helping others or giving a gift to a charity. If we had objective

proof that such a "good feeling" existed from giving a gift, would that be enough to satisfy the consideration element of a contract?

RESTATEMENT (SECOND) OF CONTRACTS, SECTIONS 17, 71

§ 17.   *Requirement of a Bargain.*

(1) . . . [T]he formation of a contract requires a bargain in which there is a manifestation of mutual assent to the exchange and a consideration.

§ 71.   *Requirement of Exchange; Types of Exchange.*

(1) To constitute consideration, a performance or a return promise must be bargained for.

(2) A performance or return promise is bargained for if it is sought by the promisor in exchange for his promise and is given by the promisee in exchange for that promise.

(3) The performance may consist of:

(a) an act other than a promise, or

(b) a forbearance, or

(c) the creation, modification, or destruction of a legal relation.

(4) The performance or return promise may be given to the promisor or to some other person. It may be given by the promisee or by some other person.

EXAMPLE: GARTH BROOKS

Garth Brooks is a successful country singer who is well-known for his charitable giving. A few years ago, Brooks began discussion with an Oklahoma hospital about a potential gift. The hospital administrators mentioned that they were thinking about opening a new wing and were seeking a naming gift. In the late 1990s, Brooks' mother had succumbed to cancer. Brooks wrote a check for $500,000 to the hospital. The hospital later claimed that Brooks had agreed to the gift with no strings attached, and the money was to be used for patient care. When the hospital failed to use Brooks' name for the new wing, however, Brooks sued for breach of contract. If you were the law clerk to the judge hearing the case, what issues might you point out to the judge in your bench memorandum?

———————

While consideration is required for a contract, there is no "set amount" of consideration that is required in any particular deal. The reason rests in freedom of contract and economic theory. Austrian economists, including Ludwig von Mises, wrote about what they termed the "subjective value of exchange." To illustrate this concept, imagine two people who have extremely different preferences for spending money. One person has collected stamps all of her life. The second person loves attending theater performances and puts a high value on great seats at opening night. The value of a stamp will be higher to the collector; likewise the theater aficionado will be more willing to pay a higher value for front row seats to *Hamilton,* the popular musical show.

The propensity to value different goods and services more or less highly is part of the idea of freedom of contract. Normally the law does not interfere in the subjective decisions about how much each part of the exchange is worth; rather, the law merely enforces the deal that the parties have reached on their own in private settings. The law thus does not inquire into the so-called "adequacy" of consideration, unless it is extremely lopsided and might give rise to a defense, such as duress or fraud. But absent a defense, contract law largely leaves the amount of consideration to the parties. The traditional way that common law judges phrased this was to say that "even a peppercorn" could be enough consideration to bind a transaction.

What about consideration that happened in the past? Let's say that a friendly neighbor, A, agrees to mow B's lawn while B is out of town. This is phrased as a friendly gesture, in other words, a gift or a favor, as nothing is requested in return. If five months from now, A confronts B and demands $30 for his labor for mowing the lawn, we could see that recognizing "past" consideration could actually lead to opportunistic, bullying behavior, and perhaps even high pressure sales tactics. As such, a past gift does not count as present consideration for legal purposes. This requirement led to some problems with pensions, where work is performed and later payments are made for the purpose of funding retirement. Legislatures, however, passed statutes to cover these instances while courts used alternate theories— including promissory estoppel—to get around the past consideration problem in these instances.

Consideration is a type of "formality," an additional requirement that the law imposes on both parties if they want their deal to be enforceable. In the past, different legal regimes have imposed different types of formalities (including wax seals, notarization of the documents, or requiring that certain types of deals be in writing) to make sure that the parties intended to make their promises binding. We will follow up with these other types of formalities in later chapters. For now, though, think about the ways that consideration differentiates deals that are enforceable from those that are not.

In a famous article, *"Consideration and Form,"* Professor Lon Fuller noted that consideration, like these other formalities, had several functions and rationales. First, consideration serves an *evidentiary* function. Striking a deal (and perhaps even taking the trouble to write out reciprocal terms) would provide evidence that a contract really did exist. Second, consideration provides a *cautionary* function. If parties took the time to affix a wax seal to a promise or arrange for a trade, they would be more careful about making a promise in return for another promise, goods, or services. Third, consideration, like other formalities, results in a *channeling* function. If the parties know what elements are required to bind them to a deal, they will know how to structure a transaction (*i.e.*, channel it) so as to make it enforceable.

That said, any time that a formality is imposed in order to justify enforcement, some transactions will be "left out" by the requirement. In the last section, we saw that the law traditionally views promises of charitable gifts as lacking in consideration. The same is true of many other promises to make a gift, especially those that involve familial promises. Without some element of exchange, these promises to make a gift are often considered unenforceable as contracts for lack of consideration. (The law of wills differs from the law of contracts; bequests are enforceable without regard to consideration but must meet other tests for validity, including specified formalities such as writings, witnesses, and signatures).

Some promises are typically seen as "social promises"—perhaps it is dishonorable not to carry through with them, but they are not enforceable in a court of law. So-called "gentlemen's agreements" are often bandied about, but would not be enforceable. Likewise, some promises seem like they should be enforceable based on notions of morality, but they technically lack the element of exchange required to make that promise binding. In the next section, we explore these tensions. Keep in mind that in saying whether consideration exists (or not), the common law judges had to engage in justice in a particular case, but also police the boundaries of what it meant to have a contract for all cases.

HAMER V. SIDWAY
27 N.E. 256 (N.Y. 1891)

PARKER, J.

The question which provoked the most discussion by counsel on this appeal, and which lies at the foundation of plaintiff's asserted right of recovery, is whether by virtue of a contract defendant's testator William E. Story became indebted to his nephew William E. Story, 2d, on his twenty-first birthday in the sum of five thousand dollars. The trial court found as a fact that 'on the 20th day of March, 1869, * * * William E. Story agreed to and with William E. Story, 2d, that if he would refrain from drinking liquor, using tobacco, swearing, and playing cards or billiards for money until he should become 21 years of age then he, the said William E. Story, would at that time pay him, the said William E. Story, 2d, the sum of $5,000 for such refraining, to which the said William E. Story, 2d, agreed,' and that he 'in all things fully performed his part of said agreement.'

The defendant contends that the contract was without consideration to support it, and, therefore, invalid. He asserts that the promisee by refraining from the use of liquor and tobacco was not harmed but benefited; that that which he did was best for him to do independently of his uncle's promise, and insists that it follows that unless the promisor was benefited, the contract was without consideration. A contention, which if well founded, would seem to leave open for controversy in many cases whether that which the promisee did or omitted to do was, in fact, of such benefit to him as to leave no consideration to support the enforcement of the promisor's agreement. Such a rule could not be tolerated, and is without foundation in the law.

The Exchequer Chamber, in 1875, defined consideration as follows: "A valuable consideration in the sense of the law may consist either in some right, interest, profit or benefit accruing to the one party, or some forbearance, detriment, loss or responsibility given, suffered or undertaken by the other." Courts "will not ask whether the thing which forms the consideration does in fact benefit the promisee or a third party, or is of any substantial value to anyone. It is enough that something is promised, done, forborne or suffered by the party to whom the promise is made as consideration for the promise made to him." (Anson's Prin. of Con. 63.) "In general a waiver of any legal right at the request of another party is a sufficient consideration for a promise." (Parsons on Contracts, 444.) "Any damage, or suspension, or forbearance of a right will be sufficient to sustain a promise." (Kent, vol. 2, 465, 12th ed.)

Pollock, in his work on contracts, page 166, after citing the definition given by the Exchequer Chamber already quoted, says: "The second branch of this judicial description is really the most important one. Consideration means not so much that one party is profiting as that the other abandons some legal right in the present or limits his legal freedom of action in the future as an inducement for the promise of the first."

Now, applying this rule to the facts before us, the promisee used tobacco, occasionally drank liquor, and he had a legal right to do so. That right he abandoned for a period of years upon the strength of the promise of the testator that for such forbearance he would give him $5,000. We need not speculate on the effort which may have been required to give up the use of those stimulants. It is sufficient that he restricted his lawful freedom of action within certain prescribed limits upon the faith of his uncle's agreement, and now having fully performed the conditions imposed, it is of no moment whether such performance actually proved a benefit to the promisor, and the court will not inquire into it, but were it a proper subject of inquiry, we see nothing in this record that would permit a determination that the uncle was not benefited in a legal sense. Few cases have been found which may be said to be precisely in point, but such as have been support the position we have taken.

In *Shadwell v. Shadwell* (9 C. B. [N. S.] 159), an uncle wrote to his nephew as follows:

> MY DEAR LANCEY—I am so glad to hear of your intended marriage with Ellen Nicholl, and as I promised to assist you at starting, I am happy to tell you that I will pay to you 150 pounds yearly during my life and until your annual income derived from your profession of a chancery barrister shall amount to 600 guineas, of which your own admission will be the only evidence that I shall require.
>
> YOUR AFFECTIONATE UNCLE,
> CHARLES SHADWELL

It was held that the promise was binding and made upon good consideration.

In *Lakota v. Newton,* an unreported case in the Superior Court of Worcester, Mass., the complaint averred defendant's promise that "if you (meaning plaintiff) will leave off drinking for a year I will give you $100," plaintiff's assent thereto, performance of the condition by him, and demanded judgment therefor. Defendant demurred on the ground, among others, that the plaintiff's declaration did not allege a valid and sufficient consideration for the agreement of the defendant. The demurrer was overruled. . . .

The cases cited by the defendant on this question are not in point. . . . In *Beaumont v. Reeve* (Shirley's L. C. 6), and *Porterfield v. Butler* (47 Miss. 165), the question was whether a moral obligation furnishes sufficient consideration to uphold a subsequent express promise. In *Duvoll v. Wilson* (9 Barb. 487), and *In re Wilber v. Warren* (104 N. Y. 192), the proposition involved was whether an executory covenant against incumbrances in a deed given in consideration of natural love and affection could be enforced.

In *Vanderbilt v. Schreyer* (91 N. Y. 392), the plaintiff contracted with defendant to build a house, agreeing to accept in part payment therefor a specific bond and mortgage. Afterwards he refused to finish his contract unless the defendant would guarantee its payment, which was done. It was held that the guarantee could not be enforced for want of consideration. For in building the house the plaintiff only did that which he had contracted to do.

And in *Robinson v. Jewett* (116 N. Y. 40), the court simply held that 'The performance of an act which the party is under a legal obligation to perform cannot constitute a consideration for a new contract.'

In further consideration of the questions presented, then, it must be deemed established for the purposes of this appeal, that on the 31st day of January, 1875, defendant's testator was indebted to William E. Story, 2d, in the sum of $5,000, and if this action were founded on that contract it would be barred by the Statute of Limitations which has been pleaded, but on that date the nephew wrote to his uncle as follows:

DEAR UNCLE,

I am now 21 years old to-day, and I am now my own boss, and I believe, according to agreement, that there is due me $5,000. I have lived up to the contract to the letter in every sense of the word.

A few days later, and on February sixth, the uncle replied, and, so far as it is material to this controversy, the reply is as follows: . . .

DEAR NEPHEW,

Your letter of the 31st ult. came to hand all right, saying that you had lived up to the promise made to me several years ago. I have no doubt but you have, for which you shall have five thousand dollars as I promised you. I had the money in the bank the day you was 21 years old that I intend for you, and you shall have the money certain. Now, Willie I do not intend to interfere with this money in any way till I think you are capable of taking care of it and the sooner that time comes the better it will please me. I would hate very much to have you start out in some adventure that you thought all right and lose this money in one year.

The first five thousand dollars that I got together cost me a heap of hard work. You would hardly believe me when I tell you that to obtain this I shoved a jackplane many a day, butchered three or four years, then came to this city, and after three months' perseverance I obtained a situation in a grocery store. I opened this store early, closed late, slept in the fourth story of the building in a room 30 by 40 feet and not a human being in the building but myself. All this I done to live as cheap as I could to save something.

I don't want you to take up with this kind of fare. I was here in the cholera season '49 and '52 and the deaths averaged 80 to 125 daily and plenty of small-pox. I wanted to go home, but Mr. Fisk, the gentleman I was working for, told me if I left then, after it got healthy he probably would not want me. I stayed. All the money I have saved I know just how I got it. It did not come to me in any mysterious way, and the reason I speak of this is that money got in this way stops longer with a fellow that gets it with hard knocks than it does when he finds it.

Willie, you are 21 and you have many a thing to learn yet. This money you have earned much easier than I did besides acquiring good habits at the same time and you are quite welcome to the money; hope you will make good use of it. I was ten long years getting this together after I was your age. Now, hoping this will be satisfactory, I stop. One thing more. Twenty-one years ago I bought you 15 sheep. These sheep were put out to double every four years. I kept track of them the first eight years; I have not heard much about them since.

Your father and grandfather promised me that they would look after them till you were of age. Have they done so? I hope they have. By this time you have between five and six hundred sheep, worth a nice little income this spring. Willie, I have said much more than I expected to; hope you can make out what I have written. To-day is the seventeenth day that I have not been out of my room, and have had the doctor as many days. Am a little better to-day; think I will get out next week. You need not mention to father, as he always worries about small matters.

TRULY YOURS,
W. E. STORY.

P. S.—You can consider this money on interest.

. . . We must now consider the effect of the letter, and the nephew's assent thereto. . . . It is essential that the letter interpreted in the light of surrounding circumstances must show an intention on the part of the uncle to become a trustee before he will be held to have become such; but in an effort to ascertain the construction which should be given to it, we are also to observe the rule that the language of the promisor is to be interpreted in the sense in which he had reason to suppose it was understood by the promisee. (*White v. Hoyt,* 73 N. Y. 505, 511.)

At the time the uncle wrote the letter he was indebted to his nephew in the sum of $5,000, and payment had been requested. The uncle recognizing the indebtedness, wrote the nephew that he would keep the money until he deemed him capable of taking care of it. He did not say "I will pay you at some other time," or use language that would indicate that the relation of debtor and creditor would continue. On the contrary, his language indicated that he had set apart the money the nephew had "earned" for him so that when he should be capable of taking care of it he should receive it with interest. He said: "I had the money in the bank the day you were 21 years old that I intended for you and you shall have the money certain."

That he had set apart the money is further evidenced by the next sentence: "Now, Willie, I don't intend to interfere with this money in any way until I think you are capable of taking care of it." Certainly, the uncle must have intended that his nephew should understand that the promise not "to interfere with this money" referred to the money in the bank which he declared was not only there when the nephew became 21 years old, but was intended for him.

True, he did not use the word "trust," or state that the money was deposited in the name of William E. Story, 2d, or in his own name in trust for him, but the language used must have been intended to assure the nephew that his money had been set apart for him, to be kept without interference until he should be capable of taking care of it, for the uncle said in substance and in effect: "This money you have earned much easier than I did * * * you are quite welcome to. I had it in the bank the day you were 21 years old and don't intend to interfere with it in any way until I think you are capable of taking care of it and the sooner that time comes the better it will please me." In this declaration there is not lacking a single element necessary for the creation of a valid trust, and to that declaration the nephew assented. . . .

NOTES AND QUESTIONS

1.   How does the court in *Hamer v. Sidway* define "consideration"? What conceptual problems does the court grapple with when trying to use the definition?

2.   In what ways does the "deal" in *Hamer* look like a bargain? A promise with a condition attached to it? A bet or a wager? A gift between family members? Which of these types of promises should the legal system enforce?

3.   Classify the cases the estate cited that the court says are "not in point." Two involve love or moral obligation (pursued further in the next case, *Mills v. Wyman*) and two involve pre-existing duty—the purported consideration was a promise to do something the promisor was already duty-bound to do.

4.   *Hamer v. Sidway* is a classic in contracts textbooks not only because of its definition of "consideration," but because of its human drama. Note differences in background and attitude between the elder and younger William. The elder William worked long hours for his money, risking health to scrimp and gather the fortune he eventually made. For more on the background, see Douglas Baird, *Reconstructing Contracts: Hamer v. Sidway*, CONTRACTS STORIES (2007).

5.   Today, many celebrities, actors, pageant contestants and others in the entertainment industry have so-called "morals clauses" in their contracts, which attempt to constrain their behavior in order to avoid scandals. Others have inserted "morals clauses" into prenuptial agreements. Doing a quick Internet search, can you find any examples of such clauses?

6.   Imagine a website that would help you plan and stick to your goals, based on binding promises ("I promise to lose 5 pounds," "I promise to increase my daily exercise"). The problem is that many people make such promises routinely, only to break them because there is no enforcement mechanism; no way to make the promise to yourself binding.

Professors Ian Ayres and Dean Karlan set out to change that with their website, www.stickK.com. The website works by allowing users to input their goals as well as their credit card information. Periodically, users must report whether they are meeting their goals; they can also set up third parties to verify their compliance. If users fail to meet their goals, the website charges a pre-set amount and donates it to a person or charity of the users' choice.

Meanwhile other website users create a community and support system for achieving goals. Rather than forfeit the money, many people choose to honor their commitments and carry through with their goals. The second "K" in the name "stickK" refers to the contract that you are making by involving the website. How and why is this form of commitment likely to be more successful than "going it alone"? What does this tell us about the power of the notion of consideration and contractual obligation?

MILLS V. WYMAN
3 Pick. 207 (Mass. 1825)

The general position, that a moral obligation is a sufficient consideration for an express promise, is to be limited in its application, to cases where a good or valuable consideration has once existed. Thus, where a son, who was of full age and had ceased to be a member of his father's family, was suddenly taken sick among strangers, and, being poor and in distress, was relieved by the plaintiff, and afterwards the father wrote to the plaintiff promising to pay him the expenses incurred, it was *held,* that such promise would not sustain an action.

[This action was] brought to recover a compensation for the board, nursing, &c., of Levi Wyman, son of the defendant, from the 5th to the 20th of February, 1821. The plaintiff then lived at Hartford, in Connecticut; the defendant, at Shrewsbury, in this county. Levi Wyman, at the time when the services were rendered, was about 25 years of age, and had long ceased to be a member of his father's family. He was on his return from a voyage at sea, and being suddenly taken sick at Hartford, and being poor and in distress, was relieved by the plaintiff in the manner and to the extent above stated.

On the 24th of February, after all the expenses had been incurred, the defendant wrote a letter to the plaintiff, promising to pay him such expenses. There was no consideration for this promise, except what grew out of the relation which subsisted between Levi Wyman and the defendant, and *Howe* J., before whom the cause was tried in the Court of Common Pleas, thinking this not sufficient to support the action, directed a nonsuit. To this direction the plaintiff filed exceptions.

PARKER, C.J.

General rules of law established for the protection and security of honest and fair-minded men, who may inconsiderately make promises without any equivalent, will sometimes screen men of a different character from engagements which they are bound in *foro conscientiæ* to perform. This is a defect inherent in all human systems of legislation. The rule that a mere verbal promise, without any consideration, cannot be enforced by action, is universal in its application, and cannot be departed from to suit particular cases in which a refusal to perform such a promise may be disgraceful.

The promise declared on in this case appears to have been made without any legal consideration. The kindness and services towards the sick son of the defendant were not bestowed at his request. The son was in no respect under the care of the defendant. He was twenty-five years old, and had long left his father's family. On his return from a foreign country, he fell sick among strangers, and the plaintiff acted the part of the good Samaritan, giving him shelter and comfort until he died. The defendant, his father, on being informed of this event, influenced by a transient feeling of gratitude, promises in writing to pay the plaintiff for the expenses he had incurred. But he has determined to break this promise, and is willing to have his case appear on record as a strong example of particular injustice sometimes necessarily resulting from the operation of general rules.

It is said a moral obligation is a sufficient consideration to support an express promise; and some authorities lay down the rule thus broadly; but upon examination of the cases we are satisfied that the universality of the rule cannot be supported, and that there must have been some preëxisting obligation, which has become inoperative by positive law, to form a basis for an effective promise. The cases of debts barred by the statute of limitations, of debts incurred by infants, of debts of bankrupts, are generally put for illustration of the rule. Express promises founded on such preëxisting equitable obligations may be enforced; there is a good consideration for them; they merely remove an impediment created by law to the recovery of debts honestly due, but which public policy protects the debtors from being compelled to pay.

In all these cases there was originally a *quid pro quo;* and according to the principles of natural justice the party receiving ought to pay; but the legislature has said he shall not be coerced; then comes the promise to pay the debt that is barred, the promise of the man to pay the debt of the infant, of the discharged bankrupt to restore to his creditor what by the law he had lost.

In all these cases there is a moral obligation founded upon an antecedent valuable consideration. These promises therefore have a sound legal basis. They are not promises to pay something for nothing; not naked pacts; but the voluntary revival or creation of obligation which before existed in natural law, but which had been dispensed with, not for the benefit of the party obliged solely, but principally for the public convenience.

If moral obligation, in its fullest sense, is a good substratum for an express promise, it is not easy to perceive why it is not equally good to support an implied promise. What a man ought to do, generally he ought to be made to do, whether he promise or refuse. But the law of society has left most of such obligations to the *interior* forum, as the tribunal of conscience has been aptly called. Is there not a moral obligation upon every son who has become affluent by means of the education and advantages bestowed upon him by his father, to relieve that father from pecuniary embarrassment, to promote his comfort and happiness, and even to share with him his riches, if thereby he will be made happy?

And yet such a son may, with impunity, leave such a father in any degree of penury above that which will expose the community in which he dwells, to the danger of being obliged to preserve him from absolute want. Is not a wealthy father under strong moral obligation to advance the interest of an obedient, well disposed son, to furnish him with the means of acquiring and maintaining a becoming rank in life, to rescue him from the horrors of debt incurred by misfortune? Yet the law will uphold him in any degree of parsimony, short of that which would reduce his son to the necessity of seeking public charity.

Without doubt there are great interests of society which justify withholding the coercive arm of the law from these duties of imperfect obligation, as they are called; imperfect, not because they are less binding upon the conscience than those which are called perfect, but because the wisdom of the social law does not impose sanctions upon them.

A deliberate promise, in writing, made freely and without any mistake, one which may lead the party to whom it is made into contracts and expenses, cannot be broken without a violation of moral duty. But if there was nothing paid or promised for it, the law, perhaps wisely, leaves the execution of it to the conscience of him who makes it. It is only when the party making the promise gains something, or he to whom it is made loses something, that the law gives the promise validity. And in the case of the promise of the adult to pay the debt of the infant, of the debtor discharged by the statute of limitations or bankruptcy, the principle is preserved by looking back to the origin of the transaction, where an equivalent is to be found. An exact equivalent is not required by the law; for there being a consideration, the parties are left to estimate its value: though here the courts of equity will step in to relieve from gross inadequacy between the consideration and the promise.

These principles are deduced from the general current of decided cases upon the subject, as well as from the known maxims of the common law. The general position, that moral obligation is a sufficient consideration for an express promise, is to be limited in its application, to cases where at some time or other a good or valuable consideration has existed.

A legal obligation is always a sufficient consideration to support either an express or an implied promise; such as an infant's debt for necessaries, or a father's promise to pay for the support and education of his minor children. But when the child shall have attained to manhood, and shall have become his own agent in the world's business, the debts he incurs, whatever may be their nature, create no obligation upon the father; and it seems to follow, that his promise founded upon such a debt has no legally binding force. . . .

Instead of citing a multiplicity of cases to support the positions I have taken, I will only refer to a very able review of all the cases in the note in 3 Bos. & Pul. 249. The opinions of the judges had been variant for a long course of years upon this subject, but there seems to be no case in which it was nakedly decided, that a promise to pay the debt of a son of full age, not living with his father, though the debt were incurred by sickness which ended in the death of the son, without a previous request by the father proved or presumed, could be enforced by action.

It has been attempted to show a legal obligation on the part of the defendant by virtue of our statute, which compels lineal kindred in the ascending or descending line to support such of their poor relations as are likely to become chargeable to the town where they have their settlement. But it is a sufficient answer to this position, that such legal obligation does not exist except in the very cases provided for in the statute, and never until the party charged has been adjudged to be of sufficient ability thereto. We do not know from the report any of the facts which are necessary to create such an obligation. Whether the deceased had a legal settlement in this commonwealth at the time of his death, whether he was likely to become chargeable had he lived, whether the defendant was of sufficient ability, are essential facts to be adjudicated by the court to which is given jurisdiction on this subject. The legal liability does not arise until these facts have all been ascertained by judgment, after hearing the party intended to be charged.

For the foregoing reasons we are all of opinion that the nonsuit directed by the Court of Common Pleas was right, and that judgment be entered thereon for costs for the defendant.

NOTES AND QUESTIONS

1.   Suppose that the Good Samaritan had taken in and cured the defendant's sick bull or cattle, and the defendant then promised to pay. Would the analysis differ? Isn't a child's health equally or more important than that of a farm animal? Is there something different about ownership versus autonomy?

2.   Does the judge writing the opinion seem to believe in it whole-heartedly? If not, then why does the court hold this way? Others have said the case illustrates a problem, formulated by Justice Oliver Wendell Holmes, that "hard cases make bad law." What do you think this phrase means? *See Northern Securities Co. v. United States*, 193 U.S. 197, 400 (1904) (Holmes, J., dissenting).

3.   Professor Geoffrey Watson researched the background of *Mills v. Wyman* and determined that events unfolded differently than reported in the case. There can be differences between how "facts" are reported or perceived by a court, and what happened in the real world in fact, due to a variety of factors ranging from the rules of evidence and the law of procedure to the practice of description and the passage of time. On the law in the case, Prof. Watson argued for evaluating the enforceability of promises not by the test of consideration but based on intention and formalities. Geoffrey R. Watson, *In the Tribunal of Conscience: Mills v. Wyman Reconsidered*, 71 TUL. L. REV. 1749 (1997).

4.   Cases such as *Mills* and the precedents it discusses can be described as posing the problem of the "trailing promise." The bargain theory of consideration applies easily to evaluate concurrent promises (buyer promises to pay cash and seller promises to deliver goods) or promises followed by performance (offeror promises to pay cash if offeree renders services). Application is more complicated when performance precedes the promise. There will be more to say about the problem of trailing promises in a Chapter Six, exploring the doctrine of restitution. There you will find a case, *Webb v. McGowan*, often usefully paired with *Mills v. Wyman*.

PROBLEMS: CONSIDERATION

In each of the problems below, is there consideration? The best answers will not be a mere "yes" or "no," but will explain the possible arguments on both sides.

1.   Bliss and Joanna met the first week of law school and rapidly became friends, since they both loved to run marathons and try out different restaurants. Since both of them were living far from home for the first time, the "besties" became each other's support network. When they realized that their birthdays were only one week apart (Bliss the first week of October, Joanna the second week), they promised each other that they would remember the dates, and would celebrate accordingly.

A.   Joanna sends Bliss a card with an adorable cat on the front who is holding a sign that says "Happy Birthday!" The card has a $20 gift certificate inside. Joanna expects a gift from Bliss a week later.

B.   Joanna promises Bliss that she will buy her a delicious chocolate cake and host a small party for her at Joanna's apartment. Bliss promises to invite some friends and eat the cake.

C.   Joanna promises Bliss that she will host a small party for her and purchase the refreshments for the party, including delicious chocolate cake. Bliss promises Joanna that in return she will give her a copy of her Contracts outline. *bargained-for exchange*

D.   Joanna promises to have a large party for Bliss, and she spends $500 on purchasing a catered dinner for 50 as well as outlays for drinks and a cleaning service. However, the day before, Bliss calls up Joanna and says "forget it." *reliance*

2.   Yesenia and Zachary were divorced ten years ago; together they have a daughter, Ximena, who has just turned nineteen. During the past ten years, both parents have shared joint custody and the financial obligations of supporting Ximena, and each has exactly followed the terms of the custody and support agreement that was filed with the court.

The entire time she was growing up, Yesenia has told Ximena about the value of education, and what a difference this will make in her life. Three years ago, when Ximena was struggling with one of her math classes, but still managed to pull off a good grade through hard work, Yesenia told her "I want you to get a good education, that is of paramount importance." Later that week as she was dropping her daughter off for time with her dad, Yesenia told Zachary "I promise to help with half of Ximena's educational costs; it is important for her to go to a good college."

Now that Ximena has graduated high school and has been accepted to the college of her choice, Zachary, who was very excited, told her that of course she should enroll and he would take care of everything. When the first tuition bill came due, he called up Yesenia and asked her for half of the tuition amount. Yesenia said, "Sorry. The support order says nothing about college expenses." Zachary told her, "I know you love your daughter, don't you want to help?" And Yesenia said, "I'm sorry, but this one's all on you." The cost of Ximena's education is $90,000 and she feels Yesenia should be held to her word. Does either Zachary or Ximena have a legal claim?

3.   Ace Garbage ran a small garbage collection business with a fleet of ten trucks. Best Garbage also ran a garbage business with ten trucks. One day, Ace lost a truck in an accident, and another was sidelined by engine trouble. Ace needed a truck badly and asked Best if it could "borrow" one for a day. Best said yes. Ace did use one of Best's trucks for a week and returned it when Ace no longer needed it. Six months later, Best needed a truck quickly when it suddenly acquired a new client. It asked Ace if it could borrow a truck for week while it looked for a new one to buy. Ace refused. Best is angry and wants to take Ace to court.

4.   DotCom, Inc. is an Internet company that raises money by attracting "eyeballs" to its home page. The more visitors ("hits") that come to the website, the more money that DotCom makes from the advertisements that they sell to their many corporate sponsors. In order to attract viewers, DotCom launches a new promotion. Every visitor to the website who signs up for their database

will receive "free" stock in the company. Signing up for the database consists of filling out a form that supplies DotCom with the user's name, address, and social security number. There is no fee. Every time repeat viewers visit the website, they earn more stock (customers are typically limited to one hit per day).

Section 5 of the Securities and Exchange Act of 1933 makes it illegal for any company not registered with the Securities and Exchange Commission to sell securities in interstate commerce. Dotcom, Inc. argues that it is exempt from registering with the SEC because they are not selling stocks; they are giving them away. What are the arguments? Who has the more convincing argument?

5.   Gorton is a hard-partying Wall Street trader from a wealthy family who has made repeated promises to Elisa, his girlfriend, that he will stop going to strip clubs and quit using cocaine. After one particularly nasty argument over his drug use, Elisa broke up with Gorton and kicked him out of their shared apartment. He then begged her to get back together, telling her repeatedly that he "would promise to be on his best behavior." Gorton told Elisa that if he visited a strip club or did drugs again, "he would give her a check for $100,000, so that she could make a new start without [him]." He even wrote out an e-mail to her, cc'd to a number of their mutual friends, saying the same thing. Elisa reluctantly accepted Gorton's apology and took him back. For one month, all was well, but then some of Gorton's buddies from work invited him out to a strip club. Upon stumbling home, he failed a drug test that Elisa administered to him. After she kicked him out of their apartment, he sent her a text message that admitted, "I didn't hold up my end of the bargain." Now Elisa would like to take Gorton to court for the $100,000. Who should prevail?

6.   Bella and Edward are two second-year law students. When Edward asked Bella to go to the Barrister's Ball, she happily agreed. However, the day before the event, she jilted Edward to go with Jacob, who spent $1000 on a corsage, dinner reservations, a limousine, and tuxedo rental. Two minutes into the Ball, however, Jacob tipped over the punch bowl and howled at the moon. Bella quickly realized that she had made a big mistake, so she jilted Jacob. Running back to Edward, she promised him that she would love him forever, and Edward, in turn, promised Bella that he would be hers until the stars fell from the sky. After graduation, Bella and Edward entered into a legal partnership specializing in human rights law, and Edward purchased Bella an expensive engagement ring. One year later, they mutually decided to call both the marriage and the business quits. What are the parties' legal obligations to each other, if any?

7.   Ronald Sump is a businessman who is running for president. So are candidates Fred Cruz and Bob Haysmitch. All three would like to be the official nominee for the Grand Old Party ("GOP"). While Cruz and Haysmitch are longtime GOP members and supporters, Sump is newer to the party. In an effort to attract support and win more votes from GOP voters, Sump makes it known that, even if he loses, he promises not to run as a third-party candidate.

some courts saying is conditional gift

He shakes hands with GOP officials and signs a "Pact of Loyalty" to the GOP. Moderates, however, like Haysmitch best and Haysmitch ends up with the highest vote totals. Faced with this loss, Sump is mulling a third-party run. Does his earlier promise legally foreclose this as an option?

8. Bob the Builder agrees with Henny Homeowner to construct an addition to an existing home in accordance with detailed plans Henny supplies in exchange for a fixed fee of $100,000. Midway through the job, without encountering any surprising conditions or challenges, Bob informs Henny that he will not complete the job unless Henny agrees to pay an additional $10,000. Henny agrees and Bob completes construction satisfactorily. What is the consideration, and what legal problems do you foresee? *preexisting duty*

9. Chad and Marc are trying to "make it big" as writers in New York City. They make what they call a "pact of perfect performance" that they will each write a blog post for a day, and if successful, at the end of the week they will go see a movie together on Friday night. If Marc completes his side of the performance by writing blog posts, but Chad does not, are there any binding legal obligations?

10. In the Lord of the Rings by J.R.R. Tolkien, a group of magical strangers convenes in an Elven City, where Elrond, as head of the Elven Council, asks the strangers if they will take up an ill-defined quest to return the "One Ring" of power to the Land of Mordor. Frodo the hobbit agrees to carry the ring, while Aragon declares that he will "pledge his sword," while Gimli the dwarf states that he will "pledge his axe." What exactly have these characters agreed to, and what is the consideration for the Council of Elrond?

The voluntary basis of contract is underscored by the further legal requisite of mutual assent. The presence or absence of assent may be ascertained in a variety of ways. The following selections from the Restatement (Second) of Contracts suggest the basic framework. Consult the case of *Lucy v. Zehmer* that appears in the Introduction, a classic case that suggests some of the salient issues. How might each of these concepts apply to that case?

RESTATEMENT (SECOND) OF CONTRACTS, SECTIONS 18, 21, 23

§ 18. *Manifestation of Mutual Assent*. Manifestation of mutual assent to an exchange requires that each party either make a promise or begin or render a performance.

§ 21. *Intention to be Legally Bound*. Neither real nor apparent intention that a promise be legally binding is essential to the formation of a contract, but a manifestation of intention that a promise shall not affect legal relations may prevent the formation of a contract.

§ 23. *Necessity that Manifestations Have Reference to Each Other.* It is essential to a bargain that each party manifest assent with reference to the manifestation of the other.

B. OFFER

Contracts are voluntary agreements freely undertaken. We have seen that the element of consideration is a necessary requirement for formation of a contract, along with mutual assent. The bargain and associated assent often follow a common pattern that contract law captures in the ideas of "offer" and "acceptance." As stated in Restatement (Second) of Contracts, Section 22, "The manifestation of mutual assent to an exchange ordinarily takes the form of an offer or proposal by one party followed by an acceptance by the other party or parties."

The steps of offer and acceptance exist so that each party can signal to each other, objectively, that they have a mutual intent to enter a contract. Offer and acceptance also provide a roadmap for the bargaining process. Following well-worn patterns, the conclusion of offer and acceptance bring some finality to the bargain.

An *offeror* makes the offer to the recipient, the *offeree*. In making the offer, the offeror is considered the "master of the offer," meaning having the power to dictate the terms. According to Restatement (Second) of Contracts, Section 29, the offeror determines to whom an offer is made, and only those to whom it is made may accept. So, hypothetically, if an offer is made and a random third-party overhears it and tries to accept, that acceptance would be ineffective. If the offeror states the offer can only be accepted in a certain way—such as by a signed writing or by the offeree standing on her head—following those instructions is the only way that an acceptance can be effective to form a contract.

According to Restatement (Second) of Contracts, Section 33, for an offer to be accepted, the terms of the contract should be reasonably certain. Reasonable certainty means that the terms "provide a basis for determining the existence of a breach and for giving an appropriate remedy." According to the Restatement (Second) of Contracts, Section 24, an offer is defined as "the manifestation of willingness to enter into a bargain, so made as to justify another person in understanding that his assent to that bargain is invited and will conclude it." Think of this as a "yes" test—will saying yes to an offer result in a completed bargain? Are there enough terms present to understand what the parties have agreed to and the basis of their deal?

Parties often spend quite a long time negotiating—they may be seeking information, haggling over the price, or they may be sending back and forth the written terms. In many large commercial transactions with drafts of different documents, the original offeror may then be turned into the offeree, and then back into the offeror again when another draft is sent. In large commercial deals, however, no one is necessarily keeping track of offers and counter-offers.

In any event, if the parties have not spelled out the terms of their intended bargain with reasonable certainty, it is implausible to believe that a court is competent to fill out those terms for them. In such circumstances, it may be fairer to conclude that the parties were engaged in discussions and ongoing negotiations rather than that one had made an offer whose acceptance could form a binding contract. That remains true even when the parties reached a preliminary agreement on some portion of the terms, or when agreeing to agree later on others. This situation is neatly illustrated by the next case, in which an enforceable contract contained a renewal term whose definiteness was contested.

JOSEPH MARTIN, JR. DELICATESSEN V. SCHUMACHER
417 N.E. 2d 541 (N.Y. 1981)

FUCHSBERG, J.

. . . In 1973, the appellant, as landlord, leased a retail store to the respondent for a five-year term at a rent graduated upwards from $500 per month for the first year to $650 for the fifth. The renewal clause stated that "(t)he Tenant may renew this lease for an additional period of five years at annual rentals to be agreed upon; Tenant shall give Landlord thirty (30) days written notice, to be mailed certified mail, return receipt requested, of the intention to exercise such right." It is not disputed that the tenant gave timely notice of its desire to renew or that, once the landlord made it clear that he would do so only at a rental starting at $900 a month, the tenant engaged an appraiser who opined that a fair market rental value would be $545.41.

The tenant thereupon commenced an action for specific performance in Supreme Court, Suffolk County, to compel the landlord to extend the lease for the additional term at the appraiser's figure or such other sum as the court would decide was reasonable. For his part, the landlord in due course brought a holdover proceeding in the local District Court to evict the tenant. On the landlord's motion for summary judgment, the Supreme Court, holding that a bald agreement to agree on a future rental was unenforceable for uncertainty as a matter of law, dismissed the tenant's complaint. . . .

It was on appeal by the tenant from these orders that the Appellate Division, expressly overruling an established line of cases in the process, reinstated the tenant's complaint and granted consolidation. In so doing, it reasoned that "a renewal clause in a lease providing for future agreement on the rent to be paid during the renewal term is enforceable if it is established that the parties' intent was not to terminate in the event of a failure to agree." It went on to provide that, if the tenant met that burden, the trial court could proceed to set a "reasonable rent." . . .

We begin our analysis with the basic observation that, unless otherwise mandated by law (e. g., residential emergency rent control statutes), a contract is a private "ordering" in which a party binds himself to do, or not to do, a particular thing (Fletcher v. Peck, 6 Cranch (10 U.S.) 87, 136; 3 L.Ed. 162. Hart and Sachs, Legal Process, 147–148 (1958)). This liberty is no right at all if it is not accompanied by freedom not to contract. The corollary is that, before one may secure redress in our courts because another has failed to honor a promise, it must appear that the promisee assented to the obligation in question.

It also follows that, before the power of law can be invoked to enforce a promise, it must be sufficiently certain and specific so that what was promised can be ascertained. Otherwise, a court, in intervening, would be imposing its own conception of what the parties should or might have undertaken, rather than confining itself to the implementation of a bargain to which they have mutually committed themselves. Thus, definiteness as to material matters is of the very essence in contract law. Impenetrable vagueness and uncertainty will not do (1 Corbin, Contracts, § 95, p. 394; 6 Encyclopedia of New York Law, Contracts, § 301; Restatement, Contracts 2d, § 32, Comment a).

Dictated by these principles, it is rightfully well settled in the common law of contracts in this State that a mere agreement to agree, in which a material term is left for future negotiations, is unenforceable (Willmott v. Giarraputo, 5 N.Y.2d 250, 253, 184 N.Y.S.2d 97, 157 N.E.2d 282; Sourwine v. Truscott, 17 Hun. 432, 434). This is especially true of the amount to be paid for the sale or lease of real property (see Forma v. Moran, 273 App. Div. 818, 76 N.Y. S.2d 232; Huber v. Ruby, 187 Misc. 967, 969, 65 N.Y.S.2d 462, app. dsmd 271 App. Div. 927, 67 N.Y.S.2d 710).

This is not to say that the requirement for definiteness in the case before us now could only have been met by explicit expression of the rent to be paid. The concern is with substance, not form. It certainly would have sufficed, for instance, if a methodology for determining the rent was to be found within the four corners of the lease, for a rent so arrived at would have been the end product of agreement between the parties themselves. Nor would the agreement have failed for indefiniteness because it invited recourse to an objective extrinsic event, condition or standard on which the amount was made to depend. All of these, inter alia, would have come within the embrace of the maxim that what can be made certain is certain . . . .

But the renewal clause here in fact contains no such ingredients. Its unrevealing, unamplified language speaks to no more than "annual rentals to be agreed upon." Its simple words leave no room for legal construction or resolution of ambiguity. Neither tenant nor landlord is bound to any formula. There is not so much as a hint at a commitment to be bound by the "fair market rental value" which the tenant's expert reported or the "reasonable rent" the Appellate Division would impose, much less any definition of either. Nowhere is there an inkling that either of the parties directly or indirectly assented, upon accepting the clause, to subordinate the figure on which it ultimately would insist, to one fixed judicially, as the Appellate Division decreed be done, or, for that matter, by an arbitrator or other third party. . . .

NOTES AND QUESTIONS

1.   A grand slogan of the common law announces that "courts do not make contracts, parties do."

2.   After stating that the omission of a material term renders an agreement to agree unenforceable, the court says this is "especially true of the amount to be paid for the sale or lease of real property." What is special about real property? How does real property differ from goods, especially commodities such as aluminum, soybeans, or steel? As we will see in Section D of this chapter, the Uniform Commercial Code takes a more nuanced approach to an open price term. It permits parties, if they so intend, to form a binding contract for the sale of goods though the price is not settled. *See* UCC § 2–305.

RESTATEMENT (SECOND) OF CONTRACTS, SECTION 33

§ 33.   *Certainty.*

(1) Even though a manifestation of intention is intended to be understood as an offer, it cannot be accepted so as to form a contract unless the terms of the contract are reasonably certain.

(2) The terms of a contract are reasonably certain if they provide a basis for determining the existence of a breach and for giving an appropriate remedy.

(3) The fact that one or more terms of a proposed bargain are left open or uncertain may show that a manifestation of intention is not intended to be understood as an offer or as an acceptance.

EXAMPLE: HOOPS COACH JIMMY WILLIAMS

The newspaper *The Minnesota Daily* detailed a $1 million jury award in favor of the plaintiff, Jimmy Williams, an assistant basketball coach:

> Jimmy Williams, a former Oklahoma State assistant coach, alleged that Minnesota men's basketball head coach Tubby Smith promised him a job in 2007. Williams testified that, when Smith was filling his coaching staff in 2007, Smith offered Williams an assistant

coaching job with a salary and benefits package of $200,000 per year. Williams quit his job at Oklahoma State and put his house up for sale.

Williams was an assistant coach with the Gophers from 1971–86 and, according to court documents, Smith knew he could help him recruit in the Midwest after coaching in the South for most of his career. Williams faxed his resume to Smith on April 2, 2007, and after a discussion about Williams coming to Minnesota that evening, Smith indicated that he could offer a $175,000 salary plus $25,000 for running Smith's basketball camp, according to deposition transcripts.

Ninety minutes after Smith allegedly offered Williams a job, Williams called then-head coach Sean Sutton and resigned as assistant coach for Oklahoma State, Williams testified. The next morning, Smith told Williams that [athletic director Joel] Maturi would have to approve the hiring but didn't anticipate any problems, according to Williams' testimony.

"He certainly did. He offered me the job. I remember it as clearly as I am sitting here today," Williams testified, according to the Pioneer Press. "There is absolutely no doubt he said that. Anyone who says anything differently is lying."

Smith testified that he never told Williams to quit his job.

NCAA reports showed that Williams had been cited for recruiting violations in 1976 and 1988 for providing financial aid, airline tickets, clothing and meals to prospective players. Williams was barred from recruiting for two years and the men's basketball program was put on two years' probation.

When Maturi learned of the violations, he called Smith and let him know hiring Williams was out of the question, citing in his testimony the history of violations the basketball program has endured in recent decades.

"The University respects the jury process, but respectfully disagrees that Joel Maturi or Tubby Smith did anything wrong," University of Minnesota General Counsel Mark Rotenberg said in a release. "Refusing to hire Jimmy Williams was the right call, and the University stands behind these officials."

Assume that you represent the University of Minnesota in the process of an appeal. What are the strongest argument(s) that you could bring in the University's favor? For more on the news story, see http://www.mndaily.com/2010/05/26/jury-rules-favor-williams-awards-1247-million.

———————

As we have seen from the materials so far, it is sometimes difficult to discern whether the parties have entered into a bargain. Large businesses sometimes have these problems too, where executives may engage in negotiations and then sit down later with attorneys to memorialize the terms of the transaction in a written document. Consider the following two cases, and think about how much certainty should be required before binding a company to a project. What reference points should be used in this determination, such as the expectations of parties generally or those involved in the case, standard business practice or those of such parties, and more general principles such as efficiency or fairness?

EMPRO MANUFACTURING CO. V. BALL-CO MANUFACTURING, INC.

870 F.2d 423 (7th Cir. 1989)

EASTERBROOK, J.

We have a pattern common in commercial life. Two firms reach concord on the general terms of their transaction. They sign a document, captioned "agreement in principle" or "letter of intent", memorializing these terms but anticipating further negotiations and decisions—an appraisal of the assets, the clearing of a title, the list is endless. One of these terms proves divisive, and the deal collapses. The party that perceives itself the loser then claims that the preliminary document has legal force independent of the definitive contract. Ours is such a dispute.

Ball-Co Manufacturing, a maker of specialty valve components, floated its assets on the market. Empro Manufacturing showed interest. After some preliminary negotiations, Empro sent Ball-Co a three-page "letter of intent" to purchase the assets of Ball-Co and S.B. Leasing, a partnership holding title to the land under Ball-Co's plant. Empro proposed a price of $2.4 million, with $650,000 to be paid on closing and a 10-year promissory note for the remainder, the note to be secured by the "inventory and equipment of Ballco." The letter stated "[t]he general terms and conditions of such proposal (which will be subject to and incorporated in a formal, definitive Asset Purchase Agreement signed by both parties)." Just in case Ball-Co might suppose that Empro had committed itself to buy the assets, paragraph four of the letter stated that "Empro's purchase shall be subject to the satisfaction of certain conditions precedent to closing including, but not limited to" the definitive Asset Purchase Agreement and, among five other conditions, "[t]he approval of the shareholders and board of directors of Empro."

Although Empro left itself escape hatches, as things turned out Ball-Co was the one who balked. The parties signed the letter of intent in November 1987 and negotiated through March 1988 about many terms. Security for the note proved to be the sticking point. Ball-Co wanted a security interest in the land under the plant; Empro refused to yield.

When Empro learned that Ball-Co was negotiating with someone else, it filed this . . . suit. Contending that the letter of intent obliges Ball-Co to sell only to it, Empro [argues] that the binding effect of a document depends on the parties' intent, which means that the case may not be dismissed—for Empro says that the parties intended to be bound, a factual issue. Empro treats "intent to be bound" as a matter of the parties' states of mind, but if intent were wholly subjective . . . no contract case could be decided without a jury trial, and no one could know the effect of a commercial transaction until years after the documents were inked. That would be a devastating blow to business. Contract law gives effect to the parties' wishes, but they must express these openly. Put differently, "intent" in contract law is objective rather than subjective . . .

Because letters of intent are written without the care that will be lavished on the definitive agreement, it may be a bit much to put dispositive weight on "subject to" in every case, and we do not read [*Interway, Inc. v. Alagna*, 407 N.E.2d 615 (1st Dist. Ill. 1980)], as giving these the status of magic words. They might have been used carelessly, and if the full agreement showed that the formal contract was to be nothing but a memorial of an agreement already reached, the letter of intent would be enforceable. *Borg-Warner Corp. v. Anchor Coupling Co.*, 16 Ill.2d 234, 156 N.E.2d 513 (1958). Conversely, Empro cannot claim comfort from the fact that the letter of intent does not contain a flat disclaimer, such as the one in [*Feldman v. Allegheny International, Inc.*, 850 F.2d 1217 (7th Cir. 1988) (Illinois law)] pronouncing that the letter creates no obligations at all. The text and structure of the letter—the objective manifestations of intent—might show that the parties agreed to bind themselves to some extent immediately. *Borg-Warner* is such a case. One party issued an option, which called itself "firm and binding"; the other party accepted; the court found this a binding contract even though some terms remained open. After all, an option to purchase is nothing if not binding in advance of the definitive contract. The parties to *Borg-Warner* conceded that the option and acceptance usually would bind; the only argument in the case concerned whether the open terms were so important that a contract could not arise even if the parties wished to be bound, a subject that divided the court. See 156 N.E.2d at 930–36 (Schaefer, J., dissenting).

A canvass of the terms of the letter Empro sent does not assist it, however. "Subject to" a definitive agreement appears twice. The letter also recites, twice, that it contains the "general terms and conditions", implying that each side retained the right to make (and stand on) additional demands. Empro insulated itself from binding effect by listing, among the conditions to which the deal was "subject", the "approval of the shareholders and board of directors of Empro." The board could veto a deal negotiated by the firm's agents for a reason such as the belief that Ball-Co had been offered too much (otherwise the officers, not the board, would be the firm's final decisionmakers, yet state law vests major decisions in the board). The shareholders could decline to give their assent for any reason (such as distrust of new business ventures) and could not even be required to look at the documents, let alone consider the merits of the deal. Empro even took care to require the return of its $5,000 in earnest money "without set off, in the event this transaction is not closed", although the seller usually gets to keep the earnest money if the buyer changes its mind. So Empro made clear that it was free to walk.

Neither the text nor the structure of the letter suggests that it was to be a one-sided commitment, an option in Empro's favor binding only Ball-Co. From the beginning Ball-Co assumed that it could negotiate terms in addition to, or different from, those in the letter of intent. The cover letter from Ball-Co's lawyer returning the signed letter of intent to Empro stated that the "terms and conditions are generally acceptable" but that "some clarifications are needed in Paragraph 3(c) (last sentence)", the provision concerning Ball-Co's security interest. "Some clarifications are needed" is an ominous noise in a negotiation, foreboding many a stalemate. Although we do not know what "clarifications" counsel had in mind, the specifics are not important. It is enough that even on signing the letter of intent Ball-Co proposed to change the bargain, conduct consistent with the purport of the letter's text and structure. . . .

PFT ROBERSON, INC. V. VOLVO TRUCKS N.A., INC.

420 F.3d 728 (7th Cir. 2005)

EASTERBROOK, J.

PFT Roberson operates a fleet of more than 1,200 long-haul trucks and trailers. Freightliner supplies, maintains, and repairs Roberson's vehicles under a fleet agreement. A "fleet agreement" is a comprehensive contract (or series of contracts) specifying the number of trucks, the price of each, how much maintenance costs per mile (a fee that increases as a truck ages and becomes more subject to breakdowns), trade-in and other repurchase details when trucks reach the end of their useful lives, and provisions for winding up the arrangement (the "exit clause"). Exit may be complex, for it can entail early and large-scale replacements, repurchases, or swaps of used trucks, as well as disputes about cause and penalties.

Late in 2001 Freightliner sent Roberson a termination notice, which activated the exit clause. Litigation erupted when the parties could not agree on how it worked; meanwhile Roberson went shopping for another supplier and approached Volvo. The parties discussed a multi-year, $84 million arrangement for the purchase and maintenance of new Volvo trucks plus the trade-in or repair of used Freightliner trucks and trailers that Freightliner did not repurchase. Lengthy drafts were exchanged from

November 2001 until late January 2002. Many "Master Agreements" were drafted; none was signed.

In March 2002 Roberson and Freightliner patched up their differences, settled the lawsuit, and extended their fleet agreement. Roberson then sued Volvo for breach of contract and fraud. According to Roberson, an email containing 572 words is the contract that Volvo breached, and the fraud consists in Volvo's efforts to negotiate additional or revised terms after sending the email. Volvo's email, dated December 6, 2001, and captioned "Confirmation of our conversation", recaps the negotiations' status. It identifies items that Roberson and Volvo had "come to agreement on" and others that the parties needed to "review and finalize."

Although the email states that the contract would be complete only when these other subjects had been resolved and the package approved by senior managers, the district judge held that a jury could find that the email constituted Volvo's assent to the items it mentioned even if a full fleet agreement had not been signed. . . .

According to the email, the parties "have come to agreement on" the number of new Volvo trucks that Roberson will purchase, the cost per mile of servicing the new trucks and some of the Freightliner trucks, and an outline of an exit clause. They had not agreed on the price per truck, on the cost per mile for all of the older trucks, on the repurchase and trade-in terms for older trucks, or on the details of the exit clause—and recall that the devil was in these details for the arrangement between Roberson and Freightliner. Roberson had not bound itself to buy a single truck; it wants to treat the email as granting it a unilateral option. No reasonable jury could conclude that the items covered in the email were independent bargains to which Volvo had bound itself. The parties were negotiating a comprehensive arrangement, not a series of stand-alone contracts. The email was not something to which Roberson could respond "I accept" and move from the negotiation to the performance stage. Nor did Roberson say "I accept" or any equivalent; the parties negotiated for another two months, and when Volvo submitted its comprehensive proposal (at least 100 times longer than the email), Roberson refused to sign.

True enough, as Roberson stresses, truck purchases can be separated from truck maintenance, and in principle many subjects could be resolved one at a time. If people choose to negotiate and agree item by item, that is their privilege. But that is not what these negotiators were doing, and the email was not an à la carte menu from which Roberson could check off the items it wanted. The email and the other writings these parties exchanged show that the negotiations were global and that Volvo wanted a complete and formal arrangement before being bound. Such caution is to be expected in a multi-million-dollar deal that would last for many years. Here, each item that Roberson and Volvo "have come to agreement on" corresponds to a missing yet required document:

- Termination clause. The email contains some elements of exit arrangements but also states that Volvo must later "provide an exit clause" and that the parties need to "review and finalize" a master agreement "w/exit clause." . . .

- Truck purchases. According to the email Roberson would purchase at least 811 new Volvo trucks, yet a purchase order or similar recitation would be required to bind Roberson to this provision (Volvo would not allow itself to be bound without a reciprocal commitment), and that was not possible until the parties agreed on the trucks' price, trade-in value, purchase and delivery schedule, and buyer and seller's remedies in case of breach, none of which the email covered.

- Maintenance cost per mile. According to the email, Volvo had agreed to maintain Roberson's trucks for a specified cost per mile, but the email added that the parties still needed to reach a "Master CPM [cost-per-mile] agreement" and approve specification sheets to catalog the preexisting damage and condition of each Roberson truck. . . .

- Trade-in value. A major source of Roberson's supposed damages was the generous (relative to Freightliner) trade-in allowance that Volvo offered for used trucks, yet the email makes the trade-in "subject to trade terms and conditions" derived not from industry practice but from a document containing "Volvo Trade Terms and conditions" that was never finalized.

Hundreds of pages eventually were needed to furnish these and other details. A telling fact about industry practice and business necessity is that the consummated fleet agreement between Roberson and Freightliner was of length and complexity similar to the final package that Volvo tendered to Roberson in January 2002—and two orders of magnitude longer than the email of December 2001.

. . . When negotiators say that agreement is subject to a more definitive document, [contract law] treats this as demonstrating intent not to be bound until that document has been prepared and signed. See, e.g., Empro Manufacturing Co., Inc. v. Ball-Co Manufacturing, Inc., 870 F.2d 423, 425 (7th Cir.1989). [The law] is averse to enforcing tentative agreements that are expressly contingent on the signing of formal or final documents.

And for good reason. Often the parties agree on some items (such as how many trucks the buyer wants) while others (such as the price) require more negotiation. If any sign of agreement on any issue exposed the parties to a risk that a judge would deem the first-resolved items to be stand-alone contracts, the process of negotiation would be more cumbersome (the parties would have to hedge every sentence with cautionary legalese), and these extra negotiating expenses would raise the effective price (for in a competitive market the buyer must cover all of the seller's costs).

[Parties can] conserve these costs by reaching agreement in stages without taking the risk that courts will enforce a partial bargain that one side or the other would have rejected as incomplete. We have recognized that contracting parties often approach agreement in stages, not that each fledged stage represents a full agreement. *See, e.g., Empro*, 870 F.2d at 426. Thus parties may reach agreement on elements A, B and C, with more negotiation required on D and E. If elements D and E are essential to the mix, Illinois does not bind the parties to A, B, or C alone. Should agreement on essential elements fail, it is a failure of negotiation not performance. And whether extra elements are essential is for the parties themselves to say—as Volvo said they were in the very email that Roberson wanted to sift for favorable terms.

A comprehensive fleet agreement depended on resolving all issues that would affect the long-term dealings. The email lists many documents that contain "more of the required details" and are necessary "for each of us to review and finalize". The email offers a few subjects that the parties agree about but principally is a negotiation tool listing the subjects that the parties agree must be agreed on in the future. Its language demonstrates that no contract has been reached.

Roberson insists that, because the email does not state that agreement is "subject to" these future negotiations and documents, the email binds Volvo on all terms it recites. This magic-words approach is not the law in Illinois; the parties need not recite a formula to demonstrate that a definitive agreement lies in the future. Words expressing contingency or dependence on a subsequent event or agreed-on element will do. Volvo and Roberson failed to agree on the details that the email listed as necessary. So clear is this that there was no need to ask a jury's view.

If Roberson had hit the reply button in the email program and said only "we accept," no contract would have been formed because the email was not a definitive offer; it called for negotiation of the many open details rather than acceptance of any contract limited to a subset of the issues. What Roberson actually did in response to the email was to show enthusiasm . . . and propose a long list of changes and additions. So even if the December 6 email was an offer, Roberson rejected it—and could not "accept" it months later by filing suit for damages. Roberson never signed anything or tried to accept by performance (as by paying for 811 tractor-trailer sets); it treats the December 6 email as an option. Yet Volvo did not give Roberson a unilateral option, least of all one that could be exercised by suit rather than by payment.

Roberson's position—that as soon as parties agree on any term, it is a jury question whether there is a contract on this term alone—would make negotiations far too risky and is not the law in Illinois or any other jurisdiction of which we are aware. The give-and-take of negotiations will leave parties with bargains on some terms that must be made up for by others that benefit the trading partner. Letting one side accept the favorable terms without the compensatory ones would be like permitting the buyer to say: "We have agreed on quantity but not price; I now accept the quantity term and am entitled to the goods at whatever price a jury thinks reasonable." Firms do not (and Volvo did not) put themselves at the mercy of their counterparts in that way. Volvo protected itself by stating in the email that many "required details" remained to be "finalize[d]"; if the details were "required," there was no agreement without them.

Suppose we treat the email as an expression of intent to reach agreement. The letter in [*Interway, Inc. v. Alagna*, 407 N.E.2d 615 (1st Dist. Ill. 1980)] was even stronger. It stated that "this will confirm our agreement" and that "we have agreed" on certain issues, yet the Illinois judiciary held that it did not create a contract on any term because it showed that negotiations remained open. Roberson's arithmetic approach—add accords, subtract discords, the remainder equals a contract—would frustrate negotiations for all but the contemporaneous exchange of commodities (a transaction that requires few preliminaries). Parties may negotiate toward closing a deal without the risk that a jury will think that some intermediate document is a contract, and without the "fear that by reaching a preliminary understanding they have bargained away their privilege to disagree on the specifics." *Empro*, 870 F.2d at 426. . . .

QUESTIONS

1. Business people often sign documents like "letter agreements," knowing that they will later return to the deal and negotiate more details. Do the opinions in *Empro v. Ball-Co* and *Volvo* provide enough guidance for business people who are entering deals?

2. Is the concept of definiteness workable? Would a bright-line rule be superior? What would the bright-line rule look like? Requiring signatures, notarization, or wax seals? What about "magic words," to use a phrase appearing in both of Judge Easterbrook's opinions? Compare the question of definiteness with the doctrine of consideration.

Aside from the challenge of distinguishing preliminary negotiations from an offer, other problems and ambiguities sometime arise during the process of "getting in." Does an advertisement typically constitute an offer or merely an invitation to make offers? Under what circumstances might an advertisement be clear enough that it could constitute an offer? What if an advertisement contains some elements or aspects of a joke or jest? Can there be an acceptance and a contract under these circumstances?

The following cases deal with these issues while working with some of the traditional tools of contract formation, including offer, acceptance, assent, and consideration. Note that the first case, *Leonard v. Pepsico*, draws on all three of the ensuing cases in this sequence (*Mesaros v. United States, Lefkowitz v. Great Minneapolis Surplus Store*, and *Carlill v. Carbolic Smoke Ball Co.*) and cites a previous case, *Lucy v. Zehmer*. Pay attention to how the court marshals and invokes or distinguishes those precedents.

LEONARD V. PEPSICO, INC.
88 F.Supp.2d 116 (S.D.N.Y. 1999)

WOOD, J.

... This case arises out of a promotional campaign conducted by defendant, the producer and distributor of the soft drinks Pepsi and Diet Pepsi. ... The promotion, entitled "Pepsi Stuff," encouraged consumers to collect "Pepsi Points" from specially marked packages of Pepsi or Diet Pepsi and redeem these points for merchandise featuring the Pepsi logo... Before introducing the promotion nationally, defendant conducted a test of the promotion in the Pacific Northwest from October 1995 to March 1996. ... A Pepsi Stuff catalog was distributed to consumers in the test market, including Washington State... Plaintiff is a resident of Seattle, Washington. While living in Seattle, plaintiff saw the Pepsi Stuff commercial that he contends constituted an offer of a Harrier Jet.

A. *The Alleged Offer*. Because whether the television commercial constituted an offer is the central question in this case, the Court will describe the commercial in detail. The commercial opens upon an idyllic, suburban morning, where the chirping of birds in sun-dappled trees welcomes a paperboy on his morning route. As the newspaper hits the stoop of a conventional two-story house, the tattoo of a military drum introduces the subtitle, "MONDAY 7:58 AM." The stirring strains of a martial air mark the appearance of a well-coiffed teenager preparing to leave for school, dressed in a shirt emblazoned with the Pepsi logo, a red-white-and-blue ball. While the teenager confidently preens, the military drumroll again sounds as the subtitle "T-SHIRT 75 PEPSI POINTS" scrolls across the screen. Bursting from his room, the teenager strides down the hallway wearing a leather jacket. The drumroll sounds again, as the subtitle

"LEATHER JACKET 1450 PEPSI POINTS" appears. The teenager opens the door of his house and, unfazed by the glare of the early morning sunshine, puts on a pair of sunglasses. The drumroll then accompanies the subtitle "SHADES 175 PEPSI POINTS." A voiceover then intones, "Introducing the new Pepsi Stuff catalog," as the camera focuses on the cover of the catalog.[2]

. . . . The scene then shifts to three young boys sitting in front of a high school building. The boy in the middle is intent on his Pepsi Stuff Catalog, while the boys on either side are each drinking Pepsi. The three boys gaze in awe at an object rushing overhead, as the military march builds to a crescendo. The Harrier Jet is not yet visible, but the observer senses the presence of a mighty plane as the extreme winds generated by its flight create a paper maelstrom in a classroom devoted to an otherwise dull physics lesson. Finally, the Harrier Jet swings into view and lands by the side of the school building, next to a bicycle rack. Several students run for cover, and the velocity of the wind strips one hapless faculty member down to his underwear. While the faculty member is being deprived of his dignity, the voiceover announces: "Now the more Pepsi you drink, the more great stuff you're gonna get."

. . . The teenager opens the cockpit of the fighter and can be seen, helmetless, holding a Pepsi. "[L]ooking very pleased with himself," . . . the teenager exclaims, "Sure beats the bus," and chortles. The military drumroll sounds a final time, as the following words appear: "HARRIER FIGHTER 7,000,000 PEPSI POINTS." A few seconds later, the following appears in more stylized script: "Drink Pepsi-Get Stuff." With that message, the music and the commercial end with a triumphant flourish.

Inspired by this commercial, plaintiff set out to obtain a Harrier Jet. Plaintiff explains that he is "typical of the 'Pepsi Generation' . . . he is young, has an adventurous spirit, and the notion of obtaining a Harrier Jet appealed to him enormously." . . . Plaintiff consulted the Pepsi Stuff Catalog. The Catalog features youths dressed in Pepsi Stuff regalia or enjoying Pepsi Stuff accessories . . . . The Catalog specifies the number of Pepsi Points required to obtain promotional merchandise. . . . The Catalog includes an Order Form which lists, on one side, fifty-three items of Pepsi Stuff merchandise redeemable for Pepsi Points . . . . Conspicuously absent from the Order Form is any entry or description of a Harrier Jet. . . . The amount of Pepsi Points required to obtain the listed merchandise ranges from 15 (for a "Jacket Tattoo" ("Sew 'em on your jacket, not your arm.")) to 3300 (for a "Fila Mountain Bike" ("Rugged. All-terrain. Exclusively for Pepsi.")). . . .

---

[2] At this point, the following message appears at the bottom of the screen: "Offer not available in all areas. See details on specially marked packages."

The rear foldout pages of the Catalog contain directions for redeeming Pepsi Points for merchandise. . . . These directions note that merchandise may be ordered "only" with the original Order Form. . . . The Catalog notes that in the event that a consumer lacks enough Pepsi Points to obtain a desired item, additional Pepsi Points may be purchased for ten cents each; however, at least fifteen original Pepsi Points must accompany each order. . . .

Although plaintiff initially set out to collect 7,000,000 Pepsi Points by consuming Pepsi products, it soon became clear to him that he "would not be able to buy (let alone drink) enough Pepsi to collect the necessary Pepsi Points fast enough." . . . Reevaluating his strategy, plaintiff "focused for the first time on the packaging materials in the Pepsi Stuff promotion," . . . and realized that buying Pepsi Points would be a more promising option. . . . Through acquaintances, plaintiff ultimately raised about $700,000.

B. *Plaintiff's Efforts to Redeem the Alleged Offer.* On or about March 27, 1996, plaintiff submitted an Order Form, fifteen original Pepsi Points, and a check for $700,008.50. . . . Plaintiff appears to have been represented by counsel at the time he mailed his check; the check is drawn on an account of plaintiff's first set of attorneys. . . . At the bottom of the Order Form, plaintiff wrote in "1 Harrier Jet" in the "Item" column and "7,000,000" in the "Total Points" column. . . . In a letter accompanying his submission, plaintiff stated that the check was to purchase additional Pepsi Points "expressly for obtaining a new Harrier jet as advertised in your Pepsi Stuff commercial." . . .

On or about May 7, 1996, defendant's fulfillment house rejected plaintiff's submission and returned the check, explaining that:

> The item that you have requested is not part of the Pepsi Stuff collection. It is not included in the catalogue or on the order form, and only catalogue merchandise can be redeemed under this program.

> The Harrier jet in the Pepsi commercial is fanciful and is simply included to create a humorous and entertaining ad. We apologize for any misunderstanding or confusion that you may have experienced and are enclosing some free product coupons for your use.

Plaintiff's previous counsel responded on or about May 14, 1996, as follows:

> Your letter of May 7, 1996 is totally unacceptable. We have reviewed the video tape of the Pepsi Stuff commercial . . . and it clearly offers the new Harrier jet for 7,000,000 Pepsi Points. Our client followed your rules explicitly. . . .

> This is a formal demand that you honor your commitment and make immediate arrangements to transfer the new Harrier

jet to our client. If we do not receive transfer instructions within ten (10) business days of the date of this letter you will leave us no choice but to file an appropriate action against Pepsi. . . .

This letter was apparently sent onward to the advertising company responsible for the actual commercial, BBDO New York ("BBDO"). In a letter dated May 30, 1996, BBDO Vice President Raymond E. McGovern, Jr., explained to plaintiff that:

> I find it hard to believe that you are of the opinion that the Pepsi Stuff commercial ("Commercial") really offers a new Harrier Jet. The use of the Jet was clearly a joke that was meant to make the Commercial more humorous and entertaining. In my opinion, no reasonable person would agree with your analysis of the Commercial.

. . . PepsiCo brought suit in this Court on July 18, 1996, seeking a declaratory judgment stating that it had no obligation to furnish plaintiff with a Harrier Jet. . . .

Advertisements as Offers. The general rule is that an advertisement does not constitute an offer. The Restatement (Second) of Contracts explains that:

> Advertisements of goods by display, sign, handbill, newspaper, radio or television are not ordinarily intended or understood as offers to sell. The same is true of catalogues, price lists and circulars, even though the terms of suggested bargains may be stated in some detail. It is of course possible to make an offer by an advertisement directed to the general public . . . , but there must ordinarily be some language of commitment or some invitation to take action without further communication.

Restatement (Second) of Contracts § 26 cmt. b (1979). Similarly, a leading treatise notes that:

> It is quite possible to make a definite and operative offer to buy or sell goods by advertisement, in a newspaper, by a handbill, a catalog or circular or on a placard in a store window. It is not customary to do this, however; and the presumption is the other way. . . . Such advertisements are understood to be mere requests to consider and examine and negotiate; and no one can reasonably regard them as otherwise unless the circumstances are exceptional and the words used are very plain and clear.

1 Arthur Linton Corbin & Joseph M. Perillo, Corbin on Contracts § 2.4, at 116–17 (rev. ed.1993) (emphasis added); see also 1 E. Allan Farnsworth, Farnsworth on Contracts § 3.10, at 239 (2d ed.1998); 1 Samuel Williston & Richard A. Lord, A Treatise on the Law of Contracts § 4:7, at 286–87 (4th ed.1990). . . .

An advertisement is not transformed into an enforceable offer merely by a potential offeree's expression of willingness to accept the offer through, among other means, completion of an order form. In Mesaros v. United States, 845 F.2d 1576 (Fed.Cir.1988), for example, the plaintiffs sued the United States Mint for failure to deliver a number of Statue of Liberty commemorative coins that they had ordered. When demand for the coins proved unexpectedly robust, a number of individuals who had sent in their orders in a timely fashion were left empty-handed. See id. at 1578–80. The court began by noting the "well-established" rule that advertisements and order forms are "mere notices and solicitations for offers which create no power of acceptance in the recipient." Id. at 1580; Restatement (Second) of Contracts § 26 ("A manifestation of willingness to enter a bargain is not an offer if the person to whom it is addressed knows or has reason to know that the person making it does not intend to conclude a bargain until he has made a further manifestation of assent."). The spurned coin collectors could not maintain a breach of contract action because no contract would be formed until the advertiser accepted the order form and processed payment. See id. at 1581 . . . Under these principles, plaintiff's letter of March 27, 1996, with the Order Form and the appropriate number of Pepsi Points, constituted the offer. There would be no enforceable contract until defendant accepted the Order Form and cashed the check.

The exception to the rule that advertisements do not create any power of acceptance in potential offerees is where the advertisement is "clear, definite, and explicit, and leaves nothing open for negotiation," in that circumstance, "it constitutes an offer, acceptance of which will complete the contract." Lefkowitz v. Great Minneapolis Surplus Store, 251 Minn. 188, 86 N.W.2d 689, 691 (1957). In Lefkowitz, defendant had published a newspaper announcement stating: "Saturday 9 AM Sharp, 3 Brand New Fur Coats, Worth to $100.00, First Come First Served $1 Each." Id. at 690. Mr. Morris Lefkowitz arrived at the store, dollar in hand, but was informed that under defendant's "house rules," the offer was open to ladies, but not gentlemen. See id. The court ruled that because plaintiff had fulfilled all of the terms of the advertisement and the advertisement was specific and left nothing open for negotiation, a contract had been formed. See id.; see also Johnson v. Capital City Ford Co., 85 So.2d 75, 79 (La.Ct.App.1955) (finding that newspaper advertisement was sufficiently certain and definite to constitute an offer).

The present case is distinguishable from Lefkowitz. First, the commercial cannot be regarded in itself as sufficiently definite, because it specifically reserved the details of the offer to a separate writing, the Catalog.[6] The commercial itself made no mention of the steps a potential offeree would be required to take to accept the alleged offer of a Harrier

---

[6]   It also communicated additional words of reservation: "Offer not available in all areas. See details on specially marked packages."

Jet. The advertisement in *Lefkowitz*, in contrast, "identified the person who could accept." Corbin, supra, § 2.4, at 119. See generally United States v. Braunstein, 75 F.Supp. 137, 139 (S.D.N.Y.1947) ("Greater precision of expression may be required, and less help from the court given, when the parties are merely at the threshold of a contract."); Farnsworth, supra, at 239 ("The fact that a proposal is very detailed suggests that it is an offer, while omission of many terms suggests that it is not.").[7]

Second, even if the Catalog had included a Harrier Jet among the items that could be obtained by redemption of Pepsi Points, the advertisement of a Harrier Jet by both television commercial and catalog would still not constitute an offer. As the *Mesaros* court explained, the absence of any words of limitation such as "first come, first served," renders the alleged offer sufficiently indefinite that no contract could be formed. *See* Mesaros, 845 F.2d at 1581. "A customer would not usually have reason to believe that the shopkeeper intended exposure to the risk of a multitude of acceptances resulting in a number of contracts exceeding the shopkeeper's inventory." Farnsworth, supra, at 242. There was no such danger in *Lefkowitz*, owing to the limitation "first come, first served."

The Court finds, in sum, that the Harrier Jet commercial was merely an advertisement. The Court now turns to the line of cases upon which plaintiff rests much of his argument.

. . . *Rewards as Offers.* In opposing the present motion, plaintiff largely relies on a different species of unilateral offer, involving public offers of a reward for performance of a specified act. Because these cases generally involve public declarations regarding the efficacy or trustworthiness of specific products, one court has aptly characterized these authorities as "prove me wrong" cases. See Rosenthal v. Al Packer Ford, 36 Md.App. 349, 374 A.2d 377, 380 (1977). The most venerable of these precedents is the case of Carlill v. Carbolic Smoke Ball Co., 1 Q.B. 256 (Court of Appeal, 1892), a quote from which heads plaintiff's memorandum of law: "[I]f a person chooses to make extravagant promises . . . he probably does so because it pays him to make them, and, if he has made them, the extravagance of the promises is no reason in law why he should not be bound by them." Carbolic Smoke Ball, 1 Q.B. at 268 (Bowen, L.J.).

Long a staple of law school curricula, *Carbolic Smoke Ball* owes its fame not merely to "the comic and slightly mysterious object involved," A.W. Brian Simpson, Quackery and Contract Law: Carlill v. Carbolic Smoke Ball Company (1893), in Leading Cases in the Common Law 259,

---

[7] The reservation of the details of the offer in this case distinguishes it from Payne v. Lautz Bros. & Co., 166 N.Y.S. 844 (N.Y.City Ct.1916). In Payne, a stamp and coupon broker purchased massive quantities of coupons produced by defendant, a soap company, and tried to redeem them for 4,000 round-trip tickets to a local beach. The court ruled for plaintiff, noting that the advertisements were "absolutely unrestricted. It contained no reference whatever to any of its previous advertising of any form." Id. At 848. In the present case, by contrast, the commercial explicitly reserved the details of the offer to the Catalog.

281 (1995), but also to its role in developing the law of unilateral offers. The case arose during the London influenza epidemic of the 1890s. Among other advertisements of the time, for Clarke's World Famous Blood Mixture, Towle's Pennyroyal and Steel Pills for Females, Sequah's Prairie Flower, and Epp's Glycerine Jube-Jubes, see Simpson, supra, at 267, appeared solicitations for the Carbolic Smoke Ball. The specific advertisement that Mrs. Carlill saw, and relied upon, read as follows:

> £100 reward will be paid by the Carbolic Smoke Ball Company to any person who contracts the increasing epidemic influenza, colds, or any diseases caused by taking cold, after having used the ball three times daily for two weeks according to the printed directions supplied with each ball. £1000 is deposited with the Alliance Bank, Regent Street, showing our sincerity in the matter.

> During the last epidemic of influenza many thousand carbolic smoke balls were sold as preventives against this disease, and in no ascertained case was the disease contracted by those using the carbolic smoke ball.

Carbolic Smoke Ball, 1 Q.B. at 256–57. "On the faith of this advertisement," id. at 257, Mrs. Carlill purchased the smoke ball and used it as directed, but contracted influenza nevertheless.[8] The lower court held that she was entitled to recover the promised reward.

Affirming the lower court's decision, Lord Justice Lindley began by noting that the advertisement was an express promise to pay £100 in the event that a consumer of the Carbolic Smoke Ball was stricken with influenza. See id. at 261. The advertisement was construed as offering a reward because it sought to induce performance, unlike an invitation to negotiate, which seeks a reciprocal promise. As Lord Justice Lindley explained, "advertisements offering rewards . . . are offers to anybody who performs the conditions named in the advertisement, and anybody who does perform the condition accepts the offer." Id. at 262; see also id. at 268 (Bowen, L.J.).[9] Because Mrs. Carlill had complied with the terms of the offer, yet contracted influenza, she was entitled to £100.

---

[8] Although the Court of Appeals's opinion is silent as to exactly what a carbolic smoke ball was, the historical record reveals it to have been a compressible hollow ball, about the size of an apple or orange, with a small opening covered by some porous material such as silk or gauze. The ball was partially filled with carbolic acid in powder form. When the ball was squeezed, the powder would be forced through the opening as a small cloud of smoke. See Simpson, supra, at 262–63. At the time, carbolic acid was considered fatal if consumed in more than small amounts. See id. at 264.

[9] Carbolic Smoke Ball includes a classic formulation of this principle: "If I advertise to the world that my dog is lost, and that anybody who brings the dog to a particular place will be paid some money, are all the police or other persons whose business it is to find lost dogs to be expected to sit down and write a note saying that they have accepted my proposal?" Carbolic Smoke Ball, 1 Q.B. at 270 (Bowen, L.J.).

Like Carbolic Smoke Ball, the decisions relied upon by plaintiff involve offers of reward. In Barnes v. Treece, 15 Wash.App. 437, 549 P.2d 1152 (1976), for example, the vice-president of a punchboard distributor, in the course of hearings before the Washington State Gambling Commission, asserted that, " 'I'll put a hundred thousand dollars to anyone to find a crooked board. If they find it, I'll pay it.' " Id. at 1154. Plaintiff, a former bartender, heard of the offer and located two crooked punchboards. Defendant, after reiterating that the offer was serious, providing plaintiff with a receipt for the punchboard on company stationery, and assuring plaintiff that the reward was being held in escrow, nevertheless repudiated the offer. See id. at 1154. The court ruled that the offer was valid and that plaintiff was entitled to his reward. See id. at 1155. The plaintiff in this case also cites cases involving prizes for skill (or luck) in the game of golf. See Las Vegas Hacienda v. Gibson, 77 Nev. 25, 359 P.2d 85 (1961) (awarding $5,000 to plaintiff, who successfully shot a hole-in-one); see also Grove v. Charbonneau Buick-Pontiac, Inc., 240 N.W.2d 853 (N.D.1976) (awarding automobile to plaintiff, who successfully shot a hole-in-one).

Other "reward" cases underscore the distinction between typical advertisements, in which the alleged offer is merely an invitation to negotiate for purchase of commercial goods, and promises of reward, in which the alleged offer is intended to induce a potential offeree to perform a specific action, often for noncommercial reasons. In Newman v. Schiff, 778 F.2d 460 (8th Cir.1985), for example, the Fifth Circuit held that a tax protestor's assertion that, "If anybody calls this show . . . and cites any section of the code that says an individual is required to file a tax return, I'll pay them $100,000," would have been an enforceable offer had the plaintiff called the television show to claim the reward while the tax protestor was appearing. See id. at 466–67. The court noted that, like Carbolic Smoke Ball, the case "concerns a special type of offer: an offer for a reward." Id. at 465.

James v. Turilli, 473 S.W.2d 757 (Mo.Ct.App.1971), arose from a boast by defendant that the "notorious Missouri desperado" Jesse James had not been killed in 1882, as portrayed in song and legend, but had lived under the alias "J. Frank Dalton" at the "Jesse James Museum" operated by none other than defendant. Defendant offered $10,000 "to anyone who could prove me wrong." See id. at 758–59. The widow of the outlaw's son demonstrated, at trial, that the outlaw had in fact been killed in 1882. On appeal, the court held that defendant should be liable to pay the amount offered. See id. at 762; see also Mears v. Nationwide Mutual Ins. Co., 91 F.3d 1118, 1122–23 (8th Cir.1996) (plaintiff entitled to cost of two Mercedes as reward for coining slogan for insurance company).

In the present case, the Harrier Jet commercial did not direct that anyone who appeared at Pepsi headquarters with 7,000,000 Pepsi Points on the Fourth of July would receive a Harrier Jet. Instead, the commercial urged consumers to accumulate Pepsi Points and to refer to the Catalog to determine how they could redeem their Pepsi Points. The commercial sought a reciprocal promise, expressed through acceptance of, and compliance with, the terms of the Order Form. As noted previously, the Catalog contains no mention of the Harrier Jet. Plaintiff states that he "noted that the Harrier Jet was not among the items described in the catalog, but this did not affect [his] understanding of the offer." (Pl. Mem. at 4.) It should have.

Carbolic Smoke Ball itself draws a distinction between the offer of reward in that case, and typical advertisements, which are merely offers to negotiate. As Lord Justice Bowen explains:

> It is an offer to become liable to anyone who, before it is retracted, performs the condition. . . . It is not like cases in which you offer to negotiate, or you issue advertisements that you have got a stock of books to sell, or houses to let, in which case there is no offer to be bound by any contract. Such advertisements are offers to negotiate—offers to receive offers—offers to chaffer, as, I think, some learned judge in one of the cases has said.

Carbolic Smoke Ball, 1 Q.B. at 268; see also Lovett, 207 N.Y.S. at 756 (distinguishing advertisements, as invitation to offer, from offers of reward made in advertisements, such as *Carbolic Smoke Ball*). Because the alleged offer in this case was, at most, an advertisement to receive offers rather than an offer of reward, plaintiff cannot show that there was an offer made in the circumstances of this case. . . .

Plaintiff's understanding of the commercial as an offer must also be rejected because the Court finds that no objective person could reasonably have concluded that the commercial actually offered consumers a Harrier Jet.

. . . . *Objective Reasonable Person Standard.* In evaluating the commercial, the Court must not consider defendant's subjective intent in making the commercial, or plaintiff's subjective view of what the commercial offered, but what an objective, reasonable person would have understood the commercial to convey. See Kay-R Elec. Corp. v. Stone & Webster Constr. Co., 23 F.3d 55, 57 (2d Cir.1994) ("[W]e are not concerned with what was going through the heads of the parties at the time [of the alleged contract]. Rather, we are talking about the objective principles of contract law."); Mesaros, 845 F.2d at 1581 ("A basic rule of contracts holds that whether an offer has been made depends on the objective reasonableness of the alleged offeree's belief that the advertisement or solicitation was intended as an offer."); Farnsworth, supra, § 3.10, at 237; Williston, supra, § 4:7 at 296–97.

If it is clear that an offer was not serious, then no offer has been made:

> What kind of act creates a power of acceptance and is therefore an offer? It must be an expression of will or intention. It must be an act that leads the offeree reasonably to conclude that a power to create a contract is conferred. This applies to the content of the power as well as to the fact of its existence. *It is on this ground that we must exclude* invitations to deal or acts of mere preliminary negotiation, and *acts evidently done in jest* or without intent to create legal relations.

Corbin on Contracts, § 1.11 at 30 (emphasis added). An obvious joke, of course, would not give rise to a contract. See, e.g., Graves v. Northern N.Y. Pub. Co., 260 A.D. 900, 22 N.Y.S.2d 537 (1940) (dismissing claim to offer of $1000, which appeared in the "joke column" of the newspaper, to any person who could provide a commonly available phone number). On the other hand, if there is no indication that the offer is "evidently in jest," and that an objective, reasonable person would find that the offer was serious, then there may be a valid offer. See Barnes, 549 P.2d at 1155 ("[I]f the jest is not apparent and a reasonable hearer would believe that an offer was being made, then the speaker risks the formation of a contract which was not intended."); see also Lucy v. Zehmer, 196 Va. 493, 84 S.E.2d 516, 518, 520 (1954) (ordering specific performance of a contract to purchase a farm despite defendant's protestation that the transaction was done in jest as "just a bunch of two doggoned drunks bluffing").

. . . *Whether the Commercial Was "Evidently Done In Jest."* Plaintiff's insistence that the commercial appears to be a serious offer requires the Court to explain why the commercial is funny. Explaining why a joke is funny is a daunting task; as the essayist E.B. White has remarked, "Humor can be dissected, as a frog can, but the thing dies in the process. . . ." The commercial is the embodiment of what defendant appropriately characterizes as "zany humor."

First, the commercial suggests, as commercials often do, that use of the advertised product will transform what, for most youth, can be a fairly routine and ordinary experience. The military tattoo and stirring martial music, as well as the use of subtitles in a Courier font that scroll terse messages across the screen, such as "MONDAY 7:58 AM," evoke military and espionage thrillers. The implication of the commercial is that Pepsi Stuff merchandise will inject drama and moment into hitherto unexceptional lives. The commercial in this case thus makes the exaggerated claims similar to those of many television advertisements: that by consuming the featured clothing, car, beer, or potato chips, one will become attractive, stylish, desirable, and admired by all. A reasonable viewer would understand such advertisements as mere puffery, not as statements of fact, see, e.g., Hubbard v. General Motors Corp., 95 Civ.

4362(AGS), 1996 WL 274018, at *6 (S.D.N.Y. May 22, 1996) (advertisement describing automobile as "Like a Rock," was mere puffery, not a warranty of quality); Lovett, 207 N.Y.S. at 756; and refrain from interpreting the promises of the commercial as being literally true.

Second, the callow youth featured in the commercial is a highly improbable pilot, one who could barely be trusted with the keys to his parents' car, much less the prize aircraft of the United States Marine Corps. Rather than checking the fuel gauges on his aircraft, the teenager spends his precious preflight minutes preening. The youth's concern for his coiffure appears to extend to his flying without a helmet. Finally, the teenager's comment that flying a Harrier Jet to school "sure beats the bus" evinces an improbably insouciant attitude toward the relative difficulty and danger of piloting a fighter plane in a residential area, as opposed to taking public transportation.

Third, the notion of traveling to school in a Harrier Jet is an exaggerated adolescent fantasy. In this commercial, the fantasy is underscored by how the teenager's schoolmates gape in admiration, ignoring their physics lesson. The force of the wind generated by the Harrier Jet blows off one teacher's clothes, literally defrocking an authority figure. As if to emphasize the fantastic quality of having a Harrier Jet arrive at school, the Jet lands next to a plebeian bike rack. This fantasy is, of course, extremely unrealistic. No school would provide landing space for a student's fighter jet, or condone the disruption the jet's use would cause.

Fourth, the primary mission of a Harrier Jet, according to the United States Marine Corps, is to "attack and destroy surface targets under day and night visual conditions." United States Marine Corps, Factfile: AV–8B Harrier II (last modified Dec. 5, 1995) <http://www.hqmc.usmc.mil/factfile. nsf>. Manufactured by McDonnell Douglas, the Harrier Jet played a significant role in the air offensive of Operation Desert Storm in 1991. See id. The jet is designed to carry a considerable armament load, including Sidewinder and Maverick missiles. See id. As one news report has noted, "Fully loaded, the Harrier can float like a butterfly and sting like a bee— albeit a roaring 14-ton butterfly and a bee with 9,200 pounds of bombs and missiles." Jerry Allegood, Marines Rely on Harrier Jet, Despite Critics, News & Observer (Raleigh), Nov. 4, 1990, at C1. In light of the Harrier Jet's well-documented function in attacking and destroying surface and air targets, armed reconnaissance and air interdiction, and offensive and defensive anti-aircraft warfare, depiction of such a jet as a way to get to school in the morning is clearly not serious even if, as plaintiff contends, the jet is capable of being acquired "in a form that eliminates [its] potential for military use." (See Leonard Aff. P 20.)

Fifth, the number of Pepsi Points the commercial mentions as required to "purchase" the jet is 7,000,000. To amass that number of points, one would have to drink 7,000,000 Pepsis (or roughly 190 Pepsis a day for the next hundred years—an unlikely possibility), or one would have to purchase approximately $700,000 worth of Pepsi Points. The cost of a Harrier Jet is roughly $23 million dollars, a fact of which plaintiff was aware when he set out to gather the amount he believed necessary to accept the alleged offer. . . . Even if an objective, reasonable person were not aware of this fact, he would conclude that purchasing a fighter plane for $700,000 is a deal too good to be true.

Plaintiff argues that a reasonable, objective person would have understood the commercial to make a serious offer of a Harrier Jet because there was "absolutely no distinction in the manner" . . . in which the items in the commercial were presented. Plaintiff also relies upon a press release highlighting the promotional campaign, issued by defendant, in which "[n]o mention is made by [defendant] of humor, or anything of the sort." (Id. at 5.) These arguments suggest merely that the humor of the promotional campaign was tongue in cheek. Humor is not limited to what Justice Cardozo called "[t]he rough and boisterous joke . . . [that] evokes its own guffaws." Murphy v. Steeplechase Amusement Co., 250 N.Y. 479, 483, 166 N.E. 173, 174 (1929). In light of the obvious absurdity of the commercial, the Court rejects plaintiff's argument that the commercial was not clearly in jest. . . .

NOTES AND QUESTIONS

1.   In *Lucy v. Zehmer*, the seller attempted to negate a contract for the sale of a farm, later claiming it was all a joke or a bluff. The court rejected that argument, calling it "bizarre." What distinguishes *Lucy v. Zehmer* from the facts of *Leonard v. Pepsico*?

2.   What elements of the Pepsi commercial led the court to view it more as a "statement made in jest" than a serious offer?

3.   For other examples of offers made in jest, that in some instances were enforceable (and in others, not), see Keith Rowley, *You Asked for it, You Got it. . . Toy Yoda Practical Jokes, Prizes, and Contract Law*, 3 NEV. L. REV. 526 (2003). Professor Rowley took the name of his article from a particular situation where waitresses at a restaurant were (orally) promised a prize for selling the most beer in a month. At the end of the month, the waitress who had sold the most was expecting a car, but instead was led out to the parking lot where she was confronted with Yoda, a toy figurine from the movie "Star Wars." That case settled (for approximately the price of a used Toyota) before it could reach the courtroom. What do these "joking" cases tell us about reasonable expectations and contract law?

LEFKOWITZ V. GREAT MINNEAPOLIS SURPLUS STORE, INC.
86 N.W.2d 689 (Minn. 1957)

MURPHY, J.

. . . This case grows out of the alleged refusal of the defendant to sell to the plaintiff a certain fur piece which it had offered for sale in a newspaper advertisement. It appears from the record that on April 6, 1956, the defendant published the following advertisement in a Minneapolis newspaper:

Saturday 9 A.M. Sharp 3 Brand New Fur Coats Worth to $100.00
First Come First Served $1 Each

On April 13, the defendant again published an advertisement in the same newspaper as follows:

Saturday 9 A.M. 2 Brand New Pastel Mink
3-Skin Scarfs Selling for.$89.50
Out they go Saturday. Each . . . $1.00
1 Black Lapin Stole Beautiful, worth $139.50 . . . $1.00
First Come First Served

The record supports the findings of the court that on each of the Saturdays following the publication of the above-described ads the plaintiff was the first to present himself at the appropriate counter in the defendant's store and on each occasion demanded the coat and the stole so advertised and indicated his readiness to pay the sale price of $1. On both occasions, the defendant refused to sell the merchandise to the plaintiff, stating on the first occasion that by a 'house rule' the offer was intended for women only and sales would not be made to men, and on the second visit that plaintiff knew defendant's house rules.

The trial court properly disallowed plaintiff's claim for the value of the fur coats since the value of these articles was speculative and uncertain. The only evidence of value was the advertisement itself to the effect that the coats were "Worth to $100.00," how much less being speculative especially in view of the price for which they were offered for sale. With reference to the offer of the defendant on April 13, 1956, to sell the "1 Black Lapin Stole * * * worth $139.50 * * * " the trial court held that the value of this article was established and granted judgment in favor of the plaintiff for that amount less the $1 quoted purchase price.

The defendant contends that a newspaper advertisement offering items of merchandise for sale at a named price is a 'unilateral offer' which may be withdrawn without notice. He relies upon authorities which hold that, where an advertiser publishes in a newspaper that he has a certain quantity or quality of goods which he wants to dispose of at certain prices and on certain terms, such advertisements are not offers which become contracts as soon as any person to whose notice they may come signifies his acceptance by notifying the other that he will take a certain quantity of them. Such advertisements have been construed as an invitation for an offer of sale on the terms stated, which offer, when received, may be accepted or rejected and which therefore does not become a contract of sale until accepted by the seller; and until a contract has been so made, the seller may modify or revoke such prices or terms. . . .

The defendant relies principally on Craft v. Elder & Johnston Co. supra. In that case, the court discussed the legal effect of an advertisement offering for sale, as a one-day special, an electric sewing machine at a named price. The view was expressed that the advertisement was (38 N.E.2d 417, 34 Ohio L.A. 605) not an offer made to any specific person but was made to the public generally. Thereby it would be properly designated as a unilateral offer and not being supported by any consideration could be withdrawn at will and without notice.' It is true that such an offer may be withdrawn before acceptance. Since all offers are by their nature unilateral because they are necessarily made by one party or on one side in the negotiation of a contract, the distinction made in that decision between a unilateral offer and a unilateral contract is not clear. On the facts before us we are concerned with whether the advertisement constituted an offer, and, if so, whether the plaintiff's conduct constituted an acceptance.

There are numerous authorities which hold that a particular advertisement in a newspaper or circular letter relating to a sale of articles may be construed by the court as constituting an offer, acceptance of which would complete a contract. J. E. Pinkham Lumber Co. v. C. W. Griffin & Co., 212 Ala. 341, 102 So. 689; Seymour v. Armstrong & Kassebaum, 62 Kan. 720, 64 P. 612; Payne v. Lautz Bros. & Co., City Ct., 166 N.Y.S. 844, affirmed, 168 N.Y.S. 369, affirmed, 185 App.Div. 904, 171 N.Y.S. 1094; Arnold v. Phillips, 1 Ohio Dec. Reprint 195, 3 West.Law J. 448; Oliver v. Henley, Tex.Civ.App., 21 S.W.2d 576; Annotation, 157 A.L.R. 744, 746.

The test of whether a binding obligation may originate in advertisements addressed to the general public is "whether the facts show that some performance was promised in positive terms in return for something requested." 1 Williston, Contracts (Rev. ed.) § 27.

The authorities above cited emphasize that, where the offer is clear, definite, and explicit, and leaves nothing open for negotiation, it constitutes an offer, acceptance of which will complete the contract. The most recent case on the subject is Johnson v. Capital City Ford Co., La.App., 85 So.2d 75, in which the court pointed out that a newspaper advertisement relating to the purchase and sale of automobiles may constitute an offer, acceptance of which will consummate a contract and create an obligation in the offeror to perform according to the terms of the published offer.

Whether in any individual instance a newspaper advertisement is an offer rather than an invitation to make an offer depends on the legal intention of the parties and the surrounding circumstances. We are of the view on the facts before us that the offer by the defendant of the sale of the Lapin fur was clear, definite, and explicit, and left nothing open for negotiation. The plaintiff having successfully managed to be the first one to appear at the seller's place of business to be served, as requested by the advertisement, and having offered the stated purchase price of the article, he was entitled to performance on the part of the defendant. We think the trial court was correct in holding that there was in the conduct of the parties a sufficient mutuality of obligation to constitute a contract of sale.

The defendant contends that the offer was modified by a "house rule" to the effect that only women were qualified to receive the bargains advertised. The advertisement contained no such restriction. This objection may be disposed of briefly by stating that, while an advertiser has the right at any time before acceptance to modify his offer, he does not have the right, after acceptance, to impose new or arbitrary conditions not contained in the published offer. Payne v. Lautz Bros. & Co., City Ct., 166 N.Y.S. 844, 848; Mooney v. Daily News Co., 116 Minn. 212, 133 N.W. 573, 37 L.R.A.,N.S., 183. Affirmed.

NOTES AND QUESTIONS

1.   In general, advertisements are not typically construed as offers, but rather invitations for those seeing the advertisement to make an offer, which the advertiser can then choose to accept. Otherwise an advertiser could be seen as making such a broad offer (with the general public) that it could not fulfill.

2.   *Lefkowitz* sets out an exception to this general rule on advertisements. What countervailing policy arguments explain why certain advertisements are treated as offers?

MESAROS V. U.S.

845 F.2d 1576 (Fed. Cir. 1988)

SKELTON, J.

On May 23, 1986, plaintiffs Mary Mesaros and husband Anthony C. Mesaros filed a class action lawsuit for themselves and others similarly situated (thirty-three of whom were named) in the United States District Court for the Southern District of Georgia, Savannah Division, against the United States of America, United States Department of the Treasury . . . (defendants) seeking damages for an alleged breach of contract by defendants in failing to deliver a quantity of Statue of Liberty commemorative coins they had ordered from defendants pursuant to an advertisement mailed to plaintiffs and published in newspapers and other news media by the United States Mint. In the alternative they sought mandamus relief for the delivery of the coins. Plaintiffs also filed a motion for certification of the class.

The defendants filed a motion to dismiss plaintiffs' suit, or in the alternative for summary judgment. On April 13, 1987, the court granted judgment for defendants on their motion in its entirety. No action was taken by the court on the class action motion because it was moot after the other action by the court. The plaintiffs filed an appeal . . . in the United States Court of Appeals for the Eleventh Circuit. On motion of defendants, the case was transferred to this court.

The facts in the case, as stated in an order of the district court dated April 13, 1987, (with a few omissions and additions), and as shown by the record are as follow[s].

In July 1985, Congress passed the Statue of Liberty-Ellis Island Commemorative Coin Act. Pub.L. No. 99–61, 99 Stat. 113 (July 9, 1985). The purpose of the Act was to provide funds, through the sale of a limited number of specially-minted commemorative coins, "to restore and renovate the Statue of Liberty and the facilities used for immigration at Ellis Island," and to establish an endowment to provide for the upkeep and maintenance of these national monuments. The Act, which by modern standards is a commendable example of brevity, instructed the Secretary of the Treasury: to mint a stated number of coins; to follow certain procedures with respect to the marketing of the coins; to disburse specified surcharges included in the price of each coin to the Statue of Liberty Foundation; and to take all actions necessary to ensure that the project would result in no net cost to the government.

Perhaps in this day and age it will surprise no one that such a laudable piece of legislation has spawned a civil action against the government. More accurately, the manner in which the coins were sold to the public, rather than the legislation itself, led to the initiation of this lawsuit by the plaintiffs. In all fairness to the plaintiffs, the court must take judicial notice that the marketing of the coins may not have been a perfectly administered process.

The provision of the Act that is directly implicated in this action is § 105(c), which reads: "The Secretary [of the Treasury] shall accept prepaid orders for [commemorative] coins prior to the issuance of the coins. Sales under this subsection shall be at a reasonable discount to reflect the benefit of prepayment." A related provision, § 105(d), authorized bulk sales of commemorative coins at a discount. Pursuant to these provisions, in November and December 1985, the Mint mailed certain advertising materials to persons, including the plaintiffs, whose names were included on a list of previous customers/coin collectors. These materials described the various coins the issuance of which was authorized by the Act,[1] and

---

[1]   At this juncture it is appropriate to note that the Act authorized the issuance of three different commemorative coins, and that different quantities of each type of coin were to be minted. The minting of no more than twenty-five million half-dollar clad coins was authorized; no more

encouraged potential purchasers to forward early payment for commemorative coins. The materials represented, inter alia, that "[i]f [the Mint] receive[s] your reservation by December 31, 1985, you will enjoy a favorable Pre-Issue Discount saving you up to 16% on your coins." Payment could be made either by check, money order, or credit card. Apparently, the Mint had not previously dealt with credit card sales, and the processing of credit card orders, which in this case turned out to be an almost impossible ordeal, was contracted to the Mellon Bank in Pittsburgh, Pennsylvania.

The materials included an order form. Directly above the space provided on this form for the customer's signature was the following:

> VERY IMPORTANT-PLEASE READ: YES, Please accept my order for the U.S. Liberty Coins I have indicated. I understand that all sales are final and not subject to refund. Verification of my order will be made by the Department of the Treasury, U.S. Mint. My coins may be delivered in multiple shipments. If my order is received by December 31, 1985, I will be entitled to purchase the coins at the Pre-Issue Discount price shown. I have read, understand and agree to the above.

On the opposite side of the form the following language appeared:

> As a special courtesy to collectors, you are receiving advance notice of the minting and issuing of three new U.S. coins authorized by Congress to commemorate the centennial of the Statue of Liberty. If you place your reservation prior to December 31, 1985, you will be eligible for a Congressionally authorized Pre-Issue Discount on all coins and sets of coins. Use this form to reserve your Liberty Coins direct from the U.S. Mint. All coins will be accompanied by a Liberty Coin presentation case and certificate.

> Please allow 6 to 8 weeks for delivery after issue date of January 1, 1986. The U.S. Mint reserves the right to limit quantities shipped, subject to availability. Mint may discontinue accepting orders should bullion prices increase significantly. Credit card orders will be billed upon receipt by the U.S. Mint.

Demand for the coins far exceeded the Mint's expectations. While supplies of the half-dollar and one-dollar coins minted pursuant to the Act were more than adequate to meet the demands of all purchasers both during the pre-issue discount period and for many months thereafter, there was an insufficient quantity of five-dollar gold coins, however, with which to fill the orders of many of those who responded to the Mint's promotional materials. According to the Mint's "knowledge and belief," the last order

---

than ten million one-dollar silver coins could be issued; and only 500,000 gold five-dollar pieces were to be produced.

for gold coins that was filled was accepted "some time between December 31, 1985, and January 6, 1986. . . . This exhausted the supply of 500,000 gold coins the issuance of which was authorized by the Act.

A great many would-be acquisitors of gold coins were disappointed by the news of the sell-out. These individuals, many of whom were coin dealers, developed a more serious case of disappointment when it became apparent that the gold coins had increased in value by approximately 200% within the first few months of 1986. Notwithstanding the foregoing facts, which understandably would be cause for tears on the part of those turned away, collectors and dealers alike, it is quite possible that no legal action against the Mint would have been contemplated had not certain matters concerning the treatment of credit card orders come to light. In this regard, the ordeal faced by plaintiffs Mary and Anthony Mesaros appears not to have been atypical.

Plaintiffs allege that on November 26, 1985, Mary Mesaros forwarded to the Mint an order for certain Statue of Liberty coins. Information concerning Anthony Mesaros' credit card was included on the order form, reflecting that the sum of $1,675 should be charged against Mr. Mesaros' credit account. Subsequently, on December 30, 1985, Anthony Mesaros forwarded orders for an additional eighteen gold coins to the Mint. These orders were placed in the names of members of the Mesaros family, and were paid for with nine separate checks.

On February 18, 1986, the Mesaroses were informed by form letter that the Mint "had tried but was unable" to process the Mesaroses' November 26, 1985, credit card order. The letter directed the plaintiffs to contact their financial institution for details relating to the rejection of their order. A new order form was forwarded to the Mesaroses along with the form letter, with which the plaintiffs were informed that they could order "the options currently available." The options then available, of course, did not include five-dollar gold coins. Investigation by Mr. Mesaros revealed that his bank had not been responsible for the rejection of his credit card order. By letter of April 7, 1986, an officer of the Columbus (Georgia) Bank and Trust Company informed Mr. Mesaros that, in fact, on December 27, 1985, that bank had given authorization to the Mellon Bank (responsible for processing credit card orders for the Mint) with respect to the coin order charged to Mr. Mesaros' account. In or about May 1986, the Mesaroses received the eighteen coins that had been paid for by checks dated December 30, 1985.

During the early months of 1986, rumors and information began to filter through the ranks of coin collectors and dealers concerning rejections of credit card orders under circumstances similar to those faced by the Mesaroses. It was becoming apparent by March or April that persons who had paid by wires, money orders or checks, dated as late as the end of

December, were receiving their coins from the Mint, while many persons who had submitted credit card orders (in November in certain cases) were not receiving their coins. These disappointed credit card customers were sent form letters by the Mint informing them either that the Mint had "tried but was unable" to process their orders (such as that received by the Mesaroses, see *supra*), or that their order could not be processed because the gold coins had sold out. According to plaintiffs, the rejection of their credit card order, and the rejection of other collectors' and dealers' credit card orders, is inexplicable on any reasonable basis, in that there existed no inaccuracies in the information provided to the Mint and no shortage of credit on the part of those submitting orders.

According to the Mint, over 756,000 orders for Statue of Liberty coins had been received as of May 30, 1986, 186,000 of which were credit card orders. According to plaintiffs, approximately 13,000 credit card orders were rejected. However, the record shows that many of the credit card orders were insufficient or incorrect for one reason or another. For instance, some were illegible or mutilated, others did not include the expiration date of the credit card, some were unsigned, and on others the standard check with the issuers (Visa and Mastercard) showed that the purchase would exceed the customer's credit limit. On still others there was no matching account number shown in the credit card companies' records. In many instances there was a discrepancy between the number of coins or sets ordered and the amounts specified by the customer. Some of the orders did not have the full credit numbers inscribed thereon.

The record does not indicate that the Mesaros order involved here had any of the above deficiencies . . . The record shows that the Mint and the Mellon Bank were simply swamped with a deluge of 756,000 orders, of which 186,000 were credit card orders. Cash orders were filled fairly promptly by the Mint, but credit card orders before being filled had to be sent by the Mint to the Mellon Bank in Pittsburgh for verification, investigation, and determination of validity. This was at best a slow process. Credit card orders, when approved by the Mellon Bank were certified as valid and returned to the Mint to be filled. Before all of the 186,000 credit card orders could be verified by the Mellon Bank and thereafter filled by the Mint, all of the gold coins had been sold by the Mint in filling cash orders, and no more coins were available. As a result, 13,000 unverified and uncertified credit card orders could not be filled, and were rejected by the Mint. The Mesaros order was in this rejected group. On February 18, 1986, the Mint advised the Mesaroses by a form letter that the Mint "had tried but was unable" to process the Mesaros credit card order, and returned the order form. Anthony Mesaros was so enraged by this turn of events that he wrote the word "bastards" across the front of the returned original order.

On May 23, 1986, plaintiffs filed suit in the district court, seeking either damages on a breach of contract theory or, in the alternative, mandamus relief in the form of a court order forcing defendants to accept plaintiffs' credit card order. Such mandamus relief would ultimately require, according to plaintiffs, the government to deliver the plaintiffs the gold coins that they ordered in November 1985. . . .

The plaintiffs claim that the Mint breached an express contract with them and that they are entitled to recover money damages from defendants for this breach. . . . The plaintiffs contend that the materials sent to them by the Mint, including the order form, constituted an offer that upon acceptance by the plaintiffs created a binding contract between them and the government whereby the government was bound and obligated to deliver the coins ordered by them. The great weight of authority is against the plaintiffs. It is well established that materials such as those mailed to prospective customers by the Mint are no more than advertisements or invitations to deal. They are mere notices and solicitations for offers which create no power of acceptance in the recipient. . . .

It is stated in Williston, A Treatise on the Law of Contracts, § 27 (3rd ed. 1957):

> Thus, if goods are advertised for sale at a certain price, it is not an offer, and no contract is formed by the statement of an intending purchaser that he will take a specified quantity of the goods at that price. The construction is rather favored that such an advertisement is a mere invitation to enter into a bargain rather than an offer. So a published price list is not an offer to sell the goods listed at the published prices.

See also Corbin, Contracts, §§ 25, 28 (1963 ed.); Lane v. Hopfeld, 160 Conn. 53, 273 A.2d 721 (1970); Montgomery Ward & Co. v. Johnson, 209 Mass. 89, 95 N.E. 290 (1911); Lovett v. Frederick Loeser & Co., 124 Misc. 81, 207 N.Y.S. 753 (1924); Osage Homestead, Inc. v. Sutphin, 657 S.W.2d 346 (Mo.App.1983).

A basic rule of contracts holds that whether an offer has been made depends on the objective reasonableness of the alleged offeree's belief that the advertisement or solicitation was intended as an offer. Generally, it is considered unreasonable for a person to believe that advertisements and solicitations are offers that bind the advertiser. Otherwise, the advertiser could be bound by an excessive number of contracts requiring delivery of goods far in excess of amounts available. That is particularly true in the instant case where the gold coins were limited to 500,000 by the Act of Congress.

We conclude that a thorough reading, construction, and interpretation of the materials sent to the plaintiffs by the Mint makes clear that the contention of the plaintiffs that they reasonably believed the materials were intended as an offer is unreasonable as a matter of law. This is especially true in view of the words "YES, Please accept my order . . ." that were printed on the credit card form, which showed that the credit card order was an offer from the plaintiffs to the Mint to buy the coins, which offer might or might not be accepted by the Mint. Accordingly, the Mint materials were intended solely as solicitations of offers from customers that were subject to acceptance by the Mint before the Mint would be bound by a contract. This is in accord with the following statement from I Corbin, Contracts, 375–76 § 88 (1963):

> Where one party solicits and receives an order or other expression of agreement from another, clearly specifying that there is to be no contract until ratification or assent by some officer or representative of the solicitor, the solicitation is not itself an offer; it is a request for an offer.

The plaintiffs rely on Lefkowitz v. Great Minneapolis Surplus Store, 251 Minn. 188, 86 N.W.2d 689 (1957). In that case a store advertised one fur stole worth $139.50 for sale for $1.00 on a first-come, first-served basis when the store opened at 9:00 a.m. The plaintiff arrived first, but the store refused to sell the stole to him. The plaintiff sued for breach of contract. The court held under these unusual facts that the advertisement constituted an offer. That case is clearly distinguishable from our case on the facts. Here the Mint had 35,500,000 coins for sale to the general public for which it received over 756,000 orders. The Mint advertisement did not state that the coins would be sold on a first-come, first-served basis, as in *Lefkowitz*, or on any other particular basis. Since the coins could be paid for with checks, money orders or credit cards, it would have been impossible for the Mint to have processed the sales on a first-come, first-served basis. The situation in *Lefkowitz* was so different that it is of no help to the plaintiffs.

We hold that the Mint advertisement materials were not an offer of sale of the coins that could be accepted by the plaintiffs to create a contract, and that no contract was made between the plaintiffs and the government with reference to the coins. [Affirmed.]

CARLILL v. CARBOLIC SMOKE BALL CO.
1 Q.B. 256 (Court of Appeal, England 1893)

LINDLEY, L.J.

The defendants, in November, 1891, caused to be published in several newspapers an advertisement to the following effect:

> £100 reward will be paid by the Carbolic Smoke Ball Company to any person who contracts the increasing epidemic influenza, colds, or any disease caused by taking cold, after having

used the ball three times daily for two weeks according to the printed directions supplied with each ball. £1,000 is deposited with the Alliance Bank, Regent Street, shewing our sincerity in the matter.

During the last epidemic of influenza, many thousand carbolic smoke balls were sold as preventives against this disease, and in no ascertained case was the disease contracted by those using the carbolic smoke ball.

One carbolic smoke ball will last a family several months, making it the cheapest remedy in the world at the price, 10s. post free. The ball can be refilled at a cost of 5s. Address, Carbolic Smoke Ball Company, 27 Princes Street, Hanover Square, London."

The plaintiff, relying upon the advertisement, bought from a chemist one of the smoke balls, and contracted influenza after using the ball for two weeks in accordance with the printed directions. She then claimed the £100 and, on the defendants refusing to pay, brought this action to recover the amount. [The plaintiffs won a judgment below and the defendants appealed.]

. . . The first observation I would make is that we are not dealing with any inferences of fact. We are dealing with an express promise to pay 100*l.* in certain events. There can be no mistake about that at all. Read this advertisement how you will, and twist it about as you will, here is a distinct promise expressed in language which is perfectly unmistakable: "100*l.* reward will be paid by the Carbolic Smoke Ball Company to any person who contracts the influenza after having use the ball three times daily," and so on.

Now one must look at it a little further, and see if this is intended to be a promise at all, or whether it is a mere puff—a sort of thing which means nothing. Is that the meaning of it? My answer to that question is No, and I base my answer upon this passage: "£1,000 is deposited with the Alliance Bank, shewing our sincerity in the matter." Now, what is that deposited for? What is that put in for, except to negative the suggestion that this is a mere puff, and means nothing at all? The deposit is called in aid by the advertiser as proof of his sincerity in the matter—that is, of his intention to pay this £100 in the events which he has specified. I make the remark, as I say, for the purpose of giving point to the observation that we are not inferring the promise from ambiguous language. Here it is, as plain as words can make it.

Then it is said that it is not binding. In the first place, it is said that it is not made with anybody in particular. Now that point is common to the words of this advertisement, as to the words of all other advertisements offering rewards. They are offers to anybody who performs the conditions named in the advertisement, and anybody who does perform the conditions accepts the offer. I take it, if you look at this advertisement in point of law, it is an offer to pay 100*l*. to anybody who will perform these conditions, and the performance of the conditions is the acceptance of the offer.

. . . Unquestionably, as a general proposition, when an offer is made, you must have it not only accepted, but the acceptance notified. But is that so in cases of this kind? I apprehend that this is rather an exception to that rule, or, if not an exception, it is open to the observation that the notification of the acceptance need not precede the performance.

. . . We have, therefore, all the elements which are necessary to form a binding contract enforceable in point of law[.] . . . It appears to me, therefore, that these defendants must perform their promise, and if they have been so unguarded and so unwary as to expose themselves to a great many actions, so much the worse for them. It appears to me it would be very little short of a scandal if we said that no action would lie on such a promise as this, acted upon as it has been.

BOWEN, L.J. [concurring].

. . . [The defendants] say that the terms are too vague to be capable of being consolidated into a contract, . . . that the vagueness of the document shews that no contract at all was intended. It seems to me that in order to arrive at a right conclusion we must read the advertisement in its plain meaning, as the public would understand it. It was intended to be issued to the public, and to be read by the public. How would an ordinary person reading this document construe it? It was intended unquestionably to have some effect, and I think the effect which it was intended to have was that by means of the use of the carbolic smoke ball the sale of the carbolic smoke ball should be increased. It was designed to make people buy the smoke ball, no doubt; but it was also designed to make them use it, because the suggestions and allegations which it contains are directed immediately to the use of the smoke ball as distinct from the purchase of it. . . .

Was it intended that the £100 should be paid? The advertisement says, £1,000 is lodged at the bank for the purpose. Therefore it cannot be said it was intended to be a mere puff. I think it was intended to be understood by the public as an offer which was to be acted upon.

But [the defendants say] there was no check on the part of the persons who made it—that it would be an insensate thing to promise £100 to a person who used the smoke ball unless you could check his using it. The answer to that seems to me to be that if a person chooses to make these extravagant promises, he probably does so because it pays him to make them; and if he has made such promises, their extravagance is no reason in law why he should not be bound by them.

But it is said the promise is made to all the world, that is, to anybody. It is not a contract made with all the world. There is the fallacy of the argument. It is an offer made to all the world, and why on earth should not an offer be made to all the world which is to ripen into a contract with anybody who comes forward and performs the condition? It is an offer to become liable to any one who, before it is retracted, performs the condition; and although the offer is made to the world, the contract is made with that limited portion of the public who come forward and perform the condition on the faith of the advertisement. It is not like cases in which you offer to negotiate, or you issue advertisements that you have got a stock of books to sell, or houses to let, in which case it is not an offer to be bound by any contract. Such advertisements are offers to negotiate—offers to receive offers—offers to chaffer, as I think some learned Judge in one of the cases has said. If this is an offer to be bound, then it is a contract the moment the person fulfils the condition. . . .

Now, if that is the law, how are you to find out whether the person who makes the offer does intimate that notification of acceptance will not be necessary in order to constitute a binding bargain? In many cases you look to the offer itself; in many cases you extract it from the character of the business that is being done; and in the advertisement cases it seems to me to follow, as an inference to be drawn from the transaction itself, that a person is not to notify his acceptance of the offer before he performs the condition; but that if he performs the condition, notification is dispensed with; and it seems to me no other conclusion could be arrived at from the point of view of common-sense.

If I advertise to the world that my dog is lost, and that anybody who brings the dog to a particular place will be paid some money, and all the police or other persons whose business it is to find lost dogs to be expected to sit down and write me a note saying that they have accepted my proposal? Why, of course, they look for the dog, and as soon as they find the dog they have performed the condition. The very essence of the transaction is that the dog should be found, and it is not necessary under such circumstances, it seems to me, to make the contract binding, that there should be any notification of acceptance at all. It follows from the nature of the thing that the performance of the condition is sufficient acceptance without the notification of it, and a person who makes an offer in an advertisement of that kind makes an offer which must be read by the light of that common-sense reflection. He does, therefore, in his offer impliedly indicate that he does not require notification of the acceptance of the offer. . . .

NOTES AND QUESTIONS

1. What is the best way to reconcile the outcomes of the foregoing line of cases? Advertisers are trying to get the "word out" about their products but

may have only limited ability to fill demand. As such, advertisements are generally seen as a solicitation or invitation for the customer to make an offer themselves, which then the seller can choose to accept. On the other hand, when an advertisement is extremely specific, perhaps this is not as much of a concern. Courts also want to protect consumer's expectations. In modern times, these issues are largely handled by state consumer protection statutes.

2.　　　What are the strongest precedents if you wanted to argue that an advertisement is an offer? What are the strongest precedents if you are an advertiser who wishes to argue that the advertisement is not an offer? See if you can put these arguments, based on the cases you have read, to use in the problem set out below.

3.　　　Today, medical devices and products of the kind that the Carbolic Smoke Ball represented are highly regulated by government agencies. In the absence of such authorities, and before the advent of modern medicine and germ theory, courts may have felt the need to protect the public from scurrilous doctors and "quack" medicines.

4.　　　The advertisement in *Carbolic Smoke Ball* is an example of what is known as a "unilateral contract." A unilateral contract invites the offeree to accept by performing, whereas a bilateral contract allows for acceptance by either performance or a return promise. Here, the advertisers did not care if someone promised to use the ball; they only wanted its use. We will come back to the distinction between unilateral and bilateral contracts later in this chapter.

EXAMPLE: DATELINE DARE

J. Cheney Mason is a high-profile and outspoken criminal defense attorney in Florida. In 2006, Mason represented Nelson Serano, a wealthy businessman, whom prosecutors alleged had orchestrated an elaborate plot to murder his former business partner, George Gonsalves, and three others in a Florida manufacturing plant. During the widely-publicized capital murder trial, Mason gave a challenge in a TV interview that aired on "Dateline NBC."

In the capital murder case, state prosecutors said Serrano, traveling under aliases, flew from Atlanta to Orlando, rented a car, then drove 66 miles to the plant and killed the four people. Then, the State said, he promptly drove 50 miles to the Tampa airport, flew back to Atlanta and, in 28 minutes, drove from the Atlanta airport five miles to a La Quinta Inn. A surveillance tape showed Serrano in the La Quinta, both at mid-day and in the evening. Serrano used the tape as an alibi. Mason argued there was no way anyone could get off a plane at Atlanta's crowded airport and be back at La Quinta 28 minutes later.

On "Dateline NBC," the host, Ann Curry, posed the vital question: whether there was enough time for Serrano to make the trip in 28 minutes. On air, an excited Mason declared:

> *And from there to be on videotape in 28 minutes? Not possible.*
> *Not possible. I challenge anybody to show me, and guess what? Did*

they bring in any evidence to say that somebody made that route, did
so? State's burden of proof. If they can do it, I'll challenge 'em. I'll pay
them a million dollars if they can do it.   unilateral

Dustin Kolodziej, a law student at South Texas College of Law living in
Houston, had been following the Serrano trial on television. He saw the
Dateline show featuring Mason. On December 10, 2007, Kolodziej made the
full trip in the required time, videotaping his steps, from Atlanta to Orlando to
Tampa and back to Atlanta and within 28 minutes, getting off the plane,
walking through the terminal, getting in a car, and arriving at La Quinta Inn.
When Kolodziej demanded payment, however, Mason refused.

Based on the precedents we have studied in this section, should the law
student be richer by $1 million?   reflect on context

C. ACCEPTANCE

Having a valid offer is the first step toward a binding agreement.
Assuming valid consideration is present, all that is then needed is the
acceptance and a binding contract will be formed. But circumstances may
intervene between the time the offer is made and before the acceptance is
tendered. Sometimes the offeror may wish to terminate an offer before it
has been accepted. According to Restatement (Second) of Contracts, Section
36, "an offeree's power of acceptance may be terminated by (a) rejection or
counter-offer by the offeree, or (b) lapse of time, or (c) revocation by the
offeror, or (d) death or incapacity of the offeror or offeree."

An offeree may choose to reject an offer. The offeree may not be
interested in the deal or have determined that it is not a good bargain. For
whatever reason, once the offeree has rejected the offer, that offer
disappears. (Of course, the parties could, at a later time, renew the offer).
Under the traditional common law "mirror image rule," an acceptance had
to match the terms of the offer precisely in order to be effective. Any
variation between the acceptance and the offer rendered the purported
acceptance ineffective and would instead be treated as a counter-offer.

The traditional common law mirror image rule has been relaxed
somewhat in more recent times. For instance, the Restatement (Second) of
Contracts, Section 61, allows for an acceptance that requests (but does not
require) a change in the terms. For transactions in goods, the Uniform
Commercial Code goes even further to effectively eliminate the mirror
image rule, as we will see in Section D of this chapter.

Another circumstance that may terminate an offer is a lapse of time.
If enough time passes, the offer is said to expire, or lapse. If no time is
specified in the offer, then it is assumed that the offeree has a reasonable
time to accept. How much time is "reasonable" depends on the
circumstances, custom, the market, and other related factors. Some offers
may only last as long as the face to face conversation in which they were

made. For example, a settlement offer in a trial may only last as long as a recess in the court hallway before a closing argument is made.

Finally, the death or incapacity of the offeror or offeree terminates the power of acceptance. As to the offeree, this reflects that only the offeree has the power of acceptance, such that their death or incapacity makes exercise of the power impossible. But as to the offeror, this rule may be a relic of the obsolete view that a contract required a "meeting of minds." While it is therefore an anomaly, it remains important. We will see an example of its doctrinal importance in a problem at the end of this section, when an offeror died as an offerree began to accept.

One basic rule that bears keeping in mind is that an offeror may choose to revoke an offer at any time before it has been accepted. The rule was established in the classic English case *Dickinson v. Dodds*, which follows.

DICKINSON V. DODDS
Court of Appeal, L.R. 2 Ch. D. 463 (1876)

On Wednesday, the 10th of June, 1874, the Defendant John Dodds signed and delivered to the Plaintiff, *George Dickinson*, a memorandum, of which the material part was as follows:

> I hereby agree to sell to Mr. *George Dickinson* the whole of the dwelling—houses, garden ground, stabling, and outbuildings thereto belonging, situate at *Croft*, belonging to me, for the sum of £800. As witness my hand this tenth day of June, 1874.
>
> "£800. (Signed) *John Dodds*
>
> P.S.—This offer to be left over until Friday, 9 o'clock, A.M. *J. D.* (the twelfth), 12th
>
> June, 1874.
>
> (Signed) *J. Dodds*

The bill alleged that Dodds understood and intended that the Plaintiff should have until Friday 9 A.M. within which to determine whether he would or would not purchase, and that he should absolutely have until that time the refusal of the property at the price of £800, and that the Plaintiff in fact determined to accept the offer on the morning of Thursday, the 11th of June, but did not at once signify his acceptance to Dodds, believing that he had the power to accept it until 9 A.M. on the Friday.

In the afternoon of the Thursday the Plaintiff was informed by a Mr. Berry that Dodds had been offering or agreeing to sell the property to Thomas Allan, the other Defendant. Thereupon the Plaintiff, at about half-past seven in the evening, went to the house of Mrs. Burgess, the mother-in-law of Dodds, where he was then staying, and left with her a formal acceptance in writing of the offer to sell the property. According to the evidence of Mrs. Burgess this document never in fact reached Dodds, she having forgotten to give it to him.

On the following (Friday) morning, at about seven o'clock, Berry, who was acting as agent for Dickinson, found Dodds at the Darlington railway station, and handed to him a duplicate of the acceptance by Dickinson, and explained to Dodds its purport. He replied that it was too late, as he had sold the property. A few minutes later Dickinson himself found Dodds entering a railway carriage, and handed him another duplicate of the notice of acceptance, but Dodds declined to receive it, saying, "You are too late. I have sold the property."

It appeared that on the day before, Thursday, the 11th of June, Dodds had signed a formal contract for the sale of the property to the Defendant Allan for £800, and had received from him a deposit of £40. The bill in this suit prayed that the Defendant Dodds might be decreed specifically to perform the contract of the 10th of June, 1874; that he might be restrained from conveying the property to Allan; that Allan might be restrained from taking any such conveyance; that, if any such conveyance had been or should be made, Allan might be declared a trustee of the property for, and might be directed to convey the property to, the Plaintiff; and for damages.

JAMES, L.J.

The document, though beginning "I hereby agree to sell," was nothing but an offer, and was only intended to be an offer, for the Plaintiff himself tells us that he required time to consider whether he would enter into an agreement or not. Unless both parties had then agreed there was no concluded agreement then made; it was in effect and substance only an offer to sell. The Plaintiff, being minded not to complete the bargain at that time, added this memorandum—"This offer to be left over until Friday, 9 o'clock A.M., 12th June, 1874." That shews it was only an offer.

There was no consideration given for the undertaking or promise, to whatever extent it may be considered binding, to keep the property unsold until 9 o'clock on Friday morning; but apparently Dickinson was of opinion, and probably Dodds was of the same opinion, that he (Dodds) was bound by that promise, and could not in any way withdraw from it, or retract it, until 9 o'clock on Friday morning, and this probably explains a good deal of what afterwards took place. But it is clear settled law, on one of the clearest principles of law, that this promise, being a mere nudum pactum, was not binding, and that at any moment before a complete acceptance by Dickinson of the offer, Dodds was as free as Dickinson himself.

Well, that being the state of things, it is said that the only mode in which Dodds could assert that freedom was by actually and distinctly saying to Dickinson, "Now I withdraw my offer." It appears to me that there is neither principle nor authority for the proposition that there must be an express and actual withdrawal of the offer, or what is called a retraction.

It must, to constitute a contract, appear that the two minds were at one, at the same moment of time, that is, that there was an offer continuing up to the time of the acceptance. If there was not such a continuing offer, then the acceptance comes to nothing.

Of course it may well be that the one man is bound in some way or other to let the other man know that his mind with regard to the offer has been changed; but in this case, beyond all question, the Plaintiff knew that Dodds was no longer minded to sell the property to him as plainly and clearly as if Dodds had told him in so many words, "I withdraw the offer." This is evident from the Plaintiff's own statements in the bill. The Plaintiff says in effect that, having heard and knowing that Dodds was no longer minded to sell to him, and that he was selling or had sold to some one else, thinking that he could not in point of law withdraw his offer, meaning to fix him to it, and endeavouring to bind him, "I went to the house where he was lodging, and saw his mother-in-law, and left with her an acceptance of the offer, knowing all the while that he had entirely changed his mind. I got an agent to watch for him at 7 o'clock the next morning, and I went to the train just before 9 o'clock, in order that I might catch him and give him my notice of acceptance just before 9 o'clock, and when that occurred he told my agent, and he told me, you are too late, and he then threw back the paper."

It is to my mind quite clear that before there was any attempt at acceptance by the Plaintiff, he was perfectly well aware that Dodds had changed his mind, and that he had in fact agreed to sell the property to Allan. It is impossible, therefore, to say there was ever that existence of the same mind between the two parties which is essential in point of law to the making of an agreement. I am of opinion, therefore, that the Plaintiff has failed to prove that there was any binding contract between Dodds and himself.

MELLISH, L.J. (concurring):

If an offer has been made for the sale of property, and before that offer is accepted, the person who has made the offer enters into a binding agreement to sell the property to somebody else, and the person to whom the offer was first made receives notice in some way that the property has been sold to another person, can he after that make a binding contract by the acceptance of the offer? I am of opinion that he cannot.

The law may be right or wrong in saying that a person who has given to another a certain time within which to accept an offer is not bound by his promise to give that time; but, if he is not bound by that promise, and may still sell the property to someone else, and if it be the law that, in order to make a contract, the two minds must be in agreement at some one time, that is, at the time of the acceptance, how is it possible that when the person to whom the offer has been made knows that the person who has made the offer has sold the property to someone else, and that, in fact, he has not remained in the same mind to sell it to him, he can be at liberty to accept the offer and thereby make a binding contract?

It seems to me that would be simply absurd. If a man makes an offer to sell a particular horse in his stable, and says, "I will give you until the day after to-morrow to accept the offer," and the next day goes and sells the horse to somebody else, and receives the purchase-money from him, can the person to whom the offer was originally made then come and say, "I accept," so as to make a binding contract, and so as to be entitled to recover damages for the non-delivery of the horse? If the rule of law is that a mere offer to sell property, which can be withdrawn at any time, and which is made dependent on the acceptance of the person to whom it is made, is a mere *nudum pactum*, how is it possible that the person to whom the offer has been made can by acceptance make a binding contract after he knows that the person who has made the offer has sold the property to some one else?

It is admitted law that, if a man who makes an offer dies, the offer cannot be accepted after he is dead, and parting with the property has very much the same effect as the death of the owner, for it makes the performance of the offer impossible. I am clearly of opinion that, just as when a man who has made an offer dies before it is accepted it is impossible that it can then be accepted, so when once the person to whom the offer was made knows that the property has been sold to some one else, it is too late for him to accept the offer, and on that ground I am clearly of opinion that there was no binding contract for the sale of this property by Dodds to Dickinson, and even if there had been, it seems to me that the sale of the property to Allan was first in point of time. However, it is not necessary to consider, if there had been two binding contracts, which of them would be entitled to priority in equity, because there is no binding contract between Dodds and Dickinson. . . .

NOTES AND QUESTIONS

1.   The classic case *Dickenson v. Dodds* stands for the proposition that the offeror may revoke the offer at any time before acceptance. However, business practice routinely involves parties keeping an offer open exclusively for a period of time. Such "holding open" is referred to as an *option contract*. Restatement (Second) of Contracts, Section 25 tells us that "an option contract is a promise which meets the requirements for the formation of a contract and limits the promisor's power to revoke an offer." Further, Restatement (Second) of Contracts, Section 37 states that an option contract survives the normal methods whereby an offer can be revoked: counter-offer, rejection, or death or incapacity of the offeror. Consider the additional selections from the Restatement on the subject of options below.

2.   Why create an option contract? An option allows the offeree an open period to think over the offer and choose whether or not to accept. During the option period, the offer remains open. By stating that an option has the same formation requirements as other contracts, the Restatement signals that *consideration* is needed in order to create an option. In other words, an option is its own contract (separate from the exchange to which it relates stated in the accompanying offer). Some amount of money or property (even if small or nominal) must be paid in order to establish an option. In some exchange transactions, an option may have economic value—which might vary with its duration and the market price volatility of the subject to be exchanged—and require that the option-holder pay accordingly, providing real not merely nominal consideration.

3.   Note that in *Dickenson v. Dodds*, nothing was paid for an option or period of contemplation. As such, no option was created and the seller was free to withdraw his offer and sell to a third party.

4.   What kind of notice to the offeree is enough to let them know that the offer has been terminated? In *Dickenson v. Dodds*, the buyer heard that the property had been sold through his agent, Mr. Berry. Is it enough that an offeree "heard it through the grapevine"? Consider Restatement (Second) of Contracts, Section 43 below.

RESTATEMENT (SECOND) OF CONTRACTS, SECTION 43

§ 43.   *Indirect Communication Of Revocation.*

An offeree's power of acceptance is terminated when the offeror takes definite action inconsistent with an intention to enter into the proposed contract and the offeree acquires reliable information to that effect.

RESTATEMENT (SECOND) OF CONTRACTS, SECTIONS 25, 87

§ 25.   *Option Contracts.*

An option contract is a promise which meets the requirements for the formation of a contract and limits the promisor's power to revoke an offer.

§ 87.   *Option Contract.*

(1)   An offer is binding as an option contract if it (a) is in writing and signed by the offeror, recites a purported consideration for the making of the offer, and proposes an exchange on fair terms within a reasonable time; or (b) is made irrevocable by statute.

(2)   An offer which the offeror should reasonably expect to induce action or forbearance of a substantial character on the part of the offeree before acceptance and which does induce such action or forbearance is binding as an option contract to the extent necessary to avoid injustice.

EXAMPLE: REVOCATION AFTER SUBSTANTIAL ACTION

John Petterson owned real estate in Brooklyn that he bought with borrowed money secured by a mortgage. The mortgage loan, which had an outstanding balance of $5,450, was to be repaid in monthly payments of $250 over the ensuing five years. On April 4, the lender wrote this letter to Petterson:

> I hereby agree to accept a full cash payoff of the entire mortgage loan for the total amount of $4,670 if you pay this full amount on or before April 25 . . .

On April 25, Petterson appeared at the lender's home and knocked at the door. The lender asked who was there and Petterson replied: "It is Mr. Petterson. I have come to pay off the mortgage." The lender answered that he had sold the mortgage to another lender. Petterson stated that he would like to speak, so the lender partly opened the door. Thereupon Petterson exhibited the cash, and said he was ready to pay off the mortgage according to the agreement. The lender refused to take the money.

Prior to this conversation, Petterson had made a contract to sell the property to a third party in a deal where he promised there would be no mortgage on it—that this loan would be paid off. But meanwhile, as the lender said, he had sold the mortgage to a third party. So Petterson was stuck and claimed breach of contract, alleging as his loss the discount on the loan the lender had promised.

Was there a contract? In *Petterson v. Pattberg*, 161 N.E. 428 (N.Y. 1928), on which this example is based, a divided New York Court of Appeals held that there was no contract. Consider the following excerpts from the majority and dissenting opinions. Which has the better of the argument? After weighing the arguments, consult the ensuing selections from the Restatement (Second) of Contracts to determine which side it takes.

Majority opinion:

> Clearly the defendant's letter proposed to Petterson the making of a unilateral contract, the gift of a promise in exchange for the performance of an act. The thing conditionally promised by the defendant was the reduction of the mortgage debt. The act requested to be done, in consideration of the offered promise, was payment in full of the reduced principal of the debt prior to the due date thereof. "If an act is requested, that very act, and no other, must be given." Williston on Contracts, § 73. . . .

> An interesting question arises when, as here, the offeree approaches the offeror with the intention of proffering performance and, before actual tender is made, the offer is withdrawn. Of such a case Williston says: "The offeror may see the approach of the offeree and know that an acceptance is contemplated. If the offeror can say "I revoke" before the offeree accepts, however brief the interval of

time between the two acts, there is no escape from the conclusion that the offer is terminated."

In this instance Petterson, standing at the door of the defendant's house, stated to the defendant that he had come to pay off the mortgage. Before a tender of the necessary moneys had been made, the defendant informed Petterson that he had sold the mortgage. That was a definite notice to Petterson that the defendant could not perform his offered promise, and that a tender to the defendant, who was no longer the creditor, would be ineffective to satisfy the debt. . . . Thus it clearly appears that the defendant's offer was withdrawn before its acceptance had been tendered. . . .

Dissenting Opinion:

The defendant's letter to Petterson constituted a promise on his part to accept payment at a discount of the mortgage he held, provided the mortgage is paid on or before [April 25]. . . Doubtless, by the terms of the promise itself, the defendant made payment of the mortgage by the plaintiff, before the stipulated time, a condition . . . to performance by the defendant of his promise to accept payment at a discount. If the condition . . . has not been performed, it is because the defendant made performance impossible by refusing to accept payment, when the plaintiff came with an offer of immediate performance. "It is a principle of fundamental justice that if a promisor is himself the cause of the failure of performance either of an obligation due him or of a condition upon which his own liability depends, he cannot take advantage of the failure." Williston on Contracts, § 677. . . .

The promise made by the defendant lacked consideration at the time it was made. Nevertheless, the promise was not made as a gift or mere gratuity to the plaintiff. It was made for the purpose of obtaining from the defendant something which the plaintiff desired. It constituted an offer which was to become binding whenever the plaintiff should give, in return for the defendant's promise, exactly the consideration which the defendant requested. Here the defendant requested no counter promise from the plaintiff. The consideration requested by the defendant for his promise to accept payment was, I agree, some act to be performed by the plaintiff. Until the act requested was performed, the defendant might undoubtedly revoke his offer. Our problem is to determine from the words of the letter, read in the light of surrounding circumstances, what act the defendant requested as consideration for his promise.

The defendant undoubtedly made his offer as an inducement to the plaintiff to "pay" the mortgage before it was due. Therefore, it is said, that "the act requested to be performed was the completed act of payment, a thing incapable of performance, unless assented to by the person to be paid." In unmistakable terms the defendant agreed to accept payment, yet we are told that the defendant intended, and the plaintiff should have understood, that the act requested by the defendant, as consideration for his promise to accept payment, included performance by the defendant himself of the very promise for which the act was to be consideration. . . .

RESTATEMENT (SECOND) OF CONTRACTS, SECTION 45

§ 45.   *Option Contract Created by Part Performance or Tender.*

(1) Where an offer invites an offeree to accept by rendering a performance and does not invite a promissory acceptance, an option contract is created when the offeree tenders or begins the invited performance or tenders a beginning of it.

(2) The offeror's duty of performance under any option contract so created is conditional on completion or tender of the invited performance in accordance with the terms of the offer.

To summarize, under the common law rule of *Dickenson v. Dodds*, an offeror may freely revoke an offer at any time before it is accepted. That rule holds true unless the parties have made a separate option contract to hold open the offer, which would require the payment of consideration. The Uniform Commercial Code, Section 2–205, however, significantly alters the common law rule for merchants. A merchant may hold open an offer without consideration, so long as certain formalities are met, creating what the UCC calls a "firm offer."

UCC SECTION 2–205

§ 2–205. *Firm Offers.*

An offer by a merchant to buy or sell goods in a signed writing which by its terms gives assurance that it will be held open is not revocable, for lack of consideration, during the time stated or if no time is stated for a reasonable time, but in no event may such period of irrevocability exceed three months; but any such term of assurance on a form supplied by the offeree must be separately signed by the offeror.

Note that the offer must be in writing by a merchant (recall the earlier definition of "merchant" from the UCC). Use these rules to help you answer the following problems.

PROBLEMS: FIRM OFFERS

1.   Javier is a skilled pet psychologist who is especially good at training dogs who have problems with persistent barking. Anna is not sure that she wants to spend so much money on dog training, but might be interested in Javier's services. Javier tells her that he has an opening next week, and that he will reserve the time for her, and that Anna has three days to decide. He lists the services he proposes to provide in writing, notes a price of $500 for the training, and signs it. The next day, Javier finds that he is actually terribly over-booked. May he revoke the offer? *can't rely on UCC b/c service contract*

2.   Lucretia is a beekeeper and manufacturer of honey, and Tom is the proprietor of Tom's Honey Treats and Baked Goods, which he plans to expand greatly over the next year with the opening of an extra annex and the addition of his Internet sales line. Tom has already made significant purchases from Lucretia but wants to make sure that his honey supply is uninterrupted. After some negotiation, Lucretia, on stationery from her business, writes out an "Official Irrevocable Offer" for 200 jars of honey, $10 per jar, good for six months, Yours Truly, /*Lucretia*/ (signature). Has Lucretia made a firm offer?

is a merchant
+ signed writing,
but she says 6mo
+ UCC says 3 mo

3.   Jimmy Williams, a basketball coach, was moving out of state. To help get organized for his move, he holds a yard sale. He wrote up a sign: "Everything must go. Make me an offer!" Along with the standard books and clothes that seem to be staples at yard sales, Jimmy was also selling some big ticket items, such as a motorcycle he had helped restore, a piano, and a washer-dryer combination set. Cedrick was very interested in the piano, and he and Jimmy discussed a price of $2,000. But Cedrick wanted to think a little more, and also call his brother, who owned a truck, which would save on the expense of hiring movers for the instrument. Cedrick asked Jimmy to "put it in writing," and Jimmy agreed, signing a note that would "keep an option open for Cedrick" to run "until the end of the day" for $2,000. Has Jimmy made a firm offer under the UCC? *No - not a merchant*

If the offer has not lapsed, been revoked, or otherwise terminated, the offeree may accept. This is the final step, and a contract is then formed. So, how may one accept an offer? Of course, sometimes the offer expressly states what needs to be done in order to accept. Because we say that the offeror is the "master of the offer," we first would look at the terms of the offer itself.

That said, there are some limits on what can constitute an acceptance. The traditional rule has been that silence, or doing nothing, cannot constitute an acceptance. The rationale is that contracts are transactions that must be entered voluntarily; so there must be some affirmative or objective manifestation of assent. To have silence operate as an acceptance would mean that some number of offerees would find themselves unwillingly pushed into contracts. However, Restatement (Second) of

Contracts, Section 69 tells us that there are some exceptions to the rule, and that silence may in these instances be considered an acceptance.

RESTATEMENT (SECOND) OF CONTRACTS, SECTION 69

§ 69. *Acceptance by Silence or Exercise of Dominion.*

(1) Where an offeree fails to reply to an offer, his silence and inaction operate as an acceptance in the following cases only:

(a) Where an offeree takes the benefit of offered services with reasonable opportunity to reject them and reason to know that they were offered with the expectation of compensation.

(b) Where the offeror has stated or given the offeree reason to understand that assent may be manifested by silence or inaction, and the offeree in remaining silent and inactive intends to accept the offer.

(c) Where because of previous dealings or otherwise, it is reasonable that the offeree should notify the offeror if he does not intend to accept.

––––––––––

For one example of the exception under Section 69, think of the "book of the month" or "CD of the month" clubs. Many of these clubs operate by giving subscribers a number of products up front, with the agreement that the subscriber will pay full price for a certain number of products later. The products are sent to the subscriber's home automatically, and doing nothing results in an acceptance. The reason these fall under the exception and are enforceable is because the subscriber assents to this arrangement at the outset, knowing that if they choose to do nothing later, they will still be bound. But both parties have assented to this arrangement in advance, and thus it is still voluntary—and an enforceable contract. More recently, this same model has been adapted for use with online meal kits.

As a matter of property law, state and federal "unsolicited merchandise statutes," mostly adopted in the 1960s and still in effect, treat unsolicited goods as gifts. *See, e.g.*, 39 U.S.C. § 3009.

PROBLEMS: ASSENT BY SILENCE

1. Sam returns home from a long day at the office, only to find a wonderfully wrapped box on his front porch. The box says that it is from "Jams Unlimited" and that something "scrumptious awaits" if he will only open the box. Sam has not ordered any products from Jams Unlimited, and he looks it over to see if there is a return address listed, but there is none. Later that night, Sam is hungry for an after-dinner sweet. His eyes alight on the package. In each instance, determine whether a contract for sale of jam has been formed.

A. Sam opens the package to find an assortment of fancy jams, including orange marmalade, mint jelly, and a strawberry-cherry blend. There is no address or other information anywhere in the package. Unable to resist temptation, Sam eats the jam.

B. Sam opens the package to find an assortment of fancy jams, including orange marmalade, mint jelly, and a strawberry-cherry blend. There is a note in the packaging that says "If you eat these jams, you will owe us $25." There is also a return postage-paid box inside with the Jams Unlimited address on it. Unable to resist temptation, Sam eats the jam.

C. Same facts as in B, except that the box for return is not postage-paid.

D. Sam opens the package to find a letter inside addressed to him. The letter contains an invitation to the "jam of the month club." As detailed in the letter, every month the jam club sends a postcard and the customer can send it back, indicating "no, I do not want the delicious jam of the month." Otherwise, hearing nothing, the customer will pay $10/jar. Sam calls the 1-800-EAT-JAMS number and agrees to join the club. The next month Sam eats the apricot, and the month after that, the peach. Each month Sam pays for the jam. However, when sent the postcard for zucchini jam, he wants to decline, but forgets about it. The zucchini jam is delivered and Sam does not want to pay. Is he liable for the $10?

2. In nice weather, Roberta enjoys walking to her office, which is located in downtown Los Angeles about ten minutes from where she lives. One day she is walking to work, although running a few minute late, when she sees a small sign in front of her. It says: "By continuing to walk down this street, you give us permission to film you as an extra for a crowd scene." Roberta does not want to be filmed, in fact she detests the idea of being on camera, but she is late to work and deviating from her normal route would make her 25 minutes late and might get her in trouble. Roberta decides to walk down the street, but the whole time says out loud "I do not agree to be filmed, I do not agree to be filmed." Is there a binding contract?

LIVINGSTONE V. EVANS

[1925] 4 D.L.R. 769 (Alberta Supreme Court)

WALSH, J.

The defendant, Thomas J. Evans, through his agent, wrote to the plaintiff offering to sell him the land in question for $1,800 on terms. On the day that he received this offer the plaintiff wired this agent as follows: "Send lowest cash price. Will give $1,600 cash. Wire." The agent replied to this by telegram as follows: "Cannot reduce price." Immediately upon the receipt of this telegram the plaintiff wrote accepting the offer. It is admitted by the defendants that this offer and the plaintiff's acceptance of it constitute a contract for the sale of this land to the plaintiff by which he is bound unless the intervening telegrams above set out put an end to his offer so that the plaintiff could not thereafter bind him to it by his acceptance of it.

It is quite clear that when an offer has been rejected it is thereby ended and it cannot be afterwards accepted without the consent of him who made it. The simple question and the only one argued before me is whether the plaintiff's counter offer was in law a rejection of the defendant's offer which freed him from it.

Hyde v. Wrench, 3 Beav. 334 (49 E.R. 132) a judgment of Lord Langdale, M.R. pronounced in 1840 is the authority for the contention that it was. The defendant offered to sell for £1,000. The plaintiff met that with an offer to pay £950 and (to quote from the judgment) "he thereby rejected the offer previously made by the Defendant. I think that it was not afterwards competent for him to revive the proposal of the Defendant, by tendering an acceptance of it."

Stevenson v. McLean, 5 Q.B.D. 346, 49 L.J.Q.B. 701, 42 L.T. 897, 28 W.R. 916, a later case relied upon by Mr. Grant is easily distinguishable from *Hyde v. Wrench* as it is in fact distinguished by Lush, J. who decided it. He held that the letter there relied upon as constituting a rejection of the offer was not a new proposal but a mere enquiry which should have been answered and not treated as a rejection but the learned Judge said that if it had contained an offer it would have likened the case to *Hyde v. Wrench*.

Hyde v. Wrench has stood without question for 85 years. It is adopted by the text writers as a correct exposition of the law and is generally accepted and recognized as such. I think it not too much to say that it has firmly established it as a part of the law of contracts that the making of a counter-offer is a rejection of the original offer.

The plaintiff's telegram was undoubtedly a counter-offer. True, it contained an inquiry as well but that clearly was one which called for an answer only if the counter-offer was rejected. In substance it said, "I will give you $1,600 cash. If you won't take that wire your lowest cash price." In my opinion it put an end to the defendant's liability under his offer unless it was revived by his telegram in reply to it.

The real difficulty in the case, to my mind, arises out of the defendant's telegram "cannot reduce price." If this was simply a rejection of the plaintiff's counter-offer it amounts to nothing. If, however, it was a renewal of the original offer it gave the plaintiff the right to bind the defendant to it by his subsequent acceptance of it.

With some doubt I think that it was a renewal of the original offer or at any rate an intimation to the plaintiff that he was still willing to treat on the basis of it. It was, of course, a reply to the counter-offer and to the enquiry in the plaintiff's telegram. But it was more than that. The price referred to in it was unquestionably that mentioned in his letter. His statement that he could not reduce that price strikes me as having but one meaning, namely, that he was still standing by it and, therefore, still open to accept it. . . .

I am, therefore, of the opinion that there was a binding contract for the sale of this land to the plaintiff of which he is entitled to specific performance. It was admitted by his counsel that if I reached this conclusion his subsequent agreement to sell the land to the defendant Williams would be of no avail as against the plaintiff's contract. . . .

RESTATEMENT (SECOND) OF CONTRACTS, SECTIONS 58, 59

§ 58.   *Necessity of Acceptance Complying with Terms of Offer.*

An acceptance must comply with the requirements of the offer as to the promise to be made or the performance to be rendered.

§ 59.   *Purported Acceptance Which Adds Qualifications.*

A reply to an offer which purports to accept it but is conditional on the offeror's assent to terms additional to or different from those offered is not an acceptance but is a counter-offer.

———————

Sometimes, the offer itself says nothing about how the offeree may accept. In that case, we must fill in the gaps. There are many instances where we will see that the contract is incomplete and we will have to turn to "default rules" in order to help fill in those gaps. Default rules can be what most people would agree to if they were asked (hypothetical consent default rules), penalty default rules (which are harsh, and serve to force information from the parties to make their own rules), or muddy default rules (complicated and therefore not what most people would think of on their own, but perhaps good rules nonetheless).

Since contracting can occur at a distance, particular rules developed about when an acceptance would become effective when sent by postal mail, for instance. Such acceptances are governed by the *mailbox rule* otherwise known as the *deposited acceptance* rule. Under this rule, an acceptance is *effective upon dispatch*. This is an unusual rule in the law, as most communications across a variety of legal contexts are deemed effective only when received.

Under contract law's mailbox rule, so long as the acceptance is properly addressed and paid for, the acceptance is effective even if the mail is lost or not delivered. In effect, this is a risk allocation default rule, putting the risk of lost communications on the offeror. It seems both a fair and efficient default rule because most offerors would be prepared to accept the risk and, as master of the offer, the offeror can change the default rule.

Despite radical transformations in the means of communication invented over the decades—from telegrams and faxes to e-mail and texting—the mailbox rule remains robust for all forms of communicating at a distance. After all, there remains risk, which must be allocated. (The mailbox rule does not apply to telephonic communications, seen as the functional equivalent of being present in the same place).

MORRISON V. THOELKE
155 So.2d 889 (App. Fla.1963)

ALLEN, ACTING CHIEF JUDGE.

. . . [A]ppellees are the owners of the subject property located in Orange County; that on November 26, 1957, appellants, as purchasers, executed a contract for the sale and purchase of the subject property and mailed the contract to appellees who were in Texas; and that on November 27, 1957, appellees executed the contract and placed it in the mails addressed to appellants' attorney in Florida. It is also undisputed that after mailing said contract, but prior to its receipt in Florida, appellees called appellants' attorney and cancelled and repudiated the execution and contract. . . .

. . . The question is whether a contract is complete and binding when a letter of acceptance is mailed, thus barring repudiation prior to delivery to the offeror, or when the letter of acceptance is received, thus permitting repudiation prior to receipt. . . .

The appellant . . . contends that this case is controlled by the general rule that insofar as the mail is an acceptable medium of communication, a contract is complete and binding upon posting of the letter of acceptance. Appellees, on the other hand, argue that the right to recall mail makes the Post Office Department the agent of the sender, and that such right coupled with communication of a renunciation prior to receipt of the acceptance voids the acceptance. In short, appellees argue that acceptance is complete only upon receipt of the mailed acceptance. . . .

Turning first to the general rule relied upon by appellant some insight may be gained by reference to the statement of the rule in leading encyclopedias and treatises. A . . . statement of the general rule is found in 1 Williston, Contracts § 81 (3rd ed. 1957):

> Contracts are frequently made between parties at some distance and therefore it is of vital importance to determine at what moment the contract is complete. If the mailing of an

acceptance completes the contract, what happens thereafter, whether the death of either party, the receipt of a revocation or rejection, or a telegraphic recalling of the acceptance, though occurring before the receipt of the acceptance, will be of no avail; whereas, if a contract is not completed until the acceptance has been received, in all the situations supposed no contract will arise.

It was early decided that the contract was completed upon the mailing of the acceptance. The reason influencing the court was evidently that when the acceptance was mailed, there had been an overt manifestation of assent to the proposal. The court failed to consider that since the proposed contract was bilateral, as is almost invariably any contract made by mail, the so-called acceptance must also have become effective as a promise to the offeror in order to create a contract. The result thus early reached, however, has definitely established the law not only in England but also in the United States, Canada and other common law jurisdictions. It is, therefore, immaterial that the acceptance never reaches its destination. . . .

A second leading treatise on the law of contracts, Corbin, Contracts §§ 78 and 80 (1950 Supp.1961), also devotes some discussion to the "rule" urged by appellants. Corbin writes:

Where the parties are negotiating at a distance from each other, the most common method of making an offer is by sending it by mail; and more often than not the offeror has specified no particular mode of acceptance. In such a case, it is now the prevailing rule that the offeree has power to accept and close the contract by mailing a letter of acceptance, properly stamped and addressed, within a reasonable time. The contract is regarded as made at the time and place that the letter of acceptance is put into the possession of the post office department.

The postal regulations have for a long period made it possible for the sender of a letter to intercept it and prevent its delivery to the addressee. This has caused some doubt to be expressed as to whether an acceptance can ever be operative upon the mere mailing of the letter, since the delivery to the post office has not put it entirely beyond the sender's control. [N]o such doubt should exist. . . . In view of common practices, in view of the difficulties involved in the process of interception of a letter, and in view of the decisions and printed discussions dealing with acceptance by post, it is believed that the fact that a letter can be lawfully intercepted by the sender should not prevent the acceptance from being operative on mailing. If the offer was made under such circumstances that the offeror should know that the offeree might reasonably regard this as a proper method of closing the deal, and the offeree does so regard it, and makes use of it, the contract is consummated even though the letter of acceptance is intercepted and not delivered. . . .

To a certain extent both appellants and appellees admit and approve the position adopted by the authorities quoted above. However, to the extent that these authorities would negative or disallow effect to appellees-offerees' power to repudiate their acceptance prior to its receipt by appellants, the appellees disagree. Their argument, and the position adopted by the lower court is succinctly expressed in the excellent memorandum opinion of the lower court as follows:

> From our examination . . . the decisions of the Courts seem to hinge upon the question of whether or not the party has lost control of the instrument prior to the time of its renunciation by him. Formerly, the Courts took the position that once a letter had been deposited in the U.S. Mail, is was beyond retrieve and the depositor no longer had control over it; that the Post Office Department became, in fact, the agent of the addressee so that any attempt to cancel or repudiate the written document was beyond the power and authority of the sender and without effect once it had been deposited in the mail. U. S. Postal Regulations, Sec. 153.5, provide, and for some years has provided, that mail deposited in a post office may be recalled by the sender before delivery to the addressee. In the Court decisions cited by the parties here, wherever this Postal Regulation has been brought to the attention of the Court, they have held that the Post Office is the agent of the sender, rather than the addressee, and his right to withdraw mail after deposit gives him the right to repudiate a document signed and mailed by him but not yet received by the addressee.

An examination of the cases relied upon by appellees sustains their contention that these decisions represent a departure from the general rule. . . . Dick v. United States, 82 F.Supp. 362, 113 Ct.Cl. 94 (1949), involved mistaken acceptance of an offer evidenced by a government purchase order. The appellant, after mailing his acceptance wired a repudiation of the acceptance. The repudiation was received prior to the acceptance. Although remanding the cause for proofs, the court inferred that the fact of a mailed acceptance did not, as a matter of law, bar subsequent repudiation. [T]he court, over a vigorous dissent, concluded that the Post Office was the sender's agent and that "delivery" was incomplete so long as the acceptance had not been received.

[The Dick v. United States opinion is] a departure from the general rule. [It rests] on the theory that the [mailbox] rule was based on a theory that the depositor lost control of his acceptance when it was deposited and that this fact rendered the acceptance complete upon deposit. To the extent that "loss of control" was the significant element in the [mailbox] rule, the logic of appellees' cases is impeccable. On the other hand, if the rule is, in fact, not based on the "loss of control" element, the fact that this element has been altered may in no way affect the validity of the rule. Determination of the question presented in this appeal cannot then be had merely by adoption or rejection of the logic of appellees' cases. Rather, the source and justification of the [mailbox] rule must be found and appellees' argument considered in light of this finding. . . .

The rule that a contract is complete upon deposit of the acceptance in the mails, [often] referred to as [the mailbox rule] and also known as the "rule in Adams v. Lindsell," had its origin, insofar as the common law is concerned, in Adams v. Lindsell, 1 Barn. & Ald. 681, 106 Eng.Rep. 250 (K.B. 1818). In that case, the defendants had sent an offer to plaintiffs on September 2nd, indicating that they expected an answer "in course of post." The offer was misdirected and was not received and accepted until the 5th, the acceptance being mailed that day and received by defendant-offerors on the 9th. However, the defendants, who had expected to receive the acceptance on or before the 7th, sold the goods offered on the 8th of September. It was conceded that the delay had been occasioned by the fault of the defendants in initially misdirecting the offer. Defendants contended that no contract had been made until receipt of the offer on the 9th.

> They relied on Payne v. Cave, 3 T.R. 148, and more particularly on Cooke v. Oxley. In that case Oxley, who had proposed to sell goods to Cooke, and given him a certain time at his request, to determine whether he would buy them or not, was held not liable to the performance of the contract, even though Cooke, within the specified time, had determined to buy them, and given Oxley notice to that effect. So here the defendants who have proposed by letter to sell this wool, are not to be held liable, even though it be now admitted that the answer did come back in due course of post. Till the plaintiffs' answer was actually received there could be no binding contract between the parties; and before then the defendants had retracted their offer by selling the wool to other persons.

> But the court said that if that were so, no contract could ever be completed by the post. For if the defendants were not bound by their offer when accepted by the plaintiffs till the answer was received, then the plaintiffs ought not to be bound till after they had received the notification that the defendants had received their answer and assented to it. And so it might go on ad infinitum. The defendants must be considered in law as making, during every instant of the time their letter was traveling, the

same identical offer to the plaintiffs, and then the contract is completed by the acceptance of it by the latter. Then as to the delay in notifying the acceptance, that arises entirely from the mistake of the defendants, and it therefore must be taken as against them that the plaintiffs' answer was received in course of post.

Examination of the decision in Adams v. Lindsell reveals three distinct factors deserving consideration. The first and most significant is the court's obvious concern with the necessity of drawing a line, with establishing some point at which a contract is deemed complete and their equally obvious concern with the thought that if communication of each party's assent were necessary, the negotiations would be interminable. A second factor, again a practical one, was the court's apparent desire to limit but not overrule the decision in Cooke v. Oxley, 3 T.R. 653 [1790] that an offer was revocable at any time prior to acceptance. In application to contracts negotiated by mail, this latter rule would permit revocation even after unqualified assent unless the assent was deemed effective upon posting. Finally, having chosen a point at which negotiations would terminate and having effectively circumvented the inequities of Cooke v. Oxley, the court, apparently constrained to offer some theoretical justification for its decision, designated a mailed offer as "continuing" and found a meeting of the minds upon the instant of posting assent. Significantly, the factor of the offeree's loss of control of his acceptance is not mentioned. . . .

The justification for the [mailbox] rule proceeds from the uncontested premise of Adams v. Lindsell that there must be, both in practical and conceptual terms, a point in time when a contract is complete. In the formation of contracts *inter praesentes* this point is readily reached upon expressions of assent instantaneously communicated. In the formation of contracts *inter absentes* by post, however, delay in communication prevents concurrent knowledge of assents and some point must be chosen as legally significant. . . .

On the one hand proponents of the rule insist that contracts *inter absentes* are *sui generis* and require consideration not in terms of the secondary principles of contract law relating to the necessity of communicating assent and the necessity of an unrecoverable expression of acceptance, but in terms of the essential concept of manifest intent and assent. . . . In support of the rule proponents urge its sanction in tradition and practice. They argue that in the average case the offeree receives an offer and, depositing an acceptance in the post, begins and should be allowed to begin reliance on the contract. . . . Finally, proponents point out that the offeror can always expressly condition the contract on his receipt of an acceptance and, should he fail to do so, the law should not afford him this advantage.

Opponents of the rule argue as forcefully that all of the disadvantages of delay or loss in communication which would potentially harm the offeree are equally harmful to the offeror. Why, they ask, should the offeror be bound by an acceptance of which he has no knowledge? Arguing specific cases, opponents of the rule point to the inequity of forbidding the offeror to withdraw his offer after the acceptance was posted but before he had any knowledge that the offer was accepted; they argue that to forbid the offeree to withdraw his acceptance, as in the instant case, scant hours after it was posted but days before the offeror knew of it, is unjust and indefensible. Too, the opponents argue, the offeree can always prevent the revocation of an offer by providing consideration, by buying an option.

In short, both advocates and critics muster persuasive argument. As Corbin indicated, there must be a choice made, and such choice may, by the nature of things, seem unjust in some cases. Weighing the arguments with reference not to specific cases but toward a rule of general application and recognizing the general and traditional acceptance of the rule as well as the modern changes in effective long-distance communication, it would seem that the balance tips . . . to continued adherence to the "Rule in Adams v. Lindsell."

RESTATEMENT (SECOND) OF CONTRACTS, SECTION 63

§ 63.   *Time When Acceptance Takes Effect.*

Unless the offer provides otherwise,

(a) an acceptance made in a manner and by a medium invited by an offer is operative and completes the manifestation of mutual assent as soon as put out of the offeree's possession, without regard to whether it ever reaches the offeror; but

(b) an acceptance under an option contract is not operative until received by the offeror.

Comment a. Rationale. It is often said that an offeror who makes an offer by mail makes the post office his agent to receive the acceptance, or that the mailing of a letter of acceptance puts it irrevocably out of the offeree's control. Under United States postal regulations, however, the sender of a letter has long had the power to stop delivery and reclaim the letter. A better explanation of the rule that the acceptance takes effect on dispatch is that the offeree needs a dependable basis for his decision whether to accept. In many legal systems, such a basis is provided by a general rule that an offer is irrevocable unless it provides otherwise. The common law provides such a basis through the rule that a revocation of an offer is ineffective if received after an acceptance has been properly dispatched. . . .

Comment f. Option contracts. An option contract provides a dependable basis for decision whether to exercise the option, and removes the primary reason for the rule of Subsection (1). Moreover, there is no objection to speculation at the expense of a party who has irrevocably assumed that risk. Option contracts are commonly subject to a definite time limit, and the usual understanding is that the notification that the option has been exercised must be received by the offeror before that time. Whether or not there is such a time limit, in the absence of a contrary provision in the option contract, the offeree takes the risk of loss or delay in the transmission of the acceptance and remains free to revoke the acceptance until it arrives. Similarly, if there is such a mistake on the part of the offeror as justifies the rescission of his unilateral obligation, the right to rescind is not lost merely because a letter of acceptance is posted.

PROBLEMS: THE MAILBOX RULE

On September 10, Vogue sent best-selling author Carrie Bradshaw an offer to publish her article, "Men and Manolos," for $10,000, to appear in the November issue. Carrie was told on the phone by her Vogue editor, as well as in the text of the letter (with signature blank), that they need an answer by September 17. However, Carrie is flummoxed about what to do, because the now half-written article criticizes her on-again-off-again boyfriend, John "Mr. Big" Preston, and she is concerned about how he will react. Carrie is also indecisive, and prone to technological meltdowns. *In each of the following scenarios, please determine whether offer and acceptance have occurred*:

Scenario A: On September 15, Carrie visits the Vogue office. She tries to speak to her editor, Candace, but Candace is in a meeting and cannot talk to Carrie face-to-face. Through the glass, Carrie gives the "thumbs up" sign, and Candace, in recognition, nods back. On September 16, Carrie signs the letter and puts it into the mailbox. She adds a post-script that says the following: "I accept your offer. I would also like two free pairs of manolos to provide inspiration." *depends on if interpreted as conditional*

Scenario B: Back to the original facts. Carrie is very excited about the Vogue offer, and decides to sign the letter and send it back via her fax machine on the morning of September 16. Everything goes smoothly on Carrie's end, and indeed, her machine prints out a page that says "sent." However, there is a problem with Vogue's receiving fax machine, and only half of the letter is printed. An intern, frightened at how her boss will react to the half-printed letter, decides to hide it and not tell anyone about it. *yes-effective on dispatch*

Scenario C: Back to the original facts. On September 15, Carrie, on the outs with Big, stays up all night to finish the column. She writes an e-mail with the title "Accept," and attaches the column as a word document, which has some disturbing content about Big. A few hours later Big appears with a flower bouquet, and he and Carrie reconcile. What happens if:

1.   On September 16, before Candace opens her e-mail inbox for the morning, Candace receives a text message that says: "Big and I are on. Article is off. xoxo Carrie."

2.   Immediately after the reconciliation on September 16, Carrie is able to recall (successfully) the e-mail message. Candace never sees it.

Scenario D: Back to the original facts. In the wake of the ever-worsening real estate slump and recession, the Vogue editors decide that Carrie's article about $800 shoes would go over poorly. Instead, the editors want to publish a piece called "Recessionista Fashion." On September 14, Carrie puts the signed offer into the mailbox. On September 15, before her editor is in receipt of Carrie's letter, Carrie hears from her friend Samantha (who threw Vogue's end of the year party and knows all the Vogue editors) that Vogue is pulling her article.

———————

There are some differences in how the mechanics of offer and acceptance work based solely on the form that acceptance takes. In a *bilateral contract*, the offeree may accept the contract by either performance or a return promise. In a *unilateral contract*, the offeree can accept only by performance. We encountered unilateral contracts in the case of *Carlill v. Carbolic Smoke Ball*, the example of rewards for lost pets, as well as in the ensuing note concerning the lender who withdrew his offer a moment before the borrower attempted to complete his act of paying early. We saw there one way that the distinction affects contract formation, including the principle, captured in Section 45 of the Restatement (Second) of Contracts, that an offeree's commencement of performance of the act forms an option contract, which terminates the offeror's power of acceptance. Determining whether an offer seeks a return promise or performance—or either—can sometimes be difficult, raising thorny interpretive questions about just what an offeror is after: some may be skeptical of promise keeping and seek only performance while others might value the security of a return promise. Compare and contrast the following case with the ensuing Problem.

BRACKENBURY V. HODGKIN

102 A. 106 (Maine 1917)

CORNISH, C.J.

The defendant Mrs. Sarah D. P. Hodgkin on the 8th day of February, 1915, was the owner of certain real estate—her home farm, situated in the outskirts of Lewiston. She was a widow and was living alone. She was the mother of six adult children, five sons, one of whom, Walter, is the codefendant, and one daughter, who is the coplaintiff. The plaintiffs were then residing in Independence, Mo. Many letters had passed between mother and daughter concerning the daughter and her husband returning to the old home and taking care of the mother, and finally on February 8, 1915, the mother sent a letter to the daughter and her husband which is the foundation of this [lawsuit].

In this letter she made a definite proposal, the substance of which was that if the Brackenburys would move to Lewiston, and maintain and care for Mrs. Hodgkin on the home place during her life, and pay the moving expenses, they were to have the use and income of the premises, together with the use of the household goods, with certain exceptions, Mrs. Hodgkin to have what rooms she might need. The letter closed, by way of postscript, with the words, "you to have the place when I have passed away."

Relying upon this offer, which was neither withdrawn nor modified, and in acceptance thereof, the plaintiffs moved from Missouri to Maine late in April, 1915, went upon the premises described and entered upon the performance of the contract. Trouble developed after a few weeks, and the relations between the parties grew most disagreeable. The mother brought two suits against her son-in-law on trifling matters, and finally ordered the plaintiffs from the place, but they refused to leave. Then on November 7, 1916, she executed and delivered to her son, Walter C. Hodgkin, a deed of the premises. . . . Walter . . . took the deed with full knowledge of the agreement between the parties and for the sole purpose of evicting the plaintiffs. [The daughter sued to] secure a reconveyance of the farm . . . . [The trial court granted the request and Walter appealed].

. . . A legal and binding contract is clearly proven. The offer on the part of the mother was in writing, and its terms cannot successfully be disputed. There was no need that it be accepted in words, nor that a counter promise on the part of the plaintiffs be made. The offer was the basis, not of a bilateral contract, requiring a reciprocal promise, a promise for a promise, but of a unilateral contract requiring an act for a promise. "In the latter case the only acceptance of the offer that is necessary is the performance of the act. In other words, the promise becomes binding when the act is performed." 6 R. C. L. 607. This is elementary law.

The plaintiffs here accepted the offer by moving from Missouri to the mother's farm in Lewiston and entering upon the performance of the specified acts, and they have continued performance since that time so far as they have been permitted by the mother to do so. The existence of a completed and valid contract is clear. . . .

RESTATEMENT (SECOND) OF CONTRACTS, SECTIONS 30, 32

§ 30.   *Form of Acceptance Invited.*

(1) An offer may invite or require acceptance to be made by an affirmative answer in words, or by performing or refraining from performing a specified act, or may empower the offeree to make a selection of terms in his acceptance.

(2) Unless otherwise indicated by the language or the circumstances, an offer invites acceptance in any manner and by any medium reasonable in the circumstances.

§ 32.   *Invitation of Promise or Performance.*

In case of doubt an offer is interpreted as inviting the offeree to accept either by promising to perform what the offer requests or by rendering the performance, as the offeree chooses.

PROBLEM: UNILATERAL OR BILATERAL?

Caro Davis was the niece of Blanche and Rupert Whitehead. Caro lived for a considerable time at the home of the Whiteheads, in California. The Whiteheads were childless and extremely fond of Caro. After Caro married, she moved to Canada and for two decades visited the Whiteheads regularly. At that point, Blanche had become seriously ill and Rupert suffered severe financial reverses and became sick as well. He wrote Caro as follows:

> Today I tried to find out what she wanted. I finally asked if she wanted to see you. She burst out crying and couldn't stop. The doctor says it would help her if you come. She needs you.

Caro's husband, Frank, wrote back:

> Sorry to hear about Blanche. Hope you are feeling better yourself. If you really want Caro to come, she can probably do it in about two weeks. Please let me know.

A short while later, Rupert wrote both Caro and Frank:

> Thanks for the assurance, which means the world to us. If you can both come, it would be wonderful. If you do, you will inherit everything. What we need is some comfort. Please let me hear from you asap. Your assurance will mean the world to us.

After both Caro and Frank Davis read this, they wrote back saying they accepted and began making arrangements to leave Canada and relocate to California. While finalizing their plans, Rupert Whitehead committed suicide. Caro and Frank were immediately notified and they at once came to California. From almost the moment of her arrival, Caro devoted herself to the care and comfort of her aunt, and she gave her aunt constant attention and care until the aunt's death several months later. It was then discovered that neither of the Whitehead's wills provided anything for Caro or Frank.

Was there a contract? How do you determine whether the offer was for a "unilateral" or "bilateral" contract? Why does that determination matter? Recall that the power of acceptance under an offer is terminated upon the death of the offeror or offeree. *See Davis v. Jacoby*, 34 P. 2d 1026 (Cal. 1934). Consult Restatement (Second) of Contracts, Section 32 above.

ELLEFSON V. MEGADETH, INC.
2005 WL 82022 (S.D.N.Y. 2005)

BUCHWALD, J.

[David Ellefson and David Mustaine are original members of the heavy metal rock band Megadeth. The band was initially formed in 1983, with Mustaine as the lead guitarist, vocalist, and songwriter, and Ellefson on bass. In 1990, the parties formed a corporation, Megadeth, Inc., with Mustaine receiving eighty percent of the stock and Ellefson twenty percent. Over the next 14 years, disagreements arose, and Ellefson alleged that Mustaine had been cutting him out of his share of the profits. In October 2003, the two men tried to resolve their disputes through negotiations led by their attorneys Kenneth Abdo (of Abdo, Abdo, Broady & Satorius for Ellefson) and Andrew Lurie (of Baker & Hostetler for Mustaine). By April of 2004, discussions focused on Mustaine buying out Ellefson's share of Megadeth, Inc. On April 16, 2004, Lurie sent Abdo an initial draft of a proposed "Settlement and General Release."]

The pace of negotiations quickened substantially during the week of May 10, 2004, due to Mustaine's imposition of a five o'clock deadline on Friday, May 14, 2004, for completion of the settlement. To that end, Abdo and Lurie began working in earnest to put together a final draft of the Agreement by the end of the week. On the morning of Thursday, May 13, Abdo received an email reminding him "that Dave Mustaine has instructed us to pull the offer to Ellefson off the table and to terminate this deal as of 5PM PST on Friday 5/14/04, if we do not have a signed agreement in hand." . . . Abdo emailed back that his client Ellefson "wants to get this behind him", but expressed some concerns that the deal might not close.

The following day, Friday, May 14, attorneys for both sides worked to finalize a draft of the Agreement in time to meet the five o'clock deadline. Early in the afternoon, . . . Abdo sent . . . Lurie an email with proposed language changes for a new draft. Later in the day, Lurie sent Abdo an email asking if his comments were complete, to which Abdo responded that he was faxing his final comments, and instructing Lurie to "[m]ake the changes and we are done." Approximately an hour later, Lurie sent Abdo a finalized, execution copy of the Agreement at 4:45 pm (PST), fifteen minutes prior to expiration of the offer. In a covering document to the final Agreement, Lurie stated that "[a]ttached is an execution copy (read only) of the above-referenced Settlement Agreement," reiterated the five o'clock deadline, and stated that [his client] reserved "the right to make further changes pending our finalizing Exhibits A and B and the full execution of the agreement early next week." In the final email of the day between the transacting attorneys, Abdo sent Lurie an email stating that "Dave Ellefson told me he signed and faxed the signature page to you. Thanks for the drafting work." Abdo's email is dated Friday, May 14, 2004 5:16 p.m.

There is no dispute that Ellefson did indeed sign and fax a completed signature page shortly after receiving the final Agreement at 4:45 p.m. on Friday. There is much dispute, however, over whether the fax was sent prior to the 5 p.m. deadline. . . .

According to . . . Lurie, he sent all the parties fully-executed copies of the Agreement by regular mail on [Thursday May 20, 2004], four business days after Ellefson's signature fax was received. [Ellefson] suggests that the alleged date of this mailing is suspicious and that the method of mailing, regular mail, is unreasonable.

[T]here was an email exchange between counsel on May 24, 2004, four days after Lurie attests he mailed the Agreement and ten days after Ellefson faxed the signed signature page. On that day, Lurie received an email from Abdo stating that Ellefson "withdraws from these negotiations and withdraws all proposals." In response to this email, Lurie stated "[w]e are not certain what you are talking about, but, as you know, there is a signed settlement agreement in place, which Dave [Ellefson] faxed to us more than a week ago." Finally, nine days later, on June 2, 2004, Abdo states that he received the finalized Agreement that Lurie mailed on May 20, 2004. . . .

The issue presented . . . is reminiscent of a first year law school contracts exam. We begin with the fundamental tenet: to have a valid contract, there must be both an offer and an acceptance. These critical elements insure that there has been mutual assent by the parties to be bound by the terms of the contract. One party makes an offer to enter into a [bargain], and the other party can either accept or reject this offer. However, once the offer has been accepted, the parties have formed a contract and are bound by the terms of that agreement, even if later events make them regret their decisions. In the case at hand, the issue is whether the exchange between Ellefson and Mustaine fulfilled the requirements of offer and acceptance.

A party making an offer can condition acceptance of that offer upon whatever terms he or she deems fit. Restatement (Second) of Contracts § 60 (1981). Many offers include terms concerning the length of time that the offer will remain open, or the method by which the offer may be accepted. Failure of the offeree to comply with the terms of the offer voids the acceptance and prevents the formation of a contract. 2 Williston on Contracts 6:12 (4th ed.2004). Without an acceptance that conforms to the terms of the offer, the parties have not mutually agreed upon what terms are binding. Therefore, courts generally find that there is no contract when an offer is followed by a defective acceptance that is equivocal or qualified in any material way.

Nonetheless, contracts are often formed after receipt of a defective acceptance. This is because an acceptance that does not unequivocally comply with the terms of original offer is considered a counteroffer. Any new terms or modified terms in the defective acceptance are treated as new terms of the counteroffer, which the original offeror may then choose to accept or reject.

A late acceptance is form of defective acceptance, and therefore is considered a counteroffer which the original offeror can decide to either accept or reject. A late acceptance is defective in two ways. First, because the acceptance is late, it is not in compliance with the terms of the offer. Second, when an offer sets a specific time for acceptance, the offer lapses upon the expiration of that time, and therefore, a late acceptance cannot result in a contract because there is no longer an existing offer to accept. Williston, supra, 5:5. Therefore, in order for a contract to exist after receipt of a late acceptance, the original offeror must accept the offeree's counteroffer. Without a communication of acceptance of the counteroffer by the original offeror, there is nothing to show the original offeror's willingness to be bound by the terms of the contract.

. . . Mustaine conditioned his offer to Ellefson on the requirement that it be accepted by Ellefson by 5 p.m. PST on Friday, May 14. . . . [T]here is no evidence to support [Mustaine's] claim that Ellefson's fax was sent within that deadline; accordingly, Ellefson did not comply with the terms of the offer and no contract was formed upon its receipt.

Because Ellefson's acceptance did not fully comply with the terms of the original offer, it was not a valid acceptance and thus is viewed as a counteroffer. Ellefson argues that his signature page was not a form of acceptance at all, but should be viewed as an invitation to continue further negotiations. Further, [Ellefson] asserts that his faxed signature page "cannot reasonably be construed as a counteroffer" since it was utterly silent as to the terms of the Agreement. We find [these] arguments unpersuasive.

First, regardless of Ellefson's subjective intent, it is the objective significance of his actions that controls. By faxing a signed signature page to an undisputed, execution version of the Agreement, plaintiff signaled his willingness to be bound by its terms, rather than, as he now claims, a desire to continue negotiations. Upon receipt of this fax, [Mustaine] could reasonably infer that Ellefson offered to bind himself to the terms of the Agreement (sent to him just minutes earlier) if [Mustaine was] willing to accept his counteroffer. The fact that the signature page did not contain all of the terms is immaterial, as the terms of the contract are not disputed and were contained in the underlying Agreement. For these reasons, once [Mustaine] received the fax, [he was] free either to accept or reject Ellefson's counteroffer.

To the extent that [Mustaine contends] that no further action on their part was required for a contract between the parties to result, we reject [the] argument. While [Mustaine] could accept or reject Ellefson's counteroffer, defendants had to manifest . . . consent to be bound by the counteroffer. Without such evidence of mutual assent, no contract had been formed. Restatement (Second) of Contracts § 70; Williston, supra, § 6:55.

We do, however, concur with the [Mustaine's] alternative contention that the mailing of the completed contract on May 20, 2004, constituted an acceptance of Ellefson's counteroffer. This act established [Mustaine's] unequivocal intention to accept Ellefson's counteroffer and be bound by the terms of the Agreement. Under the mailbox rule, . . . acceptance is considered complete upon mailing. Therefore, defendants accepted plaintiff's counteroffer prior to his May 24 withdrawal of that offer, and an enforceable contract was formed on May 20, 2004.

[Ellefson] argues that the Court should reject [Mustaine's] acceptance because the use of regular U.S. mail was an unreasonable method of acceptance in light of the parties' previous conduct. Prior communications between parties had been almost exclusively by fax or email. Therefore, "it [was] patently unreasonable . . . to mail a purported acceptance by 'snail mail' without even advising Ellefson or Abdo that it was mailed."

Whether a mode of acceptance is reasonable depends upon "what would reasonably be expected by one in the position of the contracting parties, in view of prevailing business usages and other surrounding circumstances." Williston, supra, § 6:35; see also Restatement (Second) Contracts § 65. "[A]ny reasonable and usual mode of communication may be used to accept a[n][ ] offer unless a specific mode is prescribed." Gray v. Stewart, 97 Cal.App. 4th 1394, 1397, 119 Cal.Rptr.2d 217, 220 (Cal.App. 1st Dist.2002). Further, "the use of ordinary mail [is] a reasonable mode of communication" absent special circumstances. Palo Alto Town & Country Village Inc. v. BBTC Co., 11 Cal.3d 494, 500, 521 P.2d 1097, 1100 (1974). Therefore, in the absence of any specific restriction, defendants' acceptance by mail is reasonable unless extraordinary circumstances exist.

Having examined all the surrounding circumstances, we find no impediment to [Mustaine's] acceptance by regular mail. First, the original offer and . . . counteroffer contained no restrictions on the mode of acceptance. Second, the use of fax and email to negotiate the Agreement does not preclude . . . using mail to accept [the] counteroffer by sending a fully-executed hard copy of the Agreement . . . . We therefore find that an enforceable contract was formed on May 20, 2004, prior to [Ellefson's] attempted withdrawal.

D. UCC CONTRACT FORMATION

Study the following rules of contract formation under Article 2 of the UCC. Evaluate to what degree these statutory codifications are the same as or different from the common law of contracts.

UCC SECTIONS 2–204, 2–206

§ 2–204. *Formation in General*

(1) A contract for sale of goods may be made in any manner sufficient to show agreement, including conduct by both parties which recognizes the existence of a contract.

(2) An agreement sufficient to constitute a contract for sale may be found even though the moment of its making is undetermined.

(3) Even though one or more terms are left open a contract for sale does not fail for indefiniteness if the parties have intended to make a contract and there is a reasonably certain basis for giving an appropriate remedy.

§ 2–206. *Offer and Acceptance in Formation of Contract*

(1) Unless otherwise unambiguously indicated by the language or circumstances (a) an offer to make a contract shall be construed as inviting acceptance in any manner and by any medium reasonable in the circumstances; (b) an order or other offer to buy goods for prompt or current shipment shall be construed as inviting acceptance either by a prompt promise to ship or by the prompt or current shipment of conforming or nonconforming goods, but the shipment of nonconforming goods is not an acceptance if the seller seasonably notifies the buyer that the shipment is offered only as an accommodation to the buyer.

(2) Where the beginning of a requested performance is a reasonable mode of acceptance an offeror who is not notified of acceptance within a reasonable time may treat the offer as having lapsed before acceptance.

————————

The next two cases are decided under the UCC's rules of contract formation.

UCC has "gap filling" provisions for when terms are left open

JANNUSCH V. NAFFZIGER
883 N.E.2d 711 (Ill. App. 2008)

Plaintiffs operated a business, Festival Foods, which served concessions to the general public at festivals and events throughout Illinois and Indiana from late April to late October each year. The assets of the business included a truck and servicing trailer and equipment such as refrigerators and freezers, roasters, chairs and tables, fountain service and signs and lighting equipment.

Defendants were interested in purchasing the concession business, met several times with plaintiffs, and observed the business in operation. Gene testified that on August 13, 2005, plaintiffs entered into an oral agreement to sell Festival Foods to defendants for $150,000. For the $150,000, defendants would receive the truck and trailer, all necessary equipment, and the opportunity to work at event locations secured by plaintiffs.

Defendants paid $10,000 immediately, with the balance to be paid when defendants received their loan money from the bank. Defendants took possession of Festival Foods the next day and operated Festival Foods for the remainder of the 2005 season. Gene acknowledged that the insurance and titles to the truck and trailer remained in his name because he had not yet received the purchase price from defendants.

Louann acknowledged testifying during a deposition that an oral agreement to purchase Festival Foods for $150,000 existed but later testified she could not recall specifically making an oral agreement on any particular date. Lindsey testified she and Louann met with plaintiffs on August 13, 2005, and paid the $10,000 for the right to continue to purchase the business because plaintiffs had another interested buyer. She also stated that the parties agreed defendants would run Festival Foods as they pursued buying the business.

According to Lindsey, Gene suggested the parties sign something and she replied that defendants were "in no position to sign anything" because they had not received any loan money from the bank and did not have an attorney. The following week, Lindsey consulted with an attorney regarding the legal aspects of buying and owning a business. She asked the attorney to prepare a contract for the purchase. Ultimately, the bank approved defendants for a loan. Lindsey admitted taking possession of Festival Foods, receiving the income from the business, purchasing inventory, replacing equipment, paying taxes on the business and paying employees.

Defendants operated six events, three in Indiana and three in Illinois. Gene attended the first two festivals in Valparaiso and Auburn, Indiana, with defendants, who paid him $10 an hour and paid for his lodging. Gene and Louann testified that plaintiffs' minimal involvement with the operations after August 13 was merely as advisors to defendants, who were unfamiliar with this type of business. Two days after the business season ended, defendants returned Festival Foods to the storage facility where it had been stored by Gene. Gene testified he had canceled his lease with the storage facility, telling the owner that he had sold his business.

Someone at the storage facility called Gene and reported that Festival Foods had been returned. Thereafter Gene attempted to sell Festival Foods, but was unsuccessful. Lindsey testified one of the reasons defendants returned Festival Foods was because the income from the events they operated was lower than expected. She stated Gene specifically asked defendants to run certain events for him and he ran the events where he was present. She testified Gene asked for the trailer back, stating he needed it "so he could make money on it for the end of the year," and that Gene stated he did not have money to buy back the inventory.

The trial court first held that the Uniform Commercial Code (UCC) governed the issues raised in this case, rejecting defendants' argument that a sale of goods was not involved. The trial court then found that there was a contract formed but that the evidence was insufficient to establish by a preponderance of the evidence that there was a meeting of the minds as to what that agreement was. "If this is an agreement to reach an agreement, I suspect that the action for the price must fail." . . .

Defendants argue the UCC should not apply because this case involves the sale of a business rather than just the sale of goods. The "predominant purpose" test is used to determine whether a contract for both the sale of goods and the rendition of services falls within the scope of article 2 of the UCC. A contract that is primarily for services, with the sale of goods being incidental, will not fall within the scope of article 2. *Belleville Toyota, Inc. v. Toyota Motor Sales, U.S.A., Inc.*, 199 Ill.2d 325, 352–53, 264 Ill.Dec. 283, 770 N.E.2d 177, 194–95 (2002). "[W]hether the contract was predominantly for goods or services is generally a question of fact." *Heuerman v. B & M Construction, Inc.*, 358 Ill.App.3d 1157, 1165, 295 Ill.Dec. 549, 833 N.E.2d 382, 389 (2005). Certainly significant tangible assets were involved in this case. *Cf. Fink v. DeClassis*, 745 F.Supp. 509, 516 (N.D.Ill.1990) (intangible assets accounted for $1 million of the total purchase price of $1.2 million). The evidence presented in this case was sufficient to support the conclusion that the proposed agreement was predominantly one for the sale of goods. . . .

[The court then quoted § 2–204 of the UCC, excerpted above.] Defendants argue that nothing was said in the contract about allocating a price for good will, a covenant not to compete, allocating a price for the equipment, how to release liens, what would happen if there was no loan approval, and other issues. Defendants argue these are essential terms for the sale of a business and the Internal Revenue Service requires that parties allocate the sales price. "None of these items were even discussed much less agreed to. There is not an enforceable agreement when there are so many essential terms missing."

"A contract may be enforced even though some contract terms may be missing or left to be agreed upon, but if the essential terms are so uncertain that there is no basis for deciding whether the agreement has been kept or broken, there is no contract." *Academy Chicago Publishers v. Cheever*, 144 Ill.2d 24, 30, 161 Ill.Dec. 335, 578 N.E.2d 981, 984 (1991). In Cheever, the widow of John Cheever signed an agreement to publish a collection of Cheever's short stories. *Cheever*, 144 Ill.2d at 27, 161 Ill.Dec. 335, 578 N.E.2d at 982. The Illinois Supreme Court held there was no valid and enforceable contract because there was no agreement as to the length and content of the book, who would decide which stories to include, the criteria used by the publisher in determining whether the manuscript was "satisfactory," or other terms. *Cheever*, 144 Ill.2d at 29–30, 161 Ill.Dec. 335, 578 N.E.2d at 984. "[I]n fact, all they had really agreed to was a tentative title (The Uncollected Stories of John Cheever)." *Dawson v. General Motors Corp.*, 977 F.2d 369, 373 (7th Cir.1992).

The essential terms were agreed upon in this case. The purchase price was $150,000, and the items to be transferred were specified. No essential terms remained to be agreed upon; the only action remaining was the performance of the contract. Defendants took possession of the items to be transferred and used them as their own. "Rejection of goods must be within a reasonable time after their delivery or tender. It is ineffective unless the buyer seasonably notifies the seller." [UCC 2–602(1)]. Defendants paid $10,000 of the purchase price. The fact that defendants were disappointed in the income from the events they operated is not inconsistent with the existence of a contract.

The trial court noted that "the parties have very very different views about what transpired in the course of the contract[-]formation discussions." It is not necessary that the parties share a subjective understanding as to the terms of the contract; the parties' conduct may indicate an agreement to the terms. *Steinberg v. Chicago Medical School*, 69 Ill.2d 320, 330–31, 13 Ill.Dec. 699, 371 N.E.2d 634, 640 (1977). The conduct in this case is clear. Parties discussing the sale of goods do not transfer those goods and allow them to be retained for a substantial period before reaching agreement. Defendants replaced equipment, reported income, paid taxes, and paid Gene for his time and expenses, all of which is inconsistent with the idea that defendants were only "pursuing buying the business." An agreement to make an agreement is not an agreement, but there was clearly more than that here.

The trial court believed it was significant that Lindsey told Gene that defendants were "in no position to sign anything" because they had not received any loan money from the bank and did not have any attorney. "The fact that a formal written document is anticipated does not preclude enforcement of a specific preliminary promise." *Dawson,* 977 F.2d at 374 (1992). Defendants' loan was eventually approved, they did consult with an attorney, and defendants remained in possession of and continued to operate Festival Foods. The parties' agreement could have been fleshed out with additional terms, but the essential terms were agreed upon. Louann admitted there was an agreement to purchase Festival Foods for $150,000 but could not recall specifically making an oral agreement on any particular date. "An agreement sufficient to constitute a contract for sale may be found even though the moment of its making is undetermined." [2–204(2)]. Returning the goods at the end of the season was not a rejection of plaintiffs' offer to sell, it was a breach of contract.

We conclude there was an agreement to sell Festival Foods for the price of $150,000 and that defendants breached that agreement. We reverse the circuit court's judgment and remand for the entry of an order consistent with this opinion.

NOTES AND QUESTIONS

1. Would *Jannusch* have come out differently under the common law rather than the UCC?

2. Do you agree that the facts of the case warrant classification as a transaction in goods to which Article 2 of the UCC applies?

3. Was *Cheever*, concerning the agreement to publish short stories, a transaction in goods governed by the UCC or a common law case? How does that classification affect its precedential value in *Jannusch*?

4. You will see much later in this book that the statute of frauds, which requires a signed writing to enforce certain kinds of contracts, applies to transactions in goods for the price of $500 or more. UCC § 2–201(1). It is not obvious from the *Jannusch* opinion that any such writing was made in the case or why the buyer did not make that argument.

Consider the following additional UCC sections often relevant to evaluating contract formation, and implicated by the ensuing case.

UCC SECTIONS 2–305(1), 2–306(1), 1–304

§ 2–305. *Open Price Term*

(1) The parties if they so intend can conclude a contract for sale even though the price is not settled. In such a case the price is a reasonable price

at the time for delivery if (a) nothing is said as to price; or (b) the price is left to be agreed by the parties and they fail to agree; or (c) the price is to be fixed in terms of some agreed market or other standard as set or recorded by a third person or agency and it is not so set or recorded.

§ 2–306. *Output, Requirements [Contracts]*

(1) A term which measures the quantity by the output of the seller or the requirements of the buyer means such actual output or requirements as may occur in good faith, except that no quantity unreasonably disproportionate to any stated estimate or in the absence of a stated estimate to any normal or otherwise comparable prior output or requirements may be tendered or demanded.

§ 1–304. *Obligation of Good Faith*

Every contract or duty within the Uniform Commercial Code imposes an obligation of good faith in its performance and enforcement.

———————

Most UCC provisions in the first-year course in Contracts, and this book, appear in Article 2, concerning transactions in goods. The UCC has other Articles addressing different commercial contexts, such as Article 3 on negotiable instruments, Article 8 on investment securities, and Article 9 on secured transactions, all generally taught in upper level law school classes. The last of the foregoing excerpts, Section 1–304, appears in Article 1 of the UCC and states that the obligation of good faith applies to all those Articles of the Code, not just Article 2. The common law of contracts also holds that all contracts carry within them an obligation to perform and enforce them in good faith. We will consider the meaning of these concepts in a later chapter, although for now we can safely say that good faith is almost always a question of fact that depends on the context.

BACOU DALLOZ USA V. CONTINENTAL POLYMERS, INC.
344 F.3d 22 (1st Cir. 2003)

BALDOCK, SENIOR CIRCUIT JUDGE.

In this diversity case arising out of a contract dispute, Defendant-Appellant Continental Polymers, Inc. ("Continental") appeals the district court's order granting summary judgment in favor of Bacou Dalloz USA ("Bacou") on Continental's breach of contract . . . counterclaims.

Howard Leight . . . was the sole stockholder and President of . . . Howard Leight Industries ("HLI"). HLI manufactured hearing protection products, including foam earplugs. In December 1997, Bacou, an HLI customer, sought to purchase HLI. After several days of negotiations, Leight declined to sell the company. Shortly after negotiations fell through,

Bacou co-chairman Walter Stepan and in-house counsel Philip Barr called Leight and HLI's CEO John Dean and requested they come to Rhode Island ... to explain to Bacou's chairman, Philippe Bacou, why Leight did not want to sell HLI. Leight and Dean agreed to the trip in part because Bacou was one of HLI's biggest customers.

Leight and Dean flew to Rhode Island and had dinner with Bacou, Stepan, and Barr on Saturday, January 10. During this conversation, Leight informed Bacou he would not sell because the December 1997 offer was $10 million too low. The parties began discussing terms for the sale of HLI, but decided that serious negotiations would be reserved for the next day. The parties met again on Sunday, January 11. To bridge the $10 million gap, Stepan proposed a $1 million consulting contract for Leight, as well as royalty payments, which would cut the gap in half. The parties then discussed a proposal under which Bacou would purchase all its requirements for polyurethane prepolymer, the main raw material for HLI's foam earplugs, from [Continental, a recently formed company owned by Leight and Dean] for five years. . . . Based on the then-current market price for prepolymer and HLI's volume of prepolymer, this contract would bridge the remaining $5 million price gap. The parties agreed to this arrangement and had a champagne toast.

On January 12th, Stepan and Barr presented to Leight and Dean a letter drafted by Barr and Bacou's outside counsel. [The first few paragraphs reference the asset purchase agreement and related corporate matters.] The fourth paragraph provides:

> Finally, we understand that you recently formed a new company [Continental], which will manufacture polyurethane prepolymer, the raw material used in the production of foam ear plugs by Howard S. Leight & Associates, Inc. ("HLI") and currently purchased from [Dow]. This will confirm that Bacou USA Safety, Inc. will enter into a supply agreement with [Continental] pursuant to which Bacou USA Safety, Inc. agrees to purchase its requirements for polyurethane prepolymer from [Continental] for a period of five years provided that the quality and price of such raw material are equivalent to that which is then used by HLI and available from third-party suppliers.

Stepan, Barr, and Leight signed the letter. In February, the parties met to sign the closing documents. Continental alleges that at the closing, Dean asked Stepan to incorporate the January 12th letter agreement in the asset purchase contract. Stepan allegedly responded that this was unnecessary because the January 12th letter would stand on its own and if it did not, then Bacou would not be completing the deal that day. The parties subsequently signed the asset purchase agreement without any further memorialization of a supply agreement.

Following the sale, Continental purchased property in Mexico on which it built a manufacturing plant and machinery needed to manufacture prepolymer. In January 1999, Continental informed Bacou it had completed construction and was prepared to begin shipment to Bacou. Continental and Bacou commenced negotiations for a supply agreement in February 1999. . . . The negotiations centered around . . . price, quality, [and quantity].

According to Continental, the price of prepolymer remained relatively stable, around $2 per pound both at the time of the January 12th letter and up until February 1999. In October 1998, Bacou requested a price reduction on prepolymer from its then-current supplier, Dow . . . . Dow was aware of the January 12th letter between Bacou and Continental. Within days of Dean informing Bacou that Continental was prepared to ship prepolymer, Dow agreed to reduce its prepolymer price to $1.56 per pound. According to Continental, Dow did not offer this price to other customers.

As a result of Dow's offer, Bacou took the position in negotiations with Continental that $1.56 was the price "then available" to Bacou under the January 12th letter. Continental disputed the $1.56 price. According to Continental, Bacou artificially reduced the price by telling Dow that if it could lower the price enough, Continental would not be able to match Dow's offer and Dow would remain Bacou's principal supplier.

The parties also had difficulty agreeing on the quality term. Bacou requested production of specifications and samples of Continental's prepolymer for testing to assure adequate quality. Continental refused, arguing Bacou was attempting to impose onerous testing and sampling requirements that Bacou did not require from other vendors.

The volume of prepolymer which Bacou would purchase from Continental also became a disputed issue between the parties. Bacou wanted to purchase a small percentage of prepolymer from a second source to maintain a backup supplier. Continental insisted Bacou purchase one hundred percent of its requirements from Continental. . . .

. . . Barr submitted to Continental an initial purchase order for 10,000 pounds of prepolymer at $2 per pound. The order informed Continental that a portion of this lot would be used for testing and upon qualification the balance would be used in production. The purchase order proposed that after developing a working relationship, executives from both companies could meet to work out a long-term supply agreement. Continental did not ship prepolymer to Bacou in response to this purchase order.

. . . Bacou sent Continental several draft supply agreements, all of which Continental rejected. [On] May 12, . . . Barr sent another purchase order to Continental for 10,000 pounds at $2 per pound. Continental declined to ship any product to Bacou pursuant to this purchase order.

Bacou offered Continental one last supply agreement in August 1999, but Continental again refused.

[Bacou sued Continental in state court for a declaratory judgment that it had no obligations under the January 12th letter. Continental removed to federal court and counterclaimed asserting, among other things, breach of the January 12th agreement. The district court granted Bacou's motion, saying the letter was an unenforceable "agreement to agree" and did not set out all material terms, and no reasonable criteria existed for supplying the missing terms. Continental appealed, claiming the January 12th letter is an enforceable contract.]

The district court concluded the parties did not manifest a present intent to be bound to a supply agreement in the January 12th letter. Rather, the district court held the January 12th letter was an "agreement to agree" to enter into a supply agreement in the future. The district court relied on *Centerville Builders, Inc. v. Wynne*, 683 A.2d 1340 (R.I.1996), to conclude such agreements are unenforceable under Rhode Island law.

In *Centerville Builders*, a prospective buyer entered into an agreement with the seller for the sale of a tract of land. In a document captioned "Offer to Purchase," the buyer deposited $5,000 towards the purchase of the property with a total deposit of five percent of the sale price due upon signing the purchase and sales agreement. The seller signed the Offer to Purchase after deleting the ninth condition, which would have prohibited the seller from negotiating with any other parties for the sale of the property. The agreement's sixth provision provided: "SUBJECT TO SATISFACTORY PURCHASE & SALES AGREEMENT BETWEEN SELLER AND BUYER."

Subsequently, the seller sent the buyer an unsigned purchase-and-sales agreement form. The buyer signed the agreement and returned it to the seller. The seller later notified the buyer that the seller wanted to "get more money" for the property and would therefore put the property back on the market. The buyer filed an action for breach of contract. The Rhode Island Supreme Court held no enforceable contract existed because there was no mutuality of obligation. In reaching this conclusion, the Rhode Island Supreme Court stated that—

> [W]hen the promises of the parties depend on the occurrence of some future event within the unilateral control of the promisors, the promises are illusory and the agreement is nonbinding. . . . In the instant case, . . . their promises were illusory since each party reserved the unfettered discretion to thwart the purchase and sale by unilaterally invoking condition 6 of the offer-to-purchase agreement and rejecting any purchase-and-sale agreement as "unsatisfactory."

Although it is true that the seller displayed an intent to be bound by the offer-to-purchase agreement when he signed the document and agreed to sell the property subject to the conditions specified, the inclusion of condition 6 made this an illusory promise because its occurrence depended solely on the subjective will of either party.... The seller's deletion (with the buyer's consent) of the ninth condition further evidenced the lack of mutuality of obligation. Because the seller was allowed to negotiate with other prospective buyers, the offer to purchase amounted to little more than an agreement to see if the parties could agree on a purchase-and-sale agreement at some point in the future. As such, it was not an enforceable bilateral contract.

Id. at 1341–42.

We believe the district court read *Centerville Builders* too broadly in ruling that all agreements to agree are unenforceable in Rhode Island. The Rhode Island Supreme Court's comment that the Offer to Purchase was nothing more than agreement to agree and as such was unenforceable must be viewed in the context in which it was made. The court's main concern was that the parties made illusory promises resulting in a lack of mutuality of obligation.

The January 12th letter contains no such infirmities. The letter does not condition the parties' obligations on the illusory promise that the future supply agreement be "satisfactory" to either party. The letter set forth reciprocal promises in the form of the supply agreement's material terms. Such promises are sufficient to establish mutuality of obligation. *Id.* at 1341 (noting that a bilateral contract requires mutuality of obligation which is achieved through the making of reciprocal promises). The actual supply agreement could and likely would contain payment terms, delivery terms, and other similar provisions not contained in the letter. But the fact that the parties were to negotiate these details at a future date does not render illusory the obligation incurred under the January 12th letter. The parties clearly agreed to enter into a supply agreement consistent with the terms outlined in the January 12th letter....

The district court alternatively held the January 12th letter was unenforceable because it lacked sufficiently definite material terms of price and quality. The letter describes the price and quality as follows: "the quality and price of such raw material are equivalent to that which is then used by HLI and available from third-party suppliers." The district court found this terminology too vague to provide a reasonably certain basis for giving an appropriate remedy. *See* Restatement (Second) of Contracts § 33 (1981) (endorsing the view that where the parties have intended to make a contract and there is a reasonably certain basis for granting a remedy, the court should grant that remedy). The court contended Bacou unilaterally could control the raw material HLI was using at any particular time, thus making its promise illusory.

We disagree with the district court that the price term was too vague to form an enforceable contract. The letter describes the price term as the price then available from third-party suppliers. The price term thus is readily discernible by obtaining quotes from other vendors or other evidence of the prevailing market price. Indeed, Bacou's position in negotiations with Continental was not that the price term in the January 12th letter was too vague, but that the then-available price was $1.56 per pound, Dow's last price quote to Bacou.

Whether this price was artificially deflated as Continental argues is a matter for the trier of fact. Simply because the parties disagree on the factual issue of what the then-available price actually was does not mean that the price term in the January 12th letter was vague as a matter of law. A term specifying market price or the currently available price provides a sufficiently definite basis to provide a remedy. *See The Edward S. Quirk Co., Inc. v. National Labor Relations Bd.*, 241 F.3d 41, 44 (1st Cir.2001) ("[I]f a contract for a commodity provided that a price would be 'the current market price' for the good, this might well be a figure precise enough for a court or arbitrator to enforce.").

Likewise, the quality term is not indefinite or illusory. The January 12th letter specifies that the quality must be as good as the prepolymer then used by HLI and available from third party vendors. The comparability to products available from third party vendors creates an objective and reasonably definite measure of quality. And to the extent the district court believed HLI could manipulate their prepolymer needs, under Rhode Island law, "virtually every contract contains an implied covenant of good faith and fair dealing between the parties." [*Crellin Tech., Inc. v. Equipmentlease Corp.*, 18 F.3d 1, 10 (1st Cir.1994)].

Because Bacou would have a contractual duty to determine in good faith the quality of Continental's product as compared to third party vendors, the quality term was not illusory. Consequently, we reverse the district court's grant of summary judgment in favor of Bacou on Continental's contract claim.

NOTES AND QUESTIONS

1.   The case raises questions about specificity as to price, quantity, and quality to determine whether the arrangement was a mere agreement to agree or sufficiently definite. What arguments did Bacou and the district court make on these issues? How did Continental and the appellate court find restrictions on discretion and definiteness to each term? Review the UCC provisions excerpted ahead of *Bacou Dalloz USA v. Continental Polymers, Inc.*

2.   Compare *Bacou* with *Empro Manufacturing* and *PFT Roberson v. Volvo Truck*. What factual issues distinguish these cases? Was the January 12 letter in *Bacou* more than a "letter of intent"? What facts bear on this question? Does it matter that *Empro* and *PFT* are common law cases whereas *Bacou* is a UCC case?

3.   How did the *Bacou* court distinguish *Centerville Builders*? What error did the district court commit in concluding that *Centerville Builders* compelled the conclusion that Bacou and Continental had merely made an agreement to agree?

4.   What is "mutuality of obligation"? Did the *Centerville Builders* court mean that there was no consideration? The illusory promise—in effect, "we will buy and sell this property if we decide to buy and sell this property"—meant that the parties had not exchanged promises of commitment and therefore those promises do not furnish consideration. According to the Restatement of Contracts (Second), if the requirement of consideration is met, there is no additional requirement that there be "mutuality of obligation."

5.   Consider a classic opinion written by Judge Benjamin Cardozo, *Sun Printing & Publishing Ass'n v. Remington Paper & Power Co.*, 139 N.E. 470 (N.Y. 1923). A buyer sued a seller for failure to deliver under a contract calling for the delivery of 1,000 tons of paper per month for 16 months. Prices were specified for the first four months. Thereafter, the parties were to agree on a price and the length of time that the price would apply. The price and time period were to be set fifteen days before the expiration of each period, and the price was never to exceed the contract price charged by a third party dealing in the goods.

Cardozo held that because the writing failed to provide a time term for the duration of the price that was to apply in the absence of an agreed-upon price, the contract was an unenforceable "agreement to agree." In later explaining *Sun Printing*, Cardozo emphasized the "overmastering need of certainty in the transactions of commercial life" and the attendant need to see contracts as the "will outwardly revealed in the spoken or written word" rather than some "hypothetical, imaginary will."

A dissenting judge opined that the parties thought that they had entered into a binding contract, and the duration issue could have been filled either by adopting the price in effect for one year or by doing so monthly because the contract called for monthly shipments. In the dissent's view, "the law should do here what it has done in so many other cases, apply the rule of reason and compel parties to contract in the light of fair dealing."

Who had the better argument in *Sun Printing*? How would the judges authoring the foregoing two opinions have decided the case? How would it come out under today's UCC?

6.   We will see more of the UCC rules on contract formation in Chapter Three and more on good faith, in both the UCC and common law, in Chapter Nine.

Contracts are used to shift (allocate) risks. One recurring issue in contract formation is how much risk-allocating flexibility can be retained and still result in a bargained for, bilateral contract. Risk-shifting devices abound, and include clauses such as these: (1) as to price: percentage leases, wage adjustment provisions in collective bargaining agreements, and cost-plus formulas in construction contracts and (2) as to quantity, amounts determined by the requirements of a buyer's business or the output of one or more of a seller's production facilities. As to the latter, the UCC has codified the standards. Worth noting, however, is that, despite some initial judicial hesitation with such clauses, courts eventually recognized their validity, decades before the UCC's codification.

In one prescient case, *Lima Locomotive & Machine v. National Steel Castings*, 155 F. 77 (6th Cir. 1907), the seller wrote as follows to the buyer:

> . . . We make the following proposition for furnishing all your requirements in steel castings for the remainder of the present year at the prices mentioned below, f.o.b. cars at Montpelier, the terms to be thirty days net. You agree to furnish us on or before the 15th of each month the tonnage that you wish to order during the following month. We agree to fill your orders as specified to the amount of this tonnage, and to make such deliveries as you require.

The buyer accepted and the seller later reneged, prompting the buyer's suit. The seller alleged lack of commitment or in the vocabulary of the day "want of mutuality." While a trial court had agreed with the seller, as many judges and even lawyers of the period may have done, the appellate court reversed. It explained:

> . . . the [seller] agreed to supply all of the "requirements" of the [buyer's] business for the remainder of the year 1902. The [buyer] was engaged in an established manufacturing business which required a large amount of steel castings. This was well known to the [seller], and the proposition made and accepted was made with reference to the "requirements" of that well-established business. The [sellers] were not proposing to make castings beyond the current requirements of that business, and would not have been obligated to supply castings not required in the usual course of that business. By the acceptance of the [seller]'s proposal, the [buyer] was obligated to take from the [seller] all castings which [the buyer's] business should require.

NOTE: PATTERNS OF ARGUMENT

UCC rules on contract formation can be animated by envisioning a series of fact patterns that recur and related arguments parties and their lawyers make. Start by entitling and indexing the relevant provisions, along the following lines:

conduct	2–204(1)	form of acceptance	2–206(1)(a)	open price term	2–305
definiteness	2–204(3)	notice of acceptance	2–206(2)	output/requirements	2–306
firm offers	2–205	orders	2–206(1)(b)	good faith	1–304

Imagine the following scenarios and study the related pattern of argument.

1.   Absence of Offer

Claim:	Breach of sales contract based on an order.
Defense:	There was no offer.
Reply A:	An order may be characterized as an offer under § 2–206(1)(b).
Reply B:	No distinct offer is required if party conduct manifests a contract. § 2–204(1).

2.   Revocation of Offer

Claim:	Breach of sales contract.
Defense:	The offer was revoked before acceptance.
Reply:	You promised to keep the offer open.
Defense:	There was no consideration for the promise to keep the offer open.
Reply:	No consideration is needed under § 2–205.

3.   Absence of Acceptance

Claim:	Breach of sales contract.
Defense:	There was no valid acceptance.
Reply A:	The attempted acceptance was made in a manner and medium reasonable under the circumstances. § 2–206(1)(a).
Reply B:	The acceptance was made by a promise to ship or a prompt or current shipment of conforming or nonconforming goods. § 2–206(1)(b).
Reply C:	No distinct acceptance is required if party conduct manifests a contract. § 2–204(1).

4.   Absence of Notice of Acceptance

Claim:	Breach of sales contract.
Defense:	There is no contract because the offeree did not provide notice of acceptance of the offer before it lapsed.

Reply: Notice of acceptance is not necessarily required.

Defense: Notice is required if the offeree sought to accept by beginning performance. § 2–206(2).

5. Agreement Too Indefinite to Enforce

Claim: Breach of sales contract.

Defense A: The terms are too indefinite to enforce because the obligations of the parties are unclear or amount merely to an agreement to agree.

Reply A: The contract is sufficiently definite as the facts show the parties intended to make a contract and there is a reasonably certain basis for giving an appropriate remedy. § 2–204(3).

Defense B: But the price term is missing.

Reply B: We intended a bargain with price determined as a reasonable price based on the market. § 2–305.

Defense C: But the quantity term is missing.

Reply C: We measured quantity by the seller's output / buyer's requirements, determined in good faith. § 2–306.

Defense D: You did not specify quantity in good faith. § 1–304.

Reply D: Good faith will be a question of fact to be decided in court given the specific context and details.

CHAPTER 2

RELIANCE AND PROMISSORY ESTOPPEL

■ ■ ■

Recall from *King v. Boston University* that BU prevailed in its case concerning Dr. Martin Luther King's papers under two separate legal theories. The first theory was a contract theory based on bargained-for consideration. The court reasoned that, in exchange for his papers, Dr. King could rest assured in the knowledge that they were safe from harm, and indeed, that the papers would be preserved and indexed. Consideration, therefore, had been exchanged.

The second reason for the decision rested on a reliance theory, based on BU's plans and expenditures. BU reasonably relied on the promise that it would be able to keep Dr. King's papers for the future. In other words, through reliance on King's promise, BU made itself worse off by spending money caring for the documents. The reliance theory advanced in *King v. Boston University* is known legally as *promissory estoppel*.

Promissory estoppel gradually developed in the courts in the past century to temper the perceived harshness of the rigors of traditional contract formation, especially the consideration requirement. If a party foreseeably and reasonably relied on another's promise, promissory estoppel could, in a sense, become a *substitute* for the element of consideration. In other instances, courts expanded promissory estoppel even further. Promissory estoppel might come into play whenever there was reasonable detrimental reliance by the promisee. In such settings, promissory estoppel dispenses with the traditional doctrinal tools of offer and acceptance.

While *King v. Boston University* discussed *both* traditional contract formation and promissory estoppel theory, it is more common for cases to accept one or the other theory. Contract is the more commonly-known action, based on offer, acceptance, and consideration. Damages for breach of contract are based on an expectation measure. Expectation damages give the non-breaching party the benefit of the bargain, and are typically higher than the reliance damages awarded in an action for promissory estoppel. Promissory estoppel is usually thought of as a back-up or secondary theory, if the elements of a contract cannot be shown. (We defer detailed treatment of remedies to a later chapter and include a condensed version in a "Note on Remedies" in Section B of this chapter).

Promissory estoppel is difficult to prove, and empirical evidence shows that plaintiffs asserting a promissory estoppel theory are less successful at trial than contract plaintiffs. *See* Sidney W. DeLong, *The New Requirement of Enforcement Reliance in Commercial Promissory Estoppel, Section 90 as Catch-22*, 1997 WIS. L. REV. 943 (1997); Robert A. Hillman, *Questioning the "New Consensus" on Promissory Estoppel: An Empirical and Theoretical Study*, 98 COLUM. L. REV. 580 (1998).

A. DOCTRINAL ELEMENTS

The elements of promissory estoppel are set out in the Restatement (Second) of Contracts, Section 90.

RESTATEMENT (SECOND) OF CONTACTS, SECTION 90

§ 90.   *Promise Reasonably Inducing Action or Forbearance.*

(1)   A promise which the promisor should reasonably expect to induce action or forbearance on the part of the promisee or a third person and which does induce such action or forbearance is binding if injustice can be avoided only by enforcement of the promise. The remedy granted for breach may be limited as justice requires.

––––––––––

In the following cases, ask if consideration is present. In the next case, what was the problem for the plaintiffs in arguing that a contract existed?

FEINBERG V. PFEIFFER CORP.
322 S.W. 2d 163 (St. Louis Ct. App. 1959)

DOERNER, COMMISSIONER.

This is a suit brought in the Circuit Court of the City of St. Louis by plaintiff, a former employee of the defendant corporation, on an alleged contract whereby defendant agreed to pay plaintiff the sum of $200 per month for life upon her retirement. A jury being waived, the case was tried by the court alone. Judgment below was for plaintiff for $5,100, the amount of the pension claimed to be due as of the date of the trial, together with interest thereon, and defendant duly appealed.

The parties are in substantial agreement on the essential facts. Plaintiff began working for the defendant, a manufacturer of pharmaceuticals, in 1910, when she was but 17 years of age. By 1947 she had attained the position of bookkeeper, office manager, and assistant treasurer of the defendant, and owned 70 shares of its stock out of a total of 6,503 shares issued and outstanding. Twenty shares had been given to her by the defendant or its then president, she had purchased 20, and the remaining 30 she had acquired by a stock split or stock dividend. Over the years she received substantial dividends on the stock she owned, as did all of the other stockholders. Also, in addition to her salary, plaintiff from 1937 to 1949, inclusive, received each year a bonus varying in amount from $300 in the beginning to $2,000 in the later years.

On December 27, 1947, the annual meeting of the defendant's Board of Directors was held at the Company's offices in St. Louis, presided over by Max Lippman, its then president and largest individual stockholder. The other directors present were George L. Marcus, Sidney Harris, Sol Flammer, and Walter Weinstock, who, with Max Lippman, owned 5,007 of the 6,503 shares then issued and outstanding. At that meeting the Board of Directors adopted the following resolution, which, because it is the crux of the case, we quote in full:

'The Chairman thereupon pointed out that the Assistant Treasurer, Mrs. Anna Sacks Feinberg, has given the corporation many years of long and faithful service. Not only has she served the corporation devotedly, but with exceptional ability and skill. The President pointed out that although all of the officers and directors sincerely hoped and desired that Mrs. Feinberg would continue in her present position for as long as she felt able, nevertheless, in view of the length of service which she has contributed provision should be made to afford her retirement privileges and benefits which should become a firm obligation of the corporation to be available to her whenever she should see fit to retire from active duty, however many years in the future such retirement may become effective.

It was, accordingly, proposed that Mrs. Feinberg's salary, which is presently $350.00 per month, be increased to $400.00 per month, and that Mrs. Feinberg would be given the privilege of retiring from active duty at any time she may elect to see fit so to do upon a retirement pay of $200.00 per month for life, with the distinct understanding that the retirement plan is merely being adopted at the present time in order to afford Mrs. Feinberg security for the future and in the hope that her active services will continue with the corporation for many years to come. After due discussion and consideration, and upon motion duly made and seconded, it was—

'Resolved, that the salary of Anna Sacks Feinberg be increased from $350.00 to $400.00 per month and that she be afforded the privilege of retiring from active duty in the corporation at any time she may elect to see fit so to do upon retirement pay of $200.00 per month, for the remainder of her life.'

At the request of Mr. Lippman his sons-in-law, Messrs. Harris and Flammer, called upon the plaintiff at her apartment on the same day to advise her of the passage of the resolution. Plaintiff testified on cross-examination that she had no prior information that such a pension plan was contemplated, that it came as a surprise to her, and that she would have continued in her employment whether or not such a resolution had been adopted. It is clear from the evidence that there was no contract, oral or written, as to plaintiff's length of employment, and that she was free to quit, and the defendant to discharge her, at any time.

Plaintiff did continue to work for the defendant through June 30, 1949, on which date she retired. In accordance with the foregoing resolution, the defendant began paying her the sum of $200 on the first of each month. Mr. Lippman died on November 18, 1949, and was succeeded as president of the company by his widow. Because of an illness, she retired from that office and was succeeded in October, 1953, by her son-in-law, Sidney M. Harris. Mr. Harris testified that while Mrs. Lippman had been president she signed the monthly pension check paid plaintiff, but fussed about doing so, and considered the payments as gifts.

After his election, he stated, a new accounting firm employed by the defendant questioned the validity of the payments to plaintiff on several occasions, and in the Spring of 1956, upon its recommendation, he consulted the Company's then attorney, Mr. Ralph Kalish. Harris testified that both Ernst and Ernst, the accounting firm, and Kalish told him there was no need of giving plaintiff the money. He also stated that he had concurred in the view that the payments to plaintiff were mere gratuities rather than amounts due under a contractual obligation, and that following his discussion with the Company's attorney plaintiff was sent a check for $100 on April 1, 1956. Plaintiff declined to accept the reduced amount, and this action followed. Additional facts will be referred to later in this opinion.

Appellant's first assignment of error relates to the admission in evidence of plaintiff's testimony over its objection, that at the time of trial she was sixty-five and a half years old, and that she was no longer able to engage in gainful employment because of the removal of a cancer and the performance of a colocholecystostomy operation on November 25, 1957. Its complaint is not so much that such evidence was irrelevant and immaterial, as it is that the trial court erroneously made it one basis for its decision in favor of plaintiff.

As defendant concedes, the error (if it was error) in the admission of such evidence would not be a ground for reversal, since, this being a jury-waived case, we are constrained by the statutes to review it upon both the law and the evidence, Sec. 510.310 RSMo 1949, V.A.M.S., and to render such judgment as the court below ought to have given. Section 512.160,

Minor v. Lillard, Mo., 289 S.W.2d 1; Thumm v. Lohr, Mo.App., 306 S.W.2d 604.

We consider only such evidence as is admissible, and need not pass upon questions of error in the admission and exclusion of evidence. Hussey v. Robinson, Mo., 285 S.W.2d 603. However, in fairness to the trial court it should be stated that while he briefly referred to the state of plaintiff's health as of the time of the trial in his amended findings of fact, it is obvious from his amended grounds for decision and judgment that it was not, as will be seen, the basis for his decision.

Appellant's next complaint is that there was insufficient evidence to support the court's findings that plaintiff would not have quit defendant's employ had she not known and relied upon the promise of defendant to pay her $200 a month for life, and the finding that, from her voluntary retirement until April 1, 1956, plaintiff relied upon the continued receipt of the pension installments. The trial court so found, and, in our opinion, justifiably so.

Plaintiff testified, and was corroborated by Harris, defendant's witness, that knowledge of the passage of the resolution was communicated to her on December 27, 1947, the very day it was adopted. She was told at that time by Harris and Flammer, she stated, that she could take the pension as of that day, if she wished. She testified further that she continued to work for another year and a half, through June 30, 1949; that at that time her health was good and she could have continued to work, but that after working for almost forty years she thought she would take a rest. Her testimony continued:

Q. Now, what was the reason—I'm sorry. Did you then quit the employment of the company after you—after this year and a half?

A. Yes.

Q. What was the reason that you left?

A. Well, I thought almost forty years, it was a long time and I thought I would take a little rest.

Q. Yes.

A. And with the pension and what earnings my husband had, we figured we could get along.

Q. Did you rely upon this pension?

A. We certainly did.

Q. Being paid?

A. Very much so. We relied upon it because I was positive that I was going to get it as long as I lived.

Q.   Would you have left the employment of the company at that time had it not been for this pension?

A.   No.

Mr. Allen: Just a minute, I object to that as calling for a conclusion and conjecture on the part of this witness.

The Court: It will be overruled.

Q.   (Mr. Agatstein continuing): Go ahead, now. The question is whether you would have quit the employment of the company at that time had you not relied upon this pension plan?

A.   No, I wouldn't.

Q.   You would not have. Did you ever seek employment while this pension was being paid to you—

A.   (interrupting): No.

Q.   Wait a minute, at any time prior—at any other place?

A.   No, sir.

Q.   Were you able to hold any other employment during that time?

A.   Yes, I think so.

Q.   Was your health good?

A.   My health was good.

It is obvious from the foregoing that there was ample evidence to support the findings of fact made by the court below.

We come, then, to the basic issue in the case. While otherwise defined in defendant's third and fourth assignments of error, it is thus succinctly stated in the argument in its brief: '. . . whether plaintiff has proved that she has a right to recover from defendant based upon a legally binding contractual obligation to pay her $200 per month for life.'

It is defendant's contention, in essence, that the resolution adopted by its Board of Directors was a mere promise to make a gift, and that no contract resulted either thereby, or when plaintiff retired, because there was no consideration given or paid by the plaintiff. It urges that a promise to make a gift is not binding unless supported by a legal consideration; that the only apparent consideration for the adoption of the foregoing resolution was the 'many years of long and faithful service' expressed therein; and that past services are not a valid consideration for a promise. Defendant argues further that there is nothing in the resolution which made its effectiveness conditional upon plaintiff's continued employment, that she was not under contract to work for any length of time but was free to quit whenever she wished, and that she had no contractual right to her position and could have been discharged at any time.

Plaintiff concedes that a promise based upon past services would be without consideration, but contends that there were two other elements which supplied the required element: First, the continuation by plaintiff in the employ of the defendant for the period from December 27, 1947, the date when the resolution was adopted, until the date of her retirement on June 30, 1949. And, second, her change of position, i. e., her retirement, and the abandonment by her of her opportunity to continue in gainful employment, made in reliance on defendant's promise to pay her $200 per month for life.

We must agree with the defendant that the evidence does not support the first of these contentions. There is no language in the resolution predicating plaintiff's right to a pension upon her continued employment. She was not required to work for the defendant for any period of time as a condition to gaining such retirement benefits. She was told that she could quit the day upon which the resolution was adopted, as she herself testified, and it is clear from her own testimony that she made no promise or agreement to continue in the employ of the defendant in return for its promise to pay her a pension. Hence there was lacking that mutuality of obligation which is essential to the validity of a contract.

But as to the second of these contentions we must agree with plaintiff. By the terms of the resolution defendant promised to pay plaintiff the sum of $200 a month upon her retirement. . . . As the parties agree, the consideration sufficient to support a contract may be either a benefit to the promisor or a loss or detriment to the promisee.

Section 90 of the Restatement of the Law of Contracts states that: "A promise which the promisor should reasonably expect to induce action or forbearance . . . on the part of the promisee and which does induce such action or forbearance is binding if injustice can be avoided only by enforcement of the promise." This doctrine has been described as that of 'promissory estoppel,' as distinguished from that of equitable estoppel or estoppel in pais, the reason for the differentiation being stated as follows:

> It is generally true that one who has led another to act in reasonable reliance on his representations of fact cannot afterwards in litigation between the two deny the truth of the representations, and some courts have sought to apply this principle to the formation of contracts, where, relying on a gratuitous promise, the promisee has suffered detriment. It is to be noticed, however, that such a case does not come within the ordinary definition of estoppel. If there is any representation of an existing fact, it is only that the promisor at the time of making the promise intends to fulfill it. As to such intention there is usually no misrepresentation and if there is, it is not that which has injured the promisee. In other words, he relies on a promise and

not on a misstatement of fact; and the term 'promissory' estoppel or something equivalent should be used to make the distinction.

Williston on Contracts, Rev. Ed., Sec. 139, Vol. 1. In speaking of this doctrine, Judge Learned Hand said in Porter v. Commissioner of Internal Revenue, 2 Cir., 60 F.2d 673, 675, that '. . . " 'promissory estoppel' is now a recognized species of consideration."

As pointed out by our Supreme Court in In re Jamison's Estate, Mo., 202 S.W.2d 879, 887, it is stated in the Missouri Annotations to the Restatement under Section 90 that: "There is a variance between the doctrine underlying this section and the theoretical justifications that have been advanced for the Missouri decisions."

That variance, as the authors of the Annotations point out, is that:

This § 90, when applied with § 85, means that the promise described is a contract without any consideration." In Missouri the same practical result is reached without in theory abandoning the doctrine of consideration. In Missouri three theories have been advanced as ground for the decisions:

(1) *Theory of act for promise*. The induced 'action or forbearance' is the consideration for the promise. Underwood Typewriter Co. v. Century Realty Co. (1909) 220 Mo. 522, 119 S.W. 400, 25 L.R.A., N.S., 1173. See § 76.

(2) *Theory of promissory estoppel*. The induced 'action or forbearance' works an estoppel against the promisor. (Citing School District of Kansas City v. Sheidley (1897) 138 Mo. 672, 40 S. W. 656 [37 L.R.A. 406]) . . .

(3) *Theory of bilateral contract*. When the induced 'action or forbearance' is begun, a promise to complete is implied, and we have an enforceable bilateral contract, the implied promise to complete being the consideration for the original promise.' (Citing cases.)

Was there such an act on the part of plaintiff, in reliance upon the promise contained in the resolution, as will estop the defendant . . . under the doctrine of promissory estoppel? We think there was. One of the illustrations cited under Section 90 of the Restatement is:

2.   A promises B to pay him an annuity during B's life. B thereupon resigns a profitable employment, as A expected that he might. B receives the annuity for some years, in the meantime becoming disqualified from again obtaining good employment. A's promise is binding.

This illustration is objected to by defendant as not being applicable to the case at hand. The reason advanced by it is that in the illustration B became 'disqualified' from obtaining other employment *before* A discontinued the payments, whereas in this case the plaintiff did not discover that she had cancer and thereby became unemployable until *after* the defendant had discontinued the payments of $200 per month. We think the distinction is immaterial. The only reason for the reference in the illustration to the disqualification of A is in connection with that part of Section 90 regarding the prevention of injustice. The injustice would occur regardless of when the disability occurred.

Would defendant contend that the contract would be enforceable if the plaintiff's illness had been discovered on March 31, 1956, the day before it discontinued the payment of the $200 a month, but not if it occurred on April 2nd, the day after? Furthermore, there are more ways to become disqualified for work, or unemployable, than as the result of illness. At the time she retired plaintiff was 57 years of age. At the time the payments were discontinued she was over 63 years of age. It is a matter of common knowledge that it is virtually impossible for a woman of that age to find satisfactory employment, much less a position comparable to that which plaintiff enjoyed at the time of her retirement.

The fact of the matter is that plaintiff's subsequent illness was not the 'action or forbearance' which was induced by the promise contained in the resolution. As the trial court correctly decided, such action on plaintiff's part was her retirement from a lucrative position in reliance upon defendant's promise to pay her an annuity or pension. In a very similar case, Ricketts v. Scothorn, 57 Neb. 51, 77 N.W. 365, 367, 42 L.R.A. 794, the Supreme Court of Nebraska said:

> . . . According to the undisputed proof, as shown by the record before us, the plaintiff was a working girl, holding a position in which she earned a salary of $10 per week. Her grandfather, desiring to put her in a position of independence, gave her the note accompanying it with the remark that his other grandchildren did not work, and that she would not be obliged to work any longer. In effect, he suggested that she might abandon her employment, and rely in the future upon the bounty which he promised. He doubtless desired that she should give up her occupation, but, whether he did or not, it is entirely certain that he contemplated such action on her part as a reasonable and probable consequence of his gift. Having intentionally influenced the plaintiff to alter her position for the worse on the faith of the note being paid when due, it would be grossly inequitable to permit the maker, or his executor, to resist payment on the ground that the promise was given without consideration.

 [Affirmed.]

NOTES AND QUESTIONS

1.   Why did the court turn to promissory estoppel in its analysis?

2.   Why would it make a difference if Ms. Feinberg had retired before or after she became ill? Think about the era when this case was decided. Would there be a realistic chance of Ms. Feinberg finding new employment?

3.   Think about the precedent cited at the end of the case, *Ricketts v. Scothorn*, and its facts. How does promissory estoppel expand the liability of those who make promises, either as gifts or within families? Is such expansion of promissory liability wise from a policy perspective?

4.   In what ways does promissory estoppel seem like an exception to the rule requiring consideration? In what ways does it seem like an alternative theory of liability?

5.   Times have changed since *Feinberg* in 1959, offering employees such as Ms. Feinberg recourse beyond contract law. Since 1974, promises of a pension are covered by ERISA, 29 U.S.C. ch. 18 § 1001 et seq., a federal law governing employee benefits. Once an employee's pension benefits vest, an employer must pay them under ERISA. Title VII of the Civil Rights Act of 1964, 42 U.S.C. § 2000e et seq., prohibits employment discrimination based on prohibited characteristics, such as race, religion, and gender. The Age Discrimination in Employment Act, 29 U.S.C. § 621–634, prohibits discrimination in employment on the basis of age for workers age forty and older.

EAST PROVIDENCE CREDIT UNION V. GEREMIA
239 A.2d 725 (R.I. 1968)

KELLEHER, J.

. . . On December 5, 1963, defendants, who are husband and wife, borrowed $2,350.28 from plaintiff for which they gave their promissory note. The payment of the note was secured by a chattel mortgage on defendants' 1962 ranch wagon. The mortgage contained a clause which obligated defendants to maintain insurance on the motor vehicle in such amounts as plaintiff required against loss by fire, collision, upset or overturn of the automobile and similar hazards. This provision also stipulated that if defendants failed to maintain such insurance, plaintiff could pay the premium and "any sum so paid shall be secured hereby and shall be immediately payable." The defendants had procured the required insurance and had designated plaintiff as a loss payee on its policy. The premium therefor was payable in periodic installments.

On October 11, 1965, defendants received a notice from the insurance carrier informing them that the premium then payable was overdue and that, unless it was paid within the ensuing twelve days, the policy would be cancelled. A copy of this notice was also sent by the insurer to plaintiff who thereupon sent a letter to defendants. The pertinent portion thereof reads as follows:

> We are in receipt of a cancellation notice on your Policy. If we are not notified of a renewal Policy within 10 days, we shall be forced to renew the policy for you and apply this amount to your loan.

Upon receiving this communication, defendant wife testified that she telephoned plaintiff's office and talked to the treasurer's assistant; that she told this employee to go ahead and pay the premium; that she explained to the employee that her husband was sick and they could not pay the insurance premium and the payment due on the loan; and that the employee told her [that] her call would be referred to plaintiff's treasurer. The employee testified that she told defendant to contact this officer. We deem this difference in testimony insignificant. It is clear from the record that defendants communicated their approval of an acquiescence in plaintiff's promise to pay the insurance due on the car and that this employee notified the treasurer of such fact.

On December 17, 1965, defendants' motor vehicle was demolished in a mishap the nature of which cannot be learned from the record. It is obvious, however, that the loss was within the coverage of the policy. The automobile was a total loss. The evidence shows that at the time of the loss, the outstanding balance of the loan was $987.89 and the value of the ranch wagon prior to the loss exceeded the balance due on the loan.

Sometime after this unfortunate incident, all the parties became aware that the insurer would not indemnify them for the loss because the overdue premium had not been paid and defendants' policy had been canceled prior to the accident.

The defendants had on deposit with plaintiff over $200 in savings shares. The plaintiff, in accordance with the terms of the note, had deducted therefrom certain amounts and applied them to defendants' indebtedness so that at the time this litigation was instituted defendants allegedly owed plaintiff $779.53.

In finding for defendants on their counterclaim, the trial justice awarded them all the moneys which plaintiff had applied after the date of defendants' accident to the then outstanding balance of the loan. The justice, at the conclusion of the evidence, made certain findings which were in accordance with the testimony as set forth above. He found from the evidence that plaintiff, in pursuance of its right under the mortgage contract and its letter to defendants, had agreed to renew the policy and charge and premiums paid by it on behalf of defendants to the outstanding balance on their loan.

In reaching this conclusion, the trial justice made the following observation: "it seems to me quite clear that the defendants, having been given notice that the plaintiff would do this (pay the overdue premium), and calling the plaintiff's attention to the fact that they weren't going to renew and that the plaintiff had better do this to protect everybody, seems to me at that point there was agreement on the part of the plaintiff that it would procure this insurance. Or, put it another way, that they are estopped from denying that they were exercising the right that they had under the original mortgage." The superior court further found that defendants were justified in believing in plaintiff's assurance that it would pay the overdue premium.

The sole issue raised by this appeal is whether or not plaintiff is precluded from recovering on its loan contract by reason of its failure to fulfill a promise to defendants to pay the overdue insurance premium. In urging that the trial justice erred in finding for defendants, plaintiff directs our attention to Hazlett v. First Fed. Sav. & Loan Assn., 14 Wash.2d 124, 127 P.2d 273, in which the court refused to apply the doctrine of promissory estoppel to enforce a gratuitous promise made by a mortgagee to procure fire insurance for mortgaged property even though the mortgagor suffered serious detriment in reliance on the mortgagee's promise.

Until recently it was a general rule that the doctrine of estoppel was applied only to representations made as to facts past or present. Anderson v. Polleys, 54 R.I. 296, 173 A. 114; Croce v. Whiting Milk Co., R.I., 228 A.2d 574. This doctrine is commonly known as "equitable" estoppel. Over the years, however, courts have carved out a recognized exception to this rule and applied it to those circumstances wherein one promises to do or not to do something in the future. This latter doctrine is known as 'promissory' estoppel. See Southeastern Sales & Service Co. v. T. T. Watson, Inc., Fla.App., 172 So.2d 239. See also Berarducci v. Diano, 60 R.I. 305, 198 A. 351. Promissory estoppel is defined in the . . . Restatement, Contracts, § 90, p. 110, as follows:

> A promise which the promisor should reasonably expect to induce action or forbearance . . . on the part of the promisee and which does induce such action or forbearance is binding if injustice can be avoided only by enforcement of its promise.

Although this court has not yet applied the doctrine of promissory estoppel as it is expressed in the Restatement, we have in Mann v. McDermott, 77 R.I. 142, 73 A.2d 815, implied that in appropriate circumstances we would. Traditionally, the doctrine of promissory estoppel has been invoked as a substitute for a consideration, rendering a gratuitous promise enforceable as a contract. Viewed in another way, the acts of reliance by the promisee to his detriment provided a substitute for consideration. Hoffman v. Red Owl Stores, Inc., 26 Wis.2d 683, 133 N.W.2d 267.

While the doctrine was originally recognized and most often utilized in charitable subscription cases, it presently enjoys a much wider and more expanded application. See 1 Williston, Contracts (3d. Jaeger), § 140; 1A Corbin, Contracts, §§ 193–209; 48 A.L.R.2d 1069–1088. Relative to the problem presented in this case, we have discovered several cases in which the theory of promissory estoppel has been invoked. In these cases, courts have held that a gratuitous promise made by one to procure insurance on the promisee's property is made enforceable by the promisee's reliance thereon and his forbearance to procure such insurance himself. Graddon v. Knight, 138 Cal.App.2d 577, 292 P.2d 632; see also 1A Corbin, Contracts, s 208 at 265, and cases cited therein. Our research indicates, therefore, that the contrary view expressed in Hazlett v. First Fed. Sav. & Loan Assn., supra, and relied upon by plaintiff, is a minority viewpoint on the issue before us and we are disinclined to follow it.

In the instant case, however, after a careful review of the facts, we are of the opinion that plaintiff made more than a mere gratuitous or unrecompensed promise. Instead, we believe that the promise by plaintiff to pay the insurance premium on defendants' car was one made in exchange for valid consideration. The mortgage contract provided that in the event plaintiff paid a premium for defendants, it would add such expended sums to the outstanding balance of defendants' loan. We are satisfied from a close examination of plaintiff's reply to defendants' interrogatories and of the chattel mortgage agreement that plaintiff intended to compute interest on any money it expended in keeping the insurance on defendants' car active. Hence, in our opinion, the interest due on any sums paid out by plaintiff on behalf of defendants for insurance represents valid consideration and converts their promise into a binding contract. The plaintiff's failure to successfully carry out its promise must be deemed a breach of that contract entitling defendants to assert a right of action which would at the very least offset any amount of money found owing to plaintiff on their loan.

We would point out that, even if it could be shown by plaintiff that it never intended to compute any interest on amounts paid by it for insurance premiums on defendants' car and that its promise was truly a pure gratuitous undertaking, we believe such a showing would be of no avail to it since we would not hesitate in finding from this record evidence sufficient to establish a case for the application of promissory estoppel. The conditions precedent for the invocation of this doctrine are . . . as follows: (1) Was there a promise which the promisor should reasonably expect to induce action or forbearance . . . on the part of the promisee? (2) Did the promise induce such action or forbearance? (3) Can injustice be avoided only by enforcement of the promise?

After a study of the facts in this case, our reply to each of the above inquiries is a definite 'yes.' Promissory estoppel as a legal theory is gaining in prominence as a device used by an increasing number of courts to provide a much needed remedy to alleviate the plight of those who suffer a serious injustice as a result of their good-faith reliance on the unfulfilled promises of others. As the Arkansas supreme court has so appropriately commented in Peoples Nat'l Bank of Little Rock v. Linebarger Constr. Co., 219 Ark. 11, at 17, 240 S.W.2d 12, at 16, the law of promissory estoppel exhibits "an attempt by the courts to keep remedies abreast of increased moral consciousness of honesty and fair representations in all business dealings." We subscribe to those sentiments. [Affirmed.]

NOTES AND QUESTIONS

1.   The court found consideration for the bank's promise to insure in the fact that, in exchange, it would earn interest on funds advanced to pay the insurance premium. With that finding, the case could be decided within the doctrines of traditional contract formation. The court offered an alternative holding that, absent consideration, the bank would nevertheless be liable under the theory of promissory estoppel, still a relatively novel basis of liability in the late 1960s when the opinion was written. Were these judicial observations obvious to you before reading them? Were they clear after doing so?

2.   Many courts would continue to follow this pattern—seeking to find consideration first and, only if consideration could not be found, turning to promissory estoppel. The New York Court of Appeals, thanks to the legendary Judge Benjamin Cardozo, earned a reputation for being so skillful in the art of finding consideration that it never opted to fully or formally embrace the doctrine of promissory estoppel. *See* Arthur B. Schwartz, *The Second Circuit 'Estopped': There is No Promissory Estoppel in New York*, 19 CARDOZO L. REV. 1201 (1997) (noting how many federal courts applying New York law did not always appreciate this distinction); *Allegheny College v. National Chautauqua County Bank of Jamestown*, 159 N.E. 173 (N.Y. 1927) (Cardozo, J.) (illustrating Cardozo's skillfulness along with his contemplation of the budding notion of promissory estoppel).

EXAMPLE: A PROMISED RIDE?

Consider the following story that appeared on a Silicon Valley blog:

In May, Lyft launched a program to compete with Uber's black car and SUV services. Drivers had to pony up $34,000 to purchase the "tricked-out" Lyft-branded Ford Explorers just to get into the pool. But the luxury pilot bombed, leaving "Lyft Plus" drivers with the expensive SUVs they were forced to buy.

The [problem] started from the onset, when Lyft reportedly assured their Plus drivers to "[not] worry about demand; we have that covered." But the startup's fist-bumping clientele wasn't hot for the double-priced rides, and drivers were soon assigned regular fares just to stay busy. Now the company has given up marketing the SUVs to business elites and slashed prices by 25 percent.

According to the *San Francisco Chronicle*, those cuts are causing drivers to lose money, thanks to the truck's terrible gas mileage.

"Overwhelmingly we were getting $5 or $6 rides; we can't afford it with the gas for those expensive cars," one driver said. "They get 14 (miles per gallon) in San Francisco."

SFist reports Lyft is offering to either help their Plus drivers sell the trucks or give them a $10,000 bonus (which would be subject to income tax). But the bail-out deal has been met with mixed results. Some drivers say they didn't lose money on Lyft's premium service experiment, but others claimed . . . that they got taken:

Several drivers said they had made life changes: selling existing cars, borrowing money from relatives, even forgoing other job opportunities for the chance to make more money with Lyft Plus.

"They pulled the plug, leaving us high and dry."

It's the new way "the sharing economy" lives up to its name: sharing the cost of failed product launches with 1099 contract employees. Just another cost of doing business for Silicon Valley's micro-entrepreneurs.

What do you think? Do the drivers have a legal claim?

What about an instance where consideration is arguably present, but the parties just have not yet inked a "final" deal? The intent there might be to create a final contract, but maybe the parties just "miss" and never get there. Do we need an exception for these instances? Consider the equities in the following case, concerning the obligations of Aretha Franklin, "The Queen of Soul."

ELVIN ASSOCIATES V. FRANKLIN
735 F.Supp. 1177 (S.D.N.Y. 1990)

KNAPP, J.

After a bench trial of several days, we made preliminary findings on the record in plaintiff's favor, both as to the direct claim that defendants Aretha Franklin and Crown Productions, Inc., breached a contract under which Franklin was to star in a musical production entitled "Sing Mahalia Sing" ("Mahalia"), and as to defendants' counterclaim alleging breach by plaintiff of a second contract relating to the same production. The parties have briefed several legal questions in their post-trial submissions, and in light of that briefing we have somewhat altered the tentative findings of fact and conclusions of law. While we have reconsidered and changed our view that defendants are liable for breach of contract, we do hold defendant Franklin liable to plaintiff on a theory of promissory estoppel. We adhere to our originally expressed view that the counterclaim for breach of contract should be dismissed.

The following recitation of facts is derived from the testimony and exhibits offered at trial, as well as the deposition testimony of defendant Franklin. . . In early 1984 Ashton Springer, the principal of plaintiff Elvin Associates, began efforts to mount a Broadway musical production about the life and music of Mahalia Jackson, and wrote to defendant Aretha Franklin seeking her agreement to appear in the title role. Franklin called Springer and expressed her strong interest in the production, and told Springer to contact her agents at the William Morris Agency. Springer spoke with Phil Citron and Katy Rothacker of that agency and in several conversations with the latter discussed the basic financial terms of Franklin's engagement to appear. Several proposals and counter-proposals were exchanged, in each instance relayed by Rothacker to Franklin and then back to Springer. Near the end of February 1984, Rothacker called Springer and informed him that his final proposal was acceptable.

In the interim, Springer had already set about making the necessary arrangements to get the production going. He was in frequent consultation with Franklin concerning artistic and production matters, although he negotiated the financial terms of the agreement strictly through her agents. During a conversation about rehearsal and performance dates, Franklin indicated to Springer that there were no other conflicting engagements on her schedule, stating: "This is what I am doing." After consulting with Franklin, Springer hired George Faison as director-choreographer. In the second week of March, Springer and Faison flew to Detroit to meet with Franklin to discuss various aspects of the production, including rehearsal and performance dates. Franklin agreed on a tentative schedule that called for rehearsals to begin in April and performances to begin in May.

After returning to New York, Springer began negotiating limited partnership agreements with various investors to finance the "Mahalia" production. He also began calling promoters and theaters in various cities in an effort to reserve dates for performances. During discussions with several promoters he learned for the first time that Franklin had recently cancelled several performances, purportedly due to a newly acquired fear of flying. Springer spoke with Citron at William Morris regarding these incidents, and the latter stated that the cancellations resulted from commitments made by prior agents for Franklin without her approval, and reassured Springer that there was no such problem here. Springer also spoke with Franklin, who reassured him that she wanted to do the show and that she would fly as necessary. Springer offered to make alternative arrangements for transportation to the various performance sites, and to alter the performance schedule to accommodate slower forms of transportation. Franklin told Springer that she was uncomfortable traveling more than 200 miles per day by ground transportation, but strongly assured him that she would overcome her fear of flying.

Springer had also in the interim contacted Jay Kramer, his attorney, about the proposed production and the terms he had discussed with Franklin's representatives. Kramer set up a meeting for March 23, 1984 with Franklin's representatives for the purpose of finalizing the agreement. Present at the meeting on that date were Springer, Kramer, Citron, Rothacker, Greg Pulis (an attorney at William Morris) and Andrew Feinman (Franklin's attorney). The basic financial terms that had been previously agreed upon in the Springer-Rothacker conversations were confirmed: Franklin would be paid $40,000 per week in salary, and an additional weekly amount to cover her expenses ($5000 per week while in New York; $4500 per week outside of New York). In addition, she would receive 15% of the show's gross weekly revenues exceeding $225,000 (the "break even point"), and 20% of the show's weekly profits. In return, she would commit herself to 12 weeks of performances.

Springer and Kramer asked Franklin's representatives to call her and obtain her approval of these terms. The Franklin team left the meeting room, and shortly returned indicating that she had agreed to them. The only major issue left unresolved at the close of this meeting was the location for rehearsals, Franklin's representatives having requested that they be in Detroit. Faison subsequently vetoed this proposal, stressing that the lighting and costume designers that were to be engaged were all in New York. Springer did not convey this information directly to Franklin, but she ultimately learned through her agents that the rehearsals would take place in New York.

After the March 23 meeting, Kramer drafted a contract in the form of a letter to defendant Crown Productions, Inc., the corporation through which Franklin's services were to be furnished. Crown Productions was to be the primary obligor (and obligee) under the contract, and Franklin was personally to guarantee Crown's performance.

Before drafting the contract, Kramer had obtained from William Morris a copy of a "Domestic Rider" containing various required terms for all engagement contracts involving Franklin. Among the terms listed in the rider was: "This contract/agreement shall not be deemed valid until executed by ARTIST." At the bottom of the rider was the admonition "DO NOT DEVIATE." Kramer reviewed the rider to determine which terms were appropriate for inclusion in the draft. He did not include in the first draft the term concerning validity upon execution. As he testified: "It was impractical. We were underway. From the moment we left that room, given the schedule that we outlined Mr. Springer was well on his way to making financial commitment based on the understanding we thought we had reached." Franklin's representatives never suggested that the term be inserted in any of the subsequent drafts. However, every draft began with the sentence: "This letter [addressed to Crown Productions, Inc.], when countersigned by you, shall constitute our understanding until a more formal agreement is prepared."

In the ensuing weeks a series of drafts circulated between the principals and their various agents. The basic pattern was that Kramer would first send a new draft to Springer for his approval, and would then send it to Citron, Feinman and Pulis, who would return it marked up with their comments. Franklin reviewed at least some of these drafts, but could not identify any of them with certainty as having been reviewed by her. . . . A final draft of the contract was ready for signature as of June 7, the date that Franklin was scheduled to come to New York to begin rehearsals for the show.

Springer had in the intervening weeks made all of the arrangements necessary for rehearsals to begin. He had hired set, lighting and costume designers, stage and technical crew, and had reserved dance studios. Springer was in frequent communication with Franklin during this period, as were Faison and other members of the production staff, concerning such varied matters as the compositions to be performed, the costumes she would wear, and the hiring of her own regular backup singers to be in the chorus. At one point, Franklin sang one of the production songs to Springer over the telephone. At some point during this period, Faison made final determinations as to the compositions to be performed and as to the cast and chorus.

As planned, rehearsals actually began on June 4 without Franklin, and continued for several days. Franklin did not arrive in New York on June 7 and, indeed, never came to New York for the rehearsals. Kramer immediately sought an explanation from Franklin's representatives and was informed that she would not fly. Springer paid the cast through the end of that week, but then suspended the production. He attempted to secure some other well-known performer to fill the title role, but none of the performers whom he contacted would agree to step into the role at that juncture. . . . This lawsuit ensued, with Springer (suing in the name of Elvin Associates) alleging breach of the original agreement to appear in "Mahalia," and Franklin counter-claiming for breach of the second agreement concerning the proposed Detroit-based production. In his pre-trial memorandum, Springer asserted an alternative right to recover on a theory of promissory estoppel. . . .

SEC. A   DOCTRINAL ELEMENTS   151

The central issue pertaining to plaintiff's claim for breach of contract is whether or not the parties to that proposed contract, i.e. Springer, Crown Productions, Inc., and Franklin in her capacity as guarantor of Crown's performance, evinced an intent not to be formally bound before execution of written, integrated contract. Language inserted in a draft of the agreement referring to its validity upon execution has generally been found to be strong (though not conclusive) evidence of intent not to be bound prior to execution. R.G. Group v. Horn & Hardart (2nd Cir.1984) 751 F.2d 69, 75; Reprosystem, B.V. v. SCM Corp. (2nd Cir.1984) 727 F.2d 257, 262.

Although we based our tentative findings largely on the fact that all of the incidental terms had been worked out by the final draft, and that the understanding was that Franklin would sign the agreement when she came to New York, there remains the obstacle of the preamble that Kramer drafted and that remained in every draft, namely: "This letter, when countersigned by you, shall constitute our understanding until a more formal agreement is prepared." After reviewing the above cited authorities and the post-trial submissions, we are constrained to find that such language indicates that Crown Productions, Inc. was not to be contractually bound to Springer until the draft agreement was executed. This clause is simply too close to the language held to be decisive in *Reprosystem*, *supra*, to be ignored. The cause of action for breach of contract must therefore be dismissed as against both defendants . . .

That, however, does not end the case. As above noted, plaintiff has asserted, in the alternative, a right to recover on a theory of promissory estoppel. The elements of a claim for promissory estoppel are: "[A] clear and unambiguous promise; a reasonable and foreseeable reliance by the party to whom the promise is made; and an injury sustained by the party asserting the estoppel by reason of his reliance." *Reprosystem*, *supra*, at 264 (quoting Ripple's of Clearview v. Le Havre Associates 88 A.D.2d 120, 452 N.Y.S.2d 447, 449). The " 'circumstances [must be] such as to render it unconscionable to deny' the promise upon which plaintiff has relied." Philo Smith & Co., Inc. v. USLIFE Corporation (2nd Cir.1977) 554 F.2d 34, 36 (quoting Williston on Contracts § 533A, at 801 (3d ed. 1960) (emphasis the court's)).

It is difficult to imagine a more fitting case for applying the above-described doctrine. Although for her own business purposes Franklin insisted that the formal contract be with the corporate entity through which her services were to be "furnished," in the real world the agreement was with her, and we find that she had unequivocally and intentionally committed herself to appear in the production long before the day on which it was intended that the finalized agreement with her corporation would be signed.

First, it is clear from the testimony of all of the witnesses that Franklin was enthusiastic about appearing in the production and that at all times during the relevant period gave it the highest professional priority. She early on stated to Springer: "This is what I am doing." Combined with her oral agreement, through her agents, to the basic financial terms of her engagement, her continued expression of this enthusiasm to Springer more than amply afforded Springer a reasonable basis for beginning to make the various arrangements and expenditures necessary to bring the production to fruition.

Second, Franklin could not possibly have assumed that Springer could have performed his obligations to her—which, among other things, included arranging a complicated schedule of performances to commence shortly after her arrival in New York—without committing himself to and actually spending considerable sums prior to her affixing her signature to the contract on the date of such arrival. Throughout the time that he was making those commitments and advancing the necessary sums, she accepted his performance without any disclaimer of her prior promises to him. Indeed, she actively participated in many aspects of the necessary arrangements.

Third, Franklin's expression to Springer of her fear of flying did not, as she has contended, make her promise conditional or coat it with a patina of ambiguity that should have alerted Springer to suspend his efforts to mount the production. Although Franklin rejected Springer's offer to make alternative ground transportation arrangements, her primary reason for doing so was that she was determined to overcome her fear of flying, and it was reasonable for Springer to rely on her reassurances that she would be able to fly. Moreover, it was also entirely reasonable for him to assume that if she could not overcome her fear she would travel to New York by other means, even if it meant spreading the trip over several days. In short, Franklin's fear of flying provides no basis whatsoever for avoiding liability for failing to fulfill her promise, reiterated on several occasions, to appear in "Mahalia." If she could not bring herself to fly, she should have traveled by way of ground transportation. It has not been established that she was otherwise unable to come to New York to meet her obligations.

 We conclude that under the circumstances as we have outlined them it would be unconscionable not to compensate Springer for the losses he incurred through his entirely justified reliance on Franklin's oral promises.

NOTES AND QUESTIONS

1.   Do you agree with the court's holding and reasoning? Why or why not?

2.   Aretha Franklin, the "Queen of Soul," has recorded iconic music, including "Respect," "Chain of Fools," and "Natural Woman." She has credited Mahalia Jackson with mentoring and encouraging her and her career.

3.   Franklin's aversion to flying first appeared in 1983. Stressed about her father's illness, Franklin was traveling back and forth between her family home in Detroit, and Atlanta, where she had business meetings and appearances. Franklin missed her regular flight, and the airline re-booked her onto a small prop plane. The plane faced heavy turbulence in flight, and Franklin suffered a severe panic attack.

4.   Franklin's phobia has lasted many decades, up to the present day. When she has toured, she has done so by custom bus. Her fear of flying has apparently cost her gigs in Europe and a stint as a judge on "American Idol." In your view, does this change any aspect of the case?

B. GENERAL APPLICATIONS

COSGROVE V. BARTOLOTTA
150 F.3d 729 (7th Cir. 1998)

POSNER, C.J.

A jury awarded the plaintiff damages of $135,000 in a diversity suit governed by Wisconsin law. The damages were broken down as follows: $117,000 for promissory estoppel, $1,000 for misrepresentation, and $17,000 for unjust enrichment. In response to the defendants' motion under Fed.R.Civ.P. 59(e) to alter or amend the judgment, the judge rendered judgment for the defendants on the promissory estoppel claim on the ground that the plaintiff had failed to prove reliance; but he let the jury's verdict stand with respect to the other claims. . . . Both sides appeal . . .

The principal defendant is Joseph Bartolotta, but his company—Mary-Bart, LLC—is also named as a defendant. . . Mary-Bart is neither a partnership nor a corporation, but a "limited liability company." Wis. Stat. Chapter 183. This animal is like a limited partnership; the principal difference is that it need have no equivalent to a general partner, that is, an owner who has unlimited personal liability for the debts of the firm. See generally Larry E. Ribstein & Robert R. Keatinge, *Ribstein and Keatinge on Limited Liability Companies* (1998). . . . [Discussion of jurisdiction and LLCs has been excised.—Eds.]

This brings us to the merits of the appeals. Bartolotta wanted to open a new restaurant in Milwaukee. He asked a family friend—Barry Cosgrove—for help. The help sought was a $100,000 loan from Cosgrove plus Cosgrove's business and legal advice, Cosgrove being an experienced corporate lawyer. Bartolotta promised Cosgrove not only to repay the loan with interest within three years but also to give him a 19 percent ownership interest in the restaurant. Armed with Cosgrove's pledge of the $100,000 loan, Bartolotta was able to obtain the bank financing that he needed for the venture.

In reliance on the promise of a share in the ownership of the restaurant, Cosgrove assisted Bartolotta in negotiating the lease of the restaurant premises and the loan from the bank, and it was on Cosgrove's advice that the venture was organized in the form of an LLC. But Cosgrove never actually made the loan and was never given an ownership interest in the restaurant. For after all the arrangements were complete, and though Cosgrove was willing and able to make the loan, Bartolotta obtained alternative financing and cut Cosgrove out of the deal. The restaurant opened and was a success, so the ownership interest that Cosgrove would have gotten had Bartolotta not reneged on his premise has turned out to be worth something; hence this lawsuit.

We have stated the facts as favorably to Cosgrove as the record permits, as we must do in deciding whether it was error for the district judge to take the promissory estoppel case away from the jury. Cosgrove's evidence was vigorously contested, but there was enough to enable a reasonable jury to find the facts that we have summarized. It is true that the jury found against Cosgrove on his breach of contract claim, but this was not inconsistent with its finding promissory estoppel. Cosgrove and Bartolotta never worked out the exact terms under which Cosgrove would receive a share in the restaurant, so the jury could reasonably find that there was no contract even if it believed his testimony about the promise made to him and the services that he performed in reliance on the promise.

Promissory estoppel is an alternative basis to breach of contract for seeking damages from the breakdown of a relation. If there is a promise of a kind likely to induce a costly change in position by the promisee in reliance on the promise being carried out, and it does induce such a change, he can enforce the promise even though there was no contract. *U.S. Oil Co. v. Midwest Auto Care Services, Inc.*, 150 Wis.2d 80, 440 N.W.2d 825, 828 (1989); *Skycom Corp. v. Telstar Corp.*, 813 F.2d 810, 817 (7th Cir.1987) (applying Wisconsin law).

Buried in our capsule summary of the law of promissory estoppel is an important qualification: the reliance that makes the promise legally enforceable must be induced by a reasonable expectation that the promise will be carried out. A promise that is vague and hedged about with conditions may nevertheless have a sufficient expected value to induce a reasonable person to invest time and effort in trying to maximize the likelihood that the promise will be carried out. But if he does so knowing that he is investing for a chance, rather than relying on a firm promise that a reasonable person would expect to be carried out, he cannot plead promissory estoppel. See *Major Mat Co. v. Monsanto Co.*, 969 F.2d 579, 583

(7th Cir.1992); *Gruen Industries, Inc. v. Biller,* 608 F.2d 274, 280–82 (7th Cir.1979); *Inter-Mountain Threading, Inc. v. Baker Hughes Tubular Services, Inc.,* 812 P.2d 555, 559 (Wyo.1991); *First Security Savings Bank v. Aitken,* 226 Mich.App. 291, 573 N.W.2d 307, 316–18 (1997); *Security Bank & Trust Co. v. Bogard,* 494 N.E.2d 965, 968–69 (Ind.App.1986).

Suppose a father tells his son that he is thinking of promising the son on his next birthday that if he gives up smoking the father will restore him as a beneficiary under his will. In an effort to make sure that he will be able to comply with this condition, the son enrolls in an expensive program for cigarette addicts. His birthday arrives, and the father does not make the promise that the son was hoping for. The son relied, and relied reasonably, on his father's statement, in enrolling in the anti-smoking program; but he was not relying on the carrying out of the promise (not yet made) of being restored as a beneficiary of his father's will, and therefore he has no claim of promissory estoppel. Or suppose a contractor told a subcontractor that it was thinking of hiring him for a job but wouldn't consider him unless the subcontractor had more minority workers in his employ, and the subcontractor goes out and hires some, and, as before, the contractor does not hire him. Again there would be no basis for a claim of promissory estoppel.

The defendants argue that this was such a case. But the jury was entitled to conclude differently. Bartolotta was quite definite in promising Cosgrove an ownership interest in the restaurant, though at first the size of the interest was uncertain. Bartolotta specified no contingencies that might defeat the promise. A reasonable jury could find that Cosgrove invested time and effort in the venture, and pledged to make a $100,000 loan, not because he hoped that this would induce Bartolotta to give him a share in the new company but because he thought he had already been firmly promised a share, contingent only on his honoring his pledge (if called on to do so) and providing business and legal advice as needed—all of which he did or was prepared to do.

A more difficult question is whether Cosgrove actually relied on the promise. It is dangerous to take a legal term in its lay sense. To "rely," in the law of promissory estoppel, is not merely to do something in response to the inducement offered by the promise. There must be a cost to the promisee of doing it. *Hoffman v. Red Owl Stores, Inc.,* 26 Wis.2d 683, 133 N.W.2d 267, 275 (1965); *Creative Demos, Inc. v. Wal-Mart Stores, Inc.,* 142 F.3d 367, 369 (7th Cir.1998). The pledge of $100,000 was not shown to be a cost to Cosgrove. He never actually made the loan, and there is no evidence that the making of the pledge imposed an out-of-pocket cost, as it would have done if, for example, he had had to pay a capital-gains tax in order to obtain cash needed to make the loan if asked to do so.

One could not even be certain that the personal services which Cosgrove rendered to Bartolotta cost him something without knowing what the alternative uses of his time were. If he performed these services in his spare time—time for which he had no valuable professional or even leisure use—the cost to him of performing the services for Bartolotta may have been so slight as not to count as reliance for purposes of promissory estoppel doctrine.

But this is hardly plausible; Cosgrove was a professional rendering professional services. And, if nothing else, the pledge put Cosgrove at risk, since he would have been bound—by the very doctrine of promissory estoppel that he invokes—had Bartolotta relied, and since, as the subsequent course of events proved, Bartolotta was likely to enforce the pledge only if he couldn't get better terms elsewhere, which would be a sign that the venture might be riskier than it had appeared to be originally. . . .

The defendants appeal from the part of the judgment that awarded damages for misrepresentation and unjust enrichment. The evidence that Bartolotta misrepresented a present fact—his state of mind when he made the promise—was sufficient to support the jury's verdict. So was the evidence that Cosgrove conferred on Bartolotta a benefit (the pledge of the loan, which was instrumental in enabling Bartolotta to line up bank financing, along with Cosgrove's business and legal advice) for which Cosgrove was entitled to be compensated.

When one person confers a benefit on another in circumstances in which the benefactor reasonably believes that he will be paid—that is, when the benefit is not rendered gratuitously, as by an officious intermeddler, or donatively, as by an altruist or friend or relative—then he is entitled to demand the restitution of the market value of the benefit if the recipient refuses to pay. *Ramsey v. Ellis*, 168 Wis.2d 779, 484 N.W.2d 331, 333–34 (1992); *North American Lighting, Inc. v. Hopkins Mfg. Corp.*, 37 F.3d 1253, 1259 (7th Cir.1994). That describes the present case. The jury could and did find that Cosgrove conferred benefits on Bartolotta in reliance on being compensated by the receipt of an ownership interest in the restaurant.

Where, however, the plaintiff has a good claim for either breach of contract or, as in this case, promissory estoppel, restitution is not really an alternative theory of liability, but an alternative method of computing damages. Should it turn out to be too difficult to value the restaurant business or to determine just how large an ownership interest in it Cosgrove had been promised or even to determine what it cost him in opportunities forgone to render these services, the *value* of the services that he rendered was available as an alternative measure of damages— alternative to either the opportunity or other costs to Cosgrove of the services that he rendered (the reliance measure of damages) or the value of Bartolotta's promise to him (the expectation measure of damages).

[Note that] alternative and cumulative are not synonyms and that it was triple counting for the jury to give Cosgrove the value of the promised interest in the restaurant *and* the loss that he suffered as a result of Bartolotta's misrepresentation *and* the value of the services that he rendered to Bartolotta. All that Cosgrove sought was an award of compensatory damages, which is to say an award that would put him in the position that he would have occupied had the defendant not committed wrongful acts.

Where Cosgrove would be had Bartolotta carried out his promise would be owning a chunk of Bartolotta's business, a chunk the jury valued at $117,000, presumably taking into account the risk of Cosgrove's losing his $100,000 loan should the business sour (the restaurant business is highly risky). He would not also have been paid $17,000 for services rendered or $1,000 as a kind of "kill fee" (we don't know what other sense to make of this part of the jury's award), for the ownership share was to be the full compensation for his services. So the damages awarded by the jury were excessive, but as the defendants do not object to the verdict on this ground, the point is waived.

To summarize, the judgment is affirmed in part and reversed in part with directions to reinstate the original judgment and award the plaintiff his costs.

NOTES AND QUESTIONS

1. Is the jury finding of no contract consistent with finding promissory estoppel? Explain.

2. What technique does Judge Posner use to counter the promisor's challenge to whether the promise requirement of promissory estoppel was met?

3. Future appellate attorneys of the world, heed a litigation lesson: raise your objections to trial court rulings on appeal or be seen to waive them!

NOTE ON REMEDIES

The subject of remedies, a vast and vital aspect of contract law, is considered in great detail in Chapter Seven. For now, however, it is worth identifying a few fundamental principles. First, the usual remedy for breach of contract is money damages, not an order to perform the promise. The latter remedy, called specific performance, is an extraordinary one that courts grant in narrowly delineated circumstances when money damages would be inadequate. Of money damages, there are several alternative ways to measure them.

The usual measure is the money equivalent of the promised performance, described as "expectation" damages. This remedy is designed to put the aggrieved party in the economic position that performance would have done. For example, in the case of contracts to acquire businesses, such as in *Cosgrove*, this would be based upon lost profits.

As an alternative remedy, often recognized when it is infeasible to prove such expectation damages with reasonable certainty, contract law allows aggrieved parties to recover expenses incurred in reliance on the promise, described as "reliance" damages. This remedy is designed to put the aggrieved party in the economic position it occupied before the promise was made—in *Cosgrove* the services rendered. Reliance damages are a common remedy when promissory estoppel is the basis of liability.

Yet a third alternative remedy is "restitution," measured by the value of any benefit the aggrieved party conferred on the promisor. This remedy is invoked to protect against unjust enrichment of the promisor at the other's expense, and might appear in fact patterns such as *Cosgrove* if the promissee's investments increased the value of the enterprise. We consider this topic separately in Chapter Six.

The next case, one of the earliest of the cases pioneering the modern doctrine of promissory estoppel, not only develops the contours of the doctrine as a theory of liability but engages with some questions of remedies as well.

HOFFMAN V. RED OWL STORES, INC.
133 N.W.2d 267 (Wis. 1965)

CURRIE, J.

Action by Joseph Hoffman (hereinafter 'Hoffman') and wife, plaintiffs, against defendants Red Owl Stores, Inc. (hereinafter 'Red Owl') and Edward Lukowitz. The complaint alleged that Lukowitz, as agent for Red Owl, represented to and agreed with plaintiffs that Red Owl would build a store building in Chilton and stock it with merchandise for Hoffman to operate in return for which plaintiffs were to put up and invest a total sum of $18,000; that in reliance upon the above mentioned agreement and representations plaintiffs sold their bakery building and business and their grocery store and business; also in reliance on the agreement and representations Hoffman purchased the building site in Chilton and rented a residence for himself and his family in Chilton; plaintiffs' actions in reliance on the representations and agreement disrupted their personal and business life; plaintiffs lost substantial amounts of income and expended large sums of money as expenses. Plaintiffs demanded recovery of damages for the breach of defendants' representations and agreements.

The action was tried to a court and jury. The facts hereafter stated are taken from the evidence adduced at the trial. Where there was a conflict in the evidence the version favorable to plaintiffs has been accepted since the verdict rendered was in favor of plaintiffs.

Hoffman assisted by his wife operated a bakery at Wautoma from 1956 until sale of the building late in 1961. The building was owned in joint tenancy by him and his wife. Red Owl is a Minnesota corporation having its home office at Hopkins, Minnesota. It owns and operates a number of grocery supermarket stores and also extends franchises to agency stores which are owned by individuals, partnerships and corporations. Lukowitz resides at Green Bay and since September, 1960, has been divisional manager for Red Owl in a territory comprising Upper Michigan and most of Wisconsin in charge of 84 stores. Prior to September, 1960, he was district manager having charge of approximately 20 stores.

In November, 1959, Hoffman was desirous of expanding his operations by establishing a grocery store and contacted a Red Owl representative by the name of Jansen, now deceased. Numerous conversations were had in 1960 with the idea of establishing a Red Owl franchise store in Wautoma. In September, 1960, Lukowitz succeeded Jansen as Red Owl's representative in the negotiations. Hoffman mentioned that $18,000 was all the capital he had available to invest and he was repeatedly assured that this would be sufficient to set him up in business as a Red Owl store.

About Christmastime, 1960, Hoffman thought it would be a good idea if he bought a small grocery store in Wautoma and operated it in order that he gain experience in the grocery business prior to operating a Red Owl store in some larger community. On February 6, 1961, on the advice of Lukowitz and Sykes, who had succeeded Lukowitz as Red Owl's district manager, Hoffman bought the inventory and fixtures of a small grocery store in Wautoma and leased the building in which it was operated.

After three months of operating this Wautoma store, the Red Owl representatives came in and took inventory and checked the operations and found the store was operating at a profit. Lukowitz advised Hoffman to sell the store to his manager, and assured him that Red Owl would find a larger store from him elsewhere. Acting on this advice and assurance, Hoffman sold the fixtures and inventory to his manager on June 6, 1961. Hoffman was reluctant to sell at that time because it meant losing the summer tourist business, but he sold on the assurance that he would be operating in a new location by fall and that he must sell this store if he wanted a bigger one.

Before selling, Hoffman told the Red Owl representatives that he had $18,000 for 'getting set up in business' and they assured him that there would be no problems in establishing him in a bigger operation. The makeup of the $18,000 was not discussed; it was understood plaintiff's father-in-law would furnish part of it. By June, 1961, the towns for the new grocery store had been narrowed down to two, Kewaunee and Chilton. In

Kewaunee, Red Owl had an option on a building site. In Chilton, Red Owl had nothing under option, but it did select a site to which plaintiff obtained an option at Red Owl's suggestion. The option stipulated a purchase price of $6,000 with $1,000 to be paid on election to purchase and the balance to be paid within 30 days. On Lukowitz's assurance that everything was all set plaintiff paid $1,000 down on the lot on September 15th.

On September 27, 1961, plaintiff met at Chilton with Lukowitz and Mr. Reymund and Mr. Carlson from the home office who prepared a projected financial statement. Part of the funds plaintiffs were to supply as their investment in the venture were to be obtained by sale of their Wautoma bakery building.

On the basis of this meeting Lukowitz assured Hoffman: ' * * * [E]verything is ready to go. Get your money together and we are set.' Shortly after this meeting Lukowitz told plaintiffs that they would have to sell their bakery business and bakery building, and that their retaining this property was the only 'hitch' in the entire plan. On November 6, 1961, plaintiffs sold their bakery building for $10,000. Hoffman was to retain the bakery equipment as he contemplated using it to operate a bakery in connection with his Red Owl store. After sale of the bakery Hoffman obtained employment on the night shift at an Appleton bakery.

The record contains different exhibits which were prepared in September and October, some of which were projections of the fiscal operation of the business and others were proposed building and floor plans. Red Owl was to procure some third party to buy the Chilton lot from Hoffman, construct the building, and then lease it to Hoffman. No final plans were ever made, nor were bids let or a construction contract entered. Some time prior to November 20, 1961, certain of the terms of the lease under which the building was to be rented by Hoffman were understood between him and Lukowitz. The lease was to be for 10 years with a rental approximating $550 a month calculated on the basis of 1 percent per month on the building cost, plus 6 percent of the land cost divided on a monthly basis. At the end of the 10-year term he was to have an option to renew the lease for an additional 10-year period or to buy the property at cost on an instalment basis. There was no discussion as to what the instalments would be or with respect to repairs and maintenance.

On November 22nd or 23rd, Lukowitz and plaintiffs met in Minneapolis with Red Owl's credit manager to confer on Hoffman's financial standing and on financing the agency. Another projected financial statement was there drawn up entitled, 'Proposed Financing For An Agency Store.' This showed Hoffman contributing $24,100 of cash capital of which only $4,600 was to be cash possessed by plaintiffs. Eight thousand was to be procured as a loan from a Chilton bank secured by a mortgage on the bakery fixtures, $7,500 was to be obtained on a 5 percent loan from the father-in-law, and $4,000 was to be obtained by sale of the lot to the lessor at a profit.

A week or two after the Minneapolis meeting Lukowitz showed Hoffman a telegram from the home office to the effect that if plaintiff could get another $2,000 for promotional purposes the deal could go through for $26,000. Hoffman stated he would have to find out if he could get another $2,000. He met with his father-in-law, who agreed to put $13,000 into the business provided he could come into the business as a partner. Lukowitz told Hoffman the partnership arrangement 'sounds fine' and that Hoffman should not go into the partnership arrangement with the 'front office.'

On January 16, 1962, the Red Owl credit manager teletyped Lukowitz that the father-in-law would have to sign an agreement that the $13,000 was either a gift or a loan subordinate to all general creditors and that he would prepare the agreement. On January 31, 1962, Lukowitz teletyped the home office that the father-in-law would sign one or other of the agreements. However, Hoffman testified that it was not until the final meeting some time between January 26th and February 2nd, 1962, that he was told that his father-in-law was expected to sign an agreement that the $13,000 he was advancing was to be an outright gift. No mention was then made by the Red Owl representatives of the alternative of the father-in-law signing a subordination agreement. At this meeting the Red Owl agents presented Hoffman with . . . [a projected financial statement].

Hoffman interpreted the [financial] statement to require of plaintiffs a total of $34,000 cash made up of $13,000 gift from his father-in-law, $2,000 on mortgage, $8,000 on Chilton bank loan, $5,000 in cash from plaintiff, and $6,000 on the resale of the Chilton lot. Red Owl claims $18,000 is the total of the unborrowed or unencumbered cash, that is, $13,000 from the father-in-law and $5,000 cash from Hoffman himself. Hoffman informed Red Owl he could not go along with this proposal, and particularly objected to the requirement that his father-in-law sign an agreement that his $13,000 advancement was an absolute gift. This terminated the negotiations between the parties.

The case was submitted to the jury on a special verdict with the first two questions answered by the court. This verdict, as returned by the jury, was as follows:

Question No. 1:   Did the Red Owl Stores, Inc. and Joseph Hoffman on or about mid-May of 1961 initiate negotiations looking to the establishment of Joseph Hoffman as a franchise operator of a Red Owl Store in Chilton? *Answer*: Yes. (Answered by the Court.)

Question No. 2:   Did the parties mutually agree on all of the details of the proposal so as to reach a final agreement thereon? *Answer*: No. (Answered by the Court.)

Question No. 3:   Did the Red Owl Stores, Inc., in the course of said negotiations, make representations to Joseph Hoffman that if he fulfilled certain conditions that they would establish him as franchise operator of a Red Owl Store in Chilton? *Answer*: Yes.

Question No. 4:   If you have answered Question No. 3 'Yes,' then answer this question: Did Joseph Hoffman rely on said representations and was he induced to act thereon? *Answer*: Yes.

Question No. 5:   If you have answered Question No. 4 'Yes,' then answer this question: Ought Joseph Hoffman, in the exercise of ordinary care, to have relied on said representations? *Answer*: Yes.

Question No. 6:   If you have answered Question No. 3 'Yes' then answer this question: Did Joseph Hoffman fulfill all the conditions he was required to fulfill by the terms of the negotiations between the parties up to January 26, 1962? Answer: Yes.

Question No. 7:   What sum of money will reasonably compensate the plaintiffs for such damages as they sustained by reason of:

The sale of the bakery building? *Answer*: $2,000.00.

Taking up the option on the Chilton lot? *Answer*: $1,000.00.

Expenses of moving his family to Neenah? *Answer*: $140.00.

House rental in Chilton? *Answer*: $125.00.

The sale of the Wautoma store fixtures and inventory? *Answer*: $16,735.00.

. . . The instant appeal and cross-appeal present these questions: (1) Whether this court should recognize causes of action grounded on promissory estoppel as exemplified by sec. 90 of Restatement, 1 Contracts? (2) Do the facts in this case make out a cause of action for promissory estoppel? (3) Are the jury's findings with respect to damages sustained by the evidence? . . .

Sec. 90 of Restatement, 1 Contracts, provides . . . :

A promise which the promisor should reasonably expect to induce action or forbearance . . . on the part of the promisee and which does induce such action of forbearance is binding if injustice can be avoided only by enforcement of the promise.

The Wisconsin Annotations to Restatement, Contracts, prepared under the direction of the late Professor William H. Page and issued in 1933, stated (at p. 53, sec. 90):

The Wisconsin cases do not seem to be in accord with this section of the Restatement. It is certain that no such proposition has ever been announced by the Wisconsin court and it is at least doubtful if it would be approved by the court.

Since 1933, the closest approach this court has made to adopting the rule of the Restatement occurred in the recent case of Lazarus v. American Motors Corp. (1963), 21 Wis.2d 76, 85, 123 N.W.2d 548, 553, wherein the court stated:

> We recognize that upon different facts it would be possible for a seller of steel to have altered his position so as to effectuate the equitable considerations inherent in sec. 90 of the Restatement.

While it was not necessary to the disposition of the Lazarus Case to adopt the promissory estoppel rule of the Restatement, we are squarely faced in the instant case with that issue. Not only did the trial court frame the special verdict on the theory of sec. 90 of Restatement, 1 Contracts, but no other possible theory has been presented to or discovered by this court which would permit plaintiffs to recover. Of other remedies considered that of an action for fraud and deceit seemed to be the most comparable. An action at law for fraud, however, cannot be predicated on unfulfilled promises unless the promisor possessed the present intent not to perform. Suskey v. Davidoff (1958), 2 Wis.2d 503, 507, 87 N.W.2d 306, and cases cited. Here, there is no evidence that would support a finding that Lukowitz made any of the promises, upon which plaintiffs' complaint is predicated, in bad faith with any present intent that they would not be fulfilled by Red Owl.

Many courts of other jurisdictions have seen fit over the years to adopt the principle of promissory estoppel, and the tendency in that direction continues. As Mr. Justice McFaddin, speaking in behalf of the Arkansas court, well stated, that the development of the law of promissory estoppel 'is an attempt by the courts to keep remedies abreast of increased moral consciousness of honesty and fair representations in all business dealings. Peoples National Bank of Little Rock v. Linebarger Construction Company (1951), 219 Ark. 11, 17, 240 S.W.2d 12, 16. For a further discussion of the doctrine of promissory estoppel, see 1A Corbin, Contracts, pp. 187, et seq., secs. 193–209 . . . ; 1 Williston, Contracts (Jaeger's 3d ed.), pp. 607, et seq., sec. 140; Boyer, Promissory Estoppel: Requirements and Limitations of the Doctrine 98 University of Pennsylvania Law Review (1950), 459; Seavey Reliance Upon Gratuitous Promises or Other Conduct, 64 Harvard Law Review (1951), 913; Annos. 115 A.L.R. 152, and 48 A.L.R.2d 1069.

The Restatement avoids use of the term 'promissory estoppel,' and there has been criticism of it as an inaccurate term. See 1A Corbin, Contracts, p. 232, et seq., sec. 204. On the other hand, Williston advocated the use of this term or something equivalent. 1 Williston, Contracts (1st ed.), p. 308, sec. 139. Use of the word 'estoppel' to describe a doctrine upon which a party to a lawsuit may obtain affirmative relief offends the traditional concept that estoppel merely serves as a shield and cannot serve as a sword to create a cause of action. See Utschig v. McClone (1962), 16 Wis.2d 506, 509, 114 N.W.2d 854. . . . We have employed its use in this opinion not only because of its extensive use by other courts but also since a more accurate equivalent has not been devised.

Because we deem the doctrine of promissory estoppel, as stated in sec. 90 of Restatement, 1 Contracts, is one which supplies a needed tool which courts may employ in a proper case to prevent injustice, we endorse and adopt it. . . .

Applicability of Doctrine to Facts of this Case.

The record here discloses a number of promises and assurances given to Hoffman by Lukowitz in behalf of Red Owl upon which plaintiffs relied and acted upon to their detriment.

Foremost were the promises that for the sum of $18,000 Red Owl would establish Hoffman in a store. After Hoffman had sold his grocery store and paid the $1,000 on the Chilton lot, the $18,000 figure was changed to $24,100. Then in November, 1961, Hoffman was assured that if the $24,100 figure were increased by $2,000 the deal would go through. Hoffman was induced to sell his grocery store fixtures and inventory in June, 1961, on the promise that he would be in his new store by fall. In November, plaintiffs sold their bakery building on the urging of defendants and on the assurance that this was the last step necessary to have the deal with Red Owl go through.

We determine that there was ample evidence to sustain the answers of the jury to the questions of the verdict with respect to the promissory representations made by Red Owl, Hoffman's reliance thereon in the exercise of ordinary care, and his fulfillment of the conditions required of him by the terms of the negotiations had with Red Owl.

There remains for consideration the question of law raised by defendants that agreement was never reached on essential factors necessary to establish a contract between Hoffman and Red Owl. Among these were the size, cost, design, and layout of the store building; and the terms of the lease with respect to rent, maintenance, renewal, and purchase options. This poses the question of whether the promise necessary to sustain a cause of action for promissory estoppel must embrace all essential details of a proposed transaction between promisor and promisee so as to be the equivalent of an offer that would result in a binding contract between the parties if the promisee were to accept the same.

Originally the doctrine of promissory estoppel was invoked as a substitute for consideration rendering a gratuitous promise enforceable as a contract. See Williston, Contracts (1st ed.), p. 307, sec. 139. In other words, the acts of reliance by the promisee to his detriment provided a substitute for consideration. If promissory estoppel were to be limited to only those situations where the promise giving rise to the cause of action must be so definite with respect to all details that a contract would result were the promise supported by consideration, then the defendants' instant promises to Hoffman would not meet this test. However, sec. 90 of Restatement, 1 Contracts, does not impose the requirement that the promise giving rise to the cause of action must be so comprehensive in scope as to meet the requirements of an offer that would ripen into a contract if accepted by the promisee. Rather the conditions imposed are:

(1)   Was the promise one which the promisor should reasonably expect to induce action or forbearance . . . on the part of the promisee?

(2)   Did the promise induce such action or forbearance?

(3)   Can injustice be avoided only by enforcement of the promise?

We deem it would be a mistake to regard an action grounded on promissory estoppel as the equivalent of a breach of contract action. As Dean Boyer points out, it is desirable that fluidity in the application of the concept be maintained. 98 University of Pennsylvania Law Review (1950), 459, at page 497. While the first two of the above listed three requirements of promissory estoppel present issues of fact which ordinarily will be resolved by a jury, the third requirement, that the remedy can only be invoked where necessary to avoid injustice, is one that involves a policy decision by the court. Such a policy decision necessarily embraces an element of discretion.

We conclude that injustice would result here if plaintiffs were not granted some relief because of the failure of defendants to keep their promises which induced plaintiffs to act to their detriment.

Damages.

Defendants attack all the items of damages awarded by the jury. The bakery building at Wautoma was sold at defendants' instigation in order that Hoffman might have the net proceeds available as part of the cash capital he was to invest in the Chilton store venture. The evidence clearly establishes that it was sold at a loss of $2,000. Defendants contend that half of this loss was sustained by Mrs. Hoffman because title stood in joint tenancy. They point out that no dealings took place between her and defendants as all negotiations were had with her husband.

Ordinarily only the promisee and not third persons are entitled to enforce the remedy of promissory estoppel against the promisor. However, if the promisor actually foresees, or has reason to foresee, action by a third person in reliance on the promise, it may be quite unjust to refuse to perform the promise. 1A Corbin, Contracts, p. 220, sec. 200. Here not only did defendants foresee that it would be necessary for Mrs. Hoffman to sell her joint interest in the bakery building, but defendants actually requested that this be done. We approve the jury's award of $2,000 damages for the loss incurred by both plaintiffs in this sale.

Defendants attack on two grounds the $1,000 awarded because of Hoffman's payment of that amount on the purchase price of the Chilton lot. The first is that this $1,000 had already been lost at the time the final negotiations with Red Owl fell through in January, 1962, because the remaining $5,000 of purchase price had been due on October 15, 1961. The record does not disclose that the lot owner had foreclosed Hoffman's interest in the lot for failure to pay this $5,000.

The $1,000 was not paid for the option, but had been paid as part of the purchase price at the time Hoffman elected to exercise the option. This gave him an equity in the lot which could not be legally foreclosed without affording Hoffman an opportunity to pay the balance. The second ground of attack is that the lot may have had a fair market value of $6,000, and Hoffman should have paid the remaining $5,000 of purchase price. We determine that it would be unreasonable to require Hoffman to have invested an additional $5,000 in order to protect the $1,000 he had paid. Therefore, we find no merit to defendants' attack upon this item of damages.

We also determine it was reasonable for Hoffman to have paid $125 for one month's rent of a home in Chilton after defendants assured him everything would be set when plaintiff sold the bakery building. This was a proper item of damage.

Plaintiffs never moved to Chilton because defendants suggested that Hoffman get some experience by working in a Red Owl store in the Fox River Valley. Plaintiffs, therefore, moved to Neenah instead of Chilton. After moving, Hoffman worked at night in an Appleton bakery but held himself available for work in a Red Owl store. The $140 moving expense would not have been incurred if plaintiffs had not sold their bakery building in Wautoma in reliance upon defendants' promises. We consider the $140 moving expense to be a proper item of damage.

We turn now to the damage item with respect to which the trial court granted a new trial, i. e., that arising from the sale of the Wautoma grocery store fixtures and inventory for which the jury awarded $16,735. The trial court ruled that Hoffman could not recover for any loss of future profits for the summer months following the sale on June 6, 1961, but that damages would be limited to the difference between the sales price received and fair market value of the assets sold, giving consideration to any goodwill attaching thereto by reason of the transfer of a going business.

There was no direct evidence presented as to what this fair market value was on June 6, 1961. The evidence did disclose that Hoffman paid $9,000 for the inventory, added $1,500 to it and sold it for $10,000 or a loss of $500. His 1961 federal income tax return showed that the grocery equipment had been purchased for $7,000 and sold for $7,955.96. Plaintiffs introduced evidence of the buyer that during the first eleven weeks of operation of the grocery store his gross sales were $44,000 and his profit was $6,000 or roughly 15 percent. On cross-examination he admitted that this was gross and not net profit. Plaintiffs contend that in a breach of contract action damages may include loss of profits. However, this is not a breach of contract action.

The only relevancy of evidence relating to profits would be with respect to proving the element of goodwill in establishing the fair market value of the grocery inventory and fixtures sold. Therefore, evidence of profits would be admissible to afford a foundation for expert opinion as to fair market value.

Where damages are awarded in promissory estoppel instead of specifically enforcing the promisor's promise, they should be only such as in the opinion of the court are necessary to prevent injustice. Mechanical or rule of thumb approaches to the damage problem should be avoided. . . .

At the time Hoffman bought the equipment and inventory of the small grocery store at Wautoma he did so in order to gain experience in the grocery store business. At that time discussion had already been had with Red Owl representatives that Wautoma might be too small for a Red Owl operation and that a larger city might be more desirable. Thus Hoffman made this purchase more or less as a temporary experiment. Justice does not require that the damages awarded him, because of selling these assets at the behest of defendants, should exceed any actual loss sustained measured by the difference between the sales price and the fair market value.

Since the evidence does not sustain the large award of damages arising from the sale of the Wautoma grocery business, the trial court properly ordered a new trial on this issue. . . .

NOTES AND QUESTIONS

1. What were the promises in *Cosgrove v. Bartolotta* and *Hoffman v. Red Owl*? Was reliance justified?

2. In cases like *Feinberg*, consideration is lacking because there is no "quid pro quo." Promissory estoppel serves as a substitute for consideration, exemplified by the alternative holding in *East Providence*. In cases like *Elvin v. Franklin, Cosgrove v. Bartolotta*, and *Hoffman v. Red Owl*, however, promissory estoppel enters earlier to prevent one party from detrimentally "leading on" the other. As the cases generally make clear, promissory estoppel is based on promise and reliance, not on offer and acceptance or related doctrines of traditional contract formation. In that sense, promissory estoppel is a substitute not only for consideration but for the other elements of contract formation as well.

PROBLEMS: ADMISSIONS TO PRESTIGIOUS UNIVERSITY

Admissions officers at Prestigious University have apologized after they mistakenly told nearly 1,000 high school seniors they were going to be Groundhogs next year. The students are actually still on the waiting list—despite receiving congratulatory acceptance letters from Prestigious, a highly-selective university. Prestigious said that the error happened when wait list students were sent updated notices of provisional financial aid. In the following situations, discuss whether there might be any liability under either contract or promissory estoppel. What would the damages be in either situation?

1.   In response, the school's financial aid office sent out an e-mail message on the same day that the letters went out to clarify—and apologize to students. The president of the university also wrote a letter to the 1,000 students directly, which were sent out via FedEx. The president's letter clarified each student's place on the waitlist and asked them for their forgiveness and understanding. A postage paid envelope asked the students to confirm whether they wanted to hold their place on the Prestigious University waitlist or have their name withdrawn.

2.   Imagine instead that the incorrect information was actually only sent to one individual, who lived in South Korea. No letter of correction or apology was sent. After telling all of his family, teachers, and classmates about his acceptance, the high school student visited the United States and the Prestigious University campus at his expense ($2,500), bought Prestigious college sweatshirts, t-shirts, and posters for family and friends ($500), and his family paid first month's rent and a security deposit on an apartment ($6,000 in total). Afterwards, the student sends in the $1,000 deposit (listed on the Prestigious University website) to reserve his place in the class. However, at that point the prospective student is informed that the message was sent in error; he is actually still on the waiting list.

3.   These scenarios are adapted from a real story about UCLA, though it is not the only school to have made such an error. Vassar College accidentally told more than 100 applicants that they were admitted when they were sent a "test letter" before the admissions decisions had actually been made. The University of Delaware, Penn State, UC Santa Barbara and UC San Diego are among other schools that have made similar errors in recent years.

4.   Alternately, consider that in the spring of 2017, several admitted students to Harvard had their offers revoked because of inappropriate postings in an online Facebook group. Would these applicants have a claim under breach of contract or promissory estoppel? Note that as promissory estoppel is an equitable doctrine, the party invoking it must have "clean hands." Venerable maxims of equity jurisprudence announce such general principles as "one who seeks equity must do equity" and "one who comes into equity must come with clean hands."

5.   If you were employed in the general counsel's office of Prestigious University, how might you advise the financial aid office, the admissions office, and the administration about dealing with these sorts of issues in the future?

C. CORPORATE COMMUNICATIONS

The first element of promissory estoppel in Restatement (Second) of Contracts, Section 90 is the existence of a promise. This may seem obvious but sometimes statements are made that are mere expressions of hope or are otherwise too general or vague to be a promise. Consider the next two opinions in the same case—a trial court finding promissory estoppel followed by an appellate court reversal. What promises, if any, did GM make in order to receive tax abatements?

YPSILANTI V. GENERAL MOTORS CORP.
(TRIAL COURT)
1993 WL 132385 (Cir. Ct. Mich. 1993)

SHELTON, J.

This case was begun by the Charter Township of Ypsilanti against General Motors Corporation as a result of a February 1992 announced decision to transfer automobile assembly operations at General Motors' Willow Run plant in the township to a plant in Arlington, Texas, and then to close the Willow Run facility completely. The decision followed a highly publicized earlier determination by General Motors to select either Willow Run or Arlington for the transfer. General Motors chose Arlington and announced that it would begin transfer of the Willow Run operations to Arlington and would cease Willow Run operations completely after the end of production of 1993 models there.

The township complaint alleged that General Motors had entered into agreements with the township to obtain twelve year tax abatements on property in the Willow Run plant in 1984 and 1988 and that the closing of the plant prior to the expiration of those abatement periods would violate the agreements and representations General Motors had made to obtain those abatements. The complaint alleges [both breach of contract and promissory estoppel].

Michigan, like over thirty other states, permits municipalities to offer property tax abatements to industries as a supposed means of retaining and adding employment opportunities. The statutory framework for such abatements was established in Act 198 of 1974, M.C.L. § 207.551, et seq. The intent of the statute, as codified in section 9(2)(e), is to provide tax abatements for industrial facilities which "will . . . have the reasonable likelihood to create employment, retain employment, prevent a loss of employment, or produce energy in the community in which the facility is located." . . .

For many years, General Motors has operated two adjacent plants in Ypsilanti Township, referred to as Hydra-Matic and Willow Run Assembly. Hydra-Matic employs approximately 9,000 persons and Willow Run employs approximately 4,500 persons. Within 90 days of the signing of Act 198, General Motors formed a group within the Hydra-Matic plant to seek a tax abatement. General Motors approached the State Department of Commerce and local Ypsilanti Chamber of Commerce officials to pursue such an abatement. . . .

Approval of that application was the first of what turned out to be eleven approved applications for tax abatements on the two plants over the next fifteen years. Ypsilanti Township was among the first municipalities in the State to create an industrial development district and that district eventually encompassed the area consisting of both the Hydra-Matic and Willow Run plants. From 1975 through 1990, General Motors requested and received tax abatements on facilities investments in those two plants of over $1.3 billion, with eight of the abatements in the Hydra-Matic plant and three in the Willow Run plant. . . .

Over the years, General Motors followed the example set in its first application and a course of conduct developed between General Motors and the township for the granting of tax abatements. Each time General Motors wanted an abatement to make a physical change in the plants, it would invite township officials to the plant for a briefing, a tour of the plant, and lunch. Then the formal application would be submitted and General Motors officials would appear at a public hearing before the entire Board, which would then approve the application. Each time, the Board was advised, in some specifics, of the impact of the improvements, and presumably the abatement, on production and employment levels in the plant.

In 1981, General Motors was in the process of obtaining one of its tax abatements on the Hydra-Matic plant when township trustee Wesley Prater, later to become Supervisor, expressed some concern about General Motors' commitment to retain employment at the plant. The plant manager replied with a letter to the entire Board, including the following:

> The purpose of this letter is to reassure you that it is not our intention to transfer production operations to other Hydra-Matic Division plant locations; the net effect of which would have a negative impact on the employment levels at our Ypsilanti location. *In this case, as in the past, we are dedicated to retain and/or increase jobs at Ypsilanti and will maintain this dedication in the future. We intend to keep this facility a viable operation for the community and General Motors.* If approved, the impact of this particular application will be to sustain

approximately 1,500 jobs and there will be a favorable tax impact to the Township of approximately $2.0 million per year over a twelve year period without any increase in township services . . . .

Ypsilanti Township approved every application it received from General Motors for these two plants for the maximum allowable abatement period of twelve years. The two specific abatements at issue in this case were granted in 1984 and 1988. The 1984 abatement followed the course of events which had been established by the parties' prior relationship, with a briefing, plant tour and lunch for township officials prior to the public hearing on approval of the application. The application was in connection with a $175 million project which was described in section 5e of the application:

> The introduction of a new car, in September 1985 and September 1986, which requires an additional 35,000 square foot building addition and new high technology machinery and equipment applicable to body shop processing and automation and paint, trim, and chassis processing changes.

Specifically, General Motors was changing the plant to produce its "H" model cars instead of the "X" model cars which had been produced at Willow Run. Section 10 of the application stated that the company expected to create 200 more jobs with the project and that 4,300 existing jobs would be retained as a result of the project. The township board passed a resolution approving the application for a twelve year abatement on July 17, 1984. Upon receipt of the township resolution, the State Tax Commission asked Washtenaw County to indicate whether it concurred in the abatement. The Board of Commissioners concurred in the 1984 Willow Run abatement application, but conditioned its concurrence on a letter which further explained its intent:

> The Board's approval of this application was based on its concern for economic development in Washtenaw County which results in increased job opportunities for unemployed and underemployed residents of our County. On October 8, 1984, the State Tax Commission granted the abatement and issued an Industrial Facilities Exemption Certificate for the period beginning December 30, 1984 and ending December 30, 1998.

By 1988, the demand for "H" cars had declined and General Motors decided to produce a new rear wheel "B" model of the "Caprice". The Caprice had been manufactured at plants in Arlington, Texas, and Lakewood, Georgia. General Motors decided to close the Georgia plant and modify Willow Run so it could produce rear wheel drive cars, including the Caprice. The Willow Run modification was also designed to allow the plant the flexibility to change over between rear and front wheel drive car assembly in the future.

Importantly, the decision to make this investment in Willow Run was made before General Motors pursued or even investigated the possibility of an Act 198 tax abatement for the proposed improvements. It appears that General Motors simply assumed, to the extent it considered the matter at all, that Ypsilanti Township would issue such an abatement in accordance with the prior course of conduct between General Motors and the township. The corporate decision to make the investment in Willow Run was also publicly known and widely reported in the local media before the tax abatement was ever discussed with the township. . . .

Six months after the "Caprice" announcement, General Motors pursued a tax abatement through what had become the normal course of events between it and the township. The Willow Run Comptroller, Mr. Hughes, discussed it with the outgoing township Supervisor, Mr. Allen, and the newly elected supervisor, Mr. Prater. After the usual briefing, lunch and plant tour, Mr. Prater suggested that General Motors make a public presentation to "educate" the Board since there had been a number of newly elected trustees.

The application for an abatement of taxes on the $75 million project was filed on October 7, 1988 and in Section 6c General Motors described the improvements as follows:

> Conversion of the plant to accommodate the introduction of new GM sedans and new GM station wagons. This request covers the addition of new machinery and equipment to facilitate the assembly of these automobiles. The machinery and equipment includes automation which will allow the plant to continue to be cost competitive.

Section 5 explained the proposal further:

> Willow Run Assembly is involved in the manufacture and assembly of General Motors automobiles. This application covers additional investment for machinery and equipment to assemble a new GM automobile. This requires that the plant be converted from front wheel drive to rear wheel drive assembly capability. The conversion will be such that the plant will be able to meet forward program requirements of either front wheel drive or rear wheel drive assembly with a relatively minimum additional investment.

Section 10 of the application stated that no new jobs were expected to be created by the project but that 4900 jobs "will be retained as a result of the project". Prior to the public hearing, Mr. Hughes prepared charts and graphs to show to the Board and prepared statements which both he and the Willow Run plant manager, Mr. Williams, would make to the Board. At the hearing, Mr. Williams first read his prepared statement in which he described the rear wheel drive capacity sought by the project and then read the final remark which Mr. Hughes had prepared: "Upon completion of this project and favorable market demand, it will allow Willow Run to continue production and maintain continuous employment for our employees."

Mr. Hughes then reviewed the graphs and charts and read his prepared statement which depicted General Motors' decline in market share and emphasized the relationship of that fact to employment level, both generally in the corporation and specifically at Willow Run: "What does this mean? One percent penetration that we lose at General Motors means ten thousand jobs for this corporation of our employees. In the assembly plant operation one percent means about twenty five hundred jobs throughout the US and all assembly plants." . . .

At that same public hearing, the township also considered a tax abatement application for the Hydra-Matic plant and heard from General Motors executives from that facility as well. . . . The Board of Trustees unanimously approved both the Willow Run and Hydra-Matic tax abatement applications for a twelve year period. . . .

In any event, despite some early success, General Motors did not convince people that they wanted as many Caprice cars as General Motors wanted to build. Caprice sedans were being manufactured at both the Willow Run and Arlington, Texas plants. Willow Run was also producing Buick and Cadillac station wagons. By late 1991, the demand for the Caprice had lessened and General Motors decided that the work being done at one of the plants would be transferred to the other and one would be closed.

Willow Run was operating one shift per day and Arlington was operating two shifts per day. General Motors Vice President Joseph Spielman made the decision following a short two week process which involved getting "proposals" from each of the plants and the affected communities. He recommended, and the corporation announced in February of 1992 that the work being done on the one shift at Willow Run would be transferred to the Arlington plant, which would go on three shifts per day. Importantly however, the parties to this suit have stipulated that the defendant does not rely upon "economic necessity" as a defense to this action. General Motors then gave the notice required by the federal "WARN" Act that it intends to close Willow Run entirely.

The Statute and Application as a Contract

The initial question before the Court is whether the Act 198 statutory process results in a contract between the governments involved and the industry receiving the subsidy. Clearly a State may create such a contract by statute, as the United States Supreme Court declared in *Indiana ex rel Anderson v. Brand.* . . . Whether Act 198 creates such a contract must be addressed by an examination of the statute, and the cases and administrative decisions interpreting the statute. The United States

Supreme Court noted in *United States Trust Co. v. New Jersey:* "In general, a statute is itself treated as a contract when the language and circumstances evince a legislative intent to create private rights of a contractual nature enforceable against the State."

Such an inquiry is actually no different that the initial question of whether a contract exists between two private parties, that is, whether the parties intended to enter into a contractually binding obligation. The essential elements of a contract are parties who are competent to contract, a proper subject matter, the exchange of legal consideration, mutuality of agreement and mutuality of obligation. The formation of a valid contract requires a "meeting of the minds" on all essential points of the alleged agreement, and this is to be judged objectively by looking to the expressed, not unexpressed, words of the parties and their visible acts.

The Court has concluded that, however unwisely, the state legislature did not intend to create contractual rights for the State or its subdivisions when it enacted Act 198 and that the statute does not therefore create an enforceable contract between the government and the subsidized industry. Unlike statutes which have been construed to create contractual rights, Act 198 never uses the word "contract" or any phrase which usually has a similar meaning. . . .

Most importantly, the legislature chose not to use specific contractual language or provide specific contractual remedies in the face of ample similar legislation in other states which does create and require such a contract between the government and the industries it chooses to subsidize. There are over thirty states with industrial tax subsidies and many of them require such contracts. . . . In any event, this Court is forced to read the statute as it currently stands and to hold that Act 198 does not, by itself, nor in conjunction with the completed application forms in this case, create a contract.

Promissory Estoppel

The rigid and technical rules of conventional contract law are designed to provide the framework for a Court to adjudicate the rights of parties in a contractual dispute. As with other generalized legal principles, these rigid rules sometimes fail us in our attempt to wring justice from a specific dispute between people whose expectations of each other are not fulfilled. Fortunately, our common law has also evolved concepts of equity which are designed to allow a Court the flexibility, which is the true hallmark of fairness, to do justice in such situations.

One such equitable concept in the law of contracts is the notion of promissory, or equitable, estoppel. As the Court of Appeals aptly described it:

Application of the doctrine of promissory estoppel is based on the particular factual circumstances; as an equitable remedy, it is employed to alleviate an unjust result of strict adherence to established legal principles. This doctrine is a well recognized feature of the common law of this State.

The elements of promissory, estoppel have been clearly identified: In order for a promise to be enforceable under the concept of promissory estoppel, there must be a (1) promise that the promisor should reasonably have expected to induce action . . . on the part of the promises, (2) which in fact produced reliance or forbearance of that nature, (3) in circumstances such that the promise must be enforced if injustice is to be avoided.

The plaintiffs in this case contend that, regardless whether the statute and application form created a contract by their own terms, General Motors, by its statements and conduct in connection with those and other applications, represented that it would provide continuous employment at the Willow Run plant if the government continued to provide tax abatement subsidies. The issue, in promissory estoppel terms, is whether those representations indeed constitute a promise and whether it is the type of promise that should be enforced by this Court to prevent an injustice. . . .

General Motors did not make any off-hand or casual statements to the Board at the public hearing on the abatement application. In the context of this background, when the plant manager, in the prepared statement on behalf of General Motors, stated that, subject to "favorable market demand," General Motors would "continue production and maintain continuous employment" at the Willow Run plant, it was a promise. The promise was clearly that if the township granted the abatement, General Motors would make the Caprice at Willow Run and not just transfer that work somewhere else. Our courts have accepted the following definition of a legal promise:

> The fundamental element of promise seems to be an expression of intention by the promisor that his future conduct shall be in accordance with his present expression, irrespective of what his will may be when the time for performance arrives. A statement that the granting of the abatement would enable General Motors to provide continuous employment at the plant was a *quid pro quo* type of statement that is associated in its common sense meaning with a promise.

In the context of the abatement application hearing the statement was also a promise that General Motors "should reasonably have expected to induce action . . . on the part of" the township. General Motors clearly made the statement to induce the township to cut its property taxes on the $75 million project in half. Most importantly, the promise was needed because the township otherwise had no incentive to approve the application. General Motors could not simply promise that it would make the investment in the plant *if* it was granted the abatement because it had already publicly committed to make the investment without any mention of an abatement. The only logical reason the township would have to give up half of the taxes on the project is that General Motors represented, as it had done in the past, that as long as it made those cars it was going to make them in Willow Run.

General Motors asserts that the promise was conditioned upon "favorable market demand" and therefore a totally illusory one that the township could not reasonably have relied upon. The author of the prepared statement testified at trial that when he used phrase "favorable market demand" he meant enough Caprice and station wagon sales orders to keep *both* the Willow Run and Arlington plants operating at a level of two shifts each per day, 235 days a year. Such testimony is not credible. In the context of the corporate decision to transfer the Willow Run work to Arlington and the resulting trial almost five years later, this revelation of alleged intent is suspect. As indicated earlier, the intent of the parties is to be judged objectively by looking to the expressed, not unexpressed, words of the parties. There was no mention of Arlington anywhere in the public hearing and no testimony that work levels at the Arlington plant had ever been discussed with township officials, must less been stated to be a condition of Willow Run's work level.

General Motors claims that if its view of the "favorable market demand" statement is not accepted, then the statement would be a promise to keep the plant open forever and such a promise is illogical and could never be reasonably relied upon by anyone. Certainly no one took the promise as such at the hearing and no one has suggested such a construction. The statement was made in the context of the decision to build the Caprice and the station wagons at the plant and it is apparent that "favorable market demand" referred to favorable market demand for *those* cars. General Motors' statement clearly meant that if there was a sufficient market demand to make the Caprice and the station wagons they would be made at Willow Run. The fact is that there still is market demand for those cars but General Motors has decided to transfer the assembly of a third of them from Willow run to Arlington.

The second element of promissory estoppel is that the promise produced "reliance or forbearance" .... If nothing else, and there is considerable else, the evidence that the township has given up over $2 million in local government taxes from 1988–92 for the 1988 abatement alone is sufficient to satisfy this element.

The final element is that the circumstances be such that General Motors' promise must be enforced "if injustice is to be avoided". The Court is mindful of the fact that two federal courts have refused to apply the promissory estoppel doctrine to prevent plant closings. Neither of those situations involved specific representations or representations which were made as an inducement for a local government to approve a tax abatement. More important, in each of those situations, the corporation was simply closing a plant because it was economically necessary to close it and the courts concluded that the company never promised to operate a plant when there was no demand for its product. Here, General Motors has stipulated, as it must, that economic necessity is *not* a defense. Again, General Motors is not closing this plant because there is no demand for the cars which are made there. It simply has chosen to transfer the one shift of production of those cars at Willow Run to add a new third shift at another plant in Arlington, Texas.

Aside from these distinctions in the facts of those cases, this Court, perhaps unlike the judges there, simply finds that the failure to act in this case would result in a terrible injustice and that the doctrine of promissory estoppel should be applied. Each judge who dons this robe assumes the awesome, and lonely, responsibility to make decisions about justice, and injustice, which will dramatically affect the way people are forced to live their lives. Every such decision must be the judge's own and it must be made honestly and in good conscience. There would be a gross inequity and patent unfairness if General Motors, having lulled the people of the Ypsilanti area into giving up millions of tax dollars which they so desperately need to educate their children and provide basic governmental services, is allowed to simply decide that it will desert 4500 workers and their families because it thinks it can make these same cars a little cheaper somewhere else. Perhaps another judge in another court would not feel moved by that injustice and would labor to find a legal rationalization to allow such conduct. But in this Court it is my responsibility to make that decision. My conscience will not allow this injustice to happen. . . .

YPSILANTI V. GENERAL MOTORS CORP. (APPELLATE COURT)

201 Mich. App. 128 (Mich. App. 1993)

Defendant appeals from a February 9, 1993, order of the Washtenaw Circuit Court that enjoins defendant "from transferring the production of its Caprice sedan, and Buick and Cadillac . . . station wagons, from the Willow Run plant to any other facility." We reverse.

Defendant has operated two plants in Ypsilanti for a number of years. The Hydra-Matic plant employs approximately 9,000 workers and the Willow Run plant employs more than 4,000. In 1975, the township created an industrial development district for the Hydra-Matic plant. It did the same for Willow Run in 1977. Over the years the township granted defendant eleven tax abatements under *M.C.L. § 207.551 et seq.;* M.S.A. § 7.800(1) *et seq.,* eight at Hydra-Matic and three at Willow Run. That statute authorizes municipalities to establish plant rehabilitation and industrial development districts to encourage the creation and maintenance of jobs in the state. The act provides for tax exemptions for businesses that meet the requirements of the act. *Creative Industries Group, Inc. v. Dep't of Treasury,* 187 Mich.App. 270, 272, 466 N.W.2d 311 (1991).

Two of the Willow Run abatements, for 1984 and 1988, are at issue in this case. On July 17, 1984, the township approved defendant's application for a twelve-year fifty percent abatement of personal property taxes on the corporation's $175 million investment for the introduction of a new car. The State Tax Commission later granted the exemption certificate. In April 1988, defendant announced that it would produce a new rear-wheel-drive vehicle, the Chevrolet Caprice, at Willow Run. Six months later, on October 7, 1988, defendant applied for a tax abatement for that project. The application was also for a twelve-year fifty percent abatement of personal property taxes on defendant's planned $75 million project. Following public hearings, the township approved that application, and the state tax commission issued an exemption certificate.

On December 18, 1991, defendant announced that it had decided to consolidate the work being done at Willow Run and Arlington, Texas, at Arlington. Defendant claims that the consolidation was necessary because of the company's record losses and because its Caprice sales, projected at 330,000 a year, had been running at about 275,000 a year and had slipped below 100,000 by late 1991.

The township commenced this action on April 29, 1992. The county joined voluntarily, while the state joined as an *amicus curiae,* but the trial court added the state as a party-plaintiff. The complaint alleged counts of breach of a contract created by the tax abatement statute, breach of a contract created by conduct, [and] promissory estoppel[.] Following a lengthy trial, the trial court found that the abatement statute and application did not create a contract between the township and the corporation. However, it did find that defendant was bound by promissory estoppel to retain production of the Caprice line in Willow Run, as long as the company produces that model. It concluded:

> There would be a gross inequity and patent unfairness if General Motors, having lulled the people of the Ypsilanti area into giving up millions of tax dollars which they so desperately need to educate their children and provide basic governmental services, is allowed to simply decide it will desert 4500 workers and their families because it thinks it can make these same cars cheaper somewhere else.

The trial court, relying on the background of defendant's negotiations for abatements and principally on a statement by Willow Run plant manager Harvey Williams at a public hearing, found that a promise had been made. Williams stated that "[u]pon completion of this project and favorable market demand, it will allow Willow Run to continue production and maintain continuous employment for our employees." The trial court ruled:

> In the context of this background, when the plant manager, in the prepared statement on behalf of General Motors stated that, subject to "favorable market demand," General Motors would "continue production and maintain continuous employment" at the Willow Run plant, *it was a promise*. The promise was clearly that if the Township granted the abatement, General Motors would make the Caprice at Willow Run and not just transfer that work somewhere else. [Emphasis added.]

A trial court's findings of fact in an equity action are reviewable under the clearly erroneous standard. A finding is clearly erroneous if the appellate court is left with a definite and firm conviction that a mistake has been made. *Beason v. Beason,* 435 Mich. 791, 802–804, 460 N.W.2d 207 (1990); *Attorney General v. Lake States Wood Preserving, Inc.,* 199 Mich.App. 149, 501 N.W.2d 213 (1993); *Badon v. General Motors Corp.,* 188 Mich.App. 430, 470 N.W.2d 436 (1992); MCR 2.613(C). . . .

Promissory estoppel requires an actual, clear, and definite promise. *State Bank of Standish v. Curry,* 442 Mich. 76, 84–85, 500 N.W.2d 104 (1993). Further, "reliance is reasonable only if it is induced by an actual promise." *Id.* at 84, 500 N.W.2d 104. A determination that there was a promise will be overturned if it is clearly erroneous. *Id.*

The trial court's finding that defendant promised to keep Caprice and station wagon production at Willow Run is clearly erroneous. First, the mere fact that a corporation solicits a tax abatement and persuades a municipality with assurances of jobs cannot be evidence of a promise. The very purpose of tax abatement legislation is to induce companies to locate and to continue business enterprises in the municipality. Even the trial court recognized this when it stated, "Every time, the inducement to the township was the same-jobs will be created or preserved at that plant, and it should have been, for that was the ostensible purpose of the abatement."

Second, representations of job creation and retention are a statutory prerequisite. An applicant for an industrial facilities exemption certificate must, among other things, certify that "[c]ompletion of the facility is calculated to, and will *at the time of issuance of the certificate* have the reasonable likelihood to create employment, retain employment, prevent a loss of employment, or produce energy in the community in which the facility is situated." M.C.L. § 207.559(2)(e); M.S.A. § 7.800(9)(2)(e); emphasis added.

Third, the fact that a manufacturer uses hyperbole and puffery in seeking an advantage or concession does not necessarily create a promise. For example, statements such as "We're partners" and "We look forward to growing together" were found not to constitute a promise to keep a collective bargaining agreement in force for the foreseeable future so as to create by promissory estoppel a continuing duty of the employer to honor an expired agreement. *Marine Transport Lines, Inc. v. Int'l Organization of Masters, Mates, & Pilots,* 636 F.Supp. 384 (S.D.N.Y., 1986).

Nor did exhortations for union concessions in order to keep a foundry open constitute promises under promissory estoppel to prevent a foundry from closing. *Abbington v. Dayton Malleable, Inc.,* 561 F.Supp. 1290 (S.D. Ohio, 1983), aff'd 738 F.2d 438 (CA 6, 1984). Similarly, exhortations to its employees to increase productivity and assurances that a plant would not be closed, as long as it was profitable, did not establish by promissory estoppel an obligation on a steel company to keep open a plant. *Local 1330, United Steel Workers v. United States Steel Corp.,* 631 F.2d 1264 (CA 6, 1980).

Turning to the case at bar, almost all the statements the trial court cited as foundations for a promise were, instead, expressions of defendant's hopes or expectations of continued employment at Willow Run. . . . The acts cited by the trial court were acts one would naturally expect a company to do in order to introduce and promote an abatement proposal to a municipality. The acts did not amount to a promise and, as course-of-conduct evidence, showed only efforts to take advantage of a statutory opportunity. They did not constitute assurances of continued employment. In any event, we note that the activity referred to by the trial court related to Hydra-Matic, not Willow Run.

The court cited the State Tax Commission's resolution regarding the 1984 Willow Run abatement in which the commission's approval "was based on its concern for economic development in Washtenaw County which results in increased job opportunities for unemployed and underemployed residents of our county." However, that was the commission's expectation, not defendant's promise.

In defendant's 1988 presentation, Russell Hughes, the Willow Run comptroller, recited background, including: "Since the '81, '82 time-frame you can see that we've been basically maintaining about five thousand employees each year in a very consistent pattern." However, Hughes made the statement by way of history, and not as an assurance of future employment. The circuit court also cited plant manager Harvey Williams' prepared statement:

> General Motors selected Willow Run to build these new vehicles because of our reputation for high quality, our continued harmonious relationship and our spirit of all employees working together. . . . We are asking the Board to accept our application and pass on it favorably. To join the corporation in the kind of relationship we have in the Township in assuring future investments in our plant.

However, that language is nearly identical to the puffery the federal court found not to constitute a promise in *Marine Transport Lines, Inc., supra.* The trial court referred to the township assessor's remarks:

> Needless to say I recommend approval of the petition. Based on the past history in dealing with the people at General Motors, they've always done what they said they would do and they've kept the jobs there and they kept the plant operating as an operational facility.

Again, however, that was the assessor's evaluation, not defendant's promise. The court quoted the State Tax Commission's resolution, which stated in part, "Where the facts indicate that positive results in gains in employment and taxes appear justified . . . we will support all the local unit decisions." Once again, that was the commission's assessment, not defendant's promise of continuing employment.

Defendant's statement that the lower court principally relied on to find a promise was not sufficient to constitute a promise. Plant manager Williams stated:

> Good evening, my name is Harvey Williams and I am the plant manager of the Buick Oldsmobile Cadillac groups [sic] Willow Run plant. We are pleased to have this opportunity to appear before the Ypsilanti Township Board of Trustees. This application for an industrial facilities exemption certificate is for an investment totaling $75,000,000.00 for machinery and equipment. This will enable our plant to assemble a new full size car in the 1991 model year.
>
> This new rear wheel drive car is substantially larger then [sic] our current model. And specifically it will generate major booth, oven and conveyor changes in the paint shop and assembly line process, changes in the body, trim and chassis department. This change will also provide additional flexibility at our assembly plant. Essentially we would now have the capability to produce either front or rear wheel drive cars with minimum modifications to our facility. *Upon completion of this project and favorable market demand, it will allow Willow Run to continue production and maintain continuous employment for our employees.*

I would like to introduce Russell Hughes, our controller, who will review pertinent charts pertaining to our request. [Emphasis added.]

Although the parties greatly dispute what the speaker meant by "favorable market demand" and even whether defendant should have been allowed to narrow it to Willow Run production, the fact is that the statement qualified defendant's expectation that the new abatement would allow it to continue production at the plant and maintain continuous employment for the employees. Again, even that statement was nothing more than the kind of hyperbole a corporation would use to obtain the tax abatement benefits afforded by the statute and willingly offered by the township.

The trial court clearly erred in concluding that Williams' statement, and particularly the portion emphasized in the foregoing quotation, constituted a promise of continued Caprice and station wagon production at Willow Run as long as the company produces those vehicles. Plaintiffs' reliance on *Curry* is misplaced. It merely dealt with a situation in which there was a clear promise upon which the plaintiff detrimentally relied. *Curry,* rather than compelling a conclusion in plaintiffs' favor, points to why the doctrine does not apply to this case: the promise necessary to invoke the doctrine is distinguished from a statement of opinion or mere prediction of future events. *Id.* 442 Mich. at 86, 500 N.W.2d 104.

Even if the finding of a promise could be sustained, reliance on the promise would not have been reasonable. "[T]he reliance interest protected by [Restatement] § 90 is reasonable reliance." *Curry, supra,* 442 Mich. at 84, 500 N.W.2d 104. It has never been held that an abatement carries a promise of continued employment. Indeed, the history of this case shows that persons involved in the 1988 Willow Run abatement understood that defendant was not promising continued employment.

At a township board meeting in November 1988, Dillard Craiger, chairman of the Washtenaw County Board of Commissioners, opposed a tax break for Willow Run "unless a commitment was made by General Motors to remain operating at the present facility in Ypsilanti Township for that period of time thereby securing employment for the community." Craiger also complained that defendant had not given any commitments whatsoever. Outgoing Township Supervisor Ron Allen nevertheless endorsed defendant's request for tax relief, noting that "General Motors has never been overbearing or threatening" and cautioning "the Board not to take any action that would unravel the success that the Township has had [in dealing with General Motors] over the last several years." At a subsequent work session held on December 5, 1988, at least five of the seven board members—including new Township Supervisor Wesley Prater and Township Treasurer Ruth Ann Jamnick—decided to support the application.

At the public hearing at which plant manager Harvey Williams supposedly promised "continuous employment for our employees," plant comptroller Russell Hughes almost immediately warned that "[o]ne percent [market share] penetration that we lose at General Motors means ten thousand jobs for this corporation of our employees. In the assembly plant operation one percent means about twenty five hundred jobs throughout the US and all assembly plants."

Other speakers then took the floor, several of whom specifically pointed out that defendant had not committed itself to continue operating the Willow Run plant for any particular period of time. Washtenaw County Commission Chairman Craiger, after listening to plant manager Williams' presentation, restated in detail his admonition from the previous month:

> The plant has not given us any commitments in any way that they will not "outsource" production, they will not tell you how long they are going to stay, they will not tell you that we only want it as long as we stay. Who knows, they might move tomorrow or two years from now and they will have been given three tax breaks with a hidden plan. If Georgia or Alabama gives them a hundred percent [tax abatement], don't we have a right to bid on it? Don't we have that right, or should they just say, we're closing the plant because we got a better deal. . . . I would like to be able for them to tell us how long are they going to stay.

Others echoed this concern. A Mr. Smith referred to increases in his own property taxes and added: "I have eighteen years in and I'd like to see them stay here twelve years so I can retire, but they are not promising anything." Township Supervisor Prater, who chaired the meeting, then interjected a "point of clarification," explaining to Smith that "the abatement they are asking for is not on real estate tax, it's personal property tax." But Prater did not take issue with Smith's statement that no "promise" had been made, and Smith replied that "there should be some kind of proof by them that they are not going to . . . move out." Prater made no response. Other witnesses agreed with Smith that defendant had made no commitment to continue operations at Willow Run. Mr. Debs, president of the local union at the Willow Run plant, pointed out that "nobody can tell us what the sales are going to be" and that "no plant can stay open" if sales drop. A Mr. Alford remarked that "there were some legal issues there that cannot bind [Willow Run] or Hydra-Matic to giving jobs to Ypsilanti Township."

Defendant's representatives were not asked to respond to these comments, and no member of the township board took issue with them. Instead, Supervisor Prater urged the board to approve defendant's application. The township board then voted unanimously to approve a twelve-year abatement at Willow Run; the resolution contained no suggestion that approval was conditioned on a commitment to operate the plant for any particular period.

In short, defendant made no promises. Reversed.

NOTES AND QUESTIONS

1.   Reading both the trial and appellate court decisions, do you think General Motors made a promise?

2.   What was at stake for the parties in the dispute? What were the policy issues underlying the decision?

3.   In the wake of the appellate decision, the parties settled. A contemporaneous news story, James Bennet, *GM Settles Suit Over Plant Closing*, N.Y. TIMES, April 15, 1994 captured what transpired through the settlement:

> GM has tentatively settled a lawsuit filed by a Michigan township and county over the closing of an automobile assembly plant last year. . . The suit contended that GM had promised to build cars at Willow Run through the late 1990's in return for tax abatements, and having reneged on that promise owed $13.5 million in back taxes.
>
> Under the agreement, GM will invest more than $80 million in new equipment and machinery to increase capacity at a transmission plant in the area. The investment will not result in new jobs[.] The company has also promised to clean up the closed factory to comply with state and Federal environmental laws, and to explore selling the plant or putting it to a different use. The town and county will provide 12-year tax abatements worth 50 percent of the property taxes on the new investment. . . .
>
> Of the 2,400 people once employed at Willow Run, about 200 are left in jobs maintaining the plant. Many others retired, or moved to other GM plants, including the factory in Arlington, Tex, where GM consolidated production of rear-wheel-drive cars. Twenty skilled workers employed at Willow Run have yet to be placed at other jobs . . . The transmission plant next door to Willow Run employs 5,500 people. Town officials seemed relieved to have completed the negotiations. "I have a new respect for GM and I hope they do for the township," said Wesley E. Prater, township supervisor for Ypsilanti.

What are your reactions to this news story?

4.   What should the Township Board of Ypsilanti have done at the November 1988 meeting? What options were open to them? What pressures might the Board have faced in determining an appropriate course of conduct with General Motors?

D. HANDBOOKS, MANUALS, TERMS OF USE

In addition to entering into formal contracts with their constituents, organizations publish policies or handbooks that form the background of a relationship, such as for employment or for services. While constituents are often aware of the existence of such materials, they do not always read them. Under what circumstances should such policies or handbooks nevertheless be seen to form part of the legal bargain between the parties? Under what legal theory, traditional contract formation or promissory estoppel? Consider the next case, which involves sensitive financial information and terms of use that promise privacy.

MEYER V. CHRISTIE
2007 WL 3120695 (D. Kan. 2007)

LUNGSTRUM, J.

 . . . According to the allegations in plaintiffs' complaint, plaintiffs Meyer and Pratt formed a joint venture with defendants Christie and Glen for the construction of a mixed-use residential and commercial development on certain land located in Junction City, Kansas, to be called "The Bluffs." Just months after work on the project had begun, the president of Security Savings divulged highly confidential and false information about the finances of Mr. Meyer and one of his other businesses, Engineered Roofing Products, Inc. (ERP), a business which is unrelated to the development project in Junction City. Defendants Christie and Glen learned of that confidential information and used it as a justification to terminate the joint venture. As a result, plaintiffs were denied millions of dollars in profits and unreimbursed expenses.

By way of background, plaintiffs Meyer and Pratt have considerable experience in both residential and commercial development, with particular expertise in the development, construction, and management of residential mixed-use projects which combine high quality affordable single and multi-family housing with commercial and recreational amenities. Defendant James Duff was a long-time business acquaintance of Mr. Meyer. Mr. Duff had previously helped Mr. Meyer and certain of his companies obtain financing for various commercial projects while Mr. Duff had been a loan officer of Security Savings. By 2005, Mr. Duff had moved on to become a senior officer at another bank. In February of 2005, Mr. Duff approached Mr. Meyer and suggested that plaintiffs meet defendants Christie and Glen to discuss a significant opportunity to build a residential complex in Junction City. Mr. Duff related that Messrs. Christie and Glen were established commercial developers in Junction City with many local government contacts, but who had no real experience in residential planning and development. They were therefore seeking outside partners with that expertise, so Mr. Duff suggested that they speak with Messrs. Meyer and Pratt.

Messrs. Meyer, Pratt, Christie, and Glen met and formed the joint venture in March of 2005. It was agreed that defendants Christie and Glen would contribute their contacts and expertise in the Junction City community, negotiate with local government officials for cash incentives to build the project, and coordinate the purchase of the property. Plaintiffs Meyer and Pratt, on the other hand, would contribute their expertise in residential project development to the joint venture and would be responsible to plan, develop, manage, and coordinate construction of the project. Work on the project commenced immediately. Plaintiffs Meyer and Pratt devoted substantial time and effort in planning the development of the project, including obtaining financing. In June of 2005, they formally registered their joint venture company, Junction City Partners, LLC. Work on the project continued and, in July of 2005, Junction City executed a formal Memorandum of Understanding granting the joint venture the right to develop the project.

In mid July of 2005, Mr. Meyer received a phone call from Mr. Duff about ERP, another company in which Mr. Meyer had an ownership interest and that was unrelated to The Bluffs project. Mr. Duff advised Mr. Meyer that the "word on the street" was that ERP was having financial difficulties and that its loans with Security Savings were going to be called. Mr. Duff had been the officer that had approved and accepted those loans back when he had still been employed with Security Savings and Mr. Meyer was the personal guarantor of those loans. Mr. Meyer explained to Mr. Duff that this perception was erroneous because he believed that ERP was working with Security Savings on a refinancing plan. Mr. Duff told Mr. Meyer, however, that if Mr. Christie heard about these alleged difficulties he would likely back out of The Bluffs project. When Mr. Meyer protested that this reaction would be nonsensical, Mr. Duff replied, "It's just my impression."

Shortly after this phone conversation, Messrs. Christie and Duff called Mr. Pratt to meet with them. Believing the meeting was intended to discuss The Bluffs project, Mr. Pratt was surprised when the primary topic of the meeting turned out to be the alleged financial difficulties of ERP. At the meeting, Mr. Christie told Mr. Pratt that he had sought a loan from Security Savings to buy the property for The Bluffs, but that he had been turned down because the bank would not loan money to Mr. Meyer or any entity associated with him because he allegedly had a loan with Security Savings that was in default. According to Mr. Christie, Mr. Duff had previously been on a camping trip with the president of Security Savings when he told Mr. Duff that Mr. Meyer had made fraudulent misrepresentations on a bank financing statement for ERP, and that some ERP equipment which was listed as collateral for Security Savings' loan to

ERP was missing. Mr. Duff had relayed this information to Mr. Christie. Mr. Christie continued by explaining to Mr. Pratt that, as a result of receiving this information, he no longer wanted to do business with Mr. Meyer.

According to the allegations in plaintiffs' complaint, Security Savings and Mr. Duff, who worked with Mr. Meyer to coordinate and approve Security Savings' loans to ERP while he was still an employee at that bank, had duties of care and confidentiality to both Mr. Meyer and ERP to keep financial information about Mr. Meyer and ERP private and confidential. In fact, the bank's privacy policy prohibited the disclosure of this information.

On July 21, 2005, Mr. Christie called Mr. Pratt and told him that he and Mr. Glen were terminating their partnership with Messrs. Meyer and Pratt. After the phone call ended, Mr. Pratt conducted an independent investigation of Mr. Christie's allegations about Mr. Meyer. He confirmed that none of the allegations were true. When Mr. Pratt called Mr. Christie back to inform him about those findings, Mr. Christie stated that he had already made the decision to move forward on the project without Messrs. Meyer and Pratt. Messrs. Christie and Glen did, indeed, move forward on The Bluffs project on their own. Plaintiffs now seek damages from defendants Christie and Glen, related business entities, Duff, and Security Savings arising from being cut out of The Bluffs project.

Specifically, Mr. Meyer asserts a claim against Security Savings for breach of contract. The complaint alleges that as a result of Mr. Meyer's long-term banking relationship with Security Savings, he relied on Security Savings to preserve his and his businesses' confidential customer information in its possession, in accordance with the terms of its privacy policy, its implied duty to preserve and not disclose such information without his authorization, and/or its implied contractual duty of good faith and fair dealing. The complaint alleges that Security Savings was in possession of highly confidential personal and financial information about Mr. Meyer and his associated businesses solely because of its role as a lender to Mr. Meyer and those businesses, as its customers. By providing Messrs. Christie and Duff with this highly confidential information and mischaracterizing Mr. Meyer's and ERP's finances as well as Mr. Meyer's actions regarding ERP, Security Savings breached its express and implied contractual duties to preserve and protect his confidential information.

. . . Security Savings now moves to dismiss plaintiffs' claims against it. As to plaintiffs' breach of contract claim, Security Savings argues that the complaint does not adequately allege the existence of an express or implied contract, that any such contract fails for lack of adequate consideration, and that Mr. Meyer lacks standing to assert any such claim. . .

. . . [T]he court will deny the bank's motion to dismiss plaintiffs' breach of contract claim because the factual allegations in the complaint state a claim to relief that is plausible on its face. . . . The bank's predominant argument that its privacy policy did not constitute a binding contract is that a unilateral statement of company policy does not create an express or implied contract. In support of this argument, the bank relies on cases such as *Johnson v. Nat'l Beef Packing Co.,* 220 Kan. 52, 551 P.2d 779 (1976) (company policy manual that was not published until after the plaintiff's employment began was only a unilateral expression of company policies and procedures; its terms were not bargained for by the parties and no "meeting of the minds" existed); *Berry v. General Motors Corp.,* 56 F.3d 1233, 1237 (10th Cir.1995) (applying the Kansas Supreme Court's holding in *Johnson* under similar circumstances); *Dyer v. Nw. Airlines Corps.,* 334 F.Supp.2d 1196, 1199–1200 (D.N.D.2004) (airline's privacy policy posted on its website did not constitute a contract with its customers in the absence of an allegation that passengers read and relied on the policy); and *In re Northwest Airlines Privacy Litig.,* 2004 WL 1278459, at *5–*6 (D.Minn. June 6, 2004) (same, where plaintiffs alleged that they relied on the privacy policy but not that they had actually read it).

The court finds defendants' reliance on these cases to be misplaced at this procedural juncture in light of the allegations set forth in plaintiffs' complaint. On a motion to dismiss, the court must of course accept the facts alleged in plaintiffs' complaint as true, view all reasonable inferences from those facts in favor of plaintiffs, and determine whether it is plausible based on those factual allegations that the privacy policy constituted a contract between Mr. Meyer and Security Savings.

Viewed as such, the court cannot agree with the bank's attempt to characterize its privacy policy as nothing more than a mere unilateral statement of company policy. Plaintiffs' complaint alleges that Mr. Meyer had a long-term banking business and banking relationship with Security Savings; that in the course of that relationship he relied on the bank to preserve his confidential information according to the terms of its privacy policy; and that the bank had solicited his financial information when it requested that he act as a personal guarantor on the loans that it made to ERP. Inferentially, then, the bank's privacy policy was part and parcel of its offer to make the loan to ERP, which was accepted when Mr. Meyer divulged information to the bank with the understanding that the bank would keep it confidential in accordance with its privacy policy. Under this view of the facts, the bank's privacy policy constituted part of Mr. Meyer's bargained-for exchange with the bank.

. . . In sum, the facts alleged by plaintiffs in this case sufficiently state a claim that a contract existed between the bank and Mr. Meyer based on the bank's privacy policy. . . . The bank also argues that a contract claim based on its privacy policy fails for lack of consideration because the bank was required by law under the Gramm-Leach-Bliley Act to provide notice to its consumers of its privacy policies. It is true that "an agreement to do . . . that which a person is already bound to do does not constitute a sufficient consideration for a new promise." *Apperson v. Security State Bank,* 215 Kan. 724, 734, 528 P.2d 1211, 1219 (1974); *see also* Restatement (Second) of Contracts § 73 (1981) ("Performance of a legal duty owed to a promisor . . . is not consideration. . . ."). The fallacy in the bank's argument is that the provision of the Gramm-Leach-Bliley Act that the bank relies on, 15 U.S.C. § 6803(a), only requires the bank to disclose its privacy policies. *See also* 16 C.F.R. § 313.6 (listing nine specific categories of information that must be included in privacy notices). The statute cited by the bank does not dictate what the terms of the privacy policy must be. Thus, the bank has not shown that it had a pre-existing legal duty to safeguard the confidentiality of Mr. Meyer's information. Consequently, the argument raised by the bank concerning a lack of consideration is without merit.

In sum, the facts alleged in plaintiffs' complaint state a claim for relief on a breach of contract theory that is plausible on its face. The factual allegations are sufficient to raise a right to relief above the speculative level. Accordingly, the bank's motion to dismiss Mr. Meyer's breach of contract claim against it is denied. . . .

NOTES AND QUESTIONS

1.   In its briefs, the bank cited contemporary cases noting that website polices do not constitute binding contracts. The court, however, seemed impatient with this argument, noting that Meyer had a long-term banking relationship with Security Savings; the bank requested confidential information and he provided it. As such, Meyer relied on the bank to keep the information confidential in accordance with its policies. In essence, then, the promises of confidentiality formed part of the bargained-for exchange. Is that persuasive?

2.   Would promissory estoppel have provided a firmer basis for the court's conclusion than traditional contract formation doctrine? What are the weaknesses in each of these approaches to the facts of *Meyer v. Christie*?

3.   Looking at this case from another perspective, what expectations of confidentiality does a borrower have when taking out a loan?

EXAMPLE: CLEVELAND PLAIN DEALER

Can corporate policies promising users' privacy for their comments on the Internet be enforced as contracts? In the early 2000s, the local newspaper the Cleveland Plain Dealer migrated online to provide news on the website Cleveland.com. The site allowed anyone, signed or anonymous, to post comments on news items. The site contained many governing policies, including a guarantee that would protect personal identifiable information, via a clickwrap "terms of use" that the site visitor would agree to in order to signal assent.

In 2010, eighty anonymous comments were posted, which were eventually traced back to a state court judge, who was commenting on matters pending before the court. Of course, the comments then generated a great deal of controversy over both judicial ethics and the obligation of the newspaper to follow the terms of its privacy policies.

What support do the cases in this chapter provide for website users seeking to enforce their privacy rights, either under a contractual or promissory estoppel theory? What role does the intent to be bound (or the intent not to be bound) mean in terms of legal enforceability?

McDONALD v. MOBIL COAL PRODUCING, INC.
789 P.2d 866 (Wyo. 1990)

MACY, J.

This is an appeal from a summary judgment in favor of Appellees Mobil Coal Producing, Inc., Brad Hanson, Peter Totin, and Bert Gustafson, denying the claim of Appellant Craig McDonald for wrongful discharge from employment. We reverse and remand. . . .

McDonald worked at Mobil's Caballo Rojo coal mine in Campbell County, Wyoming, from August 1987 until June 1988 as a technician in the preparation plant. Hanson was the mine superintendent, Totin was the mine supervisor of employee relations, and Gustafson was the preparation plant supervisor. McDonald contends that he resigned his position at the mine following rumors that he had sexually harassed a female co-employee. McDonald also contends the resignation resulted from a meeting with Hanson, Totin, and Gustafson where McDonald was told he had the choice of either resigning or being fired.

When McDonald applied for the position at Caballo Rojo, he signed a statement on his employment application which said in part:

> I agree that any offer of employment, and acceptance thereof, does not constitute a binding contract of any length, and that such employment is terminable at the will of either party, subject to applicable state and/or federal laws.

After he started working at the mine, McDonald received an employee handbook. The stated intention of the handbook, as addressed to Mobil employees, was "to help you understand and explain to you Mobil's policies and procedures." Despite that representation, the handbook stated that it was not a company "comprehensive policies and procedures manual, nor an employment contract."

The handbook stated that Mobil was "committed to maintaining an environment of mutual trust, understanding, and cooperation" and that Mobil encouraged communication between employees and supervisors on an informal basis. It informed the reader of the existence of "a Fair Treatment Procedure that afford [ed] an employee the opportunity to be heard, without fear of reprisal." This "Fair Treatment Procedure" was a detailed four-step procedure in which an employee discussed a problem with a supervisor. If the employee was not satisfied with the outcome of this discussion, the employee could take the matter to other supervisory personnel.

The handbook also detailed a disciplinary procedure. It included a noninclusive list of behaviors which Mobil would not condone and a five-step disciplinary process. These steps were: (1) counseling; (2) written reprimand; (3) final written reprimand; (4) three-day suspension; and (5) discharge. The handbook stated that Mobil believed "union representation [was] unnecessary for employees to enjoy job security, career opportunities, consistent treatment, and competitive wages and benefits." The handbook listed seven "fundamental obligations" for Mobil to fulfill. Among these seven were:

> 2.   To train and guide employees, allow them to develop their job abilities and regularly keep them informed of their progress.
>
> 3.   To invite constructive suggestions and criticism and guarantee the right to be heard without fear of reprisal.
>
> 4.   To give helpful consideration when an employee makes a mistake or has a personal problem with which we are asked to help.

After resigning, McDonald filed suit. . . The [trial] court noted that the "tenor" of the handbook could cause it to appear to be a contract. However, the court held that the disclaimer in the handbook defeated any claim that the handbook was part of an employment contract. Thus, despite the "tenor" of the handbook, the court held that McDonald was an at-will employee . . . . It granted summary judgment in favor of Appellees.

Summary judgment is proper only when there are no genuine issues of material fact and the prevailing party is entitled to judgment as a matter of law. . . . Disposition of this case requires us to review the revision of the employee handbook discussed in *Mobil Coal Producing, Inc. v. Parks,* 704 P.2d 702 (Wyo.1985). We held in *Parks* that the provisions in the handbook constituted part of the Mobil employee contract and that the existence of the handbook elevated the nature of the Mobil employees' status beyond simple at-will employment. *Id.* at 706–07. In an at-will employment situation, either party may terminate the relationship for any reason at any time without incurring liability . . . .

Following *Parks,* Mobil revised its handbook. The most significant revision was the addition of a statement that the handbook was not an employment contract. A contract exists when there is a meeting of the minds. *Anderson Excavating and Wrecking Company v. Certified Welding Corporation,* 769 P.2d 887 (Wyo.1988). Mobil's express disclaimer demonstrates that it had no intention to form a contract. We cannot say that the handbook was part of the employment contract; however, this determination does not end our analysis. We have recognized limited exceptions to the at-will relationship. *Nelson,* 777 P.2d at 75. *See, e.g., Leithead v. American Colloid Company,* 721 P.2d 1059 (Wyo.1986); *Alexander v. Phillips Oil Company,* 707 P.2d 1385 (Wyo.1985), *after remand* 741 P.2d 117 (Wyo.1987) (employee handbook without disclaimer is part of the employment contract); *Griess,* 776 P.2d 752 (employer cannot terminate at-will employee for seeking benefits under worker's compensation statutes); and *Parks,* 704 P.2d 702. Other provisions of the handbook require us to recognize another manner in which an employer can modify the at-will employment relationship.

As the trial court noted, if it were not for the disclaimer, the "tenor" of the handbook could cause it to be viewed as a contract, and McDonald may have believed that the handbook was a contract. Our reading of the portions of the handbook included in the record reveals language which could be understood to connote promises notwithstanding a lack of a contractual obligation. Even without a contractual obligation, some promises remain enforceable. This Court has adopted Restatement (Second) of Contracts § 90(1) . . . .

Despite the disclaimer of contract, the handbook did indicate its purpose was to explain the company's policies and procedures to Mobil's employees. Having announced the policy, presumably with a view to obtaining the benefit of improved employee attitudes and behavior and improved quality of the work force, the employer may not treat its promise as illusory. *Toussaint v. Blue Cross & Blue Shield of Michigan,* 408 Mich. 579, 292 N.W.2d 880, 895 (1980), *quoted in Damrow v. Thumb Cooperative Terminal, Inc.,* 126 Mich.App. 354, 337 N.W.2d 338, 342 (1983).

Thus, an employee is entitled to enforce a representation in an employee handbook if he can demonstrate that: (1) The employer should have reasonably expected the employee to consider the representation as a commitment from the employer; (2) the employee reasonably relied upon the representation to his detriment; and (3) injustice can be avoided only by enforcement of representation. *Cronk v. Intermountain Rural Electric Association,* 765 P.2d 619, 624 (Colo.App.), *cert. denied* (1988). These are issues for the trier of fact to determine. *Id.* Unless the employee can make this factual showing to overcome the presumption of an employment terminable at the will of either party, the employee's cause of action will fail. *Continental Air Lines, Inc. v. Keenan,* 731 P.2d 708 (Colo.1987).

Genuine issues of fact exist here. McDonald must prove that his resignation was forced and not volitional. Should McDonald meet this burden, the finder of fact must determine what effect, if any, the representations made by Mobil in its handbook had upon an otherwise at-will employment relationship. McDonald's affidavit in opposition to the motions for dismissal purported that he relied upon the procedures outlined in the handbook. Issues of whether Mobil should have expected McDonald's reliance upon these procedures, whether McDonald's reliance was reasonable, and whether the Mobil termination procedures should be enforced to avoid injustice will need to be addressed if McDonald proves his resignation was forced. The trial court improperly granted summary judgment to Appellees. Reversed and remanded . . . .

GOLDEN, J., specially concurring.

I concur only in the result, disagreeing with the application of the principles of promissory estoppel under the facts of consequence in this case.

The trial court found that the disclaimer (stating that the handbook was not a "comprehensive policies and procedural manual, nor an employment contract") was conspicuous because it was located on the handbook's first page. I disagree. The fact that the disclaimer appears on the front page does not by itself make it conspicuous. I would rule, as a matter of law, that a disclaimer's location is not the sole determinant of whether or not it is conspicuous. In this instance, the disclaimer consisted of one sentence—no different in appearance from any of the other sentences contained on the page. It is not even labeled as a disclaimer.

The United States Court for the District of Wyoming, in a case applying Wyoming law, addressed the issue whether a disclaimer in an employee handbook negates the employee's claim that the handbook constituted an employment contract. *Jimenez v. Colorado Interstate Gas Company,* 690 F.Supp. 977 (D.Wyo.1988) (Johnson, J.). The Court ruled that disclaimers are effective only if they are conspicuous, which is a question of law. *Id.* at 980. In *Jimenez,* the employer claimed that it was not bound to follow the handbook because it contained a disclaimer stating that the handbook was not an employment contract. The District Court ruled, however, that the disclaimer was "not set off in any way that would attract attention" and, therefore, was ineffective against the employee. *Id.* at 980. The Court listed the disclaimer's inadequacies: "Nothing is capitalized that would give notice of a disclaimer. The type size equals that of other provisions on the same page. No border sets the disclaimer apart from any other paragraph on the page." *Id.* 980. After review of Mobil's employee handbook, I find that its attempted disclaimer suffers from the same deficiencies found in *Jimenez. . . .* The handbook's ambiguous provisions create issues of material fact and, therefore, summary judgment is improper.

CARDINE, C.J., dissenting.

I dissent. Mobil did all it could by its disclaimer to assure there was not a contract of employment. Parties are free to contract or not as they choose. Mobil chose not to contract with its employee, and, like it or not, we should accept that decision.

THOMAS, J., dissenting.

I agree with the dissenting opinion of Chief Justice Cardine. If I count the votes correctly, it would seem that three justices do not agree on the majority disposition invoking promissory estoppel; four justices agree that there was no employment contract; and three justices agree that the summary judgment should be reversed and the case remanded for trial. There are not many moments of comfort in the life of a judge, but I find one of those in the fact that I do not have to develop the jury instructions in this case.

In prior cases, this court has critiqued employee handbooks in the context of their effect in structuring an employment contract as distinguished from an employment at will. *Leithead v. American Colloid Company,* 721 P.2d 1059 (Wyo.1986); *Alexander v. Phillips Oil Company,* 707 P.2d 1385 (Wyo.1985); and *Mobil Coal Producing, Inc. v. Parks,* 704 P.2d 702 (Wyo.1985). In this instance, Mobil Coal Producing, Inc. obtained a signed statement from McDonald that his employment was terminable at the will of either party. The handbook contained an express disclaimer of its status as an employment contract. As Chief Justice Cardine notes in his dissent, "Mobil did all it could by its disclaimer to assure there was not a contract of employment." Indeed, what more could it have done.

Now, having done its best to have its conduct comport with the prior decisions of this court, Mobil finds that, in any event, anything it may say in the employee handbook can become a binding promise under the doctrine of promissory estoppel. I apologize to my readers for being obtuse, but I cannot distinguish that from the effect of a contract, although the majority concludes that there is no contract. I fear that corporate America, as it lives in the state of Wyoming, will be forced to conclude that the court is toying with it in some cruel and peculiar game of cat and mouse. In my judgment, we offered guidance in the earlier employee at will cases and, now, when confronted with an employer who followed that advice, we should not say that we really did not mean to adhere to our earlier guidance. . . .

McDonald v. Mobil Coal Producing, Inc.
(Rehearing)
820 P.2d 986 (Wyo. 1991)

GOLDEN, J.

Following our decision [excerpted immediately above], we granted Mobil's petition for rehearing to review and clarify our earlier decision. . . .

We reaffirm our earlier decision reversing summary judgment and remanding this case for further proceedings. We hold that a question of material fact exists concerning whether the employee handbook and Mobil's course of dealing with appellant modified the terms of appellant's at-will employment. . . .

The Federal District Court of Wyoming explored the issue of effective contract disclaimers in *Jimenez v. Colorado Interstate Gas Company,* 690 F.Supp. 977 (D.Wyo.1988). The plaintiff's employer had adopted standard operating procedures relating to cause for termination. The employer had inserted a disclaimer in these procedures to the effect that they did not constitute terms of a contract. The court stated that for a disclaimer to be effective it must be conspicuous and whether it was conspicuous was a matter of law. *Jimenez,* at 980. Where the disclaimer was not set off in any way, was placed under a general subheading, was not capitalized, and contained the same type size as another provision on the same page, it was not conspicuous. *Id.*

We adopt the rule in *Jiminez* that disclaimers must be conspicuous to be effective against employees and that conspicuousness is a matter of law. The trial court erred in its statement that there was no requirement that the disclaimers be conspicuous. We examine the disclaimers in this case to see whether they were sufficiently conspicuous to be binding on appellant.

The application form which Craig McDonald signed on July 20, 1987, contained the following disclaimer:

READ CAREFULLY BEFORE SIGNING

I agree that any offer of employment, and acceptance thereof, does not constitute a binding contract of any length, and that such employment is terminable at the will of either party, subject to appropriate state and/or federal laws.

The MCPI Employee Handbook which he received contained the following disclaimer, located on its first page, which we reproduce in full to show the context in which the disclaimer was made:

WELCOME

Mobil Coal Producing Inc., Caballo Rojo Mine, is proud to welcome you as an employee. We believe you will find safety, opportunity and satisfaction while making your contribution to Mobil's growth as a major supplier of coal.

This handbook is intended to be used as a guide for our nonexempt mine technicians and salaried support personnel, to help you understand and explain to you Mobil's policies and procedures. It is not a comprehensive policies and procedures manual, nor an employment contract. More detailed policies and procedures are maintained by the Employee Relations supervisor and your supervisor. While we intend to continue policies, benefits and rules contained in this handbook, changes or improvements may be made from time to time by the company. If you have any questions, please feel free to discuss them with your supervisor, a member of our Employee Relations staff, and/or any member of Caballo Rojo's Management. We urge you to read your handbook carefully and keep it in a safe and readily available place for future reference. Sections will be revised as conditions affecting your employment or benefits change.

> Sincerely,
> /s/
> R.J. Kovacich
> Mine Manager
> Caballo Rojo Mine

The circumstances surrounding this disclaimer are nearly identical to those of the *Jiminez* case. The disclaimer in this case was not set off by a border or larger print, was not capitalized, and was contained in a general welcoming section of the handbook. Additionally, the disclaimer was unclear as to its effect on the employment relationship. For persons untutored in contract law, such clarity is essential, as stated in this apt language from a New Jersey Supreme Court opinion:

> It would be unfair to allow an employer to distribute a policy manual that makes the workforce believe that certain promises have been made and then to allow the employer to renege on those promises. What is sought here is basic honesty: if the employer, for whatever reason, does not want the manual to be capable of being construed by the court as a binding contract, there are simple ways to attain that goal. All that need be done is the inclusion in a very prominent position of an appropriate statement *that there is no promise of any kind by the employer contained in the manual; that regardless of what the manual says or provides, the employer promises nothing and remains free to change wages and all other working conditions without having to consult anyone and without anyone's agreement; and that the*

*employer continues to have the absolute power to fire anyone with
or without good cause.*

Woolley v. Hoffman-La Roche, Inc., 99 N.J. 284, 309, 491 A.2d 1257, 1271
(1985), *mod.* 101 N.J. 10, 499 A.2d 515 (1985). No explanation was given in
the disclaimer that Mobil did not consider itself bound by the terms of the
handbook. Instead, McDonald would have been led to draw inferences from
the handbook language: that it was intended to be a guide, and that Mobil
intended to continue the policies, benefits and rules contained in the
handbook. The same paragraph which disclaimed a contract also informed
Mr. McDonald that he could discuss "any questions" he might have with
his supervisor, employee relations staff and management and urged him to
read the handbook carefully and to keep it in a safe and readily available
place.

The trial court erred in finding that the disclaimer was conspicuous.
We hold that the attempted disclaimers in the employee handbook and in
the employment application were insufficiently conspicuous to be binding
on McDonald.

In our earlier opinion, this court stated: "Following *Parks,* Mobil
revised its handbook. The most significant revision was the addition of a
statement that the handbook was not an employment contract. A contract
exists when there is a meeting of the minds. Mobil's express disclaimer
demonstrates that it had no intention to form a contract."

The above quotation could be interpreted as importing an unduly
subjective element into contract analysis. *See Pine River State Bank v.
Mettille,* 333 N.W.2d 622, 630 n. 6 (Minn.1983). However, we did not mean
to say that a contract could not be formed where one party somehow lacked
"subjective intent" but nevertheless proceeded as if there were a contract.

Under the "objective theory" of contract formation, contractual
obligation is imposed not on the basis of the subjective intent of the parties,
but rather upon the outward manifestations of a party's assent sufficient
to create reasonable reliance by the other party. *See* R. Scott and D. Leslie,
Contract Law and Theory 194–95 (1988). That Mobil did not subjectively
"intend" that a contract be formed is irrelevant, provided that Mobil made
sufficient intentional, objective manifestations of contractual assent to
create reasonable reliance by McDonald.

The Restatement (Second) of Contracts § 19 (1979) puts the matter
this way:

> (1) The manifestation of assent may be made wholly or
> partly by written or spoken words or by other acts or by failure to
> act.
>
> (2) The conduct of a party is not effective as a manifestation
> of his assent unless he intends to engage in the conduct and knows

or has reason to know that the other party may infer from his conduct that he assents.

(3)   The conduct of a party may manifest assent even though he does not in fact assent. In such cases a resulting contract may be voidable because of fraud, duress, mistake, or other invalidating cause.

The Restatement (Second) of Contracts § 21 (1979) further explains: "Neither real nor apparent intention that a promise be legally binding is essential to the formation of a contract, but a manifestation of intention that a promise shall not affect legal relations may prevent the formation of a contract."

The views expressed in the above Restatements are sound and are herewith adopted in Wyoming. Mobil's subjective "intent" to contract is irrelevant, if Mobil's intentional, objective manifestations to McDonald indicated assent to a contractual relationship.

The handbook informed McDonald that "individual consideration on employee-supervisor matters provides the best method for satisfying the employees' and the Company's needs" which could not be improved on by union representation. Mobil stated that it planned to provide, *inter alia,* "free and open communications" and stated that "on those rare occasions when differences cannot be resolved, we have a Fair Treatment Procedure that affords an employee the opportunity to be heard, without fear of reprisal." Union representation, the handbook stated, is unnecessary for employees to enjoy job security or consistent treatment.

The manual stated that Mobil recognized a "fundamental obligation" to its employees to "give helpful consideration when an employee makes a mistake or has a personal problem with which we are asked to help." The handbook outlined a procedure for presenting a problem or complaint which an employee might have. The manual also set forth a progressive discipline schedule for cases in which the employee broke the company rules or failed to meet a reasonable standard of conduct and work performance. This five-step schedule could be disregarded by the company at its discretion.

The "welcoming" section, quoted above, stated that Mobil intended to continue policies, benefits and rules contained in the handbook and that changes or improvements could be made from time to time by the company. The inference favorable to McDonald is that Mobil would follow the rules unless changed, and that since they had not been changed, Mobil was bound by them.

When McDonald went to his supervisor over the rumors that he had heard, he was told that he should "just do his job and not worry about what had been said." McDonald alleges that Mobil's course of conduct led him to believe that Mobil would follow the handbook procedures concerning the complaint of his co-employee.

Examining the handbook provisions cited above and Mobil's course of dealing with McDonald on the rumor of accusation and his termination, we find ambiguity as to whether Mobil manifested intent to modify the at-will employment to an employment which could be terminated only for cause. Mobil made numerous statements which could be construed as promises to McDonald concerning communication with him and Mobil's disciplinary procedures. Mobil's handbook stated that individual consideration and open communication would be an effective substitute for unionization. All of these manifestations could suggest to a reasonable person that Mobil intended to make legally-binding promises.

"If the meaning of a contract is ambiguous, or not apparent, it may be necessary to determine the intention of the parties from evidence other than the contract itself, and interpretation becomes a mixed question of law and fact." *Parks,* 704 P.2d at 706; and *see also Leithead v. American Colloid Company,* 721 P.2d 1059, 1068 (Wyo.1986) (Thomas, J., concurring and dissenting). There, Justice Thomas, on remand, would have extended "the scope of the trial to the factual question of the effect of language in these employee handbooks which [he perceived] not to be sufficiently apparent to justify a conclusion that this was a contract of employment as a matter of law." Justice Thomas saw the effect of the employee handbooks on at-will employment as either creating a question of fact or ambiguity such as to require a determination of the parties' intention from evidence other than the contract itself.

The meaning and effect of this employment contract, a mixed question of law and fact, remains unresolved. Therefore, we must reverse summary judgment on the contract issue. The case is remanded to the trial court for determination of whether the employee handbook and Mobil's course of dealing with McDonald modified the employment relationship from one terminable at will to one terminable only for cause.

MACY, J. concurring:

. . . In *McDonald v. Mobil Coal Producing, Inc.,* 789 P.2d 866 (Wyo.1990), we stated that genuine issues of material fact existed as to the effect, if any, the representations made by Mobil in its handbook had upon an otherwise at-will employment relationship. The Court went on to state in *McDonald* that those issues were (1) whether Mobil should have expected McDonald's reliance upon the procedures outlined in the handbook, (2) whether McDonald's reliance was reasonable, and (3) whether Mobil's termination procedures should have been enforced to avoid injustice.

The majority opinion in this case holds that there was an ambiguity in the employment handbook which presented a material question of fact as to whether Mobil intended to make legally binding promises concerning Mobil's employment termination procedures. Even if the employment handbook was ambiguous, Mobil's course of conduct clearly demonstrated that Mobil intended to make legally binding promises concerning Mobil's employment termination procedures and that Mobil certainly led McDonald to rely upon the termination procedures outlined in the handbook.

It appears that the only question which should be resolved on remand is whether Mobil's termination procedures should have been enforced to avoid an injustice; i.e., whether Mobil should have been estopped from firing McDonald without cause. *See McDonald,* 789 P.2d 866.

THOMAS, J., dissenting.

I persist in my vote to affirm the trial court in this case. Like Justice Cardine, in whose dissent I join, I am at a loss to understand what more Mobil Coal Producing, Inc. could do to make it clear to an employee that he was entering into an employment-at-will arrangement. I am satisfied that this was an employment-at-will. That relationship was not modified by the handbook. I am not persuaded that there is any more solid majority support for reversal than there was with respect to the first opinion.

I see no need to reiterate what I said in my dissenting opinion in *McDonald v. Mobil Coal Producing, Inc.,* 789 P.2d 866, 872 (Wyo.1990), Thomas, J., dissenting. I simply emphasize that, in all respects, the dissenting opinion is still sound so far as it treats with the issue relating to the contract of employment.

In this new effort in which the majority reverses the summary judgment, reliance is placed upon *Alexander v. Phillips Oil Company,* 707 P.2d 1385 (Wyo.1985), and substantial reliance is placed upon *Jimenez v. Colorado Interstate Gas Company,* 690 F.Supp. 977 (D.Wyo.1988). In invoking these authorities, the majority simply fails to recognize the actual employment-at-will arrangement that was entered into between McDonald and Mobil Coal Producing, Inc. That arrangement is captured by [the] quotation [at the outset of the majority's opinion under the heading "READ CAREFULLY BEFORE SIGNING"]. From that point on, it is ignored.

I submit, however, that the fact of that specific employment-at-will arrangement serves to distinguish this case from both *Alexander* and *Jimenez.* There are other distinguishing facts. The employee handbook, in this instance, was not adopted and issued after the time that McDonald was employed. It is difficult for me to understand how it could amend, or could in some manner have changed, the clear employment-at-will that was documented. In *Jimenez,* there was no separate document articulating an employment-at-will, and the court was dealing only with the factors of employment plus the existence of a handbook. While it might be appropriate to emphasize in an employee's handbook, that was issued without a separate document articulating the employment arrangement, the caveat explaining that the handbook is not an employment contract, that requirement is far less imperative when one recognizes that the handbook was generally available to employees of Mobil Coal Producing, Inc. After the handbook already had been published and issued, McDonald signed a document that provided that the "employment is terminable at will." Under these circumstances, the subsequent delivery of the handbook simply did not make any difference.

In my opinion, this case strikes the death knell for employment-at-will in Wyoming. It says, in effect, that even though there is a clear statement by the employee that the relationship with the employer is an employment-at-will, after the employment commences, the employer cannot engage in any dialogue with the employee about the conditions and circumstances of the employment. If any such dialogue occurs, it will be considered to have amended the arrangement in such a way that the question of employment must be submitted to a jury. I lack the imagination to visualize any situation in which dialogue about the conditions and circumstances of the employment would not occur and, consequently, it is hereafter impossible to have an employment-at-will in Wyoming.

The summary judgment entered by the trial court in this case should be affirmed.

CARDINE, J., dissenting, with whom THOMAS, J., joins.

I continue my dissent to the opinion of the court and this opinion upon rehearing for the reasons previously stated. *McDonald v. Mobil Coal Producing, Inc.,* 789 P.2d 866, 871 (Wyo.1990) (Cardine, C.J., dissenting) (*McDonald I*). This opinion after rehearing merely informs Mobil of additional requirements for effective disclaimer. If Mobil should in the future satisfy these requirements, can it assume that this court will give effect to its disclaimer—or should Mobil eliminate its employee handbook? Perhaps the answer will only come with more litigation.

In *McDonald I,* the court reversed summary judgment on the basis of promissory estoppel. Despite the disclaimer in the handbook, the court said McDonald could recover if he could demonstrate that it was reasonable to rely upon the promises contained in the handbook and if enforcement of the promises was the only way to avoid an injustice. 789 P.2d at 870. The court held that no contract was formed because there was no meeting of the minds in forming a contract. *Id.* at 869, citing *Anderson Excavating and Wrecking Co. v. Certified Welding Corp.,* 769 P.2d 887 (Wyo.1988).

Now, in this opinion upon rehearing, the court holds that if it was reasonable to rely upon promises in the handbook, then a contract was formed. This opinion states a contract is formed by "outward manifestations of a party's assent sufficient to create reasonable reliance by the other party." The language is similar to the definition of a promise in *McDonald I,* wherein the court said a promise is "a manifestation of intention to act or refrain from acting in a specified way, so made as to justify a promisee in understanding that a commitment has been made." 789 P.2d at 870, quoting Restatement, Second, Contracts § 2 (1981).

A promise is not a contract. But this court now says the making of a promise alone reasonably relied upon by another creates an enforceable contract.

It is said that whether a contract was entered into depends upon the intention of the parties. 17A Am.Jur.2d Contracts § 27 (1991). For a valid contract to exist, a meeting of the minds is necessary concerning the terms of the agreement, the parties must have intended to contract, and the contract must be supported by consideration. *Anderson Excavating,* 769 P.2d at 889; *United States Through Farmers Home Administration v. Redland,* 695 P.2d 1031, 1036 (Wyo.1985); *Miller v. Miller,* 664 P.2d 39, 40 (Wyo.1983). It is clear from the disclaimer that Mobil never intended to make a contract. There was never a meeting of the minds nor was there a valid consideration. There was no contract. That is why this court in *McDonald I* rested its decision to reverse upon the doctrine of promissory estoppel. I would affirm the decision of the trial court.

NOTES AND QUESTIONS

1.   Which of the justices has the strongest argument? Weakest? Do the strengths and weaknesses vary in terms of the law, logic, or policy aspects of the case? If you were a judge on the Wyoming Supreme Court, how would you have voted on the threshold question of whether the disclaimer was sufficiently conspicuous to be effective? If you were the trial court judge to whom the case was remanded, how would you approach the questions of (a) whether a contract has been formed and (b) whether promissory estoppel should apply?

2.   Have you ever worked at a job where you had an employee handbook? Did you read the handbook? What was your sense in terms of whether the policies in the handbook were binding on either you or on your supervisors and the company? How do these insights inform your thoughts on the preceding case?

3.   The default rule in 49 American jurisdictions (Montana is the exception) is the "at will" employment rule. This means an employee may be fired or quit at any time, for a good or bad reason or no reason at all. While some "bad reasons," such as race, sex, or religious discrimination have been outlawed by Title VII of the Civil Rights Act of 1964 as the basis for an employer's decision, an employer retains wide latitude over hiring and firing, at least compared with the laws in other countries. If the at will rule is so employer-friendly, why would employers publish a handbook giving workers additional rights? Some commentators suggest that if employers are worried that their employees might unionize, they may consider granting employees

more contractual rights to "head off" that fate. How might these factors have been operating in *Mobil Coal*?

O'NEILL V. NEW YORK UNIVERSITY
97 A.D.3d 199 (2012)

MOSKOWITZ, J.

[P]laintiff-petitioner (petitioner), a research scientist, alleges that he reported suspected research misconduct of a colleague to his superiors who, in turn, fired him in retaliation. . . . According to the complaint, in July 2002, respondents New York University, NYU Hospitals Center and NYU Langone Medical Center (NYU) hired petitioner, Dr. David O'Neill, as a non-tenured, full-time faculty member, with an annual starting salary of $140,000 pursuant to an offer letter. NYU's Faculty Handbook provided that appointment to non-tenured faculty positions "shall be for a definite period of time, not exceeding one academic year unless otherwise specified."

NYU renewed petitioner's appointment annually. As recently as February 23, 2010, NYU confirmed his appointment for the 2009–2010 academic year from September 1, 2009 through August 31, 2010 in a renewal letter. The offer letter provided that petitioner's appointment with NYU was "contingent upon continued employment in good standing with the [NYU] School of Medicine and compliance with all University and School of Medicine rules and regulations and other contractual obligations." . . .

The NYU Code of Ethics states that "[e]ach member of the University is expected to uphold the standards of [NYU] and to report suspected violations of the Code or any other apparent irregularity." . . . The NYU Code of Conduct elucidates as follows: "Every member of the Medical Center has an obligation to report situations or activities that are—or even seem to be—violations of the Code. If something concerns you but you are not sure whether it is a violation of the Code, you must raise the concern and ask for advice." The Non-Retaliation Policy states that "[t]he Medical Center promises that there will be no retaliation against you if you raise concerns or questions about misconduct or report violations of this Code."

The Faculty Handbook also contains NYU's disciplinary policies that include its General Disciplinary Regulations Applicable to both Tenured and Non-Tenured Faculty Members and the Faculty Grievance Procedures. The Disciplinary Regulations apply "where a question arises concerning an alleged violation by any member of the faculty of a rule or regulation of [NYU]" and specify whether the dean or a faculty committee addresses each question. The Grievance Procedures provide a mechanism for NYU faculty members to "seek redress of their grievances."

Petitioner's appointment with NYU included his duties as Assistant Director of the Vaccine/Cell Manipulation Core Laboratory for the NYU Cancer Institute or the Vaccine Lab. His supervisor was Dr. Nina Bhardwaj. She reported to Dr. William Carroll, the Director of the Cancer Institute. In 2004 and 2005, petitioner oversaw the construction of the Vaccine Lab. The lab's first major project was a clinical trial, that Bhardwaj designed, comparing a new and relatively expensive "dentritic cell" vaccine for malignant melanoma (skin cancer) with an inexpensive, decades-old mineral oil "Montanide" vaccine. . . .

It is undisputed that the clinical trial results showed that the dendritic cell vaccine was less effective than the Montanide vaccine. Throughout the clinical trial and for months thereafter, the research team exchanged e-mails and letters and held conferences on the clinical study. During this time, petitioner believed that Bhardwaj was attempting to shape the written and oral presentation of the clinical trial results in an unethical manner to downplay and distort the negative findings about the dendritic cell vaccine. . . .

On October 29, 2009, in a meeting with Carroll and Lauren Hackett, an NYU administrator, petitioner distributed and read aloud a prepared statement that outlined his concerns over Bhardwaj's actions. Petitioner asserted that during this time, the promotion his supervisors had recommended a year earlier had stalled. On November 19, 2009, in another meeting with Hackett, Carroll handed petitioner a letter, stating that petitioner's "lingering . . . anger" impeded progress in the Vaccine Lab. Carroll cited petitioner's concerns over the research paper's new analyses as one example of a barrier to progress. The letter warned that petitioner's "[f]ailure to immediately rectify and sustain an acceptable level of behavior may lead to further disciplinary action including termination of [his] employment."

Petitioner typically arranged tours of the Vaccine Lab for outside visitors. However, in April, 2010, Bhardwaj arranged a tour. During the tour, petitioner intervened and took over from Bhardwaj. Petitioner then e-mailed Bhardwaj, advising that she first contact him with regard to any future site visits. On April 22, 2010, Carroll learned of petitioner's e-mail and telephoned him, stating that Bhardwaj was not obligated to pre-arrange lab site visits with him. The conversation became heated. Petitioner acknowledged that he intermittently raised his voice but did so to keep from being interrupted. He asserted that the only time he raised his voice to Carroll was during this brief telephone call.

On April 23, 2010, petitioner met with Associate Dean David Levy and continued to press his concerns about Bhardwaj's actions and what he perceived as Carroll's retaliation. Levy advised petitioner to consult Dr.

Steven Abramson, Vice Dean for Faculty and Academic Affairs, to file a grievance.

On the morning of May 3, 2010, petitioner requested an appointment with Abramson to begin the grievance process. That afternoon, Carroll called petitioner to a meeting and handed him a termination letter. The termination letter, dated April 25, 2010, dismissed petitioner, "effective immediately," for alleged "unprofessional behavior." The cited behavior was that, during the April 22 telephone call with Carroll, petitioner's "tone became very argumentative" and his "voice rose in anger."

On May 7, 2010, petitioner met with Abramson and requested to appeal his termination and file a grievance. Petitioner reiterated his concerns regarding Bhardwaj, Carroll's retaliation and NYU's failure to follow its disciplinary policies. Petitioner then retained counsel. Thereafter, Dr. Reginald Odom, NYU's Vice President for Medical Center Employee and Labor Relations, periodically responded to counsel's e-mails and telephone calls. However, on July 13, 2010, Odom advised petitioner's counsel that NYU would not conduct an investigation or appeal, and that NYU maintained its termination decision. In August 2010, petitioner commenced this [action for, among other things, breach of contract by retaliation for reporting research misconduct and failure to follow disciplinary policies].

NYU contended that it thoroughly investigated petitioner's research misconduct concerns and determined that the challenged research findings constituted a mere difference of opinion. NYU further argued that petitioner's claims failed because he did not allege detrimental reliance on NYU's non-retaliatory policies. NYU contended that it followed all relevant procedures before making a reasonable determination to discharge petitioner as an at-will employee based on his unprofessional behavior.

The [court below] was not persuaded by petitioner's argument that NYU appointed him to a fixed, one-year employment term or that NYU could terminate him only for cause. Referring only to the offer letter and not the renewal letter, the court held that NYU appointed petitioner as a non-tenured faculty member with an unspecified employment period. The court rejected petitioner's argument that, by referencing the NYU Faculty Handbook, it could find a definitive term of employment . . . .

[T]he court further noted that, even if a contract period is not of definite duration, a plaintiff may still maintain an action for breach of contract if "the employer made its employee aware of an express written policy limiting the right of discharge and the employee detrimentally relied on that policy in accepting employment." The court observed that other courts have strictly applied the criteria set forth in *Weiner v. McGraw-Hill, Inc.*, 57 N.Y.2d 458, 457 N.Y.S.2d 193, 443 N.E.2d 441 [1982] in determining whether an exception to the at-will arrangement applies when the employment term is indefinite. Specifically, the court noted that the *Weiner* court looked to whether there was an express provision in an employee handbook stating that employers could terminate employees only for cause, whether the employer also orally assured the employee that there would be no termination without just cause and whether the employee turned down other employment opportunities in reliance upon the assurances. . . .

Petitioner argues that his employment relationship with NYU was not at-will, but that NYU hired him for a fixed term. He further argues that NYU's policies contained express contractual promises, thus, creating binding limitations on NYU's right to terminate. He contends that factual issues exist regarding his reliance on these limitations mitigating against an at-will employment arrangement. We find merit to these arguments.

Petitioner argues that the renewal letter, "confirm[ing]" his employment "for the academic year 2009–10," combined with the Faculty Handbook, stating that non-tenured faculty appointments "shall be for a definite period of time, not exceeding one academic year, unless otherwise specified," created employment for a definite one-year period, warranting termination only for good cause. This issue requires examination of the terms of the renewal letter and whether we should interpret it in conjunction with the general terms of the Faculty Handbook that address non-tenure appointment renewals.

The Court of Appeals has noted a "two step" analysis in determining the issue of whether an employment arrangement is at-will: "(1) if the duration is definite, the at-will doctrine is inapplicable, on the other hand, (2) if the employment term is indefinite or undefined, the rebuttable at-will presumption is operative and other factors come into the equation" (*Rooney v. Tyson*, 91 N.Y.2d 685, 689, 674 N.Y.S.2d 616, 697 N.E.2d 571 [1998]). . . . The Court held that an oral contract between plaintiff trainer and defendant boxer for the plaintiff to continue as trainer "for as long as the boxer fights professionally" supported "a definite duration finding" (id. at 693, 674 N.Y.S.2d 616, 697 N.E.2d 571). The Court reasoned that "[o]nly when we discern no term of some definiteness or no express limitation does the analysis switch over to the rebuttable presumption line of cases. . . . The agreement in this case is not silent [as to duration] and manifestly provides a sufficiently limiting framework" (id. at 690, 674 N.Y.S.2d 616, 697 N.E.2d 571). . . .

Here, we hold that NYU's letters renewing petitioner's employment over specific academic years (including the offer letter and the renewal letter), read in conjunction with the non-tenure hiring provision in the Faculty Handbook, evidence an employment arrangement for a fixed duration. . . Indeed, the renewal letter "confirm[ed]" his "status as a member of the faculty of [NYU's] School of Medicine for the academic year

2009–10." The Faculty Handbook provides that appointments to non-tenured positions, as in petitioner's case, "shall be for a definite period of time, not exceeding one academic year." The Faculty Handbook also states that renewed appointments would "automatically terminate" after a year unless NYU further renewed the appointment. In instances where employers have allowed renewable annual contracts to expire and the employee to continue working, courts have construed the new arrangement between the parties as at-will . . . .

The [trial] court erred in relying on *Lobosco [v. New York Tele. Co.*, 751 N.E.2d 462 (N.Y. 2001) which stated that] "[r]outinely issued employee manuals, handbooks and policy statements should not lightly be converted into binding employment contracts" . . . . Indeed, the manual at issue in *Lobosco*, in contrast to the NYU Faculty Handbook here, expressly disclaimed that it constituted a contract: "This Code of Conduct is not a contract of employment and does not create any contractual rights of any kind between [defendant] and its employees."

[T]he [trial] court cited as "compelling" *Slue v. New York University Medical Center*, 409 F.Supp.2d 349 [S.D.N.Y.2006]. In *Slue*, NYU terminated the plaintiff from his position as a non-tenured faculty member. The plaintiff then sued NYU for failing to follow the disciplinary policies in the Faculty Handbook. The court found that the Faculty Handbook, including its disciplinary policies, created no limitation on NYU's right to discharge the plaintiff, an at-will employee (409 F.Supp.2d at 357–362). However, the *Slue* court did conclude that those disciplinary policies were applicable where, as here, a non-tenured faculty member allegedly violated a university rule or regulation. Thus, *Slue* is inapposite because, there, NYU terminated the plaintiff not for violating a university rule, but rather for inappropriate conduct in his private medical photography practice operated in an office on NYU property. Further, in contrast to *Slue*, NYU's initial offer of employment to petitioner was contingent on his compliance with University and School of Medicine rules and regulations that required reporting of research misconduct and suspected violations of the Code of Conduct as well as NYU's non-retaliation policy. . . .

Because we find petitioner has pleaded an employment arrangement for a fixed duration, analysis of the at-will doctrine is unnecessary. Nevertheless, we also hold that petitioner, for purposes of a motion to dismiss, has sufficiently stated that NYU's rules and regulations contained an express limitation on its right to discharge him on an at-will basis. . . .

In *Weiner*, the Court of Appeals held that an employer's express promise limiting its ability to discharge an employee at-will could create an enforceable contract. There, the plaintiff stated a cause of action for breach of contract when he alleged that he relied upon his employer's oral assurances that it would terminate him only for cause, the employment application and the company handbook contained the same policy, he turned down offers of employment in reliance on this assurance and supervisors advised him to be careful when discharging other employees because the company would discharge them only for cause, in accordance with the handbook. . . .

The [trial] court held that petitioner's claim fails because his pleadings contained no allegation that he was induced to leave his previous employment or turned down other offers of employment in reliance upon NYU's policies. However, this court has previously noted that *"Weiner* should not be interpreted as limiting its holding to its specific facts, especially in light of the court's formulation of a 'totality of circumstances' test" (*Lapidus v. New York City Ch. of the N.Y. State Assn. for Retarded Children*, 118 A.D.2d 122, 126, 504 N.Y.S.2d 629 [1986], quoting *Weiner*, 57 N.Y.2d at 467, 457 N.Y.S.2d 193, 443 N.E.2d 441). Moreover, in [*Mulder v. Donaldson, Lufkin & Jenrette*, 208 A.D.2d 301, 306–307, 623 N.Y.S.2d 560 (1995)], where the defendant employer argued that the plaintiff's allegations did not fit within *Weiner*, we stated:

> "[T]his argument simply seeks to portray a factual pattern present in *Weiner* as a governing principle of law. The salient and necessary prerequisite of law, set forth in *Weiner*, which is met here, is the reliance alleged by the plaintiff. While plaintiff did not leave another job, he did aggressively pursue the true facts [about alleged company wrongdoing] upon the express written promise of the employer that there would be no retribution for reports of violations.

[*Id.*]; *see also Marfia v. T.C. Ziraat Bankasi*, 147 F.3d 83, 89 [2d Cir.1998] ["The absence of the talismanic phrase 'I relied upon the Manual' does not, however, by itself preclude a reasonable jury from weighing the evidence presented and concluding that [plaintiff] relied upon the Manual"]).

Here, the NYU Code of Ethics, the Code of Conduct, the Non-Retaliation Policy and the Research Misconduct Policies, in combination, include NYU's express promise that it will protect employees from reprisal for reporting suspected research misconduct. Thus, we can infer petitioner's reliance on NYU's policies, given the complaint's allegations of his compliance with those policies by reporting his concerns of suspected research misconduct. At this early stage of the litigation, these allegations are sufficient. . . .

NOTES AND QUESTIONS

1.   Compare *O'Neill v. New York University* with *East Providence Credit Union v. Geremia*, the case finding that a bank's promise to insure a borrower's property was supported by the consideration of interest the bank would earn on funds it loaned to pay the premium. As noted after that case, New York

courts have tended to adhere to traditional principles of contract formation without resort to promissory estoppel. In *O'Neill*, a pivotal issue was whether the researcher had relied on the university's promises, usually discussed as a central element of promissory estoppel, though, in keeping with New York legal tradition, the court and the parties treated the case as one for breach of contract. Do you favor the New York concept or a fuller-throttled embrace of promissory estoppel?

2.   Compare *O'Neill v. New York University* with *McDonald v. Mobil Coal* on the contours of the employment at will doctrine and contractual or promissory exceptions to it. Suppose NYU's codes and policies all disclaimed forming any binding contractual obligation.

3.   Courts often give considerable deference to academic decisions of private universities (such as NYU). In a passage omitted from the excerpt above, the opinion said of the trial court:

> The court noted that case law had limited the role of courts in the review of controversies involving academic institutions where the exercise of highly specialized professional judgments are at issue. The court concluded that NYU's decision to terminate petitioner for unprofessional behavior was not arbitrary and capricious or shocking to the conscience.

The appellate court obviously did not feel constrained by such deference. Was that because the contract claim, including the reliance element, served to override any such professional judgment? *See Monaco v. New York University*, 43 N.Y.S.3d 328 (App. Div. 2015):

> A university's academic and administrative decisions require professional judgment and may only be reviewed . . . to ensure that such decisions are not violative of the institution's own rules and neither arbitrary nor irrational. . . However, "[i]f the claim involves a matter of contractual right it may, of course, be vindicated in an action [at] law." . . .

> For the purpose of surviving respondents' cross motion to dismiss, petitioners, tenured faculty members of respondent New York University's School of Medicine, have sufficiently alleged that the policies contained in respondent's Faculty Handbook, which "form part of the essential employment understandings between a member of the Faculty and the University," have the force of contract (*see O'Neill v. New York Univ.*, 97 A.D.3d 199, 208–210, 944 N.Y.S.2d 503 [1st Dept.2012]). Further, for the purposes of surviving respondents' cross motion to dismiss, petitioners have sufficiently alleged that they had a mutual understanding with respondent that tenured faculty members' salaries may not be involuntarily reduced. Additionally, petitioners have sufficiently alleged that they reasonably relied on oral representations by respondents that their salaries would not be involuntarily reduced.

E. CONSTRUCTION BIDDING

We have concluded our exploration of the innovation of promissory estoppel as an alternative to consideration and traditional contract formation. Now contemplate whether promissory estoppel may instead provide a supplement to the working rules of contract formation. This issue was joined in a pair of classic opinions of two of the giants of 20th century contract law, Judge Learned Hand and Chief Justice Roger Traynor. Both wrestle with a recurring challenge in the context of construction bidding: general contractors preparing bids for large construction projects seek bids from subcontractors and all participants need a reliable basis for proceeding but hesitate to make binding commitments during the bidding process.

JAMES BAIRD CO. v. GIMBEL BROTHERS
64 F.2d 344 (2d Cir. 1933)

HAND, J.

[Suit] for breach of a contract to deliver linoleum under a contract of sale; the defendant denied the making of the contract; the parties tried the case to the judge under a written stipulation and he directed judgment for the defendant. The facts as found, bearing on the making of the contract, the only issue necessary to discuss, were as follows: The defendant, a New York merchant, knew that the Department of Highways in Pennsylvania had asked for bids for the construction of a public building. It sent an employee to the office of a contractor in Philadelphia, who had possession of the specifications, and the employee there computed the amount of the linoleum which would be required on the job, underestimating the total yardage by about one-half the proper amount.

In ignorance of this mistake, on December twenty-fourth the defendant sent to some twenty or thirty contractors, likely to bid on the job, an offer to supply all the linoleum required by the specifications at two different lump sums, depending upon the quality used. These offers concluded as follows: 'If successful in being awarded this contract, it will be absolutely guaranteed, . . . and . . . we are offering these prices for reasonable' (sic), 'prompt acceptance after the general contract has been awarded.' The plaintiff, a contractor in Washington, got one of these on the twenty-eighth, and on the same day the defendant learned its mistake and telegraphed all the contractors to whom it had sent the offer, that it withdrew it and would substitute a new one at about double the amount of the old. This withdrawal reached the plaintiff at Washington on the afternoon of the same day, but not until after it had put in a bid at Harrisburg at a lump sum, based as to linoleum upon the prices quoted by the defendant. The public authorities accepted the plaintiff's bid on December thirtieth, the defendant having meanwhile written a letter of confirmation of its withdrawal, received on the thirty-first. The plaintiff formally accepted the offer on January second, and, as the defendant persisted in declining to recognize the existence of a contract, sued it for damages on a breach.

Unless there are circumstances to take it out of the ordinary doctrine, since the offer was withdrawn before it was accepted, the acceptance was too late. Restatement of Contracts, § 35. To meet this the plaintiff argues as follows: It was a reasonable implication from the defendant's offer that it should be irrevocable in case the plaintiff acted upon it, that is to say, used the prices quoted in making its bid, thus putting itself in a position from which it could not withdraw without great loss. While it might have withdrawn its bid after receiving the revocation, the time had passed to submit another, and as the item of linoleum was a very trifling part of the cost of the whole building, it would have been an unreasonable hardship to expect it to lose the contract on that account, and probably forfeit its deposit. While it is true that the plaintiff might in advance have secured a contract conditional upon the success of its bid, this was not what the defendant suggested. It understood that the contractors would use its offer in their bids, and would thus in fact commit themselves to supplying the linoleum at the proposed prices. The inevitable implication from all this was that when the contractors acted upon it, they accepted the offer and promised to pay for the linoleum, in case their bid were accepted.

It was of course possible for the parties to make such a contract, and the question is merely as to what they meant; that is, what is to be imputed to the words they used. Whatever plausibility there is in the argument, is in the fact that the defendant must have known the predicament in which the contractors would be put if it withdrew its offer after the bids went in. However, it seems entirely clear that the contractors did not suppose that they accepted the offer merely by putting in their bids. If, for example, the successful one had repudiated the contract with the public authorities after it had been awarded to him, certainly the defendant could not have sued him for a breach. If he had become bankrupt, the defendant could not prove against his estate.

It seems plain therefore that there was no contract between them. And if there be any doubt as to this, the language of the offer sets it at rest. The phrase, 'if successful in being awarded this contract,' is scarcely met by the mere use of the prices in the bids. Surely such a use was not an 'award' of the contract to the defendant. Again, the phrase, 'we are offering these prices for . . . prompt acceptance after the general contract has been awarded,' looks to the usual communication of an acceptance, and precludes the idea that the use of the offer in the bidding shall be the equivalent. It may indeed be argued that this last language contemplated no more than an early notice that the offer had been accepted, the actual acceptance being the bid, but that would wrench its natural meaning too far, especially in the light of the preceding phrase. The contractors had a ready escape from their difficulty by insisting upon a contract before they used the figures; and in commercial transactions it does not in the end promote justice to seek strained interpretations in aid of those who do not protect themselves.

But the plaintiff says that even though no bilateral contract was made, the defendant should be held under the doctrine of 'promissory estoppel.' This is to be chiefly found in those cases where persons subscribe to a venture, usually charitable, and are held to their promises after it has been completed. It has been applied much more broadly, however, and has now been generalized in section 90, of the Restatement of Contracts. We may arguendo accept it as it there reads, for it does not apply to the case at bar. Offers are ordinarily made in exchange for a consideration, either a counter-promise or some other act which the promisor wishes to secure. In such cases they propose bargains; they presuppose that each promise or performance is an inducement to the other. Wisconsin, etc., Ry. v. Powers, 191 U. S. 379, 386, 387, 24 S. Ct. 107, 48 L. Ed. 229; Banning Co. v. California, 240 U. S. 142, 152, 153, 36 S. Ct. 338, 60 L. Ed. 569.

But a man may make a promise without expecting an equivalent; a donative promise, conditional or absolute. The common law provided for such by sealed instruments, and it is unfortunate that these are no longer generally available. The doctrine of 'promissory estoppel' is to avoid the harsh results of allowing the promisor in such a case to repudiate, when the promisee has acted in reliance upon the promise. Siegel v. Spear & Co., 234 N. Y. 479, 138 N. E. 414, 26 A. L. R. 1205. Cf. Allegheny College v. National Bank, 246 N. Y. 369, 159 N. E. 173, 57 L. R. A. 980. But an offer for an exchange is not meant to become a promise until a consideration has been received, either a counter-promise or whatever else is stipulated. To extend it would be to hold the offeror regardless of the stipulated condition of his offer. In the case at bar the defendant offered to deliver the linoleum in exchange for the plaintiff's acceptance, not for its bid, which was a matter of indifference to it. That offer could become a promise to deliver only when the equivalent was received; that is, when the plaintiff promised to take and pay for it. There is no room in such a situation for the doctrine of 'promissory estoppel.'

Nor can the offer be regarded as of an option, giving the plaintiff the right seasonably to accept the linoleum at the quoted prices if its bid was accepted, but not binding it to take and pay, if it could get a better bargain elsewhere. There is not the least reason to suppose that the defendant meant to subject itself to such one-sided obligation. True, if so construed, the doctrine of 'promissory estoppel' might apply, the plaintiff having acted in reliance upon it, though, so far as we have found, the decisions are otherwise. As to that, however, we need not declare ourselves. [Affirmed.]

DRENNAN V. STAR PAVING
333 P.2d 757 (Cal. 1958)

TRAYNOR, J.

Defendant appeals from a judgment for plaintiff in an action to recover damages caused by defendant's refusal to perform certain paving work according to a bid it submitted to plaintiff.

On July 28, 1955, plaintiff, a licensed general contractor, was preparing a bid on the 'Monte Vista School Job' in the Lancaster school district. Bids had to be submitted before 8:00 p. m. Plaintiff testified that it was customary in that area for general contractors to receive the bids of subcontractors by telephone on the day set for bidding and to rely on them in computing their own bids. Thus on that day plaintiff's secretary, Mrs. Johnson, received by telephone between fifty and seventy-five subcontractors' bids for various parts of the school job. As each bid came in, she wrote it on a special form, which she brought into plaintiff's office. He then posted it on a master cost sheet setting forth the names and bids of all subcontractors. His own bid had to include the names of subcontractors who were to perform one-half of one per cent or more of the construction work, and he had also to provide a bidder's bond of ten per cent of his total bid of $317,385 as a guarantee that he would enter the contract if awarded the work.

Late in the afternoon, Mrs. Johnson had a telephone conversation with Kenneth R. Hoon, an estimator for defendant. He gave his name and telephone number and stated that he was bidding for defendant for the paving work at the Monte Vista School according to plans and specifications and that his bid was $7,131.60. At Mrs. Johnson's request he repeated his bid. Plaintiff listened to the bid over an extension telephone in his office and posted it on the master sheet after receiving the bid form from Mrs. Johnson. Defendant's was the lowest bid for the paving. Plaintiff computed his own bid accordingly and submitted it with the name of defendant as the subcontractor for the paving. When the bids were opened on July 28th, plaintiff's proved to be the lowest, and he was awarded the contract.

On his way to Los Angeles the next morning plaintiff stopped at defendant's office. The first person he met was defendant's construction engineer, Mr. Oppenheimer. Plaintiff testified: 'I introduced myself and he immediately told me that they had made a mistake in their bid to me the night before, they couldn't do it for the price they had bid, and I told him I would expect him to carry through with their original bid because I had used it in compiling my bid and the job was being awarded them. And I would have to go and do the job according to my bid and I would expect them to do the same.'

Defendant refused to do the paving work for less than $15,000. Plaintiff testified that he 'got figures from other people' and after trying for several months to get as low a bid as possible engaged L & H Paving Company, a firm in Lancaster, to do the work for $10,948.60.

The trial court found on substantial evidence that defendant made a definite offer to do the paving on the Monte Vista job according to the plans and specifications for $7,131.60, and that plaintiff relied on defendant's bid in computing his own bid for the school job and naming defendant therein as the subcontractor for the paving work. Accordingly, it entered judgment for plaintiff in the amount of $3,817.00 (the difference between defendant's bid and the cost of the paving to plaintiff) plus costs.

Defendant contends that there was no enforceable contract between the parties [because] it made a revocable offer and revoked it before plaintiff communicated his acceptance to defendant.

There is no evidence that defendant offered to make its bid irrevocable in exchange for plaintiff's use of its figures in computing his bid. Nor is there evidence that would warrant interpreting plaintiff's use of defendant's bid as the acceptance thereof, binding plaintiff, on condition he received the main contract, to award the subcontract to defendant. In sum, there was neither an option supported by consideration nor a bilateral contract binding on both parties.

Plaintiff contends, however, that he relied to his detriment on defendant's offer and that defendant must therefore answer in damages for its refusal to perform. Thus the question is squarely presented: Did plaintiff's reliance make defendant's offer irrevocable?

Section 90 of the Restatement of Contracts states: 'A promise which the promisor should reasonably expect to induce action or forbearance of a definite and substantial character on the part of the promisee and which does induce such action or forbearance is binding if injustice can be avoided only by enforcement of the promise.' This rule applies in this state.

Defendant's offer constituted a promise to perform on such conditions as were stated expressly or by implication therein or annexed thereto by operation of law. (See 1 Williston, Contracts (3rd. ed.), § 24A, p. 56, § 61, p. 196.) Defendant had reason to expect that if its bid proved the lowest, it would be used by plaintiff. It induced [action in reliance].

Had defendant's bid expressly stated or clearly implied that it was revocable at any time before acceptance we would treat it accordingly. It was silent on revocation, however, and we must therefore determine whether there are conditions to the right of revocation imposed by law or reasonably inferable in fact. In the analogous problem of an offer for a unilateral contract, the theory is now obsolete that the offer is revocable at any time before complete performance. Thus section 45 of the Restatement of Contracts provides: 'If an offer for a unilateral contract is made, and part of the consideration requested in the offer is given or tendered by the offeree in response thereto, the offeror is bound by a contract, the duty of immediate performance of which is conditional on the full consideration being given or tendered within the time stated in the offer, or, if no time is stated therein, within a reasonable time.' In explanation, comment b states that the 'main offer includes as a subsidiary promise, necessarily implied, that if part of the requested performance is given, the offeror will not revoke his offer, and that if tender is made it will be accepted. Part performance or tender may thus furnish consideration for the subsidiary promise. Moreover, merely acting in justifiable reliance on an offer may in some cases serve as sufficient reason for making a promise binding (see § 90).'

Whether implied in fact or law, the subsidiary promise serves to preclude the injustice that would result if the offer could be revoked after the offeree had acted in detrimental reliance thereon. Reasonable reliance resulting in a foreseeable prejudicial change in position affords a compelling basis also for implying a subsidiary promise not to revoke an offer for a bilateral contract.

The absence of consideration is not fatal to the enforcement of such a promise. It is true that in the case of unilateral contracts the Restatement finds consideration for the implied subsidiary promise in the part performance of the bargained-for exchange, but its reference to section 90 makes clear that consideration for such a promise is not always necessary. The very purpose of section 90 is to make a promise binding even though there was no consideration 'in the sense of something that is bargained for and given in exchange.' (See 1 Corbin, Contracts 634 et seq.) Reasonable reliance serves to hold the offeror in lieu of the consideration ordinarily required to make the offer binding.

In a case involving similar facts the Supreme Court of South Dakota stated that 'we believe that reason and justice demand that the doctrine (of section 90) be applied to the present facts. We cannot believe that by accepting this doctrine as controlling in the state of facts before us we will abolish the requirement of a consideration in contract cases, in any different sense than an ordinary estoppel abolishes some legal requirement in its application. We are of the opinion, therefore, that the defendants in executing the agreement (which was not supported by consideration) made a promise which they should have reasonably expected would induce the plaintiff to submit a bid based thereon to the Government, that such promise did induce this action, and that injustice can be avoided only by enforcement of the promise.' Northwestern Engineering Co. v. Ellerman, 69 S.D. 397, 408, 10 N.W.2d 879, 884; see also, Robert Gordon, Inc., v. Ingersoll-Rand Co., 7 Cir., 117 F.2d 654, 661; cf. James Baird Co. v. Gimbel Bros., 2 Cir., 64 F.2d 344.

When plaintiff used defendant's offer in computing his own bid, he bound himself to perform in reliance on defendant's terms. Though defendant did not bargain for this use of its bid neither did defendant make it idly, indifferent to whether it would be used or not. On the contrary it is reasonable to suppose that defendant submitted its bid to obtain the subcontract. It was bound to realize the substantial possibility that its bid would be the lowest, and that it would be included by plaintiff in his bid. It was to its own interest that the contractor be awarded the general contract; the lower the subcontract bid, the lower the general contractor's bid was likely to be and the greater its chance of acceptance and hence the greater defendant's chance of getting the paving subcontract. Defendant had reason not only to expect plaintiff to rely on its bid but to want him to. Clearly defendant had a stake in plaintiff's reliance on its bid. Given this interest and the fact that plaintiff is bound by his own bid, it is only fair that plaintiff should have at least an opportunity to accept defendant's bid after the general contract has been awarded to him.

It bears noting that a general contractor is not free to delay acceptance after he has been awarded the general contract in the hope of getting a better price. Nor can he reopen bargaining with the subcontractor and at the same time claim a continuing right to accept the original offer. See, R. J. Daum Const. Co. v. Child, Utah, 247 P.2d 817, 823. In the present case plaintiff promptly informed defendant that plaintiff was being awarded the job and that the subcontract was being awarded to defendant. . . .

NOTES AND QUESTIONS

1.   The fact patterns in *Baird* and *Drennan* are frequent and recurring. A property owner solicits project bids from general contractors to perform designated construction work involving multiple inputs from numerous subcontractors. Projects might range from highways to skyscrapers and from elementary school buildings to elaborate industrial complexes. General contractors interested in bidding on the main project solicit sub-bids from subcontractors on the various aspects of the overall project, such as excavation, concrete, steel, bricks, air conditioning, plumbing, electrical, and so on. Look at any major building project underway around your home or school and imagine how many dozens, hundreds, or even thousands of contracts were involved in the undertaking.

2.   The bid process has been described as follows:

> In such a building project there are basically three parties involved: the letting party, who calls for bids on its job [often called the "owner"]; the general contractor, who makes a bid on the whole project; and the subcontractors, who bid only on that portion of the whole job which involves the field of its specialty. The usual procedure is that when a project is announced, a subcontractor, on his own initiative or at the general contractor's request, prepares an

estimate and submits a bid to one or more of the general contractors interested in the project. The general contractor evaluates the bids made by the subcontractors in each field and uses them to compute its total bid to the letting party. After receiving bids from general contractors, the letting party ordinarily awards the contract to the lowest reputable bidder.

Maryland Supreme Corp. v. Blake Co., 369 A.2d 1017 (Md. 1977).

3. *Baird* and *Drennan* address recurring legal skirmishes that arise during the subcontractor bidding and contract formation process. Both approaches are famous, for different reasons, as the following summary of the legacies of the two prominent opinions attest:

> The problem the construction bidding process poses is the determination of the precise points on the timeline that the various parties become bound to each other. The early landmark case was *James Baird Co. v. Gimbel Bros.* . . . Judge Hand's opinion was widely criticized, but also widely influential. The effect of the *James Baird* line of cases, however, is an "obvious injustice without relief of any description." The general contractor is bound to the price submitted to the letting party, but the subcontractors are not bound, and are free to withdraw. As one commentator described it, "If the subcontractor revokes his bid before it is accepted by the general, any loss which results is a deduction from the general's profit and conceivably may transform overnight a profitable contract into a losing deal."

> The unfairness of this regime to the general contractor was addressed in *Drennan v. Star Paving*. The *Drennan* court . . . did not use "promissory estoppel" as a substitute for the entire contract, as is the doctrine's usual function. Instead, the *Drennan* court, applying the principle of § 90, interpreted the subcontractor's bid to be irrevocable. Justice Traynor's analysis used promissory estoppel as consideration for an implied promise to keep the bid open for a reasonable time. Recovery was then predicated on traditional bilateral contract, with the sub-bid as the offer and promissory estoppel serving to replace acceptance. The *Drennan* decision has been very influential. Many states have adopted the reasoning used by Justice Traynor [including Colorado, Illinois, Kentucky, Minnesota, Missouri and New Jersey].

Pavel Enterprises, Inc. v. A.S. Johnson Co., 674 A.2d 521 (Md. 1996).

4. One problem with the *Drennan* approach is the asymmetry of reliance in the bidding process, where subs are bound to generals, but generals are not bound to subs. Imagine the unsavory behavior this asymmetry invites that hurts all subs. After a general wins the main contract, it has an incentive and power to "bid shop" (use the lowest sub bid as leverage to get yet lower bids from other subs) and "bid chop" (pressure the lowest sub bidder to reduce its

bid further). All subs also have an incentive to "bid peddle": to submit nominal bids, without doing the costly research necessary to provide a reasonable estimate, and once the low-bid is known, having saved the costs of estimating work, outbid that bidder. *Pavel Enterprises, Inc.*, at 527–528.

5.   Numerous alternative legal solutions to these recurring problems might be tried. Can you think of any based on the materials we have studied, principally in Chapter One? Would the option contract provisions of Restatement (Second) of Contracts § 87(2) work? Could the firm offer provisions of Uniform Commercial Code § 2–205 be adapted to the task, at least where the sub's bid is in writing and gives some assurance of being held open? What about unilateral contract analysis contemplated by Restatement (Second) of Contracts § 45? On this and other strategies, see *Loranger Constr. Corp. v. E.F. Hauserman Co.*, 384 N.E.2d 176 (Mass. 1978).

6.   Notice Justice Traynor's judicial craftsmanship. Does he seem highly conscious of writing in the shadows of the great Learned Hand?

CHAPTER 3

PROBLEMS OF FORM CONTRACTS

■ ■ ■

This chapter considers problems that arise from many variations of standard form contracts. The contexts range from the longstanding practice of repeated use of dense legalese (called "boilerplate"), often in consumer contracts, addressing such issues as where and how disputes may be resolved, to novel problems associated with contracts formed over the Internet. Turning to the business context, we consider examples of contract formation occurring despite both parties' use of standardized forms that do not mirror each other as well as contracts found to exist even when one side is unware of the terms.

Each of these settings is problematic because, they requiring adapting contract law's traditional tools. The problems reach to deep questions of assent, as well as more patent issues such as relative bargaining power of parties and the meaning of legal language in contracts. The following materials illustrate the struggles judges often confront in establishing the parameters for boilerplate along with a selection of the diverse scholarly viewpoints attracted by so-called adhesion contracts—those peddled on a take-it-or-leave-it basis. The law and policy around this topic are subject to continued debate, as the problems of form contracts are among the most pressing in the law of modern contracts.

A. BOILERPLATE

CARNIVAL CRUISE LINES V. SHUTE
499 U.S. 585 (1991)

BLACKMUN, J.   *↱happened at sea → federal court*

In this (admiralty) case we primarily consider whether the United States Court of Appeals for the Ninth Circuit correctly refused to enforce a forum-selection clause contained in tickets issued by petitioner Carnival Cruise Lines, Inc., to respondents Eulala and Russel Shute. . . . The Shutes, through an Arlington, Wash., travel agent, purchased passage for a 7-day cruise on petitioner's ship, the *Tropicale*. Respondents paid the fare to the agent who forwarded the payment to petitioner's headquarters in Miami, Fla. Petitioner then prepared the tickets and sent them to respondents in the State of Washington. The face of each ticket, at its left-hand lower corner, contained this admonition:

SUBJECT TO CONDITIONS OF CONTRACT ON LAST PAGES IMPORTANT! PLEASE READ CONTRACT-ON LAST PAGES 1, 2, 3

The following appeared on "contract page 1" of each ticket:

TERMS AND CONDITIONS OF PASSAGE CONTRACT TICKET . . . .

    3.   (a) The acceptance of this ticket by the person or persons named hereon as passengers shall be deemed to be an acceptance and agreement by each of them of all of the terms and conditions of this Passage Contract Ticket. . . .

    8.   It is agreed by and between the passenger and the Carrier that all disputes and matters whatsoever arising under, in connection with or incident to this Contract shall be litigated, if at all, in and before a Court located in the State of Florida, U.S.A., to the exclusion of the Courts of any other state or country. *Id.,* at 16.

The last quoted paragraph is the forum-selection clause at issue.

    . . . Respondents boarded the *Tropicale* in Los Angeles, Cal. The ship sailed to Puerto Vallarta, Mexico, and then returned to Los Angeles. While the ship was in international waters off the Mexican coast, respondent Eulala Shute was injured when she slipped on a deck mat during a guided tour of the ship's galley. Respondents filed suit against petitioner in the United States District Court for the Western District of Washington, claiming that Mrs. Shute's injuries had been caused by the negligence of Carnival Cruise Lines and its employees. *Id.,* at 4.

    Petitioner moved for summary judgment, contending that the forum clause in respondents' tickets required the Shutes to bring their suit against petitioner in a court in the State of Florida. [Discussion of personal jurisdiction omitted.—Eds.]. . . . Turning to the forum-selection clause, the Court of Appeals acknowledged that a court concerned with the enforceability of such a clause must begin its analysis with *The Bremen v. Zapata Off-Shore Co., 407 U.S. 1, 92 S.Ct. 1907, 32 L.Ed.2d 513 (1972), where this Court held that forum-selection clauses, although not "historically . . . favored," are "prima facie valid." Id.,* at 9–10, 92 S.Ct., at 1913. See 897 F.2d, at 388. The appellate court concluded that the forum clause should not be enforced because it "was not freely bargained for." *Id.,* at 389. As an "independent justification" for refusing to enforce the clause, the Court of Appeals noted that there was evidence in the record to indicate that "the Shutes are physically and financially incapable of pursuing this litigation in Florida" and that the enforcement of the clause would operate to deprive them of their day in court and thereby contravene this Court's holding in *The Bremen.* 897 F.2d, at 389.

We granted certiorari to address the question whether the Court of Appeals was correct in holding that the District Court should hear respondents' tort claim against petitioner. 498 U.S. 807–808, 111 S.Ct. 39, 112 L.Ed.2d 16 (1990). Because we find the forum-selection clause to be dispositive of this question, we need not consider petitioner's constitutional argument as to personal jurisdiction. . . . [W]e do not address the question whether respondents had sufficient notice of the forum clause before entering the contract for passage. Respondents essentially have conceded that they had notice of the forum-selection provision. Additionally, the Court of Appeals evaluated the enforceability of the forum clause under the assumption, although "doubtful," that respondents could be deemed to have had knowledge of the clause. See 897 F.2d, at 389, and n. 11.

Within this context, respondents urge that the forum clause should not be enforced because, contrary to this Court's teachings in *The Bremen,* the clause was not the product of negotiation, and enforcement effectively would deprive respondents of their day in court.

Both petitioner and respondents argue vigorously that the Court's opinion in *The Bremen* governs this case, and each side purports to find ample support for its position in that opinion's broad-ranging language. This seeming paradox derives in large part from key factual differences between this case and *The Bremen,* differences that preclude an automatic and simple application of *The Bremen*'s general principles to the facts here.

In *The Bremen,* this Court addressed the enforceability of a forum-selection clause in a contract between two business corporations. An American corporation, Zapata, made a contract with Unterweser, a German corporation, for the towage of Zapata's oceangoing drilling rig from Louisiana to a point in the Adriatic Sea off the coast of Italy. The agreement provided that any dispute arising under the contract was to be resolved in the London Court of Justice. After a storm in the Gulf of Mexico seriously damaged the rig, Zapata ordered Unterweser's ship to tow the rig to Tampa, Fla., the nearest point of refuge. Thereafter, Zapata sued Unterweser in admiralty in federal court at Tampa. . . .

This Court vacated and remanded, stating that, in general, "a freely negotiated private international agreement, unaffected by fraud, undue influence, or overweening bargaining power, such as that involved here, should be given full effect." 407 U.S., at 12–13, 92 S.Ct. at 1914–1915 (footnote omitted). The Court further generalized that "in the light of present-day commercial realities and expanding international trade we conclude that the forum clause should control absent a strong showing that it should be set aside." *Id.,* at 15, 92 S.Ct., at 1916. The Court did not define precisely the circumstances that would make it unreasonable for a court to enforce a forum clause. Instead, the Court discussed a number of factors that made it reasonable to enforce the clause at issue in *The Bremen* and that, presumably, would be pertinent in any determination whether to enforce a similar clause.

. . . [T]he Court of Appeals in the present litigation took note of the foregoing "reasonableness" factors and rather automatically decided that the forum-selection clause was unenforceable because, unlike the parties in *The Bremen,* respondents are not business persons and did not negotiate the terms of the clause with petitioner. Alternatively, the Court of Appeals ruled that the clause should not be enforced because enforcement effectively would deprive respondents of an opportunity to litigate their claim against petitioner.

The Bremen concerned a "far from routine transaction between companies of two different nations contemplating the tow of an extremely costly piece of equipment from Louisiana across the Gulf of Mexico and the Atlantic Ocean, through the Mediterranean Sea to its final destination in the Adriatic Sea." *Id.,* at 13, 92 S.Ct., at 1915. These facts suggest that, even apart from the evidence of negotiation regarding the forum clause, it was entirely reasonable for the Court in *The Bremen* to have expected Unterweser and Zapata to have negotiated with care in selecting a forum for the resolution of disputes arising from their special towing contract.

In contrast, respondents' passage contract was purely routine and doubtless nearly identical to every commercial passage contract issued by petitioner and most other cruise lines. *See, e.g., Hodes v. S.N.C. Achille Lauro ed Altri-Gestione,* 858 F.2d 905, 910 (CA3 1988), cert. dism'd, 490 U.S. 1001, 109 S.Ct. 1633, 104 L.Ed.2d 149 (1989). In this context, it would be entirely unreasonable for us to assume that respondents—or any other cruise passenger—would negotiate with petitioner the terms of a forum-selection clause in an ordinary commercial cruise ticket. Common sense dictates that a ticket of this kind will be a form contract the terms of which are not subject to negotiation, and that an individual purchasing the ticket will not have bargaining parity with the cruise line. But by ignoring the crucial differences in the business contexts in which the respective contracts were executed, the Court of Appeals' analysis seems to us to have distorted somewhat this Court's holding in *The Bremen.*

In evaluating the reasonableness of the forum clause at issue in this case, we must refine the analysis of *The Bremen* to account for the realities of form passage contracts. As an initial matter, we do not adopt the Court of Appeals' determination that a nonnegotiated forum-selection clause in a form ticket contract is never enforceable simply because it is not the subject of bargaining. Including a reasonable forum clause in a form contract of this kind well may be permissible for several reasons: First, a cruise line has a special interest in limiting the fora in which it potentially could be subject to suit. Because a cruise ship typically carries passengers from many locales, it is not unlikely that a mishap on a cruise could subject the cruise line to litigation in several different fora. See *The Bremen,* 407 U.S., at 13, and n. 15, 92 S.Ct., at 1915, and n. 15; *Hodes,* 858 F.2d, at 913.

Additionally, a clause establishing *ex ante* the forum for dispute resolution has the salutary effect of dispelling any confusion about where suits arising from the contract must be brought and defended, sparing litigants the time and expense of pretrial motions to determine the correct forum and conserving judicial resources that otherwise would be devoted to deciding those motions. See *Stewart Organization,* 487 U.S., at 33, 108 S.Ct., at 2246 (concurring opinion). Finally, it stands to reason that passengers who purchase tickets containing a forum clause like that at issue in this case benefit in the form of reduced fares reflecting the savings that the cruise line enjoys by limiting the fora in which it may be sued. Cf. *Northwestern Nat. Ins. Co. v. Donovan,* 916 F.2d 372, 378 (CA7 1990).

We also do not accept the Court of Appeals' "independent justification" for its conclusion that *The Bremen* dictates that the clause should not be enforced because "[t]here is evidence in the record to indicate that the Shutes are physically and financially incapable of pursuing this litigation in Florida." 897 F.2d, at 389. . . . In the present case, Florida is not a "remote alien forum," nor—given the fact that Mrs. Shute's accident occurred off the coast of Mexico—is this dispute an essentially local one inherently more suited to resolution in the State of Washington than in Florida. In light of these distinctions, and because respondents do not claim lack of notice of the forum clause, we conclude that they have not satisfied the "heavy burden of proof," *ibid.,* required to set aside the clause on grounds of inconvenience.

It bears emphasis that forum-selection clauses contained in form passage contracts are subject to judicial scrutiny for fundamental fairness. In this case, there is no indication that petitioner set Florida as the forum in which disputes were to be resolved as a means of discouraging cruise passengers from pursuing legitimate claims. Any suggestion of such a bad-faith motive is belied by two facts: Petitioner has its principal place of business in Florida, and many of its cruises depart from and return to Florida ports. Similarly, there is no evidence that petitioner obtained respondents' accession to the forum clause by fraud or overreaching. Finally, respondents have conceded that they were given notice of the forum provision and, therefore, presumably retained the option of rejecting the contract with impunity. In the case before us, therefore, we conclude that the Court of Appeals erred in refusing to enforce the forum-selection clause.

. . . [The Court referred to a 1936 federal statute, the Limitation of Vessel Owners Liability Act, ch. 521, 49 Stat. 1480, 46 U.S.C.App. § 183c, which outlawed contractual clauses purporting to exculpate ship owners from liability for negligence.]. By its plain language, the forum-selection clause before us does not take away respondents' right to "a trial by [a] court of competent jurisdiction" and thereby contravene the explicit proscription of § 183c. Instead, the clause states specifically that actions arising out of the passage contract shall be brought "if at all," in a court "located in the State of Florida," which, plainly, is a "court of competent jurisdiction" within the meaning of the statute.

Respondents appear to acknowledge this by asserting that although the forum clause does not directly prevent the determination of claims against the cruise line, it causes plaintiffs unreasonable hardship in asserting their rights and therefore violates Congress' intended goal in enacting § 183c. . . . Because the clause before us allows for judicial resolution of claims against petitioner and does not purport to limit petitioner's liability for negligence, it does not violate § 183c. [Reversed].

STEVENS, J., dissenting:

The Court prefaces its legal analysis with a factual statement that implies that a purchaser of a Carnival Cruise Lines passenger ticket is fully and fairly notified about the existence of the choice of forum clause in the fine print on the back of the ticket. See *ante,* at 1524. Even if this implication were accurate, I would disagree with the Court's analysis. But, given the Court's preface, I begin my dissent by noting that only the most meticulous passenger is likely to become aware of the forum-selection provision. I have therefore appended to this opinion a facsimile of the relevant text, using the type size that actually appears in the ticket itself. A careful reader will find the forum-selection clause in the 8th of the 25 numbered paragraphs. [See the notes following this case for a specimen. —Eds.]

Of course, many passengers, like the respondents in this case . . . will not have an opportunity to read paragraph 8 until they have actually purchased their tickets. By this point, the passengers will already have accepted the condition set forth in paragraph 16(a), which provides that "[t]he Carrier shall not be liable to make any refund to passengers in respect of . . . tickets wholly or partly not used by a passenger." Not knowing whether or not that provision is legally enforceable, I assume that the average passenger would accept the risk of having to file suit in Florida in the event of an injury, rather than canceling—without a refund—a planned vacation at the last minute. The fact that the cruise line can reduce its litigation costs, and therefore its liability insurance premiums, by forcing this choice on its passengers does not, in my opinion, suffice to render the provision reasonable. Cf. *Steven v. Fidelity & Casualty Co. of New York,* 58 Cal.2d 862, 883, 27 Cal.Rptr. 172, 186, 377 P.2d 284, 298 (1962) (refusing to enforce limitation on liability in insurance policy because insured "must purchase the policy before he even knows its provisions").

Even if passengers received prominent notice of the forum-selection clause before they committed the cost of the cruise, I would remain persuaded that the clause was unenforceable under traditional principles of federal admiralty law and is "null and void" under the terms of Limitation of Vessel Owners Liability Act, ch. 521, 49 Stat. 1480, 46 U.S.C.App. § 183c, which was enacted in 1936 to invalidate expressly stipulations limiting shipowners' liability for negligence.

Exculpatory clauses in passenger tickets have been around for a long time. These clauses are typically the product of disparate bargaining power between the carrier and the passenger, and they undermine the strong public interest in deterring negligent conduct. For these reasons, courts long before the turn of the century consistently held such clauses unenforceable under federal admiralty law. Clauses limiting a carrier's liability or weakening the passenger's right to recover for the negligence of the carrier's employees come in a variety of forms. Complete exemptions from liability for negligence or limitations on the amount of the potential damage recovery, requirements that notice of claims be filed within an unreasonably short period of time, provisions mandating a choice of law that is favorable to the defendant in negligence cases, and forum-selection clauses are all similarly designed to put a thumb on the carrier's side of the scale of justice.

Forum-selection clauses in passenger tickets involve the intersection of two strands of traditional contract law that qualify the general rule that courts will enforce the terms of a contract as written. Pursuant to the first strand, courts traditionally have reviewed with heightened scrutiny the terms of contracts of adhesion, form contracts offered on a take-or-leave basis by a party with stronger bargaining power to a party with weaker power. Some commentators have questioned whether contracts of adhesion can justifiably be enforced at all under traditional contract theory because the adhering party generally enters into them without manifesting knowing and voluntary consent to all their terms. See, *e.g.,* Rakoff, Contracts of Adhesion: An Essay in Reconstruction, 96 Harv.L.Rev. 1173, 1179–1180 (1983); Slawson, Mass Contracts: Lawful Fraud in California, 48 S.Cal.L.Rev. 1, 12–13 (1974); K. Llewellyn, The Common Law Tradition 370–371 (1960).

The common law, recognizing that standardized form contracts account for a significant portion of all commercial agreements, has taken a less extreme position and instead subjects terms in contracts of adhesion to scrutiny for reasonableness. Judge J. Skelly Wright set out the state of the law succinctly in *Williams v. Walker-Thomas Furniture Co.,* 121

U.S.App.D.C. 315, 319–320, 350 F.2d 445, 449–450 (1965) (footnotes omitted):

> Ordinarily, one who signs an agreement without full knowledge of its terms might be held to assume the risk that he has entered a one-sided bargain. But when a party of little bargaining power, and hence little real choice, signs a commercially unreasonable contract with little or no knowledge of its terms, it is hardly likely that his consent, or even an objective manifestation of his consent, was ever given to all of the terms. In such a case the usual rule that the terms of the agreement are not to be questioned should be abandoned and the court should consider whether the terms of the contract are so unfair that enforcement should be withheld.

See also *Steven,* 58 Cal.2d, at 879–883, 27 Cal.Rptr. at 183–185, 377 P.2d, at 295–297; *Henningsen v. Bloomfield Motors, Inc.,* 32 N.J. 358, 161 A.2d 69 (1960).

The second doctrinal principle implicated by forum-selection clauses is the traditional rule that "contractual provisions, which seek to limit the place or court in which an action may . . . be brought, are invalid as contrary to public policy." . . . A forum-selection clause in a standardized passenger ticket would clearly have been unenforceable under the common law before our decision in *The Bremen,* and, in my opinion, remains unenforceable under the prevailing rule today.

The Bremen, which the Court effectively treats as controlling this case, had nothing to say about stipulations printed on the back of passenger tickets. That case involved the enforceability of a forum-selection clause in a freely negotiated international agreement between two large corporations providing for the towage of a vessel from the Gulf of Mexico to the Adriatic Sea. The Court recognized that such towage agreements had generally been held unenforceable in American courts, but held that the doctrine of those cases did not extend to commercial arrangements between parties with equal bargaining power. . . .

NOTES AND QUESTIONS

1.   The following is a specimen of the ticket involved in the case. This is from a more recent sailing of the vessel and with the paragraphs renumbered, but exhibiting similar formatting, fonts, and positioning. The original from the case is reproduced in an appendix to the dissenting opinion, as Justice Stevens noted, an excerpt that runs many pages. Justice Stevens quipped that "only the most meticulous passenger" likely would become aware of these clauses. Are these terms conspicuous? Look back to how that term was defined in *McDonald v. Mobil Coal.* Are there reasons to require a greater degree of

conspicuousness in disclaimers in employee handbooks as compared to choice of forum clauses in cruise ship passenger tickets?

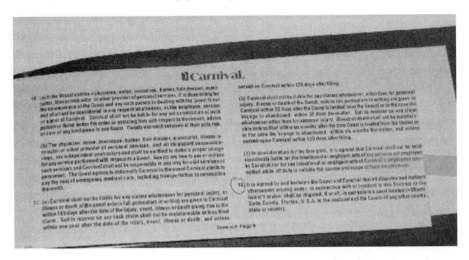

2.   List the arguments discussed by the majority and by the dissent. Which are arguments about fairness? Which are arguments about efficiency? How should the law balance these goals?

3.   The majority opinion is congruent with many of the principles favored by devotees of the economic approach to law, a school of thought dubbed law and economics. The school attempts to understand economic incentives that drive behavior and prescribe legal principles accordingly and, in contract law, often tests the appeal of legal rules in terms of their effect on overall wealth maximization or economic efficiency. While a prominent school of thought nationwide, law and economics was historically associated with the intellectual culture of the economics faculty of the University of Chicago and elaborated by Chicago law professors—and later judges—Richard Posner and Frank Easterbrook. In contract law, the general attitude is more in keeping with contract law's earliest traditions, stressing freedom of contract, private volition, and strict interpretation of contract language.

4.   The dissenting opinion is more in tune with skeptics of the law and economics school. These skeptics challenge it on many fronts, including questioning whether economic incentives dominate behavior and whether concerns in addition to efficiency deserve more weight, such as the distribution of wealth and related intuitions about fairness. In terms of broader themes in contract law, while likewise lauding freedom of contract and resulting principles, this stance may appreciate such issues as equities among parties with differing bargaining power, commercial certainty and good faith. Exemplars of this tradition include judges such as Benjamin Cardozo. The following essay encapsulates aspects of the contending positions associated with Judges Posner and Cardozo, both considered titans in the law of contracts.

LAWRENCE A. CUNNINGHAM, *CARDOZO AND POSNER: A STUDY IN CONTRACTS*
36 WM. & MARY L. REV. 1379 (1995)

Every American law student is well acquainted with the writing and thought of Benjamin N. Cardozo, the fox of American contract law. [*See* Isaiah Berlin, The Hedgehog and the Fox (1953).] For over seventy years, his opinions have formed the basis for many discussions of doctrine, method, and policy in the traditional first-year curriculum. The current generation is also becoming well acquainted with the hedgehog of American contract law—Richard A. Posner, whose opinions have been entering the domain of the core first-year curriculum in the past decade. . . .

Cardozo's judicial contributions to the law and teaching of contracts, including the good faith obligation and the doctrine of [promissory estoppel,] were achieved using a thickly textured doctrinalism involving conscious mediation amongst the competing values at stake in the law of contracts. His opinions reveal a capacious juridical framework capable of harmonizing the many contending concerns of contract law, including commercial certainty, freedom of contract, good faith, protecting the reasonable expectations of parties, and forfending interparty exploitation. Cardozo was at once master of the incremental evolution of the common law and servant of the imperative to adapt law to the needs of those it governs, evincing in his contracts opinions a fluid sense of doctrine and an animating principle of justice broadly conceived. The hallmark of his contracts opinions is balance. He was an intellectual fox.

. . . In many cases, however, Posner's views are opposed to Cardozo's, or at least in tension with them. For example, whereas Cardozo minted the implied covenant of good faith in the performance of contracts, Posner is averse to any such implication and strongly resists recognizing any obligation of good faith, even where it is imposed by statute. Posner's contracts opinions are far less textured than Cardozo's, showing a reluctance to mediate amongst the many contending values contract law has traditionally implicated and instead putting into the mix only one primary concern—efficiency through freedom of contract. Posner is an intellectual hedgehog.

Because the Posnerian framework is stricter and less capacious than [Cardozo's] framework, [a] comparison of Cardozo and Posner is primarily a study in contrasts, as a matter of doctrine, theory, and style. Contracts opinions by Posner and Cardozo resemble one another in their creativity and ingenuity, but they employ the judicial craft within very different frameworks and with distinct normative ends. Cardozo and Posner are judicial antipodes. Indeed, were Posner's contributions to the law of contracts to rise to the level of Cardozo's, many of Cardozo's contributions, both substantive and textural, would have to be jettisoned. . . .

Whether that evolution of contract law should be welcomed or thwarted ultimately depends on one's own normative views. For example, and at the risk of oversimplifying, one may prefer a conception of contract that limits itself to interests in freedom of contract and efficiency, one that presupposes that people behave, or can be made to behave, as rational economic actors and therefore prefer a Posnerian approach. Or one may prefer a conception of contract that seeks to balance values, such as good faith, fairness, or reasonable expectations, in addition to freedom of contract and efficiency and that conceives of people as socialized actors and therefore prefer [Cardozo's] approach. It should be recognized, however, that such preferences entail significant consequences for the way contract law is understood and taught and that the widespread and continued reproduction of Posner's opinions in the casebooks stands both to reflect and shape that understanding. . . .

While contract law is generally not a controversial or ideological field, the question of how much power businesses have and how much power consumers have (within their transactions as well as in society overall) does generate heated discussion. This controversy tends to center on how much government intervention or judicial oversight in the marketplace is needed. Opinions differ widely on this question. Consider the next two excerpts as counterpoints in the debate.

MARGARET JANE RADIN, *BOILERPLATE*
(2012)

Once upon a time, it was thought that "contract" referred to a bargained-for exchange transaction between two parties who each consent to the exchange. This once-upon-a-time story is the ideal of contract. The story of bargained-for exchange represents contract as it is imagined to be in a world of voluntary agreement, the world I am calling World A (for Agreement). . . . This is still how many people understand contract (with good reason). And it still animates contract theories. Contract is supposed to involve consent by each party to give up something of his or her own to obtain something he or she values more. Sally values the bicycle more than she values her $120; John values $120 more than he values his bicycle. Contract, at least in this paradigm case, is typified by a process of negotiation that results in a bargain satisfactory to both parties. The paradigm case involving negotiation is not the only kind of contract that can be valid under the basic commitment to freedom of contract; but, as we shall see, the elements of the paradigm case involving a bargain and free choice or consent are indispensable.

Once upon a time, it was also thought that when a contract is broken, there will necessarily be a remedy available to the aggrieved person. If Sally hands over her $120 but John fails to deliver the bicycle, Sally can bring John to court in a place convenient for her, and ask that John be found in breach of contract and have the court order John to make it up to Sally for his breach. Depending on the circumstances, the court will simply order John to refund Sally's money, or perhaps even to hand over the bicycle. What is important to understand is that the ideal of contract has as an important component the idea that if a contract is breached, there must be the opportunity to seek a remedy. The aggrieved party must have her day in court, and so must the party who allegedly breached. Courts, as an arm of the state, enforce contracts so that all of us may have confidence in dealing with one another. In order for the system of contract to function, there must be a viable avenue for redress of grievances in cases where the bargain fails; otherwise the trust that the ideal of contract imagines would be weakened and perhaps collapse. . . .

Alternative Legal Universes Created by Forms

. . . We are given forms to sign when we rent an automobile or an apartment, and piles of forms to sign when we buy an automobile or a house. Most of us don't read them, and most of us wouldn't understand them if we did. We are given forms to sign when we get a job, when we join a gym, when we send our kids to camp. We click "I agree" to buy products or services on the Internet, after being shown lists of fine-print terms that we don't read. We receive forms even though we don't sign them or click "I agree," such as the fine-print terms of service interior to websites, or the fine print on everything from parking lot tickets to theater tickets to sports events tickets. . . .

Arbitration clauses, choice of forum/choice of law clauses, and exculpatory clauses . . . are common components of the alternative legal universes created by firms. Most readers, I expect, are subject to one or more of them. But there are many other ways in which fine print has the effect of deleting recipients' legal rights. One common provision limits remedies for losses caused by a defective product or service to the replacement, repair, or reimbursement for the cost of the product itself, thus eliminating damages for injurious consequences of the product's failure. Another deletes ("disclaims") warranty coverage. Another says the firm will continue billing you forever for whatever you have purchased unless you notify it that you wish to terminate. . . . These are the contracts—the *purported* contracts—that belong to World B.

Standardized form contracts, when they are imposed upon consumers, have long been called "contracts of adhesion," or "take it-or-leave-it contracts," because the recipient has no choice with regard to the terms. "It's my way or the highway," says the firm to the recipient. Such paperwork is often called boilerplate, because, like the rigid metal used to construct steam boilers in the past, it cannot be altered. I have been calling boilerplate "paperwork" because "paperwork" is a neutral term, but you will have noticed that courts most often treat boilerplate as if it were a contract. The law considers boilerplate to be a method of *contract* formation. World B is the expanding universe of purported contracts that don't look or act like those of World A. World B is the world of boilerplate.

. . . Even though I know more about their legal significance than most people, I can't do anything about them, so, just like almost everyone else, I don't read them. I must, like everyone else, accept them or forego the transaction. I can't employ a financial manager for my retirement account without accepting an arbitration clause. I can't use iTunes without clicking "I agree" to its terms of service. I can't proceed with an exercise class until I've signed a form that exculpates the provider for any injury to me no matter how caused. Once I tried to tell a person presenting paperwork to me that the exculpatory clause would be unenforceable if her studio harmed me intentionally or through gross negligence rather than mere negligence. I took out a pen and offered to amend the clause, but the person presenting the form would not hear of legal niceties. It was take it or leave it.

Varieties of World B (Purported) Contracts

Here is an overview of the varieties of World B contracts we are seeing in practice. (I will stop calling them "purported" contracts, but please understand that labelling something a "contract" does not necessarily make it one.)

1.   Standardized Adhesion Contracts: of the traditional variety: An example is the parking lot ticket. . . . It's a contract of adhesion because either you "adhere" to it by taking hold of it and then driving your car into the lot, or else you don't park there. The ticket often says, "This contract limits our liability. Read it." Hardly anyone does so. The online analogue is clicking on-screen buttons to signify receipt of contractual terms. By clicking, it says, you are saying that you've read the terms and "agree" to them. It is doubtful that many people are truthful in saying this, though, because very few people read them.

2.   Offsite Terms: Refers to terms that are a part of standardized adhesion contracts but that are not stated in the document you can see. An example is the airline ticket. It says you are bound by the set of terms that make up the airline's tariff and that you can find them somewhere else—in the airline's office, perhaps, or online. Who knows what background legal rights have been given up in favor of the airline?

3. "Shrink-wrap Licenses": So called because they originated with the shrink-wrapped commercial software products that you buy in a box. The idea is that if you break the wrapper you are bound to the terms that are printed below it. By tearing cellophane you have "agreed" to a bunch of boilerplate. . .

4. "Rolling Contracts": (also called "money now, terms later"): Perhaps the earliest example of this variant is the insurance contract. The agent sells you a policy, but when the pages of fine print arrive, they contain (if you read and can understand them) a lot of exclusions and wrinkles that you didn't know about. You are still bound to the purported contract, even though you signed it *before* the terms were delivered to you. . . . A parallel example in the software world is the set of terms often called EULA ("End User License Agreement"); you see this (purported) contract when you fire up the product, which is *after* you've paid for it, not before. That is, these terms are often received under the "shrink-wrap of the second kind" procedure.

5. . . . Unwitting Contract: Most websites have a small link called something like "terms of service" (TOS). If one were to click on it, which most users don't (in fact, most probably don't even notice the link), one would see pages of boilerplate open out, telling the user that she is bound to these terms, that she has "agreed" to them simply by the act of looking at the site, and, moreover, that the owner may change the terms from time to time and that the user will then be bound by the new terms as well. This strategy has been dubbed "browsewrap." With browsewrap you are clueless unless you find and click on the link that opens it.

I am sure that most readers will recognize many of the contract varieties listed in the foregoing typology . . . It should be clear now that many interactions that are called "contracts" these days are very far from the traditional notion of a contract, the idea of bargained exchange by free choice, that still holds sway in our imaginations. Contract reality belies contract theory in many situations where consumers receive paperwork that purports to alter their legal rights. In these situations, contract theory becomes contract mythology.

Why Don't We Read Boilerplate?

Given that firms regularly use boilerplate to transport us into an alternative legal universe, why don't we read these things? Here are seven answers: (1) We wouldn't understand the terms if we did read them, so it isn't worth our time. (2) We need the product or service and have no access to a supplier that does not impose onerous clauses, so reading the terms wouldn't make any difference. (3) We are not even aware that we are becoming subject to these terms, so we don't know that there is anything to read. (4) We trust the company not to have included anything harmful. (5) We suppose that anything harmful would be unenforceable. (6) We think that the company has power over us, so that we are simply stuck with what it imposes on us. (7) Yet another reason, and an important one: we don't believe that we will ever need to exercise our background legal rights. We don't expect misfortune to befall us. . .

Boilerplate and Contract Formation

. . . Our conventional understanding of contract is at odds with this reality. Most people still think that a contract is a voluntary transaction, a consensual exchange. Indeed, contract law is itself based on the idea of free exchanges between willing parties. "Freedom of contract" is a revered ideal underlying World A, the world of voluntary exchanges, the world of Agreement. World B is another world, the world of Boilerplate. In practice some contracts reflecting voluntary exchanges between willing parties may nevertheless consist partly or wholly of a collection of form clauses, yet belong to World A. Nevertheless the archetypes of World A and World B will be useful for analysis, if only because of the large realm of purported contracts that do consist entirely of nonnegotiated boilerplate.

World B, the world of boilerplate, doesn't fit the theory, the rationale, of contract law. . . . One task . . . is to think again about whether boilerplate should be considered contractual. Indeed, I want to urge that it should not, at least not in all of its manifestations. Meanwhile, however, as long as boilerplate *is* considered contractual, as it is in our current legal system, it is regulated under contract law. Why "regulated"? Because not everything that is *called* a contract actually *is* a contract, and the law needs to be able to distinguish between those that are valid (and therefore enforceable) and those that are not. A purported contract obtained by coercion or fraud is not an enforceable contract, for example. Because boilerplate is regulated by—that is, evaluated under—contract law, those who defend boilerplate must argue that boilerplate somehow meets the requirements of contract law. Thus, they must argue that recipients somehow agree to or consent to its terms. Boilerplate is, to say the least, problematic when it comes to the issue of agreement or consent. . . .

RANDY E. BARNETT, *CONSENTING TO FORM CONTRACTS*
71 FORDHAM L. REV. 627 (2002)

There is a remarkable dissonance between contract theory and practice on the subject of form contracts. In practice, form contracts are ubiquitous. From video rentals to the sale of automobiles, form contracts are everywhere. Yet contract theorists are nothing if not suspicious of such contracts, having long ago dubbed them pejoratively "contracts of adhesion." . . . In this essay, I will identify one theoretical source of the common antipathy towards form contracts and why it is misguided. I contend that the hostility towards form contracts stems, in important part, from an implicit adoption of a promise-based conception of contractual obligation.

I shall maintain that, when one adopts (a) a consent theory of contract based not on promise but on the manifested intention to be legally bound and (b) a properly objective interpretation of this consent, form contracts can be seen as entirely legitimate—though some form terms may properly be subject to judicial scrutiny that would be inappropriate with nonform agreements. In this regard, I shall endorse the much-maligned approach of the United States Supreme Court in its decision in *Carnival Cruise Lines v. Shute*. With this account of form contracts in mind we can better appreciate the wisdom of that other maligned contracts case: *Hill v. Gateway 2000, Inc.* [excerpted below in this casebook—Eds.]

Because most terms in a form contract are rarely read, it is considered a fiction to think one has promised—either subjectively or objectively under the modern view—to perform according to a term of which the other party knows good and well one is unaware. Despite this, most contracts professors and practitioners also know that form contracts make the world go round. Psychologists tell us that the human mind will strive mightily to resolve the dissonance between two incompatible ideas. In this case, some resolve the conflict between theory and practice by rejecting form contracts because consent is lacking, while others are led to reject consent as the basis of contract and then, because consent is unnecessary, also reject form contracts in favor of government-supplied terms. By either route, then, form contracts are disdained.

[Barnett criticizes an article by Todd Rakoff that we will read, *infra*, and argues against Rakoff's suggestion that the terms in the fine print be disregarded and filled in by the courts]. . . Furthermore, the terms that will actually be imposed on the parties [by a court] are even more removed from the transaction than is a form. If anything, the problem of rational ignorance will be greatly exacerbated. Parties would no longer be weighing the probability of a suit against the cost of reading the form in front of them; they now would have to weigh this probability against the cost of hiring a lawyer to tell them what is in case law or a statute and predict, if prediction is possible, how a background rule will be applied by a future court. Surely this proposal moves an agreement much farther from the consent of the parties and towards a regime in which the legal system supplies terms that others think best.

Nevertheless, Todd Rakoff [in an excerpt below—Eds.] provided important and previously overlooked reasons why form contracts are useful and why they do not automatically implicate the same problems addressed by the doctrine of unconscionability. His unfortunate choice of terminology notwithstanding, the substance of his distinction between visible and invisible terms in forms is a highly useful one, as we shall see in the next part.

Suppose that the enforcement of private agreements is not about promising, but about manifesting consent to be legally bound. Suppose the reason why we enforce certain commitments, whether or not in the form of a promise, is because one party has manifested its consent to be legally bound to perform that commitment. According to this theory, the assent that is critical *to the issue of formation or enforceability* is not the assent to perform or refrain from performing a certain act—the promise—but the manifested assent to be legally bound to do so.

. . . [T]hink of click license agreements on web sites. When one clicks "I agree" to the terms on the box, does one usually know what one is doing? Absolutely. There is no doubt whatsoever that one is objectively manifesting one's assent to the terms in the box, whether or not one has read them. The same observation applies to signatures on form contracts. Clicking the button that says "I agree," no less than signing one's name on the dotted line indicates unambiguously: I agree to be legally bound by the terms in this agreement.

If consent to be legally bound is the basis of contractual enforcement, rather than the making of a promise, then consent to be legally bound seems to exist objectively. Even under the modem objective theory, there is no reason for the other party to believe that such subjective consent is lacking. Even if one does not want to be bound, one knows that the other party will take this conduct as indicating consent to be bound thereby.

If this sounds counterintuitive, as it will to many contracts professors, consider the following hypothetical. Suppose I say to my dearest friend, "Whatever it is you want me to do, write it down and put it into a sealed envelope, and I will do it for you." Is it categorically impossible to make such a promise? Is there something incoherent about committing oneself to perform an act the nature of which one does not know and will only learn later? To take another example, is there some reason why a soldier cannot commit himself to obey the commands of a superior (within limits perhaps), the nature of which he will only learn about some time in the future? Hardly. Are these promises *real?* I would say so and cannot think of any reason to conclude otherwise. What is true of the promises in these examples is true also of contractual consent in the case of form contracts.

If contractual enforcement is not about the promise to do or refrain from doing something, but is about legally committing oneself to perform the act described in the envelope, there is no reason, in principle, why this consent cannot be considered real. Therefore there is no reason, in principle, why such consent cannot be objectively manifested to another person. This reveals the nested nature of consent. The particular duty consented to—the promise or commitment—is nested within an overall consent to be legally bound. The consent that legitimates enforcement is the latter consent to be legally bound.

Suppose now that instead of the promise being in an unopened envelope, it is contained in an unread scroll box on a computer screen. Does this make the act of clicking "I agree" below the box any less a manifestation of consent to be bound by the unread terms therein than did the promise to perform the unknown act described in the envelope? I cannot see why. Whether or not it is a fiction to say someone is making the promise in the scroll box, it is no fiction to say that by clicking "I agree" a person is consensually committing to these (unread) promises.

True, when consenting in this manner one is running the risk of binding oneself to a promise one may regret when later learning its content. But the law does not, and should not, bar all assumptions of risk. Hard as this may be to believe, I know of people who attach waxed boards to their feet and propel themselves down slippery snow and tree covered mountains, an activity that kills or injures many people every year. Others (for fun) freely jump out of airplanes expecting their fall to be slowed by a large piece of fabric that they carry in a sack. (I am not making this up). Some ride bicycles on busy streets with automobiles whizzing past them. It seems to me that if people may legally choose to engage in such unnecessarily risky activities—and these choices are not fictions —they may legally choose to run what, to me, is the much lesser, and more necessary, risk of accepting a term in an unread agreement they may later come to regret. . . .

Does the justification for enforcing form contracts based on the existence of a manifested intention to be legally bound entail that any and every term in a form contract is enforceable? I do not think so. To begin with, as with negotiated terms, there are limits to what the obligation can be. It cannot be a commitment to violate the rights of others or (in my view) to transfer or waive an inalienable right. But the enforcement of some form terms may be subject to additional constraints that would not apply to expressly negotiated terms.

While it does manifest consent to unread terms as well as read terms, I believe there is a qualification implicit in every such manifestation of consent to be legally bound. Call it the "your-favorite-pet" qualification. If a term of the sort that Rakoff calls "invisible" (insofar as it is rational to remain ignorant of its content) specifies that in consequence of breach one must transfer custody of one's beloved dog or cat, it could surely be contended by the promisor that "while I did agree to be bound by terms I did not read, I did not agree to *that*."

. . . If, therefore, a realistic interpretation of what clicking "I agree" means is "I agree to be legally bound to (unread) terms that are not radically unexpected," then *that—and nothing more—is* what has been consented to objectively. To appreciate this better, consider the following three possible interpretations of clicking "I agree."

1. By clicking "I agree" I am expressing my intent to be bound only by the visible price and quantity terms and none of the terms in the box above. (In the case of free software, I am agreeing to nothing whatsoever when I click "I agree" though I know that the other party does not wish me to use the software without agreeing to these terms).

2. By clicking "I agree" I am expressing my intent to be bound by any term that is in the box above no matter how unexpected such a term may be.

3. By clicking "I agree" I am expressing my intent to be bound by the terms I am likely to have read (whether or not I have done so) and also by those unread terms in the agreement above that I am not likely to have read but that do not exceed some bound of reasonableness.

. . . If option 3 is the most likely meaning of clicking "I agree," as I think it is, then two things follow. First, in Rakoff's terminology, "invisible" terms that are unlikely to be read, as well as "visible" terms, can and should be enforced. Second, "invisible" terms that are beyond the pale should not be enforced unless they are brought to the attention of the other party who manifests a separate agreement to them. While option 3 does, therefore, require judicial scrutiny, it requires much less judicial scrutiny than option 1 (the option preferred by Rakoff, and probably by most contracts scholars) which permits courts to provide all the terms of the agreement beyond the few that are visible. . .

Option 3 was the approach taken by the Supreme Court in *Carnival Cruise Lines v. Shute*, a case involving a forum selection clause in a form contract on the back of a cruise ticket. While rejecting the proposition that a non-negotiated forum-selection clause is never enforceable simply because it is non-negotiated, the Court emphasized that such "clauses contained in form passage contracts are subject to judicial scrutiny for fundamental fairness." In essence, the Court rejected options 1 and 2 in favor of option 3. "Fundamental fairness" can be viewed as a surrogate for highly unexpected terms. Nobody expects the Spanish Inquisition.

NOTES AND QUESTIONS

1. What are the major points and arguments that Professors Radin and Barnett advance? Which has the most resonance for you and your own experience? For example, what is the most objectionable term you have ever seen in a form contract? How might each professor address that clause?

2. If you believe in one view more than another, play "devil's advocate" for a moment. What problems or gaps do you see in each of the arguments?

PROBLEM: THE HIP HOTEL

The Hip Hotel was originally an estate built by the Vanderbilts and Rockefellers. Recently, it has been renovated and restored, and hosts lavish weddings. The Hip Hotel posted this policy on its website:

> Please know that despite the fact that wedding couples love the Hip Hotel and our estate, your friends and families may not. If you have booked the Hip Hotel for a wedding or other type of event anywhere in the region and given us a deposit of any kind for guests to stay at the Hip Hotel there will be a $500 fine that will be deducted from your deposit for every negative review of the Hip Hotel placed on any Internet site by anyone in your party. If you stay here to attend a wedding anywhere in the area and leave us a negative review on any Internet site you agree to a $500 fine for each negative review. The Hip Hotel agrees to refund your money if the negative review is taken down.

1.   How would Professor Radin analyze the Hip Hotel's policy?

2.   How would Professor Barnett analyze the policy?

3.   Would you stay at the Hip Hotel? If not, why not? How might the market take care of the contract terms?

TODD D. RAKOFF, *CONTRACTS OF ADHESION: AN ESSAY IN RECONSTRUCTION*
96 HARVARD L. REV. 1173 (1983)

. . . A possible, perhaps common response for consumers is to concentrate on business reputation in selecting the firms with which they will deal. They consider, for example, a seller's apparent willingness to take back unsatisfactory merchandise, or an insurance company's reputation for settling claims without requiring extensive documentation or hiding behind "technical" clauses. . . . This emphasis on practice rather than terms is consistent with, and perhaps based on, an assumption that a firm's routine will often be more favorable to the adherent than the form document would require. Such an assumption may well be valid, because businessmen concerned with fostering goodwill do not always stand on a document that was from the beginning overdrafted by lawyers. Nevertheless, the adherent's recourse is now based solely on the willingness of the drafting party to process a dispute in a routine and reasonable way. The discretion of the organization has taken the place of rights enforceable by law. . .

Contract law has long been recognized as one of the most powerful statements of the nature of freedom in our society. The enforcement of contracts of adhesion certainly liberates drafting parties from legal restraints. At the same time, however, exploitation of that freedom leads to the imposition of terms on adherents. We must consider what approach to contracts of adhesion most nearly comports with the meaning and demands of freedom in modem conditions. In an earlier age, the quest for contractual freedom formed part of the historical movement by which the modern market economy grew and, often with the aid of governmental power, replaced a social order organized substantially by status and rife with legal and customary restrictions on the power to contract.

In the legal discourse of the past century or so, however, "freedom of contract" has had a much narrower and somewhat different meaning. Contract law, and the other fields of private law, are presumed adequate to prevent social coercion in the now-established market economy. The aid of the state is no longer needed to clear away the rubble of prior legal orders. "Freedom of contract" now consists in the absence of governmental meddling except when a substantial public policy justifies that intervention. It is defined in terms of the separation of the market and the state, private and public law; at its fullest reach, it is the doctrine of laissez faire.

. . . Of course, the realistic alternative to the drafter's term is not a term chosen by the individual adherent, or even by adherents as a class; a solution will be imposed by the law if not by the drafter. Compared, however, to the drafters of forms, judges, legislators, and administrative officials are impartial. They fill roles that encourage them to take a broader view of the common good. Legislators, at least, are subject to popular political control—and the decisions of administrators and judges, ultimately, to legislators. If government is at all legitimate, it is legitimate for the purpose of framing generally applicable legal rules. That cannot be said of the form draftsman.

[O]nly some of the terms contained within a standard form contract will embody the evils associated with their use. The next step, therefore, is to distinguish the form terms that are usually innocuous from those that tend to be abused even in a competitive market. The legal validity of the former set should be determined by applying the "ordinary" rules of contract law; the validity of the latter set, by applying the principle that such terms ought not to be enforced without affirmative justification.

In language an adherent might use, we must separate the "visible" terms of the contract from the "invisible" ones. Bargained terms are, of course, visible; but a term does not become invisible merely because it was presented by the drafting party on a take-it-or-leave-it basis. If we follow the dynamics of the practice we have investigated, we must also include within the set of visible terms those for which a large proportion of adherents (although not necessarily all) may be expected to have shopped; for bargaining is not essential to protect adherents as long as shopping concerning the particular term takes place. Considered by themselves, then, the visible terms of a contract of adhesion are most often those that would constitute the entire explicit contents of a very simple ordinary contract, with the price term (dickered or not) being the paradigmatic example. The invisible terms are, quite simply, all the rest.

Of course, distinguishing between the visible and invisible terms may not be a simple task. Although it is not especially difficult to identify the bargained terms in any concrete case, deciding which terms are to be considered shopped is much harder. Whether the particular adherent before the court actually shopped is not dispositive, for only when adherents in general read, understand, and shop for alternative terms do the evils associated with invisible terms disappear. Thus, the history of the actions of the parties—the most common stuff of legal proof— is not a sufficient guide; a court must consider the practices of adherents as a class.

At first blush, the task may seem hopelessly formidable. But many common legal standards assume that similar knowledge concerning social practices is accessible and manageable. "Reasonable men," "reasonable reliance," and "reasonable disclosure" simply do not exist in a social vacuum. . . . Thus, developing and applying a "customary shopper" standard is a problem of the sort typically thought fit for legal resolution. The answer, it is true, will turn in part on an appreciation of current ordinary practice that is not based on courtroom evidence, and in part— especially in changing circumstances—on a sense of what would be reasonable practice.

But these are questions informed by everyday experience; as long as any unusual facts can be introduced as evidence, there seems to be no reason to fear oversimplified or insensitive categorization. Some difficulty may arise in fields in which shopping practices are rapidly changing, perhaps under the impact of advertising. Because the purpose of demonstrating that a term is visible is to make the term more likely to be binding, it may well make sense to put the burden of persuasion on the form drafter to show that shopping practices have changed, or that sales practices have shifted to such an extent that new shopping practices are reasonable.

In the court's consideration of what constitutes the "customary shopper," the type of market will of course be relevant. For example, in commercial markets in which the adherents are typically businesses, it may well be found that a greater number of terms are visible. It is often thought—and courts sometimes assert—that doctrines concerning contracts of adhesion are only for consumers, in the popular sense of that term, and that any contract entered into by a sophisticated business should be enforced down the line. In evaluating that assertion, however, we must recognize that much turns on what constitutes "sophistication" in the matter at hand. Present law certainly does not say that only consumers, and never businesses, can take advantage of the new doctrines that temper the traditional rules. And many of the opinions that deny relief to commercial adherents do not rely on any such broad principle.

Rather, they are at pains to point out that the adherent was represented by a person likely to be knowledgeable about the types of documents used or the problems likely to arise, or that the deal was sufficiently large to make it worthwhile for the adhering party to become knowledgeable concerning the particular clause at issue. These judicial statements may overemphasize the circumstances of the case at hand, as contrasted with the shopping behavior of adherents in general, but they illustrate how the proposed analysis naturally supports the intuitive idea that deals between commercial parties should be upheld more often than consumer transactions, even if the terms appear on form documents. Commercial parties with greater expertise, and with more at stake in individual deals, can reasonably be expected to shop or bargain for a greater number of terms. When this rationale is not applicable, deals between businesses ought not to be treated differently.

The concept of the "customary shopper," as applied to consumers or to businesses, recognizes that it is not only common, but also reasonable in light of the institutional dynamics for adherents to shop only some of the terms of a prospective transaction. It is thus at odds with the traditional conceptions underlying the imposition of a "duty to read," and with some of the more recent doctrinal formulations that retain traces of that approach. For example, courts sometimes state that one of the factors helpful, or perhaps necessary, in showing that the term at issue is adhesive, is proof that no other drafting party in the same industry was offering a more favorable corresponding term. The point, presumably, is to show what would have happened had the adherent shopped for a better deal. If, however, it would be unreasonable for adherents to shop the term in question, the doctrine taxes the adhering party with the hypothetical consequences of what would have been unreasonable behavior. The asserted relevance of the inquiry depends on the erroneous assumption that the practice of using contracts of adhesion, far from having any internal logic, creates problems only when coupled with an independent distortion of the marketplace.

In most cases, the terms that a drafting party stipulates to fill in the transaction type will be invisible and hence, under the proposed analysis, presumptively unenforceable. If nothing further appears, the case should be decided by application of background law. But even if the drafting party tries to show that an invisible term should be upheld, the court cannot evaluate that showing without determining how the case would come out absent the form clause; for the showing must be particularized, and the degree of deviance from the background rule as well as the reasons supporting both the background and form terms would appear always to be relevant. Therefore, before the invisible terms can be judged, the background law and its application to the particular case must be known.

It is a routine task—not necessarily effortless, but often shouldered—for the legal system to construct the implied term applicable to a particular facet of a given type of transaction. Case law principles, statutory and administrative sources, and appropriate custom and practice furnish the building materials. In many situations, the basic outline of the implied term already exists in the law, either in the form of a generally applicable norm or as a term routinely added to simple negotiated transactions of the given type. In those cases, all that is needed is application of the rule to the particular circumstances, considered apart from the existence of a form term on point.

Nevertheless, form terms come already spelled out and applied to particular transactions. One might contend that the present proposal, if it requires such constant reference to background law, will so increase the burden of litigation for the judiciary and parties alike that it will not be worth the effort. Decision on the basis of the presumed validity of the form term might be thought to save an extended inquiry into precedent, and especially into trade usage and commercial circumstance. Moreover, one might assert that it is easier in a motion proceeding to rule on the enforceability of a form term than on the applicability of a rule of law, and therefore that the present proposal will increase the need for going to trial.

. . . If the applicable background law, once it has been determined, yields the same result as the form term, the court ought to render judgment on the basis of the legally implied rule alone and treat the form term as an irrelevancy. Exclusive reliance on the background rule has two symbolic but important purposes. First, enforcement of an invisible term, even when justified, represents acquiescence by the law in the imposition of terms on adherents. When application of the rules provided by legitimate governmental authority will give the same result, no such acquiescence should even be considered. Second, the approach taken in litigated cases becomes part of the basis on which many other claims will be abandoned, settled, or mediated. The judicial nod at the drafting party's "freedom of contract" is not harmless, even if nothing in the case turns on it. Present case law is already rife with general pronouncements favoring form draftsmen, pronouncements that when put to the test turn out to have been overstated. If the basic presumption of the law has been altered, a marked shift in approach is particularly desirable to signal the change.

If the form term differs from the legally implied term in a way that would alter the outcome of the case, it is still possible that decision should rest solely on the force of background law. There have always been rules of law beyond the reach of even the most completely dickered contract. Prohibitions on willfully harmful or grossly negligent behavior are traditional examples. Attempts to circumvent these norms are "void as against public policy." The modern cases holding "due-on-sale" clauses in mortgages void as unreasonable restraints on alienation take the same form.

However, because the use of contracts of adhesion represents a distinct social institution not adequately encapsulated by the difference between "public" policy and "private" contract, one must go beyond these generally applicable notions. That a particular background rule can be varied by a dickered term does not imply that it can be altered by a form; accordingly, it is not sufficient to assess only the degree of importance of the substantive rule in comparison to the force of a negotiated agreement. The question— or better, questions—of freedom as applied specifically to contracts of adhesion must also be addressed.

NOTES AND QUESTIONS

1. Professor Rakoff's article remains a classic in the critique of adhesion contracts. How do you evaluate his proposal for reform?

2. Many proposals for reform have been made over the years. Scholars have proposed a one-page limit and standard font sizes on forms; short rating systems, similar to the caloric and nutritional information on foods; and websites that will allow for rating terms. *See* Cheryl B. Preston, *"Please Note: You Have Waived Everything": Can Reliance Redeem Online Contracts?*, 64 AMERICAN U. L. REV. 535, 581 (2015). Some have also suggested that the United States could follow the rules in other nations, which have a separate and distinct law only for consumer transactions, which helps to level the power imbalances. *See* James R. Maxeiner, *Standard-Terms Contracting in the Global Electronic Age: European Alternatives*, 28 YALE J. INT'L L. 109 (2003). What are the strengths and weaknesses of these approaches?

3. To date, none of the proposals for reform of adhesion contracts has taken hold. Why do you think this might be?

B. ONLINE CONTRACTING

The law continues its long-standing struggle to identify what promises should be enforced as contracts and how mutual assent is manifested. This issue is arising in new and unexpected ways, as technology, computers, and the Internet change how people communicate and participate in social activities. Some of these issues are intertwined with the issues of standard form adhesion contracts that we examined previously.

The offer, acceptance, and consideration that are the elements of contract draw us back to the original, overarching concept that we started with, mutual assent. For a moment, let's consider the history of the objective and subjective notions of assent. The subjective test was illustrated by the venerable 1860s case of the *Peerless* ship. *See Raffles v.*

Wichelhaus, 2 Hurl. & C. 906, 159 Eng. Rep. 375 (English Court of Exchequer 1864). This celebrated case concerned the purchase of cotton. The buyer and seller agreed that the cotton would be delivered to Liverpool from Bombay on a ship named *Peerless*. Alas, neither party understood that there were (ironically) numerous ships named *Peerless* plying that route. As a result, each thought the cotton was to be delivered on a different *Peerless*. The error was pivotal.

In that era, the identity of a ship determined its arrival time, which in turn determined the value of goods on board. The market values of cotton were fluctuating wildly because of the cotton shortage occurring as a result of the American Civil War. Although outward manifestations of assent suggested mutual assent, subjective knowledge and intent differed. For that reason, the *Peerless* court held that the parties had not formed a contract.

Subjective manifestations are somewhat perilous, however, because people could sign contracts, exhibiting outward manifestations of intent, yet maintain a hidden intent not to be bound. If the deal turned out well, a party could insist they outwardly and inwardly intended a deal and uphold it; if it turned out poorly, a party could cite their inward intent not to be bound and escape a losing contract. *See Lucy v. Zehmer*. Thus, over the years since Peerless, courts gradually shifted to look at outward manifestations. But too much focus on objective manifestations can be perilous too, as too much emphasis on outward manifestation might hold people to bargains that they did not intend. As a result, contemporary judges use a synthesis of objective and subjective assent, but with outward manifestation the primary determinant.

In the next case, consider how the venerable principle of objective manifestation of assent can be applied to Internet transactions. Note that two cases that the court discusses—*ProCD, Inc. v. Zeidenberg* and *Hill v. Gateway*—are excerpted in Section D below.

SPECHT V. NETSCAPE COMMUNICATIONS CORP.

306 F.3d 17 (2d Cir. 2002)

SOTOMAYOR, J.

This is an appeal from a judgment of the Southern District of New York denying a motion by defendants-appellants Netscape Communications Corporation and its corporate parent, America Online, Inc. (collectively, "defendants" or "Netscape"), to compel arbitration and to stay court proceedings. In order to resolve the central question of arbitrability presented here, we must address issues of contract formation in cyberspace. Principally, we are asked to determine whether plaintiffs-appellees ("plaintiffs"), by acting upon defendants' invitation to download free software made available on defendants' webpage, agreed to be bound by the software's license terms (which included the arbitration clause at issue), even though plaintiffs could not have learned of the existence of those terms unless, prior to executing the download, they had scrolled down the webpage to a screen located below the download button.

We agree with the district court that a reasonably prudent Internet user in circumstances such as these would not have known or learned of the existence of the license terms before responding to defendants' invitation to download the free software, and that defendants therefore did not provide reasonable notice of the license terms. In consequence, plaintiffs' bare act of downloading the software did not unambiguously manifest assent to the arbitration provision contained in the license terms. . . . We therefore affirm the district court's denial of defendants' motion to compel arbitration and to stay court proceedings.

. . . [P]laintiffs alleged that, unknown to them, their use of SmartDownload transmitted to defendants private information about plaintiffs' downloading of files from the Internet, thereby effecting an electronic surveillance of their online activities in violation of two federal statutes, the Electronic Communications Privacy Act, 18 U.S.C. §§ 2510 *et seq.*, and the Computer Fraud and Abuse Act, 18 U.S.C. § 1030.

Specifically, plaintiffs alleged that when they first used Netscape's Communicator—a software program that permits Internet browsing—the program created and stored on each of their computer hard drives a small text file known as a "cookie" that functioned "as a kind of electronic identification tag for future communications" between their computers and Netscape. Plaintiffs further alleged that when they installed SmartDownload—a separate software "plug-in" that served to enhance Communicator's browsing capabilities—SmartDownload created and stored on their computer hard drives another string of characters, known as a "Key," which similarly functioned as an identification tag in future communications with Netscape. According to the complaints in this case, . . . [t]hese processes, plaintiffs claim, constituted unlawful "eavesdropping" on users of Netscape's software products as well as on Internet websites from which users employing SmartDownload downloaded files.

In the time period relevant to this litigation, Netscape offered on its website various software programs, including Communicator and SmartDownload, which visitors to the site were invited to obtain free of charge. It is undisputed that five of the six named plaintiffs . . . downloaded Communicator from the Netscape website. These plaintiffs acknowledge that when they proceeded to initiate installation of Communicator, they were automatically shown a scrollable text of that program's license agreement and were not permitted to complete the installation until they had clicked on a "Yes" button to indicate that they accepted all the license terms.[4] If a user attempted to install Communicator without clicking "Yes," the installation would be aborted. All five named user plaintiffs expressly agreed to Communicator's license terms by clicking "Yes." The Communicator license agreement that these plaintiffs saw made no mention of SmartDownload or other plug-in programs, and stated that "[t]hese terms apply to Netscape Communicator and Netscape Navigator" and that "all disputes relating to this Agreement (excepting any dispute relating to intellectual property rights)" are subject to "binding arbitration in Santa Clara County, California."

. . . Had plaintiffs scrolled down instead of acting on defendants' invitation to click on the "Download" button, they would have encountered the following invitation: "Please review and agree to the terms of the *Netscape SmartDownload software license agreement* before downloading and using the software." Plaintiffs . . . averred in their affidavits that they never saw this reference to the SmartDownload license agreement when they clicked on the "Download" button. . . . Even for a user who, unlike plaintiffs, did happen to scroll down past the download button, SmartDownload's license terms would not have been immediately displayed in the manner of Communicator's clickwrapped terms. . . .

In the district court, defendants moved to compel arbitration and to stay court proceedings pursuant to the Federal Arbitration Act ("FAA"), 9 U.S.C. § 4, arguing that the disputes reflected in the complaints, like any other dispute relating to the SmartDownload license agreement, are subject to the arbitration clause contained in that agreement. Finding that Netscape's webpage, unlike typical examples of clickwrap, neither adequately alerted users to the existence of SmartDownload's license terms nor required users unambiguously to manifest assent to those terms as a condition of downloading the product, the court held that the user plaintiffs had not entered into the SmartDownload license agreement. *Specht,* 150 F.Supp.2d at 595–96.

The district court also ruled that the separate license agreement governing use of Communicator, even though the user plaintiffs had

---

[4]   This kind of online software license agreement has come to be known as "clickwrap" (by analogy to "shrinkwrap," used in the licensing of tangible forms of software sold in packages) because it "presents the user with a message on his or her computer screen, requiring that the user manifest his or her assent to the terms of the license agreement by clicking on an icon. The product cannot be obtained or used unless and until the icon is clicked." Specht, 150 F.Supp.2d at 593–94 (footnote omitted). Just as breaking the shrinkwrap seal and using the enclosed computer program after encountering notice of the existence of governing license terms has been deemed by some courts to constitute assent to those terms in the context of tangible software, see, e.g., ProCD, Inc. v. Zeidenberg, 86 F.3d 1447, 1451 (7th Cir.1996), so clicking on a webpage's clickwrap button after receiving notice of the existence of license terms has been held by some courts to manifest an Internet user's assent to terms governing the use of downloadable intangible software, see, e.g., Hotmail Corp. v. Van$ Money Pie Inc., 47 U.S.P.Q.2d 1020, 1025 (N.D.Cal.1998).

assented to its terms, involved an independent transaction that made no mention of SmartDownload and so did not bind plaintiffs to arbitrate their claims relating to SmartDownload. *Id.* at 596. . . .

[The district court refused the Defendants' request for arbitration, concluding that users were not adequately alerted users to the existence of SmartDownload's license terms, and thus had not entered into the SmartDownload license agreement].

[U]pon the record assembled, a fact-finder could not reasonably find that defendants prevailed in showing that any of the user plaintiffs had entered into an agreement on defendants' license terms. . . . In sum, we conclude that the district court properly decided the question of reasonable notice and objective manifestation of assent as a matter of law on the record before it, and we decline defendants' request to remand for a full trial on that question. . . .

Whether governed by the common law or by Article 2 of the Uniform Commercial Code ("UCC"), a transaction, in order to be a contract, requires a manifestation of agreement between the parties. *See Windsor Mills, Inc. v. Collins & Aikman Corp.,* 25 Cal.App.3d 987, 991, 101 Cal.Rptr. 347, 350 (1972) ("[C]onsent to, or acceptance of, the arbitration provision [is] necessary to create an agreement to arbitrate."); *see also* Cal. Com.Code § 2204(1) ("A contract for sale of goods may be made in any manner sufficient to show agreement, including conduct by both parties which recognizes the existence of such a contract.").[13]

Mutual manifestation of assent, whether by written or spoken word or by conduct, is the touchstone of contract. *Binder v. Aetna Life Ins. Co.,* 75 Cal.App.4th 832, 848, 89 Cal.Rptr.2d 540, 551 (1999); *cf.* Restatement (Second) of Contracts § 19(2) (1981) ("The conduct of a party is not effective as a manifestation of his assent unless he intends to engage in the conduct and knows or has reason to know that the other party may infer from his conduct that he assents.").

Although an onlooker observing the disputed transactions in this case would have seen each of the user plaintiffs click on the SmartDownload "Download" button, *see Cedars Sinai Med. Ctr. v. Mid-West Nat'l Life Ins. Co.,* 118 F.Supp.2d 1002, 1008 (C.D.Cal.2000) ("In California, a party's intent to contract is judged objectively, by the party's outward manifestation of consent."), a consumer's clicking on a download button does not communicate assent to contractual terms if the offer did not make clear to the consumer that clicking on the download button would signify assent to those terms, *see Windsor Mills,* 25 Cal.App.3d at 992, 101

---

[13] We need not decide today whether UCC Article 2 applies to Internet transactions in downloadable products. The district court's analysis and the parties' arguments on appeal show that, for present purposes, there is no essential difference between UCC Article 2 and the common law of contracts. We therefore apply the common law, with exceptions as noted.

Cal.Rptr. at 351 ("[W]hen the offeree does not know that a proposal has been made to him this objective standard does not apply."). California's common law is clear that "an offeree, regardless of apparent manifestation of his consent, is not bound by inconspicuous contractual provisions of which he is unaware, contained in a document whose contractual nature is not obvious." *Id.; see also Marin Storage & Trucking, Inc. v. Benco Contracting & Eng'g, Inc.,* 89 Cal.App.4th 1042, 1049, 107 Cal.Rptr.2d 645, 651 (2001) (same).

Arbitration agreements are no exception to the requirement of manifestation of assent. "This principle of knowing consent applies with particular force to provisions for arbitration." *Windsor Mills,* 101 Cal.Rptr. at 351. Clarity and conspicuousness of arbitration terms are important in securing informed assent. "If a party wishes to bind in writing another to an agreement to arbitrate future disputes, such purpose should be accomplished in a way that each party to the arrangement will fully and clearly comprehend that the agreement to arbitrate exists and binds the parties thereto." *Commercial Factors Corp. v. Kurtzman Bros.,* 131 Cal.App.2d 133, 134–35, 280 P.2d 146, 147–48 (1955) (internal quotation marks omitted). Thus, California contract law measures assent by an objective standard that takes into account both what the offeree said, wrote, or did and the transactional context in which the offeree verbalized or acted. . . .

Defendants argue that plaintiffs must be held to a standard of reasonable prudence and that, because notice of the existence of SmartDownload license terms was on the next scrollable screen, plaintiffs were on "inquiry notice" of those terms.[14] We disagree with the proposition that a reasonably prudent offeree in plaintiffs' position would necessarily have known or learned of the existence of the SmartDownload license agreement prior to acting, so that plaintiffs may be held to have assented to that agreement with constructive notice of its terms. *See* Cal. Civ.Code § 1589 ("A voluntary acceptance of the benefit of a transaction is equivalent to a consent to all the obligations arising from it, so far as the facts are known, or ought to be known, to the person accepting."). It is true that "[a] party cannot avoid the terms of a contract on the ground that he or she failed to read it before signing." *Marin Storage & Trucking,* 89 Cal.App.4th at 1049, 107 Cal.Rptr.2d at 651. But courts are quick to add: "An exception to this general rule exists when the writing does not appear to be a contract and the terms are not called to the attention of the recipient. In such a case, no contract is formed with respect to the undisclosed term." . . .

Most of the cases cited by defendants in support of their inquiry-notice argument are drawn from the world of paper contracting. . . . *Walker v.*

---

[14] "Inquiry notice" is "actual notice of circumstances sufficient to put a prudent man upon inquiry." Cal. State Auto. Ass'n Inter-Ins. Bureau v. Barrett Garages, Inc., 257 Cal.App.2d 71, 64 Cal.Rptr. 699, 703 (Cal.Ct.App.1967) (internal quotation marks omitted).

Carnival Cruise Lines, 63 F.Supp.2d 1083, 1089 (N.D.Cal.1999) (under California and federal law, "conspicuous notice" directing the attention of parties to existence of contract terms renders terms binding) (quotation marks omitted); *Shacket v. Roger Smith Aircraft Sales, Inc.,* 651 F.Supp. 675, 691 (N.D.Ill.1986) (constructive notice found where "minimal investigation" would have revealed facts to offeree).

As the foregoing cases suggest, receipt of a physical document containing contract terms or notice thereof is frequently deemed, in the world of paper transactions, a sufficient circumstance to place the offeree on inquiry notice of those terms. "Every person who has actual notice of circumstances sufficient to put a prudent man upon inquiry as to a particular fact, has constructive notice of the fact itself in all cases in which, by prosecuting such inquiry, he might have learned such fact." Cal. Civ.Code § 19. These principles apply equally to the emergent world of online product delivery, pop-up screens, hyperlinked pages, clickwrap licensing, scrollable documents, and urgent admonitions to "Download Now!". What plaintiffs saw when they were being invited by defendants to download this fast, free plug-in called SmartDownload was a screen containing praise for the product and, at the very bottom of the screen, a "Download" button. Defendants argue that under the principles set forth in the cases cited above, a "fair and prudent person using ordinary care" would have been on inquiry notice of SmartDownload's license terms. *Shacket,* 651 F.Supp. at 690.

We are not persuaded that a reasonably prudent offeree in these circumstances would have known of the existence of license terms. Plaintiffs were responding to an offer that did not carry an immediately visible notice of the existence of license terms or require unambiguous manifestation of assent to those terms. Thus, plaintiffs' "apparent manifestation of . . . consent" was to terms "contained in a document whose contractual nature [was] not obvious." *Windsor Mills,* 25 Cal.App.3d at 992, 101 Cal.Rptr. at 351. Moreover, the fact that, given the position of the scroll bar on their computer screens, plaintiffs may have been aware that an unexplored portion of the Netscape webpage remained below the download button does not mean that they reasonably should have concluded that this portion contained a notice of license terms. In their deposition testimony, plaintiffs variously stated that they used the scroll bar "[o]nly if there is something that I feel I need to see that is on-that is off the page," or that the elevated position of the scroll bar suggested the presence of "mere[ ] formalities, standard lower banner links" or "that the page is bigger than what I can see." Plaintiffs testified, and defendants did not refute, that plaintiffs were in fact unaware that defendants intended to attach license terms to the use of SmartDownload.

We conclude that in circumstances such as these, where consumers are urged to download free software at the immediate click of a button, a reference to the existence of license terms on a submerged screen is not sufficient to place consumers on inquiry or constructive notice of those terms. The SmartDownload webpage screen was "printed in such a manner that it tended to conceal the fact that it was an express acceptance of [Netscape's] rules and regulations." *Larrus,* 266 P.2d at 147. Internet users may have, as defendants put it, "as much time as they need[ ]" to scroll through multiple screens on a webpage, but there is no reason to assume that viewers will scroll down to subsequent screens simply because screens are there. When products are "free" and users are invited to download them in the absence of reasonably conspicuous notice that they are about to bind themselves to contract terms, the transactional circumstances cannot be fully analogized to those in the paper world of arm's-length bargaining. In the next two sections, we discuss case law and other legal authorities that have addressed the circumstances of computer sales, software licensing, and online transacting. Those authorities tend strongly to support our conclusion that plaintiffs did not manifest assent to SmartDownload's license terms. . . .

Defendants cite certain well-known cases involving shrinkwrap licensing and related commercial practices in support of their contention that plaintiffs became bound by the SmartDownload license terms by virtue of inquiry notice. For example, in *Hill v. Gateway 2000, Inc.,* 105 F.3d 1147 (7th Cir.1997), the Seventh Circuit held that where a purchaser had ordered a computer over the telephone, received the order in a shipped box containing the computer along with printed contract terms, and did not return the computer within the thirty days required by the terms, the purchaser was bound by the contract. *Id.* at 1148–49. In *ProCD, Inc. v. Zeidenberg,* the same court held that where an individual purchased software in a box containing license terms which were displayed on the computer screen every time the user executed the software program, the user had sufficient opportunity to review the terms and to return the software, and so was contractually bound after retaining the product. *ProCD,* . . .

These cases do not help defendants. To the extent that they hold that the purchaser of a computer or tangible software is contractually bound after failing to object to printed license terms provided with the product, *Hill* [does] not differ markedly from the cases involving traditional paper contracting discussed in the previous section. Insofar as the purchaser in *ProCD* was confronted with conspicuous, mandatory license terms every time he ran the software on his computer, that case actually undermines defendants' contention that downloading in the absence of conspicuous terms is an act that binds plaintiffs to those terms. . . . In sum, the foregoing cases are clearly distinguishable from the facts of the present action. . . .

Cases in which courts have found contracts arising from Internet use do not assist defendants, because in those circumstances there was much clearer notice than in the present case that a user's act would manifest assent to contract terms. *See, e.g., Hotmail Corp. v. Van$ Money Pie Inc.,* 47 U.S.P.Q.2d 1020, 1025 (N.D.Cal.1998) (granting preliminary injunction based in part on breach of "Terms of Service" agreement, to which defendants had assented); . . . ; *Caspi v. Microsoft Network, L.L.C.,* 323 N.J.Super. 118, 732 A.2d 528, 530, 532–33 (N.J.Super.Ct.App.Div.1999) (upholding forum selection clause where subscribers to online software were required to review license terms in scrollable window and to click "I Agree" or "I Don't Agree") . . .

After reviewing the California common law and other relevant legal authority, we conclude that under the circumstances here, plaintiffs' downloading of SmartDownload did not constitute acceptance of defendants' license terms. Reasonably conspicuous notice of the existence of contract terms and unambiguous manifestation of assent to those terms by consumers are essential if electronic bargaining is to have integrity and credibility. We hold that a reasonably prudent offeree in plaintiffs' position would not have known or learned, prior to acting on the invitation to download, of the reference to SmartDownload's license terms hidden below the "Download" button on the next screen. We affirm the district court's conclusion that the user plaintiffs . . . are not bound by the arbitration clause contained in those terms. . . .

NOTES AND QUESTIONS

1.   What is the role of conspicuousness in contract formation? Justice Sotomayor notes a general rule, known as the duty to read, that people are bound to the terms of their contracts even if they did not read them; she also cites an exception for writings that do not appear to be contracts, in which case such terms must be conspicuous to be binding. Compare this with *McDonald v. Mobil Coal*, where a document that appeared to be contractual would be binding, unless containing a conspicuous disclaimer of legal liability.

2.   The *Specht* decision avoids deciding whether the UCC or the common law applies to downloadable programs on the Internet. Does it matter (in a legal sense) whether the UCC or the common law applies? Should it matter? We will examine this question in further depth in the next part of the chapter.

3.   Arbitration is a private alternative to litigation that dispenses with many aspects of civil procedure. It often includes an arbitrator instead of a jury; abbreviated discovery and hearings; no public explanation of the reasons for a ruling; and no or limited rights to appeal. When arbitration emerged as a serious alternative to litigation in the early 20th century, many judges were skeptical about the usurpation of the judicial function. That prompted Congress to pass the Federal Arbitration of 1925 to require that contracts to arbitrate be treated as are all other contracts. Since passage, and especially in

recent decades, there has been increased recognition of the validity of arbitration clauses, with many judges seeming to regard arbitration as superior to adjudication. *See* Lawrence A. Cunningham, *Rhetoric versus Reality in Arbitration Jurisprudence: How the Supreme Court Flaunts and Flunks Contracts*, 75 LAW & CONTEMPORARY PROBLEMS 129 (2012).

EXAMPLES: FACEBOOK AND GOGO

When assent is largely passive, as with electronic adhesion contracts, it is more important to probe whether the offeree had notice of the term at issue. Actual notice suffices but inquiry notice can suffice too—meaning that the offeree need not know specifics of the term but be on notice to inquire about it. The *Specht* court spoke to this issue, distinguishing a duty to read from the right of inquiry notice: "a party cannot avoid the terms of a contract on the ground that he or she failed to read it before signing, [but] an exception to this general rule exists when the writing does not appear to be a contract and the terms are not called to the attention of the recipient. In such a case no contract is formed with respect to the undisclosed terms." Two other recent cases involving prominent companies—Facebook and Gogo—point in opposite directions.

In *Fteja v. Facebook, Inc.*, 841 F.Supp.2d 829 (S.D.N.Y. 2012), a user charged emotional distress and reputational damage after Facebook disabled his account and sued in New York. Facebook, citing its terms of use that called for litigating in California, moved to transfer the case. The user countered that he had not accepted the terms. The factual situation was both similar to and different from *Carnival Cruise*.

On Facebook's web site, users are asked to provide fields of information before clicking "sign-up," whereupon a security check intervenes, after which it prompts another "sign-up," this one announcing that by clicking "you are indicating that you have read and agree to the Terms of Service"—with the latter phrase appearing as a hyperlink (underlined and italicized and leading to those terms). To have a Facebook account, a user must have so clicked; if the accompanying phrase is given effect, the user did indeed agree to the terms. Recalling *Carnival Cruise*, the *Fteja* court wondered:

> What is the difference between a hyperlink and . . . a cruise ticket [with the legend "subject to conditions" appearing on it as in *Carnival Cruise*]? The mechanics of the internet surely remain unfamiliar, even obtuse to many people. But it is not too much to expect that an internet user whose social networking was so prolific that losing Facebook access allegedly caused him mental anguish would understand that the hyperlinked phrase "Terms of Use" is really a sign that says "Click Here for Terms of Use." So understood, at least for those to whom the internet is an indispensable part of daily life, clicking the hyperlinked phrase is the twenty-first century equivalent of turning over the cruise ticket. In both cases, the consumer is

prompted to examine terms of sale that are located somewhere else. Whether or not the consumer bothers to look is irrelevant.

The facts of *Berkson v. Gogo LLC*, 97 F.Supp.3d 359 (E.D.N.Y. 2015), began on September 25, 2012, when Adam Berkson flew on Delta Airlines from New York City to Indianapolis. Needing the Internet to conduct business, he opened his laptop and followed the log-on instructions for Gogo's in-flight Wi-Fi service. Between options of $10 for the day or $35 for the month, he clicked the sign-up button for the month, entered his American Express payment information, and was surfing the web within one minute.

A few months later, however, Berkson discovered that Gogo was billing his AmEx card every month—as if he had subscribed. When he requested a refund, Gogo refused. While AmEx reversed the charges as a customer courtesy, in 2014 Berkson joined other aggrieved Gogo customers to file a federal class action lawsuit. Gogo moved to dismiss the case by citing another term on its web site, one providing that all disputes go to arbitration, not litigation.

Gogo's motion to dismiss Adam Berkson's class action complaint was decided by Judge Jack Weinstein, a distinguished then 93-year old appointed to the bench by President Lyndon Johnson. He wrote a law-review length opinion denying the motion. After quoting the foregoing passage from the *Fteja* opinion, Weinstein quarreled with his colleague in that case, as follows:

> The phrase "for those to whom the internet is an indispensable part of daily life" in *Fteja* is curious. It presupposes intensive and extensive use of the internet, an assumption not easily justifiable when the user is buying only one or a few items through this system. What of those less devoted to computers? Should a survey be taken on how they view some of these directions? Judges and law clerks tend to be sophisticated about navigating the internet and website. Are they attributing their superior knowledge to that of "read-less and run" types? A "hyperlink," which is activated by clicking on an underlined word or term, with its serious legal ramifications, may not be fully understood by many consumers.

Judge Weinstein declared that lower courts only uphold sign-in-wrap agreements, including those like Facebook's in *Fteja*, in three circumstances, all emphasizing notice of terms and access to them: (1) where the hyperlinked terms are next to the only button that lets users continue; (2) where the user signed up with a click-wrap agreement presenting hyperlinks to the terms of use on subsequent visits; or (3) where notice of the hyperlinked terms is present on multiple successive pages. Discerning governing principles from the cases, the court said that terms of use are: (1) unenforceable absent evidence that reasonably prudent users would have notice of them; (2) enforceable when users are encouraged by a site's design to examine them; and (3) unenforceable when the link to them is obscured, buried, or otherwise unlikely to be seen—as in *Specht*.

Under these cases and principles, the Gogo terms failed because: (1) there was insufficient evidence that customers knew they were binding themselves to more than a one-time deal; (2) site design did not make the terms conspicuous (e.g., large font, all caps, bold, or in multiple locations) while sign-in was both conspicuous and user-friendly; (3) the importance of the terms was accordingly obscured; and (4) nothing was said about the relative merits of arbitration versus litigation. True, the *Gogo* device closely resembled that in *Fteja*. But Judge Weinstein explained:

> But *Fteja,* and lower court cases that follow its lead, mischaracterize important Supreme Court and Court of Appeals precedent regarding contracts and the reasonable person standard that must be applied to inquiry notice of, and manifestation of assent to, the terms in a contract of adhesion. The offeror must show that a reasonable person in the position of the consumer would have known about what he was assenting to. There are significant differences between a hyperlink available near a sign-in button, which is never subsequently mailed in hardcopy or softcopy to a consumer, as is the case here, and a hardcopy cruise ticket saying in all caps [and bold that it is subject to conditions as in *Carnival Cruise*].

The court enumerated several such differences: the hyperlink is unrelated to any in-person transaction; Gogo had no practice of e-mailing or mailing its terms of use to customers; Gogo made no effort to draw Berkson's attention to its terms of use; and the passenger in *Carnival Cruise* acknowledged receiving notice of the terms—not so in Gogo. While many judges seem to assume the validity of terms of use in electronic contracts, Weinstein stressed the need for assent in contract formation that makes such an assumption irresponsible. One can hypothesize an informed minority of consumers wielding disciplining power in competitive markets against allowing offerors to sustain lopsided terms. But Weinstein found that research into the behavior of online consumers cast doubt on its efficacy.

On the other hand, a 2003 study by experts on behalf of the American Bar Association advised what offerors in electronic contracts should do to bring notice home to offerees, including using a scroll box to reveal terms of use, prominently positioning phrases calling attention to those terms, highlighting links to them, and clearly stating that the terms of use amount to a binding contract. The study opined that terms should be valid only when users are notified of the terms, have an opportunity to consider them, are told that to assent they must take a specific action, and they take that action. Many web designers followed the advice, adopting techniques such as scroll-wrap to manifest assent.

How might you reconcile *Fteja v. Facebook* and *Berkson v. Gogo*? As a matter of law, is the relative conspicuousness of the route to assent important? As to subject matter, does it matter that *Facebook* involved a forum selection clause and *Gogo* an arbitration clause?

PROBLEM: CYBER CONTRACT FORMATION

Alexandra, who lives in New York, and Bertram, who lives in California, are business people who do most of their work in cyberspace. Often the two—who have never met in person—connect in a virtual world, Second Life. In this virtual world, people use computers to create a character (an "avatar") to represent them, and they do an instant-message-like "chat" where they type back and forth, or, if they have headphones and a mic, can talk to other players in the world. One day Alexandra and Bertram encounter each other in Second Life, and Bertram sends Alexandra a message. The transcript follows:

B: Hey, how's it going? Got time to do some programming work for me?

A: What's it about?

B: Setting up an E-commerce site. Ten hours, $200/hour. Start next week? Sound ok?

A: Sure, I've done those before. Sounds good.

The next week, Bertram e-mailed Alexandra to give her more details about the work. Alexandra wrote back to say, "I'm sorry. I was just joking around on Second Life, you know, playing the game." Have Alexandra and Betram formed a contract? Explain your reasoning and make the strongest plausible arguments on both sides.

C. BATTLE OF THE FORMS

We saw at the end of Chapter One that Article 2 of the UCC, applicable to transactions in goods, is more solicitous of contract formation than the common law. The provisions we considered, Sections 2–204 and 2–206, apply generally to all transactions in goods, and may be said to echo some of the common law's own modern tendency to relax standards governing contract formation.

In the following discussion, we examine a focused UCC provision, Section 2–207, a sharp departure from the common law for particular problems arising from widespread use of standardized forms in commercial transactions in goods. The common law, especially the mirror image rule and its approach to acceptance by performance, proved inadequate to this context, which led commercial parties to disingenuous arguments as well as costly battles over whose form controlled. While the contours can be technical, the context is vast and vital.

U.S. manufacturers ship more than $5 trillion worth of goods annually to a wide variety of buyers across the globe. The bulk of this huge volume—one trillion is one thousand billion and one billion is one thousand million—is delivered pursuant to standardized written forms of agreement. These forms have been drafted by sophisticated commercial lawyers, some representing the selling manufacturers and others the buyers of the commercial world, and each attempting to craft terms as favorably as possible to their clients.

In this world, business people focus on getting orders made and filled and most transactions proceed without either haggling over the background rules or triggering any dispute. Behind the scenes, lawyers provide the written rules of the road that become relevant when disputes arise. The range and variety of resulting rules and disputes are infinite, though pivoting around a central legal framework with recurring fact patterns.

First-year law students require a grasp of the commercial context in which such forms are used for transactions in goods, why buyers and sellers may prefer different terms, and the role legal rules have played in the evolution of these transactions, particularly how the common law rules of contract formation tended to frustrate commercial realities and how the UCC was shaped to respect them. More specifically, students should gain some experience with a few of the recurring challenges the UCC's approach to this context presents.

The UCC's drafters observed that people routinely commit to buy and sell goods without haggling over terms or attentively detailing them in writing. That is especially true of companies engaged in large numbers of transactions, such as buyers acquiring parts for manufacturing products or sellers distributing goods globally. Ford Motor Co. does not dicker over each term in every automotive-parts purchase it makes nor does Intel Corp. bargain over every computer chip sale—each company's annual volume of such transactions runs billions of dollars.

Instead, one or both parties create their own standard forms to initiate, reply to, and confirm their deals. Only rarely would the terms on the forms exchanged match each other in the rigorous way required by the common law mirror image rule, except usually as to central elements such as price and quantity. Differences abound concerning other matters parties put in standard forms, such as which side bears the risk of loss while goods are in transit, warranties as to the quality of goods, or the forum in which related disputes might be resolved.

Yet despite the common law denying that a contract was formed, in untold numbers of deals, the parties intended in fact to make a legally enforceable bargain. The UCC's drafters set out to reflect this intention, making exceptions or changes to the common law to establish a framework to affirm the existence of contract and then ascertain its terms. While the world of commerce is vast and varied, there is a recurring motif that provided the UCC's drafters with a template for resolving the questions of formation and terms.

In a common pattern, a seller advertises goods in circulars, product catalogues, Internet sites, and by other means makes invitations to deal.

In response, buyers submit purchase orders stating desired goods, on terms usually sufficiently definite and intentional to satisfy the common law requirements for an offer. For most commercial parties, the purchase order is a standard form created internally for use in all the company's purchasing activities. It will accordingly tend to contain considerable boilerplate terms favorable to it as the purchaser, such as generous delivery assurances, product warranties, and dispute resolution mechanisms (*e.g.*, choosing jury trials to be held in and governed by the laws of its locale).

On receipt of the buyer's standard form of purchase order, merchandising clerks at the seller's place of business verify capacity to fulfil the order and send a confirmation to the buyer. For most commercial sellers, this confirmation would match the buyer's form as to basics such as price and quantity. It would otherwise manifest the qualities of an acceptance under common law as to intention to be bound and assent to those terms. But, as a standard form prepared for general use by other personnel at the company, sellers' acknowledgements invariably contain numerous boilerplate terms favorable to it as the seller, such as risk of loss shifting to the buyer upon shipping, disclaiming or limiting product warranties, and making arbitration the favored dispute resolution method. The terms stated by the buyer and seller, alas, would not be a mirror image.

Despite the parties plainly intending a binding contract to buy and sell the referenced quantity of goods at the agreed price, while the purchase order would qualify as a common law offer, the confirmation would fail as an acceptance, because of the mismatched terms under the mirror image rule. In most cases, the seller's subsequent act of shipping and buyer's ensuing receipt and exercise of dominion over the goods would furnish the common law's requisite manifestation to be bound and a contract formed. But on what terms?

The common law's response looked to the terms set out in the last writing exchanged by the parties before those actions: in effect, it would be classified as the offer which subsequent conduct accepted. If the last form were the seller's confirmation, then its terms ruled. This was known as the *last shot rule.* Anticipating the rule, commercial lawyers advised purchasing departments to adopt internal policies directing clerks to reply to a seller's confirmation with yet a further communication, a buyer's acknowledgement, restating all pro-buyer terms; in response to this gambit, sellers' merchandising departments established internal policies instructing clerks to include a shipping manifest with every shipment, restating all its pro-seller terms. And on it might go.

You now get the reason why this practice is called the "battle of the forms." You should also now get why the problematic doctrinal stimulus for this skirmishing of scriveners is called the "last shot rule." It was these two problems, quotidian to a degree, that UCC 2–207 set out to solve.

Summary: Rules and Problems of the Common Law. A purported acceptance with different or additional terms amounts to a rejection and counteroffer; but if both parties performed, a contract was formed on terms defined by the last document sent before performance. For commercial transactions in goods, two problems resulted: people intend binding acceptances even with additional or different terms but the law would not enforce these; and people endlessly shot forms back-and-forth before performance to make theirs the terms of the contract.

UCC SECTION 2–207 (ANNOTATED)

The text of 2–207 follows, with annotations. As you read this text, you will probably be able to identify quite a few words or phrases whose meaning is not obvious or fixed, but will require interpretation as applied to particular facts. Please do not be distracted by the extent of this challenge, which arises in part because of the huge number and wide variety of fact patterns the simple statute governs. We will focus on some of the more pivotal and instructive words and phrases, which are italicized to anticipate discussion in what follows.

§ 2–207. *Additional Terms in Acceptance or Confirmation*

(1) A *definite* and seasonable *expression of acceptance* or a written confirmation which is sent within a reasonable time operates as an acceptance even though it states terms *additional to or different* from those offered or agreed upon, *unless acceptance is expressly made conditional* on assent to the additional or different terms.

(2) The *additional* terms are to be construed as *proposals* for addition to the contract. Between *merchants* such terms become *part* of the contract *unless*: (a) the *offer* expressly *limits* acceptance to the terms of the offer; (b) they *materially alter* it; or (c) notification of *objection* to them has already been given or is given within a reasonable time after notice of them is received.

(3) Conduct by both parties which recognizes the existence of a contract is sufficient to establish a contract for sale although the writings of the parties do not otherwise establish a contract. In such case the terms of the particular contract consist of those terms on which the writings of the parties agree, together with any supplementary terms incorporated under any other provisions of this Act.

––––––––––––

Subsection (1) creates an exception to the common law's mirror image rule for transactions in goods. At common law, purported acceptances with *additional or different* terms would be rejections and counteroffers. But the first clause of subsection (1) reflects that, in most commercial transactions in goods, *definite* acceptances, while containing additional or different terms, are usually intended to form binding contracts. At the same time, the second clause of subsection (1) preserves mastery of contract formation to the parties: an offeree can make acceptance "*expressly . . . conditional* on assent to the additional or different terms."

Subsection (2) addresses what happens to "additional" terms: they are proposals to become part of the contract. The UCC then delineates between merchants and others. For merchants, additional terms become part of the contract, unless they materially alter it or, again in the spirit of party mastery over contract formation, the offeror limits acceptance to its terms or promptly objects to the offeree's additional terms. For non-merchants, the usual result is that the proposals are not part of the contract. *See Klocek v. Gateway, Inc.*, 104 F. Supp.2d 1332 (D. Kan. 2000), excerpted below in this section.

For "different" terms, courts are divided on interpreting the statute: some hold "different" terms are treated the same as "additional" terms while others hold that "different" terms knock each other out and are replaced by the UCC's default rules. The reason for the dueling stances is statutory ambiguity: subsection (1) says "different or additional" terms do not prevent an acceptance from operating as such, but subsection (2)'s disposition of such terms only references "additional" terms, not "different" terms. While drafters' official comments to statutes often help resolve such ambiguities, those of 2–207 compound them. Comment 3 states that subsection (2) addresses *both* "additional and different" terms while Comment 6 suggests that "different" terms—those that conflict—mutually knock out in favor of UCC defaults. Compare the comments (with emphasis added):

> 3.   Whether or not *additional or different* terms will become part of the agreement *depends upon* the provisions of *subsection (2)*. If they are such as materially to alter the original bargain, they will not be included unless expressly agreed to by the other party. If, however, they are terms which would not so change the bargain they will be incorporated unless notice of objection to them has already been given or is given within a reasonable time.

> 6.   If no answer is received within a reasonable time after *additional* terms are proposed, it is both fair and commercially sound to assume that their inclusion has been *assented* to. Where clauses on confirming forms sent by both parties *conflict* each party must be assumed to *object* to a clause of the other conflicting with one on the confirmation sent by himself. As a result, the requirement that there be notice of objection which is found in

subsection (2) is satisfied and the conflicting terms *do not become a part* of the contract. The contract then consists of the terms originally expressly agreed to, *terms* on which the confirmations *agree, and terms supplied* by this Act, including subsection (2).

(You will have a chance to opine on this debate in the Notes and Questions below.)

Subsection (3) negates the last shot doctrine for transactions in goods. It addresses the circumstance where party conduct manifests an intention to be bound—a shipment and receipt of delivery most often—but with documentation that does not match and is not otherwise allocated under the foregoing provisions to establish a contract. At common law, under the last shot doctrine, the last form sent ruled—it was classified as the offer that was accepted by performance. Subsection (3) removes that stimulus for the battle of the forms by directing that the contract's terms are those on which the forms agree plus, as to conflicting terms, the UCC's gap fillers.

————————

Some recurring issues under subsection (1) include: (a) whether a response to an offer is a "definite and seasonable expression of acceptance"; (b) when an acceptance is "expressly made conditional on assent to the additional or different terms"; and (3) when "a written confirmation . . . is sent within a reasonable time." Definiteness usually pivots around price and quantity, and while the mirror image rule does not apply even to those terms, wide variation in either would signal lack of acceptance, or implicit requirement of assent thereto. Example: an offer to supply 18,500 toilet paper holders would not be accepted by an order for 3,000.

To meet the requirement of conditionality, language must indicate the offeree's unwillingness to proceed with the deal unless the offeror assents to the additional or different terms. Tracking the statutory language is the cleanest method of achieving this result, though courts tend to recognize conditional acceptance as long as it provides the offeror with clear notice.

Recurring issues under subsection (2), aside from debate about "additional" versus "different" terms, center around what additional terms constitute "material" alteration so they do not become part of the contract, per (2)(b), even absent admonition or objection (under (2)(c)). Comment 4 suggests a test of materiality: whether the clause would "result in surprise or hardship if incorporated without express awareness by the other party." It instances as material:

> a clause negating such standard warranties as that of merchantability or fitness for a particular purpose in circumstances in which either warranty normally attaches; a clause requiring a guaranty of 90% or 100% deliveries in a case such as a contract by [a] cannery, where the usage of the trade

allows greater quantity leeway; a clause reserving to the seller the power to cancel upon the buyer's failure to meet any invoice when due; a clause requiring that complaints be made in a time materially shorter than customary or reasonable.

Comment 5, moreover, makes "unreasonable surprise" the core of determining materiality. It offers examples of circumstances not meeting the standard of unreasonable surprise: terms stating or enlarging a seller's exemption due to supervening events outside its control; setting a reasonable time for complaints within customary limits; providing for interest on overdue invoices; and limiting the right of rejection for defects falling within customary trade tolerances. *See generally* Timothy Davis, *U.C.C. Section 2–207: When Does an Additional Term Materially Alter a Contract*, 65 CATHOLIC U. L. REV. 489 (2016).

NOTES AND QUESTIONS

Where do you come out on the interpretive question over "additional or different" terms? To help you form your own opinion on the merits, consider what is the distinction between "additional" and "different" terms? Think of a "term" as a particularized contractual provision, such as price, quantity, payment, delivery, or warranty. If an offer states that payment is due within 30 days while an acceptance says it is due within 10 days, the terms are *different*; if the offer is silent on payment terms while the acceptance specifies the due date, that term is *additional*. One varies, the other expands, and there may be many examples and rationales for the categories, hinging around how much thought or concern either side attaches to a term.

LUNA INNOVATIONS INC. v. VERNER SCIENCE, INC.
2017 WL 1498108 (W.D. Va. 2017)

URBANSKI, D.J.

This is [an opinion denying a motion for summary judgment] in a contract dispute, centering on defendant Verner Science, Inc.'s ("Verner") rejection of plaintiff Luna Innovations Incorporated's ("Luna") shipment of certain electronic equipment. . . . Luna is a "leading manufacturer of optical technologies," while Verner is a merchant that deals in electronic test equipment in Taiwan. In late 2015, Verner entered into negotiations to purchase fiber-optic testing equipment from Luna. Pursuant to these negotiations, on December 15, 2015, Luna provided Verner with a price quote, identifying a price of $119,500 for the requested equipment and accompanying software (the "Quote"). The Quote provided for a discount of $24,500 (bringing the total cost to $95,000) if "the purchase order is received by close of business 12/16/2015." No shipping date was specified.

. . . Verner sent Luna a Purchase Order the next day. The Purchase Order differed in several respects from the Quote. It omitted the "Desktop

Analysis Software" and "Spot Scan feature" that had been included in the Quote, and accordingly authorized a purchase price of only $78,000. Moreover, the shipping date was specified as "by advice," and the purchase order asked that Luna "[e]nter this order in accordance with the prices, terms, delivery method, and specifications listed above."

. . . During . . . ensuing negotiations, Luna made clear that, in order to effectuate the sale at the discussed price, "[it] need[ed] to ship by year end." Verner re-sent its Purchase Order on December 30, 2015. In response, Luna sent Verner a Sales Order. The Sales Order specified that the shipping date as "on or before 01/15/2016," which accommodated Luna's insistence on shipment before the end of the year [*i.e.*, it could ship on December 30 or 31]. Moreover, it reincorporated the standard terms and conditions from Luna's Quote, and asked that Verner notify Luna immediately of any term of the Sales Order "is not correct in any way," so that Luna "may make the needed corrections before [the] order is processed."

Verner responded immediately, and asked that Luna "[p]lease ship the goods by our notice, not on or before 01/15/2016." Luna protested, "We need to ship your instrument today in order to meet our year-end commitments and, therefore, in order to provide your discount." Over the next day the parties continued in this vein: Luna maintained that shipping must take place before the New Year, and Verner was equally adamant that shipping should be by notice. Luna offered delayed payment terms; Verner's position did not change. Eventually, after informing Luna that its customer "will cancel the [Purchase Order] if we need the confirmation today," Verner offered Luna an ambiguously worded alternative, in lieu of cancellation of the Purchase Order: "Or you can accept return good [sic] if there is problem with our customer." . . .

Luna shipped the equipment on the last day of 2015. On January 4, 2016, Verner contacted Luna to request "the info regarding if we have to return the [equipment]." Luna responded that any return, "would require [a] reason/explanation." Verner received the equipment on January 20, 2016. The parties did not correspond again until March 9, 2016, when Verner indicated that it would need to return the equipment because Verner's customer found it unsuitable. Despite Luna's warning that it would not accept the return, Verner returned the unused equipment to Luna.

Luna filed suit on June 30, 2016, asking the court to require Verner to pay the $78,000 price of the equipment. On August 25, 2016, Verner filed its Answer and Counterclaim, in which it asked for "incurred expenses for inbound airfreight, customs clearance, outbound airfreight charges and other costs," incurred in connection with returning the equipment to Luna. . . .

Verner and Luna take different positions on the issue of contract formation. . . Verner argue[s] . . . that no binding contract existed between the parties: because Verner specified in its Purchase Order that shipment should be "by advice"—which Verner argues allows for the possibility that shipment never takes place—Luna and Verner were not obligated to ship the equipment and pay for it, respectively, and therefore no binding contract existed. Luna meanwhile, has maintained that its Quote was merely "an invitation to enter into negotiations and . . . not an offer." Thus, Luna views Verner's Purchase Order as an offer, which was accepted by Luna's Sales Order—albeit with nonconforming terms.

Ultimately, the court agrees with Luna that a binding contract was formed. To start with the Quote, it is unnecessary to decide if it should be viewed as an offer, or merely an invitation to begin negotiations. The Quote and Purchase Order differed in price, terms, equipment, and specifications. If the Quote is viewed as an invitation to enter negotiations, the Purchase Order was an initial offer; if the Quote instead represents an initial offer, then the Purchase Order was a counteroffer, not an acceptance. . . . Restatement (Second) of Contracts § 59. . . .

Thus, the Purchase Order constituted an offer. Luna's Sales Order, in turn, confirmed the price and equipment specifications in the Purchase Order, and operated as an acceptance. Accordingly, when Luna sent the Sales Order to Verner, a binding contract was formed. The Sales Order did not accept all the terms in the Purchase Order, however. As discussed, it reincorporated the terms provided in Luna's Quote, and changed the shipping term from "by advice" to "Delivery: Ship on or before 01/15/2016." The different shipping terms in the offer and acceptance did not prevent the formation of a contract, [2–207(1)] . . . but the court must now attempt to determine which shipping term, if either, controlled. . . . [under UCC 2–207(2)] . . .

Subsection (a) [of 2–207(2)] is not controlling: Verner's Purchase Order asked that Luna "[e]nter this order in accordance with" its terms, but did not expressly condition the offer on completely conforming acceptance. Subsections' (b) and (c), however, each potentially exclude both parties' shipping terms from the contract. *See Power Oaragon, Inc. v. Precision Tech. USA. Inc.*, No. 7:09CV00542, 2009 WL 700169, at *10 (W.D. Va. Mar. 17, 2009) (discussing the impact of differing terms under § 8.2–207 and holding, "[c]ourts interpreting these provisions in the UCC have applied a 'knockout rule' to 'knock out' any conflicting terms in forms such that the conflicting terms do not become part of the parties' agreement"). In such a case, the resulting contract will include "only non-conflicting terms and any others supplied by the U.C.C." (citing *Daitom, Inc. v. Pennwalt Corp.*, 741 F.2d 1569, 1579 (10th Cir. 1984)).

The shipping term in Luna's [Sales Order] may constitute a material alteration of Verner's Purchase Order. There is some precedent that supports this argument. . . . [But] the court concludes that this issue cannot be resolved solely on the exhibits and arguments submitted by the parties. Facts not before the court will bear on the materiality of the shipment terms, and it would be premature to decide this issue without further factual development. [*See In re Cotton Yarn Antitrust Litig.*, 505 F.3d 274, 296 (4th Cir. 2007)] (recognizing . . . "the importance of trade practices to the material alterations analysis"); . . . 2–207 cmt. 5 (suggesting that altered terms are material where they "involve [an] element of unreasonable surprise").

Likewise, the court is ill-equipped to determine whether Lai objected under § 2–207 (2) (c). Neither party disputes that, on the day after [Verner] received Luna's Sales Order, [Verner] requested that the "by advice" term be reinstated. However, the parties continued to correspond, and eventually, [Verner] suggested, "[o]r you can accept return good [sic] if there is problem with our customer." Verner suggests that this was meant to reserve a right of return; Luna disagrees, and suggests that [Verner] was merely insisting on a return in the event of a warranty issue, and in fact rescinded her initial objection to the Luna's shipment term. Though the court finds Verner's explanation more plausible, on summary judgment, inferences are to be drawn in favor of the non-moving party—in this case, Luna. Viewed in this light, the court cannot definitively conclude that [Verner's] correspondence operated as a notification of objection to the shipping term in Luna's Sales Order.

Even if the court could determine whether subsections (b) or (c) of § 2–207(2) operated to "knock out" the parties' differing shipment terms, questions of fact would remain. As discussed supra, if these terms are knocked out of the contract, the U.C.C. supplies the omitted term. As Luna correctly points out, 2–309 provides that "[t]he time for shipment or delivery or any other action under a contract if not provided in this title or agreed upon shall be a reasonable time." . . . 2–309 cmt. 1 elaborates,

> The reasonable time under this provision turns on the criteria as to "reasonable time" and on good faith and commercial standards set forth in Sections 1–203, 1–204 and 2–103. It thus depends upon what constitutes acceptable commercial conduct in view of the nature, purpose and circumstances of the action to be taken.

Comment 1 reinforces the conclusion that what constitutes shipment within a "reasonable time" is a factual question that is governed by the general circumstances between the parties. The court cannot decide such an issue by looking only to a series of emails between the representatives of Luna and Verner, let alone conclude as a matter of law that Verner was correct in determining that Luna's shipment date was unreasonable. . . .

Too many ambiguities remain to resolve this issue on summary judgment. . . .

NOTE: PATTERNS OF ARGUMENT

The pattern of argument between the buyer and seller in *Luna Innovations* is a familiar and recurring one in the context of contracts involving sales of goods. There are two issues: whether a contract was formed and, if so, what are the terms? On the first issue, the seller claims breach of contract and the buyer defends by denying contract formation occurred. On the second issue, the offeror seeks multiple avenues through which to claim its terms control or, failing that and if favorable, the UCC's default rules apply; in addition, the offeree urges numerous routes to argue its terms govern or, likewise, that the favorable UCC default rules govern

The available avenues and routes are those spelled out by the statutory language: for offerees, under subsection (1), that their acceptance was expressly conditional on assent to additional or different terms and, for offerors, under subsection (2), that their offer so limited acceptance, that any proposal materially alters it, or prompt objection was made. Wrangling may continue through the statutory language, including over what counts as a material alteration, whether a term is different rather than additional and the consequence thereof, and so on. The following series illustrates some of the recurring patterns—feel free to enumerate additional or different versions of this pattern as you deem productive.

1.   Section 2–207 fact patterns pose two separate analytical challenges: is there a contract and what are its terms? Concerning whether there is a contract, collate the rules concerning contract formation:

MIR	R2 § 59	MIR exception caveat	2–207(1) (clause 1)
Exception to MIR	2–207(1) (clause 1)	Contract by conduct	2–207(3)

Claim: Breach of contract for a transaction in goods.

Defense A: No contract formed because the purported acceptance was not the mirror image of the offer. R2 § 59

Reply A: A goods contract may be formed even if an acceptance contains additional or different terms. § 2–207(1) (clause 1).

Defense B: The goods exception does not apply when the offer expressly requires offeror's assent to the different or additional terms. § 2–207(1) (clause 2).

Reply B: A contract was formed by party conduct (shipping and receiving goods) despite absence of matched writings. § 2–207(3).

2.   Concerning the contract's terms, collate the rules on *additional* terms:

"additional terms"

General rule: 2–207(2) (sentence 1)   *versus*   Merchant rule: 2–207(2) (sentence 2)

Claim: Buyer alleges breach due to delayed delivery, though its offer did not specify delivery terms.

Defense: Seller's acceptance said delivery may be delayed indefinitely due to labor difficulties at its plant, a term that becomes part of the contract because the offer did not limit acceptance to its terms, is not a material alteration and Buyer did not promptly object. 2–207 Cmt. 3.

Reply A: At least one of us is not a merchant so the delayed delivery term was at best a proposal which Buyer never assented to. 2–207(2).

Reply B: Buyer's offer limited acceptance to its terms, delayed delivery term is a material alteration and/or Buyer promptly objected to the disclaimer. 2–207(2)(a)-(c).

3.   Now collate the rules—and interpretations—on *different* terms:

"different terms"

Same as "additional": Comment 3   *versus*   Knock out rule: Comment 6

Claim: Same as above except Buyer's form called for *prompt* delivery.

Defense A: Same as above.

Reply: These are "different" terms, not additional terms, and are mutually knocked out, replaced by UCC terms, which call (2–309) for shipment within a reasonable time. 2–207 Comment 6.

Defense B: "Different" terms should be treated as "additional" terms, proposals that become part of it absent admonition, alteration, or objection. 2–207 Cmt. 3.

4.   Consider facts where the parties' writings do not agree but conduct establishes a contract:

| Term on which writings agree | 2–207(3) (sentence 1) |
| UCC gap fillers | 2–207(3) (sentence 2) |

Claim: Buyer alleges breach of warranty by Seller of goods.

Defense A: Seller made no warranty.

Reply A: The contract was formed by conduct and the writings do not agree as to warranty. So the UCC warranty gap fillers (see 2–312 through 2–316) apply. UCC 2–207(3) (sentence 2).

STEP-SAVER DATA SYS. V. WYSE TECHNOLOGY
939 F.2d 91 (3d Cir. 1991)

WISDOM, J.

The growth in the variety of computer hardware and software has created a strong market for these products. It has also created a difficult choice for consumers, as they must somehow decide which of the many available products will best suit their needs. To assist consumers in this decision process, some companies will evaluate the needs of particular groups of potential computer users, compare those needs with the available technology, and develop a package of hardware and software to satisfy those needs. Beginning in 1981, Step-Saver performed this function as a value added retailer for International Business Machine (IBM) products. It would combine hardware and software to satisfy the word processing, data management, and communications needs for offices of physicians and lawyers. It originally marketed single computer systems, based primarily on the IBM personal computer.

As a result of advances in micro-computer technology, Step-Saver developed and marketed a multi-user system. With a multi-user system, only one computer is required. Terminals are attached, by cable, to the main computer. From these terminals, a user can access the programs available on the main computer. After evaluating the available technology, Step-Saver selected a program by TSL, entitled Multilink Advanced, as the operating system for the multi-user system. Step-Saver selected WY-60 terminals manufactured by Wyse, and used an IBM AT as the main computer. For applications software, Step-Saver included in the package several off-the-shelf programs, designed to run under Microsoft's Disk Operating System ("MS-DOS"), as well as several programs written by Step-Saver. Step-Saver began marketing the system in November of 1986, and sold one hundred forty-two systems mostly to law and medical offices before terminating sales of the system in March of 1987. Almost immediately upon installation of the system, Step-Saver began to receive complaints from some of its customers.

Step-Saver, in addition to conducting its own investigation of the problems, referred these complaints to Wyse and TSL, and requested technical assistance in resolving the problems. After several preliminary attempts to address the problems, the three companies were unable to reach a satisfactory solution, and disputes developed among the three concerning responsibility for the problems. As a result, the problems were never solved. At least twelve of Step-Saver's customers filed suit against Step-Saver because of the problems with the multi-user system. [This opinion concerns Step-Saver's appeal in its lawsuit against TSL for breach of warranty, which the district court dismissed as a matter of law on the grounds that TSL's box-top license disclaimed all warranties TSL might otherwise responsible for.]

The relationship between Step-Saver and TSL began in the fall of 1984 when Step-Saver asked TSL for information on an early version of the Multilink program. TSL provided Step-Saver with a copy of the early program, known simply as Multilink, without charge to permit Step-Saver to test the program to see what it could accomplish. Step-Saver performed some tests with the early program, but did not market a system based on it.

In the summer of 1985, Step-Saver noticed some advertisements in Byte magazine for a more powerful version of the Multilink program, known as Multilink Advanced. Step-Saver requested information from TSL concerning this new version of the program, and allegedly was assured by sales representatives that the new version was compatible with ninety percent of the programs available "off-the-shelf" for computers using MS-DOS. The sales representatives allegedly made a number of additional specific representations of fact concerning the capabilities of the Multilink Advanced program.

Based on these representations, Step-Saver obtained several copies of the Multilink Advanced program in the spring of 1986, and conducted tests with the program. After these tests, Step-Saver decided to market a multi-user system which used the Multilink Advanced program. From August of 1986 through March of 1987, Step-Saver purchased and resold 142 copies of the Multilink Advanced program. Step-Saver would typically purchase copies of the program in the following manner. First, Step-Saver would telephone TSL and place an order. (Step-Saver would typically order twenty copies of the program at a time.) TSL would accept the order and promise, while on the telephone, to ship the goods promptly. After the telephone order, Step-Saver would send a purchase order, detailing the items to be purchased, their price, and shipping and payment terms. TSL would ship the order promptly, along with an invoice. The invoice would contain terms essentially identical with those on Step-Saver's purchase order: price, quantity, and shipping and payment terms. No reference was made during the telephone calls, or on either the purchase orders or the invoices with regard to a disclaimer of any warranties.

Printed on the package of each copy of the program, however, would be a copy of the box-top license. The box-top license contains five terms relevant to this action: (1) The box-top license provides that the customer has not purchased the software itself, but has merely obtained a personal, non-transferable license to use the program; (2) The box-top license, in detail and at some length, disclaims all express and implied warranties except for a warranty that the disks contained in the box are free from defects; (3) The box-top license provides that the sole remedy available to a purchaser of the program is to return a defective disk for replacement; the license excludes any liability for damages, direct or consequential, caused by the use of the program; (4) The box-top license contains an integration clause, which provides that the box-top license is the final and complete expression of the terms of the parties's agreement; (5) The box-top license states: "Opening this package indicates your acceptance of these terms and conditions. If you do not agree with them, you should promptly return the package unopened to the person from whom you purchased it within fifteen days from date of purchase and your money will be refunded to you by that person."

The district court, without much discussion, held, as a matter of law, that the box-top license was the final and complete expression of the terms of the parties's agreement. Because the district court decided the questions of contract formation and interpretation as issues of law, we review the district court's resolution of these questions *de novo*.

Step-Saver contends that the contract for each copy of the program was formed when TSL agreed, on the telephone, to ship the copy at the agreed price. The box-top license, argues Step-Saver, was a material alteration to the parties's contract which did not become a part of the contract under UCC § 2–207. TSL argues that the contract between TSL and Step-Saver did not come into existence until Step-Saver received the program, saw the terms of the license, and opened the program packaging. TSL contends that too many material terms were omitted from the telephone discussion for that discussion to establish a contract for the software. Second, TSL contends that its acceptance of Step-Saver's telephone offer was conditioned on Step-Saver's acceptance of the terms of the box-top license. Therefore, TSL argues, it did not accept Step-Saver's telephone offer, but made a counteroffer represented by the terms of the box-top license, which was accepted when Step-Saver opened each package. Third, TSL argues that, however the contract was formed, Step-Saver was aware of the warranty disclaimer, and that Step-Saver, by continuing to order and accept the product with knowledge of the disclaimer, assented to the disclaimer.

As a basic principle, we agree with Step-Saver that UCC § 2–207 governs our analysis. We see no need to parse the parties' various actions to decide exactly when the parties formed a contract. TSL has shipped the product, and Step-Saver has accepted and paid for each copy of the program. The parties' performance demonstrates the existence of a contract. The dispute is, therefore, not over the existence of a contract, but the nature of its terms. When the parties' conduct establishes a contract, but the parties have failed to adopt expressly a particular writing as the terms of their agreement, and the writings exchanged by the parties do not agree, UCC § 2–207 determines the terms of the contract. . . .

... It is undisputed that Step-Saver never expressly agreed to the terms of the box-top license, either as a final expression of, or a modification to, the parties's agreement. In fact, Barry Greebel, the President of Step-Saver, testified without dispute that he objected to the terms of the box-top license as applied to Step-Saver. In the absence of evidence demonstrating an express intent to adopt a writing as a final expression of, or a modification to, an earlier agreement, we find UCC § 2–207 to provide the appropriate legal rules for determining whether such an intent can be inferred from continuing with the contract after receiving a writing containing additional or different terms.

To understand why the terms of the license should be considered under § 2–207 in this case, we review briefly the reasons behind § 2–207. Under the common law of sales, and to some extent still for contracts outside the UCC, an acceptance that varied any term of the offer operated as a rejection of the offer, and simultaneously made a counteroffer. This common law formality [is] known as the mirror image rule, because the terms of the acceptance had to mirror the terms of the offer to be effective. If the offeror proceeded with the contract despite the differing terms of the supposed acceptance, he would, by his performance, constructively accept the terms of the "counteroffer," and be bound by its terms. As a result of these rules, the terms of the party who sent the last form, typically the seller, would become the terms of the parties's contract. This result was known as the "last shot rule".

The UCC, in § 2–207, rejected this approach. Instead, it recognized that, while a party may desire the terms detailed in its form if a dispute, in fact, arises, most parties do not expect a dispute to arise when they first enter into a contract. As a result, most parties will proceed with the transaction even if they know that the terms of their form would not be enforced. The insight behind the rejection of the last shot rule is that it would be unfair to bind the buyer of goods to the standard terms of the seller, when neither party cared sufficiently to establish expressly the terms of their agreement, simply because the seller sent the last form.

Thus, UCC § 2–207 establishes a legal rule that proceeding with a contract after receiving a writing that purports to define the terms of the parties' contract is not sufficient to establish the party's consent to the terms of the writing to the extent that the terms of the writing either add to, or differ from, the terms detailed in the parties' earlier writings or discussions. In the absence of a party's express assent to the additional or different terms of the writing, section 2–207 provides a default rule that the parties intended, as the terms of their agreement, those terms to which both parties have agreed, along with any terms implied by the provisions of the UCC.

The reasons that led to the rejection of the last shot rule, and the adoption of section 2–207, apply fully in this case. TSL never mentioned during the . . . negotiations leading to the purchase of the programs, nor did it, at any time, obtain Step-Saver's express assent to, the terms of the box-top license. Instead, TSL contented itself with attaching the terms to the packaging of the software, even though those terms differed substantially from those previously discussed by the parties. Thus, the box-top license, in this case, is best seen as one more form in a battle of forms, and the question of whether Step-Saver has agreed to be bound by the terms of the box-top license is best resolved by applying the legal principles detailed in section 2–207.

TSL advances several reasons why the terms of the box-top license should be incorporated into the . . . agreement under a § 2–207 analysis. First, TSL argues that the parties' contract was not formed until Step-Saver received the package, saw the terms of the box-top license, and opened the package, thereby consenting to the terms of the license. TSL argues that a contract defined without reference to the specific terms provided by the box-top license would necessarily fail for indefiniteness. Second, TSL argues that the box-top license was a conditional acceptance and counter-offer under § 2–207(1). Third, TSL argues that Step-Saver, by continuing to order and use the product with notice of the terms of the box-top license, consented to the terms of the box-top license.

TSL argues that the parties intended to license the copies of the program, and that several critical terms could only be determined by referring to the box-top license. Pressing the point, TSL argues that it is impossible to tell, without referring to the box-top license, whether the parties intended a sale of a copy of the program or a license to use a copy. . . .

From the evidence, it appears that the following terms, at the least, were discussed and agreed to, apart from the box-top license: (1) the specific goods involved; (2) the quantity; and (3) the price. TSL argues that the following terms were only defined in the box-top license: (1) the nature of the transaction, sale or license; and (2) the warranties, if any, available. TSL argues that these two terms are essential to creating a sufficiently definite contract. We disagree.

Unlike the terms omitted by the parties in *Bethlehem Steel Corp.* [488 A.2d 581 (Pa. 1985)], the two terms cited by TSL are not "gaping holes in a multi-million dollar contract that no one but the parties themselves could fill." First, the rights of the respective parties under the federal copyright law if the transaction is characterized as a sale of a copy of the program are nearly identical to the parties's respective rights under the terms of the box-top license. Second, the UCC provides for express and implied warranties if the seller fails to disclaim expressly those warranties. Thus, even though warranties are an important term left blank by the parties, the default rules of the UCC fill in that blank. We hold that contract was sufficiently definite without the terms provided by the box-top license.

TSL advances two reasons why its box-top license should be considered a conditional acceptance under UCC § 2–207(1). First, TSL argues that the express language of the box-top license, including the integration clause and the phrase "opening this product indicates your acceptance of these terms," made TSL's acceptance "expressly conditional on assent to the additional or different terms". Second, TSL argues that the box-top license, by permitting return of the product within fifteen days if the purchaser does not agree to the terms stated in the license (the "refund offer"), establishes that TSL's acceptance was conditioned on Step-Saver's assent to the terms of the box-top license[.] While we are not certain that a conditional acceptance analysis applies when a contract is established by performance, we assume that it does and consider TSL's arguments.

[Our] approach requires the offeree to demonstrate an unwillingness to proceed with the transaction unless the additional or different terms are included in the contract. . . . Using this test, it is apparent that the integration clause and the "consent by opening" language is not sufficient to render TSL's acceptance conditional. As other courts have recognized, this type of language provides no real indication that the party is willing to forego the transaction if the additional language is not included in the contract.

The second provision provides a more substantial indication that TSL was willing to forego the contract if the terms of the box-top license were not accepted by Step-Saver. On its face, the box-top license states that TSL will refund the purchase price if the purchaser does not agree to the terms of the license. Even with such a refund term, however, the offeree/counterofferor may be relying on the purchaser's investment in time and energy in reaching this point in the transaction to prevent the purchaser from returning the item. Because a purchaser has made a decision to buy a particular product and has actually obtained the product, the purchaser may use it despite the refund offer, regardless of the additional terms specified after the contract formed. But we need not decide whether such a refund offer could ever amount to a conditional acceptance; the undisputed evidence in this case demonstrates that the terms of the license were not sufficiently important that TSL would forego its sales to Step-Saver if TSL could not obtain Step-Saver's consent to those terms.

As discussed, Mr. Greebel testified that TSL assured him that the box-top license did not apply to Step-Saver, as Step-Saver was not the end user of the Multilink Advanced program. Supporting this testimony, TSL on two occasions asked Step-Saver to sign agreements that would put in formal terms the relationship between Step-Saver and TSL. Both proposed agreements contained warranty disclaimer and limitation of remedy terms similar to those contained in the box-top license. Step-Saver refused to sign the agreements; nevertheless, TSL continued to sell copies of Multilink Advanced to Step-Saver.

Additionally, TSL asks us to infer, based on the refund offer, that it was willing to forego its sales to Step-Saver unless Step-Saver agreed to the terms of the box-top license. Such an inference is inconsistent with the fact that both parties agree that the terms of the box-top license *did not represent the parties's agreement* with respect to Step-Saver's right to transfer the copies of the Multilink Advanced program. Although the box-top license prohibits the transfer, by Step-Saver, of its copies of the program, both parties agree that Step-Saver was entitled to transfer its copies to the purchasers of the Step-Saver multi-user system. Thus, TSL was willing to proceed with the transaction despite the fact that one of the terms of the box-top license was not included in the contract between TSL and Step-Saver. We see no basis in the terms of the box-top license for inferring that a reasonable offeror would understand from the refund offer that certain terms of the box-top license, such as the warranty disclaimers, were essential to TSL, while others such as the non-transferability provision were not.

Based on these facts, we conclude that TSL did not clearly express its unwillingness to proceed with the transactions unless its additional terms were incorporated into the parties's agreement. The box-top license did not, therefore, constitute a conditional acceptance under UCC § 2–207(1). . . .

NOTES AND QUESTIONS

1.   Compare the arguments of the buyer and seller as to when their contract was formed. How do the claims about timing feed into each side's arguments?

2.   As to the *Step-Saver* dispute over definiteness, compare *Jannusch v. Naffziger* and *Baccou Dalloz USA v. Continental Polymers, Inc.*, the cases concerning, respectively, the price, quantity, and quality terms in an output contract referenced in another agreement, and the "essential" terms, such as price and the identification of goods, in connection with the sale of a festival business.

3.   UCC 2–207 is the subject of considerable litigation and criticism. Commentators appreciate the enormous problem the drafters sought to solve, and concur with the overall sense of the goal. But many are highly critical of some of the words and phrases, and especially the apparent oversight concerning the issue of "additional or different" terms. A new generation of commercial lawyers recently proposed a revision to the section, but it has not gained momentum and has not been adopted by any state. If you were a legislator, how would you re-write this section?

4.   We will consider several of the UCC's warranty provisions in a later chapter. For now, it is worth noting that warranties can be express, as when the seller represents product attributes, or implied from the circumstances and supplied by the UCC's default rules, and include such topics such as warranty of title, of merchantability, and of fitness for a particular purpose. We will also consider the UCC's rules on how warranties may be disclaimed.

PROBLEM: HAVE A SEAT

The law firm of Knights, Daze & Weekenz (KDW) is opening a new office in Tallahassee, Florida. Gustavo, the office manager, needs to order 300 new office chairs on a priority basis, hopefully by next week. The budget is $500 per chair, and for that sum the firm wants a guarantee of excellent quality and repair in the event of a problem, as well as a long return policy in case they've purchased too many chairs. As a top-flight law firm, KDW always prefers to keep its options open to sue those who have wronged the firm, regardless of the dollar amount at stake.

Office Despot is a national chain selling all manner of office equipment, including high-end office chairs that retail for $499. Despot's sales representative, Barb, seeks to sell as many chairs as possible, of course, but shipping large orders can present logistical challenges. Barb likes to have a three-week delivery window to avoid complaints about late deliveries but in a rush can probably deliver chairs within ten days. Office Despot generally prefers short periods for returns and repairs so staff can focus on filling orders. Traditionally Office Despot has used arbitration to resolve disputes with customers and suppliers.

For this exercise, work with classmates to create teams of attorneys and take turns assisting Gustavo in drafting KDW's purchase order and then assisting Barb in drafting Office Despot's invoice form. As you work on this assignment, address the following questions: What terms are essential to each side in reaching an agreement on this deal? In contrast, which terms will likely be subject to negotiation and compromise? How do you think business people resolve these competing concerns in the real world?

PROBLEMS: LET IT BURN

Arvind is the owner of Acme, a facilities management company that oversees upkeep in hundreds of factories across the United States. Due to increasing insurance rates, Arvind has started to look into upgrading the safety equipment available in the factories Acme manages. In early January, Arvind began researching a new model of fire extinguisher, the FA 357. At $100 apiece, the FA 357 is twice as expensive as a standard fire extinguisher. Its maker, First Alert, touts the FA 357 as the most reliable and easy-to-use extinguisher ever to hit the market.

After checking an industry guide and several online blogs to confirm that the FA 357 performs more reliably than existing equipment, Arvind contacted First Alert directly to gather more information. Arvind spoke at length with

Pam, Vice-President of Sales at First Alert, about the improvements and features of the FA 357. Because Arvind would be buying thousands of extinguishers for all factories Acme oversees, the two discuss a bulk discount that works out to $80 per FA 357 extinguisher.

1. On February 1, Arvind e-mailed Pam a purchase order for 15,500 FA 357 fire extinguishers at $80 per extinguisher. On February 3, Pam sent an invoice to Arvind acknowledging receipt of the purchase order, stating: "First Alert will ship 15,500 of its FA 911 Smoke Detector systems to you on March 15 for $80 per Smoke Detector." Arvind is annoyed that Pam has gotten the order so wrong, and feels cheated, because smoke detectors cost $10 per detector. Arvind would like to shop elsewhere if he does not have contractual liability. At this point, has a contract been formed under UCC 2–207? What if Pam's invoice stated instead "First Alert will ship 3,000 of its FA 357 Fire Extinguishers to you on March 15 for $80 per unit"?

→ no-no match on key terms

2. Back to the original facts of the problem. What if, on February 1, Arvind e-mails Pam a purchase order for 15,500 FA 357 fire extinguishers at $80 per extinguisher. On February 3, Pam sends an invoice to Arvind acknowledging receipt of the purchase order and stating terms identical in all aspects to the purchase order, except noting that a $1 restocking fee might apply to any returned merchandise. In the meantime, Arvind hears from a friend that First Alert isn't a particular reputable company. Arvind would like to shop elsewhere if he does not have contractual liability. At this point, has a contract been formed under UCC 2–207?

→ becomes part of contract

yes-agree on "big stuff"

3. Return again to the original facts of the problem. Safety is of paramount concern to Arvind, and given the big spending commitment Acme is making, he wants assurance of proper functioning. Pam's invoice states that the new extinguishers are being sold "AS IS" and come without any warranty. Arvind calls Pam, and says: "No dice. Either we get a product warranty or there is no deal. I'll find someone else to buy from." Pam then talks to First Alert's CEO, Katrina, who doesn't want to lose Arvind's business. Katrina personally e-mails Arvind: "No problem. We can give you a five-year warranty on all our products." Arvind writes back a nice message, and sends payment for the extinguishers. When they arrive, however, each bears a tiny sticker that reads "not warrantied." If an extinguisher malfunctions the next day (resulting in blazing consequences), is the product covered by a warranty?

→ adtl' term
→ objection (not incl.)
new agreed on term
→ breach

D. ROLLING CONTRACTS

UCC 2–207 was difficult and unwieldy enough on its own, even back in the day of pre-printed forms and invoices that were being exchanged in hard copy. Starting with a dense commercial law rule, the addition of new technologies and new forms of contracting multiplied the legal complexity too. Both business practice and commercial law continues to evolve, not always easily, as the following series of cases attest.

PROCD, INC. V. ZEIDENBERG

86 F.3d 1447 (7th Cir. 1996)

EASTERBROOK, J.

Must buyers of computer software obey the terms of shrinkwrap licenses? The district court held not, for two reasons: first, they are not contracts because the licenses are inside the box rather than printed on the outside; second, federal law forbids enforcement even if the licenses are contracts. 908 F.Supp. 640 (W.D.Wis.1996). The parties and numerous amici curiae have briefed many other issues, but these are the only two that matter—and we disagree with the district judge's conclusion on each. Shrinkwrap licenses are enforceable unless their terms are objectionable on grounds applicable to contracts in general (for example, if they violate a rule of positive law, or if they are unconscionable). Because no one argues that the terms of the license at issue here are troublesome, we remand with instructions to enter judgment for the plaintiff.

ProCD, the plaintiff, has compiled information from more than 3,000 telephone directories into a computer database. . . . ProCD sells a version of the database, called SelectPhone™, on CD-ROM discs. (CD-ROM means "compact disc—read only memory." The "shrinkwrap license" gets its name from the fact that retail software packages are covered in plastic or cellophane "shrinkwrap," and some vendors, though not ProCD, have written licenses that become effective as soon as the customer tears the wrapping from the package. Vendors prefer "end user license," but we use the more common term.) A proprietary method of compressing the data serves as effective encryption too. Customers decrypt and use the data with the aid of an application program that ProCD has written. This program, which is copyrighted, searches the database in response to users' criteria (such as "find all people named Tatum in Tennessee, plus all firms with 'Door Systems' in the corporate name"). The resulting lists (or, as ProCD prefers, "listings") can be read and manipulated by other software, such as word processing programs.

The database in SelectPhone™ cost more than $10 million to compile and is expensive to keep current. It is much more valuable to some users than to others. The combination of names, addresses, and SIC codes enables manufacturers to compile lists of potential customers. Manufacturers and retailers pay high prices to specialized information intermediaries for such mailing lists; ProCD offers a potentially cheaper alternative. People with nothing to sell could use the database as a substitute for calling long distance information, or as a way to look up old friends who have moved to unknown towns, or just as an electronic substitute for the local phone book. ProCD decided to engage in price discrimination, selling its database to the general public for personal use at a low price (approximately $150 for the set of five discs) while selling information to the trade for a higher price. . . .

If ProCD had to recover all of its costs and make a profit by charging a single price—that is, if it could not charge more to commercial users than to the general public—it would have to raise the price substantially over $150. The ensuing reduction in sales would harm consumers who value the information at, say, $200. They get consumer surplus of $50 under the current arrangement but would cease to buy if the price rose substantially. If because of high elasticity of demand in the consumer segment of the market the only way to make a profit turned out to be a price attractive to commercial users alone, then all consumers would lose out—and so would the commercial clients, who would have to pay more for the listings because ProCD could not obtain any contribution toward costs from the consumer market.

To make price discrimination work, however, the seller must be able to control arbitrage. An air carrier sells tickets for less to vacationers than to business travelers, using advance purchase and Saturday-night-stay requirements to distinguish the categories. A producer of movies segments the market by time, releasing first to theaters, then to pay-per-view services, next to the videotape and laserdisc market, and finally to cable and commercial tv. Vendors of computer software have a harder task. Anyone can walk into a retail store and buy a box. Customers do not wear tags saying "commercial user" or "consumer user." Anyway, even a commercial-user-detector at the door would not work, because a consumer could buy the software and resell to a commercial user. That arbitrage would break down the price discrimination and drive up the minimum price at which ProCD would sell to anyone.

Instead of tinkering with the product and letting users sort themselves—for example, furnishing current data at a high price that would be attractive only to commercial customers, and two-year-old data at a low price—ProCD turned to the institution of contract. Every box containing its consumer product declares that the software comes with restrictions stated in an enclosed license. This license, which is encoded on the CD-ROM disks as well as printed in the manual, and which appears on a user's screen every time the software runs, limits use of the application program and listings to non-commercial purposes.

Matthew Zeidenberg bought a consumer package of SelectPhone™ in 1994 from a retail outlet in Madison, Wisconsin, but decided to ignore the license. He formed Silken Mountain Web Services, Inc., to resell the information in the SelectPhone™ database. The corporation makes the database available on the Internet to anyone willing to pay its price—which, needless to say, is less than ProCD charges its commercial customers. Zeidenberg has purchased two additional SelectPhone™

packages, each with an updated version of the database, and made the latest information available over the World Wide Web, for a price, through his corporation. ProCD filed this suit seeking an injunction against further dissemination that exceeds the rights specified in the licenses (identical in each of the three packages Zeidenberg purchased).

[W]e treat the licenses as ordinary contracts accompanying the sale of products, and therefore as governed by the common law of contracts and the Uniform Commercial Code. Whether there are legal differences between "contracts" and "licenses" (which may matter under the copyright doctrine of first sale) is a subject for another day. See *Microsoft Corp. v. Harmony Computers & Electronics, Inc.,* 846 F.Supp. 208 (E.D.N.Y.1994). Zeidenberg does not argue that Silken Mountain Web Services is free of any restrictions that apply to Zeidenberg himself, because any effort to treat the two parties as distinct would put Silken Mountain behind the eight ball on ProCD's argument that copying the application program onto its hard disk violates the copyright laws. Zeidenberg does argue, and the district court held, that placing the package of software on the shelf is an "offer," which the customer "accepts" by paying the asking price and leaving the store with the goods. *Peeters v. State,* 154 Wis. 111, 142 N.W. 181 (1913).

In Wisconsin, as elsewhere, a contract includes only the terms on which the parties have agreed. One cannot agree to hidden terms, the judge concluded. So far, so good—but one of the terms to which Zeidenberg agreed by purchasing the software is that the transaction was subject to a license. Zeidenberg's position therefore must be that the printed terms on the outside of a box are the parties' contract—except for printed terms that refer to or incorporate other terms. But why would Wisconsin fetter the parties' choice in this way? Vendors can put the entire terms of a contract on the outside of a box only by using microscopic type, removing other information that buyers might find more useful (such as what the software does, and on which computers it works), or both.

The "Read Me" file included with most software, describing system requirements and potential incompatibilities, may be equivalent to ten pages of type; warranties and license restrictions take still more space. Notice on the outside, terms on the inside, and a right to return the software for a refund if the terms are unacceptable (a right that the license expressly extends), may be a means of doing business valuable to buyers and sellers alike. Doubtless a state could forbid the use of standard contracts in the software business, but we do not think that Wisconsin has done so.

Transactions in which the exchange of money precedes the communication of detailed terms are common. Consider the purchase of insurance. The buyer goes to an agent, who explains the essentials (amount of coverage, number of years) and remits the premium to the home office, which sends back a policy. On the district judge's understanding, the terms of the policy are irrelevant because the insured paid before receiving them. Yet the device of payment, often with a "binder" (so that the insurance takes effect immediately even though the home office reserves the right to withdraw coverage later), in advance of the policy, serves buyers' interests by accelerating effectiveness and reducing transactions costs.

Or consider the purchase of an airline ticket. The traveler calls the carrier or an agent, is quoted a price, reserves a seat, pays, and gets a ticket, in that order. The ticket contains elaborate terms, which the traveler can reject by canceling the reservation. To use the ticket is to accept the terms, even terms that in retrospect are disadvantageous. See *Carnival Cruise Lines, Inc. v. Shute,* 499 U.S. 585, 111 S.Ct. 1522, 113 L.Ed.2d 622 (1991). . . . Just so with a ticket to a concert. The back of the ticket states that the patron promises not to record the concert; to attend is to agree. A theater that detects a violation will confiscate the tape and escort the violator to the exit. One *could* arrange things so that every concertgoer signs this promise before forking over the money, but that cumbersome way of doing things not only would lengthen queues and raise prices but also would scotch the sale of tickets by phone or electronic data service.

Consumer goods work the same way. Someone who wants to buy a radio set visits a store, pays, and walks out with a box. Inside the box is a leaflet containing some terms, the most important of which usually is the warranty, read for the first time in the comfort of home. By Zeidenberg's lights, the warranty in the box is irrelevant; every consumer gets the standard warranty implied by the UCC in the event the contract is silent; yet so far as we are aware no state disregards warranties furnished with consumer products. Drugs come with a list of ingredients on the outside and an elaborate package insert on the inside. The package insert describes drug interactions, contraindications, and other vital information—but, if Zeidenberg is right, the purchaser need not read the package insert, because it is not part of the contract.

Next consider the software industry itself. Only a minority of sales take place over the counter, where there are boxes to peruse. A customer may place an order by phone in response to a line item in a catalog or a review in a magazine. Much software is ordered over the Internet by purchasers who have never seen a box. Increasingly software arrives by wire. There is no box; there is only a stream of electrons, a collection of information that includes data, an application program, instructions, many limitations ("MegaPixel 3.14159 cannot be used with BytePusher 2.718"), and the terms of sale. The user purchases a serial number, which activates the software's features. On Zeidenberg's arguments, these unboxed sales are unfettered by terms—so the seller has made a broad warranty and must pay consequential damages for any shortfalls in performance, two "promises" that if taken seriously would drive prices through the ceiling or return transactions to the horse-and-buggy age.

According to the district court, the UCC does not countenance the sequence of money now, terms later. . . . To judge by the flux of law review articles discussing shrinkwrap licenses, uncertainty is much in need of reduction—although businesses seem to feel less uncertainty than do scholars, for only three cases (other than ours) touch on the subject, and none directly addresses it. See *Step-Saver Data Systems, Inc. v. Wyse Technology,* 939 F.2d 91 (3d Cir.1991); *Vault Corp. v. Quaid Software Ltd.,* 847 F.2d 255, 268–70 (5th Cir.1988); *Arizona Retail Systems, Inc. v. Software Link, Inc.,* 831 F.Supp. 759 (D.Ariz.1993).

As their titles suggest, these are not consumer transactions. *Step-Saver* is a battle-of-the-forms case, in which the parties exchange incompatible forms and a court must decide which prevails. Our case has only one form; UCC § 2–207 is irrelevant. *Vault* holds that Louisiana's special shrinkwrap-license statute is preempted by federal law, a question to which we return. And *Arizona Retail Systems* did not reach the question, because the court found that the buyer knew the terms of the license before purchasing the software.

What then does the current version of the UCC have to say? We think that the place to start is § 2–204(1): "A contract for sale of goods may be made in any manner sufficient to show agreement, including conduct by both parties which recognizes the existence of such a contract." A vendor, as master of the offer, may invite acceptance by conduct, and may propose limitations on the kind of conduct that constitutes acceptance. A buyer may accept by performing the acts the vendor proposes to treat as acceptance. And that is what happened. ProCD proposed a contract that a buyer would accept by *using* the software after having an opportunity to read the license at leisure. This Zeidenberg did. He had no choice, because the software splashed the license on the screen and would not let him proceed without indicating acceptance.

So although the district judge was right to say that a contract can be, and often is, formed simply by paying the price and walking out of the store, the UCC permits contracts to be formed in other ways. ProCD proposed such a different way, and without protest Zeidenberg agreed. Ours is not a case in which a consumer opens a package to find an insert saying "you owe us an extra $10,000" and the seller files suit to collect. Any buyer finding such a demand can prevent formation of the contract by returning the package, as can any consumer who concludes that the terms of the license make the software worth less than the purchase price. Nothing in the UCC requires a seller to maximize the buyer's net gains.

Section 2–606, which defines "acceptance of goods," reinforces this understanding. A buyer accepts goods under § 2–606(1)(b) when, after an opportunity to inspect, he fails to make an effective rejection under § 2–602(1). ProCD extended an opportunity to reject if a buyer should find the license terms unsatisfactory; Zeidenberg inspected the package, tried out the software, learned of the license, and did not reject the goods. We refer to § 2–606 only to show that the opportunity to return goods can be important; acceptance of an offer differs from acceptance of goods after delivery, see *Gillen v. Atalanta Systems, Inc.,* 997 F.2d 280, 284 n. 1 (7th Cir.1993); but the UCC consistently permits the parties to structure their relations so that the buyer has a chance to make a final decision after a detailed review.

Some portions of the UCC impose additional requirements on the way parties agree on terms. A disclaimer of the implied warranty of merchantability must be "conspicuous." UCC § 2–316(2), incorporating UCC § 1–201(10). Promises to make firm offers, or to negate oral modifications, must be "separately signed." UCC §§ 2–205, 2–209(2). These special provisos reinforce the impression that, so far as the UCC is concerned, other terms may be as inconspicuous as the forum-selection clause on the back of the cruise ship ticket in *Carnival Lines*. Zeidenberg has not located any Wisconsin case—for that matter, any case in any state—holding that under the UCC the ordinary terms found in shrinkwrap licenses require any special prominence, or otherwise are to be undercut rather than enforced. [Reversed.]

NOTES AND QUESTIONS

1. Judge Easterbrook notes that ProCD was engaged in "price discrimination," charging varying prices to different consumers for the same good or service. Why would a business choose such a pricing strategy? How might purchasers react upon learning of different prices for the same product?

2. Zeidenberg was engaged in a form of *arbitrage*—using what we would in common parlance call a "loophole" to get around ProCD's pricing structure. Is Zeidenberg a particularly sympathetic individual? Would you wish to rule in his favor were you the judge hearing this case? How do we reconcile Zeidenberg's behavior with our (more sympathetic) feelings toward the plaintiffs in *Specht*, who unwittingly downloaded "spyware" from Netscape?

3. Here is a zen question: What is the sound of one form battling? Do you agree with Judge Easterbrook's claim that UCC 2–207 is "irrelevant" because there is only one form involved? As you will see below, in *Klocek v. Gateway*, not all courts have agreed with his analysis. Recall *Carnival Cruise*, cited in *ProCD*, and the dissent's objection that cruise passengers would buy their non-refundable ticket before learning of terms such as a forum selection clause, an objection that did not dissuade the majority from validating the clause.

4. These two cases are part of the larger policy debate about the enforceability of adhesion contracts, both on and off line. The law and economics view of the Seventh Circuit's Frank Easterbrook is generally a friendly approach for large businesses. While Zeidenberg himself seems like a "bad actor" who deserved the comeuppance of the last case, we will see in the next case how Judge Easterbrook applies this precedent to the average consumer—one not engaged in arbitrage.

HILL V. GATEWAY 2000, INC.

105 F.3d 1147 (7th Cir. 1997)

same as ProCD

EASTERBROOK, J.

A customer picks up the phone, orders a computer, and gives a credit card number. Presently a box arrives, containing the computer and a list of terms, said to govern unless the customer returns the computer within 30 days. Are these terms effective as the parties' contract, or is the contract term-free because the order-taker did not read any terms over the phone and elicit the customer's assent?

One of the terms in the box containing a Gateway 2000 system was an arbitration clause. Rich and Enza Hill, the customers, kept the computer more than 30 days before complaining about its components and performance. They filed suit in federal court arguing, among other things, that the product's shortcomings make Gateway a racketeer (mail and wire fraud are said to be the predicate offenses), leading to treble damages under RICO for the Hills and a class of all other purchasers. Gateway asked the district court to enforce the arbitration clause; the judge refused, writing that "[t]he present record is insufficient to support a finding of a valid arbitration agreement between the parties or that the plaintiffs were given adequate notice of the arbitration clause." Gateway, a now-defunct computer manufacturer that faced many similar lawsuits during the period, appealed.

The Hills say that the arbitration clause did not stand out: they concede noticing the statement of terms but deny reading it closely enough to discover the agreement to arbitrate, and they ask us to conclude that they therefore may go to court. Yet an agreement to arbitrate must be enforced "save upon such grounds as exist at law or in equity for the revocation of any contract." 9 U.S.C. § 2. *Doctor's Associates, Inc. v. Casarotto,* 517 U.S. 681, 116 S.Ct. 1652, 134 L.Ed.2d 902 (1996), holds that this provision of the Federal Arbitration Act is inconsistent with any requirement that an arbitration clause be prominent. A contract need not be read to be effective; people who accept take the risk that the unread terms may in retrospect prove unwelcome. *Carr v. CIGNA Securities, Inc.,* 95 F.3d 544, 547 (7th Cir.1996); *Chicago Pacific Corp. v. Canada Life Assurance Co.,* 850 F.2d 334 (7th Cir.1988). Terms inside Gateway's box stand or fall together. If they constitute the parties' contract because the Hills had an opportunity to return the computer after reading them, then all must be enforced.

ProCD, Inc. v. Zeidenberg, 86 F.3d 1447 (7th Cir.1996), holds that terms inside a box of software bind consumers who use the software after an opportunity to read the terms and to reject them by returning the product. Likewise, *Carnival Cruise Lines, Inc. v. Shute,* 499 U.S. 585, 111 S.Ct. 1522, 113 L.Ed.2d 622 (1991), enforces a forum-selection clause that was included among three pages of terms attached to a cruise ship ticket. *ProCD* and *Carnival Cruise Lines* exemplify the many commercial transactions in which people pay for products with terms to follow; *ProCD* discusses others. 86 F.3d at 1451–52.

The district court concluded in *ProCD* that the contract is formed when the consumer pays for the software; as a result, the court held, only terms known to the consumer at that moment are part of the contract, and provisos inside the box do not count. Although this is one way a contract could be formed, it is not the only way: "A vendor, as master of the offer, may invite acceptance by conduct, and may propose limitations on the kind of conduct that constitutes acceptance. A buyer may accept by performing the acts the vendor proposes to treat as acceptance." *Id.* at 1452.

Gateway shipped computers with the same sort of accept-or-return offer *ProCD* made to users of its software. *ProCD* relied on the Uniform Commercial Code rather than any peculiarities of Wisconsin law; both Illinois and South Dakota, the two states whose law might govern relations between Gateway and the Hills, have adopted the UCC; neither side has pointed us to any atypical doctrines in those states that might be pertinent; *ProCD* therefore applies to this dispute.

Plaintiffs ask us to limit *ProCD* to software, but where's the sense in that? *ProCD* is about the law of contract, not the law of software. Payment preceding the revelation of full terms is common for air transportation, insurance, and many other endeavors. Practical considerations support allowing vendors to enclose the full legal terms with their products. Cashiers cannot be expected to read legal documents to customers before ringing up sales. If the staff at the other end of the phone for direct-sales operations such as Gateway's had to read the four-page statement of terms before taking the buyer's credit card number, the droning voice would anesthetize rather than enlighten many potential buyers.

Others would hang up in a rage over the waste of their time. And oral recitation would not avoid customers' assertions (whether true or feigned) that the clerk did not read term X to them, or that they did not remember or understand it. Writing provides benefits for both sides of commercial transactions. Customers as a group are better off when vendors skip costly and ineffectual steps such as telephonic recitation, and use instead a simple approve-or-return device. Competent adults are bound by such documents, read or unread. For what little it is worth, we add that the box from Gateway was crammed with software. The computer came with an operating system, without which it was useful only as a boat anchor. See *Digital Equipment Corp. v. Uniq Digital Technologies, Inc.,* 73 F.3d 756, 761 (7th Cir.1996). Gateway also included many application programs. So the Hills' effort to limit *ProCD* to software would not avail them factually, even if it were sound legally—which it is not.

For their second sally, the Hills contend that *ProCD* should be limited to executory contracts (to licenses in particular), and therefore does not apply because both parties' performance of this contract was complete when the box arrived at their home. This is legally and factually wrong: legally because the question at hand concerns the *formation* of the contract rather than its *performance*, and factually because both contracts were incompletely performed. *ProCD* did not depend on the fact that the seller characterized the transaction as a license rather than as a contract; we treated it as a contract for the sale of goods and reserved the question whether for other purposes a "license" characterization might be preferable. 86 F.3d at 1450. All debates about characterization to one side, the transaction in *ProCD* was no more executory than the one here: Zeidenberg paid for the software and walked out of the store with a box under his arm, so if arrival of the box with the product ends the time for revelation of contractual terms, then the time ended in *ProCD* before Zeidenberg opened the box.

But of course ProCD had not completed performance with delivery of the box, and neither had Gateway. One element of the transaction was the warranty, which obliges sellers to fix defects in their products. The Hills have invoked Gateway's warranty and are not satisfied with its response, so they are not well positioned to say that Gateway's obligations were fulfilled when the motor carrier unloaded the box. What is more, both ProCD and Gateway promised to help customers to use their products. Long-term service and information obligations are common in the computer business, on both hardware and software sides. Gateway offers "lifetime service" and has a round-the-clock telephone hotline to fulfil this promise. Some vendors spend more money helping customers use their products than on developing and manufacturing them. The document in Gateway's box includes promises of future performance that some consumers value highly; these promises bind Gateway just as the arbitration clause binds the Hills.

Next the Hills insist that *ProCD* is irrelevant because Zeidenberg was a "merchant" and they are not. Section 2–207(2) of the UCC, the infamous battle-of-the-forms section, states that "additional terms [following acceptance of an offer] are to be construed as proposals for addition to a contract. Between merchants such terms become part of the contract unless

. . .". Plaintiffs tell us that *ProCD* came out as it did only because Zeidenberg was a "merchant" and the terms inside ProCD's box were not excluded by the "unless" clause. This argument pays scant attention to the opinion in *ProCD,* which concluded that, when there is only one form, "sec. 2–207 is irrelevant." 86 F.3d at 1452.

The question in *ProCD* was not whether terms were added to a contract after its formation, but how and when the contract was formed— in particular, whether a vendor may propose that a contract of sale be formed, not in the store (or over the phone) with the payment of money or a general "send me the product," but after the customer has had a chance to inspect both the item and the terms. *ProCD* answers "yes," for merchants and consumers alike. Yet again, for what little it is worth we observe that the Hills misunderstand the setting of *ProCD*. A "merchant" under the UCC "means a person who deals in goods of the kind or otherwise by his occupation holds himself out as having knowledge or skill peculiar to the practices or goods involved in the transaction," § 2–104(1). Zeidenberg bought the product at a retail store, an uncommon place for merchants to acquire inventory. His corporation put ProCD's database on the Internet for anyone to browse, which led to the litigation but did not make Zeidenberg a software merchant.

At oral argument the Hills propounded still another distinction: the box containing ProCD's software displayed a notice that additional terms were within, while the box containing Gateway's computer did not. The difference is functional, not legal. Consumers browsing the aisles of a store can look at the box, and if they are unwilling to deal with the prospect of additional terms can leave the box alone, avoiding the transactions costs of returning the package after reviewing its contents. Gateway's box, by contrast, is just a shipping carton; it is not on display anywhere. Its function is to protect the product during transit, and the information on its sides is for the use of handlers ("Fragile!" "This Side Up!") rather than would-be purchasers. . . .

By keeping the computer beyond 30 days, the Hills accepted Gateway's offer, including the arbitration clause. . . . The decision of the district court is vacated, and this case is remanded with instructions to compel the Hills to submit their dispute to arbitration.

KLOCEK v. GATEWAY, INC.
104 F.Supp.2d 1332 (D. Kan. 2000)

VRATIL, J.

Plaintiff brings individual and class action claims against Gateway, alleging that it induced him and other consumers to purchase computers and special support packages by making false promises of technical support . . . . Individually, plaintiff also claims breach of contract and breach of warranty, in that Gateway breached certain warranties that its computer would be compatible with standard peripherals and standard internet services ... For reasons stated below, the Court overrules Gateway's motion to dismiss ! ..

Gateway asserts that plaintiff must arbitrate his claims under Gateway's Standard Terms and Conditions Agreement ("Standard Terms"). Whenever it sells a computer, Gateway includes a copy of the Standard Terms in the box which contains the computer battery power cables and instruction manuals. At the top of the first page, the Standard Terms include the following notice:

NOTE TO THE CUSTOMER:

> This document contains Gateway 2000's Standard Terms and Conditions. By keeping your Gateway 2000 computer system beyond five (5) days after the date of delivery, you accept these Terms and Conditions.

> The notice is in emphasized type and is located inside a printed box which sets it apart from other provisions of the document. The Standard Terms are four pages long and contain 16 numbered paragraphs. Paragraph 10 provides the following arbitration clause:

> DISPUTE RESOLUTION. Any dispute or controversy arising out of or relating to this Agreement or its interpretation shall be settled exclusively and finally by arbitration. The arbitration shall be conducted in accordance with the Rules of Conciliation and Arbitration of the International Chamber of Commerce. The arbitration shall be conducted in Chicago, Illinois, U.S.A. before a sole arbitrator. Any award rendered in any such arbitration proceeding shall be final and binding on each of the parties, and judgment may be entered thereon in a court of competent jurisdiction.

Gateway urges the Court to dismiss plaintiff's claims under the Federal Arbitration Act ("FAA"), 9 U.S.C. § 1 *et seq.* The FAA ensures that written arbitration agreements in maritime transactions and transactions involving interstate commerce are "valid, irrevocable, and enforceable." 9 U.S.C. § 2 .... Gateway bears an initial summary-judgment-like burden of establishing that it is entitled to arbitration. In this case, Gateway fails to present evidence establishing the most basic facts regarding the transaction. . . .

. . . The Uniform Commercial Code ("UCC") governs the parties' transaction ... [T]he parties agree that plaintiff paid for and received a computer from Gateway. This conduct clearly demonstrates a contract for the sale of a computer. *See, e.g., Step-Saver Data Sys., Inc. v. Wyse Techn.,*

939 F.2d 91, 98 (3d Cir.1991). Thus the issue is whether the contract of sale includes the Standard Terms as part of the agreement. . . .

It appears that at least in part, the cases turn on whether the court finds that the parties formed their contract *before* or *after* the vendor communicated its terms to the purchaser. *Compare Step-Saver,* 939 F.2d at 98 (parties' conduct in shipping, receiving and paying for product demonstrates existence of contract; box top license constitutes proposal for additional terms under § 2–207 which requires express agreement by purchaser) . . . *with ProCD,* 86 F.3d at 1452 (under § 2–204 vendor, as master of offer, may propose limitations on kind of conduct that constitutes acceptance; § 2–207 does not apply in case with only one form); *Hill,* 105 F.3d at 1148–49 (same); *and Mortenson,* 998 P.2d at 311–314 (where vendor and purchaser utilized license agreement in prior course of dealing, shrinkwrap license agreement constituted issue of contract formation under § 2–204, not contract alteration under § 2–207).

Gateway urges the Court to follow the Seventh Circuit [opinions in *ProCD* and *Hill,* excerpted above]. . . . The Court is not persuaded that Kansas or Missouri courts would follow the Seventh Circuit reasoning in *Hill* and *ProCD.* In each case the Seventh Circuit concluded without support that UCC § 2–207 was irrelevant because the cases involved only one written form. *See ProCD,* 86 F.3d at 1452 (citing no authority); *Hill,* 105 F.3d at 1150 (citing *ProCD*). This conclusion is not supported by the statute or by Kansas or Missouri law. Disputes under § 2–207 often arise in the context of a "battle of forms," . . . but nothing in its language precludes application in a case which involves only one form. . . .

By its terms, § 2–207 applies to an acceptance or written confirmation. It states nothing which requires another form before the provision becomes effective. In fact, the official comment to the section specifically provides that §§ 2–207(1) and (2) apply "where an agreement has been reached orally . . . and is followed by one or both of the parties sending formal memoranda embodying the terms so far agreed and adding terms not discussed." Official Comment 1 of UCC § 2–207. Kansas and Missouri courts have followed this analysis. *See Southwest Engineering Co. v. Martin Tractor Co.,* 205 Kan. 684, 695, 473 P.2d 18, 26 (1970) (stating in dicta that § 2–207 applies where open offer is accepted by expression of acceptance in writing or where oral agreement is later confirmed in writing); *Central Bag Co. v. W. Scott and Co.,* 647 S.W.2d 828, 830 (Mo.App.1983) (§§ 2–207(1) and (2) govern cases where one or both parties send written confirmation after oral contract). Thus, the Court concludes that Kansas and Missouri courts would apply § 2–207 to the facts in this case. . . .

In addition, the Seventh Circuit provided no explanation for its conclusion that "the vendor is the master of the offer." *See ProCD,* 86 F.3d at 1452 (citing nothing in support of proposition); *Hill,* 105 F.3d at 1149 (citing *ProCD*). In typical consumer transactions, the purchaser is the offeror, and the vendor is the offeree. . . . While it is possible for the vendor to be the offeror, *see Brown Machine,* 770 S.W.2d at 419 (price quote can amount to offer if it reasonably appears from quote that assent to quote is all that is needed to ripen offer into contract), Gateway provides no factual evidence which would support such a finding in this case. The Court therefore assumes for purposes of the motion to dismiss that plaintiff offered to purchase the computer (either in person or through catalog order) and that Gateway accepted plaintiff's offer (either by completing the sales transaction in person or by agreeing to ship and/or shipping the computer to plaintiff). . . .

Under § 2–207, the Standard Terms constitute either an expression of acceptance or written confirmation. As an expression of acceptance, the Standard Terms would constitute a counter-offer only if Gateway expressly made its acceptance conditional on plaintiff's assent to the additional or different terms. [2–207(1)]. "[T]he conditional nature of the acceptance must be clearly expressed in a manner sufficient to notify the offeror that the offeree is unwilling to proceed with the transaction unless the additional or different terms are included in the contract." *Brown Machine,* 770 S.W.2d at 420. Gateway provides no evidence that at the time of the sales transaction, it informed plaintiff that the transaction was conditioned on plaintiff's acceptance of the Standard Terms.

Moreover, the mere fact that Gateway shipped the goods with the terms attached did not communicate to plaintiff any unwillingness to proceed without plaintiff's agreement to the Standard Terms. [*See Step-Saver*].

Because plaintiff is not a merchant, additional or different terms contained in the Standard Terms did not become part of the parties' agreement unless plaintiff expressly agreed to them. *See* K.S.A. § 84–2–207, Kansas Comment 2 (if either party is not a merchant, additional terms are proposals for addition to the contract that do not become part of the contract unless the original offeror expressly agrees). Gateway argues that plaintiff demonstrated acceptance of the arbitration provision by keeping the computer more than five days after the date of delivery.

Although the Standard Terms purport to work that result, Gateway has not presented evidence that plaintiff expressly agreed to those Standard Terms. Gateway states only that it enclosed the Standard Terms inside the computer box for plaintiff to read afterwards. It provides no evidence that it informed plaintiff of the five-day review-and-return period as a condition of the sales transaction, or that the parties contemplated additional terms to the agreement. *See Step-Saver,* 939 F.2d at 99 (during negotiations leading to purchase, vendor never mentioned box-top license or obtained buyer's express assent thereto). . . .

NOTES AND QUESTIONS

1.   Are the facts of *Hill v. Gateway* and *Klocek v. Gateway* distinguishable? The number of days the purchaser could keep the product differ but that does not seem legally significant. Are there reasons to be more sympathetic to the buyers in *Klocek* than to the buyer in *ProCD*? Does that help to explain the differing outcomes of the cases? Or is something else going on, such as different weight assigned to questions of fairness versus efficiency or law versus public policy?

2.   The inconsistent outcomes of *Hill v. Gateway* and *Klocek v. Gateway* trouble some commentators, who perceive ideology at play. Do you share that perception? Is it problematic? After all, the UCC is a law self-described as "uniform," judges are supposed to enforce the law, and yet we have analytically identical facts with opposed outcomes. Are ideological differences influencing these different outcomes, or is there a better explanation? *See M.A. Mortenson Co. v. Timberline Software Corp.*, 998 P.2d 305 (Wash. 2000) (following *ProCD* and *Hill* to embrace "rolling contract" theory over a vigorous dissent that asserted: "the majority abandons traditional contract principles governing offer and acceptance and relies on distinguishable cases with blind deference to software manufacturers' preferred method of conducting business.").

3.   Debate continues on the merits of rolling contract doctrine, in both courtrooms and classrooms, nationwide. Consider the following summation:

> In the waning years of the twentieth century, an influential court announced a radical change in contract formation theory. What has been labeled the "rolling" or "layered" theory proved highly controversial. Analyses of the two Seventh Circuit opinions creating the theory have revealed several of its analytical defects, but other flaws and their unintended effects have not been emphasized. Suggestions that subsequent cases have installed the rolling theory as the prevailing view are, at the least, premature. The case law progeny reveals pervasive confusion and inconsistent results.

> Beyond holdings rejecting the theory, opinions that distinguish their facts leave substantial questions as to its potential application unanswered. Without any reference to the theory, contrary holdings make it difficult to discern its current status in a given jurisdiction. The underlying purpose of the theory is the "efficacy" of form contracting, but even that alleged benefit is questionable. Commentators generally agree that the theory ignores statutory language and precedent. The majority of jurisdictions have not had the opportunity to decide the fate of the rolling theory. It is important to pursue a definitive analysis to facilitate future decisions concerning its application or rejection.

John E. Murray, Jr., *The Dubious Status of the Rolling Contract Formation Theory*, 50 DUQUESNE L.REV. 35 (2012). Compare this assessment:

> A number of courts have held that a contract is formed when deferred terms found inside the package are reviewed by the buyer and accepted by some act-usually use of the good. This "rolling" contract approach has been widely criticized by commentators as an abomination of contract law that ignores a true application of the U.C.C., as well as the spirit of that code. However, the approach is not without its allure, as it permits contracts to be formed in an efficient manner that may very well appeal to consumers. Yet too strict of an adherence to the approach threatens to impose terms upon parties that they never expected or agreed upon; but conversely, too strict of an adherence to traditional concepts of offer and acceptance threatens to displace terms that were contemplated and not objectionable. Though existing contract law does a good job of defining contract offer, the trickier issue is identifying when the offer is actually made. If parties to a contract know that there is more to the contract than simply the price and the good, then it should come as no surprise that more terms are to come, or that a more detailed offer will be forthcoming. Thus, in some scenarios, it is perfectly reasonable to assume that the contract has not been formed in-store, but rather a deferred offer will come later.

Colin P. Marks, *Not What, But When Is An Offer: Rehabilitating the Rolling Contract*, 46 CONN. L. REV. 73 (2013).

CHAPTER 4

UNENFORCEABLE BARGAINS

∎ ∎ ∎

Courts enforce contracts meeting standard tests of bargain or reliance, but will not aid parties whose contracts are unconscionable or illegal. In this chapter, we consider what principles courts reference in demarcating unenforceable bargains, which are not necessarily self-defining. True, you can imagine courts will not enforce contracts for murder or perhaps to sell a million-dollar inheritance for a dollar, but what about a contract to share lottery winnings or that repays a million dollars if the borrower of $10,000 strikes gold?

For perspective, consider that federal and state statutes police the border of marketable goods and services from those that are forbidden to be sold. On the first order are constitutional provisions and federal and state statutes that criminalize, forbid, or otherwise ban markets in a particular good or service. Constitutional provisions can be used to outlaw an entire market, such as alcohol during Prohibition. These criminal provisions—often dubbed "vice" activities—sometimes depend on context. For example, sexual activity that would otherwise be legal becomes criminalized if it involves the exchange of money.

At the same time, markets shift over the years along with changing morals. For example, many drugs that once were legal, such as cocaine, are now banned, while others, such as marijuana, go from contraband to legalized. These processes can be uneven and slow. While some states have been liberalizing state gambling laws and authorizing casino gambling, federal anti-gambling laws have cracked down on Internet gambling.

In addition to banning certain types of markets outright, many federal and state statutes either set the ground rules for participation or attempt to protect vulnerable participants. Examples include the Magnuson-Moss Warranty Act, which governs the form and structure of warranties for consumer goods, 15 U.S.C. §§ 2301–2312. Under the Securities Exchange Act, more relaxed rules are applied to investors who meet the wealth or financial knowledge tests that qualify them as accredited investors. There are also many and varied state consumer laws enacted to protect people from unsavory business practices.

In this chapter, we explore the two broad judicial policing mechanisms of unconscionability and public policy. As to the former, while courts do not usually inquire into the adequacy of consideration, some bargains are too sharp for courts to countenance, and are declared unconscionable. As to public policy, the notion is capacious, both inherently changing and unstable. Public policy provides both a judicial check on troubling contracts and creates a risk of judicial overreach.

A. UNCONSCIONABILITY

Are there any bargains that seem to be so one-sided that courts will not enforce them? Imagine, as suggested by Judge Easterbrook in *ProCD v. Zeidenberg*, that the fine print of an end user license agreement (EULA) included a clause that obligated the user to pay the software company $10,000 upon their fifth use. Such a term, buried deep in a contract's fine print, would constitute an unfair surprise, not something most computer users would expect to see. Judges would refuse to enforce it and might call it unconscionable.

In 1967, Professor Arthur Leff wrote an article about *unconscionability*, which is well-known primarily because of the distinction Leff drew between two aspects of the problem: procedural and substantive unconscionability. The following excerpt both reviews some contract law fundamentals covered earlier and anticipates additional concepts to come in the pages ahead.

ARTHUR ALLEN LEFF, *UNCONSCIONABILITY AND THE CODE—THE EMPEROR'S NEW CLAUSE*
115 U. PA. L. REV. 485 (1967)

. . . Let us begin the story the way so many good stories begin, with ritual incantation: to make a contract one needs (i) parties with capacity, (ii) manifested assent, and (iii) consideration. This is all very simple. If these criteria are met, a party to the resulting nexus who has made promises is obligated to carry them out, unless he can maintain successfully one of the standard contract-law defenses, such as fraud, duress, mistake, impossibility or illegality. These "defenses" might be classified in diverse ways to serve various analytical purposes.

For our particular needs, however, there is a simple way of grouping them which is signally illuminating: some of these defenses have to do with the *process of contracting* and others have to do with the resulting *contract*. When fraud and duress are involved, for instance, the focus of attention is on what took place between the parties at the making of the contract. With illegality, on the other hand, the material question is instead the content of the contract once "made."

The law may legitimately be interested both in the way agreements come about and in what they provide. A "contract" gotten at gunpoint may be avoided; a classic dicker over Dobbin may come to naught if horse owning is illegal. Hereafter, to distinguish the two interests, I shall often refer to bargaining naughtiness as "procedural unconscionability," and to evils in the resulting contract as "substantive unconscionability." . . .

PROBLEMS: TYPES OF UNCONSCIONABILITY

Using Professor Leff's typology of procedural and substantive unconscionability, classify each of the following examples:

1. On page 314 of a 500-page contract, in five-point type, which looks like this, a software company inserts an arbitration clause. *procedural*

2. Same facts as 1, except the clause inserted indicates that the software user must give up his or her firstborn child in order to use the software. *both*

3. Same as 2, except the child-selling term is printed in 30-point type in all bold, on page 1. *substantive*

How are unconscionability cases decided in practice? Unfortunately, economic downturns and financial crises produce many real-world cases of predatory lending and subsequent mortgage foreclosure. Consider the following case from the Arkansas Supreme Court.

GULFCO OF LOUISIANA V. BRANTLEY
430 S.W.3d 7 (Ark. 2013)

GOODSON, J.

Appellant Gulfco of Louisiana, Inc., d/b/a Tower Loan of Springhill, Louisiana (Gulfco), appeals the decision of the Columbia County Circuit Court denying its request to foreclose on the home of appellees Pamela and MacArthur Brantley. For reversal, Gulfco argues that the circuit court erred in applying Arkansas usury law to decline enforcement of the debt instruments that it contends are governed by the laws of the State of Louisiana. Gulfco also asserts that the circuit court erred in concluding that it was required to be licensed by the Arkansas Secretary of State and in ruling that the transactions were unconscionable and the product of predatory lending practices. We affirm the circuit court's decision.

. . . Gulfco is in the business of extending high-risk loans to customers with poor credit ratings. It operates primarily in Louisiana, Mississippi, and Missouri. The Brantleys, who reside in Waldo, Arkansas, obtained four loans over a two-year period from Gulfco at its location in Springhill, Louisiana, that is near the Arkansas-Louisiana border. First, on May 13, 2009, they borrowed $1,580.36 with an annual interest rate of 40.20 percent. After deductions for fees and insurance, the Brantleys received $1,031.63 in cash. Applying the stated interest rate, the finance charge amounted to $811.64, yielding a total indebtedness of $2,392, payable in twenty-six monthly installments of $92. The promissory note evidencing the debt stated that the loan was secured by "personal property."

On December 17, 2009, the Brantleys obtained another loan of $20,887.71 at an annual interest rate of 24.09 percent. Out of that sum, Gulfco satisfied the first loan and paid both a hospital bill owed by the Brantleys and their delinquent property taxes. After deducting those sums and $850 in fees, they received $17,388.32. With the finance charge of $18,784.29, the Brantleys were to pay a total of $39,672 over the course of seventy-two months at the rate of $551 per month. To secure the note for this loan, the Brantleys executed a mortgage on their home in Waldo. Gulfco appraised the value of the home at $32,000 with a quick-sale value of $27,000.

On June 2, 2010, Gulfco loaned the Brantleys an additional $2,779.82. On this loan, Gulfco charged an annual interest rate of 35.67 percent, and after deductions for fees and prepaid interest, the Brantleys received $2,501.83. Adding the finance charge of $1,250.18, the total debt amounted to $4,030 to be satisfied in twenty-six monthly installments of $155. This loan was secured by a list of personal property that included a riding lawn mower, a drill, a chainsaw, televisions, and cameras.

On March 11, 2011, the Brantleys borrowed an additional $3,345.34 with interest at 34.32 percent. Gulfco charged $400.72 in fees, and the proceeds were used to retire the June 2010 note. After these deductions, the Brantleys received cash in hand of $598.71. Including the finance charge of $1,464.66, they were obligated to pay $4,810 over twenty-six months at the rate of $185 per month. This note was secured by the same personal property as was the June 2010 loan.

The Brantleys made no payments on the loans after March 31, 2011. On July 1, 2011, Gulfco filed in the Circuit Court of Columbia County a pleading styled "Notice of Default and Intention to Sell," alleging that the mortgage on the Brantleys' home was in default and stating that a sale of the home would occur on August 19, 2011. Gulfco attached a copy of the mortgage to the notice of default. On July 14, 2011, Pamela Brantley filed a pro se answer that was followed by a response filed by the Brantleys' attorney. In the response, the Brantleys denied the substantive allegations of the notice of default, and they asserted the defenses of usury, unconscionability, estoppel, illegality, unclean hands, predatory lending practices, and a violation of the Arkansas Deceptive Trade Practices Act (ADTPA).

On August 11, 2011, the Brantleys filed a petition for a preliminary injunction to halt the proposed sale of their home. In the petition, they asserted that the promissory notes were unconscionable, as Gulfco took advantage of their lack of sophistication and induced them to mortgage their home with knowledge that they did not have stable, full-time employment. The Brantleys also alleged that the interest rates Gulfco charged were usurious under the Arkansas Constitution. Gulfco did not file a response to the petition. On August 12, 2011, the circuit court entered an order granting the Brantleys' request for a preliminary injunction.

At the trial held on May 11, 2012, MacArthur Brantley testified that he worked part-time for a moving company. He said that he learned about Gulfco through a friend and that he and Pamela took out the first loan to pay personal bills that were about to become delinquent. MacArthur said that they fell behind on their payments of $92 per month because his work was slow and because Pamela had become ill. He stated that "Dee," Gulfco's loan agent, called him about their delinquency and suggested that they take out a second loan. MacArthur said that Dee already had the papers prepared when he arrived at the office. He stated that he did not read well and that he read what he could of the loan disclosure statement and promissory note.

MacArthur testified that the money for the second loan was used to pay the first note and to buy a logging truck. He stated that he purchased the truck for $1,500 and spent $2,300 for welding in addition to buying tires and paying insurance. With regard to the June 2010 loan, MacArthur testified that the money was used to catch up the arrearages on the December-2009 loan. He said that they borrowed more money in March 2011 to again bring their loans current. MacArthur testified that they did not have the money to pay the loans and that they were faced with the choice of either accepting more loans or losing their home.

Pamela Brantley testified that she and MacArthur began construction of their home in 2000 and that they had built it a little at a time when money was available. Pamela said that she graduated from high school with a B average and that MacArthur had taken remedial classes in high school. Pamela stated that the county assessor had appraised the value of their home at $51,450. She said that she had heard from friends that Gulfco offered easy money and that she and MacArthur sought a loan because they were behind on their household bills. She said that they told the loan agent, Demetrius Wilson, that she earned $120 per week sitting for an elderly woman and that MacArthur worked part-time for a moving company and sometimes mowed yards. She said she also advised Wilson of her medical problems.

Pamela stated that Wilson knew that they had a home and about MacArthur's idea of obtaining a logging truck as a means to generate income. She testified that she advised Wilson that they were having a hard time making their payments on the first loan and that it was Wilson who suggested mortgaging their house and purchasing a logging truck. Pamela said that Wilson mentioned this idea many times in their conversations and that they finally agreed to another loan with a mortgage on their home.

She testified that having the logging truck did not work out due to problems keeping the truck running, the high cost of gasoline, and a downturn in the logging business. Pamela said that they used the June 2010 loan to make a past-due payment on the previous loan and to pay household bills. She said that she was having medical problems at the time and could not work and that they "were going in circles" and getting deeper and deeper in a hole. Pamela stated that she did not read the loan documents because she and MacArthur were broke and in need of money.

Lori Spence, Gulfco's district manager, testified that between the first loan in May 2009 and the second one in December 2009, appellees were assessed three late charges and had missed two $92 monthly payments. She acknowledged that, when the June 2010 loan was made, appellees had missed the June payment. Spence stated that with the December 2009 and June 2010 loans, appellees were paying $551 a month on the note and mortgage in addition to $155 per month on the June 2010 note. She said that they continued to miss payments and garner late charges. Introduced into evidence was a receipt [that] appellees received dated February 18, 2011, stating that "[y]ou can obtain an additional $3043.48 from us, if you need it. Just ask the manager." Spence stated that they were one payment behind on the mortgage when the final loan was made in March 2011, and the loan proceeds were used to pay that arrearage. Further, she testified that Gulfco has several offices located near the Arkansas border. . . .

The court entered an order setting forth its decision on August 12, 2012. The circuit court described what it referred to as a "disturbing pattern of lending." The court found that Gulfco made four loans to the Brantleys despite their lack of stable employment. It said that it was no surprise that they were soon behind on their payments. The court noted that subsequent loans were used to bring the former loans current, and the court called attention to the receipt that indicated that even more money was available.

The circuit court believed Pamela's testimony that Gulfco recommended the purchase of the logging truck and that the venture turned out to be one that they could not afford. It noted that with MacArthur's income level and Pamela's illness, they could not break the cycle of debt. The court considered that the fees charged for the four loans was $2,322, and it deemed significant the fact that the charges were deducted from the loan proceeds on the front end, thereby reducing the amount of money available to the Brantleys and increasing the probability of further debt. It concerned the court that Gulfco referenced a quick-sale value of the home, as it indicated that a foreclosure sale might not be conducted in a commercially reasonable manner, which would result in a deficiency judgment against the Brantleys.

In addition, the circuit court observed that Gulfco does business in three other states; that it was not licensed to do business in Arkansas; and that the interest rates would violate Arkansas usury law. In conclusion, the court found that "the loans collectively constitute predatory lending by a foreign corporation not authorized to do business in Arkansas and that the contract sought to be enforced is unconscionable and cannot be given full faith and credit. Accordingly, the contract will not be enforced against Arkansas property." Gulfco brings this appeal from the circuit court's order.

. . . Gulfco argues that the law of Louisiana applies to the debt instruments and that the circuit court erred by employing Arkansas usury law to void the agreements. It points out that the promissory note that was secured by the mortgage contains a choice-of-law provision stating that the note is governed under the provisions of Louisiana law. Further, Gulfco maintains that it is a Louisiana corporation, that the agreements were executed in Louisiana, and that the Brantleys' payments were directed to Louisiana. It contends that, under these circumstances, the validity of the agreements must be judged under Louisiana law. In response, the Brantleys assert that Gulfco waived reliance on Louisiana law because it did not give notice of its intent to rely on foreign law as required by Rule 44.1 of the Arkansas Rules of Civil Procedure.

. . . While the circuit court was indeed mindful that the loans would be usurious under Arkansas law, the court did not decline to enforce the agreements based on a violation of Arkansas usury law. Instead, the court's ruling was that the debt instruments were not enforceable because they were unconscionable and the product of predatory lending practices. Inasmuch as the circuit court did not rule that the agreements were void because they violated Arkansas usury law, Gulfco's argument presents no basis for reversal.

Gulfco takes issue with the circuit court's finding that it engaged in unconscionable and predatory lending practices. It asserts that appellees signed the documents and were aware of the interest rates being charged; that they agreed to mortgage their home; and that they wished to engage in the logging business. Gulfco argues that parties are bound by contractual provisions and may not assert ignorance of the document they have signed. It contends that a court is not to rewrite a contract but must construe it as to reflect the parties' intent. Further, Gulfco maintains that the Brantleys were not desperate or taken advantage of because it was they who sought out the first loan to help pay bills that were about to become delinquent. Gulfco also points out that the Brantleys' credit was poor and that they did not seek a loan from any other lending institution.

. . . An act is unconscionable if it affronts the sense of justice, decency, and reasonableness. *Baptist Health v. Murphy*, 2010 Ark. 358, 373 S.W.3d

269. We have stated that in assessing whether a particular contractual provision is unconscionable, the courts review the totality of the circumstances surrounding the negotiation and execution of the contract. *Jordan v. Diamond Equip. & Supply Co.*, 362 Ark. 142, 207 S.W.3d 525 (2005). Two important considerations are whether there is a gross inequality of bargaining power between the parties and whether the aggrieved party was made aware of and comprehended the provision in question. *Id.* [A]nother factor which may contribute to a finding of unconscionability is a belief by the stronger party that there is no reasonable probability that the weaker party will fully perform the contract.

Arkansas's consumer-protection law, which is an expression of this State's public policy, is consistent with the Restatement [of Contracts] § 208, which states: "If a contract or term thereof is unconscionable at the time the contract is made a court may refuse to enforce the contract, or may enforce the remainder of the contract without the unconscionable term, or may so limit the application of any unconscionable term as to avoid any unconscionable result."]

The Arkansas Home Loan Protection Act applies to high-cost home loans, which is a loan that is secured by a first lien on the structure that does not exceed $150,000, where the borrower is a natural person, and where the debt is incurred by the borrower primarily for personal, family, or household purposes. The Act prohibits practices such as lending without due regard to repayment ability. It provides,

> A creditor shall not make a high-cost home loan unless the creditor reasonably believes at the time the loan is consummated that one (1) or more of the obligors, when considered individually or collectively, will be able to make the scheduled payments to repay the obligation based upon a consideration of their current and expected income, current obligations, employment status, and other financial resources other than the borrower's equity in the dwelling that secures repayment of the loan.

. . . . Our review of the record confirms the circuit court's opinion of Gulfco's lending practices vis-a-vis the Brantleys. The Brantleys first obtained a modest loan from Gulfco to pay household bills that were about to become delinquent. They had difficulty making the $92 per month payments on this loan, as neither of them had full-time employment. Yet Gulfco, with knowledge of their employment status and Pamela's illness, loaned them approximately $20,000, taking a mortgage on the Brantleys' home as security. The proceeds of this loan were used to retire the unsecured first loan.

The testimony also indicated that Gulfco's agent persuaded the Brantleys to mortgage their home. Thereafter, the Brantleys had trouble making the monthly payments of $551. Despite this fact, Gulfco extended more credit to them, and with this third loan, they were required to pay an extra $155 per month in addition to the $551 for the second loan. Predictably, the Brantleys could not meet these obligations. Nonetheless, Gulfco made yet another loan to them after advertising in a receipt that more money was available. With this fourth loan, the third note was satisfied, and the Brantleys' monthly payments increased once again.

[The] Brantleys were not capable of making their payments from the beginning. Subsequent loans were made to pay off previous notes or to bring their payments current. Despite the Brantley's demonstrated inability to pay, Gulfco continued to loan them money. Each loan, that included built-in fees and high interest rates, placed the Brantleys in a position of ever-increasing debt, such that it was all but inevitable that they would end up in default. While the Brantleys' debt situation became more dire with each loan, Gulfco's risk was minimal, because with the mortgage, it was assured of receiving full payment on the loan. Considering the totality of the circumstances, the circuit court found that the evidence revealed an intolerable pattern of reprehensible and unconscionable conduct on the part of Gulfco that offended its sense of decency and justice. We cannot conclude that the circuit court's findings of unconscionability and predatory lending practices are clearly erroneous. . . .

NOTES AND QUESTIONS

1. What is "usury"? Does your state have a statute against usury?

2. In *Gulfco*, what specifically about the series of loans seemed problematic to the court? Which factors are unique to the particular consumers involved? Should the characteristics and capacities of the individuals involved matter when considering whether a particular deal is enforceable?

3. In *Gulfco*, the Brantleys voluntarily agreed to the loans and mortgage. Is it paternalistic to re-write this deal? This question of paternalism arises with many aspects of contract defenses. Not all deals are "good" ones, but from a meta-perspective, freedom of contract may also mean the freedom to make a "bad" deal and be free from government intervention. Where is the right line between protecting those who may be vulnerable and too much interference in freedom of contract?

4. The D.C. Court of Appeals recognized the doctrine of unconscionability in consumer transactions in *Williams v. Walker-Thomas Furniture Co.*, 350 F.2d 445 (1965). In *Williams*, a rent-to-own furniture store in the inner-city sought to replevy (repossess) household items from impoverished consumers on the basis of a "dragnet" clause: the amount owing on any one item was not considered paid unless all items were paid in full. Accepting the arguments of public interest lawyers representing the consumer, Judge J. Skelly Wright declared the dragnet clauses unconscionable.

→ absence of meaningful choice + terms unreasonably favorable to other

5. So-called "payday" lenders charge extremely high interest rates. They contend that they provide a needed service, credit to those with few assets and poor credit, but others claim they prey on vulnerable populations. Do some Internet research, and find out what options are available to those needing credit quickly from payday lenders. What are the annual percentage rates (APRs)? What are some of the contract terms?

6. In 2006, Congress passed legislation forbidding payday lenders near military bases from charging more than 36% interest on loans. 10 U.S.C. § 987. The government was concerned that members of the armed forces were being taken advantage of by exorbitant interest rates. What are the policy arguments for and against such a law?

7. As Professor Leff noted, sometimes the terms, rather than the bargaining process, are problematic. And sometimes courts will simply refuse to grant a desired remedy rather than declare a contract unconscionable or illegal. Consider the next case.

CAMPBELL SOUP CO. V. WENTZ
172 F.2d 80 (3d Cir. 1948)

GOODRICH, J.

. . . On June 21, 1947, Campbell Soup Company (Campbell), a New Jersey corporation, entered into a written contract with George B. Wentz and Harry T. Wentz, who are Pennsylvania farmers, for delivery by the Wentzes to Campbell of all the Chantenay red cored carrots to be grown on fifteen acres of the Wentz farm during the 1947 season. . . . The contract price for January, 1948 was $30 a ton.

The Wentzes harvested approximately 100 tons of carrots from the fifteen acres covered by the contract. Early in January, 1948, they told a Campbell representative that they would not deliver their carrots at the contract price. The market price at that time was at least $90 per ton, and Chantenay red cored carrots were virtually unobtainable. The Wentzes then sold approximately 62 tons of their carrots to the defendant Lojeski, a neighboring farmer. Lojeski resold about 58 tons on the open market, approximately half to Campbell and the balance to other purchasers.

On January 9, 1948, Campbell, suspecting that Lojeski was selling it "contract carrots," refused to purchase any more, and instituted these suits against the Wentz brothers and Lojeski to enjoin further sale of the contract carrots to others, and to compel specific performance of the contract. The trial court denied equitable relief. We agree with the result reached, but on a different ground from that relied upon by the District Court. . . .

Judged by the general standards applicable to determining the adequacy of the legal remedy we think that on this point the case is a proper one for [the extraordinary remedy of specific performance]. Here the goods of the special type contracted for were unavailable on the open market, the plaintiff had contracted for them long ahead in anticipation of its needs, and had built up a general reputation for its products as part of which reputation uniform appearance was important. We think if this were all that was involved in the case specific performance should have been granted.

The reason that we shall affirm instead of reversing with an order for specific performance is found in the contract itself. We think it is too hard a bargain and too one-sided an agreement to entitle the plaintiff to relief in a court of conscience. For each individual grower the agreement is made by filling in names and quantity and price on a printed form furnished by the buyer. This form has quite obviously been drawn by skilful draftsmen with the buyer's interests in mind.

Paragraph 2 provides for the manner of delivery. Carrots are to have their stalks cut off and be in clean sanitary bags or other containers approved by Campbell. This paragraph concludes with a statement that Campbell's determination of conformance with specifications shall be conclusive.

The defendants attack this provision as unconscionable. We do not think that it is, standing by itself. We think that the provision is comparable to the promise to perform to the satisfaction of another and that Campbell would be held liable if it refused carrots which did in fact conform to the specifications.

The next paragraph allows Campbell to refuse carrots in excess of twelve tons to the acre. The next contains a covenant by the grower that he will not sell carrots to anyone else except the carrots rejected by Campbell nor will he permit anyone else to grow carrots on his land. . . .

The provision of the contract which we think is the hardest is paragraph 9 . . . . Campbell is excused from accepting carrots under certain circumstances. But even under such circumstances the grower, while he cannot say Campbell is liable for failure to take the carrots, is not permitted to sell them elsewhere unless Campbell agrees. This is the kind of provision which the late Francis H. Bohlen would call "carrying a good joke too far." What the grower may do with his product under the circumstances set out is not clear. He has covenanted not to store it anywhere except on his own farm and also not to sell to anybody else.

We are not suggesting that the contract is illegal. Nor are we suggesting any excuse for the grower in this case who has deliberately broken an agreement entered into with Campbell. We do think, however, that a party who has offered and succeeded in getting an agreement as tough as this one is, should not come to a chancellor and ask court help in the enforcement of its terms. That equity does not enforce unconscionable bargains is too well established to require elaborate citation.

The plaintiff argues that the provisions of the contract are separable. We agree that they are, but do not think that decisions separating out certain provisions from illegal contracts are in point here. As already said, we do not suggest that this contract is illegal. All we say is that the sum total of its provisions drives too hard a bargain for a court of conscience to assist. . . .

NOTES AND QUESTIONS

1.   An omitted footnote in the *Campbell Soup* opinion indicates that the parties, in connection with the litigation, made "an arrangement under which Campbell received all the carrots held by the Wentzes and Lojeski, paying a stipulated market price of $90 per ton, $30 to the defendants, and the balance into the registry of the District Court pending the outcome of these appeals." As a result of the court's decision, the sellers received the full $90 per ton. Had Campbell Soup sued for damages and won, the normal rules of contract damages would award it the difference between the agreed contract price (here $30) and the higher market or "cover" price (here $90) or $60 per ton, the full amount the sellers had deposited in the court registry. So why didn't Campbell Soup simply sue for money damages? Another clause in the contract stipulated a different measure of damages for seller's breach, apparently yielding damages less than the normal rules of contract would have provided.

2.   Why would Campbell Soup have inserted the clause requiring its permission for the sellers to resell contract carrots to other buyers, even in cases when Campbell Soup did not wish to buy them? Such a clause might be viewed as legitimate if the sellers were somehow compensated for the risk that the company would refuse permission. Do you suppose the sellers were compensated?

3.   Campbell Soup got the court's message and revised its standard forms of supply contracts, which withstood a similar challenge in *Campbell Soup Co. v. Diehm*, 111 F. Supp. 211 (E.D. Pa. 1952), where the court wrote:

> The case of *Campbell Soup Company v. Wentz*, 3 Cir., 172 F.2d 80, is cited by defendants in support of their contention that the contracts in question, while valid, are unfair and therefore unenforceable in equity. The contention, we think, is without merit. The provision which the court . . . considered the severest was that which excused Campbell Soup Company from accepting carrots under certain circumstances and which prohibited the farmer even under such circumstances from selling his carrots elsewhere unless Campbell agreed. The contracts in question were altered somewhat in this respect and contained no such prohibition. All of the provisions of the contracts herein are mutual and benefit the farmers and the Company equally. For example, the provision relating to

contingencies exonerates both the growers and Campbell of default or delay in certain circumstances. The Court of Appeals ... made mention of the provision in the contract before it specifying that Campbell's determination of conformance with specifications would be conclusive. This provision has been eliminated in the present contracts. Conformance now depends on standards established by the United States Department of Agriculture, and grading is performed by graders licensed by the United States Department of Agriculture and assigned to the loading platforms by the State Department of Agriculture. The present contracts remove [the company's] discretion [about] acceptability of [product] quality.... Thus, the present contracts are not subject to the several criticisms directed at the carrot contract by the Court of Appeals. They are in our judgment fair and enforceable in equity.

FROSTIFRESH CORP. v. REYNOSO

52 Misc.2d 26 (Dist. Ct. Nassau County, N.Y. 1966)

DONOVAN, J.

Plaintiff brings this action for $1364.10, alleging that the latter amount is owed by the defendants to the plaintiff on account of the purchase of a combination-refrigerator-freezer for which they agreed to pay the sum of $1145.88. The balance of the amount consists of a claim for attorney fees in the amount of $227.35 and a late charge of $22.87. The only payment made on account of the original indebtedness is the sum of $32.00.

The contract for the refrigerator-freezer was negotiated orally in Spanish between the defendants and a Spanish speaking salesman representing the plaintiff. In that conversation, the defendant husband told the salesman that he had but one week left on his job and he could not afford to buy the appliance. The salesman distracted and deluded the defendants by advising them that the appliance would cost them nothing because they would be paid bonuses or commissions of $25.00 each on the numerous sales that would be made to their neighbors and friends. Thereafter there was submitted to and signed by the defendants a retail installment contract entirely in English. The retail contract was neither translated nor explained to the defendants. In that contract, there was a cash sales price set forth of $900.00. To this was added a credit charge of $245.88, making a total of $1145.88 to be paid for the appliance.

The plaintiff admitted that cost to the plaintiff corporation for the appliance was $348.00. No defense of fraud was set forth in the pleadings and accordingly such defense is not available. However, in the course of the trial, it did appear to the court that the contract might be unconscionable. This court therefore continued the trial at an adjourned date to afford a reasonable opportunity to the parties to present evidence as to the commercial setting, purpose and effect of the contract.

The court finds that the sale of the appliance at the price and terms indicated in this contract is . . . [unconscionable]. The service charge, which almost equals the price of the appliance is in and of itself is indicative of the oppression which was practiced on these defendants. Defendants were handicapped by a lack of knowledge, both as to the commercial situation and the nature and terms of the contract which was submitted in a language foreign to them.

The question presented in this case is simply this: Does the court have the power under section 2–302 of the Uniform Commercial Code to refuse to enforce the price and credit provisions of the contract in order to prevent an unconscionable result.

It is normally stated that the parties are free to make whatever contracts they please so long as there is no fraud or illegality (Allegheny College v. National Chautauqua County Bank, 246 N.Y. 369, 159 N.E. 173, 57 L.R.A. 980). However, it is the apparent intent of the Uniform Commercial Code to modify this general rule by giving the courts power 'to police explicitly against the contracts or clauses which they find to be unconscionable. * * * The principle is one of the prevention of oppression and unfair surprise.' (See the official comment appended to the statute in the note on page 193, McKinney's Uniform Commercial Code, volume 62 ¹/₂ Part I.)

The comment cites Campbell Soup Company v. Wentz, 3 Cir., 172 F.2d 80, to illustrate the principle. . . . The Court of Appeals said 'We think it too hard a bargain and too one-sided an agreement to entitle the plaintiff to relief in a court of conscience' (p. 83).

In the instant case the court finds that here, too, it was 'too hard a bargain' and the conscience of the court will not permit the enforcement of the contract as written. Therefore the plaintiff will not be permitted to recover on the basis of the price set forth in the retail installment contract, namely $900.00 plus $245.85 as a service charge. However, since the defendants have not returned the refrigerator-freezer, they will be required to reimburse the plaintiff for the cost to the plaintiff, namely $348.00. No allowance is made on account of any commissions the plaintiff may have paid to salesmen or for legal fees, service charges or any other matters of overhead. Accordingly the plaintiff may have judgment against both defendants in the amount of $348.00 with interest, less the $32.00 paid on account, leaving a net balance of $316.00 with interest from December 26, 1964.

B. CONSIDERATION REVISITED

Courts do not inquire into the adequacy of consideration out of deference to freedom of contract and personal autonomy along with a sense of judicial modesty. But wildly disproportionate consideration may signal neither freedom nor autonomy but coercion or worse, and be so lopsided that judicial second-guessing may be prudent.

WATERS V. MIN LTD.

587 N.E.2d 231 (Mass. 1992)

LYNCH, J.

This case arises from a contract between Gail A. Waters (plaintiff) and "the DeVito defendants" (defendants), whereby the plaintiff was to assign her annuity policy having a cash value of $189,000 to the defendants in exchange for $50,000. The plaintiff [sued] to rescind the contract on the ground of unconscionability. Defendants . . . counterclaimed seeking declaratory relief and specific enforcement of the contract. A Superior Court judge, sitting without a jury, found for the plaintiff . . . We now affirm
. . . .

. . . The plaintiff was injured in an accident when she was twelve years old. At the age of eighteen, she settled her claim and, with the proceeds, purchased the annuity contract in question from the defendant Commercial Union Insurance Company. When the plaintiff was twenty-one, she became romantically involved with the defendant Thomas Beauchemin, an ex-convict, who introduced her to drugs. Beauchemin suggested that she sell her annuity contract, introduced her to one of the defendants, and represented her in the contract negotiations. She was naive, insecure, vulnerable in contract matters, and unduly influenced by Beauchemin. The defendants drafted the contract documents with the assistance of legal counsel, but the plaintiff had no such representation. At least some portions of the contract were executed in unusual circumstances: i.e., part of the contract was signed on the hood of an automobile in a parking lot, part was signed in a restaurant. The defendants agreed to pay $50,000 for the annuity policy which would return to them as owners of the policy $694,000 over its guaranteed term of twenty-five years, and which had a cash value at the time the contract was executed of $189,000.

Beauchemin acted for himself and as agent of the defendants. For example, the defendants forgave a $100 debt of Beauchemin as deposit for the purchase of the annuity policy. From a subsequent $25,000 payment, the defendants deducted $7,000 that Beauchemin owed them.

Based on the foregoing, the judge found the contract unconscionable. . . . The defendants argue that the evidence does not support the finding that the contract was unconscionable or that they assumed no risks and therefore that the contract was oppressive. . . . The doctrine of unconscionability has long been recognized by common law courts in this country and in England. . . . "Historically, a [contract] was considered unconscionable if it was 'such as no man in his senses and not under delusion would make on the one hand, and as no honest and fair man would accept on the other.' Hume v. United States, 132 U.S. 406[, 411, 10 S.Ct. 134, 136, 33 L.Ed. 393] (1889), quoting Earl of Chesterfield v. Janssen, 38 Eng.Rep. 82, 100 (Ch. 1750). Later, a contract was determined unenforceable because unconscionable when "the sum total of its provisions drives too hard a bargain for a court of conscience to assist." Campbell Soup Co. v. Wentz, 172 F.2d 80, 84 (3d Cir.1948)." Covich v. Chambers, 8 Mass.App.Ct. 740, 750 n. 13 (1979).

The doctrine of unconscionability has also been codified in [UCC § 2–302], and, by analogy, it has been applied in situations outside the ambit of the code. See, e.g., Zapatha v. Dairy Mart, Inc., 381 Mass. 284, 291, 408 N.E.2d 1370 (1980) (termination clause in franchise agreement not considered unconscionable); Commonwealth v. DeCotis, 366 Mass. 234, 242, 316 N.E.2d 748 (1974) (extraction of resale fees for no rendered services deemed unfair act or practice under G.L. c. 93A, § 2[a]). . . . As explained in Bronstein v. Prudential Ins. Co., 390 Mass. 701, 708, 459 N.E.2d 772 (1984), "[in Zapatha] the court applied statutory policy to common law contract issues, which, for centuries have been within the province of this court." Accordingly, although we are not here concerned with a sale of goods or a commercial transaction, *Zapatha* is instructive on the principles to be applied in testing this transaction for unconscionability.

Unconscionability must be determined on a case-by-case basis, with particular attention to whether the challenged provision could result in oppression and unfair surprise to the disadvantaged party and not to allocation of risk because of "superior bargaining power." Zapatha, supra 381 Mass. at 292–293, 408 N.E.2d 1370. Courts have identified other elements of the unconscionable contract. For example, gross disparity in the consideration alone "may be sufficient to sustain [a finding that the contract is unconscionable]," since the disparity "itself leads inevitably to the felt conclusion that knowing advantage was taken of [one party]." Jones v. Star Credit Corp., 59 Misc.2d 189, 192, 298 N.Y.S.2d 264 (N.Y.Sup.Ct.1969). . . . High pressure sales tactics and misrepresentation have been recognized as factors rendering a contract unconscionable. . . . If the sum total of the provisions of a contract drive too hard a bargain, a court of conscience will not assist its enforcement. . . .

The judge found that Beauchemin introduced the plaintiff to drugs, exhausted her credit card accounts to the sum of $6,000, unduly influenced her, suggested that the plaintiff sell her annuity contract, initiated the contract negotiations, was the agent of the defendants, and benefited from the contract between the plaintiff and the defendants. The defendants were represented by legal counsel; the plaintiff was not. . . . The cash value of the annuity policy at the time the contract was executed was approximately four times greater than the price to be paid by the defendants. For payment of not more than $50,000 the defendants were to receive an asset that could be immediately exchanged for $189,000, or they could elect to hold it for its guaranteed term and receive $694,000. . . . [T]he judge could correctly conclude the contract was unconscionable.

The defendants assumed no risk and the plaintiff gained no advantage. Gross disparity in the values exchanged is an important factor to be considered in determining whether a contract is unconscionable. "[C]ourts [may] avoid enforcement of a bargain that is shown to be unconscionable by reason of gross inadequacy of consideration accompanied by other relevant factors." 1 A. Corbin, Contracts § 128 . . . See In re Estate of Vought, 76 Misc.2d 755, 351 N.Y.S.2d 816 (N.Y.Sur.Ct.1973) (assignment of interest in spendthrift trust for $66,000 under provisions which guaranteed assignees ultimate return of $1,100,000).

We are satisfied that the disparity of interests in this contract is "so gross that the court cannot resist the inference that it was improperly obtained and is unconscionable." In re Estate of Vought, supra at 760, 351 N.Y.S.2d 816. . . .

NOTES AND QUESTIONS

1. Is the standard for substantive unconscionability articulated in *Waters* objective, subjective, or a combination of both?

2. How much does the court seem to be reasoning from sympathies for the unfortunate situation of Gail Waters, who was in an accident, got romantically involved with an exploitative person, and became addicted to drugs? Is the court's approach too paternalistic?

3. The provision of lump-sum payments in situations with structured litigation settlements is controversial. In 2015, the *Washington Post* reported on several finance companies in Maryland that floated lump-sum payments to recipients of structured settlements in lead paint cases. The payments were only pennies on the dollar. The plaintiffs in the lead paint cases, mostly African American residents of inner-city Baltimore, had suffered cognitive deficits because of exposure to lead and might have had trouble understanding the terms of exchange. Lawyers were involved in drafting the settlements and meeting with the residents to secure their signatures. *See* Terrence McCoy, *How Companies Make Millions Off Lead Poisoned, Poor Blacks*, WASHINGTON POST, August 25, 2015.

EMBOLA V. TUPPELA

220 P. 789 (Wash. 1923)

PEMBERTON, J.

John Tuppela joined the gold seekers' rush to Alaska, and after remaining there a number of years prospecting was adjudged insane, and committed to an asylum in Portland, Oregon. Upon his release, after a confinement of about four years, he found that his mining properties in Alaska had been sold by his guardian. In May of 1918 Tuppela, destitute and without work, met respondent at Astoria, Oregon. They had been close friends for a period of about 30 years. Respondent advanced money for his support, and in September brought him to Seattle to the home of Herman Lindstrom, a brother-in-law of respondent. Tuppela had requested a number of people to advance money for an undertaking to recover his mining property in Alaska, but found no one who was willing to do so. The estimated value of this mining property was about $500,000. In the month of September Tuppela made the following statement to respondent:

> You have already let me have $270. If you will give me $50 more so I can go to Alaska and get my property back, I will pay you ten thousand dollars when I win my property.

Respondent accepted this offer, and immediately advanced the sum of $50. In January, 1921, after extended litigation, Tuppela recovered his property. Tuppela, remembering his agreement with respondent, requested Mr. Cobb, his trustee, to pay the full amount, and upon his refusal so to do this action was instituted to collect the same.

The answer of the appellant denies the contract, and alleges that, if it were made, it is unconscionable, not supported by adequate consideration, procured through fraud, and is usurious. The appellant also alleges that the amount advanced did not exceed $100, and he has paid $150 into the registry of the court for the benefit of respondent. The court found in favor of the respondent, and from the judgment entered this appeal is taken.

It is contended by appellant that the amount advanced is a loan, and therefore usurious, and that the sum of $300 is not an adequate consideration to support a promise to repay $10,000. It is the contention of respondent that the money advanced was not a loan, but an investment; that the transaction was in the nature of a grubstake contract, which has been upheld by this court. . . .

This is not a case wherein respondent advanced money to carry on prospecting. The money was advanced to enable appellant to recover his mining property. Appellant had already been advised by an attorney that he could not recover this property. The risk of losing the money advanced was as great in this case as if the same had been advanced under a grubstake contract. Where the principal sum advanced is to be repaid only on some contingency that may never take place, the sum so advanced is considered an investment, and not a loan, and the transaction is not usurious.

. . . The fact that the money advanced was not to be returned until appellant won his property, a contingency at that time unlikely to occur, supports the finding that the consideration was not inadequate. To the contention that the contract was procured through fraud the testimony shows that appellant voluntarily offered to pay to $10,000, and at the time was of sound and disposing mind, and considered that the contract was fair, and to his advantage.

The trial court having found that there was no fraud, and that the contract was not unconscionable, we should uphold these findings unless the evidence preponderates against them. . . We are satisfied that the evidence supports the findings. . . .

NOTES AND QUESTIONS

1.   In what sense did the deal between Embola and Tuppela look lopsided? It is not an exchange of $50 for $10,000 in the same way that *Waters* involved an exchange of $50,000 in cash for an instrument with a present cash value of $189,000. In *Embola*, there is a prospective exchange: $50 now for the chance, and only a chance, of $10,000 at some wholly unspecified future time. Why is it legally relevant to determine whether the plaintiff is a lender or a financier?

2.   Why might $50 be the most relevant figure to use when considering the exchange in *Embola*? Several other figures appear in the case: $270 already given plus $50 more for a total of $320; a contention by the prospector's trustee references $300; and the trustee deposited $150 into the court registry, arguing that the advance did not exceed $100.

3.   Consider another case where one amount of money was exchanged for another, this time in the context of war-torn Greece during the Second World War. How much do external circumstances—here, war—matter when judging the adequacy, as consideration, of an exchange of different amounts of money?

BATSAKIS V. DEMOTSIS
226 S.W.2d 673 (Tx. Ct. Civ. App. 1949)

McGILL, J.

[Batsakis sued Demotsis] to recover $2,000 with interest at the rate of 8% per annum from April 2, 1942, alleged to be due on the following instrument, being a translation from the original, which is written in . . . Greek . . . :

Peiraeus
April 2, 1942

Mr. George Batsakis
Konstantinou Diadohou #7
Peiraeus

Mr. Batsakis:

I state by my present (letter) that I received today from you the amount of two thousand dollars ($2,000.00) of United States of America money, which I borrowed from you for the support of my family during these difficult days and because it is impossible for me to transfer dollars of my own from America.

The above amount I accept with the expressed promise that I will return to you again in American dollars either at the end of the present war or even before in the event that you might be able to find a way to collect them (dollars) from my representative in America to whom I shall write and give him an order relative to this. You understand until the final execution (payment) to the above amount an eight per cent interest will be added and paid together with the principal.

I thank you and I remain yours with respects.

THE RECIPIENT,
(SIGNED) EUGENIA THE. DEMOTSIS.'

[The trial court entered] a judgment in favor of plaintiff for $750.00 principal, and interest at the rate of 8% per annum from April 2, 1942 to the date of judgment, totaling $1163.83, with interest thereon at the rate of 8% per annum until paid. [Batsakis appealed, explaining as follows.]

. . . on or about April 2, 1942 she owned money in the United States of America, but was then and there in the Kingdom of Greece in straitened financial circumstances due to the conditions produced by World War II and could not make use of her money and property and credit existing in the United States . . . . That in the circumstances the plaintiff agreed to and did lend to defendant the sum of 500,000 drachmae, which at that time, on or about April 2, 1942, had the value of $25.00 in money of the United States of America. That the said plaintiff, knowing defendant's financial distress and desire to return to the United States of America, exacted of her the written instrument plaintiff sues upon, which was a promise by her to pay to him the sum of $2,000.00. [Accordingly, the plaintiff's claim fails for want of consideration, except as to $25, which defendant hereby agrees to pay with interest.] . . .

. . . Defendant testified that she did receive 500,000 drachmas from plaintiff. It is not clear whether she received all the 500,000 drachmas or only a portion of them before she signed the instrument in question. Her testimony clearly shows that the understanding of the parties was that plaintiff would give her the 500,000 drachmas if she would sign the instrument. She testified:

Q.   [W]ho suggested the figure of $2,000.00?

A.   That was how he asked me from the beginning. He said he will give me five hundred thousand drachmas provided I signed that I would pay him $2,000.00 American money[.]

The transaction amounted to a sale by plaintiff of the 500,000 drachmas in consideration of the execution of the instrument sued on, by defendant. It is not contended that the drachmas had no value. Indeed, the judgment indicates that the trial court placed a value of $750.00 on them or on the other consideration which plaintiff gave defendant for the instrument if he believed plaintiff's testimony. . . .

Mere inadequacy of consideration will not void a contract. . . . Defendant got exactly what she contracted for according to her own testimony. The court should have rendered judgment in favor of plaintiff against defendant for the principal sum of $2,000.00 evidenced by the instrument sued on, with interest as therein provided. . . .

NOTES AND QUESTIONS

1.   Is this a harsh result? The court sees the transaction as a loan of 500,000 drachmas in exchange for signing a document, which happens to promise to repay $2,000 plus interest, and enforces the repayment of that amount. The borrower portrayed the transaction as a loan of 500,000 drachmas, worth $25, for a promise to repay a huge multiple of that, then describes that as a failure of consideration. The borrower might have described it as unconscionable on its face given the disparity in amounts. But the lender might stress that the value of the funds to facilitate escape from war is worth some huge—and unknowable—multiple of $25, which these parties pegged at $2,000 plus interest.

2.   The Nazis invaded Greece in 1941, and after the Greek resistance and subsequent surrender, there were reprisals, destruction, and price inflation. The Nazi occupiers confiscated food and cut off imports, plunging daily caloric intake to as low as 900 calories per person per day. Thousands died from malnutrition and residents were desperate to escape. One such desperate individual was Eugenia Demotsis, who used the money at issue in the case above to leave Greece.

3.   An older well-known "chestnut" case is *Fischer v. Union Trust Co.*, 101 N.W. 852 (Mich. 1904), which involved a Christmas gathering in 1895. The father, William, said to his daughter Bertha, who was mentally unstable, that:

"I want to give you, as a Christmas present, our home." He handed her the deed, which was encumbered by mortgage loans. One of her brothers handed Bertha a dollar, and she gave it to her father, who took it. Many years later, the father died, leaving few assets and unpaid mortgage loans against the home. With bank foreclosure looming, Bertha objected, saying the home was hers.

While the court agreed that delivery of the deed completed the father's gift of the home to the child, there was no consideration for his promise to discharge the mortgage loans. The court viewed the dollar Bertha handed her father as a joke. The court interpreted the dollar as *nominal* consideration, showing a lack of contractual intention.

Although the consideration doctrine is not necessarily meant as a protection against improvidently-made contracts, it helps to identify cases where there was no bargain in fact. The objectively variant sums hint that no bargain occurred. The ratio suggests jocularity, abuse or deception in the deal's procedures and invites probing the background leading to contract formation, including who proposed an exchange, who presented the terms, how they were documented, the relationship and sophistication of the parties, and ultimately, the legal conclusion of unconscionability.

PROBLEMS: HARD BARGAINS

Consider the following situations and determine whether there may be any recourse or defenses.

1. Mei is a homeowner in Stockton, California, which has the highest foreclosure rate in the entire nation. In recent years, she has been down on her luck. As an immigrant from China, she is often homesick and has become severely depressed. Her limited English skills have prevented her from advancing in her chosen profession as an accountant. In and out of work, Mei turns to alcohol to assuage her problems, but this unfortunately only exacerbates some pre-existing health issues. The roof of her home is in a state of disrepair and she is a month behind on her taxes, so Mei is rather desperate. A knock at the door reveals a "mortgage broker" who offers Mei a third mortgage on her home for the amount of the roof repair and a year's worth of taxes at what works out to 30% APR. Mei signs the papers, but later wonders if she received a bad deal. You are her legal aid attorney and must advise her as to whether this deal is enforceable.

2. Ora Williams is a graduate of the Wharton School at the University of Pennsylvania, and is a senior executive at a Fortune 500 company who earns a seven-figure salary per year. It is important for Ms. Williams to project a professional and stylish image at all times. Because of her high-pressure job, Ms. Williams does not have much time to shop, so hires a well-known personal stylist, Rachelle, who will come to her house with clothes and handbags, help her make fashionable choices, and will sell her clothes she wants. Rachelle charges Ms. Williams $500 an hour for fashion advice.

What Ms. Williams doesn't know is that Rachelle receives handbags from Yves St. Laurent at a deep discount, but resells them to clients at a significant markup over retail. Recently, YSL came out with a stylish bag, which retails for $8,000. Rachelle purchased the bag for $5,500 from YSL, but sold the bag to Ora Williams for $8,750. Ms. Williams is too busy with her high-pressure job to bother "shopping around."

Ms. Williams is happy with her new stylish YSL bag, until several months later, when in conversation with another executive who is a collector of high-end handbags, Ms. Williams realizes that she has been overcharged.

3.   After Gil received his JD degree from a California law school, he decided to join the JAG Corps as his first "real world" job. The starting salary is enough to cover his needs, but it is a government salary—rather under-funded. Suddenly, Gil's father needs major surgery, and his father's health insurance plan is not good, so expenses are mounting. Gil wants his father to concentrate on getting better, not worry about medical bills, so he visits a "payday lender" located near the army base where he is stationed. While not disclosed fully, if Gil did the math he would see that the loan came to 290% APR. However, Gil is in a rush and wants to help his father, so he doesn't inquire further into the terms.

4.   After you graduate from law school and pass the bar, you "hang out a shingle" as a solo practitioner. One day you are approached by a neighboring furniture store to help with contract drafting. Mostly the owner has you review agreements with furniture suppliers, and for the first three months all goes well.

One day, the owner tells you that furniture sales are languishing and he wants to expand his business into the "rent to own" sector. He wants your help drafting an agreement to give to potential customers. He is concerned about making sure he will be able to collect monthly payments, especially since many customers will have checkered credit histories.

The owner has done some research online to look at other contracts, and has taken a stab at writing something on his own. He doesn't understand all the details of the language, but is excited about one clause, which would allow him to repossess all merchandise he sells to a customer if that customer defaults on payments for any given item of merchandise. The owner thinks this would scare customers into paying their bills promptly. How will you advise the owner?

C. PUBLIC POLICY

Judicial refusal to enforce unconscionable bargains may be seen as an exercise of public policy. It is not the only ground on which judges often refuse to enforce a bargain. In this section, we consider several highly-charged settings in which parties have disputed the enforceability of bargains on matters of weighty policy, specifically concerning blackmail, cohabitation, gambling, and surrogacy. Can you discern a principled basis to unite these disparate cases and whether the following restatement of the law captures these examples?

RESTATEMENT (SECOND) OF CONTRACTS, SECTION 178

§ 178.   *When a Term Is Unenforceable on Grounds of Public Policy.*

(1) A promise or other term of an agreement is unenforceable on grounds of public policy if legislation provides that it is unenforceable or the interest in its enforcement is clearly outweighed in the circumstances by a public policy against the enforcement of such terms.

(2) In weighing the interest in the enforcement of a term, account is taken of (a) the parties' justified expectations, (b) any forfeiture that would result if enforcement were denied, and (c) any special public interest in the enforcement of the particular term.

(3) In weighing a public policy against enforcement of a term, account is taken of (a) the strength of that policy as manifested by legislation or judicial decisions, (b) the likelihood that a refusal to enforce the term will further that policy, (c) the seriousness of any misconduct involved and the extent to which it was deliberate, and (d) the directness of the connection between that misconduct and the term.

FIEGE V. BOEHM

123 A.2d 316 (Md. 1956)

DELAPLAINE, J.

This suit was brought in the Superior Court of Baltimore City by Hilda Louise Boehm against Louis Gail Fiege to recover for breach of a contract to pay the expenses incident to the birth of his bastard child and to provide for its support upon condition that she would refrain from prosecuting him for bastardy.

Plaintiff alleged in her declaration substantially as follows: (1) that early in 1951 defendant had sexual intercourse with her although she was unmarried, and as a result thereof she became pregnant, and defendant acknowledged that he was responsible for her pregnancy; (2) that on September 29, 1951, she gave birth to a female child; that defendant is the father of the child; and that he acknowledged on many occasions that he is its father; (3) that before the child was born, defendant agreed to pay all her medical and miscellaneous expenses and to compensate her for the loss of her salary caused by the child's birth, and also to pay her ten dollars per week for its support until it reached the age of 21, upon condition that she would not institute bastardy proceedings against him as long as he made the payments in accordance with the agreement; (4) that she placed the child for adoption on July 13, 1954, and she claimed [related sums for expenses, which defendant later refused to pay].

Defendant demurred to the declaration on the ground that it failed to allege that in September, 1953, plaintiff instituted bastardy proceedings against him in the Criminal Court of Baltimore, but since it had been found from blood tests that he could not have been the father of the child, he was acquitted of bastardy. . . .

Plaintiff, a typist, now over 35 years old, who has been employed by the Government in Washington and Baltimore for over thirteen years, testified in the Court below that she had never been married, but that at about midnight on January 21, 1951, defendant, after taking her to a moving picture theater on York Road and then to a restaurant, had sexual intercourse with her in his automobile. She further testified that he agreed to pay all her medical and hospital expenses, to compensate her for loss of salary caused by the pregnancy and birth, and to pay her ten dollars per week for the support of the child upon condition that she would refrain from instituting bastardy proceedings against him. She further testified that between September 17, 1951, and May, 1953, defendant paid her a total of $480.

Defendant admitted that he had taken plaintiff to restaurants, had danced with her several times, had taken her to Washington, and had brought her home in the country [sic]; but he asserted that he had never had sexual intercourse with her. He also claimed that he did not enter into any agreement with her. He admitted, however, that he had paid her a total of $480. His father also testified that he stated "that he did not want his mother to know, and if it were just kept quiet, kept principally away from his mother and the public and the courts, that he would take care of it."

Defendant further testified that in May, 1953, he went to see plaintiff's physician to make inquiry about blood tests to show the paternity of the child; and that those tests were made and they indicated that it was not possible that he could have been the child's father. He then stopped making payments. Plaintiff thereupon filed a charge of bastardy with the State's Attorney.

The testimony which was given in the Criminal Court by Dr. Milton Sachs, hematologist at the University Hospital, was read to the jury in the Superior Court. In recent years the blood-grouping test has been employed in criminology, in the selection of donors for blood transfusions, and as evidence in paternity cases. . . .

Although defendant was acquitted by the Criminal Court, the Superior Court overruled his motion for a directed verdict. In the charge to the jury the Court instructed them that defendant's acquittal in the Criminal Court was not binding upon them. The jury found a verdict in favor of plaintiff for $2,415.80, the full amount of her claim.

Defendant filed a motion for judgment n. o. v. or a new trial. The Court overruled that motion also, and entered judgment on the verdict of the jury. Defendant appealed from that judgment. Defendant contends that, even if he did enter into the contract as alleged, it was not enforceable, because plaintiff's forbearance to prosecute was not based on a valid claim, and hence the contract was without consideration. . . .

In Maryland it is now provided by statute that whenever a person is found guilty of bastardy, the court shall issue an order directing such person (1) to pay for the maintenance and support of the child until it reaches the age of eighteen years, such sum as may be agreed upon, if consent proceedings be had, or in the absence of agreement, such sum as the court may fix, with due regard to the circumstances of the accused person; and (2) to give bond to the State of Maryland in such penalty as the court may fix, with good and sufficient securities, conditioned on making the payments required by the court's order, or any amendments thereof. Failure to give such bond shall be punished by commitment to the jail or the House of Correction until bond is given but not exceeding two years. Code Supp.1955, art. 12, § 8.

Prosecutions for bastardy are treated in Maryland as criminal proceedings, but they are actually civil in purpose. . . . While the prime object of the Maryland Bastardy Act is to protect the public from the burden of maintaining illegitimate children, it is so distinctly in the interest of the mother that she becomes the beneficiary of it. Accordingly a contract by the putative father of an illegitimate child to provide for its support upon condition that bastardy proceedings will not be instituted is a compromise of civil injuries resulting from a criminal act, and not a contract to compound a criminal prosecution, and if it is fair and reasonable, it is in accord with the Bastardy Act and the public policy of the State.

Of course, a contract of a putative father to provide for the support of his illegitimate child must be based, like any other contract, upon sufficient consideration. The early English law made no distinction in regard to the sufficiency of a claim which the claimant promised to forbear to prosecute, as the consideration of a promise, other than the broad distinction between good claims and bad claims. No promise to forbear to prosecute an unfounded claim was sufficient consideration. In the early part of the Nineteenth Century, an advance was made from the criterion of the early authorities when it was held that forbearance to prosecute a suit which had already been instituted was sufficient consideration, without inquiring whether the suit would have been successful or not. . . .

In 1867 the Maryland Court of Appeals, in the opinion delivered by Judge Bartol in Hartle v. Stahl, 27 Md. 157, 172, held: (1) that forbearance to assert a claim before institution of suit, if not in fact a legal claim, is not of itself sufficient consideration to support a promise; but (2) that a compromise of a doubtful claim or a relinquishment of a pending suit is good consideration for a promise; and (3) that in order to support a compromise, it is sufficient that the parties entering into it thought at the time that there was a bona fide question between them, although it may eventually be found that there was in fact no such question.

We have thus adopted the rule that the surrender of, or forbearance to assert, an invalid claim by one who has not an honest and reasonable belief in its possible validity is not sufficient consideration for a contract. . . . We combine the subjective requisite that the claim be bona fide with the objective requisite that it must have a reasonable basis of support. Accordingly a promise not to prosecute a claim which is not founded in good faith does not of itself give a right of action on an agreement to pay for refraining from so acting, because a release from mere annoyance and unfounded litigation does not furnish valuable consideration.

Professor Williston was not . . . certain whether the test of reasonableness is based upon the intelligence of the claimant himself, who may be an ignorant person with no knowledge of law and little sense as to facts; but he seemed inclined to favor the view that "the claim forborne must be neither absurd in fact from the standpoint of a reasonable man in the position of the claimant, nor, obviously unfounded in law to one who has an elementary knowledge of legal principles." 1 Williston on Contracts, Rev.Ed., sec. 135. We agree that while stress is placed upon the honesty and good faith of the claimant, forbearance to prosecute a claim is insufficient consideration if the claim forborne is so lacking in foundation as to make its assertion incompatible with honesty and a reasonable degree of intelligence. Thus, if the mother of a bastard knows that there is no foundation, either in law or fact, for a charge against a certain man that he is the father of the child, but that man promises to pay her in order to prevent bastardy proceedings against him, the forbearance to institute proceedings is not sufficient consideration.

On the other hand, forbearance to sue for a lawful claim or demand is sufficient consideration for a promise to pay for the forbearance if the party forbearing had an honest intention to prosecute litigation which is not frivolous, vexatious, or unlawful, and which he believed to be well founded. . . . Thus the promise of a woman who is expecting an illegitimate child that she will not institute bastardy proceedings against a certain man is sufficient consideration for his promise to pay for the child's support, even though it may not be certain whether the man is the father or whether the prosecution would be successful, if she makes the charge in good faith. The fact that a man accused of bastardy is forced to enter into a contract to pay for the support of his bastard child from fear of exposure and the shame that might be cast upon him as a result, as well as a sense of justice to render some compensation for the injury he inflicted upon the mother, does not lessen the merit of the contract, but greatly increases it. . . .

In the case at bar there was no proof of fraud or unfairness. Assuming that the hematologists were accurate in their laboratory tests and findings, nevertheless plaintiff gave testimony which indicated that she made the charge of bastardy against defendant in good faith. For these reasons the Court acted properly in overruling the demurrer to the amended declaration and the motion for a directed verdict. . . . [Affirmed.]

NOTES AND QUESTIONS

1.   A prominent contemporary example of blackmail involved a CBS news executive, Robert Halderman, who found out that David Letterman, host of "CBS Late Night," was having extramarital affairs with staff members. Using an assortment of evidence, including letters and one woman's diary, Halderman told Letterman's limousine driver and attorney that he would go public with the evidence unless Letterman paid him $2 million. Letterman called the police, who assisted him in preparing a bogus check for $2 million.

After Halderman deposited that check, police arrested him, and he spent six months in jail. No valid contract could possibly have been formed between Halderman and Letterman in the circumstances because there was no relationship between them. The deal was based solely on a spontaneous threat from a stranger to extract cash for silence. To recognize the exchange of money for silence (and nothing else) would encourage people to engage in behavior that criminal law seeks to deter. *See* Bill Carter & Brian Stelter, *Letterman Extortion Raises Questions for CBS*, N.Y.TIMES (Oct. 2, 2009).

2.   How did the court in *Fiege v. Boehm* distinguish the facts of that case from the kind of unenforceable blackmail that later faced David Letterman? Are you convinced by the court's reasoning in *Fiege v. Boehm*? If you find the outcome problematic, articulate which specific aspects of the facts and circumstances are most troubling.

3.   *Jordan v. Knafel*, 880 N.E.2d 1061 (Ill. App. 2007) provides a modern update to *Fiege*. The case grew out of an extra-marital affair between Michael Jordan, the legendary basketball star for the Chicago Bulls, and Karla Knafel, a singer. Knafel claimed Jordan was the father of the baby she was expecting. Wanting to keep the affair and his possible paternity private, Jordan offered Knafel $5 million upon his retirement from basketball if Knafel would keep the matter confidential.

After Knafel gave birth, Jordan paid the bills and paid Knafel $250,000. In exchange, Knafel did not file a paternity suit and kept quiet. A month later, Jordan determined through blood tests that he was not the baby's father. When Jordan retired from basketball, Knafel asked him to pay up. Jordan refused and instead sued to have the alleged contract declared illegal and unenforceable. Despite the favorable precedent from *Fiege v. Boehm*, Knafel's case was problematic.

Money-for-silence deals are suspect, unless they also involve foreswearing legal action. Early English law recognized as consideration a promise not to sue, so long as the claimant held an honest and reasonable belief in the validity of the claim being sworn off. Courts refused to recognize giving entirely baseless claims as consideration but validated claims so long as they were "colorable" or "possible." But Jordan countered by arguing that the contract was unenforceable because it was induced by Knafel's fraud.

Fraud in the inducement of a contract occurs when someone knowingly misleads another into a bargain they would not likely make otherwise. Knafel argued in return that she believed in good faith that Jordan was the baby's father and that Jordan's paternity wasn't as important to his promise as was avoiding bad publicity. However, the court ultimately agreed with Jordan. To accept Knafel's claim that Jordan's agreement was not induced by the paternity issue would suggest that the two had haggled over and settled nothing by their agreement—which would make the case equivalent to blackmail.

4.   Can you reconcile *Knafel v. Jordan* and *Fiege v. Boehm*? Which seems more persuasive? Does Mr. Jordan's celebrity status matter? The social and moral context of the era of *Fiege*?

––––––––––

What about contracts between two cohabiting adults? The common law traditionally has had difficulty with such promises. Well into the twentieth century, a social stigma attached to unmarried cohabitation and law reflected that distaste by refusing to recognize bargains made in those settings as valid contracts.

Traditionally the law's main discomfort around these types of bargains stemmed from concerns about anything other than marital relationships. Early cases called this type of consideration—money for sex—"meretricious." Because prostitution was and remains illegal by statute throughout the United States (except particular counties in Nevada), courts refuse to enforce such contracts; and this repugnance extended to include deals made among unmarried cohabitants.

But social norms have evolved today. Negative labels such as "meretricious" and the association of cohabitation with prostitution are outdated and no longer reflect reality. Even so, resulting legal change is halting and varies among the states. Consider the varying approaches of New York and California in the following two cases.

TOMPKINS V. JACKSON

880 N.Y.S.2d 876 (N.Y. Sup. 2009)

EDMEAD, J.

In this unfortunate tale of a love relationship gone sour, plaintiff seeks lifetime financial support from her ex-boyfriend and the father of her child, "50 Cent," based on promises to take care of her for the rest of her life when he "made it big" in the entertainment industry. By virtue of this decision, plaintiff's claim to half of defendant's multimillion dollar estate and future income, [set at no less than $50 million dollars] is dismissed and this saga comes to an end. . . .

The parties began dating in 1995, when plaintiff was in college and defendant was recently paroled and unemployed. Defendant began living with the plaintiff on Sutphin Boulevard, Queens, New York. In 1996, while plaintiff was pregnant with defendant's son, Marquise, plaintiff relocated to Far Rockaway, Queens. It was at this time that the parties allegedly entered into the oral agreement that is the subject of this lawsuit.

Plaintiff testified at her deposition that in September 1996, "a month before" Marquise was born, when the parties were "in the bedroom," defendant began saying, "how much he loved me. And he said he always appreciated me sticking by him and supporting him in everything he does, and bearing with him. And that just to bear with him, [physically, financially, and mentally] because when he makes it big, he will take care of me for the rest of my life, and everything he owns will be mine, just as well as his." . . . This meant, "when he made it big or received a lucrative recording contract, he would—I would own everything that he owned." . . . According to plaintiff, defendant reiterated that "even if we weren't going to be together, we were down for life. That no matter what, whether we're together or not, that he would always take care of me. He said he would never see me fall. . . ."

In response, plaintiff told defendant that she "will support" him "until you get it together," including taking care of the children and the house, and "be[ing] there for [defendant] mentally . . . and financially . . . ." As far as the parties being "equal partners," defendant said that when "he made it big, that I would be equal partners in all of his earnings. . . . We never talked about losses. . . ."

Plaintiff later purchased for the defendant a diamond ring and a watch, which were "part of the makeup of him being a rapper." . . . . Plaintiff "financially supported" defendant and their joint venture agreement, by providing him money to pay for studio time, transportation to the studio, digital audio tapes . . . , reels, and tattoos on his body . . . . Between . . . 1997 [and] 2000, the parties lived in defendant's grandmother's house, where plaintiff cooked, cleaned, laundered the parties' clothing, and purchased groceries for defendant and their son [as well as working at various jobs].

In May 2000, defendant was nearly fatally shot in front of his grandmother's house. Plaintiff slept on a chair by defendant's side while he was hospitalized for 18 days . . . Upon defendant's discharge, the parties relocated to plaintiff's mother's house in Stroudsburg, Pennsylvania, where plaintiff nursed defendant back to health over . . . five months:

> He couldn't do anything. . . . He [had] a metal rod in his right hip. He couldn't walk. He couldn't feed himself . . . . I would have to make him food, blend the food, make him breakfast . . . He couldn't go to the bathroom by himself. He couldn't wash himself . . . . I would escort him. Put the walker in front of him, and you know, escort him to the bathroom. . . . I would have to massage his feet. That comforted him until he went to sleep . . . I did it because I loved him, and wanted him to be happy . . .

In October 2003, the parties moved to their own apartment at Shawnee-On-Delaware, Pennsylvania, where they resided for . . . four years.

After defendant signed a music deal in 2003, defendant began "pay[ing] some of the bills and giving plaintiff money he earned from his tours. At some later point, defendant gave plaintiff an ATM card, a "G-Unit Touring" American Express card, and blank checks drawn against the "Rotten Apple" record company plaintiff "helped him incorporate." . . .

In 2003, defendant purchased a mansion in Connecticut. The purpose of the mansion was to provide "room and board" and "a safe and secure place for him" and other artists to record music since "defendant didn't like recording at studios because people were trying to kill him." Plaintiff visited defendant in Connecticut on the weekends and during summers. However, plaintiff declined defendant's invitation to move to Connecticut, as she did not want to be "left alone," further away from her family and friends while he was "always on tour." . . . Later in 2005, defendant forced plaintiff to execute a release of life story rights to the movie "Get Rich, or Die Tryin."

Since defendant "always was telling [plaintiff] to purchase a house," plaintiff hired a real estate agent to begin looking for a house in New York. In 2005, the parties moved to Bayside, as a "way station until [plaintiff] found a house." Matters came to a critical point over the purchase of a home in Dix Hills, and in whose name the home would be placed. On December 19, 2006, defendant sent plaintiff an email message, stating:

> Neek it realy hert me to hear you say you think I wouldn't Take care of you . . . You can have the house I'll have them put it in your

name And I will give you money every month it dosent matter to me . . . .

. . . On the day of the closing, January 5, 2007, all the parties to the closing and plaintiff appeared at the closing, except for defendant. When it came time to sign the closing documents, plaintiff "stopped the whole procedure," took defendant's representative who had power of attorney, Alan Hock, out of the room, insisting that the house was "supposed to be in" plaintiff's name. When she called defendant, he instructed plaintiff to, "Put Alan on the phone. I'm going to have him put the house in your name." Mr. Hock took the phone, and said "Wait a minute, Curtis. Wait, wait, wait." Then Mr. Hock went into his office, closed the door, and came out only to advise plaintiff that "we're going to do it. Don't worry about it. We'll do it. Let's just do it this way first. And then a couple of weeks after, we'll just retransfer the house into plaintiff's name. The closing continued, and plaintiff was given the keys.

The following day, defendant expressed to plaintiff that he "want[ed] to be with her" and wanted permission to "move into the house." Plaintiff said "okay." Following the closing, plaintiff and her grandmother packed all of plaintiff's and defendant's belongings for the parties' move into the house in Dix Hills, New York ("the Dix Hills home").

Over the next two weeks, defendant drove Marquise and plaintiff's daughter to school every day. However, defendant moved out because plaintiff and defendant "got into a physical altercation where he hit [plaintiff] . . . plaintiff was upset because the house was supposed to be in [plaintiff's] name, and he—at the last minute, at the closing, he changed his mind."

In 2008, defendant filed a petition in Family Court to establish his child support obligations and later, a petition in Housing Court to evict plaintiff from the Dix Hills home. The Family Court directed that defendant pay $6,700 in child support, which includes a housing allowance. The Housing Court granted defendant possession of the Dix Hills home, and issued a warrant of eviction against plaintiff. Thereafter, plaintiff commenced the instant action seeking, *inter alia,* a temporary stay of her eviction, which this Court granted, and damages for breach of contract, unjust enrichment, and specific performance. During the pendency of the stay, the Dix Hills home was destroyed by a fire (deemed suspicious by authorities), rendering the stay moot.

Defendant now seeks summary judgment. [He] . . . maintains that plaintiff's breach of contract claim, which is actually a claim for palimony, fails because . . . no oral contract ever existed . . . [and] the purported contract lacks the requisite specificity, mutual assent, and definition.

Essentially, plaintiff was defendant's girlfriend from 1996 and then "turned into my son's mom. . . . We slept together from time to time, but she was just my son's mom." . . . Defendant denies having any conversation with the plaintiff wherein he agreed to take care of her for the rest of her or his life, and states that if he so intended he "would have married her." . . . Defendant points out that he never maintained joint accounts or held jointly titled assets with plaintiff . . . .

. . . Moreover, defendant attests that "We" did not "agree" to anything concerning the Dix Hills home, but instead, "made it clear to the plaintiff that while I would, in fact, purchase the Dix Hills house, I would not put title in her name." Defendant never discussed giving plaintiff the Dix Hills house. Defendant purchased the home in Dix Hills to "create a more comfortable space" for his son, who had been sharing a bed with his 16-year-old sister.

. . . [It] cannot be ascertained whether defendant's alleged promise "to take care of" plaintiff means that he agreed to provide plaintiff with shelter, a car, a sum certain, clothing, medical bills or to simply be there emotionally for her. Thus, his alleged promise is far too indefinite to support a contract claim. Further, plaintiff failed to indicate any actions by defendant either at the time the alleged oral contract was made or subsequent thereto, evincing his assent to the agreement. It is incredible that two then unemployed, penniless, twenty-one year olds would make such an oral contract. . . .

The deposition testimony and documentary evidence before this Court establish that none of plaintiff's causes of action have merit. As such, plaintiff's complaint is dismissed, in its entirety, with prejudice. . . .

According to plaintiff's affidavit, the parties entered into an express oral agreement "on or about September of 1996" wherein in exchange for plaintiff "providing the defendant homemaking and domestic services while we lived together, the defendant would devote his time to becoming a successful recording artist and share with me equally all his earnings from that success." Plaintiff's affidavit provides as follows:

> I agreed to continue to live with him, maintain his home, perform homemaking and domestic services for him as well as support him mentally, emotionally and financially to the best of my abilities. I also agreed to accompany him to social and other events. . . . Defendant agreed that he would vigorously pursue a professional recording career with the understanding that our combined efforts could result in the accumulation of substantial wealth and assets that we would divide and share equally.

Plaintiff admitted that she was in love with defendant when they entered into this agreement in September 1996 . . . after all, "He was a corner crack dealer parolee. He didn't have anything . . . So I was going to be with him whether he was 50 Cent, with a hundred million dollars, or Curtis Jackson, working for sanitation, making $50,000 a year. I would have been with him, because I loved him. It wasn't about him saying that he would give me everything he had. It's when you love a person, you don't—it's not about the monetary. If you're a prostitute, then it's a monetary thing. We were two people in love with each other."

While statements such as these demonstrate loving devotion and loyalty, these same statements undermine plaintiff's breach of contract . . . claim . . . for half of defendant's wealth. "As to personal services between unmarried persons living together or unmarried persons whose actions flow out of mutual friendship and reciprocal regard, there is very little difference" (Trimmer v. Van Bomel, 107 Misc.2d 201 [Sup.Ct. New York County 1980]). "An implied contract to compensate for those things which are ordinarily done by one person for another as a matter of regard and affection should not, under these well established principles, be recognized in this state" . . . . Such a claim in the context of a cohabiting relationship is against New York's public policy (as evidenced by the 1933 abolition of common-law marriages) . . .

Suits involving "unmarried persons living together who thereafter seek financial recovery frequently run afoul of the theory that a contract founded upon an agreement to live together as man and wife will not be enforced (Civ. Rts. Law, § 80–a)" (Trimmer v. Van Bomel, 107 Misc.2d 201, supra). The Court recognizes that services rendered by one paramour for the other which are non-sexual in nature and do not arise directly from such a relationship, may be deemed separable, and form the basis for compensation (Id., citing Matter of Gordon, 8 N.Y.2d 71, 202 NYS.2d 1; 6A Corbin on Contracts, § 1476, p. 622; 15 Williston on Contracts, § 1745; Restatement of Contracts § 589). However, this is not such a case.

Here, the purported agreement was made when plaintiff and defendant were living together, albeit sporadically, as lovers, and by its terms, required the defendant to support plaintiff for the rest of his and her life, even if the parties broke up and ceased cohabitating. The services for which plaintiff seeks compensation arise out of the nature of the relationship of the parties to one another. The services involved—to devote time and attention to the defendant, to act as companion, to accompany him to social events and perform household duties—are of a nature which would ordinarily be exchanged without expectation of pay.

. . . Providing loving care and assistance to her boyfriend and the father of their son before and after he was shot and seriously injured, does not transform her relationship to a one founded upon contract. To conclude otherwise would transform the parties' personal, yet informal relationship to that of a marriage.

Before a court will impose a contractual obligation, it must ascertain that a contract was made and that its terms are definite . . . . Here, it is clear that the alleged oral agreement to "take care of" plaintiff for the rest of her life, contains no specifics as to the manner in which defendant was obligated to "take care of" the plaintiff, and, assuming this included the tender of monies to plaintiff, no specifics as to the frequency and amount of payments.

Therefore, the alleged oral agreement to take care of plaintiff for the rest of her life in exchange for her promise to perform household duties and take care of the parties' children is unenforceable. And consequently, any claims based on such oral agreement, including specific performance of same, an accounting of all of defendant's assets, mandamus relief, and declaratory relief, lack merit, and are dismissed. . . .

That defendant may have derived benefit from plaintiff's acts does not mean that he was unjustly enriched. It is undisputed that the defendant provided ample economic benefits for the plaintiff over the years: he gave plaintiff money and gifts, shared in the payment of rent and utilities in Pennsylvania and Bayside, bought furniture for the plaintiff, paid her auto lease at times, paid the expenses for plaintiff's mother's funeral, gave the plaintiff's grandmother money so she could purchase and furnish an apartment, and paid plaintiff's Macy's credit card.

The Court notes that plaintiff and her daughter moved into the Dix Hills house for a couple of months prior to the date the defendant commenced the Family Court proceeding. The plaintiff locked in a higher standard of living for herself and her daughter (both living with the parties' son) than she had previously enjoyed in her Bayside apartment. . . . It cannot be ignored that the Family Court Order permits plaintiff to continue receiving child support payments from the defendant and that she will continue to do so on a monthly basis for many years to come. These payments permit plaintiff to provide a home equal in value to that of the Dix Hills home, not only for Marquise, for whom defendant is solely responsible, but for plaintiff and her own daughter, without working. In other words, plaintiff and her daughter will reap the benefits of living in a home at the expense of defendant for several years to come . . . .

NOTES AND QUESTIONS

1.   The word palimony is not a legal term but a colloquialism melding the words pal and alimony. The term was coined by celebrity divorce lawyer, Marvin Mitchelson, in 1977 when he represented Michelle Triola Marin in the next case, *Marvin v. Marvin*.

2.   Judicial approaches to palimony vary across the states, due to varying conceptions of the relevant public policy in each area, including around conceptions of marriage and related relationships. *See, e.g.*, Albertina Antognini, *The Law of Nonmarriage*, 58 BOSTON COLLEGE L. REV. 1 (2017); June Carbone & Naomi Cahn, *Nonmarriage*, 65 MARYLAND. L. REV. 55 (2016).

In comparing *Tompkins v. Jackson* with *Marvin v. Marvin*, can you detect these different approaches?

MARVIN V. MARVIN
557 P.2d 106 (Cal. 1976)

TOBRINER, J.

During the past 15 years, there has been a substantial increase in the number of couples living together without marrying. Such nonmarital relationships lead to legal controversy when one partner dies or the couple separates. Courts of Appeal, faced with the task of determining property rights in such cases, have arrived at conflicting positions: two cases (In re Marriage of Cary (1973) 34 Cal.App.3d 345 [109 Cal.Rptr. 862]; Estate of Atherley (1975) 44 Cal.App.3d 758 [119 Cal.Rptr. 41] have held that the Family Law Act (Civ.Code, § 4000 et seq.) requires division of the property according to community property principles, and one decision (Beckman v. Mayhew (1975) 49 Cal.App.3d 529 [122 Cal.Rptr. 604]) has rejected that holding. We take this opportunity to resolve that controversy and to declare the principles which should govern distribution of property acquired in a nonmarital relationship.

We conclude: (1) The provisions of the Family Law Act do not govern the distribution of property acquired during a nonmarital relationship; such a relationship remains subject solely to judicial decision. (2) The courts should enforce express contracts between nonmarital partners except to the extent that the contract is explicitly founded on the consideration of meretricious sexual services. (3) In the absence of an express contract, the courts should inquire into the conduct of the parties to determine whether that conduct demonstrates an implied contract, agreement of partnership or joint venture, or some other tacit understanding between the parties. The courts may also employ the doctrine of quantum meruit, or equitable remedies such as constructive or resulting trust, when warranted by the facts of the case.

In the instant case plaintiff and defendant [noted actress Michelle Triola and actor Lee Marvin] lived together for seven years without marrying; all property acquired during this period was taken in defendant's name. When plaintiff sued to enforce a contract under which she was entitled to half the property and to support payments, the trial court granted judgment on the pleadings for defendant, thus leaving him with all property accumulated by the couple during their relationship. Since the trial court denied plaintiff a trial on the merits of her claim, its decision conflicts with the principles stated above, and must be reversed.

. . . Plaintiff avers that in October of 1964 she and defendant 'entered into an oral agreement' that while "the parties lived together they would combine their efforts and earnings and would share equally any and all property accumulated as a result of their efforts whether individual or combined." Furthermore, they agreed to "hold themselves out to the general public as husband and wife" and that "plaintiff would further render her services as a companion, homemaker, housekeeper and cook to . . . defendant." Shortly thereafter plaintiff agreed to "give up her lucrative career as an entertainer [and] singer" in order to "devote her full time to defendant . . . as a companion, homemaker, housekeeper and cook;" in return defendant agreed to "provide for all of plaintiff's financial support and needs for the rest of her life."

Plaintiff alleges that she lived with defendant from October of 1964 through May of 1970 and fulfilled her obligations under the agreement. During this period the parties as a result of their efforts and earnings acquired in defendant's name substantial real and personal property, including motion picture rights worth over $1 million. In May of 1970, however, defendant compelled plaintiff to leave his household. He continued to support plaintiff until November of 1971, but thereafter refused to provide further support.

. . . After hearing argument the court granted defendant's motion and entered judgment for defendant. Plaintiff moved to set aside the judgment and asked leave to amend her complaint to allege that she and defendant reaffirmed their agreement after defendant's divorce was final. The trial court denied plaintiff's motion, and she appealed from the judgment.

. . . In Trutalli v. Meraviglia (1932) 215 Cal. 698 [12 P.2d 430] we established the principle that non-marital partners may lawfully contract concerning the ownership of property acquired during the relationship. We reaffirmed this principle in Vallera v. Vallera (1943) 21 Cal.2d 681, 685 [134 P.2d 761], stating that "If a man and woman [who are not married] live together as husband and wife under an agreement to pool their earnings and share equally in their joint accumulations, equity will protect the interests of each in such property." . . .

Defendant first and principally relies on the contention that the alleged contract is so closely related to the supposed "immoral" character of the relationship between plaintiff and himself that the enforcement of the contract would violate public policy. He points to cases asserting that a contract between non-marital partners is unenforceable if it is "involved in" an illicit relationship . . . . A review of the numerous California decisions concerning contracts between non-marital partners, however, reveals that the courts have not employed such broad and uncertain standards to strike down contracts. The decisions instead disclose a narrower and more precise standard: a contract between non-marital partners is unenforceable only *to the extent* that it *explicitly* rests upon the immoral and illicit consideration of meretricious sexual services.

. . . Although the past decisions hover over the issue in the somewhat wispy form of the figures of a Chagall painting, we can abstract from those decisions a clear and simple rule. The fact that a man and woman live together without marriage, and engage in a sexual relationship, does not in itself invalidate agreements between them relating to their earnings, property, or expenses. Neither is such an agreement invalid merely because the parties may have contemplated the creation or continuation of a non-marital relationship when they entered into it. Agreements between non-marital partners fail only to the extent that they rest upon a consideration of meretricious sexual services. Thus the rule asserted by defendant, that a contract fails if it is "involved in" or made "in contemplation" of a non-marital relationship, cannot be reconciled with the decisions.

. . . The principle that a contract between non-marital partners will be enforced unless expressly and inseparably based upon an illicit consideration of sexual services not only represents the distillation of the decisional law, but also offers a far more precise and workable standard than that advocated by defendant.

. . . In summary, we base our opinion on the principle that adults who voluntarily live together and engage in sexual relations are nonetheless as competent as any other persons to contract respecting their earnings and property rights. Of course, they cannot lawfully contract to pay for the performance of sexual services, for such a contract is, in essence, an agreement for prostitution and unlawful for that reason. But they may agree to pool their earnings and to hold all property acquired during the relationship in accord with the law governing community property; conversely they may agree that each partner's earnings and the property acquired from those earnings remains the separate property of the earning partner. So long as the agreement does not rest upon illicit meretricious consideration, the parties may order their economic affairs as they choose, and no policy precludes the courts from enforcing such agreements.

In the present instance, plaintiff alleges that the parties agreed to pool their earnings, that they contracted to share equally in all property acquired, and that defendant agreed to support plaintiff. The terms of the contract as alleged do not rest upon any unlawful consideration. We therefore conclude that the complaint furnishes a suitable basis upon which the trial court can render declaratory relief. . . . The trial court consequently erred in granting defendant's motion for judgment on the pleadings.

. . . [W]e believe that the prevalence of non-marital relationships in modern society and the social acceptance of them, marks this as a time when our courts should by no means apply the doctrine of the unlawfulness of the so-called meretricious relationship to the instant case. As we have explained, the non-enforceability of agreements expressly providing for meretricious conduct rested upon the fact that such conduct, as the word suggests, pertained to and encompassed prostitution. To equate the non-marital relationship of today to such a subject matter is to do violence to an accepted and wholly different practice.

We are aware that many young couples live together without the solemnization of marriage, in order to make sure that they can successfully later undertake marriage. This trial period, preliminary to marriage, serves as some assurance that the marriage will not subsequently end in dissolution to the harm of both parties. We are aware, as we have stated, of the pervasiveness of non-marital relationships in other situations.

The mores of the society have indeed changed so radically in regard to cohabitation that we cannot impose a standard based on alleged moral considerations that have apparently been so widely abandoned by so many. . . . We conclude that the judicial barriers that may stand in the way of a policy based upon the fulfillment of the reasonable expectations of the parties to a non-marital relationship should be removed. As we have explained, the courts now hold that express agreements will be enforced unless they rest on an unlawful meretricious consideration. We add that in the absence of an express agreement, the courts may look to a variety of other remedies in order to protect the parties' lawful expectations.

The courts may inquire into the conduct of the parties to determine whether that conduct demonstrates an implied contract or implied agreement of partnership or joint venture (see Estate of Thornton (1972) 81 Wn.2d 72 [499 P.2d 864]), or some other tacit understanding between the parties. The courts may, when appropriate, employ principles of constructive trust (see Omer v. Omer (1974) 11 Wash.App. 386 [523 P.2d 957]) or resulting trust (see Hyman v. Hyman (Tex.Civ.App. 1954) 275 S.W.2d 149). Finally, a non-marital partner may recover in quantum meruit for the reasonable value of household services rendered less the reasonable value of support received if he can show that he rendered services with the expectation of monetary reward. . . .

Notes and Questions

1.   Should courts treat long-term cohabiting couples as if they were effectively married in terms of dividing property, awarding support akin to alimony, and enforcing promises for care after the end of the relationship? Or should the couple be allowed to make deals but only to the extent they seem like any other commercial contract?

2.   If *Tompkins* and *Marvin* represent two prominent legal models, what are the public policies favoring or opposing these contending approaches?

3.   In *Obergefell v. Hodges*, 135 S.Ct. 2584 (2015), the United States Supreme Court recognized the right of same-sex couples to marry. Prior to this

decision, many same-sex couples used contracts to make arrangements that, while not officially "marriage," looked akin to marriage. What terms would be needed to mirror the marriage relationship? For further discussion of this history, see Craig W. Christensen, *If Not Marriage? On Securing Gay and Lesbian Family Values by a "Simulacrum of Marriage,"* 66 FORDHAM L. REV. 1699 (1998); Jennifer A. Drobac & Antony Page, *A Uniform Domestic Partnership Act: Marrying Business Partnership and Family Law*, 41 GA. L. REV. 349 (2007) (proposing business partnership model for structuring intimate relationships, whether gay or straight).

4.   These family law issues raise a perennial and longstanding question about the generality or specificity of any field of human endeavor, including contract law: is there one general field of contract law or multiple subfields, such as those applicable to different participants (such as families, consumers, or businesses) or transactions (such as construction, lending, goods or professional services)? The intellectual issue is profound and pervasive. Consider a quip by Judge Frank Easterbrook:

> the best way to learn the law applicable to specialized endeavors is to study general rules. Lots of cases deal with sales of horses; others deal with people kicked by horses; still more deal with the licensing and racing of horses, or with the care veterinarians give to horses, or with prizes at horse shows. Any effort to collect these strands into a course on "The Law of the Horse" is doomed to be shallow and to miss unifying principles.

There is a "Law of Contracts." But within it there is also Article 2 of the UCC. It seems possible to have it both ways, to classify a general law of promissory obligation within which a number of specialized rules are applicable to handle special problems, whether due to the participant types or transaction types. *See also* Lawrence Lessig, *The Law of the Horse: What Cyberlaw Might Teach*, 113 HARV. L. REV. 501 (1999).

———————

Games of chance, races, and other forms of gambling have existed as recreation and leisure activities for thousands of years. The law has tended to distinguish gambling from other forms of activity, such as investing in the stock market, based on the idea that gambling is a form of entertainment, perhaps even a vice, and that gambling involves elements of luck, randomness, or chance. Some of these distinctions between gambling and investing are artificial, socially constructed, and largely based on socioeconomic class. When the lower classes take risks, they irresponsibly engage in (immoral) gambling, but when the upper classes engage in similar activities, these activities are considered productive and classified as "investments."

Historically, gambling in the United States has either been outlawed or highly regulated, in part because gambling has traditionally been associated with vice, moral weakness, financial recklessness, and poverty. Organized crime rings have long used gambling, bookmaking, and related activities as a way to launder money from other illegal activities, such as prostitution, loan sharking, and drug sales. In addition, some individuals with susceptible personalities can become addicted to gambling, leading to emotional distress and, in extreme cases, financial ruin. When gambling occurs in the form of state-sponsored lotteries, it has been criticized as imposing a regressive tax, disproportionately taking money from the poor and uneducated to subsidize the public fisc. For all these reasons, gambling has historically been seen as an activity requiring a high level of government policing and regulation.

Currently, gambling law in the United States is a patchwork of regulation. In some states, gambling is legal, in others it is outlawed, and in still others, there is a combination, with only some forms of gambling allowed, and some forbidden. Within this patchwork, however, gambling has made recent and dramatic inroads. Native American tribes have been able to support sagging economies through revenues generated from casinos located on reservations. State governments have themselves moved toward a system where education and other vital services are often supported through state-sponsored lotteries. At the same time, in 2006, Congress passed a law directed at curbing Internet gambling. These regulatory inconsistencies point to deeply conflicted cultural views towards gambling.

SOKAITIS V. BAKAYSA

2010 WL 2383902 (Conn. Super. 2010)

SWEINTON, J.

. . . Two once-close octogenarian sisters are embroiled in a family feud over a $500,000 Powerball lottery ticket. The plaintiff, Theresa Sokaitis (Terry), brought this action for breach of contract, seeking to recover money damages from her sister, the defendant, Rose Bakaysa (Rose), alleging that Rose had breached an agreement between the parties to share equally in any winnings from, *inter alia,* lottery tickets.

This case has been characterized as one involving two sisters, both well into their eighties, "fighting" over a $500,000 lottery Powerball ticket. In reality what spurred the argument was far less than a half of a million dollars, but boils down to a loan of $250 from Rose to Terry.

The sisters grew up in a family of ten brothers and sisters in New Britain. Terry and Rose were close growing up. Both sisters married, but Rose had no children of her own while Terry had six children, one of whom suffers from disabilities. After Rose's husband died in 1981, the two became closer, and when "the casino" opened in the late 1980s, they went two or three times a week. Terry played "the cards," while Rose played the slots, and they would share what they won on an informal basis.

In January 1995, Terry "hit" the big jackpot playing Carribbean poker for $165,000. Upon receiving the check which had the taxes withheld, Terry gave it to Rose to hold for her over the weekend. The two sisters then together took the check to the bank, cashed it, and deposited it on Monday. Terry shared her winnings with Rose.

In April 1995, Terry decided that it would be a "good idea" to have a contract spelling out exactly the agreement she and Rose had about sharing their winnings. Perhaps this was to ensure that since Terry shared her big jackpot with Rose, if Rose won, she would be obligated to share in the winnings with Terry. Having made arrangements with an accountant, the two sisters went to his office, Terry told him the terms, he printed it, they both signed it, and had it notarized. It read:

THIS IS A LETTER OF AGREEMENT BETWEEN ROSE BAKAYSA AND THERESA SOKAITIS

THIS LETTER IS DATED ON 4/12/95

THIS LETTER STATES THAT WE ARE PARTNERS IN ANY WINNING WE SHALL RECEIVE, TO BE SHARED EQUALLY. (SUCH AS SLOT MACHINES, CARDS, AT FOXWOODS CASINO, AND LOTTEREY (sic) TICKETS, ETC.).

Terry and Rose continued their ventures to Foxwoods Casino, bought lottery tickets, and shared their winnings. Terry testified that "[the agreement] was supposed to last for the rest of our lives."

In 2004, Rose experienced health problems which required surgery. After she left the hospital, she went to a rehabilitation facility for several weeks, and Terry visited her every day. It was while Rose was at the facility that Terry asked her to borrow some money. Terry thought it was $100, but Rose insisted it was $250. Rose lent her the money, something Rose had repeatedly done over the years.

When Rose left the facility, she still required assistance, so she went to stay with Terry for approximately three weeks to continue her recovery. In addition to the money Terry had borrowed from Rose while Rose was at the rehabilitation facility, Terry also owed her approximately $650 from a previous loan. The two sisters decided that Rose would stay with Terry, and instead of paying Terry for food, etc., Rose would forgive the $650 debt, and they would "call it even." Rose stayed with Terry, but testified that after Terry made her breakfast, Terry left her alone for the rest of the day to recuperate on her own.

When Rose returned to her own home several weeks later, she called Terry and told Terry that she and their brother, Joe, were coming over to get the $250 that she had lent to Terry. Terry insisted it was not $250, but only $100. Terry told Rose, "Don't come, because I don't have it," and explained she would pay her the money when she did have it. It is this conversation that both parties recall differently, and it is this conversation that would determine their personal and legal relationship from then on.

Terry said that the conversation was not the heated argument that Rose recalls. Rose said that the conversation became a shouting match, and testified that Terry was "hollering on the phone, 'I don't want to be your partner anymore,' and that she (Rose) said okay." Although Rose stated at trial that their brother, Joe, was present during this telephone conversation, and Joe himself testified that he witnessed the exchange, the court does not believe Joe was present. What the court finds did happen is that Rose, upset over the heated discussion, called Joe and said, "Terry doesn't want to be my partner anymore," and Joe said, "I'll be partners with you."

After that conversation between Terry and Rose, and before Rose and Joe won the Powerball in June 2005, Terry eventually sent Rose a check for $250, but there was a significant change in their relationship. The parties did not speak or have any contact with each other, and there were no more trips together to the casino. They did not buy any lottery tickets together, nor did they share in any winnings. . . .

Rose continued to purchase lottery tickets by entering into an arrangement with her brother, Joe. Every two weeks they would purchase lottery tickets, alternating every two weeks as to who would pay the money for the tickets. The numbers were always the same, and to this day, Rose and Joe still play the same numbers. On June 15, 2005, Joe purchased their usual set of tickets at a gas station in Plainville, Connecticut, for the June 18th drawing. When he realized that they had won the Powerball for $500,000, he called Rose immediately, and told her, "we won some serious money—try a half a million!" He followed the procedure set forth by the lottery commission, signing the back of the ticket with his name, address, and social security number, and added Rose's name, social security number, and telephone number. Rose and Joe were each issued a check for approximately $175,000, on June 20, 2005. Terry later learned that Rose had won the powerball from her daughter, Eileen, who is Rose's godchild. Rose had always been very generous to Eileen, and when she won the lottery, she gave Eileen a $10,000 gift.

After the shouting match phone call, the next communication between Terry and Rose was from the state marshal who served the summons and complaint in this action on Rose, claiming the breach of contract, and seeking her share of the winnings. What came between these sisters was money.[6]

Terry is suing Rose for what she claims is a breach of contract. She contends that they had a valid written agreement, and that Rose breached the agreement when she failed to share her lottery winnings with Terry in June 2005. "The elements of a breach of contract action are the formation of an agreement, performance by one party, breach of the agreement by the other party and damages." . . . Pelletier v. Galske, 105 Conn.App. 77, 81, 936 A.2d 689 (2007), cert. denied, 285 Conn. 921, 943 A.2d 1100 (2008). A contract must be definite and certain as to its terms and requirements. Glazer v. Dress Barn, Inc., 274 Conn. 33, 51, 873 A.2d 929 (2005).

[Rose had earlier argued that the contract was void pursuant to Connecticut General Statutes § 52–553, which bars actions on wagering contracts. The question earlier had been certified to the Connecticut Supreme Court. See Sokaitis v. Bakaysa, 975 A.2d 51 (Conn. 2009). It explained that "a literal reading of the statute results in several conflicts with other, more recent, statutes related to legal wagering." Examples: a state lottery; off-track betting facilities; pari-mutuel betting at licensed events; the operation of jai alai frontons; and operation of casinos on tribal lands at which many forms of gambling occur. The statutory ban on wagering contracts is thus intended to ban only those related to illegal gambling. The contract in the present case, even if a wagering contract, did not relate to illegal gambling but to the state-authorized lottery.]

There is no dispute that there was a valid fully executed contract between Terry and Rose, which provided for the equal sharing of lottery winnings. However, Rose claims that she has a defense to the action for breach of contract because they ended the contract. Specifically, she states

---

[6] A bittersweet letter introduced at trial from Terry to Rose contains the following thoughts:

I hope you get this letter because I have plenty to say—the most important thing is I am so sick over what is happening with you and I going to court. None of this would have happened if you were not so greedy . . . All I know we should both be ashamed of our self (sic). We are sisters and goong (sic) to court is not right—All I know I am entitled to my share of the money and you know it . . .

I remember when I was pregnant. We went to Raphels and you bought me my dress. It was navy blue and it had pink flowers on it. You and I use (sic) to go to the casino all the time and to Old Saybrook and look at all the houses and get hot dogs out there at the resterants (sic) . . . Well Ro Ro, I don't know what is going to happen—but I want you to know I will always love you—But if you wanted to hurt me you did . . . My kids are so good to me and they do send me any money I need. They can't do enough for me so I guess I am rich with a lot of love and that is something you can't buy.

I hope you feel good and have good health—I have sugar and I have a desease (sic) that is incurable. It is called neurapathy (sic). I can't walk at all. It is really painful—but Ma always said other people have worse problems so I just ask God to let me be able to handle it all. Take care of yourself. Mom would be sick over all of this—it would never happen if you at least shared some of the money with me. Do you think I would have done that to you? Never . . .

See you in court. Terry

in her amended answer dated June 2, 2006, "[a]ny agreement reached by the parties as alleged has been rescinded."

Rescission is the unmaking of a contract, which "places the parties, as nearly as possible, in the same situation as existed just prior to the execution of the contract." (Internal quotation marks omitted). Winchester v. McCue, 91 Conn.App. 721, 732, 882 A.2d 143 (2005). "[T]he effect of a rescission is to extinguish the contract and to annihilate it so effectively that in contemplation of law it has never had any existence, even for the purpose of being broken. Accordingly, it has been said that a lawful rescission of an agreement puts an end to it for all purposes, not only to preclude the recovery of the contract price, but also to prevent the recovery of damages for breach of the contract. An election to rescind a contract waives the right to sue upon it. After rescission for a breach, there is no right to sue on the contract for damages for such breach." Id., at 732–33, 882 A.2d 143, citing 17 Am.Jur.2d 1002–3, Contracts § 516 (1964). "The parties to this contract could as validly agree to rescind it as they could agree to make it originally." Yale Co-operative Corporation v. Rogin, 133 Coun. 563, 567, 133 Conn. 563, 53 A.2d 383 (1947). . . .

. . . The crucial issue is what occurred in that conversation in June 2004, when Rose called Terry to tell her she wanted repayment of her $250. The evidence was clear that over the years Rose had helped Terry financially, and at that point, Rose had had enough. She wanted Terry to keep her agreement to repay the money Rose lent to her while she was at the rehabilitation facility. When Terry started to say that she did not have the money to pay her back, it is quite believable that the conversation became heated, and Terry said, as Rose testified, "I don't want to be your partner anymore," at which point Rose agreed, saying, "okay." This is backed up by Rose then telling their brother, "Terry doesn't want to be my partner anymore," to which he replied, "I'll be your partner."

The behavioral changes that occurred support Rose's position that this was a heated argument that, as her counsel argued, "clearly fractured a sibling bond and terminated the partnership." Neither party bought lottery tickets together, went to the casino together, or gambled from that day onward. Their next conversation was when Rose called Terry after being served with the lawsuit. . . .

Terry testified, "I love my sister. There was no reason to not be partners," but her conduct and Rose's conduct belie this testimony. The fact that the parties did not have any contact for over a year supports the defendant's assertions about the tenor of the conversation, and that the contract was rescinded during that conversation. The facts support her contention that during that conversation, Terry told Rose "I don't want to be your partner anymore," and Rose said, "Okay." Thus, the court finds the parties agreed to rescind their contract.

There is something in this tragedy that touches most people. While the court may be able to resolve the legal dispute, it is powerless to repair the discord and strife that now overshadows the once harmonious sisterly relationship.

For the foregoing reasons, the court finds all issues for the defendant, and enters judgment for the defendant, Rose Bakaysa. . .

NOTES AND QUESTIONS

1.   How does the Connecticut court in *Sokaitis v. Bakaysa* define "public policy"? Is there a consensus on what "public policy" means in any particular situation? To what extent is context important?

2.   Keep in mind that if a contract is declared to be void as against public policy, this creates a legal disability in the party that is seeking to enforce the agreement. Such an incursion undercuts the idea of freedom of contract. So what if, for example, you wished to sell your kidney (you have two; you only need one to live). In 2000, online auction website eBay had to take down several such advertisements for kidney sales, noting that sales of organs are illegal in the United States. Should such markets for organs be illegal? Why are such deals considered to violate public policy? The next case asks you to consider such questions in the context of surrogacy arrangements.

MATTER OF BABY M
537 A.2d 1227 (N.J. 1988)

WILENTZ, C.J.

In this matter the Court is asked to determine the validity of a contract that purports to provide a new way of bringing children into a family. For a fee of $10,000, a woman agrees to be artificially inseminated with the semen of another woman's husband; she is to conceive a child, carry it to term, and after its birth surrender it to the natural father and his wife. The intent of the contract is that the child's natural mother will thereafter be forever separated from her child. The wife is to adopt the child, and she and the natural father are to be regarded as its parents for all purposes. The contract providing for this is called a "surrogacy contract," the natural mother inappropriately called the "surrogate mother." . . .

We find no offense to our present laws where a woman voluntarily and without payment agrees to act as a "surrogate" mother, provided that she is not subject to a binding agreement to surrender her child. Moreover, our holding today does not preclude the Legislature from altering the current statutory scheme, within constitutional limits, so as to permit surrogacy contracts. Under current law, however, the surrogacy agreement before us is illegal and invalid. . . .

In February 1985, William Stern and Mary Beth Whitehead entered into a surrogacy contract. It recited that Stern's wife, Elizabeth, was infertile, that they wanted a child, and that Mrs. Whitehead was willing to provide that child as the mother with Mr. Stern as the father.

The contract provided that through artificial insemination using Mr. Stern's sperm, Mrs. Whitehead would become pregnant, carry the child to term, bear it, deliver it to the Sterns, and thereafter do whatever was necessary to terminate her maternal rights so that Mrs. Stern could thereafter adopt the child. Mrs. Whitehead's husband, Richard,[1] was also a party to the contract; Mrs. Stern was not. Mr. Whitehead promised to do all acts necessary to rebut the presumption of paternity under the Parentage Act. Although Mrs. Stern was not a party to the surrogacy agreement, the contract gave her sole custody of the child in the event of Mr. Stern's death. Mrs. Stern's status as a nonparty to the surrogate parenting agreement presumably was to avoid the application of the baby-selling statute to this arrangement.

Mr. Stern, on his part, agreed to attempt the artificial insemination and to pay Mrs. Whitehead $10,000 after the child's birth, on its delivery to him. In a separate contract, Mr. Stern agreed to pay $7,500 to the Infertility Center of New York ("ICNY"). The Center's advertising campaigns solicit surrogate mothers and encourage infertile couples to consider surrogacy. ICNY arranged for the surrogacy contract by bringing the parties together, explaining the process to them, furnishing the contractual form, and providing legal counsel.

The history of the parties' involvement in this arrangement suggests their good faith. William and Elizabeth Stern were married in July 1974, having met at the University of Michigan, where both were Ph.D. candidates. Due to financial considerations and Mrs. Stern's pursuit of a medical degree and residency, they decided to defer starting a family until 1981. Before then, however, Mrs. Stern learned that she might have multiple sclerosis and that the disease in some cases renders pregnancy a serious health risk. Her anxiety appears to have exceeded the actual risk, which current medical authorities assess as minimal. Nonetheless that anxiety was evidently quite real, Mrs. Stern fearing that pregnancy might precipitate blindness, paraplegia, or other forms of debilitation. Based on the perceived risk, the Sterns decided to forego having their own children. The decision had special significance for Mr. Stern. Most of his family had

---

[1]   Subsequent to the trial court proceedings, Mr. and Mrs. Whitehead were divorced, and soon thereafter Mrs. Whitehead remarried. Nevertheless, in the course of this opinion we will make reference almost exclusively to the facts as they existed at the time of trial, the facts on which the decision we now review was reached. We note moreover that Mr. Whitehead remains a party to this dispute. For these reasons, we continue to refer to appellants as Mr. and Mrs. Whitehead.

been destroyed in the Holocaust. As the family's only survivor, he very much wanted to continue his bloodline.

Initially the Sterns considered adoption, but were discouraged by the substantial delay apparently involved and by the potential problem they saw arising from their age and their differing religious backgrounds. They were most eager for some other means to start a family.

The paths of Mrs. Whitehead and the Sterns to surrogacy were similar. Both responded to advertising by ICNY. The Sterns' response, following their inquiries into adoption, was the result of their long-standing decision to have a child. Mrs. Whitehead's response apparently resulted from her sympathy with family members and others who could have no children (she stated that she wanted to give another couple the "gift of life"); she also wanted the $10,000 to help her family. . . .

Mrs. Whitehead had reached her decision concerning surrogacy before the Sterns, and had actually been involved as a potential surrogate mother with another couple. After numerous unsuccessful artificial inseminations, that effort was abandoned. Thereafter, the Sterns learned of the Infertility Center, the possibilities of surrogacy, and of Mary Beth Whitehead. The two couples met to discuss the surrogacy arrangement and decided to go forward. On February 6, 1985, Mr. Stern and Mr. and Mrs. Whitehead executed the surrogate parenting agreement. After several artificial inseminations over a period of months, Mrs. Whitehead became pregnant. The pregnancy was uneventful and on March 27, 1986, Baby M was born.

. . . Mrs. Whitehead realized, almost from the moment of birth, that she could not part with this child. She had felt a bond with it even during pregnancy. Some indication of the attachment was conveyed to the Sterns at the hospital when they told Mrs. Whitehead what they were going to name the baby. She apparently broke into tears and indicated that she did not know if she could give up the child. She talked about how the baby looked like her other daughter, and made it clear that she was experiencing great difficulty with the decision.

Nonetheless, Mrs. Whitehead was, for the moment, true to her word. Despite powerful inclinations to the contrary, she turned her child over to the Sterns on March 30 at the Whiteheads' home. . . . Later in the evening of March 30, Mrs. Whitehead became deeply disturbed, disconsolate, stricken with unbearable sadness. She had to have her child. She could not eat, sleep, or concentrate on anything other than her need for her baby. The next day she went to the Sterns' home and told them how much she was suffering.

The depth of Mrs. Whitehead's despair surprised and frightened the Sterns. She told them that she could not live without her baby, that she must have her, even if only for one week, that thereafter she would surrender her child. The Sterns, concerned that Mrs. Whitehead might indeed commit suicide, not wanting under any circumstances to risk that, and in any event believing that Mrs. Whitehead would keep her word, turned the child over to her. It was not until four months later, after a series of attempts to regain possession of the child, that Melissa was returned to the Sterns, having been forcibly removed from the home where she was then living with Mr. and Mrs. Whitehead, the home in Florida owned by Mary Beth Whitehead's parents.

The struggle over Baby M began when it became apparent that Mrs. Whitehead could not return the child to Mr. Stern. [The court detailed the Whitehead family's flight to Florida in order to evade legal process]. Eventually the Sterns discovered where the Whiteheads were staying, commenced supplementary proceedings in Florida, and obtained an order requiring the Whiteheads to turn over the child. Police in Florida enforced the order, forcibly removing the child from her grandparents' home. She was soon thereafter brought to New Jersey and turned over to the Sterns. The prior order of the court, issued *ex parte,* awarding custody of the child to the Sterns *pendente lite,* was reaffirmed by the trial court after consideration of the certified representations of the parties (both represented by counsel) concerning the unusual sequence of events that had unfolded. Pending final judgment, Mrs. Whitehead was awarded limited visitation with Baby M.

The Sterns' complaint, in addition to seeking possession and ultimately custody of the child, sought enforcement of the surrogacy contract. Pursuant to the contract, it asked that the child be permanently placed in their custody, that Mrs. Whitehead's parental rights be terminated, and that Mrs. Stern be allowed to adopt the child, *i.e.,* that, for all purposes, Melissa become the Sterns' child.

The trial took thirty-two days over a period of more than two months. . . . Soon after the conclusion of the trial, the trial court announced its opinion from the bench. . . . It held that the surrogacy contract was valid; ordered that Mrs. Whitehead's parental rights be terminated and that sole custody of the child be granted to Mr. Stern; and, after hearing brief testimony from Mrs. Stern, immediately entered an order allowing the adoption of Melissa by Mrs. Stern, all in accordance with the surrogacy contract. Pending the outcome of the appeal, we granted a continuation of visitation to Mrs. Whitehead, although slightly more limited than the visitation allowed during the trial.

Although clearly expressing its view that the surrogacy contract was valid, the trial court devoted the major portion of its opinion to the question of the baby's best interests. The inconsistency is apparent. The surrogacy contract calls for the surrender of the child to the Sterns, permanent and sole custody in the Sterns, and termination of Mrs. Whitehead's parental rights, all without qualification, all regardless of any evaluation of the best interests of the child. As a matter of fact the contract recites (even before the child was conceived) that it is in the best interests of the child to be placed with Mr. Stern. In effect, the trial court awarded custody to Mr. Stern, the natural father, based on the same kind of evidence and analysis as might be expected had no surrogacy contract existed. Its rationalization, however, was that while the surrogacy contract was valid, specific performance would not be granted unless that remedy was in the best interests of the child. The factual issues confronted and decided by the trial court were the same as if Mr. Stern and Mrs. Whitehead had had the child out of wedlock, intended or unintended, and then disagreed about custody. The trial court's awareness of the irrelevance of the contract in the court's determination of custody is suggested by its remark that beyond the question of the child's best interests, "[a]ll other concerns raised by counsel constitute commentary." . . . .

On the question of best interests—and we agree, but for different reasons, that custody was the critical issue—the court's analysis of the testimony was perceptive, demonstrating both its understanding of the case and its considerable experience in these matters. We agree substantially with both its analysis and conclusions on the matter of custody.

The court's review and analysis of the surrogacy contract, however, is not at all in accord with ours. . . .

We have concluded that this surrogacy contract is invalid. Our conclusion has two bases: direct conflict with existing statutes and conflict with the public policies of this State, as expressed in its statutory and decisional law.

One of the surrogacy contract's basic purposes, to achieve the adoption of a child through private placement, though permitted in New Jersey "is very much disfavored." Sees v. Baber, 74 N.J. 201, 217, 377 A.2d 628 (1977). Its use of money for this purpose—and we have no doubt whatsoever that the money is being paid to obtain an adoption and not, as the Sterns argue, for the personal services of Mary Beth Whitehead—is illegal and perhaps criminal. In addition to the inducement of money, there is the coercion of contract: the natural mother's irrevocable agreement, prior to birth, even prior to conception, to surrender the child to the adoptive couple. Such an agreement is totally unenforceable in private placement adoption.

Even where the adoption is through an approved agency, the formal agreement to surrender occurs only *after* birth . . . and then, by regulation, only after the birth mother has been offered counseling. Integral to these invalid provisions of the surrogacy contract is the related agreement, equally invalid, on the part of the natural mother to cooperate with, and not to contest, proceedings to terminate her parental rights, as well as her contractual concession, in aid of the adoption, that the child's best interests would be served by awarding custody to the natural father and his wife—all of this before she has even conceived, and, in some cases, before she has the slightest idea of what the natural father and adoptive mother are like.

The foregoing provisions not only directly conflict with New Jersey statutes, but also offend long-established State policies. These critical terms, which are at the heart of the contract, are invalid and unenforceable; the conclusion therefore follows, without more, that the entire contract is unenforceable. . . .

Conflict with Statutory Provisions . . .

Our law prohibits paying or accepting money in connection with any placement of a child for adoption. Violation is a high misdemeanor. Excepted are fees of an approved agency (which must be a non-profit entity) and certain expenses in connection with childbirth.

Considerable care was taken in this case to structure the surrogacy arrangement so as not to violate this prohibition. The arrangement was structured as follows: the adopting parent, Mrs. Stern, was not a party to the surrogacy contract; the money paid to Mrs. Whitehead was stated to be for her services—not for the adoption; the sole purpose of the contract was stated as being that "of giving a child to William Stern, its natural and biological father"; the money was purported to be "compensation for services and expenses and in no way . . . a fee for termination of parental rights or a payment in exchange for consent to surrender a child for adoption"; the fee to the Infertility Center ($7,500) was stated to be for legal representation, advice, administrative work, and other "services." Nevertheless, it seems clear that the money was paid and accepted in connection with an adoption.

The Infertility Center's major role was first as a "finder" of the surrogate mother whose child was to be adopted, and second as the arranger of all proceedings that led to the adoption. Its role as adoption finder is demonstrated by the provision requiring Mr. Stern to pay another $7,500 if he uses Mary Beth Whitehead again as a surrogate, and by ICNY's agreement to "coordinate arrangements for the adoption of the child by the wife." The surrogacy agreement requires Mrs. Whitehead to surrender Baby M for the purposes of adoption. The agreement notes that Mr. *and Mrs.* Stern wanted to have a child, and provides that the child be "placed" with Mrs. Stern in the event Mr. Stern dies before the child is born. The payment of the $10,000 occurs only on surrender of custody of the child and "completion of the duties and obligations" of Mrs. Whitehead, including termination of her parental rights to facilitate adoption by Mrs. Stern. As for the contention that the Sterns are paying only for services and not for an adoption, we need note only that they would pay nothing in the event the child died before the fourth month of pregnancy, and only $1,000 if the child were stillborn, even though the "services" had been fully rendered. Additionally, one of Mrs. Whitehead's estimated costs, to be assumed by Mr. Stern, was an "Adoption Fee," presumably for Mrs. Whitehead's incidental costs in connection with the adoption.

Mr. Stern knew he was paying for the adoption of a child; Mrs. Whitehead knew she was accepting money so that a child might be adopted; the Infertility Center knew that it was being paid for assisting in the adoption of a child. The actions of all three worked to frustrate the goals of the statute. It strains credulity to claim that these arrangements, touted by those in the surrogacy business as an attractive alternative to the usual route leading to an adoption, really amount to something other than a private placement adoption for money.

The prohibition of our statute is strong. Violation constitutes a high misdemeanor, a third-degree crime, carrying a penalty of three to five years imprisonment. The evils inherent in baby-bartering are loathsome for a myriad of reasons. The child is sold without regard for whether the purchasers will be suitable parents. N. Baker, *Baby Selling: The Scandal of Black Market Adoption* 7 (1978). The natural mother does not receive the benefit of counseling and guidance to assist her in making a decision that may affect her for a lifetime. In fact, the monetary incentive to sell her child may, depending on her financial circumstances, make her decision less voluntary. . . . Furthermore, the adoptive parents may not be fully informed of the natural parents' medical history.

Baby-selling potentially results in the exploitation of all parties involved. *Ibid.* Conversely, adoption statutes seek to further humanitarian goals, foremost among them the best interests of the child. H. Witmer, E. Herzog, E. Weinstein, & M. Sullivan, *Independent Adoptions: A Follow-Up Study* 32 (1967). The negative consequences of baby-buying are potentially present in the surrogacy context, especially the potential for placing and adopting a child without regard to the interest of the child or the natural mother.

. . . The provision in the surrogacy contract whereby the mother irrevocably agrees to surrender custody of her child and to terminate her parental rights conflicts with the settled interpretation of New Jersey statutory law. There is only one irrevocable consent, and that is the one explicitly provided for by statute: a consent to surrender of custody and a placement with an approved agency or with [the Division of Youth and Family Services]. The provision in the surrogacy contract, agreed to before conception, requiring the natural mother to surrender custody of the child without any right of revocation is one more indication of the essential nature of this transaction: the creation of a contractual system of termination and adoption designed to circumvent our statutes.

Public Policy Considerations

The surrogacy contract's invalidity, resulting from its direct conflict with the above statutory provisions, is further underlined when its goals and means are measured against New Jersey's public policy. The contract's basic premise, that the natural parents can decide in advance of birth which one is to have custody of the child, bears no relationship to the settled law that the child's best interests shall determine custody. . . . The fact that the trial court remedied that aspect of the contract through the "best interests" phase does not make the contractual provision any less offensive to the public policy of this State. . . .

The point is made that Mrs. Whitehead *agreed* to the surrogacy arrangement, supposedly fully understanding the consequences. Putting aside the issue of how compelling her need for money may have been, and how significant her understanding of the consequences, we suggest that her consent is irrelevant. There are, in a civilized society, some things that money cannot buy. In America, we decided long ago that merely because conduct purchased by money was "voluntary" did not mean that it was good or beyond regulation and prohibition. . . . Employers can no longer buy labor at the lowest price they can bargain for, even though that labor is "voluntary," or buy women's labor for less money than paid to men for the same job, or purchase the agreement of children to perform oppressive labor, or purchase the agreement of workers to subject themselves to unsafe or unhealthful working conditions. There are, in short, values that society deems more important than granting to wealth whatever it can buy, be it labor, love, or life. Whether this principle recommends prohibition of surrogacy, which presumably sometimes results in great satisfaction to all of the parties, is not for us to say. We note here only that, under existing law, the fact that Mrs. Whitehead "agreed" to the arrangement is not dispositive. . . .

In sum, the harmful consequences of this surrogacy arrangement appear to us all too palpable. In New Jersey the surrogate mother's agreement to sell her child is void. Its irrevocability infects the entire contract, as does the money that purports to buy it. . . .

Having decided that the surrogacy contract is illegal and unenforceable, we now must decide the custody question without regard to the provisions of the surrogacy contract that would give Mr. Stern sole and permanent custody. (That does not mean that the existence of the contract and the circumstances under which it was entered may not be considered to the extent deemed relevant to the child's best interests.) With the surrogacy contract disposed of, the legal framework becomes a dispute between two couples over the custody of a child produced by the artificial insemination of one couple's wife by the other's husband. Under the Parentage Act the claims of the natural father and the natural mother are entitled to equal weight, *i.e.,* one is not preferred over the other solely because he or she is the father or the mother. The applicable rule given these circumstances is clear: the child's best interests determine custody. . . .

Based on all of this we have concluded, independent of the trial court's identical conclusion, that Melissa's best interests call for custody in the Sterns. Our above-mentioned disagreements with the trial court do not, as we have noted, in any way diminish our concurrence with its conclusions. We feel, however, that those disagreements are important enough to be stated. They are disagreements about the evaluation of conduct. They also may provide some insight about the potential consequences of surrogacy. . . .

NOTES AND QUESTIONS

1.   Notice the use of legal analogy in *Baby M*. How we decide to analogize a contract is important; if the contract seems to run afoul of a statute, in this case the New Jersey adoption laws that forbid the sale of a baby, then it seems logical that the contract would be unenforceable based on public policy grounds. However, not everyone would characterize surrogacy in the same way. Is surrogacy more like "baby selling" (as the New Jersey Supreme Court reasoned), or is another analogy more apt? Some might describe surrogacy as a type of employment contract. A surrogate mother invests her time and bodily "labor" in order to gestate a child; she is paid in return for her efforts, which are valuable to those who need her services. If an employment analogy were used, and assuming fair compensation and conditions for the surrogate, does the deal look less problematic?

2.   Even though Mary Beth Whitehead succeeded in having the surrogacy contract invalidated, the "best interest of the child" inquiry did not go in her favor. When Melissa Stern was contacted about the case in 2007, she was then in college, at George Washington University, and noted that "I love my family very much and am very happy to be with them[.] I'm very happy I ended up with them. I love them, they're my best friends in the whole world, and that's all I have to say about it." By her family, she was referring to the Sterns; when she turned 18 Melissa initiated the process of allowing Elizabeth Stern to adopt her. In 2012, Melissa had moved to the United Kingdom with her husband. She received a master's from King's College London, focusing on the bioethics of surrogacy and she is now a medical writer. The trial court judge, who had originally upheld the contract as written, performed the adoption ceremony. Meanwhile, Mary Beth Whitehead remarried, had another child with her second husband, and is now a grandmother. *See* Jennifer Weiss, *Now It's Melissa's Time*, NEW JERSEY MONTHLY MAGAZINE (March 2007); Mike Kelly, *Twenty-Five Years After Baby M, Surrogacy Questions Remain Unanswered*, NORTHJERSEY.COM (March 30, 2012).

3.   In the years since *Baby M* was decided, there has been no one uniform approach to surrogacy contracts. As noted in Diane S. Hinson & Maureen McBrien, *Surrogacy Across America*, 34 FAMILY ADVOCATE 32 (2011):

> In the aftermath of the infamous *Baby M* case in the late 1980s in which a "traditional surrogate" decided to renege on her surrogacy contract and fight to keep the genetically related baby she had carried, a number of state legislatures passed laws prohibiting surrogacy to ensure that a similar scenario would never be repeated. Arizona led the pack, passing a law that made surrogacy contracts void and against public policy. Michigan and New York enacted similar statutes, with New York adding a "no compensation" provision. The District of Columbia followed soon after and upped the ante: In DC, entering into or assisting in the formation of a surrogacy contract is not just prohibited—it could land you in jail. It is noteworthy that surrogacy prohibitions, thus, did not seem to follow general political leanings, as jurisdictions such as the District of Columbia and New York are commonly perceived as politically liberal.
>
> [But] not all states jumped on the bandwagon to ban surrogacy. In fact, some states passed legislation permitting surrogacy, though often with restrictions, while others published case law authorizing surrogacy either explicitly or implicitly. As a result, what exists throughout the country is a smattering of statutes and case law to which there appears to be no rhyme or reason, and which, in any event, is often inconsistent with what happens in practice, as "intended parents" find ways to build families through surrogacy with the assistance of . . . attorneys.
>
> Even as state legislatures were busy outlawing surrogacy in response to a sensational but isolated case, medical technology was already rendering such broad-brush laws obsolete. With the advent of *in vitro* fertilization (IVF), through which embryos are fertilized outside the body and then placed back into the uterus, it became possible for a woman to become pregnant with another woman's eggs, which soon led to the advent of Gestational Surrogacy (GS). In gestational surrogacy, a "Gestational Carrier" (GC) carries a baby for someone else, but does not provide her own eggs and therefore has no genetic connection. Instead, she acts solely as a "host uterus."[1]

Times and attitudes have certainly changed as more people use these procedures to start families, including well-known celebrities. In terms of the law, U.S. jurisdictions follow a variety of approaches, which the authors above describe as ranging from one "green light" to one "red light" (criminal penalties)

---

along with one "yellow light" plus assorted states that seem to suggest "proceed at your own risk" or "okay if you satisfy specific statutory checklist requirements" or "okay under the case law" and some twenty where the law is simply unformed. Is this patchwork an example of good federalism at work or would a national approach be superior? How would you counsel a client wanting to enter a surrogacy agreement with a gestational carrier? The law at the international level beyond the U.S. is even more varied.

4.   *Baby M* concerned reproduction, but could there be instances where a person's right *not* to reproduce would be given priority over the terms of a contract? In 2000 the Supreme Judicial Court of Massachusetts tackled this issue in *A.Z. v. B.Z*, 725 N.E.2d 1051 (Mass. 2000). In that case, after the successful birth of twins through an IVF procedure, a husband and wife decided to divorce. At issue in the dispute were the extra embryos that had been frozen during the original procedure. The former husband did not wish to have further children and sought to have the contract with the fertility clinic declared void as against public policy. The Massachusetts Supreme Court sided with the former husband, noting that the divorce constituted enough of a changed circumstance to invalidate the original contract.

5.   What about contracts between spouses not to have children? An article in 2002 from the *New York Times* explored the phenomenon of wealthy men—who did not want to add to their families—requiring their second wife to sign a prenuptial agreement. These agreements would state that alimony and other property settlements would depend on a child-free marriage. *See* Jill Brooke, *A Promise to Love, Honor, and Bear No Children*, NEW YORK TIMES, Oct. 13, 2002.

6.   Decades ago, Elisabeth M. Landes and Richard Posner sparked widespread controversy when they began writing about the creation of markets for child adoption. Elisabeth M. Landes & Richard Posner, *The Economics of the Baby Shortage*, 7 J. LEGAL STUD. 323 (1978). Proposals surrounding markets for human organs have also sparked serious debate. Although there are a number of conflicting discussions and assumptions surrounding the development of commodification of the body, opponents stress two general areas of concern. First, there is a concern that markets can be coercive and play on the desperation that arises from abject poverty and economic inequality. Second, opponents argue that commodification will corrupt basic human values, meaning that "certain moral and civic goods are diminished or corrupted if bought and sold for money." In other words, particular markets might impair the value of human life and, perhaps, dignity. While the first argument looks to the ideal of consent, the dignity argument examines the type of goods on offer and questions whether the purchase and sale of those goods will produce good results for society overall.

7.   Feminist theorists have been at the forefront of this commodification discussion, perhaps because some of these markets have gender implications, concern the female body, or concern women's traditional roles, which were historically outside and apart from paid labor markets. Many theorists are

concerned with dignitary aspects of commodification, arguing that women's bodies and reproductive capacities should not be the subject of trade or market pressures. Other feminists are concerned about exploitation of poor women by the wealthy, sometimes based on racial lines or on development status of the countries in which women lived. Some are concerned that the monetization of reproductive capacity could only lead to further exploitation. For in-depth discussion of these topics, *see* RETHINKING COMMODIFICATION (MARTHA ERTMAN & JOHN C. WILLIAMS, EDS. 2005).

8. Some theorists have argued in favor of commodification more generally, proposing that familial relations might become more equitable if they were to be viewed in monetized terms. *See* Martha Ertman, *Marriage as a Trade: Bridging the Private/Private Distinction*, 36 HARV. C.R.-C.L. REV. 79 (2001); Katherine Silbaugh, *Marriage Contracts and the Family Economy*, 93 Nw. U.L. REV. 65 (1998). Indeed, Professor Kimberly Krawiec has advocated for the monetization of "taboo trades," including sex work, arguing that legalization and monetization of the sexual economy could lead to women's empowerment and more full participation in the market economy.

9. Where should the limits of contract and public policy lie? For example, think about an agreement that would allow a prisoner "good time" credit in exchange for becoming a kidney donor. Think also about a recent online auction of virginity, based at the Moonlite Bunny Ranch in Nevada. *See* Emily C. Lee, *Trading Kidneys for Prison Time: When Two Contradictory Legal Traditions Intersect, Which One has the Right-Of-Way?*, 43 U.S.F.L REV. 507, 508 (2009) (describing proposed bill in South Carolina providing credit for prisoners who became kidney donors, S.B. 480, 117th Gen. Assemb., Reg. Sess. (S.C.2007)); Kimberly D. Krawiec, *A Woman's Worth*, 88 N.C. L. REV. 1739, 1739–40 (2010) (recounting story of 2008 virginity auction). For more on commodification in the context of the Internet, see Miriam A. Cherry, *Cyber Commodification*, 72 MD. L. REV. 381 (2013).

CHAPTER 5

EXCUSES AND TERMINATION

■ ■ ■

As seen in Chapter Four, in some circumstances even properly formed contracts—deals that contain offer, acceptance, and consideration—are not enforced due to public policy concerns. We previously examined the outer boundaries of public policy and learned that the subject matter of some contracts could be scrutinized by courts, often because of worries about exploitation or overreaching or because of larger social concerns. In this chapter, we examine traditional contract law doctrines that allow a party an affirmative defense in a contract case.

Contracts can never perfectly anticipate every potential circumstance. When surprising events arise, some traditionalist lawyers would argue that we should continue to adhere to the deal, despite exceptional circumstances. That approach would reflect ancient beliefs, such as *caveat emptor*—"buyer beware" and *pacta sunt servanda*—"promises are kept." Holding the parties to their bargains may increase certainty in exchange transactions and encourage people to verify all assumptions underlying their commitments when they make them.

Time has taught, however, that such a stance can be unduly rigid, unrealistic, and myopic. It fails to appreciate how people make contracts to allocate risks. If everyone is held to technical terms of bargains with no attention to context, many arrangements will result in putting risks on people by happenstance rather than based on intention. And so there are some circumstances where courts excuse contractual obligation and permit termination of a contract. In cataloging the excuses from contract obligation, this chapter examines risk allocation in contracts, and the abiding concerns with assent and freedom of contract.

A. MISTAKE AND WARRANTY

We begin examination of contract defenses with the doctrine of mistake. Most people entering bargains are generally held to them. However, an exception applies if both parties were mistaken when they made their deal about a basic assumption that materially affects the exchange. "Mistake" does not mean a mere error or buyer's remorse; it means "a belief that is not in accord with the facts." Restatement (Second) of Contracts Section 151.

Under the doctrine of mutual mistake, either side can void the deal, so long as the risk of the basic assumption was not taken by one party alone. In the next section, we will take a closer look at this doctrine as it has developed over time. We start with a recent case that involved the vast financial scandal perpetrated by Bernard Madoff and its impact on a divorce settlement. Ensuing cases also consider the relationship between mutual mistake and warranty.

SIMKIN V. BLANK

968 N.E.2d 459 (N.Y. 2012)

GRAFFEO, JUDGE:

The primary issue before us is whether plaintiff has presented facts sufficient to support the reformation or setting aside of the parties' marital settlement agreement based on a claim of mutual mistake pertaining to an investment account. We conclude that plaintiff has failed to state a cause of action . . . and therefore dismiss the amended complaint.

Plaintiff Steven Simkin (husband) and defendant Laura Blank (wife) married in 1973 and have two children. Husband is a partner at a New York law firm and wife, also an attorney, is employed by a university. After almost 30 years of marriage, the parties separated in 2002 and stipulated in 2004 that the cut-off date for determining the value of marital assets would be September 1, 2004. The parties, represented by counsel, spent two years negotiating a detailed 22-page settlement agreement, executed in June 2006. . . .

The settlement agreement set forth a comprehensive division of marital property. Husband agreed to pay wife $6,250,000 "[a]s and for an equitable distribution of property . . . and in satisfaction of the Wife's support and marital property rights." In addition, wife retained title to a Manhattan apartment (subject to a $370,000 mortgage), an automobile, her retirement accounts and any "bank, brokerage and similar financial accounts in her name." Upon receipt of her distributive payment, wife agreed to convey her interest in the Scarsdale marital residence to husband. Husband received title to three automobiles and kept his retirement accounts, less $368,000 to equalize the value of the parties' retirement accounts. Husband further retained "bank, brokerage and similar financial accounts" that were in his name, two of which were specifically referenced—his capital account as a partner at the law firm and a Citibank account.

The agreement also contained a number of mutual releases between the parties. Each party waived any interest in the other's law license and released or discharged any debts or further claims against the other. Although the agreement acknowledged that the property division was "fair and reasonable," it did not state that the parties intended an equal distribution or other designated percentage division of the marital estate. The only provision that explicitly contemplated an equal division was the reference to equalizing the values of the parties' retirement accounts. The parties further acknowledged that the settlement constituted

> an agreement between them with respect to any and all funds, assets or properties, both real and personal, including property in which either of them may have an equitable or beneficial interest wherever situated, now owned by the parties or either of them, or standing in their respective names or which may hereafter be acquired by either of them, and all other rights and obligations arising out of the marital relationship.

At the time the parties entered into the settlement, one of husband's unspecified brokerage accounts was maintained by Bernard L. Madoff Investment Securities (the Madoff account). According to husband, the parties believed the account was valued at $5.4 million as of September 1, 2004, the valuation date for marital assets. Husband withdrew funds from this account to pay a portion of his distributive payment owed wife in 2006, and continued to invest in the account subsequent to the divorce. In December 2008, Bernard Madoff's colossal Ponzi scheme was publicly exposed and Madoff later pleaded guilty to federal securities fraud and related offenses.

As a result of the disclosure of Madoff's fraud, in February 2009—about 2 1/2 years after the divorce was finalized—husband commenced this action against wife alleging two causes of action: (1) reformation of the settlement agreement predicated on a mutual mistake and (2) unjust enrichment. The amended complaint asserts that the settlement agreement was intended to accomplish an "approximately equal division of [the couple's] marital assets," including a 50–50 division of the Madoff account.

To that end, the amended complaint states that $2,700,000 of wife's $6,250,000 distributive payment represented her "share" of the Madoff account. Husband alleges that the parties' intention to equally divide the marital estate was frustrated because both parties operated under the "mistake" or misconception as to the existence of a legitimate investment account with Madoff which, in fact, was revealed to be part of a fraudulent Ponzi scheme. The amended complaint admits, however, that funds were previously "withdrawn" from the "Account" by husband and applied to his obligation to pay wife.

In his claim for reformation, husband requests that the court "determine the couple's true assets with respect to the Madoff [a]ccount" and alter the settlement terms to reflect an equal division of the actual value of the Madoff account. The second cause of action seeks restitution from wife "in an amount to be determined at trial" based on her unjust enrichment arising from husband's payment of what the parties mistakenly believed to be wife's share of the Madoff account. Wife moved to dismiss the amended complaint on several grounds, including a defense founded on documentary evidence . . . and for failure to state a cause of action . . .

Supreme Court granted wife's motion and dismissed the amended complaint. The Appellate Division, with two Justices dissenting, reversed and reinstated the action . . . The Appellate Division granted wife leave to appeal on a certified question . . . , and we now reverse and reinstate Supreme Court's order of dismissal.

Wife argues that the Appellate Division erred in reinstating the amended complaint because the allegations, even if true, fail to appropriately establish the existence of a mutual mistake at the time the parties entered into their settlement agreement. Rather, she claims that, at most, the parties may have been mistaken as to the value of the Madoff account, but not its existence. Wife also contends that allowing husband's claims to go forward years after the division of property and issuance of a divorce decree would undermine policy concerns regarding finality in divorce cases. Husband responds that the amended complaint states a viable claim because the parties were both unaware and misled as to the legitimacy of the Madoff account, which, in husband's view, "did not in fact ever exist" due to the fraud occasioned on investors.

. . . Marital settlement agreements are judicially favored and are not to be easily set aside . . . Nevertheless, in the proper case, an agreement may be subject to rescission or reformation based on a mutual mistake by the parties . . . Similarly, a release of claims may be avoided due to mutual mistake . . . Based on these contract principles, the parties here agree that this appeal turns on whether husband's amended complaint states a claim for relief under a theory of mutual mistake.

We have explained that "[t]he mutual mistake must exist at the time the contract is entered into and must be substantial" [Matter of Gould v. Board of Educ. of Sewanhaka Cent. High School Dist., 616 N.E.2d 142 (N.Y. 1993)]. Put differently, the mistake must be "so material that . . . it goes to the foundation of the agreement" (Da Silva v. Musso, 53 N.Y.2d 543, 552, 444 N.Y.S.2d 50, 428 N.E.2d 382 [1981] . . . see also 27 Lord, Williston on Contracts § 70:12 [4th ed.] ["The parties must have been mistaken as to a basic assumption of the contract . . . Basic assumption means the mistake must vitally affect the basis upon which the parties contract"]). Court-ordered relief is therefore reserved only for "exceptional situations" (Da Silva, 53 N.Y.2d at 552, 444 N.Y.S.2d 50, 428 N.E.2d 382 . . . . The premise underlying the doctrine of mutual mistake is that "the agreement as expressed, in some material respect, does not represent the meeting of the minds of the parties" (Gould, 81 N.Y.2d at 453, 599 N.Y.S.2d 787, 616 N.E.2d 142).

Although we have not addressed mutual mistake claims in the context of marital settlement agreements, the parties cite a number of Appellate Division cases that have analyzed this issue. Husband relies on True v. True, 63 A.D.3d 1145, 1146, 882 N.Y.S.2d 261 (2d Dept.2009), where the settlement agreement provided that the husband's stock awards from his employer would be "divided 50–50 in kind" and recited that 3,655 shares were available for division between the parties. After the wife redeemed her half of the shares, the husband learned that only 150 shares remained and brought an action to reform the agreement, arguing that the parties mistakenly specified the gross number of shares (3,655) rather than the net number that was actually available for distribution. The Second Department agreed and reformed the agreement to effectuate the parties' intent to divide the shares equally, holding that the husband had established "that the parties' use of 3,655 gross shares was a mutual mistake because it undermined their intent to divide the *net* shares available for division, 50–50 in kind" . . .

Other cases relied on by husband involve marital settlement agreements that were set aside or reformed because a mutual mistake rendered a portion of the agreement impossible to perform. . . .

Wife in turn points to appellate cases denying a spouse's request to reopen a marital settlement agreement where the final value of an asset was not what the parties believed at the time of the divorce . . . In Kojovic v. Goldman, 35 A.D.3d 65, 823 N.Y.S.2d 35 (2006), lv. denied 8 N.Y.3d 804, 831 N.Y.S.2d 106, 863 N.E.2d 111 (2007), for example, the First Department dismissed the wife's reformation and rescission claims where the husband unexpectedly sold his interest in a company for $18 million after the divorce. And in Etzion v. Etzion, 62 A.D.3d 646, 880 N.Y.S.2d 79 (2009), lv. dismissed 13 N.Y.3d 824, 890 N.Y.S.2d 437, 918 N.E.2d 950 (2009), the Second Department rejected the wife's mutual mistake claim where the market value of the husband's warehouse property substantially increased in value after the city adopted a rezoning plan subsequent to the parties' settlement.

Applying these legal principles, we are of the view that the amended complaint fails to adequately state a cause of action based on mutual mistake. As an initial matter, husband's claim that the alleged mutual mistake undermined the foundation of the settlement agreement, a precondition to relief under our precedents, is belied by the terms of the agreement itself. Unlike the settlement agreement in *True* that expressly incorporated a "50–50" division of a stated number of stock shares, the settlement agreement here, on its face, does not mention the Madoff account, much less evince an intent to divide the account in equal or other proportionate shares . . . .

To the contrary, the agreement provides that the $6,250,000 payment to wife was "in satisfaction of [her] support and marital property rights," along with her release of various claims and inheritance rights. Despite the fact that the agreement permitted husband to retain title to his "bank, brokerage and similar financial accounts" and enumerated two such accounts, his alleged $5.4 million Madoff investment account is neither identified nor valued. Given the extensive and carefully negotiated nature of the settlement agreement, we do not believe that this presents one of those "exceptional situations" (Da Silva, 53 N.Y.2d at 552, 444 N.Y.S.2d 50, 428 N.E.2d 382 [internal quotation marks omitted]) warranting reformation or rescission of a divorce settlement after all marital assets have been distributed.

Even putting the language of the agreement aside, the core allegation underpinning husband's mutual mistake claim—that the Madoff account was "nonexistent" when the parties executed their settlement agreement in June 2006—does not amount to a "material" mistake of fact as required by our case law. The premise of husband's argument is that the parties mistakenly believed that they had an investment account with Bernard Madoff when, in fact, no account ever existed. In husband's view, this case is no different from one in which parties are under a misimpression that they own a piece of real or personal property but later discover that they never obtained rightful ownership, such that a distribution would not have been possible at the time of the agreement. But that analogy is not apt here. Husband does not dispute that, until the Ponzi scheme began to unravel in late 2008—more than two years after the property division was completed—it would have been possible for him to redeem all or part of the investment. In fact, the amended complaint contains an admission that husband was able to withdraw funds (the amount is undisclosed) from the account in 2006 to partially pay his distributive payment to wife. Given that the mutual mistake must have existed at the time the agreement was executed in 2006 . . . , the fact that husband could no longer withdraw funds years later is not determinative.

This situation, however sympathetic, is more akin to a marital asset that unexpectedly loses value after dissolution of a marriage; the asset had value at the time of the settlement but the purported value did not remain consistent. Viewed from a different perspective, had the Madoff account or other asset retained by husband substantially increased in worth after the divorce, should wife be able to claim entitlement to a portion of the enhanced value? The answer is obviously no. Consequently, we find this case analogous to the Appellate Division precedents denying a spouse's attempt to reopen a settlement agreement based on post-divorce changes in asset valuation. . . .

Accordingly, the order of the Appellate Division should be reversed, with costs, the order of Supreme Court reinstated, and the certified question answered in the negative. . . .

NOTES AND QUESTIONS

1.   The Ponzi scheme perpetrated by Bernard Madoff resulted in losses of more than $64 billon to investors in his so-called "hedge fund." In a Ponzi scheme, there is no actual investment. Rather, later investors' money is shuffled to fund payouts to earlier investors, with the Ponzi scheme operator taking a percentage. Other investors, seeing the returns on investment, then decide to contribute their money. At some point, when the Ponzi scheme cannot attract new investors or too many existing investors pull their money out, the scheme collapses.

Madoff's swindle was fueled by his status as the former Chairman of NASDAQ, which helped to convince investors that the promised returns were legitimate. The scheme unraveled when jittery investors withdrew funds rapidly amid the 2008 financial crisis. Simkin and Blank were two of those defrauded, along with well-known celebrities, non-profits, and charitable foundations, some of which were forced to shut down operations. For more on Madoff's fraud, *see* Miriam A. Cherry & Jarrod Wong, *Clawbacks: Prospective Contract Measures in an Age of Executive Compensation and Ponzi Schemes*, 94 MINN. L. REV. 368 (2009).

2.   One reason parties enter contracts is to divide the risk of different events (either certain or contingent) between them. As such, a contract can help the parties plan for the future. However, sometimes a material fact would not seem to be within the contemplation of the parties at the time of the contract. It is in these circumstances that we consider the doctrine of mistake.

3.   *Simkin v. Blank* was a well-publicized case, especially because the intermediate appeals court in New York had reached the opposite conclusion. How much of the outcome in this case can be ascribed to formalistic notions of contract, how much to notions of assumption of the risk, and how much to the need for finality in family law and divorce settlements? What would the policy implications have been if the court had affirmed the intermediate court? Could there have been a way to cabin such a holding to situations where there has been such a massive financial fraud, or would recognizing mutual mistake have resulted in a great deal of uncertainty and litigation?

RESTATEMENT (SECOND) OF CONTRACTS, SECTIONS 152, 154

§ 152.   *When Mistake of Both Parties Makes a Contract Voidable.*

(1)   Where a mistake of both parties at the time a contract was made as to a basic assumption on which the contract was made has a material effect on the agreed exchange of performances, the contract is voidable by

the adversely affected party unless he bears the risk of the mistake under the rule stated in Section 154.

(2)   In determining whether the mistake has a material effect on the agreed exchange of performances, account is taken of any relief by way of reformation, restitution, or otherwise.

§ 154.   *When a Party Bears the Risk of a Mistake.*

A party bears the risk of a mistake when (a) the risk is allocated to him by agreement of the parties, or (b) he is aware, at the time the contract is made, that he has only limited knowledge with respect to the facts to which the mistake relates but treats his limited knowledge as sufficient, or (c) the risk is allocated to him by the court on the ground that it is reasonable in the circumstances to do so.

EXAMPLE: THE DENVER MINT DIME

A retail dealer in coins paid a part-time coin dealer $500 for a dime purportedly minted in 1916 at Denver. Such a coin is rare so it has a market value well above its value as currency. This coin turned out to be a counterfeit, as the "D" on its face (for Denver) was forged. It is common in the coin trade for dealers buying coins to take the risk as to genuineness and to conduct related investigation.

In this case, the seller had acquired the coin for $450. The seller told the buyer $500 was the minimum sale price. The buyer examined the coin for 30 minutes and then bought it. Later a third party offered to buy it from him for $700, conditional on obtaining a certification of its genuineness by the American Numismatic Society. The Society found that the coin was a forgery. The buyer sought to rescind the contract and obtain restitution of his purchase price. Are such results likely?

Consult *Beachcomber Coins v. Boskett,* 400 A.2d 78 (N.J. Super. 1979) (granting buyer relief, rejecting assertion that buyer had taken the risk because the parties had not consciously proceeded in the face of a known risk but fully intended that the thing being exchanged was a genuine 1916 Denver mint dime, saying that "both parties were certain that the coin was genuine").

How does this fact pattern relate to that in the following case, *Sherwood v. Walker?*

SHERWOOD V. WALKER
33 N.W. 919 (Mich. 1887)

MORSE, J.J.

Replevin for a cow. . . . [J]udgment for plaintiff; appealed to circuit court of Wayne county, and verdict and judgment for plaintiff in that court. The defendants bring error . . .

The main controversy depends upon the construction of a contract for the sale of the cow. . . . The defendants reside at Detroit, but . . . have a farm at Greenfield, in Wayne county, upon which were some blooded cattle supposed to be barren as breeders. The Walkers are importers and breeders of polled Angus cattle.

The plaintiff is a banker. . . . He . . . asked to go out and look at [the defendants' cattle stock], with the statement at the time that they were probably barren, and would not breed. May 5, 1886, plaintiff went out to Greenfield, and saw the cattle. A few days thereafter, he called upon one of the defendants with the view of purchasing a cow, known as "Rose 2d of Aberlone." After considerable talk, it was agreed that defendants would telephone [plaintiff] . . . in reference to the price. The second morning after this talk he was called up by telephone, and the terms of the sale were finally agreed upon. He was to pay five and one-half cents per pound, live weight, fifty pounds shrinkage. He was asked how he intended to take the cow home, and replied that he might ship her from King's cattle-yard. He requested defendants to confirm the sale in writing, which they did by sending him the following letter [dated May 15, 1886 and addressed to T. C. Sherwood]:

> We confirm sale to you of the cow Rose 2d of Aberlone, lot 56 of our catalogue, at five and half cents per pound, less fifty pounds shrink. We inclose herewith order on Mr. Graham for the cow. You might leave check with him, or mail to us here, as you prefer.

. . . On [May 21] the plaintiff went to defendants' farm at Greenfield, and presented the order and letter[.] [An employee] informed plaintiff that the defendants had instructed him not to deliver the cow. Soon after, the plaintiff tendered to Hiram Walker, one of the defendants, $80, and demanded the cow. Walker refused to take the money or deliver the cow. The plaintiff then instituted this suit. After he had secured possession of the cow under the writ of replevin, the plaintiff caused her to be weighed by the constable who served the writ, at a place other than King's cattle-yard. She weighed 1,420 pounds.

. . . The defendants [at trial] introduced evidence tending to show that at the time of the alleged sale it was believed by both the plaintiff and themselves that the cow was barren and would not breed; that she cost $850, and if not barren would be worth from $750 to $1,000; that after the date of the letter . . . the defendants were informed . . . the cow was with calf, and therefore they instructed [their employee] not to deliver her to plaintiff, and on [May 20] telegraphed plaintiff . . . about the cow being with calf, and that consequently they could not sell her. The cow had a calf in the month of October following. . . .

. . . It appears from the record that both parties supposed this cow was barren and would not breed, and she was sold by the pound for an insignificant sum as compared with her real value if a breeder. She was evidently sold and purchased on the relation of her value for beef, unless the plaintiff had learned of her true condition, and concealed such knowledge from the defendants. . . . The circuit judge ruled that [the sale could not be rescinded] and it made no difference whether she was barren or not. I am of the opinion that the court erred in this . . . [I]t must be considered as well settled that a party who has given an apparent consent to a contract of sale may refuse to execute it, or he may avoid it after it has been completed, if the assent was founded, or the contract made, upon the mistake of a material fact—such as the subject-matter of the sale, the price, or some collateral fact materially inducing the agreement—and this can be done when the mistake is mutual. . . .

If there is a difference or misapprehension as to the substance of the thing bargained for; if the thing actually delivered or received is different in substance from the thing bargained for, and intended to be sold, then there is no contract; but if it be only a difference in some quality or accident, even though the mistake may have been the actuating motive to the purchaser or seller, or both of them, yet the contract remains binding. . . .

It seems to me, however, in the case made by this record, that the mistake or misapprehension of the parties went to the whole substance of the agreement. If the cow was a breeder, she was worth at least $750; if barren, she was worth not over $80. The parties would not have made the contract of sale except upon the understanding and belief that she was incapable of breeding, and of no use as a cow. It is true she is now the identical animal that they thought her to be when the contract was made; there is no mistake as to the identity of the creature. Yet the mistake was not of the mere quality of the animal, but went to the very nature of the thing.

A barren cow is substantially a different creature than a breeding one. There is as much difference between them for all purposes of use as there is between an ox and a cow that is capable of breeding and giving milk. If the mutual mistake had simply related to the fact whether she was with calf or not for one season, then it might have been a good sale, but the mistake affected the character of the animal for all time, and for its present and ultimate use. She was not in fact the animal, or the kind of animal, the defendants intended to sell or the plaintiff to buy. She was not a barren cow, and, if this fact had been known, there would have been no contract. The mistake affected the substance of the whole consideration, and it must be considered that there was no contract to sell or sale of the cow as she actually was. . . .

The court should have instructed the jury that if they found that the cow was sold, or contracted to be sold, upon the understanding of both parties that she was barren, and useless for the purpose of breeding, and that in fact she was not barren, but capable of breeding, then the defendants had a right to rescind . . . and the verdict should be in their favor.

The judgment of the court below must be reversed, and a new trial granted, with costs of this court to defendants. . . .

SHERWOOD, J., dissenting.

. . . The record . . . shows that the defendants, when they sold the cow, believed the cow was not with calf, and barren; that from what the plaintiff had been told by defendants (for it does not appear he had any other knowledge or facts from which he could form an opinion) he believed the cow was farrow, but still thought she could be made to breed. The foregoing shows the entire interview and treaty between the parties as to the sterility and qualities of the cow sold to the plaintiff. . . .

There is no question but that the defendants sold the cow representing her of the breed and quality they believed the cow to be, and that the purchaser so understood it. And the buyer purchased her believing her to be of the breed represented by the sellers, and possessing all the qualities stated, and even more. He believed she would breed. There is no pretense that the plaintiff bought the cow for beef, and there is nothing in the record indicating that he would have bought her at all only that he thought she might be made to breed. Under the foregoing facts—and these are all that are contained in the record material to the contract—it is held that because it turned out that the plaintiff was more correct in his judgment as to one quality of the cow than the defendants, and a quality, too, which could not by any possibility be positively known at the time by either party to exist, the contract may be annulled by the defendants at their pleasure. I know of no law, and have not been referred to any, which will justify any such holding . . .

In this case neither party knew the actual quality and condition of this cow at the time of the sale. The defendants say, or rather said, to the plaintiff, "they had a few head left on their farm in Greenfield, and asked plaintiff to go and see them, stating to plaintiff that in all probability they were sterile and would not breed." Plaintiff did go as requested, and found there these cows, including the one purchased, with a bull. The cow had been exposed, but neither knew she was with calf or whether she would breed. The defendants thought she would not, but the plaintiff says that he thought she could be made to breed, but believed she was not with calf. The defendants sold the cow for what they believed her to be, and the plaintiff bought her as he believed she was . . . I know of no precedent as authority by which this court can alter the contract thus made by these parties in writing . . .

There was no mistake of any material fact by either of the parties . . . . There was no difference between the parties, nor misapprehension, as to the substance of the thing bargained for, which was a cow supposed to be barren by one party, and believed not to be by the other. As to the quality of the animal, subsequently developed, both parties were equally ignorant, and as to this each party took his chances. If this were not the law, there would be no safety in purchasing this kind of stock. . . .

. . . I understand the law to be well settled that "there is no breach of any implied confidence that one party will not profit by his superior knowledge as to facts and circumstances" actually within the knowledge of both, because neither party reposes in any such confidence unless it be specially tendered or required, and that a general sale does not imply warranty of any quality, or the absence of any; and if the seller represents to the purchaser what he himself believes as to the qualities of an animal, and the purchaser buys relying upon his own judgment as to such qualities, there is no warranty in the case, and neither has a cause of action against the other if he finds himself to have been mistaken in judgment.

The only pretense for avoiding this contract by the defendants is that they erred in judgment as to the qualities and value of the animal. . . . The judgment should be affirmed.

NOTES AND QUESTIONS

1.   Long a casebook favorite for its barnyard antics, *Sherwood v. Walker* raises the question of how to divide an unexpected windfall. Each party to the deal expected that they were buying and selling a cow worth $80 as beef, when in reality, the cow was almost ten times more valuable as a breeder. How should courts divide such an unexpected "win"? Do you agree with the court's decision and reasoning?

2.   By contrast, in *Beachcomber Coins* (highlighted in the Example above), the court found itself having to divide an unexpected loss when what was supposedly a rare dime turned out to be a forgery. What factors in *Beachcomber Coins* might reveal that the parties thought the dime was genuine? Why are the parties' beliefs about the genuine nature of the coin important to a determination of who should bear a loss?

3.   What divides the judicial opinions in *Sherwood v. Walker*, disagreement about the facts, the law, or the application of the law to the facts?

4.   What significance, if any, should be assigned to the facts that the dissenting judge and the losing party share the same surname (Sherwood) and that the winning side and the town where they did business shared the same core name (Walker/Walkerville)?

5.   What are the competing theories on how a court might decide how to divide a loss? On the one hand, the ancient principle of *caveat emptor* (Latin for "buyer beware") would mean that purchasers have the obligation to do their own investigation and take all risks. *Caveat emptor* remains critical in contract law and American culture. But saying that all assets come with inherent risks

that every buyer must live with is a draconian, seventeenth-century relic. Absolute caveat emptor would prevent any doctrine of excuse or mutual mistake. In *Beachcomber Coins*, both parties believed that the coin was a genuine Denver-minted dime and the assumption was central to the pricing. It seems harsh in those circumstances not to recognize the doctrine of mutual mistake.

6.   For the poetry lovers in all of us, consider the following excerpt from a piece written by Duke University law professor Brainerd Currie entitled "Aberlone, Rose Of":

'Tis the middle of night on the Greenfield farm

And the creatures are huddled to keep them from harm.

Ah me!—Ah moo!

Respectively their quidsome balm

How mournfully they chew!

And one there is who stands apart

With hanging head and heavy heart.

Have pity on her sore distress,

This norm of bovine loveliness.

Her gentle limbs, her hornless brow

Proclaim no ordinary cow:

Fair as a pasture sweet with hay

Mown in the very month of May!

Nay, fairer yet! And yet more fair!

She stands alone, the short black hair

Heaving sometimes on her breast,

Shunned and despised by all the rest.

If one should ask her why she doth grieve

She would answer sadly, "I can't conceive."

SMITH V. ZIMBALIST
38 P.2d 170 (Cal.App.2 Dist. 1934)

HOUSER, J.J.

From the "findings of fact" made pursuant to the trial of the action, it appears that plaintiff, who was of the age of 86 years, although not a dealer in violins, had been a collector of rare violins for many years; "that defendant was a violinist of great prominence, internationally known, and himself the owner and collector of rare and old violins made by the old masters"; that at the suggestion of a third person, and without the knowledge by plaintiff of defendant's intention in the matter, defendant visited plaintiff at the home of the latter and there asked plaintiff if he might see plaintiff's collection of old violins; that in the course of such visit and inspection, "plaintiff showed a part of his collection to defendant; that defendant picked up one violin and asked plaintiff what he would take for the violin, calling it a 'Stradivarius'; that plaintiff did not offer his violins, or any of them, for sale, but on account of his age, after he had been asked what he would take for them, said he would not charge as much as a regular dealer, but that he would sell it for $5,000; that thereafter defendant picked up another violin, calling it a 'Guarnerius', and asked plaintiff what he would take for that violin, and plaintiff said if defendant took both violins, he could have them for $8,000; that the defendant said 'all right', thereupon stating his financial condition and asking if he could pay $2,000 cash and the balance in monthly payments of $1,000." Thereupon a memorandum was signed by defendant as follows:

> I hereby acknowledge receipt of one violin by Joseph Guarnerius and one violin by Stradivarius dated 1717 purchased by me from George Smith for the total sum of Eight Thousand Dollars toward which purchase price I have paid Two Thousand Dollars the balance I agree to pay at the rate of one thousand dollars on the fifteenth day of each month until paid in full.

In addition thereto, a "bill of sale" in the following language was signed by plaintiff:

> This certifies that I have on this date sold to Mr. Efrem Zimbalist one Joseph Guarnerius violin and one Stradivarius violin dated 1717, for the full price of $8,000.00 on which has been paid $2,000.00.

> The balance of $6,000.00 to be paid $1,000.00 fifteenth of each month until paid in full, I agree that Mr. Zimbalist shall have the right to exchange these for any others in my collection should he so desire.

That at the time said transaction was consummated each of the parties thereto "fully believed that said violins were made one by Antonius Stradivarius and one by Josef Guarnerius"; that preceding the closing of said transaction "plaintiff made no representations and warranties as to said violins, or either of them, as to who their makers were, but believed them to have been made one by Antonius Stradivarius and one by Josef Guarnerius in the early part of the eighteenth century; that plaintiff did not fraudulently make any representations or warranties to defendant at the time of said purchase"; that there was "a preponderance of evidence to the effect that said violins are not Stradivarius or Guarnerius violins, nor made by either Antonius Stradivarius or Josef Guarnerius, but were in fact made as imitations thereof, and were not worth more than $300.00."

The action which is the foundation of the instant appeal was brought by plaintiff against defendant to recover judgment for the unpaid balance of the purchase price of the two violins.

As is shown by the conclusions of law reached by the trial court from such facts, the theory upon which the case was decided was that the transaction in question was the result of "a mutual mistake on the part of plaintiff and defendant," and consequently that plaintiff was not entitled to recover judgment. From a judgment rendered in favor of defendant, plaintiff has appealed to this court.

In urging a reversal of the judgment, it is the contention of appellant that the doctrine of caveat emptor should have been applied to the facts in the case; that is to say, that in the circumstances shown by the evidence and reflected in the findings of fact, the trial court should have held that defendant bought the violins at his own risk and peril.

The substance of the argument presented by appellant is a recast of the decision at nisi prius in the case of Jendwine v. Slade (1797) 2 Espinasse, 572. The syllabus in that case is as follows:

> The putting down the name of an artist in a catalogue as the painter of any picture, is not such a warranty as will subject the party selling to an action, if it turns out that he might be mistaken, and that it was not the work of the artist to whom it was attributed.

It there appears that therein (as similarly in the instant case) "several of the most eminent artists and picture dealers were called, who differed in their opinions respecting the originality of the pictures."

Lord Kenyon (the nisi prius judge) said: "It was impossible to make this the case of a warranty; the pictures were the work of artists some centuries back, and there being no way of tracing the picture itself, it could only be matter of opinion whether the picture in question was the work of the artist whose name it bore, or not. What then does the catalogue import? That, in the opinion of the seller, the picture is the work of the artist whose name he has affixed to it. The action in its present shape must go on the ground of some fraud in the sale. "But if the seller only represents what he himself believes, he can be guilty of no fraud. The catalogue of the pictures in question leaves the determination to the judgment of the buyer, who is to exercise that judgment in the purchase. . . ."

In the case of Chandelor v. Lopus (1603) 2 Cr. Rep. 4, 79 English Rep. 3 (Full Reprint), which in the state of New York for many years was relied upon as the leading authority in situations similar to that present herein, it was held that where one sold a jewel as a bezoar stone which in truth it was not, no action would lie, unless in the complaint or declaration it was alleged that the seller knew that it was not a bezoar stone, or that he warranted the stone to be such.

In Seixas v. Woods (1805) 2 Caines (N. Y.) 48, 2 Am. Dec. 215 . . . , a sale of wood which both parties to the transaction supposed was brazilletto, when in fact it was peachum, in the absence of express warranty by the seller, was held binding on the buyer. It was also ruled that "mentioning the wood, as brazilletto wood, in the bill of parcels, and in the advertisement some days previous to the sale, did not amount to a warranty to the plaintiffs." . . .

But with reference to the first cited case (Seixas v. Woods, in which Chancellor Kent wrote a concurring opinion), in 2 Kent's Commentaries, § 479, in part it is said:

> There is no doubt of the existence of the general rule of law, as laid down in Seixas v. Woods; and the only doubt is whether it was well applied in that case, where there was a description in writing of the article by the vendor which proved not to be correct, and from which a warranty might have been inferred. But the rule fitly applies to the case where the article was equally open to the inspection and examination of both parties, and the purchaser relied on his own information and judgment, without requiring any warranty of the quality. . . .

Likewise, in 2 Blackstone's Commentaries, the exception to the general rule is there noted as follows: "But with regard to the goodness of the wares so purchased, the vendor is not bound to answer; unless he expressly warrants them to be sound and good, or unless he knew them to be otherwise, and hath used no art to disguise them, or unless they turn out to be different from what he represented them to the buyer."

In Hart v. Wright (1837) 17 Wend. (N. Y.) 267, in commenting on the rule applied in Seixas v. Woods, it is said:

> These cases have not been overruled, and their principles have not been seriously questioned anywhere. It has been doubted whether those which deny a warranty to be implied by description in a sale note, bill of parcels, etc., were not a wrong application of the common law rule, 2 Kent, Com., 479, 3d Ed.; and they have been severely criticized and generally repudiated in our sister states, whose courts hold, with the English cases, that such a description is a warranty of kind and quality, as far as it goes. . . .

. . . An American case which in principle is clearly applicable to the facts herein is that of Sherwood v. Walker, 66 Mich. 568, 33 N. W. 919, 11 Am. St. Rep. 531. It there appears that the subject of the sale was a "blooded" polled Angus cow that both parties to the transaction assumed was barren and hence useless as breeding stock. In such assumed conditions the owner agreed to sell and the purchaser agreed to buy the cow at the market price of beef cattle, to wit, 5 ½ cents per pound, or what amounted to about $80. Before the day arrived when the cow was to be delivered by the seller to the purchaser, it was discovered that the cow was with calf and consequently that the cow was worth at least $750. It was held that the owner of the cow had the right to rescind the agreement of sale. But to the contrary of such ruling on practically similar facts, see Wood v. Boynton, 64 Wis. 265, 25 N. W. 42, 54 Am. Rep. 610. . . .

In the case of Henshaw v. Robins, 9 Metc. (50 Mass.) 83, 43 Am. Dec. 367, where the authorities are reviewed, the facts and the law are indicated in the syllabus as follows: "When a bill of parcels is given, upon a sale of goods, describing the goods, or designating them by a name well understood, such bill is to be considered as a warranty that the goods sold are what they are thus described or designated to be. And this rule applies, though the goods are examined by the purchaser, at or before the sale, if they are so prepared, and present such an appearance, as to deceive skilful dealers."

Reflecting particularly upon the situation shown by the facts in the instant case, is the following language which occurs in the course of the opinion: "But we are of opinion that the examination of the article by the plaintiff, at the time of the sale, is no evidence of his intention to waive any legal right. If the spurious nature of the article might have been detected on inspection, it might have been otherwise; but we must infer, from the instruction of the court, that the jury found that the article was so disguised that the deception could not have been detected by a skilful dealer in indigo, without resorting to an analytical experiment; so that no neglect can be imputed to the plaintiff in not making a careful examination." . . .

On examination of the case of Henshaw v. Robins, supra, the similarity of the facts therein to the facts in the instant case will immediately be noted, and the language of the opinion to the effect that if "the article was so disguised that the deception could not have been detected by a [skillful] dealer" so closely applies to the situation in the instant case that the conclusion reached by the court in the cited case is particularly important in reaching a conclusion herein.

The governing principle of law to the effect that an article described in a "bill of parcels," or, as in the instant case, in a "bill of sale," amounts to a warranty that such article in fact conforms to such description and that the seller is bound by such description, has been applied in this state . . . .

. . . Although it may be that by some authorities a different rule may be indicated, it is the opinion of this court that, in accord with the weight of the later authorities . . . . , the strict rule of caveat emptor may not be applied to the facts of the instant case, but that such rule is subject to the exception thereto to the effect that on the purported sale of personal property the parties to the proposed contract are not bound where it appears that in its essence each of them is honestly mistaken or in error with reference to the identity of the subject-matter of such contract. In other words, in such circumstances, no enforceable sale has taken place.

But if it may be said that a sale, with a voidable condition attached, was the outcome of the transaction in the instant case, notwithstanding the "finding of fact" by the trial court that "plaintiff made no representations and warranties as to said violins," from a consideration of the language employed by the parties in each of the documents that was exchanged between them (to which reference hereinbefore has been had), together with the general conduct of the parties, and particularly the acquiescence by plaintiff in the declaration made by defendant regarding each of the violins and by whom it was made, it becomes apparent that, in law, a warranty was given by plaintiff that one of the violins was a Guarnerius and that the other was a Stradivarius.

The findings of fact unquestionably show that each of the parties believed and assumed that one of said violins was a genuine Guarnerius and that the other was a genuine Stradivarius; the receipt given by defendant to plaintiff for said violins so described them, and the "bill of sale" given by plaintiff to defendant certifies that plaintiff "sold to Mr. Efrem Zimbalist (defendant) one Joseph Guarnerius violin and one Stradivarius violin dated 1717 for the full price of $8,000.00 on which has been paid $2,000.00. . . ."

Without burdening this opinion with the citation of additional authorities, it may suffice to state that, although the very early decisions may hold to a different rule, all the more modern authorities, including many of those in California to which attention has been directed (besides the provision now contained in section 1734, Civ. Code), are agreed that the description in a bill of parcels or sale note of the thing sold amounts to a warranty on the part of the seller that the subject-matter of the sale conforms to such description. . . .

NOTES AND QUESTIONS

1.   The previous cases all dealt with mutual mistake. But what if the mistake of fact is only on one side of the transaction, called *unilateral mistake*? Typically in such cases, which are akin to cases of non-disclosure, issues of information asymmetries are at the forefront. In these cases, one party may actually have a great deal more knowledge of the goods and services at issue than the other does. Normally, our market economy encourages parties to use their knowledge and gain financial advantage from that knowledge, but if the deal looks extremely lopsided, the question arises whether there is a duty to disclose information. Another way of phrasing the problem is: when is non-disclosure of information wrongful? We will examine this question in more

detail below, in connection with the issues of fraud, misrepresentation, and non-disclosure.

2.   Mistake also includes a subset of cases that we might term clerical error. What if, for example, buyer and seller agree orally on a price of $50.00 for a used contracts book, but in e-mails back and forth, a decimal point is removed and neither party catches that the e-mail reads $5000 until long after the transaction has taken place? In situations like this, courts would likely analyze the problem through the doctrine of mistake and engage in *reformation* of the contract—modifying the deal to reflect the original expressed intentions of the parties.

3.   Warranty and mutual mistake are independent grounds to rescind a contract, even though they both can appear in a single case. We saw both theories at play in the dispute over the violins in *Zimbalist*. Because the papers associated with the deal showed an intention to trade violins of particular makers, the bill of sale amounted to a warranty that the seller breached. As a complementary theory, the bill of sale and the promissory note show that both parties were honestly mistaken about the identity of the subject matter, and therefore no valid contract arose.

EXAMPLE: THE PRICE FOR WINE?

Along with some friends and business colleagues, Joe Lentini was invited to dinner at a fancy steakhouse. Lentini wasn't much of a drinker, but on occasion he would have a glass of wine. Two of the other diners discussed sharing a bottle of red with Lentini, and the host of the party told them to pick out whatever they would like.

Lentini didn't have much experience ordering, so he asked if the waitress could recommend "something decent." The waitress pointed to a bottle on the menu, but since Lentini didn't have his reading glasses on him, he asked "how much?" and the waitress said "thirty-seven fifty." The drinkers at the table agreed that sounded fine.

Those ordering thought that meant $37.50. They were stunned, after the meal was over and the bill arrived, to find a charge for a bottle of wine costing $3,750. The Maitre D was summoned, and said that the table had ordered and drunk the wine, and the best he could do would be to give the wine to them at the restaurant's cost, which was $2,250. The patrons split the charge but all were angry and wished to contest the restaurant's charge.

Is there a contract? Was there a mutual mistake? A unilateral mistake?

TRIBE V. PETERSON
964 P.2d 1238 (Wyo. 1998)

TAYLOR, J.J.

Appellant, Steve Tribe, purchased his first horse, Moccasin Badger, from appellees, Mr. and Mrs. Peterson. Asserting that the sellers had expressly guaranteed that the horse would never buck, Mr. Tribe brought suit against the Petersons for breach of warranty when Moccasin Badger unceremoniously ejected Mr. Tribe from the saddle, shattering his left wrist. After the district court denied Mr. Tribe's motion for summary judgment on the issue of express warranty, the subsequent trial resulted in the jury's rejection of Mr. Tribe's claims and a "no buck" verdict. Mr. Tribe then moved for judgment as a matter of law, or in the alternative, a new trial. Both motions were denied. Finding that the jury acted reasonably, we affirm. . . .

The known history of Moccasin Badger (Badger) begins with his purchase in August 1994 by Larry Painter, a rancher who had bought and sold horses "[a]ll [his] life." When Mr. Painter bought and owned Badger, the horse was "plumb gentle * * * ." Mr. Painter brought Badger to his Uncle Oliver's in Rapid City, South Dakota in January 1995, describing him at that time: "Well, he was real gentle. And as far as we was concerned, anybody could ride him that had any experience at all riding." Oliver Painter was not called as a witness at trial, but the parties read into the record the following stipulation:

> Rather than calling Oliver Painter to testify, the parties have stipulated that if he did testify, he would testify that this horse, Moccasin Badger, was calm and gentle while he was around him. He did not have any experiences where he bucked.

In February 1995, Oliver Painter advertised the sale of Badger, and the Petersons responded. After Mrs. Peterson rode Badger and found him to be very calm and gentle, and a second visit revealed the same disposition, they purchased him for $2,200.00. During the first month the Petersons owned Badger, they rode him "two to three times a week." "[N]eeding a little money," the Petersons decided to sell Badger at the "Leo Perino sale," which attracts buyers from all over the world.

To ensure that Badger was sound and ready for sale, the Petersons twice brought Badger to Dr. Margie Jones, a board certified horse veterinarian from Sturgis, South Dakota, and Mr. Peterson trained Badger every day for a month prior to the sale. Dr. Jones testified that she found Badger to be "sound," and after performing an extensive physical examination and riding Badger, she concluded that Badger "was gentle and kind and he did what I asked him to."

The Leo Perino sale was held in Newcastle, Wyoming on June 3, 1995. Mr. Tribe and his wife attended the sale, accompanied by Steve Stoddard. The Tribes had moved to Wyoming in 1993 after selling Mr. Tribe's car dealership in northern California and purchasing a 12,000 acre ranch near Colony, Wyoming. The Tribes leased all but 400 acres to Mr. Stoddard, who they asked to assist them in recommending a place to purchase a horse which would be gentle enough for very inexperienced riders. Mr. Stoddard recommended the Leo Perino sale because it had an excellent reputation.

Badger's description in the sale brochure represented him as a "quiet . . . and extra gentle gelding . . . easy to catch, haul and shoe," and "overly kind which makes him a definite kids prospect . . . ." Mr. Stoddard initially noticed Badger while Mr. Peterson was roping with Badger in the arena. Mr. Stoddard spoke with Mr. Peterson, and Mr. Peterson told him that Badger "was five years old and that he was really gentle." Later, Mr. Stoddard approached the Petersons to get a better look at Badger, at which time Mr. Stoddard and Mrs. Tribe rode Badger. Mr. Stoddard found the horse to be "very gentle and very well-broke to ride." According to Mr. Stoddard, he asked Mr. Peterson if the horse "had any buck in him" to which Mr. Peterson responded, "No." Mr. Peterson told Mr. Stoddard that the horse had never bucked with him or any of its previous owners. The testimony conflicts, however, as to whether Mr. Peterson "guaranteed" the horse would never buck in the future. Mr. Stoddard stated he got a "guarantee" from both Petersons, while the Petersons denied they made such a guarantee, insisting it would be impossible to guarantee that any horse would not buck in the future.

Nonetheless, Mr. Tribe purchased Badger on his belief that he had been guaranteed that this horse would never buck. Upon returning to the ranch, Mrs. Tribe rode Badger without incident. The third time Mrs. Tribe rode Badger, however, she was thrown. Ten days later, after riding Badger, Mrs. Tribe asked Mr. Tribe if he wanted to ride. When he said he did, she resaddled the horse. Mr. Tribe got on the horse, and almost immediately was thrown to the ground, shattering his left wrist. Sometime later, Mr. Tribe contacted the Petersons to inform them of the injury, tape recording one conversation with Mr. Peterson. . . .

Mr. Tribe contends that, as a matter of law, the written description in the sale brochure and verbal representations of the Petersons created an express warranty that Badger was a calm and gentle horse which would never buck. "An express warranty is created by any affirmation of fact made by the seller to the buyer which relates to the goods and becomes a part of the basis of the bargain." Garriffa v. Taylor, 675 P.2d 1284, 1286 (Wyo.1984), see also Wyo. Stat. § 34.1–2–313(a)(ii) (1997) ("Any description of the goods which is made part of the basis of the bargain creates an express warranty that the goods shall conform to the description[.]"). "In order for an express warranty to exist, there must be some positive and unequivocal statement concerning the thing sold which is relied on by the buyer and which is understood to be an assertion concerning the items sold and not an opinion." Garriffa, 675 P.2d at 1286.

A representation which expresses the seller's opinion, belief, judgment or estimate does not constitute an express warranty. Id. The primary question is whether there was an affirmation of fact which amounted to an express warranty or whether the representations were merely opinions. The answer to this question results from the consideration of all the circumstances surrounding a sale and should be made by the trier of fact. Id.

The verdict form at trial asked only: "Are defendants liable to the plaintiff for damages for breach of an express warranty?" We therefore do not know if the jury determined there was no express warranty or whether a warranty was given but not breached. Either way, the jury's conclusion could reasonably be reached on the evidence presented at trial.

[Regarding] the description of Badger in the sales brochure[,] Mr. Tribe insists that this description guaranteed a gentle horse, and that the fact that he and his wife were thrown establishes that Badger was not gentle or calm. The testimony of all the witnesses, however, reveals that Badger was calm and gentle with everyone but the Tribes. The Painters and the Petersons testified that Badger was "kind" and "real gentle" throughout the time he was in their care. . . .

Moreover, Mrs. Tribe telephoned Mrs. Peterson within four or five days after the sale to say: "I want you to know I'm really getting along well with Badger. I just love him. Do you have anymore like him that we could buy?" Finally, evidence was presented which established that the disposition of a horse may be affected by the rider, the equipment, the type of feed, or a new environment. Mr. Perino affirmed that "even gentle horses" may buck. Clearly, there was evidence to support a finding that the description of Badger in the brochure was the Petersons' well-founded opinion regarding Badger's disposition. Further, even if the brochure constituted an express warranty that Badger was calm and gentle, the evidence supports the conclusion that the warranty was not breached. . . .

NOTES AND QUESTIONS

1.   How would you describe Moccasin Badger, based on all the testimony in the case? Is your description a statement of fact or an expression of opinion?

2.   Observe a theme running through the cases on mutual mistake and express warranty, concerning differences between (a) opinions and judgments on the one hand and (b) facts and definitions on the other.

3.   Why was express warranty applied in *Zimbalest* but not *Tribe*? Can a horse be both gentle and buck? Can a violin be both made by a grandmaster and by an imitator?

4.   How do the doctrinal tools of mutual mistake and express warranty help probe the way parties intended to allocate risk?

NOTE ON WARRANTIES

While breach of warranty may be an excuse from contract performance by a promisee, the breach of warranty may also entitle the aggrieved party to damages for breach of contract, a topic within the law of contract remedies addressed in Chapter Seven. Before enactment of the UCC, courts enforced disclaimers of express warranties as a simple exercise in freedom of contract. The UCC, however, takes a distinct approach to warranties.

Express warranties are addressed in 2–313; implied warranties, which encompass discrete topics such as warranty of title, of merchantability, and of fitness for a particular purpose, appear in 2–312, 2–314, and 2–315. Disclaimers are addressed in 2–316 and controversies about warranties sometimes implicate the UCC's unconscionability rules in 2–302.

Express warranties arise by volition through affirmation, description, or sample good. Implied warranties arise by virtue of law, in the UCC. These include an implied warranty of merchantability, which generally means that goods be "fit for the ordinary purposes for which such goods are used." § 2–314(2)(c). In addition, an implied warranty of fitness for a particular purpose arises where the seller has reason to know of the buyer's specific purpose or requirements and relies upon the seller's related expertise, § 2–315.

Written warranty disclaimers must be conspicuous. § 2–316(2). To disclaim the implied warranty of fitness for a particular purpose, it must be in writing and to disclaim the implied warranty of merchantability, the word "merchantability" must be used. *Id.* Warranties may be disclaimed by "language which in common understanding calls the buyer's attention to the exclusion of warranties and makes plain that there is no implied warranty." *Id.* § 2–316(3)(a). Warranties are also validly disclaimed when the buyer examines the goods or has the opportunity to do so.

UCC WARRANTY PROVISIONS

§ 2–312. *Warranty of Title . . .*

(1) Subject to subsection (2) there is in a contract for sale a warranty by the seller that (a) the title conveyed shall be good, and its transfer rightful; and (b) the goods shall be delivered free from any security interest or other lien or encumbrance of which the buyer at the time of contracting has no knowledge.

(2) A warranty under subsection (1) will be excluded or modified only by specific language or by circumstances which give the buyer reason to know that the person selling does not claim title in himself or that he is purporting to sell only such right or title as he or a third person may have. . . .

§ 2–313. *Express Warranties* . . .

(1) Express warranties by the seller are created as follows: (a) Any affirmation of fact or promise made by the seller to the buyer which relates to the goods and becomes part of the basis of the bargain creates an express warranty that the goods shall conform to the affirmation or promise. (b) Any description of the goods which is made part of the basis of the bargain creates an express warranty that the goods shall conform to the description. (c) Any sample or model which is made part of the basis of the bargain creates an express warranty that the whole of the goods shall conform to the sample or model. . . .

§ 2–314. *Implied Warranty: Merchantability* . . .

(1) Unless excluded or modified (Section 2–316), a warranty that the goods shall be merchantable is implied in a contract for their sale if the seller is a merchant with respect to goods of that kind. Under this section the serving for value of food or drink to be consumed either on the premises or elsewhere is a sale.

(2) Goods to be merchantable must be at least such as (a) pass without objection in the trade under the contract description; and (b) in the case of fungible goods, are of fair average quality within the description; and (c) are fit for the ordinary purposes for which such goods are used; and (d) run, within the variations permitted by the agreement, of even kind, quality and quantity within each unit and among all units involved; and (e) are adequately contained, packaged, and labeled as the agreement may require; and (f) conform to the promise or affirmations of fact made on the container or label if any. . .

§ 2–315. *Implied Warranty: Fitness for Particular Purpose.*

Where the seller at the time of contracting has reason to know any particular purpose for which the goods are required and that the buyer is relying on the seller's skill or judgment to select or furnish suitable goods, there is unless excluded or modified under the next section an implied warranty that the goods shall be fit for such purpose.

§ 2–316. *Exclusion or Modification of Warranties.*

(1) Words or conduct relevant to the creation of an express warranty and words or conduct tending to negate or limit warranty shall be construed wherever reasonable as consistent with each other; but . . . negation or limitation is inoperative to the extent that such construction is unreasonable.

(2) Subject to subsection (3), to exclude or modify the implied warranty of merchantability or any part of it the language must mention merchantability and in case of a writing must be conspicuous, and to exclude or modify any implied warranty of fitness the exclusion must be by

a writing and conspicuous. Language to exclude all implied warranties of fitness is sufficient if it states, for example, that "There are no warranties which extend beyond the description on the face hereof."

(3) Notwithstanding subsection (2), (a) unless the circumstances indicate otherwise, all implied warranties are excluded by expressions like "as is", "with all faults" or other language which in common understanding calls the buyer's attention to the exclusion of warranties and makes plain that there is no implied warranty; and (b) when the buyer before entering into the contract has examined the goods or the sample or model as fully as he desired or has refused to examine the goods there is no implied warranty with regard to defects which an examination ought in the circumstances to have revealed to him; and (c) an implied warranty can also be excluded or modified by course of dealing or course of performance or usage of trade. . . .

PROBLEMS: TEXAS CHAINSAW WARRANTIES

The day before Thanksgiving, Gallagher went into "Top's," a local hardware store owned by Scott Thompson, known around town as "Carrot-Top" for his bushy red hair. Gallagher purchased a TX-Model electric chainsaw for $179, about ten dollars more than the price offered at large chain retail outlets. *Analyze these problems under the UCC. Please be aware that Top's store policy does not allow for any returns or exchanges.*

1. While at Top's, no one at the store talked to Gallagher (other than the cashier who asked for his credit card). As soon as Gallagher returned home, he went outside, plugged the chainsaw into his outdoor outlet, and began using it to cut wood for a festive Thanksgiving fire. Within five minutes, the chainsaw sputtered and then went dead. Gallagher spent fifteen minutes tinkering with the chainsaw to no avail. If Gallagher wants to return the defective chainsaw, what theory and section(s) of the UCC could he invoke?

2. Change the facts. Assume that while at Top's, Gallagher spoke to Carrot-Top himself and asked for a recommendation for a "good chainsaw, that would be reliable and last at least two years." Carrot-Top discussed the options. The cheapest model they had was $69, but Carrot-Top explained that it was far from reliable. The most expensive option was $599, and Carrot-Top explained that it was the "Cadillac" of chainsaws. For his money, Carrot-Top said the best deal was the TX-Model for $170, and that it was very reliable and would "definitely last two years." Gallagher made his purchase, and happily used the chainsaw for a year, at which time, on Thanksgiving the next year, the chainsaw stopped working. If Gallagher wants to return the defective chainsaw, what theory and section(s) of the UCC could he invoke?

3. Change the facts again. When Gallagher was at Top's, he realized that not only did he need to cut wood, he also needed to carve his Thanksgiving turkey. Gallagher struck up a conversation with Carrot-Top and the two talked about how chainsaws could be used to cut through many foods, such as

watermelon and cantaloupe. Carrot-Top said he would recommend the TX-Model as the best for cutting food; and that he thought it should work about as well as an electric carving knife, except that the cut would be deeper. Gallagher made his purchase and the next day, he used the TX-Model to carve his turkey. The chainsaw effectively cut the turkey, but also cut through the plate, the wooden dining room table, and a wooden dining bench. If Gallagher wants to return the chainsaw, what theory and section(s) of the UCC could he invoke?

4.   Final set of facts. Gallagher happens into Top's and sees a TX-Model chainsaw sitting in the sale aisle. Next to it is a sign that reads: "No Warranties. Chainsaw sold AS IS." There is also tape around the chainsaw's blade that is marked "AS IS." Gallagher decides to take his chances and purchases the chainsaw. The next day, when Gallagher is using the chainsaw to cut a watermelon, it breaks. If Gallagher wants to return the chainsaw, what theory and section(s) of the UCC could he invoke?

B. FRAUD, MISREPRESENTATION, AND NON-DISCLOSURE

Judicial enforcement of a contract presupposes that manifestations of assent are freely made based on relevant information. Manifestations of assent that are instead induced by fraud, misrepresentation, or wrongful nondisclosure by the other side undercut that supposition and therefore provide an excuse from contractual obligation. Some such deceptions may provide not only an excuse from contractual obligation but create an independent tort cause of action.

Those asserting fraud must be prepared to prove their case, usually requiring evidence of the other party's intent to deceive. There are some routes around these formidable burdens, however, including the novel illustration in *Duick v. Toyota Motor Sales* that opens this section. When considering the legal analysis in *Duick*, bear in mind the contract term at issue—a mandatory arbitration clause.

DUICK V. TOYOTA MOTOR SALES
198 Cal.App.4th 1316 (2014)

ROTHSCHILD, J.J.

Defendants Toyota Motor Sales, U.S.A., Inc. (Toyota) and Saatchi & Saatchi North America, Inc. (Saatchi) appeal from the denial of their motion to compel arbitration of plaintiff Amber Duick's claims. We affirm because the putative contract is void on account of fraud in the inception. . . .

Duick's claims arise from her apparently unwitting participation in an internet-based advertising campaign launched by defendants in connection with Toyota's Matrix automobile. The campaign, known as "Your Other

You," "consisted of sending an unwitting recipient emails from an unknown individual." During the campaign, any visitor to the Toyota Matrix web site ("player 1") could designate another person ("player 2") for participation in the Your Other You "interactive experience." Player 2 would then receive an email purportedly from player 1, inviting player 2 to click a hyperlink that was in some manner "identified with Toyota." The link would direct player 2 to a web page entitled "Personality Evaluation," which displayed a drawing of a door with the word "Begin" underneath. Clicking on the door would direct player 2 to a second web page entitled "Personality Evaluation Terms and Conditions." In order to continue beyond that page, according to evidence introduced by defendants, player 2 was required to scroll through certain text (the "terms and conditions") and, at the end of that text, click a box next to the following sentence: "I have read and agree to the terms and conditions."

The first paragraph of the terms and conditions states, "You have been invited by someone who has indicated that he/she knows you to participate in Your Other You. Your Other You is a website provided by [Toyota] that offers you . . . an interactive experience." The second paragraph further states, "If you review and agree to the Terms and Conditions detailed below . . . you may participate in a 5 day digital experience through Your Other You. . . . You may receive email messages, phone calls and/or text messages during the 5-day experience." A subsequent paragraph also states, "You understand that by agreeing to these Terms, you are agreeing to receive emails, phone calls and text messages from Toyota during the 5-day experience of Your Other You." The terms and conditions contain the following arbitration provision: "You agree that . . . any and all disputes, claims, and causes of action arising out of, or connected with, Your Other You . . . shall be resolved individually, without resort to any form of class action, and exclusively by arbitration to be held solely in Los Angeles, California under the auspices of the American Arbitration Association and pursuant to its Commercial Dispute Resolution Rules and Procedures."

The record before us does not describe the further web pages (if any) to which player 2 would be directed after agreeing to the terms and conditions. Over the next several days, however, player 2 would receive emails of an unsettling nature from an "unknown individual" who appeared to have access to some personal information concerning player 2 (information that presumably was provided by player 1, without player 2's knowledge, at the initial stage).

Duick was apparently cast in the role of player 2. She received "an unsolicited email asking [her] to take a personality test." She does not remember clicking the box signifying her agreement to the terms and conditions, and she claims that for various technical reasons the text of the terms and conditions was impossible to read in its entirety.

In any event, Duick later began to receive emails from an individual identifying himself as "Sebastian Bowler." The text of the first email reads, "Amber mate! Coming 2 Los Angeles Gonna lay low at your place for a bit. Till it all blows over. Bringing Trigger." Duick received another email from Bowler the following day, accurately stating her previous home address, describing it as a "Nice place to hide out," and advising her that "Trigger don't throw up much anymore, but put some newspaper down in case." The email also provided a link to Bowler's MySpace page, which portrayed him as a 25-year-old Englishman and "a fanatical English soccer fan who enjoyed drinking alcohol to excess"; the page also displayed photographs of a pit bull dog.

Additional emails from Bowler to Duick over the next few days purported to describe his cross-country journey by car to visit her, including photos and videos of his travels and references to his efforts to evade law enforcement ("I seem to have lost the coppers for now, so I'm all good, mate"; "Had a brush with the law last night. Anyway, hopefully I'll have lost them by the time I get to your place"). One message explained that Bowler "ran into a little problem at the hotel," and Duick subsequently received an email from an individual identifying himself as "Jimmy Citro," purporting to be the manager of a motel and billing Duick for the damage Bowler had done to the motel's property. The final email included a link to a video revealing that Bowler was a fictional character and that the entire sequence of emails was an elaborate prank, all part of an advertising campaign for the Toyota Matrix.

On September 28, 2009, Duick filed suit against Toyota and Saatchi, alleging eight causes of action including intentional infliction of emotional distress, negligence, and false advertising, and seeking "compensatory damages of not less than $10,000,000" as well as other forms of relief. After defendants demurred and Duick voluntarily filed a first amended complaint, defendants moved to compel arbitration on the basis of the arbitration provision in the terms and conditions. The trial court denied defendants' motion. Defendants timely appealed. . . .

Duick contends that the arbitration provision in the terms and conditions is unenforceable because, assuming that she did agree to the terms and conditions by clicking the appropriate box, the entire agreement is void because of fraud in the inception or execution. We agree.

"California law distinguishes between fraud in the 'execution' or 'inception' of a contract and fraud in the 'inducement' of a contract. In brief, in the former case " 'the fraud goes to the inception or execution of the agreement, so that the promisor is deceived as to the nature of his act, and actually does not know what he is signing, or does not intend to enter into a contract at all, mutual assent is lacking, and [the contract] is *void*. In such a case it may be disregarded without the necessity of rescission."

Fraud in the inducement, by contrast, occurs when "the promisor knows what he is signing but his consent is *induced* by fraud, mutual assent is present and a contract is formed, which, by reason of the fraud, is *voidable*. In order to escape from its obligations the aggrieved party must *rescind* . . . ." (*Rosenthal v. Great Western Fin. Securities Corp.* (1996) 14 Cal.4th 394, 415, 58 Cal.Rptr.2d 875, 926 P.2d 1061 [hereafter *Rosenthal*].)

Fraud in the inception will render a contract "wholly void, despite the parties' apparent assent to it, when, *without negligence on his part,* a signer attaches his signature to a paper assuming it to be a paper of a different character." (*Rosenthal, supra,* 14 Cal.4th at p. 420, 58 Cal.Rptr.2d 875, 926 P.2d 1061.) Thus, "[i]f a misrepresentation as to the character or essential terms of a proposed contract induces conduct that appears to be a manifestation of assent by one who neither knows nor has a reasonable opportunity to know of the character or essential terms of the proposed contract, his conduct is not effective as a manifestation of assent." (Rest.2d Contracts, § 163.)

The terms and conditions were drafted by defendants, not by Duick. A person in the role of player 2, such as Duick, could not access the terms and conditions without first clicking "Begin" on a Web page entitled "Personality Evaluation," created by defendants. The terms and conditions themselves were entitled "Personality Evaluation Terms and Conditions." Defendants thereby led Duick to believe that she was going to participate in a personality evaluation and nothing more. In particular, a reasonable reader in Duick's position would not have known that she was signing up to be the target of a prank.

It might have been possible to draft the terms and conditions in such a way as to correct that misimpression, but defendants did not do so. We have read the terms and conditions in their entirety, and we conclude that, as written, they could not have alerted a reasonable reader in Duick's position to the true nature of what defendants proposed to do to her. Reasonable readers of the terms and conditions would not have understood that they were agreeing to be victims of a prank or were otherwise agreeing to be subjected to conduct of the kind involved in Your Other You. Because of their vagueness and opacity (such as unexplained references to an "interactive experience" and a "digital experience"), the terms and conditions made it impossible for someone in the role of player 2, such as Duick, to understand what defendants proposed to do pursuant to the putative agreement.

The only possible grounds for a contrary conclusion would be certain statements in the terms and conditions such as "You may receive email messages, phone calls and/or text messages during the 5-day experience" and "you are agreeing to receive emails, phone calls and text messages from Toyota during the 5-day experience." Those statements too, however, would not have informed a reasonable reader of the true character of the proposed contract or corrected the misimpression created by the use of the phrase "Personality Evaluation." For example, a reasonable person in Duick's position would not have understood that by agreeing that she may receive email messages, she was agreeing to receive frightening or disturbing messages (such as a bill for damages to a motel) that had no apparent or even traceable connection to the terms and conditions.

It is unsurprising, of course, that the terms and conditions were drafted in such a way as to conceal from Duick the true nature of the conduct to which she was going to be subjected-Duick was undisputedly the target of a prank, and it would make no sense for the pranksters to warn the target in advance. Our conclusion that the contract is void because of fraud in the inception is not, however, based on any alleged facts concerning defendants' intent. Rather, our conclusion is based solely on the following propositions: (1) defendants were the drafters and creators of the relevant web pages, including the full text of the terms and conditions; (2) by drafting and presenting the terms and conditions as they did, including the use of the phrase "Personality Evaluation," defendants misrepresented and concealed (whether intentionally or not) the true nature of the conduct to which Duick was to be subjected; and (3) Duick was not negligent in failing to understand the true nature of the conduct to which she was to be subjected, because no reasonable person in her position would have understood it. . . .

NOTES AND QUESTIONS

1.   Fraud in the inception is an archaic and relatively unusual doctrine while arbitration clauses in contracts have proliferated since the early 2000s, amid considerable controversy. Might the doctrine of fraud in the inception facilitate an artful means of avoiding arbitration clauses? *See DKS, Inc. v. Corporate Business Solutions, Inc.*, 675 Fed. Appx. 738 (9th Cir. 2017) (applying California law) (rejecting argument that fraud in the inception doctrine risked opening the door to subterfuge to avoid arbitration by stressing the specificity of pleadings in the case and the skill of district courts in filtering out such tactics).

2.   Fraud in the inducement is the more common type of fraud. A common formulation of its elements: (1) a material representation; (2) that was false; (3) that, when made, the speaker knew was false or recklessly disregarded the truth; (4) made with the intention to induce action; (5) that induced action; and (6) that caused injury. *See Khalaf v. United Bus. Investments, Inc.*, 615 S.W.2d 869, 871 (Tex. Civ. App. 1981).

3.   The element of materiality means that the fraud must be about an important piece of the transaction, not about a matter collateral or separate from the main subject of the contract. In other words, the plaintiff must show that fraud most likely had an influence on the decision to enter the transaction.

4.   For a straightforward case of consumer fraud, consider *Krysa v. Payne*, 176 S.W.3d 150 (Mo. Ct. App. 2005), in which a used car dealership represented to a potential purchaser that a truck on the lot could pull a trailer, had been owned by one owner, and had a clean history. After the purchase, numerous problems arose and after obtaining a "CARFAX" report for the truck, the buyers discovered that the truck had thirteen prior owners. Examination by an expert showed that the truck was actually two trucks inexpertly welded together. On these facts, the Missouri Appeals Court easily upheld a determination of fraud sounding in tort, as it was shown that this was not the first time that the dealership's agents had lied to customers about the condition of the vehicles being sold at their lot.

5.   The key difference between fraud and misrepresentation is state of mind. Fraud requires *scienter*, meaning the intent to deceive. Consider the court's formulation of the difference of these two defenses in *First Interstate Bank of Billings v. U.S.*, 61 F.3d 876 (Fed. Cir. 1995):

> The incontestability clause permits the loan guarantee to be challenged because of either fraud or misrepresentation. Although closely related, fraud and misrepresentation are distinct concepts with different elements. Fraud requires a specific intent to deceive or "a state of mind so reckless respecting consequences as to be the equivalent of intent." *J.P. Stevens & Co. v. Lex Tex Ltd., Inc.*, 747 F.2d 1553, 1559, 223 USPQ 1089, 1092 (Fed.Cir.1984), *cert. denied*, 474 U.S. 822, 106 S.Ct. 73, 88 L.Ed.2d 60 (1985). Misrepresentation does not require an intent to deceive. See *Womack v. United States*, 389 F.2d 793, 800, 182 Ct.Cl. 399 (1968) ("intent to mislead is not an essential element of actionable misrepresentation in the breach of contract context"); compare Restatement (Second) of Contracts § 159 (1979) (defining misrepresentation as "an assertion that is not in accord with the facts") with id. § 162 cmt. a (for a misrepresentation to be fraudulent, it "must not only be consciously false but must also be intended to mislead another").

6.   Both fraud and misrepresentation require that the speaker or writer made a false statement with regard to a fact (rather than a puffing statement or an opinion). Comments that a price is "low" or that a transaction is a "good deal" are generally non-actionable. The next case notes the fine line between fact and opinion.

RESTATEMENT (SECOND) OF CONTRACTS, SECTIONS 162, 164

§ 162.   *When a Misrepresentation Is Fraudulent or Material.*

(1) A misrepresentation is fraudulent if the maker intends his assertion to induce a party to manifest his assent and the maker (a) knows or believes that the assertion is not in accord with the facts, or (b) does not have the confidence that he states or implies in the truth of the assertion,

or (c) knows that he does not have the basis that he states or implies for the assertion.

(2) A misrepresentation is material if it would be likely to induce a reasonable person to manifest his assent, or if the maker knows that it would be likely to induce the recipient to do so.

§ 164.   *When a Misrepresentation Makes a Contract Voidable.*

(1) If a party's manifestation of assent is induced by either a fraudulent or material misrepresentation by the other party upon which the recipient is justified in relying, the contract is voidable by the recipient. . . .

VOKES V. ARTHUR MURRAY
212 So.2d 906 (Fla. 1968)

PIERCE, J.J.

This is an appeal by Audrey E. Vokes, plaintiff below, from a final order dismissing with prejudice, for failure to state a cause of action, her fourth amended complaint, hereinafter referred to as plaintiff's complaint.

Defendant Arthur Murray, Inc., a corporation, authorizes the operation throughout the nation of dancing schools under the name of 'Arthur Murray School of Dancing' through local franchised operators, one of whom was defendant J. P. Davenport whose dancing establishment was in Clearwater.

Plaintiff Mrs. Audrey E. Vokes, a widow of 51 years and without family, had a yen to be 'an accomplished dancer' with the hopes of finding 'new interest in life'. So, on February 10, 1961, a dubious fate, with the assist of a motivated acquaintance, procured her to attend a 'dance party' at Davenport's 'School of Dancing' where she whiled away the pleasant hours, sometimes in a private room, absorbing his accomplished sales technique, during which her grace and poise were elaborated upon and her rosy future as 'an excellent dancer' was painted for her in vivid and glowing colors. As an incident to this interlude, he sold her eight 1/2-hour dance lessons to be utilized within one calendar month therefrom, for the sum of $14.50 cash in hand paid, obviously a baited 'come on'.

Thus she embarked upon an almost endless pursuit of the terpsichorean art during which, over a period of less than sixteen months, she was sold fourteen 'dance courses' totaling in the aggregate 2302 hours of dancing lessons for a total cash outlay of $31,090.45, all at Davenport's dance emporium. All of these fourteen courses were evidenced by execution of a written 'Enrollment Agreement—Arthur Murray's School of Dancing' with the addendum in heavy black print, 'No one will be informed that you are taking dancing lessons. Your relations with us are held in strict confidence', setting forth the number of 'dancing lessons' and the 'lessons in rhythm sessions' currently sold to her from time to time, and always of course accompanied by payment of cash of the realm.

These dance lesson contracts and the monetary consideration therefor of over $31,000 were procured from her by means and methods of Davenport and his associates which went beyond the unsavory, yet legally permissible, perimeter of 'sales puffing' and intruded well into the forbidden area of undue influence, the suggestion of falsehood, the suppression of truth, and the free exercise of rational judgment, if what plaintiff alleged in her complaint was true. From the time of her first contact with the dancing school in February, 1961, she was influenced unwittingly by a constant and continuous barrage of flattery, false praise, excessive compliments, and panegyric encomiums, to such extent that it would be not only inequitable, but unconscionable, for a Court exercising inherent chancery power to allow such contracts to stand.

She was incessantly subjected to overreaching blandishment and cajolery. She was assured she had 'grace and poise'; that she was 'rapidly improving and developing in her dancing skill'; that the additional lessons would 'make her a beautiful dancer, capable of dancing with the most accomplished dancers'; that she was 'rapidly progressing in the development of her dancing skill and gracefulness', etc., etc. She was given 'dance aptitude tests' for the ostensible purpose of 'determining' the number of remaining hours [of instruction] . . . needed by her from time to time.

At one point she was sold 545 additional hours of dancing lessons to be entitled to award of the 'Bronze Medal' signifying that she had reached 'the Bronze Standard', a supposed designation of dance achievement by students of Arthur Murray, Inc. Later she was sold an additional 926 hours in order to gain the 'Silver Medal', indicating she had reached 'the Silver Standard', at a cost of $12,501.35.

At one point, while she still had to her credit about 900 unused hours of instructions, she was induced to purchase an additional 24 hours of lessons to participate in a trip to Miami at her own expense, where she would be 'given the opportunity to dance with members of the Miami Studio'. She was induced at another point to purchase an additional 123 hours of lessons in order to be not only eligible for the Miami trip but also to become 'a life member of the Arthur Murray Studio', carrying with it certain dubious emoluments, at a further cost of $1,752.30.

At another point, while she still had over 1,000 unused hours of instruction she was induced to buy 151 additional hours at a cost of $2,049.00 to be eligible for a 'Student Trip to Trinidad', at her own expense as she later learned. Also, when she still had 1100 unused hours to her credit, she was prevailed upon to purchase an additional 347 hours at a cost of $4,235.74, to qualify her to receive a 'Gold Medal' for achievement, indicating she had advanced to 'the Gold Standard'.

On another occasion, while she still had over 1200 unused hours, she was induced to buy an additional 175 hours of instruction at a cost of $2,472.75 to be eligible 'to take a trip to Mexico'. Finally, sandwiched in between other lesser sales promotions, she was influenced to buy an additional 481 hours of instruction at a cost of $6,523.81 in order to 'be classifies as a Gold Bar Member, the ultimate achievement of the dancing studio'.

All the foregoing sales promotions, illustrative of the entire fourteen separate contracts, were procured by defendant Davenport and Arthur Murray, Inc., by false representations to her that she was improving in her dancing ability, that she had excellent potential, that she was responding to instructions in dancing grace, and that they were developing her into a beautiful dancer, whereas in truth and in fact she did not develop in her dancing ability, she had no 'dance aptitude', and in fact had difficulty in 'hearing that musical beat'. The complaint alleged that such representations to her 'were in fact false and known by the defendant to be false and contrary to the plaintiff's true ability, the truth of plaintiff's ability being fully known to the defendants, but withheld from the plaintiff for the sole and specific intent to deceive and defraud the plaintiff and to induce her in the purchasing of additional hours of dance lessons'. It was averred that the lessons were sold to her 'in total disregard to the true physical, rhythm, and mental ability of the plaintiff'. In other words, while she first exulted that she was entering the 'spring of her life', she finally was awakened to the fact there was 'spring' neither in her life nor in her feet.

The complaint prayed that the Court decree the dance contracts to be null and void and to be cancelled, that an accounting be had, and judgment entered against, the defendants 'for that portion of the $31,090.45 not charged against specific hours of instruction given to the plaintiff'. The Court held the complaint not to state a cause of action and dismissed it with prejudice. We disagree and reverse.

The material allegations of the complaint must, of course, be accepted as true for the purpose of testing its legal sufficiency. Defendants contend that contracts can only be rescinded for fraud or misrepresentation when the alleged misrepresentation is as to a material fact, rather than an opinion, prediction or expectation, and that the statements and representations set forth at length in the complaint were in the category of 'trade puffing', within its legal orbit.

It is true that 'generally a misrepresentation, to be actionable, must be one of fact rather than of opinion'. Tonkovich v. South Florida Citrus Industries, Inc., Fla.App.1966, 185 So.2d 710; Kutner v. Kalish,

Fla.App.1965, 173 So.2d 763. But this rule has significant qualifications, applicable here. It does not apply where there is a fiduciary relationship between the parties, or where there has been some artifice or trick employed by the representor, or where the parties do not in general deal at 'arm's length' as we understand the phrase, or where the representee does not have equal opportunity to become apprised of the truth or falsity of the fact represented. 14 Fla.Jur. Fraud and Deceit, § 28; Kitchen v. Long, 1914, 67 Fla. 72, 64 So. 429. As stated by Judge Allen of this Court in Ramel v. Chasebrook Construction Company, Fla.App.1961, 135 So.2d 876:

> . . . A statement of a party having . . . superior knowledge may be regarded as a statement of fact although it would be considered as opinion if the parties were dealing on equal terms.

It could be reasonably supposed here that defendants had 'superior knowledge' as to whether plaintiff had 'dance potential' and as to whether she was noticeably improving in the art of terpsichore. And it would be a reasonable inference from the undenied averments of the complaint that the flowery eulogiums heaped upon her by defendants as a prelude to her contracting for 1944 additional hours of instruction in order to attain the rank of the Bronze Standard, thence to the bracket of the Silver Standard, thence to the class of the Gold Bar Standard, and finally to the crowning plateau of a Life Member of the Studio, proceeded as much or more from the urge to 'ring the cash register' as from any honest or realistic appraisal of her dancing prowess or a factual representation of her progress.

Even in contractual situations where a party to a transaction owes no duty to disclose facts within his knowledge or to answer inquiries respecting such facts, the law is if he undertakes to do so he must disclose the whole truth. Ramel v. Chasebrook Construction Company, supra; Beagle v. Bagwell, Fla.App.1964, 169 So.2d 43. From the face of the complaint, it should have been reasonably apparent to defendants that her vast outlay of cash for the many hundreds of additional hours of instruction was not justified by her slow and awkward progress, which she would have been made well aware of if they had spoken the 'whole truth'.

In Hirschman v. Hodges, etc., 1910, 59 Fla. 517, 51 So. 550, it was said that—

> . . . what is plainly injurious to good faith ought to be considered as a fraud sufficient to impeach a contract, and that an improvident agreement may be avoided— . . . because of surprise, or mistake, Want of freedom, undue influence, the suggestion of falsehood, or the suppression of truth. . . .

We repeat that where parties are dealing on a contractual basis at arm's length with no inequities or inherently unfair practices employed, the Courts will in general 'leave the parties where they find themselves'. But in the case sub judice, from the allegations of the unanswered complaint, we cannot say that enough of the accompanying ingredients, as mentioned in the foregoing authorities, were not present which otherwise would have barred the equitable arm of the Court to her. In our view, from the showing made in her complaint, plaintiff is entitled to her day in Court.

It accordingly follows that the order dismissing plaintiff's last amended complaint with prejudice should be and is reversed.

NOTES AND QUESTIONS

1. Why does the court allow Audrey Vokes to escape performance? Is it based on undue influence, lowered capacity, or some sort of fraud? See if you can articulate the elements that the court applies.

2. Does the court seem to have a paternalistic attitude toward Ms. Vokes? In other words, if Ms. Vokes is having a fun time and enjoying spending her money on dance lessons, is it really the court's business to go back and dispute this deal? Are some of these issues gendered? Consider the following argument by Professor Deborah Threedy:

> In order to prevail under the contract defenses, a plaintiff must assume the position of pleading special protection. The contract defenses are all based, to a greater or lesser extent, on paternalism: the plaintiff pleading a contract defense should be granted an exception from contract liability due to an impaired ability to protect herself in the marketplace. For subordinated social groups, such as women or minorities, such special pleading presents a dilemma.
>
> One horn of the dilemma runs as follows: In order to qualify for protection, the plaintiff must prove that she is less able to protect herself than the ordinary contract bargainer. If successful, she has established that she is less qualified to participate in contract activity. In other words, she has established herself as being on the margins of contract, as in some sense "less." That, in turn, can serve to reinforce the subordination of her social category, which may have contributed to her need for protection in the first place. In other words, such special pleading, if based on gender, tends to reinforce the very subordination that feminists seek to overcome. That is the first horn of the dilemma.
>
> The other horn is that, because gender subordination has real consequences (including lower pay, impaired access to social goods such as education due to child care responsibilities, etc.), to ignore gender, to be gender-blind, to say that gender merits no special concern or treatment, leaves untouched the existing gender subordination.

Deborah L. Threedy, *Dancing Around Gender: Lessons from Arthur Murray on Gender and Contracts*, 45 WAKE FOREST L. REV. 749, 754–55 (2010).

3.   Does the case turn on whether Ms. Vokes was actually improving as a dancer? Is this a question of fact or a matter of opinion?

4.   Is this case problematic from a teaching standpoint? If a student is learning slowly, but with some progress, should they be offered positive affirmation and encouragement, or should they be told that they are not doing well? Which approach is likely to yield better results? Did the dance teachers here have an obligation to be brutally honest about Ms. Vokes's apparent lack of talent?

5.   Complicating matters further, it turns out that many dance studios were sued for overzealous sales, preying on lonely and vulnerable women as well as men. *See, e.g. Syester v. Banta*, 133 N.W. 2d 666 (Iowa 1965) (noting a list of high pressure sales techniques used by Arthur Murray, including flattery, not allowing the prospective student time to think it over, or to consult with a financial advisor).

While *Vokes* involved a series of affirmative false misstatements, sometimes nothing at all is said. Can a seller stay silent even when they have important information? When does a party to a sale have a duty to disclose information? Or, put another way, when is non-disclosure wrongful?

STAMBOVSKY V. ACKLEY
169 A.D.2d 254 (N.Y. App. Div. 1991)

RUBIN, J.J.

Plaintiff, to his horror, discovered that the house he had recently contracted to purchase was widely reputed to be possessed by poltergeists, reportedly seen by defendant seller and members of her family on numerous occasions over the last nine years. Plaintiff promptly commenced this action seeking rescission of the contract of sale. Supreme Court reluctantly dismissed the complaint, holding that plaintiff has no remedy at law in this jurisdiction.

The unusual facts of this case, as disclosed by the record, clearly warrant a grant of equitable relief to the buyer who, as a resident of New York City, cannot be expected to have any familiarity with the folklore of the Village of Nyack. Not being a "local," plaintiff could not readily learn that the home he had contracted to purchase is haunted. Whether the source of the spectral apparitions seen by defendant seller are parapsychic or psychogenic, having reported their presence in both a national publication ("Readers' Digest") and the local press (in 1977 and 1982, respectively), defendant is estopped to deny their existence and, as a matter of law, the house is haunted.

More to the point, however, no divination is required to conclude that it is defendant's promotional efforts in publicizing her close encounters with these spirits which fostered the home's reputation in the community.

In 1989, the house was included in a five-home walking tour of Nyack and described in a November 27th newspaper article as "a riverfront Victorian (with ghost)." The impact of the reputation thus created goes to the very essence of the bargain between the parties, greatly impairing both the value of the property and its potential for resale. The extent of this impairment may be presumed for the purpose of reviewing the disposition of this motion to dismiss the cause of action for rescission (*Harris v. City of New York,* 147 A.D.2d 186, 188–189, 542 N.Y.S.2d 550) and represents merely an issue of fact for resolution at trial.

While I agree with Supreme Court that the real estate broker, as agent for the seller, is under no duty to disclose to a potential buyer the phantasmal reputation of the premises and that, in his pursuit of a legal remedy for fraudulent misrepresentation against the seller, plaintiff hasn't a ghost of a chance, I am nevertheless moved by the spirit of equity to allow the buyer to seek rescission of the contract of sale and recovery of his downpayment. New York law fails to recognize any remedy for damages incurred as a result of the seller's mere silence, applying instead the strict rule of caveat emptor. Therefore, the theoretical basis for granting relief, even under the extraordinary facts of this case, is elusive if not ephemeral.

"Pity me not but lend thy serious hearing to what I shall unfold" (William Shakespeare, Hamlet, Act I, Scene V [Ghost]).

From the perspective of a person in the position of plaintiff herein, a very practical problem arises with respect to the discovery of a paranormal phenomenon: "Who you gonna' call?" as the title song to the movie "Ghostbusters" asks. Applying the strict rule of caveat emptor to a contract involving a house possessed by poltergeists conjures up visions of a psychic or medium routinely accompanying the structural engineer and Terminix man on an inspection of every home subject to a contract of sale. It portends that the prudent attorney will establish an escrow account lest the subject of the transaction come back to haunt him and his client—or pray that his malpractice insurance coverage extends to supernatural disasters. In the interest of avoiding such untenable consequences, the notion that a haunting is a condition which can and should be ascertained upon reasonable inspection of the premises is a hobgoblin which should be exorcised from the body of legal precedent and laid quietly to rest.

It has been suggested by a leading authority that the ancient rule which holds that mere non-disclosure does not constitute actionable misrepresentation "finds proper application in cases where the fact undisclosed is patent, or the plaintiff has equal opportunities for obtaining information which he may be expected to utilize, or the defendant has no reason to think that he is acting under any misapprehension" (Prosser, Law of Torts § 106, at 696 [4th ed., 1971]). However, with respect to transactions in real estate, New York adheres to the doctrine of caveat emptor and imposes no duty upon the vendor to disclose any information concerning the premises (*London v. Courduff,* 141 A.D.2d 803, 529 N.Y.S.2d 874) unless there is a confidential or fiduciary relationship between the parties (*Moser v. Spizzirro,* 31 A.D.2d 537, 295 N.Y.S.2d 188, *affd.,* 25 N.Y.2d 941, 305 N.Y.S.2d 153, 252 N.E.2d 632; *IBM Credit Fin. Corp. v. Mazda Motor Mfg. (USA) Corp.,* 152 A.D.2d 451, 542 N.Y.S.2d 649) or some conduct on the part of the seller which constitutes "active concealment" (*see, 17 East 80th Realty Corp. v. 68th Associates,* 173 A.D.2d 245, 569 N.Y.S.2d 647 [dummy ventilation system constructed by seller]; *Haberman v. Greenspan,* 82 Misc.2d 263, 368 N.Y.S.2d 717 [foundation cracks covered by seller]).

Normally, some affirmative misrepresentation (*e.g., Tahini Invs., Ltd. v. Bobrowsky,* 99 A.D.2d 489, 470 N.Y.S.2d 431 [industrial waste on land allegedly used only as farm]; *Jansen v. Kelly,* 11 A.D.2d 587, 200 N.Y.S.2d 561 [land containing valuable minerals allegedly acquired for use as campsite]) or partial disclosure (*Junius Constr. Corp. v. Cohen,* 257 N.Y. 393, 178 N.E. 672 [existence of third unopened street concealed]; *Noved Realty Corp. v. A.A.P. Co.,* 250 App.Div. 1, 293 N.Y.S. 336 [escrow agreements securing lien concealed]) is required to impose upon the seller a duty to communicate undisclosed conditions affecting the premises (*contra, Young v. Keith,* 112 A.D.2d 625, 492 N.Y.S.2d 489 [defective water and sewer systems concealed]).

Caveat emptor is not so all-encompassing a doctrine of common law as to render every act of non-disclosure immune from redress, whether legal or equitable. "In regard to the necessity of giving information which has not been asked, the rule differs somewhat at law and in equity, and while the law courts would permit no recovery of *damages* against a vendor, because of mere concealment of facts *under certain circumstances,* yet if the vendee refused to complete the contract because of the concealment of a material fact on the part of the other, equity would refuse to compel him so to do, because equity only compels the specific performance of a contract which is fair and open, and in regard to which all material matters known to each have been communicated to the other" (*Rothmiller v. Stein,* 143 N.Y. 581, 591–592, 38 N.E. 718 [emphasis added]). Even as a principle of law, long before exceptions were embodied in statute law (*see, e.g.,* UCC 2–312, 2–313, 2–314, 2–315 . . .), the doctrine was held inapplicable to contagion among animals, adulteration of food, and insolvency of a maker of a promissory note and of a tenant substituted for another under a lease (*see, Rothmiller v. Stein, supra,* at 592–593, 38 N.E. 718 and cases cited therein). Common law is not moribund. *Ex facto jus oritur* (law arises out of facts). Where fairness and common sense dictate that an exception should be created, the evolution of the law should not be stifled by rigid application of a legal maxim.

The doctrine of caveat emptor requires that a buyer act prudently to assess the fitness and value of his purchase and operates to bar the purchaser who fails to exercise due care from seeking the equitable remedy of rescission (*see, e.g., Rodas v. Manitaras,* 159 A.D.2d 341, 552 N.Y.S.2d 618). For the purposes of the instant motion to dismiss the action . . . , plaintiff is entitled to every favorable inference which may reasonably be drawn from the pleadings, specifically, in this instance, that he met his obligation to conduct an inspection of the premises and a search of available public records with respect to title. It should be apparent, however, that the most meticulous inspection and the search would not reveal the presence of poltergeists at the premises or unearth the property's ghoulish reputation in the community. Therefore, there is no sound policy reason to deny plaintiff relief for failing to discover a state of affairs which the most prudent purchaser would not be expected to even contemplate (*see, Da Silva v. Musso,* 53 N.Y.2d 543, 551, 444 N.Y.S.2d 50, 428 N.E.2d 382).

The case law in this jurisdiction dealing with the duty of a vendor of real property to disclose information to the buyer is distinguishable from the matter under review. The most salient distinction is that existing cases invariably deal with the physical condition of the premises (*e.g., London v. Courduff, supra* [use as a landfill]; *Perin v. Mardine Realty Co.,* 5 A.D.2d 685, 168 N.Y.S.2d 647 *affd.* 6 N.Y.2d 920, 190 N.Y.S.2d 995, 161 N.E.2d 210 [sewer line crossing adjoining property without owner's consent]), defects in title (*e.g., Sands v. Kissane,* 282 App.Div. 140, 121 N.Y.S.2d 634 [remainderman]), liens against the property (*e.g., Noved Realty Corp. v. A.A.P. Co., supra*), expenses or income (*e.g., Rodas v. Manitaras, supra* [gross receipts]) and other factors affecting its operation. No case has been brought to this court's attention in which the property value was impaired as the result of the reputation created by information disseminated to the public by the seller (or, for that matter, as a result of possession by poltergeists).

Where a condition which has been created by the seller materially impairs the value of the contract and is peculiarly within the knowledge of the seller or unlikely to be discovered by a prudent purchaser exercising due care with respect to the subject transaction, nondisclosure constitutes a basis for rescission as a matter of equity. Any other outcome places upon the buyer not merely the obligation to exercise care in his purchase but rather to be omniscient with respect to any fact which may affect the bargain. No practical purpose is served by imposing such a burden upon a purchaser. To the contrary, it encourages predatory business practice and offends the principle that equity will suffer no wrong to be without a remedy. . . .

To the extent New York law may be said to require something more than "mere concealment" to apply even the equitable remedy of rescission, the case of *Junius Construction Corporation v. Cohen,* 257 N.Y. 393, 178

N.E. 672, *supra,* while not precisely on point, provides some guidance. In that case, the seller disclosed that an official map indicated two as yet unopened streets which were planned for construction at the edges of the parcel. What was not disclosed was that the same map indicated a third street which, if opened, would divide the plot in half. The court held that, while the seller was under no duty to mention the planned streets at all, having undertaken to disclose two of them, he was obliged to reveal the third (*see also, Rosenschein v. McNally,* 17 A.D.2d 834, 233 N.Y.S.2d 254).

In the case at bar, defendant seller deliberately fostered the public belief that her home was possessed. Having undertaken to inform the public at large, to whom she has no legal relationship, about the supernatural occurrences on her property, she may be said to owe no less a duty to her contract vendee. It has been remarked that the occasional modern cases which permit a seller to take unfair advantage of a buyer's ignorance so long as he is not actively misled are "singularly unappetizing" (Prosser, Law of Torts § 106, at 696 [4th ed. 1971]). Where, as here, the seller not only takes unfair advantage of the buyer's ignorance but has created and perpetuated a condition about which he is unlikely to even inquire, enforcement of the contract (in whole or in part) is offensive to the court's sense of equity. Application of the remedy of rescission, within the bounds of the narrow exception to the doctrine of caveat emptor set forth herein, is entirely appropriate to relieve the unwitting purchaser from the consequences of a most unnatural bargain.

Accordingly, the judgment of the Supreme Court, New York County (Edward H. Lehner, J.), entered April 9, 1990, which dismissed the complaint pursuant to CPLR 3211(a)(7), should be modified, on the law and the facts and in the exercise of discretion, and the first cause of action seeking rescission of the contract reinstated, without costs. . . .

SMITH, J., dissenting:

I would affirm the dismissal of the complaint by the motion court. Plaintiff seeks to rescind his contract to purchase defendant Ackley's residential property and recover his down payment. Plaintiff alleges that Ackley and her real estate broker, defendant Ellis Realty, made material misrepresentations of the property in that they failed to disclose that Ackley believed that the house was haunted by poltergeists. Moreover, Ackley shared this belief with her community and the general public through articles published in *Reader's Digest* (1977) and the local newspaper (1982). In November 1989, approximately two months after the parties entered into the contract of sale but subsequent to the scheduled October 2, 1989 closing, the house was included in a five-house walking tour and again described in the local newspaper as being haunted.

Prior to closing, plaintiff learned of this reputation and unsuccessfully sought to rescind the $650,000 contract of sale and obtain return of his

$32,500 down payment without resort to litigation. The plaintiff then commenced this action for that relief and alleged that he would not have entered into the contract had he been so advised and that as a result of the alleged poltergeist activity, the market value and resaleability of the property was greatly diminished. Defendant Ackley has counterclaimed for specific performance.

"It is settled law in New York that the seller of real property is under no duty to speak when the parties deal at arm's length. The mere silence of the seller, without some act or conduct which deceived the purchaser, does not amount to a concealment that is actionable as a fraud (*see Perin v. Mardine Realty Co., Inc.,* 5 A.D.2d 685, 168 N.Y.S.2d 647, *aff'd.,* 6 N.Y.2d 920, 190 N.Y.S.2d 995, 161 N.E.2d 210; *Moser v. Spizzirro,* 31 A.D.2d 537, 295 N.Y.S.2d 188, *aff'd.,* 25 N.Y.2d 941, 305 N.Y.S.2d 153, 252 N.E.2d 632). The buyer has the duty to satisfy himself as to the quality of his bargain pursuant to the doctrine of caveat emptor, which in New York State still applies to real estate transactions." *London v. Courduff,* 141 A.D.2d 803, 804, 529 N.Y.S.2d 874, *app. dism'd.,* 73 N.Y.2d 809, 537 N.Y.S.2d 494, 534 N.E.2d 332 (1988).

The parties herein were represented by counsel and dealt at arm's length. This is evidenced by the contract of sale which, *inter alia,* contained various riders and a specific provision that all prior understandings and agreements between the parties were merged into the contract, that the contract completely expressed their full agreement and that neither had relied upon any statement by anyone else not set forth in the contract. There is no allegation that defendants, by some specific act, other than the failure to speak, deceived the plaintiff. Nevertheless, a cause of action may be sufficiently stated where there is a confidential or fiduciary relationship creating a duty to disclose and there was a failure to disclose a material fact, calculated to induce a false belief. *County of Westchester v. Welton Becket Assoc.,* 102 A.D.2d 34, 50–51, 478 N.Y.S.2d 305, *aff'd.,* 66 N.Y.2d 642, 495 N.Y.S.2d 364, 485 N.E.2d 1029 (1985). However, plaintiff herein has not alleged and there is no basis for concluding that a confidential or fiduciary relationship existed between these parties to an arm's length transaction such as to give rise to a duty to disclose. In addition, there is no allegation that defendants thwarted plaintiff's efforts to fulfill his responsibilities fixed by the doctrine of caveat emptor. *See London v. Courduff, supra,* 141 A.D.2d at 804, 529 N.Y.S.2d 874.

Finally, if the doctrine of caveat emptor is to be discarded, it should be for a reason more substantive than a poltergeist. The existence of a poltergeist is no more binding upon the defendants than it is upon this court. . . .

NOTES AND QUESTIONS

1.   On which party, the buyer or the seller, should the risk of property defects be allocated to as a matter of the legal default rule? In most modern property transactions, many risks are allocated to the seller by default, so that sellers wishing to reallocate this risk to the buyer must expressly so state, using such language as selling the property "as is." Examples of such risks are hazards and defects such as termites or lead paint that may be difficult to verify without a formal inspection. What is the rationale for this default rule?

2.   Apart from those standard disclosures about hazardous conditions, how many aspects of a house purchase should sellers be required to provide assurance about? Some might argue that the *Stambovsky* court went too far. For a counterpoint, consider the decision of the Pennsylvania Supreme Court in *Milliken v. Jacono*, 96 A.3d 997 (Pa. 2014), refusing to provide relief to the buyer when the seller knew of (but did not disclose) a murder-suicide on the property that had happened two years earlier.

As the court noted, "the varieties of traumatizing events that could occur on a property are endless. Efforts to define those that would warrant mandatory disclosure would be a Sisyphean task. One cannot quantify the psychological impact of different genres of murder, or suicide—does a bloodless death by poisoning or overdose create a less significant "defect" than a bloody one from a stabbing or shooting? How would one treat other violent crimes . . .? What if the killings were elsewhere, but the sadistic serial killer lived there? What if satanic rituals were performed in the house?"

In your opinion, which of these past events, if any, should be disclosed? What might be the problem with trying to draw a bright line?

3.   For an older, yet colorful, case on the duty to disclose in the context of real property, see *Ikeda v. Curtis*, 261 P.2d 684 (Wash. 1953). In that case, the seller reported $1900/month in income from a hotel. What the seller failed to disclose, however, was that the income was almost entirely derived from prostitution-related activity. The court therefore found the statement of income to be fraudulently inflated and awarded damages to the buyer.

WAL-MART STORES, INC. V. COUGHLIN

369 Ark. 365 (2007)

BROWN, J.

. . . Wal-Mart Stores, Inc., appeals from an order dismissing its First Amended Complaint filed against appellee, Thomas Coughlin. Wal-Mart raises issues on appeal relating to (1) Coughlin's duty as a fiduciary to disclose material facts before entering into a self-dealing contract, and (2) his fraudulent inducement of Wal-Mart to enter into the Retirement Agreement, which incorporated a Mutual General Release . . . between the parties, by his failure to disclose material facts and by his affirmative misrepresentations. We agree with Wal-Mart that it sufficiently pled

Coughlin's duty, as a fiduciary, to disclose material facts as well as fraudulent inducement by Coughlin's affirmative misrepresentations so as to withstand a motion to dismiss . . . .

In 1978, Coughlin began working for Wal-Mart as the Director for Loss Prevention, where he had the responsibility to investigate theft, fraud, and abuse by Wal-Mart associates, suppliers, and others who may have committed these offenses against the company. From 1983 until 2003, Coughlin held various executive positions within Wal-Mart and the company's Sam's Club division. He also eventually became a member of the Wal-Mart Board of Directors. During this time, he retained responsibility for management of the Loss Prevention Department. In 2003, Coughlin assumed the position of Executive Vice President and Vice Chairman of the Board of Wal-Mart Stores, Inc. (USA), and later became Vice Chairman of Wal-Mart's Board of Directors.

In 2004, Wal-Mart announced that Coughlin would retire in 2005. On January 22, 2005, Wal-Mart and Coughlin entered into a Retirement Agreement, which included the Release between the parties, under which Coughlin was to receive millions of dollars in benefits over the ensuing years. In February 2005, after the execution of the agreement, Wal-Mart learned of Coughlin's fraudulent conduct after a store associate alerted Wal-Mart's internal investigations group that Coughlin had used a Wal-Mart gift card, issued internally for associate relations, for personal purchases. Through the internal investigation that followed, Wal-Mart learned that Coughlin had abused his position of authority and conspired with subordinates to misappropriate hundreds of thousands of dollars in cash and property through various fraudulent schemes. Three months after Wal-Mart signed the Retirement Agreement and Release with Coughlin, Wal-Mart suspended Coughlin's retirement benefits.

. . . Wal-Mart filed suit against Coughlin to void the Retirement Agreement and Release . . . . Coughlin moved to dismiss the complaint for failure to state a claim upon which relief could be granted . . . . [T]he circuit court dismissed Wal-Mart's complaint with respect to all allegations occurring prior to the execution of the Retirement Agreement and Release. The circuit court ruled in its order that Wal-Mart had failed to plead specifically that it was fraudulently induced to sign the Retirement Agreement and Release. The court further stated that whether Coughlin had a duty to disclose material facts to Wal-Mart before signing the Retirement Agreement and Release was an issue of first impression in Arkansas and that it would not reach such a conclusion, particularly in light of the Release. In its order, the circuit court said: "the Arkansas trial court is the wrong venue in which to make new case law."

. . . Wal-Mart filed [an] Amended Complaint and added fraudulent inducement of the Retirement Agreement and Release as a new claim for relief. Wal-Mart alleged in that new claim that Coughlin had made repeated misrepresentations to Wal-Mart about his conduct by his execution of Certifications and Disclosures pursuant to [federal securities] regulations and Wal-Mart's internal policies, which attested to no wrongdoing. Wal-Mart asserted that these misrepresentations induced it to enter into the Retirement Agreement and Release. [T]he circuit court entered its final order, which found that "Wal-Mart failed to specifically plead a nex[u]s between Coughlin's alleged fraud and the signing of the Release" and dismissed the . . . Amended Complaint.

Wal-Mart concedes that the issue of a fiduciary's duty to disclose improper conduct to the corporation has never been decided in Arkansas. It urges, nonetheless, that this court should bring Arkansas in line with the view held by the vast majority of other state and federal courts. It asserts that this court has long held that corporate officers and directors owe a fiduciary duty to their corporations, but it contends that we now should take the additional step and hold that this duty obligates officers and directors to disclose material facts of past fraud to the corporation before entering into a self-dealing contract. This fiduciary duty, according to Wal-Mart, applies to directors and officers when entering into agreements with the corporation, and it is those directors and officers who have the burden of proving good faith and fairness with respect to the agreement with the corporation. Wal-Mart maintains that Coughlin breached his fiduciary duty of disclosure by concealing his prior theft from Wal-Mart when negotiating and signing his Retirement Agreement and Release.

Coughlin, for his part, does not dispute that he breached his fiduciary duty by stealing from Wal-Mart but rather . . . contends that Arkansas case law does not support Wal-Mart's position that fiduciaries have a duty to disclose past fraud to corporations before entering into an agreement with those corporations. Rather, he argues that this state strongly supports freedom of contract between two sophisticated parties and that the general principles of contract law must apply to this case. He contends that Wal-Mart, which insisted that he sign the Release as part of the Retirement Agreement, was capable of excluding claims arising from a breach of the fiduciary's duty to disclose but chose not to do so. . . .

Arkansas jurisprudence "imposes a high standard of conduct upon an officer or director of a corporation. . . ." *Raines v. Toney*, 228 Ark. 1170, 1178, 313 S.W.2d 802, 808 (1958). This court has held that an officer or director of a corporation owes a fiduciary duty to the corporation and its shareholders. *See Raines, supra.* The high standard of conduct owed by an officer to his corporation has also been codified in the Arkansas Business Corporation Act . . .

The Release included in the Retirement Agreement provides:

> The Associate and Wal-Mart hereby release, acquit and forever discharge each other and (to the extent applicable) their respective directors, officers, shareholders, employees, successors and assigns, of and from any and all liability for claims, causes of actions, demands, damages, attorneys fees, expenses, compensation, or other costs or losses of any nature whatsoever, whether known or unknown, which the Associate or Wal-Mart may have arising out of or in any way related to the Associate's employment with Wal-Mart, including, but not limited to, claims for wages, back pay, front pay, promotion or reinstatement opportunities. This release does not, however, preclude the Associate or Wal-Mart from pursuing a claim for breach of the Agreement or the Non-Compete Agreement.

. . . We address then the question of a fiduciary's failure to disclose fraud perpetrated against the corporation and the impact it has on the validity of a subsequent Retirement Agreement and Release. As an initial matter, we conclude that the language of the Release is clear and unambiguous. Despite that clear language, a significant majority of other jurisdictions, both state and federal, have held that a fiduciary owes a duty of full disclosure when entering into a transaction with the fiduciary's corporation and that the fiduciary's failure to disclose material facts relating to a mutual release of claims between the parties is sufficient to set aside the release. . . .

Wal-Mart sufficiently stated a claim for relief in its . . . Amended Complaint that Coughlin had a duty as a fiduciary to disclose material facts . . . We are persuaded, in addition, that the majority view is correct, which is that the failure of a fiduciary to disclose material facts of his fraudulent conduct to his corporation prior to entering into a self-dealing contract with that corporation will void that contract and that material facts are those facts that could cause a party to act differently had the party known of those facts. We emphasize, however, that this duty of a fiduciary to disclose is embraced within the obligation of a fiduciary to act towards his corporation in good faith, which has long been the law in Arkansas. Stated differently, we are not adopting a new principle of fiduciary law by our holding today but simply giving voice to an obvious element of the fiduciary's duty of good faith. We reverse the order of dismissal on this point and remand the matter for further proceedings. . . .

In holding as we do, we have considered . . . Coughlin's contention that Arkansas has strong jurisprudence favoring freedom of contract. Nevertheless, we conclude that it is for a jury to decide whether Coughlin breached his fiduciary duty to disclose material facts to Wal-Mart and whether the parties intended the Release to bar claims of fraudulent inducement related to that duty to disclose.

. . . Wal-Mart contends that the circuit court erred in giving effect to the terms of the Release before resolving the question of whether Coughlin, by his failure to disclose material facts and his affirmative misrepresentations, fraudulently induced Wal-Mart into signing the contract. Wal-Mart claims that circuit courts should not give effect to the terms of a contract if there is a factual or legal question regarding the contract's validity. It urges that a contract, which is the product of fraudulent inducement, is void and that the terms of a release in that contract cannot bar a claim by one of the parties who was fraudulently induced into executing the contract. . . .

Coughlin's response centers . . . on the fact that Wal-Mart released all "known and unknown" claims against him, which, he argues, includes any affirmative misrepresentations. He adds that the circuit court correctly found that Wal-Mart failed to plead a specific nexus between Coughlin's alleged fraud in executing those documents and the signing of the Retirement Agreement and Release.

This court has held that a misrepresentation of facts amounting to fraud can render a release of claims ineffective and, in addition, present a question of fact for the jury. Furthermore, we have said that releases contained in contracts do not relieve a party of liability for fraud if that party obtained the contract by fraud.

In order to prove fraud, a plaintiff must prove five elements under Arkansas law: (1) that the defendant made a false representation of material fact; (2) that the defendant knew that the representation was false or that there was insufficient evidence upon which to make the representation; (3) that the defendant intended to induce action or inaction by the plaintiff in reliance upon the representation; (4) that the plaintiff justifiably relied on the representation; and (5) that the plaintiff suffered damage as a result of the false representation. *See Bomar v. Moser*, 369 Ark. 123, 251 S.W.3d 234 (2007). This court has further said regarding fraudulent inducement:

> Fraud cannot be an agreement. It is an imposture practiced by one upon another. It may be used as an inducement to enter into an agreement. Defendant does not claim that he entered into an agreement that affects the validity of the contract, but that he was induced by false representations to enter into the contract. If that be true the validity of the contract is not assailed, but its very existence is destroyed. To constitute fraud by false representation there must be a representation of alleged existing fact; that representation must be false in fact; it must be made with intent to deceive, and the person to whom it is made must believe it.

[*Allen v. Overturf,* 353 S.W.2d 343, 345 (1962)] (quoting *Scarsdale Pub. Co. v. Carter,* 63 Misc. 271, 116 N.Y.S. 731, 735 (1909)).

The circuit court ruled in its final order that Wal-Mart failed to plead fraudulent inducement with particularity, as required by Rule 9(b) of the Arkansas Rules of Civil Procedure. We disagree. Wal-Mart clearly pled the following facts supporting fraud in its ... Amended Complaint: (1) Coughlin made false representations in the Certifications and Disclosures ... pursuant to [federal securities regulations] and Wal-Mart's internal control policy, when he stated that neither he nor the members of his family had received personal benefits from Wal-Mart and that he was not aware of any officer who had committed acts of fraud or violated Wal-Mart's ethics policy; (2) Coughlin knew that the representations ... were false as Coughlin had stolen hundreds of thousands of dollars in money and property from Wal-Mart; (3) Coughlin intended to induce Wal-Mart to act in reliance on these misrepresentations in making decisions regarding Coughlin's executive responsibilities and his compensation and benefits ...; (4) Wal-Mart justifiably relied on these misrepresentations ... to promote Coughlin both as an officer and director and in making the decision to offer Coughlin a lucrative Retirement Agreement; and (5) Wal-Mart suffered damages as a result of the misrepresentations as Wal-Mart would not have entered into the Retirement Agreement and Release except for Coughlin's misrepresentations. . . . Reversed and remanded.

NOTES AND QUESTIONS

1. Some legal relationships are effective only when one party is able to repose trust and confidence in the other to act in the first party's best interests. Besides corporate officers and directors, who owe duties to their shareholders, as in *Wal-Mart,* examples are attorney-client, doctor-patient, trustee-beneficiary, executor-estate, and partners to one another. To promote the efficacy of such confidential relationships and to support the beneficiary's trust, the common law imposes special duties on such fiduciaries that restrict the ambit of freedom of contract with beneficiaries. For one, fiduciaries owe their beneficiaries a duty of candor not required of contracting parties operating at arms'-length. For another, while courts do not inquire into the adequacy of consideration in contracts made at arms'-length, they scrutinize the terms of fiduciary contracts for fundamental fairness to the beneficiary.

2. The status relationship between fiduciaries and their beneficiaries may permit beneficiaries to rescind innocently unfair transactions that might be upheld between parties dealing at arms' length. In the classic case of *Jackson v. Seymour,* 71 S.E.2d 181 (Va. 1952), a land sale contract conveyed 31 acres for $275 that subsequent facts revealed had a market value of between $3,200 and $5,000. The acreage was contiguous to other property both parties were familiar with but neither had set foot on the subject property. Both assumed it was only useful as pasture when in fact it boasted substantial

timberland. The buyer alleged the seller represented the limited utility and said $275 was a good price though the seller disputed that.

Absent any special relationship between the buyer and seller, the contract probably would have been upheld. But the parties were brother and sister and the brother also served as the sister's business manager—the sister stressing that she had reposed "utmost confidence" in this role. The court ordered rescission and restitution, couching the substance of its ruling in "constructive fraud" proxied by the vast disparity between price and value given the confidential relationship. The court explained:

> This is not the ordinary case in which the parties dealt at arm's length and the shrewd trader was entitled to the fruits of his bargain. The parties were brother and sister. He was a successful business man and she a widow in need of money and forced by circumstances, according to the defendant's own testimony, to sell a part of the lands which she had inherited. Because of their friendly and intimate relations, she entrusted to him and he assumed the management and renting of a portion of this very land. He engaged tenants for such of the land as could be cultivated and collected the rents. She accepted his settlements without question. Moreover, it is undisputed that neither of the parties knew of the timber on the land and we have from the defendant's own lips the admission that as it turned out "afterwards" he had paid a grossly inadequate price for the property and that he would not have bought it from her for the small amount paid if he had then known of the true situation. To hold that under these circumstances the plaintiff is without remedy would be a reproach to the law. Nor do we think that a court of equity is so impotent.

3.   In contrast, a classic opinion establishing the privilege of silence in arms'-length transactions was written by Chief Justice Marshall for the U.S. Supreme Court in *Laidlaw v. Organ*, 15 U.S. 178 (1817). A contract for the sale of 111,000 pounds of tobacco was made in the morning on February 18, 1815 in New Orleans, just a few hours before news circulated of a peace treaty ending the War of 1812 and with it a naval embargo that had reduced the price of tobacco by nearly half. The buyer was aware of the forthcoming peace treaty and concomitant doubling of the contract's value, while the seller was not. The seller alleged that it asked the buyer whether there was any news that might affect the contract's value and the buyer said nothing. Chief Justice Marshall's opinion was but one paragraph long, with these key points:

> The question [is] whether the intelligence of extrinsic circumstances, which might influence the price of the commodity, and which was exclusively within the knowledge of the [buyer], ought to have been communicated by him to the [seller]? The court is of opinion that he was not bound to communicate it. It would be difficult to circumscribe the contrary doctrine within proper limits, where the means of intelligence are equally accessible to both parties. But at

the same time, each party must take care not to say or do anything tending to impose upon the other. [That] question, whether any imposition was practised by the [buyer] upon the [seller] ought to [be] submitted to the jury.

Deception—fraud and misrepresentation as we have seen—may warrant voiding a contract on equitable grounds, as would nondisclosure by a fiduciary or other person having a duty to disclose—but commercial buyers and sellers like those in *Laidlaw* are not so bound. Legal historians point to *Laidlaw* as a foundational statement of caveat emptor in the United States, containing as it does both the general grant of freedom to be silent along with limitations on concealment. For trivia buffs, the buyer was represented in the case by Francis Scott Key, author of the poem that formed the basis for the U.S. national anthem.

4. We will encounter two additional cases involving fiduciaries later in this chapter and further stress the contrast between fiduciary relationships and contractual relationships in Chapter Nine when examining contract law's duty of good faith.

C. IMPOSSIBILITY, FRUSTRATION, IMPRACTICABILITY

The doctrine of mutual mistake deals with errors of presently existing fact—but what happens if the facts and circumstances surrounding the transaction change *after* the deal has already been struck? Three related doctrines—impossibility, impracticability, and frustration of purpose—deal with these types of issues. Key to all of these defenses is that the changed circumstance must be a situation that was not the fault of either party and that was remote in possibility or else unforeseen.

During the Middle Ages, the developing law was not sympathetic to these types of changed circumstance defenses. So, for example, in the landmark case of *Paradine v. Jane*, Aleyn 26, 82 Eng. Rep. 897 (King's Bench, England, 1647), the court ruled that despite the fact that an army headed by the alien Prince Rupert had invaded the land, the tenant still had to pay. The stance was rigid. "Yet, he ought to pay his rent," is a famous legal conclusion from that ancient case. The law at that time did not take into account that there was a legitimate reason for non-payment—that the land was non-productive as it was occupied by hostile forces—instead ruling that contract liability was *absolute*. To the courts of that era, the changed circumstances behind non-performance did not matter.

The law, however, has since evolved past that rigid formalism. Instead, these defenses based on changed circumstances bend more toward pragmatic compromise. If due to unforeseen circumstances a performance that formed the basis of a contract becomes practically valueless to a party, *frustration of purpose* might come into play. And in situations where changed circumstances render performance unduly difficult or burdensome, we might consider the doctrine of *impracticability*.

In this section, we examine the development of the doctrines of frustration of purpose, impossibility, and impracticability. We will see how parties in modern disputes often allocate the risk of unforeseen events between each other using what is known as a force majeure clause. Turning to modern times, we will ask whether a roller rink can keep operating without its promised insurance.

TAYLOR V. CALDWELL
122 Eng. Rep. 309 (King's Bench, England 1863)

. . . The judgment of the Court was now delivered by Blackburn J. In this case the plaintiffs and defendants had, on the 27th May, 1861, entered into a contract by which the defendants agreed to let the plaintiffs have the use of The Surrey Gardens and Music Hall on four days then to come, viz., the 17th June, 15th July, 5th August and 19th August, for the purpose of giving a series of four grand concerts, and day and night fêtes at the Gardens and Hall on those days respectively; and the plaintiffs agreed to take the Gardens and Hall on those days, and pay £100 for each day.

. . . The agreement . . . [sets] out various stipulations between the parties as to what each was to supply for these concerts and entertainments, and as to the manner in which they should be carried on. The effect of the whole is to shew that the existence of the Music Hall in the Surrey Gardens in a state fit for a concert was essential for the fulfilment of the contract—such entertainments as the parties contemplated in their agreement could not be given without it.

After the making of the agreement, and before the first day on which a concert was to be given, the Hall was destroyed by fire. This destruction, we must take it on the evidence, was without the fault of either party, and was so complete that in consequence the concerts could not be given as intended. And the question we have to decide is whether, under these circumstances, the loss which the plaintiffs have sustained is to fall upon the defendants. The parties when framing their agreement evidently had not present to their minds the possibility of such a disaster, and have made no express stipulation with reference to it, so that the answer to the question must depend upon the general rules of law applicable to such a contract.

There seems no doubt that where there is a . . . contract to do a thing, not in itself unlawful, the contractor must perform it or pay damages for not doing it, although in consequence of unforeseen accidents, the performance of his contract has become unexpectedly burthensome or even impossible. The law is so laid down in 1 Roll. Abr. 450, Condition (G), and in the note (2) to *Walton* v. *Waterhouse* (2 Wms. Saund. 421 a. 6th ed.), and is recognised as the general rule by all the Judges in the much discussed case of *Hall* v. *Wright* (E. B. & E. 746).

But this rule is only applicable when the contract is positive and absolute, and not subject to any condition either express or implied: and there are authorities which, as we think, establish the principle that where, from the nature of the contract, it appears that the parties must from the beginning have known that it could not be fulfilled unless when the time for the fulfilment of the contract arrived some particular specified thing continued to exist, so that, when entering into the contract, they must have contemplated such continuing existence as the foundation of what was to be done; there, in the absence of any express or implied warranty that the thing shall exist, the contract is not to be construed as a positive contract, but as subject to an implied condition that the parties shall be excused in case, before breach, performance becomes impossible from the perishing of the thing without default of the contractor.

. . . There is a class of contracts in which a person binds himself to do something which requires to be performed by him in person; and such promises, e.g. promises to marry, or promises to serve for a certain time, are never in practice qualified by an express exception of the death of the party; and therefore in such cases the contract is in terms broken if the promisor dies before fulfilment. Yet it was very early determined that, if the performance is personal, the executors are not liable . . . Crompton J., in his judgment, puts another case. "Where a contract depends upon personal skill, and the act of God renders it impossible, as, for instance, in the case of a painter employed to paint a picture who is struck blind, it may be that the performance might be excused."

It seems that in those cases the only ground on which the parties or their executors, can be excused from the consequences of the breach of the contract is, that from the nature of the contract there is an implied condition of the continued existence of the life of the contractor, and, perhaps in the case of the painter of his eyesight.

. . . These are instances where the implied condition is of the life of a human being, but there are others in which the same implication is made as to the continued existence of a thing. For example, where a contract of sale is made amounting to a bargain and sale, transferring presently the property in specific chattels, which are to be delivered by the vendor at a future day; there, if the chattels, without the fault of the vendor, perish in the interval, the purchaser must pay the price and the vendor is excused from performing his contract to deliver, which has thus become impossible.

. . . In none of these cases is the promise in words other than positive, nor is there any express stipulation that the destruction of the person or thing shall excuse the performance; but that excuse is by law implied, because from the nature of the contract it is apparent that the parties contracted on the basis of the continued existence of the particular person or chattel. In the present case, looking at the whole contract, we find that the parties contracted on the basis of the continued existence of the Music Hall at the time when the concerts were to be given; that being essential to their performance.

We think, therefore, that the Music Hall having ceased to exist, without fault of either party, both parties are excused, the plaintiffs from taking the gardens and paying the money, the defendants from performing their promise to give the use of the Hall and Gardens and other things. Consequently the rule must be absolute to enter the verdict for the defendants.

NOTES AND QUESTIONS

1.   Did the *Taylor* court agree with the venerable principle of *pact sunt servanda*—that "promises are kept"? How did it respond to that argument?

2.   The *Taylor* court implies a condition to the owner's obligation to provide the Music Hall. What is that condition? What is the basis for making the implication?

3.   When, according to the *Taylor* court, is one justified implying a condition concerning the continued existence of a structure or state of affairs? Does the phrase "nature of a contract" help evaluate that question? What about the necessity of such continuity to the performance of the contract?

4.   What does it mean to say that the parties contemplated the continued existence of the Music Hall? Did the parties mention fire as a possibility and agree on its effects on their bargain? How does one determine whether something is contemplated by the parties? Consider the following variations on the *Taylor* deal:

A.   Suppose during negotiations, tenant says to owner: "If the Music Hall burns down, I want to be repaid for my expenses and lost profit." Owner says nothing in reply and all other facts are the same as in the *Taylor* case.

no express assent to risk allocation but fire is now foreseeable

B.   Suppose tenant makes the same comment to owner and owner replies saying "that's the most ridiculous proposition I have ever heard."

C.   Suppose tenant makes the same comment to owner, which of the following responses do you surmise are likely or reasonable: (i) "I can only do that if the rental price is triple what we've been discussing." (ii) "I can only do that if my fire liability insurance policy will cover such a commitment."

D.   Suppose there is no discussion about fire risk but there has been a rash of theater arsons during the most reason entertainment season in the district where the Music Hall is located.

5.   Suppose a different set of contracts, such as these: Owner promises tenant to undertake substantial advertising and promotion for the concert and incurred significant expenses doing so when the destructive fire occurred. Can owner recover such costs from tenant?

6.   Is "contemplation of the parties" the same as foreseeability or different? What is the relationship between those concepts and risk? To what extent is it sensible in evaluating excuse based on impossibility and related doctrines to talk about the "intention" of the parties? Consider these variations:

A.   The fire is due to owner's negligence. Can tenant recover?

B.   Suppose no fire occurred but that tenant was unable to sell tickets to the performance and seeks to be excused from the contract.

C.   Owner warrants the continued existence of the theater and yet a fire destroys it.

KRELL V. HENRY

2 K.B. 740 (Court of Appeal, England 1903)

The plaintiff, Paul Krell, sued the defendant, C. S. Henry, for £50, being the balance of a sum of £75., for which the defendant had agreed to hire a flat at 56A, Pall Mall on the days of June 26 and 27, for the purpose of viewing the processions to be held in connection with the coronation of His Majesty. The defendant denied his liability, and counter-claimed for the return of the sum of £25, which had been paid as a deposit, on the ground that, the processions not having taken place owing to the serious illness of the King, there had been a total failure of consideration for the contract entered into by him.

The facts, which were not disputed, were as follows. The plaintiff on leaving the country in March, 1902, left instructions with his solicitor to let his suite of chambers at 56A, Pall Mall on such terms and for such period (not exceeding six months) as he thought proper. On June 17, 1902, the defendant noticed an announcement in the windows of the plaintiff's flat to the effect that windows to view the coronation processions were to be let. The defendant interviewed the housekeeper on the subject, when it was pointed out to him what a good view of the processions could be obtained from the premises, and he eventually agreed with the housekeeper to take the suite for the two days in question for a sum of £75.

On June 20 the defendant wrote the following letter to the plaintiff's solicitor:—

I am in receipt of yours of the 18th instant, inclosing form of agreement for the suite of chambers on the third floor at 56A, Pall Mall, which I have agreed to take for the two days, the 26th and 27th instant, for the sum of £75. For reasons given you I cannot enter into the agreement, but as arranged over the telephone I

> inclose herewith cheque for £25 as deposit, and will thank you to
> confirm to me that I shall have the entire use of these rooms
> during the days (not the nights) of the 26th and 27th instant. You
> may rely that every care will be taken of the premises and their
> contents. On the 24th inst. I will pay the balance, viz., £50, to
> complete the £75 agreed upon.

On the same day the defendant received the following reply from the
plaintiff's solicitor:

> I am in receipt of your letter of to-day's date inclosing cheque for
> £25. deposit on your agreeing to take Mr. Krell's chambers on the
> third floor at 56A, Pall Mall for the two days, the 26th and 27th
> June, and I confirm the agreement that you are to have the entire
> use of these rooms during the days (but not the nights), the
> balance, £50., to be paid to me on Tuesday next the 24th instant.

The processions not having taken place on the days originally
appointed, namely, June 26 and 27, the defendant declined to pay the
balance of £50 alleged to be due from him under the contract in writing of
June 20 constituted by the above two letters. Hence the present action.

Darling J., on August 11, 1902, held, upon the authority of Taylor v.
Caldwell and The Moorcock, that there was an implied condition in the
contract that the procession should take place, and gave judgment for the
defendant on the claim and counter-claim. The plaintiff appealed.

WILLIAMS, L. J.J.

The real question in this case is the extent of the application in English
law of the principle of the Roman law which has been adopted and acted on
in many English decisions, and notably in the case of Taylor v.
Caldwell. . . .

The doubt in the present case arises as to how far this principle
extends. . . . I do not think that the principle of the civil law as introduced
into the English law is limited to cases in which the event causing the
impossibility of performance is the destruction or non-existence of
something which is the subject-matter of the contract or of some condition
or state of things expressly specified as a condition of it. I think that you
first have to ascertain, not necessarily from the terms of the contract, but,
if required, from necessary inferences, drawn from surrounding
circumstances recognised by both contracting parties, what is the
substance of the contract, and then to ask the question whether that
substantial contract needs for its foundation the assumption of the
existence of a particular state of things. If it does, this will limit the
operation of the general words, and in such case, if the contract becomes
impossible of performance by reason of the non-existence of the state of

things assumed by both contracting parties as the foundation of the contract, there will be no breach of the contract thus limited.

Now what are the facts of the present case? The contract is contained in two letters of June 20 which passed between the defendant and the plaintiff's agent, Mr. Cecil Bisgood. These letters do not mention the coronation, but speak merely of the taking of Mr. Krell's chambers, or, rather, of the use of them, in the daytime of June 26 and 27, for the sum of £75, £25 then paid, balance £50 to be paid on the 24th. But the affidavits, which by agreement between the parties are to be taken as stating the facts of the case, shew that the plaintiff exhibited on his premises, third floor, 56A, Pall Mall, an announcement to the effect that windows to view the Royal coronation procession were to be let, and that the defendant was induced by that announcement to apply to the housekeeper on the premises, who said that the owner was willing to let the suite of rooms for the purpose of seeing the Royal procession for both days, but not nights, of June 26 and 27.

In my judgment the use of the rooms was let and taken for the purpose of seeing the Royal procession. It was not a demise of the rooms, or even an agreement to let and take the rooms. It is a licence to use rooms for a particular purpose and none other. And in my judgment the taking place of those processions on the days proclaimed along the proclaimed route, which passed 56A, Pall Mall, was regarded by both contracting parties as the foundation of the contract; and I think that it cannot reasonably be supposed to have been in the contemplation of the contracting parties, when the contract was made, that the coronation would not be held on the proclaimed days, or the processions not take place on those days along the proclaimed route; and I think that the words imposing on the defendant the obligation to accept and pay for the use of the rooms for the named days, although general and unconditional, were not used with reference to the possibility of the particular contingency which afterwards occurred.

It was suggested in the course of the argument that if the occurrence, on the proclaimed days, of the coronation and the procession in this case were the foundation of the contract, and if the general words are thereby limited or qualified, so that in the event of the non-occurrence of the coronation and procession along the proclaimed route they would discharge both parties from further performance of the contract, it would follow that if a cabman was engaged to take someone to Epsom on Derby Day at a suitable enhanced price for such a journey, say £10, both parties to the contract would be discharged in the contingency of the race at Epsom for some reason becoming impossible; but I do not think this follows, for I do not think that in the cab case the happening of the race would be the foundation of the contract.

No doubt the purpose of the engager would be to go to see the Derby, and the price would be proportionately high; but the cab had no special qualifications for the purpose which led to the selection of the cab for this particular occasion. Any other cab would have done as well. Moreover, I think that, under the cab contract, the hirer, even if the race went off, could have said, "Drive me to Epsom; I will pay you the agreed sum; you have nothing to do with the purpose for which I hired the cab," and that if the cabman refused he would have been guilty of a breach of contract, there being nothing to qualify his promise to drive the hirer to Epsom on a particular day.

Whereas in the case of the coronation, there is not merely the purpose of the hirer to see the coronation procession, but it is the coronation procession and the relative position of the rooms which is the basis of the contract as much for the lessor as the hirer; and I think that if the King, before the coronation day and after the contract, had died, the hirer could not have insisted on having the rooms on the days named. It could not in the cab case be reasonably said that seeing the Derby race was the foundation of the contract, as it was of the licence in this case. Whereas in the present case, where the rooms were offered and taken, by reason of their peculiar suitability from the position of the rooms for a view of the coronation procession, surely the view of the coronation procession was the foundation of the contract, which is a very different thing from the purpose of the man who engaged the cab—namely, to see the race—being held to be the foundation of the contract. Each case must be judged by its own circumstances.

In each case one must ask oneself, first, what, having regard to all the circumstances, was the foundation of the contract? Secondly, was the performance of the contract prevented? Thirdly, was the event which prevented the performance of the contract of such a character that it cannot reasonably be said to have been in the contemplation of the parties at the date of the contract? If all these questions are answered in the affirmative (as I think they should be in this case), I think both parties are discharged from further performance of the contract.

I think that the coronation procession was the foundation of this contract, and that the non-happening of it prevented the performance of the contract; and, secondly, I think that the non-happening of the procession, to use the words of Sir James Hannen in Baily v. De Crespigny, was an event "of such a character that it cannot reasonably be supposed to have been in the contemplation of the contracting parties when the contract was made, and that they are not to be held bound by general words which, though large enough to include, were not used with reference to the possibility of the particular contingency which afterwards happened." The test seems to be whether the event which causes the impossibility was or might have been anticipated and guarded against. It seems difficult to say, in a case where both parties anticipate the happening of an event, which anticipation is the foundation of the contract, that either party must be taken to have anticipated, and ought to have guarded against, the event which prevented the performance of the contract. . . .

It is not essential to the application of the principle of Taylor v. Caldwell that the direct subject of the contract should perish or fail to be in existence at the date of performance of the contract. It is sufficient if a state of things or condition expressed in the contract and essential to its performance perishes or fails to be in existence at that time.

In the present case the condition which fails and prevents the achievement of that which was, in the contemplation of both parties, the foundation of the contract, is not expressly mentioned either as a condition of the contract or the purpose of it; but I think for the reasons which I have given that the principle of Taylor v. Caldwell ought to be applied. This disposes of the plaintiff's claim for £50 unpaid balance of the price agreed to be paid for the use of the rooms. The defendant at one time set up a cross-claim for the return of the 25£ he paid at the date of the contract. As that claim is now withdrawn it is unnecessary to say anything about it. . . . I think this appeal ought to be dismissed. . . .

NOTES AND QUESTIONS

1.   Does *Taylor v. Caldwell* resolve the issue in *Krell v. Henry*?

2.   What is the difference between the room in *Krell v. Henry* and the cab in the Epsom race hypothetical? What role does price play in the analysis? Note how the court references a "suitably enhanced" price in the Epsom hypothetical.

3.   Can you restate the three questions that *Krell v. Henry* seems to require asking to determine whether the doctrine of frustration of purpose excuses a contractual obligation?

PROBLEM: CANCELLED INAUGURATIONS

Landlord rented a room to let Tenant observe the inauguration parade honoring the next President of the United States on inauguration day in January. Tenant paid a 10% deposit.

1.   Inclement weather led the organizers to cancel the parade. Landlord proposes to retain the deposit and seek the balance due. What result?

2.   A sharp decline in the President-elect's popularity, due to his surprising support for a regressive tax bill, suggests that the audience for the inauguration parade will be dismal. Tenant does not want to attend. Can Tenant rescind?

RESTATEMENT (SECOND) OF CONTRACTS, SECTIONS 261, 265

§ 261. *Discharge by Supervening Impracticability.* Where, after a contract is made, a party's performance is made impracticable without his fault by the occurrence of an event the non-occurrence of which was a basic assumption on which the contract was made, his duty to render that performance is discharged, unless the language or the circumstances indicate the contrary.

§ 265. *Discharge by Supervening Frustration.* Where, after a contract is made, a party's principal purpose is substantially frustrated without his fault by the occurrence of an event the non-occurrence of which was a basic assumption on which the contract was made, his remaining duties to render performance are discharged, unless the language or the circumstances indicate the contrary.

Comment a. Rationale. Section [265] deals with the problem that arises when a change in circumstances makes one party's performance virtually worthless to the other, frustrating his purpose in making the contract. It is distinct from the problem of impracticability dealt with in [Section 261] because there is no impediment to performance by either party. . . . The rule stated in this Section sets out the requirements for the discharge of . . . duty. First, the purpose that is frustrated must have been a principal purpose of that party in making the contract. It is not enough that he had in mind some specific object without which he would not have made the contract. The object must be so completely the basis of the contract that, as both parties understand, without it the transaction would make little sense.

Second, the frustration must be substantial. It is not enough that the transaction has become less profitable for the affected party or even that he will sustain a loss. The frustration must be so severe that it is not fairly to be regarded as within the risks that he assumed under the contract. Third, the non-occurrence of the frustrating event must have been a basic assumption on which the contract was made. This involves essentially the same sorts of determinations that are involved under the general rule on impracticability. The foreseeability of the event is here, as it is there, a factor in that determination, but the mere fact that the event was foreseeable does not compel the conclusion that its non-occurrence was not such a basic assumption.

Illustrations:

1.   A and B make a contract under which B is to pay A $1,000 and is to have the use of A's window on January 10 to view a parade that has been scheduled for that day. Because of the illness of an important official, the parade is cancelled. B refuses to use the window or pay the $1,000. B's duty to pay $1,000 is discharged, and B is not liable to A for breach of contract.

2.   A contracts with B to print an advertisement in a souvenir program of an international yacht race, which has been scheduled by a yacht club, for a price of $10,000. The yacht club cancels the race because of the outbreak of war. A has already printed the programs, but B refuses to pay the $10,000. B's duty to pay $10,000 is discharged, and B is not liable to A for breach of contract.

3.   A, who owns a hotel, and B, who owns a country club, make a contract under which A is to pay $1,000 a month and B is to make the club's membership privileges available to the guests in A's hotel free of charge to them. A's building is destroyed by fire without his fault, and A is unable to remain in the hotel business. A refuses to make further monthly payments. A's duty to make monthly payments is discharged, and A is not liable to B for breach of contract.

4.   A leases neon sign installations to B for three years to advertise and illuminate B's place of business. After one year, a government regulation prohibits the lighting of such signs. B refuses to make further payments of rent. B's duty to pay rent is discharged, and B is not liable to A for breach of contract.

LLOYD V. MURPHY

153 P.2d 47 (Cal. 1944)

TRAYNOR, J.

On August 4, 1941 plaintiffs leased to defendant for a five-year term beginning September 15, 1941, certain premises located at the corner of Almont Drive and Wilshire Boulevard in the city of Beverly Hills, Los Angeles County, "for the sole purpose of conducting thereon the business of displaying and selling new automobiles (including the servicing and repairing thereof and of selling the petroleum products of a major oil company) and for no other purpose whatsoever without the written consent of the lessor" except "to make an occasional sale of a used automobile." Defendant agreed not to sublease or assign without plaintiffs' written consent. On January 1, 1942 the federal government ordered that the sale of new automobiles be discontinued. It modified this order on January 8, 1942 to permit sales to those engaged in military activities, and on January 20, 1942, it established a system of priorities restricting sales to persons having preferential ratings . . .

On March 10, 1942, defendant explained the effect of these restrictions on his business to one of the plaintiffs authorized to act for the others, who orally waived the restrictions in the lease as to use and subleasing and offered to reduce the rent if defendant should be unable to operate profitably. Nevertheless defendant vacated the premises on March 15, 1942, giving oral notice of repudiation of the lease to plaintiffs, which was followed by a written notice on March 24, 1942. Plaintiffs affirmed in writing on March 26th their oral waiver and, failing to persuade defendant to perform his obligations, they rented the property to other tenants pursuant to their powers under the lease in order to mitigate damages.

On May 11, 1942, plaintiffs brought this action praying for declaratory relief to determine their rights under the lease, and for judgment for unpaid rent. Following a trial on the merits, the court found that the leased premises were located on one of the main traffic arteries of Los Angeles County; that they were equipped with gasoline pumps and in general adapted for the maintenance of an automobile service station; that they contained a one-story storeroom adapted to many commercial purposes; that plaintiffs had waived the restrictions in the lease and granted defendant the right to use the premises for any legitimate purpose and to sublease to any responsible party; that defendant continues to carry on the business of selling and servicing automobiles at two other places.

Defendant testified that at one of these locations he sold new automobiles exclusively and when asked if he were aware that many new automobile dealers were continuing in business replied: 'Sure. It is just the location that I couldn't make a go, though, of automobiles.' Although there was no finding to that effect, defendant estimated in response to inquiry by his counsel, that 90 per cent of his gross volume of business was new car sales and 10 per cent gasoline sales.

The trial court held that war conditions had not terminated defendant's obligations under the lease and gave judgment for plaintiffs, declaring the lease as modified by plaintiffs' waiver to be in full force and effect, and ordered defendant to pay the unpaid rent with interest, less amounts received by plaintiffs from re-renting. Defendant brought this appeal, contending that the purpose for which the premises were leased was frustrated by the restrictions placed on the sale of new automobiles by the federal government, thereby terminating his duties under the lease.

Although commercial frustration was first recognized as an excuse for nonperformance of a contractual duty by the courts of England (Krell v. Henry, C.A., 1903, 2 K.B. 740; Blakely v. Muller, K.B., 19 T.L.R. 186; see McElroy and Williams, The Coronation Cases, 4 Mod.L.Rev. 241) its soundness has been questioned by those courts (see Maritime National Fish, Ltd., v. Ocean Trawlers, Ltd., (1935) A. C. 524, 528–29; 56 L.Q.Rev. 324, arguing that Krell v. Henry, supra, was a misapplication of Taylor v. Caldwell, 1863, 3 B.&S. 826, the leading case on impossibility as an excuse for nonperformance[.]

. . . Although the doctrine of frustration is akin to the doctrine of impossibility of performance (see Civ.Code, § 1511; 6 Cal.Jur. 435–450; 4 Cal.Jur. Ten-year Supp. 187–192; Taylor v. Caldwell, supra) since both have developed from the commercial necessity of excusing performance in cases of extreme hardship, frustration is not a form of impossibility even under the modern definition of that term, which includes not only cases of physical impossibility but also cases of extreme impracticability of performance . . . . Performance remains possible but the expected value of performance to the party seeking to be excused has been destroyed by a fortuitous event, which supervenes to cause an actual but not literal failure of consideration. Krell v. Henry supra; . . . Williston . . . §§ . . . 1935, 1954 . . . ; Restatement, Contracts, § 288.

The question in cases involving frustration is whether the equities of the case, considered in the light of sound public policy, require placing the risk of a disruption or complete destruction of the contract equilibrium on defendant or plaintiff under the circumstances of a given case . . . See Smith, Some Practical Aspects of the Doctrine of Impossibility, 32 Ill.L.Rev. 672, 675; Patterson, Constructive Conditions in Contracts, 42 Columb.L.Rev. 903, 949. and the answer depends on whether an unanticipated circumstance, the risk of which should not be fairly thrown on the promisor, has made performance vitally different from what was reasonably to be expected . . . .

The purpose of a contract is to place the risks of performance upon the promisor, and the relation of the parties, terms of the contract, and circumstances surrounding its formation must be examined to determine whether it can be fairly inferred that the risk of the event that has supervened to cause the alleged frustration was not reasonably foreseeable. If it was foreseeable there should have been provision for it in the contract, and the absence of such a provision gives rise to the inference that the risk was assumed.

The doctrine of frustration has been limited to cases of extreme hardship so that businessmen, who must make their arrangements in advance, can rely with certainty on their contracts. . . . The courts have required a promisor seeking to excuse himself from performance of his obligations to prove that the risk of the frustrating event was not reasonably foreseeable and that the value of counterperformance is totally or nearly totally destroyed, for frustration is no defense if it was foreseeable or controllable by the promisor, or if counterperformance remains valuable. . . .

Thus laws or other governmental acts that make performance unprofitable or more difficult or expensive do not excuse the duty to perform a contractual obligation . . . It is settled that if parties have contracted with reference to a state of war or have contemplated the risks arising from it, they may not invoke the doctrine of frustration to escape their obligations . . .

At the time the lease in the present case was executed the National Defense Act [of 1940], authorizing the President to allocate materials and mobilize industry for national defense, had been law for more than a year.

The automotive industry was in the process of conversion to supply the needs of our growing mechanized army and to meet lend-lease commitments. Iceland and Greenland had been occupied by the army. Automobile sales were soaring because the public anticipated that production would soon be restricted.

These facts were commonly known and it cannot be said that the risk of war and its consequences necessitating restriction of the production and sale of automobiles was so remote a contingency that its risk could not be foreseen by defendant, an experienced automobile dealer. Indeed, the conditions prevailing at the time the lease was executed, and the absence of any provision in the lease contracting against the effect of war, gives rise to the inference that the risk was assumed. Defendant has therefore failed to prove that the possibility of war and its consequences on the production and sale of new automobiles was an unanticipated circumstance wholly outside the contemplation of the parties.

Nor has defendant sustained the burden of proving that the value of the lease has been destroyed. The sale of automobiles was not made impossible or illegal but merely restricted and if governmental regulation does not entirely prohibit the business to be carried on in the leased premises but only limits or restricts it, thereby making it less profitable and more difficult to continue, the lease is not terminated or the lessee excused from further performance. . . . Defendant may use the premises for the purpose for which they were leased. New automobiles and gasoline continue to be sold. Indeed, defendant testified that he continued to sell new automobiles exclusively at another location in the same county.

Defendant contends that the lease is restrictive and that the government orders therefore destroyed its value and frustrated its purpose. Provisions that prohibit subleasing or other uses than those specified affect the value of a lease and are to be considered in determining whether its purpose has been frustrated or its value destroyed. See Owens, The Effect of the War Upon the Rights and Liabilities of Parties to a Contract, 19 California State Bar Journal 132, 143. It must not be forgotten, however, that "The landlord has not covenanted that the tenant shall have the right to carry on the contemplated business or that the business to which the premises are by their nature or by the terms of the lease restricted shall be profitable enough to enable the tenant to pay the rent but has imposed a condition for his own benefit; and, certainly, unless and until he chooses to take advantage of it, the tenant is not deprived of the use of the premises." 6 Williston, Contracts . . . § 1955 . . .

In the present lease plaintiffs reserved the rights that defendant should not use the premises for other purposes than those specified in the lease or sublease without plaintiffs' written consent. Far from preventing other uses or subleasing they waived these rights, enabling defendant to use the premises for any legitimate purpose and to sublease them to any responsible tenant. This waiver is significant in view of the location of the premises on a main traffic artery in Los Angeles County and their adaptability for many commercial purposes. The value of these rights is attested by the fact that the premises were rented soon after defendants vacated them. It is therefore clear that the governmental restrictions on the sale of new cars has not destroyed the value of the lease. Furthermore, plaintiffs offered to lower the rent if defendant should be unable to operate profitably, and their conduct was at all times fair and cooperative.

The consequences of applying the doctrine of frustration to a leasehold involving less than a total or nearly total destruction of the value of the leased premises would be undesirable. Confusion would result from different decisions purporting to define 'substantial' frustration. Litigation would be encouraged by the repudiation of leases when lessees found their businesses less profitable because of the emergency.

Many leases have been affected in varying degrees by the widespread governmental regulations necessitated by war conditions.

The cases that defendant relies upon are consistent with the conclusion reached herein. In Industrial Development & Land Co. v. Goldschmidt, supra, the lease provided that the premises should not be used other than as a saloon. When national prohibition made the sale of alcoholic beverages illegal, the court excused the tenant from further performance on the theory of illegality or impossibility by a change in domestic law. The doctrine of frustration might have been applied, since the purpose for which the property was leased was totally destroyed and there was nothing to show that the value of the lease was not thereby totally destroyed. In the present case the purpose was not destroyed but only restricted, and plaintiffs proved that the lease was valuable to defendant.

In Grace v. Croninger . . . (12 Cal.App.2d 603, 55 P.2d 941), the lease was for the purpose of conducting a 'saloon and cigar store, and for no other purpose' with provision for subleasing a portion of the premises for bootblack purposes. The monthly rental was $650. It was clear that prohibition destroyed the main purpose of the lease, but since the premises could be used for bootblack and cigar store purposes, the lessee was not excused from his duty to pay the rent. In the present case new automobiles and gasoline may be sold under the lease as executed and any legitimate business may be conducted or the premises may be subleased under the lease as modified by plaintiff's waiver. . . . [Affirmed.]

NOTES AND QUESTIONS

1. Can you draw sharp distinctions among the excuses based on supervening events: impossibility, frustration of purpose, and

impracticability? Might more than one of these excuses apply to cases involving post-formation surprise and changed circumstances? Did Justice Traynor draw sharp distinctions between frustration of purpose and impracticability?

2.   What is the role of waiver in *Lloyd v. Murphy*? Note that waiver, a general legal concept of common use across the law of contracts and beyond, is the voluntary relinquishment of a known right. The landlord surrendered its right to enforce the use and subleasing clauses. It presumably had negotiated for these and were for its benefit rather than that of the tenant. The landlord's waiver helps put it in a good light as to the equities of the case, demonstrating flexibility and effort to accommodate. Doctrinally, however, would the elements of impractacibility still have been met absent the waivers?

PROBLEMS: IMPRACTICABILITY

1.   (a) Waterways Vessel Co. ("Owner") agrees to ship Mighty Manufacturer's freight from Miami, Florida to Kuwait City, Kuwait. A terrorist-inspired war unexpectedly breaks out in Kuwait and the terrorists announce that they will try to sink all vessels bound for Kuwait ports. Owner refuses to perform. Is Owner bound or discharged? (b) Suppose instead that the terrorists announce only that they will confiscate all vessels found in Kuwait ports and suppose further that the freight are commercial goods that can be bought and sold on markets throughout the world. Is Owner excused due to impracticability? (c) Finally, suppose that the goods are medical supplies being shipped by the International Red Cross, and they might coincidentally prove extremely valuable in the conflict.

2.   (a) Several months after the nationalization of the Suez Canal, during the international crisis resulting from its seizure, Owner agrees to carry a cargo of Fanny Farmer's wheat on Owner's ship from Galveston, Texas to Bandar Shapur, Iran for a flat rate. The contract does not specify the route, but the voyage would normally be through the Straits of Gibraltar and the Suez Canal, a distance of 10,000 miles. A month later, and several days after the ship departed Galveston, the Suez Canal is closed by an outbreak of hostilities, so that the only route to Bandar Shapur is the longer 13,000-mile voyage around the Cape of Good Hope. May Owner lawfully refuse to complete the voyage unless Farmer pays additional compensation? Consult *American Trading and Prod. Corp. v. Shell Int'l Marine, Ltd.*, 453 F.2d 939 (2d Cir.1972). (b) Suppose instead that, after Owner's vessel entered into the Suez Canal, the blockade was imposed and the vessel could not exit the Canal.

3.   All-Mart Milk Distributor and Elsie Dairy agree that Dairy will sell and Distributor will buy all the latter's requirements of milk in its distribution system, but not less than 200 quarts a day, for one year. Dairy may deliver milk from any source but expects to deliver milk from his own herd. Dairy's herd is destroyed by hoof-and-mouth-disease and Dairy fails to deliver any milk. May Dairy be excused? Consult *Bunge Corp. v. Recker*, 519 F.2d 449 (8th Cir.1975).

4.   Sweet Seller agrees to sell and Buyer Bakery to buy on credit 1,500,000 gallons of molasses "of the usual run from the Domino Sugar refinery in Brooklyn, New York." Domino delivers molasses to others but fails to deliver any to Seller, and Seller fails to deliver any to Buyer. Is Seller's duty to Buyer discharged? Consult *Canadian Indus. Alcohol Co. v. Dunbar Molasses Co.*, 258 N.Y. 194, 179 N.E. 383 (1932).

KEL KIM CORP. V. CENTRAL MARKETS, INC.
519 N.E.2d 295 (N.Y. 1987)

[PER CURIAM.] In early 1980, plaintiff Kel Kim Corporation leased a vacant supermarket in Clifton Park, New York, from defendants. The lease was for an initial term of 10 years with two 5-year renewal options. The understanding of both parties was that plaintiff would use the property as a roller skating rink open to the general public, although the lease did not limit use of the premises to a roller rink.

The lease required Kel Kim to "procure and maintain in full force and effect a public liability insurance policy or policies in a solvent and responsible company or companies . . . of not less than Five Hundred Thousand Dollars . . . to any single person and in the aggregate of not less than One Million Dollars . . . on account of any single accident." Kel Kim obtained the required insurance coverage and for six years operated the facility without incident. In November 1985 its insurance carrier gave notice that the policy would expire on January 6, 1986 and would not be renewed due to uncertainty about the financial condition of the reinsurer, which was then under the management of a court-appointed administrator. Kel Kim transmitted this information to defendants and, it asserts, thereafter made every effort to procure the requisite insurance elsewhere but was unable to do so on account of the liability insurance crisis. Plaintiff ultimately succeeded in obtaining a policy in the aggregate amount of $500,000 effective March 1, 1986 and contends that no insurer would write a policy in excess of that amount on any roller skating rink. As of August 1987, plaintiff procured the requisite coverage.

On January 7, 1986, when plaintiff's initial policy expired and it remained uninsured, defendants sent a notice of default, directing that it cure within 30 days or vacate the premises. Kel Kim and the individual guarantors of the lease then began this declaratory judgment action, urging that they should be excused from compliance with the insurance provision either because performance was impossible or because the inability to procure insurance was within the lease's *force majeure* clause.*

---

*   The clause reads: "If either party to this Lease shall be delayed or prevented from the performance of any obligation through no fault of their own by reason of labor disputes, inability to procure materials, failure of utility service, restrictive governmental laws or regulations, riots, insurrection, war, adverse weather, Acts of God, or other similar causes beyond the control of such party, the performance of such obligation shall be excused for the period of the delay."

Special Term granted defendants' motion for summary judgment, nullified the lease, and directed Kel Kim to vacate the premises. A divided Appellate Division affirmed. [We affirm.]

PH

Generally, once a party to a contract has made a promise, that party must perform or respond in damages for its failure, even when unforeseen circumstances make performance burdensome; until the late nineteenth century even impossibility of performance ordinarily did not provide a defense . . . . While such defenses have been recognized in the common law, they have been applied narrowly, due in part to judicial recognition that the purpose of contract law is to allocate the risks that might affect performance and that performance should be excused only in extreme circumstances . . . . Impossibility excuses a party's performance only when the destruction of the subject matter of the contract or the means of performance makes performance objectively impossible. Moreover, the impossibility must be produced by an unanticipated event that could not have been foreseen or guarded against in the contract . . . .

Applying these principles, we conclude that plaintiff's predicament is not within the embrace of the doctrine of impossibility. Kel Kim's inability to procure and maintain requisite coverage could have been foreseen and guarded against when it specifically undertook that obligation in the lease, and therefore the obligation cannot be excused on this basis.

For much the same underlying reason, contractual *force majeure* clauses—or clauses excusing nonperformance due to circumstances beyond the control of the parties—under the common law provide a similarly narrow defense. Ordinarily, only if the *force majeure* clause specifically includes the event that actually prevents a party's performance will that party be excused. . . . Here, of course, the contractual provision does not specifically include plaintiff's inability to procure and maintain insurance. Nor does this inability fall within the catchall "or other similar causes beyond the control of such party." The principle of interpretation applicable to such clauses is that the general words are not to be given expansive meaning; they are confined to things of the same kind or nature as the particular matters mentioned (*see,* 18 Williston, Contracts § 1968, at 209 [3d ed. 1978]).

We agree with the conclusion reached by the majority below that the events listed in the *force majeure* clause here are different in kind and nature from Kel Kim's inability to procure and maintain public liability insurance. The recited events pertain to a party's ability to conduct day-to-day commercial operations on the premises. While Kel Kim urges that the same may be said of a failure to procure and maintain insurance, such an event is materially different. The requirement that specified amounts of public liability insurance at all times be maintained goes not to frustrated expectations in day-to-day commercial operations on the premises—such as interruptions in the availability of labor, materials and utility services—but to the bargained-for protection of the landlord's unrelated economic interests where the tenant chooses to continue operating a public roller skating rink on the premises . . . . [Affirmed.]

NOTE: TRUMP V. DEUTSCHE BANK

In the first decade of the 2000s, Donald Trump, the billionaire real estate developer elected president of the U.S. in 2016, was in the midst of building what would be Chicago's tallest skyscraper, a combination of a luxury hotel and condominiums. To finance the project, in 2005 Trump had borrowed $640 million from lenders led by Deutsche Bank. But with the downturn in real estate and the financial crisis of 2008, also known as the Great Recession, Trump found himself short on buyers and long on debt.

Trump cited the Great Recession as an excuse to delay making his monthly payments, over $40 million per month. The banks refused to accept the excuse, so Trump—a prolific litigant—went to court. What follows is a short excerpt from Trump's complaint seeking excuse from his contractual obligations. A discussion of the merits of the complaint follows. (We have renumbered the paragraphs of the complaint to facilitate readability and discussion.)

[1]   Pursuant to the Construction Loan Agreement, Deutsche Bank was to serve as the Initial Lender and thereafter as the administrative agent for the consortium of lenders which would take participation interest in the loan made . . . [in the amount of] $640,000,000.00. . .

[2]   As contemplated under the Construction Loan Agreement, Plaintiffs entered into contracts with architects, construction managers, contractors and various other entities, including ultimate purchasers of units who have made down payments in anticipation of the completion of the Project.

[3]   Plaintiffs proceeded diligently to construct and develop the Project, proceeding first with the hotel portion of the Project. . . .

[4]   Notwithstanding the initial success of the sales efforts with respect to the Project, the real estate market in Chicago suffered a severe downturn in parallel with the real estate downward spiral in the United States, slowing sales and sharply decreasing market prices for real estate of all kinds. . . .

[5]   The parties to the Construction Loan Agreement contemplated that the Deutsche Bank Loan would be paid on the Maturity Date . . . However, because of the aforesaid financial crisis, characterized as a "once-in-a-century credit tsunami" by the Federal Reserve Chairman and the fact that, as Deutsche Bank itself characterized it, "the global financial system has been pushed to the brink of collapse," satisfaction of the Deutsche Bank Loan on November 7, 2008 has become impossible to perform.

[6]   Due to the unprecedented financial crisis in the credit markets now prevailing, in part due to acts Deutsche Bank itself participated in, and the

consequent severe downturn in the U.S. real estate markets, including in particular the Chicago real estate market, Plaintiffs properly noticed a force majeure event pursuant to a specially negotiated force majeure clause set forth in the parties' Construction Loan Agreement[.]

[7] . . . The Construction Loan Agreement provided as follows:

Force Majeure Event shall mean any of the following . . . : (i) acts of declared or undeclared war by a foreign enemy or terrorist acts; (ii) riots, civil commotion or insurrection; (iii) casualty or condemnation; (iv) fire, floods, hurricanes or other casualty; (v) earthquakes; (vi) acts of god; (vii) governmental preemption in the case of a national emergency; (viii) unavailability of labor or materials to the extent not within the reasonable control of Borrower or any Trade Contractor; (ix) strikes, lockouts or other labor trouble, (x) the suspension of governmental operations, which suspension affects real estate development in the City of Chicago generally . . . *and (xi) any other event or circumstance not within the reasonable control of Borrower.* . . . (emphasis added).

[8] Deutsche Bank, however, has wrongfully refused to acknowledge the force majeure event and the consequent extension of the maturity date mandated under the plain and unambiguous terms of the Construction Loan Agreement. . . .

[9] As a result of the above wrongful conduct, as set forth in greater detail below, Plaintiffs have been damaged in the form of damage to reputation, lost profits, and increased costs . . . and which continue to accrue but which are believed to be in an amount no less than Three Billion ($3,000,000,000.00) Dollars.

Despite Trump's arguments, there was no mutual mistake between him and the banks that would excuse payment. We have seen that in extreme cases, Acts of God—such as fire, flood, lightening, famine, or deep freezes—may destroy the subject matter of a contract and the parties may be excused from performance. Such Acts of God would also be covered by the force majeure clause in the contract at issue. We have also seen that in extreme cases, a party can be excused when the economics of a deal make performance impracticable. But that excuse is usually limited. As one example, it did not cover a bargain to transport goods like oil from Texas to India, although a wartime blockade was preventing the shippers from taking the cheapest route through the Suez Canal and the alternative cost twice as much. *See American Trading & Prod. Corp. v. Shell Int'l Marine, Ltd.*, 453 F.2d 939 (2nd Cir. 1972).

And so Deutsche Bank and Trump's other lenders stressed the narrowness of these excuses, reflected in the long-standing principle of contract law, *pacta sunt servanda*, "promises must be kept."

Despite the weakness in Trump's legal arguments, he was able to use the litigation as a negotiation tactic, which allowed him to receive accommodation from Deutsche Bank in his repayment schedule. Trump stretched the case out through settlement in July 2010, which gave him some breathing room as the financial storm passed. The common person, who may have been struggling with his or her mortgage during that time, would not have the leverage to receive such accommodation. Partly this is because of a lack of resources, but partly this is also because regular individuals lack the advantages that come from large scale operations. Banks compete vigorously for Trump's billions in business. So the banks had every incentive to settle their dispute with him and allow a change to the terms, even though they were not technically legally required to make those changes.

The law, therefore, is clear. To paraphrase the court in the seventeenth-century case of *Paradine v. Jane*, even Donald Trump must pay his debts.

NOTES AND QUESTIONS

1.   Financial exigency of one party is not normally considered a legal excuse or defense. If Buyer enters into a contract to purchase with Seller, and then Buyer has a sudden financial loss from an investment, that loss does not relieve Buyer of the obligation to continue with the sale. Buyer could decide it is better to breach the contract, but that will entail paying damages, as we will see in the chapter on remedies.

2.   Just as a party's financial circumstance is not a legally-defensible excuse or reason for escaping a contract, neither is a general economic downturn seen as an excuse. The housing market collapse of 2008 did not give homeowners an "out" to stop paying loans, and indeed, as we saw above, legally even Donald Trump did not have such an escape clause.

3.   Sometimes it may seem that a party *should have* a defense or excuse to a contract, even though such a defense is not recognized by law. This was the case when several firms that accepted money in the 2008 government bailout were simultaneously offering executive bonuses. The public, perhaps rightly, responded with outrage and demands that the bonuses not be paid. But without a careful examination of the contracts and analysis of the possible legal claims involved, including perhaps fraud or changed circumstances, an immediate knee-jerk reaction is far from a reasoned legal argument or conclusion. *See* Lawrence A. Cunningham, *A.I.G.'s Bonus Blackmail*, N.Y. TIMES (March 18, 2009).

4.   To get at some of the perceived excesses of executive compensation through contract law, one of the casebook authors has suggested the idea of "clawback provisions," contracts that require the payback of bonuses or other compensation if a company's financial condition worsens or there has been fraud. *See* Miriam A. Cherry & Jarrod Wong, *Clawbacks: Prospective Contract Measures in an Era of Excessive Executive Compensation and Ponzi Schemes*, 94 MINN. L. REV. 368 (2009).

5.   Another similar situation occurred when Citigroup and other financial institutions that were rescued by government bailouts were rebuked by members of Congress for lavish spending on branding rights associated with

The New York Mets team's new stadium. In one sense, the decision to go forward with the contract did seem outlandish, given the financial position of Citigroup and the amount of money spent on bailing out the company.

At the same time, others thought that this was a marketing strategy and that it was not Congress's place to micromanage these types of spending decisions. Amid the political rhetoric, few appreciated the need to read the terms of the contract and figure out whether there really was a right of termination, and if not, what breach of the agreement would have cost Citigroup. In such a situation, examining the language of the contract and thinking through all possible defenses is crucial.

PROBLEMS: SUPERVENING EVENTS

1. Beyonce Knowles, movie star of *Dream Girls* and the hit maker behind the album *I Am Sasha Fierce,* was scheduled to perform a three-night concert in Cairo's main stadium in February. The concert was planned for the better part of a year, in order to promote her album, and is part of Beyonce's worldwide tour. The local promoters have contracted to secure the stadium as well as to secure all local and operational logistics for the tour.

   A. Analyze what happens to the obligations to perform if, at the end of February, Egypt descends into civil war.

   B. Analyze what happens to the obligations to perform if, at the end of February, a cloud of locusts descends onto the main stadium.

2. Three years ago, Riley Myrus was a well-known child star extremely popular with the "tween" viewing audience. Since she has reached the age of majority, however, she has begun "acting out" in part to try to show that she is mature enough for grown-up roles.

   At her direction, her manager hired out the "Good Time Lounge" in California to celebrate Riley's March record release. In advance, her manager had to pay a $50,000 non-refundable charge to the Good Time Lounge. The Good Time Lounge is a bar, but 80% of its profits come from its sale of salvia, an herb smoked like tobacco. Salvia is a mild hallucinogen. Although salvia is legal, everyone is aware that it is on the "watch" list for the Drug Enforcement Agency (DEA).

   A. The day before the party, the DEA issues a pronouncement making salvia illegal. Riley's manager would like the deposit back. What result?

   B. The owners of the Good Time Lounge have noticed an 80% dropoff in their business since salvia was made illegal. They are two years into a four-year lease of the bar, and they would now like to break the lease without penalty if at all possible. Do they have any recourse?

Bride and Groom contracted with Pantagis Renaissance to hold a banquet for a wedding reception for 150 people, to be held between 6 p.m. and 11 p.m. on Saturday, August 3. The total contract price was $10,578, paid in advance. The contract contained a force majeure clause, which stated: "Pantagis will be excused from performance under this contract if it is prevented from doing so by an Act of God (such as flood, fire, hail, windstorm, etc.), or other unforeseen events or circumstances."

On the big day, temperatures rose to 90 degrees and, less than forty-five minutes after the reception began, a power failure occurred in the area. At the time, Bride and Groom were in an upstairs room with the bridal party, and their guests were downstairs being served alcoholic beverages and hors d'oeuvres. The power failure caused all the lights, except emergency lights, to go out and the air conditioning system to shut off. In the circumstances, it was not possible for the band to play or the photographer to take pictures. Is the Pantagis excused? Consult *Facto v. Pantagis*, 915 A.2d 59 (N.J. Super. 2007).

D. CAPACITY: MINORS, MENTAL ILLNESS

What about defenses that—rather than the presence or absence of existing facts or extreme changes in markets, or Acts of God—are needed because of one party's disability or weakness? The infancy doctrine is a way for a minor, in most states meaning a person less than eighteen years old, to disaffirm a contract. The ancient doctrine limits the freedom to contract with minors. It reflects the idea that allowing someone to exercise freedom of contract depends on an exercise of maturity, judgment and experience— traits not every child can be presumed to possess. A similar somewhat paternalistic impulse governs contracts made by mentally ill people (defined in more detail below), who may likewise elect to disaffirm otherwise valid contracts.

The infancy doctrine also reflects a general principle that parents bear considerable, albeit not absolute, responsibility for their minor children. The public policy impulse to protect children is paramount, so that it applies even when it imposes hardship on another party to a minor's contract. Sell a car on credit to a minor who defaults, and the law will not help you recover. The law's position helps protect minors against adults who may intentionally seek to exploit them, although as a practical result it means that minors have the right to disaffirm even the fairest contracts made with the most scrupulous adults.

Judges have for centuries been prepared to intervene on behalf of minors and the mentally ill who wish to disaffirm a contract. A minor or mentally ill person may, on the other hand, choose to go forward with the contract and bind their counterparty. The election rests with the party who labors under a disability, whether of youth or of mental illness.

After looking at a deal involving the sale of a car, we turn to the case of Craig Traylor, the American actor known for his role as best friend of the title character in the hit television show *Malcolm in the Middle*. Some of the more well-known cases dealing with the infancy doctrine have arisen around litigation brought by or about deals involving child performers. We then turn to a classic case, *Ortelere*, that presents vexing questions about mental illness and the standard for disaffirming a contract.

RESTATEMENT (SECOND) OF CONTRACTS, SECTION 14

§ 14.   *Infants*. Unless a statute provides otherwise, a natural person has the capacity to incur only voidable contractual duties until the beginning of the day before the person's eighteenth birthday.

HALBMAN V. LEMKE
298 N.W.2d 562 (Wis. 1980)

CALLOW, J. . . .

On or about July 13, 1973, James Halbman, Jr. (Halbman), a minor, entered into an agreement with Michael Lemke (Lemke) whereby Lemke agreed to sell Halbman a 1968 Oldsmobile for the sum of $1,250. Lemke was the manager of L & M Standard Station in Greenfield, Wisconsin, and Halbman was an employe at L & M. . . . Halbman paid Lemke $1,000 cash and took possession of the car. Arrangements were made for Halbman to pay $25 per week until the balance was paid, at which time title would be transferred. About five weeks after the purchase agreement, and after Halbman had paid a total of $1,100 of the purchase price, a connecting rod on the vehicle's engine broke. Lemke, while denying any obligation, offered to assist Halbman in installing a used engine in the vehicle if Halbman, at his expense, could secure one. Halbman declined the offer and in September took the vehicle to a garage where it was repaired at a cost of $637.40. Halbman did not pay the repair bill.

In October of 1973 Lemke endorsed the vehicle's title over to Halbman, although the full purchase price had not been paid by Halbman, in an effort to avoid any liability for the operation, maintenance, or use of the vehicle. On October 15, 1973, Halbman returned the title to Lemke by letter which disaffirmed the purchase contract and demanded the return of all money theretofore paid by Halbman. Lemke did not return the money . . . .

The repair bill remained unpaid, and the vehicle remained in the garage where the repairs had been made. In the spring of 1974, in satisfaction of a garageman's lien for the outstanding amount, the garage elected to remove the vehicle's engine and transmission and then towed the vehicle to the residence of James Halbman, Sr., the father of the plaintiff minor. Lemke was asked several times to remove the vehicle from the senior Halbman's home, but he declined to do so, claiming he was under no legal obligation to remove it. During the period when the vehicle was at the garage and then subsequently at the home of the plaintiff's father, it was subjected to vandalism, making it unsalvageable.

Halbman [sued for] return of the $1,100 he had paid toward the purchase of the vehicle [and] Lemke counterclaimed for $150, the amount still owing on the contract [and also claimed restitution for depreciation of the car]. . . . [T]he trial court granted judgment [to] Halbman, concluding that when a minor disaffirms a contract for the purchase of an item, he need only offer to return the property remaining in his hands without making restitution for any use or depreciation. . . . [T]he court also allowed interest to the plaintiff dating from the disaffirmance of the contract. . . . The appellate court affirmed . . . .

Neither party challenges the absolute right of a minor to disaffirm a contract for the purchase of items which are not necessities. That right, variously known as the doctrine of incapacity or the "infancy doctrine," is one of the oldest and most venerable of our common law traditions. . . . [I]ts purpose is the protection of minors from foolishly squandering their wealth through improvident contracts with crafty adults who would take advantage of them in the marketplace. . . . Thus . . . a contract of a minor for items which are not necessities is void or voidable at the minor's option. . . .

Once there has been a disaffirmance, however, . . . problems arise regarding the rights and responsibilities of the parties relative to the disposition of the consideration exchanged on the contract. As a general rule a minor who disaffirms a contract is entitled to recover all consideration he has conferred incident to the transaction. . . . In return the minor is expected to restore as much of the consideration as, at the time of disaffirmance, remains in the minor's possession. . . . The minor's right to disaffirm is not contingent upon the return of the property, however, as disaffirmance is permitted even where such return cannot be made. . . . Olson v. Veum, 197 Wis. 342, 345, 222 N.W. 233 (1928).

The return of property remaining in the hands of the minor is not the issue presented here. In this case we have a situation where the property cannot be returned to the vendor in its entirety because it has been damaged and therefore diminished in value, and the vendor seeks to recover the depreciation. Although this court has been cognizant of this issue on previous occasions, we have not heretofore resolved it. . . .

The law regarding the . . . consideration exchanged on a disaffirmed contract is characterized by confusion, inconsistency, and a general lack of uniformity as jurisdictions attempt to reach a fair application of the infancy doctrine in today's marketplace. See Walter D. Navin, Jr., The Contracts of Minors Viewed from the Perspective of Fair Exchange, 50 N.C.L.Rev.

517 (1972). . . . That both parties rely on this court's decision in Olson v. Veum, supra, is symptomatic of the problem.

In Olson a minor, with his brother, an adult, purchased farm implements and materials, paying by signing notes payable at a future date. Prior to the maturity of the first note, the brothers ceased their joint farming business, and the minor abandoned his interest in the material purchased by leaving it with his brother. The vendor initiated an action against the minor to recover on the note, and the minor (who had by then reached majority) disaffirmed. . . . [We held] that the contract of a minor for the purchase of items which are not necessities may be disaffirmed even when the minor cannot make restitution. Lemke calls our attention to the following language in that decision:

> [There is a] substantial distinction between a mere denial by an infant of contract liability where the other party is seeking to enforce it and those cases where he who was the minor not only disaffirms such contract but seeks the aid of the court to restore to him that with which he has parted at the making of the contract. In the one case he is using his infancy merely as a shield, in the other also as a sword. . . .

From this Lemke infers that when a minor, as a plaintiff, seeks to disaffirm a contract and recover his consideration, different rules should apply than if the minor is defending against an action on the contract by the other party. . . .

Additionally, Lemke [draws on the dissenting opinion in Olson to argue] that a disaffirming minor's obligation to make restitution turns upon his ability to do so [and that obligations are excused only when] restitution is not possible. Here Lemke holds Halbman's $1,100, and accordingly there is no question as to Halbman's ability to make restitution.

Halbman argues in response that, while the "sword-shield" dichotomy may apply where the minor has misrepresented his age to induce the contract, that did not occur here and he may avoid the contract without making restitution notwithstanding his ability to do so.

The principal problem is the use of the word "restitution" in Olson. A minor, as we have stated, is under an enforceable duty to return to the vendor, upon disaffirmance, as much of the consideration as remains in his possession. When the contract is disaffirmed, title to that part of the purchased property which is retained by the minor revests in the vendor; it no longer belongs to the minor. . . . The rationale for the rule is plain: a minor who disaffirms a purchase and recovers his purchase price should not also be permitted to profit by retaining the property purchased. The infancy doctrine is designed to protect the minor, sometimes at the expense of an innocent vendor, but it is not to be used to bilk merchants out of property as well as proceeds of the sale. Consequently, it is clear that, when the minor no longer possesses the property which was the subject matter of the contract, the rule requiring the return of property does not apply.[1] The minor will not be required to give up what he does not have. . . . Olson does no more than set forth the foregoing rationale and that the word "restitution" as it is used in that opinion is limited to the return of the property to the vendor. . . .

Here Lemke seeks restitution of the value of the depreciation by virtue of the damage to the vehicle prior to disaffirmance. Such a recovery would require Halbman to return more than that remaining in his possession. It seeks compensatory value for that which he cannot return. Where there is misrepresentation by a minor or willful destruction of property, the vendor may be able to recover damages in tort. . . . But absent these factors, as in the present case, we believe that to require a disaffirming minor to make restitution for diminished value is, in effect, to bind the minor to a part of the obligation which by law he is privileged to avoid.' . . .

The cases upon which the petitioner relies for the proposition that a disaffirming minor must make restitution for loss and depreciation . . . would at some point force the minor to bear the cost of the very improvidence from which the infancy doctrine is supposed to protect him, [so] we cannot follow them.

. . . [M]odifications of the rules governing the capacity of infants to contract are best left to the legislature. Until such changes are forthcoming, however, we hold that, absent misrepresentation or tortious damage to the property, a minor who disaffirms a contract for the purchase of an item which is not a necessity may recover his purchase price without liability for use, depreciation, damage, or other diminution in value. . . . We believe this result is consistent with the purpose of the infancy doctrine. The decision of the court of appeals is affirmed. ✳

BERG v. TRAYLOR
148 Cal.App.4th 809 (Cal.App.2 Dist. 2007)

TODD, J.J.

On January 18, 1999, Berg entered into a two-page "Artist's Manager's Agreement" (agreement) with . . . Craig . . . who was then 10 years old [and Craig's mother, Meshiel]. Meshiel signed the agreement and wrote Craig's

---

[1]   Although we are not presented with the question here, we recognize there is considerable disagreement among the authorities on whether a minor who disposes of the property should be made to restore the vendor with something in its stead. The general rule appears to limit the minor's responsibility for restoration to specie only. . . . [Other approaches include the "status quo" approach which] requires the minor to restore the precontract status quo, even if it means returning proceeds or other value; [one] requiring the minor to restore only the property remaining in the hands of the minor; [and the] benefits theory which requires the disaffirming minor to pay for the contract to the extent he benefited from it. . . .

name on the signature page where he was designated "Artist." Craig did not sign the agreement. Pursuant to the agreement, Berg was to act as Craig's exclusive personal manager in exchange for a commission of 15 percent of all gross monies or other consideration paid to him as an artist during the three-year term of the agreement, as well as income from merchandising or promotional efforts or offers of employment made during the term of the agreement, regardless of when Craig received such monies. The agreement expressly provided that any action Craig "may take in the future pertaining to disaffirmance of this agreement, whether successful or not," would not affect Meshiel's liability for any commissions due Berg. The agreement also provided that any disputes concerning payment or interpretation of the agreement would be determined by arbitration in accordance with the rules of Judicial Arbitration and Mediation Services, Inc. (JAMS).

. . . On or about June 13, 2001, Craig obtained a recurring acting role on the Fox Television Network show "Malcolm in the Middle" (show). On September 11, 2001, four months prior to the expiration of the agreement, Meshiel sent a certified letter to Berg stating that while she and Craig appreciated her advice and guidance, they no longer needed her management services and could no longer afford to pay Berg her 15 percent commission because they owed a "huge amount" of taxes. On September 28, 2001, Berg responded, informing appellants that they were in breach of the agreement. . . .

. . . The arbitration hearing commenced on February 7, 2005. Because appellants had failed to pay their share of the arbitration fees, Berg did not anticipate their appearance and did not retain a court reporter. . . . Meshiel and Craig's counsel failed to appear at the hearing . . . Craig did not appear. According to Meshiel, the arbitrator denied her request for a two-week continuance.

. . . On February 11, 2005, the arbitrator issued his award, which was served on the parties on February 14, 2005. Noting that Craig had not appeared at the hearing "despite personal service of summons and notice from JAMS," the arbitrator stated that the award was "issued against him through prove-up and default as provided for in the JAMS Rules" incorporated by reference. . . . The arbitrator awarded Berg commissions and interest of $154,714.15, repayment of personal loans and interest of $5,094, and attorney fees and costs of $13,762. He also awarded Berg $405,000 "for future earnings projected on a minimum of 6 years for national syndication earnings," and stated that this part of the award would "vest and become final, as monies earned after February 7, 2005, become due and payable." . . .

[Meshiel and Craig had a series of attorneys work for them]. On August 8, 2005, the Law Offices of Robert N. Pafundi substituted in as appellants' fourth counsel. The same day, appellants filed a "Notice of Disaffirmance of Arbitration Award by Minor," which stated that in addition to his disaffirmance of the agreement on September 11, 2001, Craig was also disaffirming the arbitration award and all other proceedings and orders arising out of the parties' dispute, including the stipulation to submit the action to binding arbitration . . .

On August 18, 2005, appellants filed a petition/response seeking to vacate the arbitration award. The petition to vacate was based primarily on the grounds that Craig had exercised his statutory right to disaffirm both the original agreement with Berg and the arbitration award and that Berg was illegally practicing as an unlicensed talent agent. Following a hearing, the trial court took the matter under submission and the next day issued an order denying the petition to vacate the arbitration award as untimely and granting Berg's petition to confirm the award. Thereafter, the trial court entered a judgment in favor of Berg consistent with the arbitrator's award. [This appeal followed].

Simply stated, one who provides a minor with goods and services does so at her own risk. . . . The agreement here expressly contemplated this risk, requiring that Meshiel remain obligated for commissions due under the agreement regardless of whether Craig disaffirmed the agreement. Thus, we have no difficulty in reaching the conclusion that Craig is permitted to and did disaffirm the agreement and any obligations stemming therefrom, while Meshiel remains liable under the agreement and resulting judgment. Where our difficulty lies is in understanding how counsel, the arbitrator and the trial court repeatedly and systematically ignored Craig's interests in this matter. From the time Meshiel signed the agreement, her interests were not aligned with Craig's. That no one— counsel, the arbitrator or the trial court—recognized this conflict and sought appointment of a guardian ad litem for Craig is nothing short of stunning. It is the court's responsibility to protect the rights of a minor who is a litigant in court. . . .

"As a general proposition, parental consent is required for the provision of services to minors for the simple reason that minors may disaffirm their own contracts to acquire such services." (*Ballard v. Anderson* (1971) 4 Cal.3d 873, 878, 95 Cal.Rptr. 1, 484 P.2d 1345.) According to Family Code section 6700, "a minor may make a contract in the same manner as an adult, subject to the power of disaffirmance" provided by Family Code section 6710. In turn, Family Code section 6710 states: "Except as otherwise provided by statute, a contract of a minor may be disaffirmed by the minor before majority or within a reasonable time afterwards or, in case of the minor's death within that period, by the minor's heirs or personal representative." Sound policy considerations support this provision: "The law shields minors from their lack of judgment and experience and under certain conditions vests in them the right to disaffirm their contracts. Although in many instances such disaffirmance may be a hardship upon those who deal with an infant, the right to avoid his contracts is conferred by law upon a minor 'for his protection against his own improvidence and the designs of others.' It is the policy of the law to protect a minor against himself and his indiscretions and immaturity as well as against the machinations of other people and to discourage adults from contracting with an infant. Any loss occasioned by the disaffirmance of a minor's contract might have been avoided by declining to enter into the contract." (*Niemann v. Deverich* (1950) 98 Cal.App.2d 787, 793, 221 P.2d 178; accord *Burnand v. Irigoyen* (1947) 30 Cal.2d 861, 866, 186 P.2d 417.)

Berg offers two reasons why the plain language of Family Code section 6710 is inapplicable, neither of which we find persuasive. First, she argues that a minor may not disaffirm an agreement signed by a parent. She relies on two cases to support her position, both of which are inapposite because they address discrete public policy concerns not at issue here. In *Doyle v. Giuliucci* (1965) 62 Cal.2d 606, 43 Cal.Rptr. 697, 401 P.2d 1, the court rejected a minor's attempt to disaffirm a healthcare contract containing an arbitration provision signed by the minor's father. The court explained that a minor's statutory power to disaffirm a contract "does not apply to contracts between adults and is therefore not controlling on the question of a parent's power to bind his child to arbitrate by entering into a contract of which the child is a third party beneficiary." (*Id.* at p. 609, 43 Cal.Rptr. 697, 401 P.2d 1.)

The court found "compelling reasons" for recognizing that "the power to enter into a contract for medical care that binds the child to arbitrate any dispute arising thereunder is implicit in a parent's right and duty to provide for the care of his child." (*Id.* at p. 610, 43 Cal.Rptr. 697, 401 P.2d 1; see also *Pietrelli v. Peacock* (1993) 13 Cal.App.4th 943, 947, 16 Cal.Rptr.2d 688 [a parent's power to bind a minor child to arbitration of claims arising from the minor's health care contract is implied from the parent's duties and rights as the child's guardian].) Because it was unlikely that medical groups would contract directly with minors who could disaffirm their own contracts to pay for medical services, minors could therefore only be assured of the benefits of a group medical service if their parents contracted on their behalf. (*Ibid.*) Moreover, the arbitration provision did not unreasonably restrict a minor's rights, "for it does no more than specify a forum for the settlement of disputes." (*Doyle v. Giuliucci, supra,* at p. 610, 43 Cal.Rptr. 697, 401 P.2d 1.)

Here, in contrast, Craig was not a third party beneficiary of the agreement signed by his mother, but a principal.* Moreover, there are no compelling reasons justifying binding Craig to the agreement. An agreement for personal management services does not implicate a parent's

---

* [Third party beneficiary doctrine is taken up in the last chapter of this book. It addresses when non-parties to a contract may enforce it, based upon whether the parties so intended.]

fundamental duty to provide for the care and health of a child. Further, because there is a statutory procedure governing contracts in which minors agree to render artistic or creative services, there is no danger that talent managers will decline to contract with minors absent their parents contracting on their behalf. (See Fam.Code, §§ 6750, 6751, subd. (a).) Finally, the agreement here did not merely require Craig to arbitrate his disputes, but created significant obligations on his part, notably, the payment of substantial monies to Berg.

In the other case relied on by Berg, *Hohe v. San Diego Unified Sch. Dist.* (1990) 224 Cal.App.3d 1559, 274 Cal.Rptr. 647, the court rejected a minor's attempt to disaffirm a liability release signed by her father relating to the minor's participation in a school program. Relying on *Doyle,* the *Hohe* court reasoned that a parent may contract on behalf of his or her children and that former Civil Code section 35 (now Family Code section 6710) was not intended to affect contracts entered into by adults on behalf of their children. (*Hohe v. San Diego Unified Sch. Dist., supra,* at p. 1565, 274 Cal.Rptr. 647.) It has become "well established that a parent may execute a release on behalf of his or her child." (*Aaris v. Las Virgenes Unified School Dist.* (1998) 64 Cal.App.4th 1112, 1120, 75 Cal.Rptr.2d 801.) Here, in contrast, Meshiel did not sign an agreement on Craig's behalf that merely obligated him to release another party from liability. Thus, the state's public policy to enforce releases signed by parents on behalf of their children is not implicated. There is no public policy barring a minor from disaffirming a contract that imposes significant affirmative responsibilities on him.

Second, Berg argues that Craig cannot disaffirm the agreement because it was for his and his family's necessities. Family Code section 6712 provides that a valid contract cannot be disaffirmed by a minor if all of the following requirements are met: the contract is to pay the reasonable value of things necessary for the support of the minor or the minor's family, the things have actually been furnished to the minor or the minor's family, and the contract is entered into by the minor when not under the care of a parent or guardian able to provide for the minor or the minor's family. These requirements are not met here.

The agreement was not a contract to pay for the necessities of life for Craig or his family. While such necessities have been held to include payment for lodging (*Burnand v. Irigoyen, supra,* 30 Cal.2d at pp. 867–868, 186 P.2d 417) and even payment of attorneys' fees (*Leonard v. Alexander* (1942) 50 Cal.App.2d 385, 387–389, 122 P.2d 984), we cannot conclude that a contract to secure personal management services for the purpose of advancing Craig's acting career constitutes payment for the type of necessity contemplated by Family Code section 6712. Nor is there any evidence that Meshiel was unable to provide for the family in 1999 at the time of the agreement. As such, Family Code section 6712 does not bar the minor's disaffirmance of the contract.

No specific language is required to communicate an intent to disaffirm. "A contract (or conveyance) of a minor may be avoided by any act or declaration disclosing an unequivocal intent to repudiate its binding force and effect." (*Spencer v. Collins* (1909) 156 Cal. 298, 303, 104 P. 320.) Express notice to the other party is unnecessary. (*Celli v. Sports Car Club of America, Inc.* (1972) 29 Cal.App.3d 511, 517, 105 Cal.Rptr. 904.) We find that the "Notice of Disaffirmance of Arbitration Award by Minor" filed on August 8, 2005 was sufficient to constitute a disaffirmance of the agreement by Craig. Although the notice assumed that Meshiel's September 11, 2001 letter to Berg stating that Meshiel and Craig were no longer going to honor their obligations under the agreement acted as a prior disaffirmance of the agreement, the notice further stated that Craig "disaffirms all other documents filed under his name or affecting him as a minor in this litigation. . . ." This language adequately conveyed Craig's intent to repudiate the binding force and effect of the agreement. . . .

We find that Craig was entitled to and did disaffirm the agreement which, among other things, required him to arbitrate his disputes with Berg. On this basis alone, therefore, the judgment confirming the arbitration award must be reversed. . . . Although it is unnecessary to our disposition, we further find that Craig was entitled to and did disaffirm the arbitration award because he was never represented by an appointed guardian ad litem.

. . . Appellants do not generally distinguish their arguments between mother and son, apparently assuming that if Craig disaffirms the agreement and judgment, Meshiel would be permitted to escape liability as well. But a disaffirmance of an agreement by a minor does not operate to terminate the contractual obligations of the parent who signed the agreement. . . The agreement Meshiel signed provided that Craig's disaffirmance would not serve to void or avoid Meshiel's obligations under the agreement and that Meshiel remained liable for commissions due Berg regardless of Craig's disaffirmance. Accordingly, we find no basis for Meshiel to avoid her independent obligations under the agreement.

The judgment is reversed as to Craig and affirmed as to Meshiel. . . .

NOTES AND QUESTIONS

1.   The common law that lets a minor disaffirm a contract also allows for exceptions to the rule. A minor might elect a judicial proceeding to become emancipated, which would allow for binding contracts. Some states allow minors to make binding contracts for "necessaries," although how "necessaries" are defined may depend on the minor's parents and what they are able to provide. For example, most people would think that an apartment rental would

be part of "necessaries," but some courts have held otherwise, because a parent may be offering free shelter. *See Webster Street Partnership Ltd. v. Sheridan*, 368 N.W.2d 439 (Neb. 1985). A contract with an attorney, however, may be seen as "necessaries," if needed to enforce a minor's rights.

2.   Like other common law claims and defenses, statutes may modify or change the infancy defense. For example, many college students take out educational loans even though they are minors. According to Section 484A(b)(2) of the Higher Education Act of 1965 (20 U.S.C. 1091a(b)(2)), the defense of infancy is not valid against the collection of a student loan.

3.   Many courts seem to agree with both the judicial ruling in *Lemke* and wish for a legislative solution that would abolish the escape hatch for infants. What are your thoughts? Does the development of enhanced communication technology and the Internet influence your position? Consider the following commentary.

CHERYL B. PRESTON, *CYBERINFANTS*
39 PEPP. L. REV. 225 (2012)

The past two decades have seen life in America dramatically altered by the digital revolution. Minors, including both small children and mature adolescents, are increasingly involved in online activities that generate profits for online service providers (OSPs). According to recent studies, approximately ninety-five percent of teens ages twelve to seventeen were online in 2011, seventy percent go online daily, and nearly fifty percent go online several times a day. Eighty percent of those online teens used social network sites. Providers of such "free" web services do so intending to recover their costs and make significant profit from advertisements and other monetized features. Economic incentives drive OSPs to increase their teen user base, as well as their adult user base. In addition, because of youths' widespread online presence, combined with increasing access to money, "children comprise a significant segment of online consumers, a segment that is rapidly enlarging." According to a 2010 Pew Research Center Internet study, "48% of wired teens have bought things online like books, clothing or music." The most popular sites for minors include eBay, Amazon, Barnes & Noble, and MySpace, and almost three million minors make purchases online every month.

OSPs almost universally present their potential online customer or user with an adhesive contract containing extensive administrative terms. These ongoing licensing agreements—intended to govern use of e-mail, online games, and other forms of intellectual property services, as well as commitments made in creating an account for purchasing goods—are typically identified as "Terms of Service," "Terms of Use," "Conditions of Use," "Terms and Conditions," "End User License Agreements," and so forth (hereinafter collectively and singularly "TOS"). These contracts may be characterized as "clickwrap," "browsewrap," or other "wrap" contracts, referring to the method of formation. . . . [M]inors can frequently void TOS under the traditional infancy doctrine.

The infancy doctrine, although subject to some narrow defenses, permits avoidance of any contract entered into by a minor. Avoidance is permitted throughout minority and for a reasonable time after reaching adulthood, so long as the minor has not ratified the contract as an adult. Disaffirmance does require that the minor return any benefit received as consideration on the contract, to the extent it is still in the minor's possession. In most jurisdictions, the minor is also entitled to restitution of the consideration already conferred on the adult pursuant to the contract. In a dozen states, the adult has a right to offset the depreciation of the consideration from the amount paid back to the minor. But in most states, the minor is entitled to repayment without deduction.

Online markets are increasingly dependent on minors. With the threat of the infancy doctrine, one would think merchants would be extremely reluctant to deal with minors for any transaction that is not de minimus or for food, clothing, or shelter (and even then, most minors providing these goods for themselves are not providing "necessities"). And yet, the lure of profits appears to have overcome the fear of legal disaffirmance, at least so far. But the infancy doctrine cannot be dismissed as an insignificant risk. Once minors, and their parents, catch on to the fact that the legislatures of almost every state and the vast majority of courts still strictly affirm the doctrine, the impact on businesses targeted largely at minors may be severe.

. . . [T]he emergence of a significant market relying on unemancipated teens to consume purely discretionary goods and services, and various other changes in the way we think about teens, may warrant a serious reassessment of the infancy doctrine and its existing exceptions. The doctrine may be unwarranted when asserted by a minor to evade the payment of a standard, publicized price in a part of the market that is truly competitive and for which information is readily available. But this does not mean the doctrine need be thrown out entirely. Any reassessment must be thoughtful and limited unless and until we have current evidence establishing that minors no longer need some or all of the doctrine's protections or that the doctrine is being regularly abused. Such a reassessment must be sensitive to context and consider whether changes in the infancy doctrine should be undertaken first with brick-and-mortar transactions or TOS, and whether changes should be experimental and incremental or encompassing.

At this point, the infancy doctrine is the law, and it is one mechanism for encouraging online businesses to [rein] in their greed both in targeting children and in catching all users with hidden, overreaching contract terms.

It is often said that having two parties of the requisite capacity is one of the essential elements of a contract. But another way of putting it is that the lack of such capacity can render a contract voidable, under an affirmative defense. Consider in the ensuing case the defense that rests on mental state. Recall, again, that defenses are the unusual case, the exception to the general rule of contract enforceability and damages.

RESTATEMENT (SECOND) OF CONTRACTS, SECTION 15

§ 15. *Mental Illness or Defect.*

(1) A person incurs only voidable contractual duties by entering into a transaction if by reason of mental illness or defect [a] He is unable to understand in a reasonable manner the nature and consequences of the transaction or [b] He is unable to act in a reasonable manner in relation to the transaction and the other party has reason to know of his condition.

(2) Where the contract is made on fair terms and the other party is without knowledge of the mental illness or defect, the power of avoidance under Subsection (1) terminates to the extent that the contract has been so performed in whole or in part or the circumstances have so changed that avoidance would be unjust. In such a case a court may grant relief as justice requires.

ORTELERE V. TEACHERS' RETIREMENT BOARD
25 N.Y.2d 196 (N.Y. 1969)

BREITEL, J.J.

. . . The husband and executor of Grace W. Ortelere, [a] deceased New York City schoolteacher, sues to set aside her application for retirement without option, in the event of her death. It is alleged that Mrs. Ortelere, on February 11, 1965, two months before her death from natural causes, was not mentally competent to execute a retirement application. By this application, effective the next day, she elected the maximum retirement allowance . . . She thus revoked her earlier election of benefits under which she named her husband a beneficiary of the unexhausted reserve upon her death. Selection of the maximum allowance extinguished all interests upon her death.

Following a nonjury trial in Supreme Court, it was held that Grace Ortelere had been mentally incompetent at the time of her February 11 application, thus rendering it "null and void and of no legal effect." The Appellate Division, by a divided court, reversed the judgment of the

Supreme Court and held that, as a matter of law, there was insufficient proof of mental incompetency as to this transaction . . . .

Mrs. Ortelere's mental illness [is] undisputed. It is not seriously disputable, however, that she had complete cognitive judgment or awareness when she made her selection. A modern understanding of mental illness, however, suggests that incapacity to contract or exercise contractual rights may exist, because of volitional and affective impediments or disruptions in the personality, despite the intellectual or cognitive ability to understand. It will be recognized as the civil law parallel to the question of criminal responsibility which has been the recent concern of so many and has resulted in statutory and decisional changes in the criminal law . . . .

Mrs. Ortelere, an elementary schoolteacher since 1924, suffered a "nervous breakdown" in March, 1964 and went on a leave of absence expiring February 5, 1965. She was then 60 years old and had been happily married for 38 years. On July 1, 1964 she came under the care of Dr. D'Angelo, a psychiatrist, who diagnosed her breakdown as involutional psychosis, melancholia type. Dr. D'Angelo prescribed, and for about six weeks decedent underwent, tranquilizer and shock therapy. Although moderately successful, the therapy was not continued since it was suspected that she also suffered from cerebral arteriosclerosis, an ailment later confirmed. However, the psychiatrist continued to see her at monthly intervals until March, 1965. On March 28, 1965 she was hospitalized after collapsing at home from an aneurysm. She died two days later; the cause of death was "Cerebral thrombosis due to H(ypertensive) H(eart) D(isease)."

As a teacher she had been a member of the Teachers' Retirement System of the City of New York . . . . This entitled her to certain annuity and pension rights, preretirement death benefits, and empowered her to exercise various options concerning the payment of her retirement allowance.

Some years before, on June 28, 1958, she had executed a "Selection of Benefits under Option One" naming her husband as beneficiary of the unexhausted reserve. Under this option upon retirement her allowance would be less by way of periodic retirement allowances, but if she died before receipt of her full reserve the balance of the reserve would be payable to her husband. On June 16, 1960, two years later, she had designated her husband as beneficiary of her service death benefits in the event of her death prior to retirement.

Then on February 11, 1965, when her leave of absence had just expired and she was still under treatment, she executed a retirement application, the one here involved, selecting the maximum retirement allowance payable during her lifetime with nothing payable on or after death. She also, at this time, borrowed from the system the maximum cash withdrawal permitted, namely, $8,760. Three days earlier she had written the board, stating that she intended to retire on February 12 or 15 or as soon as she received "the information I need in order to decide whether to take an option or maximum allowance." She then listed eight specific questions, reflecting great understanding of the retirement system, concerning the various alternatives available.

An extremely detailed reply was sent, by letter of February 15, 1965, although by that date it was technically impossible for her to change her selection. However, the board's chief clerk, before whom Mrs. Ortelere executed the application, testified that the questions were "answered verbally by me on February 11th." Her retirement reserve totaled $62,165 (after deducting the $8,760 withdrawal), and the difference between electing the maximum retirement allowance (no option) and the allowance under "option one" was $901 per year or $75 per month. That is, had the teacher selected "option one" she would have received an annual allowance of $4,494 or $375 per month, while if no option had been selected she would have received an annual allowance of $5,395 or $450 per month. Had she not withdrawn the cash the annual figures would be $5,247 and $6,148 respectively.

Following her taking a leave of absence for her condition, Mrs. Ortelere had become very depressed and was unable to care for herself. As a result her husband gave up his electrician's job, in which he earned $222 per week, to stay home and take care of her on a full-time basis. She left their home only when he accompanied her. Although he took her to the Retirement Board on February 11, 1965, he did not know why she went, and did not question her for fear "she'd start crying hysterically that I was scolding her. That's the way she was. And I wouldn't upset her."

The Orteleres were in quite modest circumstances. They owned their own home, valued at $20,000, and had $8,000 in a savings account. They also owned some farm land worth about $5,000. Under these circumstances, as revealed in this record, retirement for both of the Orteleres or the survivor of them had to be provided, as a practical matter, largely out of Mrs. Ortelere's retirement benefits.

According to Dr. D'Angelo, the psychiatrist who treated her, Mrs. Ortelere never improved enough to "warrant my sending her back (to teaching)." A physician for the Board of Education examined her on February 2, 1965 to determine her fitness to return to teaching. Although not a psychiatrist but rather a specialist in internal medicine, this physician "judged that she had apparently recovered from the depression" and that she appeared rational. However, before allowing her to return to teaching, a report was requested from Dr. D'Angelo concerning her condition. It is notable that the Medical Division of the Board of Education on February 24, 1965 requested that Mrs. Ortelere report to the board's "panel psychiatrist" on March 11, 1965.

Dr. D'Angelo stated "(a)t no time since she was under my care was she ever mentally competent"; that "(m)entally she couldn't make a decision of any kind, actually, of any kind, small or large." He also described how involutional melancholia affects the judgment process:

> They can't think rationally, no matter what the situation is. They will even tell you, 'I used to be able to think of anything and make any decision. Now,' they say, 'even getting up, I don't know whether I should get up or whether I should stay in bed.' Or, 'I don't even know how to make a slice of toast any more.' Everything is impossible to decide, and everything is too great an effort to even think of doing. They just don't have the effort, actually, because their nervous breakdown drains them of all their physical energies.

> . . . The well-established rule is that contracts of a mentally incompetent person who has not been adjudicated insane are voidable. . . . Traditionally, in this State and elsewhere, contractual mental capacity has been measured by what is largely a cognitive test . . . . Under this standard the "inquiry" is whether the mind was "so affected as to render him wholly and absolutely incompetent to comprehend and understand the nature of the transaction" (Aldrich v. Bailey, Supra, at p. 89, 30 N.E. at p. 265). . . . Conversely, it is also well recognized that contractual ability would be affected by insane delusions intimately related to the particular transaction . . . .

These traditional standards governing competency to contract were formulated when psychiatric knowledge was quite primitive. They fail to account for one who by reason of mental illness is unable to control his conduct even though his cognitive ability seems unimpaired. . . . This is no longer the prevailing view . . . .

Of course, the greatest movement in revamping legal notions of mental responsibility has occurred in the criminal law. . . . While the policy considerations for the criminal law and the civil law are different, both share in common the premise that policy considerations must be based on a sound understanding of the human mind and, therefore, its illnesses.

Hence, because the cognitive rules are, for the most part, too restrictive and rest on a false factual basis they must be re-examined. Once it is understood that, accepting plaintiff's proof, Mrs. Ortelere was psychotic and because of that psychosis could have been incapable of making a voluntary selection of her retirement system benefits, there is an issue that a modern jurisprudence should not exclude, merely because her mind could pass a 'cognition' test based on nineteenth century psychology.

There has also been some movement on the civil law side to achieve a modern posture. . . . It is quite significant that Restatement, 2d, Contracts, states the modern rule on competency to contract. This is in evident recognition, and the Reporter's Notes support this inference, that, regardless of how the cases formulated their reasoning, the old cognitive test no longer explains the results. Thus, the new Restatement section reads: "(1) A person incurs only voidable contractual duties by entering into a transaction if by reason of mental illness or defect . . . (b) he is unable to act in a reasonable manner in relation to the transaction and the other party has reason to know of his condition." (Restatement, 2d, Contracts (T.D. No. 1, April 13, 1964), § 18C.) . . .

The avoidance of duties under an agreement entered into by those who have done so by reason of mental illness, but who have understanding, depends on balancing competing policy considerations. There must be stability in contractual relations and protection of the expectations of parties who bargain in good faith. On the other hand, it is also desirable to protect persons who may understand the nature of the transaction but who, due to mental illness, cannot control their conduct. Hence, there should be relief only if the other party knew or was put on notice as to the contractor's mental illness. Thus, the Restatement provision for avoidance contemplates that "the other party has reason to know" of the mental illness (Id.).

When, however, the other party is without knowledge of the contractor's mental illness and the agreement is made on fair terms, the proposed Restatement rule is: "The power of avoidance under subsection (1) terminates to the extent that the contract has been so performed in whole or in part or the circumstances have so changed that avoidance would be inequitable. In such a case a court may grant relief on such equitable terms as the situation requires." (Restatement, 2d, Contracts, Supra, § 18C, subd. (2).)

The system was, or should have been, fully aware of Mrs. Ortelere's condition. They, or the Board of Education, knew of her leave of absence for medical reasons and the resort to staff psychiatrists by the Board of Education. Hence, the other of the conditions for avoidance is satisfied.

Lastly, there are no significant changes of position by the system other than those that flow from the barest actuarial consequences of benefit selection.

Nor should one ignore that in the relationship between retirement system and member, and especially in a public system, there is not involved a commercial, let alone an ordinary commercial, transaction. Instead the nature of the system and its announced goal is the protection of its members and those in whom its members have an interest. It is not a sound scheme which would permit 40 years of contribution and participation in the system to be nullified by a one-instant act committed by one known to be mentally ill. This is especially true if there would be no substantial harm to the system if the act were avoided. On the record none may gainsay that her selection of a 'no option' retirement while under psychiatric care, ill with cerebral arteriosclerosis, aged 60, and with a family in which she had always manifested concern, was so unwise and foolhardy that a factfinder might conclude that it was explainable only as a product of psychosis.

On this analysis it is not difficult to see that plaintiff's evidence was sufficient to sustain a finding that, when she acted as she did on February 11, 1965, she did so solely as a result of serious mental illness, namely, psychosis. Of course, nothing less serious than medically classified psychosis should suffice or else few contracts would be invulnerable to some kind of psychological attack. Mrs. Ortelere's psychiatrist testified quite flatly that as an involutional melancholiac in depression she was incapable of making a voluntary 'rational' decision. Of course, as noted earlier, the trial court's finding and perhaps some of the testimony attempted to fit into the rubrics of the traditional rules. For that reason rather than reinstatement of the judgment at Trial Term there should be a new trial under the proper standards frankly considered and applied.

Accordingly, the order of the Appellate Division should be reversed, without costs, and the action remanded to Special Term for a new trial.

JASEN, J., dissenting:

Where there has been no previous adjudication of incompetency, the burden of proving mental incompetence is upon the party alleging it. I agree with the majority at the Appellate Division that the plaintiff, the husband of the decedent, failed to sustain the burden incumbent upon him of proving deceased's incompetence.

The evidence conclusively establishes that the decedent, at the time she made her application to retire, understood not only that she was retiring, but also that she had selected the maximum payment during her lifetime.

Indeed, the letter written by the deceased to the Teachers' Retirement System prior to her retirement demonstrates her full mental capacity to understand and to decide whether to take on option or the maximum allowance. The full text of the letter reads as follows:

February 8, 1965

Gentlemen:

I would like to retire on Feb. 12 or Feb. 15. In other words, just as soon as possible after I receive the information I need in order to decide whether to take an option or maximum allowance. Following are the questions I would like to have answered:

1.   What is my 'average' five-year salary?

2.   What is my maximum allowance?

3.   I am 60 years old. If I select option four—a with a beneficiary (female) 27 years younger, what is my allowance?

4.   If I select four-a on the pension part only, and take the maximum annuity, what is my allowance?

5.   If I take a loan of 89% of my year's salary before retirement, what would my maximum allowance be?

6.   If I take a loan of $5,000 before retiring, and select option four-a on both the pension and annuity, what would my allowance be?

7.   What is my total service credit? I have been on a leave without pay since Oct. 26, 1964.

8.   What is the 'factor' used for calculating option four-a with the above beneficiary?

Thank you for your promptness in making the necessary calculations. I will come to your office on Thursday afternoon of this week.

It seems clear that this detailed, explicit and extremely pertinent list of queries reveals a mind fully in command of the salient features of the Teachers' Retirement System. Certainly, it cannot be said that the decedent could possess sufficient capacity to compose a letter indicating such a comprehensive understanding of the retirement system, and yet lack the capacity to understand the answers.

As I read the record, the evidence establishes that the decedent's election to receive maximum payments was predicated on the need for a higher income to support two retired persons—her husband and herself. Since the only source of income available to decedent and her husband was decedent's retirement pay, the additional payment of $75 per month which she would receive by electing the maximal payment was a necessity. Indeed, the additional payments represented an increase of 20% over the benefits payable under option 1. Under these circumstances, an election of maximal income during decedent's lifetime was not only a rational, but a necessary decision.

Further indication of decedent's knowledge of the financial needs of her family is evidenced by the fact that she took a loan for the maximum amount ($8,760) permitted by the retirement system at the time she made application for retirement.

Moreover, there is nothing in the record to indicate that the decedent had any warning, premonition, knowledge or indication at the time of retirement that her life expectancy was, in any way, reduced by her condition.

Decedent's election of the maximum retirement benefits, therefore, was not so contrary to her best interests so as to create an inference of her mental incompetence. . . .

Nor can I agree with the majority's view that the traditional rules governing competency to contract "are, for the most part, too restrictive and rest on a false factual basis."

The issue confronting the courts concerning mental capacity to contract is under what circumstances and conditions should a party be relieved of contractual obligations freely entered. This is peculiarly a legal decision, although, of course, available medical knowledge forms a datum which influences the legal choice. It is common knowledge that the present state of psychiatric knowledge is inadequate to provide a fixed rule for each and every type of mental disorder. Thus, the generally accepted rules which have evolved to determine mental responsibility are general enough in application to encompass all types of mental disorders, and phrased in a manner which can be understood and practically applied by juries composed of laymen.

. . . As in every situation where the law must draw a line between liability and nonliability, between responsibility and nonresponsibility, there will be borderline cases, and injustices may occur by deciding erroneously that an individual belongs on one side of the line or the other. To minimize the chances of such injustices occurring, the line should be drawn as clearly as possible.

. . . I fear that the majority's refinement of the generally accepted rules will prove unworkable in practice, and make many contracts vulnerable to psychological attack. Any benefit to those who understand what they are doing, but are unable to exercise self-discipline, will be outweighed by frivolous claims which will burden our courts and undermine the security of contracts. The reasonable expectations of those who innocently deal with persons who appear rational and who understand what they are doing should be protected.

Accordingly, I would affirm the order appealed from. [The vote was 5 to 2.]

NOTES AND QUESTIONS

1.   How did the retirement benefits system work in *Ortelere* and what is the effect of disallowing an election *ex post*? If the decision that Ms. Ortelere made was such a foolish choice, why were employees allowed to make that election at all? Are "slippery slope" arguments implicated here? In other words, if an exception is made for the family of Ms. Ortelere, and they may disaffirm

her choice, what is the result for the other teachers who are also part of the risk sharing system?

2.   The courts in *Traylor* and *Ortelere* treated the contracts as voidable, giving the vulnerable party the election to disaffirm or affirm the contract. By contrast, contracts that are illegal or against public policy, as we saw in the last chapter, are void in that neither party can enforce the deal under any circumstances. What might be the rationale for the different treatment of these classes of defenses?

3.   What was the old "cognitive" test described by the *Ortelere* court? What is the difference between the old test and more modern notions of mental illness? According to the National Institute of Mental Health, major depression affects approximately 14.8 million American adults. Depression is the leading cause of disability in the United Sates for those in the age group 15–44. What does the large number of people who suffer from mental health problems and the increased awareness of their importance mean for courts? Should judges be more understanding of excuse under this defense, or does the prevalence of mental health problems instead mean that courts should ignore the issue except in extreme cases?

4.   Does it matter what the other party thinks or knows about the party who has a mental illness? Consider Restatement (Second) of Contracts, Section 15, excerpted earlier.

5.   In *Ortelere*, the teacher's employer knew quite a lot about her health status, including the fact that she was on a leave from work due to major depression. But in some instances, the health problem might not be as clear, and the outcome might depend on objective manifestations and how reasonable it might be to think that a person could exercise their ability to contract. The Restatement (Second) of Contracts, Section 15 attempts to strike a balance between protecting the party who is suffering from mental illness, while at the same time respecting that individual's freedom to enter contracts. Another policy implicated is the interest of the person on the other side of the transaction, who may not know that the other party suffers from mental illness and who may be counting on the contract being binding.

PROBLEMS

In each problem, analyze the contractual rights and liabilities of the parties.

1.   Dylan is busy both with work as an attorney (primarily contract litigation and drafting) and shares custody of his fourteen year-old son, Chad, with his ex-wife. Chad is going through a somewhat "difficult" stage, where he is not interested in talking to people, but he loves computers. Normally, Dylan limits Chad's computer use strictly, as they only have one "shared" computer in the living room and Dylan only rarely leaves Chad unsupervised since he is immature for his age. One Saturday, however, Dylan was having trouble with the computer and realized a good deal of basic software was erased.

Short on time, Dylan asked Chad to reinstall his software, which was a product of BigSoft, Inc. Chad was happy to get more computer time, so he cheerfully re-installed the program, using the access code Dylan got when he paid for the product. Chad did so in his own name, and in every instance where he was presented with the terms of the website, he clicked "I AGREE." Chad did not read any of the terms of the agreements. Three days later, Dylan is upset to find out that the BigSoft software product is responsible for all of his computer troubles and has (just yesterday) corrupted part of his computer's drive, costing $400 to repair. Apparently the most recent version of the "clickwrap" agreement limits liability for any fault of the product to only $1, although Dylan does not remember this clickwrap being a part of the old version that he installed.   minor can disaffirm   agent?

2.   Ashley Arrows is a supermodel and actress who has often graced the cover of leading magazines. Lately, however, that attention has been less for her acting and more for her hard-partying lifestyle and stints in rehab. Lisa Hernandez is a store owner on Rodeo Drive, in Beverly Hills, and she often has celebrities as her clients. Lisa's store is packed with beautiful chandeliers, lighting fixtures, and expensive and rare lamps.

Because so many celebrities come in, and because she lives so close to Hollywood, Lisa is an avid reader of *We*, *Persons*, and other news/celebrity gossip magazines. For months last year, she followed with baited breath the question of whether Ashley would lose custody of her child due to her somewhat bizarre and erratic public behavior. There have been rumors and speculations in these publications that Ashley's real problem stems from bi-polar (manic depressive) disorder. However, the latest issue of "*We*" said that with therapy and the right medication, Ashley was doing better and might soon recover her acting career.

It was one of Lisa's most exciting days when one afternoon, Ashley appeared in her store. Ashley told Lisa that she was going to redecorate her entire Hollywood mansion immediately and needed "exquisite lighting" to go along with it. When Lisa asked why Ashley was alone, she told Lisa that "I needed to get away from that ridiculous crowd" and "lose some of the noise from my head." The two had some reasonable conversation about Ashley's upcoming movie, as Lisa showed Ashley some of her most precious chandeliers. After about twenty minutes of looking, Ashley declared, "I've shopped everywhere and these are best chandeliers I've seen. Ring them up and I'll take them all."

Quickly, Lisa calculates that this is going to be one of her best sales days in a long time. Lisa hands Ashley a detailed accounting and work order, which Ashley signs. The chandeliers come to $90,000, and Ashley hands over her platinum card. While there is some markup because of the ritzy location on Rodeo Drive, Lisa's prices are comparable to the deals other stores offer on chandeliers. The terms posted on the receipt say that all sales are final and when told about the store policy, Ashley nods her head and says "I understand." Lisa's store delivers the chandeliers and her workers have installed two of them, when, a week later, Ashley sends Lisa a note. Ashley is seeking to be released from the contract because during the past week she was in a "manic" phase and completely blew her budget on shopping.

If Lisa refuses to release Ashley from the contract, present the arguments on either side, and then present a conclusion as to how a judge might decide this case.

3.   Chip is a 43-year old well-off business owner who is depressed and spends a great deal of time thinking about his own mortality. Realizing he is unhappy in his marriage, he divorced his wife of the last 18 years, even though she pleads with him to attend counseling before such a drastic step. Further, he decides to sell off a large stock investment that he had originally planned for use for his son's college education and instead uses the money to purchase a red sports car that costs $175,000.

When he went to the dealership, Chip began by talking to the salesman about needing a new car since he was recently divorced. Sizing Chip up as a "midlife crisis," the salesman gave him a "hard sell," telling him about all the attention he will receive if he drives the car around town and how women find this type of car almost irresistible. Chip is very excited about the car and purchased it on the spot, since he thinks it may relieve his crushing anxiety and make him happy.

Only a month later, however, Chip receives help for depression, including therapy and medication, and realizes that he has made some poor choices. Now that he is feeling better, he would like to mend his relationships with his ex-wife and son. Further, he regrets purchasing the sports car and believes that it was extremely selfish and short-sighted. He realizes that it is more important to help his son attend college. If Chip were to resell the car on the open market, it would be "used" (he's driven it 1,500 miles) and he would lose $50,000. Chip would vastly prefer to rescind the transaction.

What is your assessment of Chip's chances of success in disaffirming the deal?

4.   In order to purchase items through a cell phone app, users can establish a password or use a fingerprint in order to provide positive identification that shows they are authorized to make a purchase. On previous occasions, Cassie, who is six years old, has used her dad Holden's cell phone to play various games, including "Candy Crush." Yesterday, Holden was tired from work and nodded asleep while he was watching Cassie. Bored, Cassie used Holden's finger in order to unlock his phone and purchase $452 worth of items in a game that she was playing. What are Holden's legal options?

E. DURESS

There are a series of contract defenses that concentrate on the misbehavior of one of the parties to the contract. Under Restatement (Second) of Contracts, Section 175, "If a party's manifestation of assent is induced by an improper threat by the other party that leaves the victim no reasonable alternative, the contract is voidable by the victim." The commentary to this section notes that "Courts originally restricted duress to threats involving loss of life, mayhem or imprisonment, but these restrictions have been greatly relaxed[.]"

The Restatement goes on, in Section 176, to define an improper threat as one that "threatens a crime or tort" or abuse of legal process, whether criminal or civil, or a violation of the contractual duty of good faith and fair dealing. An improper threat would also include instances where the "resulting exchange is not on fair terms" and where there was harm to the recipient of the threat, but no benefit to the individual making the threat, or when "what is threatened is otherwise a use of power for illegitimate ends."

Courts have discussed duress in both the context of *physical duress* (or threats that amount to such) and improper threats or pressure that amount to *economic duress*. Physical duress is the literal "gun to the head" situation where a party's life or physical well-being is put in jeopardy. While these situations seem straightforward, there can also be third-party duress that operates on a subtler level.

Economic duress encompasses significantly more behavior and defining it precisely is a thorny question. Economics is the study of scarcity. Most everyone (but perhaps the wealthiest citizens) in a market economy is subject to some degree of financial constraint and limitation, but we do not consider that a "duress" situation. So striking a deal to perform labor to pay for living expenses is accepted as a normal, and in fact almost universally required tradeoff, rather than seen as the product of economic duress.

Likewise, in a capitalist economy, business people are encouraged to jump on a good deal and to take advantage of good prices in the market. But the doctrine of economic duress reminds us that there are some limits to how much one party can "take advantage" of the other in a contractual relationship. After all, once in a contract the parties owe each other a duty of good faith to work toward the completion of the contract. Especially if one party attempts to set up the other party or creates an exploitative or "high pressure" situation for the other, courts may find this overreaching. The following cases seek to set out when opportunistic behavior crosses the line into economic duress.

ALASKA PACKERS' ASS'N V. DOMENICO
54 C.C.A. 485 (9th Cir. 1902)

ROSS, J.J.

The [breach] in this case was based upon a contract alleged to have been entered into between the [fishermen] and the appellant corporation on the 22d day of May, 1900, at Pyramid Harbor, Alaska, by which it is claimed the appellant promised to pay each of the [fishermen], among other things, the sum of $100 for services rendered and to be rendered. In its answer the [corporation] denied the execution, on its part, of the contract sued upon, averred that it was without consideration, and for a third defense alleged that the work performed by the [fishermen] for it was performed under other and different contracts than that sued on, and that, prior to the filing of the [action], each of the [fishermen] was paid by the respondent the full amount due him thereunder, in consideration of which each of them executed a full release of all his claims and demands[.]

The evidence shows without conflict that on March 26, 1900, at the city and county of San Francisco, the [fishermen] entered into a written contract with the [corporation], whereby they agreed to go from San Francisco to Pyramid Harbor, Alaska, and return, on board such vessel as might be designated by the [corporation], and to work for the [corporation] during the fishing season of 1900, at Pyramid Harbor, as sailors and fishermen, agreeing to do 'regular ship's duty, both up and down, discharging and loading; and to do any other work whatsoever when requested to do so by the captain or agent of the Alaska Packers' Association.' By the terms of this agreement, the appellant was to pay each of the [fishermen] $50 for the season, and two cents for each red salmon in the catching of which he took part.

On the 15th day of April, 1900, 21 of the [fishermen] signed shipping articles by which they shipped as seamen on the Two Brothers, a vessel chartered by the appellant for the voyage between San Francisco and Pyramid Harbor, and also bound themselves to perform the same work for the [corporation] provided for by the previous contract of March 26th; the appellant agreeing to pay them therefor the sum of $60 for the season, and two cents each for each red salmon in the catching of which they should respectively take part. Under these contracts, the [fishermen] sailed on board the Two Brothers for Pyramid Harbor, where the [corporation] had about $150,000 invested in a salmon cannery. The [fishermen] arrived there early in April of the year mentioned, and began to unload the vessel and fit up the cannery.

A few days thereafter, to wit, May 19th, they stopped work in a body, and demanded of the company's superintendent there in charge $100 for services in operating the vessel to and from Pyramid Harbor, instead of the sums stipulated for in and by the contracts; stating that unless they were paid this additional wage they would stop work entirely, and return to San Francisco. The evidence showed, and the court below found, that it was impossible for the [corporation] to get other men to take the places of the [fishermen], the place being remote, the season short and just opening; so that, after endeavoring for several days without success to induce the [fishermen] to proceed with their work in accordance with their contracts, the company's superintendent, on the 22d day of May, so far yielded to their demands as to instruct his clerk to copy the contracts executed in San Francisco, including the words 'Alaska Packers' Association' at the end, substituting, for the $50 and $60 payments, respectively, of those contracts, the sum of $100, which document, so prepared, was signed by the [fishermen] before a shipping commissioner whom they had requested to be brought from Northeast Point; the superintendent, however, testifying that he at the time told the [fishermen] that he was without authority to enter into any such contract, or to in any way alter the contracts made between them and the company in San Francisco.

Upon the return of the [fishermen] to San Francisco at the close of the fishing season, they demanded pay in accordance with the terms of the alleged contract of May 22d, when the company denied its validity, and refused to pay other than as provided for by the contracts of March 26th and April 5th, respectively. Some of the [fishermen], at least, consulted counsel, and, after receiving his advice, those of them who had signed the shipping articles before the shipping commissioner at San Francisco went before that officer, and received the amount due them thereunder, executing in consideration thereof a release in full, and the others paid at the office of the company, also receipting in full for their demands.

On the trial in the court below, the [fishermen] undertook to show that the fishing nets provided by the respondent were defective, and that it was on that account that they demanded increased wages. On that point, the evidence was substantially conflicting, and the finding of the court was against the [fishermen] the court saying:

> The contention of [the fishermen] that the nets provided them were rotten and unserviceable is not sustained by the evidence. The defendants' interest required that [the fishermen] should be provided with every facility necessary to their success as fishermen, for on such success depended the profits defendant would be able to realize that season from its packing plant, and the large capital invested therein. In view of this self-evident fact, it is highly improbable that the defendant gave [the fishermen] rotten and unserviceable nets with which to fish. It follows from this finding that [fishermen] were not justified in refusing performance of their original contract. . . .

The evidence being sharply conflicting in respect to these facts, the conclusions of the court, who heard and saw the witnesses, will not be disturbed. The Alijandro, 6 C.C.A. 54, 56 Fed. 621; The Lucy, 20 C.C.A. 660, 74 Fed. 572; The Glendale, 26 C.C.A. 500, 81 Fed. 633. The Coquitlam, 23 C.C.A. 438, 77 Fed. 744; Gorham Mfg. Co. v. Emery-Bird-Thayer Dry Goods Co., 43 C.C.A. 511, 104 Fed. 243.

The real questions in the case as brought here are questions of law, and, in the view that we take of the case, it will be necessary to consider but one of those. Assuming that the appellant's superintendent at Pyramid Harbor was authorized to make the alleged contract of May 22d, and that he executed it on behalf of the appellant, was it supported by a sufficient consideration? From the foregoing statement of the case, it will have been seen that the [fishermen] agreed in writing, for certain stated compensation, to render their services to the appellant in remote waters where the season for conducting fishing operations is extremely short, and in which enterprise the appellant [corporation] had a large amount of money invested; and, after having entered upon the discharge of their contract, and at a time when it was impossible for the appellant to secure other men in their places, the [fishermen], without any valid cause, absolutely refused to continue the services they were under contract to perform unless the [corporation] would consent to pay them more money. Consent to such a demand, under such circumstances, if given, was, in our opinion, without consideration, for the reason that it was based solely upon the [fishermen's] agreement to render the exact services, and none other, that they were already under contract to render. The case shows that they willfully and arbitrarily broke that obligation. As a matter of course, they were liable to the [corporation] in damages, and it is quite probable, as suggested by the court below in its opinion, that they may have been unable to respond in damages. But we are unable to agree with the conclusions there drawn, from these facts, in these words:

> Under such circumstances, it would be strange, indeed, if the law would not permit the defendant to waive the damages caused by the [fishermen's] breach, and enter into the contract sued upon,— a contract mutually beneficial to all the parties thereto, in that it gave to the [fishermen] reasonable compensation for their labor, and enabled the defendant to employ to advantage the large capital it had invested in its canning and fishing plant.

Certainly, it cannot be justly held, upon the record in this case, that there was any voluntary waiver on the part of the appellant of the breach of the original contract. The company itself knew nothing of such breach until the expedition returned to San Francisco, and the testimony is uncontradicted that its superintendent at Pyramid Harbor, who, it is claimed, made on its behalf the contract sued on, distinctly informed the [fishermen] that he had no power to alter the original or to make a new contract, and it would, of course, follow that, if he had no power to change the original, he would have no authority to waive any rights thereunder. The circumstances of the present case bring it, we think, directly within the sound and just observations of the supreme court of Minnesota in the case of King v. Railway Co., 61 Minn. 482, 63 N.W. 1105:

No astute reasoning can change the plain fact that the party who refuses to perform, and thereby coerces a promise from the other party to the contract to pay him an increased compensation for doing that which he is legally bound to do, takes an unjustifiable advantage of the necessities of the other party. Surely it would be a travesty on justice to hold that the party so making the promise for extra pay was estopped from asserting that the promise was without consideration. A party cannot lay the foundation of an estoppel by his own wrong, where the promise is simply a repetition of a subsisting legal promise. There can be no consideration for the promise of the other party, and there is no warrant for inferring that the parties have voluntarily rescinded or modified their contract. The promise cannot be legally enforced, although the other party has completed his contract in reliance upon it.

In Lingenfelder v. Brewing Co., 103 Mo. 578, 15 S.W. 844, the court, in holding void a contract by which the owner of a building agreed to pay its architect an additional sum because of his refusal to otherwise proceed with the contract, said:

> It is urged upon us by respondents that this was a new contract. New in what? Jungenfeld was bound by his contract to design and supervise this building. Under the new promise, he was not to do anything more or anything different. What benefit was to accrue to Wainwright? He was to receive the same service from Jungenfeld under the new, that Jungenfeld was bound to tender under the original, contract. What loss, trouble, or inconvenience could result to Jungenfeld that he had not already assumed?

> No amount of metaphysical reasoning can change the plain fact that Jungenfeld took advantage of Wainwright's necessities, and extorted the promise of five per cent. on the refrigerator plant as the condition of his complying with his contract already entered into. Nor had he even the flimsy pretext that Wainwright had violated any of the conditions of the contract on his part. Jungenfeld himself put it upon the simple proposition that 'if he, as an architect, put up the brewery, and another company put up the refrigerating machinery, it would be a detriment to the Empire Refrigerating Company,' of which Jungenfeld was president.

> To permit plaintiff to recover under such circumstances would be to offer a premium upon bad faith, and invite men to violate their most sacred contracts that they may profit by their own wrong. That a promise to pay a man for doing that which he

is already under contract to do is without consideration is conceded by respondents. The rule has been so long imbedded in the common law and decisions of the highest courts of the various states that nothing but the most cogent reasons ought to shake it. (Citing a long list of authorities.)

But it is 'carrying coals to Newcastle' to add authorities on a proposition so universally accepted, and so inherently just and right in itself. The learned counsel for respondents do not controvert the general proposition. They contention is, and the circuit court agreed with them, that, when Jungenfeld declined to go further on his contract, the defendant then had the right to sue for damages, and not having elected to sue Jungenfeld, but having acceded to his demand for the additional compensation defendant cannot now be heard to say his promise is without consideration. While it is true Jungenfeld became liable in damages for the obvious breach of his contract, we do not think it follows that defendant is estopped from showing its promise was made without consideration. . . . * * *

What we hold is that, when a party merely does what he has already obligated himself to do, he cannot demand an additional compensation therefor; and although, by taking advantage of the necessities of his adversary, he obtains a promise for more, the law will regard it as nudum pactum, and will not lend its process to aid in the wrong.

[The Supreme Court] of Vermont in the subsequent case of Cobb v. Cowdery, 40 Vt. 25, 94 Am.Dec. 370, . . . held that:

A promise by a party to do what he is bound in law to do is not an illegal consideration, but is the same as no consideration at all, and is merely void; in other words, it is insufficient, but not illegal. Thus, if the master of a ship promise his crew an addition to their fixed wages in consideration for and as an incitement to, their extraordinary exertions during a storm, or in any other emergency of the voyage, this promise is nudum pactum; the voluntary performance of an act which it was before legally incumbent on the party to perform being in law an insufficient consideration; and so it would be in any other case where the only consideration for the promise of one party was the promise of the other party to do, or his actual doing, something which he was previously bound in law to do. Chit. Cont. (10th Am.Ed.) 51; Smith, Cont. 87; 3 Kent, Com. 185.

It results from the views above expressed that the judgment must be reversed, and the cause remanded, with directions to the court below to enter judgment for the respondent, with costs. It is so ordered.

NOTES AND QUESTIONS

1. In the area of labor relations, both management and workers implicitly have power to halt production. What aspect of the fishermen's actions in this case did the court seem to think was coercive?

2. Is *Alaska Packers v. Domenico* a case about economic duress or a case about past consideration and the pre-existing duty rule?

3. Interestingly, after researching this case extensively, Professor Deborah Threedy has argued that in fact the nets provided to the fishermen did cause them actual problems. The fishermen, who were Italian, were not used to these nets and complained that the nets were not serviceable. While the company supervisor attempted to explain why their facility used these particular types of nets, his explanation did not make it through to the fishermen—the supervisor did not speak Italian. *See* Deborah Threedy, *A Fish Story: Alaska Packers' Association v. Domenico*, 2000 UTAH L. REV. 185 (2000).

4. If the fishermen truly believed that the nets were not serviceable, in your mind should that change the outcome of the case?

———

Normally, if circumstances have legitimately changed, a party may choose to modify the terms of a deal. And so under the Restatement (Second) of Contracts, Section 89, a contract modification is binding: "(a) if the modification is fair and equitable in view of circumstances not anticipated by the parties when the contact was made; or (b) to the extent provided by statute; or (c) to the extent that justice requires enforcement in view of material change of position in reliance on the promise." Note that U.C.C. Section 2–209 has abandoned the idea of needing consideration in order to make a contract modification binding, but has instead added (in the comments) the requirement that any contract modifications that have been made must be done so in "good faith." The good faith requirement protects the other party from coercive or exploitative contract modifications that do look more like economic duress. Consider the following case.

AUSTIN INSTRUMENT V. LORAL CORP.
29 N.Y.2d 124 (N.Y. 1971)

FULD, C.J.

The defendant, Loral Corporation, seeks to recover payment for goods delivered under a contract which it had with the plaintiff Austin Instrument, Inc., on the ground that the evidence establishes, as a matter of law, that it was forced to agree to an increase in price on the items in question under circumstances amounting to economic duress.

In July of 1965, Loral was awarded a $6,000,000 contract by the Navy for the production of radar sets. The contract contained a schedule of deliveries, a liquidated damages clause applying to late deliveries and a cancellation clause in case of default by Loral. The latter thereupon solicited bids for some 40 precision gear components needed to produce the radar sets, and awarded Austin a subcontract to supply 23 such parts. That party commenced delivery in early 1966.

In May, 1966, Loral was awarded a second Navy contract for the production of more radar sets and again went about soliciting bids. Austin bid on all 40 gear components but, on July 15, a representative from Loral informed Austin's president, Mr. Krauss, that his company would be awarded the subcontract only for those items on which it was low bidder. The Austin officer refused to accept an order for less than all 40 of the gear parts and on the next day he told Loral that Austin would cease deliveries of the parts due under the existing subcontract unless Loral consented to substantial increases in the prices provided for by that agreement—both retroactively for parts already delivered and prospectively on those not yet shipped—and placed with Austin the order for all 40 parts needed under Loral's second Navy contract.

Shortly thereafter, Austin did, indeed, stop delivery. After contacting 10 manufacturers of precision gears and finding none who could produce the parts in time to meet its commitments to the Navy, Loral acceded to Austin's demands; in a letter dated July 22, Loral wrote to Austin that 'We have feverishly surveyed other sources of supply and find that because of the prevailing military exigencies, were they to start from scratch as would have to be the case, they could not even remotely begin to deliver on time to meet the delivery requirements established by the Government. * * * Accordingly, we are left with no choice or alternative but to meet your conditions.'

Loral thereupon consented to the price increases insisted upon by Austin under the first subcontract and the latter was awarded a second subcontract making it the supplier of all 40 gear parts for Loral's second contract with the Navy. Although Austin was granted until September to resume deliveries, Loral did, in fact, receive parts in August and was able to produce the radar sets in time to meet its commitments to the Navy on both contracts. After Austin's last delivery under the second subcontract in July, 1967, Loral notified it of its intention to seek recovery of the price increases.

On September 15, 1967, Austin instituted this action against Loral to recover an amount in excess of $17,750 which was still due on the second subcontract. On the same day, Loral commenced an action against Austin claiming damages of some $22,250—the aggregate of the price increases under the first subcontract—on the ground of economic duress. The two actions were consolidated and, following a trial, Austin was awarded the sum it requested and Loral's complaint against Austin was dismissed on the ground that it was not shown that 'it could not have obtained the items in question from other sources in time to meet its commitment to the Navy under the first contract.' A closely divided Appellate Division affirmed (35 A.D.2d 387, 316 N.Y.S.2d 528, 532). There was no material disagreement concerning the facts; as Justice Steuer stated in the course of his dissent below, '(t)he facts are virtually undisputed, nor is there any serious question of law. The difficulty lies in the application of the law to these facts.' (35 A.D.2d 392, 316 N.Y.S.2d 534.)

The applicable law is clear and, indeed, is not disputed by the parties. A contract is voidable on the ground of duress when it is established that the party making the claim was forced to agree to it by means of a wrongful threat precluding the exercise of his free will. The existence of economic duress or business compulsion is demonstrated by proof that 'immediate possession of needful goods is threatened' (Mercury Mach. Importing Corp. v. City of New York, 3 N.Y.2d 418, 425, 165 N.Y.S.2d 517, 520, 144 N.E.2d 400) or, more particularly, in cases such as the one before us, by proof that one party to a contract has threatened to breach the agreement by withholding goods unless the other party agrees to some further demand. However, a mere threat by one party to breach the contract by not delivering the required items, though wrongful, does not in itself constitute economic duress. It must also appear that the threatened party could not obtain the goods from another source of supply and that the ordinary remedy of an action for breach of contract would not be adequate.

We find without any support in the record the conclusion reached by the courts below that Loral failed to establish that it was the victim of economic duress. On the contrary, the evidence makes out a classic case, as a matter of law, of such duress.

It is manifest that Austin's threat—to stop deliveries unless the prices were increased—deprived Loral of its free will. As bearing on this, Loral's relationship with the Government is most significant. As mentioned above, its contract called for staggered monthly deliveries of the radar sets, with clauses calling for liquidated damages and possible cancellation on default. Because of its production schedule, Loral was, in July, 1966, concerned with meeting its delivery requirements in September, October and November, and it was for the sets to be delivered in those months that the withheld gears were needed. Loral had to plan ahead, and the substantial liquidated damages for which it would be liable, plus the threat of default, were genuine possibilities. Moreover, Loral did a substantial portion of its business with the Government, and it feared that a failure to deliver as agreed upon would jeopardize its chances for future contracts. These genuine concerns do not merit the label "self-imposed, undisclosed and subjective" which the Appellate Division majority placed upon them. It was perfectly reasonable for Loral, or any other party similarly placed, to consider itself in an emergency, duress situation.

Austin, however, claims that the fact that Loral extended its time to resume deliveries until September negates its alleged dire need for the parts. A Loral official testified on this point that Austin's president told him he could deliver some parts in August and that the extension of deliveries was a formality. In any event, the parts necessary for production of the radar sets to be delivered in September were delivered to Loral on September 1, and the parts needed for the October schedule were delivered in late August and early September. Even so, Loral had to 'work * * * around the clock' to meet its commitments. Considering that the best offer Loral received from the other vendors it contacted was commencement of delivery sometime in October, which, as the record shows, would have made it late in its deliveries to the Navy in both September and October, Loral's claim that it had no choice but to accede to Austin's demands is conclusively demonstrated.

We find unconvincing Austin's contention that Loral, in order to meet its burden, should have contacted the Government and asked for an extension of its delivery dates so as to enable it to purchase the parts from another vendor. Aside from the consideration that Loral was anxious to perform well in the Government's eyes, it could not be sure when it would obtain enough parts from a substitute vendor to meet its commitments. The only promise which it received from the companies it contacted was for Commencement of deliveries, not full supply, and, with vendor delay common in this field, it would have been nearly impossible to know the length of the extension it should request. It must be remembered that Loral was producing a needed item of military hardware. Moreover, there is authority for Loral's position that nonperformance by a subcontractor is not an excuse for default in the main contract. (See, e.g., McBride & Wachtel, Government Contracts, § 35.10, (11).) In light of all this, Loral's claim should not be held insufficiently supported because it did not request an extension from the Government.

Loral, as indicated above, also had the burden of demonstrating that it could not obtain the parts elsewhere within a reasonable time, and there can be no doubt that it met this burden. The 10 manufacturers whom Loral contacted comprised its entire list of 'approved vendors' for precision gears, and none was able to commence delivery soon enough. As Loral was producing a highly sophisticated item of military machinery requiring parts made to the strictest engineering standards, it would be unreasonable to hold that Loral should have gone to other vendors, with whom it was either unfamiliar or dissatisfied, to procure the needed parts. As Justice Steuer noted in his dissent, Loral 'contacted all the manufacturers whom it believed capable of making these parts' (35 A.D.2d at p. 393, 316 N.Y.S.2d at p. 534), and this was all the law requires.

It is hardly necessary to add that Loral's normal legal remedy of accepting Austin's breach of the contract and then suing for damages would have been inadequate under the circumstances, as Loral would still have had to obtain the gears elsewhere with all the concomitant consequences mentioned above. In other words, Loral actually had no choice, when the prices were raised by Austin, except to take the gears at the 'coerced' prices and then sue to get the excess back.

Austin's final argument is that Loral, [even if] it did enter into the contract under duress, lost any rights it had to a refund of money by waiting until July, 1967, long after the termination date of the contract, to disaffirm it. It is true that one who would recover moneys allegedly paid under duress must act promptly to make his claim known. (See Oregon Pacific R.R. Co. v. Forrest, 128 N.Y. 83, 93, 28 N.E. 137, 139; Port Chester Elec. Constr. Corp. v. Hastings Terraces, 284 App.Div. 966, 967, 134 N.Y.S.2d 656, 658.) In this case, Loral delayed making its demand for a refund until three days after Austin's last delivery on the second subcontract. Loral's reason—for waiting until that time—is that it feared another stoppage of deliveries which would again put it in an untenable situation. Considering Austin's conduct in the past, this was perfectly reasonable, as the possibility of an application by Austin of further business compulsion still existed until all of the parts were delivered.

In sum, the record before us demonstrates that Loral agreed to the price increases in consequence of the economic duress employed by Austin. Accordingly, the matter should be remanded to the trial court for a computation of its damages. The order appealed from should be modified, with costs, by reversing so much thereof as affirms the dismissal of defendant Loral Corporation's claim and, except as so modified, affirmed.

BERGAN, J., dissenting:

Whether acts charged as constituting economic duress produce or do not produce the damaging effect attributed to them is normally a routine type of factual issue. Here the fact question was resolved against Loral both by the Special Term and by the affirmance at the Appellate Division. It should not be open for different resolution here.

In summarizing the Special Term's decision and its own, the Appellate Division decided that 'the conclusion that Loral acted deliberately and voluntarily, without being under immediate pressure of incurring severe business reverses, precludes a recovery on the theory of economic duress' (35 A.D.2d 387, 391, 316 N.Y.S.2d 528, 532).

When the testimony of the witnesses who actually took part in the negotiations for the two disputing parties is examined, sharp conflicts of fact emerge. Under Austin's version the request for a renegotiation of the existing contract was based on Austin's contention that Loral had failed to carry out an understanding as to the items to be furnished under that contract and this was the source of dissatisfaction which led both to a revision of the existing agreement and to entering into a new one.

This is not necessarily and as a matter of law to be held economic duress. On this appeal it is needful to look at the facts resolved in favor of Austin most favorably to that party. Austin's version of events was that a threat was not made but rather a request to accommodate the closing of its plant for a customary vacation period in accordance with the general understanding of the parties.

Moreover, critical to the issue of economic duress was the availability of alternative suppliers to the purchaser Loral. The demonstration is replete in the direct testimony of Austin's witnesses and on cross-examination of Loral's principal and purchasing agent that the availability of practical alternatives was a highly controverted issue of fact. On that issue of fact the explicit findings made by the Special Referee were affirmed by the Appellate Division. Nor is the issue of fact made the less so by assertion that the facts are undisputed and that only the application of equally undisputed rules of law is involved.

Austin asserted and Loral admitted on cross-examination that there were many suppliers listed in a trade registry but that Loral chose to rely only on those who had in the past come to them for orders and with whom they were familiar. It was, therefore, at least a fair issue of fact whether under the circumstances such conduct was reasonable and made what might otherwise have been a commercially understandable renegotiation an exercise of duress. . . .

NOTES AND QUESTIONS

1.   Could the majority in *Austin v. Loral* have invoked the preexisting duty rule? What doctrinal difficulties would the facts pose? In the same vein, could the *Alaska Packers* court have invoked the doctrine of duress? What doctrinal difficulties would the facts of that case have posed for that excuse?

2.   Did the *Austin v. Loral* majority adequately address whether the subcontractor's threat was improper?

3.   Which opinion in *Austin v. Loral* is more persuasive, the majority or dissent? Explain your reasoning.

4.   Professor Meredith Miller's research into the background of the *Austin v. Loral* dispute reveals that the facts were actually more complicated than the New York Court of Appeals makes them out to be. In fact, Austin had alleged that it lost money under the first contract and also had seen increases in its costs. As Professor Miller explains:

> "Framing" describes the technique attorneys use to present the facts and the law in terms most favorable to their clients. The same technique has alternatively been described as "characterizing." The idea of framing is not new or novel; it is one of the bases of legal education and the practice of law. Framing occurs at two general levels in any dispute. First, the legal question is framed. Second, the

answers to that question, or the facts, are characterized to fit within the doctrinal framework of the question. . . . The ability to "frame the legal issue" is among the basic skills that law students develop to "think more like a lawyer." It is the process of defining the parameters of a legal dispute in terms of a more doctrinally sustainable theory based on the facts.

Likewise, "characterizing the facts" is the attorney's rhetorical process of presenting a client's perspective of a set of circumstances. In *Austin v. Loral*, the parties perceived and, thus, characterized the same events in a different manner. Austin took steps to characterize the events as a matter of commercially understandable renegotiation, while Loral took the steps to characterize the same set of circumstances as coercive. Both sides made efforts to favorably characterize the facts; however, Austin failed to frame the legal issue in a manner that made its characterization of the facts doctrinally relevant. Tellingly, the market shifts and Austin's losses under the First Subcontract were not even mentioned in the Court of Appeals decision."

Meredith R. Miller, *Revisiting Austin v. Loral: A Study in Economic Duress, Contract Modification and Framing*, 2 HASTINGS BUS. L.J. 357, 393–94 (2006). How might framing be important for an attorney trying to make out a claim of economic duress?

UCC SECTION 2–209

§ 2–209. *Modification, Rescission and Waiver*.

(1) An agreement modifying a contract within this Article needs no consideration to be binding.

(2) A signed agreement which excludes modification or rescission except by a signed writing cannot be otherwise modified or rescinded, but except as between merchants such a requirement on a form supplied by the merchant must be separately signed by the other party.

(3) The requirements of the statute of frauds section of this Article (Section 2–201) must be satisfied if the contract as modified is within its provisions.

(4) Although an attempt at modification or rescission does not satisfy the requirements of subsection (2) or (3) it can operate as a waiver.

WISCONSIN KNIFE WORKS v. NATIONAL METAL CRAFTERS
781 F.2d 1280 (7th Cir. 1986)

POSNER, J.

. . . Wisconsin Knife Works, [a subsidiary of Black & Decker], sent National Metal Crafters a series of purchase orders [for tool components called spade bit blanks] on the back of each of which was printed, "Acceptance of this Order, either by acknowledgment or performance, constitutes an unqualified agreement to the following." A list of "Conditions of Purchase" follows, of which the first is, "No modification of this contract, shall be binding upon Buyer [Wisconsin Knife Works] unless made in writing and signed by Buyer's authorized representative. Buyer shall have the right to make changes in the Order by a notice, in writing, to Seller." There were six purchase orders in all, each with the identical conditions. . . .

Delivery was due in October and November 1981. National Metal Crafters missed the deadlines. But Wisconsin Knife Works did not immediately declare a breach, cancel the contract, or seek damages for late delivery. Indeed, on July 1, 1982, it issued a new batch of purchase orders (later rescinded). By December 1982 National Metal Crafters was producing spade bit blanks for Wisconsin Knife Works under the original set of purchase orders in adequate quantities, though this was more than a year after the delivery dates in the orders. But on January 13, 1983, Wisconsin Knife Works notified National Metal Crafters that the contract was terminated. By that date only 144,000 of the more than 281,000 spade bit blanks that Wisconsin Knife Works had ordered in the six purchase orders had been delivered.

Wisconsin Knife Works brought this breach of contract suit, charging that National Metal Crafters had violated the terms of delivery in the contract that was formed by the acceptance of the six purchase orders. National Metal Crafters replied that the delivery dates had not been intended as firm dates [and] the contract had been modified and not broken. [After a jury trial, the court below agreed and dismissed Wisconsin Knife's complaint, and the latter appealed.]

The principal issue is the effect of the provision in the purchase orders that forbids the contract to be modified other than by a writing signed by an authorized representative of the buyer. The theory on which the judge sent the issue of modification to the jury was that the contract could be modified orally or by conduct as well as by a signed writing. National Metal Crafters had presented evidence that Wisconsin Knife Works had accepted late delivery of the spade bit blanks and had cancelled the contract not because of the delays in delivery but because it could not produce spade bits at a price acceptable to Black & Decker.

Section 2–209(2) of the Uniform Commercial Code provides that "a signed agreement which excludes modification or rescission except by a signed writing cannot be otherwise modified or rescinded, but except as between merchants such a requirement on a form supplied by the merchant must be separately signed by the other party." . . . The meaning of this provision and its proviso is not crystalline and there is little pertinent case law. One might think that an agreement to exclude modification except by a signed writing must be signed in any event by the party against whom the requirement is sought to be enforced, that is, by National Metal Crafters, rather than by the party imposing the requirement.

But if so the force of the proviso ("but except as between merchants . . .") becomes unclear, for it contemplates that between merchants no separate signature by the party sought to be bound by the requirement is necessary. A possible reconciliation, though not one we need embrace in order to decide this case, is to read the statute to require a separate signing or initialing of the clause forbidding oral modifications, as well as of the contract in which the clause appears. There was no such signature here; but it doesn't matter; this was a contract "between merchants." Although in ordinary language a manufacturer is not a merchant, "between merchants" is a term of art in the Uniform Commercial Code. It means between commercially sophisticated parties . . . which these were.

Of course there must still be a "signed agreement" containing the clause forbidding modification other than by a signed writing, but there was that. National Metal Crafters' signed acknowledgments of the first two purchase orders signified its assent to the printed conditions and naturally and reasonably led Wisconsin Knife Works to believe that National Metal Crafters meant also to assent to the same conditions should they appear in any subsequent purchase orders that it accepted. Those subsequent orders were accepted, forming new contracts on the same conditions as the old, by performance—that is, by National Metal Crafters' beginning the manufacture of the spade bit blanks called for by the orders. See UCC § 2–207(3). So there was an agreement, signed by National Metal Crafters, covering all the purchase orders. The fact that the delivery dates were not on the purchase orders when received by National Metal Crafters is nothing of which it may complain; it was given carte blanche to set those dates.

When National Metal Crafters had difficulty complying with the original specifications for the spade bit blanks, Wisconsin Knife Works modified them; and National Metal Crafters argues that the engineering drawings containing those modifications are the written modification that section 2–209(2), if applicable, calls for. In fact these particular modifications seem to fall within the clause of the contract that allows the buyer (Wisconsin Knife Works) to modify the specifications by notice. The context of this clause makes clear that such notice is not the written modification to which the previous sentence refers. But in any event there was no modification of the delivery dates.

We conclude that the clause forbidding modifications other than in writing was valid and applicable . . . [However,] Section 2–209(4) of the Uniform Commercial Code provides that an "attempt at modification" which does not satisfy a contractual requirement that modifications be in writing nevertheless "can operate as a waiver." . . .

Because the performance of the parties to a contract is typically not simultaneous, one party may find himself at the mercy of the other unless the law of contracts protects him. Indeed, the most important thing which that law does is to facilitate exchanges that are not simultaneous by preventing either party from taking advantage of the vulnerabilities to which sequential performance may give rise. If A contracts to build a highly idiosyncratic gazebo for B, payment due on completion, and when A completes the gazebo B refuses to pay, A may be in a bind—since the resale value of the gazebo may be much less than A's cost—except for his right to sue B for the price. Even then, a right to sue for breach of contract, being costly to enforce, is not a completely adequate remedy. B might therefore go to A and say, "If you don't reduce your price I'll refuse to pay and put you to the expense of suit"; and A might knuckle under. If such modifications are allowed, people in B's position will find it harder to make such contracts in the future, and everyone will be worse off.

The common law dealt with this problem by refusing to enforce modifications unsupported by fresh consideration. *See, e.g., Alaska Packers' Ass'n v. Domenico*, 117 Fed. 99 (9th Cir.1902). Thus in the hypothetical case just put B could not have enforced A's promise to accept a lower price. But this solution is at once overinclusive and underinclusive—the former because most modifications are not coercive and should be enforceable whether or not there is fresh consideration, the latter because, since common law courts inquire only into the existence and not the adequacy of consideration, a requirement of fresh consideration has little bite. B might give A a peppercorn, a kitten, or a robe in exchange for A's agreeing to reduce the contract price, and then the modification would be enforceable and A could no longer sue for the original price.

The draftsmen of the Uniform Commercial Code took a fresh approach, by making modifications enforceable even if not supported by consideration (see section 2–209(1)) and looking to the doctrines of duress and bad faith for the main protection against exploitive or opportunistic attempts at modification, as in our hypothetical case. See UCC § 2–209, official comment 2. But they did another thing as well. In section 2–209(2) they allowed the parties to exclude oral modifications. National Metal Crafters argues that two subsections later they took back this grant of power by allowing an unwritten modification to operate as a waiver.

The common law did not enforce agreements such as section 2–209(2) authorizes. The "reasoning" was that the parties were always free to agree orally to cancel their contract and the clause forbidding modifications not in writing would disappear with the rest of the contract when it was cancelled. . . . This is not reasoning; it is a conclusion disguised as a metaphor. It may have reflected a fear that such clauses, buried in the fine print of form contracts, were traps for the unwary . . . . But the framers of the Uniform Commercial Code, as part and parcel of rejecting the requirement of consideration for modifications, must have rejected the traditional view; must have believed that the protection which the doctrines of duress and bad faith give against extortionate modifications might need reinforcement—if not from a requirement of consideration, which had proved ineffective, then from a grant of power to include a clause requiring modifications to be in writing and signed. An equally important point is that with consideration no longer required for modification, it was natural to give the parties some means of providing a substitute for the cautionary and evidentiary function that the requirement of consideration provides; and the means chosen was to allow them to exclude oral modifications.

If section 2–209(4), which as we said provides that an attempted modification which does not comply with subsection (2) can nevertheless operate as a "waiver," is interpreted so broadly that any oral modification is effective as a waiver notwithstanding section 2–209(2), both provisions become superfluous and we are back in the common law—only with not even a requirement of consideration to reduce the likelihood of fabricated or unintended oral modifications. A conceivable but unsatisfactory way around this result is to distinguish between a modification that substitutes a new term for an old, and a waiver, which merely removes an old term.

On this interpretation National Metal Crafters could not enforce an oral term of the allegedly modified contract but could be excused from one of the written terms. This would take care of a case such as *Alaska Packers*, where seamen attempted to enforce a contract modification that raised their wages, but would not take care of the functionally identical case where seamen sought to collect the agreed-on wages without doing the agreed-on work. Whether the party claiming modification is seeking to impose an onerous new term on the other party or to wriggle out of an onerous term that the original contract imposed on it is a distinction without a difference. We can see that in this case. National Metal Crafters, while claiming that Wisconsin Knife Works broke their contract as orally modified to extend the delivery date, is not seeking damages for that breach. But this is small comfort to Wisconsin Knife Works, which thought it had a binding contract with fixed delivery dates. Whether called modification or waiver, what National Metal Crafters is seeking to do is to nullify a key term other than by a signed writing. If it can get away with this merely by testimony about an oral modification, section 2–209(2) becomes very nearly a dead letter.

The path of reconciliation with subsection (4) is found by attending to the precise wording of (4). It does not say that an attempted modification "is" a waiver; it says that "it can operate as a waiver." It does not say in what circumstances it can operate as a waiver; but if an attempted modification is effective as a waiver only if there is reliance, then both sections 2–209(2) and 2–209(4) can be given effect. Reliance, if reasonably induced and reasonable in extent, is a common substitute for consideration in making a promise legally enforceable, in part because it adds something in the way of credibility to the mere say-so of one party. The main purpose of forbidding oral modifications is to prevent the promisor from fabricating a modification that will let him escape his obligations under the contract; and the danger of successful fabrication is less if the promisor has actually incurred a cost, has relied. There is of course a danger of bootstrapping— of incurring a cost in order to make the case for a modification. But it is a risky course and is therefore less likely to be attempted than merely testifying to a conversation; it makes one put one's money where one's mouth is. . . .

The statute could be clearer; but the draftsmen were making a big break with the common law in subsections (1) and (2), and naturally failed to foresee all the ramifications of the break. . . . [Its] draftsmanship was not flawless—what human product is? . . . We know that the draftsmen of section 2–209 wanted to make it possible for parties to exclude oral modifications. They did not just want to give "modification" another name—"waiver." Our interpretation gives effect to this purpose. It is also consistent with though not compelled by the case law. . .

Missing from the jury instruction . . . in this case is any reference to reliance, that is, to the incurring of costs by National Metal Crafters in reasonable reliance on assurances by Wisconsin Knife Works that late delivery would be acceptable. And although there is evidence of such reliance, it naturally was not a focus of the case, since the issue was cast as one of completed (not attempted) modification, which does not require reliance to be enforceable. [Remanded.]

EASTERBROOK, J., dissenting.

. . . The majority holds that no "attempt at modification" may be a "waiver" within the meaning of § 2–209(4) unless the party seeking to enforce the waiver has relied to its detriment. I do not think that detrimental reliance is an essential element of waiver under § 2–209(4).

"Waiver" is not a term the UCC defines. At common law "waiver" means an intentional relinquishment of a known right. A person may relinquish a right by engaging in conduct inconsistent with the right or by a verbal or written declaration. I do not know of any branch of the law— common, statutory, or constitutional—in which a renunciation of a legal entitlement is effective only if the other party relies to his detriment. True, the law of "consideration" imposed something like a reliance rule; payment of a pine nut (the peppercorn of nouvelle cuisine) is a tiny bit of detriment, and often the law of consideration is expressed in terms of detriment. But

§ 2–209(1) of the UCC provides that consideration is unnecessary to make a modification effective. The introduction of a reliance requirement into a body of law from which the doctrine of consideration has been excised is novel. . . .

This novelty encounters an obstacle within § 2–209. Section 2–209(5) states that a person who "has made a waiver affecting an executory portion of the contract may retract the waiver" on reasonable notice "unless the retraction would be unjust in view of a material change of position in reliance on the waiver." Section 2–209 therefore treats "waiver" *and "reliance" as different. Under § 2–209(4) a waiver may be effective; under § 2–209(5) a waiver may be effective prospectively only if there was also detrimental reliance.

"Waiver" . . . ought to mean the same in subsections (4) and (5). Unsuccessful attempts at modification may be waivers under § 2–209(4). Then § 2–209(5) deals with a subset of these "waivers," the subset that affects the executory portion of the contract. Waivers affecting executory provisions are enforceable or not depending on reliance. We know from the language and structure of § 2–209 that there is a difference between waivers that affect the executory portions of contracts and waivers that do not. Under the majority's reading, however, there is no difference. No waiver is effective without detrimental reliance. It is as if the majority has eliminated § 2–209(4) from the UCC and rewritten § 2–209(5) to begin: "A party who has made [an ineffectual attempt at modification] affecting [any] portion of the contract may retract. . . ."

Repair work of this kind sometimes is necessary. A legislature has many minds, and as years pass these different people may use the same word in different ways; so, too, the shifting coalitions that create a complex statute may contribute to it multiple meanings of a single word, the more so because amendments may be added to a statute after other portions have been bargained out. Section 2–209 of the UCC is not a slapdash production or the work of competing committees unaware of each other's words, however. The UCC is one of the most carefully assembled statutes in American history. It was written under the guidance of a few people, all careful drafters, debated for a decade by the American Law Institute and committees of commercial practitioners, and adopted en bloc by the states. Vague and uncertain in places the Code is; no one could see all of the problems that would come within its terms, and in some cases foreseen problems were finessed rather than solved. But "waiver" did not call for finesses, and § 2–209 was drafted and discussed as a single unit. "Waiver" in § 2–209(4) and "waiver" in § 2–209(5) are six words apart, which is not so great a gap that the mind loses track of meaning.

The subsections read well together if waiver means "intentional relinquishment of a known right" in both. Section 2–209(4) says that a failed attempt at modification may be a waiver and so relinquish a legal entitlement (such as the entitlement to timely delivery); § 2–209(5) adds that a waiver cannot affect the executory portion of the contract (the time of future deliveries, for example) if the waiving party retracts, unless there is also detrimental reliance. But for § 2.209(2) the oral waiver could affect the executory portion of the contract even without reliance. It is not necessary to vary the meaning of the word to make sense of each portion of the statute.

The majority makes reliance an ingredient of waiver not because the structure of the UCC demands this reading, but because it believes that otherwise the UCC would not deal adequately with the threat of opportunistic conduct. The drafters of the UCC chose to deal with opportunism not through a strict reading of waiver, however, but through a statutory requirement of commercial good faith. See § 2–103 and comment 2 to § 2–209. The modification-only-in-writing clause has nothing to do with opportunism. A person who has his contracting partner over a barrel, and therefore is able to obtain a concession, can get the concession in writing. The writing will be the least of his worries. . . .

A modification-only-in-writing clause may permit the parties to strengthen the requirement of commercial good faith against the careless opportunist, but its principal function is to make it easier for business to protect their agreement against casual subsequent remarks and manufactured assertions of alteration. . . .

A requirement of reliance will not make a difference very often— certainly not in this case. Any waiver that is more than a condonation of an existing default will induce some reliance. The buyer who asks a seller of fungible goods to defer delivery induces reliance even though the waiver of timely delivery will not affect the production of the goods. When the goods have a custom design, as the spade bit blanks do, some reliance is close to a certainty. I doubt that National Metal Crafters would have produced the same goods in the same quantity but for a belief that Wisconsin Knife Works wanted to have them. A change of position in reliance on the frequent discussions is all the majority requires. Summary judgment cannot be far away. Still, it is better not to ask unnecessary questions even when the questions have ready answers.

PROBLEM: GOTTA CATCH 'EM ALL

Kathy Kidsitter is a highly sought-after nanny in Los Angeles, with a degree in early childhood education. She has an impressive A-list Hollywood clientele, who sometimes have unusual dietary requests for their children. On occasion, she is asked to "live in" with her clients for a period, and accompany clients on family vacations to provide childcare. Kathy is widely accepted as one of the best in the industry, and routinely charges upwards of $100 per hour for her services.

Jack Nidoran and Joyce Caterpie, founding partners of the Nidoran, Caterpie, & Weedel law firm, have been married for fifteen years and have a cute, but rambunctious ten-year-old daughter named Joules nearing completion of the fourth grade at Coddled Kids Academy. Only a few weeks ago, Joules' summer break was about to begin, but her parents were having no luck finding a replacement nanny.

Fortunately, Kathy Kidsitter came to the rescue. She was contacted by Joyce Caterpie on May 25, after a referral by a shared acquaintance, and showed up for the interview the following day. Both Jack and Joyce were impressed by Kathy's educational background and experience with children of privilege. They wanted to hire her immediately, so they quickly drew up a contract outlining the terms of her employment. Kathy's celebrity clientele routinely asked her to sign contracts, which protected their confidentiality and outlined her duties.

The essential terms of the contract, which all parties signed, are: (1) Kathy Kidsitter agrees to provide care of Joules Nidoran during business hours from May 28 to July 27; (2) care includes all basic needs (such as food, water, clothing, transportation) as well as educational opportunities, outdoor recreation and travel, and social interaction with similarly-situated peers; and (3) in exchange for all of these services, Mr. Jack Nidoran and Mrs. Joyce Caterpie agree to pay Kathy Kidsitter $48,000 in three monthly installments of $16,000 each, to be paid on the 27th day of each calendar month covered by the agreement.

The first few days were relatively quiet. Joules spent much of the day at school and much of the afternoon and evening doing homework. However, when school ended a couple weeks later, Kathy's duties increased. A week into summer vacation, a game called PokémonGo was released that was very popular with Joules and her friends. Initially, Kathy found the game to be fun and enjoyed spending time outdoors, capturing pocket monsters (through the artificial reality interface on her cell phone) with Joules. A week later, Kathy and Joules had just placed a lure at the local Starbucks Pokéstop to attract more Pokémon when Joules received a text from her school nemesis, Mercedes Hilton. It was a screenshot of her nearly-filled Pokédex, an index of her captures. Mercedes was missing only five Pokémon!

Joules immediately turned into a Pokéfreak. She routinely woke Kathy at 3:00 am to go on hunts that would often last sixteen straight hours and cover distances, by foot, that even marathoners would shy away from. Joules refused to eat or sleep and threw screaming tantrums if Kathy even suggested taking a break from the hunt.

Even Jack and Joyce became obsessed with winning, referring to young Mercedes Hilton as "C-Class," the entry-level vehicle for Mercedes-Benz. They committed all necessary resources to Joules' Pokédreams, buying several airline tickets for Joules and Kathy when the elusive Articuno, Zapdos, and Moltres were rumored to be roosting near Sidney, Australia and also in the Democratic Republic of Congo. On these international Pokéhunts, Kathy, who became easily airsick, suffered tremendously. At one point, while Joules was safely sleeping in a Brazzaville hotel room, Kathy was restocking Joules' Pokéballs at a Pokéstop across from the hotel when Kathy was kidnapped. On that trip Kathy contracted both malaria and a form of dengue fever simultaneously. Joules' parents paid the ransom and all hospital bills but at no point showed any signs of letting her end the hunt.

After nearly plummeting to her death from a high mountain pass in Nepal, Kathy borrowed a satellite phone from a local NGO to call Joules' parents. She demanded more money or else she would not fulfill the contract. After all, Kathy was putting her life on the line every single day "in a quest to be the very best" so Joules would have bragging rights over Mercedes. After a little deliberation, Jack and Joyce agreed to triple Kathy's compensation for the remaining month of the contract. Kathy continued her globe-trotting Pokéhunt, risking life and limb on numerous occasions. After collecting all the remaining Pokémon, Kathy and Joules returned home and sent Little Miss "C-Class" a Pokédex screenshot that would lead the young Ms. Hilton to months of therapy and eventually a new pony. On July 27, Mr. Nidoran and Mrs. Caterpie wrote the final check to Kathy Kidsitter in the amount of $16,000 instead of $48,000 as agreed via sat phone, refusing to pay a penny more.

Analyze the rights and obligations of the parties.

YUK FUNG MA V. J.C. SAKE INC.
2011 WL 2175913 (N.Y.Sup.)

DEMAREST, J.J.

Following a framed-issue bench trial on plaintiff's allegations that he was forced by economic duress to sell his shares in defendant J.C. Sake, Inc. (Sake) to his fellow shareholders, the individual defendants named herein, for less than the value he believes was attributable to his interest, the court makes the following findings of fact and reaches the following conclusions of law.

The essential facts are substantially undisputed. Plaintiff Yuk Fung Ma (Ma) entered into an agreement with defendant Gee Wai Chan ("Alex") and his brother Gee On Chan ("Adam") in or about late December of 2006 to open a restaurant in which plaintiff would be the cook and primary manager. Alex, who owned other restaurants, would come by to assist and advise. Adam was present at the opening of the restaurant, but otherwise did not appear, although, according to the pleadings, both Alex and Adam hold an ownership interest in the building at 2087 Coney Island Avenue in which the restaurant is located. Plaintiff (who is related to Alex's wife) would receive compensation for his daily labors at the rate of approximately $3000 a month for six days a week, plus overtime, which was represented to be the market rate for "head cook". Initially, plaintiff was asked to invest $100,000, but was permitted to contribute only

$46,414.50 in cash for what plaintiff believed was a one-third ownership interest in the business.

Following formation of the corporate defendant, plaintiff, Alex and Adam opened a bank account at TD Bank and, after renovating the premises, opened the restaurant in May of 2007. Soon thereafter, Alex left the country and did not return until late in May 2008. In the interim, plaintiff, together with his wife and sister, managed the business. It is not disputed that the restaurant was not profitable for the first several months of operation and, according to plaintiff, he was unable to take a salary for the first ten months, although he was able to begin to recoup the loss beginning in 2008.

Upon Alex's return from China, in June 2008, he visited the restaurant and, according to his own testimony, found the situation not to his liking, including the presence of plaintiff's wife, child and sister on the premises and unsanitary conditions. Plaintiff testified that Alex demanded that he purchase supplies for the restaurant through a distributor owned by Alex, but that plaintiff declined because he wanted competitive prices. Plaintiff testified that Alex threatened to "kick [him] out" if he refused. Plaintiff testified that he responded "OK," that upon a calculation of what was owed to him, and payment thereof, he would get out.

Together with plaintiff, on July 7, 2008, Adam calculated plaintiff's interest based upon the records and receipts, to which plaintiff also had full access, but plaintiff did not agree with defendants' offer of $47,000 for his shares. Part of the reason for plaintiff's rejection of the numbers was apparently his contention that there were several other investors, the other defendants herein, of which plaintiff claims to have had no prior notice, whose interests were factored into the computation. Alex contended that he had supplied at least some of the names to plaintiff early on so that plaintiff was aware of the other investors. Plaintiff took the written calculation home to consult with his wife and an uncle.

The following day, July 8, 2008, Adam telephoned the plaintiff after 10 P.M. regarding the $47,000 offer, which plaintiff again rejected as "incorrect". Plaintiff closed the restaurant and went home. When he arrived at the restaurant the next day, July 9, he found that the locks had been changed and he was unable to open. At approximately 11:30 P.M. that night, plaintiff received a call from his uncle directing him to call Adam. In a telephone conversation with Adam close to midnight, plaintiff complained of the store closing. Adam responded that the offer that had been $47,000 was being reduced by $12,000, to $35,000, because of the closing and that, if plaintiff did not take it, the restaurant would continue to be closed and plaintiff would get nothing. Plaintiff agreed to meet Adam at another restaurant owned by Adam located on Ocean Avenue, the next day at 11:00 A.M.

Adam and Alex described the negotiations with plaintiff somewhat differently, claiming that the arguments between Alex and plaintiff, which included plaintiff's sister and an incident in late June in which police were summoned to the restaurant, had created an irreconcilable rift that precluded a continuing business relationship. Both testified that the initial proposal was that either plaintiff could buy out the other shareholders or be bought out by them. The suggested price for the restaurant, the "total amount," was $160,000, which had been discussed and agreed among all of the investing defendants. Alex testified that, in the beginning of July, plaintiff was told that he could have the "five shares" belonging to the defendant shareholders for $113,000 ($160,000 less the approximately $47,000 invested by plaintiff), or could be bought out for $47,000, but that plaintiff never responded. Thereafter, Alex left the negotiations to Adam.

Plaintiff denied that he had been given the alternative to purchase defendants' interest in the restaurant. Plaintiff stated that the $160,000 value was not consistent with the numbers contained in Adam's original calculations which indicated $230,000. It is not clear where this number came from, but it may have included the investments of the other shareholder defendants which were not known to plaintiff in advance of the falling out between himself and Alex.

When plaintiff met Adam on July 10, negotiations resumed, with plaintiff complaining that he was being "robbed" of his efforts in managing the restaurant through its early stages of loss to the point of profitability and having "a gun to [his] head," and Adam demanding that he accept the $35,000 or face further closing and get "nothing". Ultimately, Adam paid plaintiff $38,000 for his shares in Sake and a written agreement was prepared, in Chinese, by defendant Wong Chi Kong, who was also present, acknowledging plaintiff's sale of "all equity" in Sake and indicating he would have nothing further to do with the restaurant. The additional $3,000 was based upon profits for the month of June which had been omitted from earlier calculations.

Plaintiff testified that he had accepted the $38,000 in cash, at the urging of his uncle and upon consultation with his wife because, at the time, his wife was not employed, he was about to be unemployed, and he needed the money to support his family and feared that, if he did not accept, he would get "nothing" based on defendants' threats to keep the restaurant closed.

Both of the above-captioned actions initiated by plaintiff Ma require a threshold determination regarding plaintiff's status as a shareholder of Sake. Defendants contend that the document executed by Ma on July 10, 2008, constitutes unequivocal and binding evidence that Ma sold his shares in Sake on that date for $38,000 and that petitioner Ma had no standing as a shareholder to bring the petition for dissolution of Sake under Index no.

23704/08, filed August 13, 2008, or to prosecute those causes of action set forth in Index no. 28887/10 which are derivative in nature regarding alleged diversion of corporate assets to the private purpose of Alex in improving his building. Plaintiff contends that he executed the sale document and accepted $38,000 under economic duress and that the sale should, therefore, be voided.

Economic duress requires proof by the party making such claim that he was compelled to agree to the terms of a contract "because of a wrongful threat by the other party which precluded the exercise of [his] free will" (*805 Third Ave Co. v. M.W. Realty Assoc.,* 58 N.Y.2d 447, 451 [1983]). "A valid claim of duress has two components, (1) threats of an unlawful act by one party which (2) compels performance by the other party of an act which it had a legal right to abstain from performing" (*Chase Manhattan Bank v. State of New York,* 13 AD3d 873 [3d Dept 2004]).

The undisputed evidence here is that defendants forced plaintiff to accede to a price for his interest in Sake against his own will by changing the locks on the restaurant and forcing plaintiff out of work. It was acknowledged that plaintiff was the authorized manager of the restaurant and that both plaintiff and his wife were employed there. Plaintiff testified to his economic distress at the prospect of being unemployed. Clearly defendants' actions were preemptive and were designed to coerce plaintiff to accept defendants' calculations as to the value of his interest despite his own reservations about their accuracy. Plaintiff took prompt action to repudiate the agreement in commencing suit.

However, it is apparent from the testimony of plaintiff that he had agreed to a severance of his business relationship with defendants in light of the extreme animosity between Alex and plaintiff and his family members and the various disputes concerning business judgments. Initially offered basically the refund of his investment in exchange for his shares, plaintiff believed this sum did not represent a fair return, although he never made a counter-demand as he contended he did not have enough time to do so. The reduction of defendants' offer to $35,000 was based on defendants' unilateral and unjustified closing of the restaurant.

Plaintiff capitulated to defendants' threat to keep the restaurant closed indefinitely and to thus deprive plaintiff, not only of a fair return on his shares, but also of gainful employment and the means to support his family. Such coercion, though perhaps not *per se* illegal, is certainly unconscionable. The court finds defendants' actions constituted economic duress which precluded plaintiff's exercise of free will and compelled him to agree to a purchase price that was not consistent with the value of his shares. *See Art Stone Theatrical Corp. v. Tech. Programming & Sys. Support of Long Is., Inc.,* 157 A.D.2d 689, 691 [2d Dept 1990].

Although plaintiff seeks to void the sale of his shares so as to restore himself to the status of a shareholder, the passage of nearly three years since the date of the transaction, during which period Alex has managed the restaurant, and more particularly, the undisputed fact that the parties had essentially agreed to a sale of plaintiff's interest in light of their irreconcilable differences regarding the operation of the restaurant, support the conclusion that the sale itself is not void, but that the appropriate equitable remedy here is the voidance of the price and an award of money damages based upon an assessment of the value of plaintiff's shares on July 8, 2008. *See Doyle v. Allstate Ins. Co.,* 1 N.Y.2d 439, 443 [1956]; *Ungewitter v. Toch,* 31 A.D.2d 583 [3d Dept 1968]. . . .

NOTES AND QUESTIONS

1.   Which aspect of the defendant's behavior seemed particularly coercive? Do you think the plaintiff's own economic situation played a role in the court's decision? Should it have?

2.   The fact pattern posed in *Yuk Fung Ma v. J.C. Sake Inc.* is common in the life of closely held corporations (closely held or privately held businesses are ones that are not traded on a public exchange like the New York Stock Exchange or NASDAQ).

Often arising in small business settings, the problem is commonplace: one or two majority shareholders who control more than 51% of the shares will "freeze out" a minority shareholder. This is problematic in close corporations where oftentimes the shares are not liquid—there is no ready market for valuation, and where the minority shareholders are paid a salary. Apart from "economic duress" such "freeze out" situations may implicate an "abuse of control" wherein the majority shareholder or shareholders may be found to have violated a fiduciary duty to the minority shareholder.

For a classic case on abuse of control, see *Wilkes v. Springdale Nursing Home,* 353 N.E.2 657 (Mass. 1976).

3.   To paraphrase an apocryphal yet colorful saying by a successful business person, "I have a company and it has different valuations. The first 51% is worth millions of dollars, the last 49% isn't worth a damn." Many deal with this problem ex-ante by writing in contractual protections or a buy-sell agreement with their co-venturers. These contractual rights can be used to clarify and shore up the minority shareholder's position within the company, and many such agreements provide for arbitration or other forms of alternative dispute resolution in the event there is a conflict over valuation.

EXAMPLE: HURRICANE SANDY

In the wake of Hurricane Sandy, many in the New Jersey-New York area were hard hit with storm damage, and many essential services were off-line for long periods. Gas stations, taxicabs, and other services raised their prices.

Many condemned these practices, saying that jacking up prices was taking advantage of people's desperation during an emergency. Many customers were angry at the "hold up" and noted that increasing the prices during a stressful time was unethical. Some even called it "reverse looting."

Others, however, including prominent economists, defended the behavior, noting that it is nothing more than a response to the laws of supply and demand. After a disaster, there may be limited supply and increased demand for transportation, batteries, or drinking water. Rising prices are a way of getting these goods and services to those who place the greatest value on them or of encouraging people to prepare for disasters in advance.

1.   Are price increases an illegal form of economic duress or just a reasonable business response to a shortage? How should the law respond?

2.   In some states, statutes exist to prevent price gouging. Are these types of laws sound policy? Does your state have such a statute?

F. UNDUE INFLUENCE

As we have seen, some defenses, such as economic duress, concentrate on the overreaching or bad behavior of market actors. Other defenses, such as mental capacity, focus on questions of vulnerability. The defense of undue influence focuses on *both* bad behavior and one party's vulnerability.

ODORIZZI V. BLOOMFIELD SCHOOL DISTRICT
246 Cal. App. 2d 123 (Cal. App. 1966)

FLEMING, J.

... Plaintiff Donald Odorizzi was employed during 1964 as an elementary school teacher by defendant Bloomfield School District and was under contract with the district to continue to teach school the following year as a permanent employee. On June 10 he was arrested . . . for certain alleged crimes [relating to homosexual activity] that a month later were dismissed by a judge as unsupported by reasonable or probable cause; and on June 11 he signed and delivered to his superiors his written resignation as a teacher, a resignation which the district accepted on June 13. . . . [I]n September he sought to resume his employment with the district. On the district's refusal to reinstate him he filed suit for declaratory and other relief.

Odorizzi's amended complaint asserts his resignation was invalid because obtained through duress, fraud, mistake, and undue influence and given at a time when he lacked capacity to make a valid contract. Specifically, Odorizzi declares he was under such severe mental and emotional strain at the time he signed his resignation, having just completed the process of arrest, questioning by the police, booking, and release on bail, and having gone for 40 hours without sleep, that he was incapable of rational thought or action. While he was in this condition and unable to think clearly, the superintendent of the district and the principal of his school came to his apartment.

They said they were trying to help him and had his best interests at heart, that he should take their advice and immediately resign his position with the district, that there was no time to consult an attorney, that if he did not resign immediately the district would suspend and dismiss him from his position and publicize the proceedings, his "aforedescribed arrest" and cause him "to suffer extreme embarrassment and humiliation"; but that if he resigned at once the incident would not be publicized and would not jeopardize his chances of securing employment as a teacher elsewhere. Odorizzi pleads that because of his faith and confidence in their representations they were able to substitute their will and judgment in place of his own and thus obtain his signature to his purported resignation. A demurrer to his amended complaint was sustained without leave to amend.

[The court reversed the trial court as to undue influence but not the other four excuses her asserted.] Undue influence . . . is a shorthand legal phrase used to describe persuasion which tends to be coercive in nature, persuasion which overcomes the will without convincing the judgment. . . . The hallmark of such persuasion is high pressure, a pressure which works on mental, moral, or emotional weakness to such an extent that it approaches the boundaries of coercion. In this sense, undue influence has been called overpersuasion. . . .

Misrepresentations of law or fact are not essential to the charge, for a person's will may be overborne without misrepresentation. By statutory definition undue influence includes "taking an unfair advantage of another's weakness of mind, or . . . taking a grossly oppressive and unfair advantage of another's necessities or distress." . . . While most reported cases of undue influence involve persons who bear a confidential relationship to one another, a confidential or authoritative relationship between the parties need not be present when the undue influence involves unfair advantage taken of another's weakness or distress. . . .

We paraphrase the summary of undue influence given the jury by Sir James P. Wilde in Hall v. Hall, L.R. 1, P. & D. 481, 482 (1868): To make a good contract a man must be a free agent. Pressure of whatever sort which overpowers the will without convincing the judgment is a species of restraint under which no valid contract can be made. Importunity or threats, if carried to the degree in which the free play of a man's will is overborne, constitute undue influence, although no force is used or threatened. A party may be led but not driven, and his acts must be the offspring of his own volition and not the record of someone else's. . . .

Undue susceptibility may consist of total weakness of mind which leaves a person entirely without understanding . . . ; or, a lesser weakness which destroys the capacity of a person to make a contract even though he is not totally incapacitated . . . ; or, the first element in our equation, a still lesser weakness which provides sufficient grounds to rescind a contract for undue influence . . . . Such lesser weakness need not be long-lasting nor wholly incapacitating, but may be merely a lack of full vigor due to age . . . , physical condition . . . , emotional anguish . . . , or a combination of such factors. The reported cases have usually involved elderly, sick, senile persons alleged to have executed wills or deeds under pressure. . . . In some of its aspects this lesser weakness could perhaps be called weakness of spirit. But whatever name we give it, this first element of undue influence resolves itself into a lessened capacity of the object to make a free contract. . . .

Undue influence in its second aspect involves an application of excessive strength by a dominant subject against a servient object. Judicial consideration of this second element in undue influence has been relatively rare, for there are few cases denying persons who persuade but do not misrepresent the benefit of their bargain. Yet logically, the same legal consequences should apply to the results of excessive strength as to the results of undue weakness. Whether from weakness on one side, or strength on the other, or a combination of the two, undue influence occurs whenever there results "that kind of influence or supremacy of one mind over another by which that other is prevented from acting according to his own wish or judgment, and whereby the will of the person is overborne and he is induced to do or forbear to do an act which he would not do, or would do, if left to act freely." (Webb v. Saunders, 79 Cal.App.2d 863, 871 [181 P.2d 43].) Undue influence involves a type of mismatch which our statute calls unfair advantage. (Civ. Code, § 1575.) Whether a person of subnormal capacities has been subjected to ordinary force or a person of normal capacities subjected to extraordinary force, the match is equally out of balance. If will has been overcome against judgment, consent may be rescinded.

The difficulty, of course, lies in determining when the forces of persuasion have overflowed their normal banks and become oppressive flood waters. There are second thoughts to every bargain, and hindsight is still better than foresight. Undue influence cannot be used as a pretext to avoid bad bargains or escape from bargains which refuse to come up to expectations. . . . If we are temporarily persuaded against our better judgment to do something about which we later have second thoughts, we must abide the consequences of the risks inherent in managing our own affairs. . . .

However, overpersuasion is generally accompanied by certain characteristics which tend to create a pattern. The pattern usually involves several of the following elements: (1) discussion of the transaction at an unusual or inappropriate time, (2) consummation of the transaction in an unusual place, (3) insistent demand that the business be finished at once, (4) extreme emphasis on untoward consequences of delay, (5) the use of multiple persuaders by the dominant side against a single servient party, (6) absence of third-party advisers to the servient party, (7) statements that there is no time to consult financial advisers or attorneys. If a number of these elements are simultaneously present, the persuasion may be characterized as excessive. . . .

The difference between legitimate persuasion and excessive pressure, like the difference between seduction and rape, rests to a considerable extent in the manner in which the parties go about their business. For example, if a day or two after Odorizzi's release on bail the superintendent of the school district had called him into his office during business hours and directed his attention to those provisions of the Education Code compelling his leave of absence and authorizing his suspension on the filing of written charges, had told him that the district contemplated filing written charges against him, had pointed out the alternative of resignation available to him, had informed him he was free to consult counsel or any adviser he wished and to consider the matter overnight and return with his decision the next day, it is extremely unlikely that any complaint about the use of excessive pressure could ever have been made against the school district.

But, according to the allegations of the complaint, this is not the way it happened, and if it had happened that way, plaintiff would never have resigned. Rather, the representatives of the school board undertook to achieve their objective by overpersuasion and imposition to secure plaintiff's signature but not his consent to his resignation through a high-pressure carrot-and-stick technique—under which they assured plaintiff they were trying to assist him, he should rely on their advice, there wasn't time to consult an attorney, if he didn't resign at once the school district would suspend and dismiss him from his position and publicize the proceedings, but if he did resign the incident wouldn't jeopardize his chances of securing a teaching post elsewhere.

Plaintiff has thus pleaded both subjective and objective elements entering the undue influence equation and stated sufficient facts to put in issue the question whether his free will had been overborne by defendant's agents at a time when he was unable to function in a normal manner. It was sufficient to pose ". . . the ultimate question . . . whether a free and competent judgment was merely influenced, or whether a mind was so dominated as to prevent the exercise of an independent judgment." (Williston on Contracts, § 1625 [rev. ed.]; Rest., Contracts, § 497, com. c.) The question cannot be resolved by an analysis of pleading but requires a finding of fact.

We express no opinion on the merits of plaintiff's case, or the propriety of his continuing to teach school (Ed. Code, § 13403), or the timeliness of his rescission (Civ. Code, § 1691). We do hold that his pleading, liberally construed, states a cause of action for rescission of a transaction to which his apparent consent had been obtained through the use of undue influence. [Reversed.]

NOTES AND QUESTIONS

1.   The appellate court in *Odorizzi* reversed as to undue influence only, not the other grounds asserted—duress, fraud, mistake or lack of capacity. Please make the strongest possible argument to support excuse on each of those grounds. Which, if any, of these is persuasive?

2.   Background research by University of Washington Law School Dean Kellye Testy reveals that even though, technically Odorizzi "won" this portion of the case, the overall result was not positive. After this "victory," Odorizzi still had to plead his case for reinstatement with the school board. After years of legal wrangling and high attorney's fees, Odorizzi ultimately gave up on his career as a teacher. *See* KELLYE Y. TESTY, RELATIONAL BACKGROUND: DONALD ODORIZZI'S STORY, IN RANDY E. BARNETT, CONTRACTS: CASES AND DOCTRINE 1122–29 (2d ed. Aspen 1999).

3.   As noted at the outset, the allegations against the teacher in the case concerned homosexual activity. Since the time of the *Odorizzi* decision, the Supreme Court decided *Obergefell v. Hodges*, 576 U.S. ___, 135 S.Ct. 2584 (2015), which held that same-sex couples have a fundamental right to marry. Approximately thirty-five states have passed laws prohibiting employment discrimination on the basis of sexual orientation. Approximately fifteen states, however, have yet to take any legislative action. A federal law (ENDA) has been proposed in Congress on sexual orientation discrimination in employment, but has yet to garner requisite support for passage.

RESTATEMENT (SECOND) OF CONTRACTS, SECTION 177

§ 177.   *When Undue Influence Makes a Contract Voidable.*

(1)   Undue influence is unfair persuasion of a party who is under the domination of the person exercising the persuasion or who by virtue of the relation between them is justified in assuming that that person will not act in a manner inconsistent with his welfare.

(2)   If a party's manifestation of assent is induced by undue influence by the other party, the contract is voidable by the victim.

(3)   If a party's manifestation of assent is induced by one who is not a party to the transaction, the contract is voidable by the victim unless the other party to the transaction in good faith and without reason to know of the undue influence either gives value or relies materially on the transaction.

IN RE ESTATE OF BURREN
994 N.E.2d 1022 (Il. App. 2013)

NEVILLE, J.J.

In 2004, Glenn Burren signed a will that named his attorney, Steven Miner, as executor. In the will, Glenn named his three children and Steven's two children as the principal legatees of the estate. When Glenn died, Steven filed the will in the probate court. Glenn's children contested the will and petitioned to recover sums of money Glenn gave Steven in the years before Glenn's death. The trial court, after a bench trial, held the will invalid and ordered Steven to pay to the estate almost $500,000, plus prejudgment interest in excess of $200,000. Steven appeals from both the order declaring the will invalid and the order directing Steven to repay the estate more than $700,000.

We find that the evidence raises presumptions that Steven exercised undue influence over Glenn when Glenn signed checks transferring money from Glenn's accounts to Steven. [The following omits discussion and analysis concerning the successful challenge to the execution of the will]. . . . We also find the evidence sufficient to support the trial court's finding that Steven failed to rebut the presumption of undue influence. . . .

In 1976, Marion Burren brought her date, Steven, home to meet her parents. Marion's father, Glenn, got along well with Steven, who called Glenn "Pops." They continued to visit each other after Steven and Marion broke up in 1978. Glenn divorced Marion's mother in 1978, and that same year he started dating Steven's mother, Nancy Miner.

Steven graduated from law school and obtained his license to practice law in 1981. He represented Glenn in several real estate transactions, and he represented Marion in her divorce. In June 2003, Steven, acting as attorney for Glenn's sister, Pearl Burren, prepared a power of attorney in which Pearl appointed Glenn as her agent with the power to conduct financial transactions for her. Glenn wrote several checks to Steven on Pearl's account. When Pearl died in November 2003, Glenn inherited an investment account worth about $620,000, and real estate which Glenn sold, with Steven acting as his attorney, for more than $187,000. Glenn made his bank account a joint account, giving Steven the power to sign checks drawn on Glenn's account.

Glenn came to Steven's home for a birthday party for Steven's son, Steven Miner II, in January 2004. Before leaving, Glenn signed a typewritten will which named Steven as the estate's executor. The will split the bulk of Glenn's estate into five equal parts, with one-fifth going to each of Glenn's three children, Marion Stewart, Linda Kemp and Glenn Burren, Jr., and one-fifth going to each of Steven's children, Steven II and Katy Miner.

Glenn made out many checks to Steven over the course of the following years. The checks totaled almost $500,000. At Steven's behest, Glenn signed a number of letters, on Steven's letterhead and addressed to Glenn, regarding the checks. One dated June 2004 says:

> Re: receipt of $70,000.00
> Pops:
> Please allow this letter to acknowledge the receipt of $70,000.00 in cash and checks. I remain
> Respectfully,
> Steven A. Miner
> SAM/sm
>
> APPROVED:
> Glenn Burren /s/

Other letters, phrased identically except for the amount of the check, acknowledged checks for $50,000 in September 2004, and $50,000 in October 2004. A similar letter dated December 2003 confirmed receipt of $62,000. In 2006, Glenn signed forms Steven prepared that gave Steven a power of attorney to act on Glenn's behalf for both health care decisions and for Glenn's property.

When Glenn died, on July 20, 2007, his net assets, which exceeded $800,000 in 2004, had dwindled to less than $350,000. Steven petitioned for probate of the will and for letters of office naming him executor of the estate. The court appointed Steven as executor. Marion and Linda contested the will and petitioned for removal of Steven from his position as executor. In October 2008, Marion and Linda filed a citation to recover assets, asking the court to order Steven to pay to the estate $492,779.75, for the checks Glenn gave Steven after May 2003.

At the trial . . . Marion introduced into evidence a letter Glenn received in September 2004 from his investment advisor, advising Glenn not to increase his withdrawals from his account, which Glenn had limited to $2,000 per month. The letter indicated that as long as Glenn used only $2,000 per month, he reduced the balance in his account by only $3,500 per year. [This is presumably because interest on the principal balance would have approximated $27,000.—Eds.]

Steven testified that Glenn treated him as a father would treat a son, and Glenn treated Steven's children as though they were Glenn's grandchildren. Steven said Glenn made him a joint owner of the bank account because Glenn did not trust his children, and Glenn wanted assurance that if anything happened to him, someone would pay his bills. Steven admitted that he cashed the checks on which Glenn listed him as payee. The checks Steven cashed totaled $498,659.75. Steven did not remember why Glenn paid Steven money out of Pearl's account. Steven testified that he cashed the other checks for Glenn, returning almost all of the money from the checks directly to Glenn.

Steven never asked Glenn why he needed so much cash. Steven claimed that the four letters Glenn approved showed that Steven gave the cash back to Glenn. Steven also prepared the letters that Glenn signed directing his investment advisor to issue checks to Steven for $70,000 in April 2004, $49,881 in August 2004, and $49,881 in September 2004. Steven explained that he typed the letters for Glenn because Glenn had no typewriter. Steven admitted that he did not advise Glenn to seek independent legal advice before writing him the checks or adding him onto the joint bank account.

. . . The trial court found that Glenn relied on Steven for legal and financial advice. The court did not believe Steven's testimony that he gave to Glenn all of the money he received from cashing the checks Glenn gave him, especially because Steven presented "no independent credible evidence to corroborate" his testimony. The court held that Marion and Linda showed that Steven had a fiduciary relationship with Glenn, and Steven benefitted from the transactions with Glenn, so the evidence raised a presumption that Steven exercised undue influence over Glenn. The court concluded that Steven failed to rebut the presumption of undue influence. The court entered a judgment against Steven for $498,659.75 plus interest.

. . . .

Steven claims that the trial court should not have found that he exercised undue influence over Glenn when Glenn signed checks made out to Steven. Courts closely scrutinize transactions between attorneys and their clients. *Klaskin,* 126 Ill.2d at 386, 128 Ill.Dec. 526, 534 N.E.2d 971. "When an attorney engages in a transaction with a client and is benefited thereby, a presumption arises that the transaction proceeded from undue influence. * * * [C]ourts require clear and convincing evidence to rebut this presumption." *Klaskin,* 126 Ill.2d at 386–87, 128 Ill.Dec. 526, 534 N.E.2d 971.

Steven claims first that he did not benefit from the transactions with Glenn, because he gave Glenn back all of the cash he received from cashing the checks. Steven's exhibits prove the assertion false, as he provides no accounting for $10,000, even assuming that Glenn used none of the checks he received to pay any of his expenses. Cashing checks he received from Glenn benefitted Steven, giving rise to the presumption of undue influence. See *Klaskin,* 126 Ill.2d at 386, 128 Ill.Dec. 526, 534 N.E.2d 971.

Next, Steven argues that he rebutted the presumption of undue influence with evidence of his close relationship with Glenn, Glenn's mental competence, and Steven's repayment to Glenn of most of the amounts Steven received from the cashed checks. Steven asks us to apply the holding of *In re Marriage of Pagano,* 154 Ill.2d 174, 180 Ill.Dec. 729, 607 N.E.2d 1242 (1992), where the court said:

> The presumption of undue influence applied to agreements between attorneys and their clients is not conclusive, however, and may be rebutted by the attorney. This court has looked to several factors in determining whether such a presumption is overcome, including whether: (1) the attorney made a full and frank disclosure of all relevant information; (2) the client's agreement was based on adequate consideration, and (3) the client had independent advice before completing the transaction. [Citations.] Other Illinois decisions have applied slightly different factors, including whether: (1) the agreement was offered by the lawyer with unquestionable good faith and with complete disclosure, (2) the client entered into the agreement with a full understanding of all facts and their legal importance, and (3) the client's decision was free from undue influence and was fair.

Steven admits that Glenn had no independent legal advice about the many checks Glenn wrote to Steven. Steven's relationship with Glenn has little bearing here, as "an affectionate relationship between the testator and a preferred beneficiary is not sufficient to rebut a presumption of undue influence." *In re Estate of Mooney,* 117 Ill.App.3d 993, 998, 73 Ill.Dec. 169, 453 N.E.2d 1158 (1983). Neither does Glenn's mental competence prove a lack of undue influence. See *Pagano,* 154 Ill.2d at 186, 180 Ill.Dec. 729, 607 N.E.2d 1242.

Steven relies on the letters Glenn signed on Steven's letterhead, concerning four transactions involving a total of $232,000. Steven claims that in the letters Glenn admitted that Steven gave him the entire amount in cash. But the letters do not support Steven's argument. In the letters, addressed to Glenn, Steven "acknowledge[d] the receipt" of the amount of the checks associated with each letter. Glenn signed on a line indicating his approval of the transactions. Giving the letters their most natural interpretation, the letters indicate that Steven received the cash, and Glenn approved the transactions. While the letters help somewhat with the argument that Steven disclosed all the transactions to Glenn, they show no consideration for the sums Steven received, and extremely generous gifts from Glenn to Steven, rather than fair transactions.

Thus, the evidence shows some disclosure, but no independent advice, no consideration, and no fairness. We cannot say that the trial court's finding, that Steven failed to present clear and convincing evidence to rebut the presumption of undue influence, is contrary to the manifest weight of the evidence. . . .

EXAMPLE: SCOUT'S HONOR

In 1960, writer Harper Lee published the classic legal novel *To Kill a Mockingbird*, featuring saintly small-town attorney Atticus Finch as protagonist. The plot is told from the point of view of Finch's young daughter, Scout, and follows the story of the family as Atticus defends of a black man wrongly accused of a crime in the segregated South. The book was a runaway bestseller and garnered widespread critical acclaim, winning the Pulitzer Prize. The book was later made into a movie starring Gregory Peck. Monroeville, the small Alabama town where Ms. Lee lived, staged a dramatization of a scene from the book every year in her honor.

In the years that followed publication and success of *To Kill a Mockingbird*, Ms. Lee rarely gave interviews and became increasingly reclusive. When asked about further writing, she made statements to the effect that she had perfected her message in her first book, and that it would be her last. Ms. Lee's sister, Alice, was an attorney in Montgomery, Alabama, who helped shelter the author as she withdrew from everyday life. Harper Lee said she was done with writing; she had said what she had to in her one jewel of a book.

At least that was the case until 2015, two months after sister Alice died. The attorney who assumed Alice's clients announced that a formerly lost manuscript entitled *Go Set a Watchman* had been discovered in Harper Lee's safe deposit box. This manuscript was alternately described as a separate book and as a rough draft of *To Kill a Mockingbird*. By that time, Harper Lee was blind and lived in an assisted living institution. The publisher of *To Kill a Mockingbird* decided to print the new Harper Lee book, and it sold millions of copies. The new book cast a critical light on the character of Atticus Finch, who, it was revealed, was a virulent racist.

What ethical obligations would Harper Lee's attorney or publishers have in regard to the *Go Set a Watchman* contracts?

LUTGERT V. LUTGERT
338 So.2d 1111 (Fla. App. 1976)

McNULTY, C.J.

We void this day an antenuptial agreement because of involuntariness on the part of the wife. The ten-year marriage of the parties hereto was dissolved upon the petition of the husband. An antenuptial agreement which, among other things, provided for the matter of support or alimony and a waiver by the wife of attorneys' fees in the event of separation or divorce was sustained by the trial court and the questions relating to alimony and attorneys fees were adjudicated accordingly. The relevant portions of the agreement are as follows:

> FIRST: The said RAYMOND L. LUTGERT represents that his present estate consists of approximately Three Million Dollars

($3,000,000.00) in value. The nature of his assets are such that precise valuation is impossible, but this is believed to be a reasonable and conservative figure at this time.

* * *

THIRD: All the personal and real estate now owned by the said RAYMOND L. LUTGERT shall be his own personal estate to be dealt with by him during his lifetime or by will as freely as though this agreement had not been executed in all respects except as indicated immediately hereinafter, namely:

* * *

C. The foregoing provisions hereof are in contemplation of the parties remaining married to and living with each other until the death of one of them. However, it is the desire of the parties to recognize the possibility of presently unanticipated separation or divorce.

Each of the parties has been previously married and is aware of the expense and possible publicity with resultant personal embarrassment, which may result from court controversy in a divorce or separate maintenance action over financial matters, in addition to great emotional strain.

The parties therefore further agree as follows:

In the event of the separation of the parties with or without divorce the said RAYMOND L. LUTGERT will pay to the said MURIEL STEVENSON the sum of One Thousand Dollars ($1,000.00) per month so long as she shall live, and not remarry.

Such payments shall be in full of any support money or alimony from the said RAYMOND L. LUTGERT to the said MURIEL STEVENSON, and Each party shall pay his or her own attorneys fees and other expenses in any separation or divorce proceeding. . . .

While the testimony relating to the execution of the agreement is conflicting in several particulars, we accept the husband's version except as to the undenied portions of the wife's version. A narrative of significant events follows:

The parties, and their then spouses, were acquainted socially for a considerable period of time before their marriage in Chicago, where they previously resided. Their relationship ripened into a love affair after their respective former spouses became illicitly involved with each other and two divorces ensued. They kept company for approximately a year and became engaged some four weeks prior to their marriage herein at 12:30 in the early morning hours of Friday, April 30, 1965.

An understanding of the odd hour of the marriage can be had from the events which began on Monday evening of that fateful week, April 26, when appellee husband called and suggested that they be married shortly after midnight on Thursday, April 29, provided they could book passage for an extended honeymoon cruise on the SS Constitution, scheduled to sail from New York later on that same day. The wife ecstatically agreed.

On Tuesday morning, April 27, the husband advised appellant by telephone that he had succeeded in getting passage on the Constitution and that the wedding plans could go ahead. The parties met shortly thereafter and spent the rest of that day purchasing a sable stole for her and a wedding outfit for him; getting their passports straightened out; getting blood tests; arranging for a state Court of Appeals judge to marry them; acquiring the use of V.I.P. facilities, called the 'Topflight Room' of Northwest Airlines, at the O'Hare Airport in Chicago; and inviting family and friends to the wedding.

On Wednesday, April 28, the wife purchased her trousseau, after which the parties met at their jewelers to select and fit wedding rings. Thereafter, a marriage license was procured.

The following day, Thursday, April 29, is the critical date concerning the execution of the antenuptial agreement. That afternoon the parties met again at the jewelers to finalize the sizing of the wedding rings. While they were being readied the husband took the antenuptial agreement out of his pocket and for the first time presented it to appellant and asked her to sign it. She objected, saying that it indicated lack of trust on his part and that she didn't want the marriage to start out on such a weak footing. He made light of that suggestion, proclaiming that the agreement was of no consequence anyway since they wouldn't be getting a divorce. He joked about being married for some 80 years, getting married at their age. The wife still objected; so the husband called his Chicago lawyers, Cummings and Wyman, while still at the jewelers and apparently some conversation ensued between the lawyers and the wife after the husband put her on the telephone. While the evidence is conflicting as to whether this phone conversation resulted in any change in the wording of the agreement (the husband contends it did), the documentary evidence itself irrefutably demonstrates that the document was in fact drawn up and finally drafted the preceding Monday, April 26, and was not changed in any respect thereafter.

As a further insight into the events leading up to the agreement herein, it is agreed that the subject of an antenuptial agreement had been brought up on more than one occasion for perhaps up to a year before the marriage herein. The husband testified that he wanted such an agreement because his father had advised it and because he had had extreme difficulty during his first divorce. No specific agreement nor draft thereof was made, however, until the instant agreement was prepared on April 26 of that eventful week in 1965 as aforesaid. The wife insists that she consistently objected to such an agreement, whatever its terms, and the sole testimony in rebuttal of this is the husband's statement that 'there was no refutation of any willingness to sign such an agreement.'

In any case, following the aforementioned phone call, the wife finally agreed reluctantly to sign the agreement after the husband insisted that the wedding would otherwise be called off. She contends that she signed the agreement then and there at the jewelers; but we can accept the husband's version that it wasn't signed until just before the wedding that night (i.e., about 12:30 a.m. on Friday) when the minute hand of the clock was on the rise 'for luck,' as several of the witnesses testified. Two witnesses corroborated the husband's version that the agreement was indeed signed at the airport shortly before the wedding, one Williams, the husband's nephew, who also was a notary public and who appears to have taken the acknowledgment of the parties, and one of the husband's attorneys who was a member of the aforementioned Cummings and Wyman firm. Each additionally testified that he did not hear the wife voice any objections to the agreement as she executed it.

After the marriage, as may be gleaned from the admitted wealth of the husband the parties enjoyed a lifestyle reserved only to the fabulously rich. While the trial court found that during the times material herein the husband was worth from approximately $3,100,000 at the beginning to $3,900,000 at the present time, the wife points to much of the record tending to the conclusion that he is really presently worth nearer to $25,000,000. Indeed the admitted opulent lifestyle would appear to be supportable only if the latter figure were found to be the fact. For example, the present homeplace in Naples, Florida, is a palatial mansion directly on the Gulf of Mexico. It has eight bedrooms, twelve baths, a five-car garage, a guest house and servants' quarters and is surrounded by some four and a half acres of formal gardens with a gate house at its entrance. The parties owned at least three luxury motor yachts, one of them a 50-footer custom built in North Carolina, and one a 63-footer custom built in Japan. They at one time owned a private turbojet airplane. They drove only luxury cars, including Rolls Royces and Lincoln Continentals. They took at least one round-the-world cruise and several extended cruises to Europe and other parts of the world. They had staffs of servants and gardeners. He gave expensive gifts of valuable jewelry. The husband has a hobby of collecting classic automobiles, his present collection having a value in excess of $900,000; and on one occasion he bid for and purchased an original Duesenberg automobile for some $207,000.

The wife was fully aware before the marriage, of course, that the husband was a man of great wealth—and lived it. But all this, it seems to us, should only point up the expectancy of security on the part of the wife at the time of her acceptance of the marriage proposal, as well as the disproportionate relative positions of the parties, when it is emphasized that she had only a relatively small amount of cash in her own right at that time, together with some interest in the marital home of her prior marriage, and approximately $600 a month alimony (for only 10 years) as a result of a prior divorce. Clearly, since the agreement herein limits her simply to $1,000 a month alimony in the event of separation or divorce, and no attorneys fees, a grossly disproportionate benefit to the husband as a result of the agreement is startlingly patent.

[I]t is black letter law that the parties to an antenuptial agreement do not deal at arms' length with each other. Their relationship is one of mutual trust and confidence. While such agreements are not per se suspect in the law, the courts nevertheless scrutinize them with care; and the parties must exercise the highest degree of good faith, candor and sincerity in all matters bearing on the terms and execution of the proposed agreement, with *fairness* being the ultimate measure. Moreover, a presumption of undue influence or overreaching arises in transactions or contracts between persons in such a confidential relationship when it is clear that the dominant party thereto is the grossly disproportionate beneficiary of the transaction. It is well settled, for example, that with respect to the issue of full disclosure of the prospective husband's wealth, a disproportionate benefit to the husband in an antenuptial agreement casts upon him the burden of showing that the wife in fact did have full or sufficient knowledge of the husband's wealth.

The presumption which arises in these cases operates against the party receiving such benefit and imposes upon him the burden of coming forth with evidence sufficient to rebut it to the extent necessary to avoid its preponderating on the issue to which it relates. We see no reason why the burden on the part of the husband ought be any less with respect to the issue of voluntariness on the part of the wife in entering into such an agreement, than it is with respect to the issue of full disclosure, when there is a grossly disproportionate benefit to him. Together with sufficient coercive circumstances surrounding the execution of the agreement as to give rise to a presumption of undue influence or overreaching.

Here, it appears that the wife was in her middle or late thirties at the time of the agreement. The instant marriage was her third, following one of approximately seventeen years during which she bore three children. Her first marriage was of very short duration having been entered into when she was seventeen years old. Concededly, therefore, it can hardly be said that she was mesmerized by prehymeneal ardor when she entered into the agreement. But that doesn't mean that her volition could not still have been overcome by circumstances sufficiently coercive in nature. . . .

[A]ll the circumstances surrounding the execution of the agreement in this case, including its disproportionate terms, militate against fairness and are sufficient to support a presumption, as a matter of law, of undue influence and overreaching which bore adversely on the free exercise of the wife's will. We certainly couldn't indulge a contrary presumption; the wife could hardly say more in rebuttal. Nor need we go so far as to say that the wife proved [i]nvoluntariness as a matter of law. The device of a presumption such as that we employ here is the prevalent judicial tool commonly used in the determination vel non of undue influence or overreaching in transactions arising out of confidential relationships.

The burden thus shifted to the husband to rebut this presumption by coming forth with some competent evidence to the contrary. We have searched the record in vain to find it—it simply isn't there. The mere statement by the husband that 'there was no refutation of any willingness (on the part of the wife) to sign such an agreement,' which alluded to prior discussions of an antenuptial agreement generally and not to the specific one involved here which was objected to, will not alone suffice. . . .

NOTES AND QUESTIONS

1.   Using the factor test set out in *Odorizzi*, what facts seem to lend credence to the presence of undue influence in the previous two cases?

2.   What role does the value of trust play in these decisions? Is it significant that the last two cases involve familial promises?

3.   What role does vulnerability (or protecting the weaker party) play in the defense of undue influence? Think back to Gail Waters in *Waters v. Min Ltd.* (the case involving the lopsided annuity exchange). Might Waters have argued undue influence as well as unconscionability to avoid the contract?

4.   Prenuptial agreements gained widespread legal recognition beginning with a landmark Florida case, *Posner v. Posner*, 257 So.2d 530 (Fla. 1972). Today, nearly all states recognize their validity and a majority have enacted the 1983 Uniform Premarital Agreement Act (UPAA). Section 6(a) of the UPAA provides:

A premarital agreement is not enforceable if the party against whom enforcement is sought proves that: (1) that party did not execute the agreement voluntarily; or (2) the agreement was unconscionable when it was executed and, before execution of the agreement, that party: (i) was not provided a fair and reasonable disclosure of the property or financial obligations of the other party; (ii) did not voluntarily and expressly waive, in writing, any right to disclosure of the property or financial obligations of the other party beyond the disclosure provided; and (iii) did not have, or reasonably could not have had, an adequate knowledge of the property or financial obligations of the other party.

How would this legislation apply to *Lutgert v. Lutgert*? Consult Barbara Ann Atwood, *Ten Years Later: Lingering Concerns About the Uniform Premarital Agreement Act*, 19 JOURNAL OF LEGISLATION 127 (1993).

EXAMPLE: T-REX APTLY NAMED SUE

In August 1990, commercial fossil hunters from the Black Hills Geologic Institute ("Black Hills") discovered the remains of an almost-complete Tyrannosaurus Rex skeleton located in the Badlands of South Dakota. Named "Sue" after her discoverer, the fossil immediately became the subject of controversy. The collectors gave the purported owner of the land, a Native American rancher named Maurice Williams, a check for $5,000, which he cashed, and the collectors excavated Sue. The fair market value of a T-Rex skeleton with that degree of completeness was over $8 million.

As the discovery garnered publicity, Williams began a fierce court battle to rescind the contract with Black Hills, claiming that the $5,000 was merely a payment to inspect the property for potential fossils. He was not the only one with a bone to pick. At one point, the parties claiming ownership of Sue included Black Hills, Williams, the Cheyenne River Sioux tribe (Williams' land was within the boundaries of their reservation), and the federal government (the government had held the land in trust for Williams so it was not subject to tax forfeiture).

On these facts, which contract defenses might be available to Williams? *See* Miriam A. Cherry, *A Tyrannosaurus-Rex Aptly Named "Sue": Using A Disputed Dinosaur to Teach Contract Defenses*, 81 N.D. L. REV. 295, 295–96 (2005).

CHAPTER 6

RESTITUTION

■ ■ ■

The law of restitution is a separate body of law, independent of contract. But the law of restitution also overlaps with contract law. For that matter, restitution is also independent of but overlapping with tort law. Section 1 of the Restatement (Third) of Restitution announces the fundamental principle: "A person who is unjustly enriched at the expense of another is subject to liability in restitution." While it is correct and conventional to view contract and tort as the principal sources of common law civil liability, restitution is a close third.

Some fact patterns commonly appearing in first year law school classes are easy to classify—a breached promise creates an issue of contract law or negligence causes an issue of tort law. Other fact patterns defy tidy classification and that is often where restitution enters. While an entire course on restitution could be designed, it is customary in U.S. law schools to incorporate some of its quasi-contractual aspects in the first-year course on contracts and we follow that custom here. It is useful to begin with the following official comment to Section 1 of the Restatement (Third) of Restitution before examining some of the principal contexts in which restitution interacts with contract law principles.

RESTATEMENT (THIRD) OF RESTITUTION, COMMENT TO SECTION 1

Liability in restitution derives from the receipt of a benefit whose retention without payment would result in the unjust enrichment of the defendant at the expense of the claimant. While the paradigm case of unjust enrichment is one in which the benefit on one side of the transaction corresponds to an observable loss on the other, the consecrated formula "at the expense of another" can also mean "in violation of the other's legally protected rights," without the need to show that the claimant has suffered a loss. The usual consequence of a liability in restitution is that the defendant must restore the benefit in question or its traceable product, or else pay money in the amount necessary to eliminate unjust enrichment.

The identification of unjust enrichment as an independent basis of liability in common-law legal systems—comparable in this respect to a liability in contract or tort—was the central achievement of the 1937 Restatement of Restitution.... The use of the word "restitution" to

describe the cause of action as well as the remedy is likewise inherited from
the original Restatement, despite the problems this usage creates. There
are cases in which the essence of a plaintiff's right and remedy is the
reversal of a transfer, and thus a literal "restitution," without regard to
whether the defendant has been enriched by the transfer in question.
Conversely, there are cases in which the remedy for unjust enrichment
gives the plaintiff something—typically, the defendant's wrongful gain—
that the plaintiff did not previously possess.

Such is the inherent flexibility of the concept of unjust enrichment that
almost every instance of a recognized liability in restitution might be
referred to the broad rule of the present section [quoted in the opening
paragraph above]. The same flexibility means that the concept of unjust
enrichment will not, by itself, yield a reliable indication of the nature and
scope of the liability imposed by this part of our legal system. It is by no
means obvious, as a theoretical matter, how "unjust enrichment" should
best be defined; whether it constitutes a rule of decision, a unifying theme,
or something in between; or what role the principle would ideally play in
our legal system. Such questions preoccupy much academic writing on the
subject. This Restatement has been written on the assumption that the law
of restitution and unjust enrichment can be usefully described without
insisting on answers to any of them.

———————

Ordinarily, contract law enforces bargains when they are made before
performance is rendered. The opposite sequence, with performance before
the bargain, is problematic for contract law. People conferring benefits
(without a bargain) are normally thought to be acting gratuitously. And if
people are acting gratuitously, that signals a gift, not a binding contract.

There is a valid reason that contract law frowns upon performance
before a bargain. Any other rule would mean that people could impose
contract duties on others simply by conferring benefits on them. One could
imagine companies shipping goods that were not ordered and later
demanding payment. It would mean that squeegee windshield washers
could render performance and make an enforceable contract even without
a car driver's consent. It might even permit a neighbor making
improvements to a nearby home to recover money for unwanted services.

Therefore, while the general rule of contract law is that the bargain
must precede the performance, the law of restitution reflects a limited
exception. In some situations, denying compensation would be unjust, such
as where someone confers benefits on another who has requested or
accepted them. But this exception is construed narrowly so as not to
condone such "officious" or unwanted types of meddling behavior. Courts
deny recovery to so-called *capricious intermeddlers* or *officious*

intermeddlers. People conferring unwanted benefits are not entitled to compensation, no matter how valuable or beneficial their actions might be.

A. GRATUITY OR EXCHANGE

RESTATEMENT (SECOND) OF CONTRACTS, SECTION 86

§ 86. *Promise for Benefit Received.*

(1) A promise made in recognition of a benefit previously received by the promisor from the promisee is binding to the extent necessary to prevent injustice.

(2) A promise is not binding under Subsection (1): (a) if the promisee conferred the benefit as a gift or for other reasons the promisor has not been unjustly enriched; or (b) to the extent that its value is disproportionate to the benefit.

ESTATE OF CLEVELAND v. GORDEN
837 S.W.2d 68 (Tenn. App. 1992)

Koch, J.

This appeal involves a niece's efforts to obtain reimbursement from her deceased aunt's estate for expenditures made during her aunt's lifetime for medical and other expenses. The Davidson County Probate Court denied the niece's claim because the aunt had never specifically agreed to reimburse her niece for these expenditures. The niece has appealed. We have determined that the niece should be reimbursed for the expenditures made on her aunt's behalf and, therefore, reverse the probate court.

Frances Cleveland was originally from Wartrace. She later moved to Nashville where she lived in a small house on Linden Avenue owned jointly with her sister. Ms. Cleveland supported herself with her social security benefits, some modest investment income, and the income from a trust fund established by a deceased sister. She lived alone in her later years, although her nieces and nephews occasionally stayed with her when she became ill.

Ms. Cleveland prepared a will in March 1976 leaving most of her antique furniture to her nephew and her two nieces, Elizabeth Watson of Raleigh, North Carolina and Jane C. Gorden of Houston, Texas. She left her house, several items of furniture, and a 1932 Ford automobile to the Bethsalem Presbyterian Church in Wartrace. She also named the church as the residuary beneficiary of her estate and designated Third National Bank as executor.

Ms. Cleveland became seriously ill in January 1984. One of her neighbors telephoned Ms. Gorden in Houston, and Ms. Gorden immediately traveled to Nashville because Ms. Cleveland was then 92-years-old and had no one else to take care of her. Ms. Gorden tried to look after her aunt for approximately three weeks but eventually realized that she was not up to the task because Ms. Cleveland required continuous skilled care. In February 1984, Ms. Gorden placed Ms. Cleveland in a nursing home in Shelbyville where she could be near her friends and other more distant relatives.

When her aunt entered the nursing home, Ms. Gorden discussed Ms. Cleveland's finances with the officers at the Third National Bank in Nashville where Ms. Cleveland maintained her accounts, including the trust account established for her by her sister. The bank officers advised Ms. Gorden that she would be able to obtain full reimbursement for any expenditures she made on her aunt's behalf if she opened a separate account for that purpose and maintained detailed expense records. Ms. Gorden accordingly opened a checking account and made arrangements with Third National Bank to deposit into that account all the income from a trust her mother had established for her years earlier.

Beginning in February 1984, Ms. Gorden used her own funds to pay most of her aunt's bills. These expenses included Ms. Cleveland's nursing home bills, her other medical expenses, the utilities for her Linden Avenue house, and occasional small personal sundries purchased for Ms. Cleveland. At the same time, all of Ms. Cleveland's social security benefits and other income, including rental income from her house, continued to be deposited into Ms. Cleveland's own account. Third National Bank occasionally deposited some of Ms. Cleveland's funds in the account maintained by Ms. Gorden when Ms. Gorden's own funds were insufficient to pay all of her aunt's expenses.

Ms. Cleveland's health stabilized after she entered the nursing home. Ms. Gorden visited her occasionally and received periodic reports from the nursing home about her aunt's health. Ms. Cleveland was aware that Ms. Gorden was using her own money to pay the nursing home bills and told a companion that Ms. Gorden "would get everything she had, if there was anything left." In January 1989, Ms. Cleveland finally gave Ms. Gorden a limited power of attorney authorizing Ms. Gorden to write checks on Ms. Cleveland's account to pay for her medical and living expenses.

Ms. Cleveland died in the nursing home on March 15, 1989. Her 1976 will was admitted to probate, and the probate court appointed a substitute administrator after Third National Bank declined to serve as executor. Ms. Gorden filed a timely claim seeking reimbursement for the $99,741 she spent on Ms. Cleveland's behalf from 1984 through 1989. She did not seek payment for all the other services she had rendered to her aunt. The administrator opposed the claim on the grounds that these expenditures were gifts since Ms. Cleveland had never agreed to reimburse her niece.

The probate court agreed and denied the claim. Ms. Gorden has perfected this appeal.

This case requires us to decide whether Ms. Gorden was a capricious intermeddler who is not entitled to reimbursement for her expenditures on Ms. Cleveland's behalf because of her kinship with Ms. Cleveland. Far from being an intermeddler, we find that Ms. Gorden was acting out of a sense of family obligation. We also find, contrary to the probate court, that Ms. Cleveland knew that Ms. Gorden expected to be reimbursed for the expenditures she was making on Ms. Cleveland's behalf.

A person who voluntarily and officiously pays another's debts is not entitled to reimbursement. Restatement of Restitution §§ 2, 112 (1936); see also Walker v. Walker, 138 Tenn. 679, 681–82, 200 S.W. 825, 825 (1918) (person voluntarily paying another's debt without fraud, accident, mistake, or agreement is not entitled to subrogation); Goodfriend v. United American Bank, 637 S.W.2d 870, 872 (Tenn.Ct.App.1982) (a mere volunteer, intermeddler, or stranger, or one acting officiously in paying another's debt is not entitled to subrogation).

The general rule is not applicable when the payment is made under the compulsion of a moral obligation, in ignorance of the real state of facts, or under an erroneous impression of one's legal duty. . . . Thus, a person who pays another's debt because of a moral obligation is not an officious intermeddler and is entitled to reimbursement unless the payment was gratuitous.

A moral obligation is a duty that cannot be legally enforced. . . . It springs from the common sense of justice and fairness shared by all honorable persons and is more than a desire to be charitable or to give a gift. . . .

A moral obligation is perhaps best epitomized by the obligation family members commonly feel to support each other. Accordingly, the Tennessee Supreme Court has held that a woman who voluntarily undertook to care for her [dependent] sister

> was not only moved by sisterly affection, and by that feeling of compassion which would arise in the breast of any one possessed of normal sympathies; but she was, in a sense, under a form of moral compulsion. The burden had been cast on her, and she would not throw it off without a gross violation of duty and a shock of the moral sense.

Key v. Harris, 116 Tenn. 161, 171–72, 92 S.W. 235, 237 (1905).

Even though they are not intermeddlers, family members are generally precluded from recovering for services provided to their close relatives because the law presumes that the services were a gratuitous part of the relationship when the relatives live together as part of the same family. . . . The reasons for the presumption are that "family life abounds in acts of reciprocal kindness which tend to promote the comfort and convenience of the family, and that the introduction of commercial considerations into the relations of persons so closely bound together would expel this spirit of mutual beneficence and to that extent mar family unity." Key v. Harris, 116 Tenn. at 171, 92 S.W. at 237.

The presumption that family members' services are gratuitous is not conclusive. It can be rebutted by proof of an express agreement to pay for the services or by proof of circumstances showing that the relative accepting the benefit of the services knew or should have known that the relative performing them expected compensation or reimbursement. Gorrell v. Taylor, 107 Tenn. at 570, 64 S.W. at 888; In re Estate of Hicks, 510 S.W.2d 263, 265 (Tenn.Ct.App.1972).

We concur with the probate court's conclusion that Ms. Gorden did not intend her expenditures on Ms. Cleveland's behalf to be a gift. We do not concur, however, with its conclusion that the record does not contain proof of circumstances demonstrating that Ms. Cleveland knew or should have known that Ms. Gorden expected to be reimbursed.

The proof quickly dispels any notion that Ms. Gorden undertook to support her aunt gratuitously. The responsibility was thrust upon her, and she responded partly because of her family obligations and partly because no other relative was willing to take on the task. Ms. Cleveland's bankers told Ms. Gorden that she could be reimbursed, and from the outset, Ms. Gorden manifested her desire for reimbursement by maintaining detailed records of her expenditures as the bankers requested. While her arrangement with her aunt could have been better structured with the assistance of counsel, Ms. Gorden should not be penalized for failing to seek legal advice when she decided to help Ms. Cleveland.

Ms. Gorden's assistance to her aunt went beyond what would normally have been expected of family members in similar circumstances. The ladies were not close relatives and had never lived together in a family relationship. Gorrell v. Taylor, 107 Tenn. at 570, 64 S.W. at 888. Since she was disabled, Ms. Cleveland was never able to return Ms. Gorden's kindness and was unable to perform her share of the normal familial responsibilities. Key v. Harris, 116 Tenn. at 171, 92 S.W. at 237.

Even though the ladies had no express agreement to reimburse Ms. Gorden for her expenditures, Ms. Cleveland knew that Ms. Gorden was supporting her and accepted the support. . . . Since Ms. Cleveland had left Ms. Gorden only a portion of her furniture, her statement that Ms. Gorden "would get everything she had, if there was anything left" indicates her expectation that Ms. Gorden would be compensated with a larger share of her estate.

We reverse the denial of Ms. Gorden's claim and remand the case to the probate court for further proceedings consistent with this opinion. We tax the costs to Frances Cleveland's estate for which execution, if necessary, may issue.

NOTES AND QUESTIONS

1.   What was the problem with finding an enforceable contract in *Estate of Cleveland v. Gorden*? Was there a formal offer or acceptance? What was the intent of the parties? Did Jane Gorden believe she was making a gift, or that she was making a loan to her aunt? On the other side, did Frances Cleveland consider these payments a gift, or did she expect to pay her niece back for medical and nursing home expenses? Even without the technical elements of the contract, did the parties intend for an exchange?

2.   What is the "family member rule"? How can an advocate overcome its presumption? *See Lund v. Lund*, 848 N.W.2d 266 (N.D. 2014) (invoking family member rule to deny claims for breach of contract or restitution to son seeking $750,000 from parents for help, along with siblings, working their 22-acre farm for most of his life). Does the rule seem reasonable or fair? Is it still apt given contemporary family arrangements or does it appear to be a relic from a different era? *See* Jonathan S. Henes, *Compensating Caregiving Relatives: Abandoning the Family Member Rule in Contracts*, 17 CARDOZO L. REV. 705 (1996).

3.   How did the advice that the bank gave to the niece, Jane Gorden, contribute to this litigation? Should Gorden have taken the bank's advice? What are the risks of accepting legal advice from non-lawyers?

4.   Imagine that you were a legal advisor to Jane Gorden at the time that her aunt became ill and needed assisted living care. How would you advise Gorden so as to avoid or eliminate the problems with the estate that arose in this case?

5.   What is a "capricious intermeddler"? Does this seem to be a positive, neutral, or negative term? Why would being classified as such work to bar recovery? Consider the following well-known case about the care and feeding of a homeless racehorse.

BAILEY V. WEST
249 A.2d 414 (R. I. 1969)

PAOLINO, J.

This is a civil action wherein the plaintiff alleges that the defendant is indebted to him for the reasonable value of his services rendered in connection with the feeding, care and maintenance of a certain race horse named "Bascom's Folly" from May 3, 1962 through July 3, 1966. The case was tried before a justice of the superior court sitting without a jury, and resulted in a decision for the plaintiff for his cost of boarding the horse for the five months immediately subsequent to May 3, 1962, and for certain expenses incurred by him in trimming its hoofs. The cause is now before us on the plaintiff's appeal and defendant's cross appeal from the judgment entered pursuant to such decision.

The facts material to a resolution of the precise issues raised herein are as follows. In late April 1962, defendant, accompanied by his horse trainer, went to Belmont Park in New York to buy race horses. On April 27, 1962, defendant purchased "Bascom's Folly" from a Dr. Strauss and arranged to have the horse shipped to Suffolk Downs in East Boston, Massachusetts. Upon its arrival defendant's trainer discovered that the horse was lame, and so notified defendant, who ordered him to reship the horse by van to the seller at Belmont Park. The seller refused to accept delivery at Belmont on May 3, 1962, and thereupon, the van driver, one Kelly, called defendant's trainer and asked for further instructions. Although the trial testimony is in conflict as to what the trainer told him, it is not disputed that on the same day Kelly brought "Bascom's Folly" to plaintiff's farm where the horse remained until July 3, 1966, when it was sold by plaintiff to a third party.

While "Bascom's Folly" was residing at his horse farm, plaintiff sent bills for its feed and board to defendant at regular intervals. According to testimony elicited from defendant at the trial, the first such bill was received by him some two or three months after "Bascom's Folly" was placed on plaintiff's farm. He also stated that he immediately returned the bill to plaintiff with the notation that he was not the owner of the horse nor was it sent to plaintiff's farm at his request. The plaintiff testified that he sent bills monthly to defendant and that the first notice he received from him disclaiming ownership was '. . . maybe after a month or two or so' subsequent to the time when the horse was left in plaintiff's care.

In his decision the trial judge found that defendant's trainer had informed Kelly during their telephone conversation of May 3, 1962, that ". . . he would have to do whatever he wanted to do with the horse, that he wouldn't be on any farm at the defendant's expense . . . ." He also found, however, that when "Bascom's Folly" was brought to his farm, plaintiff was not aware of the telephone conversation between Kelly and defendant's trainer, and hence, even though he knew there was a controversy surrounding the ownership of the horse, he was entitled to assume that ". . . there is an implication here that, 'I am to take care of this horse.' "

Continuing his decision, the trial justice stated that in view of the result reached by this court in a recent opinion [Strauss v. West, 100 R.I. 388, 216 A.2d 366] wherein we held that the instant defendant was liable to the original seller, Dr. Strauss, for the purchase price of this horse, there was a contract 'implied in fact' between the plaintiff and defendant to board "Bascom's Folly" and that this contract continued until plaintiff received notification from defendant that he would not be responsible for the horse's board. The trial justice further stated that ". . . I think there was notice given at least at the end of the four months, and I think we must add another month on there for a reasonable disposition of his property."

In view of the conclusion we reach with respect to defendant's first two contentions, we shall confine ourselves solely to a discussion and resolution of the issues necessarily implicit therein, and shall not examine other subsidiary arguments advanced by plaintiff and defendant.

The defendant alleges in his brief and oral argument that the trial judge erred in finding a contract "implied in fact" between the parties. We agree. . . .

The source of the obligation in a contract "implied in fact," as in express contracts, is in the intention of the parties. We hold that there was no mutual agreement and "intent to promise" between the plaintiff and defendant so as to establish a contract "implied in fact" for defendant to pay plaintiff for the maintenance of this horse. From the time Kelly delivered the horse to him plaintiff knew there was a dispute as to its ownership, and his subsequent actions indicated he did not know with whom, if anyone, he had a contract. After he had accepted the horse, he made inquiries as to its ownership and, initially, and for some time thereafter, sent his bills to both defendant and Dr. Strauss, the original seller.

There is also uncontroverted testimony in the record that prior to the assertion of the claim which is the subject of this suit neither defendant nor his trainer had ever had any business transactions with plaintiff, and had never used his farm to board horses. Additionally, there is [uncontroverted] evidence that this horse, when found to be lame, was shipped by defendant's trainer not to plaintiff's farm, but back to the seller at Belmont Park. What is most important, the trial justice expressly stated that he believed the testimony of defendant's trainer that he had instructed Kelly that defendant would not be responsible for boarding the horse on any farm.

From our examination of the record we are constrained to conclude that the trial justice overlooked and misconceived material evidence which establishes beyond question that there never existed between the parties an element essential to the formulation of any true contract, namely, an "intent to contract." . . .

The defendant's second contention is that, even assuming the trial justice was in essence predicating defendant's liability upon a quasi-contractual theory, his decision is still unsupported by competent evidence and is clearly erroneous.

The following discussion of quasi-contracts appears in 12 Am.Jur., Contracts, § 6 (1938) at pp. 503 to 504:

> . . . A quasi contract has no reference to the intentions or expressions of the parties. The obligation is imposed despite, and frequently in frustration of, their intention. For a quasi-contract neither promise nor privity, real or imagined, is necessary. In quasi contracts the obligation arises, not from consent of the parties, as in the case of contracts, express or implied in fact, but from the law of natural immutable justice and equity. The act, or acts, from which the law implies the contract must, however, be voluntary. Where a case shows that it is the duty of the defendant to pay, the law imputes to him a promise to [fulfill] that obligation. The duty, which thus forms the foundation of a quasi-contractual obligation, is frequently based on the doctrine of unjust enrichment. . . .
>
> . . . The law will not imply a promise against the express declaration of the party to be charged, made at the time of the supposed undertaking, unless such party is under legal obligation paramount to his will to perform some duty, and he is not under such legal obligation unless there is a demand in equity and good conscience that he should perform the duty.
>
> [E]ssential elements of a quasi-contract are a benefit conferred upon defendant by plaintiff, appreciation by defendant of such benefit, and acceptance and retention by defendant of such benefit under such circumstances that it would be inequitable to retain the benefit without payment of the value thereof. . . .

The key question raised by this appeal with respect to the establishment of a quasi-contract is whether or not plaintiff was acting as a "volunteer" at the time he accepted the horse for boarding at his farm. There is a long line of authority which has clearly enunciated the general rule that ". . . if a performance is rendered by one person without any request by another, it is very unlikely that this person will be under a legal duty to pay compensation." 1A Corbin, Contracts § 234.

The Restatement of Restitution, § 2 (1937) provides: "A person who officiously confers a benefit upon another is not entitled to restitution therefor." Comment a in the above-mentioned section states in part as follows:

> . . . Policy ordinarily requires that a person who has conferred a benefit . . . by way of giving another services . . . should not be permitted to require the other to pay therefor, unless the one conferring the benefit had a valid reason for so doing. A person is not required to deal with another unless he so desires and,

ordinarily, a person should not be required to become an obligor unless he so desires.

Applying those principles to the facts in the case at bar it is clear that plaintiff cannot recover. The plaintiff's testimony on cross-examination is the only evidence in the record relating to what transpired between Kelly and him at the time the horse was accepted for boarding. The defendant's attorney asked plaintiff if he had any conversation with Kelly at that time, and plaintiff answered in substance that he had noticed that the horse was very lame and that Kelly had told him: "That's why they wouldn't accept him at Belmont Track." The plaintiff also testified that he had inquired of Kelly as to the ownership of "Bascom's Folly," and had been told that "Dr. Strauss made a deal and that's all I know."

It further appears from the record that plaintiff acknowledged receipt of the horse by signing a uniform livestock bill of lading, which clearly indicated on its face that the horse in question had been consigned by defendant's trainer not to plaintiff, but to Dr. Strauss's trainer at Belmont Park. Knowing at the time he accepted the horse for boarding that a controversy surrounded its ownership, plaintiff could not reasonably expect remuneration from defendant, nor can it be said that defendant acquiesced in the conferment of a benefit upon him. The undisputed testimony was that defendant, upon receipt of plaintiff's first bill, immediately notified him that he was not the owner of "Bascom's Folly" and would not be responsible for its keep.

It is our judgment that the plaintiff was a mere volunteer who boarded and maintained "Bascom's Folly" at his own risk and with full knowledge that he might not be reimbursed for expenses he incurred incident thereto.

The plaintiff's appeal is denied and dismissed, the defendant's cross appeal is sustained, and the cause is remanded to the superior court for entry of judgment for the defendant.

NOTES AND QUESTIONS

1. So goes the story of Bascom's Folly, the unfortunately-named racehorse without a home. If no one claimed responsibility for the horse's boarding bill, did Bailey act at his own peril? Conversely, after he had accepted the horse into his farm, would refusing to provide care also create legal risks? What, if anything, should Bailey have done differently in this situation?

2. What motivation did Bailey have to care for the horse if he was unable to ascertain the horse's owner? Is it not desirable to reward such caregivers? Does the law reflect such a desire? Recall *Mills v. Wyman,* the case of the caregiver for the adult son of a fleetingly-grateful father. While Good Samaritans are so-called because they act out of kindness, not profit, many activities blur the line between altruism and profit-seeking.

3.   Shifting from a moral perspective to an economic efficiency viewpoint, why might Bailey's behavior make sense? If there is a business in boarding horses and someone shows up with a horse at the gate, it might be reasonable to take care of it, even in the face of paperwork or confusion over ownership. In the vast majority of real life cases, this might work out fine. Therefore, this case might be something of an outlier, even if it establishes a legal rule.

4.   What are the doctrinal elements of a claim for restitution? Why did Bailey fail to meet the elements?

5.   For an even older case regarding similar issues, consider *Boothe v. Fitzpatrick*, 36 Vt. 681, 1864 WL 2408 (Vt. 1864). A farmer found a bull that had escaped from a neighbor's property. While caring for the bull, the farmer did not know who owned it until the neighbor later visited the farm, saw the bull, and said he would pay the farmer for the costs of care. The farmer kept the bull through winter, when the neighbor recovered it. The neighbor refused to pay for any expenses incurred and the farmer sued. The court found for the farmer, noting that it was clear that after the promise to pay was made, everything that followed was a binding contract, and the neighbor was required to pay for the bull's upkeep. But the court also held that the neighbor was retroactively responsible for the bull's expenses even before his promise to pay. While acknowledging that it might be past consideration, the court noted:

> If the consideration, even without request, moves directly from the plaintiff to the defendant and [inures] directly to the defendant's benefit, the promise is binding, though made upon a past consideration. In this case there was such consideration. The plaintiff parted with what was of value to him, and it [inured] directly to the benefit of the defendant. A promise upon such past consideration is binding. This principle is fundamental and elementary, and is sustained by abundant authority.

Despite aversion to imposing debts without assent, the *Boothe* court reasoned that the neighbor's trailing promise negated that concern. In addition, the court noted, there was little doubt that the neighbor had "received a valuable pecuniary benefit at the [farmer's] expense."

6.   For more on officious intermeddlers, see John P. Dawson, *The Self-Serving Intermeddler*, 87 HARV. L. REV. 1409, 1409–10 (1974). For more on *Bailey v. West*, see Mark P. Gergen, *Restitution As A Bridge over Troubled Contractual Waters*, 71 FORDHAM L. REV. 709 (2002).

7.   What if we could go back in time and ask the parties what deal they wanted to take care of Bascom's Folly? This idea is called a "hypothetical bargain." Is it clear then that there would have been no contract, and no benefit to be gained from the parties' dealings? Or, in theory, could the parties have agreed, directly or indirectly, to allocate the risk of the horse's lameness? What happens if we hypothetically rewind the clock in the next case?

COTNAM V. WISDOM

104 S.W. 164 (Ark. 1907)

[In accordance with a common practice of the period, the facts and procedural posture of the following case are provided by a court official, called a reporter, rather than the judge.—Eds.]

F.L. Wisdom and George C. Abel presented a claim against the estate of A.M. Harrison, deceased, of which T. T Cotnam is [administrator], for $2,000 on account of surgical attention to the deceased, who was killed by being thrown from a street car. The probate court allowed the account in the sum of $400, and the administrator appealed to the circuit court.

The evidence showed that deceased received fatal injuries in a street car wreck; that while he was unconscious some person summoned Dr. Wisdom to attend him; that Dr. Wisdom called in Dr. Abel, an experienced surgeon, to assist him; that they found that the patient was suffering from a fracture of the temporal and parietal bones, and that it was necessary to perform the operation of trephining; that the patient lived only a short time after the operation, and never recovered consciousness.

Dr. Abel testified, over defendant's objection, that the charge of $2,000 was based on the result of inquiry as to the financial condition of deceased's estate. It was further proved, over defendant's objection, that deceased was a bachelor, and that his estate, which amounted to about $18,500, including $10,000 of insurance, would go to collateral heirs.

Various physicians testified as to the customary fees of doctors in similar cases, and fixed the amount at various sums ranging from $100 to $2,000. There was also evidence that the ability of the patient to pay is usually taken into consideration by surgeons in fixing their fee. At the plaintiff's request the court charged the jury as follows:

    1. If you find from the evidence that plaintiffs rendered professional services as physicians and surgeons to the deceased, A.M. Harrison, in a sudden emergency following the deceased's injury in a street car wreck, in an endeavor to save his life, then you are instructed that plaintiffs are entitled to recover from the estate of the said A.M. Harrison such sum as you may find from the evidence is a reasonable compensation for the services rendered.

    2. The character and importance of the operation, the responsibility resting upon the surgeon performing the operation, his experience and professional training, and the ability to pay of the person operated upon, are elements to be considered by you in determining what is a reasonable charge for the services performed . . . .

In his opening statement to the jury, counsel for claimants stated that "Harrison was worth $8,000, and had insurance, and his estate was left to collateral heirs, to nephews and nieces." Counsel for defendant objected to such argument, but the court overruled the objection; and the defendant saved his exceptions. Verdict for $650 was returned in plaintiff's favor. Defendant has appealed. . . .

HILL, C. J.

. . . The first question is as to the correctness of this instruction. . . . The appellant says:

> Harrison was never conscious after his head struck the pavement. He did not and could not, expressly or impliedly, assent to the action of the appellees. He was without knowledge or will power. However merciful or benevolent may have been the intention of the appellees, a new rule of law, of contract by implication of law, will have to be established by this court in order to sustain the recovery.

Appellant is right in saying that the recovery must be sustained by a contract by implication of law, but is not right in saying that it is a new rule of law, for such contracts are almost as old as the English system of jurisprudence. They are usually called "implied contracts." More properly they should be called "quasi contracts" or "constructive contracts." . . .

The following excerpts from *Sceva v. True*, 53 N. H. 627, are peculiarly applicable here:

> We regard it as well settled by the cases referred to in the briefs of counsel, many of which have been commented on at length by Mr. Shirley for the defendant, that an insane person, an idiot, or a person utterly bereft of all sense and reason by the sudden stroke of an accident or disease may be held liable, in assumpsit, for necessaries furnished to him in good faith while in that unfortunate and helpless condition. And the reasons upon which this rest are too broad, as well as too sensible and humane, to be overborne by any deductions which a refined logic may make from the circumstances that in such cases there can be no contract or promise, in fact, no meeting of the minds of the parties.

> The cases put it on the ground of an implied contract; and by this is not meant, as the defendant's counsel seems to suppose, an actual contract—that is, an actual meeting of the minds of the parties, an actual, mutual understanding, to be inferred from language, acts, and circumstances by the jury—but a contract and promise, said to be implied by the law, where, in point of fact, there was no contract, no mutual understanding, and so no promise. The defendant's counsel says it is usurpation for the

court to hold, as a matter of law, that there is a contract and a promise, when all the evidence in the case shows that there was not a contract, nor the semblance of one. It is doubtless a legal fiction, invented and used for the sake of the remedy. If it was originally usurpation, certainly it has now become very inveterate, and firmly fixed in the body of the law. . . .

In its practical application it sustains recovery for physicians and nurses who render services for infants, insane persons, and drunkards. . . . And services rendered by physicians to persons unconscious or helpless by reason of injury or sickness are in the same situation as those rendered to persons incapable of contracting. . . . The court was therefore right in giving the instruction in question.

2. The defendant sought to require the plaintiff to prove, in addition to the value of the services, the benefit, if any, derived by the deceased from the operation, and alleges error in the court refusing to so instruct the jury. The court was right in refusing to place this burden upon the physicians. The same question was considered in *Ladd v. Witte*, 116 Wis. 35, 92 N. W. 365, where the court said:

> That is not at all the test. So that a surgical operation be conceived and performed with due skill and care, the price to be paid therefor does not depend upon the result. The event so generally lies with the forces of nature that all intelligent men know and understand that the surgeon is not responsible therefor. In absence of express agreement, the surgeon, who brings to such a service due skill and care, earns the reasonable and customary price therefor, whether the outcome be beneficial to the patient or the reverse. . . .

NOTES AND QUESTIONS

1. Were the doctors acting out of a charitable impulse or perhaps because of their obligations to help a dying man based upon medical ethics? The era's common law did not impute an obligation to assist a stranger. *Compare Hurley v. Eddingfield*, 59 N.E. 1058 (Ind. 1901) (no duty for physician to render aid).

2. If we could turn back the hands of time to ten minutes before the accident and inquired whether Mr. Harrison would be willing to pay to have doctors attempt to save his life in the event of an accident on the streetcar, what do you imagine his answer would be? Would their services be unwanted, or would they be highly desired at any price? *See* Robert A. Long, Jr., *A Theory of Hypothetical Contract*, 94 YALE L.J. 415, 429–31 (1984).

3. Suppose that while the doctors were treating Mr. Harrison, he regained consciousness, told the doctors to "leave me alone," and then lost consciousness again, now more gravely ill than before. Same analysis and

result? What if the patient's firmly-held religious beliefs require refusing medical treatment?

PROBLEM: IT'S COLD OUTSIDE

Alice, who lives at 113 Manchester Road, has a longstanding contract with Harrison, who runs a snow and ice removal company. Alice pays a flat fee of $100 per month, and in return Harrison and his crew remove snow and ice as conditions warrant. (The charge is $50 per visit, if done on a per job basis). If there is no snow and ice, Harrison makes out like a bandit; but if it snows six times in one month, it is a sweet deal for Alice.

In the winter of 2017, Alice decided she had enough of the cold weather in St. Louis and decided to spend a few months in Bermuda. Alice was in a hurry to leave town and start her vacation, so she never called Harrison to cancel the service or tell him that she would be out of town.

On the date of the worst snowstorm in memory, Harrison came down with a cold and fever and couldn't work. Harrison put one of his best employees, Janel, in charge of his crew. However, Janel had never been to Alice's house. During the storm, Janel went to what she thought was 113 Manchester Road. In reality, she showed up at 118 Manchester Road (part of the last "3" on the sign was covered by snow). She and another worker spent half an hour clearing snow and ice at 118 Manchester.

The entire time, the homeowner, Billy, was inside. He had a couple beers and from within his darkened house Billy enjoyed watching Janel and the other worker from Harrison's company clear the snow from his driveway and front walk. Meanwhile, all the way in Bermuda, Alice heard from a neighbor that snow was piling up all around her house and creating hazardous conditions. Alice e-mailed Harrison asking what was going on. After a bit of detective work, Harrison discovered the mix-up and sent a bill for $100 to Billy.

Meanwhile, Harrison was feeling so feverish that he figured he should probably drive himself to the local emergency room. Upon arriving in the ER, Harrison slipped into an unresponsive state before he could tell anyone what was wrong. Luckily, since he was at the ER, doctors were able to treat Harrison and he left the hospital the next day. A week later, a bill for $3,000 was sent to the address on his driver's license.

Analyze the liabilities of the parties (Alice, Billy, and Harrison), both in contract and also under unjust enrichment/restitution.

B. MERE VOLUNTEERS

The following materials continue the discussion of "mere volunteers" started in the previous section while also pursuing the doctrine of restitution as a remedy. Notice that the remedy of restitution differs from traditional contract remedies. Contract remedies seek primarily to protect the expectations of aggrieved parties by putting them in the economic

[handwritten margin note:] unjust b/c he could have stopped them

[handwritten margin note:] recovery would be value of benefit b/c no contractual price + Billy

position they would have been in as a result of performance. Restitution, in contrast, aims to reverse unjust enrichment, awarding the economic value of the benefit conferred.

BRADY V. ALASKA
965 P.2d 1 (Alaska 1998)

COMPTON, J.

A [northern spruce bark] beetle epidemic is decimating forests in Alaska. Steven Brady and Terry Brady generally oppose the State of Alaska's policy response to the epidemic. They particularly decry the State's treatment of them in denying their application to buy the right to harvest dead and dying trees near Moose Pass. They had hoped to show that such harvesting can help stanch the epidemic. The Bradys brought a broad array of claims against the State and two State forestry officials. . . . They appeal two summary judgments dismissing all claims in their consolidated suits. We affirm.

. . . In 1992 the State formed a Forest Health Initiative, directed by Daniel Golden, to address the [beetle epidemic]. In April 1993 Golden suggested to Terry Brady that he apply to the Department of Natural Resources (DNR), Division of Forestry (Forestry), for a negotiated timber sale—i.e., a sale without public advertisement of or competitive bidding for the right to harvest a limited amount of timber. . . . Terry could then conduct a model timber-salvage project to demonstrate his belief that harvesting and reforestation can fight the epidemic.

In May 1993 Terry twice unsuccessfully applied for a sale in a 200-acre area near Moose Pass. Kenai-Kodiak Area Forester Jim Peterson rejected his applications. Peterson noted that a forestry regulation barred a sale until DNR's Division of Lands (DOL) had classified the land. . . He also noted Forestry's policy of not making negotiated timber sales in areas of competitive interest in timber. Terry offered to help DNR prepare a site-specific Forest Land-Use Plan [called an FLUP] for the area by gathering data "for the 200 acres." (In addition to the regulation that Peterson had noted requiring classification, the timber-sale statute bars sales of more than ten acres of timber before such an FLUP is in effect.) . . .

The Bradys and other timber-sale applicants met with State Forester Tom Boutin on June 30, 1993. He agreed to "entertain" six applications for negotiated sales. Terry again offered to gather data for an FLUP. The State accepted this offer in a July 21 letter from Peterson:

We would like to take you up on your offer to help prepare the site-specific plan as required [by Alaska statute]. You indicated your willingness to do the research, compile and report the required data[,] and submit this information to us. Due to our present workload, this assistance would help expedite the sale.

Terry began collecting data, and submitted two draft FLUPs in September.

The July 21 letter also acknowledged the Bradys' renewed application for a sale and requested $3,000 "as a presale deposit." Peterson wrote that Forestry was working with DOL and hoped to finish classifying the area "expeditiously." "In the meantime," he concluded, "we will begin preparation of a sale in the area requested upon receipt of the presale deposit. We look forward to working with you on successful completion of this proposal." Terry sent the $3,000, deeming it a "down payment."

On October 4 the public met to discuss forest issues in Moose Pass; Peterson and State Forester Boutin attended. At the meeting, Sherman (Red) Smith, another negotiated-sale applicant and a close business associate of Terry Brady, said, "As far as we're concerned he's [Boutin's] made a contract with us." Boutin did not reply; he has [sworn] that he did not hear the comment. On October 7 DNR Commissioner Harry Noah told the Bradys that DNR "might . . . reject[ ]" the proposed sales as not being in the State's best interest.

A week later Peterson toured the proposed sale area with the Bradys and other applicants and said that Forestry had sent DOL "a copy of the Forest Land Use Plan. It's the best site-specific [data] that we have." Peterson also said, in response to a question about timing: "We can be prepared to sign . . . make that contract . . . sign that contract . . . on the day they [DOL] sign the classification order."

On October 20 Terry submitted his final report and an invoice for professional services for $26,250. Peterson declined to pay, writing that, "[i]n all our discussions with you, never at any time was there an indication of our entering into a professional-services contract with you."

The parties agree that DOL used Terry's work in preparing a draft FLUP in October. The State deems the use "paraphrasing" that appeared only in a draft, not the final plan; the DOL employee who wrote the plans affied "that no time or money savings resulted [from the use]." Terry disputes this claim.

On November 12 Peterson wrote Terry Brady that "[a]fter considerable review, [Boutin] has decided that . . . negotiated timber sales in the Moose Pass area would not be in the best interest of the state." Peterson gave two reasons. One was that there was "competitive interest" in the Moose Pass timber. The other was that the Bradys and their associates had applied for four contiguous sales, each of the maximum size for a negotiated sale. To grant their applications would effectively "circumvent[ ] the mandated public processes"—i.e., public notice and competitive bidding—for large timber sales. The Bradys exhaustively pursued administrative appeals. They each then filed similar suits. . . .

The Bradys made three sets of claims: (1) constitutional, statutory, and tort claims assailing the State's forest management policy in general; (2) takings claims based on the State's dealings with them; and (3) common-law and equitable claims based on those dealings. [The court rejected all such claims; only the discussion of claim (3) follows]. . . .

Terry claims that the State owes him $26,250 on a contract or quantum meruit theory for his professional services in researching an FLUP. . . . The State does not dispute that Terry offered to do the disputed work, and that it accepted his offer. [But there] was no written contract for Terry's work, and he said in an administrative appeal, "I admit there was no agreement as to compensation." There was thus no enforceable contract for want of an essential term—price.[36] . . . This alone would suffice to bar enforcement, but we also note that, as the State pointed out to Terry, it can only make professional services contracts in writing and after bidding and formal approval [under applicable state statutory requirements]. . . .

To gain restitution of the value of his services in quantum meruit, Terry need not show an actual promise or agreement,[38] but instead that: (1) he conferred a benefit on the State; (2) the State appreciated the benefit; and (3) the State accepted and retained it under circumstances making it inequitable to do so without paying him. . . . While the State disputes all three elements, we need address only the last, inequity, which is the most significant. . . .

We refer to Terry's cause of action as quantum meruit. "Courts generally treat actions brought upon theories of unjust enrichment, quasi-contract, contracts implied in law, and quantum meruit as essentially the same." Alaska Sales & Serv., Inc. v. Millet, 735 P.2d 743, 746 n. 6 (Alaska 1987).

It is not unjust to retain a benefit given without expectation of payment. . . . We have noted in dictum that this is true in a business as well as a friendly context if [services were rendered to gain a business advantage]. That is the State's view: Brady offered to do the work; the State accepted; neither mentioned compensation; and he did the work in his self-interest, hoping to facilitate a contract.

The Restatement of Restitution provides, and many non-Alaskan cases have held, that one who renders services in the expectation of gaining a

---

[36] . . . . The alleged timber-sale contract could include an open price term under the UCC . . . but professional services do not come within the UCC.

[38] See, e.g., White v. Alaska Ins. Guar. Ass'n, 592 P.2d 367, 371 (Alaska 1979) (describing quasi-contract as legal fiction " 'based on the maxim that one who is unjustly enriched at the expense of another is required to make restitution,' " and noting that "an agreement between the parties is not . . . necessary.") (quoting Hill v. Waxberg, 237 F.2d 936, 939 (9th Cir.1956)).

future business advantage ordinarily cannot recover the value of those services in quantum meruit, even if her expectation goes unrealized. . . . We adopt that rule. We note that it has two exceptions: a plaintiff may be entitled to restitution if she manifested an expectation that the recipient would pay for her services, or if she rendered services in reliance on the recipient's promise to enter a contract, or to negotiate in good faith to form one, and the recipient then broke that promise.[44] Thus, if the State had promised to execute a timber-sale contract, or breached its promise to negotiate in good faith, restoring to Terry the value of his services might be a viable theory. But the State . . . did neither.

An inquiry into whether a plaintiff manifested an expectation of payment has two aspects. It is objective—i.e., a court must ask whether a reasonable person in the recipient's position would have realized from the plaintiff's words and acts that she expected to be paid. . . . And it is equitable, as the 1983 draft Second Restatement stresses by asking whether, if the recipient retains the benefit of the services without paying, his conduct will appear "unconscionable in purpose or effect." . . . A comment to the 1983 draft makes a point relevant to both aspects of the inquiry: a party negotiating a contract usually realizes that she is venturing time and effort at the risk that negotiations may fail. . . . Thus, when a disappointed plaintiff seeks restitution of the value of services that she provided during negotiations, a court must decide whether, under all the circumstances, the recipient knew or should have known that the plaintiff expected to be paid, or whether, as is usually fair to say, the plaintiff should have known that she was taking a chance.

Terry never said, until he submitted his invoice, that he expected to be paid. He seemed to have volunteered to do the work in order to gain a business advantage by expediting the land classification. His brief does not discuss whether a reasonable entity in the State's position would have inferred that he expected to be paid. (He did argue below that the project's economic realities made that expectation apparent, but he has not argued this on appeal.) He identifies no genuine dispute of fact material to the issue of whether the State should have realized that he expected to be paid. Given his silence, and the reasonable alternate explanation for his efforts, officials had little or no reason to think that he did. There is no evidence to support a finding that their acts were unconscionable in purpose or effect. . . .

---

[44] In one case, Hill, a developer, asked Waxberg, a contractor, to help prepare a building project, promising to give Waxberg the contract if financing materialized. See Hill v. Waxberg, 237 F.2d 936, 938 (9th Cir.1956). Waxberg did the work, and the financing went through, but he and Hill could not agree on a contract, so Hill hired another contractor. The court awarded Waxberg restitution of the value of his work. See id. at 938–40. . . .

NOTES AND QUESTIONS

1.   Was Terry Brady a volunteer? An officious intermeddler? Are these characterizations accurate depictions of Brady's actions? For a classic discussion of the officious intermeddler or mere volunteer, see John P. Dawson, *Negotiorum Gestio: The Altruistic Intermeddler*, 74 HARVARD L. REV. 1 (1961).

2.   One might also say that Terry Brady volunteered to do the survey work in order to gain an advantage for himself and his business partners. What did Brady hope to gain by doing the survey? Is the time that he took to work on the survey part of "business negotiations" completed in the hope that a contract will follow?

3.   Have you worked in sales or know anyone who has? Often those who work in sales must spend money and expend effort in order to convince the other party to ink a deal. Those expenses of putting together a pitch are part of doing business, and they are not usually considered to be recoverable, either in contract, reliance, or unjust enrichment.

4.   The court talks about Brady's actions not being conducted with the expectation of payment. Why is the expectation of payment important to achieving a recovery in unjust enrichment? Should it be? This issue is explored further in the next case.

MARTIN V. LITTLE, BROWN & CO.
450 A.2d 984 (Pa. Super. 1981)

WIEAND, J.

This appeal was taken from an order sustaining preliminary objections in the nature of a demurrer to appellant's pro se complaint in assumpsit. The trial court held that a contract had not been made and that there could be no recovery on quantum meruit where appellant had volunteered information which enabled appellee, a publisher of books, to effect a recovery against a third person for copyright infringement. We agree and, accordingly, affirm.

. . . [O]n September 28, 1976, the appellant, James L. Martin [who the court identified as a law student], directed a letter to Bantam Books, Inc. in which he advised the addressee that portions of a paperback publication entitled "How to Buy Stocks" had been plagiarized by the authors of a later book entitled "Planning Your Financial Future." Appellant's letter offered to provide a copy of the book, in which appellant had highlighted the plagiarized passages, with marginal references to the pages and paragraphs of the book from which the passages had been copied.

By letter dated October 21, 1976 and signed by Robin Paris, Editorial Assistant, the appellee, Little, Brown and Company, Inc., invited appellant to send his copy of "Planning Your Financial Future." This was done, and appellee acknowledged receipt thereof in writing. Thereafter, appellant made inquiries about appellee's investigation but received no response. Appellant was persistent, however, and upon learning that appellee had agreed with his assertions and was pursuing a claim of copyright infringement, he demanded compensation for his services. Appellee denied that it had contracted with appellant or was otherwise obligated to compensate appellant for his work or for his calling the infringement to the publisher's attention. Nevertheless, appellee offered an honorarium in the form of a check for two hundred dollars, which appellant retained but did not cash. Instead, he filed suit to recover one-third of the recovery [obtained] by appellee.

These facts and all reasonable inferences therefrom have been admitted by appellee's demurrer. . . . In determining whether they are sufficient to state a cause of action we are guided by the rule that a demurrer may be sustained only in clear cases, and all doubts must be resolved in favor of the sufficiency of the complaint. . . .

The facts alleged . . . are insufficient to establish a contractual relationship between appellant and appellee. Appellant's initial letter did not expressly or by implication suggest a desire to negotiate. Neither did appellee's letter of October 21, 1976, which invited appellant to send his copy of the offending publication, constitute an offer to enter a unilateral contract. It was no more than a response to an initial letter by appellant in which he notified appellee of a copyright infringement and expressed a willingness to forward a copy of the infringing work in which he had highlighted copied portions and cited pages of appellee's work which had been copied. Appellant's letter did not suggest that he intended to be paid, and appellee's response did not contain an offer to pay appellant if he forwarded his copy of the infringing work. In brief, payment to appellant was not discussed in any of the [correspondence] which preceded the forwarding of appellant's work to appellee.

"A contract, implied in fact, is an actual contract which arises where the parties agree upon the obligations to be incurred, but their intention, instead of being expressed in words, is inferred from their acts in the light of the surrounding circumstances." [Home Protection Building & Loan Association Case, 143 Pa.Super. 96, 98, 17 A.2d 755, 756 (1941).] An implied contract is an agreement which legitimately can be inferred from the intention of the parties as evidenced by the circumstances and "the ordinary course of dealing and the common understanding of men." Hertzog v. Hertzog, 29 Pa. 465, 468 (1857).

> Generally, there is an implication of a promise to pay for valuable services rendered with the knowledge and approval of the recipient, in the absence of a showing to the contrary. A promise to pay the reasonable value of the service is implied where one performs for another, with the other's knowledge, a useful service

of a character that is usually charged for, and the latter expresses no dissent or avails himself of the service. A promise to pay for services can, however, only be implied when they are rendered in such circumstances as authorized the party performing to entertain a reasonable expectation of their payment by the party benefited. The service or other benefit must not be given as a gratuity or without expectation of payment, and the person benefited must do something from which his promise to pay may be fairly inferred.

Home Protection Building & Loan Association Case, supra .... When a person requests another to perform services, it is ordinarily inferred that he intends to pay for them, unless the circumstances indicate otherwise. Restatement Restitution § 107(2) (1937). However, where the circumstances evidence that one's work effort has been voluntarily given to another, an intention to pay therefor cannot be inferred. In the instant case, the facts alleged in the complaint disclose a submission of information from appellant to appellee without any discussion pertaining to appellee's payment therefor. Clearly, there was no basis upon which to infer the existence of a unilateral contract.

Similarly, there is no factual premise to support a finding that appellee is entitled to recover in quasi-contract for the information supplied by appellant. Where one person has been unjustly enriched at the expense of another he or she must make restitution to the other. .... However, unjust enrichment is the key to an action for restitution.... The vehicle for achieving restitution is a quasi-contract, or contract implied in law. "Unlike true contracts, quasi-contracts are not based on the apparent intention of the parties to undertake the performances in question, nor are they promises. They are obligations created by law for reasons of justice." Schott v. Westinghouse Electric Corporation, 436 Pa. 279, 290, 259 A.2d 443, 449 (1969), quoting Restatement (Second) of Contracts, § 5, comment b. at 24. "Quasi-contracts may be found in the absence of any expression of assent by the party to be charged and may indeed be found in spite of the party's contrary intention." Schott v. Westinghouse Electric Corporation, supra .... To sustain a claim of unjust enrichment, it must be shown by the facts pleaded that a person wrongly secured or passively received a benefit that it would be unconscionable to retain. ...

As a general rule, volunteers have no right to restitution.... Appellant was a volunteer. It was he who made the unsolicited suggestion that he would be willing to submit to appellee his copy of "Planning Your Financial Future" with notations to show which portions had been purloined from "How to Buy Stocks." His offer to do so was not conditioned upon payment of any kind. He did not suggest, either expressly or by implication, that he expected to be paid for this information or for time spent in reducing the same to writing. Thus, the facts averred in the complaint establish that he was purely a volunteer and cannot properly be reimbursed for unjust enrichment.[2] . . .

QUESTIONS

1. What might have motivated Martin in this case? Was it chiefly financial gain, or might he have had other reasons for writing to the publisher?

2. If money was the object, what should Martin (a law student) have done differently to obtain payment? What might Martin's initial letter to the publisher have stated to improve his chances of receiving compensation?

EXAMPLE: ROD STEWART AT THE RIO

The British rock star Rod Stewart, singer of "Maggie May," "Reason to Believe," and many other hits, was scheduled to play a concert at the Las Vegas Rio Hotel & Casino on New Year's Eve, December 31, 2000. The Rio advanced Stewart an impressive $2 million payment. Unfortunately, in the spring of 2000, Stewart was diagnosed with thyroid cancer, and related surgery damaged his vocal chords. While Stewart and the Rio discussed rescheduling, they were unable to reach agreement. The Rio saw this as an example of Stewart's intransigence, while the rock star thought the Rio feared losing money if the date were changed. They disagreed about what their bargain required and under what circumstances it might be excused. As negotiations broke down, the parties headed to court.

The case was a difficult one. While both parties seemed to have agreed to the price and to be contractually bound, the judge noted that there was no agreement on what would happen in the particular circumstances of Rod Stewart's inability to perform. If wounded vocal chords were an "Act of God," they were within the contract's force majeure clause, but if merely an illness, no clause in the contract provided an excuse.

The court found that nothing in the contract determined who should be entitled to the $2 million advance, so the judge turned to restitution principles instead. Make the arguments on both sides.

EXAMPLE: IN THE RUNNING

Yvette is a bicyclist and runner who enjoys participating in athletic events on weekends, to meet fitness goals, give back to the community, and spend time with friends. Many races she runs are sponsored by charities or organizations that donate some portion of admission fees to non-profit organizations that perform good works in the community.

---

[2] The parties have not briefed and our decision makes it unnecessary that we consider the damages which appellant would otherwise be entitled to recover. It is clear, however, that such damages are measured by the reasonable value of services rendered and not by a percentage of the recovery achieved by the appellee as a result of the copyright infringement first described by appellant. . . .

On days when she takes time off from athletics or is injured, Yvette volunteers at races to do work such as checking athletes in, passing out free gear, supporting water bottle refilling stations, and serving food after the event. She appreciates the other volunteers who provide these services when she is racing and believes in the spirit of reciprocity and everyone chipping in for good charitable causes.

Recently, an exposé in a local newspaper discussed how a leading sponsor of many races gives only a tiny fraction of its proceeds to charity. In fact, it is a for-profit promotion company that does not pay those who staff its events, registering participants, distributing water, or serving food. Yvette calculates that she has spent 10 days last year working events for the for-profit promotions company, without pay.

1.   What theories of liability we have studied might Yvette pursue? Contract? Promissory estoppel? Unjust enrichment? What are the arguments for and against these three theories of liability?

2.   If Yvette can convince a court to entertain such theories of liability, then what theories of remedy can she sustain? What would be the measure of damages under contract, promissory estoppel, and unjust enrichment?

3.   What other legal arguments might Yvette have? (Hint: In addition to common-law theories under tort law, consider statutory arguments. For example, think about minimum wage laws).

C. TRAILING PROMISES

Fact patterns eliciting analysis under the law of restitution often pose challenging questions of timing. What if the promise to pay follows the performance? Recall *Mills v. Wyman* from Chapter One, and consider the following case as a companion.

WEBB V. MCGOWIN (APPEALS COURT)
168 So. 196 (Ala. App. 1935)

BRICKEN, J.

. . . The complaint as originally filed was amended. The demurrers to the complaint as amended were sustained, and because of this adverse ruling by the court the plaintiff took a non-suit, and the assignment of errors on this appeal are predicated upon said action or ruling of the court. A fair statement of the case presenting the questions for decision is set out in appellant's brief, which we adopt.

On the 3d day of August, 1925, [Joe Webb, the plaintiff and appellant in the case] while in the employ of the W.T. Smith Lumber Company, a corporation, and acting within the scope of his employment, was engaged in clearing the upper floor of mill No. 2 of the company. While so engaged he was in the act of dropping a pine block from the upper floor of the mill to the ground below; this being the usual and ordinary way of clearing the floor, and it being the duty of the plaintiff in the course of his employment to so drop it. The block weighed about 75 pounds.

As appellant [Webb] was in the act of dropping the block to the ground below, he was on the edge of the upper floor of the mill. As he started to turn the block loose so that it would drop to the ground, he saw J. Greeley McGowin, testator of the defendants, on the ground below and directly under where the block would have fallen had appellant turned it loose. Had he turned it loose it would have struck McGowin with such force as to have caused him serious bodily harm or death. Appellant could have remained safely on the upper floor of the mill by turning the block loose and allowing it to drop, but had he done this the block would have fallen on McGowin and caused him serious injuries or death.

The only safe and reasonable way to prevent this was for appellant to hold to the block and divert its direction in falling from the place where McGowin was standing and the only safe way to divert it so as to prevent its coming into contact with McGowin was for appellant to fall with it to the ground below. Appellant did this, and by holding to the block and falling with it to the ground below, he diverted the course of its fall in such way that McGowin was not injured. In thus preventing the injuries to McGowin appellant himself received serious bodily injuries, resulting in his right leg being broken, the heel of his right foot torn off and his right arm broken. He was badly crippled for life and rendered unable to do physical or mental labor.

On September 1, 1925, in consideration of appellant having prevented him from sustaining death or serious bodily harm and in consideration of the injuries appellant had received, McGowin agreed with him to care for and maintain him for the remainder of appellant's life at the rate of $15 every two weeks from the time he sustained his injuries to and during the remainder of appellant's life; it being agreed that McGowin would pay this sum to appellant for his maintenance. Under the agreement McGowin paid or caused to be paid to appellant the sum so agreed on up until McGowin's death on January 1, 1934. After his death the payments were continued to and including January 27, 1934, at which time they were discontinued. Thereupon plaintiff brought suit to recover the unpaid installments accruing up to the time of the bringing of the suit.

The material averments of the different counts of the original complaint and the amended complaint are predicated upon the foregoing statement of facts. . . .

1. [Webb] saved McGowin from death or grievous bodily harm. This was a material benefit to him of infinitely more value than any financial aid he could have received. Receiving this benefit, McGowin became morally bound to compensate appellant for the services rendered. Recognizing his moral obligation, he expressly agreed to pay appellant as alleged in the complaint and complied with this agreement up to the time of his death; a period of more than 8 years.

Had McGowin been accidentally poisoned and a physician, without his knowledge or request, had administered an antidote, thus saving his life, a subsequent promise by McGowin to pay the physician would have been valid. Likewise, McGowin's agreement . . . to compensate appellant for saving him from death or grievous bodily injury is valid and enforceable.

Where the promisee cares for, improves, and preserves the property of the promisor, though done without his request, it is sufficient consideration for the promisor's subsequent agreement to pay for the service, because of the material benefit received. . . .

In Boothe v. Fitzpatrick, 36 Vt. 681, the court held that a promise by defendant to pay for the past keeping of a bull which had escaped from defendant's premises and been cared for by plaintiff was valid, although there was no previous request, because the subsequent promise obviated that objection; it being equivalent to a previous request. On the same principle, had the promisee saved the promisor's life or his body from grievous harm, his subsequent promise to pay for the services rendered would have been valid. Such service would have been far more material than caring for his bull. Any holding that saving a man from death or grievous bodily harm is not a material benefit sufficient to uphold a subsequent promise to pay for the service, necessarily rests on the assumption that saving life and preservation of the body from harm have only a sentimental value. The converse of this is true. Life and preservation of the body have material, pecuniary values, measurable in dollars and cents. Because of this, physicians practice their profession charging for services rendered in saving life and curing the body of its ills, and surgeons perform operations. The same is true as to the law of negligence, authorizing the assessment of damages in personal injury cases based upon the extent of the injuries, earnings, and life expectancies of those injured.

In the business of life insurance, the value of a man's life is measured in dollars and cents according to his expectancy, the soundness of his body, and his ability to pay premiums. The same is true as to health and accident insurance.

It follows that if . . . appellant saved J. Greeley McGowin from death or grievous bodily harm, and McGowin subsequently agreed to pay him for the service rendered, it became a valid and enforceable contract.

2.   It is well settled that a moral obligation is a sufficient consideration to support a subsequent promise to pay where the promisor has received a material benefit, although there was no original duty or liability resting on the promisor. . . .

[This case] is clearly distinguishable from that class of cases where the consideration is a mere moral obligation or conscientious duty unconnected with receipt by promisor of benefits of a material or pecuniary nature. . . . Here the promisor received a material benefit constituting a valid consideration for his promise.

3.   Some authorities hold that, for a moral obligation to support a subsequent promise to pay, there must have existed a prior legal or equitable obligation, which for some reason had become unenforceable, but for which the promisor was still morally bound. This rule, however, is subject to qualification in those cases where the promisor, having received a material benefit from the promisee, is morally bound to compensate him for the services rendered and in consideration of this obligation promises to pay. In such cases the subsequent promise to pay is an affirmance or ratification of the services rendered carrying with it the presumption that a previous request for the service was made. . . .

4.   . . . [I]n saving McGowin from death or grievous bodily harm, appellant was crippled for life. This was part of the consideration of the contract declared on. McGowin was benefited. Appellant was injured. Benefit to the promisor or injury to the promisee is a sufficient legal consideration for the promisor's agreement to pay. . . .

5.   . . . [T]he services rendered by appellant were not gratuitous. The agreement of McGowin to pay and the acceptance of payment by appellant conclusively shows the contrary. . . .

. . . [T]he court below erred in the ruling complained of; that is to say, in sustaining the demurrer, and for this error the case is reversed and remanded. . . .

SAMFORD, J. (concurring).

The questions involved in this case are not free from doubt, and perhaps the strict letter of the rule, as stated by judges, though not always in accord, would bar a recovery by plaintiff, but following the principle announced by Chief Justice Marshall in Hoffman v. Porter, Fed.Cas. No. 6,577, 2 Brock. 156, 159, where he says, "I do not think that law ought to be separated from justice, where it is at most doubtful," I concur in the conclusions reached by the court.

WEBB V. MCGOWIN (SUPREME COURT)
168 So. 199 (Ala. 1935)

FOSTER, J.

[This is the Supreme Court of Alabama's subsequent opinion in Webb v. McGowin refusing to hear an appeal of the lower court's ruling, or more technically, denying a petition for a writ of certiorari to the Court of Appeals.] We do not in all cases in which we deny a petition for certiorari to the Court of Appeals approve the reasoning and principles declared in the opinion, even though no opinion is rendered by us. It does not always seem to be important that they be discussed, and we exercise . . . discretion in that respect. But when the opinion of the Court of Appeals asserts important principles or their application to new situations, and it may be uncertain whether this court agrees with it in all respects, we think it advisable to be specific in that respect when the certiorari is denied. We think such a situation here exists. . . .

The opinion of the Court of Appeals . . . recognizes and applies the distinction between a supposed moral obligation of the promisor, based upon some refined sense of ethical duty, without material benefit to him, and one in which such a benefit did in fact occur. We agree with that court that if the benefit be material and substantial, and was to the person of the promisor rather than to his estate, it is within the class of material benefits which he has the privilege of recognizing and compensating either by an executed payment or an executory promise to pay. . . . The reason is emphasized when the compensation is not only for the benefits which the promisor received, but also for the injuries either to the property or person of the promisee by reason of the service rendered.

Writ denied.

NOTES AND QUESTIONS

1.   Abstractly, what moral issues arise when one life is saved at great harm to another? Do those saved have moral duties to their rescuers? Are these moral obligations the sort of promises the law of contract or unjust enrichment should recognize?

2.   Today, most workplace accidents such as that in *Webb v. McGowin* would be addressed by worker's compensation programs. In the era of *Webb*, not only were such financial risk-spreading devices undeveloped, the country was in the grip of the Great Depression, physical injuries could be career-ending, and disabled people enjoyed few of the legal and medical protections recognized today. Might these factors have influenced the court's legal judgment? Might enforcing the employer's promise be the employee's only financial recourse in that day and age?

3. Recall that "moral consideration" generally does not count as legal consideration. Recall the facts of *Mills v. Wyman*, where a father's trailing promise to pay for his son's medical bills was unenforceable. Are there any factual or doctrinal differences that account for the opposite result in *Webb v. McGowin*? For an interesting discussion and comparison of the two cases, see Geoffrey R. Watson, *In the Tribunal of Conscience: Mills v. Wyman Reconsidered*, 71 TULANE L. REV. 1749 (1997).

4. For another classic often paired in casebooks, see *Harrington v. Taylor*, 36 S.E.2d 227 (N.C. 1945). In this case, a husband assaulted his wife, who took refuge in a neighbor's house. The next day the husband gained access to the house and again assaulted his wife. The wife responded by striking the husband with an axe; she was about to kill her husband when the neighbor intervened, catching the blow and saving the husband's life, but injuring the neighbor's own hand badly in the process.

Subsequently, the husband orally promised to pay the neighbor's damages but, after paying a small sum, failed to pay anything more. The court treated this as a consideration case, holding that while saving someone's life was a humanitarian act, the neighbor was not entitled to recovery as she was a mere volunteer. As the court stated, "however much the [husband] should be impelled by common gratitude to alleviate the [neighbor's] misfortune, a humanitarian act of this kind, voluntarily performed, is not such consideration as would entitle her to recover at law."

5. For more on trailing promises, see Stanley Henderson, *Promises Grounded in the Past: The Idea of Unjust Enrichment and the Law of Contracts*, 57 VIRGINIA L. REV. 1115 (1971).

PROBLEM: SAVE THE BAKER

Michel, who immigrated to the United States from France, is in his mid-sixties and owns a successful French bakery, La Chou Chou, in San Francisco, California. For eight years Michel has sold traditional French baked goods such as croissants and baguettes. Depending on how business goes, Michel will either work by himself or hire a part-time helper or two, at a cost of about $35,000 per year per helper. The bakery typically nets about $200,000 per year in profit after expenses are paid.

A few months ago, Michel wanted to expand his bakery's business, to add an economic buffer toward travel and retirement. He began experimenting with frying up croissant dough and layering the dough with jam and cream. Michel named his creation a "cronut," a cross between a doughnut and a croissant with a hole in the middle. Within hours of offering these items for sale, word spread on social media that they were delicious. Every day Michel opened the bakery a long line of customers stretched around the block.

During this time, Michel struck up a friendship with a young man named Jerome who hung around La Chou Chou. Jerome was virtually homeless, as he had no steady job due to past health problems. Jerome would sometimes earn a few dollars by holding a place in line for a wealthy person who wanted to buy a cronut. Michel offered Jerome coffee on a regular basis and when they saw each other they would talk about cooking and baked goods.

Jerome would often show up outside the bakery at 5 a.m. when the line was forming to offer his services for holding someone's place. One morning, Jerome showed up before anyone else. He noticed Michel slumped over a counter inside the bakery. An oven had malfunctioned, and Michel inhaled carbon monoxide, became unconscious, and collapsed. Jerome broke a window with a rock, hauled Michel to safety, and called an ambulance. Doctors noted that if Michel had not received fresh air when he did, most likely he would have suffered brain damage or died.

Grateful to Jerome for saving him, Michel told Jerome he would provide him a place to live and train him for part-time work in the bakery, paying him the starting salary (minimum wage). With training, Jerome excelled at his job, and Michel was delighted. Having only one estranged daughter with no interest in the bakery business, Michel promised, in front of several customers, to leave the business and the building to Jerome two years in the future (Michel's planned retirement) in exchange for $1. Jerome tendered the $1, but nothing was ever put in writing. Motivated by his stake in the business, Jerome worked even harder at the bakery. Given the long lines of customers, Jerome helped the bakery be more productive, and between that help and the popularity of the cronuts, profits for La Chou Chou increased to $400,000 that year.

One day not long after, Michel left Jerome in charge of the bakery while he went to run an errand. Upon returning to the bakery a few hours later, Michel was surprised to find Jerome hosting a drinking game for some of his friends. When Michel chided Jerome that this was improper during working hours, Jerome (who was drunk) told him that he was "an overbearing boss" and began swearing at him in French, a language Michel knows quite well.

Michel told Jerome to leave, and that he had ruined his chance at success. Before Jerome stormed out, he swore to sue for what he considered unlawful termination, his rightful share of the bakery's earnings, as well as a declaration that he would have ownership rights to the building and the business in two years. He ended this tirade by again insulting Michel in French and slamming the door. It looks like their working relationship is ruined.

Analyze the causes of action arising from these facts.

D. NOVEL IDEAS

BAER V. CHASE
2007 WL 1237850 (D.N.J. 2007)

PISANO, J.

. . . Proving to be every bit as resilient as Tony Soprano, the fictional mob boss and central figure of The Sopranos, this action returns to the Court for a third time. In two prior opinions, this Court has set forth a comprehensive summary of the facts of this case. See Baer v. Chase, No. 02–2334, 2005 WL 1106487, at *1–3 (D.N.J. Apr. 29, 2005); Baer v. Chase, No. 02–2334, 2004 WL 350050, at *2–4 (D.N.J. Feb. 20, 2004); see also Baer v. Chase, 392 F.3d 609, 612–15 (3d Cir.2004). In the interest of brevity, the Court will discuss only those facts that are relevant to Defendants' motion.

[Robert] Baer, a former prosecutor in the Union County Prosecutor's Office in Elizabeth, New Jersey, and [David] Chase, a writer, director, producer and creator of television programs, met in June 1995, around the time Chase was developing an idea for a television series about a mob boss in therapy. During their initial meeting, Baer told Chase some New Jersey crime stories, all of which were factual and true. Baer, apparently unaware of the fact that Chase had previously worked on projects involving northern New Jersey mobsters, suggested that Chase shoot movies or television shows about crime in New Jersey and the northern New Jersey mob. Also, according to Baer, he mentioned some facts and locations concerning organized crime in New Jersey, but provided no "detail or drama."

In July 1995, as Chase began to devote more attention to the "mob boss in therapy idea," he contacted Baer to see if he would be willing to help Chase compile information about the inner workings of the mob. To obtain some of the desired information, Baer reached out to Detective Lieutenant Robert Jones ("Jones"), an organized crime expert in the Union County Prosecutor's Office. After speaking with Jones, Baer sent Chase some notes discussing mob involvement in gambling and in the garbage business, and Morris Levy, the Jewish mobster and record producer who had been jailed for defrauding MCA Records. In August 1995, Chase pitched the idea for a show about a mob boss in therapy to Fox Broadcasting ("Fox") and, in early September, Fox agreed to finance the creation of a pilot story.

In October, Chase visited New Jersey for three days to conduct research for the show. During his visit, Chase spent many hours with Baer, who arranged for Chase to meet with individuals whom Baer thought could provide useful information about organized crime. Specifically, Chase and Baer met with Jones, Detective Thomas Koczur ("Koczur"), an Elizabeth homicide detective and close friend to Baer, and Antonio Spirito ("Spirito"), a waiter at an Italian restaurant, whom Koczur knew to be a good storyteller. . . . Baer and Koczur, who served as tour guide, drove Chase to several locations in northern New Jersey, including local landmarks, known mob hangouts, and locations of mob significance in Elizabeth and Newark. Additionally, Koczur arranged for the group to have lunch with Spirito, who shared some true and sometimes personal crime stories. Finally, Chase met with Jones who provided him with access to wiretaps that were used in local criminal trials and information about organized crime, including facts about Morris Levy and the mob's infiltration of MCA Records. As Baer has acknowledged, virtually all of the information provided to Chase during his visit exists in the public record.

At the end of October 1995, Chase returned to Los Angeles and completed a draft pilot of The Sopranos, which he delivered to Fox in early December 1995. After completing the pilot script, Chase sent a copy to Baer. Fourteen months later, Baer sent Chase his written comments on the script, but had no further involvement with Chase or The Sopranos. Though the issue of compensation came up on a few occasions, Chase never paid Baer for his services and the two never entered into a contract of any kind. Chase, recognized as creator, writer, director and producer of the series, continued working on The Sopranos, which first aired on HBO in 1999. The Sopranos, now in its final season, has enjoyed widespread critical and financial success. . . .

Baer's Complaint . . . asserts claims . . . for: (1) breach of contract; (2) breach of implied contract; (3) breach of quasi-contract; [and six other claims including fraud, misrepresentation, misappropriation and unfair competition].

[This court previously] granted summary judgment to [Chase and his company] and dismissed Baer's Complaint in its entirety. Notably, the Court found as a matter of law that the ideas that Baer allegedly conveyed to Chase were not novel because the so-called ideas consisted of facts and locations that exist in the public domain. Further, the stories told to Chase during his three-day visit to New Jersey were not Baer's stories, nor did he tell them. . . . The stories, told by Koczur, Jones and Spirito, were thus not original to Baer. . . . As such, the Court concluded (and Baer conceded the point) that the "locations, stories and information" discussed during Chase's October 1995 visit "either existed in the public domain or came from one of [Baer]'s associates." Id. . . .

On appeal, the Third Circuit reversed this Court's dismissal of Baer's quasi-contract claim, but affirmed dismissal of the other nine claims in Baer's Complaint. Discussing Baer's ideas in the context of his claim for misappropriation, the Third Circuit found that "[i]t is clear that virtually all of Baer's alleged contributions either existed in the public domain or concerned stories and facts that he did not provide." Baer, 392 F.3d at 629.

In response to Baer's claim that he selected which stories his associates would tell and that this unique combination of stories made them original despite their existence in the public domain, the Circuit Court stated that "[a]ggregation of ideas and expression do not by themselves create novelty." Id. On remand, this Court granted summary judgment in favor of Defendants on the quasi-contract claim on the basis that the statute of limitations barred the claim. The Third Circuit, however, reversed that finding and the parties are back before this Court to litigate Baer's quasi-contract claim, the only surviving claim . . . .

A quasi-contract, which is not a contract at all, is based upon an equitable principle through which courts "prevent unjust enrichment or unconscionable benefit or advantage." Duffy v. Charles Schwab & Co., 123 F.Supp.2d 802, 814 (D.N.J. 2000) (quotation omitted) . . . . The quasi-contract theory permits a plaintiff to recover damages "even though the parties' words and actions are insufficient to manifest an intention" to enter into a contract. Weichert Co. Realtors v. Ryan, 128 N.J. 427, 608 A.2d 280, 285 (1992) . . . . As such, quasi-contract and contract, whether express or implied, are mutually exclusive theories of recovery. Duffy, 123 F.Supp.2d at 814.

Under New Jersey law, to recover in quasi-contract for the use of an idea, the plaintiff must demonstrate that the idea for which he seeks compensation was novel. Id. at 815 (denying plaintiff's quasi-contract claim for non-novel idea) . . . . Indeed, it is not "unjust" to use a non-novel idea without compensating the one who supplied the idea. . . . In earlier opinions, both this Court and the Third Circuit concluded that Baer did not communicate any novel ideas to Chase. . . . Baer relies on a case from the Alaska Supreme Court, Reeves v. Alyeska Services Co., 926 P.2d 1130, 1144 (Alaska 1996), for the proposition that the sharing of a non-novel idea can give rise to a quasi-contract claim. In addition to the fact that a case from the Alaska Supreme Court is not binding upon this Court, Reeves involves an application of Alaska law, which is simply not relevant to the issue presented here: whether Baer may recover, under New Jersey law, for Chase's use of non-novel ideas. [But] Courts interpreting New Jersey law on quasi-contract have concluded that novelty is required for a quasi-contract claim involving the use of ideas. . . . Moreover, the Reeves Court, much like courts applying New Jersey law, stated that novelty and originality "distinguish protectable ideas from ordinary ideas that are freely available for others to use" and the use of a non-novel idea "cannot satisfy the requirements of a quasi-contract claim." Reeves, 926 P.2d at 1143. Thus, Baer's reliance on Reeves is unavailing.

Next, Baer argues that his ideas are compensable in quasi-contract because the ideas, though not novel in an absolute sense, were novel to Chase. New Jersey law, however, does not recognize the "novelty to the buyer" theory for idea submission claims that are not contract-based. In

Johnson v. Benjamin Moore & Co., 347 N.J.Super. 71, 788 A.2d 906, 919 (App.Div.2002), the New Jersey Appellate Division adopted the standard announced in Nadel v. Play-by-Play Toys & Novelties, Inc., 208 F.3d 368 (2d Cir.2000). The Nadel, or New York, standard distinguishes between idea submission claims that are property-based, which "can only arise from the taking of an idea that is original or novel in absolute terms," and claims that are contract-based, which must only satisfy a "novelty to the buyer" standard. . . . Under the Nadel standard, Baer's quasi-contract claim, which by its very nature is not based in contract, fails because, as he has conceded, he cannot make a showing of absolute novelty.

Nor can Baer recover under a theory that he shaped, developed and combined ideas that were not his or existed in the public domain. "An idea will not satisfy [the novelty] requirement if it is not significantly different from, or is an obvious adaptation or combination of ideas in the public domain." Duffy, 123 F.Supp.2d at 810. Further, as the Third Circuit stated in response to Baer's argument that he is entitled to recovery for shaping and adapting ideas that existed in the public record or were based on real-life stories, "[a]ggregation of ideas and expression do not by themselves create novelty." Baer, 392 F.3d at 629. Relying on Duffy, the Third Circuit added that the presentation or adaptation of ideas goes "more to an idea's expression than to the idea itself" and the expression of an idea is not entitled to protection. Id. Thus, even if Baer had shaped or developed facts and ideas that existed in the public domain, that would not entitle him to any recovery in this case. . . .

Under New Jersey law, "quasi-contractual recovery for services rendered when a party confers a benefit with a reasonable expectation of payment . . . is known as quantum meruit [which] entitles the performing party to recoup the reasonable value of services rendered." Weichert Co. Realtors, 608 A.2d at 285 (citations omitted). "The New Jersey Supreme Court has not definitively articulated the competent methods of establishing damages in a quantum meruit action." See West v. IDT Corp., No. 01–4372, 2006 WL 1459971, at *3 (D.N.J. May 25, 2006). Nonetheless, the New Jersey Supreme Court has recognized the following two methods as appropriate for calculating damages in a quantum meruit action: (1) the market value method, in which damages are calculated according to industry custom or practice for similar services, see Weichert Co. Realtors, 608 A.2d at 287; and (2) the cost method, in which damages are limited to the costs a plaintiff incurs in providing the service . . . . The prevailing view among courts is that the market value method is the proper measure for damages "in quantum meruit cases where the defendant requests services from the plaintiff." [Candace S. Kovacic, A Proposal to Simplify Quantum Meruit Litigation, 35 Am. U.L.Rev. 547, 551 (1986)].[8]

---

[8] According to Professor Kovacic, "the reasonable market value of plaintiff's services can be viewed as the correct remedy in most quantum meruit cases . . . because reasonable value can be

. . . Baer's quantum meruit claims arise from Chase's requests for services, namely that Baer conduct research on organized crime, introduce Chase to individuals with knowledge of the northern New Jersey Mafia, and generally help Chase gather information about the mob. This, in other words, is a quantum meruit case in which the defendant requested services from the plaintiff. [Accordingly,] the Court finds that the proper measure of damages in this case is the market value method. . . .

NOTES AND QUESTIONS

1. *The Sopranos* was a runaway hit for HBO, garnering critical attention and commercial success during its run from 1999 to 2007. Its stars became well-known, and two former writers went on to write and produce the hit shows *Boardwalk Empire* and *Mad Men*.

2. Chase had a long career before *The Sopranos*, working on the shows *Northern Exposure* and *The Rockford Files*. It is safe to say, though, that *The Sopranos* was his largest success; he has had several other projects since but none of the same high profile.

3. Was the subject of *The Sopranos* truly novel? In 1999, the movie *Analyze This* was released. Starring Robert De Niro, the movie centered on a mob boss and his treatment in therapy. The movie, however, was a comedy, not a serious character study or glimpse into the world of organized crime.

4. Note that the court does not rule out the idea of some measure of recovery for Baer. What damages are possible for Baer under a restitution / unjust enrichment theory? Why are the damages so limited?

5. In the aftermath of the ruling, both sides claimed victory. Chase said he won, as Baer would not be allowed a share of the profits from *The Sopranos*. Baer claimed a "moral victory" from acknowledgement of his time and work toward *The Sopranos*. Who was correct?

6. Are there truly any "novel" ideas? In T.S. Eliot's *The Wasteland*, culture is endlessly recycling itself. In the language of post-modern literary criticism, the best a creator can do is *bricolage*—tinkering—to select the best and most interesting pieces of what has come before. Or, in the words of philosopher Umberto Eco, culture is a type of palimpsest, a scroll over-written by other scroll writers. Anyone writing or conducting research benefits from those who have gone before.

7. An entrepreneur or artist with an idea for a business or product often needs to share it with others in order to receive advice or financial backing. It is a well-known practice to ask others to sign a confidentiality or non-disclosure

---

viewed as the defendant's gain in certain situations. The value of plaintiff's services measures the defendant's gain when the defendant requests the work: the defendant's benefit is receiving what he or she requested; those requested services have a market value." Kovacic, 35 Am. U.L.Rev. at 557.

agreement (commonly known as an NDA). Could such an agreement be used to reduce the risk of disputes like the one in *Baer v. Chase?*

APFEL V. PRUDENTIAL-BACHE SECURITIES, INC.
616 N.E.2d 1095 (N.Y. 1993)

SIMONS, J.

Defendant, an investment bank, seeks to avoid an agreement to purchase plaintiffs' idea for issuing and selling municipal bonds. Its principal contention is that plaintiffs had no property right in the idea because it was not novel and, therefore, consideration for the contract was lacking. For reasons which follow, we conclude that a showing of novelty is not required to validate the contract. The decisive question is whether the idea had value, not whether it was novel. . . .

In 1982, plaintiffs, an investment banker and a lawyer, approached defendant's predecessor with a proposal for issuing municipal securities through a system that eliminated paper certificates and allowed bonds to be sold, traded, and held exclusively by means of computerized "book entries". Initially, the parties signed a confidentiality agreement that allowed defendant to review the techniques as detailed in a 99-page summary. Nearly a month of negotiations followed before the parties entered into a sale agreement under which plaintiffs conveyed their rights to the techniques and certain trade names and defendant agreed to pay a stipulated rate based on its use of the techniques for a term from October 1982 to January 1988. Under the provisions of the contract, defendant's obligation to pay was to remain even if the techniques became public knowledge or standard practice in the industry and applications for patents and trademarks were denied. Plaintiffs asserted that they had not previously disclosed the techniques to anyone and they agreed to maintain them in confidence until they became public.

From 1982 until 1985, defendant implemented the contract, although the parties dispute whether amounts due were fully paid. Defendant actively encouraged bond issuers to use the computerized "book entry" system and, for at least the first year, was the sole underwriter in the industry employing such a system. However, in 1985, following a change in personnel, defendant refused to make any further payments. It maintained that the ideas conveyed by plaintiffs had been in the public domain at the time of the sale agreement and that what plaintiffs sold had never been theirs to sell. Defendant's attempts to patent the techniques proved unsuccessful. By 1985, investment banks were increasingly using computerized systems, and by 1990 such systems were handling 60% of the dollar volume of all new issues of municipal securities.

Plaintiffs commenced this litigation seeking $45 million in compensatory and punitive damages. They asserted 17 causes of action based on theories of breach of contract, breach of a fiduciary duty, fraud, various torts arising from defendant's failure to obtain patents, and unjust enrichment. Defendant's answer interposed defenses and counterclaims for breach of contract, breach of warranty, waiver, fraud, estoppel, laches, mutual mistake, rescission, and a lack of consideration. Plaintiffs then moved for partial summary judgment, defendant cross-moved for summary judgment dismissing the complaint, and plaintiffs responded with a motion seeking dismissal of the affirmative defenses.

Supreme Court concluded that triable issues existed on the questions of whether defendant breached the contract by refusing to make payments and whether plaintiffs committed a breach by allegedly disclosing the techniques to another company. The court also found defendant had raised a triable issue on whether plaintiffs had partially waived their right to payment by forgoing certain claims to compensation. The remainder of the pleadings were found to be legally insufficient. Accordingly, the court dismissed all the causes of action except the first, which alleges breach of contract, and struck all defendant's defenses and counterclaims except those relating to breach of contract and the partial defense of waiver. The Appellate Division modified the order by reinstating defendant's claim that the sale agreement lacked consideration. It held that novelty was required before an idea could be valid consideration but concluded that the question was one of fact to be decided at trial. It also reinstated the cause of action for unjust enrichment, holding that the presence of an express contract did not foreclose recovery on a theory of quasi contract.

On this appeal, defendant's principal contention is that no contract existed between the parties because the sale agreement lacked consideration. Underlying that argument is its assertion that an idea cannot be legally sufficient consideration unless it is novel. Defendant supports that proposition by its reading of such cases as Downey v. General Foods Corp., 31 N.Y.2d 56, 334 N.Y.S.2d 874, 286 N.E.2d 257 [and] Soule v. Bon Ami Co., 201 App.Div. 794, 195 N.Y.S. 574, affd. 235 N.Y. 609, 139 N.E. 754 . . . . Plaintiffs insist that their system was indeed novel, but contend that, in any event, novelty is not required to validate the contract at issue here. . . . Defendant's cross motion for summary judgment insofar as it sought to dismiss the first cause of action alleging breach of contract was properly denied. Additionally, plaintiffs' motion to dismiss the lack of consideration defenses and counterclaims should be granted.

Under the traditional principles of contract law, the parties to a contract are free to make their bargain, even if the consideration exchanged is grossly unequal or of dubious value (see, . . . Hamer v. Sidway, 124 N.Y. 538, 27 N.E. 256 . . .). Absent fraud or unconscionability, the adequacy of consideration is not a proper subject for judicial scrutiny . . . . It is enough that something of "real value in the eye of the law" was exchanged (see, Mencher v. Weiss, 306 N.Y. 1, 8, 114 N.E.2d 177 . . .). The fact that the sellers may not have had a property right in what they sold does not, by itself, render the contract void for lack of consideration . . . .

Manifestly, defendant received something of value here; its own conduct establishes that. After signing the confidentiality agreement, defendant thoroughly reviewed plaintiffs' system before buying it. Having done so, it was in the best position to know whether the idea had value. It decided to enter into the sale agreement and aggressively market the system to potential bond issuers. For at least a year, it was the only underwriter to use plaintiffs' "book entry" system for municipal bonds, and it handled millions of such bond transactions during that time. Having obtained full disclosure of the system, used it in advance of competitors, and received the associated benefits of precluding its disclosure to others, defendant can hardly claim now the idea had no value to its municipal securities business. Indeed, defendant acknowledges it made payments to plaintiffs under the sale agreement for more than two years, conduct that would belie any claim it might make that the idea was lacking in value or that it had actually been obtained from some other source before plaintiffs' disclosure.

Thus, defendant has failed to demonstrate on this record that the contract was void or to raise a triable issue of fact on lack of consideration. . . . Defendant . . . [contends that cases such as Downey v. General Foods Corp. and Soule v. Bon Ami Co.], . . . establish an exception to traditional principles of contract law and require that the idea must be novel before it can constitute valid consideration for a contract. . . .

In Downey, plaintiff submitted an idea for an advertising campaign. A short time later, defendant General Foods mounted a campaign that was similar to the one plaintiff had suggested and plaintiff sought damages in a complaint alleging several theories for recovery. We ordered the dismissal of the complaint on two separate grounds: first, the lack of novelty and, second, defendant's prior possession of the idea—i.e., its lack of novelty as to defendant. To the extent plaintiff's causes of action were grounded on assertions of a property right, we found that they were untenable "if the elements of novelty and originality [were] absent, since the property right in an idea is based upon these two elements." Second, we concluded that the defendant possessed plaintiff's ideas prior to plaintiff's disclosure. Thus, the ideas could have no value to defendant and could not supply consideration for any agreement between the parties.

In Soule v. Bon Ami Co., plaintiff made an express contract with Bon Ami to disclose a way to increase profits. The idea consisted largely of a proposal to raise prices. The Appellate Division, in a frequently cited opinion, denied plaintiff any recovery, finding that the bargain lacked consideration because the idea was not novel. This Court affirmed but it did so on a different basis: it held that plaintiff had failed to show that profits resulted from the disclosure.

These decisions do not support defendant's contention that novelty is required in all cases involving disclosure of ideas. Indeed, we have explicitly held that it is not (see, Keller v. American Chain Co., 255 N.Y. 94, 174 N.E. 74). Downey, Soule and cases in that line of decisions involve a distinct factual pattern: the buyer and seller contract for disclosure of the idea with payment based on use, but no separate post-disclosure contract for use of the idea has been made. Thus, they present the issue of whether the idea the buyer was using was, in fact, the seller's.

Such transactions pose two problems for the courts. On the one hand, how can sellers prove that the buyer obtained the idea from them, and nowhere else, and that the buyer's use of it thus constitutes misappropriation of property? Unlike tangible property, an idea lacks title and boundaries and cannot be rendered exclusive by the acts of the one who first thinks it. On the other hand, there is no equity in enforcing a seemingly valid contract when, in fact, it turns out upon disclosure that the buyer already possessed the idea. In such instances, the disclosure, though freely bargained for, is manifestly without value. A showing of novelty, at least novelty as to the buyer, addresses these two concerns. Novelty can then serve to establish both the attributes of ownership necessary for a property-based claim and the value of the consideration—the disclosure—necessary for contract-based claims.

There are no such concerns in a transaction such as the one before us. Defendant does not claim that it was aware of the idea before plaintiffs disclosed it but, rather, concedes that the idea came from them. When a seller's claim arises from a contract to use an idea entered into after the disclosure of the idea, the question is not whether the buyer misappropriated property from the seller, but whether the idea had value to the buyer and thus constitutes valid consideration. In such a case, the buyer knows what he or she is buying and has agreed that the idea has value, and the Court will not ordinarily go behind that determination. The lack of novelty, in and of itself, does not demonstrate a lack of value (see, Keller v. American Chain Co., 255 N.Y. 94, 174 N.E. 74, supra). To the contrary, the buyer may reap benefits from such a contract in a number of ways—for instance, by not having to expend resources pursuing the idea through other channels or by having a profit-making idea implemented sooner rather than later. The law of contracts would have to be substantially rewritten were we to allow buyers of fully disclosed ideas to disregard their obligation to pay simply because an idea could have been obtained from some other source or in some other way. . . .

Having found that defendant's counterclaims and defenses challenging the existence of a valid contract should be stricken, we further conclude that the Appellate Division erred in reinstating plaintiffs' seventh cause of action, which alleged unjust enrichment on a quasi-contract theory. The transaction is controlled by the express agreement of the parties and their rights and liabilities are to be determined solely on theories of breach of contract and the partial defense of waiver (see, Miller v. Schloss, 218 N.Y. 400, 408–409, 113 N.E. 337). . . .

NOTES AND QUESTIONS

1.   Was the idea in *Apfel v. Prudential-Bache Securities* novel? Does it matter in this case? If not, why not?

2.   How was *Apfel* about the adequacy of consideration? Recall your study of consideration. Should the court assume there is consideration because there was a signed agreement between the parties? Does the commercial setting justify assuming that the parties are sophisticated business people?

3.   Should *Apfel* have been decided under a contract theory or under a restitution/unjust enrichment theory?

E. UNJUST ENRICHMENT

Several interesting cases about unjust enrichment involve unpaid labor on the Internet. Sometimes those who perform the work are not even aware of it. Consider the following example, thinking about the expectation of profit from commercial activity. Also keep in mind the idea that many people now do work for free in the hopes of "gaining exposure," and making a future profit from that. Yet others may do so only for political purposes. Should the motivation for work matter in relation to whether website operators are unjustly enriched?

TASINI V. AOL, INC.
851 F.Supp.2d 734 (S.D.N.Y.)
aff'd, 505 Fed. Appx. 45 (2d Cir. 2012)

KOELTIL, J.

The plaintiffs, Jonathan Tasini ("Tasini"), Molly Secours ("Secours"), Tara Dublin ("Dublin"), Richard Laermer ("Laermer"), and Billy Altman ("Altman"), individually and on behalf of all others similarly situated, . . . bring this proposed class action under the common law doctrine of unjust enrichment . . . . The plaintiffs have sued AOL, Inc. ("AOL"), TheHuffingtonPost.com, Inc., Arianna Huffington ("Huffington"), and Kenneth Lerer ("Lerer") (collectively "the defendants"), alleging that the defendants unjustly . . . denied the plaintiffs compensation for submitting content to and promoting content on The Huffington Post (www.the huffington post. com), . . . a website owned and operated by the defendants. . . .

The Huffington Post launched its www.huffington post.com website as a for-profit enterprise on May 9, 2005. . . . The Huffington Post was ostensibly created by defendants Huffington and Lerer . . . . The website has become quite popular, receiving more than 26 million unique visitors per month as of January 2011. . . . The website provides a mix of content that is written by paid staff members, collected from other websites, or submitted by unpaid bloggers . . . who have been selected or recruited to blog for the website. . . .

The named plaintiffs and prospective class members are members of the last group: the website's unpaid content providers. . . . The majority of these content providers are "professional or quasi-professional writers." . . . The named plaintiffs are all repeat-providers, having submitted significant volumes of content over varying periods of time. For example, plaintiff Tasini, described in the Complaint as a professional author, politician, union leader, and successful United States Supreme Court litigant, submitted content 216 times over the course of more than 5 years and publicized that content through social networking media such as Facebook and Twitter. . . .

Rather than monetary compensation, the unpaid content providers are offered exposure—namely, visibility, promotion, and distribution, for themselves and their work. . . . Although the defendants have, at times, considered compensating the unpaid content providers by, for example, allowing content providers to choose charities with which advertising revenue generated by their content would be shared, the defendants otherwise made clear to the plaintiffs from the beginning that they never intended to pay content providers such as the plaintiffs for submissions. . . . The unpaid submissions are arguably the website's most valuable content, both because of their effect of "optimizing" the website's ranking in search engines such as Google (thus attracting more viewers to the website) and because they allow The Huffington Post to keep production costs low. . . . Additionally, The Huffington Post encourages the bloggers to promote their own submissions via their social networks such as by sending emails, sharing their posts on Facebook or MySpace, responding to reader comments, and contacting other blogs. . . . As a result, the Complaint alleges that The Huffington Post gains more both in terms of exposure and monetary value from the unpaid submissions than do the authors. . . .

From its inception, The Huffington Post has generated revenue by, among other things, selling advertising targeted towards visitors to the website. . . . Advertising revenues increase in proportion to the amount of page views a website receives, which in turn is a function of the quality of the content provided, as well as the website's ability to attract visitors either through its own marketing or via the social networks of others. . . . The Huffington Post allegedly keeps track of the number of page views of, and thus the revenue generated by, each piece of content (including unpaid submissions) on the website. . . . This information was never provided to the plaintiffs or other content providers. . . .

The Complaint alleges that, while the "guidelines" distributed by The Huffington Post to the plaintiffs and other content providers suggest that this page-view information is unavailable, the data is in fact generated and retained by The Huffington Post and is readily accessible. . . . Keeping this data hidden prevents the plaintiffs and others from knowing the exact monetary value The Huffington Post generates from their submissions. . . . Stated in other terms, this prevents the plaintiffs from knowing how much exposure their submissions generate for The Huffington Post as compared to the level of exposure the plaintiffs acquire from being published by The Huffington Post. . . . Nowhere does the Complaint allege that the plaintiffs were promised any monetary compensation. . . .

In early 2011, AOL purchased The Huffington Post for around $315 million. . . . The Complaint asserts that The Huffington Post "was an attractive merger target for AOL because of [The Huffington Post's] ability to obtain high quality content from [the plaintiffs] at no cost." . . . The Complaint alleges that at least $105 million of the purchase price is properly traceable to the plaintiffs, including "the value created by the content provided by [the plaintiffs]," the plaintiffs' "efforts to publicize the content provided," and "the value created by [the plaintiffs] in lowering the cost of content production for AOL. . . ." . . . Following the purchase, AOL has ostensibly hopped on the unpaid-content bandwagon, reducing its volume of paid submissions in favor of unpaid submissions. . . .

After the merger, the plaintiffs brought this suit claiming . . . that The Huffington Post was unjustly enriched as a result of this practice. . . . Under the doctrine of unjust enrichment, the plaintiffs seek damages in the form of compensation for the alleged monetary value of their submissions, specifically at least $105 million (the plaintiffs' alleged contribution to The Huffington Post's purchase price). . . . The plaintiffs allege that they added value by submitting content to the website and promoting that content. The defendants argue that the plaintiffs' claim should be dismissed for failure to demonstrate that equity and good conscience require restitution and, in the alternative, that the plaintiffs' unjust enrichment claim is barred by the existence of an implied contract between the plaintiffs and the defendants. . . .

The equitable doctrine of unjust enrichment rests on the principle that a party should not be allowed to enrich itself at the expense of another. . . . In order to establish a claim for unjust enrichment under New York law, a plaintiff must establish: "(1) that the defendant benefitted; (2) at the plaintiff's expense; and (3) that equity and good conscience require restitution." In re Mid-Island Hosp., Inc., 276 F.3d 123, 129–30 (2d Cir.2002) (citation omitted) . . . If the plaintiffs fail to demonstrate that equity and good conscience require restitution, their claim should be dismissed. . . .

Here, the plaintiffs claim that the defendants have been unjustly enriched by generating profit from the submissions of the plaintiffs to The Huffington Post and not paying the plaintiffs for those submissions, while enticing the plaintiffs with misleading promises of exposure. However, the plaintiffs entered into their transactions with the defendants with full knowledge of the facts and no expectation of compensation other than exposure. In such circumstances, equity and good conscience counsel against retroactively altering the parties' clear agreements.

There is no question that the plaintiffs submitted their materials to The Huffington Post with no expectation of monetary compensation and that they got what they paid for—exposure in The Huffington Post. . . . Courts applying New York law require a plaintiff to allege some expectation of compensation that was denied in order to demonstrate that equity requires restitution. . . .

The plaintiffs argue that an expectation of compensation is not always required for an unjust enrichment claim. The plaintiffs point to cases where it was not initially clear to the plaintiff that the plaintiff actually enriched the defendant, such as where it was uncertain whether the defendant would ultimately use what the plaintiff had provided. See, e.g., News World Commc'ns, Inc. v. Thompsen, 878 A.2d 1218, 1224–25 (D.C.2005). At best, these cases stand for the proposition that plaintiffs who are unsure of whether they will be compensated if their services are not used may still sue if the services they render do ultimately benefit a defendant who then denies compensation. See Thompsen, 878 A.2d at 1224–26 (noting that defendant "obviously would not be unjustly enriched if it refused to pay for the unsolicited material" that it never used). Stated in other terms, the plaintiffs in these cases expected compensation but the exact terms of the compensation were unclear. These cases therefore fail to support the plaintiffs' argument that unjust enrichment does not require an expectation of compensation. Indeed, in this case, the plaintiffs expected only exposure rather than monetary compensation if their submissions were used, and those terms were clear from the outset. . . . Therefore, under New York law, a plaintiff must plead some expectation of compensation that was denied in order to recover under a theory of unjust enrichment. The Complaint fails to do so and the claim for unjust enrichment must therefore be dismissed.

Moreover, equity and good conscience plainly do not support the plaintiffs in this matter. No one forced the plaintiffs to give their work to The Huffington Post for publication and the plaintiffs candidly admit that they did not expect compensation. The principles of equity and good conscience do not justify giving the plaintiffs a piece of the purchase price when they never expected to be paid, repeatedly agreed to the same bargain, and went into the arrangement with eyes wide open. . . . Quite simply, the plaintiffs offered a service and the defendants offered exposure in return, and the transaction occurred exactly as advertised. The defendants followed through on their end of the agreed-upon bargain. That the defendants ultimately profited more than the plaintiffs might have expected does not give the plaintiffs a right to change retroactively their clear, up-front agreement. That is an effort to change the rules of the game after the game has been played, and equity and good conscience require no such result.

The Complaint fails to demonstrate that the principles of equity and good conscience require restitution and thus fails to allege a proper claim for unjust enrichment. For the reasons explained above, the plaintiffs' claim for unjust enrichment must be dismissed.[4]

NOTES AND QUESTIONS

1. The lead plaintiff in the case, Jonathan Tasini, is a journalist focusing on labor and employment issues in the news. A former president of the National Writers' Union, he has been involved in other court cases seeking payment for writers and journalists. In *New York Times v. Tasini*, 533 U.S. 483 (2001), he was the lead plaintiff for a group of writers claiming that publishers violated their copyrights by posting print articles in digital databases without permission or payment. That case ultimately resulted in an $18 million payment to the journalists.

2. Is the dispute in *Tasini v. AOL* about conflicting expectations of whether a particular activity will be volunteer or for-profit, or whether the forum, in this case a blog, is for-profit or non-profit? Before the purchase of the blog by AOL, many people saw the Huffington Post as a liberal online community dedicated to sharing news and a place for members of the Democratic Party to write and voice their views about issues of the day. Many writers did not necessarily want payment when they started because they viewed the blog as a community, not a profit-making enterprise. As such, they were outraged when they saw that their free efforts were used by the blog's organizers to make hundreds of millions of dollars. The expectation was that their efforts would remain an act of volunteerism, and that if the context changed, they wanted fair payment for their work. *See* Miriam A. Cherry, *Cyber Commodification*, 72 MARYLAND L. REV. 381 (2013).

3. There are other contexts when there is no expectation of payment but the law nonetheless requires it, because of the applicability of minimum wage laws. The issue has become more salient in recent years due to the growth of unpaid internships. Federal guidelines allow unpaid internships as an

---

[4] The defendants argue in the alternative that the plaintiffs and defendants had an agreement amounting to an implied contract, such that the unjust enrichment claim must fail because a quasi-contract claim cannot exist when there is an actual contract. It is unnecessary to reach this argument because the plaintiffs have failed to state a claim for unjust enrichment.

exemption to minimum wage laws, but internships must provide educational training, the internship cannot displace paid workers, and there must be no "immediate advantage" from an intern's help. In other words, the internship must benefit the intern, not the organization. *See* Steven Greenhouse, *The Unpaid Intern, Legal or Not*, N.Y.TIMES, April 2, 2010; ROSS PERLIN, INTERN NATION (2011). Recently in response to several prominent lawsuits, publishers and Hollywood companies have begun paying for previously unpaid internships.

EXAMPLE: CHARITY FOR GOOGLE

A "recaptcha" is a code that Internet users are asked to enter to prove they are human, not automated programs (called bots). Internet users are often asked to enter a recaptcha if they desire to post a comment to a blog or to sign into an Internet account.

Most people insert the code and think no more of it. But some users became curious when many requested codes looked like street signs or address numbers from the sides of buildings. Some sleuthing revealed that the company making these recaptchas had been acquired by the dominant Internet search company, Google.

Google had keyed the captchas to match fuzzy photos of street signs and pictures of houses taken for use in its Google Earth mapping project. These were signs and numbers that Google's optical recognition software could not identify. Google was also using recaptcha software to reduce typographical errors in books it scanned into its Google Books project. In both contexts, Internet users entering these numbers were helping to improve Google's projects—without compensation and without their knowledge.

Imagine a group of these users have come to talk to you about any causes of action they might bring. How might you advise them? Does it matter that the recaptcha users might have free access to Google Earth or Google Books?

PROBLEM: PANTSUIT NATION

In October of 2016, a "secret" privately-run Facebook group called "Pantsuit Nation" formed on Facebook. The idea was to show support for presidential candidate Hillary Rodham Clinton by wearing a pantsuit to the polls when voting in the national election. The invitation-only Facebook group proved popular, swelling to four million members. In days leading up to the election, a variety of posts emerged online, some hewing to the original idea of wearing a pantsuit and expressing support for Clinton, but others telling stories about facing down sexism or engaging in longstanding activism in the Democratic party.

After Mrs. Clinton lost the election in a surprise upset, "Pantsuit Nation" evolved into a space where members could write about their take on that outcome and resulting challenges. Some wrote of standing up to sexism, racism, or other intolerance. Some posted family pictures including interracial marriages, and still other stories presented "feel-good" tales about random acts of kindness. Many found support in the website to process the surprising election results. Some speculated that the Facebook group could create a motivated base that might help Democratic candidates in state and local elections.

On December 19, 2016, Libby Chamberlain, creator of the Facebook group, announced she had landed a contract to publish a coffee table book based on posts appearing on Pantsuit Nation. While some members applauded and many committed to buying the book, thousands of critical comments appeared. Many thought that they were participating in a "secret" group, which implied that the posts would not be shared, let alone published. Others were concerned about pictures or stories being published without permission. Many who commented on the post were outraged and offended by what they saw as exploitation of the group's content for the profit of one group member.

Asha is a member of the Pantsuit Nation group who shared a story about her family as well as several photos. She is concerned that these materials will be published, and is upset that she would receive nothing for her efforts. If you represent Asha (and other members of the Facebook Group), what are your strongest arguments? What counterarguments might you expect?

NOTE ON RESTITUTION AND COMPARATIVE LAW

The concepts behind restitution and unjust enrichment are ancient, tracing back to notions first expressed in Roman law. In modern times, an attempt at organization, categorization, and modernization of the doctrine came from the American Law Institute, which in 1937 published the *Restatement of the Law of Restitution*. After this innovation, however, the field of restitution languished in the United States. As Professor John Langbein noted, it was "as though a neutron bomb has hit the field—the monuments have been left standing, but the people have been killed off. . . . What restitution is taught in American law schools today turns up mostly in snippits in the remedy units of contracts and trust books . . . ." John H. Langbein, *The Later History of Restitution, in* RESTITUTION: PAST, PRESENT, AND FUTURE 57, 61 (W.R. Cornish et al. eds., 1998); *see also* Chaim Saiman, *Restitution in America: Why the U.S. Refuses to Join the Global Restitution Party*, 28 OXFORD J. LEGAL STUD. 99, 100–02 (2008).

In contrast, a great deal more theoretical development of the doctrine occurred within the law of the United Kingdom, where in 1966 an expansive, influential, and canonical discussion of the subject appeared. In U.K. law, restitution is seen as its own separate doctrinal area apart from contract law. As one commentator put it, restitution is "the area of law concerned with relieving a defendant of wealth which, in the eyes of the law, he should not be entitled to retain." ANDREW TETTENBORN, LAW OF RESTITUTION IN ENGLAND AND IRELAND 1 (2d ed. 1996).

To a foreign reader, these accounts all seem to be searching for an underlying unifying concept or philosophy behind the award of remedies.

English cases have recognized the existence of unjust enrichment and restitution theories. As noted by Professor Gerhard Dannemann, "Preceded and helped by scholarly work, English courts have unfrozen the law of restitution and have . . . achieved a rapid development which might have taken a century in other areas of law." Gerhard Dannemann, *Unjust Enrichment by Transfer: Some Comparative Remarks*, 79 TEXAS L. REV. 1837, 1843 (2001) (footnote omitted).

The elements of a restitution claim in the U.K. are encapsulated in a series of questions: "(1) has the defendant been *benefited* (i.e. enriched)? (2) was the enrichment *at the claimant's expense*? (3) was the enrichment *unjust*? (4) are there any *defences*?" As Professor Burrows goes on to explain, the bulk of the law coalesces around the concepts of "benefit," the idea of "the claimant's expense," "unjust factors," and "defenses." The rest of Burrows' treatise expands upon each of these questions and issues in turn, providing discussion of theoretical problems as well as sample cases along the way. ANDREW BURROWS, THE LAW OF RESTITUTION (2d ed. 2002).

Although the United States has recently seen a resurgence of interest in the study of unjust enrichment and restitution, along with the articulation of the Restatement (Third) of Restitution in 2011, these theories are not generally taught in law school classes and many practicing lawyers and judges are wholly unaware of them. Nonetheless, if we are to think about new types of labor and unpaid work on the Internet, some of the more complex nuances of unjust enrichment and restitution under U.K. law may provide the intellectual tools to process and resolve any such claim.

CHAPTER 7

REMEDIES

■ ■ ■

A theory of contractual liability—such as bargain, reliance, restitution—is necessary to sustain a judgment, but equally important is a theory of the remedy: what a court should do about a judgment of contractual liability. The question of remedies for breach of contract has appeared in the background of many of the previous cases we have examined. The materials have mentioned specific performance as an extraordinary remedy, along with references to other equitable remedies such as rescission and the broad general category of money damages.

As a preliminary matter of fundamentals, the theories of liability themselves may suggest a remedial implication: the bargain principle measured as the expected benefit of the bargain; the reliance interest measured by out-of-pocket expenses in reliance; and the restitution interest in disgorging unjust enrichment. As a further fundamental matter, the principal goal of contract remedies is to *compensate* aggrieved parties for breach, and this single principle can be used to explain virtually all aspects of the law of contract remedies.

Among implications of the compensation principle, it rules out punitive damages for breach of contract, such as those that appear in tort cases, which are not intended to compensate but rather to punish and deter. The compensation principle also suggests why specific performance is an extraordinary remedy: money damages will often suffice to achieve the compensation objective so that the remedy of specific performance is only available when money damages would be inadequate to do so. Finally, the compensation principle suggests the need for legal limitations on money awards to avoid over-compensating.

This chapter explores each of these fundamental principles and their implications. We start with the recognized interests protected (expectancy, reliance, restitution), followed by three doctrinal limitations on contract damages (certainty, foreseeability, and mitigation), and judicial evaluation of party efforts to stipulate damages themselves. The penultimate section takes up specific performance and the concluding section highlights several distinct issues of contract remedies raised by UCC Article 2 and transactions in goods.

A. INTERESTS

The standard measure of damages for breach of contract is a monetary award designed to protect the aggrieved party's expectations. This is done by awarding the money equivalent to what performance of a breached promise would have provided. This measure, known as *expectation damages* or *expectancy damages*, is intended to give the aggrieved party the "expected benefit of the bargain." In other words, it is to pay the difference between what the party received and what they would have received had the promise been performed. Lost profits are a common method of measuring the expectation interest.

Sometimes the aggrieved party is unable to prove damages to a reasonable certainty. Maybe they are speculative, coming as they do from anticipated sales or expected profits, hardly a guarantee. Or perhaps the parties never got a final contract signed, or are bound not through a traditional contractual obligation but by promissory estoppel. In these instances, the alternate measure of *reliance damages* may be more appropriate. It seeks to compensate the aggrieved party for expenses incurred by actions induced by the other party's promises or conduct. Reliance damages are generally less than expectation damages, but they will at least compensate the aggrieved party by putting them back into the position they would have been in if the promise had not been made and the aggrieved party had not relied.

A third alternative remedy is called *quantum meruit* or *restitution* and is closely related to unjust enrichment theory. Unjust enrichment is technically not a contractual theory; the idea is that sometimes, even lacking a contract, one party has been enriched unfairly at the expense of the other. Restitution compels the enriched party to disgorge the amount of their unjust gain. Despite the name "restitution," which sounds punitive or like a tort, normally the restitution interest is lower than either reliance or expectation damages. This is actually a remedy of last resort because it normally provides the least compensation.

To illustrate these three kinds of interests, take a simple hypothetical. Antique Publishing Company hires best-selling author and comedian Bettina Brown to complete writing a popular, for all-audiences humor book. The book incorporates jokes, word play, and other humorous aspects of puns throughout the ages. Titled "Cruel and Unusual PUNishment," Antique provides Brown a $500,000 publishing advance for her 50% share of the anticipated profits. In ensuing months, it spends another $50,000 on media promotions, and another $25,000 in organizing a book/comedy tour and paying to reserve venues.

Based on previous book sales by Brown on similar topics, this book is anticipated to be a best-seller; her last best seller brought in $1 million in profits to the publishing company. One year after signing the contract,

Brown repudiates her obligations under the contract and abandons the book because she has received a better offer to perform the lead role in a comedy film.

Expectancy. Antique's first theory of liability for Brown's breach of contract will be for expectation damages. There will be no book so Antique will seek to recover its expected benefit of the bargain, which are the profits it would have generated from the book publication. Profits, in turn, would be the revenue from sales minus the expenses incurred to generate them. Based on the previous book, these might reach around the range of $1 million. Antique, however, would have the burden of proving the expected benefit of the bargain with reasonable certainty, which can be difficult to do.

Reliance. If Antique is unable to prove lost profits with reasonable certainly, it will seek instead to recover the costs incurred in reliance on Brown's promises. In this example, reliance damages would be the amounts expended for the advance, publicity, and the reservations ($575,000). Antique is still obliged to prove its losses with reasonable certainty, but since these payments are easy to document, this should prove to be no obstacle.

Restitution. But suppose Brown can defend against liability for breach of contract, as well as promissory estoppel, due to some doctrinal defect, such as that the written agreement contained numerous mistakes or that her promises were always qualified by saying that she would only write the book if she was unable to land the lead in the comedy film. While Antique might not legitimately be entitled to profits and it is reasonable to let Antique bear most of its reliance expenses, it would appear to be a windfall to let Brown retain the advance. Under that reasoning, Antique would be entitled to recover, in restitution, the $500,000 paid to Brown as an advance.

As noted above, in discussing Antique's possible lost profits for an as-yet unwritten book, there may be issues with collecting lost profits. There is a basic limiting principle of contract law that requires that the aggrieved party seeking damages for breach must prove their losses with a degree of reasonable certainty. This sounds easy, but in dealing with elements like lost profits, the damages may be difficult to calculate. Sometimes when faced with uncertainty, courts will reduce damage awards if they are feared to be speculative.

Tidy as these examples may seem, and useful as the doctrinal categories are, consider some real-world examples of how they play out.

GOLDBERG V. PARIS HILTON ENTERTAINMENT, INC.
2009 WL 2525482 (S.D. Fla. 2009)

MORENO, J.

Plaintiff Michael I. Goldberg, as a court appointed Receiver, has been assigned any claims and causes of action that Pledge This, LLC may have against Defendants Paris Hilton Entertainment, Inc. and Paris Hilton individually. In his capacity as a Receiver, Goldberg filed a complaint for breach of contract against both Defendants. Goldberg claims that Paris Hilton, a celebrity promoter, failed to keep her end of the bargain, set in a written contract, where Ms. Hilton promised to promote the film *National Lampoon's Pledge This!.*, in which she played the lead role. The Court conducted a two-day bench trial to resolve the factual dispute on whether Paris Hilton breached the promotion and publicity clause of the agreement, for which Ms. Hilton received $1 million.

The film, independently produced and hardly destined for critical acclaim, nevertheless appeared likely to, at least to the investors, make money due to the "Paris Hilton" brand. The movie first enjoyed a short, limited theatrical release before going to DVD distribution on December 19, 2006, but never made money. Thus the Receiver, on behalf of the investors, seeks to recoup the $8.3 million cost of producing the film, including the $1 million paid to Paris Hilton for "acting" and "executive producer services" . . .

The Defendants argue that Ms. Hilton promoted the film prior to the movie hitting the theaters, and that the producers of the film made requests for promotional interviews and appearances in Japan and Europe while she was not professionally available. Paris Hilton further contends that *Pledge This!* flopped economically because of the inexperience of the producers, and for their failure to properly and successfully market the movie. Thus, she contends that any economic loss was not due to her failure to promote. Rather, she strenuously argues she did promote the film, and no further appearances by her would have overcome the producers' failure to properly promote it.

In any event, even if Ms. Hilton had breached the contract, the damages claimed—the cost of production—are based on speculation. One never knows how much a movie may make, and in fact most independent films not tied to the well-known studios fail to make money.

Voluminous emails have been introduced into evidence regarding the requests for Paris Hilton to be interviewed in Japan, Austria, the United Kingdom, and at talk shows in the United States and even in Russian publications. The Receiver specifically alleges breaches of the promotion clause on the failure to promote on:

- December 5, 2006, for failure to agree to publicize the film while in Japan, or upon her return to the Los Angeles area;

- December 15, 2006, for failure to agree to publicize the film while in Japan;

- December 21, 2006, for failure to agree to an interview with the Russian edition of FHM magazine;

- January 5, 2007, for failure to agree to appear on either The Late Show with David Letterman or The Tonight Show with Jay Leno;

- January 29, 2007, for failure to agree to interviews with Austrian and German television outlets while in Vienna;

- February 23, 2007, for failure to agree to telephone interviews in connection with an MTV/VH1 satellite radio tour;

- February 27, 2007, for failure to agree to provide interviews to eight United Kingdom publications;

- March 8 and 14, 2007, for failure to agree to provide interviews with two specific British publications, through written questions and answers;

- April 5, 2007, for failure to agree to an appearance in Japan in May 2007 to publicize the DVD release in that country; and

- February 23, 2007, for failure to agree to a proposed MTV/VH1 interview.

There are specific allegations for each one of these requests for Ms. Hilton to promote *Pledge This!,* namely her failure to comply within the 72 hours provided in the contract. There are also specific responses and defenses to each request, all invoking either Paris Hilton's availability or the reasonableness of the requests.[1] The Court is asked to make specific findings of fact and separate conclusions of law on the reasonableness of the requests, or whether Paris Hilton's "handlers" and agents intentionally breached the contract by not notifying her of the requests and not responding to the requests on a timely basis, i.e. within 72 hours. In making those findings the Court would have to assess the credibility of Ms. Hilton, who testified live and that of her handlers, Jason Moore, Lori Glass and Alanna McCarthy, who testified by deposition.

The Court is indeed prepared to make those findings pursuant to Fed. R. Civ. P. 52(a). However, the Court finds that even if the Receiver were to show that some of the requests for promotion were indeed reasonable and

---

[1] Much time was spent on Paris Hilton's busy schedule, including how long it takes for Paris Hilton to do her hair (over 3 hours), whether she could promote *Pledge This!* while visiting Japan and Austria to promote other products, or whether she should have spent Christmas with her family in Hawaii instead of promoting the movie.

that Paris Hilton and her "handlers" appeared to be less than enthusiastic in promoting the film *Pledge This!* and instead failed to timely respond, the Receiver simply cannot prove his reliance theory of damages. Nevertheless, the Receiver posits an alternative theory of restitution damages. The Court therefore directs the Plaintiff to further brief which portion of the $1 million paid to Ms. Hilton specifically compensated her for the promotion of the DVD release only. In doing so, the Receiver must specify where in the record in the bench trial or in the discovery process there is support for an allocation of promotional damages linked to the DVD distribution only. . . .

Reliance Damages

Goldberg premises his primary theory of damages on reliance; he posits that the producers *of Pledge This!* relied on Ms. Hilton's future promotion of a DVD release when they spent $8.3 million making the film. After conducting a bench trial in this case and reviewing the evidence before it, the Court finds this theory entirely speculative and unsupported by the facts.

"Although not the normal measure of damages," New York law does award damages where a plaintiff incurred expenses in "reasonable" reliance on the defendant's performance. See, e. g., V.S. Intern., S.A. v. Boyden World Corp., 862 F.Supp. 1188, 1198 (S.D.N.Y.1994). Nevertheless, a plaintiff must demonstrate that "damages were caused by and are directly traceable to the [defendant's] breach." Bausch & Lomb Inc. v. Bressler, 977 F.2d 720, 731 (2nd Cir.1992) (applying New York law) (internal citations omitted). Even plaintiffs seeking reliance damages must establish this causal link. Lifewise Master Funding et al. v. Telebank, 374 F.3d 917, 933 (10th Cir.2004) (applying New York law). "When a plaintiff fails to come forward with evidence sufficient to demonstrate damages flowing from the alleged breach and relies instead upon wholly speculative theories of damages, dismissal of the breach of contract claim may be in order." 28 N.Y. Pr., Contract Law § 22:5.

Goldberg argues that the Defendants actually bear the burden of proof on causation. He points to American Capital Corp. v. FDIC, 472 F.3d 859 (Fed.Cir.2006), under which the Federal Circuit upheld reliance damages for a plaintiff that "demonstrated the [defendant] had reason to know the loss would occur if it breached the contract, and the [defendant's] breach did, in fact, result in significant losses." Id. at 869. Nevertheless, American Capital Corp. merely shows that causation can be inferred from a breach committed in the face of a foreseeable loss. This harmonizes with the requirement that a plaintiff prove reliance damages were foreseeable at the time of the breach. See, e.g., 24/7 Records, Inc. v. Sony Music Entertainment, Inc., 566 F.Supp.2d 305, 319 (S.D.N.Y. 2008).

In this case, Goldberg has failed to satisfy the Court that any of his alleged reliance damages were foreseeable. He set forth no compelling evidence that the Defendants' various alleged breaches caused foreseeable damages. Crucially, Goldberg could point to no actual contractual provision, and could proffer no specific testimony from anyone who actually decided to invest in the movie, that Ms. Hilton's prospective promotion of the DVD release, in particular, induced their investment.

Mr. DiLorenzo, one of seven executive producers for the film, testified that Pledge This LLC and Pledge This Holdings relied on Ms. Hilton later doing DVD promotion when they produced the film. Nevertheless, Mr. DiLorenzo could not and did not argue that he specifically was induced to invest $8.3 million. Neither could Mr. DiLorenzo demonstrate in any compelling manner the precise extent to which *Pledge This!* lost money directly because of Ms. Hilton's alleged failure to promote. For his part, Mr. Goldberg argued by affidavit that he directed $137,000 to be spent from receivership funds on post-production work, in reliance on Ms. Hilton's future DVD promotion. This argument also fails to establish direct causation. Mr. Goldberg may show that he directed expenditures, but he can only speculate that the film failed to recoup that expenditure because Ms. Hilton failed to adequately promote the DVD release. Furthermore, he certainly cannot show that any such speculative failure was foreseeable to Ms. Hilton. This is especially true given that the film's limited theatrical release netted revenue far in excess of the expenditures Goldberg directed, and that the theatrical release itself depended on the very post-production work Goldberg agreed to fund. In short, Goldberg's reliance theory necessarily speculates that Ms. Hilton's promotion of the DVD would have lead to a recoupment of costs. Not only is this speculation disallowed by the law on reliance damages, it also flies in the face of the facts of the case.

Contrary to Goldberg's speculative theory, the Court finds compelling evidence in the record that *Pledge This!* lost money because the film's inexperienced producers hastily cobbled together a wholly inadequate marketing plan. The inexperience and relative ineffectiveness of the film's producers starkly clarifies the speculative nature of Goldberg's reliance theory. Had the producers of the film actually *relied* on Ms. Hilton promoting the DVD release of the film when they invested and spent money, logically they would have developed a more comprehensive program of DVD promotion. In fact, Ms. Hilton's testimony forcefully contrasted the producers' marketing of this film with other films she has appeared in during her career. *Pledge This!* enjoyed a very limited theatrical release and no standard press junket. It therefore performed poorly in theaters and went straight to DVD. At that point, the producers still had no comprehensive, effective marketing plan in place. Instead, they sent scatter-shot requests to their principal star in the hopes that she could find time to promote a sinking ship.

In short, Mr. Goldberg's reliance theory cannot overcome the facts of the case. Any causal connection between Ms. Hilton's alleged breaches and the financial ruin of the film are wholly speculative, and therefore cannot entitle Goldberg to recovery.

Restitution Damages

Goldberg proffers restitution as an alternative theory of recovery. Accordingly, he argues that the Court should disgorge the Defendants of the $1 million Ms. Hilton received under the contract. Prior to the trial, Goldberg submitted a supplemental expert report on this theory of damages, and the Defendants filed a motion *in limine* to disallow it as untimely and inadmissible. The Court denied that motion *in limine* in its Omnibus Order, with leave to reargue after the trial on liability.

The Court has concluded the trial on liability and foreclosed recovery on a reliance theory. Although these "Restitution" damages may also be speculative, the Court will allow the Receiver to describe the evidentiary grounds to determine which portions of the $1 million paid to Ms. Hilton were in consideration for her various roles in this project, including, for example, her acting services ($65,000 according to Plaintiff's Exhibit 2) and her executive producer services ($935,000 according to Plaintiff's Exhibit # 2).

If the Receiver were to be successful on this restitution claim, the Court would need to decide how much of the $935,000 was for the use of her name and likeness in promoting the DVD immediately before and within a reasonable time after the DVD release on December 19, 2006 versus the promotion she performed leading up to the theatrical release of the movie. The Court will allow the Receiver to submit the list of witnesses and the short description of their testimony plus the exhibits previously described in this order no later than August 26, 2009. In that submission the Receiver shall include the methodology requested of the Court in assessing a portion of the damages. For example, if the Court were to find that Ms. Hilton breached the contract on one of the requests made, how much restitution is the Receiver entitled to for that one event missed?

Thus, before it issues specific findings of fact and conclusions of law on the credibility of the various witnesses and the liability of the Defendants generally, the Court will provide the parties an opportunity to submit briefs on Goldberg's restitution theory. The parties should limit their briefs to this discrete issue, including whether Goldberg's restitution theory and supplemental expert report should be excluded as untimely and inadmissible, but also and especially the specific factual and legal merits of the theory itself. . . .

NOTES AND QUESTIONS

1.   Given the facts of *Goldberg v. Hilton*, classify the measures of damages: expectation, reliance, and restitution. What interests of the aggrieved party do each of these measures protect?

2.   As noted, contract law remedies are designed to compensate, not punish, and therefore exclude punitive awards such as may be available in tort actions. The following case, colloquially known as the "hairy hand case," is the classic illustration of the differences between contract and tort liability and related damages.

HAWKINS V. MCGEE
146 A. 641 (N.H. 1929)

[A father sued a surgeon who had performed primitive experimental skin-grafting surgery on his son's hand, alleging claims in both contract (warranty) and tort (negligence). A jury trial resulted in a verdict on the contract claim for the father of $3,000 while the court had dismissed the negligence claim before trial. At the trial, the surgeon's lawyers lodged several objections concerning instructions the judge gave the jury concerning the proper measure of damages. The surgeon moved to set aside the verdict, as contrary to the evidence or on the grounds that the damages were excessive. The trial court denied the former motion but found the damages excessive and ordered the verdict set aside unless the father agreed to accept damages of $500. The father refused so the trial court set the verdict aside. The father appealed.]

BRANCH, J.

1.   The operation in question consisted in the removal of a considerable quantity of scar tissue from the palm of the plaintiff's right hand and the grafting of skin taken from the plaintiff's chest in place thereof. The scar tissue was the result of a severe burn caused by contact with an electric wire, which the plaintiff received about nine years before the time of the transactions here involved. There was evidence to the effect that before the operation was performed the plaintiff and his father went to the defendant's office, and that the defendant, in answer to the question, "How long will the boy be in the hospital?" replied, "Three or four days, not over four; then the boy can go home and it will be just a few days when he will go back to work with a good hand."

Clearly this and other testimony to the same effect would not justify a finding that the doctor contracted to complete the hospital treatment in three or four days or that the plaintiff would be able to go back to work within a few days thereafter. The above statements could only be construed as expressions of opinion or predictions as to the probable duration of the treatment and plaintiff's resulting disability, and the fact that these estimates were exceeded would impose no contractual liability upon the defendant. The only substantial basis for the plaintiff's claim is the testimony that the defendant also said before the operation was decided upon, "I will guarantee to make the hand a hundred per cent perfect hand or a hundred per cent good hand." The plaintiff was present when these words were alleged to have been spoken, and, if they are to be taken at their face value, it seems obvious that proof of their utterance would establish the giving of a warranty in accordance with his contention.

The defendant argues, however, that, even if these words were uttered by him, no reasonable man would understand that they were used with the intention of entering "into any contractual relation whatever," and that they could reasonably be understood only "as his expression in strong language that he believed and expected that as a result of the operation he would give the plaintiff a very good hand." It may be conceded, as the defendant contends, that, before the question of the making of a contract should be submitted to a jury, there is a preliminary question of law for the trial court to pass upon, i. e. "whether the words could possibly have the meaning imputed to them by the party who founds his case upon a certain interpretation," but it cannot be held that the trial court decided this question erroneously in the present case.

It is unnecessary to determine at this time whether the argument of the defendant, based upon "common knowledge of the uncertainty which attends all surgical operations," and the improbability that a surgeon would ever contract to make a damaged part of the human body "one hundred per cent perfect," would, in the absence of countervailing considerations, be regarded as conclusive, for there were other factors in the present case which tended to support the contention of the plaintiff. There was evidence that the defendant repeatedly solicited from the plaintiff's father the opportunity to perform this operation, and the theory was advanced by plaintiff's counsel in cross-examination of defendant that he sought an opportunity to "experiment on skin grafting," in which he had had little previous experience. If the jury accepted this part of plaintiff's contention, there would be a reasonable basis for the further conclusion that, if defendant spoke the words attributed to him, he did so with the intention that they should be accepted at their face value, as an inducement for the granting of consent to the operation by the plaintiff and his father, and there was ample evidence that they were so accepted by them. The question of the making of the alleged contract was properly submitted to the jury.

2.   The substance of the charge to the jury on the question of damages appears in the following quotation: "If you find the plaintiff entitled to anything, he is entitled to recover for what pain and suffering he has been made to endure and for what injury he has sustained over and above what injury he had before." To this instruction the defendant seasonably

excepted. By it, the jury was permitted to consider two elements of damage: (1) Pain and suffering due to the operation; and (2) positive ill effects of the operation upon the plaintiff's hand. Authority for any specific rule of damages in cases of this kind seems to be lacking, but, when tested by general principle and by analogy, it appears that the foregoing instruction was erroneous.

"By 'damages,' as that term is used in the law of contracts, is intended compensation for a breach, measured in the terms of the contract." Davis v. New England Cotton Yarn Co., 77 N. H. 403, 404, 92 A. 732, 733. The purpose of the law is "to put the plaintiff in as good a position as he would have been in had the defendant kept his contract." 3 Williston Cont. § 1338; Hardie-Tynes Mfg. Co. v. Easton Cotton Oil Co., 150 N. C. 150, 63 S. E. 676, 134 Am. St. Rep. 899. The measure of recovery "is based upon what the defendant should have given the plaintiff, not what the plaintiff has given the defendant or otherwise expended." 3 Williston Cont. § 1341. . . .

The present case is closely analogous to one in which a machine is built for a certain purpose and warranted to do certain work. In such cases, the usual rule of damages for breach of warranty in the sale of chattels is applied, and it is held that the measure of damages is the difference between the value of the machine, if it had corresponded with the warranty and its actual value, together with such incidental losses as the parties knew, or ought to have known, would probably result from a failure to comply with its terms. . . .

The rule thus applied is well settled in this state. "As a general rule, the measure of the vendee's damages is the difference between the value of the goods as they would have been if the warranty as to quality had been true, and the actual value at the time of the sale, including gains prevented and losses sustained, and such other damages as could be reasonably anticipated by the parties as likely to be caused by the vendor's failure to keep his agreement, and could not by reasonable care on the part of the vendee have been avoided." Union Bank v. Blanchard, 65 N. H. 21, 23, 18 A. 90 . . . . We therefore conclude that the true measure of the plaintiff's damage in the present case is the difference between the value to him of a perfect hand or a good hand, such as the jury found the defendant promised him, and the value of his hand in its present condition, including any incidental consequences fairly within the contemplation of the parties when they made their contract. 1 Sutherland, Damages (4th Ed.) § 92. Damages not thus limited, although naturally resulting, are not to be given.

The extent of the plaintiff's suffering does not measure this difference in value. The pain necessarily incident to a serious surgical operation was a part of the contribution which the plaintiff was willing to make to his joint undertaking with the defendant to produce a good hand. It was a legal detriment suffered by him which constituted a part of the consideration given by him for the contract. It represented a part of the price which he was willing to pay for a good hand, but it furnished no test of the value of a good hand or the difference between the value of the hand which the defendant promised and the one which resulted from the operation.

It was also erroneous and misleading to submit to the jury as a separate element of damage any change for the worse in the condition of the plaintiff's hand resulting from the operation, although this error was probably more prejudicial to the plaintiff than to the defendant. Any such ill effect of the operation would be included under the true rule of damages set forth above, but damages might properly be assessed for the defendant's failure to improve the condition of the hand, even if there were no evidence that its condition was made worse as a result of the operation.

It must be assumed that the trial court, in setting aside the verdict, undertook to apply the same rule of damages which he had previously given to the jury, and, since this rule was erroneous, it is unnecessary for us to consider whether there was any evidence to justify his finding that all damages awarded by the jury above $500 were excessive.

3.   Defendant's requests for instructions were loosely drawn, and were properly denied. A considerable number of issues of fact were raised by the evidence, and it would have been extremely misleading to instruct the jury in accordance with defendant's request No. 2, that "the only issue on which you have to pass is whether or not there was a special contract between the plaintiff and the defendant to produce a perfect hand." Equally inaccurate was defendant's request No. 5, which reads as follows: "You would have to find, in order to hold the defendant liable in this case, that Dr. McGee and the plaintiff both understood that the doctor was guaranteeing a perfect result from this operation." If the defendant said that he would guarantee a perfect result, and the plaintiff relied upon that promise, any mental reservations which he may have had are immaterial. The standard by which his conduct is to be judged is not internal, but external. . . .

Defendant's request No. 7 was as follows: "If you should get so far as to find that there was a special contract guaranteeing a perfect result, you would still have to find for the defendant unless you also found that a further operation would not correct the disability claimed by the plaintiff." In view of the testimony that the defendant had refused to perform a further operation, it would clearly have been erroneous to give this instruction. The evidence would have justified a verdict for an amount sufficient to cover the cost of such an operation, even if the theory underlying this request were correct. . . .

NOTES AND QUESTIONS

1.   Given the facts of *Hawkins v. McGee*, classify the measures of damages as applied to the facts: expectation, reliance, and restitution.

2.   Would any of these measures adequately compensate the victim in *Hawkins*? Subsequent materials on *Hawkins v. McGee* tell us that the victim in this case was "scarred for life," unable to use his hand for manual labor and ashamed of its appearance in an era when those with disabilities were treated poorly, often with fear, hostility, and discrimination.

3.   Why was *Hawkins v. McGee* brought as a contracts case rather than a tort case? Think about issues like statutes of limitations as well as the difficulty of assessing malpractice in a small rural community home to few physicians.

4.   For another classic case on contract remedies—this one involving a botched plastic surgery on an actor's nose and a challenging setting to measure damages—see *Sullivan v. O'Connor*, 296 N.E.2d 183 (Mass. 1973).

5.   Why are punitive damages not available for breach of contract? Think about the nature of the harm in a breach of contract cases versus the harm in a tort case. What role does risk allocation play? What about the interest in deterrence? Should there be such a distinction between contract and tort?

6.   For more on the question of tort-like remedies for contract breaches, see Timothy J. Sullivan, *Punitive Damages in the Law of Contract: The Reality and the Illusion of Legal Change*, 61 MINN. L. REV. 207 (1977); Douglas J. Whaley, *Paying for the Agony: The Recovery of Emotional Distress Damages in Contract Actions*, 26 SUFFOLK U. L. REV. 935 (1992). For more on the famous case of *Hawkins v. McGee*, see Jorie Roberts, *Hawkins Case: A Hair-Raising Experience*, 66 HARV. L. RECORD 1 (1978).

EXAMPLE: THE BEATLES

Probing the blurry line between damages based on a breach of contract and damages based on the commission of a tort is a case that the Beatles brought against their long-time producers, EMI and Capitol Records, in 1979. *Apple Records, Inc. v. Capitol Records, Inc.*, 529 N.Y.S.2d 279 (N.Y. 1st Dept. 1988). After the companies allegedly distributed Beatles' recordings wrongfully for their own promotional purposes, not to help Beatles' sales, and then lied about their actions, the Beatles charged breach of the contract's payment terms plus fraud. The companies objected to letting the Beatles pursue both claims, saying the fraud allegation was merely a contract claim wrapped in tort clothing, only to rack up extra damages.

Because contract and tort claims in situations like this are often intertwined, it is more useful to ask whether the alleged tort asserts an invasion of rights that existed apart from contract than to try to separate harms into neat categories of contract and tort. The Beatles persuaded a court that the record companies had both breached the contract by mishandling payments and separately committed a tort by lying about how they distributed the band's music. Such success is rare though. Most courts analyzing claims arising from a bargain view them as breaches of contract, rather than as separate torts.

PROBLEM: PARIS HILTON REDUX

In December 2006, Hilton agreed to endorse Hairtech products exclusively, not touting competing brands, and authorized it to use her images in product promotions. In exchange, Hairtech would pay Hilton $3.5 million plus a 10% royalty on sales. Hairtech expected the arrangement to generate $35 million in revenue. Hairtech later sued Hilton for breach of contract and fraud, a tort claim.

The breach of contract claim asserted Hilton's failure to appear at promotional events and the endorsement of competing products. The company said Hilton failed to appear at a June 2007 Hairtech product launch party because she was in jail for drunk driving. Hairtech said it spent $130,000 on that event and expected it to generate $900,000 in direct revenue plus $5.6 million in indirect revenue.

The company's fraud claim (sounding in tort) alleged that Hilton deceived it by making misrepresentations and false promises about her intention to honor the contract. For that, the company claimed tens of millions of dollars in punitive damages (amounts on top of any awards for actual loss, intended to punish). What is the probability of success?

B. CERTAINTY

MINDGAMES, INC. v. WESTERN PUB. CO., INC.
218 F.3d 652 (7th Cir. 2000)

POSNER, C.J.

This is a diversity suit for breach of contract, governed by Arkansas law because of a choice of law provision in the contract. The plaintiff, MindGames, was formed in March of 1988 by Larry Blackwell to manufacture and sell an adult board game, "Clever Endeavor," that he had invented. The first games were shipped in the fall of 1989 and by the end of the year, 75 days later, 30,000 had been sold. In March of 1990, MindGames licensed the game to the defendant, Western, a major marketer of games. Western had marketed the very successful adult board games "Trivial Pursuit" and "Pictionary" and thought "Clever Endeavor" might be as successful. The license contract, on which this suit is premised, required Western to pay MindGames a 15 percent royalty on all games sold. The contract was by its terms to remain in effect until the end of January of 1993, or for another year if before then Western paid MindGames at least $1.5 million in the form of royalties due under the contract or otherwise, and for subsequent years as well if Western paid an annual renewal fee of $300,000.

During the first year of the contract, Western sold 165,000 copies of "Clever Endeavor" and paid MindGames $600,000 in royalties. After that, sales fell precipitously (though we're not told by how much) but the parties continued under the contract through January 31, 1994, though Western did not pay the $900,000 ($1.5 million minus $600,000) that the contract would have required it to pay in order to be entitled to extend the contract for a year after its expiration. In February of 1994 the parties finally parted. Later that year MindGames brought this suit, which seeks $900,000, plus lost royalties of some $40 million that MindGames claims it would have earned had not Western failed to carry out the promotional obligations that the contract imposed on it, plus $300,000 on the theory that Western renewed the contract for a third year, beginning in February of 1994; Western sold off its remaining inventory of "Clever Endeavor" in that year.

The district court granted summary judgment for Western, holding that the contract did not entitle MindGames to a renewal fee and that Arkansas's "new business" rule barred any recovery of lost profits. Although the victim of a breach of contract is entitled to nominal damages, MindGames does not seek them; and so if it is not entitled to either type of substantial damages that it seeks, judgment was correctly entered for Western. By not seeking nominal damages, incidentally, MindGames may have lost a chance to obtain significant attorneys' fees, to which Arkansas law entitles a prevailing party in a breach of contract case.

The rejection of MindGames' claim to the renewal fee for the second year (and a fortiori the third) was clearly correct. . . .

The more difficult issue is MindGames' right to recover lost profits for Western's alleged breach of its duty to promote "Clever Endeavor." A minority of states have or purport to have a rule barring a new business, as distinct from an established one, from obtaining damages for lost profits as a result of a tort or a breach of contract. . . . Arkansas is said to be one of the "new business" rule states on the strength of a case decided by the state's supreme court many years ago. The appellants in Marvell Light & Ice Co. v. General Electric Co., 162 Ark. 467, 259 S.W. 741 (1924), sought to recover the profits that they claimed to have lost as a result of a five and a half month delay in the delivery of icemaking machinery; the delay, the appellants claimed, had forced them to delay putting their ice factory into operation.

The court concluded, however, that because there was no indication "that the manufacture and sale of ice by appellants was an established business so that proof of the amount lost on account of the delay . . . might be made with reasonable certainty," "the anticipated profits of the new business are too remote, speculative, and uncertain to support a judgment for their loss." It quoted an earlier decision in which another court had said that "he who is prevented from embarking [on] a new business can recover no profits, because there are no provable data of past business from which the fact that anticipated profits would have been realized can be legally deduced." Central Coal & Coke Co. v. Hartman, 111 Fed. 96, 99 (8th Cir.1901).

That quotation is taken to have made Arkansas a "new business" state, although the rest of the *Marvell* opinion indicates that the court was concerned that the anticipated profits of the *particular* new business at issue, rather than of every new business, were too speculative to support an award of damages. . . . *Marvell* has never been overruled; and federal courts ordinarily take a nonoverruled decision of the highest court of the state whose law governs a controversy by virtue of the applicable choice of law rule to be conclusive on the law of the state. But this is a matter of practice or presumption, not of rule. The rule is that in a case in federal court in which state law provides the rule of decision, the federal court must predict how the state's highest court would decide the case, and decide it the same way. Law, Holmes said, in a controversial definition that is, however, a pretty good summary of how courts apply the law of other jurisdictions, is just a prediction of what the courts of that jurisdiction would do with the case if they got their hands on it. Oliver Wendell Holmes, "The Path of the Law," 10 Harv. L.Rev. 457, 461 (1897). Since state courts like federal courts do occasionally overrule their decisions, there will be occasional, though rare, instances in which the best prediction of what the state's highest court will do is that it will *not* follow its previous decision.

That is the best prediction in this case. *Marvell* was decided more than three quarters of a century ago, and the "new business" rule which it has been thought to have announced has not been mentioned in a published Arkansas case since. The opinion doesn't make a lot of sense on its facts, as we have seen, and the Eighth Circuit case on which it relied has long been superseded in that circuit. . . . The Arkansas cases decided since *Marvell* that deal with damages issues exhibit a liberal approach to the estimation of damages that is inconsistent with a flat rule denying damages for lost profits to all businesses that are not well established. [*E.g.*, Ozark Gas Transmission Systems v. Barclay, 662 S.W.2d 188, 192 (Ark. 1983).] The *Ozark* decision, for example, allowed an orchard farmer to recover for the damages to a *new* orchard. The "new business" rule has, moreover, been abandoned in most states that once followed it . . . and it seems to retain little vitality even in states like Virginia, which purport to employ the hard-core per se approach.

Western tries to distinguish *Ozark* by pointing to the fact that the plaintiff there was an established orchard farmer, albeit the particular orchard represented a new venture for him. This effort to distinguish that case brings into view the primary objection to the "new business" rule, an objection of such force as to explain its decline and make it unlikely that Arkansas would follow it if the occasion for its supreme court to choose, arose. The objection has to do with the difference between *rule* and *standard* as methods of legal governance.

A rule singles out one or a few facts and makes it or them conclusive of legal liability; a standard permits consideration of all or at least most facts that are relevant to the standard's rationale. A speed limit is a rule; negligence is a standard. Rules have the advantage of being definite and of limiting factual inquiry but the disadvantage of being inflexible, even arbitrary, and thus over-inclusive, or of being under-inclusive and thus opening up loopholes (or of being *both* over- and under-inclusive!). Standards are flexible, but vague and open-ended; they make business planning difficult, invite the sometimes unpredictable exercise of judicial discretion, and are more costly to adjudicate-and yet when based on lay intuition they may actually be more intelligible, and thus in a sense clearer and more precise, to the persons whose behavior they seek to guide than rules would be. No sensible person supposes that rules are always superior to standards, or vice versa, though some judges are drawn to the definiteness of rules and others to the flexibility of standards. But that is psychology; the important point is that some activities are better governed by rules, others by standards. States that have rejected the "new business" rule are content to control the award of damages for lost profits by means of a standard-damages may not be awarded on the basis of wild conjecture, they must be proved to a reasonable certainty, . . . that is applicable to proof of damages generally. . . . The "new business" rule is an attempt now widely regarded as failed to control the award of such damages by means of a rule.

The rule doesn't work because it manages to be at once vague and arbitrary. One reason is that the facts that it makes determinative, "new," "business," and "profits," are not facts, but rather are the conclusions of a reasoning process that is based on the rationale for the rule and that as a result turns the rule into an implicit standard. What, for example, is a "new" business? What, for that matter, is a "business"? And are royalties what the rule means by "profits"? MindGames was formed more than a year before it signed the license agreement with Western, and it sold 30,000 games in the six months between the first sales and the signing of the contract. MindGames' only "business," moreover, was the licensing of intellectual property. An author who signs a contract with a publisher for the publication of his book would not ordinarily be regarded as being engaged in a "business," or his royalties or advance described as "profits." He would be surprised to learn that if he sued for unpaid royalties he could not get them because his was a "new business." Suppose a first-time author sued a publisher for an accounting, and the only issue was how many copies the publisher had sold. Under the "new business" rule as construed by Western, the author could not recover his lost royalties even though there was no uncertainty about what he had lost. So construed and applied, the rule would have no relation to its rationale, which is to prevent the award of speculative damages.

Western goes even further, arguing that even if it, Western, a well-established firm, were the plaintiff, it could not recover its lost profits because the sale of "Clever Endeavor" was a new business. On this construal of the rule, "business" does not mean the enterprise; it means any business activity. So Western's sale of a new game is a new business, yet we know from the *Ozark* decision that an orchard farmer's operation of a new orchard is an old business.

The rule could be made sensible by appropriate definition of its terms, but we find it hard to see what would be gained, given the existence of the serviceable and familiar standard of excessive speculativeness. The rule may have made sense at one time; the reduction in decision costs and uncertainty brought about by avoiding a speculative mire may have swamped the increased social costs resulting from the systematically inadequate damages that a "new business" rule decrees. But today the courts have become sufficiently sophisticated in analyzing lost-earnings claims, and have accumulated sufficient precedent on the standard of undue speculativeness in damages awards, to make the balance of costs and benefits tip against the rule. In any event we are far in this case, in logic as well as time, from the ice factory whose opening was delayed by the General Electric Company. We greatly doubt that there is a "new business" rule in the common law of Arkansas today, but if there is it surely does not extend so far beyond the facts of the only case in which the rule was ever invoked to justify its invocation here. There is no authority for, and no common sense appeal to, such an extension.

But that leaves us with the question of undue speculation in estimating damages. Abrogation of the "new business" rule does not produce a free-for-all. What makes MindGames' claim of lost royalties indeed dubious is not any "new business" rule but the fact that the success of a board game, like that of a book or movie, is so uncertain. Here newness enters into judicial consideration of the damages claim not as a rule but as a factor in applying the standard. Just as a start-up company should not be permitted to obtain pie-in-the-sky damages upon allegations that it was snuffed out before it could begin to operate (unlike the ice factory in *Marvell,* which did begin production, albeit a little later than planned), capitalizing fantasized earnings into a huge present value sought as damages, so a novice writer should not be permitted to obtain damages from his publisher on the premise that but for the latter's laxity he would have had a bestseller, when only a tiny fraction of new books achieve that success. Damages must be proved, and not just dreamed . . . .

This is not to suggest that damages for lost earnings on intellectual property can never be recovered; that "entertainment damages" are not recoverable in breach of contract cases. That would just be a variant of the discredited "new business" rule. What is important is that Blackwell had no track record when he created "Clever Endeavor." He could not point to other games that he had invented and that had sold well. He was not in the position of the bestselling author who can prove from his past success that his new book, which the defendant failed to promote, would have been likely-not certain, of course-to have enjoyed a success comparable to that of the average of his previous books if only it had been promoted as promised. That would be like a case of a new business launched by an entrepreneur with a proven track record.

In the precontract sales period and the first year of the contract a total of 195,000 copies of "Clever Endeavor" were sold; then sales fizzled. The public is fickle. It is possible that if Western had marketed the game more vigorously, more would have been sold, but an equally if not more plausible possibility is that the reason that Western didn't market the game more vigorously was that it correctly sensed that demand had dried up.

Even if that alternative is rejected, we do not see how the number of copies that would have been sold but for the alleged breach could be determined given the evidence presented in the summary judgment proceedings (a potentially important qualification, of course); and so MindGames' proof of damages is indeed excessively speculative. Those proceedings were completed with no evidence having been presented from which a rational trier of fact could conclude *on this record* that some specific quantity, or for that matter some broad but bounded range of alternative estimates, of copies of "Clever Endeavor" would have been sold had Western honored the contract. MindGames obtained $600,000 in royalties on sales of 165,000 copies of the game, implying that Western would have had to sell more than 10 million copies to generate the $40 million in lost royalties that MindGames seeks to recover.

When the breach occurred, MindGames should have terminated the contract and sought distribution by other means. See Farnsworth, *supra,* § 12.12, pp. 806–08. The fact that it did not do so—that so far as appears it has made no effort to market "Clever Endeavor" since the market for the game collapsed in 1991—is telling evidence of a lack of commercial promise unrelated to Western's conduct.

Although Western in its brief in this court spent most of its time misguidedly defending the "new business" rule, clinging to *Marvell* for dear life (a case seemingly on point, however vulnerable, is a security blanket that no lawyer feels comfortable without), it did argue that in any event MindGames' claim for lost royalties was too speculative to ground an award of damages for that loss. The argument was brief but not so brief as to fail to put MindGames on notice of a possible alternative ground for upholding the district court's judgment; we may of course affirm an award of summary judgment on any ground that has not been forfeited or waived in the district court. MindGames did not respond to the argument in its reply brief. It pointed to no evidence from which lost royalties could be calculated to even a rough approximation. We find its silence eloquent and Western's argument compelling, and so the judgment in favor of Western is [affirmed].

NOTES AND QUESTIONS

1.   What is the "new business rule"? Does it make sense from a doctrinal or economic standpoint? How would you assess Judge Posner's discussion of the rule?

2.   Does *MindGames* illustrate the lament about "win the battle, but lose the war?" What else did MindGames need to anticipate in its reply brief in order to have a successful outcome?

3.   What is the difference between a rigid rule and a more flexible standard? In your law school studies to date, you probably have encountered numerous examples of both as well as some laws that defy tidy classification of rules versus standards. As you continue to refine your legal skills, think about whether particular circumstances are better served by laws that resemble rules versus standards.

4.   Note that the court in dicta suggested that MindGames may have lost a chance to recover substantial attorney's fees under state law by failure to seek nominal damages for breach of contract. If you ever find yourself advising on contract disputes or conducting contract litigation, definitely be aware of any such possibilities.

5.   In an omitted portion, the *MindGames* opinion refers to the doctrine of foreseeability, a further limitation on contract damages, discussed in an ensuing section, and the famous case reproduced there, *Hadley v. Baxendale*. Said the court: "The rule of *Hadley v. Baxendale*, 9 Ex. 341, 156 Eng. Rep. 145 (1854), often prevents the victim of a breach of contract from obtaining lost profits, but that rule is not invoked here. Neither the 'new business' rule nor the rule of *Hadley v. Baxendale* stands for the general proposition that lost profits are never a recoverable item of damages in a tort or breach of contract case."

CHICAGO COLISEUM CLUB v. DEMPSEY
265 Ill.App. 542 (Ill. App. 1st Dist. 1932)

WILSON, J.

Chicago Coliseum Club, a corporation, as plaintiff, brought its action against William Harrison Dempsey, known as Jack Dempsey, to recover damages for breach of a written contract executed March 13, 1926, but bearing date of March 6 of that year.

Plaintiff was incorporated as an Illinois corporation for the promotion of general pleasure and athletic purposes and to conduct boxing, sparring and wrestling matches and exhibitions for prizes or purses. The defendant William Harrison Dempsey was well known in the pugilistic world and, at the time of the making and execution of the contract in question, held the title of world's Champion Heavy Weight Boxer.

Under the terms of the written agreement, the plaintiff was to promote a public boxing exhibition in Chicago, or some suitable place to be selected by the promoter, and had engaged the services of one Harry Wills, another well-known boxer and pugilist, to engage in a boxing match with the defendant Dempsey for the championship of the world. By the terms of the agreement Dempsey was to receive $10, receipt of which was acknowledged, and the plaintiff further agreed to pay to Dempsey the sum of $300,000 on the 5th day of August 1926—$500,000 in cash at least 10 days before the date fixed for the contest, and a sum equal to 50 per cent of the net profits over and above the sum of $2,000,000 in the event the gate receipts should exceed that amount. In addition the defendant was to receive 50 per cent of the net revenue derived from moving picture concessions or royalties received by the plaintiff, and defendant agreed to have his life and health insured in favor of the plaintiff in a manner and at a place to be designated by the plaintiff. Defendant further agreed not to engage in any boxing match after the date of the agreement and prior to the date on which the contest was to be held. . . .

March 6, 1926, the plaintiff entered into an agreement with Harry Wills, in which Wills agreed to engage in a boxing match with the Jack Dempsey named in the agreement hereinbefore referred to. Under this agreement the plaintiff, Chicago Coliseum Club was to deposit $50,000 in escrow in the National City Bank of New York City, New York, to be paid over to Wills on the 10th day prior to the date fixed for the holding of the boxing contest. Further conditions were provided in said contract with Wills, which, however, are not necessary to set out in detail. There is no evidence in the record showing that the $50,000 was deposited nor that it has ever been paid, nor is there any evidence in the record showing the financial standing of the Chicago Coliseum Club, a corporation, plaintiff in this suit. This contract between the plaintiff and Wills appears to have been entered into several days before the contract with Dempsey.

March 8, 1926, the plaintiff entered into a contract with one Andrew C. Weisberg, under which it appears that it was necessary for the plaintiff to have the services of an experienced person skilled in promoting boxing exhibitions and that the said Weisberg was possessed of such qualifications and that it was necessary for the plaintiff to procure his help in the promoting of the exhibition. It appears further from the agreement that it was necessary to incur expenditures in the way of traveling expenses, legal services and other costs in and about the promotion of the boxing match, and Weisberg agreed to investigate, canvass and organize the various hotel associations and other business organizations for the purpose of securing accommodations for spectators and to procure subscriptions and contributions from such hotels and associations and others for the erection of an arena and other necessary expense in order to carry out the enterprise and to promote the boxing match in question. Under these agreements Weisberg was to furnish the funds for such purposes and was to be reimbursed out of the receipts from the sale of tickets for the expenses incurred by him, together with a certain amount for his services.

Both the Wills contract and the Weisberg contract are referred to at some length, inasmuch as claims for damages by plaintiff are predicated upon these two agreements. Under the terms of the contract between the plaintiff and Dempsey and the plaintiff and Wills, the contest was to be held during the month of September, 1926.

July 10, 1926, plaintiff wired Dempsey at Colorado Springs, Colorado, stating that representatives of life and accident insurance companies would call on him for the purpose of examining him for insurance in favor of the Chicago Coliseum Club, in accordance with the terms of his contract, and also requesting the defendant to begin training for the contest not later than August 1, 1926. In answer to this communication plaintiff received a telegram from Dempsey, as follows:

> BM Colorado Springs Colo   July 10th 1926
>
> B. E. Clements
>
> President Chicago Coliseum Club Chgo Entirely too busy training for my coming Tunney match to waste time on insurance representatives stop as you have no contract suggest you stop kidding yourself and me also
>
>   Jack Dempsey

We are unable to conceive upon what theory the defendant could contend that there was no contract, as it appears to be admitted in the proceeding here and bears his signature and the amounts involved are sufficiently large to have created a rather lasting impression on the mind of anyone signing such an agreement. It amounts, however, to a repudiation of the agreement and from that time on Dempsey refused to take any steps to carry out his undertaking. It appears that Dempsey at this time was engaged in preparing himself for a contest with Tunney to be held at Philadelphia, Pennsylvania, sometime in September, and on August 3, 1926, plaintiff, as complainant, filed a bill in the superior court of Marion county, Indiana, asking to have Dempsey restrained and enjoined from engaging in the contest with Tunney, which complainant was informed and believed was to be held on the 16th day of September, and which contest would be in violation of the terms of the agreement entered into between the plaintiff and defendant at Los Angeles, March 13, 1926.

Personal service was had upon the defendant Dempsey in the proceeding in the Indiana court and on August 27, 1926, he entered his general appearance, by his attorneys, and filed his answer in said cause. September 13, 1926, a decree was entered in the superior court of Marion county, finding that the contract was a valid and subsisting contract between the parties, and that the complainant had expended large sums of money in carrying out the terms of the agreement, and entering a decree that Dempsey be perpetually restrained and enjoined from in any way, wise, or manner, training or preparing for or participating in any contracts or engagements in furtherance of any boxing match, prize fight or any exhibition of like nature, and particularly from engaging or entering into any boxing match with one Gene Tunney, or with any person other than the one designated by plaintiff.

It is insisted among other things that the costs incurred by the plaintiff in procuring the injunctional order in Marion County, Indiana, were properly chargeable against Dempsey for his breach of contract and recoverable in this proceeding. Under the evidence in the record in this proceeding there appears to have been a valid subsisting agreement between the plaintiff and Dempsey, in which Dempsey was to perform according to the terms of the agreement and which he refused to do, and the plaintiff, as a matter of law, was entitled at least to nominal damages. For this reason, if for no other, judgment should have been for the plaintiff.

During the proceeding in the circuit court of this county it was sought to introduce evidence for the purpose of showing damages, other than nominal damages, and in view of the fact that the case has to be retried, this court is asked to consider the various items of expense claimed to have been incurred and various offers of proof made to establish damages for breach of the agreement. Under the proof offered, the question of damages naturally divides itself into the four following propositions:

1st. Loss of profits which would have been derived by the plaintiff in the event of the holding of the contest in question;

2nd. Expenses incurred by the plaintiff prior to the signing of the agreement between the plaintiff and Dempsey;

3rd. Expenses incurred in attempting to restrain the defendant from engaging in other contests and to force him into a compliance with the terms of his agreement with the plaintiff; and

4th. Expenses incurred after the signing of the agreement and before the breach of July 10, 1926.

Proposition 1.   Plaintiff offered to prove by one Mullins that a boxing exhibition between Dempsey and Wills held in the City of Chicago on September 22, 1926, would bring a gross receipt of $3,000,000, and that the expense incurred would be $1,400,000, leaving a net profit to the promoter of $1,600,000. The court properly sustained an objection to this testimony. The character of the undertaking was such that it would be impossible to produce evidence of a probative character sufficient to establish any amount which could be reasonably ascertainable by reason of the character of the undertaking. The profits from a boxing contest of this character, open to the public, is dependent upon so many different circumstances that they are not susceptible of definite legal determination.

The success or failure of such an undertaking depends largely upon the ability of the promoters, the reputation of the contestants and the conditions of the weather at and prior to the holding of the contest, the accessibility of the place, the extent of the publicity, the possibility of other and counter attractions and many other questions which would enter into consideration. Such an entertainment lacks utterly the element of stability which exists in regular organized business. This fact was practically admitted by the plaintiff by the allegation of its bill filed in the Marion county court of Indiana asking for an injunction against Dempsey. Plaintiff in its bill in that proceeding charged, as follows:

> That by virtue of the premises aforesaid, the plaintiff will, unless it secures the injunctive relief herein prayed for, suffer great and irreparable injury and damages, not compensable by any action at law in damages, the damages being incapable of commensuration, and plaintiff, therefore, has no adequate remedy at law.

Compensation for damages for a breach of contract must be established by evidence from which a court or jury are able to ascertain the extent of such damages by the usual rules of evidence and to a reasonable degree of certainty. We are of the opinion that the performance in question is not susceptible of proof sufficient to satisfy the requirements and that the damages, if any, are purely speculative. . . .

Proposition 2:   Expenses incurred by the plaintiff prior to the signing of the agreement between the plaintiff and Dempsey. The general rule is that in an action for a breach of contract a party can recover only on damages which naturally flow from and are the result of the act complained of. . . . The Wills contract was entered into prior to the contract with the defendant and was not made contingent upon the plaintiff's obtaining a similar agreement with the defendant Dempsey. Under the circumstances the plaintiff speculated as to the result of his efforts to procure the Dempsey contract. It may be argued that there had been negotiations pending between plaintiff and Dempsey which clearly indicated an agreement between them, but the agreement in fact was never consummated until sometime later. The action is based upon the written agreement which was entered into in Los Angeles. Any obligations assumed by the plaintiff prior to that time are not chargeable to the defendant. Moreover, an examination of the record discloses that the $50,000 named in the contract with Wills, which was to be payable upon a signing of the agreement, was not and never has been paid. There is no evidence in the record showing that the plaintiff is responsible financially, and, even though there were, we consider that it is not an element of damage which can be recovered for breach of the contract in question.

Proposition 3:   Expenses incurred in attempting to restrain the defendant from engaging in other contests and to force him into a compliance with the terms of his agreement with the plaintiff. After the repudiation of the agreement by the defendant, plaintiff was advised of defendant's match with Tunney which, from the evidence, it appears, was to take place in Philadelphia in the month of September and was in direct conflict with the terms of the agreement entered into between plaintiff and defendant. Plaintiff's bill, filed in the superior court of Marion county, Indiana, was an effort on the part of the plaintiff to compel defendant to live up to the terms of his agreement. The chancellor in the Indiana court entered his decree, which apparently is in full force and effect, and the defendant in violating the terms of that decree, after personal service, is answerable to that court for a violation of the injunctional order entered in said proceeding.

The expenses incurred, however, by the plaintiff in procuring that decree are not collectible in an action for damages in this proceeding; neither are such similar expenses as were incurred in the trips to Colorado and Philadelphia, nor the attorney's fees and other expenses thereby incurred. Cuyler Realty Co. v. Teneo Co., Inc., 188 N. Y. S. 340. The plaintiff having been informed that the defendant intended to proceed no further under his agreement, took such steps at its own financial risk. There was nothing in the agreement regarding attorney's fees and there was nothing in the contract in regard to the services of the defendant from which it would appear that the action for specific performance would lie. After the clear breach of contract by the defendant, the plaintiff proceeded with this character of litigation at its own risk. We are of the opinion that the trial court properly held that this was an element of damages which was not recoverable.

Proposition 4:   Expenses incurred after the signing of the agreement and before the breach of July 10, 1926. After the signing of the agreement plaintiff attempted to show expenses incurred by one Weisberg in and about the furtherance of the project. Weisberg testified that he had taken an active part in promoting sports for a number of years and was in the employ of the Chicago Coliseum Club under a written contract during all of the time that his services were rendered in furtherance of this proposition. This contract was introduced in evidence and bore the date of March 8, 1926. Under its terms Weisberg was to be reimbursed out of the gate receipts and profits derived from the performance. His compensation depended entirely upon the success of the exhibition. Under his agreement with the plaintiff there was nothing to charge the plaintiff unconditionally with the costs and expenses of Weisberg's services. The court properly ruled against the admissibility of the evidence.

We find in the record, however, certain evidence which should have been submitted to the jury on the question of damages sustained by the plaintiff. The contract on which the breach of the action is predicated shows a payment of $10 by the plaintiff to the defendant and the receipt acknowledged. It appears that the stadium located in the South Park District, known as Soldier's Field, was considered as a site for the holding of the contest and plaintiff testified that it paid $300 to an architect for plans in the event the stadium was to be used for the performance. This item of damage might have been made more specific and may not have been the best evidence in the case but, standing alone, it was sufficient to go to the jury. There were certain elements in regard to wages paid assistant secretaries which may be substantiated by evidence showing that they were necessary in furtherance of the undertaking. If these expenses were incurred they are recoverable if in furtherance of the general scheme. The defendant should not be required to answer in damages for salaries paid regular officials of the corporation who were presumed to be receiving such salaries by reason of their position, but special expenses incurred are recoverable.

The expenses of Hoffman in going to Colorado for the purpose of having Dempsey take his physical examination for insurance, if before the breach and reasonable, are recoverable. The railroad fares for those who went to Los Angeles for the purpose of procuring the signing of the agreement are not recoverable as they were incurred in a furtherance of the procuring of the contract and not after the agreement was entered into. The services of Shank in looking after railroad facilities and making arrangements with the railroad for publicity and special trains and accommodations were items which should be considered and if it develops that they were incurred in a furtherance of the general plan and properly proven, are items for which the plaintiff should be reimbursed.

The items recoverable are such items of expense as were incurred between the date of the signing of the agreement and the breach of July 10, 1926, by the defendant and such as were incurred as a necessary expense in furtherance of the performance. Proof of such items should be made subject to the usual rules of evidence.

For the reasons stated in this opinion the judgment of the circuit court is reversed and the cause remanded for a new trial.

Judgment reversed and cause remanded.

NOTES AND QUESTIONS

1.   Given the facts of *Chicago Colliseum*, classify the measures of damages: expectation, reliance, and restitution.

2.   Do we have any idea of what prompted Dempsey's repudiation of the contract? During the 1920s, there was still a discriminatory "color line" in boxing. Harry Wills (known as the "Black Panther"), a powerful and talented fighter, may have been denied the opportunity to contend for the heavyweight championship because of his race. In the decade before, fights between white and black fighters had resulted in heightened racial tensions and violence. In the ensuing years, some venues and promoters refused to book matches between fighters of different races. Others alleged that Dempsey knew how strong Wills was and did not want to lose his boxing title to a black man. While there are many rumors, we may never know the real reasons behind Dempsey's contractual breach.

3.   Jack Dempsey led a fascinating life, starting when he left his family to live as a hobo at age 15. After Dempsey started to win fights, boxing promoters played up his unpredictable and angry personality to attract large crowds to the ring. After losing the championship a second time to Gene Tunney (the upcoming match referenced in the case), Dempsey retired from prizefighting. In a sudden twist of fate, Dempsey lost all of the money he had made in the ring in the stock market crash and the Great Depression. He recouped his losses by opening a restaurant, working in support around the boxing ring, and even joining the Coast Guard during World War II. Hearing of fellow World War II veteran heavy-weight Joe Louis' financial problems and fight with the IRS, Dempsey formed a committee to raise funds for the "Brown Bomber."

4.   In a notable English case, after incurring expenses, a film company agreed with the American actor, Robert Reed, that he would perform in a new film. *Anglia Television Ltd. v. Reed*, 1 Queen's Bench 60 (1972). Reed breached his promise to perform. The company was entitled to recover, in addition to its reliance expenses, expenses incurred before it made the contract. The rationale: by making the contract, it appeared that Reed, not the company, accepted the risk of loss due to his breach. After all, the company could have hired any number of other actors to perform the role but chose him.

In contrast, the promoter in Jack Dempsey's case was denied pre-contract expenses. In that case, the making of the contract did not suggest that Dempsey accepted the risk of loss due to his breach. After all, the promoter could not have hired anyone other than Jack to defend his heavyweight champion title.

Although the "Pledge This" film company did not claim pre-contract reliance, its right to recover them would depend on whether Paris Hilton's celebutante status makes her more like the one-of-a-kind heavyweight champion of the world or a dime-a-dozen actor. For more on this topic, see Mitchell L. Engler & Susan Schwab, *Rethinking Contract Damages*, 84 TEMPLE L. REV. 119 (2011).

5.   When expectation or reliance damages cannot be obtained, aggrieved parties may seek restitution. This is a claim to recover damages to prevent the other party from keeping an undeserved windfall, called "unjust enrichment." In the *Pledge This!* case, the film company argued it was unjust to let Hilton keep $1 million—or at least the $935,000 for non-acting services—after she failed to uphold her end of the bargain concerning promotion. But unjust enrichment usually applies only when someone confers a benefit on someone else without also expressing an agreement about the exchange. It does not apply when people have an express contract and an aggrieved party simply cannot prove the losses as contract law requires.

6.   On the other hand, restitution is known as an "equitable remedy." That means courts tailor vague principles to meet what justice merits in particular cases. In the Pledge-Hilton dispute, the court entertained the film company's restitution claim. But the judge insisted it would have to show exactly what dollar amount was unfair for Hilton to keep—which the company simply could not do. That, ultimately, left it empty-handed. The film, which the judge wryly noted was "never destined for critical acclaim," flopped financially, both in the market and in court.

NOTE: ANTICIPATORY REPUDIATION

Jack Dempsey had no legal excuse for avoiding his contractual duty to fight. Since the time for the fight had not yet arrived, Dempsey's advance announcement of his desire to breach the contract is known as an *anticipatory repudiation*. Generally if an anticipatory repudiation happens, then the contract is treated as breached and the aggrieved party can sue immediately for damages.

This may seem like a commonsense result, but it took the common law some time to get to that point. In the early common law, there was doubt about whether the aggrieved party had to wait for the time of performance to arrive, and then for a breach to occur, before the ability to sue for damages would arise. Technically, even if a party *said* they wouldn't perform, they could change their mind and actually end up performing. The result was inefficiency.

In the landmark case of *Hochester v. De La Tour*, 2 E&B 678 (1853), the Queen's Bench resolved the matter. In that case, De La Tour hired Hochester as a courier and servant for a trip around Europe. Before the trip was to begin, however, De La Tour indicated he changed his mind and no longer desired to go on the trip. Hochester sued, but De La Tour moved to dismiss because the time for the trip had not yet arrived. The Queen's Bench sided with the servant, Hochester, ruling that in the face of an anticipatory repudiation the aggrieved party had no need to hold themselves ready to perform; rather upon receiving an anticipatory repudiation aggrieved parties can suspend performance and immediately sue for breach.

A common problem is determining whether a wavering party has repudiated or is merely grumbling about prospective performance. Jack Dempsey was clear in saying that he would not perform, but not all manifestations are so clear. What if someone says they are "rethinking their commitments" or "need time to assess" whether they will continue with a contract?

STILES FAMILY LTD. V. RIGGS AND STILES, INC.
2016 WL 6819788 (W. Va. 2016)

MEMORANDUM DECISION.

. . . This case centers on whether respondents, tenants to a farm lease that limits the use of the subject property to agricultural purposes, breached the lease when they permitted a music concert promoter [Walther Productions] to apply to the Jefferson County Board of Zoning Appeals ("Zoning Board") for approval to host a music festival on the property, but where the application was subsequently withdrawn after petitioner (the landlord on the lease) objected, and the festival never took place. Stated another way, the issue is whether the filing of the application, which was later withdrawn, constituted a breach of the lease. We agree with the circuit court that it did not.

The parties in this case are wholly comprised of parents and siblings of the Stiles family. . . . In October of 2006, the parties entered into a "Farm Lease" wherein respondents agreed to farm the subject property. Respondents have done so continuously since 2006. In 2013, with respondents' permission, Walther Productions filed an application for a seasonal use permit with the Zoning Board to explore whether it was feasible under the Zoning Board's regulations to hold a five-day music festival on the farm property. In November of 2013, petitioner learned of the application and submitted a written objection to the Zoning Board. Shortly thereafter, petitioner attempted to terminate the Farm Lease, citing [a provision stating]: "The Tenant shall be leasing the Premises for the purpose of planting, maintaining, and cultivating farm crops and/or other vegetation thereon, and the use of the Premises for any other purpose without Landlord's written approval shall be a breach by Tenant of the terms of this lease." . . .

In December of 2013, the application before the Zoning Board was withdrawn. It is undisputed that the music festival never occurred. In November of 2014, petitioner filed a complaint in circuit court alleging that respondents' unapproved permission for Walther Productions to apply to the Zoning Board for approval to hold a music festival on the property constituted a prohibited "use" of property under the terms of the lease. Petitioner sought a declaratory judgment that respondents breached the Farm Lease and that the lease was terminated by virtue of the above-cited lease provisions. . . . [T] circuit court granted summary judgment in favor of respondents, concluding in relevant part as follows:

> The [c]ourt finds that under the plain language of the Farm Lease, it is clear that the "use" of the property for some act other than agricultural use is required to constitute a breach. That simply did not occur. An application for a variance is just that, an application. None of the conditions precedent for such an event, including a contract between [respondents] and the third party seeking to hold the event, ever came to fruition. As a result, the event never made it past the early stages of consideration. As these conditions did not occur, and the application was subsequently withdrawn, the terms of the Lease were not breached. . . .

. . . Petitioner contends that the circuit court erroneously focused on the fact that the music festival never occurred, and consequently it ignored the doctrine of "anticipatory breach." An "anticipatory breach" is defined as "one committed before the time has come when there is a present duty of performance and is the outcome of words or acts evincing an intention to refuse performance in the future." 17A Am. Jur. 2d Contracts, § 448. We have held that

> [t]he general rule in cases of anticipatory breach of contract is that where one party repudiates the contract and refuses longer to be bound by it, the injured party has an election to pursue any of three remedies: he may treat the contract as rescinded and recover on quantum meruit so far as he has performed; or he may keep the contract alive for the benefit of both parties, being at all times ready and able to perform, and at the end of the time specified in the contract for performance, sue and recover under the contract; or he may treat the repudiation as putting an end to the contract for all purposes of performance, and sue for the profits he would have realized, if he had not been prevented from performing.

Annon v. Lucas, 155 W.Va. 368, 185 S.E.2d 343 (1971).

Petitioner argues that respondents repudiated the lease by knowingly allowing the concert promoter to apply for the approvals needed to hold the festival. Petitioner argues that, even though the festival did not occur, respondents' actions were so clear and unequivocal that they did not intend to abide by the lease restrictions on the use of the property that the circuit court should have ruled that respondents breached the lease, rather than force petitioner to wait until several thousand concert-goers show up on the property.

[W]e do not find that there was a breach, anticipatory or otherwise, of the Farm Lease by respondents. This Court has held that "[a]nticipatory repudiation and breach of contract, sufficient to give a cause of action, or to use as a defense to suit by the repudiating party, must be *unequivocal, absolute and positive*." *Mollohan v. Black Rock Contracting, Inc.*, 160 W.Va. 446, 235 S.E.2d 813 (1977) (emphasis added). Moreover, in addition to being unequivocal, we have held that the repudiation of the contract in question must "deal with the entire performance to which the contract binds the party which it is claimed has renounced the same." *Id.*

[T]hree undeniable facts . . . foreclose petitioner's anticipatory breach argument: (1) respondents continually farmed the property consistent with the lease since 2006; (2) respondents did not cease farming the property with the filing of the application to the Zoning Board; and (3) the application was ultimately withdrawn. . . . Continuing to farm the property under the lease is entirely inconsistent with the type of conduct required to establish a breach of the lease; respondents continued to do the very thing that the lease required them to do. Therefore, there was no repudiation or compromise of the "entire performance" required under the Farm Lease.

Second, and possibly more damaging to petitioner's argument, is the fact that the application was withdrawn after petitioner and respondents could not reach a compromise regarding the music festival. Withdrawal of the application demonstrated precisely the type of equivocation that showed that respondents lacked an absolute and positive intent to breach the lease. Therefore, we reject petitioner's argument that respondents' conduct constituted an anticipatory breach of the Farm Lease. . . .

NOTES AND QUESTIONS

1. The *Stiles* decision also rejected the lessor/petitioner's argument that the lessee's agreement with Walther Productions to allow the filing of the Zoning Board application was a breach of the lease's limitation on use or at the very least an anticipatory repudiation of that limitation. Suppose Walther's application was not withdrawn but approved. At what point would the lessee commit breach or repudiation? Would signing a sublease with Walther suffice? Would it be necessary for the lessee to communicate its intentions clearly to the lessor?

2. To count as an anticipatory repudiation that excuses performance and creates a claim for breach, the declaration must be clear and unequivocal in expressing a lack of willingness to perform. In response to equivocating comments, however, the other party would likely want to find out more information. In such cases, the law allows the other party to ask for *adequate assurances* of performance. If those are not forthcoming, then it may transform

the equivocal statement into a repudiation of the contract. Communication between the parties assumes great importance in such situations.

MARVEL ENTERTAINMENT V. ARP FILMS
684 F.Supp. 818 (S.D.N.Y. 1988)

CONBOY, J.

Marvel Entertainment Group, Inc. [owns] the copyrights to Spiderman and other fictional cartoon characters. . . . Marvel entered into [an] agreement (the 1976 Agreement) with ARP Films, Inc., a Delaware corporation, and Claude S. Hill, the principal of ARP. The 1976 Agreement permitted Hill, through ARP, to [market] Marvel properties. In return, ARP and Hill were obligated to remit certain specified percentages of their gross receipts back to Marvel and to provide Marvel with records. . . .

In July, 1986, ARP commenced an action against Marvel claiming that Marvel breached the 1976 Agreement by distributing the cartoons on videocassettes in disregard of ARP's allegedly exclusive right to do so. . . . Marvel [counterclaimed] seeking damages and a declaration that the contract had been terminated. . . . Marvel claims that, based upon undisputed facts, and as a matter of law, plaintiffs materially breached the 1976 Agreement by . . . refusing, since March of 1987, to report the results . . . and withholding Marvel's share . . . .

On November 12, 1986, James E. Galton, the President of Marvel, sent Hill a letter which purported to terminate all rights granted in connection with the 1976 Agreement. Despite the letter, plaintiffs continued to distribute the animated films but, since March of 1987, have neither paid Marvel its share of the distribution receipts nor accounted for such distribution as required under the contract.

Marvel claims that notwithstanding Marvel's arguably wrongful repudiation of the contract in 1986, plaintiffs' decision to continue the contract and exploit their rights thereunder bound them to continue their obligations as well. Marvel contends that plaintiffs' failure to remit monies due and account for their distribution activities is a material breach of the agreement justifying Marvel's termination of the contract.

Relying on the principles of anticipatory breach, plaintiffs contend that they had the right to withhold their own performance "to give Marvel an incentive to repent its repudiation."

When a party to a contract materially breaches that contract, the aggrieved party has two choices. He can cancel the contract and sue for total breach, or . . . affirm the contract and sue for partial breach. When the aggrieved party chooses to affirm the contract "in spite of a known excuse, the defense thereupon is lost and the injured party is himself liable if he subsequently fails to perform." 22 N.Y.Jur.2d § 375. See also 5 Williston On Contracts, § 688 at p. 300 (3d ed. 1961).

The innocent party can affirm the contract by his conduct and, in this regard, "[t]he continued acceptance of benefits under the contract is the most common and clearest case of election [to affirm the contract] by conduct." Cities Service Helex, Inc. v. United States, 543 F.2d 1306, 211 Ct.Cl. 222 (1976). In the present case, plaintiffs have affirmed the contract by continuing to distribute the Marvel cartoons, but have failed, since March, 1987, to pay Marvel its share of the proceeds and to account to Marvel for the same.

Relying on the principles of anticipatory breach, see §§ 251–57 of the Restatement Contracts 2d, plaintiffs contend that they were entitled to continue distribution under the 1976 Agreement and withhold their own performance until Marvel withdrew its repudiation. Plaintiffs' reliance on the principles of anticipatory breach is misplaced for several reasons. First, a brief explanation of those principles would be helpful. Section 251 of the Restatement of Contracts 2d provides:

> (1) Where reasonable grounds arise to believe that the obligor will commit a breach by non-performance that would of itself give the obligee a claim for damages for total breach . . . , the obligee may demand adequate assurance of due performance and may, if reasonable, suspend any performance for which he has not already received the agreed exchange until he receives such assurance.

> (2) The obligee may treat as a repudiation the obligor's failure to provide within a reasonable time such assurance of due performance as is adequate in the circumstances of the particular case.

Without the alternative provided in Section 251 of the Restatement, an innocent obligee, confronted with an obligor's prospective unwillingness or inability to perform, would be placed in the difficult position of guessing whether the obligor will perform. If the obligee believes that the obligor will not perform and it turns out that he is wrong, the obligee's own failure to perform may subject him to liability.

If the obligee ignores the obligor's apparent unwillingness to perform and continues his own performance, he runs the risk of never receiving the agreed upon return performance when that performance comes due. See Farnsworth, Contracts § 8.23 at 643–45 (1982). Under the Restatement, the obligor's failure to give adequate assurances that he will perform may be treated as a repudiation giving the obligee an immediate right to sue for total breach even though the obligor's performance is not yet due. . . .

Assuming that plaintiffs were in a position to treat Marvel's repudiation as a total breach, plaintiffs had the right, as with any other material breach, to either terminate the contract or affirm it:

> When a promisor repudiates a contract, the injured party faces an election of remedies; he can treat the repudiation as an anticipatory breach and immediately seek damages for breach of contract, thereby terminating the contractual relation between the parties, or he can treat the repudiation as an empty threat, wait until the time for performance arrives and exercise his remedies for actual breach if a breach does in fact occur at such time.

Silver Air v. Aeronautic Development Corp. Ltd., 656 F.Supp. 170 (S.D.N.Y.1987) (quoting Taylor v. Johnston, 15 Cal.3d 130, 123 Cal.Rptr. 641, 539 P.2d 425 (1975)).

However, a contract that is not treated as broken continues to exist for the benefit of both parties. There is no specific time limit within which the non-repudiating party must elect his remedy, but if the non-repudiating party himself defaults on the contract before he elects to accept the breach, the other party has the right to act upon his default. Id. See also North Country Rocky Point, Inc. v. Lewyt-Patchogue Co., 60 A.D.2d 258, 401 N.Y.S.2d 258 (2d Dep't 1978). Thus, even if plaintiffs were entitled to suspend their performance pending adequate assurances from Marvel, they forfeited their defense to performance by electing to affirm the contract.

Furthermore, under § 251 of the Restatement, an obligee can only suspend a performance "for which he has not already received the agreed exchange." See First Nat'l Bank of Aberdeen v. Indian Industries, 600 F.2d 702, 709 (8th Cir.1979) (non-defaulting party need not perform when it is clearly established that the promised equivalent will not be forthcoming); Long Island R. Co. v. Northville Industries, 41 N.Y.2d 455, 393 N.Y.S.2d 925, 362 N.E.2d 558 (1977) (for doctrine of anticipatory breach to apply, there must be some dependency of performances). Under the 1976 Agreement, plaintiffs receive the gross receipts from the distribution directly, and then pay Marvel its share. In effect, payments are due Marvel after plaintiffs have received the agreed exchange for such payments: the right to distribute Marvel properties and to receive a percentage of the proceeds therefrom. Thus, the principles of anticipatory breach are not applicable to the present dispute.

Accordingly, plaintiffs were not entitled to affirm and exploit their rights under the contract and at that the same time withhold their own performance indefinitely pending adequate assurances. Such a windfall is not sanctioned by any of the authorities cited by plaintiffs. The Court concludes, therefore, that to the extent plaintiffs affirmed the 1976

Agreement by exploiting Marvel properties and receiving the proceeds therefrom, plaintiffs breached the Agreement by failing to pay Marvel its share of such proceeds and by failing to provide records of the same. The Court, however, cannot say, as a matter of law, that the breach gives Marvel the right to terminate the contract. Materiality of breach is ordinarily a question of fact to be determined at trial.

NOTES AND QUESTIONS

1.　The murkiness of the circumstances that might give rise to repudiation makes it advisable for parties uncertain of the other side's performance to reach out and determine the facts before taking action. To adapt a classic case teaching this lesson, *Hathaway v. Sabin*, 22 A. 633 (Vt. 1891), suppose that Venue, a concert hall in New York, agrees to let Band, based in California, perform on the night of May 7 in exchange for a percentage of ticket sales. The contract states that Band is liable whether or not members are able to appear. On May 6, an unexpected airline strike occurs.

Venue reasonably supposes Band will be unable to reach New York. Venue therefore rents the space to another band. Absent consulting with Band, however, Venue's action is a repudiation, giving Band the right to damages. On the other hand, if Band is unable to appear, it is in breach of contract, giving Venue the right to damages. *See* Restatement (Second) of Contracts, Section 251, Illustration 1. Suppose, alternatively, that Band owns a private jet and has no problem arriving May 7, only to find the other band using the hall. *See id.* Illustration 2.

2.　We will see more of anticipatory repudiation later in this chapter under the heading UCC Remedies. Topics include further reference to the right to seek adequate assurance of due performance and the additional challenges of at what point in time to measure damages for breach by anticipatory repudiation.

C. FORESEEABILITY

Contract law's compensation principle is limited not only by the certainty requirement but an additional requirement that damages be "foreseeable." Exactly what this general vague phrase means has been a source of contention since at least 1854 and the famous case of *Hadley v. Baxendale*. Consider that there seem to be two strands of the limitation, one general or law-imposed and one specific or imposed by the parties' contract.

HADLEY V. BAXENDALE

9 Ex Ch 341, 156 ER 145 (1854)

[In accordance with a common practice of the period, the facts and procedural posture of the following case are provided by a court official, called a reporter, rather than the judge.—Eds.]

. . . At the trial before Crompton, J., at the last Gloucester Assizes, it appeared that the plaintiffs carried on an extensive business as millers at Gloucester; and that, on the 11th of May, their mill was stopped by a breakage of the crank shaft by which the mill was worked. The steam-engine was manufactured by Messrs. Joyce & Co., the engineers, at Greenwich, and it became necessary to send the shaft as a pattern for a new one to Greenwich. The fracture was discovered on the 12th, and on the 13th the plaintiffs sent one of their servants to the office of the defendants, who are the well-known carriers trading under the name of Pickford & Co., for the purpose of having the shaft carried to Greenwich.

The plaintiffs' servant told the clerk that the mill was stopped, and that the shaft must be sent immediately; and in answer to the inquiry when the shaft would be taken, the answer was, that if it was sent up by twelve o'clock an day, it would be delivered at Greenwich on the following day. On the following day the shaft was taken by the defendants, before noon, for the purpose of being conveyed to Greenwich, and the sum of 2l. 4s. was paid for its carriage for the whole distance; at the same time the defendants' clerk was told that a special entry, if required, should be made to hasten its delivery. The delivery of the shaft at Greenwich was delayed by some neglect; and the consequence was, that the plaintiffs did not receive the new shaft for several days after they would otherwise have done, and the working of their mill was thereby delayed, and they thereby lost the profits they would otherwise have received.

On the part of the defendants, it was objected that these damages were too remote, and that the defendants were not liable with respect to them. The learned Judge left the case generally to the jury, who found a verdict with 25l. damages beyond the amount paid into Court.

Whateley, in last Michaelmas Term, obtained a rule nisi for a new trial, on the ground of misdirection.

ALDERSON, B. We think that there ought to be a new trial in this case; but, in so doing, we deem it to be expedient and necessary to state explicitly the rule which the Judge, at the next trial, ought, in our opinion, to direct the jury to be governed by when they estimate the damages.

It is, indeed, of the last importance that we should do this; for, if the jury are left without any definite rule to guide them, it will, in such cases as these, manifestly lead to the greatest injustice. The Courts have done this on several occasions; and in Blake v. Midland Railway Company (18

Q. B. 93), the Court granted a new trial on this very ground, that the rule had not been definitely laid down to the jury by the learned Judge at Nisi Prius.

"There are certain establishing rules," this Court says, in Alder v. Keighley (15 M. & W. 117), "according to which the jury ought to find". And the Court, in that case, adds: "and here there is a clear rule, that the amount which would have been received if the contract had been kept, is the measure of damages if the contract is broken."

Now we think the proper rule is such as the present is this: Where two parties have made a contract which one of them has broken, the damages which the other party ought to receive in respect of such breach of contract should be such as may fairly and reasonably be considered either arising naturally, i.e., according to the usual course of things, from such breach of contract itself, or such as may reasonably be supposed to have been in the contemplation of both parties, at the time they made the contract, as the probable result of the breach of it. Now, if the special circumstances under which the contract was actually made where communicated by the plaintiffs to the defendants, and thus known to both parties, the damages resulting from the breach of such a contract, which they would reasonably contemplate, would be the amount of injury which would ordinarily follow from a breach of contract under these special circumstances so known and communicated.

[O]n the other hand, if these special circumstances were wholly unknown to the party breaking the contract, he, at the most, could only be supposed to have had in his contemplation the amount of injury which would arise generally, and in the great multitude of cases not affected by any special circumstances, from such a breach of contract. For, had the special circumstances been known, the parties might have specially provided for the breach of contract by special terms as to the damages in that case; and of this advantage it would be very unjust to deprive them. Now the above principles are those by which we think the jury ought to be guided in estimating the damages arising out of any breach of contract. It is said, that other cases such as breaches of contract in the nonpayment of money, or in the not making a good title of land, are to be treated as exceptions from this, and as governed by a conventional rule.

But as, in such cases, both parties must be supposed to be cognizant of that well-known rule, these cases may, we think, be more properly classed under the rule above enunciated as to cases under known special circumstances, because there both parties may reasonably be presumed to contemplate the estimation of the amount of damages according to the conventional rule. Now, in the present case, if we are to apply the principles above laid down, we find that the only circumstances here communicated by the plaintiffs to the defendants at the time of the contract was made, were, that the article to be carried was the broken shaft of a mill, and that the plaintiffs were the millers of the mill.

But how do these circumstances shew reasonably that the profits of the mill must be stopped by an unreasonable delay in the delivery of the broken shaft by the carrier to the third person? Suppose the plaintiffs had another shaft in their possession put up or putting up at the time, and that they only wished to send back the broken shaft to the engineer who made it; it is clear that this would be quite consistent with the above circumstances, and yet the unreasonable delay in the delivery would have no effect upon the intermediate profits of the mill.

Or, again, suppose that, at the time of the delivery to the carrier, the machinery of the mill had been in other respects defective, then, also, the same results would follow. Here it is true that the shaft was actually sent back to serve as a model for the new one, and that the want of a new one was the only cause of the stoppage of the mill, and that the loss of profits really arose from not sending down the new shaft in proper time, and that this arose from the delay in delivering the broken one to serve as a model. But it is obvious that, in the great multitude of cases of millers sending off broken shafts to third persons by a carrier under ordinary circumstances, such consequences would not, in all probability, have occurred; and these special circumstances were here never communicated by the plaintiffs to the defendants.

It follows therefore, that the loss of profits here cannot reasonably be considered such a consequence of the breach of contract as could have been fairly and reasonably contemplated by both the parties when they made this contract. For such loss would neither have flowed naturally from the breach of this contract in the great multitude of such cases occurring under ordinary circumstances, nor were the special circumstances, which, perhaps, would have made it a reasonable and natural consequence of such breach of contract, communicated to or known by the defendants.

The Judge ought, therefore, to have told the jury, that, upon the facts then before them, they ought not to take the loss of profits into consideration at all in estimating the damages. There must therefore be a new trial in this case. Rule absolute.

NOTES AND QUESTIONS

1.   *Hadley v. Baxendale* states a now-canonical limitation on contract damages. The court announced two rules regarding remedies for breach of contract amounting to a requirement of foreseeability: (1) damages include those that arise naturally, in the usual course of things, from breach and (2) damages beyond those must have been in the contemplation of the parties, at the time they made the contract, as the probable result of breach. The latter are denominated as "consequential damages."

2.   A contract price includes, in effect, an insurance premium for the cost of breach, damages payable. Promisors need a basis to gauge probable damages, including information that distinguishes between ordinary circumstances flowing from a breach and special factors that warrant adjusting the contract price. Contract law's limitation on consequential damages induces parties to reveal such information about any special factors at the time of contract formation. Some scholars see the rule of *Hadley* as inducing such disclosure, which they refer to as a "penalty default rule." *See* Ian Ayres & Robert Gertner, *Filling Gaps in Incomplete Contracts: An Economic Theory of Default Rules*, 99 YALE L.J. 87 (1989).

3.   Is there an argument that the carrier knew the mill would be stopped without the essential component? Why would this knowledge be important to the outcome of the case?

4.   To celebrate the 150th anniversary of *Hadley*, a group of contract law professors gathered at the site of the mill to discuss the implications of the decision. Articles resulting from the conference can be found in Volume 11 of the Texas Wesleyan Law Review. *See* Frank Snyder et al, *Hadley v. Baxendale: Still Crazy After All These Years*, 11 TEX. WES. L. REV. 707 (2005).

5.   From the same conference comes some more information about the defendant in the case:

> The defendant . . . is Joseph Baxendale, managing partner of Pickford and Co., the common carrier that delayed the delivery of the Hadley's shaft. Baxendale was named the defendant, because Pickfords was a partnership . . . . The Pickford family retained control until 1817 when over expansion and accumulated debt threatened bankruptcy. Baxendale joined Pickfords at that time. He and two other partners brought a needed capital infusion to the firm, which Baxendale obtained the old fashioned way—from his wife's dowry. As the catalyst of Pickfords' recovery, Baxendale transformed the firm from a family-run canal carrier into a national enterprise. He had the foresight to discern the future impact of the railroad on freight carriage and oversaw the firm's switch from canal to rail traffic. Through his efforts Pickfords became a national rail agent, a highly complex transportation enterprise, and a modern specialized firm operating on a gigantic scale at a time of England's economic growth[.]

James J. Fishman, *Joseph Baxendale*, 11 TEX. WESLEYAN L. REV. 249 (2005).

6.   What aspects of the case seem to be related to the prevailing onset of the industrial revolution? With modern air and freight travel as well as package-tracking technology, does the *Hadley* rule still make sense in the context of package tracking? What options are available at the post office, FedEx, or UPS to make sure a valuable package arrives in time and/or is properly insured against loss and damage? Imagine you have an industrial

part that needs to get sent to a mechanic immediately. Look online to find your shipping options.

7.   How does *Hadley v. Baxendale* apply to the *MindGames* fact pattern? Would lost profits from breach of a board game contract "arise naturally"? Were such damages within the contemplation of the parties?

REDGRAVE V. BOSTON SYMPHONY ORCHESTRA

855 F.2d 888 (1st Cir. 1988)

COFFIN, J.

. . . The plaintiffs, actress Vanessa Redgrave and Vanessa Redgrave Enterprises, Ltd. (hereinafter Redgrave), brought suit against the Boston Symphony Orchestra (hereinafter the BSO) for cancelling a contract for Redgrave's appearance as narrator in a performance of Stravinsky's "Oedipus Rex." The cancellation occurred in the wake of protests over Redgrave's participation because of her support of the Palestine Liberation Organization. She sought recovery both for breach of contract . . . .

A jury awarded Redgrave $100,000 in consequential damages caused by the BSO's breach of contract . . . . On the BSO's motion for judgment notwithstanding the verdict on the consequential damages issue, the district court held that the evidence of consequential damages was sufficient . . . . BSO [agues] that the evidence of consequential damages was insufficient We conclude . . . that Redgrave has presented sufficient evidence to prove only $12,000 in consequential damages, minus certain expenses. . . .

In March 1982, the Boston Symphony Orchestra (BSO) engaged Vanessa Redgrave to narrate Stravinsky's "Oedipus Rex" in a series of concerts in Boston and New York. Following announcement of the engagement, the BSO received calls from its subscribers and from community members protesting the engagement because of Redgrave's political support for the Palestine Liberation Organization and because of her views regarding the state of Israel. On or about April 1, 1982, the BSO cancelled its contract with Redgrave and its performances of "Oedipus Rex."

Redgrave sued the BSO for breach of contract and for violation of the MCRA. The BSO argued at trial that the contract rightfully was cancelled because the cancellation was the result of "a cause or causes beyond the reasonable control" of the BSO. . . . BSO agents testified that they had not cancelled the performances in order to punish Redgrave for her past speech or repress her future speech, but because it was felt that potential disruptions, given the community reaction, would implicate the physical safety of the audience and players and would detract from the artistic qualities of the production.

Following a sixteen-day trial, the jury found that the BSO wrongfully had breached its contract with Redgrave. On that basis, the district court awarded Redgrave her stipulated performance fee of $27,500. The jury also found that the BSO's cancellation had damaged Redgrave's career by causing loss of future professional opportunities, and awarded Redgrave $100,000 in consequential damages. The district court found that the question whether there was sufficient evidence to support a finding of $100,000 in consequential damages was a "close and debatable" one, but concluded that there was sufficient evidence to support the award. . . .

In response to special interrogatories, the jury found that the BSO's cancellation of the "Oedipus Rex" concerts caused consequential harm to Redgrave's professional career and that this harm was a foreseeable consequence within the contemplation of the parties at the time they entered the contract. . . . A threshold question is whether Massachusetts contract law allows the award of such consequential damages for harm to a claimant's professional career.

Redgrave's consequential damages claim is based on the proposition that a significant number of movie and theater offers that she would ordinarily have received in the years 1982 and following were in fact not offered to her as a result of the BSO's cancellation in April 1982. The BSO characterizes this claim as one for damage to Redgrave's reputation, and argues that the . . . Massachusetts state court decisions in McCone v. New England Telephone & Telegraph Co., 393 Mass. 231, 471 N.E.2d 47 (1984), and Daley v. Town of West Brookfield, 19 Mass.App.Ct. 1019, 476 N.E.2d 980 (1985), establish that Massachusetts law does not permit plaintiffs in breach of contract actions to recover consequential damages for harm to reputation.

In McCone v. New England Telephone & Telegraph Co., plaintiffs alleged that their employer's breach of an implied covenant of good faith had caused them loss of salary increases, loss of pension benefits, and "damage to their professional reputations, disruption of their personal lives, and great pain of body and mind." The Massachusetts Supreme Judicial Court held that the claims for damages to reputation and other emotional injury could not be sustained in the suit because "these additional damages are not contract damages." Id. In Daley v. Town of West Brookfield, a Massachusetts appellate court observed that "[d]amages for injury to reputation are usually not available in contract actions," noting that the rationale most often given is that "such damages are remote and not within the contemplation of the parties." 19 Mass.App.Ct. at 1019 n. 1, 476 N.E.2d at 980 n. 1.

The BSO notes that Massachusetts is in agreement with virtually all other jurisdictions in holding that damages for reputation are not available in contract actions. See, e.g., Volkswagen Interamericana, S.A. v. Rohlsen,

360 F.2d 437, 446 (1st Cir.1966) (applying federal law); Stancil v. Mergenthaler Linotype Co., 589 F.Supp. 78, 84–85 (D.Haw.1984); O'Leary v. Sterling Extruder Corp., 533 F.Supp. 1205, 1209 (E.D.Wis.1982); Skagway City School Board v. Davis, 543 P.2d 218, 225–27 (Ala.1975); Tousley v. Atlantic City Ambassador Hotel Corp., 25 N.J.Misc. 88, 50 A.2d 472, 474–75 (N.J.Sup.Ct.1947). This impressive line of cases, however, becomes less impressive for our purposes when the reasoning in these cases is analyzed with reference to the particular claim put forth by Redgrave.

In cases that have analyzed the reasons for disallowing a contract claim for reputation damages, courts have identified two determinative factors. First, courts have observed that attempting to calculate damages for injury to reputation is "unduly speculative." Skagway City School Board, 543 P.2d at 225. See O'Leary, 533 F.Supp. at 1209; Tousley, 50 A.2d at 474–75. In many cases, the courts have viewed the claims for damages to reputation as analogous to claims for physical or emotional distress and have noted the difficulty in ascertaining such damages for contract purposes. See, e.g., Westwater v. Rector, Warden and Vestry of Grace Church, 140 Cal. 339, 342, 73 P. 1055 (1903) ("Damages to health, reputation, or feelings are not clearly ascertainable either in their nature or origin."). As the court in *Skagway* noted, an estimate of injury to reputation "must rest upon a number of imprecise variables," including the causal connection between the breach of contract and the injury to reputation and the amount by which any future earnings would be decreased by causes other than the breach.

The second factor that courts identify is that damages for injury to reputation "cannot reasonably be presumed to have been within the contemplation of the parties when they entered into the contract." Skagway City School Board, 543 P.2d at 225. These courts state that the basic rule of Hadley v. Baxendale, 9 Ex. 341, 156 Eng.Rep. 145 (1854), which requires that contract damages be of the kind that arise naturally from the breach of a contract or be of a kind that reasonably may have been in the contemplation of the parties when they entered the contract, cannot possibly be met in a claim for general damages to reputation occurring as the result of a breach of contract. . . . The Massachusetts Supreme Judicial Court seems to have accepted this rationale as a legitimate one for disallowing claims for injury to reputation as a contract damage. . . .

The claim advanced by Redgrave is significantly different, however, from a general claim of damage to reputation. Redgrave is not claiming that her general reputation as a professional actress has been tarnished by the BSO's cancellation. Rather, she claims that a number of specific movie and theater performances that would have been offered to her in the usual course of events were not offered to her as a result of the BSO's cancellation. This is the type of specific claim that, with appropriate evidence, can meet the Hadley v. Baxendale rule, as adopted by the

Massachusetts Supreme Judicial Court in John Hetherington & Sons, Ltd. v. William Firth Co., 210 Mass. 8, 21; 95 N.E. 961, 964 (1911) (in breach of contract action, injured party receives compensation for any loss that follows as a natural consequence from the breach, was within the contemplation of reasonable parties as a probable result of breach, and may be computed by "rational methods upon a firm basis of facts"). . . .

The jury was given appropriate instructions to help it determine whether Redgrave had suffered consequential damages through loss of future professional opportunities. They were told to find that the BSO's cancellation was a proximate cause of harm to Redgrave's professional career only if they determined that "harm would not have occurred but for the cancellation and that the harm was a natural and probable consequence of the cancellation." In addition, they were told that damages should be allowed for consequential harm "only if the harm was a foreseeable consequence within the contemplation of the parties to the contract when it was made." In response to special interrogatories, the jury found that the BSO's cancellation caused consequential harm to Redgrave's career and that the harm was a foreseeable consequence within the contemplation of the parties.

Although we find that Redgrave did not present sufficient evidence to establish that the BSO's cancellation caused consequential harm to her professional career in the amount of $100,000, . . . we hold that, as a matter *BUT* of Massachusetts contract law, a plaintiff may receive consequential damages if the plaintiff proves with sufficient evidence that a breach of contract proximately caused the loss of identifiable professional opportunities. This type of claim is sufficiently different from a nonspecific allegation of damage to reputation that it appropriately falls outside the general rule that reputation damages are not an acceptable form of contract damage.

NOTES AND QUESTIONS

1.   If you are counsel for a non-profit organization negotiating to host an individual who may be politically controversial, what can you learn from this case? Should an engagement contract address the possibility of protests or other political pressure? If so, what do you want the clause to say? Can the language allocate those risks to the performer rather than to the host?

2.   On occasion, universities have withdrawn speaking invitations after learning of political opposition to a selected speaker. If a speaking contract were breached, what should the speaker's damages be? Should the university be liable for damages from the loss of prospective speaking engagements that breach may occasion? Does this outcome create a disincentive to contract with any politically controversial figure?

PROBLEM: LADY AGATHA'S ORCHIDS

Lady Agatha is an avid orchid collector, gathering rare specimens from around the world to keep throughout the interior of her lavish home. Some of her orchids have taken years to find on various orchid hunting and buying trips. To accommodate the orchids in the depth of the frigid English winter, Lady Agatha recently commissioned the building of a greenhouse to showcase her collection. After the greenhouse was almost complete in August, Lady Agatha moved her entire collection into the structure. She then entered into a contract with a heating and cooling contractor, Alexander Siberia, to install a foolproof heating system for the greenhouse. The heating system was of paramount importance because orchids normally grow in warm jungle environments in countries such as Costa Rica. Orchids are delicate, and cold breezes can result in their injury or death.

Siberia agreed that he would install the greenhouse heating system at a cost of $30,000, and that it would be finished and the heat turned on before October 15. While Lady Agatha did not communicate the value of the orchids in question, she made it known that time was of the essence and that the onset of cold weather would jeopardize the health of the orchids. Siberia indicated that he understood her needs with the orchid collection and that the price for completion of the project would cover a backup generator and timely workmanship.

On October 1, Lady Agatha left the country for an orchid gathering trip in the Amazon River basin, leaving just one maid working as a skeleton crew to attend to caretaking her estate. When she then returned to her estate in England on November 15, Lady Agatha found a frigid greenhouse and all of her orchids were, sadly, "pushing up the daisies." Despite Siberia's assurances, he had attended to a $250,000 job with Lord Crawley and had delayed working on Lady Agatha's greenhouse. While many would say that Lady Agatha's collection was priceless, as it has been collected personally from many areas of the world, a market value of the collection would be $125,000.

If Lady Agatha sues Alexander Siberia in the Court of the Exchequer, what facts will be important to bring to a jury? What might serve to limit the damages Lady Agatha may be able to collect? Should it make a difference that Alexander Siberia had breached the contract to take on a better-paying commission from Lord Crawley?

D. MITIGATION

There are times when a party announces an intention to breach a contract. If announced before performance has begun, this may amount to anticipatory repudiation. But sometimes performance has already started when one party announces its intention to breach. Upon hearing of the other party's intention to breach, what obligations does the other party have? Can they carry on with their contractual duties as if nothing has happened? Under the doctrine of mitigation, explained in the following classic case, the performing party would carry on at his or her peril.

ROCKINGHAM COUNTY V. LUTEN BRIDGE CO.
35 F.2d 301 (4th Cir. 1929)

PARKER, J.

This was an action at law instituted in the court below by the Luten Bridge Company, as plaintiff, to recover of Rockingham county, North Carolina, an amount alleged to be due under a contract, but contends that notice of cancellation was given the bridge company before the erection of the bridge was commenced, and that it is liable only for the damages which the company would have sustained, if it had abandoned construction at that time. The judge below . . . excluded evidence offered by the county in support of its contentions as to notice of cancellation and damages, and instructed a verdict for plaintiff for the full amount of its claim. From judgment on this verdict the county has appealed.

The facts . . . are as follows: On January 7, 1924, the board of commissioners of Rockingham county voted to award to plaintiff a contract for the construction of the bridge in controversy. Three of the five commissioners favored the awarding of the contract and two opposed it. Much feeling was engendered over the matter, with the result that on February 11, 1924, W. K. Pruitt, one of the commissioners who had voted in the affirmative, sent his resignation to the clerk of the superior court of the county. The clerk received this resignation on the same day, and immediately accepted same and noted his acceptance thereon. Later in the day, Pruitt called him over the telephone and stated that he wished to withdraw the resignation, and later sent him written notice to the same effect. The clerk, however, paid no attention to the attempted withdrawal, and proceeded on the next day to appoint one W. W. Hampton as a member of the board to succeed him.

After his resignation, Pruitt attended no further meetings of the board, and did nothing further as a commissioner of the county. Likewise Pratt and McCollum, the other two members of the board who had voted with him in favor of the contract, attended no further meetings. Hampton, on the other hand, took the oath of office immediately upon his appointment and entered upon the discharge of the duties of a commissioner. He met regularly with the two remaining members of the board, Martin and Barber, in the courthouse at the county seat, and with them attended to all of the business of the county. Between the 12th of February and the first Monday in December following, these three attended, in all, 25 meetings of the board.

At one of these meetings, a regularly advertised called meeting held on February 21st, a resolution was unanimously adopted declaring that the contract for the building of the bridge was not legal and valid, and directing the clerk of the board to notify plaintiff that it refused to recognize same as a valid contract, and that plaintiff should proceed no further thereunder. This resolution also rescinded action of the board theretofore taken looking to the construction of a hard-surfaced road, in which the bridge was to be a mere connecting link. The clerk duly sent a certified copy of this resolution to plaintiff.

At the regular monthly meeting of the board on March 3d, a resolution was passed directing that plaintiff be notified that any work done on the bridge would be done by it at its own risk and hazard, that the board was of the opinion that the contract for the construction of the bridge was not valid and legal, and that, even if the board were mistaken as to this, it did not desire to construct the bridge, and would contest payment for same if constructed. A copy of this resolution was also sent to plaintiff. At the regular monthly meeting on April 7th, a resolution was passed, reciting that the board had been informed that one of its members was privately insisting that the bridge be constructed. It repudiated this action on the part of the member and gave notice that it would not be recognized. At the September meeting, a resolution was passed to the effect that the board would pay no bills presented by plaintiff or anyone connected with the bridge. At the time of the passage of the first resolution, very little work toward the construction of the bridge had been done, it being estimated that the total cost of labor done and material on the ground was around $1,900; but, notwithstanding the repudiation of the contract by the county, the bridge company continued with the work of construction.

On November 24, 1924, plaintiff instituted this action against Rockingham county, and against Pruitt, Pratt, McCollum, Martin, and Barber, as constituting its board of commissioners. Complaint was filed, setting forth the execution of the contract and the doing of work by plaintiff thereunder, and alleging that for work done up until November 3, 1924, the county was indebted in the sum of $18,301.07. . . .

At the trial, . . . [t]he county elicited on cross-examination proof as to the state of the work at the time of the passage of the resolutions to which we have referred. It then offered these resolutions in evidence; but . . . this evidence was excluded, and the jury was instructed to return a verdict for plaintiff for the full amount of its claim. The county preserved exceptions to the rulings which were adverse to it, and contends that there was error on the part of the judge below . . . in excluding the evidence offered . . . of the resolutions attempting to cancel the contract and the notices sent plaintiff pursuant thereto; and in directing a verdict for plaintiff in accordance with its claim.

As the county now admits the execution and validity of the contract, and the breach on its part, the ultimate question in the case is one as to the measure of plaintiff's recovery . . . . [W]e do not think that, after the county had given notice, while the contract was still executory, that it did not desire the bridge built and would not pay for it, plaintiff could proceed to build it and recover the contract price. It is true that the county had no right to rescind the contract, and the notice given plaintiff amounted to a breach on its part; but, after plaintiff had received notice of the breach, it was its duty to do nothing to increase the damages flowing therefrom. If A enters into a binding contract to build a house for B, B, of course, has no right to rescind the contract without A's consent.

But if, before the house is built, he decides that he does not want it, and notifies A to that effect, A has no right to proceed with the building and thus pile up damages. His remedy is to treat the contract as broken when he receives the notice, and sue for the recovery of such damages, as he may have sustained from the breach, including any profit which he would have realized upon performance, as well as any other losses which may have resulted to him. In the case at bar, the county decided not to build the road of which the bridge was to be a part, and did not build it. The bridge, built in the midst of the forest, is of no value to the county because of this change of circumstances. When, therefore, the county gave notice to the plaintiff that it would not proceed with the project, plaintiff should have desisted from further work. It had no right thus to pile up damages by proceeding with the erection of a useless bridge.

The contrary view was expressed by Lord Cockburn in Frost v. Knight, L.R. 7 Ex. 111, but, as pointed out by Prof. Williston (Williston on Contracts, vol. 3, p. 2347), it is not in harmony with the decisions in this country. The American rule and the reasons supporting it are well stated by Prof. Williston as follows:

> There is a line of cases running back to 1845 which holds that, after an absolute repudiation or refusal to perform by one party to a contract, the other party cannot continue to perform and recover damages based on full performance. This rule is only a particular application of the general rule of damages that a plaintiff cannot hold a defendant liable for damages which need not have been incurred; or, as it is often stated, the plaintiff must, so far as he can without loss to himself, mitigate the damages caused by the defendant's wrongful act. The application of this rule to the matter in question is obvious. If a man engages to have work done, and afterwards repudiates his contract before the work has been begun or when it has been only partially done, it is inflicting damage on the defendant without benefit to the plaintiff to allow the latter to insist on proceeding with the contract. The work may be useless to the defendant, and yet he would be forced to pay the full contract price. On the other hand, the plaintiff is interested

only in the profit he will make out of the contract. If he receives this it is equally advantageous for him to use his time otherwise.

The leading case on the subject in this country is . . . Clark v. Marsiglia, 1 Denio (N.Y.) 317, 43 Am.Dec. 670. In that case defendant had employed plaintiff to paint certain pictures for him, but countermanded the order before the work was finished. Plaintiff, however, went on and completed the work and sued for the contract price. In reversing a judgment for plaintiff, the court said:

> The plaintiff was allowed to recover as though there had been no countermand of the order; and in this the court erred. The defendant, by requiring the plaintiff to stop work upon the paintings, violated his contract, and thereby incurred a liability to pay such damages as the plaintiff should sustain. Such damages would include a recompense for the labor done and materials used, and such further sum in damages as might, upon legal principles, be assessed for the breach of the contract; but the plaintiff had no right, by obstinately persisting in the work, to make the penalty upon the defendant greater than it would otherwise have been.

. . . . It follows that there was error in directing a verdict for plaintiff for the full amount of its claim. The measure of plaintiff's damage, upon its appearing that notice was duly given not to build the bridge, is an amount sufficient to compensate plaintiff for labor and materials expended and expense incurred in the part performance of the contract, prior to its repudiation, plus the profit which would have been realized if it had been carried out in accordance with its terms. . . . The judgment below will accordingly be reversed, and the case remanded for a new trial. . . .

NOTES AND QUESTIONS

1.   Why might the construction company continue work on the bridge despite the board's resolutions? What might have been happening with local politics that seems to have increased the amount of uncertainty? For more of the backstory of this case, see Barak D. Richman, et al., *A Bridge, a Tax Revolt, and the Struggle to Industrialize: The Story and Legacy of Rockingham County v. Luten Bridge Co.*, 84 N.C. L. REV. 1841 (2006).

2.   Do you see any analogies between the context of *Rockingham County v. Luten Bridge* and the volunteers or "officious intermeddlers" discussed in Chapter Six on restitution?

PARKER V. TWENTIETH CENTURY FOX

474 P.2d 689 (Cal. 1970)

BURKE, J.

Defendant Twentieth Century-Fox Film Corporation appeals from a summary judgment granting to plaintiff the recovery of agreed compensation under a written contract for her services as an actress in a motion picture. As will appear, we have concluded that the trial court correctly ruled in plaintiff's favor and that the judgment should be affirmed.

Plaintiff [Shirley MacLaine] is well known as an actress, and in the contract between plaintiff and defendant is sometimes referred to as the 'Artist.' Under the contract, dated August 6, 1965, plaintiff was to play the female lead in defendant's contemplated production of a motion picture entitled 'Bloomer Girl.' The contract provided that defendant would pay plaintiff a minimum 'guaranteed compensation' of '53,571.42 per week for 14 weeks commencing May 23, 1966, for a total of $750,000. Prior to May 1966 defendant decided not to produce the picture and by a letter dated April 4, 1966, it notified plaintiff of that decision and that it would not 'comply with our obligations to you under' the written contract.

By the same letter and with the professed purpose 'to avoid any damage to you,' defendant instead offered to employ plaintiff as the leading actress in another film tentatively entitled 'Big Country, Big Man' (hereinafter, 'Big Country'). The compensation offered was identical, as were 31 of the 34 numbered provisions or articles of the original contract.[1] Unlike 'Bloomer Girl,' however, which was to have been a musical production, 'Big Country' was a dramatic 'western type' movie. 'Bloomer Girl' was to have been filmed in California; 'Big Country' was to be produced in Australia. Also, certain terms in the proffered contract varied from those of the original.[2] Plaintiff was given one week within which to

---

[1] Among the identical provisions was the following found in the last paragraph of Article 2 of the original contract: "We [20th Century Fox] shall not be obligated to utilize your [MacLaine's] services in or in connection with the Photoplay hereunder, our sole obligation, subject to the terms and conditions of this Agreement, being to pay you the guaranteed compensation herein provided for."

[2] Article 29 of the original contract specified that plaintiff approved the director already chosen for 'Bloomer Girl' and that in case he failed to act as director plaintiff was to have approval rights of any substitute director. Article 31 provided that plaintiff was to have the right of approval of the 'Bloomer Girl' dance director, and Article 32 gave her the right of approval of the screenplay. Defendant's letter of April 4 to plaintiff, which contained both defendant's notice of breach of the 'Bloomer Girl' contract and offer of the lead in 'Big Country,' eliminated or impaired each of those rights. It read in part as follows:

The terms and conditions of our offer of employment are identical to those set forth in the 'BLOOMER GIRL' Agreement, Articles 1 through 34 and Exhibit A to the Agreement, except as follows:

1. Article 31 of said Agreement will not be included in any contract of employment regarding 'BIG COUNTRY, BIG MAN' as it is not a musical and it thus will not need a dance director.'

accept; she did not and the offer lapsed. Plaintiff then commenced this action seeking recovery of the agreed guaranteed compensation.

The complaint sets forth two causes of action. The first is for money due under the contract; the second, based upon the same allegations as the first, is for damages resulting from defendant's breach of contract. Defendant in its answer admits the existence and validity of the contract, that plaintiff complied with all the conditions, covenants and promises and stood ready to complete the performance, and that defendant breached and 'anticipatorily repudiated' the contract. It denies, however, that any money is due to plaintiff either under the contract or as a result of its breach, and pleads as an affirmative defense to both causes of action plaintiff's allegedly deliberate failure to mitigate damages, asserting that she unreasonably refused to accept its offer of the leading role in 'Big Country.'

Plaintiff moved for summary judgment . . . , the motion was granted, and summary judgment for $750,000 plus interest was entered in plaintiff's favor. This appeal by defendant followed. . . .

As stated, defendant's sole defense to this action which resulted from its deliberate breach of contract is that in rejecting defendant's substitute offer of employment plaintiff unreasonably refused to mitigate damages.

The general rule is that the measure of recovery by a wrongfully discharged employee is the amount of salary agreed upon for the period of service, less the amount which the employer affirmatively proves the employee has earned or with reasonable effort might have earned from other employment. . . . However, before projected earnings from other employment opportunities not sought or accepted by the discharged employee can be applied in mitigation, the employer must show that the other employment was comparable, or substantially similar, to that of which the employee has been deprived; the employee's rejection of or failure to seek other available employment of a different or inferior kind may not be resorted to in order to mitigate damages. . . .

In the present case defendant has raised no issue of *reasonableness of efforts* by plaintiff to obtain other employment; the sole issue is whether plaintiff's refusal of defendant's substitute offer of 'Big Country' may be used in mitigation. Nor, if the 'Big Country' offer was of employment

---

2.   In the 'BLOOMER GIRL' agreement, in Articles 29 and 32, you were given certain director and screenplay approvals and you had preapproved certain matters. Since there simply is insufficient time to negotiate with you regarding your choice of director and regarding the screenplay and since you already expressed an interest in performing the role in 'BIG COUNTRY, BIG MAN,' we must exclude from our offer of employment in 'BIG COUNTRY, BIG MAN' any approval rights as are contained in said Articles 29 and 32; however, we shall consult with you respecting the director to be selected to direct the photoplay and will further consult with you with respect to the screenplay and any revisions or changes therein, provided, however, that if we fail to agree . . . [our] decision . . . with respect to the selection of a director and to revisions and changes in the said screenplay shall be binding . . . .

different or inferior when compared with the original 'Bloomer Girl' employment, is there an issue as to whether or not plaintiff acted reasonably in refusing the substitute offer. Despite defendant's arguments to the contrary, no case cited or which our research has discovered holds or suggests that reasonableness is an element of a wrongfully discharged employee's option to reject, or fail to seek, different or inferior employment lest the possible earnings therefrom be charged against him in mitigation of damages.[5]

Applying the foregoing rules to the record in the present case, with all intendments in favor of the party opposing the summary judgment motion—here, defendant—it is clear that the trial court correctly ruled that plaintiff's failure to accept defendant's tendered substitute employment could not be applied in mitigation of damages because the offer of the 'Big Country' lead was of employment both different and inferior, and that no factual dispute was presented on that issue. The mere circumstance that 'Bloomer Girl' was to be a musical review calling upon plaintiff's talents as a dancer as well as an actress, and was to be produced in the City of Los Angeles, whereas 'Big Country' was a straight dramatic role in a 'Western Type' story taking place in an opal mine in Australia, demonstrates the difference in kind between the two employments; the female lead as a dramatic actress in a western style motion picture can by no stretch of imagination be considered the equivalent of or substantially similar to the lead in a song-and-dance production.

Additionally, the substitute 'Big Country' offer proposed to eliminate or impair the director and screenplay approvals accorded to plaintiff under the original 'Bloomer Girl' contract, and thus constituted an offer of inferior employment. No expertise or judicial notice is required in order to hold that the deprivation or infringement of an employee's rights held under an original employment contract converts the available 'other employment' relied upon by the employer to mitigate damages, into inferior employment which the employee need not seek or accept. . . .

---

[5]   Instead, in each case the reasonableness referred to was that of the *efforts* of the employee to obtain other employment that was not different or inferior; his right to reject the latter was declared as an unqualified rule of law. Thus, Gonzales v. Internat. Assn. of Machinists, Supra, 213 Cal.App.2d 817, 823–824, 29 Cal.Rptr. 190, 194, holds that the trial court correctly instructed the jury that plaintiff union member, a machinist, was required to make 'such *efforts* as the average (member of his union) desiring employment would make at that particular time and place' (italics added); but, further, that the court *properly rejected defendant's offer of proof of the availability of other kinds of employment* at the same or higher pay than plaintiff usually received and all outside the jurisdiction of his union, as plaintiff could not be required to accept different employment or a nonunion job.

In Harris v. Nat. Union, etc., Cooks and Stewards, Supra, 116 Cal.App.2d 759, 761, 254 P.2d 673, 676, the issues were stated to be, inter alia, whether comparable employment was open to each plaintiff employee, and if so whether each plaintiff made a *reasonable effort to secure such employment. It was held that the trial court properly sustained an objection to an offer to prove a custom of accepting a job in a lower rank when work in the higher rank* was not available, as 'The duty of mitigation of damages . . . does not require the plaintiff 'to seek or to accept other employment of a different or inferior kind." (p. 764(5), 254 P.2d p. 676.) . . . .

Statements found in affidavits submitted by defendant in opposition to plaintiff's summary judgment motion, to the effect that the 'Big Country' offer was not of employment different from or inferior to that under the 'Bloomer Girl' contract, merely repeat the allegations of defendant's answer to the complaint in this action, constitute only conclusionary assertions with respect to undisputed facts, and do not give rise to a triable factual issue so as to defeat the motion for summary judgment. . . .

In view of the determination that defendant failed to present any facts showing the existence of a factual issue with respect to its sole defense—plaintiff's rejection of its substitute employment offer in mitigation of damages—we need not consider plaintiff's further contention that for various reasons, including the provisions of the original contract set forth in footnote 1, *ante*, plaintiff was excused from attempting to mitigate damages. . . .

SULLIVAN, C.J. (dissenting).

The basic question in this case is whether or not plaintiff acted reasonably in rejecting defendant's offer of alternate employment. The answer depends upon whether that offer (starring in 'Big Country, Big Man') was an offer of work that was substantially similar to her former employment (starring in 'Bloomer Girl') or of work that was of a different or inferior kind. To my mind this is a factual issue which the trial court should not have determined on a motion for summary judgment. The majority have not only repeated this error but have compounded it by applying the rules governing mitigation of damages in the employer-employee context in a misleading fashion. Accordingly, I respectfully dissent.

The familiar rule requiring a plaintiff in a tort or contract action to mitigate damages embodies notions of fairness and socially responsible behavior which are fundamental to our jurisprudence. Most broadly stated, it precludes the recovery of damages which, through the exercise of due diligence, could have been avoided. Thus, in essence, it is a rule requiring reasonable conduct in commercial affairs. This general principle governs the obligations of an employee after his employer has wrongfully repudiated or terminated the employment contract. Rather than permitting the employee simply to remain idle during the balance of the contract period, the law requires him to make a reasonable effort to secure other employment.[1] He is not obliged, however, to seek or accept any and

---

[1] The issue is generally discussed in terms of a duty on the part of the employee to minimize loss. The practice is long-established and there is little reason to change despite Judge Cardozo's observation of its subtle inaccuracy. 'The servant is free to accept employment or reject it according to his uncensored pleasure. What is meant by the supposed duty is merely this: That if he unreasonably reject, he will not be heard to say that the loss of wages from then on shall be deemed the jural consequence of the earlier discharge. He has broken the chain of causation, and loss resulting to him thereafter is suffered through his own act.' (McClelland v. Climax Hosiery Mills (1930) 252 N.Y. 347, 359, 169 N.E. 605, 609, concurring opinion.)

all types of work which may be available. Only work which is in the same field and which is of the same quality need be accepted.[2]

Over the years the courts have employed various phrases to define the type of employment which the employee, upon his wrongful discharge, is under an obligation to accept. Thus in California alone it has been held that he must accept employment which is 'substantially similar' . . . ; 'comparable employment' . . . ; employment 'in the same general line of the first employment' . . . ; 'equivalent to his prior position' . . . ; 'employment in a similar capacity' . . . ; employment which is 'not . . . of a different or inferior kind'. . . .

For reasons which are unexplained, the majority cite several of these cases yet select from among the various judicial formulations which contain one particular phrase, 'Not of a different or inferior kind,' with which to analyze this case. I have discovered no historical or theoretical reason to adopt this phrase, which is simply a negative restatement of the affirmative standards set out in the above cases, as the exclusive standard. Indeed, its emergence is an example of the dubious phenomenon of the law responding not to rational judicial choice or changing social conditions, but to unrecognized changes in the language of opinions or legal treatises. However, the phrase is a serviceable one and my concern is not with its use as the standard but rather with what I consider its distortion.

The relevant language excuses acceptance only of employment which is of a *different kind*. . . . It has never been the law that the mere existence of *differences between two jobs in the same field* is sufficient, as a matter of law, to excuse an employee wrongfully discharged from one from accepting the other in order to mitigate damages. Such an approach would effectively eliminate any obligation of an employee to attempt to minimize damage arising from a wrongful discharge. The only alternative job offer an employee would be required to accept would be an offer of his former job by his former employer.

Although the majority appear to hold that there was a difference 'in kind' between the employment offered plaintiff in 'Bloomer Girl' and that offered in 'Big Country', an examination of the opinion makes crystal clear that the majority merely point out differences between the two *films* (an obvious circumstance) and then [apodictically] assert that these constitute a difference in the *kind of employment*. The entire rationale of the majority boils down to this: that the '*mere circumstances*' that 'Bloomer Girl' was to be a musical review while 'Big Country' was a straight drama 'demonstrates the difference in kind' since a female lead in a western is not

---

[2]   This qualification of the rule seems to reflect the simple and humane attitude that it is too severe to demand of a person that he attempt to find and perform work for which he has no training or experience. Many of the older cases hold that one need not accept work in an inferior rank or position nor work which is more menial or arduous. This suggests that the rule may have had its origin in the bourgeois fear of resubmergence in lower economic classes.

'the equivalent of or substantially similar to' a lead in a musical. This is merely attempting to prove the proposition by repeating it. It shows that the vehicles for the display of the star's talents are different but it does not prove that her employment as a star in such vehicles is of necessity different in kind and either inferior or superior.

I believe that the approach taken by the majority (a superficial listing of differences with no attempt to assess their significance) may subvert a valuable legal doctrine.[5] The inquiry in cases such as this should not be whether differences between the two jobs exist (there will always be differences) but whether the differences which are present are substantial enough to constitute differences in the *kind* of employment or, alternatively, whether they render the substitute work employment of an *inferior kind.*

It seems to me that *this* inquiry involves, in the instant case at least, factual determinations which are improper on a motion for summary judgment. Resolving whether or not one job is substantially similar to another or whether, on the other hand, it is of a different or inferior kind, will often (as here) require a critical appraisal of the similarities and differences between them in light of the importance of these differences to the employee. This necessitates a weighing of the evidence, and it is precisely this undertaking which is forbidden on summary judgment. . . .

This is not to say that summary judgment would never be available in an action by an employee in which the employer raises the defense of failure to mitigate damages. No case has come to my attention, however, in which summary judgment has been granted on the issue of whether an employee was obliged to accept available alternate employment. Nevertheless, there may well be cases in which the substitute employment is so manifestly of a dissimilar or inferior sort, the declarations of the plaintiff so complete and those of the defendant so . . . inadequate that no factual issues exist for which a trial is required. This, however, is not such a case.

It is not intuitively obvious, to me at least, that the leading female role in a dramatic motion picture is a radically different endeavor from the leading female role in a musical comedy film. Nor is it plain to me that the rather qualified rights of director and screenplay approval contained in the first contract are highly significant matters either in the entertainment industry in general or to this plaintiff in particular. Certainly, none of the declarations introduced by plaintiff in support of her motion shed any light

---

[5] The values of the doctrine of mitigation of damages in this context are that it minimizes the unnecessary personal and social (e.g., nonproductive use of labor, litigation) costs of contractual failure. If a wrongfully discharged employee can, through his own action and without suffering financial or psychological loss in the process, reduce the damages accruing from the breach of contract, the most sensible policy is to require him to do so. I fear the majority opinion will encourage precisely opposite conduct.

on these issues. . . . Nor do they attempt to explain why she declined the offer of starring in 'Big Country, Big Man.' Nevertheless, the trial court granted the motion, declaring that these approval rights were 'critical' and that their elimination altered 'the essential nature of the employment.'. . .

I cannot accept the proposition that an offer which eliminates *any* contract right, regardless of its significance, is, as a matter of law, an offer of employment of an inferior kind. Such an absolute rule seems no more sensible than the majority's earlier suggestion that the mere existence of differences between two jobs is sufficient to render them employment of different kinds. Application of such per se rules will severely undermine the principle of mitigation of damages in the employer-employee context.

I remain convinced that the relevant question in such cases is whether or not a particular contract provision is so significant that its omission create employment of an inferior kind. This question is, of course, intimately bound up in what I consider the ultimate issue: whether or not the employee acted reasonably. This will generally involve a factual inquiry to ascertain the importance of the particular contract term and a process of weighing the absence of that term against the countervailing advantages of the alternate employment. In the typical case, this will mean that summary judgment must be withheld. . . .

NOTES AND QUESTIONS

1.   The dissent in *Parker* noted that the case was decided without a trial, meaning that as a matter of law "Big Country, Big Man" was an "inferior" offer of employment. Do you agree with this conclusion, or should a trial have been conducted?

2.   Note that "Bloomer Girl" was a musical that also contained social commentary. The plot of "Bloomer Girl" centers on Evelina Applegate, who comes of age during the turbulent period leading up to the U.S. Civil War in the 1860s. Evelina is the daughter of a skirt manufacturer who defies her father by wearing bloomers instead of skirts to assert her independence. Evelina is also an abolitionist and refuses to marry her suitor until he manumits his family's slaves. As noted in Mary Joe Frug, *Re-Reading Contracts: A Feminist Analysis of a Contracts Casebook*, 34 AM. U. L. REV. 1114 (1985), the musical "Bloomer Girl" dealt with gender, race, and cultural issues in a way that "Big Country, Big Man," a straight-up Western, simply could not address.

3.   How might a contrary result in *Parker* have affected the balance of power between star actors and movie studios in other situations? In other words, if a studio had the power to mitigate a contractual breach by substituting a different project of its choosing, could actors ever really have a "say" in which roles they were selecting?

E. STATED REMEDIES

Some contracts contain a provision stating (in advance) what will happen in the event that one of the parties breaches. We call these terms *stated damages, liquidated damages,* or *stipulated damages.* While many lay people believe that these stated remedies will be enforced exactly as written, that is a misconception. Before enforcing a stated damage provision, a court will analyze the provision to determine if it is punitive. As noted earlier, in contract law punitive measures are disfavored, especially if harsh or far out of line with the amount of money normally awarded as expectation damages.

If a court decides that the stated damages diverge too far from expectation damages and become punitive, then the court will call the provision a *penalty clause,* and deem it unenforceable. Any term in a contract that is called a "fine" or "penalty" may receive a hard look because of how it is denominated in the contract. In short, if a contract contains a stated damages clause, that is only the beginning of the analysis, rather than the end.

MULDOON V. LYNCH
6 P. 417 (Cal. 1885)

MYRICK, J.

The question involved in this appeal is whether a sum named in a contract as a forfeiture is to be regarded as liquidated damages or as a penalty. The plaintiffs and defendant executed a written contract, by which the plaintiffs were to furnish and complete certain improvements on the cemetery lot of defendant in a cemetery in San Francisco, viz., grading, brick-work, stone-work, monument, sarcophagus, etc., in which lot the remains of defendant's deceased husband had been interred. The monument was to be of the best article of hard Ravaccioni Italian marble. The amount to be paid for the whole was $18,788—four installments, of $1,725 each, to be paid as the work progressed to the point of being ready for the reception of the monument, and the balance, $11,887, on the completion of the whole. The contract contained the following clause:

> All the work, with the exception of monument, to be completed within four months from date of contract, and the balance in twelve months from the date of this contract, under forfeiture of ten dollars per day for each and every day beyond the stated time for completion.

The monument was procured in Italy, but was delayed nearly two years in reaching the point of destination for the following reason: The monument was of four large blocks of marble; one of them was of the weight of 20 tons. The marble was transported from the quarry to a sea-port in

Italy for shipment, and was there delayed waiting for a vessel. As one of the plaintiffs testified:

> We had to wait until we got a ship. We got the Ottilio. It was the first vessel that left there for two years for this port. Owing to the size of the blocks the only way to bring them here was by ships directly from Italy; the largest block would not have been allowed on a railroad car.

As soon as the marble reached San Francisco it was set up, and everything was according to the contract, without question being made, except as to the matter of time; that was the only point of controversy. The plaintiffs claim that defendant is indebted to them in the sum of $11,887, with interest from the day of the completion of the monument, and that the sum of $10 per day mentioned in the contract as a forfeiture is a penalty, and not matter of defense or setoff without proof of actual damage; while the defendant claims that the said sum of $10 per day is to be taken as liquidated damages, and, the same amounting to $7,820, is to be deducted from the sum of $11,887, leaving defendant indebted in the sum of $4,067 only.

There is no doubt that parties to a contract may agree upon the amount which shall constitute the damage for its breach. It is declared in section 3301, Civil Code, that "no damages can be recovered for a breach of contract which are not clearly ascertainable in both their nature and origin;" but section 1671 of the same Code declares that "the parties to a contract may agree therein upon an amount which shall be presumed to be the amount of damages sustained by a breach thereof, when, from the nature of the case, it would be impracticable, or extremely difficult, to fix the actual damage."

When parties have endeavored to contract with reference to damages—when they have explicitly declared that a sum named by them shall be taken as stipulated damages—it may be that such declaration would be taken as conclusive, and that courts would not attempt to relieve the losing party from his unfortunate or ill-advised engagement. But where it appears on the face of the contract that the sum named was intended by the parties to be considered as a penalty—a spur—courts will not enforce another construction, especially when the result would be the payment of a sum largely disproportionate to any reasonable idea of actual damage.

The contract reads, "under forfeiture of ten dollars per day for each and every day beyond the stated time for completion." The general rule is that damages are and ought to be purely compensatory; they should be commensurate with the injury, neither more nor less. There is nothing in this case to indicate that the defendant has suffered any actual damage which can be measured or compensated by money. It is true, she had the right to contract to have the monument erected in memory of her deceased husband, and to have it at a certain time; and possibly the agreement might have been so drawn that her disappointment should have received adequate compensation; but, referring to the words used by the parties, we are not prepared to say that either had thought of compensation as such. The word "forfeiture" is the equivalent of the word "penalty;" it imports a penalty. . . .

It has been held that in an agreement to convey land, and on default to pay a certain sum of money, or where the contractor agreed to do certain work, with a provision to pay a certain sum for each day's delay beyond the day fixed, or an agreement not to carry on a certain business at a named place, with a promise to pay a sum in case of violation of the agreement (Streeter v. Rush, 25 Cal. 67) if it appears that the parties intended the sum named to be considered liquidated damages, courts will not interfere with the contract, even if it might seem to have been an improvident agreement. But where it appears that the parties intended the sum named to be a forfeiture or penalty, it has been generally held that the party in whose favor the penalty or forfeiture exists must prove his damage.

In the case before us there is no claim of special damage. It might have been quite difficult for the defendant to show any damage of a pecuniary nature for the non-completion of the monument at the time specified, though its completion might have been of great comfort and consolation to her affectionate remembrance. . . .

[W]e are of opinion that the sum named is to be regarded as a penalty, and that the plaintiffs were entitled to recover the whole of the balance unpaid. [Affirmed.]

NOTES AND QUESTIONS

1.   What if the delay had been only ten days? In the court's analysis, what is the role of proportionality?

2.   Suppose the contract had not called the payment "forfeiture upon breach" but rather "compensation for breach." Same result?

3.   What interests did the delay implicate other than expectancy or reliance? Are interests such as comfort, consolation, or affectionate remembrance cognizable in contract remedies? *See Valentine v. General American Credit, Inc.*, 362 N.W.2d 628 (Michigan 1984).

4.   What are the policy concerns associated with liquidated damages clauses? On one hand, there is the contract doctrine of compensation damages and an associated aversion to penalties and forfeiture. On the other hand, there is the fundamental principle of freedom of contract and party autonomy. Which is the more compelling policy interest?

VANDERBILT UNIVERSITY V. DINARDO
174 F.3d 751 (6th Cir. 1999)

GIBSON, CIRCUIT JUDGE.

Gerry DiNardo resigned as Vanderbilt's head football coach to become the head football coach for Louisiana State University. As a result, Vanderbilt University brought this breach of contract action. The district court entered summary judgment for Vanderbilt, awarding $281,886.43 pursuant to a damage provision in DiNardo's employment contract with Vanderbilt. DiNardo appeals, arguing that the district court erred in concluding: (1) that the contract provision was an enforceable liquidated damage provision and not an unlawful penalty under Tennessee law; (2) that Vanderbilt did not waive its right to liquidated damages; (3) that the Addendum to the contract was enforceable; and (4) that the Addendum applied to the damage provision of the original contract. DiNardo also argues that there are disputed issues of material fact precluding summary judgment. We affirm the district court's ruling that the employment contract contained an enforceable liquidated damage provision and the award of liquidated damages under the original contract. We conclude, however, that there are genuine issues of material fact as to whether the Addendum was enforceable. We therefore reverse the judgment awarding liquidated damages under the Addendum and remand the case to the district court. . . .

On December 3, 1990, Vanderbilt and DiNardo executed an employment contract hiring DiNardo to be Vanderbilt's head football coach. Section one of the contract provided:

> The University hereby agrees to hire Mr. DiNardo for a period of five (5) years from the date hereof with Mr. DiNardo's assurance that he will serve the entire term of this Contract, a long-term commitment by Mr. DiNardo being important to the University's desire for a stable intercollegiate football program. . . .

The contract also contained reciprocal liquidated damage provisions. Vanderbilt agreed to pay DiNardo his remaining salary should Vanderbilt replace him as football coach, and DiNardo agreed to reimburse Vanderbilt should he leave before his contract expired. Section eight of the contract stated:

> Mr. DiNardo recognizes that his promise to work for the University for the entire term of this 5-year Contract is of the essence of this Contract to the University. Mr. DiNardo also recognizes that the University is making a highly valuable investment in his continued employment by entering into this Contract and its investment would be lost were he to resign or otherwise terminate his employment as Head Football Coach with

the University prior to the expiration of this Contract. Accordingly, Mr. DiNardo agrees that in the event he resigns or otherwise terminates his employment as Head Football Coach (as opposed to his resignation or termination from another position at the University to which he may have been reassigned), prior to the expiration of this Contract, and is employed or performing services for a person or institution other than the University, he will pay to the University as liquidated damages an amount equal to his Base Salary, less amounts that would otherwise be deducted or withheld from his Base Salary for income and social security tax purposes, multiplied by the number of years (or portion(s) thereof) remaining on the Contract.

During contract negotiations, section eight was modified at DiNardo's request so that damages would be calculated based on net, rather than gross, salary.

Vanderbilt initially set DiNardo's salary at $100,000 per year. DiNardo received salary increases in 1992, 1993, and 1994.

[We omit the court's ensuing discussion about whether the parties had extended the contract for another two years or not, which are not relevant to the legal issues discussed below.]

In November 1994, Louisiana State University contacted Vanderbilt in hopes of speaking with DiNardo about becoming the head football coach for L.S.U. Hoolahan gave DiNardo permission to speak to L.S.U. about the position. On December 12, 1994, DiNardo announced that he was accepting the L.S.U. position.

Vanderbilt sent a demand letter to DiNardo seeking payment of liquidated damages under section eight of the contract. Vanderbilt believed that DiNardo was liable for three years of his net salary: one year under the original contract and two years under the Addendum. DiNardo did not respond to Vanderbilt's demand for payment.

Vanderbilt brought this action against DiNardo for breach of contract. DiNardo removed the action to federal court, and both parties filed motions for summary judgment. The district court held that section eight was an enforceable liquidated damages provision, not an unlawful penalty, and that the damages provided under section eight were reasonable. . . .

DiNardo . . . claims that section eight of the contract is an unenforceable penalty under Tennessee law. DiNardo argues that the provision is not a liquidated damage provision but a "thinly disguised, overly broad non-compete provision," unenforceable under Tennessee law. . . .

Contracting parties may agree to the payment of liquidated damages in the event of a breach. See Beasley v. Horrell, 864 S.W.2d 45, 48

(Tenn.Ct.App.1993). The term "liquidated damages" refers to an amount determined by the parties to be just compensation for damages should a breach occur. See id. Courts will not enforce such a provision, however, if the stipulated amount constitutes a penalty. See id. A penalty is designed to coerce performance by punishing default. See id. In Tennessee, a provision will be considered one for liquidated damages, rather than a penalty, if it is reasonable in relation to the anticipated damages for breach, measured prospectively at the time the contract was entered into, and not grossly disproportionate to the actual damages. See Beasley, 864 S.W.2d at 48; Kimbrough & Co. v. Schmitt, 939 S.W.2d 105, 108 (Tenn.Ct.App.1996). When these conditions are met, particularly the first, the parties probably intended the provision to be for liquidated damages. However, any doubt as to the character of the contract provision will be resolved in favor of finding it a penalty. See Beasley, 864 S.W.2d at 48.

The district court held that the use of a formula based on DiNardo's salary to calculate liquidated damages was reasonable "given the nature of the unquantifiable damages in the case." 974 F.Supp. at 642. The court held that parties to a contract may include consequential damages and even damages not usually awarded by law in a liquidated damage provision provided that they were contemplated by the parties. . . . The court explained:

> The potential damage to [Vanderbilt] extends far beyond the cost of merely hiring a new head football coach. It is this uncertain potentiality that the parties sought to address by providing for a sum certain to apply towards anticipated expenses and losses. It is impossible to estimate how the loss of a head football coach will affect alumni relations, public support, football ticket sales, contributions, etc. . . . As such, to require a precise formula for calculating damages resulting from the breach of contract by a college head football coach would be tantamount to barring the parties from stipulating to liquidated damages evidence in advance.

Id. at 642.

DiNardo contends that there is no evidence that the parties contemplated that the potential damage from DiNardo's resignation would go beyond the cost of hiring a replacement coach. He argues that his salary has no relationship to Vanderbilt's damages and that the liquidated damage amount is unreasonable and shows that the parties did not intend the provision to be for liquidated damages.

DiNardo's theory of the parties' intent, however, does not square with the record. The contract language establishes that Vanderbilt wanted the five-year contract because "a long-term commitment" by DiNardo was "important to the University's desire for a stable intercollegiate football program," and that this commitment was of "essence" to the contract. Vanderbilt offered the two-year contract extension to DiNardo well over a year before his original contract expired. Both parties understood that the extension was to provide stability to the program, which helped in recruiting players and retaining assistant coaches. Thus, undisputed evidence, and reasonable inferences therefrom, establish that both parties understood and agreed that DiNardo's resignation would result in Vanderbilt suffering damage beyond the cost of hiring a replacement coach.

This evidence also refutes DiNardo's argument that the district court erred in presuming that DiNardo's resignation would necessarily cause damage to the University. That the University may actually benefit from a coaching change (as DiNardo suggests) matters little, as we measure the reasonableness of the liquidated damage provision at the time the parties entered the contract, not when the breach occurred, Kimbrough & Co., 939 S.W.2d at 108, and we hardly think the parties entered the contract anticipating that DiNardo's resignation would benefit Vanderbilt.

The stipulated damage amount is reasonable in relation to the amount of damages that could be expected to result from the breach. As we stated, the parties understood that Vanderbilt would suffer damage should DiNardo prematurely terminate his contract, and that these actual damages would be difficult to measure. See Kimbrough & Co., 939 S.W.2d at 108. . . .

. . . Vanderbilt hired DiNardo for a unique and specialized position, and the parties understood that the amount of damages could not be easily ascertained should a breach occur. Contrary to DiNardo's suggestion, Vanderbilt did not need to undertake an analysis to determine actual damages, and using the number of years left on the contract multiplied by the salary per year was a reasonable way to calculate damages considering the difficulty of ascertaining damages with certainty. See Kimbrough & Co., 939 S.W.2d at 108. The fact that liquidated damages declined each year DiNardo remained under contract, is directly tied to the parties' express understanding of the importance of a long-term commitment from DiNardo. Furthermore, the liquidated damages provision was reciprocal and the result of negotiations between two parties, each of whom was represented by counsel.

We also reject DiNardo's argument that a question of fact remains as to whether the parties intended section eight to be a "reasonable estimate" of damages. The liquidated damages are in line with Vanderbilt's estimate of its actual damages. See Kimbrough & Co., 939 S.W.2d at 108–09. Vanderbilt presented evidence that it incurred expenses associated with recruiting a new head coach of $27,000.00; moving expenses for the new coaching staff of $86,840; and a compensation difference between the coaching staffs of $184,311. The stipulated damages clause is reasonable under the circumstances, and we affirm the district court's conclusion that the liquidated damages clause is enforceable under Tennessee law. . . .

NELSON, C.J. (dissenting in part).

If section eight of the contract was designed primarily to quantify, in an objectively reasonable way, damages that the university could be expected to suffer in the event of a breach, such damages being difficult to measure in the absence of an agreed formula, the provision is enforceable as a legitimate liquidated damages clause. If section eight was designed primarily to punish Coach DiNardo for taking a job elsewhere, however, the provision is a penalty unenforceable under Tennessee law. My colleagues on the panel and I are in agreement, I believe, on both of these propositions. We disagree, however, as to section eight's primary function.

It seems to me that the provision was designed to function as a penalty, not as a liquidation of the university's damages. . . . My principal reasons for viewing section eight as a penalty are these: (1) although the damages flowing from a premature resignation would normally be the same whether or not Coach DiNardo took a job elsewhere, section eight does not purport to impose liability for liquidated damages unless the coach accepts another job; (2) the section eight formula incorporates other variables that bear little or no relation to any reasonable approximation of anticipated damages; and (3) there is no evidence that the parties were attempting, in section eight, to come up with a reasonable estimate of the university's probable loss if the coach left. I shall offer a few words of explanation on each of these points.

Section eight does not make Coach DiNardo liable for any liquidated damages at all, interestingly enough, unless, during the unexpired term of his contract, he "is employed or performing services for a person or institution other than the University. . . ." But how the coach spends his post-resignation time could not reasonably be expected to affect the university's damages; should the coach choose to quit in order to lie on a beach somewhere, the university would presumably suffer the same damages that it would suffer if he quit to coach for another school. The logical inference, therefore, would seem to be that section eight was intended to penalize the coach for taking another job, and was not intended to make the university whole by liquidating any damages suffered as a result of being left in the lurch.

This inference is strengthened, as I see it, by a couple of other anomalies in the stipulated damages formula. First, I am aware of no reason to believe that damages arising from the need to replace a prematurely departing coach could reasonably be expected to vary in direct proportion to the number of years left on the coach's contract. Section eight, however, provides that for every additional year remaining on the contract, the stipulated damages will go up by the full amount of the annual take-home pay contemplated under the contract. Like the "other employment" proviso, this makes the formula look more like a penalty than anything else.

Second, the use of a "take-home pay" measuring stick suggests that the function of the stick was to rap the coach's knuckles and not to measure the university's loss. Such factors as the number of tax exemptions claimed by the coach, or the percentage of his pay that he might elect to shelter in a 401(k) plan, would obviously bear no relation at all to the university's anticipated damages.

Finally, the record before us contains no evidence that the contracting parties gave any serious thought to attempting to measure the actual effect that a premature departure could be expected to have on the university's bottom line. On the contrary, the record affirmatively shows that the university did not attempt to determine whether the section eight formula would yield a result reasonably approximating anticipated damages. The record shows that the university could not explain how its anticipated damages might be affected by the coach's obtaining employment elsewhere, this being a subject that the draftsman of the contract testified he had never thought about. And the record shows that the question of why the number of years remaining on the contract would have any bearing on the amount of the university's damages was never analyzed either.

In truth and in fact, in my opinion, any correspondence between the result produced by the section eight formula and a reasonable approximation of anticipated damages would be purely coincidental. What section eight prescribes is a penalty, pure and simple, and a penalty may not be enforced under Tennessee law. On remand, therefore, in addition to instructing the district court to try the factual questions identified in Judge Gibson's opinion, I would instruct the court to determine the extent of any actual damages suffered by the university as a result of Coach DiNardo's breach of his contract. Whether more than the section eight figure or less, I believe, the university's actual damages should be the measure of its recovery. . . .

NOTES AND QUESTIONS

1.   Restatement (Second) of Contracts Section 356(1) clarifies several aspects of the stated damages doctrine: "Damages for breach by either party may be liquidated in the agreement but only at an amount that is reasonable in light of the anticipated or actual loss caused by the breach and the difficulties of proof of loss. A term fixing unreasonably large liquidated damages is unenforceable on grounds of public policy as a penalty."

2.   The judicial concern about compensation exhibits an aversion to penalties and forfeiture, meaning that judges police clauses that over-compensate. Is there any basis for judicial supervision of clauses that under-

compensate? For instance, the manufacturer and servicer of a burglar detection system proffers a clause limiting its liability for breach of the service contract to the monthly subscription fee, rather than covering losses due to burglary. The clause operates to under-compensate a store owner for loss upon servicer breach. Is it valid? Is it correct to classify such a limitation on liability as a liquidated damages clause? *See Samson Sales v. Honeywell*, 465 N.E.2d 392 (Ohio 1984).

3.   Earlier cases, and the Restatement (First), tested a clause's validity at the time of contract formation, asking whether the forecast of damages was reasonable. The Restatement (Second) follows the UCC in its more flexible approach that upholds clauses reasonable in light of what eventually happened. *See* UCC § 2–718(1). Is there some tension between the two prongs of the test—requiring a comparison to losses and some difficulty in proving losses? Might insisting on showing both the loss and the difficulty of proving loss constrain strategic incentives?

4.   Standard legal doctrine puts the burden on the opponent of a clause to show that a clause is not a reasonable forecast of actual damages (measured either prospectively or given the outcome) and that measuring the exact damages is not difficult. But consider another, less legalistic way, to evaluate the legitimacy of a liquidated damages clause, by asking whether the party proposing it has a rational business purpose for doing so.

EXAMPLE: SUMMER CAMP

Parents sign up their children for summer camp in Maine with the cost of $8,000. The camp rewards those who pay early with a discount and has a corresponding declining scale of refunds as the summer approaches. Anyone who enrolls before February 1 gets a price discount to $5,000 and must pay a $500 deposit. The cancellation schedule provides that those cancelling: (a) before February 1 are entitled to a full refund of the $500 deposit less a $25 processing fee; (b) between then and May 1 forfeits the full deposit; and (c) after May 1 surrenders the deposit and is liable for the full price.

On June 14, parents called the camp to inform them that their child would not be attending because the child had failed Spanish and therefore had to attend summer school. The camp apparently failed to adduce evidence showing that the arrangement was a reasonable forecast of actual damages or that actual damages were difficult to prove. *See Pacheco v. Scoblionko*, 532 A.2d 1036 (Me. 1987).

Do you agree with this result? Can you identify legitimate business reasons for the fee structure, such as the frequency of last-minute withdrawals from camp, staffing commitments, and allocations of camp capacity? Note also that the clause varied with the gravity of breach and consider what role such a feature should play in the analysis.

PROBLEM: EXECUTIVE COMPENSATION

A company executive signed a two-year employment agreement containing a severance clause stating that if the company breaches within that period it will pay the remaining salary due. Company breaches at a time when the remaining salary due is $75,000. The executive obtains another job paying a salary of $50,000 for the rest of the time period covered by the original contract. Consider the following questions:

1.   Are the substitute earnings probative of the clause's validity?

2.   Can the executive recover the entire $75,000 from the company?

3.   Suppose the substitute amount had been $150,000 instead of $50,000.

EXAMPLE: CELL PHONE TERMINATION FEES

The market for cell phones took off in the early 2000s, with mobile plans becoming ubiquitous. To keep the market growing, many cellular network providers tossed in incentives for new customers: when signing up for a plan, a new mobile phone was included. At least one-third of cell phone service customers signed up for these kinds of deals, which granted them a new phone to go along with a fixed period of service, usually lasting two years.

Built into the pricing of the contract, however, were early termination fees (ETFs). These fixed flat fees, ranging around $200, remained the same no matter when in the contract the customer terminated service. The networks justified ETFs by pointing to their need for customer continuity and upfront costs of phones. Customers were frustrated, however, at being "locked in" to a particular carrier if the cell service was sub-par. ETFs prompted numerous class-action lawsuits and investigations by state attorney generals.

Are the ETFs valid as reasonable liquidated damages, or are they unenforceable as a form of penalty clause?

PROBLEM: LESS CANDY, MORE FRUIT

Seller, Inc. produces a lemon-flavored hard candy that has achieved widespread popularity. Buyer, Corp. is a candy merchant that operates over fifty retail stores in Massachusetts and also is a substantial wholesaler to companies with vending machines in public school systems throughout the state. In 2003, Seller negotiated a valid signed three-year contract with Buyer for lemon-flavored hard candy under which Buyer obligated itself to purchase 1000 boxes monthly at $10.00 per box. For the first 24 months, all went well. Buyer ordered 1000 boxes per month and resold them both in its own stores and to the vending machine operators at a handsome profit.

While the first 24 months of the contract had gone well, that was about to change quite suddenly. At the beginning of the third year, the state superintendent of public schools unexpectedly issued a directive requiring all school districts to remove candy machines from their premises and replace them with machines selling fruit and nuts. Consequently, sales plummeted, and over the next six months, Buyer began to accumulate a surplus of lemon-flavored candies that it was forced to warehouse rather than market. In early June, Buyer asked Seller to relieve it of its obligations under the contract for the remaining six months. Seller declined to do so.

The Buyer/Seller contract contained the following provision in small print on the back of the document. "Should Buyer fail to take the agreed upon minimum quantity [1,000 boxes monthly for three years @ $10.00 per box], the parties agree that Seller shall be entitled to damages calculated on the difference between the amount actually paid by Buyer for purchases of the product and the total minimum price payable per month for the full period of this contract."

Buyer, believing it was no longer obligated to perform, informed Seller that it would not accept deliveries for the remaining six months of the contract. Seller responded that it had more of these candies than it could sell and was holding Buyer to its contract and the damages provision. Please analyze the contractual obligations (along with any damages) for Buyer and Seller.

F. SPECIFIC PERFORMANCE

Sometimes, aggrieved parties request the actual benefit of the bargain, a demand that the breaching party go through with a promise. Courts have been more receptive to such requests for specific performance when the contract involves the transfer of land, as each parcel of land is considered unique and irreplaceable. The notion of making a party go through with their deal is at first intuitively appealing, especially to those who believe that breaching a promise is morally problematic.

Specific performance, however, is considered an exceptional remedy, an alternative to the normal measure of paying monetary damages. One reason is that specific performance requires time and judicial resources to supervise compliance. In addition, in some instances specific performance would be too intrusive or invasive to a party's autonomy interests. This is especially true for contracts for personal services or contracts that take place over a period of time.

VAN WAGNER ADVERTISING CORP. V. S&M ENTERPRISES
492 N.E.2d 756 (N.Y. 1986)

KAYE, J.

Specific performance of a contract to lease "unique" billboard space is properly denied when damages are an adequate remedy to compensate the tenant and equitable relief would impose a disproportionate burden on the defaulting landlord. . . .

By agreement dated December 16, 1981, Barbara Michaels leased to plaintiff, Van Wagner Advertising, for an initial period of three years plus option periods totaling seven additional years space on the eastern exterior wall of a building on East 36th Street in Manhattan. Van Wagner was in the business of erecting and leasing billboards, and the parties anticipated that Van Wagner would erect a sign on the leased space, which faced an exit ramp of the Midtown Tunnel and was therefore visible to vehicles entering Manhattan from that tunnel.

In early 1982 Van Wagner erected an illuminated sign and leased it to Asch Advertising, Inc. for a three-year period commencing March 1, 1982. However, by agreement dated January 22, 1982, Michaels sold the building to defendant S & M Enterprises. Michaels informed Van Wagner of the sale in early August 1982, and on August 19, 1982 S & M sent Van Wagner a letter purporting to cancel the lease as of October 18 pursuant to section 1.05, which provided:

> Notwithstanding anything contained in the foregoing provisions to the contrary, Lessor (or its successor) may terminate and cancel this lease on not less than 60 days prior written notice in the event and only in the event of: (a) a bona fide sale of the building to a third party unrelated to Lessor.

Van Wagner abandoned the space under protest and in November 1982 commenced this action for declarations that the purported cancellation was ineffective and the lease still in existence, and for specific performance and damages.

In the litigation the parties differed sharply on the meaning of section 1.05 of the lease. Van Wagner contended that the lease granted a right to cancel only to the owner as it was about to sell the building—not to the new purchaser—so that the building could be conveyed without the encumbrance of the lease. S & M, in contrast, contended that the provision clearly gave it, as Michaels' successor by virtue of a bona fide sale, the right to cancel the lease on 60 days' notice. . . .

At a nonjury trial, both parties introduced parol evidence, in the form of testimony about negotiations, to explain the meaning of section 1.05. Additionally, one of S & M's two partners testified without contradiction that, having already acquired other real estate on the block, S & M purchased the subject building in 1982 for the ultimate purpose of demolishing existing buildings and constructing a mixed residential-commercial development. The project is to begin upon expiration of a lease of the subject building in 1987, if not sooner.

Trial Term concluded that Van Wagner's position on the issue of contract interpretation was correct, either because the lease provision unambiguously so provided or, if the provision were ambiguous, because the parol evidence showed that the "parties to the lease intended that only an owner making a bona fide sale could terminate the lease. They did not intend that once a sale had been made that any future purchaser could terminate the lease at will." Trial Term declared the lease "valid and subsisting" and found that the "demised space is unique as to location for the particular advertising purpose intended by Van Wagner and Michaels, the original parties to the Lease."

However, the court declined to order specific performance in light of its finding that Van Wagner "has an adequate remedy at law for damages". Moreover, the court noted that specific performance "would be inequitable in that its effect would be disproportionate in its harm to the defendant and its assistance to plaintiff." Concluding that "[t]he value of the unique qualities of the demised space has been fixed by the contract Van Wagner has with its advertising client, Asch for the period of the contract," the court awarded Van Wagner the lost revenues on the Asch sublease for the period through trial, without prejudice to a new action by Van Wagner for subsequent damages if S & M did not permit Van Wagner to reoccupy the space. On Van Wagner's motion to resettle the judgment to provide for specific performance, the court adhered to its judgment.

On cross appeals the Appellate Division affirmed, without opinion. We granted both parties leave to appeal.

Whether or not a contract provision is ambiguous is a question of law to be resolved by a court. . . . In our view, section 1.05 is ambiguous. Reasonable minds could differ as to whether the lease granted a purchaser of the property a right to cancel the lease, or limited that right to successive sellers of the property . . . However, Trial Term's alternate finding—that the parol evidence supported Van Wagner's interpretation of the provision—was one of fact. That finding, having been affirmed by the Appellate Division and having support in the record, is beyond the scope of our review . . . . Thus, S & M's cancellation of Van Wagner's lease constituted a breach of contract.

Given defendant's unexcused failure to perform its contract, we next turn to a consideration of remedy for the breach: Van Wagner seeks specific performance of the contract, S & M urges that money damages are adequate but that the amount of the award was improper.[2]

---

[2] We note that the parties' contentions regarding the remedy of specific performance in general, mirror a scholarly debate that has persisted throughout our judicial history, reflecting fundamentally divergent views about the quality of a bargained-for promise. While the usual remedy in Anglo-American law has been damages, rather than compensation "in kind" (see, Holmes, The Path of the Law, 10 Harv.L.Rev. 457, 462 [1897]; Holmes, The Common Law, at 299–301 [1881]; and Gilmore, The Death of Contract, at 14–15), the current trend among commentators appears to favor the remedy of specific performance (see, Farnsworth, Legal Remedies for Breach of Contract, 70 Colum.L.Rev. 1145, 1156 [1970]; Linzer, On the Amorality of Contract Remedies—Efficiency, Equity, and the Second Restatement, 81 Colum.L.Rev. 111 [1981]; and Schwartz, The Case for Specific Performance, 89 Yale L.J. 271 [1979]), but the view is not unanimous (see, Posner, Economic Analysis of Law § 4.9, at 89–90 [2d ed 1977]; Yorio, In Defense of Money Damages for Breach of Contract, 82 Colum.L.Rev. 1365 [1982]).

Whether or not to award specific performance is a decision that rests in the sound discretion of the trial court, and here that discretion was not abused. Considering first the nature of the transaction, specific performance has been imposed as the remedy for breach of contracts for the sale of real property . . . , but the contract here is to lease rather than sell an interest in real property. While specific performance is available, in appropriate circumstances, for breach of a commercial or residential lease, specific performance of real property leases is not in this State awarded as a matter of course. . . .

Van Wagner argues that specific performance must be granted in light of the trial court's finding that the "demised space is unique as to location for the particular advertising purpose intended". The word "uniqueness" is not, however, a magic door to specific performance. A distinction must be drawn between physical difference and economic interchangeability. The trial court found that the leased property is physically unique, but so is every parcel of real property and so are many consumer goods. Putting aside contracts for the sale of real property, where specific performance has traditionally been the remedy for breach, uniqueness in the sense of physical difference does not itself dictate the propriety of equitable relief.

By the same token, at some level all property may be interchangeable with money. . . . Even a rare manuscript has an economic substitute in that there is a price for which any purchaser would likely agree to give up a right to buy it, but a court would in all probability order specific performance of such a contract on the ground that the subject matter of the contract is unique.

The point at which breach of a contract will be redressable by specific performance thus must lie not in any inherent physical uniqueness of the property but instead in the uncertainty of valuing it . . . . [T]he fact that the subject of the contract may be "unique as to location for the particular advertising purpose intended" by the parties does not entitle a plaintiff to the remedy of specific performance.

Here, the trial court correctly concluded that the value of the "unique qualities" of the demised space could be fixed with reasonable certainty and without imposing an unacceptably high risk of undercompensating the injured tenant. Both parties complain: Van Wagner asserts that while lost revenues on the Asch contract may be adequate compensation, that contract expired February 28, 1985, its lease with S & M continues until 1992, and the value of the demised space cannot reasonably be fixed for the balance of the term. S & M urges that future rents and continuing damages are necessarily conjectural, both during and after the Asch contract, and that Van Wagner's damages must be limited to 60 days—the period during which Van Wagner could cancel Asch's contract without consequence in the event Van Wagner lost the demised space. S & M points out that Van

Wagner's lease could remain in effect for the full 10-year term, or it could legitimately be extinguished immediately, either in conjunction with a bona fide sale of the property by S & M, or by a reletting of the building if the new tenant required use of the billboard space for its own purposes. Both parties' contentions were properly rejected.

First, it is hardly novel in the law for damages to be projected into the future. Particularly where the value of commercial billboard space can be readily determined by comparisons with similar uses—Van Wagner itself has more than 400 leases—the value of this property between 1985 and 1992 cannot be regarded as speculative. Second, S & M having successfully resisted specific performance on the ground that there is an adequate remedy at law, cannot at the same time be heard to contend that damages beyond 60 days must be denied because they are conjectural. If damages for breach of this lease are indeed conjectural, and cannot be calculated with reasonable certainty, then S & M should be compelled to perform its contractual obligation by restoring Van Wagner to the premises.

Moreover, the contingencies to which S & M points do not, as a practical matter, render the calculation of damages speculative. While S & M could terminate the Van Wagner lease in the event of a sale of the building, this building has been sold only once in 40 years; S & M paid several million dollars, and purchased the building in connection with its plan for major development of the block. The theoretical termination right of a future tenant of the existing building also must be viewed in light of these circumstances. If any uncertainty is generated by the two contingencies, then the benefit of that doubt must go to Van Wagner and not the contract violator. Neither contingency allegedly affecting Van Wagner's continued contractual right to the space for the balance of the lease term is within its own control; on the contrary, both are in the interest of S & M . . . . Thus, neither the need to project into the future nor the contingencies allegedly affecting the length of Van Wagner's term render inadequate the remedy of damages for S & M's breach of its lease with Van Wagner.

The trial court, additionally, correctly concluded that specific performance should be denied on the ground that such relief "would be inequitable in that its effect would be disproportionate in its harm to defendant and its assistance to plaintiff" (see, Matter of Burke v. Bowen, 40 N.Y.2d 264, 267, 386 N.Y.S.2d 654, 353 N.E.2d 567; Cox v. City of New York, 265 N.Y. 411, 193 N.E. 251; Restatement [Second] of Contracts § 364 [1] [b]). It is well settled that the imposition of an equitable remedy must not itself work an inequity, and that specific performance should not be an undue hardship . . . . This conclusion is "not within the absolute discretion of the Supreme Court" (McClure v. Leaycraft, 183 N.Y. 36, 42, 75 N.E. 961; see, Trustees of Columbia Col. v. Thacher, 87 N.Y. 311; cf. Forstmann v. Joray Holding Co., 244 N.Y. 22, 154 N.E. 652). Here, however, there was no abuse of discretion; the finding that specific performance would disproportionately harm S & M and benefit Van Wagner has been affirmed by the Appellate Division and has support in the proof regarding S & M's projected development of the property.

While specific performance was properly denied, the court erred in its assessment of damages. . . . [T]he court fashioned relief for S & M's breach of contract only to the time of trial, and expressly contemplated that "[i]f defendant continues to exclude plaintiff from the leased space action for continuing damages may be brought." In requiring Van Wagner to bring a multiplicity of suits to recover its damages the court erred. Damages should have been awarded through the expiration of Van Wagner's lease.

Accordingly, the order of the Appellate Division should be modified, with costs to plaintiff, and the case remitted to Supreme Court, New York County, for further proceedings in accordance with this opinion and, as so modified, affirmed.

NOTES AND QUESTIONS

1. Examine the sources found in Footnote 2 of *Van Wagner*. Why are opinions so divided around the wisdom of specific performance as a remedy? What interests are at stake?

2. How does the court define "uniqueness"? What makes something "unique"?

3. Is the real problem here the difficulty of assigning a monetary value to objects or performances? Under the court's reasoning, if everything could be accurately and objectively valued, say by supercomputer artificial intelligence, would any rationale for specific performance exist? If not, would this legal world make sense to you? Does money strike you as a universally adequate remedy, if only we could value items or services accurately?

AMERICAN BROADCASTING COMPANIES V. WOLF
420 N.E.2d 363 (N.Y. 1981)

COOKE, C.J.

This case provides an interesting insight into the fierce competition in the television industry for popular performers and favorable ratings. It requires legal resolution of a rather novel employment imbroglio.

The issue is whether plaintiff American Broadcasting Companies, Incorporated (ABC), is entitled to equitable relief against defendant Warner Wolf, a New York City sportscaster, because of Wolf's breach of a good faith negotiation provision of a now expired broadcasting contract with ABC. In the present circumstances, it is concluded that the equitable relief sought by plaintiff—which would have the effect of forcing Wolf off the air—may not be granted. . . .

Warner Wolf, a sportscaster who has developed a rather colorful and unique on-the-air personality, had been employed by ABC since 1976. In February, 1978, ABC and Wolf entered into an employment agreement which, following exercise of renewal option, was to terminate on March 5, 1980. The contract contained a clause, known as a good-faith negotiation and first-refusal provision, that is at the crux of this litigation:

> You agree, if we so elect, during the last ninety (90) days prior to the expiration of the extended term of this agreement, to enter into good faith negotiations with us for the extension of this agreement on mutually agreeable terms. You further agree that for the first forty-five (45) days of this renegotiation period, you will not negotiate for your services with any other person or company other than WABC-TV or ABC. In the event we are unable to reach an agreement for an extension by the expiration of the extended term hereof, you agree that you will not accept, in any market for a period of three (3) months following expiration of the extended term of this agreement, any offer of employment as a sportscaster, sports news reporter, commentator, program host, or analyst in broadcasting (including television, cable television, pay television and radio) without first giving us, in writing, an opportunity to employ you on substantially similar terms and you agree to enter into an agreement with us on such terms.

Under this provision, Wolf was bound to negotiate in good faith with ABC for the 90-day period from December 6, 1979 through March 4, 1980. For the first 45 days, December 6 through January 19, the negotiation with ABC was to be exclusive. Following expiration of the 90-day negotiating period and the contract on March 5, 1980, Wolf was required, before *accepting* any other offer, to afford ABC a right of first refusal; he could comply with this provision either by refraining from accepting another offer or by first tendering the offer to ABC. The first-refusal period expired on June 3, 1980 and on June 4 Wolf was free to accept any job opportunity, without obligation to ABC.

Wolf first met with ABC executives in September, 1979 to discuss the terms of a renewal contract. Counterproposals were exchanged, and the parties agreed to finalize the matter by October 15. Meanwhile, unbeknownst to ABC, Wolf met with representatives of CBS in early October. Wolf related his employment requirements and also discussed the first refusal-good faith negotiation clause of his ABC contract. Wolf furnished CBS a copy of that portion of the ABC agreement. On October 12, ABC officials and Wolf met, but were unable to reach agreement on a renewal contract. A few days later, on October 16 Wolf again discussed employment possibilities with CBS.

Not until January 2, 1980 did ABC again contact Wolf. At that time, ABC expressed its willingness to meet substantially all of his demands. Wolf rejected the offer, however, citing ABC's delay in communicating with him and his desire to explore his options in light of the impending expiration of the 45-day exclusive negotiation period.

On February 1, 1980, after termination of that exclusive period, Wolf and CBS orally agreed on the terms of Wolf's employment as sportscaster for WCBS-TV, a CBS-owned affiliate in New York. During the next two days, CBS informed Wolf that it had prepared two agreements and divided his annual compensation between the two: one covered his services as an on-the-air sportscaster, and the other was an off-the-air production agreement for sports specials Wolf was to produce. The production agreement contained an exclusivity clause which barred Wolf from performing "services of any nature for" or permitting the use of his "name, likeness, voice or endorsement by, any person, firm or corporation" during the term of the agreement, unless CBS consented. The contract had an effective date of March 6, 1980.

Wolf signed the CBS production agreement on February 4, 1980. At the same time, CBS agreed in writing, in consideration of $100 received from Wolf, to hold open an offer of employment to Wolf as sportscaster until June 4, 1980, the date on which Wolf became free from ABC's right of first refusal. The next day, February 5, Wolf submitted a letter of resignation to ABC.

Representatives of ABC met with Wolf on February 6 and made various offers and promises that Wolf rejected. Wolf informed ABC that they had delayed negotiations with him and downgraded his worth. He stated he had no future with the company. He told the officials he had made a "gentlemen's agreement" and would leave ABC on March 5. Later in February, Wolf and ABC agreed that Wolf would continue to appear on the air during a portion of the first-refusal period, from March 6 until May 28. . . .

ABC commenced this action on May 6, 1980, by which time Wolf's move to CBS had become public knowledge. The complaint alleged that Wolf, induced by CBS breached both the good-faith negotiation and first-refusal provisions of his contract with ABC. ABC sought specific enforcement of its right of first refusal and an injunction against Wolf's employment as a sportscaster with CBS.

After a trial, Supreme Court found no breach of the contract, and went on to note that, in any event, equitable relief would be inappropriate. A divided Appellate Division, while concluding that Wolf had breached both the good-faith negotiation and first-refusal provisions, nonetheless affirmed on the ground that equitable intervention was unwarranted. There should be an affirmance.

[We] agree with the Appellate Division that defendant Wolf breached his obligation to negotiate in good faith with ABC from December, 1979 through March, 1980. When Wolf signed the production agreement with CBS on February 4, 1980, he obligated himself not to render services "of any nature" to any person, firm or corporation on and after March 6, 1980. Quite simply, then, beginning on February 4 Wolf was unable to extend his contract with ABC; his contract with CBS precluded him from legally serving ABC in any capacity after March 5. Given Wolf's existing obligation to CBS, any negotiations he engaged in with ABC, without the consent of CBS, after February 4 were meaningless and could not have been in good faith.

At the same time, there is no basis in the record for the Appellate Division's conclusion that Wolf violated the first-refusal provision by entering into an oral sportscasting contract with CBS on February 4. The first-refusal provision required Wolf, for a period of 90 days after termination of the ABC agreement, either to refrain from accepting an offer of employment or to first submit the offer to ABC for its consideration. By its own terms, the right of first refusal did not apply to offers accepted by Wolf prior to the March 5 termination of the ABC employment contract. It is apparent, therefore, that Wolf could not have breached the right of first refusal by accepting an offer during the term of his employment with ABC. . . . Rather, his conduct violates only the good-faith negotiation clause of the contract. The question is whether this breach entitled ABC to injunctive relief that would bar Wolf from continued employment at CBS. . . . To resolve this issue, it is necessary to trace the principles of specific performance applicable to personal service contracts. . . .

Courts of equity historically have refused to order an individual to perform a contract for personal services . . . . Originally this rule evolved because of the inherent difficulties courts would encounter in supervising the performance of uniquely personal efforts.[4] . . . During the Civil War era, there emerged a more compelling reason for not directing the performance of personal services: the Thirteenth Amendment's prohibition of involuntary servitude. It has been strongly suggested that judicial compulsion of services would violate the express command of that

---

[4] The New York Court of Chancery in De Rivafinoli v. Corsetti (4 Paige Chs. 264, 270) eloquently articulated the traditional rationale for refusing affirmative enforcement of personal service contracts: "I am not aware that any officer of this court has that perfect knowledge of the Italian language, or possesses that exquisite sensibility in the auricular nerve which is necessary to understand, and to enjoy with a proper zest, the peculiar beauties of the Italian opera, so fascinating to the fashionable world. There might be some difficulty, therefore, even if the defendant was compelled to sing under the direction and in the presence of a master in chancery, in ascertaining whether he performed his engagement according to its spirit and intent. It would also be very difficult for the master to determine what effect coercion might produce upon the defendant's singing, especially in the livelier airs; although the fear of imprisonment would unquestionably deepen his seriousness in the graver parts of the drama. But one thing at least is certain; his songs will be neither comic, or even semi-serious, while he remains confined in that dismal cage, the debtor's prison of New York."

amendment . . . . For practical, policy and constitutional reasons, therefore, courts continue to decline to affirmatively enforce employment contracts.

Over the years, however, in certain narrowly tailored situations, the law fashioned other remedies for failure to perform an employment agreement. Thus, where an employee refuses to render services to an employer in violation of an existing contract, and the services are unique or extraordinary, an injunction may issue to prevent the employee from furnishing those services to another person for the duration of the contract (see, e. g., Shubert Theatrical Co. v. Gallagher, 206 App.Div. 514, 201 N.Y.S. 577). Such "negative enforcement" was initially available only when the employee had expressly stipulated not to compete with the employer for the term of the engagement (see, e.g., Lumley v. Wagner, 1 De G.M.&G. 604, 42 Eng.Rep. 687; Shubert Theatrical Co. v. Rath, 271 F. 827, 830–833; 4 Pomeroy, Equity Jurisprudence [5th ed.], § 1343, at p. 944). Later cases permitted injunctive relief where the circumstances justified implication of a negative covenant (see, e. g., Montague v. Flockton, L.R. 16 Eq. 189 [1873], 4 Pomeroy, Equity Jurisprudence [5th ed.], § 1343; 5A Corbin, Contracts, § 1205). In these situations, an injunction is warranted because the employee either expressly or by clear implication agreed not to work elsewhere for the period of his contract. And, since the services must be unique before negative enforcement will be granted, irreparable harm will befall the employer should the employee be permitted to labor for a competitor . . . .

After a personal service contract terminates, the availability of equitable relief against the former employee diminishes appreciably. Since the period of service has expired, it is impossible to decree affirmative or negative specific performance. Only if the employee has expressly agreed not to compete with the employer following the term of the contract, or is threatening to disclose trade secrets or commit another tortious act, is injunctive relief generally available at the behest of the employer . . . . Even where there is an express anticompetitive covenant, however, it will be rigorously examined and specifically enforced only if it satisfies certain established requirements . . . . Indeed, a court normally will not decree specific enforcement of an employee's anticompetitive covenant unless necessary to protect the trade secrets, customer lists or good will of the employer's business, or perhaps when the employer is exposed to special harm because of the unique nature of the employee's services . . . . And, an otherwise valid covenant will not be enforced if it is unreasonable in time, space or scope or would operate in a harsh or oppressive manner . . . . There is, in short, general judicial disfavor of anticompetitive covenants contained in employment contracts . . . .

Underlying the strict approach to enforcement of these covenants is the notion that, once the term of an employment agreement has expired, the general public policy favoring robust and uninhibited competition should not give way merely because a particular employer wishes to insulate himself from competition. . . . Important, too, are the "powerful considerations of public policy which militate against sanctioning the loss of a man's livelihood" (Purchasing Assoc. v. Weitz, 13 N.Y.2d at p. 272, 246 N.Y.S.2d 600, 196 N.E.2d 245, . . .). At the same time, the employer is entitled to protection from unfair or illegal conduct that causes economic injury. The rules governing enforcement of anticompetitive covenants and the availability of equitable relief after termination of employment are designed to foster these interests of the employer without impairing the employee's ability to earn a living or the general competitive mold of society. . . .

Specific enforcement of personal service contracts thus turns initially upon whether the term of employment has expired. If the employee refuses to perform during the period of employment, was furnishing unique services, has expressly or by clear implication agreed not to compete for the duration of the contract and the employer is exposed to irreparable injury, it may be appropriate to restrain the employee from competing until the agreement expires. Once the employment contract has terminated, by contrast, equitable relief is potentially available only to prevent injury from unfair competition or similar tortious behavior or to enforce an express and valid anticompetitive covenant. In the absence of such circumstances, the general policy of unfettered competition should prevail. . . .

Applying these principles, it is apparent that ABC's request for injunctive relief must fail. There is no existing employment agreement between the parties; the original contract terminated in March, 1980. Thus, the negative enforcement that might be appropriate during the term of employment is unwarranted here. Nor is there an express anticompetitive covenant that defendant Wolf is violating, or any claim of special injury from tortious conduct such as exploitation of trade secrets. In short, ABC seeks to premise equitable relief after termination of the employment upon a simple, albeit serious, breach of a general contract negotiation clause. . . . To grant an injunction in that situation would be to unduly interfere with an individual's livelihood and to inhibit free competition where there is no corresponding injury to the employer other than the loss of a competitive edge. Indeed, if relief were granted here, any breach of an employment contract provision relating to renewal negotiations logically would serve as the basis for an open-ended restraint upon the employee's ability to earn a living should he ultimately choose not to extend his employment. . . . Our public policy, which favors the free exchange of goods and services through established market mechanisms, dictates otherwise.

Equally unavailing is ABC's request that the court create a noncompetitive covenant by implication. Although in a proper case an implied-in-fact covenant not to compete for the term of employment may be found to exist, anticompetitive covenants covering the postemployment period will not be implied. Indeed, even an express covenant will be scrutinized and enforced only in accordance with established principles.

This is not to say that ABC has not been damaged in some fashion or that Wolf should escape responsibility for the breach of his good-faith negotiation obligation.[10] Rather, we merely conclude that ABC is not entitled to equitable relief. Because of the unique circumstances presented, however, this decision is without prejudice to ABC's right to pursue relief in the form of monetary damages, if it be so advised. . . . [Affirmed.]

FUCHSBERG, J. (dissenting).

I agree with all the members of this court, as had all the Justices at the Appellate Division, that the defendant Wolf breached his undisputed obligation to negotiate in good faith for renewal of his contract with ABC. Where we part company is in the majority's unwillingness to mold an equitable decree, even one more limited than the harsh one the plaintiff proposed, to right the wrong.

Central to the disposition of this case is the first-refusal provision. Its terms are worth recounting. They plainly provide that, in the 90-day period immediately succeeding the termination of his ABC contract, before Wolf could accept a position as sportscaster with another company, he first had to afford ABC the opportunity to engage him on like terms. True, he was not required to entertain offers, whether from ABC or anyone else, during that period. In that event he, of course, would be off the air for that 90 days, during which ABC could attempt to orient its listeners from Wolf to his successor. On the other hand, if Wolf wished to continue to broadcast actively during the 90 days, ABC's right of first refusal put it in a position to make sure that Wolf was not doing so for a competitor. One way or the other, however labeled, the total effect of the first refusal agreement was that of an express conditional covenant under which Wolf could be restricted from appearing on the air other than for ABC for the 90-day posttermination period.

One need not be in the broadcasting business to understand that the restriction ABC bargained for, and Wolf granted, when they entered into the original employment contract was not inconsequential. The earnings of broadcasting companies are directly related to the "ratings" they receive. This, in turn, is at least in part dependent on the popularity of personalities

---

[10] It should be noted that the dissenter would ground relief upon the first-refusal clause, a provision of the contract that defendant did not breach. The dissenting opinion fails to specify why the first-refusal clause—or for that matter any other provision of the contract that defendant did not breach—is relevant in [determining] the availability of equitable relief. And, while the dissent correctly noted the flexibility of equitable remedies, this does not mean that courts of equity totally dispense with governing rules. Our analysis of the relevant principles, guided by important underlying policy considerations, reveals that this case falls well beyond the realm where equitable intervention would be permissible.

like Wolf. It therefore was to ABC's advantage, once Wolf came into its employ, especially since he was new to the New York market, that it enhance his popularity by featuring, advertising and otherwise promoting him. This meant that the loyalty of at least part of the station's listening audience would become identified with Wolf, thus enhancing his potential value to competitors, as witness the fact that, in place of the $250,000 . . . he was receiving during his last year with ABC, he was able to command $400,000 to $450,000 per annum in his CBS "deal". A reasonable opportunity during which ABC could cope with such an assault on its good will had to be behind the clause in question.

Moreover, it is undisputed that, when in late February Wolf executed the contract for an extension of employment during the 90-day hiatus for which the parties had bargained, ABC had every right to expect that Wolf had not already committed himself to an exclusivity provision in a producer's contract with CBS in violation of the good-faith negotiation clause . . . . Surely, had ABC been aware of this gross breach, had it not been duped into giving an uninformed consent, it would not have agreed to serve as a self-destructive vehicle for the further enhancement of Wolf's potential for taking his ABC-earned following with him.

In the face of these considerations, the majority rationalizes its position of powerlessness to grant equitable relief by choosing to interpret the contract as though there were no restrictive covenant, express or implied. However, as demonstrated, there is, in fact, an express three-month negative covenant which, because of Wolf's misconduct, ABC was effectively denied the opportunity to exercise. Enforcement of this covenant, by enjoining Wolf from broadcasting for a three-month period, would depart from no entrenched legal precedent. Rather, it would accord with equity's boasted flexibility . . . .

NOTES AND QUESTIONS

1.   The history of forced labor is a long and shameful one. In modern times, discussion seems to focus more on the issue of enforcing a negative covenant (a promise not to do something otherwise permitted), rather than forcing someone to work against his or her will. What policy concerns arise with a negative covenant? Explicit negative covenants are embodied in covenants not to compete. Some have questioned the wisdom of enforcing such provisions from a policy perspective.

At one time, such covenants were illegal bargains in restraint of trade and courts refused to enforce them. In the modern era, courts scrutinize them for reasonableness in scope, in terms of job type, geography, and duration. States take different approaches upon the identification of impermissible clauses, some invalidating the contract, others excising the objectionable portions, and yet others rewriting the terms to render them reasonable. Some states make such covenants enforceable only if the employee is paid additional consideration for signing the agreement. Why might additional consideration be an important factor in a court's analysis of enforceability?

2.   Non-compete clauses can prevent workers from earning a livelihood, and research suggests that they may be harmful overall for a region's economy. Professor Alan Hyde compares the economy and employment laws in Boston, Massachusetts to Silicon Valley in California. Hyde suggests that Silicon Valley's enormous economic growth is due in part to California's statutory prohibition on non-competition clauses. Hyde believes that this difference is crucial, leading to more business opportunities for workers in California. ALAN HYDE, WORKING IN SILICON VALLEY: ECONOMIC AND LEGAL ANALYSIS OF A HIGH-VELOCITY LABOR MARKET (2003). If your client wanted to include a non-competition clause in a contract with a worker who was a California resident, how would you have to advise the client?

3.   The majority opinion in *ABC v. Wolf* cites *Lumley v. Wagner*, a classic opinion on equitable remedies for breach of a personal services contract. In *Lumley*, a noted opera singer, Johanna Wagner, contracted with Benjamin Lumley to sing exclusively at Her Majesty's Theatre on designated nights during the 1852 season. A rival theater manager, Frederick Gye of the Covent Garden Theatre, offered Wagner more money to breach and sing at his theater. Wagner breached the contract and Lumley sued for specific performance. The court found breach but declined to grant specific performance. An order to sing at Her Majesty's Theatre would be difficult to supervise—tonal quality, color of the voice, vocal technique—so the court fashioned another remedy. It enjoined Wagner from performing elsewhere. Explained the court: "the injunction may . . . tend to the fulfilment of her engagement; though, in continuing the injunction, I disclaim doing indirectly what I cannot do directly." Separately, Lumley won a judgment against Gye for tortious interference with contract, a topic we consider in Chapter Eleven. *Lumley v. Gye*, 2 El. & Bl. 216 (1853).

4.   The difficulty of judicial supervision remains an important rationale for denying requests for specific performance in certain cases, such as the construction contract in the following case.

NORTHERN DELAWARE INDUSTRIAL V. E. W. BLISS CO.

245 A.2d 431 (Del. Ch. 1968)

MARVEL, VICE CHANCELLOR.

Plaintiffs and defendant are parties to a contract dated May 26th, 1966, under the terms of which defendant agreed to furnish all labor, services, materials and equipment necessary to expand and modernize a steel fabricating plant owned by the plaintiff Phoenix Steel Corporation at Claymont, Delaware. A massive undertaking is called for in the contract, the total price for the work to be performed by the defendant being set in the contract at $27,500,000 and the area of contract performance extending over a plant site of approximately sixty acres.

Work on the project has not progressed as rapidly as contemplated in the contract and what plaintiffs now seek is an order compelling defendant to requisition 300 more workmen for a night shift, thus requiring defendant to put on the job, as it allegedly contracted to do, the number of men required to make up a full second shift at the Phoenix plant site during the period when one of the Phoenix mills must be shut down in order that its modernization may be carried out under the contract. And while the present record is sparse, there seems to be no doubt but that defendant has fallen behind the work completion schedules set forth in such contract. What plaintiffs apparently seek is a speeding up of work at the site by means of a court-ordered requisitioning by defendant of more laborers.

The basis for plaintiffs' application for equitable relief is found in a work proposal made by defendant's prime subcontractor . . . to the Bliss Company, the terms of which are made part of the contract between plaintiffs and defendant. Such proposal stipulates inter alia:

> T. Working Schedule. All work is quoted on a normal 40 hour basis-5 days per week except for necessary service tie-ins. The only additional premium time included is that required during the shut-down of #1 mill when two turn-week work is contemplated.

According to plaintiffs, the phrase 'two turn-week work' is a term used in the steel industry to designate the employment of day and night shifts over a full seven day work week, and defendant does not deny this. Plaintiffs therefor reason that inasmuch as at or about the time of the filing of the complaint defendant was operating one shift at the site ranging in size from 192 to 337 workers per day, whereas paragraph 'T' above referred to contemplates two daily shifts, that they are entitled to a court order directing defendant to employ not less than 300 construction workers on each of two shifts, seven days per week. Plaintiffs seek other relief, including damages, but consideration of such other requested relief will be deferred for the present. Defendants earlier moved for dismissal or a stay [because] the parties are allegedly contractually bound to arbitrate their differences.

However, the sole matter now for decision is a question raised by the Court at argument on defendant's motion, namely whether or not this Court should exercise its jurisdiction to grant plaintiffs' application for an order for specific performance of an alleged contractual right to have more workers placed on the massive construction project here involved, and order the requisitioning of 300 workers for a night shift, this being the number of laborers deemed by plaintiffs to be appropriate properly to bring about prompt completion of the job at hand.

On the basis of the record before me, viewed in the light of the applicable law, I am satisfied that this Court should not, as a result of granting plaintiffs' prayer for specific performance of an alleged term of a building contract, become committed to supervising the carrying out of a massive, complex, and unfinished construction contract, a result which would necessarily follow as a consequence of ordering defendant to requisition laborers as prayed for, 13 Am.Jur.2nd, Building and Construction Contracts, § 112. Parenthetically, it is noted that if such laborers are in fact available (which appears not to be the case), their presence at the Claymont site might well impede rather than advance the orderly completion of the steel mill renovation work now under way.

It is not that a court of equity is without jurisdiction in a proper case to order the completion of an expressly designed and largely completed construction project, particularly where the undertaking to construct is tied in with a contract for the sale of land and the construction in question is largely finished, *Valley Builders, Inc. v. Stein*, 41 Del.Ch. 259, 193 A.2d 793, and *Lee Builders v. Wells*, 33 Del.Ch. 315, 92 A.2d 710, *rev'd on other grounds*, 34 Del.Ch. 107, 99 A.2d 620. Furthermore, this is not a case which calls for a building plan so precisely definite as to make compliance therewith subject to effective judicial supervision, *Wilmont Homes, Inc. v. Weiler*, 42 Del.Ch. 8, 202 A.2d 576, but rather an attempt to have the Court as the result of ordering a builder to speed up general work by hiring a night shift of employees (a proposal which was merely 'contemplated' by the subcontractor . . .) to become deeply involved in supervision of a complex construction project located on plaintiffs' property.

The point is that a court of equity should not order specific performance of any building contract in a situation in which it would be impractical to carry out such an order, *Jones v. Parker*, 163 Mass. 564, 40 N.E. 1044, and Restatement, Contracts § 371, unless there are special circumstances or the public interest is directly involved. In the case of *City Stores v. American* (D.C.D.C.) 266 F.Supp. 766, which plaintiffs cite to support their application, specific performance was sought of an agreement which contemplated that plaintiff would become a tenant in a designated section of a shopping center to be constructed by defendant. The plans for such center were quite definite and the court was obviously impressed by the fact that unless the relief sought were to be granted, plaintiff would lose out on a promised opportunity to share in the expected profits of a shopping center located in a burgeoning North Virginia suburb. The ruling while perhaps correct under the circumstances of the case has no application here.

I conclude that to grant specific performance, as prayed for by plaintiffs, would be inappropriate in view of the imprecision of the contract provision relied upon and the impracticability if not impossibility of effective enforcement by the Court of a mandatory order designed to keep a specific number of men on the job at the site of a steel mill which is undergoing extensive modernization and expansion. If plaintiffs have sustained loss as a result of actionable building delays on defendant's part at the Phoenix plant at Claymont, they may, at an appropriate time, resort to law for a fixing of their claimed damages. . . .

ON REARGUMENT. . . . In their motion for reargument plaintiffs argue that what they actually seek is not an order which would make the Court the supervisor of a vast building project but rather one directing the performance of a ministerial act, namely the hiring by defendant of more workers. Plaintiffs also contend that they should have an opportunity to supplement the record for the purpose of demonstrating that construction labor is available in the area as well as establishing that perhaps fewer than 300 additional workers could adequately insure defendant's performance of the contract here in issue. These contention, if factually sustainable, do not, of course, affect the Court's power to decline to exercise its jurisdiction to order specific performance of a construction contract.

Plaintiffs, in seeking specific performance of what they now term defendant's ministerial duty to hire a substantial number of additional laborers, run afoul of the well-established principle that performance of a contract for personal services, even of a unique nature, will not be affirmatively and directly enforced, *Lumley v. Wagner*, 1 De G.M. & G. 404. This is so, because, as in the closely analogous case of a construction contract, the difficulties involved in compelling performance are such as to make an order for specific performance impractical. . . .

NOTES AND QUESTIONS

1.   What difficulties is the *Northern Delaware* court referring to that makes an order of specific performance "impractical"?

2.   Of the contracts cases you have read where money damages would be inadequate to warrant specific performance, which would pose such difficulties to render specific performance impractical? Might a judge enlist experts in the field to mitigate such difficulties?

3.   Despite perceived difficulties of judicial supervision of decrees granting specific performance, courts have on important occasions ordered far-reaching, ongoing, and systemic remedies for large-scale injustices. Consider, for example, court supervision of school desegregation orders or to remediate appalling conditions in prisons. *See, e.g.*, *Jenkins v. Missouri*, 807 F.2d 657 (8th Cir. 1986) (en banc) (overseeing opening of magnet schools in Kansas City as well as directing for tax increase to pay for school desegregation); *Brown v. Plata*, 563 U.S. 493 (2011) (court supervision to reduce prison overcrowding).

IN RE IBP, INC. SHAREHOLDERS LITIGATION
789 A.2d 14 (Del. Ch. 2001)

[Tyson Foods, a large purveyor of poultry, wanted to acquire IBP, a large purveyor of pork, and to assure that its rival, Smithfield Foods, another large pork producer, from doing so. After an intense auction with escalating bids, Tyson outbid Smithfield, agreeing to pay more than $3 billion, at $30 per share, to IBP stockholders. It would pay shareholders using a combination of cash and stock in the merged company. The Merger Agreement, signed January 1, 2001, permitted Tyson to terminate if a "material adverse change" in IBP's business occurred between the time of signing the contract and completing all the required steps to complete the merger, which would take several months. Tyson subsequently argued that such a "material adverse change" had occurred and sought to terminate. IBP successfully objected to Tyson's assertion, meaning Tyson was in breach of contract. IBP sought specific performance; Tyson preferred to pay cash, the standard remedy for breach of contract.]

STRINE, CHANCELLOR.

Having determined that the Merger Agreement is a valid and enforceable contract that Tyson had no right to terminate, I now turn to the question of whether the Merger Agreement should be enforced by an order of specific performance. Although Tyson's voluminous post-trial briefs argue the merits fully, its briefs fail to argue that a remedy of specific performance is unwarranted in the event that its position on the merits is rejected.

This gap in the briefing is troubling. A compulsory order will require a merger of two public companies with thousands of employees working at facilities that are important to the communities in which they operate. The impact of a forced merger on constituencies beyond the stockholders and top managers of IBP and Tyson weighs heavily on my mind. The prosperity of IBP and Tyson means a great deal to these constituencies. I therefore approach this remedial issue quite cautiously and mindful of the interests of those who will be affected by my decision.

I start with a fundamental question: is this is a truly unique opportunity that cannot be adequately monetized? If the tables were turned and Tyson was seeking to enforce the contract, a great deal of precedent would indicate that the contract should be specifically enforced. In the more typical situation, an acquiror argues that it cannot be made whole unless it can specifically enforce the acquisition agreement, because the target company is unique and will yield value of an unquantifiable nature, once combined with the acquiring company. In this case, the sell-side of the transaction is able to make the same argument, because the Merger Agreement provides the IBP stockholders with a choice of cash or Tyson stock, or a combination of both. Through this choice, the IBP stockholders were offered a chance to share in the upside of what was touted by Tyson as a unique, synergistic combination. This court has not found, and Tyson has not advanced, any compelling reason why sellers in mergers and acquisitions transactions should have less of a right to demand specific performance than buyers, and none has independently come to my mind.

In addition, the determination of a cash damages award will be very difficult in this case. And the amount of any award could be staggeringly large. No doubt the parties would haggle over huge valuation questions, which (Tyson no doubt would argue) must take into account the possibility of a further auction for IBP or other business developments. A damages award can, of course, be shaped; it simply will lack any pretense to precision. An award of specific performance will, I anticipate, entirely eliminate the need for a speculative determination of damages. . . .

Finally, there is no doubt that a remedy of specific performance is practicable. Tyson itself admits that the combination still makes strategic sense. At trial, [a senior Tyson executive] John Tyson was asked by his own counsel to testify about whether it was fair that Tyson should enter any later auction for IBP . . . . This testimony indicates that Tyson Foods is still interested in purchasing IBP, but wants to get its original purchase price back and then buy IBP off the day-old goods table. I consider John Tyson's testimony an admission of the feasibility of specific performance. . . .

Probably the concern that weighs heaviest on my mind is whether specific performance is the right remedy in view of the harsh words that have been said in the course of this litigation. Can these management teams work together? The answer is that I do not know. [Some of the executives involved testified that they can.] I am not convinced, although Tyson's top executives continue to respect the managerial acumen of [those senior executives], if not that of their financial subordinates.

What persuades me that specific performance is a workable remedy is that Tyson will have the power to decide all the key management questions itself. It can therefore hand-pick its own management team. While this may be unpleasant for the top level IBP managers who might be replaced, it was a possible risk of the Merger from the get-go and a reality of today's M & A market.

The impact on other constituencies of this ruling also seems tolerable. Tyson's own investment banker thinks the transaction makes sense for Tyson, and is still fairly priced at $30 per share. One would think the Tyson constituencies would be better served on the whole by a specific performance remedy, rather than a large damages award that did nothing but cost Tyson a large amount of money.

In view of these factors, I am persuaded that an award of specific performance is appropriate, regardless of what level of showing was required by IBP. That is, there is clear and convincing evidence to support this award. Such an award is decisively preferable to a vague and imprecise damages remedy that cannot adequately remedy the injury to IBP's stockholders. . . .

NOTES AND QUESTIONS

1.   The Delaware Chancery Court is among the most sophisticated commercial courts, with a special expertise in corporate law, including an expertise around corporate merger agreements. The Chancellor in IBP obviously struggles with this vexing fact pattern. The doctrinal review reflects settled law and the discretionary factors a clear-eyed view of both the limits of money damages as well as the hazards and prospects of specific performance.

2.   Remedies for breach of merger agreements are often stated in the contract. Many include express termination fees, often called break-up fees, akin to liquidated damages clauses for the corporate context. Such clauses often state that specific performance is unavailable.

3.   The Delaware Chancery Court declined to order specific performance of a merger agreement whose remedy provisions were ambiguous, but where evidence showed that the defendant understood that it barred specific performance and the plaintiff knew or should have known of that understanding. *United Rental v. RAM Holdings, Inc.*, 937 A.2d 810, 813 (Del. Ch. 2007).

4.   In another case, the court ordered specific performance of various contractual covenants and duties expressed in the merger agreement but declined to order a buyer to consummate the merger. *Hexicon Specialty Chemicals v. Huntsman Corp.*, 965 A.2d 715, 759 (Del. Ch. 2008).

G. UCC REMEDIES

The Uniform Commercial Code embraces most of the fundamental principles of the common law of contracts on remedies, particularly the compensation principle and the expectancy measure. The UCC specifically embraces those principles in its treatment of liquidated damages clauses in Section 2–718(1), which expresses principles similar to those of the common law: "Damages for breach by either party may be liquidated in the agreement but only at an amount which is reasonable in the light of the anticipated or actual harm caused by the breach, the difficulties of proof of loss, and the inconvenience or non-feasibility of otherwise obtaining an adequate remedy. A term fixing unreasonably large liquidated damages is void as a penalty."

But the UCC also contains numerous specific commercial law concepts and articulates an index of specific damages measures for specified settings. The statute organizes these UCC contract remedies according to which side is aggrieved, buyer or seller, and denominates these as buyer's damages and seller's damages, respectively. The statutory approach first provides an index of remedies available in general to buyers and to sellers with cross-references to other sections where the specifics of each remedy are detailed. Following is a summary of the general indexing of remedies and highlights of the specifics. Ensuing cases quote the relevant UCC sections in context.

Buyer's remedies are indexed in Section 2–711. It empowers aggrieved buyers either to (x) "cover"—meaning buy substitute goods from other vendors—and have damages measured under Section 2–712 by the difference between the contract price and cover price (the "contract-cover difference") or (y) simply have damages measured under Section 2–713 by the difference between the contract price and prevailing market price (the "contract-market difference"). Section 2–711 also authorizes specific performance in "proper cases," generally those warranting that extraordinary remedy under the common law.

Buyer's remedies can be animated preliminarily by the following illustration. Suppose Anoushka needs 100 red balloons as decorations for a 1980s-themed party occurring in three weeks. Anoushka makes a contract with Just Add Helium, Inc. (JAH) to pay $1 each for the red balloons or a total of $100. Two days after making the contract, JAH determines that it cannot fill the order, and lets Anoushka know. At the time, red balloons were selling on the open market for $3 each or a total of $300 for 100.

Under UCC Section 2–713, Anoushka could recover damages measured by the difference between the prevailing market price for balloons and the contract price (the contract-market difference, equaling $200). But Anoushka still needs the balloons to make her party a success. Anoushka could scour the market for an alternative supplier. Suppose she can and does and finally buys 100 balloons from Nena, Inc., but now at a cost of $4 balloon or $400 total. Under UCC Section 2–712, Anoushka could recover the $300 contract-cover difference. Specific performance is probably not warranted, given the fungible character of this good and an active market for it, suggesting that these monetary remedies adequately compensate for the breach.

Seller's remedies are indexed in Section 2–703, which besides entitling aggrieved sellers to withhold or stop delivery or cancel the contract, empowers them either to (x) resell the goods—akin to buyer's cover—and have damages measured under Section 2–706 by the difference between the contract price and resale price or (y) simply have damages measured under 2–708, again parallel to buyer's remedies, by the difference between the contract price and prevailing market price or, if that would undercompensate the seller, for lost profits. Section 2–703 also authorizes an "action for the price" under Section 2–709 in "proper cases," akin to buyer's remedy of specific performance, and likewise an extraordinary remedy.

To illustrate seller's remedies, start over with our red balloons example. Suppose that, after Anoushka signs the contract to buy 100 balloons for $1 each from JAH, Anoushka breaches, having found another vendor offering balloons for 50 cents each or $50 total. JAH has numerous options to assure its compensation for breach, including: selling the contracted balloons to another buyer and collecting the contract-resale difference; if the contracted balloons cannot be sold to another party, say because they have been tailored to the 1980's theme party, seeking the contract price; the contract-market difference; or if the latter would undercompensate, say because JAH has the capacity to sell as many balloons as customers might order, collecting lost profits on the breached contract. Of course, these remedies are not cumulative, but alternatives, and sellers are to choose that which best compensates for breach.

The following cases explore several prominent remedial provisions under Article 2 of the UCC, specifically buyer's remedies in general and upon anticipatory repudiation in *Cosden Oil.*; seller's action for the price in *Foxco Industries v. Fabric World*; and seller's action for lost profits in *Neri v. Retail Marine.* These are prominent, and chosen for presentation here, because they recur frequently in commercial practice, and because they present challenging legal issues that offer valuable training for new lawyers.

In *Cosden Oil*, below, the buyer seeks damages upon seller's anticipatory repudiation, raising vexing issues of measurement under the UCC and commercial practice. In our earlier treatment of anticipatory repudiation at common law, in cases such as *Stiles Family Ltd.* and *Marvel Entertainment*, we stressed the challenging threshold question of what words or conduct constitute anticipatory repudiation and how parties unsure of others' intentions may address the uncertainty. While in *Cosden Oil* there is no dispute about the seller's repudiation, the UCC delineates express rights to address cases where there is doubt. Compare and contrast this UCC provision with this topic's treatment in the Restatement (Second) of Contracts, quoted in *Marvel Entertainment*.

UCC SECTION 2–609

§ 2–609. *Right to Adequate Assurance of Performance*

(1) ... When reasonable grounds for insecurity arise with respect to the performance of either party the other may in writing demand adequate assurance of due performance and until he receives such assurance may if commercially reasonable suspend any performance for which he has not already received the agreed return.

(2) Between merchants the reasonableness of grounds for insecurity and the adequacy of any assurance offered shall be determined according to commercial standards. ...

(4) After receipt of a justified demand failure to provide within a reasonable time not exceeding thirty days such assurance of due performance as is adequate under the circumstances of the particular case is a repudiation of the contract.

COSDEN OIL & CHEMICAL CO. V. HELM
736 F.2d 1064 (5th Cir. 1984)

REAVLEY, J.

We must address one of the most difficult interpretive problems of the Uniform Commercial Code—the appropriate time to measure buyer's damages where the seller anticipatorily repudiates a contract and the buyer does not cover. The district court applied the Texas version of Article 2 and measured buyer's damages at a commercially reasonable time after seller's repudiation. We affirm . . .

This contractual dispute arose out of events and transactions occurring in the first three months of 1979, when the market in polystyrene, a petroleum derivative used to make molded products, was steadily rising. During this time Iran, a major petroleum producer, was undergoing political turmoil. [Helm or Buyer], an international trading company based in Hamburg, West Germany, anticipated a tightening in the world petrochemical supply and decided to purchase a large amount of polystyrene. [Buyer] initiated negotiations with Cosden Oil & Chemical Company (Cosden) [or Seller], a Texas-based producer of chemical products, including polystyrene.

[Buyer] contacted [Seller's] national sales coordinator, to inquire about the possibility of purchasing quantities of polystyrene. Negotiating over the telephone and by telex, the parties agreed to the purchase and sale of 1250 metric tons of high impact polystyrene at $.2825 per pound and 250 metric tons of general purpose polystyrene at $.265 per pound. [During January, the parties agreed to a series of four purchase-and-sale transactions, constituting separate elements of a single contract, referred to as 04, 05, 06, and 07, and specifying varying terms, as to price, quantity, quality (impact-level), delivery and other matters].

Cosden shipped 90,000 pounds of high impact polystyrene to Helm on or about January 26. Cosden then sent an invoice for that quantity to Helm on or about January 31. The front of the invoice stated, "This order is subject to the terms and conditions shown on the reverse hereof." Among the "Conditions of Sale" listed on the back of the invoice was a force majeure provision. Helm paid for the first shipment in accordance with the agreement.

As Helm had expected, polystyrene prices began to rise in late January, and continued upward during February and March. Cosden also experienced problems at two of its plants in late January. Normally, Cosden supplied its Calumet City, Illinois, production plant with styrene monomer, the "feed stock" or main ingredient of polystyrene, by barges that traveled from Louisiana up the Mississippi and Illinois Rivers to a canal that extended to Cosden's plant. Due to the extremely cold winter of 1978–79, however, the Illinois River and the canal froze, suspending barge traffic for a few weeks.

A different problem beset Cosden's Windsor, New Jersey, production plant. A new reactor, used in the polystyrene manufacturing process, had recently been installed at the Windsor plant. A manufacturing defect soon became apparent, however, and Cosden returned the reactor to the manufacturer for repair, which took several weeks. At the time of the reactor breakdown, Cosden was manufacturing only general purpose at the Windsor plant. Cosden had planned on supplying Helm's high impact orders from the Calumet City plant.

Late in January Cosden notified Helm that it was experiencing problems at its production facilities and that the delivery under 04 might be delayed. On February 6, [Seller called Buyer to report that it was] cancelling orders 05, 06, and 07 because two plants were "down" and it did not have sufficient product to fill the orders. Cosden, however, would continue to honor order 04. [Seller] confirmed the cancellation in a letter dated February 8, which [Buyer] received on or about February 12. After Helm learned of Cosden's cancellation, [it developed] a strategy [to] urge that Cosden continue to perform under 04 and, after receiving the high impact polystyrene, would offset amounts owing under 04 against Helm's damages for nondelivery of the balance of polystyrene. . . .

In mid-February Cosden shipped approximately 1,260,000 pounds of high impact to Helm under order 04. This shipment's invoice, which also included the force majeure provision . . ., specified that Helm owed $355,950, due by March 15 or 16. After this delivery Helm requested that Cosden deliver the balance under order 04 for shipment on a vessel departing March 16. Cosden informed Helm that a March 16 delivery was not possible. On March 15, citing production problems with the 04 balance, Cosden offered to sell 1000 metric tons of styrene monomer at $.41 per pound. . . . Helm refused the offer, insisting on delivery of the balance of 04 polystyrene by March 31 at the latest. Around the end of March, [Seller told Buyer] it was cancelling the balance of order 04.

Cosden sued Helm, seeking damages for Helm's failure to pay for delivered polystyrene. Helm counterclaimed for Cosden's failure to deliver polystyrene as agreed. The jury found on special verdict that Cosden had agreed to sell polystyrene to Helm under all four orders. The jury also found that Cosden anticipatorily repudiated orders 05, 06, and 07 and that Cosden cancelled order 04 before Helm's failure to pay for the second 04 delivery constituted a repudiation. The jury fixed the per pound market prices for polystyrene under each of the four orders at three different times: when Helm learned of the cancellation, at a commercially reasonable time thereafter, and at the time for delivery.

The district court, viewing the four orders as representing one agreement, determined that Helm was entitled to recover $628,676 in damages representing the difference between the contract price and the market price at a commercially reasonable time after Cosden repudiated its polystyrene delivery obligations and that Cosden was entitled to an offset of $355,950 against those damages for polystyrene delivered, but not paid for, under order 04.

Both parties find fault with the time at which the district court measured Helm's damages for Cosden's anticipatory repudiation of orders 05, 06, and 07. Cosden argues that damages should be measured when Helm learned of the repudiation. Helm contends that market price as of the last day for delivery—or the time of performance—should be used to compute its damages under the contract-market differential. We reject both views, and hold that the district court correctly measured damages at a commercially reasonable point after Cosden informed Helm that it was cancelling the three orders.

Article 2 of the Code has generally been hailed as a success for its comprehensiveness, its deference to mercantile reality, and its clarity. Nevertheless, certain aspects of the Code's overall scheme have proved troublesome in application. The interplay among sections 2.610, 2.711, 2.712, 2.713, and 2.723 [is] one of those areas, and has been described as "an impossible legal thicket." J. White & R. Summers, *Uniform Commercial Code* § 6–7 at 242 (2d ed. 1980). The aggrieved buyer seeking damages for seller's anticipatory repudiation presents the most difficult interpretive problem. Section 2.713 describes the buyer's damages remedy:

> *Buyer's Damages for Non-Delivery or Repudiation.* (a) Subject to the provisions of this chapter with respect to proof of market price (Section 2.723), the measure of damages for non-delivery or repudiation by the seller is the difference between the market price *at the time when the buyer learned of the breach* and the contract price together with any incidental and consequential damages provided in this chapter (Section 2.715), but less expenses saved in consequence of the seller's breach. (emphasis added).

Courts and commentators have identified three possible interpretations of the phrase "learned of the breach." If seller anticipatorily repudiates, buyer learns of the breach: (1) When he learns of the repudiation; (2) When he learns of the repudiation plus a commercially reasonable time; or (3) When performance is due under the contract. *See, e.g., First National Bank of Chicago v. Jefferson Mortgage Co.,* 576 F.2d 479 (3d Cir.1978); *Cargill, Inc. v. Stafford,* 553 F.2d 1222 (10th Cir.1977); J. White & R. Summers § 6–7 at 240–52; Note, *U.C.C. § 2–713: Anticipatory Repudiation and the Measurement of an Aggrieved Buyer's Damages,* 19 Wm. & Mary L.Rev. 253 (1977). . . .

We do not doubt, and Texas law is clear, that market price at the time buyer learns of the breach is the appropriate measure of section 2.713 damages in cases where buyer learns of the breach at or after the time for performance. This will be the common case, for which section 2.713 was designed. *See* Peters, *Remedies for Breach of Contracts Relating to the Sale of Goods Under the Uniform Commercial Code: A Roadmap for Article Two,* 73 Yale L.J. 199, 264 (1963). In the relatively rare case where seller anticipatorily repudiates and buyer does not cover, the specific provision for anticipatory repudiation cases, section 2.610, authorizes the aggrieved party to await performance for a commercially reasonable time before resorting to his remedies of cover or damages.

In the anticipatory repudiation context, the buyer's specific right to wait for a commercially reasonable time before choosing his remedy must be read together with the general damages provision of section 2.713 to extend the time for measurement beyond when buyer learns of the breach. Comment 1 to section 2.610 states that if an aggrieved party "awaits performance beyond a commercially reasonable time he cannot recover resulting damages which he should have avoided." This suggests that an aggrieved buyer can recover damages where the market rises during the commercially reasonable time he awaits performance. To interpret 2.713's "learned of the breach" language to mean the time at which seller first communicates his anticipatory repudiation would undercut the time that 2.610 gives the aggrieved buyer to await performance.

The buyer's option to wait a commercially reasonable time also interacts with section 2.611, which allows the seller an opportunity to retract his repudiation. Thus, an aggrieved buyer "learns of the breach" a commercially reasonable time after he learns of the seller's anticipatory repudiation. The weight of scholarly commentary supports this interpretation. *See* J. Calamari & J. Perillo, *Contracts* § 14–20 (2d ed. 1977); Sebert, *Remedies Under Article Two of the Uniform Commercial Code: An Agenda for Review,* 130 U.Pa.L.Rev. 360, 372–80 (1981); Wallach, *Anticipatory Repudiation and the UCC,* 13 U.C.C.L.J. 48 (1980); Peters, *supra,* at 263–68.

Typically, our question will arise where parties to an executory contract are in the midst of a rising market. To the extent that market decisions are influenced by a damages rule, measuring market price at the time of seller's repudiation gives seller the ability to fix buyer's damages and may induce seller to repudiate, rather than abide by the contract. By contrast, measuring buyer's damages at the time of performance will tend to dissuade the buyer from covering, in hopes that market price will continue upward until performance time.

Allowing the aggrieved buyer a commercially reasonable time, however, provides him with an opportunity to investigate his cover possibilities in a rising market without fear that, if he is unsuccessful in obtaining cover, he will be relegated to a market-contract damage remedy measured at the time of repudiation. The Code supports this view. While cover is the preferred remedy, the Code clearly provides the option to seek damages. *See* § 2.712(c) & comment 3. . . .

Persuasive arguments exist for interpreting "learned of the breach" to mean "time of performance," consistent with the pre-Code rule. *See* J. White & R. Summers, *supra,* § 6–7; Anderson, *supra.* If this was the intention of the Code's drafters, however, phrases in section 2.610 and 2.712 lose their meaning. If buyer is entitled to market-contract damages measured at the time of performance, it is difficult to explain why the anticipatory repudiation section limits him to a commercially reasonable time to await performance. *See* § 2.610 comment 1. Similarly, in a rising market, no reason would exist for requiring the buyer to act "without unreasonable delay" when he seeks to cover following an anticipatory repudiation. *See* § 2.712(a).

The interplay among the relevant Code sections does not permit, in this context, an interpretation that harmonizes all and leaves no loose ends. We therefore acknowledge that our interpretation fails to explain the language of section 2.723(a) insofar as it relates to aggrieved buyers. We note, however, that the section has limited applicability—cases that come to trial before the time of performance will be rare. Moreover, the comment to section 2.723 states that the "section is not intended to exclude the use of any other reasonable method of determining market price or of measuring damages. . . ." In light of the Code's persistent theme of commercial reasonableness, the prominence of cover as a remedy, and the time given an aggrieved buyer to await performance and to investigate cover before selecting his remedy, we agree with the district court that "learned of the breach" incorporates section 2.610's commercially reasonable time.

NOTES AND QUESTIONS

1.   Would the force majeure clauses in seller's sales documents have excused its performance obligations? Recall *Kel-Kim* and related materials in Chapter Five. Would that clause and the related problems have a bearing on what constitutes a commercially reasonable time for measuring buyer's damages? What other factors might bear on delineating a commercially reasonable time in the context of a seller's anticipatory repudiation?

2.   The rest of the *Cosden* opinion, omitted from this book, contains rich additional analysis of many UCC issues.

3.   Among other opinions that engage clearly with the difficult question of buyer's damages upon anticipatory repudiation, consider *Oloffson v. Coomer*, 296 N.E.2d 871 (Ill. 1973); *Cargill Inc. v. Stafford*, 553 F.2d 1222 (10th Cir. 1977); and *Trinidad Bean v. Frush*, 494 N.W.2d 347 (Neb. App. 1992). These opinions do not always reach the same conclusions on how to interpret these vexing UCC provisions.

4.   *Cosden Oil* cites Peters, *Remedies for Breach of Contracts Relating to the Sale of Goods Under the Uniform Commercial Code: A Roadmap for Article Two*, 73 YALE L.J. 199 (1963), a classic of continuing reliability in this difficult area. The piece was written by Professor Ellen Ash Peters, as her tenure piece at Yale Law School, where she taught from 1956 to 1978. In 1978, she was appointed to the Supreme Court of Connecticut, where she served with distinction and wrote important commercial law opinions, including one appearing later in this book, *Plataq Corp. v. Machlett Labs*.

FOXCO INDUSTRIES V. FABRIC WORLD
595 F.2d 976 (5th Cir. 1979)

TJOFLAT, J.

In this diversity action Foxco Industries, Ltd. (Foxco), a Delaware corporation, following a jury trial recovered a $26,000 judgment against Fabric World, Inc. (Fabric World), an Alabama corporation, for breaching a contract to purchase certain knitted fabric goods and refusing to pay for merchandise previously purchased. Fabric World [contends that] the district court erred in its instructions to the jury on damages . . . .

Foxco is in the business of manufacturing knitted fabrics for sale to retail fabric stores and the garment industry. . . . Fabric World is engaged in the retail fabric business and operates a chain of stores in a number of states; its headquarters is in Huntsville, Alabama.

There are two seasons in the fabric industry, a spring season and a fall season. Before the beginning of each season Foxco displays for customers samples of the line of fabrics it will manufacture that season. Customer orders are accepted only from the fabric shown on display. Foxco's manufacturing operation is limited to filling these orders; no fabrics are manufactured merely to be held as inventory. There was some conflict in the testimony as to whether fabric specially knit for one customer, such as Fabric World, could be resold to another customer.

Foxco sells some of its goods to retail fabric stores through manufacturers' representatives, operating on a commission basis, who sell the lines of numerous manufacturers. Foxco furnishes each representative with samples and a price list. Larger retail store customers, such as Fabric

World, are handled personally by Foxco's sales manager, Allen Feller, a salaried employee, who supervises all retail fabric store sales. He has responsibility over the approximately twenty-six manufacturers' representatives carrying the Foxco line.

... On April 22, 1974, Feller traveled to Huntsville to show Fabric World the new fall line. His meeting with Glenn Jameson, Fabric World's president, culminated in a written order for "first quality" goods. A dispute subsequently arose regarding the quality of the goods sent to fill the order, and Fabric World refused to pay for the portion of the goods it considered defective.

On October 21, 1974, Feller returned to Huntsville to show Jameson the line for the following spring season. Jameson voiced no complaint about the quality of the goods received pursuant to the previous April 22 order. In fact, he gave Feller a new order, in writing, for 12,000 yards of first quality fabric, at a price of $36,705, to be delivered by January 15, 1975.

A few weeks after the October 21 order was placed, the textile industry began to experience a precipitous decline in the price of yarn. Because of a drop in the price of finished goods, Fabric World wrote Foxco on November 15, 1974, and cancelled its October 21 order. Foxco immediately replied, stating that the manufacture of the order was substantially completed and that it could not accept the cancellation. On November 27, 1974, Foxco's attorney wrote Fabric World that if the goods were not accepted they would be finished and sold and Fabric World sued for the difference between the contract price and the sales price received by Foxco. On December 3, 1974, Fabric World agreed to accept the order, but threatened to return the entire shipment if it contained one flaw. Foxco, believing that it was impossible to produce an order of this magnitude without a single flaw, decided it would not ship the order (which was completed a short time later).

Fabric World established that in December 1974 the fair market value of the October order was approximately 20% less than the contract price. However, Foxco make no attempt to sell the goods from the time Fabric World cancelled the order until September 1975, when the goods had dropped 50% in value. In that month Foxco sold at a private sale without notice to Fabric World approximately 7,000 yards from the order for an average price of between $1.50 and $1.75 per yard, a total consideration of $10,119.50. By the time of trial in April 1976, Foxco had on hand about 5,000 yards of the order worth between $1.25 and $1 per yard, or about $6,250. . . .

The court . . . instructed the jury that, if it found that Fabric World was liable to Foxco, it was free to calculate Foxco's damages under either section 2–708 or 2–709 of the Alabama Uniform Commercial Code. Fabric World objected, asserting that section 2–709 is inapplicable in this case, and now argues that the verdict resulted from an application of that section.

[We have been unable to locate any Alabama cases construing UCC Sections 2–708 or 2–709.] Accordingly, we must anticipate the decision of an Alabama court faced with the questions now presented. We have no reason to believe that an Alabama court would not study relevant precedents from the other 48 jurisdictions which have adopted the U.C.C.; therefore, we look to those precedents for guidance.

Fabric World maintains that the $26,000 verdict awarded to Foxco cannot be supported by the district court's instruction under U.C.C. section 2–708, allowing the difference between the market and contract price as the measure of damages. Fabric World calculates that, in view of the market price at the time the October 1974 contract was breached, the maximum amount the jury could have given Foxco under the section 2–708 instruction was approximately $16,000, [being] $10,000 less than its $26,000 verdict. Accordingly, it reasons that the verdict must have been fashioned pursuant to the section 2–709 charge and the verdict cannot stand unless that charge was proper. As we now discuss, the jury was appropriately instructed, and Foxco's damage award must be approved.

U.C.C. section 2–703 . . . sets out the remedies available to the seller of goods against a defaulting purchaser:

> Seller's remedies in general. Where the buyer wrongfully rejects or revokes acceptance of goods or fails to make a payment due on or before delivery or repudiates with respect to a part or the whole, then with respect to any goods directly affected and, if the breach is of the whole contract (section 2–612), then also with respect to the whole undelivered balance, the aggrieved seller may:
>
> (a) Withhold delivery of such goods;
>
> (b) Stop delivery by any bailee as hereafter provided (section 2–705);
>
> (c) Proceed under section 2–704 respecting goods still unidentified to the contract;
>
> (d) Resell and recover damages as hereafter provided (section 2–706);
>
> (e) Recover damages for nonacceptance (section 2–708) or in a proper case the price (section 2–709);
>
> (f) Cancel.

As Fabric World correctly argues, notwithstanding section 2–703(d) Foxco cannot invoke section 2–706, . . . because, following Fabric World's breach, Foxco privately sold some of the goods without notice to Fabric

World. Thus, Foxco, having elected not to pursue the relief available under section 2–703(a), (b), and (f), is limited to its remedies under section 2–703(e), i.e., either section 2–708 or 2–709. The district court charged the jury under both of these latter provisions, leaving to the jury the determination of which was more appropriately applicable under the facts developed at trial. Since Fabric World properly concedes that a section 2–708 instruction was warranted on the state of the record before the trial judge, we may reverse only if the evidence was insufficient for the jury to invoke section 2–709 as a measure of Foxco's damages.

When Fabric World cancelled its October 1974 order on November 15, 1974, Foxco had not yet fully completed the manufacture of the contracted-for fabric. Under U.C.C. section 2–704, a seller aggrieved by a buyer's repudiation of unfinished goods may, in the exercise of reasonable commercial judgment and in order to avoid loss, either complete the manufacture and wholly identify the goods to the contract or cease their manufacture and resell them at their salvage value. As stated in the Official Comment to this section,

> This section gives an aggrieved seller the right at the time of breach to identify to the contract any conforming finished goods, regardless of their resalability, and to use reasonable judgment as to completing unfinished goods. It thus makes the goods available for resale under the resale section, the seller's primary remedy, and *in the special case in which resale is not practicable*, allows the action for the price which would then be necessary to give the seller the value of his contract.

(Emphasis added). The jury obviously decided that Foxco acted in a commercially reasonable manner when it decided to process to a conclusion the manufacture of the already substantially completed Fabric World order. Foxco was then entitled to the appropriate seller's breach of contract remedy.

U.C.C. section 2–709(1)(b) . . . provides that an action for the price of goods may be maintained "if the seller is unable after Reasonable effort to resell them at a Reasonable price or the circumstances Reasonably indicate that such effort will be unavailing." The Official Comment to section 2–709 states, in pertinent part, that:

> 2.   The action for the price is now generally limited to those cases where resale of the goods is impracticable . . . .

> 3.   This section substitutes an objective test by action for the former "not readily resalable" standard. An action for the price under subsection (1)(b) can be sustained only after a "reasonable effort to resell" the goods "at reasonable price" has actually been made or where the circumstances "reasonably indicate" that such an effort will be unavailing.

. . . The evidence at trial clearly established that all of Foxco's goods were specially manufactured for the customer who ordered them and that it was difficult for Foxco to resell fabric manufactured for one purchaser to another buyer. Further, it was normally very difficult to sell Foxco's spring fabric after the spring buying season had ended; the precipitous decline of the knitted fabric market presented an additional barrier to resale. It was not until the next spring buying season returned that Foxco, in September 1975, finally sold a portion of the goods identified to Fabric World's October 1974 order.

Fabric World argues that Foxco made no effort whatsoever to resell the goods during the months that intervened (between the contract breach and Foxco's eventual disposition of the fabric in September 1975) despite the presence of some market for the goods in that interim period. Thus, Fabric World concludes, the requisites of section 2–709(1)(b) were not satisfied. Under section 2–709(1)(b), however, Foxco was required only to use reasonable efforts to resell its goods at a Reasonable price. From the time of Fabric World's breach to September 1975 there was a 50% Decline in the market price of this material. We cannot say that the jury was precluded from finding that Foxco acted reasonably under the circumstances or that there was no reasonable price at which Foxco could sell these goods. Fabric World breached its contract with Foxco, and the jury was entitled to a charge which gave Foxco the full benefit of its original bargain.

NOTES AND QUESTIONS

1.   In what ways are the buyer's remedy of specific performance and seller's remedy of an action for the price parallel or different?

2.   In what ways are the UCC's remedial provisions on these subjects akin to or different from those developed at common law? Can the similarities and differences be justified given the respective contexts these laws govern?

NERI V. RETAIL MARINE
285 N.E.2d 311 (N.Y. 1972)

GIBSON, J.

The appeal concerns the right of a retail dealer to recover loss of profits and incidental damages upon the buyer's repudiation of a contract governed by the Uniform Commercial Code. This is, indeed, the correct measure of damage in an appropriate case and to this extent the code [§ 2–708] effected a substantial change from prior law, whereby damages were ordinarily limited to "the difference between the contract price and the market or current price". Upon the record before us, the courts below erred in declining to give effect to the new statute and so the order appealed from must be reversed.

The plaintiffs contracted to purchase from defendant a new boat of a specified model for the price of $12,587.40, against which they made a deposit of $40. They shortly increased the deposit to $4,250 in consideration of the defendant dealer's agreement to arrange with the manufacturer for immediate delivery on the basis of "a firm sale", instead of the delivery within approximately four to six weeks originally specified. Some six days after the date of the contract plaintiffs' lawyer sent to defendant a letter rescinding the sales contract for the reason that plaintiff Neri was about to undergo hospitalization and surgery, in consequence of which, according to the letter, it would be "impossible for Mr. Neri to make any payments". The boat had already been ordered from the manufacturer and was delivered to defendant at or before the time the attorney's letter was received. Defendant declined to refund plaintiffs' deposit and this action to recover it was commenced. Defendant counterclaimed, alleging plaintiffs' breach of the contract and defendant's resultant damage in the amount of $4,250, for which sum defendant demanded judgment. Upon motion, defendant had summary judgment on the issue of liability tendered by its counterclaim; and Special Term directed an assessment of damages, upon which it would be determined whether plaintiffs were entitled to the return of any portion of their down payment.

Upon the trial so directed, it was shown that the boat ordered and received by defendant in accordance with plaintiffs' contract of purchase was sold some four months later to another buyer for the same price as that negotiated with plaintiffs. From this proof the plaintiffs argue that defendant's loss on its contract was recouped, while defendant argues that but for plaintiffs' default, it would have sold two boats and have earned two profits instead of one. Defendant proved, without contradiction, that its profit on the sale under the contract in suit would have been $2,579 and that during the period the boat remained unsold incidental expenses aggregating $674 for storage, upkeep, finance charges and insurance were incurred. Additionally, defendant proved and sought to recover attorneys' fees of $1,250.

The trial court found "untenable" defendant's claim for loss of profit, inasmuch as the boat was later sold for the same price that plaintiffs had contracted to pay; found, too, that defendant had failed to prove any incidental damages; further found "that the terms of [2–718(2)(b)] of the Uniform Commercial Code are applicable and same make adequate and fair provision to place the sellers in as good a position as performance would have done" and, in accordance with paragraph (b) of subsection (2) thus relied upon, awarded defendant $500 upon its counterclaim and directed that plaintiffs recover the balance of their deposit, amounting to $3,750. The ensuing judgment was affirmed, without opinion, at the Appellate Division, 37 A.D.2d 917, 326 N.Y.S.2d 984, and defendant's appeal to this court was taken by our leave.

The issue is governed in the first instance by section 2–718 of the Uniform Commercial Code which provides, among other things, that the buyer, despite his breach, may have restitution of the amount by which his payment exceeds: (a) reasonable liquidated damages stipulated by the contract or (b) absent such stipulation, 20% Of the value of the buyer's total performance or $500, whichever is smaller [§ 2–718(2)(a) & (b)]. As above noted, the trial court awarded defendant an offset in the amount of $500 under paragraph (b) and directed restitution to plaintiffs of the balance. Section 2–718, however, establishes, in paragraph (a) of subsection (3), an alternative right of offset in favor of the seller, as follows: "(3) The buyer's right to restitution under subsection (2) is subject to offset to the extent that the seller establishes (a) a right to recover damages under the provisions of this Article other than subsection (1)".

Among "the provisions of this Article other than subsection (1)" are those to be found in section 2–708, which the courts below did not apply. [Section 2–708 provides as follows:

§ 2–708. *Seller's Damages for Non-acceptance or Repudiation.*

(1) . . . the measure of damages for non-acceptance or repudiation by the buyer is the difference between the market price at the time and place for tender and the unpaid contract price together with any incidental damages provided in this Article (Section 2–710), but less expenses saved in consequence of the buyer's breach.

(2) If the measure of damages provided in subsection (1) is inadequate to put the seller in as good a position as performance would have done then the measure of damages is the profit (including reasonable overhead) which the seller would have made from full performance by the buyer, together with any incidental damages provided in this Article (Section 2–710), due allowance for costs reasonably incurred and due credit for payments or proceeds of resale.]

The buyer's right to restitution was established at Special Term upon the motion for summary judgment, as was the seller's right to proper offsets, in each case pursuant to section 2–718; and, as the parties concede, the only question before us, following the assessment of damages at Special Term, is that as to the proper measure of damage to be applied. The conclusion is clear from the record—indeed with mathematical certainty— that "the measure of damages provided in subsection (1) is inadequate to put the seller in as good a position as performance would have done" (Uniform Commercial Code, § 2–708, subsection (2)) and hence—again under subsection (2)—that the seller is entitled to its "profit (including reasonable overhead) . . . together with any incidental damages . . . , due allowance for costs reasonably incurred and due credit for payments or proceeds of resale."

It is evident, first, that this retail seller is entitled to its profit and, second, that the last sentence of subsection (2), as hereinbefore quoted, referring to "due credit for payments or proceeds of resale" is inapplicable to this retail sales contract.[2] Closely parallel to the factual situation now before us is that hypothesized by Dean Hawkland as illustrative of the operation of the rules:

> Thus, if a private party agrees to sell his automobile to a buyer for $2,000, a breach by the buyer would cause the seller no loss (except incidental damages, i.e., expense of a new sale) if the seller was able to sell the automobile to another buyer for $2000. But the situation is different with dealers having an unlimited supply or standard-priced goods.
>
> Thus, if an automobile dealer agrees to sell a car to a buyer at the standard price of $2000, a breach by the buyer injures the dealer, even though he is able to sell the automobile to another for $2000. If the dealer has an inexhaustible supply of cars, the resale to replace the breaching buyer costs the dealer a sale, because, had the breaching buyer performed, the dealer would have made two sales instead of one. The buyer's breach, in such a case, depletes the dealer's sales to the extent of one, and the measure of damages should be the dealer's profit on one sale. Section 2–708 recognizes this, and it rejects the rules developed under the Uniform Sales Act by many courts that the profit cannot be recovered in this case.

(Hawkland, Sales and Bulk Sales (1958 ed.), pp. 153–154; and see Comment, 31 Fordham L.Rev. 749, 755–756.)

The record which in this case establishes defendant's entitlement to damages in the amount of its prospective profit, at the same time confirms defendant's cognate right to "any incidental damages provided in this Article . . . . [T]he seller's right to recover loss of profits is not exclusive and that he may recoup his "incidental" expenses as well . . . Although the trial court's denial of incidental damages in the uncontroverted amount of $674 was made in the context of its erroneous conclusion that [2–718(2)(b)] was applicable and was "adequate . . . to place the sellers in as good a position

---

[2]   The concluding clause, 'due credit for payments or proceeds of resale', is intended to refer to 'the privilege of the seller to realize junk value when it is manifestly useless to complete the operation of manufacture' . . . The commentators who have considered the language have uniformly concluded that 'the reference is to a resale as scrap under . . . Section 2–704' (1956 Report of N.Y.Law Rev.Comm., p. 397; . . .). Another writer, reaching the same conclusion, after detailing the history of the clause, says that 'proceeds of resale' previously meant the resale value of the goods in finished form; now it means the resale value of the components on hand at the time plaintiff learns of breach' (Harris, Seller's Damages, 18 Stan.L.Rev. 66, 104).

as performance would have done", the denial seems not to have rested entirely on the court's mistaken application of the law, as there was an explicit finding "that defendant completely failed to show that it suffered any incidental damages." We find no basis for the court's conclusion with respect to a deficiency of proof inasmuch as the proper items of the $674 expenses (being for storage, upkeep, finance charges and insurance for the period between the date performance was due and the time of the resale) were proven without objection and were in no way controverted, impeached or otherwise challenged, at the trial or on appeal. Thus the court's finding of a failure of proof cannot be supported upon the record and, therefore, and contrary to plaintiffs" contention, the affirmance at the Appellate Division was ineffective to save it.

The trial court correctly denied defendant's claim for recovery of attorney's fees incurred by it in this action. Attorney's fees incurred in an action such as this are not in the nature of the protective expenses contemplated by the statute [1–106(1); 2–710; § 2–708(2)] . . . .

It follows that plaintiffs are entitled to restitution of the sum of $4,250 paid by them on account of the contract price less an offset to defendant in the amount of $3,253 on account of its lost profit of $2,579 and its incidental damages of $674. . . .

NOTES AND QUESTIONS

1. *Neri* is considered to be the leading case on the subject of lost volume sellers and the meaning of 2–708(2). What is the rationale behind the lost volume seller doctrine? What are the doctrine's advantages and disadvantages? How does the doctrine of the lost volume seller interact with the common law's mitigation limitation on contract remedies?

2. Should it matter whether any given seller or types of seller have the capacity to bear the costs of a lost sale? Are large commercial entities better able to bear the costs of a lost sale than smaller sellers?

3. What other conditions must a seller meet to qualify as a lost volume seller? Is it necessary that the second sale be profitable? Must the seller be able to trace the particular good to be sold under the repudiated contract as the one resold under a subsequent contract? The following case addresses such questions.

R.E. DAVIS CHEMICAL CORP. V. DIASONICS, INC.

924 F.2d 709 (7th Cir. 1991)

CUDAHY, J.

. . . R.E. Davis Chemical Corporation (Davis), an Illinois business, contracted to purchase [a] magnetic resonance instrument (MRI), from Diasonics [for] $1,500,000 . . . Davis advanced a $300,000 deposit for the

MRI but failed to take delivery, thereby breaching the contract. After Davis repudiated the contract, Diasonics resold the MRI to a third party at the contract price.

When Diasonics refused to refund the $300,000 deposit, Davis filed suit demanding return of the downpayment pursuant to section 2–718(2) of the Uniform Commercial Code (the UCC). Diasonics counterclaimed, alleging that it was entitled to recover the profit it lost on the sale under UCC 2–708(2) because it was a lost volume seller. The district court entered summary judgment for Davis, holding that lost volume sellers are not eligible for recovery of lost profits but rather are limited to damages measured by the difference between the resale price and the contract price together with incidental damages under UCC 2–706(1). Concluding that the Illinois Supreme Court would follow the majority of jurisdictions, which allow lost volume sellers to recoup their lost profits under UCC 2–708(2), we reversed and remanded the case with instructions that

> the district court calculate Diasonics' damages under 2–708(2) if Diasonics can establish, not only that it had the capacity to make the sale to Davis as well as the sale to the resale buyer, but also that it would have been profitable for it to make both sales . . . [and that Diasonics] probably would have made the second sale absent the breach.

. . . Concluding that Diasonics had adequately established damages for its lost profit amounting to $453,050, the district court ultimately entered judgment for Diasonics in the sum of $153,050 ($453,050 less the $300,000 deposit which Diasonics retained). . . Davis challenges the district court's verdict [and] would prohibit Diasonics from recovering the profit it lost on the sale because Diasonics failed to precisely identify the buyer to whom it resold the MRI.

Ordinarily, a seller's damages for a buyer's breach of contract are measured by the difference between the contract price and the market price. In some situations, however, this sum is inadequate to place the seller in as good a position as performance would have done. For example, a broken contract costs a lost volume seller—one with a finite quantity of customers and the capacity to make an additional sale—its profit on one sale. To be made whole, a lost volume seller must thus recover damages equal to the profit it lost on the sale.

In accordance with this reasoning, in Diasonics I, 826 F.2d at 681, we adopted for the first time in Illinois the rule that a lost volume seller is entitled to recoup its lost profit. We held that in order to qualify as a lost volume seller, a plaintiff must establish the following three factors: (1) that it possessed the capacity to make an additional sale, (2) that it would have been profitable for it to make an additional sale, and (3) that it probably would have made an additional sale absent the buyer's breach.

Diasonics has adduced ample evidence to establish its status as a lost volume seller. The evidence is undisputed that Diasonics possessed the capacity to manufacture one more MRI. Diasonics also demonstrated that it was, in the words of Judge Kocoras, "beating the bushes for all possible sales." Douglas McCutcheon, controller of Diasonics' MRI Division, testified at trial that Diasonics' sales force pursued "every possible lead" and attempted to "identify every possible qualified customer" in 1984. The fact that Diasonics was still a young company struggling to acquire business in an extremely competitive market at the time of Davis' breach lends independent corroboration to McCutcheon's statements. Based upon this evidence, the district court's finding that Diasonics probably would have made an additional sale but for Davis' breach is not clearly erroneous.

Davis offers no evidence to controvert the proof adduced by Diasonics that it both possessed the capacity to manufacture additional MRIs and was actively soliciting every possible customer for MRI sales in 1984. Instead, Davis clutches at one footnote in our previous opinion to justify its contention that Diasonics must precisely identify the resale buyer. In this case, it appears that the generic MRI units manufactured by Diasonics were interchangeable and thus were not identified to any particular customer until just prior to delivery. The mere fact that Diasonics was unable to specify the particular unit Davis contracted to buy and trace the exact resale buyer for that unit thus should not foreclose it from recovering lost profits. Without more evidence, we decline to impose upon Diasonics the burden of proving the exact buyer who purchased this particular system in order to qualify as a lost volume seller.

NOTES AND QUESTIONS

1. In the opening paragraph, the court declares that "Diasonics resold the MRI to a third party at the contract price" yet in the final paragraph it appears that Diasonics could not say to whom it had resold the MRI. Is there a conflict there?

2. Under what circumstances should the lost volume seller doctrine extend to settings other than goods? Can the lost volume seller idea be extended to services? The celebrity athlete Michael Jordan argued it should apply to him in the context of a company that breached his product endorsement contracts. The court's opinion in that case follows.

IN RE WORLDCOM, INC.
361 B. R. 675 (Bankr. S.D.N.Y. 2007)

GONZALEZ, BANKRUPTCY JUDGE.

. . . On or about July 10, 1995, [Michael] Jordan [the star basketball player] and [WorldCom, Inc., a defunct telecommunications company that became part of MCI] entered into an endorsement agreement (the

"Agreement"). At that time, Jordan was considered to be one of the most popular athletes in the world. The Agreement granted MCI a ten-year license to use Jordan's name, likeness, "other attributes," and personal services to advertise and promote MCI's telecommunications products and services beginning in September 1995 and ending in August 2005. The Agreement did not prevent Jordan from endorsing most other products or services, although he could not endorse the same products or services that MCI produced. In addition to a $5 million signing bonus, the Agreement provided an annual base compensation of $2 million for Jordan.

The Agreement provided that Jordan would be treated as an independent contractor and that MCI would not withhold any amount from Jordan's compensation for tax purposes. The Agreement provided that Jordan was to make himself available for four days, not to exceed four hours per day, during each contract year to produce television commercials and print advertising and for promotional appearances. The parties agreed that the advertising and promotional materials would be submitted to Jordan for his approval, which could not be unreasonably withheld, fourteen days prior to their release to the general public. From 1995 to 2000, Jordan appeared in several television commercials and a large number of print ads for MCI.

[MCI filed for bankruptcy and Jordan sought to recover in that proceeding under the Agreement.] He claimed $2 million for each of the payments that were due in June of 2002, 2003, 2004, and 2005. MCI does not object to the Claim to the extent Jordan seeks $4 million for the 2002 and 2003 payments under the Agreement. As of the rejection in July 2003, two years remained under the Agreement.

. . . MCI argues that Jordan had an obligation to mitigate his damages and failed to do so. MCI argues that . . . as a result of Jordan's failure to mitigate damages following [MCI's] rejection, the Claim should be reduced to $4 million. MCI argues that it is under no obligation to pay Jordan for contract years 2004 and 2005. . . . Jordan argues that [he is] a "lost volume seller" and thus mitigation does not apply . . .

. . . The doctrine of avoidable consequences, which has also been referred to as the duty to mitigate damages, "bars recovery for losses suffered by a non-breaching party that could have been avoided by reasonable effort and without risk of substantial loss or injury." Edward M. Crough, Inc. v. Dep't of Gen. Servs. of D.C., 572 A.2d 457, 466 (D.C.1990). The burden of proving that the damages could have been avoided or mitigated rests with the party that committed the breach. See Obelisk Corp. v. Riggs Nat'l Bank of Washington, D.C., 668 A.2d 847, 856 (D.C.1995). The efforts to avoid or mitigate the damages do not have to be successful, as long as they are reasonable. See Edward M. Crough, 572 A.2d at 467.

Jordan argues that as a "lost volume seller" he was under no obligation to mitigate damages. Alternatively, Jordan argues that MCI failed to establish that Jordan could have entered a "substantially similar" endorsement contract and that Jordan acted reasonably in not entering another endorsement agreement after MCI's breach. MCI counters that Jordan is not a lost volume seller and that MCI has shown that Jordan failed to take reasonable steps to mitigate damages. . . .

Jordan argues that MCI's mitigation defense does not apply here because Jordan is akin to a "lost volume seller." Jordan points to testimony demonstrating that he could have entered into additional endorsement contracts even if MCI had not rejected the Agreement. Thus, he argues, any additional endorsement contracts would not have been substitutes for the Agreement and would not have mitigated the damages for which MCI is liable.

"A lost volume seller is one who has the capacity to perform the contract that was breached in addition to other potential contracts due to unlimited resources or production capacity." Precision Pine & Timber, Inc. v. United States, 72 Fed.Cl. 460, 490 (Fed.Cl.2006). A lost volume seller does not minimize its damages by entering into another contract because it would have had the benefit of both contracts even if the first were not breached. . . . The lost volume seller has two expectations, the profit from the breached contract and the profit from one or more other contracts that it could have performed at the same time as the breached contract. . . .

This case offers a twist on the typical lost volume seller situation. In what the Court regards as the typical situation, the non-breaching seller has a near-inexhaustible supply of inventory. See, e.g., Katz Commc'ns, Inc. v. Evening News Ass'n, 705 F.2d 20, 26 (2d Cir.1983). In the typical situation, when a buyer breaches an agreement to buy a good or service from the seller, the item is returned to inventory and the lost volume seller continues in its efforts to sell its goods or services. However, the transactions that occur following the breach are not necessarily the result of the breach but fundamentally the result of the seller continuing efforts to market its goods and services. It is this continuous effort coupled with a virtually limitless supply that warrants the lost volume exception to mitigation. As stated above, the transactions that may occur after the breach would in the context of the lost volume seller have occurred independent of the breach. Here, Jordan lacked a nearly limitless supply and had no intention of continuing to market his services as a product endorser. . . .

To claim lost volume seller status, Jordan must establish that he would have had the benefit of both the original and subsequent contracts if MCI had not rejected the Agreement. See Ullman-Briggs, 754 F.Supp. at 1008. Although there is no definitive set of elements that the non-breaching party must show, many cases seem to follow the language from the Restatement (2d), Section 347, that the non-breaching party must show that it "could and would have entered into" a subsequent agreement. See . . . Green Tree Financial, 2002 WL 31163072, at *9 ("[t]o recover lost profits under this theory, a non-breaching party must prove three things: (1) that the seller of services had the capability to perform both contracts simultaneously; (2) that the second contract would have been profitable; and (3) that the seller of service would have entered into the second contract if the first contract had not been terminated").

. . . Jordan focuses primarily on his capacity to enter subsequent agreements, arguing that the loss of MCI's sixteen-hour annual time commitment hardly affected his ability to perform additional endorsement services. On this prong alone, Jordan likely would be considered a lost volume seller of endorsement services because he had sufficient time to do multiple endorsements. Although he does not have the "infinite capacity" that some cases discuss, a services provider does not need unlimited capacity but must have the requisite capacity and intent to perform under multiple contracts at the same time. See Gianetti, 266 Conn. at 561–62, 833 A.2d 891 (plastic surgeon could be considered a lost volume seller if it were determined that he had the capacity and intent to simultaneously work out of three or four hospitals profitably).

Contrary to Jordan's analysis, courts do not focus solely on the seller's capacity. The seller claiming lost volume status must also demonstrate that it would have entered into subsequent transactions. . . . Jordan has not shown he could and would have entered into a subsequent agreement. Rather, the evidence shows that Jordan did not have the "subjective intent" to take on additional endorsements. . . . The testimony from Jordan's representatives establishes that although Jordan's popularity enabled him to obtain additional product endorsements in 2003, Jordan desired to scale back his level of endorsements. Jordan's financial and business advisor, Curtis Polk ("Polk"), testified that at the time the Agreement was rejected, Jordan's desire was "not to expand his spokesperson or pitchman efforts with new relationships."

. . . Polk testified that had Jordan wanted to do additional endorsements after the 2003 rejection, he could have obtained additional deals. Jordan's agent, David Falk ("Falk"), testified that "there might have been twenty more companies that in theory might have wanted to sign him" but that Jordan and his representatives wanted to avoid diluting his image. . . . [A]t the time the Agreement was rejected, Jordan had implemented a strategy of not accepting new endorsements because of a belief that new deals would jeopardize his ability to achieve his primary goal of National Basketball Association ("NBA") franchise ownership. . . .

One of the classic examples of the lost volume seller is found in *Neri v. Retail Marine Corp.* [Referring to the automobile dealership example excerpted in the *Neri* opinion, the court commented as follows.] This example would surely have a different result if the car dealership was winding down its business and had agreed to sell one of its last cars to a buyer. If that buyer subsequently breached the contract and did not purchase the car, the dealership could hardly be expected to recover lost profits damages if the dealer put the car back onto a deserted car lot, made no attempts to sell it, and kept the dealership shuttered to new customers. Those modifications are analogous to Jordan's situation, with his stated desire to withdraw his services from the endorsement marketplace, and the lost volume seller theory accordingly does not apply to his circumstances.

Jordan states that it is a "red herring" to speculate under the lost volume analysis on what he would have done because that:

> ignores the central point of the lost volume principle: if Jordan had ... accepted a substantially similar endorsement opportunity—exactly what [MCI] argues he was required to do to mitigate damages—the damages for which [MCI] is liable would not have been reduced by one penny because the lost volume principle would allow Jordan to retain the benefits of both the [MCI] Agreement and the hypothetical additional endorsement.

Jordan overlooks an important point about the lost volume seller theory—that the "original sale and the second sale are independent events," [Snyder v. Herbert Greenbaum & Associates, 380 A.2d 618, 625 (Md. Ct. Spec. App. 1977], because the lost volume seller's intent to enter into new contracts is the same before and after a purchaser's breach. The lost volume seller's desire to sell more units of goods or services is virtually unaffected by the loss of a single sale or agreement.

Next, even if Jordan had mitigated damages by entering one subsequent endorsement agreement, this, without more, does not mean that Jordan was a lost volume seller. The lost volume seller has the intent and capacity to sell multiple units despite the breach of a contract for one transaction.

Finally, if Jordan had entered into a subsequent agreement or agreements, and if he had showed both the capacity and the intent to make subsequent sales, that might have had the effect of helping him to establish his status as a lost volume seller, which generally would relieve him of the duty to mitigate. This would not be a novel situation but it ignores the fact that he did not do so. . . .

Because the evidence establishes, among other things, that Jordan would not have entered into subsequent agreements, Jordan has not established that he is a lost volume seller. This theory thus does not relieve Jordan from the duty to mitigate damages. . . .

NOTES AND QUESTIONS

1. The court also rejected Jordan's alternative argument, based on *Parker v. Twentieth Century-Fox Film Corp.*, that MCI had to show he could have entered "substantially similar" endorsement contracts to count in mitigation of damages. The court distinguished *Parker* as "analyzed under employment law and one that presented a completely different factual and procedural background."

2. Suppose an attorney-client retainer agreement called for the client to advance fees to the attorney and, upon termination by the client, let the lawyer retain all such fees as liquidated damages, even if the lawyer did not render any particular service to earn them. These so-called nonrefundable retainers have been outlawed in most states on public policy grounds, primarily because they impair client rights to terminate their lawyers freely. But reaching that legal conclusion required considerable litigation and debate over whether there might be ways to validate such clauses. *E.g.*, *Matter of Cooperman*, 633 N.E.2d 1069 (N.Y. 1994). One line of argument portrayed the device as equivalent to the lost volume seller of commercial law. For a statement and rejection of this argument, see Lester Brickman & Lawrence A. Cunningham, *Nonrefundable Retainers: Impermissible Under Fiduciary, Statutory and Contract Law*, 57 FORDHAM L. REV. 149 (1988):

> In the rare case when a nonrefundable retainer is a valid liquidated damages clause, the avoidable consequences doctrine is implicated upon breach. This doctrine requires an attorney to make reasonable efforts to mitigate damages. Like other employees, an attorney is not entitled to "live in voluntary idleness" upon discharge but must seek alternative employment. Damages are reduced by the amount the lawyer earned or could have earned doing comparable work. The extent to which mitigation reduces damages depends on the injured lawyer's elasticity of capacity—the extent to which the lawyer's practice can accommodate additional services for new or additional clients.

> If elasticity is infinite, then a lawyer is equivalent to the lost volume seller of commercial law, whose damages are the lost profits from the broken contract not offset by the profits on the resale of the item in question. This is because he would have benefited from two sales instead of one but for the breach. Whether an attorney has a capacity that is both liberated and idled by the breach, therefore requiring him to mitigate, is a question of fact. But since most attorneys keep their plates full, they often will be unable to satisfy the conditions of the lost volume seller; they will rarely have high elasticities of capacity.

> The most likely candidate for the lost volume lawyer category would be the large law firm that routinely recruits new associates; that minority of firms can plausibly argue that they can render services without limitation and thus avoid the obligation to mitigate

damages. In all cases, the client's liability upon breach would be determined by reducing the lawyer's contract damages, usually based on expectancy, by his avoidable damages, based on comparable alternatives. In the lost volume case, this mitigation obligation will be zero. Unless a lawyer is able to show lost volume and difficulty in ascertaining damages, however, then the extent of [the] duty to mitigate is considered in determining the reasonableness of the sum fixed as a liquidated damages clause. The lawyer thus cannot use liquidated damages provisions to [negate] the obligation to mitigate.

However, the same considerations that yield zero mitigation also limit if not preclude nonrefundable retainers from being good faith estimates of damages. Thus, in the case of the law firm equivalent to the lost volume seller, damages for breach would be limited to the profits lost as a consequence of the breach. Lost profits would be measured as lost revenue less the cost that would have been incurred for hiring associates to undertake the work. Accordingly, even if mitigation is zero, damages are less than the amount of the price for the service. Therefore, for a nonrefundable retainer to be a reasonable estimate of damages, it would have to be conceived as a lost profit rather than a lost revenue.

EXAMPLE: SEASON TICKETS

Ticket sales provide big-time sports teams with a steady revenue stream that can be used to finance long-term investment. During the economic boom of the early and mid-2000s, many franchises, like the Washington Redskins football team, built expensive new stadiums.

Partly to obtain long-term construction loans, teams sold season tickets for up to 10 years, promising seats in exchange for fan agreements to make annual payments. Amid the late 2008–09 economic recession, however, many fans could not afford to maintain the luxury of better times and breached their contracts with the stadiums. In response, some teams sued fans.

One such defendant was Redskins fan Pat Hill, a 72-year-old real estate agent who lived outside Washington, D.C. She had held season tickets since the early 1960s and renewed them when the team built its new stadium. But after property values plunged during the recession, her business faltered, and she could no longer afford the $5,300 annual sales price for two seats.

Though Hill asked the team for a grace period, it declined and sued her for ten years' worth of season tickets. Unable to pay for a lawyer but believing she had a duty to pay her debts, she let the Redskins win a default judgment against her in court for about $60,000.

The Washington Post identified Pat Hill as one of 125 similar Redskins' fans the team sued that year, claiming millions of dollars in damages. The team's general counsel, David Donovan, acknowledged the suits but said they were a last resort and a small fraction of the 20,000 annual team season ticket contracts, most of which were honored or renegotiated.

Some fans saw it differently, saying the team's renegotiation proposals often came with stinging penalties. They complained that even as the team was recovering ticket prices from breaching fans, it was reselling the same tickets to other spectators, amounting to double dipping. The team denied that.

Discuss the arguments on both sides.

CHAPTER 8

PROBLEMS OF WRITTEN CONTRACTS

■ ■ ■

In this chapter, we consider some of the problems associated with written agreements, organized around three topics: (1) the meaning to be given written expressions, an often surprisingly challenging subject of *interpretation*; (2) how contract law determines which of multiple written or oral expressions constitute the final contract of the parties, by an intricate set of doctrines collectively dubbed the *parol evidence rule*; and (3) the relatively small subset of contracts that law requires be memorialized in writing, governed by an ancient law called the *statute of frauds*.

A. INTERPRETATION

Over many years, courts developed principles of contract interpretation that help contract drafters structure bargains, providing a sense of how what they write will be interpreted. These canons of interpretation reflect both a sense of tradition and an attitude of pragmatism. A primary principle of interpretation is to determine what parties intended and enforce the resulting bargain.

At the same time, other norms and standards play a role in construing contractual meaning. For example, the tenet *contra proferentem* holds that ambiguities are resolved against the interests of the party that drafted an agreement. This rule of construction diminishes incentives to conceal or downplay objectionable content in vague language. Instead, it encourages the drafting party (having greater control over the content of the document), to communicate clearly to the other side. Another fundamental judicial tenet of "construction" is to treat agreements as a whole, not isolating discrete words. Courts try to get a sense of what the overall intent was of the parties to the contract, rather than myopically fixating on separate single aspects.

Even so, interpretive challenges also arise when people attach different meanings to the same word or words in a contract. Consider the following classic case, in which the plaintiff cried "fowl."

FRIGALIMENT IMPORTING CO. V.
B.N.S. INTERN. SALES CORP.
190 F.Supp. 116 (S.D.N.Y. 1960)

FRIENDLY, J.

The issue is, what is chicken? Plaintiff says 'chicken' means a young chicken, suitable for broiling and frying. Defendant says 'chicken' means any bird of that genus that meets contract specifications on weight and quality, including what it calls 'stewing chicken' and plaintiff pejoratively terms 'fowl'. Dictionaries give both meanings, as well as some others not relevant here. To support its, plaintiff sends a number of volleys over the net; defendant essays to return them and adds a few serves of its own. Assuming that both parties were acting in good faith, the case nicely illustrates Holmes' remark 'that the making of a contract depends not on the agreement of two minds in one intention, but on the agreement of two sets of external signs—not on the parties' having meant the same thing but on their having said the same thing.' The Path of the Law, in Collected Legal Papers, p. 178. I have concluded that plaintiff has not sustained its burden of persuasion that the contract used 'chicken' in the narrower sense.

The action is for breach of the warranty that goods sold shall correspond to the description, New York Personal Property Law, McKinney's Consol. Laws, c. 41, § 95. Two contracts are in suit. In the first, dated May 2, 1957, defendant, a New York sales corporation, confirmed the sale to plaintiff, a Swiss corporation, of

> "US Fresh Frozen Chicken, Grade A, Government Inspected, Eviscerated 2 1/2–3 lbs. and 1 1/2–2 lbs. each all chicken individually wrapped in cryovac, packed in secured fiber cartons or wooden boxes, suitable for export

75,000 lbs. 2 1/2–3 lbs.	@$33.00
25,000 lbs. 1 1/2–2 lbs.	@$36.50

> per 100 lbs. FAS New York

> scheduled May 10, 1957 pursuant to instructions from Penson & Co., New York.'

The second contract, also dated May 2, 1957, was identical save that only 50,000 lbs. of the heavier 'chicken' were called for, the price of the smaller birds was $37 per 100 lbs., and shipment was scheduled for May 30. The initial shipment under the first contract was short but the balance was shipped on May 17. When the initial shipment arrived in Switzerland, plaintiff found, on May 28, that the 2 1/2–3 lbs. birds were not young chicken suitable for broiling and frying but stewing chicken or 'fowl'; indeed, many of the cartons and bags plainly so indicated. Protests ensued.

Nevertheless, shipment under the second contract was made on May 29, the 2 1/2–3 lbs. birds again being stewing chicken. Defendant stopped the transportation of these at Rotterdam.

This action followed. Plaintiff says that, notwithstanding that its acceptance was in Switzerland, New York law controls under the principle of Rubin v. Irving Trust Co., 1953, 305 N.Y. 288, 305, 113 N.E.2d 424, 431; defendant does not dispute this, and relies on New York decisions. I shall follow the apparent agreement of the parties as to the applicable law.

Since the word 'chicken' standing alone is ambiguous, I turn first to see whether the contract itself offers any aid to its interpretation. Plaintiff says the 1 1/2–2 lbs. birds necessarily had to be young chicken since the older birds do not come in that size, hence the 2 1/2–3 lbs. birds must likewise be young. This is unpersuasive—a contract for 'apples' of two different sizes could be filled with different kinds of apples even though only one species came in both sizes. Defendant notes that the contract called not simply for chicken but for 'US Fresh Frozen Chicken, Grade A, Government Inspected.' It says the contract thereby incorporated by reference the Department of Agriculture's regulations, which favor its interpretation; I shall return to this after reviewing plaintiff's other contentions.

The first hinges on an exchange of cablegrams which preceded execution of the formal contracts. The negotiations leading up to the contracts were conducted in New York between defendant's secretary, Ernest R. Bauer, and a Mr. Stovicek, who was in New York for the Czechoslovak government at the World Trade Fair. A few days after meeting Bauer at the fair, Stovicek telephoned and inquired whether defendant would be interested in exporting poultry to Switzerland. Bauer then met with Stovicek, who showed him a cable from plaintiff dated April 26, 1957, announcing that they 'are buyer' of 25,000 lbs. of chicken 2 1/2–3 lbs. weight, Cryovac packed, grade A Government inspected, at a price up to 33¢ per pound, for shipment on May 10, to be confirmed by the following morning, and were interested in further offerings. After testing the market for price, Bauer accepted, and Stovicek sent a confirmation that evening.

Plaintiff stresses that, although these and subsequent cables between plaintiff and defendant, which laid the basis for the additional quantities under the first and for all of the second contract, were predominantly in German, they used the English word 'chicken'; it claims this was done because it understood 'chicken' meant young chicken whereas the German word, 'Huhn,' included both 'Brathuhn' (broilers) and 'Suppenhuhn' (stewing chicken), and that defendant, whose officers were thoroughly conversant with German, should have realized this. Whatever force this argument might otherwise have is largely drained away by Bauer's testimony that he asked Stovicek what kind of chickens were wanted, received the answer 'any kind of chickens,' and then, in German, asked whether the cable meant 'Huhn' and received an affirmative response. . . .

Plaintiff's next contention is that there was a definite trade usage that 'chicken' meant 'young chicken.' Defendant showed that it was only beginning in the poultry trade in 1957, thereby bringing itself within the principle that 'when one of the parties is not a member of the trade or other circle, his acceptance of the standard must be made to appear' by proving either that he had actual knowledge of the usage or that the usage is 'so generally known in the community that his actual individual knowledge of it may be inferred.' 9 Wigmore, Evidence (3d ed. § 1940) 2464. Here there was no proof of actual knowledge of the alleged usage; indeed, it is quite plain that defendant's belief was to the contrary. In order to meet the alternative requirement, the law of New York demands a showing that 'the usage is of so long continuance, so well established, so notorious, so universal and so reasonable in itself, as that the presumption is violent that the parties contracted with reference to it, and made it a part of their agreement.' Walls v. Bailey, 1872, 49 N.Y. 464, 472–473.

Plaintiff endeavored to establish such a usage by the testimony of three witnesses and certain other evidence. Strasser, resident buyer in New York for a large chain of Swiss cooperatives, testified that 'on chicken I would definitely understand a broiler.' However, the force of this testimony was considerably weakened by the fact that in his own transactions the witness, a careful businessman, protected himself by using 'broiler' when that was what he wanted and 'fowl' when he wished older birds. . . . While Wigmore thinks this goes too far, a witness' consistent failure to rely on the alleged usage deprives his opinion testimony of much of its effect. Niesielowski, an officer of one of the companies that had furnished the stewing chicken to defendant, testified that 'chicken' meant 'the male species of the poultry industry. That could be a broiler, a fryer or a roaster', but not a stewing chicken; however, he also testified that upon receiving defendant's inquiry for 'chickens', he asked whether the desire was for 'fowl or frying chickens' and, in fact, supplied fowl, although taking the precaution of asking defendant, a day or two after plaintiff's acceptance of the contracts in suit, to change its confirmation of its order from 'chickens,' as defendant had originally prepared it, to 'stewing chickens.'

Dates, an employee of Urner-Barry Company, which publishes a daily market report on the poultry trade, gave it as his view that the trade meaning of 'chicken' was 'broilers and fryers.' In addition to this opinion testimony, plaintiff relied on the fact that the Urner-Barry service, the Journal of Commerce, and Weinberg Bros. & Co. of Chicago, a large supplier of poultry, published quotations in a manner which, in one way or another, distinguish between 'chicken,' comprising broilers, fryers and certain other categories, and 'fowl,' which, Bauer acknowledged, included stewing chickens. This material would be impressive if there were nothing to the contrary. However, there was, as will now be seen.

Defendant's witness Weininger, who operates a chicken eviscerating plant in New Jersey, testified 'Chicken is everything except a goose, a duck, and a turkey. Everything is a chicken, but then you have to say, you have to specify which category you want or that you are talking about.' Its witness Fox said that in the trade 'chicken' would encompass all the various classifications. Sadina, who conducts a food inspection service, testified that he would consider any bird coming within the classes of 'chicken' in the Department of Agriculture's regulations to be a chicken. The specifications approved by the General Services Administration include fowl as well as broilers and fryers under the classification 'chickens.' Statistics of the Institute of American Poultry Industries use the phrases 'Young chickens' and 'Mature chickens,' under the general heading 'Total chickens.' and the Department of Agriculture's daily and weekly price reports avoid use of the word 'chicken' without specification.

Defendant advances several other points which it claims affirmatively support its construction. Primary among these is the regulation of the Department of Agriculture, 7 C.F.R. § 70.300–70.370, entitled, 'Grading and Inspection of Poultry and Edible Products Thereof.' and in particular 70.301 which recited [The following are the various classes of chickens: (a) Broiler or fryer; (b) Roaster; (c) Capon; (d) Stag); (e) Hen or stewing chicken or fowl; (f) Cock or old rooster. . . .]

Defendant argues, as previously noted, that the contract incorporated these regulations by reference. Plaintiff answers that the contract provision related simply to grade and Government inspection and did not incorporate the Government definition of 'chicken,' and also that the definition in the Regulations is ignored in the trade. However, the latter contention was contradicted by Weininger and Sadina; and there is force in defendant's argument that the contract made the regulations a dictionary, particularly since the reference to Government grading was already in plaintiff's initial cable to Stovicek.

Defendant makes a further argument based on the impossibility of its obtaining broilers and fryers at the 33¢ price offered by plaintiff for the 2 1/2–3 lbs. birds. There is no substantial dispute that, in late April, 1957, the price for 2 1/2–3 lbs. broilers was between 35 and 37¢ per pound, and that when defendant entered into the contracts, it was well aware of this and intended to fill them by supplying fowl in these weights. It claims that plaintiff must likewise have known the market since plaintiff had reserved shipping space on April 23, three days before plaintiff's cable to Stovicek, or, at least, that Stovicek was chargeable with such knowledge. It is scarcely an answer to say, as plaintiff does in its brief, that the 33¢ price offered by the 2 1/2–3 lbs. 'chickens' was closer to the prevailing 35¢ price for broilers than to the 30¢ at which defendant procured fowl. Plaintiff must have expected defendant to make some profit— certainly it could not have expected defendant deliberately to incur a loss.

When all the evidence is reviewed, it is clear that defendant believed it could comply with the contracts by delivering stewing chicken in the 2 ½–3 lbs. size. Defendant's subjective intent would not be significant if this did not coincide with an objective meaning of 'chicken.' Here it did coincide with one of the dictionary meanings, with the definition in the Department of Agriculture Regulations to which the contract made at least oblique reference, with at least some usage in the trade, with the realities of the market, and with what plaintiff's spokesman had said. Plaintiff asserts it to be equally plain that plaintiff's own subjective intent was to obtain broilers and fryers; the only evidence against this is the material as to market prices and this may not have been sufficiently brought home. In any event it is unnecessary to determine that issue. For plaintiff has the burden of showing that 'chicken' was used in the narrower rather than in the broader sense, and this it has not sustained. . . .

NOTES AND QUESTIONS

1. What factors caused the confusion that seems to abound in *Frigaliment*? Would the word "chicken" have seemed ambiguous to you before reading this case?

2. The dispute involved conflicting information presented by the parties. Ultimately, the court looked, as a default rule, to the burden of proof to reach its determination. Had the court not been constrained by this burden, would the outcome be different? What would a dissenting opinion in this case look like? What arguments would be presented?

3. What role did expert witnesses play in helping the court to resolve the case? How can experts be useful in determining contract interpretation?

4. Notice the *Frigaliment* court's use of the market price of young chickens and the market price of stewing chickens. Normally, absent unconscionability or other rare contexts, courts do not inquire into the adequacy of consideration. Why does the court here analyze the substance of the transaction? How might the amount of an exchange aid the interpretation of a contract?

5. How could the drafters of the contract have avoided this problem? In general, what lessons can this case teach about contract negotiation and drafting?

6. The *Frigaliment* opinion opens by saying, "The issue is, what is chicken?" Was that the issue in the case?

EXAMPLE: WTC AND 9/11—ONE OCCURRENCE OR TWO?

On September 11, 2001, terrorists hijacked commercial aircraft and flew two of them into the World Trade Center in New York—another hit the Pentagon in Washington and a fourth was overtaken by passengers, forcing it to nosedive into a Pennsylvania field. Beyond the loss of 3,000 lives and many personal injuries, the assaults in New York destroyed or damaged twenty buildings, including the total collapse of five of the buildings that comprised the World Trade Center (WTC).

The insurance industry incurred an unprecedented $40 billion in claims, all pursuant to thousands of insurance contracts, including aviation, life, workers' compensation, and liability policies. *See* Scott G. Johnson, *Ten Years After 9/11*, 46 TORT TRIAL & INSURANCE PRACTICE L.J. 685 (Spring-Summer 2011); *World Trade Center Properties, L.L.C. v. Hartford Fire Insurance Co.*, 345 F.3d 154, 180 (2d Cir. 2003). While many claims were filed and paid without incident, some generated significant litigation. One issue was particularly vexing: how many occurrences were there on 9/11 at the WTC: one, encompassing the destruction of the entire unitary complex, or two, given that two planes struck separate towers?

Commercial property insurance policies typically address claims on a per occurrence basis, including in terms of overall policy limits (the maximum payable) and the applicable deductible (in effect, the minimum loss before any coverage applies). When losses are within limits, the question of occurrences relates only to the deductibles and insurers tend to classify events into multiple occurrences to generate multiple deductibles; but when losses exceed policy limits, the number of occurrences defines that cap and insurers generally prefer to classify events as involving a single occurrence to cap liability. In the case of the destruction of the WTC on 9/11, losses vastly exceeded policy limits, turning what may have seemed like a semantic question into a $3.5 billion disagreement.

The WTC was owned by the Port Authority of New York and New Jersey, which had recently leased it to Silverstein Properties, Inc. The lease agreement required Silverstein to insure the WTC, and on September 11 it was in the process of putting insurance in place. Given the WTC's size and scope, the insurance was large and complex, involving more than thirty insurers, each offering varying layers of coverage that aggregated $3.5 billion—"per occurrence." Silverstein claimed there had been two occurrences, meaning $7 billion in total coverage; the insurers said there had been but one occurrence, meaning $3.5 billion in total coverage.

Despite posing the same question—what is an occurrence?—the answer differed for different insurers because the insurers were bound by different contract policies using different contract language. One group had bound itself to a policy (called the Willis form) which defined "occurrence" to mean "all losses or damages that are attributable directly or indirectly to one cause or to one series of similar causes." Other policies either did not define the term occurrence or defined it differently. Court proceedings followed accordingly.

Interpreting policies using the Willis form's definition of occurrence was relatively easy for the judges, with both the trial and appellate courts finding that the 9/11 attacks amounted to one occurrence. The reasoning was closely tied to the specific definition: "no finder of fact could reasonably fail to find that the intentional crashes into the WTC of two hijacked airplanes sixteen minutes apart as a result of a single, coordinated plan of attack, was, at the least, a 'series of similar causes.'" *World Trade Center Properties*, 345 F.3d 154, 180. The liability of such insurers was therefore limited to the respective policy cap. The conclusion was reached on summary judgment—meaning as a matter of law without need for any trial.

Such an easy interpretation was impossible under the other policies, however. For those that lacked a definition of occurrence, both courts concluded that the concept was sufficiently ambiguous to require considering extrinsic evidence to determine contractual intention. This requires studying context: meaning is to be interpreted given the specific policy and facts of the case, not broad generalities or legal principles. The issue was therefore a matter for a jury. After listening to competing evidence and views, the jury decided that the 9/11 assault on the WTC amounted to two occurrences for purposes of coverage under the policies.

The jury was apparently persuaded by evidence offered at trial by Silverstein's expert witness on the insurance business. Concerning policies that did not define occurrence, he explained that insurers generally take occurrence to have a narrow meaning—giving rise to multiple occurrences from given scenarios—principally because that increases the number of deductibles that apply. Insurers only prefer a broad conception of occurrence—one-occurrence interpretations—in total loss situations such as this, which are rarer. For policies that defined occurrence differently than in the Willis form—such as any loss or series of losses arising out of one "event"—the expert explained that the word event should likewise be construed narrowly.

The policy language is the starting point for making a deal and interpreting it. Want a specific definition, then supply it, and courts will enforce it accordingly; absent a specific definition, courts must dig into context, get all the facts, and let the fact finder decide. The latter setting obviously entails greater uncertainty, subjectivity, and contingency. Indeed, while some courts urge juries to contemplate the dictionary definition of occurrence, others adopt a logical perspective, which can vary according to emphasizing the causes of a loss (where all damage from a single, proximate cause is a single occurrence) or the effects (each separate incident of loss is a separate occurrence).

F.B.T. PRODUCTIONS, LLC V. AFTERMATH RECORDS

621 F.3d 958 (9th Cir. 2010)
cert. denied, 562 U.S. 1286 (2011)

SILVERMAN, C.J.

. . . This dispute concerns the percentage of royalties due to Plaintiffs F.B.T. Productions, LLC, and Em2M, LLC, under their contracts with Defendant Aftermath in connection with the recordings of Marshal B. Mathers, III, professionally known as the rap artist Eminem. Specifically, F.B.T. and Aftermath disagree on whether the contracts' "Records Sold" provision or "Masters Licensed" provision sets the royalty rate for sales of Eminem's records in the form of permanent downloads and mastertones. Before trial, F.B.T. moved for summary judgment that the Masters Licensed provision unambiguously applied to permanent downloads and mastertones. The district court denied the motion. At the close of evidence, F.B.T. did not move for judgment as a matter of law, and the jury returned a verdict in favor of Aftermath. On appeal, F.B.T. reasserts that the Masters Licensed provision unambiguously applies to permanent downloads and mastertones. We agree that the contracts are unambiguous and that the district court should have granted summary judgment to F.B.T. . . .

. . . F.B.T. signed Eminem in 1995, gaining exclusive rights to his recordings. In 1998, F.B.T. signed an agreement transferring Eminem's exclusive recording services to Aftermath. The "Records Sold" provision of that agreement provides that F.B.T. is to receive between 12% and 20% of the adjusted retail price of all "full price records sold in the United States . . . through normal retail channels." The agreement further provides that "[n]otwithstanding the foregoing," F.B.T. is to receive 50% of Aftermath's net receipts "[o]n masters licensed by us . . . to others for their manufacture and sale of records or for any other uses." The parties refer to this provision as the "Masters Licensed" provision. The contract defines "master" as a "recording of sound, without or with visual images, which is used or useful in the recording, production or manufacture of records." The agreement does not contain a definition of the terms "licensed" or "normal retail channels."

In 2002, Aftermath's parent company, Defendant UMG Recordings, Inc., concluded an agreement with Apple Computer, Inc., that enabled UMG's sound recordings, including the Eminem masters, to be sold through Apple's iTunes store as permanent downloads. Permanent downloads are digital copies of recordings that, once downloaded over the Internet, remain on an end-user's computer or other device until deleted. The contract between UMG and Apple is but one example of the many agreements that Aftermath has concluded to sell sound recordings in digital formats since approximately 2001. Since 2003, Aftermath has also concluded contracts with major cellular telephone network carriers to sell sound recordings as mastertones, which are short clips of songs that can be purchased by users to signal incoming calls, popularly known as ringtones.

In 2003, F.B.T. and Aftermath entered into a new agreement that terminated the 1998 agreement. The 2003 agreement increased some royalty rates, but incorporated the wording of the Records Sold and Masters Licensed provisions from the 1998 agreement. In 2004, the parties amended the agreement to provide that "Sales of Albums by way of permanent download shall be treated as [U.S. Normal Retail Channel] Net Sales for the purposes of escalations." Escalations are increases in the royalty rate when total album sales surpass certain targets. The amendment further provides, "Except as specifically modified herein, the Agreement shall be unaffected and remain in full force and effect."

F.B.T. brought suit after a 2006 audit showed that Aftermath had been applying the Records Sold provision to calculate the royalties due to F.B.T. for sales of Eminem's recordings in the form of permanent downloads and mastertones. Before trial, F.B.T. moved for summary judgment that the Masters Licensed provision unambiguously applied to those sales. Aftermath cross-moved for summary judgment. It argued, in part, that the 2004 amendment showed that the parties intended the Records Sold provision to apply to permanent downloads.

After provisionally reviewing the undisputed extrinsic evidence, the district court concluded that the agreements were reasonably susceptible to either party's interpretation and denied both motions for summary judgment. At trial, only Aftermath moved for judgment as a matter of law at the close of the evidence. The court denied the motion. The jury returned a verdict in favor of Aftermath, and the district court awarded Aftermath its attorneys' fees of over $2.4 million. F.B.T. timely appealed the district court's final judgment and award of attorneys' fees. We . . . reverse.

. . . [T]he Records Sold provision contains the royalty rate for "full price records sold in the United States . . . through normal retail channels." On summary judgment, Aftermath argued that the Records Sold provision applied because permanent downloads and mastertones are records, and because iTunes and other digital music providers are normal retail channels in the United States.

However, the agreements also provide that "notwithstanding" the Records Sold provision, F.B.T. is to receive a 50% royalty on "masters licensed by [Aftermath] . . . to others for their manufacture and sale of records or for any other uses." The parties' use of the word "notwithstanding" plainly indicates that even if a transaction arguably falls within the scope of the Records Sold provision, F.B.T. is to receive a 50% royalty if Aftermath licenses an Eminem master to a third party for "any" use. A contractual term is not ambiguous just because it is broad.

Here, the Masters Licensed provision explicitly applies to (1) masters (2) that are licensed to third parties for the manufacture of records "or for any other uses," (3) "notwithstanding" the Record Sold provision. This provision is admittedly broad, but it is not unclear or ambiguous.

Accordingly, to determine whether the Masters Licensed provision applies, we must decide whether Aftermath licensed the Eminem masters to third parties. Aftermath argues that there was no evidence that it or F.B.T. used the term "licensed" in a technical sense. See Cal. Civ.Code § 1644 ("The words of a contract are to be understood in their ordinary and popular sense, rather than according to their strict legal meaning; unless used by the parties in a technical sense. . . ."). In the ordinary sense of the word, a license is simply "permission to act." Webster's Third New International Dictionary of the English Language 1304 (2002). Aftermath did not dispute that it entered into agreements that permitted iTunes, cellular phone carriers, and other third parties to use its sound recordings to produce and sell permanent downloads and mastertones. Those agreements therefore qualify as licenses under Aftermath's own proposed construction of the term.

The conclusion that Aftermath licensed the Eminem masters to third parties also comports well with and finds additional support in federal copyright law. When one looks to the Copyright Act, the terms "license" and "sale" have well differentiated meanings, and the differences between the two play an important role in the overall structures and policies that govern artistic rights. For example, under the language of the Act and the Supreme Court's interpretations, a "sale" of a work may either be a transfer in title of an individual copy of a work, or a sale of all exclusive intellectual property rights in a work. See 17 U.S.C. § 109 (describing the "first sale" doctrine); Quality King Distribs. v. L'anza Research Int'l, 523 U.S. 135, 145 . . . (1998) (describing the transfer of an individual copy of a work as a sale) . . . .

There is no dispute that Aftermath was at all relevant times the owner of the copyrights to the Eminem recordings at issue in this case, having obtained those rights through the recording contracts in exchange for specified royalty payments. Pursuant to its agreements with Apple and other third parties, however, Aftermath did not "sell" anything to the download distributors. The download distributors did not obtain title to the digital files. The ownership of those files remained with Aftermath, Aftermath reserved the right to regain possession of the files at any time, and Aftermath obtained recurring benefits in the form of payments based on the volume of downloads. . . . Under our case law interpreting and applying the Copyright Act, too, it is well settled that where a copyright owner transfers a copy of copyrighted material, retains title, limits the uses to which the material may be put, and is compensated periodically based on the transferee's exploitation of the material, the transaction is a license! . . .

Furthermore, the sound recordings that Aftermath provided to third parties qualify as masters. The contracts define a "master" as a "recording of sound . . . which is used or useful in the recording, production or manufacture of records." Aftermath admitted that permanent downloads and mastertones are records. The sound recordings that Aftermath supplied to third parties were "used or useful" in the production of permanent downloads and mastertones, so those sound recordings were masters. Because Aftermath permitted third parties to use the Eminem masters to produce and sell records, in the form of permanent downloads and mastertones, F.B.T. is entitled to a 50% royalty under the plain terms of the agreements.

Aftermath argues that the 2004 amendment to the agreements clarified that the Records Sold provision sets the royalty for permanent downloads. However, the 2004 amendment states only that albums sold as permanent downloads are to be counted "for purposes of escalations" under the Records Sold provision, and that "[e]xcept as specifically modified herein, the Agreement shall be unaffected and remain in full force and effect." Read in context, the plain language of the amendment provides that sales of permanent downloads by third parties count towards escalations on the royalty owed when Aftermath itself sells records through normal retail channels. It does not state, and in no way implies, that the royalty rate for the sale of the permanent downloads by third parties is set by the Records Sold provision.

NOTES AND QUESTIONS

1.   The rapper Eminem is a controversial figure who has received a considerable amount of press for some of the litigation he was involved in, most characterized by public feuding and court battles with his mother and ex-wife. This case raised interesting issues around technology and contract interpretation, but drew far less media attention than his divorce and the defamation lawsuit brought by his mother. For one journalistic account of the instant case, see Ben Sisario, *Eminem Lawsuit May Raise Pay for Older Artists*, N.Y. TIMES (March 27, 2011).

2.   Although the outcome in *F.B.T. Productions* is sensible based on the court's reading of the contract, the district court had reached the opposite conclusion. What arguments could have influenced the district court?

3.   The issue of technological change is vexing and recurring. Even when anticipated, technology sometimes changes settled deals in unpredictable ways. Those who drafted the Eminem contract may not have envisioned iTunes, but they did include all future forms of masters within the bargain's reach. The case shows that it pays to think through plausible future scenarios

and negotiate some parameters for how to handle them in the contract. A failure to do so can be costly.

4. *F.B.T. Productions* illustrates the importance of linguistic structure and cues in written contracts. It is common for contracts with many and complex provisions to bring clarity to particularly important deal points through use of key terms. Lawyers use key terms to cue judges to specific preferences, and judicial ears are attuned to such legal music. Such cues are particularly valuable considering that the limits of language often make it difficult, years later, to determine what people intended when they agreed to a written bargain. What language plays this role in *F.B.T. Productions*?

What happens when two provisions of a contract are inharmonious or out-of-sync with each other? The following case, involving CBS News anchor Dan Rather's employment agreement, explores this issue.

RATHER V. CBS CORP.

886 N.Y.S.2d 121 (N.Y. App. Div. 2009)

CATTERSON, J.

This action asserting breach of contract . . . arises out of a September 8, 2004 broadcast that plaintiff Dan Rather narrated on the CBS 60 Minutes II television program about then President George W. Bush's service in the Texas Air National Guard. Rather alleges that CBS disavowed the broadcast after it was attacked by Bush supporters . . . . Rather alleges that, following President Bush's re-election, CBS informed him that he would be removed as anchor of the CBS Evening News. Rather claims that although his employment agreement required that, in the event he was removed as anchor, CBS would make him a regular correspondent on 60 Minutes or immediately pay all amounts due under the agreement and release him to work elsewhere, CBS kept him on the payroll while denying him the opportunity to cover important news stories until May 2006 when it terminated his contract, effective June 2006.

Rather commenced this action against CBS Corporation [and other corporate and individual defendants] in September 2007. He asserted, inter alia, claims of breach of contract and breach of fiduciary duty. . . . [T]his Court finds that the motion court erred in denying the defendants' motion to dismiss the claims for breach of contract and breach of fiduciary duty, and therefore we find the complaint must be dismissed in its entirety. . . .

Rather alleges that he delivered his last broadcast as anchor of the CBS Evening News on March 9, 2005, and that, since he was only nominally assigned to 60 Minutes II and then 60 Minutes, he should have received the remainder of his compensation under the agreement in March

2005. Rather claims that, in effect, CBS "warehoused" him, and that, when he was finally terminated and paid in June 2006, CBS did not compensate him for the 15 months "when he could have worked elsewhere." This claim attempts to gloss over the fact that Rather continued to be compensated at his normal CBS salary of approximately $6 million a year until June 2006 when the compensation was accelerated upon termination, consistent with his contract.

Contractually, CBS was under no obligation to "use [Rather's] services or to broadcast any program" so long as it continued to pay him the applicable compensation. This "pay or play" provision of the original 1979 employment agreement was specifically reaffirmed in the 2002 Amendment to the employment agreement.

That Amendment also provided, in subparagraph 1(g), that if CBS removed Rather as anchor or co-anchor of the CBS Evening News and failed to assign him as a correspondent on 60 Minutes II or another mutually agreed upon position, the agreement would be terminated, Rather would be free to seek employment elsewhere, and CBS would pay him immediately the remainder of his weekly compensation through November 25, 2006.

We agree that subparagraph 1(g) must be read together with the subparagraph 1(f), which provided that if CBS removed Rather from the CBS Evening News, it would assign him to 60 Minutes II "as a full-time Correspondent," and if 60 Minutes II were canceled, it would assign him to 60 Minutes as a correspondent "to perform services on a regular basis." However, this construction does not render any language of the agreement inoperative, since, consistent with the "pay or play" clause, neither subparagraph 1(g) nor 1(f) requires that CBS actually use Rather's services or broadcast any programs on which he appears, but simply retains the option of accelerating the payment of his compensation under the agreement if he is not assigned to either program.

It is clear that subparagraph 1(g) applies only to a situation where CBS removed Rather as anchor of CBS Evening News and then failed to assign him "as a Correspondent on 60 Minutes II." The amended complaint alleges that when Rather no longer performed anchor duties at CBS, he was assigned to 60 Minutes II. Thus, Rather implicitly concedes that CBS fully complied with subparagraph 1(g).

The [lower court] erred in finding that subparagraph 1(g) modified the "pay or play" provision when it ignored the initial prefatory clause to the rest of that subparagraph, which states "[e]xcept as otherwise specified in this Agreement." As the defendants correctly assert, the seven words are crucial because they require subparagraph 1(g) to be read together with the "pay or play" provision, and thus, subparagraph 1(g) cannot modify the "pay or play" provision to mean that CBS must utilize Rather in accordance with some specific standard by featuring him in a sufficient number or types of broadcasts. As the defendants aptly observed, "the notion that a network would cede to a reporter editorial authority to decide what stories will be aired is absurd." . . .

Rather's cause of action for breach of fiduciary duty must also be dismissed. [The lower court] held that the issue of "whether a fiduciary duty has been created in the course of the long relationship between Rather and CBS is really a question of fact." Previously, the court determined that "the length of [Rather's] contractual relationship with [CBS], and the nature of the service that [Rather] performed under his contracts" created an issue of fact that could not be resolved on motion. This was error.

Rather claims that his "four-decade history" with CBS constituted a "special relationship that imposed fiduciary duties upon CBS toward [Rather]." The law in this Department, and indeed enunciated in every reported appellate-division-level case, is that employment relationships do not create fiduciary relationships. . . . The length of Rather's tenure at CBS is irrelevant to, and does not support, this claim of a fiduciary relationship . . . , nor does Rather's status as "the public face of CBS News after Walter Cronkite retired [. . .]." . . .

NOTES AND QUESTIONS

1. The court tried to decide this case based on "plain meaning." The pay-or-play clause in the contract dated to 1979 and is standard in many industries, including broadcast journalism and entertainment. While networks such as CBS like to protect themselves from ceding managerial control to staff, on-air personalities command leverage in contract negotiations based on fame and abilities.

2. The 2002 amendments to the CBS-Rather contract were made when Dan Rather personified CBS News and enjoyed commanding stature. It would be unsurprising if Rather used his leverage to get the terms as he interpreted the contract: keep him in high-level posts or let him out of the deal and accelerate his pay.

3. Just as in the Eminem litigation, linguistic cues played a role in the *Rather* opinion. Which linguistic cues did the court analyze in deciding how the contract should be interpreted?

4. It is tempting to compare the method and philosophy of interpretation of contracts to those involving the interpretation of statutes. They may seem similar in the sense of involving the discernment of intention or meaning and application of abstract principles to concrete facts. But they differ in fundamental ways, starting with how contract is an exercise of volition by private actors while statutes are public enactments by bodies of elected officials coordinating action in a constitutional system. For a critical assessment of efforts to push the analogy, see Mark L. Movsesian, *Are Statutes*

Really "Legislative Bargains"? The Failure of the Contract Analogy in Statutory Interpretation, 76 NORTH CAROLINA L. REV. 1146 (1998).

———————

As courts frequently look to linguistic cues in specific contracts, they tend to invoke recurring principles of interpretation. Some of these are collected in various sections of the Restatement (Second) of Contracts, such as those that follow.

RESTATEMENT (SECOND OF CONTRACTS), SECTION 202

§ 202.   *Rules in Aid of Interpretation.*

(1) Words and other conduct are interpreted in the light of all the circumstances, and if the principal purpose of the parties is ascertainable it is given great weight.

(2) A writing is interpreted as a whole, and all writings that are part of the same transaction are interpreted together.

(3) Unless a different intention is manifested, (a) where language has a generally prevailing meaning, it is interpreted in accordance with that meaning; (b) technical terms and words of art are given their technical meaning when used in a transaction within their technical field.

(4) Where an agreement involves repeated occasions for performance by either party with knowledge of the nature of the performance and opportunity for objection to it by the other any course of performance accepted or acquiesced in without objection is given great weight in the interpretation of the agreement.

(5) Wherever reasonable, the manifestations of intention of the parties to a promise or agreement are interpreted as consistent with each other and with any relevant course of performance, course of dealing or usage of trade.

———————

The court in *Aftermath Records* also addressed such arguments in passages omitted from the excerpt above, as follows:

> Nor did any of the evidence regarding industry custom or the parties' course of performance support Aftermath's interpretation that the Records Sold provision applies. Aftermath's expert explained that the Masters Licensed provision had in the past been applied "only to compilation records and incorporation into movies, TV shows, and commercials." It was, however, undisputed that permanent downloads and mastertones only came into existence from 2001 to 2003. Consequently, the fact that the Masters Licensed provision had never previously been applied to

those forms of licensing is immaterial. There is no indication that the parties intended to confine the contract to the state of the industry in 1998. To the contrary, the contract contemplated advances in technology. It provided that Aftermath had the right to exploit the "masters in any and all forms of media now known and hereinafter developed." Aftermath's evidence of how the Masters Licensed provision had been applied in the past therefore did not cast doubt on its application to permanent downloads and mastertones.

Furthermore, Aftermath renewed its agreement with F.B.T. in 2003, by which time permanent downloads and mastertones were coming into existence. Aftermath argued that subsequent to renewal, F.B.T. had "never objected to Defendants' payment of royalties under the Records Sold provision until the auditor raised the issue in 2006." However, Aftermath provided no evidence that F.B.T. knowingly acquiesced to payment under the Records Sold provision between 2003 and 2006. It showed that F.B.T. had received statements that included royalties for permanent downloads and mastertones, but it was uncontroverted that F.B.T. did not audit those royalty statements until 2006. F.B.T. had no obligation to audit the statements any earlier than it did, and it immediately raised the issue with Aftermath after the audit. Accordingly, Aftermath cannot use F.B.T.'s lack of objection to payments made before 2006 to prove how it interpreted the agreements. . . . The undisputed extrinsic evidence provisionally reviewed by the district court therefore did not support Aftermath's interpretation that the Records Sold provision applies. . . .

The UCC provides statutory directives for the judicial interpretation of contracts concerning transactions in goods. These center around important concepts in commercial law: course of dealing and usage of trade, which are set forth in Article I of the UCC, the main article of the overall Code, and course of performance, contained in Article II on transactions in goods. Consider the following statutory excerpts.

UCC SECTIONS 1–205, 2–208

§ 1–205. *Course of Dealing and Usage of Trade*

(1) A course of dealing is a sequence of previous conduct between the parties to a particular transaction which is fairly to be regarded as establishing a common basis of understanding for interpreting their expressions and other conduct.

(2) A usage of trade is any practice or method of dealing having such regularity of observance in a place, vocation or trade as to justify an

expectation that it will be observed with respect to the transaction in question. The existence and scope of such a usage are to be proved as facts. If it is established that such a usage is embodied in a written trade code or similar writing the interpretation of the writing is for the court.

(3) A course of dealing between parties and any usage of trade in the vocation or trade in which they are engaged or of which they are or should be aware given particular meaning to and supplement or qualify terms of an agreement.

(4) The express terms of an agreement and an applicable course of dealing or usage or trade shall be construed wherever reasonable as consistent with each other; but when such construction is unreasonable express terms control both course of dealing and usage or trade and course of dealing controls usage of trade. . . .

§ 2–208. *Course of Performance or Practical Construction*

(1) Where the contract for sale involves repeated occasions for performance by either party with knowledge of the nature of the performance and opportunity for objection to it by the other, any course of performance accepted or acquiesced in without objection shall be relevant to determine the meaning of the agreement.

(2) The express terms of the agreement and any such course of performance, as well as any course of dealing and usage of trade, shall be construed whenever reasonable as consistent with each other; but when such construction is unreasonable, express terms shall control course of performance and course of performance shall control both course of dealing and usage of trade (Section 1–205).

FOXCO INDUSTRIES V. FABRIC WORLD
595 F.2d 976 (5th Cir. 1979)

TJOFLAT, J.

[The facts of this case and the court's opinion on the measure of damages are excerpted in Chapter Seven: Remedies. The following excerpt includes additional factual background on trade usage and the court's opinion concerning that aspect of the seller's argument. Recall that the case involved a seller, Foxco, suing a buyer, Fabric World, of knitted fabric goods, for the contract price.]

Fabric World [contends that] the district court erred in admitting into evidence published standards of the Knitted Textile Association to establish the meaning of a disputed contract term.

During the course of the trial there was much testimony regarding the meaning of the term first quality goods used in the contracts between Foxco and Fabric World. The testimony on behalf of Fabric World was that it meant fabric containing no flaws. Foxco introduced evidence, over the objection of Fabric World, in the form of an exhibit containing standards for finished knitted goods promulgated by the Knitted Textile Association, a large textile industry group to which Foxco belongs. These standards indicated that certain types and amounts of flaws were permissible in first quality fabric. Fabric World is not a member of that association and claimed it had no knowledge of the standards adopted by the association's members. One ground for Fabric World's present appeal is its contention that the standards of a trade association of which it had no knowledge are not admissible to show the meaning of the undefined and disputed contract term "first quality" goods. . . .

Fabric World's . . . claim is that the district court erred in admitting into evidence the definition of first quality goods contained in the Standards for Finished Knitted Fabrics of the Knitted Textile Association. It contends that it is not a member of the Knitted Textile Association, was unaware of its existence until the time of trial, and that that group's standards were inadmissible because they were a custom or usage of the trade of which Fabric World had no knowledge. We find no error in the trial court's ruling.

A major issue in this case is what was meant by the term "first quality." Under the traditional [common law], Fabric World's contention may have merit: the private, subjective intent of one party to a contract may well be irrelevant in determining the meaning of a contract term unless it is shown that that intent was communicated to the other party. In this case there is no direct evidence, as Fabric World argues, that it was put on notice that usage and custom, as embodied in the industry standards, would be used to define the meaning of first quality.

Under Alabama sales law, however, that Fabric World did not know of the industry's usage and custom or of the standards in question is of no moment; the parties to a contract such as the one in issue are *presumed* to have intended the incorporation of trade usage in striking their bargain. Section 1–205(2) defines trade usages. It provides in part that

> A usage of trade is any practice or method of dealing having such regularity of observance in a place, vocation or trade as to justify an expectation that it will be observed with respect to the transaction in question. The existence and scope of such a usage are to be proved as facts.

It further states: "A course of dealing between parties and any usage of trade in the vocation or trade in which they are engaged or of which they are or should be aware give particular meaning to and supplement or qualify terms of an agreement." There was uncontroverted testimony that the Knitted Textile Association is an industry group with over 1500 members. Its standards could certainly qualify as trade usages, and thus were admissible notwithstanding Fabric World's unawareness of them. . . .

PROBLEM: PANERA'S LEASE

Panera, Inc. owns and operates 25 Panera restaurants in northern California. Panera is a café style chain that sells sandwiches, coffee, salads, and soup in a casual atmosphere. Two years ago, Panera negotiated to open a new franchise in an area of South Sacramento that borders on the city of Elk Grove. According to a recent survey by Panera's marketing department, demographics reveal a population that is predominantly middle to upper class, $1/3$ Latino, $1/3$ white, and $1/3$ African American, Asian American, and other, and that, regardless of ethnic background, all were hungry for the type of dining experience the Panera franchise offers. Panera negotiated the ten-year lease with Landlord, Inc., which included the following language Panera drafted:

> Landlord, Inc. agrees not to enter into a lease, occupancy agreement or license affecting space in the Shopping Center or consent to an amendment to an existing lease permitting use. . . for a bakery or restaurant reasonably expected to have annual sales of sandwiches greater than ten percent (10%) of its total sales or primarily for the sale of high quality coffees or teas, such as, but not limited to, Starbucks or Peet's Coffee and Tea.

The Panera restaurant opened and has been operating at a consistently high profit for two years. However, approximately two months ago, Panera learned that Landlord, Inc. had entered into negotiations with Qdoba, LLC, who was planning to construct and operate a Qdoba Mexican grill in the same shopping center as the Panera restaurant. Qdoba serves mostly lunch fare, including tacos, burritos, and quesadillas. Both Qdoba and Panera target the same "fast casual" market, those seeking a tasty quality meal but with quick counter service and reasonable prices.

The general manager of Panera, Inc. became concerned about the possible loss of business from a competing chain in the same plaza and contacted Landlord, Inc. to express displeasure. After some conversation, the general manager of Panera voiced his contention that the terms of the lease were being violated. Over the objection, however, Landlord, Inc. entered into a new lease with Qdoba LLC. Qdoba knew nothing of the fuss, in the meantime (a) hiring a construction engineer and accruing $85,000 in planning costs and (b) binding itself to spend $300,000 for construction of its new Mexican grill. Panera decided that it was time to go to court.

In their respective court filings, it came to light that none of the terms in the original Panera lease agreement were defined. However, according to the *New Webster Third International Dictionary*, a "sandwich" is "two thin pieces of bread, usually buttered with a thin layer (as of meat, cheese, or savory mixture) spread between them." Chef Carlo Ortega, a world-famous gastronomic expert who has appeared on the Food Network program "Iron Chef," states in his affidavit that "a sandwich is commonly known as the staple lunch food of the region, which includes a meat, cheese, vegetable and/or starch, depending on the surrounding community." Qdoba LLC has not actually opened the doors to its Elk Grove restaurant yet.

The Hon. Judge Melissa Wisdom is set to try the case. You are her law clerk, and she has asked you for a memorandum of law setting forth the issues. She wants a thorough analysis of the issues, including your advice on how to decide the case.

B. PAROL EVIDENCE RULE

The process of contract interpretation is sometimes intertwined with the parol evidence rule and its exceptions, a set of doctrines that help determine the scope of the parties' agreement to be interpreted. A recurring pattern appears: oral negotiations lead to a deal, which is then memorialized in writing. Later, when a conflict arises, one party wants to rely on the strict words of the agreement. The other party, however, may try to re-introduce the earlier oral negotiations or prior drafts of the contract. These oral negotiations, prior drafts, or indeed, anything outside the "four corners" of the pages of the contract, are dubbed "parol evidence."

Under the parol evidence rule, if the contract's written terms are meant as complete, final, and unambiguous, then the contract is considered "integrated." If the contract is integrated in the writing, then that written document *cannot* be supplemented by the parol evidence—those prior agreements or oral statements. Instead, the parol evidence rule holds that execution of the complete and final contract supersedes negotiations or stipulations about its subject matter that led up to it. While this "rule" sounds straightforward, the parol evidence rule is subject to many exceptions. The following two cases illustrate the rules around application of the parol evidence rule in two leading jurisdictions, California and New York. As you will see, these approaches diverge. In your opinion, which jurisdiction has the most sensible rules about parol evidence?

PACIFIC GAS & ELEC. v. G.W. THOMAS DRAYAGE & RIGGING CO.
442 P.2d 641 (Cal. 1968)

TRAYNOR, C.J.

Defendant appeals from a judgment for plaintiff in an action for damages for injury to property under an indemnity clause of a contract.

In 1960 defendant entered into a contract with plaintiff to furnish the labor and equipment necessary to remove and replace the upper metal cover of plaintiff's steam turbine. Defendant agreed to perform the work "at (its) own risk and expense' and to 'indemnify' plaintiff 'against all loss, damage, expense and liability resulting from . . . injury to property, arising

out of or in any way connected with the performance of this contract."
Defendant also agreed to procure not less than $50,000 insurance to cover
liability for injury to property. Plaintiff was to be an additional named
insured, but the policy was to contain a cross-liability clause extending the
coverage to plaintiff's property.

During the work the cover fell and injured the exposed rotor of the
turbine. Plaintiff brought this action to recover $25,144.51, the amount it
subsequently spent on repairs. During the trial it dismissed a count based
on negligence and thereafter secured judgment on the theory that the
indemnity provision covered injury to all property regardless of ownership.

Defendant offered to prove by admissions of plaintiff's agents, by
defendant's conduct under similar contracts entered into with plaintiff, and
by other proof that in the indemnity clause the parties meant to cover
injury to property of third parties only and not to plaintiff's property.
Although the trial court observed that the language used was "the classic
language for a third party indemnity provision' and that 'one could very
easily conclude that . . . its whole intendment is to indemnify third parties,"
it nevertheless held that the "plain language" of the agreement also
required defendant to indemnify plaintiff for injuries to plaintiff's property.
Having determined that the contract had a plain meaning, the court
refused to admit any extrinsic evidence that would contradict its
interpretation.

When a court interprets a contract on this basis, it determines the
meaning of the instrument in accordance with the ". . . extrinsic evidence
of the judge's own linguistic education and experience." (3 Corbin on
Contracts (1960 ed.) . . . . The exclusion of testimony that might contradict
the linguistic background of the judge reflects a judicial belief in the
possibility of perfect verbal expression. . . . This belief is a remnant of a
primitive faith in the inherent potency . . . and inherent meaning of words
. . . .

The test of admissibility of extrinsic evidence to explain the meaning
of a written instrument is not whether it appears to the court to be plain
and unambiguous on its face, but whether the offered evidence is relevant
to prove a meaning to which the language of the instrument is reasonably
susceptible. . . .

A rule that would limit the determination of the meaning of a written
instrument to its four-corners merely because it seems to the court to be
clear and unambiguous, would either deny the relevance of the intention of
the parties or presuppose a degree of verbal precision and stability our
language has not attained.

Some courts have expressed the opinion that contractual obligations
are created by the mere use of certain words, whether or not there was any
intention to incur such obligations. [The court instances Hotchkiss v.

National City Bank of New York, 200 F. 287, 293 (S.D.N.Y. 1911) ("A contract has, strictly speaking, nothing to do with the personal, or individual, intent of the parties. A contract is an obligation attached by the mere force of law to certain acts of the parties, usually words, which ordinarily accompany and represent a known intent.").] Under this view, contractual obligations flow, not from the intention of the parties but from the fact that they used certain magic words. Evidence of the parties' intention therefore becomes irrelevant.

In this state, however, the intention of the parties as expressed in the contract is the source of contractual rights and duties. . . . A court must ascertain and give effect to this intention by determining what the parties meant by the words they used. Accordingly, the exclusion of relevant, extrinsic evidence to explain the meaning of a written instrument could be justified only if it were feasible to determine the meaning the parties gave to the words from the instrument alone.

If words had absolute and constant referents, it might be possible to discover contractual intention in the words themselves and in the manner in which they were arranged. Words, however, do not have absolute and constant referents. . . . The meaning of particular words or groups of words varies with the ". . . verbal context and surrounding circumstances and purposes in view of the linguistic education and experience of their users and their hearers or readers (not excluding judges). . . . A word has no meaning apart from these factors; much less does it have an objective meaning, one true meaning." (Corbin, The Interpretation of Words and the Parol Evidence Rule (1965) 50 Cornell L.Q. 161, 187.) Accordingly, the meaning of a writing ". . . can only be found by interpretation in the light of all the circumstances that reveal the sense in which the writer used the words. The exclusion of parol evidence regarding such circumstances merely because the words do not appear ambiguous to the reader can easily lead to the attribution to a written instrument of a meaning that was never intended." . . . Universal Sales Corp. v. Cal. Press Mfg. Co., . . . 128 P.2d 665, 679 [1942] (concurring opinion) . . .

Although extrinsic evidence is not admissible to add to, detract from, or vary the terms of a written contract, these terms must first be determined before it can be decided whether or not extrinsic evidence is being offered for a prohibited purpose. The fact that the terms of an instrument appear clear to a judge does not preclude the possibility that the parties chose the language of the instrument to express different terms. That possibility is not limited to contracts whose terms have acquired a particular meaning by trade usage,[6] but exists whenever the parties'

---

[6] Extrinsic evidence of trade usage or custom has been admitted to show that the term "United Kingdom" in a motion picture distribution contract included Ireland . . . ; that the word "ton" in a lease meant a long ton or 2,240 pounds and not the statutory ton of 2,000 pounds . . . ; that the word "stubble" in a lease included not only stumps left in the ground but everything "left on the ground after the harvest time" . . . ; that the term "north" in a contract dividing mining

understanding of the words used may have differed from the judge's understanding.

Accordingly, rational interpretation requires at least a preliminary consideration of all credible evidence offered to prove the intention of the parties. . . . Such evidence includes testimony as to the "circumstances surrounding the making of the agreement . . . including the object, nature and subject matter of the writing . . ." so that the court can "place itself in the same situation in which the parties found themselves at the time of contracting." . . . Universal Sales Corp. v. Cal. Press Mfg. Co., supra, 20 Cal.2d 751, 761, 128 P.2d 665, 671. . . . If the court decides, after considering this evidence, that the language of a contract, in the light of all the circumstances, is "fairly susceptible of either one of the two interpretations contended for . . . ." Balfour v. Fresno C. & I. Co. (1895) 109 Cal. 221, 225, 41 P. 876, 877 . . . , extrinsic evidence relevant to prove either of such meanings is admissible. . . .

In the present case the court erroneously refused to consider extrinsic evidence offered to show that the indemnity clause in the contract was not intended to cover injuries to plaintiff's property. Although that evidence was not necessary to show that the indemnity clause was reasonably susceptible of the meaning contended for by defendant, it was nevertheless relevant and admissible on that issue. Moreover, since that clause was reasonably susceptible of that meaning, the offered evidence was also admissible to prove that the clause had that meaning and did not cover injuries to plaintiff's property. . . . Accordingly, the judgment must be reversed. . . .

W.W.W. ASSOCIATES, INC. V. GIANCONTIERI
566 N.E.2d 639 (N.Y. 1990)

KAYE, J.

In this action for specific performance of a contract to sell real property, the issue is whether an unambiguous reciprocal cancellation provision should be read in light of extrinsic evidence, as a contingency clause for the sole benefit of plaintiff purchaser, subject to its unilateral waiver. Applying the principle that clear, complete writings should generally be enforced according to their terms, we reject plaintiff's reading of the contract and dismiss its complaint.

Defendants, owners of a two-acre parcel in Suffolk County, on October 16, 1986 contracted for the sale of the property to plaintiff, a real estate investor and developer. The purchase price was fixed at $750,000—$25,000 payable on contract execution, $225,000 to be paid in cash on closing (to

---

claims indicated a boundary line running along the "magnetic and not the true meridian" . . . ; and that a form contract for purchase and sale was actually an agency contract . . . .

take place "on or about December 1, 1986"), and the $500,000 balance secured by a purchase-money mortgage payable two years later.

The parties signed a printed form Contract of Sale, supplemented by several of their own paragraphs. Two provisions of the contract have particular relevance to the present dispute—a reciprocal cancellation provision (para. 31) and a merger clause (para. 19). Paragraph 31, one of the provisions the parties added to the contract form, reads: "The parties acknowledge that Sellers have been served with process instituting an action concerned with the real property which is the subject of this agreement. In the event the closing of title is delayed by reason of such litigation it is agreed that closing of title will in a like manner be adjourned until after the conclusion of such litigation provided, *in the event such litigation is not concluded, by or before 6–1–87 either party shall have the right to cancel this contract whereupon the down payment shall be returned and there shall be no further rights hereunder.*" (Emphasis supplied.) Paragraph 19 is the form merger provision, reading: "All prior understandings and agreements between seller and purchaser are merged in this contract [and it] completely expresses their full agreement. It has been entered into after full investigation, neither party relying upon any statements made by anyone else that are not set forth in this contract."

The Contract of Sale, in other paragraphs the parties added to the printed form, provided that the purchaser alone had the unconditional right to cancel the contract within 10 days of signing (para. 32), and that the purchaser alone had the option to cancel if, at closing, the seller was unable to deliver building permits for 50 senior citizen housing units (para. 29).

The contract in fact did not close on December 1, 1986, as originally contemplated. As June 1, 1987 neared, with the litigation still unresolved, plaintiff on May 13 wrote defendants that it was prepared to close and would appear for closing on May 28; plaintiff also instituted the present action for specific performance. On June 2, 1987, defendants canceled the contract and returned the down payment, which plaintiff refused. Defendants thereafter sought summary judgment dismissing the specific performance action, on the ground that the contract gave them the absolute right to cancel.

Plaintiff's claim to specific performance rests upon its recitation of how paragraph 31 originated. Those facts are set forth in the affidavit of plaintiff's vice-president, submitted in opposition to defendants' summary judgment motion.

As plaintiff explains, during contract negotiations it learned that, as a result of unrelated litigation against defendants, a lis pendens had been filed against the property. Although assured by defendants that the suit was meritless, plaintiff anticipated difficulty obtaining a construction loan (including title insurance for the loan) needed to implement its plans to build senior citizen housing units. According to the affidavit, it was therefore agreed that paragraph 31 would be added for plaintiff's sole benefit, as contract vendee. As it developed, plaintiff's fears proved groundless—the lis pendens did not impede its ability to secure construction financing. However, around March 1987, plaintiff claims it learned from the broker on the transaction that one of the defendants had told him they were doing nothing to defend the litigation, awaiting June 2, 1987 to cancel the contract and suggesting the broker might get a higher price.

Defendants made no response to these factual assertions. Rather, its summary judgment motion rested entirely on the language of the Contract of Sale, which it argued was, under the law, determinative of its right to cancel. . . .

Critical to the success of plaintiff's position is consideration of the extrinsic evidence that paragraph 31 was added to the contract solely for its benefit. . . . In that a party for whose sole benefit a condition is included in a contract may waive the condition prior to expiration of the time period set forth in the contract and accept the subject property "as is," . . . plaintiff's undisputed factual assertions—if material—would defeat defendants' summary judgment motion.

We conclude, however, that the extrinsic evidence tendered by plaintiff is not material. In its reliance on extrinsic evidence to bring itself within the "party benefited" cases, plaintiff ignores a vital first step in the analysis: before looking to evidence of what was in the parties' minds, a court must give due weight to what was in their contract.

A familiar and eminently sensible proposition of law is that, when parties set down their agreement in a clear, complete document, their writing should as a rule be enforced according to its terms. Evidence outside the four corners of the document as to what was really intended but unstated or misstated is generally inadmissible to add to or vary the writing . . . . That rule imparts "stability to commercial transactions by safeguarding against fraudulent claims, perjury, death of witnesses . . . infirmity of memory . . . [and] the fear that the jury will improperly evaluate the extrinsic evidence." (Fisch, New York Evidence § 42, at 22 [2d ed].) Such considerations are all the more compelling in the context of real property transactions, where commercial certainty is a paramount concern.

Whether or not a writing is ambiguous is a question of law to be resolved by the courts . . . . In the present case, the contract, read as a whole to determine its purpose and intent, . . . plainly manifests the intention that defendants, as well as plaintiff, should have the right to cancel after June 1, 1987 if the litigation had not concluded by that date; and it further plainly manifests the intention that all prior understandings be merged into the contract, which expresses the parties' full agreement (see, 3 Corbin, Contracts § 578, at 402–403). Moreover, the face of the contract reveals a "logical reason" (152 A.D.2d, at 341, 548 N.Y.S.2d 580) for the explicit provision that the cancellation right contained in paragraph 31 should run to the seller as well as the purchaser. A seller taking back a purchase-money mortgage for two thirds of the purchase price might well wish to reserve its option to sell the property for cash on an "as is" basis if third-party litigation affecting the property remained unresolved past a certain date.

Thus, we conclude there is no ambiguity as to the cancellation clause in issue, read in the context of the entire agreement, and that it confers a reciprocal right on both parties to the contract.

The question next raised is whether extrinsic evidence should be considered in order to create an ambiguity in the agreement. That question must be answered in the negative. It is well settled that "extrinsic and parol evidence is not admissible to create an ambiguity in a written agreement which is complete and clear and unambiguous upon its face." . . . Intercontinental Planning v. Daystrom, Inc., 24 N.Y.2d 372, 379, 300 N.Y.S.2d 817, 248 N.E.2d 576 [1969]. . .

Plaintiff's rejoinder—that defendants indeed had the specified absolute right to cancel the contract, but it was subject to plaintiff's absolute prior right of waiver—suffers from a logical inconsistency that is evidence in a mere statement of the argument. But there is an even greater problem. Here, sophisticated businessmen reduced their negotiations to a clear, complete writing. In the paragraphs immediately surrounding paragraph 31, they expressly bestowed certain options on the purchaser alone, but in paragraph 31 they chose otherwise, explicitly allowing both buyer and seller to cancel in the event the litigation was unresolved by June 1, 1987. By ignoring the plain language of the contract, plaintiff effectively rewrites the bargain that was struck. An analysis that begins with consideration of extrinsic evidence of what the parties meant, instead of looking first to what they said and reaching extrinsic evidence only when required to do so because of some identified ambiguity, unnecessarily denigrates the contract and unsettles the law. . . .

NOTES AND QUESTIONS

1.   The California and New York courts reflect conflicting views of the parol evidence rule. Articulate these views and state the principal policy justifications for each.

2.   Chief Justice Traynor's approach in *Pacific Gas* has drawn many critics. For example the Ninth Circuit wrote: "*Pacific Gas* casts a long shadow of uncertainty over all transactions negotiated and executed under the law of California. . . . Be that as it may. While we have our doubts about the wisdom

of *Pacific Gas*, we have no difficulty in understanding its meaning, even without extrinsic evidence to guide us." *Trident Center v. Connecticut General Life Insurance Co.*, 847 F.2d 564 (9th Cir. 1988).

3.   The United Nations Convention on Contracts for the International Sale of Goods (CISG), which governs the international sale of goods, does not contain a parol evidence rule. Courts hearing a case governed by the CISG will allow in all prior evidence, whether oral or written, in order to help determine a contract's meaning. CISG Section 8(3). What is the wisdom of such a rule for cross-border transactions?

4.   For additional analysis of contract interpretation and the parol evidence rule, including examples of judicial error and suggestions for improvement, see E. Allan Farnsworth, *"Meaning" in the Law of Contracts*, 76 YALE L. J. 939 (1967); John D. Calamari & Joseph M. Perillo, *A Plea for a Uniform Parol Evidence Rule and Principles of Contract Interpretation*, 42 INDIANA L. J. 333 (1967). *See also Taylor v. State Farm Mutual Automobile Ins. Co.*, 854 P.2d 1134 (Ariz. 1993).

The intertwining of interpretation and the parol evidence rule arises from practical guidelines that have been developed based on experience concerning such matters as whether the parties to an agreement intended it to *integrate* their entire agreement, only part of it, or none of it. "Integration" refers to the idea of the written document being the final expression of the terms of the agreement. Many contracts will contain an *"integration clause,"* a statement toward the end of the written contract stating that the writing is the only item to be considered in determining the parties' deal.

Note that the ruling about whether a contract is "integrated" is one for the judge, not for the jury. In general, the parol evidence rule (and its exceptions, which will be covered later) provide the judge a great deal of discretion to admit or exclude the prior oral statements or drafts. Case law on the parol evidence rule is complex and vast—one of the most litigated areas of contract law—and the enormity is reflected in the extensive scope of treatment of the subject in the Restatement (Second) of Contracts. Note the headings under which the following excerpts appear: "The Scope Of Contractual Obligations" and the "Effect of Adoption Of a Writing." These provisions are technical and interactive, so it is necessary to read through the entire excerpt once and then return to the beginning to re-read it.

RESTATEMENT (SECOND) OF CONTRACTS, SECTIONS 209–210, 212–216

§ 209.   *Integrated Agreements.*

(1) An integrated agreement is a writing or writings constituting a final expression of one or more terms of an agreement.

(2) Whether there is an integrated agreement is to be determined by the court as a question preliminary to determination of a question of interpretation or to application of the parol evidence rule.

(3) Where the parties reduce an agreement to a writing which in view of its completeness and specificity reasonably appears to be a complete agreement, it is taken to be an integrated agreement unless it is established by other evidence that the writing did not constitute a final expression.

§ 210.   *Completely and Partially Integrated Agreements.*

(1) A completely integrated agreement is an integrated agreement adopted by the parties as a complete and exclusive statement of the terms of the agreement.

(2) A partially integrated agreement is an integrated agreement other than a completely integrated agreement.

(3) Whether an agreement is completely or partially integrated is to be determined by the court as a question preliminary to determination of a question of interpretation or to application of the parol evidence rule.

Comment:

a.   Complete integration. The definition in Subsection (1) is to be read with the definition of integrated agreement in § 209, to reject the assumption sometimes made that because a writing has been worked out which is final on some matters, it is to be taken as including all the matters agreed upon. Even though there is an integrated agreement, consistent additional terms not reduced to writing may be shown, unless the court finds that the writing was assented to by both parties as a complete and exclusive statement of all the terms. Upon such a finding, however, evidence of the alleged making of consistent additional terms must be kept from the trier of fact. . . .

b.   Proof of complete integration. That a writing was or was not adopted as a completely integrated agreement may be proved by any relevant evidence. A document in the form of a written contract, signed by both parties and apparently complete on its face, may be decisive of the issue in the absence of credible contrary evidence. But a writing cannot of itself prove its own completeness, and wide latitude must be allowed for inquiry into circumstances bearing on the intention of the parties.

§ 212. *Interpretation of Integrated Agreement*

(1) The interpretation of an integrated agreement is directed to the meaning of the terms of the writing or writings in the light of the circumstances, in accordance with the rules stated in this Chapter.

(2) A question of interpretation of an integrated agreement is to be determined by the trier of fact if it depends on the credibility of extrinsic evidence or on a choice among reasonable inferences to be drawn from extrinsic evidence. Otherwise a question of interpretation of an integrated agreement is to be determined as a question of law.

Comment:

a. "Objective" and "subjective" meaning. Interpretation of contracts deals with the meaning given to language and other conduct by the parties rather than with meanings established by law. But the relevant intention of a party is that manifested by him rather than any different undisclosed intention. . . . The meaning of one party may prevail as to one term and the meaning of the other as to another term; thus the contract as a whole may not be entirely in accordance with the understanding of either. When a party is thus held to a meaning of which he had reason to know, it is sometimes said that the "objective" meaning of his language or other conduct prevails over his "subjective" meaning. Even so, the operative meaning is found in the transaction and its context rather than in the law or in the usages of people other than the parties. . . .

b. Plain meaning and extrinsic evidence. It is sometimes said that extrinsic evidence cannot change the plain meaning of a writing, but meaning can almost never be plain except in a context. Accordingly, the rule stated in Subsection (1) is not limited to cases where it is determined that the language used is ambiguous. Any determination of meaning or ambiguity should only be made in the light of the relevant evidence of the situation and relations of the parties, the subject matter of the transaction, preliminary negotiations and statements made therein, usages of trade, and the course of dealing between the parties. . . . But after the transaction has been shown in all its length and breadth, the words of an integrated agreement remain the most important evidence of intention. . . .

§ 213. *Effect of Integrated Agreement On Prior Agreements (Parol Evidence Rule)*

(1) A binding integrated agreement discharges prior agreements to the extent that it is inconsistent with them.

(2) A binding completely integrated agreement discharges prior agreements to the extent that they are within its scope.

(3) An integrated agreement that is not binding or that is voidable and avoided does not discharge a prior agreement. But an integrated

agreement, even though not binding, may be effective to render inoperative a term which would have been part of the agreement if it had not been integrated.

Comment:

a. Parol evidence rule. This Section states what is commonly known as the parol evidence rule. It is not a rule of evidence but a rule of substantive law. Nor is it a rule of interpretation; it defines the subject matter of interpretation. It renders inoperative prior written agreements as well as prior oral agreements. Where writings relating to the same subject matter are assented to as parts of one transaction, both form part of the integrated agreement. Where an agreement is partly oral and partly written, the writing is at most a partially integrated agreement. See § 209.

b. Inconsistent terms. Whether a binding agreement is completely integrated or partially integrated, it supersedes inconsistent terms of prior agreements. To apply this rule, the court must make preliminary determinations that there is an integrated agreement and that it is inconsistent with the term in question. *See* § 209. Those determinations are made in accordance with all relevant evidence, and require interpretation both of the integrated agreement and of the prior agreement. The existence of the prior agreement may be a circumstance which sheds light on the meaning of the integrated agreement, but the integrated agreement must be given a meaning to which its language is reasonably susceptible when read in the light of all the circumstances.

§ 214. *Evidence of Prior or Contemporaneous Agreements and Negotiations*

Agreements and negotiations prior to or contemporaneous with the adoption of a writing are admissible in evidence to establish: (a) that the writing is or is not an integrated agreement; (b) that the integrated agreement, if any, is completely or partially integrated; (c) the meaning of the writing, whether or not integrated; (d) illegality, fraud, duress, mistake, lack of consideration, or other invalidating cause; (e) ground for granting or denying rescission, reformation, specific performance, or other remedy.

§ 215. *Contradiction of Integrated Terms*

Except as stated in the preceding Section, where there is a binding agreement, either completely or partially integrated, evidence of prior or contemporaneous agreements or negotiations is not admissible in evidence to contradict a term of the writing.

§ 216.   *Consistent Additional Terms*

(1) Evidence of a consistent additional term is admissible to supplement an integrated agreement unless the court finds that the agreement was completely integrated.

(2) An agreement is not completely integrated if the writing omits a consistent additional agreed term which is (a) agreed to for separate consideration, or (b) such a term as in the circumstances might naturally be omitted from the writing.

The parol evidence rule's exclusion of extrinsic evidence in the face of a fully integrated agreement yields to several exceptions. For one, as seen in *Pacific Gas*, if terms in the contract are considered *ambiguous*, evidence of their meaning may be admissible despite the parol evidence rule. In addition, courts generally admit evidence to show excuse from contractual obligation, despite the parol evidence rule, such as showing fraud or mistake. Yet another exception admits evidence of a collateral or separate matter—an often vexing exception, as the classic case that follows attests.

MITCHILL V. LATH
160 N.E. 646 (N.Y. 1928)

ANDREWS, J.

In the fall of 1923 the Laths owned a farm. This they wished to sell. Across the road, on land belonging to Lieutenant Governor Lunn, they had an icehouse which they might remove. Mrs. Mitchill looked over the land with a view to its purchase. She found the icehouse objectionable. Thereupon 'the defendants orally promised and agreed, for and in consideration of the purchase of their farm by the plaintiff, to remove the said icehouse in the spring of 1924.' Relying upon this promise, she made a written contract to buy the property for $8,400 . . . Later receiving a deed, she entered into possession, and has spent considerable sums in improving the property for use as a summer residence. The defendants have not fulfilled their promise as to the icehouse, and do not intend to do so. We are not dealing, however, with their moral delinquencies. The question before us is whether their oral agreement may be enforced in a court of equity.

This requires a discussion of the parol evidence rule—a rule of law which defines the limits of the contract to be construed. . . . It is more than a rule of evidence, and oral testimony, even if admitted, will not control the written contract . . . , unless admitted without objection Brady v. Nally, 151 N. Y. 258, 45 N. E. 547. It applies, however, to attempts to modify such a contract by parol. It does not affect a parol collateral contract distinct from and independent of the written agreement. It is, at times, troublesome to draw the line. Williston, in his work on Contracts . . . points out the difficulty. "Two entirely distinct contracts," he says, "each for a separate consideration, may be made at the same time, and will be distinct legally. Where, however, one agreement is entered into wholly or partly in consideration of the simultaneous agreement to enter into another, the transactions are necessarily bound together. . . . Then if one of the agreements is oral and the other in writing, the problem arises whether the bond is sufficiently close to prevent proof of the oral agreement." That is the situation here. It is claimed that the defendants are called upon to do more than is required by their written contract in connection with the sale as to which it deals.

The principal may be clear, but it can be given effect by no mechanical rule. As so often happens it is a matter of degree, for, as Prof. Williston also says, where a contract contains several promises on each side it is not difficult to put any one of them in the form of a collateral agreement. If this were enough, written contracts might always be modified by parol. Not form, but substance, is the test.

In applying this test, the policy of our courts is to be considered. We have believed that the purpose behind the rule was a wise one, not easily to be abandoned. Notwithstanding injustice here and there, on the whole it works for good. Old precedents and principles are not to be lightly cast aside, unless it is certain that they are an obstruction under present conditions. New York has been less open to arguments that would modify this particular rule, than some jurisdictions elsewhere. Thus in Eighmie v. Taylor, 98 N. Y. 288, it was held that a parol warranty might not be shown, although no warranties were contained in the writing.

Under our decisions before such an oral agreement as the present is received to vary the written contract, at least three conditions must exist: (1) The agreement must in form be a collateral one; (2) it must not contradict express or implied provisions of the written contract; (3) it must be one that parties would not ordinarily be expected to embody in the writing, or, put in another way, an inspection of the written contract, read in the light of surrounding circumstances, must not indicate that the writing appears "to contain the engagements of the parties, and to define the object and measure the extent of such engagement." Or, again, it must not be so clearly connected with the principal transaction as to be part and parcel of it.

The respondent does not satisfy the third of these requirements. It may be, not the second. We have a written contract for the purchase and sale of land. The buyer is to pay $8,400 in the way described. She is also to pay her portion of any rents, interest on mortgages, insurance premiums, and water meter charges. She may have a survey made of the premises. On their part, the sellers are to give a full covenant deed of the premises as described, or as they may be described by the surveyor, if the survey is had, executed, and acknowledged at their own expense; they sell the personal property on the farm and represent they own it; they agree that all amounts paid them on the contract and the expense of examining the title shall be a lien on the property; they assume the risk of loss or damage by fire until the deed is delivered; and they agree to pay the broker his commissions. Are they to do more? Or is such a claim inconsistent with these precise provisions? It could not be shown that the plaintiff was to pay $500 additional. Is it also implied that the defendants are not to do anything unexpressed in the writing?

That we need not decide. At least, however, an inspection of this contract shows a full and complete agreement, setting forth in detail the obligations of each party. On reading it, one would conclude that the reciprocal obligations of the parties were fully detailed. Nor would his opinion alter if he knew the surrounding circumstances. The presence of the icehouse, even the knowledge that Mrs. Mitchill thought it objectionable, would not lead to the belief that a separate agreement existed with regard to it. Were such an agreement made it would seem most natural that the inquirer should find it in the contract. Collateral in form it is found to be, but it is closely related to the subject dealt with in the written agreement—so closely that we hold it may not be proved.

Where the line between the competent and the incompetent is narrow the citation of authorities is of slight use. Each represents the judgment of the court on the precise facts before it. How closely bound to the contract is the supposed collateral agreement is the decisive factor in each case. . . . [Reversed.]

LEHMAN, J. (dissenting).

I accept the general rule as formulated by Judge Andrews. I differ with him only as to its application to the facts shown in the record. The plaintiff contracted to purchase land from the defendants for an agreed price. A formal written agreement was made between the sellers and the plaintiff's husband. It is on its face a complete contract for the conveyance of the land. It describes the property to be conveyed. It sets forth the purchase price to be paid. All the conditions and terms of the conveyance to be made are clearly stated. I concede at the outset that parol evidence to show additional conditions and terms of the conveyance would be inadmissible. There is a conclusive presumption that the parties intended to integrate in that written contract every agreement relating to the nature or extent of the property to be conveyed, the contents of the deed to be delivered, the consideration to be paid as a condition precedent to the delivery of the deeds, and indeed all the rights of the parties in connection with the land. The conveyance of that land was the subject-matter of the written contract, and the contract completely covers that subject.

The parol agreement which the court below found the parties had made was collateral to, yet connected with, the agreement of purchase and sale. It has been found that the defendants induced the plaintiff to agree to purchase the land by a promise to remove an icehouse from land not covered by the agreement of purchase and sale. No independent consideration passed to the defendants for the parol promise. To that extent the written contract and the alleged oral contract are bound together. The same bond usually exists wherever attempt is made to prove a parol agreement which is collateral to a written agreement. . . .

Judge Andrews has formulated a standard to measure the closeness of the bond. Three conditions, at least, must exist before an oral agreement may be proven to increase the obligation imposed by the written agreement. I think we agree that the first condition that the agreement 'must in form be a collateral one' is met by the evidence. I concede that this condition is met in most cases where the courts have nevertheless excluded evidence of the collateral oral agreement. The difficulty here, as in most cases, arises in connection with the two other conditions.

The second condition is that the "parol agreement must not contradict express or implied provisions of the written contract." Judge Andrews voices doubt whether this condition is satisfied. The written contract has been carried out. The purchase price has been paid; conveyance has been made; title has passed in accordance with the terms of the written contract. The mutual obligations expressed in the written contract are left unchanged by the alleged oral contract. When performance was required of the written contract, the obligations of the parties were measured solely by its terms. By the oral agreement the plaintiff seeks to hold the defendants to other obligations to be performed by them thereafter upon land which was not conveyed to the plaintiff. The assertion of such further obligation is not inconsistent with the written contract, unless the written contract contains a provision, express or implied, that the defendants are not to do anything not expressed in the writing.

Concededly there is no such express provision in the contract, and such a provision may be implied, if at all, only if the asserted additional obligation is "so clearly connected with the principal transaction as to be part and parcel of it," and is not "one that the parties would not ordinarily be expected to embody in the writing." The hypothesis so formulated for a conclusion that the asserted additional obligation is inconsistent with an implied term of the contract is that the alleged oral agreement does not comply with the third condition as formulated by Judge Andrews. In this case, therefore, the problem reduces itself to the one question whether or not the oral agreement meets the third condition.

I have conceded that upon inspection the contract is complete. . . . That engagement was on the one side to convey land; on the other to pay the price. The plaintiff asserts further agreement based on the same consideration to be performed by the defendants after the conveyance was complete, and directly affecting only other land. It is true, as Judge Andrews points out, that 'the presence of the icehouse, even the knowledge that Mrs. Mitchill though it objectionable, would not lead to the belief that a separate agreement existed with regard to it'; but the question we must decide is whether or not, assuming an agreement was made for the removal of an unsightly icehouse from one parcel of land as an inducement for the purchase of another parcel, the parties would ordinarily or naturally be expected to embody the agreement for the removal of the icehouse from one parcel in the written agreement to convey the other parcel.

Exclusion of proof of the oral agreement on the ground that it varies the contract embodied in the writing may be based only upon a finding or presumption that the written contract was intended to cover the oral negotiations for the removal of the icehouse which lead up to the contract of purchase and sale. To determine what the writing was intended to cover, "the document alone will not suffice. What it was intended to cover cannot be known till we know what there was to cover. The question being whether certain subjects of negotiation were intended to be covered, we must compare the writing and the negotiations before we can determine whether they were in fact covered." Wigmore on Evidence (2d Ed.) § 2430.

The subject-matter of the written contract was the conveyance of land. The contract was so complete on its face that the conclusion is inevitable that the parties intended to embody in the writing all the negotiations covering at least the conveyance. The promise by the defendants to remove the icehouse from other land was not connected with their obligation to convey except that one agreement would not have been made unless the other was also made. The plaintiff's assertion of a parol agreement by the defendants to remove the icehouse was completely established by the great weight of evidence. It must prevail unless that agreement was part of the agreement to convey and the entire agreement was embodied in the writing.

The fact that in this case the parol agreement is established by the overwhelming weight of evidence is, of course, not a factor which may be considered in determining the competency or legal effect of the evidence. Hardship in the particular case would not justify the court in disregarding or emasculating the general rule. It merely accentuates the outlines of our problem. The assumption that the parol agreement was made is no longer obscured by any doubts. The problem, then, is clearly whether the parties are presumed to have intended to render that parol agreement legally ineffective and nonexistent by failure to embody it in the writing. Though we are driven to say that nothing in the written contract which fixed the terms and conditions of the stipulated conveyance suggests the existence of any further parol agreement, an inspection of the contract, though it is complete on its face in regard to the subject of the conveyance, does not, I think, show that it was intended to embody negotiations or agreements, if any, in regard to a matter so loosely bound to the conveyance as the removal of an icehouse from land not conveyed.

The rule of integration undoubtedly frequently prevents the assertion of fraudulent claims. Parties who take the precaution of embodying their oral agreements in a writing should be protected against the assertion that other terms of the same agreement were not integrated in the writing. The limits of the integration are determined by the writing, read in the light of the surrounding circumstances. A written contract, however complete, yet covers only a limited field. I do not think that in the written contract for the conveyance of land here under consideration we can find an intention to cover a field so broad as to include prior agreements, if any such were made, to do other acts on other property after the stipulated conveyance was made. . . .

[The vote was 5 to 2, with Cardozo and other judges joining the majority.]

NOTES AND QUESTIONS

1. Consider the following account of the jurisprudential context of *Mitchill v. Laith*, from Lawrence A. Cunningham, *Toward a Prudential and Credibility-Centered Parol Evidence Rule*, 68 U. CINCINNATI L. REV. 279–281 (2000):

> The divide between the majority and the dissent in *Mitchill v. Lath* reflected the parol evidence rule in transition. The majority approached the problem in reverse chronological order, starting with the writing; the dissent approached it in direct chronological order, starting with the prior agreement and moving forward toward the writing. Judge Andrews, writing for the majority, reflected the views of Williston and the Restatement (First). Judge Lehman, writing for the dissent, reflected the views of Corbin and anticipated the Restatement (Second) approach. As a result of these diametric approaches, the majority determined that the writing, based solely upon an inspection and reading of it, was integrated, whereas the dissent, assuming that the separate bargain actually occurred, concluded that it was not. . . .

> Which approach is superior has been the source of endless debate. The highest level of that debate is showcased in the duel between the Restatement (First) and the Restatement (Second). Under the Restatement (First), one asks "is the writing integrated" and answers that question by looking at evidence inside the writing as to the state of mind of the parties. If that evidence suggests that the parties did not intend the writing to be final—there is no evidence inside the writing indicating that the writing was intended to be

integrated—the inquiry ends and evidence of the prior agreement is admissible. If it does "look" final and complete, the inquiry also ends and the extrinsic evidence is excluded.

Andrews' test, and the Restatement (First), are versions of the approach propounded by Williston. Beginning with the writing, it focuses on the contents within its "four corners." The inspection and reading of the writing limited by its four corners asks, as the Mitchill majority did, whether the terms of a separate bargain would naturally have been included in the one written up. Under Williston's formulation, this determination is asked not of the particularized parties to the bargain but of abstracted, reasonable parties in the positions of the actual parties. If reasonable parties would have naturally included the separate bargain in the writing, then the writing is integrated. No evidence about the other terms can be admitted.

A principal rationale of the Andrews-Williston approach is the warning made by early courts against a "circle of interpretation," a worry that allowing a party to admit evidence by introducing the evidence is to "work in a circle." Against this rationale was the invocation by Corbin of that very circle, when he emphasized Wigmore's point that "a writing cannot prove its own completeness." Proof of its completeness, Corbin contended (and the Restatement (Second) follows), must come from the parol evidence so examining it is necessary to decide whether it is admissible.

Corbin defined the purpose of contract law as the realization of the reasonable expectations of contracting parties—actual contracting parties, not abstracted ones. In the parol evidence rule context, this purpose required rejecting Williston's test and its emphasis on what abstracted reasonable parties would naturally have included when reducing their bargains to writing. Corbin's test of integration was whether the parties—the actual parties—intended their writing to be an integration. Making that determination requires not only going beyond the four corners of the writing, but also permits the trial judge to evaluate all relevant evidence, including the evidence whose admissibility is in dispute.

Building on the insights of Lehman and of Corbin, the Restatement (Second) directs that one no longer ask "is the writing integrated," but whether it is completely or partially integrated. This distinction drives the architecture of Sections 213, 215, and 216 of the Restatement (Second), which calls for applying the parol evidence rule differently for completely and partially integrated agreements, although there is a good argument that it is virtually impossible for any agreement to be completely integrated.

Under the Restatement (Second), a writing that contains a final expression of a bargain is still called an integrated agreement. A partially integrated agreement is one that is final but not complete. The parol evidence rule consequence of a partially integrated writing is that no evidence of a prior agreement is admissible that would contradict the writing, though that evidence is admissible to supplement the writing by consistent additional terms. A completely integrated agreement is one that is final and also complete. The parol evidence rule consequence of a final and complete agreement is that no evidence of a prior agreement is admissible period (whether to contradict or to supplement the writing).

2. Which opinion in *Mitchill v. Laith* is more persuasive?

EXAMPLE: MARK ZUCKERBERG'S DEVELOPER

In 2012, real estate developer Mircea Voskerician claimed that he approached Facebook founder Mark Zuckerberg with a great deal. Voskerician alleged that he gave Zuckerberg a 40 percent discount on the price of the property behind Zuckerberg's existing Palo Alto house. In return for the lowered price, Zuckerberg allegedly promised him introductions and referrals that would boost Voskerician's real estate business. The closing took place at the discounted $4.3 million price, but the contract of sale was silent on the subject of further business, referrals, or introductions to Zuckerberg's friends and contacts. The alleged introductions and further business never materialized, and so Voskerician brought suit.

As part of discovery in the case, e-mails from Facebook employees surfaced that seemed to show that Zuckerberg had promised to help the developer in a "light" way. E-mails also showed that a Facebook security official ran interference with Voskerician, discouraging him from contacting Zuckerberg.

Imagine that you are the judicial clerk to the judge hearing this case in the California trial courts. The judge would like you to analyze the parol evidence rule and its exceptions as applied to these facts. Would Mark Zuckerberg's alleged promise to help the developer in a "light" way be considered part of the contract? *See* Joel Rosenblatt, *Zuckerberg's Neighbors Join Backyard Brawl with Developer*, BLOOMBERG NEWS (June 2, 2015).

PROBLEM: JAVIER'S PAY

Etienne owns a business selling half-deflated footballs to NFL teams. Due to increased demand for his product, Etienne hires an assistant, Javier, to help with administrative work. After the two bargain about yearly salary via e-mail and agree upon $40,000, Etienne has Javier sign a five page "employment agreement" that retains the at-will rule, but includes a covenant not-to-compete. At the bottom of the last page, the document says: "This is a complete and integrated agreement and constitutes the final agreement of the parties hereto on all matters."

After several months, unbeknownst to Javier, Etienne does some clerical work himself; he "whites-out" the amount of salary and writes in $35,000 instead. He carefully alters the document to make it look like this was the original. Then Etienne reduces the amount he is paying Javier in his monthly check. Upon objection from Javier, Etienne throws the (altered) contract at him and says "sue me." Javier does sue Etienne, and he would like to enter evidence of his oral negotiations with Etienne as well as an e-mail that Etienne sent him that mentions $40,000. What result?

PROBLEM: TAKE ME OUT TO THE BALLGAME

Koji Tanaka grew up around baseball and wanted to be a baseball player all his life. With a singular sense of dedication, Koji distinguished himself in college baseball and was recruited by minor league teams. In 2000, Koji hit the big time, being picked up by Big League Baseball (BLB) as a first baseman and designated hitter by the Pittsburgh Mercenaries and then the Washington Generals. Koji Tanaka had great success with his career, but toward the end of his time with the Generals in 2011, Koji's priorities had shifted.

Right after starting with BLB, Koji Tanaka and his wife Juniata had a son who they named Hiroki. As soon as Hiroki could walk, he showed a fascination with the game of baseball. After Juniata's death in 2011, Koji realized that his priority had to be raising eleven-year-old Hiroki. Despite losing his mother, Hiroki was generally a well-adjusted boy, who practiced non-stop with his little league team.

In 2011 Koji Tanaka was a free agent, and started looking for a deal that would be more accommodating to his enhanced family responsibilities. Koji ended up talking to the Chicago Greystockings, a BLB club that billed itself as "family friendly" within player circles. The Greystockings put a deal on the table for Koji Tanaka to play for them for four years at $14 million per year, nearly double the amount offered by the Generals. Apart from compensation, Koji asked whether he could bring Hiroki with him to workouts, practices, and spring training. Some of the time Hiroki could stay in the clubhouse with his school tutor, but for a part of the day, he would assist players on the field and watch Koji play.

The assistant manager agreed with the arrangement, stating "We'd be happy to have Hiroki. We will consider him a member of the team along with you." This statement won over Koji and after the meeting he told his agent: "This is the deal I want." Although the lawyers for the team, as well as Koji's agent and attorney, had all heard the promise about Hiroki, the standard form contract used by the Greystockings for every player (which they said they rarely altered) did not address the issue of player's children or family as it was a bit "out of the box." Offer, acceptance, and consideration were all present and the contract was duly signed.

The next year was extremely successful for both Greystockings and Koji Tanaka. The team improved its record substantially. Hiroki came along with Koji to every practice, and had his own locker in the clubhouse as an honorary "member of the team." When he wasn't with his tutor, Hiroki would run errands for the players, bringing them water or a towel if they needed it. Most players thought Hiroki was a diligent and polite boy. However, some grumbled privately that they had to "watch their language," and that on occasion they felt like they had to "babysit." No one "officially" complained, however.

Koji's second year with the Greystockings, however, was a disaster. The Greystockings had a long losing streak, and Koji had an injury at the start of the season. While before the complaints about young Hiroki being around had been subtle, now several members of the Greystockings began to "razz" Koji and his "shadow," Hiroki, for always being underfoot. Only one such complaint made it to the general manager, as most of the players had a positive impression of Hiroki.

As the losing season ended, the team's assistant manager called Koji in for a sit-down. He asked Koji to "dial it back" on Hiroki's clubhouse visits, and "only bring him in half of the time" or "a lot less." The assistant manager felt the players were distracted and that Hiroki was "becoming a bit of a sideshow." When Koji mentioned that this wasn't what he had been promised during contract negotiations, the assistant manager didn't try to deny what he'd said. He just pointed out that team performance always had to come before "side promises" to any one player.

The talk seemed to have been prompted by another player who wanted to bring his behaviorally-disturbed child to work with him. After the meeting, Koji met with the general manager and the owner. In these meetings, Koji pointed out that his son's presence at the ballpark was in fact a large part of what had attracted him to the team in the first place, but they sided with the assistant coach. At an impasse, Koji decided to consider early retirement but also look into his legal options.

How would you advise Koji? What are his strongest arguments, and what are the weak points?

The following three opinions wrestle with a vexing and recurring problem arising from integration clauses (also called merger clauses). While usually valid and enforceable, trouble arises when parties swap assertions of fraud or misrepresentation.

DANANN REALTY CORP. v. HARRIS
157 N.E.2d 597 (N.Y. 1959)

BURKE, J.

The plaintiff . . . alleges . . . that it was induced to enter into a contract of sale of a lease of a building held by defendants because of oral representations, falsely made by the defendants, as to the operating expenses of the building and as to the profits to be derived from the investment. Plaintiff, affirming the contract, seeks damages for fraud. . . . [The trial court dismissed the complaint and an intermediate appellate court unanimously reversed, certifying as the issue whether the complaint stated a cause of action.]

The contract . . . contains the following language pertaining to the particular facts of representations:

> The Purchaser has examined the premises agreed to be sold and is familiar with the physical condition thereof. The Seller has not made and does not make any representations as to the physical condition, rents, leases, expenses, operation or any other matter or thing affecting or related to the aforesaid premises, except as herein specifically set forth, and the Purchaser hereby expressly acknowledges that no such representations have been made, and the Purchaser further acknowledges that it has inspected the premises and agrees to take the premises 'as is' . . . , neither party relying upon any statement or representation, not embodied in this contract . . .

Were we dealing solely with a general and vague merger clause, our task would be simple. A reiteration of the fundamental principle that a general merger clause is ineffective to exclude parol evidence to show fraud in inducing the contract would then be dispositive of the issue (Sabo v. Delman, 3 N.Y.2d 155, 164 N.Y.S.2d 714). To put it another way, where the complaint states a cause of action for fraud, the parol evidence rule is not a bar to showing the fraud either in the inducement or in the execution despite an omnibus statement that the written instrument embodies the whole agreement, or that no representations have been made.

Here, however, plaintiff has in the plainest language announced and stipulated that it is not relying on any representations as to the very matter as to which it now claims it was defrauded. Such a specific disclaimer destroys the allegations in plaintiff's complaint that the agreement was executed in reliance upon these contrary oral representations . . .

In this case, of course, the plaintiff made a representation in the contract that it was not relying on specific representations not embodied in the contract, while, it now asserts, it was in fact relying on such oral representations. Plaintiff admits then that it is guilty of deliberately misrepresenting to the seller its true intention. To condone this fraud would place the purchaser in a favored position. Cf. Riggs v. Palmer, 115 N.Y. 506, 511, 512, 22 N.E. 188, 190, 5 L.R.A. 340. This is particularly so, where, as here, the purchaser confirms the contract, but seeks damages. If the plaintiff has made a bad bargain he cannot avoid it in this manner.

If the language here used is not sufficient to estop a party from claiming that he entered the contract because of fraudulent representations, then no language can accomplish that purpose. To hold otherwise would be to say that it is impossible for two businessmen dealing at arm's length to agree that the buyer is not buying in reliance on any representations of the seller as to a particular fact. . . .

FULD, J. (dissenting).

If a party has actually induced another to enter into a contract by means of fraud and so the complaint before us alleges I conceive that language may not be devised to shield him from the consequences of such fraud. The law does not temporize with trickery or duplicity, and this court, after having weighed the advantages of certainty in contractual relations against the harm and injustice which result from fraud, long ago unequivocally declared that

> a party who has perpetrated a fraud upon his neighbor may (not) contract with him, in the very instrument by means of which it was perpetrated, for immunity against its consequences, close his mouth from complaining of it, and bind him never to seek redress. Public policy and morality are both ignored if such an agreement can be given effect in a court of justice. The maxim that fraud vitiates every transaction would no longer be the rule, but the exception.

Bridger v. Goldsmith, 143 N.Y. 424, 428, 38 N.E. 458, 459. It was a concern for similar considerations of policy which persuaded Massachusetts to repudiate the contrary rule which it had initially espoused. 'The same public policy that in general sanctions the avoidance of a promise obtained by deceit', wrote that state's Supreme Judicial Court in Bates v. Southgate, 308 Mass. 170, 182, 31 N.E.2d 551, 558, 133 A.L.R. 1349,

> strikes down all attempts to circumvent that policy by means of contractual devices. In the realm of fact it is entirely possible for a party knowingly to agree that no representations have been made to him, while at the same time believing and relying upon representations which in fact have been made and in fact are false but for which he would not have made the agreement. To deny this possibility is to ignore the frequent instances in everyday experience where parties accept . . . and act upon agreements containing . . . exculpatory clauses in one from or another, but where they do so, nevertheless, in reliance upon the honesty of supposed friends, the plausible and disarming statements of salesmen, or the customary course of business. To refuse relief would result in opening the door to a multitude of frauds and in thwarting the general policy of the law.

It is impossible, on either principle or reasoning, to distinguish the present case from the many others which this court has decided. . . .

Although the clause in the contract before us may be differently worded from those in the agreements involved in the other cases decided by this court, it undoubtedly reflects the same thought and meaning, and the reasoning and the principles which the court deemed controlling in those cases are likewise controlling in this one. Their application, it seems plain to me, compels the conclusion that the complaint herein should be sustained and the plaintiff accorded a trial of its allegations.

It is said, however, that the provision in this contract differs from those heretofore considered in that it embodies a specific and deliberate exclusion of a particular subject. The quick answer is that the clause now before us is not of such a sort. On the contrary, instead of being limited, it is all-embracing, encompassing every representation that a seller could possibly make about the property being sold and, instead of representing a special term of a bargain, is essentially 'boiler plate.' The more elaborate verbiage in the present contract cannot disguise the fact that the language which is said to immunize the defendants from their own fraud is no more specific than the general merger clause in Sabo v. Delman. . . .

In any event, though, I cannot believe that the outcome of a case such as this, in which the defendant is charged with fraud, should turn on the particular language employed in the contract. As Judge Augustus Hand, writing for the Federal Court of Appeals, observed,

> the ingenuity of draftsmen is sure to keep pace with the demands of wrongdoers, and if a deliberate fraud may be shielded by a clause in a contract that the writing contains every representation made by way of inducement, or that utterances shown to be untrue were not an inducement to the agreement,

a fraudulent seller would have a simple method of obtaining immunity for his misconduct. Arnold v. National Aniline & Chem. Co., 2 Cir., 20 F.2d 364, 369.

The guiding rule that fraud vitiates every agreement which it touches has been well expressed not only by the courts of this state, but by courts throughout the country and by the House of Lords in England. And, in recognizing that the plaintiff may assert a cause of action in fraud, the courts have not differentiated between the type or form of exculpatory provision inserted in the contract. It matters not, the cases demonstrate, whether the clause simply recites that no representations have been made or more fully stipulates that the seller has not made any representations concerning certain enumerated subjects and that the purchaser has made his own investigation and has not relied upon any representation by the seller, not embodied in the writing. See, e. g., Sabo v. Delman . . . .

The rule heretofore applied by this court presents no obstacle to honest business dealings, and dishonest transactions ought not to receive judicial protection. The clause in the contract before us may lend support to the defense and render the plaintiff's task of establishing its claim more difficult, but it should not be held to bar institution of an action for fraud.

Whether the defendants made the statements attributed to them and, if they did, whether the plaintiff relied upon them, whether, in other words, the defendants were guilty of fraud, are questions of fact not capable of determination on the pleadings alone. The plaintiff in entitled to its day in court. [The vote was 6 to 1.]

NOTES AND QUESTIONS

1.   Which opinion is more persuasive, the majority or Judge Fuld's dissent? Which do you suppose has been more influential with courts in other states?

2.   How shall we distinguish between general merger clauses and specific disclaimers? Will all contract language be neatly classifiable into one category or the other? Suppose a single paragraph of a contract contains both a "merger-and-disclaimer clause"?

LaFAZIA V. HOWE
575 A.2d 182 (R.I. 1990)

FAY, C.J.

This [is an] appeal from a Superior Court order granting the plaintiffs' motion for summary judgment. We affirm.

The facts relevant to this appeal are as follows. The defendants, James and Theresa Howe (the Howes), entered into a contract with plaintiffs, Arthur LaFazia and Dennis Gasrow, to purchase Oaklawn Fruit and Produce (Oaklawn), a delicatessen, on July 6, 1987. . . . The Howes had no experience in the business of running a delicatessen, although they had owned a jewelry business for over twenty years.

The Howes met with plaintiffs to discuss the sale for the first time in the middle of June 1987. At that time it had been represented to them that it was an extremely profitable business, that plaintiffs had operated it for eight years, and that they were "burned out." . . . After the first meeting the Howes asked plaintiffs for the tax returns, accounts payable, and other records so they could determine the business's profitability and the amount plaintiffs were spending on inventory. The plaintiffs told the Howes that since they always paid cash and did not keep very good books, there were no records except tax returns, which, they said, did not reflect the true figures. The Howes reviewed the tax returns and had a manager of a sandwich shop with whom they were friendly review the returns as well.

Relying on the information they received, they decided that this was not a viable business. The Howes met with plaintiffs again and questioned them regarding the low figures of their tax returns and their previous representation that the business brought in between $450,000 and $500,000 a year. The plaintiffs pointed out to the Howes that they both had fancy cars, lived in fancy houses, and that Dennis Gasrow supported a family with three children. James Howe said he was convinced by their representations that the tax returns did not reflect the true value of the business . . . . In addition Theresa Howe and her brother visited the store a few times before the Howes decided to purchase it and observed what appeared to be a fairly busy sandwich trade.

The Howes agreed to buy the business for $90,000. At the closing the Howes paid plaintiffs $60,000 and signed a promissory note for $30,000. The defendants were represented at the closing by their son, a Providence attorney. Included in the Memorandum of Sale were merger and disclaimer clauses:

> 9.   The Buyers rely on their own judgment as to the past, present or prospective volume of business or profits of the business of the Seller and does not rely on any representations of the Seller with respect to the same.

> 10. No representations or warranties have been made by the Seller, or anyone in its behalf, to the Buyers as to the condition of the assets which are the subject of this sale, and it is understood and agreed that said assets are sold 'as is' at the time of sale. . . .

> 12. This agreement constitutes the entire agreement between the parties hereto.

this alone may have been too general, vague (Danann)

[Neither Howe remembers] reading paragraph 9 or 10 when they signed the documents at the closing. They assumed that their son had reviewed the documents beforehand. The Howes took over the management of the business the day after the closing. James Howe stated that after approximately one month his business experience told him that "there was a problem." He spoke to plaintiffs, and they told him that in September and October, after the vacation months, business would increase.

The promissory note was due in October, and the Howes, who claimed that the business had lost money from the first day, could not make the payment on time. In an attempt to keep his bargain, James Howe said he gave plaintiffs two payments for $10,000, "even though [he] knew [he] had been taken." To make matters worse, the fruit-basket business around the Christmas season did not materialize as plaintiffs had said it would. Consequently the $10,000 outstanding on the promissory note has never been paid. In February 1988 the Howes sold the business for $45,000.

On February 2, 1988, plaintiffs instituted this suit for breach of a promissory note. The Howes counterclaimed that plaintiffs made specific misrepresentations for the purpose of inducing defendants to enter into the contract. On March 2, 1989, plaintiffs filed a motion for summary judgment on the claim and the counterclaim. The motion was heard on April 18, 1989,

and a decision was entered for plaintiffs on both claims on April 25, 1989. PH
At the hearing the trial justice addressed defendants:

> I reviewed the contract in this case, and the only action left
> to you on your counter-claim is to prove that there was deceit; and
> it seems to me he gave you the tax returns. You came to an opinion
> that . . . the tax returns didn't justify the asking price. The
> provisions of the contract clearly indicate that the parties are
> making their own judgment. The contract is complete and regular
> on its face. I see no ability in the face of that contract for you to
> show a fraudulent misrepresentation. The contract d[i]sallows
> any representations. The parties were acting upon their own.

The defendants appealed the judgment to this court on May 3, 1989.
[They argue] that summary judgment was inappropriate because plaintiffs'
misrepresentations raised an issue of material fact concerning whether
such misrepresentations were intended to induce defendants to purchase a
failing business. The defendants argue that plaintiffs' material
misrepresentations, even if innocently made, were a basis for rescinding
the contract. The plaintiffs [argue] that the . . . specific disclaimer destroys
the allegation in defendants' claim that the agreement had been executed
in reliance on any oral representations. . . .

The trial justice [concluded] that defendants' only recourse on their
counterclaim was an action for deceit, yet defendants argue that they are
entitled to a rescission of the contract. In McGovern v. Crossley, 477 A.2d
101, 103 (R.I.1984), we stated that a person " 'who has been induced by
fraud to enter into a contract may pursue either one of two remedies.' "
That person "may rescind the contract or affirm the contract and sue for
damages in an action for deceit." Id. The tort claim and the claim for
rescission afford alternative sources of relief in which, if one is granted, the
other is withheld. Thus one cannot recover on both theories.

This court has also ruled that the right to rescind a contract must be
exercised with "reasonable promptness" after the discovery of the facts that
give rise to the right. The Howes attest to the fact that they discovered by
October 1987, when the promissory note was due, that they had been
"taken." Instead of maintaining an action for abrogation or undoing of the
contract, they made $20,000's worth of payments on the contract, and a few
months later, in February 1988, they sold the business. The evidence is
clear and unambiguous that the Howes did not declare by word or act that
the contract had been rescinded. They elected to affirm the contract
instead. Even in the counterclaim . . . defendants never brought up their
claim for rescission. Instead they asked for relief in the form of "costs,
interest and attorney's fees as well as punitive damages." They also argued
the elements of an action for deceit in the counterclaim.

In Halpert v. Rosenthal, 107 R.I. 406, 267 A.2d 730 (1970), we illustrated the difference between a claim for damages for intentional deceit and a claim for rescission. "Deceit is a tort action, and it requires some degree of culpability on the misrepresenter's part." Id. at 412, 267 A.2d at 733. It is fundamental to actions predicated on the theory of deceit that the party claiming deceit present evidence that shows that he or she was induced to act because of his or her reliance upon the alleged false representations.

We find that there was no issue of material fact in the instant case and that summary judgment was appropriate because the merger and disclaimer clauses preclude defendants from asserting that plaintiffs made material misrepresentations regarding the profitability of the business. The clauses prevent defendants from successfully claiming reliance on prior representations.

Although we have previously held that fraud vitiates all contracts, Bloomberg v. Pugh Brothers Co., 45 R.I. 360, 364, 121 A. 430, 431 (1923), we emphasized in Bloomberg that one could not "by such a provision as is contained in the contract in this case" escape liability for fraudulent misrepresentations. Id. The merger and disclaimer clause in Bloomberg was of a general, nonspecific nature:

> The foregoing contains the whole agreement between the parties to this contract and they, and each of them, shall be estopped from asserting, as an inducement to make said contract, any misrepresentation upon the part of either of the parties hereto, or any agent or servant of either of the parties hereto.

. . . [This case] is factually more closely similar to Danann Realty Corp. v. Harris, 5 N.Y.2d 317, 157 N.E.2d 597, 184 N.Y.S.2d 599 (1959), wherein the purchaser initiated an action for damages for fraud because of alleged false representations by the sellers regarding the operating expenses of the building the plaintiff sought to purchase and the profits to be derived from the investment. . . .

The [Dannan court] wrote: "Were we dealing solely with a general and vague merger clause, our task would be simple. . . . Here, however, plaintiff has in the plainest language announced and stipulated that it is not relying on any representations as to the very matter as to which it now claims it was defrauded." Id. at 320, 157 N.E.2d at 598–99, 184 N.Y.S.2d at 602. The court held that "[s]uch a specific disclaimer destroys the allegations in the complaint that the agreement was executed in reliance upon these contrary oral representations."

[W]e are also confronted with such specific language regarding the very matter concerning which defendants now claim they were defrauded- the profitability of the business. Clause 9 of the Memorandum of Sale declares specifically that the buyers are to rely on their own judgment and not on any representations of the sellers regarding the past, present, or prospective volume of business, or profits of the business. Clause 10 states that no warranties have been made by the sellers regarding the condition of the assets and that the assets are sold "as is" at the time of the sale.

Like the complaint in *Danann* ..., defendants' counterclaim contained no allegations that the contract had not been read by the purchaser or that the merger and disclaimer provisions had not been understood or had been procured by fraud. James Howe said he certainly understood the documents when he signed them, although both he and his wife no longer remember seeing the merger and disclaimer clauses. Moreover, at trial it was established that both parties were represented by counsel at the closing. Although plaintiffs' counsel drew up the sales contract, defendants' counsel admitted reviewing the document with his clients and making some initial changes.

For these reasons we find that defendants' asserted reliance on the oral representations of plaintiffs is not justifiable. We agree with the court in *Danann* . . . when it stated that "[t]o hold otherwise would be to say that it is impossible for two businessmen dealing at arm's length to agree that the buyer is not buying in reliance on any representations of the seller as to a particular fact."

NOTES AND QUESTIONS

1.   Would sustaining the buyer's claim in *LaFazia* allow it to, in effect, win by deceit—saying it is relying on itself when that is, as asserted, not so?

2.   Can you think of any other ways to resolve the apparent, and recurring, tension between the competing values of justice and freedom of contract?

SNYDER V. LOVERCHECK
992 P.2d 1079 (Wyo. 1999)

TAYLOR, J.

Believing himself to have been shortchanged in the purchase of a wheat farm, appellant [sued] the sellers, both real estate agents, and his agent's employer. The district court granted summary judgment in favor of all defendants on all of appellant's claims. . . . [W]e affirm. . . .

In the fall of 1995, [Loren] Snyder began searching for a suitable wheat farm. To facilitate his search, he contacted and employed [Jeremy] Hayek, a real estate agent employed by The Property Exchange. Hayek contacted Ron Lovercheck of Bear Mountain Land Company (Ron) and discussed O.W. and Margaret Lovercheck's (the Loverchecks) farm in Goshen County. Hayek, Ron, and Snyder toured the farm on November 5, 1995. The crops were planted but not growing when they toured the farm. Ron did mention that there had been some problems with rye in the past, expressing his belief that the problem was minor. Snyder left the meeting with the understanding that the problem was confined to about 100 of the 1,960 acres.

The following day, Ron, through Hayek, informed Snyder that he had spoken with the former owner of the farm, Ray Headrick (Headrick). Headrick stated that the acreage in question had always produced more wheat than the county average. Headrick also showed Ron the areas where the rye problem was at its worst. Those areas comprised about 100 acres total, and Headrick said that those areas could grow as much as twenty to twenty-five percent rye. Snyder returned to view the property on ten to twelve occasions after the initial tour.

Eventually, Snyder made an offer on the property, and negotiations ensued. On February 16, 1996, Snyder and the Loverchecks entered into a contract for sale of the farm. The contract, drafted by Hayek on Wyoming Real Estate Commission Forms, expressly provided that:

> Purchaser is not relying upon any representations of the Seller or Seller's agents or sub-agents as to any condition which Purchaser deems to be material to Purchaser's decision to purchase this property[.]

This language mirrors the language in a statement of condition of the property completed by the Loverchecks at Snyder's request. The contract also contained an "as is" clause, a merger clause, a liberal inspection clause, and a specific objection procedure. Snyder stated in his deposition that he read parts of the contract, but not the above-quoted language.

The purchase price for the farm was $526,500.00, and the parties closed on May 10, 1996. According to Snyder, when the crops came up the rye problem was not minor, but rather he estimates that there is rye on 1,800 acres, over a third of which was 100% infected. The affidavit of Snyder's expert stated that the extensive rye problem decreased the value of the farm to only $392,000.00.

Snyder [sued] alleging that the Loverchecks breached the contract for sale, that Ron and the Loverchecks negligently and fraudulently misrepresented the extent of the rye problem, that Ron's fraudulent misrepresentations entitled Snyder to punitive damages, and that Hayek and The Property Exchange breached their duty to delete and/or explain the waiver language. . . .

The district court found that neither Ron nor the Loverchecks had breached the contract, and that the punitive damages claim fell with the underlying claims. Snyder makes no argument to this Court that such determinations were erroneous; rather, he relies solely on the contention that the Loverchecks, through Ron, negligently and fraudulently represented to Snyder that the rye problem was minor and manageable. The Loverchecks respond that the disclaimer clause in the contract for sale precludes Snyder from asserting such claims. . . .

The effect of merger and disclaimer clauses on pre-contractual misrepresentations poses significant questions of public policy. There are two prevailing views on the subject. One school of thought focuses on the sanctity of the right to contract, and holds that a party is bound by a specific disclaimer even if the contract was fraudulently obtained. The other school of thought latches on to the age-old proposition that fraud vitiates all contracts, and holds that a party to a contract is not bound by a disclaimer if it was fraudulently obtained. Wyoming subscribes to the latter view.

The Loverchecks ask us to adopt the reasoning of [*Danann*], where the New York Court of Appeals considered "whether the plaintiff can possibly establish from the facts alleged in the complaint . . . reliance upon the misrepresentations . . ." That court recognized a difference between a general merger clause and a specific disclaimer of reliance, noting that general merger clauses do not preclude a claim of fraud in the inducement. . . .

Danann . . . has been followed by other courts, but has been limited in its applicability to situations where the disclaimer is specifically tailored. In *LaFazia v. Howe,* 575 A.2d 182, 186 (R.I.1990), the Supreme Court of Rhode Island applied the reasoning of *Danann Realty Corp.* to a disclaimer specifically denying reliance upon the seller's representations as to the profitability of the business being sold. However, in *Travers v. Spidell,* 682 A.2d 471, 473 (R.I.1996) (per curiam), the court found that a merger-and-disclaimer clause was insufficient to invoke the rule where it did not specifically discuss the location or boundaries of the well in issue. Another path of evolution has been to dilute *Danann* . . . into a balancing test where the disclaimer is a factor to be considered in determining reliance. *See Flakus v. Schug,* 213 Neb. 491, 329 N.W.2d 859, 863 (1983), *overruled on other grounds sub nom., Nielsen v. Adams,* 223 Neb. 262, 388 N.W.2d 840 (1986).

Although not cited by the parties, we found that this issue is not unprecedented in Wyoming, and we choose to follow our long-established rule. Our decision to do so is not solely based on consideration of the doctrine of stare decisis, but also our finding that the rule in Wyoming more appropriately balances the competing interests of justice and freedom of contract.

In *Baylies v. Vanden Boom,* 40 Wyo. 411, 278 P. 551, 552 (1929), the parties negotiated an exchange of a hotel in Kansas City, Missouri for a ranch in Uinta County. The parties entered into an agreement which provided:

> In the telegram of acceptance of proposition of the exchange of properties said telegram mentioned certain representations made by Bert L. Cook, Henry J. Vanden Boom, having no way of knowing whether to concur in his agents' representations, said representations are herewith set out, and constitute the only representations made.

Baylies, 278 P. at 553–54. The memorandum went on to list several representations, and was signed by both parties. *Id.* at 554. After taking over management of the hotel, Baylies discovered that several of the representations made to him, and not contained within the agreement, were untrue. *Id.* at 552. Baylies sued to rescind the contract, and Vanden Boom asserted that Baylies was precluded from asserting reliance upon any representations not contained within the memorandum. *Id.* at 551–52. [We] considered the rule analogous to *Danann* . . . that was in use at the time in several jurisdictions, and exemplified by Massachusetts cases.

> The Massachusetts cases emphasize the desirability of certainty in the contractual relations of those who have made a definite agreement, and if they say that they contract without regard to prior representations and that prior utterances have not been an inducement to their consent, any occasional damage to the individual caused by antecedent fraud is thought to be outweighed by the advantage of certainty and freedom from attacks, which would in the majority of cases be unfounded where such provisions were in the agreement.

Baylies, 278 P. at 555 (*quoting Arnold v. National Aniline & Chemical Co.,* 20 F.2d 364 (2nd Cir.1927)). We found, however, that competing considerations outweighed any interest in certainty. "A perpetrator of fraud cannot close the lips of his innocent victim by getting him blindly to agree in advance not to complain against it." *Baylies,* 278 P. at 556 (*quoting Webster v. Palm Beach Ocean Realty Co.,* 16 Del.Ch. 15, 139 A. 457 (1927)). We held that Baylies was not precluded from proving that he relied upon the fraudulent misrepresentations notwithstanding the fact that he had signed the memorandum. *Baylies,* 278 P. at 557.

The Massachusetts Supreme Court has subsequently adopted the rule to which we subscribe, and has succinctly stated the policy behind the rule:

> In the realm of fact it is entirely possible for a party knowingly to agree that no representations have been made to him, while at the same time believing and relying upon representations which in fact have been made and in fact are false but for which he would not have made the agreement. To deny this possibility is to ignore the frequent instances in everyday experience where parties accept, often without critical examination, and act upon agreements containing somewhere

within their four corners exculpatory clauses in one form or another, but where they do so, nevertheless, in reliance upon the honesty of supposed friends, the plausible and disarming statements of salesmen, or the customary course of business. To refuse relief would result in opening the door to a multitude of frauds and in thwarting the general policy of the law.

Bates v. Southgate, 308 Mass. 170, 31 N.E.2d 551, 558 (1941).

Moreover, such a rule comports with the well-established exceptions to the parol evidence rule. That rule dictates that when the meaning of a contract is unambiguous, extrinsic evidence is not admitted to contradict the plain meaning of the terms used by the parties. *Union Pacific Resources Co. v. Texaco, Inc.,* 882 P.2d 212, 220 (Wyo.1994). We depart from the parol evidence rule only if parol evidence is used to establish a separate and distinct contract, a condition precedent, *fraud,* mistake or repudiation. Restatement of Contracts (Second) § 214 (1981).

Therefore, we decline to adopt the reasoning of *Danann Realty Corp.,* and hold that Snyder is not precluded from asserting a claim for fraudulent misrepresentation by either the merger or disclaimer clauses. While the district court's decision on this issue was incorrect, it is well established that a district court judgment may be affirmed on any proper legal grounds supported by the record. *Bird v. Rozier,* 948 P.2d 888, 892 (Wyo.1997).

"A plaintiff who alleges fraud must do so clearly and distinctly, and fraud will not be imputed to any party when the facts and circumstances out of which it is alleged to arise are consistent with honesty and purity of intention." *Duffy v. Brown,* 708 P.2d 433, 437 (Wyo.1985). Fraud must be established by clear and convincing evidence, and will never be presumed. *Id.*

In the present case, Snyder presented no evidence to the district court consistent with fraud. Ron expressed his belief about the extent of the rye problem, and immediately sought a more informed opinion. No accusation has been made that Headrick's appraisal of the rye problem was based on anything other than his observations or was intentionally misleading. No one prevented Snyder from inspecting the land, and, in fact, he visited the land at least ten times before he agreed to the purchase. The facts of this case do not even approach the elevated burden of proof necessary to establish a claim of fraud. Summary judgment was properly granted on this issue.

NOTES AND QUESTIONS

1. What is your position on the relative persuasiveness of *Dannan* or *Snyder*? Is your position influenced by your stance on the parol evidence rule generally—such as your views on whether a strong parol evidence rule or a weak parol evidence rule is superior?

2.   Courts following *Danann* have referred to this problem as a "double liar scenario." *See Abry Partners V, L.P. v. F&W Acquisition LLC*, 891 A.2d 1032, 1058 (Del. Ch. 2006):

> To fail to enforce non-reliance clauses is not to promote a public policy against lying. Rather, it is to excuse a lie made by one contracting party in writing—the lie that it was relying only on contractual representations and that no other representations had been made—to enable it to prove that another party lied orally or in a writing outside the contract's four corners. For the plaintiff in such a situation to prove its fraudulent inducement claim, it proves itself not only a liar, but a liar in the most inexcusable of commercial circumstances: in a freely negotiated written contract. Put colloquially, this is necessarily a "Double Liar" scenario. To allow the buyer to prevail on its claim is to sanction its own fraudulent conduct.

3.   For more on this subject, see *MBIA Insurance Corp. v. Royal Indemnity Co.*, 426 F.3d 204, 218 (3d Cir. 2005) (Alito, J.) (applying Delaware law and predicting that "when sophisticated parties have inserted clear anti-reliance language . . . Delaware's highest court will enforce it to bar a subsequent fraud claim."); Kevin E. Davis, *Licensing Lies: Merger Clauses, the Parol Evidence Rule and Pre-Contractual Misrepresentations*, 33 VALPARAISO L. REV. 485 (1998); and Russell Korobkin, *The Borat Problem in Negotiation: Fraud, Assent, and the Behavioral Law and Economics of Standard Form Contracts*, 101 CALIFORNIA L. REV. 51 (2013). The latter poses and addresses the following example, based on a case that has become a modern law school staple.

EXAMPLE: BORAT

In the wildly popular movie *Borat: Cultural Learnings of America for Make Benefit Glorious Nation of Kazakhstan*, English comedian Sacha Baron Cohen played an outrageously inappropriate Kazakhstani reporter, Borat Sagdiyev, who traveled the U.S. filming a documentary about American culture. In his travels, the title character adopts a bizarre persona to elicit offensive statements and self-humiliating behavior from many ordinary Americans clearly not in on the joke. The movie was a critical and commercial worldwide success for Cohen and the movie's producer, Twentieth Century Fox.

Michael Psenicska, a Maryland driving instructor, was one unwitting stooge. In the movie, Psenicska, hired for a lesson, was trapped in the passenger seat as Kazakhstani careened through streets while endorsing rape and shouting obscenities at other drivers. Discombobulated by this shocking behavior, Psenicska anxiously ignored, deflected, or tittered at Borat's antics while trying to prevent an accident.

In Alabama, etiquette expert Kathie Martin attempted to teach social graces to Borat, who made bigoted, racist and sexist comments and showed Martin nude pictures, leaving her uncomfortable and speechless. Excerpts from Martin's coaching session are interspersed with scenes from a dinner party that etiquette instructor Cynthia Streit hosted for Borat and her friends. The boorish Borat shocked the guests with sexual innuendos and put-downs.

As Borat continued his travels, he encountered a recreational vehicle populated by a trio of university fraternity brothers. In the ensuing alcohol-enhanced conversation, the men disparaged women and rued the abolition of slavery.

These and others interviewed alleged in a lawsuit that production assistants had solicited their interest by portraying the project as a documentary about immigration and assimilation in America. On filming day, the assistants supplied a small sum of cash along with a "Standard Consent Agreement," which they insisted be signed, and many said they had not read. The document indicates the signatory's consent to appear in a "documentary-style film" using "entertaining content and formats." Lengthy waivers renounce any legal claims, including any claims of fraud, and conclude that the signatory "is not relying upon any promises or statements made by anyone about the nature of the film."

The Borat plaintiffs alleged they were induced to participate in the video sessions by the producer's representation that the footage would be used for a documentary film about American life made for an Eastern European audience. They claimed they did not consent to playing stooges in a Sacha Baron Cohen comedy routine as part of a studio-produced, major motion picture run worldwide. Twentieth Century Fox pointed to the signed Standard Consent Agreements. Who has the better of it and why?

NOTE AND PROBLEM ON SCRIVENER'S ERROR

Language is unruly enough without people making mistakes in writing or copying, but such error is a fact of life. Some of these issues arise in the context of invoking the excuse of mutual mistake, and are worth revisiting from the perspective of what to do when a written document diverges from the intent of the parties. Often called "scrivener's error," reflecting its ancient roots dating to the old days before typewriters or computers, when scriveners made copies of documents by hand, the label denominates a wide range of drafting and other clerical errors. Consider the following problem involving scrivener's error.

A prominent Boston lawyer represented a wealthy couple, Frank and Jamie, in a post-nuptial agreement years after they were married. By then, the parties owned many residences and several businesses, including the Los Angeles Dodgers major league baseball team. They had suffered negative experiences when the two asset types were commingled. For example, business creditors once threatened foreclosure on a family residence when some of Frank's heavily-indebted commercial ventures could not repay loans.

To prevent recurrence, their attorney drafted the spousal agreement to allocate title to the assets between the couple. The parties intended Jamie to have all residential property and Frank to have all commercial property. This allocation would not give lenders recourse to the residential property if riskier commercial operations, funded with debt, went awry. The two later disputed how they intended to allocate the Dodgers.

The post-nuptial agreement depended on an attached exhibit that showed which assets belonged to whom. Their lawyer, Silverstein, initially proposed that the parties sign a total of three original duplicates of the deal, to be held by each of the parties and by him. Late in the process, just before signing, Silverstein elected to double the number to six—out of what he called an "abundance of caution" to have a "set of protective documents."

Both parties signed all six. The exhibits, however, were mismatched in the process so that the final documents said different things: three said Frank alone owned the Dodgers while three said the two shared ownership of the Dodgers equally.

By 2010, the value of the Dodgers had risen to $700 million; meanwhile, the financial crisis that began in 2008 caused the value of the residential property to plummet. Though the property values allocated between Frank and Jamie were never equal, the discrepancy was, by then, acute. Also acute was the acrimony between the spouses, whose divorce battle, paraded on the front pages of tabloids, traded incendiary allegations of infidelity and power-mongering within the Dodgers organization.

In the midst of all of this, it was revealed that the couple's lawyer made an honest clerical error when preparing the documents. Silverstein accidently created two versions, one declaring the Dodgers to be Frank's alone and another making the Dodgers joint property. Silverstein noticed this error at the last minute and tried to correct it, though he never explained the error or his correction to either Frank or Jamie.

Despite that clerical error, Frank contended, there was no question what the parties intended: to allocate the Dodgers (and all commercial property) to him and the residences to Jamie. That made sense for both. Though the asset values differ greatly, Jamie was insulated from the downside that acquiring the Dodgers—or any commercial property using debt—entails.

Jamie stressed how the value discrepancy suggested something suspicious about the case. She portrayed the clerical garbling skeptically, insinuating that Silverstein and Frank had tricked her into signing documents whose content she had not agreed to.

Jamie laid out a simple case of logic: there were two opposite versions of the contract, it was infeasible to enforce both, and there was no basis to choose which to enforce. Ergo: neither should be enforced. Without an enforceable contract, then, state divorce law applied and prescribed an equitable split of all the couple's assets.

1.   Who has the better argument? How should the court decide this dispute?

2.   Why did Jamie and Frank use the same lawyer? What risks did that create?

3.   If there had been two lawyers, does that abate the risk of scrivener's error?

4.   What are some of the professionalism and ethical issues that the attorney in this case must confront?

PROBLEM: EREHWON CONSULTATION

Erehwon is a newly formed city state located in the jungle of Honduras, settled by libertarian immigrants that come in equal numbers from California and New York. As libertarians, the immigrants support only the most minimal role of government and instead favor freedom of contract as a way for individuals to provide for mutual services and aid. The city state of Erehwon has hired you as a consultant. Regardless of your own personal political beliefs, how will you guide them in deciding how their judicial system should handle parol evidence?

C. STATUTE OF FRAUDS

The statute of frauds is ancient. First adopted in England in 1677, the statute remains in place throughout the United States—despite being repealed in its native UK in 1954. The statute of frauds requires that certain types of contracts be memorialized in a writing signed by the party defending against enforcement.

The original reasons for the statute of frauds sound antiquated to modern ears. It was adopted in a feudal era when court trials were primitive. Juries decided outcomes based on firsthand knowledge of the facts, as opposed to testimony of other witnesses. The result was a spate of perjury occurring in court. To address these problems, the statute of frauds required signed writings to bind certain deals that seemed particularly susceptible to frauds and perjuries.

Although today's rules vary by state, most statutes of frauds apply to the same six types of transactions, three of which occur regularly in general practice and three of which are more arcane. The three regularly recurring categories are those involving land or real property, the sale of goods priced at $500 or more, and contracts that cannot be fully performed within one year (as opposed to merely terminated). The three archaic or odder categories are contracts where the consideration is marriage (such as when parents paid the royal family of a prince to marry their child, and excluding reciprocal promises to marry); promises of executors of estates to pay the estate's debts from their own pockets; and promises of sureties to pay a debtor's obligations to a creditor.

These delineations create the threshold issue: is a transaction within the statute or not? If so, the next question is what form of writing will satisfy the statute's requirement of a signed memorial. Again, the statutes vary, but typically require the defendant's promise be evidenced by a writing that states the essential terms of the promise with reasonable certainty and is signed by the defendant. Recall *Lucy v. Zehmer*: the purchase and sale of the farm would be within the land sale clause of the statute with the restaurant counter check satisfying its requirements, as it stated the essential terms (description, price, satisfactory title) and was signed by the defendant.

Similar to the requirement of consideration, the writing requirement of the statute of frauds is a type of formality. Such requirements create bright lines that signify—objectively—when a party is serious about creating a legal obligation. At the same time, formal requirements may seem in some instances harsh or unfair and courts urged to overlook what many perceive to be a mere technical requirement.

While the land sale and goods clauses of the statute sometimes raise challenging issues at the margins, the one-year clause poses often-fiendish puzzles. A vexing question is whether the one-year test should be interpreted literally, so that any period beyond one year falls within the statute, or practically, appreciating how deals can end early, with many nominal multiyear deals not exceeding one year. Beyond the threshold question of whether the statute of frauds applies to a transaction, the materials that follow also explore what counts as a "writing" that would satisfy the statute of frauds.

RESTATEMENT (SECOND) OF CONTRACTS, SECTION 130

§ 130.   *Contract Not to Be Performed Within a Year.*

(1)   Where any promise in a contract cannot be fully performed within a year from the time the contract is made, all promises in the contract are within the Statute of Frauds until one party to the contract completes his performance.

(2)   When one party to a contract has completed his performance, the one-year provision of the Statute does not prevent enforcement of the promises of other parties.

ROSENTHAL V. FONDA
862 F.2d 1398 (9th Cir. 1988)

CANBY, J.

Richard Rosenthal appeals the district court's grant of summary judgment in favor of Jane Fonda and four of her related corporations. The district court determined that New York law controlled this dispute and that New York's statute of frauds barred Rosenthal's claim against Fonda for breach of an oral contract. On appeal, Rosenthal contends that California, not New York, law should control this action and that California's statute of frauds does not bar his oral contract claim against Fonda. In addition, Rosenthal contends that even if New York law does properly control, his contract with Fonda is not barred by New York's statute of frauds. We affirm the district court's holding that New York's statute of frauds controls and that it serves to bar Rosenthal from enforcing this oral contract against Fonda.

. . . This action arises out of the twelve year relationship between Jane Fonda and her former attorney and general business manager, Richard Rosenthal. In 1968, Fonda, a California resident, retained the services of a New York law firm. She entered into an oral agreement with the firm that she would pay five percent of her earnings as compensation for the firm's services. Rosenthal, an attorney with the firm, assumed responsibility for a large share of the firm's activities on Fonda's behalf. In 1971, the law firm dissolved and in 1972, Rosenthal began to represent Fonda as an independent private practitioner. Rosenthal alleges that in April of 1972, he and Fonda entered into an oral contract whereby he agreed to continue performing a variety of services for Fonda and she, in turn, agreed to pay him ten percent of all gross professional income derived from the projects that were initiated during his tenure.

Rosenthal continued to represent Fonda from his New York office. In 1978, Rosenthal and his family moved to California, at Fonda's request, so that he could be closer to her and represent her more efficiently. Despite relocating, Rosenthal maintained a home and an office in New York. Fonda discharged Rosenthal approximately two years later, on May 30, 1980. Rosenthal [sued] Fonda in California district court to recover commissions on projects that were initiated during his tenure and produced or continued to produce income after his termination. . . .

. . . Rosenthal contends that the district court should have applied California, not New York, law to resolve this dispute. The district court correctly recognized that a federal court sitting in diversity must apply the conflict of law rules of the forum. Klaxon Co. v. Stentor Electric Mfg. Co., 313 U.S. 487, 496, 61 S.Ct. 1020, 1021, 85 L.Ed. 1477 (1941). This case comes from the United States District Court for the Central District of California; therefore, California's conflict of law rules apply to determine whether California or New York law should properly control this case. California utilizes the "governmental interest" analysis in deciding conflicts of law. See Liew v. Official Receiver and Liquidator, 685 F.2d 1192, 1195–96 (9th Cir.1982).

The application of California's governmental interest analysis requires three steps. Liew, 685 F.2d at 1196. First, the substantive law of each state must be examined to assure that the laws differ as applied to this transaction. Second, if the laws do differ, the court must determine whether a "true conflict" exists in that both New York and California have an interest in having its law applied. Finally, if a true conflict exists, the court must determine which state's interest would be more impaired if its policy were subordinated to the policy of the other. Id. The conflict is resolved by applying the law of the state whose interest would be most impaired if its law were not applied. Id.

I.   *Do The Laws of the Two States Differ?* The principal issue in this dispute is whether Rosenthal's breach of oral contract claim is barred under the statute of frauds provision that requires that all contracts not to be performed within one year be in writing. Textually, the relevant New York and California provisions of the statute of frauds are essentially identical. New York's statute of frauds provides that "[e]very agreement, promise or undertaking is void or unenforceable unless it or some note or memorandum thereof be in writing and subscribed by the party to be charged therewith, or his agent, if such agreement, promise or undertaking, by its terms is not to be performed within one year from making thereof . . ." N.Y.Gen.Oblig.Law § 5–701. Similarly, California's statute provides that "[t]he following contracts are invalid, unless the same, or some note or memorandum thereof, is in writing and subscribed by the party to be charged or by his agent: 1. An agreement that by its terms is not to be performed within a year from the making thereof. . .". Cal.Civ.Code § 1624.1.

The district court found that while these two provisions are facially identical, they are interpreted differently. The court correctly determined that in California, Rosenthal's employment contract with Fonda, terminable at the will of either party, would fall outside the bar of the state's statute of frauds because it is capable of being performed within a year. . . . California's one year provision is interpreted literally and narrowly. Plumlee v. Poag, 150 Cal.App.3d 541, 198 Cal.Rptr. 66, 71 (1984). Only those oral contracts which "expressly preclude performance within one year" or that "cannot possibly be performed within one year" are unenforceable. Id. . . . In this case, Fonda could have discharged Rosenthal after he had worked for her for six months; therefore, this contract was capable of being performed within one year. Moreover, California's statute of frauds does not invalidate oral employment contracts that call for the payment of commissions after one year or upon termination of the employment relationship. . . . Thus, Rosenthal's oral contract with Fonda would not be barred under California's statute of frauds.

In New York, however, while a typical employment contract with no fixed term is not barred by the statute of frauds, Fisher v. Ken Carter

Industries, Inc., 127 A.D.2d 817, 512 N.Y.S.2d 408, 409 (1987), a commission sales arrangement that extends beyond the employee's termination or that has no specific time frame has repeatedly been held to be one that cannot be performed within one year. See Zupan v. Blumberg, 2 N.Y.2d 547, 161 N.Y.S.2d 428, 429, 141 N.E.2d 819, 822 (1957); Urvant v. Imco Poultry, Inc., 325 F.Supp. 677, 683–85 (E.D.N.Y.1970), aff'd, 440 F.2d 1355 (2d Cir.1971) (summarizing New York case law applying the one year provision to continuing commission arrangements). The New York rule was enunciated in McCollester v. Chisholm, 104 A.D.2d 361, 478 N.Y.S.2d 691 (1984), aff'd, 65 N.Y.2d 891, 493 N.Y.S.2d 310, 482 N.E.2d 1226 (1985):

> A service contract of indefinite duration, in which one party agrees to procure customers, or accounts, or orders on behalf of the second party, is not by its terms performable within one year— and hence must be in writing and signed by the party to be charged—since performance is dependent, not upon the will of the parties to the contract, but on that of a third party. Id. at 692.

The key element in deciding whether New York's statute of frauds applies to bar a commission sales agreement is whether the defendant can unilaterally terminate the contract, discharging all promises made to the plaintiff including the promise to make commission payments. . . . If commission payments are due under the contract after one party has fully performed, the contract, by its own terms, cannot be performed within a year because there is no way the defendant can unilaterally terminate the contract. . . .

In the present case, Rosenthal contends that Fonda promised him a percentage fee every time a project initiated during his tenure generated income. Fonda could not unilaterally terminate this contract once Rosenthal performed because she would continue to owe Rosenthal money under the contract for as long as his projects generated income. Moreover, Fonda's liability to perform under the contract and make commission payments to Rosenthal is dependent not upon her will, but upon the will of others who may elect, for example, to exhibit her works. This contract, therefore, would be barred under New York's statute of frauds as one that by its own terms could not be performed within a year.

II. *Does A "True Conflict" Exist?.* Because the substantive law of California and that of New York differ when applied to this oral contract, we must next determine whether both New York and California have an interest in having their own law applied. . . . If only one state has a legitimate interest in the application of its law, there is no real problem; the law of the interested state should control. . . .

California, as the forum state, has an interest in having its law applied to this case. . . . As the forum, a California court will conclude that a conflict is "false" and apply its own law unless the application of the foreign law will "significantly advance the interests of the foreign state." . . . California presumably also has an interest in the enforcement of oral contracts involving one of its domiciliaries, although it may be questioned whether it is interested in applying its rule to protect a domiciliary of New York when New York would not protect him.

New York can be said to have an interest if the policies underlying its statute of frauds would be advanced when the law is applied to this transaction. . . . The district court correctly found that New York's statute of frauds is meant to protect not only the state's residents, but also nonresidents who employ New York agents. . . . In O'Keeffe v. Bry, 456 F.Supp. 822 (S.D.N.Y.1978), the court found that Georgia O'Keeffe, a New Mexico resident who had employed the services of a New York agent, had brought her business to New York and was thus entitled to the protections of New York's statute of frauds. Id. at 828. . . . Thus, New York has an expressed interest in extending the protections of its statute of frauds to nonresidents, like Fonda, who choose to employ or do business with New York residents.

In addition, New York has sufficient contacts with this transaction to justify a significant interest in having its own law applied. . . . Rosenthal was a New York resident, licensed to practice law only in New York, at the time he entered into the contract with Fonda. In addition, he performed many years of service under the contract from his New York office; it was not until 1978 that Rosenthal became licensed to practice law in California and moved to Los Angeles. Even after he moved, Rosenthal maintained a home and office in New York. These contacts with New York serve to support New York's interest in having its own law apply to govern this transaction. Thus, both California and New York have a legitimate interest in having their own law apply to this case.

III. *The "Comparative Impairment" Analysis.* Under the third step in California's governmental interest analysis, the conflict between New York and California law must be resolved by applying the law of the state whose interest would be most impaired if its law were not applied. Liew, 685 F.2d at 1196. The district court held that New York's stricter statute of frauds should be applied because New York has an interest in protecting more people than California and California's interest would not be frustrated by the application of New York law.

New York courts have made it clear that New York has a strong interest in protecting out-of-state residents, even while making it easier to prove liability against its own residents, in order to encourage the national use of New York services. See O'Keeffe, 456 F.Supp. at 828.

It is true that California has some interest in applying the one year provision of the statute of frauds very narrowly to promote the enforceability of otherwise valid oral contracts. . . . It is also true that one of the parties to the oral agreement is a domiciliary of California. Nevertheless, California does not have a strong interest in applying its policy against its domiciliary in order to protect a New York plaintiff that New York has no interest in protecting. . . .

In addition, the parties' reasonable expectations were probably that New York law would apply to their contract. . . . Fonda sought out a New York law firm to represent her interests and Rosenthal was a New York resident, licensed to practice law in New York, when he entered into this agreement. The contract was "substantially performed" by Rosenthal from his New York office. . . . Rosenthal entered into the oral agreement with Fonda in April, 1972 and carried out his services from New York until 1978, when he moved to Los Angeles. Fonda terminated his services approximately two years later. Thus, the bulk of their agreement was performed by Rosenthal in New York. These facts indicate that the parties would have reasonably expected New York law to govern their agreement. Thus, the district court correctly concluded that New York's policies would be most impaired if its law were not applied. . . . AFFIRMED.

NOTES AND QUESTIONS

1. Opinions about the statute of frauds have long been sharply divided, with the statute called variously the "wisest" and "the most mischievous law" ever. *Compare* Hugh F. Willis, *The Statute of Frauds: A Legal Anachronism*, INDIANA L. J. 3 (1928) *with* Karl N. Llewellyn, *What Price Contract? An Essay in Perspective*, YALE L. J. 40 (1931). In what ways might the statue of frauds be "mischievous"?

2. The statute of frauds was created to address a problem of systemic over-enforcement in that people lied to claim deals existed when none were struck. But requiring a writing leads to the opposite problem of under-enforcement. Any time that a requirement of a formality is imposed, some agreements that parties actually intended will go unenforced, because of what could be seen as a technicality.

3. The statute of frauds contains exceptions developed over hundreds of years. There have been circumstances where, even though a bargain is of the type that comes within the statute of frauds, courts have chosen to excuse compliance. Usually that occurs when the circumstances supply other protections against the fraud and perjury that the state was aimed to neutralize.

4. Under the UCC, the statute of frauds applies to a sale of goods for $500 or more. Exceptions to the statute of frauds under the UCC include part performance of a contract, where someone has acted in a manner referencing a valid bargain, and admission in court as to the existence of a contract. *E.g.,* UCC 2–201(2). There is a further exception for specially manufactured goods. UCC 2–201(3).

5. In recent decades, promissory estoppel has emerged as another possible exception to the statute of frauds, at least in some states. Promissory estoppel is, after all, an equitable doctrine focused on reliance rather than technical elements of traditional contract formation. But some courts have rejected a promissory estoppel approach to the statute of frauds. To these courts, promissory estoppel is a limited doctrine, best viewed as an alternative route to contractual liability when consideration is lacking. In other respects, according to these courts, promissory estoppel follows contract law doctrines, including the statute of frauds. *Cf. Alaska Democratic Party v. Rice*, 934 P.2d 1313 (Alaska 1997) (presenting what amounts to a multi-factor inquiry suggesting that the facts of a case, and especially remedies available, may warrant embracing or rejecting a promissory estoppel exception rather than seeing the decision as an either-or test that varies by state).

UCC 2–201

§ 2–201. *Formal Requirements; Statute of Frauds.*

(1) Except as otherwise provided in this section a contract for the sale of goods for the price of $500 or more is not enforceable by way of action or defense unless there is some writing sufficient to indicate that a contract for sale has been made between the parties and signed by the party against whom enforcement is sought or by his authorized agent or broker. . . .

(2) Between merchants if within a reasonable time a writing in confirmation of the contract and sufficient against the sender is received and the party receiving it has reason to know its contents, it satisfies the requirements of subsection (1) against such party unless written notice of objection to its contents is given within 10 days after it is received. . . .

(3) A contract which does not satisfy the requirements of subsection (1) but which is valid in other respects is enforceable

(a) if the goods are to be specially manufactured for the buyer and are not suitable for sale to others in the ordinary course of the seller's business and the seller, before notice of repudiation is received and under circumstances which reasonably indicate that the goods are for the buyer, has made either a substantial beginning of their manufacture or commitments for their procurement; or

(b) if the party against whom enforcement is sought admits in his pleading, testimony or otherwise in court that a contract for sale was made, but the contract is not enforceable under this provision beyond the quantity of goods admitted; or

(c) with respect to goods for which payment has been made and accepted or which have been received and accepted (Sec. 2–206).

PROBLEM: LINDSAY'S GORILLAS

Lindsay, an amusement park proprietor, is interested in buying ten 50-foot giant mechanical gorillas for display in her parks, located in ten different states. She begins talking to John, a gifted metalworker who runs a machine shop and who has done commissions for museums, parks, and businesses. Over the course of one month, John and Lindsay speak for five hours on the telephone about specifications for the gorillas. Each will cost $100,000 and take considerable expertise and labor to complete. John anticipates making a handsome profit, $300,000, above his costs.

Lindsay says, "Great—we have a deal. A contract and purchase order is coming your way from my attorney." John, eager to get to work on this exciting project, buys $50,000 worth of equipment. After two weeks, not having heard from Lindsay, John e-mails her asking for the contract, but does not receive a reply. Finally, after three more phone messages, Lindsay sends a handwritten note from her fax machine that says these exact words, no more, no less: "Let's get those monkeys out!"

John figured that Lindsay is just behind on her work and hasn't had time to consult with her attorney or draw up the contract. Since this is a big order for his shop, he calls an attorney he has used occasionally and asks her to write up a contract memorializing the terms he had discussed with Lindsay. He signs it and e-mails it to Lindsay, but doesn't hear anything from her. In the meantime, John continues work on the mechanical gorillas, since he doesn't want to get behind on the job. He hires an experienced welder, at a cost of $80,000, to help.

Nine days later, Lindsay changes her mind about the gorillas. She thinks they are too scary for some children likely to visit the parks and decides that instead she would prefer to go with an Atlantis/ Mermaid theme. She drops a note in the mail that says: "Forget the gorillas," and faxes the same to John. At that point, John has completed work on three of the giant mechanical gorillas and has three more underway.

In the case of *John v. Lindsay*, what are the arguments on either side for enforcement or non-enforcement, and who has the better arguments?

———————

While the previous section explored the threshold question of whether the statute of frauds applies, the following materials concentrate on the question of what is needed in order to meet the requirements of a writing.

RESTATEMENT (SECOND) OF CONTRACTS, SECTION 131

§ 131.　　*General Requisites of a Memorandum.*

Unless additional requirements are prescribed by the particular statue, a contract within the Statute of Frauds is enforceable if it is evidenced by any writing, signed by or behalf of the party to be charged which (a) reasonably identifies the subject matter of the contract; (b) is sufficient to indicate that a contract with respect thereto has been made between the parties or offered by the signer to the other party and (c) states with reasonable certainty the essential terms of the unperformed promises in the contract.

CRABTREE V. ELIZABETH ARDEN SALES CORP.
110 N.E.2d 551 (N.Y. 1953)

FULD, JUDGE.

In September of 1947, Nate Crabtree entered into preliminary negotiations with Elizabeth Arden Sales Corporation, manufacturers and sellers of cosmetics, looking toward his employment as sales manager. Interviewed on September 26th, by Robert P. Johns, executive vice-president and general manager of the corporation, who had apprised him of the possible opening, Crabtree requested a three-year contract at $25,000 a year. Explaining that he would be giving up a secure well-paying job to take a position in an entirely new field of endeavor which he believed would take him some years to master he insisted upon an agreement for a definite term. And he repeated his desire for a contract for three years to Miss Elizabeth Arden, the corporation's president.

When Miss Arden finally indicated that she was prepared to offer a two-year contract, based on an annual salary of $20,000 for the first six months, $25,000 for the second six months and $30,000 for the second year, plus expenses of $5,000 a year for each of those years, Crabtree replied that that offer was 'interesting'. Miss Arden thereupon had her personal secretary make this memorandum on a telephone order blank that happened to be at hand:

EMPLOYMENT AGREEMENT WITH NATE CRABTREE

Date Sept. 26-1947 6: PM   At 681-5th Ave * * *

Begin 20000.

6 months 25000.   6 months 30000.

5000. per year   Expense money

(2 years to make good)

Arrangement with Mr Crabtree

By Miss Arden

A few days later, Crabtree 'phoned Mr. Johns and telegraphed Miss Arden; he accepted the 'invitation to join the Arden organization', and Miss Arden wired back her 'welcome'. When he reported for work, a 'pay-roll change' card was made up and initialed by Mr. Johns, and then forwarded to the payroll department. Reciting that it was prepared on September 30,

1947, and was to be effective as of October 22d, it specified the names of the parties, Crabtree's 'Job Classification' and, in addition, contained the notation that 'This employee is to be paid as follows:

> First six months of employment $20,000. per annum
>
> Next six months of employment 25,000. per annum
>
> After one year of employment 30,000. per annum
>
> Approved by RPJ (initialed)

After six months of employment, Crabtree received the scheduled increase from $20,000 to $25,000, but the further specified increase at the end of the year was not paid. Both Mr. Johns and the comptroller of the corporation, Mr. Carstens, told Crabtree that they would attempt to straighten out the matter with Miss Arden, and, with that in mind, the comptroller prepared another 'pay-roll change' card, to which his signature is appended, noting that there was to be a 'Salary increase' from $25,000 to $30,000 a year, 'per contractual arrangements with Miss Arden'. The latter, however, refused to approve the increase and, after further fruitless discussion, plaintiff left defendant's employ and commenced this action for breach of contract.

At the ensuing trial, defendant denied the existence of any agreement to employ plaintiff for two years, and further contended that, even if one had been made, the statute of frauds barred its enforcement. The trial court found against defendant on both issues and awarded plaintiff damages of about $14,000, and the Appellate Division, two justices dissenting, affirmed. Since the contract relied upon was not to be performed within a year, the primary question for decision is whether there was a memorandum of its terms, subscribed by defendant, to satisfy the statute of frauds, Personal Property Law, § 31. . . .

Each of the two payroll cards the one initialed by defendant's general manager, the other signed by its comptroller unquestionably constitutes a memorandum under the statute. That they were not prepared or signed with the intention of evidencing the contract, or that they came into existence subsequent to its execution, is of no consequence . . . ; it is enough, to meet the statute's demands, that they were signed with intent to authenticate the information contained therein and that such information does evidence the terms of the contract. . . . Those two writings contain all of the essential terms of the contract the parties to it, the position that plaintiff was to assume, the salary that he was to receive except that relating to the duration of plaintiff's employment. Accordingly, we must consider whether that item, the length of the contract, may be supplied by reference to the earlier unsigned office memorandum, and, if so, whether its notation, '2 years to make good', sufficiently designates a period of employment.

The statute of frauds does not require the 'memorandum . . . to be in one document. It may be pieced together out of separate writings, connected with one another either expressly or by the internal evidence of subject-matter and occasion.' Marks v. Cowdin, supra, 226 N.Y. 138, 145, 123 N.E. 139, 141. . . . Where each of the separate writings has been subscribed by the party to be charged, little if any difficulty is encountered. . . . Where, however, some writings have been signed, and others have not as in the case before us there is basic disagreement as to what constitutes a sufficient connection permitting the unsigned papers to be considered as part of the statutory memorandum. The courts of some jurisdictions insist that there be a reference, of varying degrees of specificity, in the signed writing to that unsigned, and, if there is no such reference, they refuse to permit consideration of the latter in determining whether the memorandum satisfies the statute. . . . That conclusion is based upon a construction of the statute which requires that the connection between the writings and defendant's acknowledgment of the one not subscribed, appear from examination of the papers alone, without the aid of parol evidence. The other position which has gained increasing support over the years is that a sufficient connection between the papers is established simply by a reference in them to the same subject matter or transaction. . . . The statute is not pressed "to the extreme of a literal and rigid logic," Marks v. Cowdin, supra, 226 N.Y. 138, 144, 123 N.E. 139, 141, and oral testimony is admitted to show the connection between the documents and to establish the acquiescence, of the party to be charged, to the contents of the one unsigned. . . .

The view last expressed impresses us as the more sound, and, indeed although several of our cases appear to have gone the other way, see, e. g., Newbery v. Wall, 65 N.Y. 484; Wilson v. Lewiston Mill Co., 150 N.Y. 314, 44 N.E. 959 this court has on a number of occasions approved the rule, and we now definitively adopt it, permitting the signed and unsigned writings to be read together, provided that they clearly refer to the same subject matter or transaction. . . .

. . . As the United States Supreme Court declared, in sanctioning the admission of parol evidence to establish the connection between the signed and unsigned writings. "There may be cases in which it would be a violation of reason and common sense to ignore a reference which derives its significance from such (parol) proof. If there is ground for any doubt in the matter, the general rule should be enforced. But where there is no ground for doubt, its enforcement would aid, instead of discouraging, fraud." Beckwith v. Talbot, supra, 95 U.S. 289, 292, 24 L.Ed. 496 . . .

Turning to the writings in the case before us, the unsigned office memo, the payroll change form initialed by the general manager Johns, and the paper signed by the comptroller Carstens it is apparent, and most patently, that all three refer on their face to the same transaction. The parties, the position to be filled by plaintiff, the salary to be paid him, are all identically set forth; it is hardly possible that such detailed information could refer to another or a different agreement. Even more, the card signed by Carstens notes that it was prepared for the purpose of a 'Salary increase per contractual arrangements with Miss Arden'. That certainly constitutes a reference of sorts to a more comprehensive 'arrangement,' and parol is permissible to furnish the explanation.

The corroborative evidence of defendant's assent to the contents of the unsigned office memorandum is also convincing. Prepared by defendant's agent, Miss Arden's personal secretary, there is little likelihood that that paper was fraudulently manufactured or that defendant had not assented to its contents. Furthermore, the evidence as to the conduct of the parties at the time it was prepared persuasively demonstrates defendant's assent to its terms. Under such circumstances, the courts below were fully justified in finding that the three papers constituted the 'memorandum' of their agreement within the meaning of the statute.

Nor can there be any doubt that the memorandum contains all of the essential terms of the contract. . . . Only one term, the length of the employment, is in dispute. The September 26th office memorandum contains the notation, '2 years to make good'. What purpose, other than to denote the length of the contract term, such a notation could have, is hard to imagine. Without it, the employment would be at will . . . and its inclusion may not be treated as meaningless or purposeless. Quite obviously, as the courts below decided, the phrase signifies that the parties agreed to a term, a certain and definite term, of two years, after which, if plaintiff did not 'make good', he would be subject to discharge. And examination of other parts of the memorandum supports that construction. Throughout the writings, a scale of wages, increasing plaintiff's salary periodically, is set out; that type of arrangement is hardly consistent with the hypothesis that the employment was meant to be at will. The most that may be argued from defendant's standpoint is that '2 years to make good', is a cryptic and ambiguous statement. But, in such a case, parol evidence is admissible to explain its meaning. . . . Having in mind the relations of the parties, the course of the negotiations and plaintiff's insistence upon security of employment, the purpose of the phrase or so the trier of the facts was warranted in finding was to grant plaintiff the tenure he desired. [Affirmed.]

NOTES AND QUESTIONS

1.   Just how much writing is enough writing to satisfy the statute of frauds? In *Rosenfeld v. Basquiat*, 78 F.3d 84 (2d Cir. 1996), the court held that the signature requirement of the statute of frauds was satisfied by a scrawl of an artist in crayon in a short memo on a larger piece of paper. Whether the writing counted was an important question because the writing exchanged

three paintings for $12,000, and the paintings were later valued at over $350,000.

2.   The UCC allows several exceptions to the statute of frauds. Examine Section 2–201. What are some of the reasons for allowing a "merchant exception" to the statute of frauds? Why provide an exemption for specially manufactured goods or for situations where performance has already begun? What do these exceptions tell us about the policy reasons behind the statute of frauds? What do these exceptions tell us about the policies behind the UCC?

3.   How does the statute of frauds interact with modern technology? Recent laws have been enacted to recognize electronic signatures and treat them as binding. *See* Electronic Signatures in Global and National Commerce Act of 2000, 15 U.S.C. 7001 (2000). To similar effect is the Uniform Electronic Transactions Act, adopted in the vast majority of states. For more on this topic, see Margaret Jane Radin, *Online Standardization and the Integrating of Text and Machine*, 70 FORDHAM L. REV. 1125 (2002).

EXAMPLE: CLIFF DUMAS

Country music personality Cliff Dumas wanted a new job and set his sights on Infinity Broadcasting's Chicago affiliate, US-99. Dumas discussed a five-year contract with US-99's program director, Justin Case. Talks in 2000 broke down over differences about salary.

When discussions resumed two years later, they still haggled over money. Case e-mailed Dumas several different annual salary ranges, from $125,000 to $250,000, and Dumas replied by e-mail that the range beginning with $175,000 "seems right."

Case followed with further e-mails noting matters to discuss, including Dumas' radio personality, the show's format, and the duration of any deal. Dumas recalled ironing out such things in later phone calls. Piecing together various e-mails, Dumas thought terms had emerged: a five-year deal starting August 4, 2002 at $175,000 per year. He also believed they agreed to a deal by phone on May 20, 2002, reinforced by a follow-up e-mail from Case saying the station's ratings had fallen and they wanted Dumas to turn things around. On May 30, Dumas quit his job at a station in New Mexico and told Case that a week later.

Case then stressed that a final hiring decision had not been made and that the decision was up to station manager Eric Logan. So Dumas followed up with Logan. Though Logan signaled willingness to "move forward," he gave no firm answers, despite many e-mails from Dumas that summer. On July 23 Dumas turned tempestuous, demanding an immediate response and threatening legal action. At that point, station officials stopped returning Dumas's calls or e-mails. A year later, after no response, Dumas sued.

If you were an attorney for Dumas what arguments would you make in the lawsuit against the radio station? If you were an attorney for the radio station, how would you answer these arguments?

CHAPTER 9

PERFORMANCE AND MODIFICATION

■ ■ ■

Contract performance almost always presents questions, large and small, about who is supposed to do what, and when. This often provokes disputes that prompt modifications, settlements, or other adjustments. The parties should be free to revise their deals during the course of performance, but only when done in good faith based on changed circumstances, not when one side exploits the circumstances to induce the other to accede to threats. If economic duress, rather than free will, drives a modification, contract law should no more enforce such a bargain than it would enforce those that result from mutual mistake or fraud, as we examined in Chapter Five.

In this chapter, we will examine issues that arise during contract performance, which are deeply intertwined with the question of good faith. A duty of good faith is sometimes necessary to fill gaps in incomplete contracts. These deals, despite being incomplete, seem to have been intended by the parties as a bargain. The concept of good faith is elastic, stretching to play many roles in the performance, modification, settlement, and adjustment of deals. It is useful in a broad range of settings, such as making midcourse modifications, settling disputes, and exercising discretion. Good faith is both changeable and modest, helping to fill gaps and to police abuses while letting the parties to a deal allocate power as they wish.

A. IMPLIED DUTY OF GOOD FAITH

We start with a classic opinion, written by Judge Cardozo, involving a clothing designer who survived the Titanic disaster. We will follow with a modern day application of the duty of good faith by examining a legal dispute involving greeting cards penned by the late Dr. Maya Angelou, author of *I Know Why the Caged Bird Sings*, who was a mentor to media mogul Oprah Winfrey.

WOOD v. LUCY, LADY DUFF-GORDON

118 N.E. 214 (N.Y. 1917)

CARDOZO, J.

The defendant styles herself 'a creator of fashions.' Her favor helps a sale. Manufacturers of dresses, millinery, and like articles are glad to pay for a certificate of her approval. The things which she designs, fabrics, parasols, and what not, have a new value in the public mind when issued in her name. She employed the plaintiff to help her to turn this vogue into money. He was to have the exclusive right, subject always to her approval, to place her indorsements on the designs of others. He was also to have the exclusive right to place her own designs on sale, or to license others to market them. In return she was to have one-half of 'all profits and revenues' derived from any contracts he might make. The exclusive right was to last at least one year from April 1, 1915, and thereafter from year to year unless terminated by notice of 90 days. The plaintiff says that he kept the contract on his part, and that the defendant broke it. She placed her indorsement on fabrics, dresses, and millinery without his knowledge, and withheld the profits. He sues her for the damages, and the case comes here on demurrer.

The agreement of employment is signed by both parties. It has a wealth of recitals. The defendant insists, however, that it lacks the elements of a contract. She says that the plaintiff does not bind himself to anything. It is true that he does not promise in so many words that he will use reasonable efforts to place the defendant's indorsements and market her designs. We think, however, that such a promise is fairly to be implied. The law has outgrown its primitive stage of formalism when the precise word was the sovereign talisman, and every slip was fatal. It takes a broader view today. A promise may be lacking, and yet the whole writing may be 'instinct with an obligation,' imperfectly expressed (Scott, J., in McCall Co. v. Wright, 133 App. Div. 62, 117 N. Y. Supp. 775; Moran v. Standard Oil Co., 211 N. Y. 187, 198, 105 N. E. 217). If that is so, there is a contract.

The implication of a promise here finds support in many circumstances. The defendant gave an exclusive privilege. She was to have no right for at least a year to place her own indorsements or market her own designs except through the agency of the plaintiff. The acceptance of the exclusive agency was an assumption of its duties. Phoenix Hermetic Co. v. Filtrine Mfg. Co., 164 App. Div. 424, 150 N. Y. Supp. 193; W. G. Taylor Co. v. Bannerman, 120 Wis. 189, 97 N. W. 918; Mueller v. Mineral Spring Co., 88 Mich. 390, 50 N. W. 319. We are not to suppose that one party was to be placed at the mercy of the other. Hearn v. Stevens & Bro., 111 App. Div. 101, 106, 97 N. Y. Supp. 566; Russell v. Allerton, 108 N. Y.

288, 15 N. E. 391. Many other terms of the agreement point the same way. We are told at the outset by way of recital that:

'The said Otis F. Wood possesses a business organization adapted to the placing of such indorsements as the said Lucy, Lady Duff-Gordon, has approved.'

The implication is that the plaintiff's business organization will be used for the purpose for which it is adapted. But the terms of the defendant's compensation are even more significant. Her sole compensation for the grant of an exclusive agency is to be one-half of all the profits resulting from the plaintiff's efforts. Unless he gave his efforts, she could never get anything. Without an implied promise, the transaction cannot have such business 'efficacy, as both parties must have intended that at all events it should have.' Bowen, L. J., in the Moorcock, 14 P. D. 64, 68. But the contract does not stop there. The plaintiff goes on to promise that he will account monthly for all moneys received by him, and that he will take out all such patents and copyrights and trade-marks as may in his judgment be necessary to protect the rights and articles affected by the agreement. It is true, of course, as the Appellate Division has said, that if he was under no duty to try to market designs or to place certificates of indorsement, his promise to account for profits or take out copyrights would be valueless. But in determining the intention of the parties the promise has a value. It helps to enforce the conclusion that the plaintiff had some duties. His promise to pay the defendant one-half of the profits and revenues resulting from the exclusive agency and to render accounts monthly was a promise to use reasonable efforts to bring profits and revenues into existence. . . .

The judgment of the Appellate Division should be reversed, and the order of the Special Term affirmed, with costs in the Appellate Division and in this court.

NOTES AND QUESTIONS

1. What were the terms of the proposed deal that Lady Lucy Duff-Gordon and Wood seemed to have agreed on? What were the uncertainties that were apparently left open by their agreement?

2. What aspects of the deal in *Wood* were uncertain, vague, or illusory? How did the court resolve these ambiguities?

3. A volume of essays in the *Pace Law Review* commemorated the ninetieth anniversary of the *Lucy, Lady Duff-Gordon* case, a reminder of the case's prominent role in contract law. The essays covered the role of default terms, the context of the case and its implications, the meaning of good faith, and the use of the case in the classroom. An accompanying fashion exhibition celebrated Lucy's role as a designer and fashion celebrity. She was, in fact, a type of precursor for "reality stars" today who seem to be famous for being

famous. For an overview of the conference on *Wood*, see James J. Fishman, *The Enduring Legacy of* Wood v. Lucy, Lady Duff-Gordon, 28 PACE L. REV. 162 (2008).

4.   Some have wondered why Justice Cardozo seemed to express antipathy toward Lady Duff-Gordon. The essays from the *Pace Law Review* note that she and her husband, Sir Cosmo, were survivors of the Titanic disaster. The allegation was that even though there was room in their lifeboat, the couple and ship personnel rowed past drowning passengers and ignored their pleas for aid. Such callous behavior brought a rebuke from the court convened by the British Board of Trade charged with investigating the disaster, and it perhaps brought about an unofficial rebuke (and *sub rosa* dislike) from Justice Cardozo. *See* STEPHEN COX, MYSTERIES OF THE TITANIC 24 (1997). The common law seems to be the richer for Cardozo's enmity.

5.   What did Cardozo mean when he wrote, "The law has outgrown its primitive stage of formalism when the precise word was the sovereign talisman, and every slip was fatal. It takes a broader view today"? How would you define "formalism," and what aspects of it still constitute part of the contract law you have studied in this course?

EXAMPLE: O. HENRY

The implied covenant of good faith played an important role in a famous case involving a play adapted from a novel by O. Henry: the play was called *Alias Jimmy Valentine* based on the novel *A Retrieved Reformation. The Kirk La Shelle Company v. Paul Armstrong Co.*, 188 N.E. 163 (N.Y. 1933). The play was often performed in the early 1900s and was turned into a silent movie in the 1920s. The playwright, Paul Armstrong, transferred the rights to a private company shortly before his death in 1918, prompting a creditor to sue the company. In 1921, the two settled the dispute on terms calling for the company to share control rights and economic royalties on future productions of the play (as well as another called *Salomy Jane*), but not in motion pictures.

Later, the company transferred the rights to create talking pictures of the play to MGM, a major filmmaker, cutting out the creditor from oversight or payment. The creditor sued, alleging breach of contract. While no express provision applied, and the parties could not have contemplated the invention of talking pictures when they made their deal, the court found an implied promise not to take actions that would impair the value of the deal they had made. Since production and sale of the talking picture would compete with marketing of other dramatic adaptations of the work, the company breached its contract by cutting the creditor out of that production. The court explained the concept this way:

> the principle that in every contract there is an implied covenant that neither party shall do anything which will have the effect of destroying or injuring the right of the other party to receive the fruits of the contract, which means that in every contract there exists an implied covenant of good faith and fair dealing.

On the facts, the court held that in granting half the benefits of the production of the play, the company undertook "an implied obligation . . . not to render valueless the right conferred by the contract." The court also spoke of the origins of this concept in fiduciary duties, elaborating as follows: "By entering into the contract and accepting and retaining the consideration therefor, the respondents assumed a fiduciary relationship which had its origin in the contract, and which imposed upon them the duty of utmost good faith."

NOTE ON CONTRACTUAL GOOD FAITH

Contract law's implied covenant of good faith is deliberately vague, general, and contextual: what good faith requires varies with context. It is Protean and normally intended to flesh out express performance obligations left under-specified (in a common contemporary formulation, to fill gaps in incomplete contracts). Courts have declared that good faith requires punctuality and diligence, for instance, and bars dilatory conduct or deliberate shoddiness in performance. In these respects, good faith mimics other generalized contractual obligations, such as standards of commercial reasonableness referenced in multiple sections of the UCC. These are likewise context-dependent and incorporate into the contract such features as the timing and conduct recognized as norms in given commercial settings.

To be distinguished from such contract-based doctrines of good faith and commercial reasonableness are the elevated standards of fiduciary duty that significantly restrict the ambit of a fiduciary's freedom of contract with a beneficiary (*e.g.*, *Wal-Mart v. Coughlin* in Chapter Five). Fiduciaries—agents such as attorneys, corporate directors, physicians, or trustees and executors— are obliged to subordinate their interests to those their beneficiaries— principals such as clients, shareholders, patients, or trusts and estates. Fiduciary duties require candor, confidentiality, and loyalty, all far more demanding than covenants among arms'-length contracting parties and imposed due to the status of the parties rather than their volition. These fiduciary duties are organized within the law of agency, as encapsulated in the Restatement (Third) of Agency and, in law school, are examined in various upper level courses such as Professional Responsibility and Corporations.

In the first year of law school, you might ask a fundamental, though complex, question: whether fiduciary duties—and the broader law of agency where they reside—appear to have their origins more in contract or in tort. They are tort-like in that they are imposed as a matter of law based on status, yet they are contract-like in that they attach to relationships that are volitional at heart. Complicating such a question further is history: fiduciary duties are of ancient origin whereas contract law's covenant of good faith dates only to around the period of *Kirk La Shelle*. This may explain what might otherwise be a curious statement in *Kirk La Shelle*, that "the respondents assumed a fiduciary relationship which had its origin in the contract, and which imposed upon them the duty of utmost good faith." We will encounter the borderline between contractual good faith and fiduciary duty in two more cases ahead— *Rather v. CBS* and *Dalton v. ETS*.

Consider how the contractual duty of good faith relates to the compensation principle of contract remedies. To paraphrase Justice Holmes, a contract obliges a promisor either to perform or pay damages, and there is no penalty for choosing to breach and pay rather than perform. Holmes, *The Path of the Law*, 10 HARVARD L. REV. 457, 462 (1897). The good faith duty does not alter this framework or ask more of contracting parties. Its role is more supplemental, in filling gaps in incomplete contracts as well as to assure that parties not take actions that would impair the reasonable value of the promised performance, whether delivered in fact or compensated for in money damages. But while good faith is therefore a subtle contractual notion, its effects are far-reaching.

B. LEWIS PRODUCTIONS, INC. V. ANGELOU
2005 WL 1138474 (S.D.N.Y.)

MUKASEY, J.

Plaintiff B. Lewis Productions, Inc. (BLP) sues defendant Maya Angelou for breach of contract and breach of the duty of good faith and fair dealing . . . .

Butch Lewis is the president and sole owner of plaintiff corporation B. Lewis Productions, Inc. BLP's business consists primarily of promoting boxing and other sports and entertainment events. Defendant Maya Angelou, a resident of North Carolina, is a renowned poet. Defendant Hallmark Cards, Incorporated, a Missouri corporation, manufactures greeting cards and related products. In this action, BLP claims that Angelou breached an agreement in which she granted BLP the exclusive right to exploit her original literary works for publication in greeting cards and similar products. Angelou claims that no enforceable contract existed. . . .

Lewis and Angelou became acquainted in early 1994 when, at Lewis's request, Angelou visited Mike Tyson at an Indiana prison. . . . At that meeting, Angelou and Lewis discussed how she might reach a broader base of readers by publishing her works in greeting cards. . . . Several months after this initial meeting, Lewis met with Angelou at her North Carolina home to discuss a potential collaboration between Angelou and BLP to market Angelou's works to greeting card companies. . . . In November 1994, Lewis and Angelou signed a "letter agreement" that established what the letter called a "Joint Venture" to publish Angelou's writings in greeting cards and other media forms. The letter agreement, dated November 22, 1994 and signed by both parties, reads as follows:

> This letter agreement made between B. LEWIS PRODUCTIONS, INC. (BLP) with offices at 250 West 57th Street, New York, N.Y. 10019 and MAYA ANGELOU (ANGELOU) whose address is 2720 Reynolda Road, Suite # 1, Winston-Salem, NC

27106, sets forth the understandings of the parties with reference to the following:

1.   The parties will enter into a Joint Venture (Venture), wherein ANGELOU will exclusively contribute original literary works (Property) to the Venture and BLP will seek to exploit the rights for publishing of said Property in all media forms including, but not limited to greeting cards, stationery and calendars, etc.

2.   BLP will contribute all the capital necessary to fund the operation of the Venture.

3.   ANGELOU will contribute, on an exclusive basis, original literary works to the Venture after consultations with and mutual agreement of Butch Lewis, who will be the managing partner of the Venture.

4.   The Venture shall own the copyrights to all of ANGELOU's contributions to the Venture.

(a) If any of the subject copyrights do not produce any income for a consecutive five (5) year period as a result of the exploitation referred to [in] paragraph 1 herein then the ownership of these copyrights shall revert to Angelou exclusively.

5.   The name of the Venture shall be mutually agreed upon.

6.   Gross Revenue shall be distributed and applied in the following order:

(a)   Return of BLP's capital contribution.

(b)   Reimbursement of any and all expenses of the Venture.

(c)   Balance (net profits) to be shared equally between BLP and ANGELOU.

(d) ANGELOU shall have the right at any time, upon reasonable notice, to inspect all records including but not limited to the financial records of the Venture.

This Agreement shall be binding upon the parties until a more formal detailed agreement is signed.

In late 1994, BLP began to market Angelou's work to Hallmark and several other greeting card companies. Lewis began to negotiate a license agreement with Hallmark on Angelou's behalf. When Hallmark asked Lewis for confirmation that he was indeed authorized to act on Angelou's behalf, on June 19, 1996, Lewis sent Hallmark a letter signed by Angelou that stated:

This will confirm that BUTCH LEWIS PRODUCTIONS, INC. (BLP) has the exclusive right to represent DR. MAYA ANGELOU for the exploitation of her work product in the area of greeting cards, stationery, calendars, etc. as per the contract executed by BLP and Dr. Angelou dated November 22, 1994 which is still in full force and effect.

. . . In March 1997, after extended negotiations, Hallmark sent BLP a license agreement for the use of Angelou's future exclusive works which would have paid her and BLP 9% of gross revenues from sales of licensed products, with a $50,000 advance payment and a guaranteed minimum $100,000 in royalties. . . Angelou's greeting cards would be administered through Hallmark's Ethnic Business Center. . . .

Also in March 1997, Lewis and Angelou encountered one another at an event in Las Vegas, where Angelou saw Lewis, who is black, punctuate a conversation with white people by grabbing his crotch. . . . After she witnessed Lewis's behavior, Angelou "burned up his ears." . . . She claims that she told him that the "venture" between them was off, and that she no longer wanted to work with him. . . . Lewis denies that Angelou made any such comment at the time. . . .

However, when Lewis forwarded the Hallmark license agreement to Angelou, she did not sign it, and later told her literary agent Helen Brann to "start putting a little cold water on the prospect of this deal with Hallmark. . . After meeting with Lewis and his associate Joy Farrell, Brann sent a letter to Lewis on May 5, 1997, informing him "that it is not going to work out now for Dr. Maya Angelou to make any deal with Hallmark Cards." . . . In her letter, Brann cited Angelou's commitment to Random House as the publisher of all of Angelou's "major work" as a reason for not proceeding with Hallmark. Brann noted that "[n]either Dr. Angelou nor I like to say never, and I suppose that sometime in the future we might all figure out a way, in cooperation with Random House and Hallmark and us, to launch some kind of greeting card program, but this year is definitely not the year to contemplate such a move." . . .

Lewis claims that at a later meeting in 1997, Angelou told him that she would sign the licensing agreement with Hallmark "after the New Year," and that in February 1998, she told him she was planning to sign the agreement "as soon as she [got] everything off her table." . . . However Angelou did not sign the Hallmark licensing agreement, and according to Lewis's associate Farrell, when Farrell left BLP in mid-1998, in her opinion the deal was "dead," and the project was over. . . . Additionally, because Hallmark did not hear from Lewis after it sent him the licensing agreement in 1997, Hallmark executives eventually concluded that the collaboration between BLP and Angelou was "dead." . . .

Hallmark wrote Angelou's agent Brann in March 1998 to inquire whether Angelou was still interested in pursuing a program of greeting cards, stating that its "discussions with Mr. Lewis ended in early 1997 when he could not deliver a program." . . . Brann responded that Angelou was not interested in entering into an agreement with Hallmark at that time. . . . However, in June 1999, Angelou's close friend Amelia Parker, who was acquainted with an executive at Hallmark, convinced Angelou to have lunch with Hallmark executives at the company's St. Louis headquarters when Angelou was in town for an unrelated speaking engagement. . . . Angelou was encouraged by this meeting and decided to try to arrange a licensing deal with Hallmark.

Simultaneously, Angelou sought to assure that her ties to Lewis were severed. On June 16, 1999 Angelou's North Carolina counsel sent a letter to BLP stating that "any business relationship that you may have had or contemplated pursuant to a letter dated November 22, 1994 from you to Dr. Angelou, has been terminated." . . . Lewis claims that he never received this letter, and that as far as he was concerned, the November 1994 letter agreement was still in force in 1999. . . . According to Lewis, he contacted Angelou in 1999 about the Hallmark licensing agreement and she put him off again; at this point Lewis stopped trying to communicate with Angelou about Hallmark, and instead kept abreast of her views on the matter by communicating with her close friend Bob Brown, who did not tell Lewis that the "venture" had been terminated. Lewis learned that Hallmark and Angelou had reached an agreement without his assistance when he saw a press release about the deal in November 2000. . . .

On June 28, 2000, after more than a year of negotiations and discussions, Hallmark and Angelou signed a licensing agreement which featured a sliding royalty scale based on net revenues, guaranteed Angelou a minimum payment of $2 million, and gave her a $1 million advance. This agreement allowed Hallmark to use Angelou's previously published work as well as future works she would create for the project; additionally, the marketing of Angelou's products would not be restricted to ethnic consumers. . .

. . . Angelou claims that as a matter of law, no bilateral contract existed between her and BLP because the Agreement was vague, indefinite, and lacking in essential terms. . . . "In order for an agreement to be enforced, it must be sufficiently 'definite and explicit so [that the parties'] intention may be ascertained to a reasonable degree of certainty.'" *Best Brands Beverage, Inc. v. Falstaff Brewing Corp.,* 842 F.2d 578, 587 (2d Cir.1987) . . . Moreover, an agreement cannot be enforced if it lacks essential terms, and if the court is unable to supply such missing terms in a reasonable fashion that is consistent with the parties' intent. . . . A court may not "rewrite the contract and impose liabilities not bargained for." *A/S Atlantica v. Moran Towing & Transp. Co.,* 498 F.2d 158, 161 (2d Cir.1974). . . .

A term is essential if "it seriously affects the rights and obligations of the parties and there is a significant evidentiary dispute as to its content."

Ginsberg Machine Co. v. J. & H. Label Processing Corp., 341 F.2d 825, 828 (2d Cir.1965). Terms that may be considered essential in any agreement include the price to be paid, the work to be done, and the time of performance. *See* 1 Williston on Contracts § 4.18; *Schenk v. Red Sage,* No. 91 Cv. 7868, 1994 U.S. Dist. LEXIS 399, at *35 (S.D.N.Y. Jan. 20, 1994). When a court encounters indefinite terms, but finds that the parties did intend to form a contract, as the court found in its first decision in this case, the court then must attempt to "attach a sufficiently definite meaning to [the] bargain." 1 Williston § 4.18. A court should be especially willing to do so if the plaintiff has fully or partly performed under the agreement "since the performance may either remove the uncertainty or militate in favor of recovery even if the uncertainty continues." *Id.* . . . Of course, the court may not make a contract for the parties, *see* 1 Corbin § 4.1. However, because the parties in this case did intend a contract, the court is obligated to fill any gaps their Agreement contains, if it reasonably is able to do so. Voiding an agreement for lack of essential terms "is a step that courts should take only in rare and extreme circumstances." *Shann v. Dunk,* 84 F.3d 73, 81 (2d Cir.1996).

Angelou claims that the Agreement in this case is unenforceable because it lacks multiple essential terms. She notes that the Agreement does not specify or describe: what "original literary works" she would be contributing to the project; whether these literary works would be new or chosen from her previously published works; the quantity of works Angelou was to produce; when she was to contribute these works; the duration of the Agreement; or the extent of BLP's substantive or financial obligations under the Agreement. . . . Further, Angelou argues that the Agreement's designation of BLP's right to exploit Angelou's work in "all media forms" is overbroad and does not express the parties' intent, because this provision would have affected Angelou's agreement with her literary publisher Random House. *Id.* at 20. As explained below, these allegedly indefinite or missing terms are capable of reasonable interpretation.

1.   *Price.* The general rule is that price is "an essential ingredient" of every contract, and that a compensation clause is enforceable only if payment can be determined from the agreement without any "further expression by the parties." *Van Diepen v. Baeza,* No. 96 Cv. 8731, 1998 U.S. Dist. LEXIS 5763, at *21–*22 (S.D.N.Y. Feb. 26, 1998) . . . . Angelou notes that the Agreement does not state how much capital, if any, BLP was obligated to contribute to the project, and argues that this constitutes a failure to specify the essential term of price. . . . The Agreement does state, however, that BLP will contribute "all the capital necessary." The Agreement further specifies how gross revenue generated by the "Venture" was to be distributed: BLP's capital is returned, any of the Venture's expenses are reimbursed, and any net profits are shared equally between BLP and Angelou. . . . There is at least a material question of fact as to

whether this payment and distribution scheme was sufficiently definite. BLP was obligated under the Agreement to contribute "all" capital-an arrangement with a meaning that arguably is capable of enforcement. Moreover, the capital necessary to a "Venture" of the sort at issue here would be modest, if indeed any capital expenditures would have been necessary. Even expense items were likely to be limited to funds required to produce greeting card mock-ups, postage, and perhaps some travel.

If Angelou had signed the Hallmark license agreement that Lewis had negotiated on her behalf, and if revenue had been generated from Angelou's line of greeting cards, the Agreement between BLP and Angelou would have provided clear guidelines for distribution of that revenue. A compensation clause need not specify dollar figures to be definite.

BLP's part performance too shows that the parties had a meeting of the minds on the financial aspects of the Agreement. *See* Restatement (Second) of Contracts § 34; 1 Corbin § 4.1. BLP paid all initial expenses as Lewis began to negotiate licensing deals with various greeting card companies, and Angelou raised no objection during that time. The price terms of the Agreement are capable of reasonable interpretation, and therefore arguably are sufficiently definite for enforcement.

2. *Duration*. Angelou claims also that the Agreement's lack of a duration term renders it too vague for enforcement. . . . However, the court need decide this issue because the Agreement's lack of a duration term is not material. Under both New York and North Carolina law, a duration clause is not necessary in a contract for services. If such a contract makes no provision for duration, the contract is presumed to be terminable at will. . . .

3. *Subject Matter*. Angelou argues that the Agreement insufficiently defined the works she would supply to the project and the form in which her works would be exploited. The Agreement provides that Angelou will "exclusively contribute original literary works (Property) to the Venture and BLP will seek to exploit the rights for publishing of said Property in all media forms including, but not limited to greeting cards, stationery and calendars, etc."

BLP claims that the Agreement's subject matter was sufficiently definite because the Agreement stated that the details of the work would be mutually agreed upon, and could not be finalized until a licensing agreement with a specific greeting card company had been reached. . . . Angelou claims that this admission confirms her argument that the Agreement was merely an "agreement to agree," and not a binding Agreement in and of itself. However, this court has already held that the Agreement was more than simply an "agreement to agree"-the parties intended a binding contract here, . . . The parties understood that they were agreeing to work together to publish Angelou's writings in greeting cards, and potentially in related media forms such as calendars and stationery. The details of the arrangement would become final as individual projects were undertaken. . . When the Agreement was signed, there was a meeting of the minds as to its subject matter, and given the expressed intent of the parties, the court reasonably would be able to supply missing details, if necessary. (could argue against this)

Duty of Good Faith and Missing Terms

The above discussion of missing essential terms intersects with the issue of whether the parties here owed one another an obligation of good faith and fair dealing. New York and North Carolina courts have held that every contract contains an implied covenant of good faith and fair dealing, in which each party agrees not to injure the rights of the other to receive benefits under that agreement. *Dalton v. Educ. Testing Serv.,* 87 N.Y.2d 384, 396, 639 N.Y.S.2d 977, 984 (1995). In this case, BLP argues that each party's duty of good faith and fair dealing served to supply any missing terms relating to their respective obligations under the Agreement, and that Angelou breached her implied covenant of good faith when she failed to contribute any works to the project. . . .

Then-Judge Cardozo's opinion in *Wood v. Lucy, Lady Duff Gordon,* 222 N.Y. 88, 118 N.E. 214 (1917), underpins the analysis here. In that case, the defendant Lady Duff Gordon, a self-styled "creator of fashions," agreed with the plaintiff Otis Wood that he would have the exclusive right, subject to her approval, to sell her designs, to license others to market them, and to place her endorsement on the designs of others. As Cardozo phrased it, "[s]he employed the plaintiff to turn this vogue into money." *Id.* at 90. Under the agreement, Lady Duff Gordon was to receive one half of "all profits and revenues" derived from contracts made by the defendant involving her work. *Id.* at 90. The defendant sued Lady Duff Gordon, claiming that she had placed her endorsement on various products without his knowledge and kept the profits for herself. Lady Duff Gordon claimed in response that the original agreement between herself and Wood was unenforceable and illusory because it failed to specify Wood's obligation to sell and market her designs. The facts here strongly resemble those in Cardozo's classic. As in that case, we have here an artistic defendant, a 50–50 arrangement to market her creations, and an alleged behind-the-back breach, with Ms. Angelou cast as a Lady Duff Gordon for the modern age.

In *Wood,* the Court held that although the contract between the parties did not spell out each party's obligations,

> [t]he law has outgrown its primitive stage of formalism when the precise word was the sovereign talisman, and every slip was fatal. It takes a broader view to-day. A promise may be lacking, and yet the whole writing may be instinct with an obligation, imperfectly expressed. If that is so, there is a contract.

Id. at 91 (internal quotation marks omitted). The Court found the implication of a binding promise between the parties from numerous aspects of the agreement. Lady Duff Gordon gave Wood the "exclusive" right to market her creations; she must have expected him to perform, because her business would have ceased to exist without him. Additionally, Lady Duff Gordon's sole compensation was to be one-half of the profits: Therefore unless Wood made reasonable efforts under the agreement, she could recover nothing under its terms, defeating the "business efficacy" that both parties must have desired when they made the agreement. *Id.* The contract between Wood and Lady Duff Gordon was upheld, and generated a body of law in which the duty of good faith upheld binding agreements with scant details. 2 Corbin § 5.27 ("The finding of implied promises is more common today than in the era before the *Wood* case. Courts recognize that if the parties intend a contract, rather than a nullity, implying promises to avoid the finding of illusoriness or indefiniteness protects the reasonable expectation of the parties engendered by the agreement.").

Angelou claims that the Agreement is unenforceable because it fails to define either party's obligations. She argues that the Agreement does not specify a quantity of work to be supplied by her, nor does it state what effort BLP was required to expend in furtherance of the Agreement. . . . According to Angelou, the Agreement was so vague that she could have complied with its terms and never provided any work to the project; similarly, BLP could have complied simply by making a few telephone inquiries. . . . Indeed, both Lewis and Angelou testified that Angelou was under no obligation to provide any works to the project. . . . Perhaps, but consider what might have occurred if Angelou had accepted some version of the proposal that Hallmark made to BLP. If Angelou had failed thereafter to contribute some works, but had published other works on her own that could have been used in greeting cards, BLP might have sued for damages stemming from Angelou's nonperformance. . . .

As . . . in *Wood,* it appears that the parties here intended to form a binding contract. Deficiencies or gaps in the Agreement regarding the parties' obligations may be filled by the obligation of good faith that each incurred upon signing it. As in *Wood,* the profit-sharing arrangement between the parties here meant that Angelou and BLP had nothing to gain from the Agreement if either failed to perform or gave minimal effort. Therefore we must assume that each party arguably had an obligation to make "reasonable efforts" in furtherance of the Agreement in order to vindicate the "business efficacy" that both parties must have contemplated when they entered the Agreement. *Wood,* 222 N.Y. at 90, 92.

Angelou cites *Ginsberg,* 341 F.2d at 828, for the proposition that some contractual voids are too great to fill by implication. In *Ginsberg,* an oral contract followed by an exchange of letters between two businessmen for an exclusive agency in the selling of machine labels was found unenforceable for lack of any duration term in the agreement and other important omissions. The *Ginsberg* Court acknowledged *Wood's* "classic principle," but found too many terms missing, and held that "the risk of ensnaring a party in a set of contractual obligations that he never knowingly assumed [wa]s too serious." *Id.*

In this case, the evidence shows that Lewis and Angelou agreed on the terms of the contract and on the meaning of those terms. Angelou and BLP never argued over the substance of the Agreement, and as Lewis marketed the Angelou project to greeting card companies, Angelou never protested. To the contrary, she signed a confirmation of the Agreement on June 19, 1996, which was sent to Hallmark. . . . Angelou did eventually refuse to deal with BLP, but this decision was not motivated by any contractual dispute. Angelou testified that she did not like the mock-ups of the greeting cards that BLP presented to her . . . that she was disgusted by Lewis's behavior at the event in Las Vegas . . . and that she felt it was morally wrong to compromise her relationship with Random House by publishing her work elsewhere . . . None of these reservations had anything to do with the terms of the contract Angelou signed with BLP. Angelou articulated no concerns about the nature or scope of the Agreement, and did not complain that she had been ensnared into contractual obligations she had unknowingly assumed. Angelou's plight does not resemble that of the merchant in *Ginsberg* who made an oral contract and signed an informal letter confirming a vague arrangement. Her case more closely parallels that of Lady Duff Gordon, who signed a binding agreement that she later came to regret.

The repeated use of the language of exclusivity in the dealings between Angelou and BLP is further evidence that each party had a good faith obligation to perform under the Agreement. The Agreement twice uses the word "exclusive" in describing Angelou's contributions to the "Venture"— "Angelou will exclusively contribute original literary works," and "Angelou will contribute, on an exclusive basis, original literary works" . . . As in *Wood,* "[w]e are not to suppose that one party was to be placed at the mercy of the other," 222 N.Y. at 91; rather, Angelou committed to work only with BLP to accomplish her contractual goal, and trusted that BLP would fulfill his obligations under the Agreement. . . . [The] Agreement at least arguably contains most if not all required essential terms for enforcement. Any remaining vagueness or uncertainty regarding the parties' obligations may be found immaterial, because the parties' reciprocal duty of good faith under the Agreement ensured that they would make reasonable efforts to perform.

For the reasons set forth above, [the motion for summary judgment is] denied.

NOTES AND QUESTIONS

1. What terms does the court note are essential to finding a binding contract? How are *Lewis v. Angelou* and the duty of good faith related to the materials that we studied in our very first chapter, on contract formation?

2. As seen in *Lewis v. Angelou*, once parties have entered a contract, the law instills an implied legal duty for each party to act in good faith toward fulfilling the bargain—or at least protecting the value of the exchange upon breach. As a matter of private autonomy, this duty of good faith is intended to reflect law's sense of what most people forming contracts expect from themselves and others; as a matter of public policy, the good-faith duty encourages people to expect integrity and reliability in legally recognized contractual relations.

3. Despite the seeming simplicity of the good-faith obligation, however, this duty has both aided and vexed courts. The concept of good faith helps fill in gaps when a contract does not address some contingency that arises later. But an expansive conception of an implied good-faith duty could put courts in the business of rewriting the bargains people make, and courts generally try to resist such interventions. *See generally* STEVEN J. BURTON & ERIC G. ANDERSEN, CONTRACTUAL GOOD FAITH: FORMATION, PERFORMANCE, BREACH, ENFORCEMENT (Boston: Little, Brown & Co. 1995).

PROBLEM: THE FALLING STAR

Ari Silver, a hot-shot Hollywood agent, is approached to represent a D-List celebrity. Ari, who is quite confident in his own abilities, thinks he can resuscitate or create anyone's reputation in the entertainment industry. Ari agrees to sign a deal in which he will give "his best efforts" to represent the celebrity and do a career re-boot.

1. Under a "best efforts" clause, how much work and effort would Ari Silver have to perform in order to comply with his obligations under the contract? Would there be any reference points for such "best efforts"?

2. If you were the attorney for the celebrity, what else might you want to insert into such a representation agreement?

3. If you were the attorney for Ari Silver, what might you want to insert into such a representation agreement?

NOTE ON OUTPUT AND REQUIREMENTS CONTRACTS

Recall from the materials on contract formation the concepts of output and requirements contracts addressed by UCC Section 2–306 as applied in *Bacou Dalloz USA v. Continental Polymers, Inc.* In these contracts, the quantity term is unenumerated, identified as all the buyer's needs ("requirements contract") or all the seller's production ("output contract"). The absence of an enumeration of such an important term might doom such agreements as too indefinite to enforce. But commercial parties find such arrangements appealing to assure sources of supply or of sale and invariably intend them to be legally binding. The concept of good faith assists in doing so. It delineates the quantity term in relation to actual needs or production, determined in good faith.

EASTERN AIRLINES V. GULF OIL
415 F.Supp. 429 (S.D. Fla. 1975)

KING, J.

[A leading airline of the period, Eastern, formed a jet fuel requirements contract with a leading supplier, Gulf Oil. The parties faithfully performed for many years, with Eastern receiving a steady and uninterrupted supply, at a set price, and Gulf being assured of recurring revenue, likewise at a set price. Both parties stood to gain and also to lose: lower market prices made the deal better for Gulf while higher market prices made it better for Eastern. However, partway into the contract, a fuel shortage arose in the Middle East due to war and the cartel-like behavior of OPEC. Market prices rose dramatically and Gulf sought out, seeking additional payments under the threat of terminating supply.]

Gulf has taken the position in this case that the contract between it and Eastern is not a valid document in that it lacks mutuality of obligation; it is vague and indefinite; and that it renders Gulf subject to Eastern's whims respecting the volume of jet fuel Gulf would be required to deliver to the purchaser Eastern.

The contract talks in terms of fuel "requirements." The parties have interpreted this provision to mean that any aviation fuel purchased by Eastern at one of the cities covered by the contract, must be bought from Gulf. Conversely, Gulf must make the necessary arrangements to supply Eastern's reasonable good faith demands at those same locations. This is the construction the parties themselves have placed on the contract and it has governed their conduct over many years and several contracts.

In early cases, requirements contracts were found invalid for want of the requisite definiteness, or on the grounds of lack of mutuality. Many such cases are collected and annotated at 14 A.L.R. 1300. As reflected in the foregoing annotation, there developed rather quickly in the law the view that a requirements contract could be binding where the purchaser had an operating business. The "lack of mutuality" and "indefiniteness" were resolved since the court could determine the volume of goods provided for under the contract by reference to objective evidence of the volume of goods required to operate the specified business. Therefore, well prior to the adoption of the Uniform Commercial Code, case law generally held requirements contracts binding. See 26 A.L.R.2d 1099, 1139. . . .

Reasonable elasticity in the requirements is expressly envisaged by this section and good faith variations from prior requirements are permitted even when the variation may be such as to result in discontinuance. A shut-down by a requirements buyer for lack of orders might be permissible when a shut-down merely to curtail losses would not. The essential test is whether the party is acting in good faith. Similarly, a sudden expansion of the plant by which requirements are to be measured would not be included within the scope of the contract as made but normal expansion undertaken in good faith would be within the scope of this section. One of the factors in an expansion situation would be whether the market price has risen greatly in a case in which the requirements contract contained a fixed price. . . .

The parties have consistently over the years relied upon each other to act in good faith in the purchase and sale of the required quantities of aviation fuel specified in the contract. During the course of the contract, various estimates have been exchanged from time to time, and, since the advent of the petroleum allocations programs, discussions of estimated requirements *have been on a monthly (or more frequent) basis. The court concludes that the document is a binding and enforceable requirements contract.

Gulf suggests that Eastern violated the contract between the parties by manipulating its requirements through a practice known as 'fuel freighting' in the airline industry. Requirements can vary from city to city depending on whether or not it is economically profitable to freight fuel. This fuel freighting practice in accordance with price could affect lifting from Gulf stations by either raising such liftings or lowering them. If the price was higher at a Gulf station, the practice could have reduced liftings there by lifting fuel in excess of its actual operating requirements at a prior station, and thereby not loading fuel at the succeeding high price Gulf station. Similarly where the Gulf station was comparatively cheaper, an aircraft might load more heavily at the Gulf station and not load at other succeeding non-Gulf stations.

The court however, finds that Eastern's performance under the contract does not constitute a breach of its agreement with Gulf and is consistent with good faith and established commercial practices as required by U.C.C. 2–306. "Good Faith" means "honesty in fact in the conduct or transaction concerned." U.C.C. 1–201(19). Between merchants, "good faith" means "honesty in fact and the observance of reasonable commercial standards of fair dealing in the trade." U.C.C. 2–103(1)(b) and Official Comment 2 of U.C.C. 2–306. The relevant commercial practices are courses of performance, courses of dealing and usages of trade.

Throughout the history of commercial aviation, including 30 years of dealing between Gulf and Eastern, airlines' liftings of fuel by nature have been subject to substantial daily, weekly, monthly and seasonal variations, as they are affected by weather, schedule changes, size of aircraft, aircraft load, local airport conditions, ground time, availability of fueling facilities, whether the flight is on time or late, passenger convenience, economy and efficiency of operation, fuel taxes, into-plane fuel service charges, fuel price, and ultimately, the judgment of the flight captain as to how much fuel he wants to take.

All these factors are, and for years have been, known to oil companies, including Gulf, and taken into account by them in their fuel contracts, Gulf's witnesses at trial pointed to certain examples of numerically large 'swings' in monthly liftings by Eastern at various Gulf stations. Gulf never complained of this practice and apparently accepted it as normal procedure. Some of the 'swings' were explained by the fueling of a single aircraft for one flight, or by the addition of one schedule in mid-month. The evidence establishes that Eastern, on one occasion, requested 500,000 additional gallons for one month at one station, without protest from Gulf, and that Eastern increased its requirements at another station more than 50 percent year to year, from less than 2,000,000 to more than 3,000,000 gallons, again, without Gulf objection.

The court concludes that fuel freighting is an established industry practice, inherent in the nature of the business. The evidence clearly demonstrated that the practice has long been part of the established courses of performance and dealing between Eastern and Gulf. As the practice of 'freighting' or 'tankering' has gone on unchanged and unchallenged for many years accepted as a fact of life by Gulf without complaint, the court is reminded of Official Comment 1 to U.C.C. 2–208: "The parties themselves know best what they have meant by their words of agreement and their action under that agreement is the best indication of what that meaning was."

From a practical point of view, 'freighting' opportunities are very few, according to the uncontradicted testimony, as the airline must perform its schedules in consideration of operating realities. There is no suggestion here that Eastern is operating at certain gulf stations but taking no fuel at all. The very reason Eastern initially desired a fuel contract was because the airline planned to take on fuel, and had to have an assured source of supply.

If a customer's demands under a requirements contract become excessive, U.C.C. 2–306 protects the seller and, in the appropriate case, would allow him to refuse to deliver unreasonable amounts demanded (but without eliminating his basic contract obligation); similarly, in an appropriate case, if a customer repeatedly had no requirements at all, the seller might be excused from performance if the buyer suddenly and without warning should descend upon him and demand his entire inventory, but the court is not called upon to decide those cases here.

Rather, the case here is one where the established courses of performance and dealing between the parties, the established usages of the trade, and the basic contract itself all show that the matters complained of for the first time by Gulf after commencement of this litigation are the fundamental given ingredients of the aviation fuel trade to which the parties have accommodated themselves successfully and without dispute over the years. . . . The court concludes that Eastern has not violated the contract.

Most courts recognize an implied duty of good faith as an element of every contract, even ones in which the quantity, price, and effort expended are enumerated. In the negotiation of a contract, each side may focus solely on their own best interest; once in a contract, however, discretion is constrained to require at least some degree of looking out for the contractual interests of the other side. But what, exactly, does that mean? The following case attempts an answer—and illustrates some of the challenges.

DALTON V. EDUCATIONAL TESTING SERVICE
663 N.E.2d 289 (N.Y. 1995)

KAYE, C.J.

The primary question before us is whether defendant, Educational Testing Service (ETS), a standardized testing firm, complied with procedures specified in its contract with high school senior Brian Dalton in refusing to release Dalton's Scholastic Aptitude Test (SAT) score. Because the factual findings underlying the trial court's determination that ETS failed to act in good faith in following those procedures were affirmed by the Appellate Division, have support in the record and are consequently beyond the scope of our review, we conclude—as did the trial court and Appellate Division—that ETS breached its contract with Dalton. Though we agree, moreover, with the courts below that specific performance is the appropriate remedy, we nevertheless conclude that the promised performance was good-faith compliance with the stated procedures, not release of the questioned scores as ordered by those courts.

In May 1991, Brian Dalton took the SAT . . . Six months later, in November, he took the examination a second time, as a senior . . . and his combined score increased 410 points. Because Dalton's score increased by more than 350 points, his test results fell within the ETS category of "Large Score Differences" or "discrepant scores." In accordance with ETS policy, members of the ETS Test Security Office therefore reviewed his May and November answer sheets. Upon a finding of disparate handwriting, the answer sheets were submitted to a document examiner, who opined that they were completed by separate individuals. Dalton's case was then forwarded to the Board of Review, which preliminarily decided that substantial evidence supported cancelling Dalton's November score.

Upon registering for the November SAT, Dalton had signed a statement agreeing to the conditions in the New York State edition of the Registration Bulletin, which reserved to ETS "the right to cancel any test score * * * if ETS believes that there is reason to question the score's validity." The Registration Bulletin further provided that, if "the validity of a test score is questioned because it may have been obtained unfairly, ETS [will] notif[y] the test taker of the reasons for questioning the score" and offer the test-taker the following five options: (1) the opportunity to provide additional information, (2) confirmation of the score by taking a free retest, (3) authorization for ETS to cancel the score and refund all fees, (4) third-party review by any institution receiving the test score or (5) arbitration.

As specified in the Registration Bulletin, ETS apprised Dalton of its preliminary decision to cancel his November SAT score in a letter from Test Security Specialist Celeste M. Eppinger. Noting the handwriting disparity and the substantial difference between his May and November test results, Eppinger informed Dalton that "[t]he evidence suggests that someone else may have completed your answer sheet and that the questioned scores may be invalid." She advised him that he could supply "any additional information that will help explain" this or, alternatively, elect one of the other options.

. . . Dalton opted to present additional information to the Board of Review, including the following: verification that he was suffering from mononucleosis during the May examination; diagnostic test results from a preparatory course he took prior to the November examination (he had taken no similar course prior to the May SAT) that were consistent with his performance on that test; a statement from an ETS proctor who remembered Dalton's presence during the November examination; and statements from two students—one previously unacquainted with Dalton—that he had been in the classroom during that test. Dalton further provided ETS with a report from a document examiner obtained by his family who concluded that Dalton was the author of both sets of answer sheets.

ETS, after several Board of Review meetings, submitted the various handwriting exemplars to a second document examiner who, like its first, opined that the May and November tests were not completed by the same individual. As a result, ETS continued to question the validity of Dalton's November score.

At this point plaintiff Peter Dalton, father and natural guardian of Brian Dalton [sued] to prohibit ETS from cancelling Dalton's November

SAT score and to compel immediate release of the score. Following a 12-day nonjury trial, the trial court found that ETS failed "to make even rudimentary efforts to evaluate or investigate the information" furnished by Dalton and thus concluded that ETS failed to act in good faith in determining the legitimacy of Dalton's score, thereby breaching its contract. The trial court premised this conclusion on its determination that the ETS Board of Review members failed to evaluate the information submitted because they believed Dalton's presence at the November SAT to be wholly irrelevant to the handwriting issue and that he could controvert the Board's preliminary finding that the score was invalid solely by taking a retest. As a remedy for the contractual breach, the trial court ordered ETS to release the November SAT score.

The Appellate Division affirmed. It too found that ETS ignored the documentation provided by Dalton and considered only the reports of its own document examiners. Like the trial court, the Appellate Division concluded that this failure to evaluate as well as to investigate Dalton's information constituted a breach of contract. In light of these factual determinations, we agree that ETS breached its contract with Dalton but differ as to the scope of the relief.

. . . Implicit in all contracts is a covenant of good faith and fair dealing in the course of contract performance (see, *Van Valkenburgh, Nooger & Neville v. Hayden Publ. Co.,* 30 N.Y.2d 34, 45, 330 N.Y.S.2d 329, 281 N.E.2d 142, *cert denied* 409 U.S. 875, 93 S.Ct. 125, 34 L.Ed.2d 128). Encompassed within the implied obligation of each promisor to exercise good faith are " 'any promises which a reasonable person in the position of the promisee would be justified in understanding were included' " (*Rowe v. Great Atl. & Pac. Tea Co.,* 46 N.Y.2d 62, 69, 412 N.Y.S.2d 827, 385 N.E.2d 566, quoting 5 Williston, Contracts § 1293, at 3682 [rev ed 1937]). This embraces a pledge that "neither party shall do anything which will have the effect of destroying or injuring the right of the other party to receive the fruits of the contract" (*Kirke La Shelle Co. v. Armstrong Co.,* 263 N.Y. 79, 87, 188 N.E. 163). Where the contract contemplates the exercise of discretion, this pledge includes a promise not to act arbitrarily or irrationally in exercising that discretion (see, *Tedeschi v. Wagner Coll.,* 49 N.Y.2d 652, 659, 427 N.Y.S.2d 760, 404 N.E.2d 1302). The duty of good faith and fair dealing, however, is not without limits, and no obligation can be implied that "would be inconsistent with other terms of the contractual relationship" (*Murphy v. American Home Prods. Corp.,* 58 N.Y.2d 293, 304, 461 N.Y.S.2d 232, 448 N.E.2d 86).

The parties here agreed to the provisions in the Registration Bulletin, which expressly permit cancellation of a test score so long as ETS found "reason to question" its validity after offering the test-taker the five specified options. Nothing in the contract compelled ETS to prove that the test-taker cheated. Nor did the invitation to the test-taker to furnish ETS with relevant information reasonably and realistically translate into any requirement that ETS conduct a field investigation or gather evidence to verify or counter the test-taker's documentation. Indeed, such an obligation would be inconsistent with the contractual language placing the burden squarely on the test-taker to overcome the ETS finding of score invalidity. ETS, therefore, was under no duty, express or implied, to initiate an external investigation into a questioned score.

The contract, however, did require that ETS consider any relevant material that Dalton supplied to the Board of Review. The Registration Bulletin explicitly afforded Dalton the option to provide ETS with relevant information upon notification that ETS questioned the legitimacy of his test score. Having elected to offer this option, it was certainly reasonable to expect that ETS would, at the very least, consider any relevant material submitted in reaching its final decision.

Dalton triggered this implied-in-law obligation on the part of ETS by exercising his contractual option to provide ETS with information [.] . . . Significantly, Dalton heeded the advice in the Procedures for Questioned Scores and tendered numerous documents that did more than simply deny allegations of wrongdoing or attest to his good character, such as medical evidence regarding his physical condition, statements by fellow test-takers, the statement of a classroom proctor and consistent diagnostic test results . . .

Nevertheless, with the exception of the document examiner's report, ETS disputes the relevancy of this information. Specifically, ETS maintains that the sole issue before the Board of Review was the disparate handwriting and that evidence regarding Dalton's health (apart from a damaged arm) or presence during both examinations is irrelevant to resolving that issue.

To be sure, the Procedures for Questioned Scores warned Dalton "to provide only additional information that is relevant to the questions being raised." The Eppinger letter to Dalton, however, informed him that his November score was possibly invalid precisely because ETS believed "that someone else may have completed [his] answer sheet." Thus, ETS expressly framed the dispositive question as one of suspected impersonation. Because the statements from the classroom proctor and November test-takers corroborated Dalton's contention that he was present at and in fact took the November examination, they were relevant to this issue.

Likewise, inasmuch as the medical documentation concerning Dalton's health at the time of the May SAT provided an explanation for his poor performance on that examination, and the consistent diagnostic test results demonstrated his ability to achieve such a dramatic score increase, these items were also germane to the question whether it was Dalton or an imposter who completed the November examination. Indeed, in its manual,

Policies and Procedures Concerning Scores of Questionable Validity—which details internal ETS procedure regarding questioned scores—ETS offers several examples of "relevant information" that a test-taker might provide, including "a doctor's report that the candidate was under the influence of medication at the time the low score was earned." Regarding "a case of possible impersonation" in particular, the manual suggests that "other test results might demonstrate that the questioned score is not inconsistent with other measures of the candidate's abilities." Thus, Dalton's material fell within ETS' own definition of relevancy, as expressed in its manual and letter to Dalton.

The critical question then is whether the Board of Review made any effort to consider this relevant information submitted by Dalton. That is a factual inquiry. Both the trial court and the Appellate Division concluded that the Board utterly failed to evaluate the material. Given these affirmed findings, "our scope of review is narrow. This Court is without power to review findings of fact if such findings are supported by evidence in the record" (*Humphrey v. State of New York,* 60 N.Y.2d 742, 743, 469 N.Y.S.2d 661, 457 N.E.2d 767).

Several Board of Review members—each member alone had the power to order release of Dalton's November score—testified that they believed information establishing Dalton's presence during the November examination to be irrelevant to their determination and, moreover, that only a successful retest would validate Dalton's score. Thus, there is support in the record for the factual determinations of the trial court and Appellate Division and they are binding on us. This is so notwithstanding inconsistent testimony by Board members that the Board did review Dalton's information but found it unpersuasive. In light of the affirmed findings, the Court of Appeals simply does not have authority to weigh conflicting evidence and make its own factual determinations, as the dissent would do.

Consequently, this case is factually distinct from those relied upon by ETS, where the testing service considered but then rejected information provided by the test-taker (*see, e.g., Langston v. ACT,* 890 F.2d 380; *Denburg v. Educational Testing Serv.,* No. C–1715–83 [NJ Super Ct]; *cf., Johnson v. Educational Testing Serv.,* 754 F.2d 20, 26, *cert. denied* 472 U.S. 1029, 105 S.Ct. 3504, 87 L.Ed.2d 635 [noting that ETS provided test-taker with opportunity to be heard and to be represented by counsel]). When ETS fulfills its contractual obligation to consider relevant material provided by the test-taker and otherwise acts in good faith, the testing service—not the courts—must be the final arbiter of both the appropriate weight to accord that material and the validity of the test score. This Court will not interfere with that discretionary determination unless it is performed arbitrarily or irrationally.

Where, however, ETS refuses to exercise its discretion in the first instance by declining even to consider relevant material submitted by the test-taker, the legal question is whether this refusal breached an express or implied term of the contract, not whether it was arbitrary or irrational. Here, the courts below agreed that ETS did not consider the relevant information furnished by Dalton. By doing so, ETS failed to comply in good faith with its own test security procedures, thereby breaching its contract with Dalton.

The dissent urges that because the trial court and Appellate Division relied in part on ETS' failure to investigate Dalton's information, they arguably employed an erroneous legal standard. Overlooked, however, is that both courts also concluded that ETS' refusal to evaluate the material breached the contract with Dalton and, thus, employed a correct legal standard. Moreover, the crucial factual inquiry under the correct standard—whether ETS considered Dalton's relevant material—has already been resolved by those courts. Because this factual finding dictates the legal conclusion that ETS breached the contract, remittal is unnecessary.

We agree with the trial court and Appellate Division that Dalton is entitled to specific performance of the contract. Dalton is not, however, entitled to release of his score as though fully validated. The goal of specific performance is to produce "as nearly as is practicable, the same effect as if the contract had been performed" (Farnsworth, Contracts § 12.5, at 823 [1982]). Had the contract here been performed, ETS would have considered the information provided by Dalton in reaching a final decision. ETS never promised to release a score believed to be invalid, and the validity of Dalton's November SAT score has yet to be determined. Indeed, the trial court specifically noted that it was not resolving the question whether Dalton in fact took the November test. . . .

Dalton is entitled to relief that comports with ETS' contractual promise—good-faith consideration of the material he submitted to ETS. We cannot agree with Dalton's assumption that ETS will merely rubber-stamp its prior determination without good-faith attention to his documentation and that reconsideration by ETS will be an empty exercise. Our conclusion that the contract affords Dalton a meaningful remedy rests also on the provision in the Procedures for Questioned Scores allowing Dalton to utilize one or more of the remaining four options in combination with renewed consideration by the Board of Review. Those options—including third-party review by any institution receiving the test score as well as arbitration—remain available should ETS determine that the information submitted fails to resolve its concerns about the validity of the November score.

Accordingly, the Appellate Division order should be modified in accordance with this opinion and, as so modified, affirmed, without costs.

LEVINE, J. (dissenting).

I agree with the majority that the Educational Testing Service (ETS) had no duty, express or implied, to investigate the information submitted by Brian Dalton. However, I do not agree that we are bound by the factual determinations of the lower courts, which are based on an erroneous legal standard, or that the record contains any evidence that ETS arbitrarily failed to consider the materials submitted by Dalton. I, therefore, respectfully dissent.

A primary obligation of ETS as administrator of the SAT and other scholastic aptitude tests heavily relied upon by institutions of higher education is to certify that released scores accurately reflect the performance on the test of the identified test taker. The college admission process is highly dependent on the authenticity of the SAT scores released by ETS, as are other test takers whose scores are valued in relation to those of all others who take the exam and are competing for admission. In order to ensure the reliability of its certification process, ETS has established elaborate procedures that balance the harms to institutions and other candidates of the release of possibly invalid scores against the detriment to students whose scores are challenged as potentially invalid. The procedures established by ETS are unquestionably fair; they give test takers whose scores are questioned opportunity after opportunity to validate their scores. In the end, however, ETS as a practical necessity must be the final arbiter of whether it can honestly certify the validity of a student's score. Thus, the standard contract between ETS and test takers reserves to ETS the right "to cancel any test score * * * if ETS believes that *there is reason to question* the score's validity [emphasis supplied]."

. . . My colleagues in the majority here, however, correctly conclude that ETS had no express or implied duty to investigate. Thus, it seems indisputable that the ultimate determinations of the courts below—that ETS breached its implied covenant of good faith and fair dealing—were reached at least in significant part by reliance on an erroneous legal standard, that ETS had a duty to investigate. Thus, at a minimum, reversal and remittal for new findings based on the proper legal standard is required here.

However, applying the correct legal standard to the record evidence, it is my conclusion that ETS fulfilled its contractual obligations as a matter of law and, therefore, we should reverse and dismiss the Daltons' complaint. As the Chief Judge concludes, ETS was contractually obligated to consider any relevant material that Dalton supplied the Board of Review (majority opn, at 390, at 980 of 639 N.Y.S.2d, at 292 of 663 N.E.2d). After considering that evidence, ETS had the stated right to cancel Dalton's test score if it possessed "a reason to question" the score's validity. Thus, it seems self-evident that ETS expressly reserved to itself substantial discretion on whether to refuse to certify a test score.

To be sure, there is a covenant of good faith and fair dealing implicit in the contract between Dalton and ETS . . . It requires that "neither party shall do anything which will have the effect of destroying or injuring the right of the other party to receive the fruits of the contract" (*Kirke La Shelle Co. v. Armstrong Co.,* 263 N.Y. 79, 87, 188 N.E. 163). In this way, the implied covenant "is in aid and furtherance of other terms of the agreement of the parties. No obligation can be implied, however, which would be inconsistent with other terms of the contractual relationship" (*Murphy v. American Home Prods. Corp.,* 58 N.Y.2d 293, 304, 461 N.Y.S.2d 232, 448 N.E.2d 86 [rejecting application of implied covenant to at-will employment contracts]). Where good faith is an *express* condition of a contract that contemplates a wide scope of discretion on the part of one party, there is no breach if the discretionary act performed is "not arbitrary and capricious" (*Smith v. Robson,* 148 N.Y. 252, 255, 42 N.E. 677; *see also,* 3A Corbin, Contracts § 647, at 104–106). The implied covenant does no more; it works only to ensure that a party with whom discretion is vested does not act arbitrarily or irrationally (*see, e.g., Tedeschi v. Wagner Coll.,* 49 N.Y.2d 652, 659, 427 N.Y.S.2d 760, 404 N.E.2d 1302).

Thus, the issue here is whether there is evidence that ETS performed its discretionary functions arbitrarily or irrationally, or with bad faith in fact . . . Here, there was no evidence of bad faith in fact. Moreover, ETS had two definitive reports of highly qualified handwriting experts, of proven reliability, that the November 1991 answer sheet was filled out by someone other than the person who filled out the May 1991 exam answer sheet and the documents known to have been signed or produced by Brian Dalton. Surely it was not irrational or arbitrary for ETS to find that the unexplained disparate handwriting on the November 1991 answer sheet gave it reason to question the validity of the second test score. The courts below did not find otherwise. Nor can it be said that, as a matter of law, the evidence submitted by Dalton totally obviated the reasons ETS had to question the test score. It was, therefore, not a breach of the implied covenant of good faith to refuse to certify Dalton's scores after consideration of the evidence submitted, and the majority does not so hold.

Rather the majority holds that there is evidence that ETS breached its implied covenant of good faith in its deliberative process in failing "to consider" Dalton's submissions (majority opn, at 391, at 980–981 of 639 N.Y.S.2d, at 292–293 of 663 N.E.2d). However, the uncontroverted evidence accepted by the courts below and the majority here is that when ETS received the information submitted by Dalton it did not totally disregard it. Rather, it considered it and judged it weighty enough to merit further evaluation. Thus, it is undeniable that ETS responded to the submissions by retaining another handwriting expert to get a third evaluation of the documents. In addition, ETS submitted Dalton's additional handwriting samples to its first handwriting expert for a second evaluation.

To overcome this concrete evidence of consideration, the majority points to selectively narrow portions of the record in which ETS Board of Review members testified that they deemed irrelevant Dalton's evidence that tended to show he was in the room on the day the test was given as evidence that ETS "failed to consider" Dalton's submissions, which in turn supported the determination of its breach of the implied covenant of good faith and fair dealing. I disagree.

. . . Each Board member testified that the evidence did not explain their one lingering crucial doubt, the disparate handwriting, which was the exact doubt communicated to Dalton by ETS—"someone else may have completed [the] answer sheet" (Dec. 11, 1991 letter to Brian Dalton). Because the reason to deem irrelevant Dalton's evidence of presence was not irrational, arbitrary or capricious it cannot, as a matter of law, form the basis of a breach of the implied covenant of good faith. It is only by substituting its judgment for that of ETS as to what should have been deemed relevant evidence that the majority finds evidence of bad faith. . . .

. . . Accordingly, I would reverse the order of the Appellate Division and dismiss.

NOTES AND QUESTIONS

1.   *ETS v. Dalton* poses the question "just *how much* good faith is necessary"? The majority and the dissent have a different view of what good faith required. As good faith is a malleable concept, its precise definition may remain elusive. Which do you believe has the stronger argument, the majority or the dissent? Why?

2.   If you believed that "good faith" required more investigation than ETS did in this instance, is your opinion influenced by the relative power imbalance of the parties or the fact that the testing company seemed to have written its own rules unilaterally?

3.   Conversely, if you believe that ETS fulfilled its contractual duty of good faith, did efficiency, cost, and administrative convenience enter into your analysis? As in civil procedure, the values of fairness and efficiency may at times conflict.

4.   What did this lawsuit ultimately accomplish for Dalton? Did he have better options? How might you have advised him and his parents if they came to you for legal advice in his senior year of high school?

5.   In light of the last question, why do you think Dalton and his parents pursued multiple levels of litigation? Notice that the Daltons did not seek money damages but specific performance, which the Court of Appeals defined

not as the requested release of the score but good faith consideration of the materials submitted.

B. DISCRETION AND GOOD FAITH

The dissenting opinion in *Dalton v. ETS* focuses on good faith as a limitation on discretion, a common function for the doctrine at work in the following cases. Absent the doctrine, unbridled discretion may render promises illusory, lacking consideration, and therefore unenforceable under principles of traditional contract formation discussed in Chapter One.

THIRD STORY MUSIC, INC. V. WAITS

48 Cal.Rptr.2d 747 (Cal.App.2 Dist. 1995)

EPSTEIN, J.

This case involves a dispute between a company which owned the rights to the musical output of singer/songwriter Tom Waits from 1972 to 1983 and the party which purchased those rights. The issue is whether a promise to market music, or to refrain from doing so, at the election of the promisor is subject to the implied covenant of good faith and fair dealing where substantial consideration has been paid by the promisor. We conclude that the implied covenant does not apply.

. . . According to the complaint, Waits agreed to render his services as a recording artist and songwriter exclusively to Third Story Productions (predecessor-in-interest to plaintiff and appellant Third Story Music, Inc.) from 1972 to 1983, pursuant to written agreements dated July 1, 1972 and July 1, 1977. Third Story Productions transferred its rights in Waits' music to Asylum Records (predecessor-in-interest to defendant/respondent Warner Communications, Inc.) on August 31, 1972, and to Elektra/Asylum Records (currently a division of Warner Communications, Inc.) pursuant to an agreement dated June 15, 1977.

Under these agreements, TSM was to produce master recordings featuring performances by Waits. Warner obtained from TSM the worldwide right to "manufacture, sell, distribute and advertise records or other reproductions (visual or nonvisual) embodying such recordings, to lease, license, convey or otherwise use or dispose of the recordings by any method now or hereafter known, in any field of use, to release records under any trademarks, trade names or labels, to perform the records or other reproductions publicly and to permit the public performance thereof by radio broadcast, television or any other method now or hereafter known, all upon such terms and conditions as we may approve, and to permit others to do any or all of the foregoing. . . ." This clause of the agreements also specifically stated that Warner "may at our election refrain from any or all of the foregoing."

TSM was to receive as a royalty a percentage of the amount earned by Warner from its exploitation of the music. In addition, Warner was required to pay TSM a specific dollar amount as an advance on royalties.[3]

So far as can be ascertained from the record, the parties operated under these agreements without controversy until 1993. At that time, an affiliate of TSM known as Bizarre/Straight Records sought to compile and market an album of previously-released Waits compositions, including four which were the subject of the TSM/Warner agreement: On the Nickel, Jitterbug Boy, Invitation to the Blues, and Ruby's Arms. Bizarre/Straight presented a licensing proposal to Warner through its agent Warner Special Products. During negotiations, Bizarre/Straight and TSM learned that Warner had no objection to the deal, but that it would not be made final unless Waits personally approved the licensing request.

For reasons unknown, but which TSM claims have to do with Waits' desire to maximize profit on music created after his association with TSM, Waits refused consent. TSM brought suit for contract damages based on breach of the implied covenant of good faith and fair dealing, claiming that Warner "has created an impediment to [TSM] receiving material benefits under the [parties'] agreements and has wrongfully interjected that requirement [the requirement of Waits' approval] into an unknown number of potentially lucrative licensing arrangements, in so doing preventing at least the issuance of the four licenses described above, and other licenses, which TSM will ascertain through discovery."

Warner . . . [alleged] that the clause in the agreement permitting it to "at [its] election refrain" from doing anything to profitably exploit the music is controlling and precludes application of any implied covenant. The demurrer was sustained on those grounds. TSM contends on appeal, and argued below, that when a party to a contract is given this type of discretionary power, that power must be exercised in good faith, and that permitting the artist to decide whether a particular licensing arrangement was or was not acceptable did not represent a good faith exercise. . . .

---

[3] Paragraph 34 of the 1972 agreement provides: "Conditioned upon your and the Artist's full and faithful performance of all of the terms hereof, we shall pay you the following amounts: (a) Four Thousand Dollars ($4,000.00) concurrently with the execution hereof and Four Thousand Dollars ($4,000.00) upon the commencement of each renewal term hereof, if any; and (b) Four Thousand Eight Hundred Dollars ($4,800.00) during the initial term hereof and during each renewal term hereof, if any, payable in twelve (12) equal monthly installments during each such term. All such amount shall constitute non-returnable advances against any and all royalties hereunder." The 1978 agreement provided for a payment of $100,000 for each LP produced and delivered by TSM during the first two terms of the agreement, $50,000 of which was to be paid immediately and unconditionally, and $150,000 for each LP produced and delivered by TSM during the third renewal term.

When an agreement expressly gives to one party absolute discretion over whether or not to perform, when should the implied covenant of good faith and fair dealing be applied to limit its discretion? Both sides rely on different language in the recent Supreme Court decision in *Carma Developers (Cal.), Inc. v. Marathon Development California, Inc.* (1992) 2 Cal.4th 342, 6 Cal.Rptr.2d 467, 826 P.2d 710 to answer that question. In *Carma,* the parties had entered into a lease agreement which stated that if the tenant procured a potential sublessee and asked the landlord for consent to sublease, the landlord had the right to terminate the lease, enter into negotiations with the prospective sublessee, and appropriate for itself all profits from the new arrangement. In the passage relied on by TSM, the court recognized that "[t]he covenant of good faith finds particular application in situations where one party is invested with a discretionary power affecting the rights of another." (2 Cal.4th at 372, 6 Cal.Rptr.2d 467, 826 P.2d 710.) The court expressed the view that "[s]uch power must be exercised in good faith." (*Id.*)

At the same time, the *Carma* court upheld the right of the landlord to freely exercise its discretion to terminate the lease in order to claim for itself—and deprive the tenant of—all profit from the expected sublease. In this regard, the court stated: "We are aware of no reported case in which a court has held the covenant of good faith may be read to prohibit a party from doing that which is expressly permitted by an agreement. On the contrary, as a general matter, implied terms should never be read to vary express terms. [Citations.] 'The general rule [regarding the covenant of good faith] is plainly subject to the exception that the parties may, by express provisions of the contract, grant the right to engage in the very acts and conduct which would otherwise have been forbidden by an implied covenant of good faith and fair dealing. . . . This is in accord with the general principle that, in interpreting a contract "an implication . . . should not be made when the contrary is indicated in clear and express words." 3 Corbin, Contracts, § 564, p. 298 (1960). . . . As to acts and conduct authorized by the express provisions of the contract, no covenant of good faith and fair dealing can be implied which forbids such acts and conduct. And if the defendants were given the right to do what they did by the express provisions of the contract there can be no breach.' " (2 Cal.4th at p. 374, 6 Cal.Rptr.2d 467, 826 P.2d 710, quoting *VTR, Incorporated v. Goodyear Tire & Rubber Company* (S.D.N.Y.1969) 303 F.Supp. 773, 777–778.)

. . . In situations such as the present one, where a discretionary power is expressly given by the contractual language, the quoted passages from *Carma* set up an apparent inconsistency between the principle that the covenant of good faith should be applied to restrict exercise of a discretionary power and the principle that an implied covenant must never vary the express terms of the parties' agreement. We attempt to reconcile the two.

We first emphasize a long-established rule concerning implied covenants. To be imposed " '(1) the implication must arise from the language used or it must be indispensable to effectuate the intention of the parties; (2) it must appear from the language used that it was so clearly within the contemplation of the parties that they deemed it unnecessary to express it; (3) implied covenants can only be justified on the grounds of legal necessity; (4) a promise can be implied only where it can be rightfully assumed that it would have been made if attention had been called to it; (5) there can be no implied covenant where the subject is completely covered by the contract.' " (*Lippman v. Sears, Roebuck & Co.* (1955) 44 Cal.2d 136, 142, 280 P.2d 775; *City of Glendale v. Superior Court* (1993) 18 Cal.App.4th 1768, 1778, 23 Cal.Rptr.2d 305.)

With this in mind, we review the authorities cited in *Carma* for the proposition that a discretionary power must be exercised in good faith. . . . [I]n *Cal. Lettuce Growers v. Union Sugar Co.* (1955) 45 Cal.2d 474, 289 P.2d 785, . . . it was alleged that a contract permitting the buyer of sugar beets to set the price to be paid was illusory. The court implied an obligation to set the price fairly in accordance with the covenant of good faith and fair dealing, thus protecting the enforceability of the agreement. (*Id.* at p. 484, 289 P.2d 785.) . . .

The latest edition to the Corbin treatise on contracts puts it more poetically:

> If what appears to be a promise is an illusion, there is no promise. Like the mirage of the desert with its vision of flowing water which yet lets the traveler die of thirst, there is nothing there. By the phrase 'illusory promise' is meant words in promissory form that promise nothing. They do not purport to put any limitation on the freedom of the alleged promisor. If A makes an illusory promise, A's words leave A's future action subject to A's own future whim, just as it would have been had A said nothing at all. (2 Corbin, Contracts (rev. ed. 1995) § 5.28, p. 142.)

. . . In the same vein, covenants to use "good faith" or "best efforts" to generate profits for the licensor are routinely implied where the licensor grants exclusive promotional or licensing rights in exchange for a percentage of profits or royalties, but the licensee does not expressly promise to do anything. (See, e.g., *Zilg v. Prentice-Hall, Inc.* (2d Cir.1983) 717 F.2d 671, 679–681 [discussing the difference between "best efforts" and "good faith"].) As Justice Cardozo put it in one of the earliest cases involving this type of arrangement, *Wood v. Lucy, Lady Duff-Gordon* (1917) 222 N.Y. 88, 118 N.E. 214, "It is true that [the licensee] does not promise in so many words that he will use reasonable efforts to place the [licensor's] indorsements and market her designs. We think, however, that such a promise is fairly to be implied. The law has outgrown its primitive stage of formalism when the precise word was the sovereign talisman, and every slip was fatal. It takes a broader view today. A promise may be lacking, and yet the whole writing may be 'instinct with an obligation,' imperfectly expressed. [Citations omitted.] If that is so, there is a contract." (222 N.Y. at pp. 90–91, 118 N.E. 214.)

In each of these cases, the courts were forced to resolve contradictory expressions of intent from the parties: the intent to give one party total discretion over its performance and the intent to have a mutually binding agreement. In that situation, imposing the duty of good faith creates a binding contract where, despite the clear intent of the parties, one would not otherwise exist. Faced with that choice, courts prefer to imply a covenant at odds with the express language of the contract rather than literally enforce a discretionary language clause and thereby render the agreement unenforceable. As was said in the most recent edition of Corbin's treatise on contracts: "The complaint that a promise is illusory often comes in rather poor grace from the addressee of the allegedly illusory promise, particularly where the addressor is ready and willing to carry out the expression of intention. For this reason, courts are quite properly prone to examine the context to conclude that the escape hatch was intended to be taken only 'in good faith' or in the 'exercise of a reasonable discretion' or upon some other condition not wholly within the control of the promisor. In which case, the conclusion is that the promise is not illusory." (1 Corbin, Contracts (rev. ed. 1995), § 1.17, p. 49.) "The tendency of the law is to avoid the finding that no contract arose due to an illusory promise when it appears that the parties intended a contract. . . . An implied obligation to use good faith is enough to avoid the finding of an illusory promise." (2 Corbin, Contracts, *supra,* § 5.28 at pp. 149–150.)

We turn to the question of whether it is necessary in this case to imply a covenant of good faith to protect the enforceability of the contract, or otherwise to effectuate the clear and obvious intent of the parties. The TSM/Warner agreement states that Warner may market the Waits recordings, or "at [its] election" refrain from all marketing efforts. Read literally, as the trial court did and respondent would have us do, this is a textbook example of an illusory promise. At the same time, there can be no question that the parties intended to enter into an enforceable contract with binding promises on both sides. Were this the only consideration given by Warner, a promise to use good faith would necessarily be implied under the authorities discussed.

The illusory promise was not, however, the only consideration given by the licensee. Under paragraph 33 of the 1977 agreement and paragraph 34 of the 1972 agreement, Warner promised to pay TSM a guaranteed minimum amount no matter what efforts were undertaken. It follows that, whether or not an implied covenant is read into the agreement, the agreement would be supported by consideration and would be binding. . . . The guaranteed payments involved do not appear to be large in relation to what might be earned from the music of a successful recording artist. But unless the consideration given was so one-sided as to create an issue of unconscionability, the courts are not in a position to decide whether legal consideration agreed to by the parties is or is not fair. The $8,800 annual payments due under the 1972 agreement and the $50,000 minimum payment, plus $100,000 to $150,000 for each LP produced by TSM, due under the 1978 agreement amounted to more than the peppercorn of consideration the law requires.

. . . Warner bargained for and obtained all rights to Waits' 1972 to 1983 musical output, and paid legally adequate consideration. That it chose not to grant a license in a particular instance cannot be the basis for complaint on the part of TSM as long as Warner made the agreed minimum payments and paid royalties when it did exploit the work. "The courts cannot make better agreements for parties than they themselves have been satisfied to enter into or rewrite contracts because they operate harshly or inequitably. It is not enough to say that without the proposed implied covenant, the contract would be improvident or unwise or would operate unjustly. Parties have the right to make such agreements. The law refuses to read into contracts anything by way of implication except upon grounds of obvious necessity." (*Walnut Creek Pipe Distributors, Inc. v. Gates Rubber Co.* (1964) 228 Cal.App.2d 810, 815, 39 Cal.Rptr. 767.) TSM was free to accept or reject the bargain offered and cannot look to the courts to amend the terms that prove unsatisfactory. . . . As we agree with the trial court that no such duty existed, demurrer was properly sustained . . . The judgment is affirmed.

CUSSLER v. CRUSADER ENTERTAINMENT, LLC

2010 WL 718007 (Cal.App.2 Dist. 2010)

KITCHING, J.

Plaintiff and appellant Clive Cussler, a widely read novelist, entered into a contract with defendant and respondent Crusader Entertainment, LLC (Crusader), a film producer. Under the contract, if certain conditions were satisfied, Crusader had the option of purchasing certain Clive Cussler books for the purpose of producing films. Crusader exercised its initial option and produced a film based on the novel Sahara. Prior to the release of the film, however, the relationship between the parties soured and Cussler filed suit against Crusader. Crusader in turn filed a cross-complaint against Cussler.

Both parties accused each other of breaching the contract and committing various torts. After a 14-week trial, the jury returned a special verdict rejecting most of the causes of action asserted by both parties. The jury, however, found that Cussler breached the implied covenant of good faith and fair dealing and that Crusader incurred damages in the amount of $5 million as a result of that breach. The trial court then entered a judgment for that amount in favor of Crusader. Cussler appeals the judgment and requests that we enter a new judgment in his favor in the amount of $8,571,429.

We affirm the judgment with respect to Cussler's claims against Crusader. But we reverse the judgment with respect to Crusader's claim for breach of the implied covenant against Crusader. For reasons we shall explain, Crusader's breach of the implied covenant claim is barred as a matter of law. . . .

Cussler and Crusader entered into a Memorandum of Agreement for Option and Purchase of Literary Material dated May 9, 2001. The contract contemplated that Crusader would produce a film franchise, i.e., a series of films, based on Cussler's novels featuring the character Dirk Pitt.

The contract provided that Crusader could exercise an initial option to produce a film based on Cussler's novel Sahara and a second novel to be designated by Crusader. It further provided that, if certain conditions were satisfied, Crusader "shall pay [Cussler] the sum of Twenty Million Dollars ($20,000,000) payable in seven equal annual instalments [sic] over a period of seven (7) years beginning on [the date the initial option is exercised] which shall constitute the Fixed Purchase Price for the novel entitled 'Sahara' which shall be the Initial Picture and one additional Theatrical Picture ('the Second Picture') based on the 'Second Novel.'"

Under the contract, Crusader also had the option of purchasing a third Dirk Pitt novel for a third film. This option could not be exercised unless certain conditions were satisfied. One condition was that Crusader was required to commence "principal photography" of Sahara within 24 months of the date it exercised its initial option. If Crusader failed to do so, then Cussler in its discretion could elect not to sell the rights to the third novel to Crusader.

. . . On November 6, 2001, Crusader exercised its initial option to acquire from Cussler film rights to Sahara and a second novel. Accordingly, in order to preserve its option of purchasing the rights to a third novel, Crusader was required to, inter alia, commence principal photography of the film Sahara on or before November 6, 2003.

. . . Before the contract was signed, Cussler approved a screenplay (the Approved Screenplay) for the film Sahara. The contract provided that Crusader would "not . . . change the Approved Screenplay . . . without Cussler's written approval exercisable in his sole and absolute discretion." However, once actual production of the film began, Cussler could not prevent the director of the film "from making the type of on[-]set changes . . . customarily made in the ordinary course of the production of a motion picture[.]" Cussler also could not prohibit the producers of the film from "making changes required by the exigencies of production" or "making changes required by the company that issues the completion bond for the picture pursuant to customary provisions contained in completion bonds. . . ."

After the contract was executed, Crusader sought to change the Approved Screenplay. It hired and fired and sometimes hired again at least 10 different screenwriters who submitted more than two dozen screenplays.

Cussler disapproved of most of the screenplays submitted by Crusader, often without much consideration. In one instance, Cussler disapproved a screenplay before he read it. After Crusader urged Cussler to review the document, he read the first 35 pages then threw it in the garbage. At a meeting with Crusader, Cussler flung the screenplay over his head and referred to it as "crap."

Meanwhile Cussler began writing his own drafts of the screenplay. Crusader did not approve of Cussler's scripts for creative and budgetary reasons. Further, Crusader was concerned that its use of a screenplay written by Cussler, who was not a member of the Writer's Guild, would violate Crusader's contract with the Writer's Guild. In addition, the film's distributor, Paramount, opposed Cussler writing the screenplay. Crusader thus asked Cussler to stop writing screenplays, but Cussler continued to do so.

Cussler's conduct made it difficult for Crusader to obtain the services of new screenwriters because it became known in Hollywood that Cussler would rewrite screenplays. Crusader also allegedly had difficulty recruiting actors because they did not like Cussler's proposed screenplays. This allegedly delayed the production of the film.

By April 2003, Cussler began to . . . press for the use of *his* screenplay. Cussler advised Crusader that he did not trust other writers and that the only way to move forward with the production of the film was for Crusader to use Cussler's screenplay. When Crusader refused Cussler's demand, the relationship between the parties further deteriorated. Beginning in the Spring of 2003, Cussler stopped communicating with Crusader for several months. Although Crusader continued to send Cussler screenplays, even after Crusader hired a director and began filming, Cussler stopped reading the screenplays he received because he felt that Crusader would not listen to his input. . .

Paragraph 17 of the contract expressly prohibited Cussler and his agents from publicly speaking about the subject matter of the contract without Crusader's approval, which could not be "unreasonably withheld." However, in the fall of 2003, about a month before the first scene of Sahara was filmed, Cussler's publicist Carole Bartholomeaux began a campaign on

Cussler's website requesting Cussler's fans to pressure Crusader to use Cussler's screenplay. In response to Bartholomeaux's campaign, Crusader began receiving about 20 emails a day from Cussler's fans.

At about the same time, Cussler began speaking about Sahara in radio and newspaper interviews. In these interviews, Cussler repeatedly made disparaging remarks about the film's screenplay. For example, in October 2003, Cussler said in a radio interview that Crusader had "gutted a lot of the dramatic scenes." Similarly, Cussler was quoted in the Denver Post in December 2003, as stating, "They've sent me seven scripts, and I've inserted each one in the trash can." . . . A few weeks later, in an article in the Contra Costa Times, Cussler stated: "Right now, it looks like they might go forward with a screenplay [for Sahara] that I have not approved. Which means my readers are going to get disappointed because the screenplay I've seen is just awful." . . .

In December 2003, Cussler's fans started an internet petition stating that Crusader was using a screenplay that Cussler did not approve in violation of Crusader's contract, and demanding that Crusader use a screenplay written by Cussler. The petition repeated Cussler's criticisms of the screenplay made in the Denver Post article. . . . In January 2004, Cussler commenced this action by filing a complaint against Crusader in the superior court. Crusader, in turn, filed a cross-complaint against Cussler. Prior to the trial, on or about April 8, 2005, the film Sahara was released.

. . . In his breach of contract claim, Cussler alleged that Crusader breached the contract by, inter alia, using a screenplay for Sahara that was not approved by Cussler [and] defaulting on its obligations due under the contract . . . In its operative pleading, the fourth amended and supplemental cross-complaint, Crusader alleged that Cussler "arbitrarily, irrationally, and destructively pursued his consultation and approval rights" relating to the screenplay for Sahara in violation of the implied covenant of good faith and fair dealing. Crusader further alleged that Cussler's disparaging statements about Sahara breached the implied covenant, as well as paragraph 17 of the contract. . . .

On May 15, 2007, after a 14-week trial and 9 days of deliberations, the jury rendered a special verdict. The jury found that Crusader had breached the contract but also found that Cussler was not harmed by that breach. . . . All but one of Crusader's claims was also rejected. . . . [The jury also] found that Cussler breached the implied covenant of good faith and fair dealing, and awarded Crusader $2.5 million for past economic loss and $2.5 million for future economic loss, for a total of $5 million in damages. . . . The judgment deemed Crusader the prevailing party and awarded Crusader $5 million in damages, costs, and prejudgment interest. This appeal followed.

[Cussler made several arguments resting on the idea that several of the jury's findings were internally inconsistent, that he should not be obligated to pay Crusader's attorney's fees, and that he did not breach the duty of good faith. We turn to the last of these issues.—Eds.]

. . . "It has long been recognized in California every contract contains an implied covenant of good faith and fair dealing that neither party will do anything which will injure the right of the other to receive the benefits of the agreement." . . . This covenant is read into contracts "in order to protect the express covenants or promises of the contract, not to protect some general public policy interest not directly tied to the contract's purpose." (*Wolf v. Walt Disney Pictures & Television* (2008) 162 Cal.App.4th 1107, 1120, 76 Cal.Rptr.3d 585 (*Wolf*).)

The implied covenant cannot vary the express terms of the contract (*Carma Developers (Cal.) Inc. v. Marathon Development California, Inc.* (1992) 2 Cal.4th 342, 374, 6 Cal.Rptr.2d 467, 826 P.2d 710 (*Carma*)) or impose duties or limits beyond the express terms. (*Guz v. Bechtel National, Inc.* (2000) 24 Cal.4th 317, 349–350, 100 Cal.Rptr.2d 352, 8 P.3d 1089 (*Gu*).) The parties to a contract " 'may, by express provisions of the contract, grant the right to engage in the very acts and conduct which would otherwise have been forbidden by an implied covenant of good faith and fair dealing. . . .' " (*Carma*, at p. 374, 6 Cal.Rptr.2d 467, 826 P.2d 710.) The implied covenant "will only be recognized to further the contract's purpose; it will not be read into a contract to prohibit a party from doing that which is expressly permitted by the agreement itself." (*Wolf, supra*, 162 Cal.App.4th at p. 1120, 76 Cal.Rptr.3d 585.)

The implied covenant cannot be imposed on a subject that is completely covered by the contract's express terms. (*Third Story Music, Inc. v. Waits* (1995) 41 Cal.App.4th 798, 804, 48 Cal.Rptr.2d 747 (*Third Story Music*).) Thus, to the extent an implied covenant claim "seeks simply to invoke terms to which the parties *did* agree, it is superfluous." (*Guz, supra*, 24 Cal.4th at p. 352, 100 Cal.Rptr.2d 352, 8 P.3d 1089.) In other words, if the allegations supporting a breach of the implied covenant claim "do not go beyond the statement of a mere contract breach and, relying on the same alleged acts, simply seek the same damages or other relief already claimed in a companion contract cause of action, they may be disregarded as superfluous as no additional claim is actually stated." . . .

. . . Crusader argues that Cussler breached the implied covenant in "numerous ways," but does not articulate any specific conduct that supports its claim apart from (1) Cussler's alleged bad faith disapproval of screenplays and associated delays in the production of the film Sahara, (2) Cussler's public statements regarding the film Sahara, and (3) Cussler's alleged unreasonable delay in approving actor Steve Zahn. Applying the principles of *Carma, Third Story Music,* and the other cases we have cited, we shall conclude that Crusader's cause of action for breach of the implied covenant of good faith and fair dealing fails as a matter of law.

Crusader's implied covenant claim is based mainly on Cussler's failure to approve Crusader's numerous proposed screenplays. As stated, Crusader expressly promised to *not* change the Approved Screenplay unless Cussler, in his sole and absolute discretion, approved. We cannot excuse Crusader from its express obligation to use the Approved Screenplay and take away Cussler's express right to reject unapproved screenplays unless, contrary to the parties' intention, a literal interpretation of the contract would render it illusory and unenforceable. (*Third Story Music, supra,* 41 Cal.App.4th at p. 808, 48 Cal.Rptr.2d 747.)

Under the plain and literal terms of the contract, Cussler could reject unapproved screenplays for unreasonable reasons (e.g., a desire to write the screenplay himself) or for no reason at all.[10] Nonetheless, Crusader received consideration under the contract regardless of how Cussler exercised his discretion. That is because Crusader could have, if it chose, used the Approved Screenplay to produce the film Sahara. Thus the contract is not illusory even if Cussler unreasonably exercised his discretion to withhold approval of a different screenplay. The implied covenant therefore should not be imposed.

The bargain struck by Crusader and Cussler did not require Cussler to act reasonably or in good faith in approving screenplays. Rather, the agreement expressly gave Cussler the right to approve screenplays "in his sole and absolute discretion." The parties were free to grant Cussler by express terms such discretion even if such discretion would otherwise be forbidden by the implied covenant. (*Carma, supra,* 2 Cal.4th at p. 374, 6 Cal.Rptr.2d 467, 826 P.2d 710.) Indeed, the parties clearly understood the difference between "absolute" and "reasonable" discretion because another provision of the contract prohibited Crusader from "unreasonably" withholding approval of Cussler's public statements regarding the film Sahara. We cannot rewrite the contract simply because Crusader believes, with hindsight, that using the Approved Screenplay or giving Cussler unfettered discretion to reject other screenplays was not a commercially wise endeavor. *Third Story Music, supra,* 41 Cal.App.4th at p. 809, 48 Cal.Rptr.2d 747; *Wolf, supra,* 162 Cal.App.4th at p. 1122, 76 Cal.Rptr.3d 585.) . . .

Crusader argues that Cussler's negative public statements regarding the film Sahara were a breach of the implied covenant of good faith and fair dealing. At trial, however, Crusader argued that these statements

---

[10] In its pleadings, at trial and on appeal Crusader argued that Cussler had a bad motive to withhold his approval of proposed screenplays, namely pressuring Crusader to allow Cussler to write the screenplay. The law, however, generally does not distinguish between good and bad motives for breaching a contract. (Applied Equipment Corp. v. Litton Saudi Arabia Ltd. (1994) 7 Cal.4th 503, 516, 28 Cal.Rptr.2d 475, 869 P.2d 454.)

were a breach of the *express* contract, specifically paragraph 17 of the contract. We agree with Crusader's position at trial.

[P]aragraph 17 provided that Cussler and his agents shall not "circulate, publish, or otherwise disseminate any news stories or articles, books, or other publicity containing [Cussler's] name and relating directly or indirectly" to the film Sahara "unless the same are first approved by [Crusader], such approval not to be unreasonably withheld." We hold that, as a matter of law, this provision prohibited Cussler from making *any* public statements-good or bad-regarding Sahara without Crusader's approval. Cussler's alleged disparaging statements about Sahara on the radio, in newspapers and on the internet, therefore, were a breach of the express terms of the contract. Accordingly, to the extent Crusader's breach of the implied covenant cause of action was based on the public statements of Cussler and his agents regarding Sahara, the cause of action is superfluous and should be disregarded.

The trial court determined that Crusader was the prevailing party. In light of our reversal of the $5 million award to Crusader, the trial court must reexamine that issue. [This issue was crucial to the question of attorney's fees.—Eds.] . . . Except as provided herein, the judgment is affirmed. The judgment is reversed with respect the $5 million award to Crusader in connection with its cause of action for breach of the implied covenant and good faith and fair dealing. The judgment is also reversed with respect to the trial court's findings that Crusader is the prevailing party and that Crusader is entitled to recover costs. The case is remanded to the trial court so that it can determine whether there is a prevailing party and, if so, whether that party is Cussler or Crusader. If the trial court determines that there is a prevailing party, it should also determine the amount of costs, if any, that party should recover. The parties are to bear their own costs on appeal.

NOTES AND QUESTIONS

1.   How are *Third Story Music, Inc. v. Waits* and *Cussler* similar? How much discretion did each contract grant Warner and Cussler, respectively?

2.   Note that despite all of this behind-the-scenes drama, *Sahara* was eventually made into a movie, starring Matthew McConaughey and Penelope Cruz. While the movie earned more than $122 million in box office receipts and should have been a success, its huge production budget and distribution costs meant that overall the film lost over $80 million. Due to the shortfall, no sequels have been released.

3.   The *Cussler* case offers lessons for preparing contracts to anticipate possible impasses. Less obvious, but just as important, is the case's fundamental lesson: be careful when you are choosing a partner in a business venture. Cussler and Crusader did not seem to trust one another even at the

very beginning of the relationship. The same could be said for Lewis and Angelou; a rough-and-tumble boxing promoter and an eloquent poet were unlikely to see eye-to-eye on a greeting card line.

Mistrust is not a good foundation for any deal that will be carried out over a period of years, but mistrust is particularly problematic in a deal that concerns any kind of artistic matter, such as creating a film based on a popular novel. In addition, the litigation in *Cussler* emphasizes that the transaction costs of attorney's fees can, if allowed, consume far more than the gains from the deal itself.

4.   For more on good faith in contracts, see Teri J. Dobbins, *Losing Faith: Extracting the Implied Covenant of Good Faith from (Some) Contracts*, 84 OREGON L. REV. 227 (2005); Harold Dubroff, *The Implied Covenant of Good Faith in Contract Interpretation and Gap-Filling: Reviling a Revered Relic*, 80 ST. JOHN'S L. REV. 559 (2006); Michael P. Van Alstine, *Of Textualism, Party Autonomy and Good Faith*, 40 WILLIAM & MARY L. REV. 1223 (1999).

C. MODIFICATION

The implied duty of good faith is also implicated in contract modification. Often, parties decide midstream to re-negotiate some aspect of their deal. While in some instances this seems a perfectly natural way for the parties to solve differences or resolve some of the unanticipated contingencies that may arise in the course of performance, in other situations a contract modification may look more opportunistic and more like the product of coercion. Once parties have locked themselves into a deal, they may have forgone other market opportunities and thus exposed their vulnerability.

Contract law has policed the issue of coerced or exploitative contract modification in three ways: through requiring additional consideration for a re-negotiated contract, i.e. essentially making a new contract through some additional payment or effort on behalf of the parties; through the defense of economic duress; and through the idea, centered in UCC Section 2–209, that all contract modifications must be made in good faith. Even though these are different doctrinal methods of policing contract modification, what they all have in common is the desire to protect the original bargain from changes that are coerced or extorted.

Recall the *Alaska Packers v. Domenico* case in Chapter Three, where the court held that despite the company's agreement to pay the fishermen more money, the parties were both still bound by the original agreement. The court viewed the matter as one of pre-existing duty and lack of any fresh consideration, but the court could also have analyzed the agreement under economic duress. As noted in the materials accompanying *Alaska Packers*, the condition of the nets was a pivotal fact—had the court believed the company provided faulty nets, the issue of good faith would have been joined.

BRIAN CONSTRUCTION & DEVELOPMENT COMPANY V. BRIGHENTI

405 A.2d 72 (Conn. 1978)

LOISELLE, J.

The plaintiff, a contractor, brought this action for damages against the defendant, a subcontractor, alleging that the defendant had breached a contract under which he had promised to perform certain excavation work for the plaintiff. The defendant counterclaimed. The court rendered judgment for the defendant on the plaintiff's claim and for the plaintiff on the defendant's counterclaim. From the judgment for the defendant, the plaintiff has appealed.

The relevant facts as found by the court are as follows: In early 1968, Joseph E. Bennett, doing business as Joseph E. Bennett Company, entered into a contract with Seymour B. Levine (hereinafter the owner) for the construction of a post office building in Bristol. Shortly thereafter, Bennett assigned the contract to the plaintiff, who, on October 10, 1968, entered into a written subcontract with the defendant. Pursuant to that contract, consisting of a standard subcontract agreement plus specifications, the defendant agreed to perform "all Excavation, Grading, Site Work, Asphalt Pavement, Landscaping, and Concrete Work" and "everything requisite and necessary to finish the entire work properly." In return, the defendant was to receive $104,326.

The defendant commenced excavation of the premises on October 15, 1968, at which time he discovered considerable debris below the surface, consisting in part of concrete foundation walls, slab floors, underground tanks, twisted metals and various combustible materials. Apparently, the discovered walls and floor had been part of the basement of an old factory which had previously been located on the site. The plaintiff had previously taken test borings of the excavation site, the results of which had been given to the defendant prior to the execution of the subcontract. The defendant had relied upon those results, although they proved to be grossly inaccurate. Neither party had been aware of the rubble and, consequently, its removal was not specifically called for by the plans and specifications included in the subcontract, nor was the cost of its removal included in the contract price. Nonetheless, the existence of the rubble necessitated excavation beyond the depth anticipated in the plans and specifications and the post office building could not be constructed without its removal.

A provision of the general contract between the owner and Bennett provided that "no extra work or change shall be made unless in pursuance of a written order from the Owner signed or countersigned by the Architect, or a written order from the Architect stating that the Owner has authorized the extra work or change." A separate provision of the contract specified that each subcontractor was to make all claims for extras "to the Contractor in the manner provided in the General Conditions of the Contract . . . for like claims by the Contractor upon the Owner." A provision of the subcontract reiterated this requirement, adding that "no extra work or other change will be commenced by the Sub-Contractor without the Contractor's prior approval in writing." Similarly, both contracts included provisions under which the subcontractor agreed to be bound to the contractor by the terms of the general contract and to assume toward the contractor all those obligations which he, under the contract, assumed towards the owner.

Upon discovery of the unanticipated debris, the plaintiff notified the architect, the attorney for the owner, representatives of the Bristol redevelopment agency, which owned the building site, and representatives of the postal service of the existence of the rubble. All agreed that removal of the rubble was requisite for completion of the building, yet none would issue written authorization for its removal. . . . The plaintiff sought to notify the owner, but because the owner was ill, the plaintiff was unable to reach him.

On October 21, 1968, the defendant ceased working on the excavation site and notified the plaintiff of his refusal to continue. Subsequently, the defendant offered to complete the subcontract if the plaintiff would have the unsuitable material removed. The plaintiff refused this offer. He then ordered the defendant to remove the rubble as part of "everything requisite and necessary" under the subcontract. The defendant refused. When the plaintiff was confronted with this situation, and no one would take the responsibility to authorize the removal of the rubble, although its removal was necessary for the contractor to complete his contract, he chose to enter into a further agreement with the defendant for work not included in the subcontract.

The plaintiff and the defendant orally agreed that the defendant would be paid his costs for removing the unanticipated rubble, plus 10 percent. By letter dated November 7, 1968, the plaintiff confirmed this oral agreement. Although requested in the letter to do so, the defendant failed to sign and return a copy of the letter to the plaintiff. Nonetheless, the defendant returned to work, continuing until about November 13, 1968, at which point he left the job, refusing to return despite the plaintiff's request that he complete the work. The plaintiff completed his own contract with the owner, suffering, as a result of the defendant's abandonment, considerable damages.

. . . It is an accepted principle of law in this state that when a party agrees to perform an obligation for another to whom that obligation is already owed, although for lesser remuneration, the second agreement does not constitute a valid, binding contract. See, e. g., Dahl v. Edwin Moss & Son, Inc., 136 Conn. 147, 69 A.2d 562; Gruber v. Klein, 102 Conn. 34, 127 A. 907; Warren v. Skinner, 20 Conn. 559. "The basis of the rule is generally made to rest upon the proposition that in such a situation he who promises the additional compensation receives nothing more than that to which he is already entitled and he to whom the promise is made gives nothing that he was not already under legal obligation to give. 1 Williston on Contracts, § 130." Blakeslee v. Board of Water Commissioners, 106 Conn. 642, 652, 139 A. 106, 110. Where, however, the subsequent agreement imposes upon the one seeking greater compensation an additional obligation or burden not previously assumed, the agreement, supported by consideration, is valid and binding upon the parties. See, e. g., Simone v. Kirschner, 100 Conn. 427, 124 A. 20.

In Blakeslee v. Board of Water Commissioners, supra, 106 Conn. 656, 139 A. 111, this court, in analyzing these traditional principles, articulated the evolving rule that "where a contract must be performed under burdensome conditions not anticipated, and not within the contemplation of the parties at the time (when) the contract was made, and the promisee measures up to the right standard of honesty and fair dealing, and agrees, in view of the changed conditions, to pay what is then reasonable, just, and fair, such new contract is not without consideration within the meaning of that term, either in law or in equity." . . .

This principle has received recognition by courts of other jurisdictions confronted with situations comparable to that now before this court. In Evergreen Amusement Corporation v. Milstead, 206 Md. 610, 112 A.2d 901, the Maryland Court of Appeals found a subsequent oral agreement of the parties to a written construction contract valid, relying, in part, upon the theory of unforeseen circumstances. In that case, the plaintiff, operator of a drive-in movie theater, had entered into a written contract with the defendant, a contractor, pursuant to which the latter agreed to supply all the necessary materials and to perform the work needed to clear the theater site of timber, stumps, and waste material, and to grade the site as indicated on the accompanying plans.

Once the work was underway, it became apparent that substantial, additional fill would be needed to complete the project, although neither party had anticipated this, both relying upon a topographical map which proved to be of doubtful accuracy. The court found that the parties, upon this discovery, entered into an oral agreement whereby the defendant would bring in the fill for additional compensation. On appeal, the plaintiff claimed that this agreement lacked consideration since the defendant promised only to do that which he had already agreed to do, i. e., to furnish all materials needed to grade the theater site. Relying upon the theory of unforeseen circumstances, the court held the agreement to be binding.

In another case involving facts similar to those now before us, a California Court of Appeal in Bailey v. Breetwor, 206 Cal.App.2d 287, 23 Cal.Rptr. 740, without reference to the theory of unforeseen circumstances, determined that a subsequent oral agreement of parties to a written contract was valid where unanticipated, burdensome conditions, not contemplated by the parties at the time the written contract was executed, were encountered. In that case, the defendant owner had entered into a written contract with a construction company to grade and compact a building site for $2600. The work was subcontracted to the plaintiff, who agreed to perform the work in accordance with the general contract.

Upon commencing his work, the plaintiff discovered, below the surface, an extensive amount of wet clay. The owner was notified of this and was advised that, although removal of this clay was not included in the subcontract, its removal was necessary for compliance with the city building code. In return for costs plus 10 percent, the plaintiff orally agreed to remove the clay. Determining that the oral agreement constituted a separate, binding contract, the court noted that "(t)his performance was clearly beyond the scope of the original contract. Bailey (the plaintiff) thus incurred a new detriment and Breetwor (the owner) received a new benefit constituting sufficient consideration for Breetwor's promise." Id., 292, 23 Cal.Rptr. 743.

Although the technical terminology apparent in these two cases differs, the underlying reasoning is similar. In each case, an unforeseen, burdensome condition was discovered during the performance of the original contract. The promise of additional compensation in return for the promise that the additional work required would be undertaken was held to constitute a separate, valid agreement. Such reasoning is applicable to the facts of this case. The unchallenged findings of the court reveal that the substantial rubble found beneath the surface of the site was not anticipated by either party, that its presence necessitated excavation beyond the depths required in the plans and specifications, that the cost of removing this rubble was not included in the contract price and that the parties entered into a separate oral agreement for the removal of the rubble. Under these circumstances, the subsequent oral agreement, that the defendant would remove this rubble in return for additional compensation, was binding as a new, distinct contract, supported by valid consideration. See Restatement (Second) Contracts § 89D (Tentative Draft No. 2, 1965). The defendant's failure to comply with this agreement constitutes a breach of contract. Because of our disposition of this issue, we need not address the question of whether the subcontract incorporated the provision of the contract requiring written authorization by the architect or owner for extra work.

. . . There is error, the judgment for the defendant on the complaint is set aside and the case is remanded with direction to render judgment for the plaintiff to recover such damages as he may prove on a new trial limited to the issue of damages.

NOTES AND QUESTIONS

1.   What approach does the court take to contract modification in *Brian Construction*? Does the court's approach seem sensible?

2.   In all cases, one concern is whether a contract modification has been coerced by a party once performance has begun. Another path, and the one taken by UCC Section 2–209, is to rely on the duty of good faith to police exploitive behavior.

3.   How does the duty of good faith work in connection with contract modification? Courts wish, rightfully so, to discourage exploitative behavior. At the same time, however, it may benefit the parties to be able to adjust their bargain if it turns out that more or less effort or expense is required or requested. And so the doctrine of good faith performs the "heavy lifting," functioning as a check on one party getting carried away by the other's vulnerability in the bargain.

EXAMPLE: EXTRA WORK AT THE WORLD TRADE CENTER

When the South Tower of the World Trade Center was destroyed on September 11, 2001, debris struck the 41-story Deutsche Bank building, opening it up to soot, dirt, and dust. A state agency, the Lower Manhattan Development Corporation (LMDC), acquired the building in 2004. Shortly thereafter, they realized that the building had been so badly damaged that it would need to be demolished. LMDC put out the demolition for a competitive bidding process.

The winning bidder was Bovis, Inc., a leading construction company. During bidding, LMDC made available its environmental study which showed that hazardous materials, including asbestos, were contaminating the building. Both sides knew the project was perilous.

The parties used an elaborate and negotiated contract to allocate the risks. LMDC would pay Bovis a fixed price of $81 million to demolish the building. There would be additional payments, at cost plus a fixed profit, for "extra work" that the two might agree on. The contract allocated to Bovis all risks from hazardous materials. The concept of "extra work" was defined as things beyond the project's initial scope or addressing hazardous materials not known to be in the building. The concept excluded work arising from Bovis's errors or negligence or legal requirements.

Bovis subcontracted part of the job to another contractor, John Galt Corp., on terms that mirrored the contract between LMDC and Bovis. Almost immediately after work began, however, Bovis and Galt ran into tremendous problems, many of which Bovis claimed were unanticipated and outside its contract with LMDC. Bovis asked for additional payments, but LMDC declined, stating that the work was within the contract. Slowdowns and manpower reductions followed.

The Governor of New York and Mayor of New York City coordinated a meeting to try to resolve the issue. LMDC agreed to pay Bovis a $10 million extra payment and advanced a refundable $28 million in the event these contested claims were "extra work" under the contract.

Though Bovis and Galt resumed work, there were serious problems with the project. Pedestrians were injured when a pipe and crowbar fell from the site. Because Galt workers were smoking, a fire engulfed the building, and two firefighters were killed. The fire was more severe because Bovis had dismantled the water supply earlier in contravention of state law. Bovis paid the firefighters' families $5 million each and had to pay various regulatory fines. After the fire, Bovis terminated the contract with Galt.

Bovis claimed that many of the costs were due to extra work and sought more money. LMDC balked. They signed a truce just to keep the project moving. Net result: LMDC paid Bovis $150 million, and the project was four years late. Bovis claimed another $80 million, while LMDC claimed that Bovis should have to refund it $100 million for the refundable advance, advances paid in the peace treaties, and damages for delay.

Which side has the better argument?

————————

A related issue to contract modification arises under the doctrine known as "accord and satisfaction." This is a contract law concept addressing attempts by parties to excuse or release a debt. One party offers a payment less than the amount claimed to be owed. The accord allows the discharge of the earlier debt, and the "satisfaction" binds the parties to the new agreement for a lesser amount.

MARTON REMODELING V. JENSEN

706 P.2d 607 (Utah 1985)

HOWE, J.

These appeals are from a judgment entered in an action brought by the plaintiff, Marton Remodeling, to foreclose a mechanic's lien which it had filed against a house and lot owned by the defendant, Mark Jensen, for $6,538.12 which it claimed was due it for remodeling. Judgment was entered on a jury verdict for $1,538, together with $1,000 punitive damages, and attorney fees of $5,950.24. The trial court remitted the award of punitive damages and reduced the attorney fees by 50 percent to $2,976.12. Jensen appeals from that judgment in case No. 18400, and in case No. 18401, Marton appeals, seeking to reinstate the award of punitive damages and recover the full amount of attorney fees awarded by the jury.

Jensen engaged Marton Remodeling in a "time and materials" contract to remodel his house. When Marton presented the final bill for $6,538.12, Jensen contended that the number of hours claimed was excessive. He offered to pay $5,000 because he considered the services were worth that amount, but Marton refused the offer. Nevertheless, Jensen sent Marton a $5,000 check with the following condition placed thereon: "Endorsement hereof constitutes full and final satisfaction of any and all claims payee may have against Mark S. Jensen, or his property, arising from any circumstances existing on the date hereof." Marton wrote a letter to Jensen refusing to accept the check in full payment and demanded the balance. When Jensen made no further payment, Marton filed a mechanic's lien on Jensen's property and cashed the check after writing "not full payment" below the condition. This action was then brought by Marton to recover the $1,538 balance plus punitive damages and attorney fees.

Jensen contends that the trial court erred in refusing to direct a verdict in his favor because, as a matter of law, Marton's cashing of the $5,000 check constituted an accord and satisfaction that could not be altered by the words added to the condition placed thereon by Jensen. We agree. Viewing the evidence in the light most favorable to Marton Remodeling, there was an accord and satisfaction as we have defined that term in the previous cases decided by this Court. . . . Marton asserts that there was not an accord and satisfaction because Marton was unquestionably entitled to the $5,000 represented by the check, and the only dispute was whether any further amount was owing.

Marton is not aided by *Allen-Howe Specialties v. U.S. Construction, Inc.,* Utah, 611 P.2d 705 (1980). There, the cashing of a check representing a progress payment on a contract was held not to be an accord and satisfaction of all amounts owing up to that time. At the time the progress payment was made, there was no dispute and, unlike the instant case, it was not tendered as the last payment of the contract where finality and settlement is usually sought and intended.

[The case is not] . . . dispositive here where we are confronted with a single unliquidated claim, *viz.,* the balance owing on a "time and materials" contract. Instead, the general rule applies, which is that an accord and satisfaction of a single claim is not avoided merely because the amount paid and accepted is only that which the debtor concedes to be due or that his view of the controversy is adopted in making the settlement. . . . Corbin on Contracts § 1289 approves the rule and states that it is supported by the greater number of cases, citing as good examples *Miller v. Prince Street Elevator Co.,* 41 N.M. 330, 68 P.2d 663 (1937), *Treat v. Price,* 47 Neb. 875, 66 N.W. 834 (1896), and *Fuller v. Kemp,* 138 N.Y. 231, 33 N.E. 1034 (1893).

It is of no legal consequence that Marton told Jensen upon receipt of the $5,000 check that he did not regard it as payment in full. Marton could not disregard with immunity the condition placed on the check by Jensen by writing "not full payment" under the condition. It is true that there is not an automatic accord and satisfaction every time a creditor cashes a check bearing a "paid in full" notation. *Smoot v. Checketts*, 41 Utah 211, 125 P. 412 (1912). An accord and satisfaction requires that there be an unliquidated claim or a bona fide dispute over the amount due. *Ashton v. Skeen, supra.* Payment must be tendered in full settlement of the entire dispute and not in satisfaction of a separate undisputed obligation, as in *Bennett v. Robinson's Medical Mart, Inc., supra.* Payment cannot be given merely as a progress payment, as in *Allen-Howe v. U.S. Construction, Inc., supra.* However, when a bona fide dispute arises (the existence of which Marton does not dispute in this appeal) and a check is tendered in full payment of an unliquidated claim as we have here, arising out of a "time and materials" contract, the creditor may not disregard the condition attached. Corbin on Contracts § 1279 explains:

> The fact that the creditor scratches out the words "in full payment," or other similar words indicating that the payment is tendered in full satisfaction, does not prevent his retention of the money from operating as an assent to the discharge. The creditor's action in such case is quite inconsistent with his words. It may, indeed, be clear that he does not in fact assent to the offer made by the debtor, so that there is no actual "meeting of the minds." But this is merely another illustration of the fact that the making of a contract frequently does not require such an actual meeting.

Restatement (Second) of Contracts § 281 is to the same effect and provides the following illustration:

> 6.   A contracts with B to have repairs made on A's house, no price being fixed. B sends A a bill for $1,000. A honestly disputes this amount and sends a letter explaining that he thinks the amount excessive and is enclosing a check for $800 as payment in full. B, after reading the letter, indorses the check and deposits it in his bank for collection. B is bound by an accord under which he promises to accept payment of the check in satisfaction of A's debt for repairs. The result is the same if, before indorsing the check, B adds the words "Accepted under protest as part payment." The result would be different, however, if B's claim were liquidated, undisputed and matured.

(Citation omitted.) See *Miller v. Prince Street Elevator Co., supra, Wilmeth v. Lee*, Okla., 316 P.2d 614 (1957), and *Graffam v. Geronda*, Me., 304 A.2d 76 (1973), for cases where it was held that a creditor cannot avoid the consequences of his exercise of dominion by a declaration that he does not assent to the condition attached by the debtor. The last cited case succinctly stated the law to be, "The law gave the plaintiffs the choice of accepting the check on defendant's terms or of returning it."

. . . Several courts have stated that if they were to construe the statute to limit accord and satisfaction, it would jeopardize a convenient and valuable means of achieving informal settlements. . . . The law favors compromise in order to limit litigation. Accord and satisfaction serves this goal. . . . Our determination that there was an accord and satisfaction obviates the necessity of our consideration of any of the other points raised in either appeal. The judgment in favor of the plaintiff is reversed, and the case is remanded to the trial court to enter judgment in favor of the defendant. Costs on appeal are awarded to defendant.

COMPLAINT: FUSARI INC. V. MERMAID LLC
Index No. 2010–650179 (N.Y. Sup. 2010)

Heaven has no rage like love to hatred turned,
Nor hell a fury like a woman scorned.

All business is personal. When those personal relationships evolve into romantic entanglements, any corresponding business relationship usually follows the same trajectory so that when one crashes they all burn. That is what happened here.

THE PARTIES

. . . Plaintiff is 100% owned and operated by Rob Fusari, a talented, multi-platinum song writer and producer, recently selected and featured as one of Billboard Magazine's Top Ten Music Producers of 2009. Mr. Fusari's extensive track record as a songwriter and producer includes three number 1 hits: "Bootylicious" by Destiny's Child, "Wild, Wild West" by Will Smith and "Love That Man" by Whitney Houston. Mr. Fusari has also worked with such successful artists as the Jonas Brothers, Jessica Simpson, Kelly Rowland, and Britney Spears. . . . Upon information and belief, Mermaid is equally owned and operated by its members, Stephani Germanotta p/k/a "Lady Gaga" and her father, Joe Germanotta. Ms. Germanotta's talent and meteoric rise to fame as an entertainer and recording star is well documented and incontestable. . . .

BACKGROUND

On the night of March 23, 2006, before the then Stefani Germanotta's performance at a New Writers' Showcase at New York's The Cutting Room, she approached singer-songwriter Wendy Starland and asked if Starland remembered her from Germanotta's days working as an intern at Famous Music Publishing. It turned out that the two were both on the venue's roster to perform that night.

At the time, Starland had been musically collaborating regularly with Rob Fusari for over 2 years. Starland knew that Fusari had been searching for months for a dynamic female rock-n-roller with garage band chops to front an all girl version of The Strokes. Starland was blown away by

Germanotta's performance and immediately called Fusari and told him she had found him his girl.

Starland then put Germanotta on the phone with Fusari. While the two talked, Fusari listened to some of Germanotta's music on her PureVolume web page. While not overwhelmed by Germanotta's song selections, he could tell she had more to offer creatively and invited her out to his production studio in Parsippany, New Jersey.

The next day Germanotta took the bus to Parsippany from the Port Authority depot and then hiked a quarter-mile to reach Rob Fusari's 150 Studios. Fusari was expecting someone a little more grunge-rocker than the young Italian girl "guidette" that arrived at his doorstep and was worried that he had made a mistake. Fusari then asked her to play one of her songs on the studio piano and within seconds realized that Germanotta had star potential. The trick would be coaxing it out of her.

Before long, Germanotta was riding the bus to Jersey every day to work with Fusari at his studio. Fusari thought Germanotta's songs were brilliant but lacked commercial appeal. He pushed her to explore different musical genres. Over the course of the next several months, Germanotta commuted from New York to Jersey seven days a week, radically reshaping her approach. They put their focus on writing music and finding a sound for her. Fusari finally convinced Germanotta to abandon rock riffs and add dance beats. He demonstrated how the sound of a drum machine would not hurt the integrity of her music.

That day the two finished writing "Beautiful, Dirty, Rich," a song that later appeared on Germanotta's debut album, and the die was cast. They went on to co-write a number of what later turned out to be hits, including "Papparazzi," "Brown Eyes" and "Disco Heaven." Fusari also created the name "Lady Gaga" for his protege. During those early days the two worked out of his Parsippany studio, Fusari likened Germanotta's dramatic personality to Queen's Freddy Mercury, and would always greet Germanotta's arrival with his rendition of Queen's "Radio Ga Ga". One day when Fusari addressed a cell phone text to Germanotta under the moniker "Radio Ga Ga" his cell phone's spell check converted "Radio" to "Lady." Germanotta loved it and "Lady Gaga" was born.

Working intensely in such close emotional quarters over a sustained period nurtured Fusari and Germanotta's relationship to a new, personal and romantic level, and the two began to spend all of their time together as a couple. Germanotta started staying over at Fusari's home and Fusari, in turn, began socializing with Germanotta's family, regularly dining with Germonatta's parents and siblings at their home in Manhattan.

Fusari began shopping the CD they produced with the songs they had co-written to a number of record companies with which Fusari had a relationship. In or about May of 2006, Fusari and Germanotta formalized their business relationship as well. Fusari, then doing business as Fusari Productions, Inc., entered into an agreement with defendant Mermaid to form and organize what is now defendant TLC for the purpose of exclusively professionally exploiting Germanotta and the songs that Fusari co-wrote and or produced. It was then that Fusari first learned about the extensive involvement of Joe Germanotta in the business dealings of his talented daughter. . . .

The Production Agreement provides that Fusari Inc. and Defendant Mermaid, among other things, formed Defendant TLC, a New Jersey limited liability company that would furnish the exclusive recording services of Stefani Germonatta a/k/a "Lady Gaga" (the "Artist"), to a major record label/distributor, for the Artist to furnish her exclusive recording services to the contemplated New Jersey limited liability company upon its formation, and for Fusari Inc. to furnish the production services of Rob Fusari to the contemplated New Jersey limited liability company upon its formation. Fusari owned twenty percent (20%) of TLC and Mermaid owned eighty percent (80%). . . .

During this same period, Fusari, who was then represented by his personal manager Laurent Besencon of New Heights Entertainment LLC pursuant to a Personal Management Agreement dated October 21, 2004 ("2004 Management Agreement"), introduced Besencon to Lady Gaga. Besencon, realizing after hearing the recorded results of Fusari's work with the young artist, requested that he be allowed to represent Lady Gaga as well as Fusari, making the argument at the time that it would keep their burgeoning enterprise all under one roof. Fusari relented.

Fusari then played Germanotta's music for Joshua Sarubin, Vice President of A&R for Island Def Jam ("IDJ") and Sarubin immediately brought Fusari and Germanotta into IDJ to hear her play live. During that session, L.A. Ried, then President of IDJ, who heard Germanotta performing from his office, came into the audition and decided on the spot to sign her to a record deal. Her first album was tentatively scheduled for release in May 2007. At this point, Fusari and Mermaid decided to renegotiate their Production Agreement in order to address such areas of exploitation as merchandising rights. Also, the IDJ deal had refused to guaranty Fusari's rights as producer on any of Germanotta's albums, so the parties also made sure to address those rights in their new agreement. The end result was the TLC Amendment.

. . . Pursuant to paragraph 1(b) of the TLC Amendment, the ownership percentages of the members of TLC are as follows: Mermaid—80%; Plaintiff—20%. . . . As contemplated by paragraph 2(a) of the TLC Amendment, the Furnishing Agreement provides that Mermaid is entitled to the Artist's exclusive recording services, and in turn, Mermaid will furnish to TLC the exclusive recording services of the Artist for the purpose of TLC furnishing said Artist's services to a "Distributor." . . .

[However] L.A. Ried's capriciousness struck . . . when Germanotta was unexplainably dropped from IDJ after only three months. . . . Germanotta's confidence was bruised, but Fusari encouraged her to keep writing and recording. Unfortunately, the stress of the set-back with IDJ also negatively impacted the personal relationship between Fusari and Germanotta. The couple was now constantly bickering as Germanotta became more and more verbally abusive towards Fusari. Fusari wanted to return their relationship to a purely professional level, so in January 2007, he ended their romantic involvement.

. . . At this point, Laurent Besencon, started pairing Germanotta with a number of New Heights' other songwriter-producers such as "Red One," with whom Germanotta co-wrote "Poker Face," "Just Dance" and "Boys, Boys, Boys". As a result, Fusari soon found himself being involuntarily relegated by TLC to the fringe on all musical creative decisions being made on behalf of Germanotta.

. . . At the same time, Fusari found that he was being frozen out of the actual negotiations that were taking place between TLC and Interscope. Fusari kept demanding that he remain directly involved in any new distribution agreement. After a while, Germanotta and her father stopped taking his telephone calls or otherwise responding to Fusari's texts and emails. . . . By May 30, 2007, Germanotta had signed a new distribution deal with Interscope Records (the "Second Distribution Agreement").

. . . Lady Gaga's debut album on Interscope, The Fame, was co-produced by Fusari. He also co-wrote and produced four songs on that album, including "Paparazzi," "Beautiful, Dirty, Rich," "Brown Eyes" and "Disco Heaven". The European version of the album The Fame also includes two more of Fusari's songs "Retro, Dance, Freak" and "Again Again". . . .

[BREACH OF CONTRACT]

. . . Plaintiff has performed all of its obligations to both Mermaid and TLC as set forth within the TLC Amendment. . . . As a 20% member of TLC, Plaintiff owns a 20% interest in and to the results and proceeds of the exclusive recording artist services of Stephani Germanotta p/k/a "Lady Gaga" furnished by TLC to a Distributor, including without limitation, Interscope.

. . . Accordingly, pursuant to said 20% interest, Plaintiff is entitled to compensation under the TLC Amendment in the amount of 20% of all advances, royalties or other proceeds derived from the exploitation of master recordings subject to the TLC Amendment including all master recordings embodying the performances of Stephani Germanotta p/k/a

"Lady Gaga" (without deductions of any kind except as specifically set forth in subparagraph 4 (a) and 4(b) of the TLC Amendment) and whether distributed by IDJ, Interscope or any substitute distributor (the "Fusari Interest").

. . . Defendants have acknowledged Plaintiff's entitlement to the Fusari Interest. On June 18, 2009, TLC issued a check (#2010) in the amount of $203,000.00 to Plaintiff. The payment description states: "Lady Gaga Interscope Deal 20% Commission." . . . Moreover, on or about December 29, 2009, TLC issued a second check (#2017) in the amount of $394,965.00 to Plaintiff. On the back of the check, immediately beneath the endorser's signature line, Defendants caused to have written "Endorsed In Accord And Satisfaction Of All Sums Due To Undersigned". . . . By adding this endorsement to the back of the check, Defendants had attempted to trick Plaintiff into depositing said check and thereby settle all outstanding debts due him by Defendants under the TLC Amendment and to bar Plaintiff from seeking any additional payments of the Fusari Interest as they came due in the future.

. . . Plaintiff has refused to endorse and/or deposit the check and has returned it to TLC. . . . Other than the above described payments, Defendants have failed to make additional payments to Plaintiff that would constitute compensation owed to Plaintiff of the Fusari Interest. . . . As a result of Defendants' actions, Defendants have materially breached the TLC Amendment to Plaintiff's detriment. . . . Therefore, and by reason of Defendants' foregoing breach, Plaintiff is entitled to an award of damages in an amount to be determined at trial, but not less than $5,000,000. . . .

NOTES AND QUESTIONS

1. *Marton Remodeling* and the complaint against Lady Gaga demonstrate how some people seek an informal settlement of dispute by sending a check with an endorsement. Why might such a tactic be effective in settling a dispute? Why might it be problematic?

2. In general an accord and satisfaction is a contract governed by the general principles of contract formation, including offer, acceptance and consideration as well as mutual manifestation of assent. Concerning consideration, the good faith disagreement over the amount owed suffices. In the case of Lady Gaga, her check would be a valid offer of settlement if there were a genuine dispute about the debt that Fusari claimed. As such, Fusari was correct in his concern that accepting the check from Lady Gaga might bind him to a lower settlement amount.

3. Given the millions at stake, Fusari wisely decided not to cash Lady Gaga's check and instead filed the complaint above. By not cashing it, Fusari preserved his rights. In the wake of his lawsuit, Lady Gaga filed her own complaint against Fusari. Eventually the former paramours settled their

dispute out of court. As part of the deal, both promised to keep the terms of the settlement confidential.

4.   More intricate aspects of the doctrine of accord and satisfaction are treated in upper-level courses on commercial law. For academic treatment of the doctrine, see Bryan D. Hull & Aalok Sharma, *Satisfaction Not Guaranteed: California's Conflicting Law on the Use of Accord and Satisfaction* Checks, 33 LOYOLA L.A. REV. 1 (1999); Michael D. Floyd, *How Much Satisfaction Should You Expect from an Accord?*, 26 LOYOLA CHICAGO L. J. 1 (1994).

EXAMPLE: CONAN O'BRIEN

In the early 2000s, Conan O'Brien was a promising comic and talk show host who caught the eye of the major television networks, including NBC. In 2004, they entered into a contract that in six years had Conan hosting "The Tonight Show," the iconic evening show airing at 11:30 pm, immediately after the local news. The show had been hosted for decades by Johnny Carson and at the time was hosted by Jay Leno, who agreed to an orderly succession to Conan. At the time, ratings were at a peak.

When the time arrived for the transition, Conan took over the show and performed for seven months. However, in month eight NBC decided on a switch: they would air the show Conan was hosting to 12:05 a.m., moving to the earlier slot a show hosted by none other than Jay Leno. Conan objected, claiming breach of contract.

NBC asserted that the contract was silent about what time "The Tonight Show" would air. One reason for such silence could be that operational decisions must be left with the network to enable programming management. On the other hand, for sixty years the "The Tonight Show" aired at the same time—immediately after the local news.

While the parties ended up settling their dispute out of court, how would you analyze the legal issues and the question of good faith if they decided to litigate?

CHAPTER 10

CONDITIONS

■ ■ ■

This chapter examines the concept of conditions. Conditions are important features of many contracts. Parties may be willing to make a promise but only if some event occurs or does not occur—"I promise to buy your farm but only if interest rates remain below 5%." Contracts can be used to express both promises and conditions, and drafters and interpreters must develop a basis for distinguishing between them. It is not always easy to interpret contractual expressions, but the difference between classifying an uncertain expression as a promise or a condition are like night and day—finding or excusing liability. The stakes are high. Promises must be performed, or else a remedy paid; conditions limit the scope of a promise. If a condition does not occur, then the obligation never ripens—it need not be performed.

Conditions also arise even when parties do not expressly invoke them. Judges are often asked to determine whether one party's performance is a condition to the other party's duty and language is not always clear about that. *Equity abhors a forfeiture*, goes an old legal saying, so interpretative doubts are resolved in favor of treating uncertain expressions as promises, not conditions. The anti-forfeiture principle—which is a principle of judicial construction rather than of contract interpretation—helps solve problems that occur when contracts extend over multiple periods or involve many steps. One challenge is determining which party must perform first so that failure to do so spells breach, and contract law offers a set of "constructive" conditions to navigate this process.

The chapter starts with some definitions of conditions, in contrast to promises, and illustrates some techniques of both interpretation and construction used to distinguish between promises or conditions. It then considers two recurring fact settings where the interpretation and construction of conditions appear: conditions of party satisfaction and constructive conditions associated with sequential performance. The final two sections consider the common law's doctrine of substantial performance and the UCC's perfect tender rule, highlighting another context where the common law and UCC diverge.

A. EXPRESS CONDITIONS

MERRITT HILL VINEYARDS V. WINDY HEIGHTS VINEYARD
460 N.E.2d 1077 (N.Y. 1984)

KAYE, J.

. . . In September, 1981, plaintiff, Merritt Hill Vineyards, entered into a written agreement with defendants, Windy Heights Vineyard and its sole shareholder Leon Taylor, to purchase a majority stock interest in respondents' Yates County vineyard, and tendered a $15,000 deposit. The agreement provides that "[i]f the sale contemplated hereby does not close, Taylor shall retain the deposit as liquidated damages unless Taylor or Windy Heights failed to satisfy the conditions specified in Section 3 thereof."

Section 3, in turn, lists several "conditions precedent" to which the obligation of purchaser to pay the purchase price and to complete the purchase is subject. Among the conditions are that, by the time of the closing, Windy Heights shall have obtained a title insurance policy in a form satisfactory to Merritt Hill, and Windy Heights and Merritt Hill shall have received confirmation from the Farmers Home Administration that certain mortgages on the vineyard are in effect and that the proposed sale does not constitute a default.

In April, 1982, at the closing, plaintiff discovered that neither the policy nor the confirmation had been issued. Plaintiff thereupon refused to close and demanded return of its deposit. When defendants did not return the deposit, plaintiff instituted this action . . . . Special Term denied plaintiff's motion for summary judgment . . . . The Appellate Division unanimously reversed. [We affirm.]

A promise is "a manifestation of intention to act or refrain from acting in a specified way, so made as to justify a promisee in understanding that a commitment has been made." (Restatement, Contracts 2d, § 2, subd. [1].) A condition, by comparison, is "an event, not certain to occur, which must occur, unless its non-occurrence is excused, before performance under a contract becomes due." (Restatement, Contracts 2d, § 224.)

Here, the contract requirements of a title insurance policy and mortgage confirmation are expressed as conditions of plaintiff's performance rather than as promises by defendants. The requirements are contained in a section of the agreement entitled "Conditions Precedent to Purchaser's Obligation to Close," which provides that plaintiff's obligation to pay the purchase price and complete the purchase of the vineyard is "subject to" fulfillment of those requirements. No words of promise are employed. Defendants' agreement to sell the stock of the vineyard, not those conditions, was the promise by defendants for which plaintiff's promise to pay the purchase price was exchanged.

Defendants' failure to fulfill the conditions of section 3 entitles plaintiff to a return of its deposit but not to consequential damages. While a contracting party's failure to fulfill a condition excuses performance by the other party whose performance is so conditioned, it is not, without an independent promise to perform the condition, a breach of contract subjecting the nonfulfilling party to liability for damages (Restatement, Contracts 2d, § 225, subds. [1], [3]; 3A Corbin, Contracts, § 663; 5 Williston, Contracts [Jaeger–3d ed.], § 665). This is in accord with the parties' expressed intent, for section 1 of their agreement provides that if defendants fail to satisfy the conditions of section 3 plaintiff's deposit will be returned. It does not provide for payment of damages.

NOTES AND QUESTIONS

1.   The threshold challenging in addressing conditions is often to determine whether a contractual expression is a promise or a condition. The techniques of interpretation examined in Chapter Eight can be adapted. The ultimate issue is what the parties intended. Linguistic cues aid the effort, at both the drafting and interpretation stages. What linguistic cues appeared in *Merritt Hill Vineyards*?

2.   State the legal consequences of concluding that a contractual expression is a "promise" and those that follow from denominating it a "condition."

HOWARD V. FEDERAL CROP INSURANCE CORP.

540 F.2d 695 (5th Cir. 1976)

WIDENER, J.

. . . Federal Crop Insurance Corporation, an agency of the United States, in 1973, issued three policies to the Howards, insuring their tobacco crops, to be grown on six farms, against weather damage and other hazards. The Howards (plaintiffs) established production of tobacco on their acreage, and have alleged that their 1973 crop was extensively damaged by heavy rains, resulting in a gross loss to the three plaintiffs in excess of $35,000. The plaintiffs harvested and sold the depleted crop and timely filed notice and proof of loss with FCIC, but, prior to inspection by the adjuster for FCIC, the Howards had either plowed or disked under the tobacco fields in question to prepare the same for sowing a cover crop of rye to preserve the soil.

When the FCIC adjuster later inspected the fields, he found the stalks had been largely obscured or obliterated by plowing or disking and denied the claims, apparently on the ground that the plaintiffs had violated a portion of the policy which provides that the stalks on any acreage with respect to which a loss is claimed shall not be destroyed until the corporation makes an inspection. The holding of the district court is best capsuled in its own words:

> The inquiry here is whether compliance by the insureds with this provision of the policy was a condition precedent to the recovery. The court concludes that it was and that the failure of the insureds to comply worked a forfeiture of benefits for the alleged loss.

There is no question but that apparently after notice of loss was given to defendant, but before inspection by the adjuster, plaintiffs plowed under the tobacco stalks and sowed some of the land with a cover crop, rye. The question is whether, under paragraph 5(f) of the tobacco endorsement to the policy of insurance, the act of plowing under the tobacco stalks forfeits the coverage of the policy. Paragraph 5 of the tobacco endorsement is entitled *Claims*. Pertinent to this case are subparagraphs 5(b) and 5(f), which are as follows:

> 5(b) *It shall be a condition precedent* to the payment of any loss that the insured establish the production of the insured crop on a unit and that such loss has been directly caused by one or more of the hazards insured against during the insurance period for the crop year for which the loss is claimed, and furnish any other information regarding the manner and extent of loss as may be required by the Corporation. (Emphasis added)

> 5(f) The tobacco stalks on any acreage of tobacco of types 11a, 11b, 12, 13, or 14 with respect to which a loss is claimed *shall not be destroyed until the Corporation makes an inspection*. (Emphasis added)

The arguments of both parties are predicated upon the same two assumptions. First, if subparagraph 5(f) creates a condition precedent, its violation caused a forfeiture of plaintiffs' coverage. Second, if subparagraph 5(f) creates an obligation (variously called a promise or covenant) upon plaintiffs not to plow under the tobacco stalks, defendant may recover from plaintiffs (either in an original action, or, in this case, by a counterclaim, or as a matter of defense) for whatever damage it sustained because of the elimination of the stalks. However, a violation of subparagraph 5(f) would not, under the second premise, standing alone, cause a forfeiture of the policy.

Generally accepted law provides us with guidelines here. There is a general legal policy opposed to forfeitures. Insurance policies are generally construed most strongly against the insurer. When it is doubtful whether words create a promise or a condition precedent, they will be construed as creating a promise. Harris and Harris Const. Co. v. Crain and Denbo, Inc.,

256 N.C. 110, 123 S.E.2d 590, 595 (1962). The provisions of a contract will not be construed as conditions precedent in the absence of language plainly requiring such construction. Harris, 123 S.E.2d at 596.

Plaintiffs rely most strongly upon the fact that the term "condition precedent" is included in subparagraph 5(b) but not in subparagraph 5(f). It is true that whether a contract provision is construed as a condition or an obligation does not depend entirely upon whether the word "condition" is expressly used. However, the persuasive force of plaintiffs' argument in this case is found in the use of the term "condition precedent" in subparagraph 5(b) but not in subparagraph 5(f). Thus, it is argued that the ancient maxim to be applied is that the expression of one thing is the exclusion of another. . . .

The Restatement of the Law of Contracts states: § 261. INTERPRETATION OF DOUBTFUL WORDS AS PROMISE OR CONDITION. "Where it is doubtful whether words create a promise or an express condition, they are interpreted as creating a promise; but the same words may sometimes mean that one party promises a performance and that the other party's promise is conditional on that performance." Two illustrations (one involving a promise, the other a condition) are used in the Restatement:

> 2.   A, an insurance company, issues to B a policy of insurance containing promises by A that are in terms conditional on the happening of certain events. The policy contains this clause: 'provided, in case differences shall arise touching any loss, *the matter shall be submitted to impartial arbitrators*, whose award shall be binding on the parties.' This is a promise to arbitrate and does not make an award a condition precedent of the insurer's duty to pay.

> 3.   A, an insurance company, issues to B an insurance policy in usual form containing this clause: 'In the event of disagreement as to the amount of loss it shall be ascertained by two appraisers and an umpire. The loss shall *not be payable until 60 days after the award of the appraisers when such an appraisal is required.'* This provision is not merely a promise to arbitrate differences but makes an award a condition of the insurer's duty to pay in case of disagreement. (Emphasis added)

We believe that subparagraph 5(f) in the policy here under consideration fits illustration 2 rather than illustration 3. Illustration 2 specifies something to be done, whereas subparagraph 5(f) specifies something not to be done. Unlike illustration 3, subparagraph 5(f) does not state any conditions under which the insurance shall "not be payable," or use any words of like import. We hold that the district court erroneously held, on the motion for summary judgment, that subparagraph 5(f)

established a condition precedent to plaintiffs' recovery which forfeited the coverage.

From our holding that defendant's motion for summary judgment was improperly allowed, it does not follow the plaintiffs' motion for summary judgment should have been granted, for if subparagraph 5(f) be not construed as a condition precedent, there are other questions of fact to be determined. At this point, we merely hold that the district court erred in holding, on the motion for summary judgment, that subparagraph 5(f) constituted a condition precedent with resulting forfeiture.

The explanation defendant makes for including subparagraph 5(f) in the tobacco endorsement is that it is necessary that the stalks remain standing in order for the Corporation to evaluate the extent of loss and to determine whether loss resulted from some cause not covered by the policy. However, was subparagraph 5(f) inserted because without it the Corporation's opportunities for proof would be more difficult, or because they would be impossible? Plaintiffs point out that the Tobacco Endorsement, with subparagraph 5(f), was adopted in 1970, and crop insurance goes back long before that date. . . . [Remanded.]

NOTES AND QUESTIONS

1. Compare and contrast *Merritt Hill Vineyards* with *Howard*. What linguistic cues appeared in *Howard* and were they dispositive?

2. Explain why the farmer's public policy argument was persuasive. What is forfeiture? Why favor construing ambiguous contractual expressions as promises rather than conditions?

3. What is the difference between a *condition precedent* and a *condition subsequent*? As a great comedian once said, "it's all in the timing." A condition precedent involves the need for an event to happen before a party is required to perform; the obligation does not ripen until the condition is satisfied. In contrast, a condition subsequent is one discharged by a later event occurring after the contract. True conditions subsequent are rare; almost all conditions that you will see in practice are conditions precedent. The Restatement (Second) of Contracts, Section 224, Comment e, has eliminated this distinction, treating all conditions the same way. Nevertheless, some jurisdictions (and their bar examiners) retain these two categories, so it is approrpiate to distinguish them. In *Howard,* how would you classify the conditions?

4. The common law once put great emphasis on the distinction between a condition precedent and a condition subsequent. The distinction had an impact on the burden of proof in bringing a case. Whereas the plaintiff had the burden of pleading and proving a condition precedent, the defendant carried the burden of pleading and proving a condition subsequent. *See Gray v. Gardner*, 17 Mass. 188 (1821) (illustration of condition subsequent, where arrival of whale oil on any ship entering Nantucket harbor extinguished the obligation between buyer and seller to transact for whale oil).

RESTATEMENT (SECOND) OF CONTRACTS, SECTIONS 224–226

§ 224.   *Condition Defined*.

A condition is an event, not certain to occur, which must occur, unless its non-occurrence is excused, before performance under a contract becomes due.

§ 225.   *Effects of the Non-Occurrence of a Condition*.

(1) Performance of a duty subject to a condition cannot become due unless the condition occurs or its non-occurrence is excused.

(2) Unless it has been excused, the non-occurrence of a condition discharges the duty when the condition can no longer occur.

(3) Non-occurrence of a condition is not a breach by a party unless he is under a duty that the condition occur.

§ 226.   *How an Event May be Made a Condition*.

An event may be made a condition either by the agreement of the parties or by a term supplied by the court.

———————

In the 1990 film "Dances with Wolves," Kevin Costner cemented his leadership in the Hollywood scene by starring as Lt. John J. Dunbar. The film, which Costner also produced, inspired Costner's fantasy of developing a luxury hotel in the Black Mountains of South Dakota named The Dunbar. For the centerpiece of his plans, Costner commissioned 18 massive bronze sculptures, assembled as the "Lakota Bison Jump," from noted local artist Peggy Detmers. Despite buying 1,000 acres of South Dakota land and spending two decades and millions of dollars trying to build the Dunbar, Costner never completed the resort.

While reading the following case, see if you can list the terms of the deal and whether a term in the contract is a promise, a condition, or an insignificant term. How does the court resolve the matter? Did it reach the right decision?

DETMERS V. COSTNER

Civ. 09–60 (Fourth Judicial Circuit, South Dakota, 2011)

MACY, J.

. . . Beginning in the 1990s, Kevin Costner envisioned building a resort in Deadwood. The resort was to be named The Dunbar and originally included plans for a five-star hotel, walking trails, golf course, and tennis courts. Costner also planned to include bison sculptures as the centerpiece at the entryway to the hotel instead of having "the proverbial fountain in front of a hotel." Costner purchased 1,000 acres of real property north of Deadwood with these plans in mind.

In the mid-1990s Costner commissioned Peggy Detmers to build the bison sculptures for The Dunbar. The final plans called for 14 bison and 3 Lakota warriors mounted on horseback, all of which are 25 percent larger than life scale. Detmers claims that she reduced her fee from approximately $1,000,000 to $250,000 on this project in exchange for royalty rights in reproductions of the sculptures that could be sold at The Dunbar. Costner disputes that Detmers reduced her fee in exchange for royalty rights, but does acknowledge that it was his intention to market reproductions at The Dunbar hotel.

In the late-1990s and the early part of 2000, Detmers became concerned because The Dunbar had not been built. Detmers stopped working on the sculptures. On May 5, 2000, Detmers and Costner entered into an express written contract whereby in exchange for completing the sculptures, Detmers would receive $60,000 in additional payment, royalty rights on reproductions, and display of the sculptures. This contract is at the center of the parties' current dispute. In pertinent part, the contract provides:

> 3.   Although I do not anticipate this will ever arise, if The Dunbar is not built within ten(10)years or the sculptures are not agreeably displayed elsewhere, I will give you 50% of the profits from the sale of the one and one-quarter life scale sculptures after I have recouped all my costs incurred in the creation of the sculptures and any such sale. The sale price will be at our [sic] above standard bronze market pricing. All accounting will be provided. In addition, I will assign back to you the copyright of the sculptures so sold (14 bison, 3 Lakota horse and riders).

Costner has expended considerable sums and made significant efforts, but to date, The Dunbar has not been built. Because the resort had not been built in the early 2000s, both parties began looking for alternative locations for the placement of the sculptures. Detmers considered locations in Hill City while Costner considered locations in and around Deadwood. Ultimately, Costner realized that he could place the sculptures on a portion of the real property he owned and intended for The Dunbar. Costner testified that he called Detmers on January 23 or 24, 2002 to let her know that he was considering placing the sculptures at a site on The Dunbar property. At that location, Costner knew he could dedicate a site for the sculptures and provide them with protection, something that several of the temporary locations he considered could not. Costner further alleges that Detmers was aware of his plans and approved of that location. Detmers acknowledged receiving a phone call from Costner on January 23 or 24, 2002, but she disputes that she approved that location and claims that she was not aware of Costner's intent to place the sculptures there until she read about it in a newspaper article on April 23, 2002.

On January 29, 2002, the project's architect, Patrick Wyss, sent a letter to Costner confirming the beginning of the design process. After the decision was made to construct Tatanka, Detmers' involvement increased. Wyss was instructed by Costner to keep Detmers informed and involved. Beginning in June 2002, Detmers was influential in the placement of the sculptures on the Tatanka property. In March 2003, the "mock-up" of the sculpture placement began. Numerous photos were admitted into evidence depicting Detmers' involvement in the "mock-up" and final placement of the sculptures. Moreover, Costner indicated that he ceded many decisions to Detmers because, as the artist, she "had a place of authority" and "heavy influence" regarding sculpture placement. Lastly, numerous media articles from 2002 and 2003 quote Detmers as being "excited" and "relieved" about the sculptures placement at Tatanka. Those same articles characterize Tatanka as a "stand-alone" entity, completely separate from The Dunbar.

In the end, Tatanka consisted of a visitor's center with a gift shop and café, interactive museum, nature walkways, and the sculptures. Costner spent approximately $6,000,000 building this attraction. Tatanka was dedicated and had its public grand opening on June 21, 2003. Both Costner and Detmers spoke at the grand opening.

There is conflicting testimony regarding statements and promises made to Detmers throughout the process of placing the sculptures at Tatanka. Detmers claims that one of the reasons that she agreed to create the sculptures for a reduced fee was because they were planned to be part of the five-star hotel at The Dunbar where fine art reproductions could be marketed. She also claims that when the sculptures were being placed at Tatanka, Costner and his associates were representing that The Dunbar would still be built and that her sculptures would still be part of the resort. Costner claims that it has always been his intention to build The Dunbar and that he still hopes to one day be able to build The Dunbar. He also claims that neither he nor any of his associates ever promised Detmers that The Dunbar would be built.

In December 2008, Detmers brought suit against Costner alleging breach of contract. In her prayer for relief she requested specific performance. She alleges that because The Dunbar was not built within ten years and the sculptures are not agreeably displayed elsewhere she is entitled to 50 percent of the proceeds from the sale of the sculptures. Following the close of evidence, Detmers made a motion to amend her pleadings to conform to the evidence and requests the additional and alternative remedies of money damages in the amount of $690,000 and transfer of copyright in all fine art reproductions life size or smaller. . . .

In the Plaintiffs' pre-trial submission, the issue to be resolved was, "[w]hether Detmers agreed to the monument being placed somewhere other than the Dunbar." The Defendants' pre-trial submission stated the issue similarly, "[w]hether or not Detmers acquiesced or otherwise agreed to display the sculptures at the Tatanka location." Interestingly, the Plaintiffs substantially change the issue to be determined after the trial, stating the issue as, "can Kevin Costner avoid any obligation to Peggy Detmers by claiming that back in 2002 Detmers agreeably displayed her sculptures elsewhere, i.e., somewhere other than the resort?" The Court has continuously stated that the issue for trial was whether the sculptures were "agreeably displayed elsewhere" because The Dunbar was not built by 2010.

. . . Leading up to and during trial, both parties agreed that the issue to be determined was whether the sculptures were "agreeably displayed elsewhere" pursuant to the contract. However, the Plaintiffs' post-trial brief focuses primarily on whether the sculptures were placed "elsewhere." The Plaintiffs claim that because the property dedicated to Tatanka was originally part of plan for The Dunbar and because Tatanka was strategically built so that The Dunbar could still potentially be constructed in the future, the sculptures have not been placed "elsewhere." Instead, they have been placed on the same property as The Dunbar.

The Court finds this argument . . . unpersuasive. As this Court has previously ruled, the terms of this contract are clear and unambiguous. . . . When terms are unambiguous, courts construe contract terms using the plain and ordinary meaning of the words. "Elsewhere," as used in the contract, clearly means at a site other than The Dunbar. This is in accord with the regular meaning of that term. See BLACK'S LAW DICTIONARY 468 (5th ed. 1979) (defining elsewhere as "in another place; in any other place"); WEBSTER'S NEW COLLEGIATE DICTIONARY 404 (9th ed. 1986) (defining elsewhere as "in or to another place").

Because The Dunbar has not been built, any site is elsewhere, i.e., somewhere other than The Dunbar. Furthermore, it is apparent from the trial testimony and from the media articles concerning Tatanka, that this site was always considered its own, stand-alone entity, completely separate and apart from The Dunbar. Costner built Tatanka because he knew that he could provide a permanent and safe place to display these sculptures apart from any potential resort. It was upon this assumption that he spent significant sums in building a separate attraction to display these sculptures for the long term. The placement of the sculptures at Tatanka is elsewhere. It is "in another place[,]" separate and distinct, from the non-existent Dunbar hotel and resort.

Because the sculptures have been placed "elsewhere" the only issue remaining is whether the sculptures are also "agreeably displayed." In making this determination, the conduct of the parties is controlling. Detmers' trial testimony reveals that her understanding was that The Dunbar was definitely going to be built, and based in large part on that promise, she created the sculptures at an allegedly reduced fee in exchange for royalty rights in fine art reproductions. She claims that even at the time the sculptures were being placed at Tatanka, Costner or his associates were telling her that they still intended to build The Dunbar. She testified that without the exposure provided by a five-star hotel, she would not have agreed to the terms of the May 5, 2000 contract, because her compensation was largely tied to royalties on fine art reproductions. Ultimately, she testified that she did not agree to Tatanka as a permanent home for the sculptures in the absence of The Dunbar. However, the facts presented at trial belie her assertions.

First, and most importantly, the very language of the contract contemplates that The Dunbar may not be built. The contract states, "[a]lthough I do not anticipate this will ever arise, if The Dunbar is not built within ten (10) years . . . ." Therefore, the contract acknowledges the fact that The Dunbar may not be built. In addition, Costner's testimony indicates that although he has been attempting to build The Dunbar for years, and continues to try to build it, he never promised Detmers or anyone else that it would actually be built. Clearly, Costner intended to build The Dunbar, but at no time did Costner, nor anyone associated with Costner, promise Detmers that The Dunbar would be built. Therefore, any reliance by Detmers on a promise or guarantee that The Dunbar would be built is unreasonable.

Second, Detmers' actions following the decision to place the sculptures on the stand-alone site that later became known as Tatanka indicate that she agreed to display them at that location. The evidence is clear that Detmers was notified of the plan to place the sculptures at Tatanka in January 2002, that she was involved as part of the construction team, that she had significant involvement in the "mock-up" and placement of the sculptures in early 2003, and that she gave a speech at the Tatanka grand opening in June 2003. Significantly, Detmers testified that she never told Costner that she disagreed with the placement of the sculptures at Tatanka. These are not the actions of someone that protested the placement of the sculptures at Tatanka. Rather, her significant involvement clearly indicates that she was agreeable to the sculptures' placement at Tatanka for the long term.

Third, Costner's funding and building of Tatanka is further evidence of an agreeable display. In January of 2002, Costner was aware that he needed to find a suitable display for the sculptures. After looking at potential sites, he realized that he could create a permanent display area for the sculptures on a part of the property he purchased for The Dunbar. It is unreasonable to think that Costner would expend millions of dollars in creating this attraction if the parties did not agree that this would be the final display area for the sculptures. This project required landscape architecture, building construction, "mock-up" of the sculptures, anchored placement of the sculptures, and significant other expenditures of time, labor, and money. This type of undertaking is inconsistent with a unilateral placement of the sculptures for only seven years before they would have to be moved again or sold if The Dunbar was not built. To conclude that this was a unilateral decision by Costner that was not agreed upon by Detmers would cause an absurd result; namely that Costner would have spent $6,000,000 to place the sculptures for a few years until Detmers could require that he have them moved someplace else that was agreeable to them both or demand that they be sold. This Court cannot endorse such an absurd result. See *Nelson v. Schellpfeffer,* 2003 SD.7, ¶ 8, 656 NW2d 740, 743.

Based on the foregoing, the Court concludes that the parties "agreeably displayed" the sculptures "elsewhere" when they were placed at the stand-alone, independent site of Tatanka. Although Detmers characterizes the parties' agreement as a build it and they will come guarantee for sculpture royalties based on the intended existence of The Dunbar by 2010, the parties agreement expressly negates such a characterization. Furthermore, the actions of the parties in funding, building, placing, and dedicating the sculptures at Tatanka leads to only one logical conclusion: they agreed to display the sculptures at that location. The Court finds that the parties agreed to display the sculptures somewhere other than at The Dunbar and that Costner has not breached the contract. Therefore, the Plaintiffs' prayer for relief is DENIED.

NOTES AND QUESTIONS

1.   Detmers appealed to the South Dakota Supreme Court, which in 2012 affirmed the judgment in favor of Costner. *See Detmers v. Costner,* 814 N.W.2d 146 (S.D. 2012).

2.   What is Detmers' argument concerning the placement of her sculptures? While this court seems skeptical, are there any economic reasons or arguments based on custom that might support her position?

3.   Could this case actually be classified as a case about "interpretation" rather than strictly as a "conditions" case? What methods of interpretation does the court use in this case to help resolve the dispute between Costner and Detmers?

RESTATEMENT (SECOND) OF CONTRACTS, SECTIONS 227, 229

§ 227. *Standards of Preference with Regard to Conditions.*

(1) In resolving doubts as to whether an event is made a condition of an obligor's duty, and as to the nature of such an event, an interpretation is preferred that will reduce the obligee's risk of forfeiture, unless the event is within the obligee's control or the circumstances indicate that he has assumed the risk.

(2) Unless the contract is of a type under which only one party generally undertakes duties, when it is doubtful whether (a) duty is imposed on an oblige that an event occur, or (b) the event is made a condition of the obligor's duty, or (c) the event is made a condition of the obligor's duty and a duty is imposed on the oblige that the event occur, the first interpretation is preferred in the event is within the obligee's control.

(3) In case of doubt, an interpretation under which an event is a condition of an obligor's duty is preferred over an interpretation under which the non-occurrence of the event is a ground for discharge of that duty after it has become a duty to perform.

§ 229. *Excuse of a Condition to Avoid Forfeiture.*

To the extent that the non-occurrence of a condition would cause disproportionate forfeiture, a court may excuse the nonoccurrence of that condition unless its occurrence was a material party of the agreed exchange.

PROBLEM: MONEY DON'T MATTER TONIGHT

Nobel Prize-winning climatologist, Dr. Raj Damson, had a longstanding spiritual connection with music of the recording artist formerly known as Prince. Even as a boy, Raj was routinely disciplined by his teachers for trying to look like Prince by cutting out small portions from his pants during lunch breaks at his primary school in Hydrabad, India. Over the years, as Dr. Damson studied the mechanisms behind global warming, he continued to be one of Prince's biggest fans. With winnings from his Nobel Prize, Dr. Damson bought signed and rare edition Prince albums, traveled the globe to hear Prince in concert, and even got to meet Prince once backstage as part of a concert promotion.

In 2016, Dr. Damson mourned Prince's death. A week after Prince's passing, Dr. Damson honored Prince's memory by launching 200 weather balloons rigged with a combination of silver-iodide and *trachelomonas* algae. When the balloons reached specified altitudes, small explosive charges scattered the silver-algae combination throughout the troposphere, seeding clouds across 400 square kilometers above the city center. The result was 30 minutes of perfectly purple rain that drenched denizens of Hydrabad.

The province of Andhra Pradesh was in a frenzy. Before government officials and local police could bring Dr. Damson in for questioning, he had packed up and, along with his wife and daughter, Appolonia, boarded a flight bound for the U.S. The family was excited to arrive in Prince's hometown, Minneapolis, Minnesota, where Dr. Damson had arranged for a visiting research position and had already purchased a red Corvette.

After settling in Minnesota and the family taking turns to volunteer at Prince's Paisley Park estate, Dr. Damson felt he needed to do more as one of Prince's "SuperFans." Dr. Damson spoke with management of the Minnesota cemetery where Prince had been laid to rest and told them of his desire to rest near his hero. There was still a family burial area in the same cemetery that was available, but space was at a premium. It would cost over $40,000 to buy the burial area. Nonetheless, Dr. Damson believed it was worthwhile, given his lifelong commitment to his idol, Prince. Indeed, the cemetery management had shown him that the plot was within eyesight of his hero's grave. Dr. Damson signed the papers and paid, by check, for the burial plot for him and his family.

Approximately one month later, Prince's sister determined that there was so little room in the cemetery that it would be impossible for the whole Nelson family to be laid to rest together. (The late artist was born Prince Rogers Nelson). She decided to relocate Prince's gravesite to a less-developed part of the city. Upon hearing this news, Dr. Damson requested that the cemetery refund his money, but the cemetery refused, noting that the plot was still perfectly useable as a burial site.

What are the conditions in this problem? How might they lead to legal arguments?

B. CONDITIONS OF SATISFACTION

Some express conditions qualify a duty based upon whether a party finds some result satisfactory, such as the other party's performance. Judges must interpret the related contractual expression, but given the discretion this might otherwise create, judges also must determine the legal effects of their interpretation. In contrast to the interpretation of contracts, this is often referred to as the judicial construction of contracts.

MATTEI V. HOPPER
330 P.2d 625 (Cal. 1958)

SPENCE, J.

Plaintiff brought this action for damages after defendant allegedly breached a contract by failing to convey her real property in accordance with the terms of a deposit receipt which the parties had executed. After a trial without a jury, the court concluded that the agreement was 'illusory' and lacking in 'mutuality.' From the judgment accordingly entered in favor of defendant, plaintiff appeals.

Plaintiff was a real estate developer. He was planning to construct a shopping center on a tract adjacent to defendant's land. For several months, a real estate agent attempted to negotiate a sale of defendant's property under terms agreeable to both parties. After several of plaintiff's proposals had been rejected by defendant because of the inadequacy of the price offered, defendant submitted an offer. Plaintiff accepted on the same day.

The parties' written agreement was evidenced on a form supplied by the real estate agent, commonly known as a deposit receipt. Under its terms, plaintiff was required to deposit $1,000 of the total purchase price of $57,500 with the real estate agent, and was given 120 days to 'examine the title and consummate the purchase.' At the expiration of that period, the balance of the price was 'due and payable upon tender of a good and sufficient deed of the property sold.' The concluding paragraph of the deposit receipt provided: 'Subject to Coldwell Banker & Company obtaining leases satisfactory to the purchaser.' This clause and the 120-day period were desired by plaintiff as a means for arranging satisfactory leases of the shopping center buildings prior to the time he was finally committed to pay the balance of the purchase price and to take title to defendant's property.

Plaintiff took the first step in complying with the agreement by turning over the $1,000 deposit to the real estate agent. While he was in the process of securing the leases and before the 120 days had elapsed, defendant's attorney notified plaintiff that defendant would not sell her land under the terms contained in the deposit receipt. Thereafter, defendant was informed that satisfactory leases had been obtained and that plaintiff had offered to pay the balance of the purchase price. Defendant failed to tender the deed as provided in the deposit receipt.

Initially, defendant's thesis that the deposit receipt constituted no more than an offer by her, which could only be accepted by plaintiff notifying her that all of the desired leases had been obtained and were satisfactory to him, must be rejected. Nowhere does the agreement mention the necessity of any such notice. Nor does the provision making the agreement 'subject to' plaintiff's securing 'satisfactory' leases necessarily constitute a condition to the existence of a contract. Rather, the whole purchase receipt and this particular clause must be read as merely making plaintiff's performance dependent on the obtaining of 'satisfactory' leases. Thus a contract arose, and plaintiff was given the power and privilege to terminate it in the event he did not obtain such leases. (See 3 Corbin, Contracts (1951), s 647, pp. 581–585.) . . .

However, the inclusion of this clause, specifying that leases 'satisfactory' to plaintiff must be secured before he would be bound to perform, raises the basic question whether the consideration supporting the contract was thereby vitiated. When the parties attempt, as here, to make a contract where promises are exchanged as the consideration, the promises must be mutual in obligation. In other words, for the contract to bind either party, both must have assumed some legal obligations. Without this mutuality of obligation, the agreement lacks consideration and no enforceable contract has been created. Or, if one of the promises leaves a party free to perform or to withdraw from the agreement at his own unrestricted pleasure, the promise is deemed illusory and it provides no consideration. Whether these problems are couched in terms of mutuality of obligation or the illusory nature of a promise, the underlying issue is the same consideration.

While contracts making the duty of performance of one of the parties conditional upon his satisfaction would seem to give him wide latitude in avoiding any obligation and thus present serious consideration problems, such 'satisfaction' clauses have been given effect. They have been divided into two primary categories and have been accorded different treatment on that basis. First, in those contracts where the condition calls for satisfaction as to commercial value or quality, operative fitness, or mechanical utility, dissatisfaction cannot be claimed arbitrarily, unreasonably, or capriciously (Collins v. Vickter Manor, Inc., 47 Cal.2d 875, 882–883, 306 P.2d 783), and the standard of a reasonable person is used in determining whether satisfaction has been received.

[Some cases] expressly rejected the arguments that such clauses either rendered the contracts illusory or deprived the promises of their mutuality of obligation. The remaining cases tacitly assumed the creation of a valid contract. However, it would seem that the factors involved in determining whether a lease is satisfactory to the lessor are too numerous and varied to permit the application of a reasonable man standard as envisioned by this line of cases. Illustrative of some of the factors which would have to be considered in this case are the duration of the leases, their provisions for renewal options, if any, their covenants and restrictions, the amounts of the rentals, the financial responsibility of the lessees, and the character of the lessees' businesses.

This multiplicity of factors which must be considered in evaluating a lease shows that this case more appropriately falls within the second line of authorities dealing with 'satisfaction' clauses, being those involving fancy, taste, or judgment. Where the question is one of judgment, the promisor's determination that he is not satisfied, when made in good faith, has been held to be a defense to an action on the contract. Although [the precedents] do not expressly discuss the issues of mutuality of obligation or illusory promises, they necessarily imply that the promisor's duty to exercise his judgment in good faith is an adequate consideration to support the contract. None of these cases voided the contracts on the ground that they were illusory or lacking in mutuality of obligation.

Defendant's attempts to distinguish these cases are unavailing, since they are predicated upon the assumption that the deposit receipt was not a contract making plaintiff's performance conditional on his satisfaction. As seen above, this was the precise nature of the agreement. Even though the 'satisfaction' clauses discussed in the . . . cases dealt with performances to be received as parts of the agreed exchanges, the fact that the leases here which determined plaintiff's satisfaction were not part of the performance to be rendered is not material. The standard of evaluating plaintiff's satisfaction [in terms of] good faith applies with equal vigor to this type of condition and prevents it from nullifying the consideration otherwise present in the promises exchanged.

Moreover, the secondary authorities are in accord with the California cases on the general principles governing 'satisfaction' contracts. 'It has been questioned whether an agreement in which the promise of one party is conditioned on his own or the other party's satisfaction contains the elements of a contract whether the agreement is not illusory in character because conditioned upon the whim or caprice of the party to be satisfied. Since, however, such a promise is generally considered as requiring a performance which shall be satisfactory to him in the exercise of an honest judgment, such contracts have been almost universally upheld.' (3 Williston, Contracts (rev. ed. 1936), s 675A, p. 1943; see also 3 Corbin, Contracts (1951), ss 644, 645, pp. 560–572.) 'A promise conditional upon the promisor's satisfaction is not illusory since it means more than that validity of the performance is to depend on the arbitrary choice of the promisor. His expression of dissatisfaction is not conclusive. That may show only that he has become dissatisfied with the contract; he must be dissatisfied with the performance, as a performance of the contract, and his dissatisfaction must be genuine.' (Restatement, Contracts (1932), § 265, comment a.)

. . . We conclude that the contract here was neither illusory nor lacking in mutuality of obligation because the parties inserted a provision in their contract making plaintiff's performance dependent on his satisfaction with the leases to be obtained by him.

OMNI GROUP V. SEATTLE FIRST NATIONAL BANK

645 P.2d 727 (Wash. App. 1982)

JAMES, J.

Plaintiff Omni Group, Inc. (Omni), a real estate development corporation, appeals entry of a judgment in favor of John B. Clark, individually, and as executor of the estate of his late wife, in Omni's action to enforce an earnest money agreement for the purchase of realty owned by the Clarks. We reverse.

In December 1977, Mr. and Mrs. Clark executed an exclusive agency listing agreement with the Royal Realty Company of Bellevue (Royal) for the sale of approximately 59 acres of property. The list price was $3,000 per acre.

In early May, Royal offered the Clark property to Omni. On May 17, following conversations with a Royal broker, Omni signed an earnest money agreement offering $2,000 per acre. Two Royal brokers delivered the earnest money agreement to the Clarks. The Clarks signed the agreement, but directed the brokers to obtain further consideration in the nature of Omni's agreement to make certain improvements on adjacent land not being offered for sale. Neither broker communicated these additional terms to Omni. In pertinent part, the earnest money agreement provides:

> This transaction is subject to purchaser receiving an engineer's and architect's feasibility report prepared by an engineer and architect of the purchaser's choice. Purchaser agrees to pay all costs of said report. If said report is satisfactory to purchaser, purchaser shall so notify seller in writing within fifteen (15) days of seller's acceptance of this offer. If no such notice is sent to seller, this transaction shall be considered null and void.

Exhibit A, p. 6. Omni's purpose was to determine, prior to actual purchase, if the property was suitable for development. On June 2, an Omni employee personally delivered to the Clarks a letter advising that Omni had decided to forgo a feasibility study. They were further advised that a survey had revealed that the property consisted of only 50.3 acres. The Clarks agreed that if such were the case, they would accept Omni's offer of $2,000 per acre but with a minimum of 52 acres ($104,000). At this meeting, the Clarks' other terms (which had not been disclosed by Royal nor included in the earnest money agreement signed by the Clarks) were discussed. By a letter of June 8, Omni agreed to accept each of the Clarks' additional terms. The Clarks, however, refused to proceed with the sale after consulting an attorney.

The Clarks argued and the trial judge agreed, that by making its obligations subject to a satisfactory "engineer's and architect's feasibility report" in paragraph 6, Omni rendered its promise to buy the property illusory. Omni responds that paragraph 6 created only a condition precedent to Omni's duty to buy, and because the condition was for its benefit, Omni could waive the condition and enforce the agreement as written. We conclude Omni's promise was not illusory.

A promise for a promise is sufficient consideration to support a contract. If, however, a promise is illusory, there is no consideration and therefore no enforceable contract between the parties. Consequently, a party cannot create an enforceable contract by waiving the condition which renders his promise illusory. But that a promise given for a promise is dependent upon a condition does not necessarily render it illusory or affect its validity as consideration. Furthermore,

> a contractor can, by the use of clear and appropriate words, make his own duty expressly conditional upon his own personal satisfaction with the quality of the performance for which he has bargained and in return for which his promise is given. Such a limitation on his own duty does not invalidate the contract as long as the limitation is not so great as to make his own promise illusory.

3A A. Corbin, Contracts s 644 at 78–79 (1960).

Paragraph 6 may be analyzed as creating two conditions precedent to Omni's duty to buy the Clarks' property. First, Omni must receive an "engineer's and architect's feasibility report." Undisputed evidence was presented to show that such "feasibility reports" are common in the real estate development field and pertain to the physical suitability of the property for development purposes. Such a condition is analogous to a requirement that a purchaser of real property obtain financing, which imposes upon the purchaser a duty to make a good faith effort to secure financing. In essence, this initial language requires Omni to attempt, in good faith, to obtain an "engineer's and architect's feasibility report" of a type recognized in the real estate trade.

The second condition precedent to Omni's duty to buy the Clarks' property is that the feasibility report must be "satisfactory" to Omni. A condition precedent to the promisor's duty that the promisor be "satisfied" may require performance personally satisfactory to the promisor or it may require performance acceptable to a reasonable person. Whether the promisor was actually satisfied or should reasonably have been satisfied is a question of fact. In neither case is the promisor's promise rendered illusory. 3A A. Corbin, Contracts s 644 (1960).

In Mattei v. Hopper, 51 Cal.2d 119, 121, 330 P.2d 625 (1958), plaintiff real estate developer contracted to buy property for a shopping center " '[s]ubject to Coldwell Banker & Company obtaining leases satisfactory to the purchaser.' " Plaintiff had 120 days to consummate the purchase, including arrangement of satisfactory leases for shopping center buildings, before he was committed to purchase the property. The trial judge found the agreement "illusory." The California Supreme Court reversed [stating]:

> [I]t would seem that the factors involved in determining whether a lease is satisfactory to the lessor are too numerous and

varied to permit the application of a reasonable man standard as envisioned by this line of cases. Illustrative of some of the factors which would have to be considered in this case are the duration of the leases, their provisions for renewal options, if any, their covenants and restrictions, the amounts of the rentals, the financial responsibility of the lessees, and the character of the lessees' businesses.

Comparable factors doubtless determine whether an "engineer's and architect's feasibility report" is satisfactory. But

> [t]his multiciplicity of factors which must be considered in evaluating a lease shows that this case more appropriately falls within the second line of authorities dealing with "satisfaction" clauses, being those involving fancy, taste, or judgment. Where the question is one of judgment, the promisor's determination that he is not satisfied, when made in good faith, has been held to be a defense to an action on the contract. . .

Further,

> . . . The standard of evaluating plaintiff's satisfaction—good faith—applies with equal vigor to this type of condition and prevents it from nullifying the consideration otherwise present in the promises exchanged.

Mattei v. Hopper, supra at 123–24, 330 P.2d 625. . . . We conclude that the condition precedent to Omni's duty to buy requiring receipt of a "satisfactory" feasibility report does not render Omni's promise to buy the property illusory.

Paragraph 6 further provides, "If said report is satisfactory to purchaser, purchaser shall so notify seller in writing within fifteen (15) days of seller's acceptance of this offer"; otherwise, the transaction "shall be considered null and void." We read this language to mean that Omni is required ("shall") to notify the Clarks of its acceptance if the feasibility report was "satisfactory." As we have stated, this determination is not a matter within Omni's unfettered discretion.

Omni has, by the quoted language, reserved to itself a power to cancel or terminate the contract. See generally 1A A. Corbin, Contracts § 265 (1963). Such provisions are valid and do not render the promisor's promise illusory, where the option can be exercised upon the occurrence of specified conditions. Here, Omni can cancel by failing to give notice only if the feasibility report is not "satisfactory." Otherwise, Omni is bound to give notice and purchase the property. Accordingly, we conclude paragraph 6 does not render Omni's promise illusory, . . .

NOTES AND QUESTIONS

1. If buyer argued only that "subject to" receiving the feasibility report was a condition, not a negation of duty, would that suffice? Does there need to be some additional commitment, even if a limited one? Is that why the court spoke of good faith? *Compare Wood v. Lucy, Lady-Duff Gordon*; *Paul v. Rosen*, 122 N.E.2d 603 (Ill.App.2d 1954).

2. If the buyer made an unconditional promise to buy, it would be bound; if it makes a conditional promise to buy, then waives that condition, should that not be recognized as binding just the same? Why or why not?

3. What does it mean for the buyer to be satisfied with the feasibility report? Does it mean that the report is a solid work of professional quality? Or does it mean that it contains a favorable conclusion about the parcel's suitability for development? Is the court clear on what standard governs the buyer's satisfaction—an honest but subjective judgment or an objective reasonableness standard?

MORIN BUILDING PRODUCTS V. BAYSTONE CONSTRUCTION, INC.

717 F.2d 413 (7th Cir. 1983)

POSNER, J.

This appeal from a judgment for the plaintiff in a diversity suit requires us to interpret Indiana's common law of contracts. General Motors, which is not a party to this case, hired Baystone Construction, Inc., the defendant, to build an addition to a Chevrolet plant in Muncie, Indiana. Baystone hired Morin Building Products Company, the plaintiff, to supply and erect the aluminum walls for the addition. The contract required that the exterior siding of the walls be of "aluminum type 3003, not less than 18 B & S gauge, with a mill finish and stucco embossed surface texture to match finish and texture of existing metal siding." The contract also provided "that all work shall be done subject to the final approval of the Architect or Owner's [General Motors'] authorized agent, and his decision in matters relating to artistic effect shall be final, if within the terms of the Contract Documents"; and that "should any dispute arise as to the quality or fitness of materials or workmanship, the decision as to acceptability shall rest strictly with the Owner, based on the requirement that all work done or materials furnished shall be first class in every respect. What is usual or customary in erecting other buildings shall in no wise enter into any consideration or decision."

Morin put up the walls. But viewed in bright sunlight from an acute angle the exterior siding did not give the impression of having a uniform finish, and General Motors' representative rejected it. Baystone removed Morin's siding and hired another subcontractor to replace it. General Motors approved the replacement siding. Baystone refused to pay Morin the balance of the contract price ($23,000) and Morin brought this suit for the balance, and won.

The only issue on appeal is the correctness of a jury instruction which, after quoting the contractual provisions requiring that the owner (General Motors) be satisfied with the contractor's (Morin's) work, states: "Notwithstanding the apparent finality of the foregoing language, however, the general rule applying to satisfaction in the case of contracts for the construction of commercial buildings is that the satisfaction clause must be determined by objective criteria. Under this standard, the question is not whether the owner was satisfied in fact, but whether the owner, as a reasonable person, should have been satisfied with the materials and workmanship in question."

There was much evidence that General Motors' rejection of Morin's exterior siding had been totally unreasonable. Not only was the lack of absolute uniformity in the finish of the walls a seemingly trivial defect given the strictly utilitarian purpose of the building that they enclosed, but it may have been inevitable; "mill finish sheet" is defined in the trade as "sheet having a nonuniform finish which may vary from sheet to sheet and within a sheet, and may not be entirely free from stains or oil." If the instruction was correct, so was the judgment. But if the instruction was incorrect—if the proper standard is not whether a reasonable man would have been satisfied with Morin's exterior siding but whether General Motors' authorized representative in fact was—then there must be a new trial to determine whether he really was dissatisfied, or whether he was not and the rejection therefore was in bad faith.

Some cases hold that if the contract provides that the seller's performance must be to the buyer's satisfaction, his rejection—however unreasonable—of the seller's performance is not a breach of the contract unless the rejection is in bad faith. See, e.g., Stone Mountain Properties, Ltd. v. Helmer, 139 Ga.App. 865, 869, 229 S.E.2d 779, 783 (1976). But most cases conform to the position stated in section 228 of the Restatement (Second) of Contracts (1979): if "it is practicable to determine whether a reasonable person in the position of the obligor would be satisfied, an interpretation is preferred under which the condition [that the obligor be satisfied with the obligee's performance] occurs if such a reasonable person in the position of the obligor would be satisfied." . . .

We do not understand the majority position to be paternalistic; and paternalism would be out of place in a case such as this, where the subcontractor is a substantial multistate enterprise. The requirement of reasonableness is read into a contract not to protect the weaker party but to approximate what the parties would have expressly provided with respect to a contingency that they did not foresee, if they had foreseen it. Therefore the requirement is not read into every contract, because it is not always a reliable guide to the parties' intentions. In particular, the presumption that the performing party would not have wanted to put himself at the mercy of the paying party's whim is overcome when the nature of the performance contracted for is such that there are no objective standards to guide the court. It cannot be assumed in such a case that the parties would have wanted a court to second-guess the buyer's rejection. So "the reasonable person standard is employed when the contract involves commercial quality, operative fitness, or mechanical utility which other knowledgeable persons can judge .... The standard of good faith is employed when the contract involves personal aesthetics or fancy." Indiana Tri-City Plaza Bowl, Inc. v. Estate of Glueck, supra, 422 N.E.2d at 675; see also Action Engineering v. Martin Marietta Aluminum, 670 F.2d 456, 460–61 (3d Cir. 1982).

We have to decide which category the contract between Baystone and Morin belongs in. The particular in which Morin's aluminum siding was found wanting was its appearance, which may seem quintessentially a matter of "personal aesthetics," or as the contract put it, "artistic effect." But it is easy to imagine situations where this would not be so. Suppose the manager of a steel plant rejected a shipment of pig iron because he did not think the pigs had a pretty shape. The reasonable-man standard would be applied even if the contract had an "acceptability shall rest strictly with the Owner" clause, for it would be fantastic to think that the iron supplier would have subjected his contract rights to the whimsy of the buyer's agent. At the other extreme would be a contract to paint a portrait, the buyer having reserved the right to reject the portrait if it did not satisfy him. Such a buyer wants a portrait that will please him rather than a jury, even a jury of connoisseurs, so the only question would be his good faith in rejecting the portrait. Gibson v. Cranage, 39 Mich. 49 (1878).

This case is closer to the first example than to the second. The building for which the aluminum siding was intended was a factory—not usually intended to be a thing of beauty. That aesthetic considerations were decidedly secondary to considerations of function and cost is suggested by the fact that the contract specified mill-finish aluminum, which is unpainted. There is much debate in the record over whether it is even possible to ensure a uniform finish within and among sheets, but it is at least clear that mill finish usually is not uniform. If General Motors and Baystone had wanted a uniform finish they would in all likelihood have ordered a painted siding. Whether Morin's siding achieved a reasonable uniformity amounting to satisfactory commercial quality was susceptible of objective judgment; in the language of the Restatement, a reasonableness standard was "practicable."

But this means only that a requirement of reasonableness would be read into this contract if it contained a standard owner's satisfaction clause, which it did not; and since the ultimate touchstone of decision must be the intent of the parties to the contract we must consider the actual language they used. The contract refers explicitly to "artistic effect," a choice of words that may seem deliberately designed to put the contract in the "personal aesthetics" category whatever an outside observer might think. But the reference appears as number 17 in a list of conditions in a general purpose form contract. And the words "artistic effect" are immediately followed by the qualifying phrase, "if within the terms of the Contract Documents," which suggests that the "artistic effect" clause is limited to contracts in which artistic effect is one of the things the buyer is aiming for; it is not clear that he was here. The other clause on which Baystone relies, relating to the quality or fitness of workmanship and materials, may seem all-encompassing, but it is qualified by the phrase, "based on the requirement that all work done or materials furnished shall be first class in every respect"—and it is not clear that Morin's were not. This clause also was not drafted for this contract; it was incorporated by reference to another form contract (the Chevrolet Division's "Contract General Conditions"), of which it is paragraph 35. We do not disparage form contracts, without which the commercial life of the nation would grind to a halt. But we are left with more than a suspicion that the artistic-effect and quality-fitness clauses in the form contract used here were not intended to cover the aesthetics of a mill-finish aluminum factory wall.

If we are right, Morin might prevail even under the minority position, which makes good faith the only standard but presupposes that the contract conditioned acceptance of performance on the buyer's satisfaction in the particular respect in which he was dissatisfied. Maybe this contract was not intended to allow General Motors to reject the aluminum siding on the basis of artistic effect. It would not follow that the contract put Morin under no obligations whatsoever with regard to uniformity of finish. The contract expressly required it to use aluminum having "a mill finish . . . to match finish . . . of existing metal siding." The jury was asked to decide whether a reasonable man would have found that Morin had used aluminum sufficiently uniform to satisfy the matching requirement. This was the right standard if, as we believe, the parties would have adopted it had they foreseen this dispute. It is unlikely that Morin intended to bind itself to a higher and perhaps unattainable standard of achieving whatever perfection of matching that General Motors' agent insisted on, or that General Motors would have required Baystone to submit to such a standard. Because it is difficult—maybe impossible—to achieve a uniform finish with mill-finish aluminum, Morin would have been running a considerable risk of rejection if it had agreed to such a condition, and it therefore could have been expected to demand a compensating increase in the contract price. This would have required General Motors to pay a premium to obtain a freedom of action that it could not have thought terribly important, since its objective was not aesthetic. If a uniform finish was important to it, it could have gotten such a finish by specifying painted siding.

All this is conjecture; we do not know how important the aesthetics were to General Motors when the contract was signed or how difficult it really would have been to obtain the uniformity of finish it desired. The fact that General Motors accepted the replacement siding proves little, for there is evidence that the replacement siding produced the same striped effect, when viewed from an acute angle in bright sunlight, that Morin's had. When in doubt on a difficult issue of state law it is only prudent to defer to the view of the district judge, Murphy v. White Hen Pantry Co., 691 F.2d 350, 354 (7th Cir. 1982), here an experienced Indiana lawyer who thought this the type of contract where the buyer cannot unreasonably withhold approval of the seller's performance.

Lest this conclusion be thought to strike at the foundations of freedom of contract, we repeat that if it appeared from the language or circumstances of the contract that the parties really intended General Motors to have the right to reject Morin's work for failure to satisfy the private aesthetic taste of General Motors' representative, the rejection would have been proper even if unreasonable. But the contract is ambiguous because of the qualifications with which the terms "artistic effect" and "decision as to acceptability" are hedged about, and the circumstances suggest that the parties probably did not intend to subject Morin's rights to aesthetic whim. [Affirmed.]

NOTES AND QUESTIONS

1.   Does Judge Posner's *Morin* opinion evince paternalism? Were stern judicial denials of doing so necessary? When would a requirement of reasonableness be paternalistic? When is it merely an aid to interpretation? Is it "fantastic" to believe that a buyer of pig iron, for example, could reject a shipment "because he did not think the pigs had a pretty shape"? What if the contract so stated, or used phrases such as "artistic effect," "quality or fitness" and "decision as to acceptability"? When should those words be given their ordinary meaning and when reinterpreted?

2.   Does Judge Posner's opinion undermine freedom of contract? How is freedom of contract exercised? How do contracting parties express themselves?

3.   Corbin wrote, long ago, that courts sometimes set aside an express condition calling for personal satisfaction:

> by indulging in a process of pseudo-interpretation, finding that the language used means the "satisfaction of a reasonable man." When this is in fact what is done, it is a substitution by the court of a reasonable condition precedent in place of what seems to the court an unreasonable condition precedent. Such pseudo-interpretation as

this constitutes a judicial limitation upon the freedom of contract of the parties.

Corbin might have tolerated the fashioning of some remedy in cases where the condition arose as a result of inequality in bargaining power, but he emphasized that this remedy would still constitute judicial restriction on freedom of contract.

4.   Is Judge Posner's opinion a manifestation of judicial pragmatism?

C. CONSTRUCTIVE CONDITIONS

In many complex transactions, the contract documentation contemplates that all of the respective duties are to be performed simultaneously. A good example is the purchase and sale of a business. The agreement may expressly state a closing date at which each side will perform their various obligations: the buyer providing cash or delivering other consideration and the seller transferring title and making other representations about the property's condition. Making the obligations concurrent solves otherwise thorny problems about who must go first: must the buyer tender cash to trigger the seller's duty to tender the deed or must the seller tender the deed to trigger the buyer's duty to pay?

Determining whether one side or the other must perform first often hinges on whether either accepted the other's credit risk in choosing to deal with them. If not, it is best to view promises as mutually conditional, so that each side must tender its performance as a condition to the other being bound to perform. People sometimes accept other people's credit risk, of course, such as when employees must work for a period of time before receiving their first paycheck. In these cases, one party must go first, rather than both at the same time. Either way, contract law encourages the parties to come together and perform their bargains rather than stand back and declare the other party has breached. The following three classic opinions of the New York Court of Appeals, contributed by three generations of jurists, suggest some of the problems and related solutions.

ZIEHEN V. SMITH
42 N.E. 1080 (N.Y. 1896)

O'BRIEN, J.

The plaintiff, as vendee, under an executory contract for the sale of real estate, has recovered of the defendant, the vendor, damages for a breach of the contract to convey, to the extent of that part of the purchase money paid at the execution of the contract, and for certain expenses in the examination of the title. The question . . . is whether the plaintiff established at the trial such a breach of the contract as entitled him to recover.

By the contract, which bears date August 10, 1892, the defendant agreed to convey to the plaintiff, by good and sufficient deed, the lands described therein, being a country hotel with some adjacent land. The plaintiff was to pay for the same the sum of $3,500, as follows: $500 down, . . . paid [upon] execution of the contract; $300 more on the 15th day of September, 1892. He was to assume an existing mortgage on the property of $1,000, and the balance, of $1,700, he was to secure by his bond and mortgage on the property, payable, with interest, one year after date. The courts below have assumed that the payment of the $300 by the plaintiff, the execution of the bond and mortgage, and the delivery of the conveyance by the defendant, were intended to be concurrent acts, and therefore the day designated by the contract for mutual performance was the 15th of September, 1892. Since no other day is mentioned in the contract for the payment of the money or the exchange of the papers, we think that this construction was just and reasonable . . . . It is not alleged or claimed that the plaintiff on that day, or at any other time, offered to perform on his part, or demanded performance on the part of the defendant; and this presents the serious question in the case, and the only obstacle to the plaintiff's recovery.

It is, no doubt, the general rule that, in order to entitle a party to recover damages for the breach of an executory contract of this character, he must show performance, or tender of performance, on his part. He must show in some way that the other party is in default, in order to maintain the action, or that performance or tender has been waived. But a tender of performance on the part of the vendee is dispensed with in a case where it appears that the vendor has disabled himself from performance, or that he is on the day fixed by the contract for that purpose, for any reason, unable to perform. The judgment in this case must stand, if at all, upon the ground that on the 15th day of September, 1892, the defendant was unable to give to the plaintiff any title to the property embraced in the contract; and hence any tender of performance on the part of the plaintiff, or demand of performance on his part, was unnecessary, because, upon the facts appearing, it would be an idle or useless ceremony.

It appeared upon the trial that at the time of the execution of the contract there was another mortgage upon the premises of $1,500, which fact was not disclosed to the plaintiff, and of the existence of which he was then ignorant. That on or prior to the 21st of July, 1892, some 20 days before the contract was entered into, an action was commenced to foreclose this mortgage, and notice of the pendency of the action filed in the county clerk's office; that on the 30th of September, following, judgment of foreclosure was granted, and entered on the 31st of October, thereafter, and on the 28th of December the property was sold to a third party by virtue of the judgment, and duly conveyed by deed from the referee. It appears that the defendant was not the maker of this mortgage, and was not aware of its existence, but it was made by a former owner, and the defendant's title was subject to it when he contracted to sell the property to the plaintiff.

The decisions on the point involved do not seem to be entirely harmonious. In some of them it is said that the existence, at the date fixed for performance, of liens or incumbrances upon the property, is sufficient to sustain an action by the vendee to recover the part of the purchase money paid upon the contract. Morange v. Morris, 42 N. Y. 48; Ingalls v. Hahn, 47 Hun, 104. The general rule, however, . . . seems to be that in cases where, by the terms of the contract, the acts of the parties are to be concurrent, it is the duty of him who seeks to maintain an action for a breach of the contract, either by way of damages for the nonperformance, or for the recovery of money paid thereon, not only to be ready and willing to perform on his part, but he must demand performance from the other party.

The qualifications to this rule are to be found in cases where the necessity of a formal tender or demand is obviated by the acts of the party sought to be charged, as by his express refusal in advance to comply with the terms of the contract in that respect, or where it appears that he has placed himself in a position in which performance is impossible. If the vendor of real estate, under an executory contract, is unable to perform on his part, at the time provided by the contract, a formal tender or demand on the part of the vendee is not necessary in order to enable him to maintain an action to recover the money paid on the contract, or for damages.

In this case there was no proof that the defendant waived tender or demand, either by words or conduct. The only difficulty in the way of the performance on his part was the existence of the mortgage, which the proof tends to show was given by a former owner, and its existence on the day of performance was not known to either party. In order to sustain the judgment, we must hold that the defendant, on the day of performance, was [not true] unable to convey to the plaintiff the title which the contract required, simply because of the existence of the incumbrance.

[T]he defendant had [not] placed himself in such a position that he was unable to perform the contract on his part, and that his title was destroyed, or that it was impossible for him to convey, within the meaning of the rule which dispenses with the necessity of tender and demand in order to work a breach of an executory contract for the sale of land. It cannot be affirmed, under the circumstances, that, if the plaintiff had made the tender and demand on the day provided in the contract, he would not have received the title which the defendant had contracted to convey. The contract is not broken by the mere fact of the existence on the day of performance of some lien or incumbrance which it is in the power of the vendee to remove. That is all that was shown in this case . . . All concur. Judgment reversed.

STEWART V. NEWBURY
115 N.E. 984 (N.Y. 1917)

CRANE, J.

    The defendants [own a] pipe fitting business under the name of Newbury Manufacturing Company. The plaintiff is a contractor [in] Tuxedo, N. Y. The parties had . . . correspondence about the erection . . . of a concrete mill building at Monroe, N.Y. [On July 18, 1911 the contractor wrote to the owner as follows:]

    With reference to the proposed work on the new foundry building I had hoped to be able to get up and see you this afternoon, but find that impossible and am, in consequence, sending you these prices, which I trust you will find satisfactory.

    I will agree to do all excavation work required at sixty-five ($.65) cents per cubic yard.

    I will put in the concrete work, furnishing labor and forms only, at two and 05–100 ($2.05) dollars per cubic yard.

    I will furnish labor to put in reenforcing at four ($4.00) dollars per ton.

    I will furnish labor only to set all window and door frames, window sash and doors, including the setting of hardware for one hundred twelve ($112) dollars. As alternative I would be willing to do any or all of the above work for cost plus 10 per cent., furnishing you with first class mechanics and giving the work considerable of my personal time.

    Hoping to hear favorably from you . . .

[On July 22, 1911, owner replied as follows:]

    Confirming the telephone conversation of this morning we accept your bid of July the 18th to do the concrete work on our new building. We trust that you will be able to get at this the early part of next week.

Nothing was said in writing about the time or manner of payment. The plaintiff, however, claims that after sending his letter, and before receiving that of the defendant, he had a telephone communication with Mr. Newbury and said: "I will expect my payments in the usual manner," and Newbury said, "All right, we have got the money to pay for the building." This conversation over the telephone was denied by the defendants. The custom, the plaintiff testified, was to pay 85 per cent. every 30 days or at the end of each month, 15 per cent. being retained till the work was completed.

In July the plaintiff commenced work and continued until September 29th, at which time he had progressed with the construction as far as the first floor. He then sent a bill for the work done up to that date for $896.35. The defendants refused to pay the bill and work was discontinued. The plaintiff claims that the defendants refused to permit him to perform the rest of his contract, they insisting that the work already done was not in accordance with the specifications. The defendants claimed upon the trial that the plaintiff voluntarily abandoned the work after their refusal to pay his bill. On October 5, 1911, the defendants wrote the plaintiff a letter containing the following:

> Notwithstanding you promised to let us know on Monday whether you would complete the job or throw up the contract, you have not up to this time advised us of your intention. . . . Under the circumstances, we are compelled to accept your action as being an abandonment of your contract and of every effort upon your part to complete your work on our building. As you know, the bill which you sent us and which we declined to pay is not correct, either in items or amount, nor is there anything due you under our contract as we understand it until you have completed your work on our building.

To this letter the plaintiff replied the following day. In it he makes no reference to the telephone communication agreeing, as he testified, to make "the usual payments," but does say this:

> There is nothing in our agreement which says that I shall wait until the job is completed before any payment is due, nor can this be reasonably implied. . . . As to having given you positive date as to when I should let you know what I proposed doing, I did not do so; on the contrary, I told you that I would not tell you positively what I would do until I had visited the job, and I promised that I would do this at my earliest convenience and up to the present time I have been unable to get up there.

The defendant Herbert Newbury testified that the plaintiff "ran away and left the whole thing." And the defendant F. A. Newbury testified that he was told by Mr. Stewart's [agent] that Stewart was going to abandon the job; that he thereupon telephoned Mr. Stewart, who replied that he would let him know about it the next day, but did not.

In this action . . . to recover the amount of the [invoice sent plus] $95.68 damages for breach of contract, the plaintiff had a verdict for the amount stated in the [invoice], but not for the other damages claimed, and the judgment entered thereon has been affirmed by the Appellate Division. The appeal to us is upon exceptions to the judge's charge. The court charged the jury as follows:

> Plaintiff says that he was excused from completely performing the contract by the defendants' unreasonable failure to pay him for the work he had done during the months of August and September. . . .

> Was it understood that the payments were to be made monthly? If it was not so understood, the defendants only obligation was to make payments at reasonable periods, in view of the character of the work, the amount of work being done, and the value of it.

> In other words, if there was no agreement between the parties respecting the payments, the defendants' obligation was to make payments at reasonable times. . . . But whether there was such an agreement or not, you may consider whether it was reasonable or unreasonable for him to exact a payment at that time and in that amount.

The court further said, in reply to a request to charge: "I will say in that connection, if there was no agreement respecting the time of payment, and if there was no custom that was understood by both parties, and with respect to which they made the contract, then the plaintiff was entitled to payments at reasonable times." . . .

The jury was plainly told that if there were no agreement as to payments, yet the plaintiff would be entitled to part payment at reasonable times as the work progressed, and if such payments were refused he could abandon the work and recover the amount due for the work performed.

This is not the law. Counsel for the plaintiff omits to call our attention to any authority sustaining such a proposition and our search reveals none. In fact, the law is very well settled to the contrary. This was an entire contract. Ming v. Corbin, 142 N. Y. 334, 340, 341, 37 N. E. 105. Where a contract is made to perform work and no agreement is made as to payment, the work must be substantially performed before payment can be demanded.

This case was also submitted to the jury upon the ground that there may have been a breach of contract by the defendants in their refusal to permit the plaintiff to continue with his work, claiming that he had departed from the specifications, and there was some evidence justifying this view of the case; but it is impossible to say upon which of these two theories the jury arrived at its conclusion. The above errors, therefore, cannot be considered as harmless and immaterial. As the verdict was for the amount of the [invoice] and did not include the damages for a breach of contract, which would be the loss of profits, it may well be presumed that the jury adopted the first ground of recovery charged by the court as above quoted and decided that the plaintiff was justified in abandoning work for nonpayment of the installment. [Reversed.]

COHEN V. KRANZ

189 N.E.2d 473 (N.Y. 1963)

BURKE, J.

On September 22, 1959 plaintiff contracted to [buy] defendants' one-family house in Nassau County for $40,000. Four thousand dollars was paid on the signing of the contract and the balance due upon delivery of the deed was in the form of $24,500 cash and the assumption of an $11,500 first mortgage. Closing was set for November 15. Plaintiff obtained an adjournment of the closing date to December 15 without any indication that title would be rejected. On November 30, plaintiff's attorney sent defendants' attorney a letter stating: "An investigation has disclosed that the present structure of the premises is not legal and thus title is unmarketable. Unless a check to the order of Lester Cohen, as attorney in fact, for Sarah Cohen is received in five days, we shall be obligated to commence proceedings against your client."

Plaintiff's attorney appeared at the office of defendants' attorney on the adjourned law date [December 15] and demanded return of the $4,000 deposit, which was refused . . . . Neither party was then able to perform and neither made any tender. Plaintiff thereafter commenced this action for return of the deposit plus the costs of searching title; defendants counterclaimed for damages for breach of contract.

[The trial court] gave judgment for plaintiff. The court found that the premises were subject to protective covenants filed in the Nassau County Clerk's office and that the insurability clause of the contract was not complied with because a swimming pool on the premises, installed under a permit, lacked a certificate of occupancy from the Oyster Bay Architectural Control Committee. Further, a split rail fence projected beyond the front line of the dwelling. The court also found that plaintiff had notified defendants of the claimed defects prior to the December 15 closing date and that defendants had taken no steps to remedy the defects, nor had it been established that the violations were minor. The court held, therefore, that the defective title excused plaintiff from tender of payment and awarded plaintiff judgment in the amount of her deposit.

The Appellate Division . . . unanimously reversed . . . on the law and facts and directed judgment on the counterclaim for $1,500. It is from this judgment that plaintiff appeals. In reversing Trial Term's findings of fact, the Appellate Division expressly found that plaintiff's letter of November 30 rejecting title and demanding return of the deposit failed to specify the claimed illegality, and that specific objections to title were not raised until

January 25, 1960. The letter speaks for itself and the Appellate Division is obviously correct.

Plaintiff's arguments directed at the Appellate Division's finding of January 25th as the date when specific objections were first communicated to defendants are unavailing inasmuch as the earliest further communication of objections supported by the evidence took place upon the commencement of this action by plaintiff on December 31st, still more than two weeks after the law date. It was also found, contrary to the trial court, that the objections to title were curable upon proper and timely notice and demand.

We think the weight of the evidence supports the Appellate Division here too. The swimming pool was constructed with a permit and lacked only a certificate of occupancy (which was in fact obtained before defendants sold the house to a third person). The fence projection likewise could clearly be found to be a readily curable objection. These were the only two objections that possibly violated the 'DECLARATION OF PROTECTIVE COVENANTS' recorded in the Nassau County Clerk's office and to which the title insurer excepted.

The Appellate Division also found that defendants had not waived a tender by plaintiff and that plaintiff's rejection of title in advance was a default precluding her from recovery of the deposit. Since it is undisputed that defendants made no tender, the Appellate Division's award of damages for breach of contract necessarily implies that no such tender was required. We agree.

While a vendee can recover his money paid on the contract from a vendor who defaults on law day [the date set for closing the transaction] without a showing of tender or even of willingness and ability to perform where the vendor's title is incurably defective, a tender and demand are required to put the vendor in default where his title could be cleared without difficulty in a reasonable time. Further, the vendor in such a case is entitled to a reasonable time beyond law day to make his title good. It is, therefore, clear that plaintiff's advance rejection of title and demand for immediate return of the deposit was unjustified and an anticipatory breach of contract. This position, adhered to throughout, prevented defendants' title defects from ever amounting to a default. Consequently, plaintiff is barred from recovering the deposit from a vendor whose title defects were curable and whose performance was never demanded on law day. . . .

Defendants obtained an affirmative recovery on their counterclaim for breach of contract based on the loss they sustained when they sold the house to a third person for what the courts below found to be its fair market value. This recovery stands on a different footing from their right to retain the deposit. . . . [W]hile the vendee's right to recover the deposit from a defaulting vendor can rest solely upon the latter's default, an action for damages for breach of contract requires a showing that the plaintiff himself . . . has performed all conditions precedent and concurrent, unless excused. In the case of a purchase of real estate, this would be a showing of tender and demand or, if that be unnecessary, an idle gesture, because of the incurable nature of the title defect, then at least a showing at the trial that the plaintiff vendee was in a position to perform had the vendor been willing and able to perform his part. . . .

Not only did plaintiff's unjustified attempt to cancel the contract and recover her deposit before the adjourned law date render unnecessary and wasteful any attempt by defendants to cure the minor defects before that date, but the failure to specify the objections rendered it impossible. The finding of the Appellate Division, supported by the weight of the evidence, that the defects were curable, means that defendants were basically able to perform and whatever technical inability existed in this regard on the law date was caused by plaintiff and is excused fully as much as the lack of formal tender.

NOTES AND QUESTIONS

1.   State the holding in each of the foregoing cases: *Ziehen*, *Stuart*, and *Cohen*. State the most general legal principles possible to account for all three opinions. What values do the opinions, individually and collectively, seem to stress? Freedom of contract? Protecting and enforcing exchanges manifestly intended to be performed, despite post-formation wiggling and wrangling by parties in light of subsequent events?

2.   State the issue of waiver raised in each of *Ziehen* and *Cohen*. How did each side argue the issue and each opinion resolve it?

3.   In *Ziehen*, was the order of performance explicit? Was the fact of stating a closing date probative of when the parties intended their respective performances to be due? The buyer argued that its promise was conditional on the seller being ready, willing, and able to perform. Did the mortgage affect that ability? Did it negate that ability?

4.   In *Stewart*, the contract (or series of communications) did not specify which payment scheme the owner preferred. Is there anything in the texts that suggests which side had the stronger argument? Is the contractor's delineation of the separate steps probative? Why did the court seem to deny that?

EXAMPLE: CHARLIE SHEEN

A common question in the performance of contracts that break down is: "who's to blame for breach?" Unlike the fight between an older and younger sibling where both are punished with a "time out," with breach, the courts do care "who started it." This seems to be one of the central issues in the Charlie Sheen–Warner Brothers litigation over the making of the television series *Two and a Half Men*. While this is a rich scenario for contract law, one major issue in the litigation boils down to a fact question: was Sheen able or unable to act in *Two and a Half Men*? Determining Sheen's acting ability might be difficult as a substantive matter, involving opinions of artistic taste and judgment. But contract law provides ways to frame issues that help probe the reasonableness of Warner's and Sheen's conflicting opinions about his ability to perform.

Warner Brothers and Chuck Lorre produced *Two and Half Men*, and for seven seasons, Sheen successfully played the lead character, with whom he had much in common, both being middle-aged bachelors engaging in irresponsible behavior and prone to abusing alcohol, drugs, and women. Despite Sheen's lurid off-air antics, Warner renewed his contract in May 2010 for the popular show. The updated contract, heavily negotiated with extensive provisions, called for Sheen to perform two dozen episodes in each season with Warner to pay him $1.2 million per episode.

The relationship between the parties had been rocky for a while, due to Sheen's personal life. He endured a public divorce that culminated in physical and drug abuse charges in an incident in Aspen in December 2009 and an encounter with a prostitute in New York City's Plaza Hotel in October 2010, also involving allegations of substance abuse. Sheen lost about 20 pounds in the last few months of 2010, attributed to illegal drug consumption. Meanwhile, Warner went on with the show, creating and airing episodes starring Sheen. At the same time, Chuck Lorre began poking fun at Sheen for his out-of-control behavior.

In January 2011, Warner grew worried. Its senior executives suspected that Sheen needed medical treatment for his addictions and visited him at his home, warning him that a failure to clean up his act would end the show. At first, Sheen agreed to enter rehab, but he later reneged, claiming he had kicked his habit. Lorre decided that fewer episodes would be made that season. Warner's agreement with Lorre's decision to reduce the episodes, along with Sheen's heightening animosity toward Lorre because of his wise-cracking, brought Sheen to the boiling point. On February 24, Sheen began a media blitz in which he lambasted Lorre and Warner, made bizarre statements to the media, and boasted of super-human powers to win his battle with drugs by blinking his eyes.

Warner announced it was suspending production of the show. It expressed continuing concern about Sheen's health and stressed that it had demanded assurances that Sheen would seek treatment, which he rebuffed. On February 28, Sheen claimed that Warner was in breach of contract for suspending the show without justification. Sheen demanded to be paid for all contract episodes, whether produced or not, citing a so-called "play or pay" clause in their contract.

In a letter of March 7, Warner responded by terminating its agreement with Sheen, calling his objectionable conduct a breach. Warner cited several promises it said Sheen breached and portrayed his fulfillment of them as conditions to its duties to use or pay Sheen. One authorized Warner to suspend or terminate Sheen's employment based on his incapacity. This included "physical or mental disabilities" that rendered Sheen unable to perform essential duties, including significant changes in physical appearance. A similar clause covered any "serious health condition" lasting more than a couple of weeks. Warner said Sheen's appearance, condition, conduct, and statements triggered its rights to suspend or terminate under these clauses.

Sheen denied this, claiming he was clean and sober. Sheen claimed Warner cancelled the series in retaliation for Sheen criticizing Lorre, not because of Sheen's abilities. Sheen claimed he was ready, willing, and able to perform his obligations under the contract.

Sheen asserted and Warner acknowledged the "play or pay" clause requiring paying Sheen even if episodes were not made. But while Sheen thought this clause closed the case, his belief was premature. Even an expansive play-or-pay clause does not automatically mean payment is due without regard to why an episode goes unproduced. These clauses, common in entertainment contracts, require a producer to pay an entertainer an agreed sum even if the parties do not create art—but they are not unconditional. Like any other promise, they are often subject to conditions, most often the receiving party fulfilling its side of the deal.

Warner cited an express limit on Sheen's rights concerning publicity. The contract made Warner officials the exclusive publicists for the show, prohibiting Sheen from publicizing it other than by "normal, incidental, non-derogatory publicity relating solely to" Sheen's role. Warner classified Sheen's media rants containing derogatory remarks as violating this clause. The clause was not obviously applicable, however, as it restricted publicity (in the sense of promotion or advertising), which Sheen did not pursue, and did not squarely bar him from commentary or disparagement. The question remained: Who had breached first?

Following is a part of the complaint filed by Charlie Sheen against producer Chuck Lorre and Warner Brothers for breach of contract. Keep in mind that the complaint sets out Sheen's view of the case and thus is only one side of the story. What do you think are the merits and problems with Charlie Sheen's complaint? If you were the law clerk to the judge hearing this case, would you advise allowing this complaint to proceed?

COMPLAINT: SHEEN V. LORRE
Docket No. SC111794 (Cal. Super. Ct. Mar. 10, 2011)

Plaintiffs Charlie Sheen and 9th Step Productions (collectively sometimes referred to as "Plaintiffs"), for their Complaint against Defendants Chuck Lorre, Chuck Lorre Productions, Inc. and WB Studio Enterprises, Inc. (sometimes collectively referred to as "Defendants") hereby allege as follows: . . .

23. As of May 17, 2010, Plaintiff 9th Step Productions entered into a written letter agreement with WB, through a division of WB called Warner

Bros. Television, for the acting services of Plaintiff Charlie Sheen with respect to the 2010/2011 and 2011/2012 production seasons of the Series (the "Acting Agreement"). The Acting Agreement provides for, among other things, payment to 9th Step Productions of a specified fee per episode for Mr. Sheen's acting services, on a "pay or play" basis, with a minimum guarantee of 24 episodes per season. The Acting Agreement incorporated provisions from previous written agreements relating to earlier seasons of the Series.

24. Plaintiffs are informed and believe and thereon allege that Defendants Lorre and/or CLPI have also entered into an agreement with WB pursuant to which Defendants agreed to act as show runner and to timely write and develop scripts for episodes of the Series, in which it was always contemplated that Charlie Sheen would star pursuant to the Acting Agreement (the "Show Runner Agreement"). The Show Runner Agreement was entered into expressly for the benefit of Plaintiffs in that, among other things, the services of both Mr. Sheen and Lorre were necessary in order for the Series to succeed. It was necessary for Lorre to fully and timely discharge the obligations specified in the Show Runner Agreement in order for both WB and Plaintiffs to obtain the rights and benefits of, and to properly discharge their respective obligations under, the Acting Agreement.

25. In early February 2011, production of the Series was briefly postponed due to Mr. Sheen's hospitalization. On February 14, 2011, Mr. Sheen attempted to return to the set in accordance with the agreed production schedule. However, he was informed that production could not proceed because Lorre had not supervised or arranged for production of shooting scripts, notwithstanding the fact that it was contemplated that Mr. Sheen would return shortly to work. Mr. Sheen was informed that he should return to work the week of February 28, 2011, when production of the Series would resume.

26. The conduct of Lorre, on his own behalf and on behalf of CLPI, in refusing to arrange for production of shooting scripts for the Series so that production could be continued in mid-February, 2011 was a unilateral breach of the Show Runner Agreement, as well as a direct interference with the Acting Agreement. Lorre had no right to unilaterally discontinue the production of shooting scripts, and thereby interrupt the production schedule. His conduct, moreover, significantly damaged not only Plaintiffs but the crew and other cast members working on the series. Plaintiffs are informed and believe and thereon allege that Defendants Lorre and CLPI took this action to satisfy their own egotistical desires and damage Mr. Sheen.

27. Even with postponing production until the delayed February 28, 2011 data, there was still adequate time under the agreed production

schedule (which was to terminate on or about April 8, 2011) to complete an additional six to eight episodes of the Series under the original production schedule and the Acting Agreement. However, in mid-February, 2011, Plaintiffs were informed that the production schedule would arbitrarily be terminated on or about March 25, 2011, and that only four additional episodes of the Series would be produced under the revised schedule. This arbitrary determination, which Plaintiffs are informed and believe and thereon allege was at the urging and insistence of Defendants Lorre and CLPI and agreed to by Defendant WB, constituted a breach by WB, and an unlawful and intentional interference by Defendants Lorre end CLPI, of Plaintiffs' rights under the Acting Agreement. Once again, this action also adversely affected numerous innocent people working on the Series including the cast and crew.

28. From time to time during the production of the Series, Defendant Chuck Lorre, on his own behalf and on behalf of Defendant CLPI, engaged in conduct and made statements to Mr. Sheen and publicly to others, including the media, in order to intentionally harass, annoy and damage Plaintiffs. For no legitimate reason whatsoever, Lorre required Mr. Sheen to perform multiple takes of scenes during filming solely to harass and frustrate Mr. Sheen and exhibit that Lorre was in control. Lorre also engaged in a pattern and practice of disseminating harassing, derogatory and highly inflammatory comments about Mr. Sheen through the media and through the use of "vanity cards" broadcast at the end of each episode of the Series.

29. Among the numerous harassing, derogatory and damaging statements that Defendants Lorre and CLPI have publicly disseminated via the internationally broadcast vanity cards that obviously refer to Mr. Sheen are the following:

- Under the heading "To Do List," Lorre wrote "Meditate using new mantra, 'High ratings do not equate to high self-esteem,' " "Go to Al-Anon meeting," and "Write a country song entitled, 'Hooker in the closet.' (Chorus: 'There's a hooker in the closet, 'neath the monogrammed robes, don't know how she got there and I can't find my clothes. Officer Krupke, how are you tonight? I've misplaced my watch but I'm feeling alright.')"

- Following statements about his own healthy lifestyle, Lorre wrote: "If Charlie Sheen outlives me, I'm gonna be really pissed."

- Lorre suggested that persons viewing the show not drink to excess and "avoid degrading yourself by having meaningless sex with strangers in a futile attempt to fill the emptiness in your soul."

- Lorre suggested that the audience extend prayers to people working on the Series and that viewers should "Feel free to pick whomever you think is most in need. Just hurry."

- He also wrote, "We employ a highly-paid Hollywood professional who has years of experience with putting his life at risk. And sadly no, I'm not talking about our stunt man."

30. When Mr. Sheen finally responded to Lorre's unrelenting derogatory statements in the media during the week of February 21, 2011, Defendants Lorre and CLPI retaliated by using their influence to prevail upon WB to terminate production of the Series for the remainder of the 2010/2011 Season. On or about February 24, 2011, WB and CBS issued the following joint statement: "Based on the totality of Charlie Sheen's statements, conduct and condition, CBS and Warner Bros. Television have decided to discontinue production of Two and a Half Men for the remainder of the season." On March 7, 2011, Plaintiffs were informed that WB terminated the Acting Agreement and does not intend to pay Plaintiffs the compensation due thereunder.

31. Notwithstanding the attempt to premise the cancellation of production of the Series and the termination of the Acting Agreement upon Mr. Sheen's alleged conduct, including his response to the campaign of harassment and derogatory statements by Lorre about Mr. Sheen in the media, Defendants Lorre and CLPI had already refused to perform their obligations under the Show Runner Agreement by, among other things, (a) refusing to supervise production of shooting scripts in January and February in anticipation of Mr. Sheen's imminent return to the set, and (b) demanding that production of the Series terminate on March 25 instead of April 8, 2011, long before Mr. Sheen made any public statements about Lorre. . . .

32. Plaintiffs are informed and believe and thereon allege that the actions of Defendants Lorre and CTPI as alleged herein were fueled not only by Lorre's ego, but also by a material conflict of interest between the involvement of Lorre and CLPI on the Series and their other projects at Warner Bros. and CBS. Among other things, Plaintiffs are informed and believe that Lorre and CLPI have a significantly higher profit participation on their other projects at WB and CBS than they do on the Series, and that writers who they originally hired to work on the Series are now writing for their other shows, such that they were incentivized to focus on their other shows as opposed to continuing their involvement on the Series as required under the Show Runner Agreement. . . .

47. Pursuant to the Acting Agreement between Plaintiff 9th Step Productions and WB, 9th Step is entitled to be paid for Mr. Sheen's services on the Series on a pay-or-play basis at a specified rate per episode, with a minimum guarantee of 24 episodes per production season. In addition,

Plaintiff 9th Step Productions is entitled to be paid back end Compensation and other amounts specified in the Acting Agreement.

48. Plaintiffs are informed and believe that WB intends to pay 9th Step Productions for a maximum of 16 episodes for the 2010/2011 season of the Series, and in any event does not intend to pay the episodic fee for a minimum of 24 episodes as required under the Acting Agreement. WB has also stated that it is refusing to pay the back end Compensation and other amounts due and owing to Plaintiff under the Acting Agreement. WB's conduct in refusing to pay the episodic fees owed under the Acting Agreement constitutes a breach of the Acting Agreement, and its statements indicating that it does not intend to pay the back end compensation due and owing to 9th Step despite the fact that Plaintiffs have faithfully rendered services and fully performed their obligations on 177 episodes of the Series constitutes an anticipatory breach of the Acting Agreement.

49. Plaintiffs have performed all conditions, covenants and promises required pursuant to the Acting Agreement, except for those conditions, covenants and promises which have been prevented or otherwise excused by WB's conduct.

50. WB has materially breached the Acting Agreement by, among other things, failing and refusing to pay the episodic fee payments for 24 episodes of the Series and other payments, including back end compensation required under the Acting Agreement.

51. As a proximate result of WB's breaches of contract, Plaintiff 9th Step Productions has sustained damages in an amount in excess of one Hundred Million Dollars, together with interest thereon at the maximum legal rate. In addition, the Acting Agreement provides for recovery of "all costs, fees and expenses, including attorneys fees" incurred in enforcing an award obtained pursuant to the Acting Agreement. Plaintiff seeks those amounts as well. When Plaintiff has ascertained the full amount of its damages, it will seek leave of Court to amend this Complaint accordingly.

NOTES AND QUESTIONS

1. The Sheen dispute reveals some interesting aspects of constructive conditions of exchange. Sheen seems to argue that Lorre, like the buyer in *Ziehen*, had to tender performance and show readiness, willingness, and ability to perform, not merely assume or declare Sheen's prospective inability. Like the hotel seller with a potentially cloudy title, nothing prevented Sheen from delivering his lines on the set (despite a potentially cloudy mind and body). In Sheen's view, however, Warner acted precipitously and without justification. From his perspective, Warner was in breach.

2. Warner might argue that the case was more like the construction case *Stewart v. Newbury*. In construction contracts, it is common and practical for

services to be rendered before payment is due. True, the Warner–Sheen contract specifically addressed the timing of payment by stating separate amounts per episode, a way to distinguish construction and employment cases silent about that. But Warner did not commit to pay for episodes that were unproduced due to Sheen's problematic behavior.

The question remains whether Warner waived its rights. Acting and personal services contracts, including that between Sheen and Warner, typically contain clauses addressing the actor's behavior. The one in Sheen's contract authorized Warner to suspect or terminate the contract if Sheen committed "felony" offenses involving moral turpitude and another if he engaged in "extra hazardous activity." Warner asserted that Sheen triggered these clauses by furnishing cocaine to others and taking extraordinary amounts of it himself. Those activities interfered with Sheen's ability to perform the contract, Warner argued. Sheen responded that Warner had acquiesced in his hazardous behavior the previous season, as they had renewed the contract while drug charges were pending against him. Sheen thus asserted that Warner had waived its right to insist on these clauses addressing his personal behavior.

In legal terms, "waiver" is the voluntary relinquishment of a known right. It can be effective absent reliance or consideration and is usually irrevocable. (For discussion of waiver in this book, consult *Lloyd v. Murphy* and the majority and dissenting opinions in *Wisconsin Knife Works v. National Metal Crafters*, all in Chapter Five.)

For a waiver to be effective, though, the right in question cannot be the material part of an exchange. Otherwise, the whole idea of consideration would be worthless—people could formally agree to an exchange but then waive (or be forced to waive) their rights. So material promises made in exchanges cannot simply be waived but require a bargained-for-exchange to modify them. (The concept of good faith may enter into the analysis as well.) Other terms, like conditions or minor promises, can be waived.

At issue in the Sheen–Warner dispute, then, was whether the personal behavior provisions were material promises Sheen made to Warner, which could not be waived without consideration, or conditions of Warner's duties, which could be waived without consideration. Naturally, Sheen characterized them as conditions that Warner had waived; Warner claimed that they were vital parts of the agreed exchange that could not be relinquished without getting something in return, which it had not received.

This aspect of the Sheen dispute was a modern replay of a famous older case involving an "abstinence clause" in a book contract. Professor William Clark, then affiliated with Washington & Lee University, was a prolific writer of law books. He signed a multi-year contract with West Publishing, a powerhouse publisher of law books then and now. The contract stated that Clark would abstain from drinking alcohol during its term and that payment was $2 per page plus $4 per page if Clark abstained. Clark imbibed while writing but yet wanted his additional $4/page anyway. Clark asserted that West knew he was drinking but that West acquiesced.

CLARK V. WEST
86 N.E. 1 (N.Y. 1908)

WERNER, J.

The contract before us, stripped of all superfluous verbiage, binds the plaintiff to total abstention from the use of intoxicating liquors during the continuance of the work which he was employed to do. The stipulations relating to the plaintiff's compensation provide that if he does not observe this condition he is to be paid at the rate of $2 per page, and if he does comply therewith he is to receive $6 per page. The plaintiff has written one book under the contract, known as 'Clark & Marshall on Corporations,' which has been accepted, published, and copies sold in large numbers by the defendant. The plaintiff admits that while he was at work on this book he did not entirely abstain from the use of intoxicating liquors. He has been paid only $2 per page for the work he has done. He claims that, despite his breach of this condition, he is entitled to the full compensation of $6 per page, because the defendant, with full knowledge of plaintiff's nonobservance of this stipulation as to total abstinence, has waived the breach thereof and cannot now insist upon strict performance in this regard. This plea of waiver presents the underlying question which determines the answers to the questions certified.

Briefly stated, the defendant's position is that the stipulation as to plaintiff's total abstinence is the consideration for the payment of the difference between $2 and $6 per page, and therefore could not be waived except by a new agreement to that effect based upon a good consideration; that the so-called waiver alleged by the plaintiff is not a waiver, but a modification of the contract in respect of its consideration. The plaintiff, on the other hand, argues that the stipulation for his total abstinence was merely a condition precedent, intended to work a forfeiture of the additional compensation in case of a breach, and that it could be waived without any formal agreement to that effect based upon a new consideration.

The subject-matter of the contract was the writing of books by the plaintiff for the defendant. The duration of the contract was the time necessary to complete them all. The work was to be done to the satisfaction of the defendant, and the plaintiff was not to write any other books except those covered by the contract, unless requested so to do by the defendant, in which latter event he was to be paid for that particular work by the year. The compensation for the work specified in the contract was to be $6 per page, unless the plaintiff failed to totally abstain from the use of intoxicating liquors during the continuance of the contract, in which event he was to receive only $2 per page.

That is the obvious import of the contract construed in the light of the purpose for which it was made, and in accordance with the ordinary meaning of plain language. It is not a contract to write books in order that the plaintiff shall keep sober, but a contract containing a stipulation that he shall keep sober so that he may write satisfactory books. When we view the contract from this standpoint, it will readily be perceived that the particular stipulation is not the consideration for the contract, but simply one of its conditions which fits in with those relating to time and method of delivery of manuscript, revision of proof, citation of cases, assignment of copyrights, keeping track of new cases and citations for new editions, and other details which might be waived by the defendant, if he saw fit to do so.

This is made clear, it seems to us, by the provision that, 'in consideration of the above promises,' the defendant agrees to pay the plaintiff $2 per page on each book prepared by him, and if he 'abstains from the use of intoxicating liquor and otherwise fulfills his agreements as hereinbefore set forth, he shall be paid an additional $4 per page in manner hereinbefore stated.' The compensation of $2 per page, not to exceed $250 per month, was an advance or partial payment of the whole price of $6 per page, and the payment of the two-thirds, which was to be withheld pending the performance of the contract, was simply made contingent upon the plaintiff's total abstention from the use of intoxicants during the life of the contract.

It is possible, of course, by segregating that clause of the contract from the context, to give it a wider meaning and a different aspect than it has when read in conjunction with other stipulations; but this is also true of other paragraphs of the contract. The paragraph, for instance, which provides that after the publication of any of the books written by the plaintiff he is to receive an amount equal to one-sixth of the net receipts from the combined sales of all the books which shall have been published by the defendant under the contract, less any and all payments previously made, 'until the amount of $6 per page of each book shall have been paid, after which the first party (plaintiff) shall have no right, title, or interest in said books or the receipts from the sales thereof.'

That section of the contract, standing alone, would indicate that the plaintiff was to be entitled, in any event, to the $6 per page to be paid out of the net receipts of the copies of the book sold. The contract, read as a whole, however, shows that it is modified by the preceding provisions, making the compensation in excess of the $2 per page dependent upon the plaintiff's total abstinence, and upon the performance by him of the other conditions of the contract. It is obvious that the parties thought that the plaintiff's normal work was worth $6 per page. That was the sum to be paid for the work done by the plaintiff, and not for total abstinence. If the plaintiff did not keep to the condition as to total abstinence, he was to lose part of that sum.

Precisely the same situation would have risen if the plaintiff had disregarded any of the other essential conditions of the contract. The fact that the particular stipulation was emphasized did not change its character. It was still a condition which the defendant could have insisted upon, as he has apparently done in regard to some others, and one which he could waive just as he might have waived those relating to the amount of the advance payments, or the number of pages to be written each month. A breach of any of the substantial conditions of the contract would have entailed a loss or forfeiture similar to that consequent upon a breach of the one relating to total abstinence, in case of the defendant's insistence upon his right to take advantage of them.

This, we think, is the fair interpretation of the contract, and it follows that the stipulation as to the plaintiff's total abstinence was nothing more nor less than a condition precedent. If that conclusion is well founded, there can be no escape from the corollary that this condition could be waived; and, if it was waived, the defendant is clearly not in a position to insist upon the forfeiture which his waiver was intended to annihilate. The forfeiture must stand or fall with the condition. If the latter was waived, the former is no longer a part of the contract. Defendant still has the right to counterclaim for any damages which he may have sustained in consequence of the plaintiff's breach, but he cannot insist upon strict performance. Dunn v. Steubing, 120 N. Y. 232, 24 N. E. 315; Parke v. Franco-American Trading Co., 120 N. Y. 51, 56, 23 N. E. 996; Brady v. Cassidy, 145 N. Y. 171, 39 N. E. 814.

This whole discussion is predicated, of course, upon the theory of an express waiver. We assume that no waiver could be implied from the defendant's mere acceptance of the books and his payment of the sum of $2 per page without objection. It was the defendant's duty to pay that amount in any event after acceptance of the work. The plaintiff must stand upon his allegation of an express waiver, and if he fails to establish that he cannot maintain his action.

The theory upon which the defendant's attitude seems to be based is that, even if he has represented to the plaintiff that he would not insist upon the condition that the latter should observe total abstinence from intoxicants, he can still refuse to pay the full contract price for his work. The inequity of this position becomes apparent when we consider that this contract was to run for a period of years, during a large portion of which the plaintiff was to be entitled only to the advance payment of $2 per page; the balance being contingent, among other things, upon publication of the books and returns from sales.

Upon this theory the defendant might have waived the condition while the first book was in process of production, and yet, when the whole work was completed, he would still be in a position to insist upon the forfeiture because there had not been strict performance. Such a situation is possible in a case where the subject of the waiver is the very consideration of a contract . . . but not where the waiver relates to something that can be waived. In the case at bar, as we have seen, the waiver is not of the consideration or subject-matter, but of an incident to the method of performance. The consideration remains the same. The defendant has had the work he bargained for, and it is alleged that he has waived one of the conditions as to the manner in which it was to have been done. He might have insisted upon literal performance, and then he could have stood upon the letter of his contract. If, however, he has waived that incidental condition, he has created a situation to which the doctrine of waiver very precisely applies.

The cases which present the most familiar phases of the doctrine of waiver are those which have arisen out of litigation over insurance policies where the defendants have claimed a forfeiture because of the breach of some condition in the contract, but it is a doctrine of general application which is confined to no particular class of cases. A 'waiver' has been defined to be the intentional relinquishment of a known right. It is voluntary and implies an election to dispense with something of value, or forego some advantage which the party waiving it might at its option have demanded or insisted upon . . . and this definition is supported by many cases in this and other states.

In the recent case of Draper v. Oswego Co. Fire R. Ass'n, 190 N. Y. 12, 16, 82 N. E. 755, Chief Judge Cullen, in speaking for the court upon this subject, said: 'While that doctrine and the doctrine of equitable estoppel are often confused in insurance litigation, there is a clear distinction between the two. A 'waiver' is the voluntary abandonment or relinquishment by a party of some right or advantage. As said by my Brother Vann in the Kiernan Case, 150 N. Y. 190, 44 N. E. 698: 'The law of waiver seems to be a technical doctrine, introduced and applied by the court for the purpose of defeating forfeitures.'

While the principle may not be easily classified, it is well established that, if the words and acts of the insurer reasonably justify the conclusion that with full knowledge of all the facts it intended to abandon or not to insist upon the particular defense afterwards relied upon, a verdict or finding to that effect establishes a waiver, which, if it once exists, can never

814 CONDITIONS CH. 10

be revoked.' The doctrine of equitable estoppel, or estoppel in pais, is that a party may be precluded by his acts and conduct from asserting a right to the detriment of another party who, entitled to rely on such conduct, has acted upon it. * * * As already said, the doctrine of waiver is to relieve against forfeiture. It requires no consideration for a waiver, nor any prejudice or injury to the other party.' To the same effect, see Knarston v. Manhattan Life Ins. Co., 140 Cal. 57, 73 Pac. 740.

It remains to be determined whether the plaintiff has alleged facts which, if proven, will be sufficient to establish his claim of an express waiver by the defendant of the plaintiff's breach of the condition to observe total abstinence. In the 12th paragraph of the complaint, the plaintiff alleges facts and circumstances which we think, if established, would prove defendant's waiver of plaintiff's performance of that contract stipulation. These facts and circumstances are that, long before the plaintiff had completed the manuscript of the first book undertaken under the contract, the defendant had full knowledge of the plaintiff's nonobservance of that stipulation, and that with such knowledge he not only accepted the completed manuscript without objection, but 'repeatedly avowed and represented to the plaintiff that he was entitled to and would receive said royalty payments (i.e., the additional $4 per page), and plaintiff believed and relied upon such representations, * * * and at all times during the writing of said treatise on Corporations, and after as well as before publication thereof as aforesaid, it was mutually understood, agreed, and intended by the parties hereto that, notwithstanding plaintiff's said use of intoxicating liquors, he was nevertheless entitled to receive and would receive said royalty as the same accrued under said contract.'

[W]e think it cannot be doubted that the allegations contained in the twelfth paragraph of the complaint, if proved upon the trial, would be sufficient to establish an express waiver by the defendant of the stipulation in regard to plaintiff's total abstinence. [Reversed.]

NOTES AND QUESTIONS

1. The court faced an interpretive question: was the clause a promise, which could not be waived, or a condition, which could? Which was it and why?

2. If West had a concern about Clark's sobriety, was this contract provision the best way to achieve its objectives? What were some potential alternatives, both then and today?

3. Apply *Clark v. West* to the Sheen dispute. Note that the Sheen dispute ultimately went to arbitration, per another clause in their contract and application of *AT&T v. Concepcion,* 563 U.S. 333 (2011). *See Sheen v. Lorre,* 2011 WL 2349074 (Superior Ct. Cal. June 15, 2011) (ordering case to arbitration). Details and results of the arbitration are confidential, so we are left to speculate about how the Sheen case would be decided in a court.

D. SUBSTANTIAL PERFORMANCE

Actress Sandra Bullock, who starred in hit films such as *Miss Congeniality* and *The Blind Side*, hired a developer, DCI, to build her a fashionable lake house in Austin, Texas. Unfortunately, costs on the project rapidly escalated. Bullock complained about the costs and defects in workmanship, including a leaky roof and windows, faulty wiring, defective masonry, and other problems. DCI blamed Bullock for ordering too many changes to the plans. In May 2000, after paying over $6.5 million, Bullock asked the builders to stop construction. DCI sued. The jury eventually found in Bullock's favor, but determining the damages became a difficult question; the parties eventually settled for an undisclosed amount.

The contractual dispute over Sandra Bullock's lake house highlights an important issue in contract law. What is the proper measure of damages if there is a deviation from the exact terms spelled out in the contract? Should the breaching party have to pay for the cost of completion of the project as it was exactly spelled out in the contract or instead for the resulting diminution in market value that is due to the deviation? But, first, in dealing with a contract for services, we must ask the question of whether the breach itself is material, or whether the contract has actually been substantially performed. Consider the following building case, a classic statement of the issue in the context of services.

JACOB & YOUNGS V. KENT
129 N.E. 889 (N.Y. 1921)

CARDOZO, J.

The plaintiff built a country residence for the defendant at a cost of upwards of $77,000, and now sues to recover a balance of $3,483.46, remaining unpaid. The work of construction ceased in June, 1914, and the defendant then began to occupy the dwelling. There was no complaint of defective performance until March, 1915. One of the specifications for the plumbing work provides that "All wrought-iron pipe must be well galvanized, lap welded pipe of the grade known as 'standard pipe' of Reading manufacture."

The defendant learned in March, 1915, that some of the pipe, instead of being made in Reading, was the product of other factories. The plaintiff was accordingly directed by the architect to do the work anew. The plumbing was then encased within the walls except in a few places where it had to be exposed. Obedience to the order meant more than the substitution of other pipe. It meant the demolition at great expense of substantial parts of the completed structure. The plaintiff left the work untouched, and asked for a certificate that the final payment was due. Refusal of the certificate was followed by this suit.

The evidence sustains a finding that the omission of the prescribed brand of pipe was neither fraudulent nor willful. It was the result of the oversight and inattention of the plaintiff's subcontractor. Reading pipe is distinguished from Cohoes pipe and other brands only by the name of the manufacturer stamped upon it at intervals of between six and seven feet. Even the defendant's architect, though he inspected the pipe upon arrival, failed to notice the discrepancy. The plaintiff tried to show that the brands installed, though made by other manufacturers, were the same in quality, in appearance, in market value, and in cost as the brand stated in the contract—that they were, indeed, the same thing, though manufactured in another place. The evidence was excluded, and a verdict directed for the defendant. The Appellate Division reversed, and granted a new trial.

We think the evidence, if admitted, would have supplied some basis for the inference that the defect was insignificant in its relation to the project. The courts never say that one who makes a contract fills the measure of his duty by less than full performance. They do say, however, that an omission, both trivial and innocent, will sometimes be atoned for by allowance of the resulting damage, and will not always be the breach of a condition to be followed by a forfeiture. Spence v. Ham, 163 N. Y. 220, 57 N. E. 412, Woodward v. Fuller, 80 N. Y. 312; Glacius v. Black, 67 N. Y. 563, 566; Bowen v. Kimbell, 203 Mass. 364, 370, 89 N. E. 542, 133 Am. St. Rep. 302. The distinction is akin to that between dependent and independent promises, or between promises and conditions. Anson on Contracts (Corbin's Ed.) § 367; 2 Williston on Contracts, § 842.

Some promises are so plainly independent that they can never by fair construction be conditions of one another. Rosenthal Paper Co. v. Nat. Folding Box & Paper Co., 226 N. Y. 313, 123 N. E. 766; Bogardus v. N. Y. Life Ins. Co., 101 N. Y. 328, 4 N. E. 522. Others are so plainly dependent that they must always be conditions. Others, though dependent and thus conditions when there is departure in point of substance, will be viewed as independent and collateral when the departure is insignificant. 2 Williston on Contracts, §§ 841, 842; Eastern Forge Co. v. Corbin, 182 Mass. 590, 592, 66 N. E. 419; Robinson v. Mollett, L. R., 7 Eng. & Ir. App. 802, 814; Miller v. Benjamin, 142 N. Y. 613, 37 N. E. 631. Considerations partly of justice and partly of presumable intention are to tell us whether this or that promise shall be placed in one class or in another. The simple and the uniform will call for different remedies from the multifarious and the intricate. The margin of departure within the range of normal expectation upon a sale of common chattels will vary from the margin to be expected upon a contract for the construction of a mansion or a 'skyscraper.'

There will be harshness sometimes and oppression in the implication of a condition when the thing upon which labor has been expended is incapable of surrender because united to the land, and equity and reason in the implication of a like condition when the subject-matter, if defective, is in shape to be returned. From the conclusion that promises may not be treated as dependent to the extent of their uttermost minutiae without a sacrifice of justice, the progress is a short one to the conclusion that they may not be so treated without a perversion of intention. Intention not otherwise revealed may be presumed to hold in contemplation the reasonable and probable. If something else is in view, it must not be left to implication. There will be no assumption of a purpose to visit venial faults with oppressive retribution.

Those who think more of symmetry and logic in the development of legal rules than of practical adaptation to the attainment of a just result will be troubled by a classification where the lines of division are so wavering and blurred. Something, doubtless, may be said on the score of consistency and certainty in favor of a stricter standard. The courts have balanced such considerations against those of equity and fairness, and found the latter to be the weightier. The decisions in this state commit us to the liberal view, which is making its way, nowadays, in jurisdictions slow to welcome it. Dakin & Co. v. Lee, 1916, 1 K. B. 566, 579. Where the line is to be drawn between the important and the trivial cannot be settled by a formula. 'In the nature of the case precise boundaries are impossible.' 2 Williston on Contracts, § 841.

The same omission may take on one aspect or another according to its setting. Substitution of equivalents may not have the same significance in fields of art on the one side and in those of mere utility on the other. Nowhere will change be tolerated, however, if it is so dominant or pervasive as in any real or substantial measure to frustrate the purpose of the contract. Crouch v. Gutmann, 134 N. Y. 45, 51, 31 N. E. 271, 30 Am. St. Rep. 608. There is no general license to install whatever, in the builder's judgment, may be regarded as 'just as good.' Easthampton L. & C. Co., Ltd., v. Worthington, 186 N. Y. 407, 412, 79 N. E. 323. The question is one of degree, to be answered, if there is doubt, by the triers of the facts (Crouch v. Gutmann; Woodward v. Fuller, supra), and, if the inferences are certain, by the judges of the law (Easthampton L. & C. Co., Ltd., v. Worthington, supra).

We must weigh the purpose to be served, the desire to be gratified, the excuse for deviation from the letter, the cruelty of enforced adherence. Then only can we tell whether literal fulfillment is to be implied by law as a condition. This is not to say that the parties are not free by apt and certain words to effectuate a purpose that performance of every term shall be a condition of recovery. That question is not here. This is merely to say that the law will be slow to impute the purpose, in the silence of the parties, where the significance of the default is grievously out of proportion to the oppression of the forfeiture. The willful transgressor must accept the penalty of his transgression. Schultze v. Goodstein, 180 N. Y. 248, 251, 73 N. E. 21; Desmond-Dunne Co. v. Friedman-Doscher Co., 162 N. Y. 486, 490,

Should've made express

56 N. E. 995. For him there is no occasion to mitigate the rigor of implied conditions. The transgressor whose default is unintentional and trivial may hope for mercy if he will offer atonement for his wrong. . . .

In the circumstances of this case, we think the measure of the allowance is not the cost of replace replacement, which would be great, but the difference in value, which would be either nominal or nothing. Some of the exposed sections might perhaps have been replaced at moderate expense. The defendant did not limit his demand to them, but treated the plumbing as a unit to be corrected from cellar to roof. In point of fact, the plaintiff never reached the stage at which evidence of the extent of the allowance became necessary. The trial court had excluded evidence that the defect was unsubstantial, and in view of that ruling there was no occasion for the plaintiff to go farther with an offer of proof.

We think, however, that the offer, if it had been made, would not of necessity have been defective because directed to difference in value. It is true that in most cases the cost of replacement is the measure. . . . The owner is entitled to the money which will permit him to complete, unless the cost of completion is grossly and unfairly out of proportion to the good to be attained. When that is true, the measure is the difference in value. Specifications call, let us say, for a foundation built of granite quarried in Vermont. On the completion of the building, the owner learns that through the blunder of a subcontractor part of the foundation has been built of granite of the same quality quarried in New Hampshire.

The measure of allowance is not the cost of reconstruction. 'There may be omissions of that which could not afterwards be supplied exactly as called for by the contract without taking down the building to its foundations, and at the same time the omission may not affect the value of the building for use or otherwise, except so slightly as to be hardly appreciable.' Handy v. Bliss, 204 Mass. 513, 519, 90 N. E. 864, 134 Am. St. Rep. 673. Cf. Foeller v. Heintz, 137 Wis. 169, 178, 118 N. W. 543, 24 L. R. A. (N. S.) 321; Oberlies v. Bullinger, 132 N. Y. 598, 601, 30 N. E. 999; 2 Williston on Contracts, § 805, p. 1541. The rule that gives a remedy in cases of substantial performance with compensation for defects of trivial or inappreciable importance has been developed by the courts as an instrument of justice. The measure of the allowance must be shaped to the same end.

The order should be affirmed, and judgment absolute directed in favor of the plaintiff upon the stipulation, with costs in all courts.

MCLAUGHLIN, J.

I dissent. The plaintiff did not perform its contract. Its failure to do so was either intentional or due to gross neglect which, under the uncontradicted facts, amounted to the same thing, nor did it make any proof of the cost of compliance, where compliance was possible.

Under its contract it obligated itself to use in the plumbing only pipe (between 2,000 and 2,500 feet) made by the Reading Manufacturing Company. The first pipe delivered was about 1,000 feet and the plaintiff's superintendent then called the attention of the foreman of the subcontractor, who was doing the plumbing, to the fact that the specifications annexed to the contract required all pipe used in the plumbing to be of the Reading Manufacturing Company. They then examined it for the purpose of ascertaining whether this delivery was of that manufacture and found it was.

Thereafter, as pipe was required in the progress of the work, the foreman of the subcontractor would leave word at its shop that he wanted a specified number of feet of pipe, without in any way indicating of what manufacture. Pipe would thereafter be delivered and installed in the building, without any examination whatever. Indeed, no examination, so far as appears, was made by the plaintiff, the subcontractor, defendant's architect, or any one else, of any of the pipe except the first delivery, until after the building had been completed.

Plaintiff's architect then refused to give the certificate of completion, upon which the final payment depended, because all of the pipe used in the plumbing was not of the kind called for by the contract. After such refusal, the subcontractor removed the covering or insulation from about 900 feet of pipe which was exposed in the basement, cellar, and attic, and all but 70 feet was found to have been manufactured, not by the Reading Company, but by other manufacturers, some by the Cohoes Rolling Mill Company, some by the National Steel Works, some by the South Chester Tubing Company, and some which bore no manufacturer's mark at all. The balance of the pipe had been so installed in the building that an inspection of it could not be had without demolishing, in part at least, the building itself.

I am of the opinion the trial court was right in directing a verdict for the defendant. The plaintiff agreed that all the pipe used should be of the Reading Manufacturing Company. Only about two-fifths of it, so far as appears, was of that kind. If more were used, then the burden of proving that fact was upon the plaintiff, which it could easily have done, since it knew where the pipe was obtained. The question of substantial performance of a contract of the character of the one under consideration depends in no small degree upon the good faith of the contractor. If the plaintiff had intended to, and had, complied with the terms of the contract except as to minor omissions, due to inadvertence, then he might be allowed to recover the contract price, less the amount necessary to fully compensate the defendant for damages caused by such omissions. Woodward v. Fuller, 80 N. Y. 312; Nolan v. Whitney, 88 N. Y. 648.

But that is not this case. It installed between 2,000 and 2,500 feet of pipe, of which only 1,000 feet at most complied with the contract. No explanation was given why pipe called for by the contract was not used, nor that any effort made to show what it would cost to remove the pipe of other manufacturers and install that of the Reading Manufacturing Company. The defendant had a right to contract for what he wanted. He had a right before making payment to get what the contract called for. It is no answer to this suggestion to say that the pipe put in was just as good as that made by the Reading Manufacturing Company, or that the difference in value between such pipe and the pipe made by the Reading Manufacturing Company would be either 'nominal or nothing.'

Defendant contracted for pipe made by the Reading Manufacturing Company. What his reason was for requiring this kind of pipe is of no importance. He wanted that and was entitled to it. It may have been a mere whim on his part, but even so, he had a right to this kind of pipe, regardless of whether some other kind, according to the opinion of the contractor or experts, would have been 'just as good, better, or done just as well.' He agreed to pay only upon condition that the pipe installed were made by that company and he ought not to be compelled to pay unless that condition be performed. . . .

What was said by this court in Smith v. Brady, supra, is quite applicable here:

> I suppose it will be conceded that every one has a right to build his house, his cottage or his store after such a model and in such style as shall best accord with his notions of utility or be most agreeable to his fancy. The specifications of the contract become the law between the parties until voluntarily changed. If the owner prefers a plain and simple Doric column, and has so provided in the agreement, the contractor has no right to put in its place the more costly and elegant Corinthian. If the owner, having regard to strength and durability, has contracted for walls of specified materials to be laid in a particular manner, or for a given number of joists and beams, the builder has no right to substitute his own judgment or that of others. Having departed from the agreement, if performance has not been waived by the other party, the law will not allow him to allege that he has made as good a building as the one he engaged to erect. He can demand payment only upon and according to the terms of his contract, and if the conditions on which payment is due have not been performed, then the right to demand it does not exist. To hold a different doctrine would be simply to make another contract, and would be giving to parties an encouragement to violate their engagements, which the just policy of the law does not permit.

(17 N. Y. 186, 72 Am. Dec. 422).

I am of the opinion the trial court did not err in ruling on the admission of evidence or in directing a verdict for the defendant. For the foregoing reasons I think the judgment of the Appellate Division should be reversed and the judgment of the Trial Term affirmed.

NOTES AND QUESTIONS

1.   If you own a home (or, say, have watched a home-buying program on HGTV), was the brand of pipe a significant consideration for you (or most prospective homebuyers)? Most house purchasers care about price, location, square footage, and condition of a property. Few would know the name or brand of any particular pipe used in their home, and most could probably care less, provided that the plumbing generally met a standard of quality approved of by their home inspector. This commonsense notion bears out the wisdom of Justice Cardozo's approach, which emphasizes that the builder did substantially perform and the buyer did, for the most part, receive the mansion that he had paid for.

2.   Note the dissent's forceful argument that if the buyer contracted for a certain pipe and noted it in the contract, he should receive it, thereby gaining the benefit of the bargain. Do you think that this case is correctly decided?

3.   Would it make a difference to the outcome of the case if we change the facts so that the buyer was one of the major shareholders and a member of the board of directors of the Reading Pipe Company? What if the buyer had, in fact, designed the house to be a type of "Reading Pipe Showcase" home to be viewed by prospective customers looking to install new plumbing systems in their homes?

4.   In a case that took place in the 1960s, a builder built a home on an empty lot using stock architectural drawings. The contract was for a fixed price of $27,000 (about $200,000 today) and the buyer had made progress payments of $20,000. However, there were deviations from the plan, including cracked patio tiles, the omission of a bench, and a misplaced living room wall. The question, the court asked, was whether the builder had substantially performed, and the court said yes, fundamentally the buyer was to receive the promised home. Accordingly, the damage caused by the deviations could be compensated for in money, but the deviations did not excuse the buyer from his end of the deal. *See Plante v. Jacobs*, 103 N.W.2d 296 (Wisconsin 1960).

5.   Cardozo wrote that "The willful transgressor must accept the penalty of his transgression." What do you suppose he meant?

PROBLEM: KROJB

Krojb, the global singing sensation from Nuuk, Greenland, is an appointed United Nations Goodwill Ambassador for the promotion of environmental awareness. As such, he takes care to ensure that his carbon footprint is minimized in everything he does.

This concern extended to the written contract he had entered into with Xerxes Corporation ("Xerxes") to build him a house for $2.3 million in Los Angeles, which he felt he needed given the increasing amount of time he was spending in the United States. Wanting to ensure that the house would be environmentally sound, Krojb specified in the contract an extensive list of materials that would be used for its construction, including that "all wall insulation material must be of Insula manufacture." The contract does not define the term "Insula."

It turned out that Insula came in two varieties: Insula Green, which was manufactured from recycled materials, and Insula Black, which was cheaper and more effective as insulation, but whose manufacture generated a fair amount of greenhouse gases. Assuming that the contract referred to the latter, Xerxes had used Insula Black in constructing the house. Unfortunately, Krojb only realized this was the case after the house was completed. Incensed, Krojb brings an action for breach of contract against Xerxes.

1.   Did Xerxes breach its contract?

2.   For purposes of this next question, assume that the court determined that Xerxes breached its contract. Assuming further that it will cost $500,000 to replace Insula Black with Insula Green, what measure of damages might Krojb seek and the court award?

———————

Note that the damages awarded in *Jacob & Youngs v. Kent* are for diminution in market value, i.e. the difference between a house with Reading pipe and the pipe that was used. The difference in market value, the court noted, was negligible or next to zero. Had the court instead decided to award the cost of completion, that would have been an extremely expensive remedy. In order to replace the pipe, the already-completed walls would have had to have been torn down, the pipes changed out, and then the plaster redone. Such a remedy might in fact be seen as economically wasteful.

Not only was this an issue in the previous case, the question of the correct measure of damages also was at the forefront of the Sandra Bullock lake house dispute. The issue was similar: What is the proper measure of damages if there is a deviation from the exact terms that are spelled out in the contract? Should the breaching party have to pay for the cost of completion of the project as it was exactly spelled out in the contract or instead for the resulting diminution in market value that is due to the deviation? Here, the difficulty of determining damages may have pushed the parties toward settlement.

RESTATEMENT (SECOND) OF CONTRACTS, SECTION 348

§ 348. *Alternatives to Loss in Value of Performance.*

(2) If a breach results in defective or unfinished construction and the loss in value to the injured party is not proved with sufficient certainty, he may recover damages based on (a) the diminution in the market price of the property caused by the breach, or (b) the reasonable cost of completing performance or of remedying the defects if that cost is not clearly disproportionate to the probable loss of value to him.

GROVES V. JOHN WUNDER CO.
286 N.W. 235 (Minn. 1939)

STONE, J.

Action for breach of contract. Plaintiff got judgment for a little over $15,000. Sorely disappointed by that sum, he appeals.

In August, 1927, S. J. Groves & Sons Company, a corporation (hereinafter mentioned simply as Groves), owned a tract of 24 acres of Minneapolis suburban real estate. It was served or easily could be reached by railroad trackage. It is zoned as heavy industrial property. But for lack of development of the neighborhood its principal value thus far may have been in the deposit of sand and gravel which it carried. The Groves company had a plant on the premises for excavating and screening the gravel. Nearby defendant owned and was operating a similar plant.

In August, 1927, Groves and defendant made the involved contract. For the most part it was a lease from Groves, as lessor, to defendant, as lessee; its term seven years. Defendant agreed to remove the sand and gravel and to leave the property 'at a uniform grade, substantially the same as the grade now existing at the roadway * * * on said premises, and that in stripping the overburden * * * it will use said overburden for the purpose of maintaining and establishing said grade.'

Under the contract defendant got the Groves screening plant. The transfer thereof and the right to remove the sand and gravel made the consideration moving from Groves to defendant, except that defendant incidentally got rid of Groves as a competitor. On defendant's part it paid Groves $105,000. So that from the outset, on Groves' part the contract was executed except for defendant's right to continue using the property for the stated term. (Defendant had a right to renewal which it did not exercise.)

Defendant breached the contract deliberately. It removed from the premises only 'the richest and best of the gravel' and wholly failed, according to the findings, 'to perform and comply with the terms, conditions, and provisions of said lease * * * with respect to the condition in which the surface of the demised premises was required to be left.'

Defendant surrendered the premises, not substantially at the grade required by the contract 'nor at any uniform grade.' Instead, the ground was 'broken, rugged, and uneven.' Plaintiff sues as assignee and successor in right of Groves.

As the contract was construed below, the finding is that to complete its performance 288,495 cubic yards of overburden would need to be excavated, taken from the premises, and deposited elsewhere. The reasonable cost of doing that was found to be upwards of $60,000. But, if defendant had left the premises at the uniform grade required by the lease, the reasonable value of the property on the determinative date would have been only $12,160. The judgment was for that sum, including interest, thereby nullifying plaintiff's claim that cost of completing the contract rather than difference in value of the land was the measure of damages. The gauge of damage adopted by the decision was the difference between the market value of plaintiff's land in the condition it was when the contract was made and what it would have been if defendant had performed. The one question for us arises upon plaintiff's assertion that he was entitled, not to that difference in value, but to the reasonable cost to him of doing the work called for by the contract which defendant left undone.

1. Defendant's breach of contract was wilful. There was nothing of good faith about it. Hence, that the decision below handsomely rewards bad faith and deliberate breach of contract is obvious. That is not allowable. Here the rule is well settled, and has been since Elliott v. Caldwell, 43 Minn. 357, 45 N.W. 845, 9 L.R.A. 52, that, where the contractor wilfully and fraudulently varies from the terms of a construction contract, he cannot sue thereon and have the benefit of the equitable doctrine of substantial performance. That is the rule generally. See Annotation, 'Wilful or intentional variation by contractor from terms of contract in regard to material or work as affecting measure of damages,' 6 A.L.R. 137.

Jacob & Youngs, Inc. v. Kent, 230 N.Y. 239, 243, 244, 129 N.E. 889, 891, 23 A.L.R. 1429, is typical. It was a case of substantial performance of a building contract. (This case is distinctly the opposite.) Mr. Justice Cardozo, in the course of his opinion, stressed the distinguishing features. 'Nowhere,' he said, 'will change be tolerated, however, if it is so dominant or pervasive as in any real or substantial measure to frustrate the purpose of the contract.' Again, 'the willful transgressor must accept the penalty of his transgression.'

2. In reckoning damages for breach of a building or construction contract, the law aims to give the disappointed promisee, so far as money will do it, what he was promised. 9 Am.Jur. Building and Construction Contracts, § 152. It is so ruled by a long line of decisions in this state, beginning with Carli v. Seymour, Sabin & Co., 26 Minn. 276, 3 N.W. 348,

where the contract was for building a road. There was a breach. Plaintiff was held entitled to recover what it would cost to complete the grading as contemplated by the contract. For our other similar cases, see 2 Dunnell, Minn. Dig. (2 ed. & Supp.) §§ 2561, 2565.

Never before, so far as our decisions show, has it even been suggested that lack of value in the land furnished to the contractor who had bound himself to improve it any escape from the ordinary consequences of a breach of the contract. . . .

Even in case of substantial performance in good faith, the resulting defects being remediable, it is error to instruct that the measure of damage is 'the difference in value between the house as it was and as it would have been if constructed according to contract.' The 'correct doctrine' is that the cost of remedying the defect is the 'proper' measure of damages. Snider v. Peters Home Building Co., 139 Minn. 413, 414, 416, 167 N.W. 108.

Value of the land (as distinguished from the value of the intended product of the contract, which ordinarily will be equivalent to its reasonable cost) is no proper part of any measure of damages for wilful breach of a building contract. The reason is plain. . . .

The owner's right to improve his property is not trammeled by its small value. It is his right to erect thereon structures which will reduce its value. If that be the result, it can be of no aid to any contractor who declines performance. As said long ago in Chamberlain v. Parker, 45 N.Y. 569, 572: 'A man may do what he will with his own, * * * and if he chooses to erect a monument to his caprice or folly on his premises, and employs and pays another to do it, it does not lie with a defendant who has been so employed and paid for building it, to say that his own performance would not be beneficial to the plaintiff.' To the same effect is Restatement, Contracts, § 346, p. 576, Illustrations of Subsection (1), par. 4. . . .

To diminish damages recoverable against him in proportion as there is presently small value in the land would favor the faithless contractor. It would also ignore and so defeat plaintiff's right to contract and build for the future. To justify such a course would require more of the prophetic vision than judges possess. This factor is important when the subject matter is trackage property in the margin of such an area of population and industry as that of the Twin Cities. . . .

It is suggested that because of little or no value in his land the owner may be unconscionably enriched by such a reckoning. The answer is that there can be no unconscionable enrichment, no advantage upon which the law will frown, when the result is but to give one party to a contract only what the other has promised; particularly where, as here, the delinquent has had full payment for the promised performance.

3.   It is said by the Restatement, Contracts, § 346, comment b: 'Sometimes defects in a completed structure cannot be physically remedied without tearing down and rebuilding, at a cost that would be imprudent and unreasonable. The law does not require damages to be measured by a method requiring such economic waste. If no such waste is involved, the cost of remedying the defect is the amount awarded as compensation for failure to render the promised performance.'

The 'economic waste' declaimed against by the decisions applying that rule has nothing to do with the value in money of the real estate, or even with the product of the contract. The waste avoided is only that which would come from wrecking a physical structure, completed, or nearly so, under the contract. The cases applying that rule go no further. Illustrative are Buchholz v. Rosenberg, 163 Wis. 312, 156 N.W. 946; Burmeister v. Wolfgram, 175 Wis. 506, 185 N.W. 517. Absent such waste, as it is in this case, the rule of the Restatement, Contracts, § 346, is that 'the cost of remedying the defect is the amount awarded as compensation for failure to render the promised performance.' That means that defendants here are liable to plaintiff for the reasonable cost of doing what defendants promised to do and have wilfully declined to do. . . .

The judgment must be reversed with a new trial to follow.

OLSON, J. (dissenting).

. . . We have here then a situation where, concededly, if the contract had been performed, plaintiff would have had property worth, in round numbers, no more than $12,000. If he is to be awarded damages in an amount exceeding $60,000 he will be receiving at least 500 per cent more than his property, properly leveled to grade by actual performance, was intrinsically worth when the breach occurred. To so conclude is to give him something far beyond what the parties had in mind or contracted for.

There is no showing made, nor any finding suggested, that this property was unique, specially desirable for a particular or personal use, or of special value as to location or future use different from that of other property surrounding it. Under the circumstances here appearing, it seems clear that what the parties contracted for was to put the property in shape for general sale. And the lease contemplates just that, for by the terms thereof defendant agreed 'from time to time, as the sand and gravel are removed from the various lots * * * leased, it will surrender said lots to the lessor' if of no further use to defendant 'in connection with the purposes for which this lease is made.'

The theory upon which plaintiff relies for application of the cost of performance rule must have for its basis cases where the property or the improvement to be made is unique or personal instead of being of the kind ordinarily governed by market values. His action is one at law for damages, not for specific performance. As there was no affirmative showing of any peculiar fitness of this property to a unique or personal use, the rule to be applied is, I think, the one applied by the court. The cases bearing directly upon this phase so hold. Briefly, the rule here applicable is this: Damages recoverable for breach of a contract to construct is the difference between the market value of the property in the condition it was when delivered to and received by plaintiff and what its market value would have been if defendant had fully complied with its terms . . .

The principle for which I contend is not novel in construction contract cases. It is well stated in McCormick, Damages, § 168, pp. 648, 649, as follows: 'In whatever way the issue arises, the generally approved standards for measuring the owner's loss from defects in the work are two: First, in cases where the defect is one that can be repaired or cured without undue expense, so as to make the building conform to the agreed plan, then the owner recovers such amount as he has reasonably expended, or will reasonably have to spend, to remedy the defect. Second, if, on the other hand, the defect in material or construction is one that cannot be remedied without an expenditure for reconstruction disproportionate to the end to be attained, or without endangering unduly other parts of the building, then the damages will be measured not by the cost of remedying the defect, but by the difference between the value of the building as it is and what it would have been worth if it had been built in conformity with the contract.'

And the same thought was expressed by Mr. Justice Cardozo in Jacob & Youngs, Inc. v. Kent, 230 N.Y. 239, 244, 129 N.E. 889, 891, 23 A.L.R. 1429, 1433, thus: 'The owner is entitled to the money which will permit him to complete, unless the cost of completion is grossly and unfairly out of proportion to the good to be attained. When that is true, the measure is the difference in value.' . . .

PEEVYHOUSE v. GARLAND COAL & MINING COMPANY

382 P.2d 109 (Okla. 1963)

JACKSON, J.

In the trial court, plaintiffs Willie and Lucille Peevyhouse sued the defendant, Garland Coal and Mining Company, for damages for breach of contract. Judgment was for plaintiffs in an amount considerably less than was sued for. Plaintiffs appeal and defendant cross-appeals.

In the briefs on appeal, the parties present their argument and contentions under several propositions; however, they all stem from the basic question of whether the trial court properly instructed the jury on the measure of damages.

Briefly stated, the facts are as follows: plaintiffs owned a farm containing coal deposits, and in November, 1954, leased the premises to defendant for a period of five years for coal mining purposes. A 'stripmining' operation was contemplated in which the coal would be taken from pits on the surface of the ground, instead of from underground mine shafts. In addition to the usual covenants found in a coal mining lease, defendant specifically agreed to perform certain restorative and remedial work at the end of the lease period. It is unnecessary to set out the details of the work to be done, other than to say that it would involve the moving of many thousands of cubic yards of dirt, at a cost estimated by expert witnesses at about $29,000.00. However, plaintiffs sued for only $25,000.00.

During the trial, it was stipulated that all covenants and agreements in the lease contract had been fully carried out by both parties, except the remedial work mentioned above; defendant conceded that this work had not been done.

Plaintiffs introduced expert testimony as to the amount and nature of the work to be done, and its estimated cost. Over plaintiffs' objections, defendant thereafter introduced expert testimony as to the 'diminution in value' of plaintiffs' farm resulting from the failure of defendant to render performance as agreed in the contract-that is, the difference between the present value of the farm, and what its value would have been if defendant had done what it agreed to do.

At the conclusion of the trial, the court instructed the jury that it must return a verdict for plaintiffs, and left the amount of damages for jury determination. On the measure of damages, the court instructed the jury that it might consider the cost of performance of the work defendant agreed to do, 'together with all of the evidence offered on behalf of either party'.

It thus appears that the jury was at liberty to consider the 'diminution in value' of plaintiffs' farm as well as the cost of 'repair work' in determining the amount of damages.

It returned a verdict for plaintiffs for $5000.00—only a fraction of the 'cost of performance', *but more than the total value of the farm even after the remedial work is done.*

On appeal, the issue is sharply drawn. Plaintiffs contend that the true measure of damages in this case is what it will cost plaintiffs to obtain performance of the work that was not done because of defendant's default. Defendant argues that the measure of damages is the cost of performance 'limited, however, to the total difference in the market value before and after the work was performed'. . .

Plaintiffs rely on Groves v. John Wunder Co., 205 Minn. 163, 286 N.W. 235, 123 A.L.R. 502. In that case, the Minnesota court, in a substantially similar situation, adopted the 'cost of performance' rule as-opposed to the 'value' rule. The result was to authorize a jury to give plaintiff damages in the amount of $60,000, where the real estate concerned would have been worth only $12,160, even if the work contracted for had been done.

It may be observed that Groves v. John Wunder Co., supra, is the only case which has come to our attention in which the cost of performance rule has been followed under circumstances where the cost of performance greatly exceeded the diminution in value resulting from the breach of contract. Incidentally, it appears that this case was decided by a plurality rather than a majority of the members of the court. . .

The explanation may be found in the fact that the situations presented are artificial ones. It is highly unlikely that the ordinary property owner would agree to pay $29,000 (or its equivalent) for the construction of 'improvements' upon his property that would increase its value only about ($300) three hundred dollars. The result is that we are called upon to apply principles of law theoretically based upon reason and reality to a situation which is basically unreasonable and unrealistic.

In Groves v. John Wunder Co., supra, in arriving at its conclusions, the Minnesota court apparently considered the contract involved to be analogous to a building and construction contract, and cited authority for the proposition that the cost of performance or completion of the building as contracted is ordinarily the measure of damages in actions for damages for the breach of such a contract.

In an annotation following the Minnesota case beginning at 123 A.L.R. 515, the annotator places the three cases relied on by defendant (Sandy Valley, Bigham and Sweeney) under the classification of cases involving 'grading and excavation contracts'.

We do not think either analogy is strictly applicable to the case now before us. The primary purpose of the lease contract between plaintiffs and defendant was neither 'building and construction' nor 'grading and excavation'. It was merely to accomplish the economical recovery and marketing of coal from the premises, to the profit of all parties. The special provisions of the lease contract pertaining to remedial work were incidental to the main object involved.

Even in the case of contracts that are unquestionably building and construction contracts, the authorities are not in agreement as to the factors to be considered in determining whether the cost of performance rule or the value rule should be applied. The American Law Institute's Restatement of the Law, Contracts, Volume 1, Sections 346(1)(a)(i) and (ii) submits the proposition that the cost of performance is the proper measure of damages 'if this is possible and does not involve *unreasonable economic waste';* and that the diminution in value caused by the breach is the proper measure 'if construction and completion in accordance with the contract would involve *unreasonable economic waste'.* (Emphasis supplied.) In an explanatory comment immediately following the text, the Restatement makes it clear that the 'economic waste' referred to consists of the destruction of a substantially completed building or other structure. Of course no such destruction is involved in the case now before us.

On the other hand, in McCormick, Damages, Section 168, it is said with regard to building and construction contracts that ' * * * in cases where the defect is one that can be repaired or cured without *undue expense*' the cost of performance is the proper measure of damages, but where ' * * * the defect in material or construction is one that cannot be remedied without *an expenditure for reconstruction disproportionate to the end to be attained*' (emphasis supplied) the value rule should be followed. The same idea was expressed in Jacob & Youngs, Inc. v. Kent, 230 N.Y. 239, 129 N.E. 889, 23 A.L.R. 1429, as follows:

'The owner is entitled to the money which will permit him to complete, unless the cost of completion is grossly and unfairly out of proportion to the good to be attained. When that is true, the measure is the difference in value.'

It thus appears that the prime consideration in the Restatement was 'economic waste'; and that the prime consideration in McCormick, Damages, and in Jacob & Youngs, Inc. v. Kent, supra, was the relationship between the expense involved and the 'end to be attained'-in other words, the 'relative economic benefit'.

. . . We therefore hold that where, in a coal mining lease, lessee agrees to perform certain remedial work on the premises concerned at the end of the lease period, and thereafter the contract is fully performed by both parties except that the remedial work is not done, the measure of damages in an action by lessor against lessee for damages for breach of contract is ordinarily the reasonable cost of performance of the work; however, where the contract provision breached was merely incidental to the main purpose in view, and where the economic benefit which would result to lessor by full performance of the work is grossly disproportionate to the cost of performance, the damages which lessor may recover are limited to the diminution in value resulting to the premises because of the non-performance.

. . . Under the most liberal view of the evidence herein, the diminution in value resulting to the premises because of non-performance of the remedial work was $300.00. After a careful search of the record, we have found no evidence of a higher figure, and plaintiffs do not argue in their briefs that a greater diminution in value was sustained. It thus appears that the judgment was clearly excessive, and that the amount for which judgment should have been rendered is definitely and satisfactorily shown by the record. . . . We are of the opinion that the judgment of the trial court for plaintiffs should be, and it is hereby, modified and reduced to the sum of $300.00, and as so modified it is affirmed.

IRWIN, J. (dissenting).

By the specific provisions in the coal mining lease under consideration, the defendant agreed as follows:

> 7b Lessee agrees to make fills in the pits dug on said premises on the property line in such manner that fences can be placed thereon and access had to opposite sides of the pits.

> 7c Lessee agrees to smooth off the top of the spoil banks on the above premises.

> 7d Lessee agrees to leave the creek crossing the above premises in such a condition that it will not interfere with the crossings to be made in pits as set out in 7b.

> 7f Lessee further agrees to leave no shale or dirt on the high wall of said pits.

Following the expiration of the lease, plaintiffs made demand upon defendant that it carry out the provisions of the contract and to perform those covenants contained therein.

Defendant admits that it failed to perform its obligations that it agreed and contracted to perform under the lease contract and there is nothing in the record which indicates that defendant could not perform its obligations. Therefore, in my opinion defendant's breach of the contract was wilful and not in good faith.

Although the contract speaks for itself, there were several negotiations between the plaintiffs and defendant before the contract was executed. Defendant admitted in the trial of the action, that plaintiffs insisted that the above provisions be included in the contract and that they would not agree to the coal mining lease unless the above provisions were included.

In consideration for the lease contract, plaintiffs were to receive a certain amount as royalty for the coal produced and marketed and in addition thereto their land was to be restored as provided in the contract. . . Therefore, defendant had knowledge, when it prevailed upon the plaintiffs to execute the lease, that the cost of performance might be disproportionate to the value or benefits received by plaintiff for the performance. . . Defendant has received its benefits under the contract and now urges, in substance, that plaintiffs' measure of damages for its failure to perform should be the economic value of performance to the plaintiffs and not the cost of performance.

In my judgment, we should follow the case of Groves v. John Wunder Company, 205 Minn. 163, 286 N.W. 235, 123 A.L.R. 502, which defendant agrees 'that the fact situation is apparently similar to the one in the case at bar[.]'

I therefore respectfully dissent to the opinion promulgated by a majority of my associates.

NOTES AND QUESTIONS

1.   The *Groves* and *Peevyhouse* holdings conflict. Both cite *Jacob & Youngs v. Kent* for support. Which outcome would Justice Cardozo agree with? Which case is the better-reasoned decision?

2.   Professor Judith Maute of the University of Oklahoma has written several articles about the *Peevyhouse* case and filmed Willie and Lucille Peevyhouse as part of an oral history documentary. Her work reveals that the Peevyhouses cared about the land, as it had long been in their family, and only agreed to lease to the mining company on the condition that the land would be restored. Professor Maute's work reveals that there was more to the story than was reported in the case, notably differences in the quality of attorney representation each side could afford, as well as allegations of political corruption. Judith L. Maute, *Peevyhouse v. Garland Coal Co. Revisited: The Ballad of Willie and Lucille*, 89 Nw. U. L. REV. 1341 (1995).

3.   Economic efficiency arguments may make some sense in this context. However, given the modern-day concern over environmental destruction caused by strip mining (and more recent attempts at conservation and acknowledgment that we have finite natural resources), should the value of economic efficiency win the day? Does Restatement (Second) of Contracts, Section 348 (excerpted above) shed any light on this topic?

4.   Can you make an argument that both *Groves* and *Peevyhouse* were wrongly decided? In *Groves*, a business owner recovered damages for breach of contract in circumstances where it seems unlikely that the damages would be used to complete the promised performance; in *Peevyhouse*, farm owners were denied damages for breach of contract in circumstances where they may well have used the money to restore the land. If neither of these cases was decided correctly, what would be the best rule to draw from them?

5.   When there is doubt about whether an aggrieved party values a breached promise at the cost of completion and the difference in value is slight, might other contract remedies help? What about specific performance? If a court is prepared to order a breaching party to perform, might that induce both parties to reveal their true preferences? Or at the very least to induce bargaining toward dispute resolution?

EXAMPLE: THE FEDEX-KINKO'S MERGER

In many transactions, a buyer (of a home, business, etc.) will desire to include many different conditions in the contract and retain some measure of subjectivity that they have some control over. This means that if the buyer performs due diligence, and a problem arises, the buyer will have more discretion to back out of the deal. The seller, on the other hand, will prefer as few conditions as possible, and with a preference for more objective conditions, making the agreement more difficult for the buyer to escape. Use these observations, as well as what you have learned about conditions, to assist you in the following exercise.

In 2003, the private shipping company Federal Express (FedEx) wanted to acquire Kinko's, a popular chain for office services and supplies. Customers would patronize Kinko's if they needed self-serve copies, or they could request assistance for larger copying and printing jobs; they could also receive or send faxes or have documents or photos scanned into various formats. FedEx announced that it would pay $2.4 billion cash to acquire the 1,200 Kinko's locations across the country. FedEx was betting that customers would appreciate the synergy between having an office where they would be able to fax, e-mail, print, photocopy, and send documents via overnight delivery.

1.   You are a junior associate on a team of corporate attorneys representing FedEx. What items would FedEx want to include in the contract (i.e. what are important factors to making sure that the acquisition will close)? Are there any practical considerations in the merger that the other attorneys might overlook? Are there certain risks that the contract should allocate between the parties?

2.   One factor that management has stressed is the necessity of an independent audit of Kinko's books. Why might this be so important to FedEx management?

3.   Perhaps you can assist your client by drafting the language in the FedEx-Kinko's merger agreement in a certain way. How would you draft the language so that FedEx could receive the independent audit that it wants of Kinko's books and still retain the deal?

E. UCC: PERFECT TENDER RULE

While the common law doctrine of substantial performance enjoys a venerable tradition and much to commend it for a wide range of transactions from construction to personal services, the law of sales has always imposed a strict requirement of performance. Dubbed the *perfect tender rule*, any variation in the tender of performance—as to quantity, description, delivery time, or otherwise—permits the other party to reject the tender outright. While surely efficient, fair, and useful in many cases, the perfect tender rule can produce harsh effects. These led commercial actors and laws to build a variety of ameliorating devices, including permitting acceptance of deviating performances and providing the right to cure imperfect tenders. The related legal machinery under the UCC can be intricate and complex. The following cases explore some of the mechanics. For reference, relevant statutory provisions are excerpted after each case.

RAMIREZ V. AUTOSPORT

440 A.2d 1345 (N.J. 1982)

POLLOCK, J.

This case raises several issues under the Uniform Commercial Code ("the Code" and "UCC") concerning whether a buyer may reject a tender of goods with minor defects and whether a seller may cure the defects. . . . The main issue is whether plaintiffs, Mr. and Mrs. Ramirez, could reject the tender by defendant, Autosport, of a camper van with minor defects and cancel the contract for the purchase of the van.

The trial court ruled that Mr. and Mrs. Ramirez rightfully rejected the van and awarded them the fair market value of their trade-in van. The Appellate Division affirmed in a brief per curiam decision which, like the trial court opinion, was unreported. We affirm the judgment of the Appellate Division.

Following a mobile home show at the Meadowlands Sports Complex, Mr. and Mrs. Ramirez visited Autosport's showroom in Somerville. On July 20, 1978 the Ramirezes and Donald Graff, a salesman for Autosport, agreed on the sale of a new camper and the trade-in of the van owned by Mr. and Mrs. Ramirez. Autosport and the Ramirezes signed a simple contract reflecting a $14,100 purchase price for the new van with a $4,700 trade-in allowance for the Ramirez van, which Mr. and Mrs. Ramirez left with Autosport. After further allowance for taxes, title and documentary fees, the net price was $9,902. Because Autosport needed two weeks to prepare the new van, the contract provided for delivery on or about August 3, 1978.

On that date, Mr. and Mrs. Ramirez returned with their checks to Autosport to pick up the new van. Graff was not there so Mr. White, another salesman, met them. Inspection disclosed several defects in the van. The paint was scratched, both the electric and sewer hookups were missing, and the hubcaps were not installed. White advised the Ramirezes not to accept the camper because it was not ready.

Mr. and Mrs. Ramirez wanted the van for a summer vacation and called Graff several times. Each time Graff told them it was not ready for delivery. Finally, Graff called to notify them that the camper was ready. On August 14 Mr. and Mrs. Ramirez went to Autosport to accept delivery, but workers were still touching up the outside paint. Also, the camper windows were open, and the dining area cushions were soaking wet. Mr. and Mrs. Ramirez could not use the camper in that condition, but Mr. Leis, Autosport's manager, suggested that they take the van and that Autosport would replace the cushions later. Mrs. Ramirez counteroffered to accept the van if they could withhold $2,000, but Leis agreed to no more than $250, which she refused. Leis then agreed to replace the cushions and to call them when the van was ready.

On August 15, 1978 Autosport transferred title to the van to Mr. and Mrs. Ramirez, a fact unknown to them until the summer of 1979. Between August 15 and September 1, 1978 Mrs. Ramirez called Graff several times urging him to complete the preparation of the van, but Graff constantly advised her that the van was not ready. He finally informed her that they could pick it up on September 1.

When Mr. and Mrs. Ramirez went to the showroom on September 1, Graff asked them to wait. And wait they did-for one and a half hours. No one from Autosport came forward to talk with them, and the Ramirezes left in disgust.

On October 5, 1978 Mr. and Mrs. Ramirez went to Autosport with an attorney friend. Although the parties disagreed on what occurred, the general topic was whether they should proceed with the deal or Autosport should return to the Ramirezes their trade-in van. Mrs. Ramirez claimed they rejected the new van and requested the return of their trade-in. Mr. Lustig, the owner of Autosport, thought, however, that the deal could be salvaged if the parties could agree on the dollar amount of a credit for the Ramirezes. Mr. and Mrs. Ramirez never took possession of the new van and repeated their request for the return of their trade-in. Later in October, however, Autosport sold the trade-in to an innocent third party for $4,995. . . . On November 20, 1978 the Ramirezes sued Autosport seeking, among other things, rescission of the contract. Autosport counterclaimed for breach of contract.

Our initial inquiry is whether a consumer may reject defective goods that do not conform to the contract of sale. The basic issue is whether under the UCC a seller has the duty to deliver goods that conform precisely to the contract. We conclude that the seller is under such a duty to make a "perfect tender" and that a buyer has the right to reject goods that do not conform to the contract. That conclusion, however, does not resolve the entire dispute between buyer and seller. A more complete answer requires a brief statement of the history of the mutual obligations of buyers and sellers of commercial goods.

In the nineteenth century, sellers were required to deliver goods that complied exactly with the sales agreement. See Filley v. Pope, 115 U.S. 213, 220, 6 S.Ct. 19, 21, 29 L.Ed. 372, 373 (1885) (buyer not obliged to accept otherwise conforming scrap iron shipped to New Orleans from Leith, rather than Glasgow, Scotland, as required by contract); Columbian Iron Works & Dry-Dock Co. v. Douglas, 84 Md. 44, 47, 34 A. 1118, 1120–1121 (1896) (buyer who agreed to purchase steel scrap from United States cruisers not obliged to take any other kind of scrap). That rule, known as the "perfect tender" rule, remained part of the law of sales well into the twentieth century. By the 1920's the doctrine was so entrenched in the law that Judge Learned Hand declared "(t)here is no room in commercial contracts for the doctrine of substantial performance." Mitsubishi Goshi Kaisha v. J. Aron & Co., Inc., 16 F.2d 185, 186 (2 Cir. 1926).

The harshness of the rule led courts to seek to ameliorate its effect and to bring the law of sales in closer harmony with the law of contracts, which allows rescission only for material breaches. Nevertheless, a variation of the perfect tender rule appeared in the Uniform Sales Act. N.J.S.A. 46:30–75 (purchasers permitted to reject goods or rescind contracts for any breach of warranty); N.J.S.A. 46:30–18 to –21 (warranties extended to include all the seller's obligations to the goods). The chief objection to the continuation of the perfect tender rule was that buyers in a declining market would reject goods for minor nonconformities and force the loss on surprised sellers.

To the extent that a buyer can reject goods for any nonconformity, the UCC retains the perfect tender rule. . . . Section 2–601 authorizes a buyer to reject goods if they "or the tender of delivery fail in any respect to conform to the contract". 2–601. The Code, however, mitigates the harshness of the perfect tender rule and balances the interests of buyer and seller. See Restatement (Second), Contracts, § 241 comment (b) (1981). The Code achieves that result through its provisions for revocation of acceptance and cure. 2–608, 2–508.

Initially, the rights of the parties vary depending on whether the rejection occurs before or after acceptance of the goods. Before acceptance, the buyer may reject goods for any nonconformity. 2–601. Because of the seller's right to cure, however, the buyer's rejection does not necessarily discharge the contract. 2–508. Within the time set for performance in the contract, the seller's right to cure is unconditional. Some authorities recommend granting a breaching party a right to cure in all contracts, not merely those for the sale of goods. Underlying the right to cure in both kinds of contracts is the recognition that parties should be encouraged to communicate with each other and to resolve their own problems.

The rights of the parties also vary if rejection occurs after the time set for performance. After expiration of that time, the seller has a further reasonable time to cure if he believed reasonably that the goods would be acceptable with or without a money allowance. 2–508(2). The determination of what constitutes a further reasonable time depends on the surrounding circumstances, which include the change of position by and the amount of inconvenience to the buyer. Those circumstances also include the length of time needed by the seller to correct the nonconformity and his ability to salvage the goods by resale to others. Thus, the Code balances the buyer's right to reject nonconforming goods with a "second chance" for the seller to conform the goods to the contract under certain limited circumstances.

After acceptance, the Code strikes a different balance: the buyer may revoke acceptance only if the nonconformity substantially impairs the value of the goods to him. 2–608. See Herbstman v. Eastman Kodak Co., 68 N.J. 1, 9, 342 A.2d 181 (1975). This provision protects the seller from revocation for trivial defects. It also prevents the buyer from taking undue advantage of the seller by allowing goods to depreciate and then returning them because of asserted minor defects. Because this case involves rejection of goods, we need not decide whether a seller has a right to cure substantial defects that justify revocation of acceptance.

A further problem, however, is identifying the remedy available to a buyer who rejects goods with insubstantial defects that the seller fails to cure within a reasonable time. The Code provides expressly that when "the buyer rightfully rejects, then with respect to the goods involved, the buyer may cancel." 2–711. "Cancellation" occurs when either party puts an end to the contract for breach by the other. . . .

Underlying the Code provisions is the recognition of the revolutionary change in business practices in this century. The purchase of goods is no longer a simple transaction in which a buyer purchases individually-made goods from a seller in a face-to-face transaction. Our economy depends on a complex system for the manufacture, distribution, and sale of goods, a system in which manufacturers and consumers rarely meet. Faceless manufacturers mass-produce goods for unknown consumers who purchase those goods from merchants exercising little or no control over the quality of their production. In an age of assembly lines, we are accustomed to cars with scratches, television sets without knobs and other products with all kinds of defects. Buyers no longer expect a "perfect tender". If a merchant sells defective goods, the reasonable expectation of the parties is that the buyer will return those goods and that the seller will repair or replace them.

Recognizing this commercial reality, the Code permits a seller to cure imperfect tenders. Should the seller fail to cure the defects, whether substantial or not, the balance shifts again in favor of the buyer, who has the right to cancel or seek damages. 2–711. In general, economic considerations would induce sellers to cure minor defects. Assuming the seller does not cure, however, the buyer should be permitted to exercise his remedies under 2–711. . . .

The trial court found that Mr. and Mrs. Ramirez had rejected the van within a reasonable time under 2–602. The court found that on August 3, 1978 Autosport's salesman advised the Ramirezes not to accept the van and that on August 14, they rejected delivery and Autosport agreed to replace the cushions. . . . Although the trial court did not find whether Autosport cured the defects within a reasonable time, we find that Autosport did not effect a cure. Clearly the van was not ready for delivery during August, 1978 when Mr. and Mrs. Ramirez rejected it, and Autosport had the burden of proving that it had corrected the defects. Although the Ramirezes gave Autosport ample time to correct the defects, Autosport did not demonstrate that the van conformed to the contract on September 1. In fact, on that date, when Mr. and Mrs. Ramirez returned at Autosport's invitation, all they received was discourtesy. . . .

UCC SECTIONS 2–601, 602, 608, 508

§ 2–601. *Buyer's Rights on Improper Delivery.*

. . . if the goods or the tender of delivery fail in any respect to conform to the contract, the buyer may (a) reject the whole; or (b) accept the whole; or (c) accept any commercial unit or units and reject the rest.

§ 2–602. *Manner and Effect of Rightful Rejection.*

(1) Rejection of goods must be within a reasonable time after their delivery or tender. It is ineffective unless the buyer seasonably notifies the seller.

(2) . . . (a) after rejection any exercise of ownership by the buyer with respect to any commercial unit is wrongful as against the seller . . . [buyer] is under a duty after rejection to hold them with reasonable care at the seller's disposition for a time sufficient to permit the seller to remove them . . .

§ 2–608. *Revocation of Acceptance in Whole or in Part.*

(1) The buyer may revoke his acceptance of a lot or commercial unit whose non-conformity substantially impairs its value to him if he has accepted it (a) on the reasonable assumption that its non-conformity would be cured and it has not been seasonably cured; or (b) without discovery of such non-conformity if his acceptance was reasonably induced either by the difficulty of discovery before acceptance or by the seller's assurances.

(2) Revocation of acceptance must occur within a reasonable time after the buyer discovers or should have discovered the ground for it and before any substantial change in condition of the goods which is not caused by their own defects. It is not effective until the buyer notifies the seller of it.

(3) A buyer who so revokes has the same rights and duties with regard to the goods involved as if he had rejected them.

§ 2–508. *Cure by Seller of Improper Tender or Delivery; Replacement.*

(1) Where any tender or delivery by the seller is rejected because non-conforming and the time for performance has not yet expired, the seller may seasonably notify the buyer of his intention to cure and may then within the contract time make a conforming delivery.

(2) Where the buyer rejects a non-conforming tender which the seller had reasonable grounds to believe would be acceptable with or without money allowance the seller may if he seasonably notifies the buyer have a further reasonable time to substitute a conforming tender.

PLATEQ CORP. v. MACHLETT LABS, INC.
456 A.2d 786 (Conn. 1983)

PETERS, J.

In this action by a seller of specially manufactured goods to recover their purchase price from a commercial buyer, the principal issue is whether the buyer accepted the goods before it attempted to cancel the contract of sale. The [seller], Plateq Corporation of North Haven, sued the [buyer], The Machlett Laboratories, Inc., to recover damages, measured by the contract price and incidental damages, arising out of the defendant's allegedly wrongful cancellation of a written contract for the manufacture and sale of two leadcovered steel tanks . . . . The defendant denied liability and counterclaimed for damages. After a full hearing, the trial court found for the plaintiff both on its complaint and on the defendant's counterclaim. The defendant has appealed.

The trial court . . . found the following facts. On July 9, 1976, the defendant ordered from the plaintiff two leadcovered steel tanks to be constructed by the plaintiff according to specifications supplied by the defendant. The parties understood that the tanks were designed for the special purpose of testing x-ray tubes and were required to be radiation-proof within certain federal standards. Accordingly, the contract provided that the tanks would be tested for radiation leaks after their installation on the defendant's premises. The plaintiff undertook to correct, at its own cost, any deficiencies that this post-installation test might uncover. The plaintiff had not previously constructed such tanks, nor had the defendant previously designed tanks for this purpose. . . . All the goods were to be delivered to the defendant at the plaintiff's place of business.

Although the plaintiff encountered difficulties both in performing according to the contract specifications and in completing performance within the time required, the defendant did no more than call these deficiencies to the plaintiff's attention during various inspections in September and early October, 1976. By October 11, 1976, performance was belatedly but substantially completed. On that date, Albert Yannello, the defendant's engineer, noted some remaining deficiencies which the plaintiff promised to remedy by the next day, so that the goods would then be ready for delivery. Yannello gave no indication to the plaintiff that this arrangement was in any way unsatisfactory to the defendant. Not only did Yannello communicate general acquiescence in the plaintiff's proposed tender but he specifically led the plaintiff to believe that the defendant's truck would pick up the tanks . . . within a day or two. Instead of sending its truck, the defendant sent a notice of total cancellation which the plaintiff received on October 14, 1976. That notice failed to particularize the grounds upon which cancellation was based.

On this factual basis, the trial court, having concluded that the transaction was a contract for the sale of goods falling within the Uniform Commercial Code, considered whether the defendant had accepted the goods. The court determined that the defendant had accepted the tanks, primarily by signifying its willingness to take them despite their nonconformities, in accordance with § 2–606(1)(a), and secondarily by failing to make an effective rejection, in accordance with § 2–606(1)(b).

Once the tanks had been accepted, the defendant could rightfully revoke its acceptance under § 2–608 only by showing substantial impairment of their value to the defendant. In part because the defendant's conduct had foreclosed any post-installation inspection, the court concluded that such impairment had not been proved. Since the tanks were not readily resaleable on the open market, the plaintiff was entitled, upon the defendant's wrongful revocation of acceptance, to recover their contract price, minus salvage value, plus interest. §§ 2–703; 2–709(1)(b). Accordingly, the trial court awarded the plaintiff damages . . . .

[The defendant buyer] maintains that the trial court erred: (1) in invoking the "cure" section, § 2–508, when there had been no tender by the plaintiff seller; (2) in concluding, in accordance with the acceptance section, § 2–606(1), that the defendant had "signified" to the plaintiff its willingness to take the contract goods; (3) in misconstruing the defendant's statutory and contractual rights of inspection; and (4) in refusing to find that the defendant's letter of cancellation was occasioned by the plaintiff's breach. We find no error.

Upon analysis, all of the defendant's claims of error are variations upon one central theme. The defendant claims that on October 11, when its engineer Yannello conducted the last examination on the plaintiff's premises, the tanks were so incomplete and unsatisfactory that the defendant was rightfully entitled to conclude that the plaintiff would never make a conforming tender. From this scenario, the defendant argues that it was justified in cancelling the contract of sale. It denies that the seller's conduct was sufficient to warrant a finding of tender, or its own conduct sufficient to warrant a finding of acceptance.

The difficulty with this argument is that it is inconsistent with the underlying facts . . . [The trial court found that] by October 11, 1976, performance was in substantial compliance with the terms of the contract. The trial court further found that on that day the defendant was notified that the goods would be ready for tender the following day and that the defendant responded to this notification by promising to send its truck to pick up the tanks in accordance with the contract.

[T]he trial court . . . was warranted in concluding, on two independent grounds, that the defendant had accepted the goods it had ordered from the plaintiff. Under the [UCC], § 2–606(1) "[a]cceptance of goods occurs when the buyer (a) after a reasonable opportunity to inspect the goods signifies to the seller . . . that he will take . . . them in spite of their nonconformity; or (b) fails to make an effective rejection."

In concluding that the defendant had "signified" to the plaintiff its willingness to "take" the tanks despite possible remaining minor defects, the trial court necessarily found that the defendant had had a reasonable opportunity to inspect the goods. The defendant does not maintain that its engineer, or the other inspectors on previous visits, had inadequate access to the tanks, or inadequate experience to conduct a reasonable examination. It recognizes that inspection of goods when the buyer undertakes to pick up the goods is ordinarily at the seller's place of tender.

The defendant argues, however, that its contract, in providing for inspection for radiation leaks after installation of the tanks at its premises, necessarily postponed its inspection rights to that time. The trial court considered this argument and rejected it, and so do we. It was reasonable, in the context of this contract for the special manufacture of goods with which neither party had had prior experience, to limit this clause to adjustments to take place after tender and acceptance.

After acceptance, a buyer may still, in appropriate cases, revoke its acceptance, § 2–608, or recover damages for breach of warranty, § 2–714. The trial court reasonably concluded that a post-installation test was intended to safeguard these rights of the defendant as well as to afford the plaintiff a final opportunity to make needed adjustments. The court was therefore justified in concluding that there had been an acceptance within § 2–606(1)(a). A buyer may be found to have accepted goods despite their known nonconformity; and despite the absence of actual delivery to the buyer.

The trial court's alternate ground for concluding that the tanks had been accepted was the defendant's failure to make an effective rejection. Pursuant to § 2–606(1)(b), an acceptance occurs when, after a reasonable opportunity to inspect, a buyer has failed to make "an effective rejection as provided by subsection (1) of section 2–602." The latter subsection, in turn, makes a rejection "ineffective unless the buyer seasonably notifies the seller." § 2–605(1)(a) goes on to provide that a buyer is precluded from relying, as a basis for rejection, upon unparticularized defects in his notice of rejection, if the defects were such that, with seasonable notice, the seller could have cured by making a substituted, conforming tender.

The defendant does not question the trial court's determination that its telegram of cancellation failed to comply with the requirement of particularization contained in § 2–605(1). Instead, the defendant argues that the plaintiff was not entitled to an opportunity to cure, under § 2–508, because the plaintiff had never made a tender of the tanks. That argument founders, however, on the trial court's finding that the seller was ready to make a tender on the day following the last inspection by the defendant's engineer and would have done so but for its receipt of the defendant's telegram of cancellation. The trial court furthermore found that the defendant's unparticularized telegram of cancellation wrongfully interfered with the plaintiff's contractual right to cure any remaining post-installation defects. In these circumstances, the telegram of cancellation constituted both a wrongful and an ineffective rejection on the part of the defendant.

Once the conclusion is reached that the defendant accepted the tanks, its further rights of cancellation under the contract are limited by the [UCC]. After acceptance, the buyer must pay for the goods at the contract rate; § 2–607(1); and bears the burden of establishing their nonconformity. § 2–607(4); *Stelco Industries, Inc. v. Cohen,* 438 A.2d 759 (1980). After acceptance, the buyer may only avoid liability for the contract price by invoking the provision which permits revocation of acceptance. That provision, § 2–608(1), requires proof that the "nonconformity [of the goods] substantially impairs [their] value to him." On this question, which is an issue of fact, the trial court again found against the defendant. Since the defendant has provided no basis for any argument that the trial court was clearly erroneous in finding that the defendant had not met its burden of proof to show that the goods were substantially nonconforming, we can find no error in the conclusion that the defendant's cancellation constituted an unauthorized and hence wrongful revocation of acceptance.

Finally, the defendant . . . challenges the trial court's conclusion about the remedial consequences of its earlier determinations. Although the trial court might have found the plaintiff entitled to recover the contract price because of the defendant's acceptance of the goods; §§ 2–703(e) and 2–709(1)(a); the court chose instead to rely on § 2–709(1)(b), which permits a price action for contract goods that cannot, after reasonable effort, be resold at a reasonable price. Since the contract goods in this case were concededly specially manufactured for the defendant, the defendant cannot and does not contest the trial court's finding that any effort to resell them on the open market would have been unavailing. In the light of this finding, the defendant can only reiterate its argument, which we have already rejected, that the primary default was that of the plaintiff rather than that of the defendant. The trial court's conclusion to the contrary supports both its award to the plaintiff and its denial of the defendant's counterclaim.

UCC SECTIONS 2–605, 606, 607

§ 2–605. *Waiver of Buyer's Objections by Failure to Particularize.*

(1) The buyer's failure to state in connection with rejection a particular defect which is ascertainable by reasonable inspection precludes [it] from relying on the unstated defect to justify rejection or to establish breach (a) where the seller could have cured it if stated seasonably; or (b) between merchants when the seller has after rejection made a request in writing for a full and final written statement of all defects on which the buyer proposes to rely.

§ 2–606. *What Constitutes Acceptance of Goods.*

(1) Acceptance of goods occurs when the buyer (a) after a reasonable opportunity to inspect the goods signifies to the seller that the goods are conforming or that he will take or retain them in spite of their non-conformity; or (b) fails to make an effective rejection (subsection (1) of Section 2–602), but such acceptance does not occur until the buyer has had a reasonable opportunity to inspect them; or (c) does any act inconsistent with the seller's ownership; but if such act is wrongful as against the seller it is an acceptance only if ratified by him. . . .

§ 2–607. *Effect of Acceptance . . . Burden of Establishing Breach After Acceptance . . .*

(1) The buyer must pay at the contract rate for any goods accepted. . . .

(4) The burden is on the buyer to establish any breach with respect to the goods accepted.

NOTES AND QUESTIONS

1. Compare and contrast the common law doctrine of substantial performance and the sales law (UCC) perfect tender rule. Is one doctrinal approach superior to the other in all cases?

2. Are the alternative approaches specially suited to their respective domains—perfect tenders for goods, substantial performance for non-goods?

CHAPTER 11

THIRD PARTIES

■ ■ ■

In this final chapter we consider the interests of non-parties to contracts, organized around four topics: (a) under what circumstances third parties have the right to enforce contracts to which they are strangers, called *third-party beneficiary doctrine*; (b) to what extent contracting parties may transfer their rights or duties to third parties, the law of *assignment and delegation*; (c) the limits on third party rights to impede the existing or prospective contract rights of others, established by the tort law doctrine proscribing *tortious interference* with contract relations; and (d) the power of contracting parties to alter the laws of tort to limit liability for wrongs such as negligence, attempted principally through the contractual use of *exculpation clauses*.

A. THIRD-PARTY BENEFICIARIES

In many situations, contracts radiate benefits to people other than the direct parties. In the distant past, doctrines addressing third-party effects were limited by the notion of "privity," meaning that only the parties to the contract held any legal obligations, rights, or duties. However, the law gradually moved to a more permissive approach, recognizing that contract parties often intend to create enforcement rights in third parties. A classic example are life insurance contracts, in which a person's family or heirs will be taken care of financially if the person whose life is insured passes away. While the contract is between the insured and the insurance company, the contract is made for the express benefit of the beneficiaries.

The phrase "third-party beneficiary" describes people who are entitled to enforce promises made between others when those promises were intended for their benefit. We will explore the classic judicial opinions providing the doctrinal basis for this innovation, but let's begin with a colorful illustration of recent vintage.

DETROIT INSTITUTE OF ARTS V. ROSE
127 F.Supp.2d 117 (D. Conn. 2001)

DRONEY, D.J.

"The Howdy Doody Show" was a television program beloved by millions of children now known as "the baby boom generation." It was produced and broadcast by the National Broadcasting Company, Inc. ("NBC") from 1947 to 1960. Hosted by Robert "Buffalo Bob" Smith, the show's main character was Howdy Doody, a puppet in the image of a freckled-faced boy in cowboy clothing. For most of its run, the show aired every afternoon after school. In that era, television programming—especially for children—was very limited, which contributed to the show's immense popularity. . . .

Howdy Doody [including older models of Howdy Doody, Double Doody, and Canadian Howdys, used on the show that aired in Canada], like the many other puppets used in the show, were maintained and operated by several puppeteers, including Rufus C. Rose and his wife, Margaret ("Margo") Rose. Beginning in 1952, Rufus Rose served as the puppet master, puppeteer, and caretaker for many of the puppets that appeared on the American broadcast of the "The Howdy Doody Show." He also created some puppets and made repairs at his workshop in Waterford, Connecticut. While the American show was on the air, Rufus Rose received $75.00 per week from NBC for "storing and servicing" the puppets at his workshop as part of his compensation. Like her husband, Margo Rose repaired puppets that appeared on the show; she also designed some of the show's characters and modeled and painted their heads.

When "The Howdy Doody Show" went off the air in December 1960, Rufus Rose ended his employment by NBC but kept possession of many of the puppets used in the show, including Howdy Doody, Double Doody, and the Canadian Howdys. Pursuant to an informal agreement made at the end of the show's run with Roger Muir, the show's executive producer, Rufus Rose continued to store the puppets in his Connecticut workshop until final arrangements were made for them.

[I]n late 1965 . . . Rufus Rose . . . began a series of correspondence with NBC about payment for his maintenance and storage of the puppets since the end of the show in 1960, and about the future of the puppets, including Howdy Doody. In a June 3, 1966 letter to NBC General Manager William J. Schmitt, Rufus Rose proposed that: (1) NBC pay him for the storage and upkeep of all the puppets since the end of the show; (2) NBC allow him to keep the minor puppets (but with the understanding that he would not use them as Howdy Doody show characters); and (3) the main puppets from the show, including Howdy Doody, be turned over to a museum known as the Detroit Institute of Arts ("DIA"). Rufus Rose indicated in his letter that the DIA "houses the recognized museum of Puppetry in America." Schmitt turned Rose's letter and the matter over to Howard Singer of NBC's legal department.

On March 20, 1967, after some negotiations, Singer sent Rufus Rose a proposed general release and a cover letter which set forth an amount for the past storage and maintenance fees, agreed that Rose would send

Howdy Doody to the DIA, and agreed that Rose could keep the "minor puppets." Rose returned the executed release with a cover letter on March 23, 1967. For the next few years, Rufus Rose kept the Howdy Doody puppet at his Waterford workshop.

The next chapter in the travels of Howdy Doody began in 1970. In response to a request from his friend Buffalo Bob, who was then making public appearances throughout the country in his role from the show, Rufus Rose agreed in a letter to send Howdy Doody to Buffalo Bob. In that letter, dated September 11, 1970, Rufus Rose explained to Buffalo Bob that he had agreed with NBC that the puppet would "eventually" be placed in the DIA, and it never would be used in a commercial manner. Rufus Rose went on to say that he was sending the "one and only original HOWDY DOODY" to Buffalo Bob "with this mutual understanding and responsibility." Rufus Rose died in 1975, while Howdy Doody was still in Buffalo Bob's possession. Through the next fifteen years or so, Buffalo Bob kept Howdy Doody and used him in his public appearances.

Beginning in 1992, Buffalo Bob's attorney, Edward Burns, wrote to NBC, Margo Rose (Rufus Rose's widow), and the DIA, requesting that they waive the requirement that Howdy Doody be placed in the DIA. Burns indicated that Buffalo Bob had fallen on difficult financial times, and now wished to sell the puppet and keep the proceeds. In a reply written on behalf of his mother, Margo Rose, Christopher Rose stated that it was his father's intention that Buffalo Bob honor the "condition" that Howdy be given to the DIA. NBC wrote Buffalo Bob that it also refused to release Howdy Doody to him. The DIA also declined to allow Buffalo Bob to sell the puppet. As a result, in a July 24, 1995 letter, Buffalo Bob informed the DIA that he would transfer Howdy Doody to the museum when he no longer wished to keep the puppet.

Eventually, Buffalo Bob and Christopher Rose changed their minds about Howdy Doody. On April 19, 1998, they executed an agreement to sell the puppet and split the profits. . . . According to the DIA, on June 19, 1998, Christopher Rose entered into a consignment agreement with Leland's Collectibles, Inc., an auction house, for the sale of the "original Howdy Doody" and other puppets from "The Howdy Doody Show." A few days later, Buffalo Bob died. The DIA then brought this case to prevent the Rose family from selling the puppet and also to gain possession of it. . . .

The DIA argues that it was a third party beneficiary of the 1966–1967 agreement between NBC and Rufus Rose and thus is entitled to ownership of Howdy Doody. . . .

Third-Party Beneficiary Contracts. Two parties may enter into a contract to benefit a third party beneficiary who is then entitled to enforce contractual obligations without being a party to the contract and thus may sue the obligor for breach. To be valid, there need not be express language in the contract creating a direct obligation to the third party beneficiary. However, a contract can only result in an obligation to a third party if both parties to the contract intended to created a direct obligation from the promisor to the third party. In other words, [that] a third party may gain an incidental benefit is not enough to support third-party beneficiary status. . . .

To recover on a contract made for his benefit, the third party beneficiary need not consent to the contract, as long as he or she knows of the contract and accepts it when he or she begins an action to enforce it. *See Data Gen. Corp., Inc. v. Citizens Nat'l Bank*, 502 F.Supp. 776, 785 (D.Conn.1980). Generally, a third party beneficiary is subject to the defenses that the promisor could raise in a suit by the promisee. *See Benson v. Brower's Moving & Storage, Inc.*, 907 F.2d 310, 313 (2d Cir.1990). The parties to a contract to benefit a third party may discharge or alter the promisor's obligations under that contract if the terms of the original agreement do not prohibit such changes, the third party has not relied upon the contract, or the third party has not yet brought suit based on the contract. See Restatement (Second) of Contracts § 311. Any modification of such a contract must be accomplished by a subsequent agreement between the parties. *Id.*

The plaintiff has produced evidence to establish as a matter of law that three of the letters between Rufus Rose and NBC from 1966 and 1967 created a binding contract. The evidence also shows that the parties agreed that Rufus Rose would transfer Howdy Doody to the DIA, a third party beneficiary of the contract. Although the parties did not specify when this transfer would occur, a reasonable time for such performance is implied by law, and thus the DIA is now entitled to Howdy Doody. The three letters which constitute this contract are discussed below.

Rufus Rose's June 3, 1966, letter to NBC General Manager William J. Schmitt followed the Connecticut Supreme Court's decision of November 30, 1965, which affirmed the trial court judgment in Rose's favor as to his care of the puppets which had been damaged in [a] fire. In that June letter, Rose first proposes that the NBC litigation be "finally resolved" and then proposes that NBC pay him $11,062.50 for his storage and maintenance of the puppets at his Waterford workshop since 1960.

As to the future of all the puppets, Rufus Rose made the following proposal in his letter:

> In the matter of the final disposition of the HOWDY DOODY puppets I would like to propose that the main characters such as HOWDY DOODY, MR. BLUSTER, DILLY DALLY, JOHN J. FEDOOZLE, FLUB-A-DUB and several others, be turned over to the Detroit Art Institute wich [sic] houses the recognized museum of Puppetry in America. . . . As for the balance of the puppets,

many of which have considerable fire damage, I feel they have little if any commercial value. However, I could use them up in my own future private work, without of course keeping or using their identities as HOWDY DOODY characters, if you would allow.

Oral and written negotiations over the course of the next few months apparently concerned the amount to be paid to Rufus Rose for the storage fees, and the disposition of puppets other than Howdy. NBC's Howard Singer wrote to Rufus Rose on March 20, 1967, memorializing the results of these negotiations: (1) NBC would pay Rufus Rose $3,500.00 "in settlement of our past differences" and Rose would sign a general release; (2) Rose and Roger Muir would "arrange for the disposition of the various Howdy Doody puppets (except for 'HOWDY DOODY,' of course)"; (3) none of the puppets to be kept by Rose or Muir could be used commercially; and (4) Rose would inform Singer which puppets would be "going into the PUPPET MUSEUM," along with Howdy Doody. It is clear from Singer's letter that even though these terms had been agreed to orally, he wished to set them out specifically in writing in the form of a counteroffer to Rose's written offer of June 3, 1966. In a March 23, 1967, letter, Rose accepted Singer's terms, indicated that he enclosed the signed general release, and stated that he would "at least" send Howdy Doody and the two other "main characters" to the DIA . . . .

In addition to setting forth the terms of the agreement between Rufus Rose and NBC, these letters also show that the agreement was supported by consideration. [An] exchange of promises is sufficient consideration to support a contract if the promises are capable of being performed. Here, NBC paid Rufus Rose $3,500.00, permitted Rufus Rose and Roger Muir to keep the minor puppets from "The Howdy Doody Show," and agreed that Howdy Doody and the other main characters be given to the DIA. In return, Rufus Rose promised to comply with these terms and agreed to release NBC from any claims that he might have had against it concerning the storage and maintenance of the puppets since 1960. These commitments were all capable of being performed and therefore constitute valid consideration. Consequently, the 1966–1967 agreement was valid and enforceable.

The Rose defendants attempt to construe the contract as concerning only the parties' agreement as to the storage and maintenance fees and the "settlement of . . . past differences," and argue that the language concerning the future of the puppets was not a subject of the contract. In particular, they point to the language of the general release, which does not discuss the future of the puppets, but instead mentions only the fire damage and payment for past storage and maintenance of the puppets. However, while the general release may have been so limited, the contract between the parties encompassed more than just the issues covered by the general release. The three letters show that the parties intended not only to resolve their past dispute over these charges, but also to resolve how the puppets would be handled in the future. This was an essential part of the agreement between Rufus Rose and NBC, not merely an afterthought or a separate topic from the contract. It also makes sense that the release only specifically mentioned the past dispute over the fire damage and the maintenance charges; that dispute was the subject of the of the Connecticut state court litigation, not the future disposition of the puppets.

The three letters also show that NBC was committed to assuring that Howdy Doody be given to the DIA. As to the other puppets, Singer was not as concerned or as specific as to whether they were sent to the DIA or kept by Rose and Muir, so long as they were not commercially exploited and so long as NBC was informed by Rose as to their fate. However, it is clear from the letters that NBC specifically intended that the Howdy Doody puppet go to the museum. For example, the March 20, 1967, letter of Singer singles out Howdy Doody from the other puppets for the purpose of making clear that it would be sent to the DIA. Rose's intent, as expressed in his letters, was the same as to Howdy. There was a special significance and status of Howdy Doody, and the letters recognize it and deal with it. . . .

The evidence further shows that there is no genuine issue of material fact that the DIA was a third party beneficiary of the agreement between Rufus Rose and NBC. First, even though Singer, in his letter of March 20, 1967, does not specifically name the DIA as the "beneficiary," his reference to the "Puppet Museum" indicates that he was describing and confirming his understanding of the entity to which Rufus Rose referred in his letter of June 3. Second, while the defendants argue that the language of the March 20, 1967, Singer letter indicates that Howdy Doody is "excepted" from the agreement, when read in light of Rufus Rose' two letters to NBC described above, it is clear that Singer's statement does not except Howdy Doody from the puppets to be donated to the DIA, but instead excludes Howdy from the group of minor puppets to be kept by Rufus Rose and Muir to make sure that it would go to the DIA. Third, although it is not clear whether the DIA knew about the agreement at the time of its formation, the museum is now aware of the contract and has certainly accepted it or endorsed it by bringing this action to enforce it, which is all that is required. *See Data Gen. Corp., Inc.*, 502 F.Supp. at 785.

The interpretation of the third-party beneficiary arrangement between Rufus Rose and NBC is reinforced when the terms of the contract are considered in light of the circumstances attending the making of the contract, as well as the parties' motives. The correspondence from NBC indicates that it was not only concerned with the past dispute with Rufus Rose and settling the future of the puppets, but also with commercial exploitation of all of the puppets from the show, especially Howdy Doody. The two "conditions" it placed on Rufus Rose—that all of the puppets not be used in a commercial manner and that Howdy Doody be displayed in a museum—show an intent to guard Howdy's image. NBC's apparent failure later to confirm delivery of the puppet to the DIA, or the fact that current NBC employees may not have been aware of this arrangement does not raise a genuine issue of material fact as to whether a contract existed. There is uncontested evidence of the intent of NBC—through Howard Singer's letters—at the time of the contract.

Rufus Rose' letters evidence a motivation similar to that of NBC. As Howdy Doody's primary caretaker, he was the first to propose sending the puppet to the DIA. This shows his selfless desire to preserve Howdy Doody in a public place he considered to "house[ ] the recognized museum of Puppetry in America," so that future generations could still see and enjoy Howdy Doody, rather than keep the puppet for his own profit. . . .

The DIA has shown that it is the owner of the Howdy Doody puppet as a matter of law. It was a third party beneficiary of the contract between Rufus Rose and NBC from 1967. The clear intent of Rufus Rose and NBC, as expressed in that contract, was that the puppet be placed in the museum. . . .

NOTES AND QUESTIONS

1.   In many ways, engagement with third-party beneficiary law entails a complete review of the entire course on contracts, from formation and excuses through interpretation, performance, and conditions. While it is neither necessary nor possible to reexamine all those topics within the framework of third-party beneficiary law, be on the lookout for both how those topics arise in third-party beneficiary doctrine and how third parties might assert themselves into disputes you have examined as two-party affairs.

2.   Why does the Howdy Doody court permit the DIA to enforce the Rose-NBC contract? What is the court's reasoning that justifies viewing DIA as a third-party beneficiary? Recall fundamental principles of contract formation such as intent.

3.   If the parties to a contract refuse to enforce it, die, or are neglectful of their duties, why should strangers be entitled to enforce it? Is the question solely a matter of the intent of the original parties? Are there any social goals furthered by allowing third party enforcement?

4.   Stories of Buffalo Bob's comeback tour do not mention difficult financial times. Rather, they note that many members of the "The Peanut Gallery" were eager for the nostalgic opportunity to replay their childhood memories of the show. See, e.g. John Bordsen, *If Buffalo Bob Has His Way. . . It'll Be 'Howdy Doody' Time Again!*, TULSA WORLD, Dec. 24, 1991.

5.   The DIA is world-famous for its puppetry collection. In 2013, the City of Detroit declared bankruptcy, stoking fears for the fate of the museum, including concerns about pressure to sell its collection to satisfy $18 billion

owed to creditors. *See Detroit Institute of Arts Puppet Collection*, CNN.COM, July 19, 2013.

DIA v. Rose is a modern statement of settled third-party beneficiary doctrine, but the doctrine's origins were anything but easy and reveal much about the process of the common law. To illustrate, let's examine two early well-known cases that set the stage for today's third-party beneficiary law. The first, *Lawrence v. Fox*, established that creditor beneficiaries could enforce contracts of others, on the grounds that the creditor relationship supported an inference that the parties intended such parties to be able to enforce the contract. The second, *Seaver v. Ransom*, extended the privilege of enforcement to donee beneficiaries, so long as similar evidence warranting such an inference appeared.

LAWRENCE V. FOX
20 N.Y. 268 (1859)

[In accordance with a common practice of the period, the facts of the following case are provided by someone other than the judge. The majority opinion, moreover, was set forth in lengthy paragraphs which have been subdivided into additional paragraphs below to enable easier reading.— Eds.]

. . . [O]ne Holly, in November, 1857, at the request of the defendant [Fox], loaned and advanced to him $300, stating at the time that he [Holly] owed that sum to the plaintiff [Lawrence] for money borrowed of him, and had agreed to pay it to him the then next day; that the defendant in consideration thereof, at the time of receiving the money, promised to pay it to the plaintiff the then next day. . . . [Fox] moved for a nonsuit [on the] grounds . . . that the agreement by the defendant with Holly to pay the plaintiff was void for want of consideration, and that there was no privity between the plaintiff and defendant. The court overruled the motion, and . . . the jury . . . found . . . for the plaintiff [in] the amount of the loan and interest, $344.66, upon which judgment was entered; from which the defendant appealed to the Superior Court, at general term, where the judgment was affirmed, and the defendant appealed to this court. . . .

GRAY, J.

. . . [I]t is claimed that notwithstanding [that Fox's] promise was established by competent evidence, it was void for the want of consideration. It is now more than a quarter of a century since it was settled by the Supreme Court of this State . . . that a promise in all material respects like the one under consideration was valid; and the judgment of that court was unanimously affirmed by the Court for the Correction of Errors. (Farley v. Cleaveland, 4 Cow., 432; same case in error, 9 id., 639.)

In that case one Moon owed Farley and sold to Cleaveland a quantity of hay, in consideration of which Cleaveland promised to pay Moon's debt to Farley; and the decision in favor of Farley's right to recover was placed upon the ground that the hay received by Cleaveland from Moon was a valid consideration for Cleaveland's promise to pay Farley, and that the subsisting liability of Moon to pay Farley was no objection to the recovery.

The fact that the money advanced by Holly to the defendant was a loan to him for a day, and that it thereby became the property of the defendant, seemed to impress the defendant's counsel with the idea that because the defendant's promise was not a trust fund placed by the plaintiff in the defendant's hands, out of which he was to realize money as from the sale of a chattel or the collection of a debt, the promise although made for the benefit of the plaintiff could not enure to his benefit. The hay which Cleaveland delivered to Moon was not to be paid to Farley, but the debt incurred by Cleaveland for the purchase of the hay, like the debt incurred by the defendant for money borrowed, was what was to be paid.

That case . . . puts to rest the objection that the defendant's promise was void for want of consideration. [There] the promise was not only made to Moon but to the plaintiff Farley. [Here] the promise was made to Holly and not expressly to the plaintiff; and this difference between the two cases presents the question . . . as to the want of privity between the plaintiff and defendant. As early as 1806 it was announced by the Supreme Court of this State, upon what was then regarded as the settled law of England, "That where one person makes a promise to another for the benefit of a third person, that third person may maintain an action upon it." Schermerhorn v. Vanderheyden (1 John. R., 140), has often been re-asserted by our courts and never departed from. . . .

The same principle is adjudged in several cases in Massachusetts. . . . In Hall v. Marston [1822, 17 Mass. 575] the court [said]: "It seems to have been well settled that if A promises B for a valuable consideration to pay C, the latter may maintain assumpsit for the money;" and in Brewer v. Dyer, [1851, 7 Cush. 337, 340,] the recovery was upheld, as the court said, ". . . not . . . upon the ground of any actual or supposed relationship between the parties as some of the earlier cases would seem to indicate, but upon the broader and more satisfactory basis, that the law operating on the act of the parties creates the duty, establishes a privity, and implies the promise and obligation on which the action is founded." . . .

But it is urged that because the defendant was not in any sense a trustee of the property of Holly for the benefit of the plaintiff, the law will not imply a promise. I agree that many of the cases where a promise was implied were cases of trusts, created for the benefit of the promiser. The case of Felton v. Dickinson (10 Mass., 189, 190), and others that might be cited, are of that class; but concede them all to have been cases of trusts, and it proves nothing against the application of the rule to this case. The duty of the trustee to pay the *cestuis que trust*, according to the terms of the trust, implies his promise to the latter to do so.

In this case the defendant, upon ample consideration received from Holly, promised Holly to pay his debt to the plaintiff; the consideration received and the promise to Holly made it as plainly his duty to pay the plaintiff as if the money had been remitted to him for that purpose, and as well implied a promise to do so as if he had been made a trustee of property to be converted into cash with which to pay. The fact that a breach of the duty imposed in the one case may be visited, and justly, with more serious consequences than in the other, by no means disproves the payment to be a duty in both. The principle illustrated by the example so frequently quoted (which concisely states the case in hand) "that a promise made to one for the benefit of another, he for whose benefit it is made may bring an action for its breach," has been applied to trust cases, not because it was exclusively applicable to those cases, but because it was a principle of law, and as such applicable to those cases.

It was also insisted that Holly could have discharged the defendant from his promise, though it was intended by both parties for the benefit of the plaintiff, and therefore the plaintiff was not entitled to maintain this suit for the recovery of a demand over which he had no control. It is enough that [Holly] did not release [Fox] from his promise, and whether he could or not is a question not now necessarily involved; but if it was, I think it would be found difficult to maintain the right of Holly to discharge a judgment recovered [Lawrence] upon confession or otherwise, for the breach of [Fox's] promise . . . .

. . . Suppose the defendant had given his note in which, for value received of Holly, he had promised to pay the plaintiff and the plaintiff had accepted the promise, retaining Holly's liability. Very clearly Holly could not have discharged that promise, be the right to release the defendant as it may. No one can doubt that he owes the sum of money demanded of him, or that in accordance with his promise it was his duty to have paid it to the plaintiff; nor can it be doubted that whatever may be the diversity of opinion elsewhere, the adjudications in this State, from a very early period, approved by experience, have established the defendant's liability; if, therefore, it could be shown that a more strict and technically accurate application of the rules applied, would lead to a different result (which I by no means concede), the effort should not be made in the face of manifest justice. [Affirmed.]

JOHNSON, CHIEF JUDGE, DENIO, SELDEN, ALLEN and STRONG, JUDGES, concurred. Johnson and Denio were of opinion that [Fox's] promise was to be regarded as made to [Lawrence] through the medium of his agent

[Holly], whose action he could ratify when it came to his knowledge, though taken without his being privy thereto.

COMSTOCK, J. (dissenting).

The plaintiff had nothing to do with the promise on which he brought this action. It was not made to him, nor did the consideration proceed from him. If he can maintain the suit, it is because an anomaly has found its way into the law .... In general, there must be privity of contract. The party who sues upon a promise must be the promisee, or he must have some legal interest in the undertaking. In this case, it is plain that Holly, who loaned the money to the defendant, and to whom the promise in question was made, could at any time have claimed that it should be performed to himself personally. He had lent the money to the defendant, and at the same time directed the latter to pay the sum to the plaintiff. This direction he could countermand, and if he had done so, manifestly the defendant's promise to pay according to the direction would have ceased to exist. The plaintiff would receive a benefit by a complete execution of the arrangement, but the arrangement itself was between other parties, and was under their exclusive control. If the defendant had paid the money to Holly, his debt would have been discharged thereby. So Holly might have released the demand or assigned it to another person, or the parties might have annulled the promise now in question, and designated some other creditor of Holly as the party to whom the money should be paid. It has never been claimed, that in a case thus situated, the right of a third person to sue upon the promise rested on any sound principle of law. . . .

The cases in which some trust was involved are also frequently referred to as authority for the doctrine now in question, but they do not sustain it. If A delivers money or property to B, which the latter accepts upon a trust for the benefit of C, the latter can enforce the trust by an appropriate action for that purpose. (Berly v. Taylor, 5 Hill, 577.) If the trust be of money, I think the beneficiary may assent to it and bring the action for money had and received to his use. If it be of something else than money, the trustee must account for it according to the terms of the trust, and upon principles of equity. There is some authority even for saying that an express promise founded on the possession of a trust fund may be enforced by an action at law in the name of the beneficiary, although it was made to the creator of the trust.

. . . The case of The Delaware and Hudson Canal Company v. The Westchester County Bank (4 Denio, 97), involved a trust because the defendants had received from a third party a bill of exchange under an agreement that they would endeavor to collect it, and would pay over the proceeds when collected to the plaintiffs. A fund received under such an agreement does not belong to the person who receives it. He must account for it specifically; and perhaps there is no gross violation of principle in permitting the equitable owner of it to sue upon an express promise to pay it over. Having a specific interest in the thing, the undertaking to account for it may be regarded as in some sense made with him through the author of the trust. But further than this we cannot go without violating plain rules of law. In the case before us there was nothing in the nature of a trust or agency. The defendant borrowed the money of Holly and received it as his own. The plaintiff had no right in the fund, legal or equitable. The promise to repay the money created an obligation in favor of the lender to whom it was made and not in favor of any one else. . . .

GROVER, JUDGE, also dissented.

NOTES AND QUESTIONS

1. It seems Holly's debt to Lawrence arose from illegal gambling so that Lawrence could not have enforced his own contract with Holly. *See* Anthony Jon Waters, *The Property in the Promise: A Study of the Third Party Beneficiary Rule*, 98 HARVARD L. REV. 1109 (1985) (providing a rich factual background on the case).

2. There was little or no applicable New York law on third-party beneficiaries at the time of *Lawrence v. Fox*. The closest factual precedent was *Farley*, but all three parties in *Farley* had signed the contract. Various other cases had dabbled in the rhetoric of third-party beneficiaries, but it is difficult to discern in them a clear statement and application of the principles. Nevertheless, a number of scholars have seized on such earlier statements to claim that *Lawrence v. Fox* did not break new legal ground. Melvin Aron Eisenberg, *Third-Party Beneficiaries*, 92 COLUMBIA L. REV. 1358, 1363 (1992); Peter Karsten, *The "Discovery" of Law by English and American Jurists of the Seventeenth, Eighteenth, and Nineteenth Centuries: Third-Party Beneficiary Contracts as a Test Case*, 9 LAW & HISTORY REV. 327 (1991). For a study of *Lawrence v. Fox* attributing its status as a leading case to its treatment by contracts casebook editors who were seeking to advance normative agendas, see M.H. Hoeflich & E. Perelmuter, *The Anatomy of a Leading Case: Lawrence v. Fox in the Courts, the Casebooks, and the Commentaries*, 21 U. MICHIGAN J.L. REFORM 721 (1988).

3. Yet doctrinal hurdles surmounted in *Lawrence v. Fox* are clear from the separate dissenting and concurring opinions in the case. Judge Comstock seemed to accept the majority's position on the consideration question but could not accept the disposition or analysis of the privity claim. Comstock observed that the majority was using trust concepts that were inapplicable and that the majority could cite no authority for the conclusion it reached. The trust concepts had never before been used in the way the majority was using them.

The concurring judges argued another route for enforcing the contract: an agency theory, treating the promisee as the agent, with legal authority to bind his principal, and the beneficiary as the principal. The conceptual problem of how the beneficiary could be the principal if he had not made the promisee his agent was handled by deciding that the promisee created the relationship by his actions and that the beneficiary ratified them. For a study of *Lawrence v. Fox* and what the evolution of the third-party beneficiary says about the majesty of the common law, see Lawrence A. Cunningham, *The Common Law as an Iterative Process*, 81 NOTRE DAME L. REV. 747 (2006).

SEAVER V. RANSOM
120 N.E. 639 (N.Y. 1918)

POUND, J.

Judge Beman and his wife were advanced in years. Mrs. Beman was about to die. She had a small estate, consisting of a house and lot in Malone and little else. Judge Beman drew his wife's will according to her instructions. It gave $1,000 to plaintiff, $500 to one sister, plaintiff's mother, and $100 each to another sister and her son, the use of the house to her husband for life, and remainder to the American Society for the Prevention of Cruelty to Animals. She named her husband as residuary legatee and executor. Plaintiff was her niece, 34 years old in ill health sometimes a member of the Beman household. When the will was read to Mrs. Beman, she said that it was not as she wanted it. She wanted to leave the house to plaintiff. She had no other objection to the will, but her strength was waning, and, although the judge offered to write another will for her, she said she was afraid she would not hold out long enough to enable her to sign it. So the judge said, if she would sign the will, he would leave plaintiff enough in his will to make up the difference. He avouched the promise by his uplifted hand with all solemnity and his wife then executed the will. When he came to die, it was found that his will made no provision for the plaintiff.

This action was brought, and plaintiff recovered judgment in the trial court, on the theory that Beman had obtained property from his wife and induced her to execute the will in the form prepared by him by his promise to give plaintiff $6,000, the value of the house, and that thereby equity impressed his property with a trust in favor of plaintiff. Where a legatee promises the testator that he will use property given him by the will for a particular purpose, a trust arises. . . . Beman received nothing under his wife's will but the use of the house in Malone for life. Equity compels the application of property thus obtained to the purpose of the testator, but equity cannot so impress a trust, except on property obtained by the promise. Beman was bound by his promise, but no property was bound by it; no trust in plaintiff's favor can be spelled out.

An action on the contract for damages, or to make the executors trustees for performance, stands on different ground. . . . The Appellate Division properly passed to the consideration of the question whether the judgment could stand upon the promise made to the wife, upon a valid consideration, for the sole benefit of plaintiff. The judgment of the trial court was affirmed by a return to the general doctrine laid down in the great case of *Lawrence v. Fox*, 20 N. Y. 268, which has since been limited as herein indicated.

Contracts for the benefit of third persons have been the prolific source of judicial and academic discussion. Williston, *Contracts for the Benefit of a Third Person*, 15 Harvard Law Review, 767; Corbin, *Contracts for the Benefit of Third Persons*, 27 Yale Law Review, 1008. The general rule, both in law and equity . . . , was that privity between a plaintiff and a defendant is necessary to the maintenance of an action on the contract. The consideration must be furnished by the party to whom the promise was made. The contract cannot be enforced against the third party, and therefore it cannot be enforced by him. On the other hand, the right of the beneficiary to sue on a contract made expressly for his benefit has been fully recognized in many American jurisdictions, either by judicial decision or by legislation, and is said to be "the prevailing rule in this country." *Hendrick v. Lindsay*, 93 U. S. 143. . . . It has been said that "the establishment of this doctrine has been gradual, and is a victory of practical utility over theory, of equity over technical subtlety." Brantly on Contracts (2d Ed.) p. 253. The reasons for this view are that it is just and practical to permit the person for whose benefit the contract is made to enforce it against one whose duty it is to pay. Other jurisdictions still adhere to the present English rule . . . that a contract cannot be enforced by or against a person who is not a party. . . .

In New York the right of the beneficiary to sue on contracts made for his benefit is not clearly or simply defined. It is at present confined: First. To cases where there is a pecuniary obligation running from the promisee to the beneficiary, "a legal right founded upon some obligation of the promisee in the third party to adopt and claim the promise as made for his benefit." Farley v. Cleveland, 4 Cow. 432 . . . ; Lawrence v. Fox, supra; . . . Secondly, to cases where the contract is made for the benefit of the wife (Buchanan v. Tilden, 158 N. Y. 109. . . affianced wife (De Cicco v. Schweizer, 221 N. Y. 431 . . . , or child . . . of a party to the contract. The close relationship cases go back to the early King's Bench case (1677), long since repudiated in England, of Dutton v. Poole, 2 Lev. 211 . . . . The natural and moral duty of the husband or parent to provide for the future of wife or child sustains the action on the contract made for their benefit. . . .

The right of the third party is also upheld in, thirdly, the public contract cases . . . where the municipality seeks to protect its inhabitants by covenants for their benefit; and, fourthly, the cases where, at the request of a party to the contract, the promise runs directly to the beneficiary although he does not furnish the consideration . . . . It may be safely said that a general rule sustaining recovery at the suit of the third party would include but few classes of cases not included in these groups, either categorically or in principle.

The desire of the childless aunt to make provision for a beloved and favorite niece differs imperceptibly in law or in equity from the moral duty of the parent to make testamentary provision for a child. The contract was made for the plaintiff's benefit. She alone is substantially damaged by its breach. The representatives of the wife's estate have no interest in enforcing it specifically. It is said in Buchanan v. Tilden that the common law imposes moral and legal obligations upon the husband and the parent not measured by the necessaries of life. It was, however, the love and affection or the moral sense of the husband and the parent that imposed such obligations in the cases cited, rather than any common-law duty of husband and parent to wife and child.

If plaintiff had been a child of Mrs. Beman, legal obligation would have required no testamentary provision for her, yet the child could have enforced a covenant in her favor identical with the covenant of Judge Beman in this case. De Cicco v. Schweizer, *supra*. The constraining power of conscience is not regulated by the degree of relationship alone. The dependent or faithful niece may have a stronger claim than the affluent or unworthy son. No sensible theory of moral obligation denies arbitrarily to the former what would be conceded to the latter. We might consistently either refuse or allow the claim of both, but I [cannot] reconcile a decision in favor of the wife in *Buchanan v. Tilden*, based on the moral obligations arising out of near relationship, with a decision against the niece here on the ground that the relationship is too remote for equity's ken. No controlling authority depends upon so absolute a rule. [One judge had written that:] "The doctrine of *Lawrence v. Fox* is progressive, not retrograde. The course of the late decisions is to enlarge, not to limit, the effect of that case." . . .

. . . If Mrs. Beman had left her husband the house on condition that he pay the plaintiff $6,000, and he had accepted the devise [then] he would have become personally liable to pay the legacy, and plaintiff could have recovered in an action at law against him, whatever the value of the house. . . . That would be because the testatrix had in substance bequeathed the promise to plaintiff, and not because close relationship or moral obligation sustained the contract. The distinction between an implied promise to a testator for the benefit of a third party to pay a legacy and an unqualified promise on a valuable consideration to make provision for the third party by will is discernible, but not obvious. The tendency of American authority is to sustain the gift in all such cases and to permit the donee beneficiary to recover on the contract. . . . The equities are with the plaintiff, and they may be enforced in this action, whether it be regarded as an action for damages or an action for specific performance to convert the defendants into trustees for plaintiff's benefit under the agreement. . . .

NOTES AND QUESTIONS

1.   What is the concept of "privity"? Why is it important in *Seaver v. Ransom*? In contract doctrine? Have you encountered this concept in other doctrinal areas of law? Why is the concept important in those doctrinal areas?

2.   What is the triangular nature of the promises in *Seaver v. Ransom*? Who are the actors and their relationships to each other? Who did the aunt intend to benefit through her will? Should her niece have the power to enforce that promise even though the legal (formal) technicalities were not complied with?

3.   Once again, we see the role of formalities, in this case, recording a gift in a signed will, versus the equities or moralities of enforcing a promise. In what other contexts has this tension arisen throughout our course materials?

4.   During its time, *Seaver v. Ransom* was considered a "pivotal" case, and the type of contract at issue came to be known as part of a line of "donee-beneficiary" cases. A donee-beneficiary case is one where "a performance objective of the contracting parties, as manifested in the contract read in the light of surrounding circumstances, is to give effect to a donative intention of the promisee by obliging the promisor to render a performance that will benefit the third party." *See* Melvin A. Eisenberg, *Third Party Beneficiaries*, 92 COLUMBIA L. REV. 1358, 1371 (1992).

EXAMPLE: HEINZ

In 2013, H.J. Heinz Company, the condiment maker, with an abiding loyalty to its hometown community of Pittsburgh, was sold in a corporate merger to a buyer group that included 3G, a Brazilian financial firm, and Berkshire Hathaway, the U.S. conglomerate overseen by Warren Buffett. The merger agreement devoted an entire section to the company's cultural connection to Pittsburgh. It declared that "after the Closing, the Company's current headquarters in Pittsburgh, Pennsylvania will be the Surviving Corporation's headquarters."

A covenant, which survives the closing and was made by the corporate subsidiary the buyers created for the acquisition and jointly owned (called the "Parent"), promises: "[A]fter the Closing, Parent shall cause the Surviving Corporation to preserve the Company's heritage and continue to support philanthropic and charitable causes in Pittsburgh." The contractual language is less precise than one might expect of a long-term corporate promise. For instance, there is no time frame (just repeatedly saying from and after "Closing") or benchmarks (only vague references to preserving "heritage" and supporting charities). The contract referenced the company's contractual right to name Pittsburgh's professional athletic stadium, called Heinz Field, and required keeping that name.

Interestingly, the promises are made by the buyer which, upon closing, owns the seller, and will not sue itself for breach. The agreement declares that there are no third-party beneficiaries, other than specific stated exceptions such as option holders and personnel covered by indemnification. There is no mention of, say, Pittsburgh headquarters' personnel, Pittsburgh charities, or the Heinz family. The contract, however, required the parties to reference these commitments in their press releases about the deal.

Within a year of the Heinz deal, the company, led by managers appointed by 3G, cut more than 300 jobs at Pittsburgh headquarters. A further Pittsburgh dilution occurred soon thereafter, when Heinz merged with Chicago-based Kraft to form The Kraft Heinz Company. While the company adopted dual headquarters and asserted it was keeping its Pittsburgh covenants, locals perceived a hollowing out and migration of the company to Chicago. Are the commitments in this contract enforceable as a practical matter? Could any third party credibly claim standing—at least without the contractual disclaimer? Were these provisions simply a publicity stunt?

———

After the nineteenth century, the class of creditor beneficiaries came to seem relatively simple. The class grew to include promises bargained for by those owing the third party any other legal obligation too, beyond money. In the early twentieth century the doctrine expanded, allowing third parties to enforce contracts intended for the beneficiaries of promises, even though the person getting the promise did not have any legal obligation to the third party.

Some courts flirted with permitting citizens to enforce contracts against service providers who had contracts with the government. A common setting involved water supply contracts for municipal fire hydrants. Citizens harmed by a water company's breach of its government contract could recover damages from the company. This class, however, was kept narrower than the classes of creditor and donee beneficiaries. Courts recognized that cities and their suppliers often do not intend for citizens to have enforcement rights—lest that result in staggering liability. Accordingly, although a few cases upheld the rights of citizens to enforce government contracts, most did not, and the category remains narrow at best. Consider this example.

H.R. MOCH CO. V. RENSSELAER WATER CO.
159 N.E. 896 (N.Y. 1928)

CARDOZO, C.J.

The defendant, a waterworks company under the laws of this state, made a contract with the city of Rensselaer for the supply of water during a term of years. Water was to be furnished to the city for sewer flushing and street sprinkling; for service to schools and public buildings; and for service at fire hydrants, the latter service at the rate of $42.50 a year for each hydrant. Water was to be furnished to private takers within the city at their homes and factories and other industries at reasonable rates, not exceeding a stated schedule. While this contract was in force, a building caught fire. The flames, spreading to the plaintiff's warehouse [nearby], destroyed it and its contents. The defendant, according to the complaint, was promptly notified of the fire, but omitted and neglected after such notice, to supply or furnish sufficient or adequate quantity of water, with adequate pressure to stay, suppress, or extinguish the fire before it reached the warehouse of the plaintiff, although the pressure and supply which the defendant was equipped to supply and furnish, and had agreed by said contract to supply and furnish, was adequate and sufficient to prevent the spread of the fire to and the destruction of the plaintiff's warehouse and its contents.

By reason of the failure of the defendant to "fulfill the provisions of the contract between it and the city of Rensselaer," the plaintiff is said to have suffered damage, for which judgment is demanded. A motion, in the nature of a demurrer, to dismiss the complaint, was denied at Special Term. The Appellate Division reversed by a divided court.

. . . The complaint, we are told, is to be viewed as stating: (1) A cause of action for breach of contract within *Lawrence v. Fox*, 20 N. Y. 268; (2) a cause of action for a common-law tort, within *MacPherson v. Buick Motor Co.*, 217 N. Y. 382 . . . .

We think the action is not maintainable as one for breach of contract.

No legal duty rests upon a city to supply its inhabitants with protection against fire. . . . That being so, a member of the public may not maintain an action under *Lawrence v. Fox* against one contracting with the city to furnish water at the hydrants, unless an intention appears that the promisor is to be answerable to individual members of the public as well as to the city for any loss ensuing from the failure to fulfill the promise. No such intention is discernible here. On the contrary, the contract is significantly divided into two branches: One a promise to the city for the benefit of the city in its corporate capacity, in which branch is included the service at the hydrants; and the other a promise to the city for the benefit of private takers, in which branch is included the service at their homes and factories.

In a broad sense it is true that every city contract, not improvident or wasteful, is for the benefit of the public. More than this, however, must be shown to give a right of action to a member of the public not formally a party. The benefit, as it is sometimes said, must be one that is not merely incidental and secondary. . . . It must be primary and immediate in such a sense and to such a degree as to bespeak the assumption of a duty to make reparation directly to the individual members of the public if the benefit is lost. The field of obligation would be expanded beyond reasonable limits if less than this were to be demanded as a condition of liability.

[A] promisor undertakes to supply fuel for heating a public building. He is not liable for breach of contract to a visitor who finds the building without fuel, and thus contracts a cold. The list of illustrations can be indefinitely extended. The carrier of the mails under contract with the government is not answerable to the merchant who has lost the benefit of a bargain through negligent delay. The householder is without a remedy against manufacturers of hose and engines, though prompt performance of their contracts would have stayed the ravages of fire. "The law does not spread its protection so far." Robins Dry Dock & Repair Co. v. Flint, 275 U. S. 303 . . . .

So with the case at hand. By the vast preponderance of authority, a contract between a city and a water company to furnish water at the city hydrants has in view a benefit to the public that is incidental rather than immediate, an assumption of duty to the city and not to its inhabitants. Such is the ruling of the Supreme Court of the United States. . . . Such has been the ruling in this state . . . , though the question is still open in this court. Such with few exceptions has been the ruling in other jurisdictions. . . . The diligence of counsel has brought together decisions to that effect from 26 states. . . . Only a few states have held otherwise. . . .

An intention to assume an obligation of indefinite extension to every member of the public is seen to be the more improbable when we recall the crushing burden that the obligation would impose. . . . The consequences invited would bear no reasonable proportion to those attached by law to defaults not greatly different. A wrongdoer who by negligence sets fire to a building is liable in damages to the owner where the fire has its origin, but not to other owners who are injured when it spreads. The rule in our state is settled to that effect, whether wisely or unwisely. . . . If the plaintiff is to prevail, one who negligently omits to supply sufficient pressure to extinguish a fire started by another assumes an obligation to pay the ensuing damage, though the whole city is laid low. A promisor will not be deemed to have had in mind the assumption of a risk so overwhelming for any trivial reward.

The cases that have applied the rule of *Lawrence v. Fox* to contracts made by a city for the benefit of the public are not at war with this conclusion. Through them all there runs as a unifying principle the presence of an intention to compensate the individual members of the public in the event of a default. For example, in *Pond v. New Rochelle Water Co.*, 183 N. Y. 330 . . . the contract with the city fixed a schedule of rates to be supplied, not to public buildings, but to private takers at their homes. In *Matter of International R. Co. v. Rann*, 224 N. Y. 83, 85, 120 N. E. 153, the contract was by street railroads to carry passengers for a stated fare. In *Smyth v. City of New York*, 203 N. Y. 106, 96 N. E. 409, and Rigney v. New York Cent. & H. R. R. Co., 217 N. Y. 31, 111 N. E. 226, covenants were made by contractors upon public works, not merely to indemnify the city, but to assume its liabilities. These and like cases come within the third group stated in the comprehensive opinion in *Seaver v. Ransom*, 224 N. Y. 233, 238. . . . The municipality was contracting in behalf of its inhabitants by covenants intended to be enforced by any of them severally as occasion should arise.

We think the action is not maintainable as one for a common-law tort.

"It is ancient learning that one who assumes to act, even though gratuitously, may thereby become subject to the duty of acting carefully, if he acts at all." Glanzer v. Shepard, 233 N. Y. 236, 239 . . . . The plaintiff would bring its case within the orbit of that principle. The hand once set to a task may not always be withdrawn with impunity though liability would fail if it had never been applied at all. A time-honored formula often phrases the distinction as one between misfeasance and nonfeasance. Incomplete the formula is, and so at times misleading. Given a relation involving in its existence a duty of care irrespective of a contract, a tort may result as well from acts of omission as of commission in the fulfillment of the duty thus recognized by law. . . .

What we need to know is not so much the conduct to be avoided when the relation and its attendant duty are established as existing. What we need to know is the conduct that engenders the relation. It is here that the formula, however incomplete, has its value and significance. If conduct has gone forward to such a stage that in action would commonly result, not negatively merely in withholding a benefit, but positively or actively in working an injury, there exists a relation out of which arises a duty to go forward. . . .

So the surgeon who operates without pay is liable, though his negligence is in the omission to sterilize his instruments (cf. *Glanzer v. Shepard, supra*); the engineer, though his fault is in the failure to shut off steam (*Kelly v. Metropolitan Ry. Co.*, [1 Q. B. 944 (1895)]; the maker of automobiles, at the suit of someone other than the buyer, though his negligence is merely in inadequate inspection (*MacPherson v. Buick Motor Co.*, 217 N. Y. 382 . . .). The query always is whether the putative wrongdoer has advanced to such a point as to have launched a force or instrument of harm, or has stopped where inaction is at most a refusal to become an instrument for good. . . .

The plaintiff would have us hold that the defendant, when once it entered upon the performance of its contract with the city, was brought into such a relation with [everyone] who might potentially be benefited through the supply of water at the hydrants as to give to negligent performance, without reasonable notice of a refusal to continue, the quality of a tort. . . . [L]iability would be unduly and indeed indefinitely extended by this enlargement of the zone of duty. The dealer in coal who is to supply fuel for a shop must then answer to the customers if fuel is lacking.

The manufacturer of goods, who enters upon the performance of his contract, must answer, in that view, not only to the buyer, but to those who to his knowledge are looking to the buyer for their own sources of supply. Every one making a promise having the quality of a contract will be under a duty to the promisee by virtue of the promise, but under another duty, apart from contract, to an indefinite number of potential beneficiaries when performance has begun. The assumption of one relation will mean the involuntary assumption of a series of new relations, inescapably hooked together. . . . The failure in such circumstances to furnish an adequate supply of water is at most the denial of a benefit. It is not the commission of a wrong. . . .

NOTES AND QUESTIONS

1.   The type of argument Judge Cardozo uses in *Moch* would be classified as a "slippery slope" argument. If a citizen could bring an action as a third-party beneficiary when government services are not provided, where would the liability end? Is the real concern that such a liability rule would result in too much litigation? Is that a valid concern in this context?

2.   Viewed broadly, *Moch* and similar cases raise philosophical and political questions about how much, if any, governmental services are owed by a municipality to the citizens that live there and pool their resources through tax revenue for the provision of such services. Certain basic municipal services such as clean water, streets and roadways, and garbage pickup are seen by many as part of the social contract, and an expectation of what citizens get in return for their tax dollars. As a philosophical and political matter, how far should responsibilities, duties, and obligations of local governments extend? Do those obligations change if some of these government services are outsourced to private organizations?

3.   Consider what happens when basic services are not provided and fundamental notions of public responsibility are breached. In Flint, Michigan, the water service provided to residents was contaminated, but local health officials and politicians told constituents that the water was safe to drink. Sara Ganim & Linh Tran, *How Tap Water Became Toxic in Flint, Michigan*, CNN.COM, January 13, 2016. Is this a matter for redress by contract law, tort law, or criminal law? What reasoning underlies your answer?

PROBLEM: CITIZEN BENEFICIARIES

Ascot is a town of approximately 1 million that has seen the loss of many manufacturing jobs from its inner city. Many of Ascot's residents have migrated to larger cities in other states, while others have moved far out to the Ascot suburbs in search of jobs and lower housing prices. This has largely destroyed the economic life of Ascot's inner city, which during the past two decades has had the highest poverty rates in the state.

Ascot's local leaders have noted that in other cities around the country of a similar size, including the neighboring city of Bowtie, life has been turning around in the past five years. Increasingly, younger people are moving back to urban areas, noting the easy commute to work, as well as the presence of libraries, museums, and public transportation. Ascot's leaders decided to get an "urban revitalization" initiative underway. They used public municipal funds to hire a strategic and grant writing consulting company, Windsor, Inc. that would seek funding for business and job creation as well as economic development within the Ascot inner city.

Windsor was extremely successful, identifying a federal government grant focused on urban core revitalization. Under the federal government program, if an urban area met the criteria for an "urban entrepreneurial economic zone" and had a functioning job placement center for residents, then assistance would be given to those starting businesses. Assistance would also be given to establish community health plans and daycare centers that would benefit the residents. Other urban areas that had been named "urban entrepreneurial economic zones" saw a growth in local businesses and a dramatic decline in unemployment.

Not only did Windsor identify the program, but the company, with the permission of its supervising city official in charge of the urban revitalization effort, also applied for the grant on the City of Ascot's behalf. The federal government determined that Ascot had met all of the criteria in order to be named an urban entrepreneurial zone, and all relevant documents were signed. The residents were happy and excited. When it came time to pay for the programs, however, it was revealed that Ascot did not have a qualifying job placement center. The federal government asked Ascot to establish such a center, but Ascot's city council declined to pay for it, with the loss of the grant funding as a result.

The residents are furious at this result and would like to sue in order to enforce the terms of the grant with the federal government or the terms of the contract between Ascot and Windsor. Alternatively, to solve the problem, they would ask the court to require the City of Ascot to build the qualifying job placement center. Do the residents have a cause of action? What are their strategic options?

———————

Consider how the Restatement deals with third-party beneficiaries. Afterward, we'll look at a case involving whether foreign workers of a U.S. company may have rights and benefits under a supply contract.

RESTATEMENT (SECOND) OF CONTRACTS, SECTIONS 302, 313

§ 302.   *Intended and Incidental Beneficiaries.*

(1) Unless otherwise agreed between promisor and promisee, a beneficiary of a promise is an intended beneficiary if recognition of a right to performance in the beneficiary is appropriate to effectuate the intention of the parties and either

(a) the performance of the promise will satisfy an obligation of the promisee to pay money to the beneficiary; or

(b) the circumstances indicate that the promisee intends to give the beneficiary the benefit of the promised performance.

(2) An incidental beneficiary is a beneficiary who is not an intended beneficiary.

Comments: . . .

d.   Other intended beneficiaries. Either a promise to pay the promisee's debt to a beneficiary or a gift promise involves a manifestation of intention by the promisee and promisor sufficient, in a contractual setting, to make reliance by the beneficiary both reasonable and probable. Other cases may be quite similar in this respect. Examples are a promise to perform a supposed or asserted duty of the promisee, a promise to discharge a lien on the promisee's property, or a promise to satisfy the duty of a third person. In such cases, if the beneficiary would be reasonable in relying on the promise as manifesting an intention to confer a right on him, he is an intended beneficiary. Where there is doubt whether such reliance would be reasonable, considerations of procedural convenience and other factors not strictly dependent on the manifested intention of the parties may affect the question whether under Subsection (1) recognition of a right in the beneficiary is appropriate. In some cases an overriding policy, which may be embodied in a statute, requires recognition of such a right without regard to the intention of the parties.

Illustrations:

10. A, the operator of a chicken processing and fertilizer plant, contracts with B, a municipality, to use B's sewage system. With the purpose of preventing harm to landowners downstream from its system, B obtains from A a promise to remove specified types of waste from its deposits into the system. C, a downstream landowner, is an intended beneficiary under Subsection (1)(b).

12. B contracts to build a house for A. Pursuant to the contract, B and his surety S execute a payment bond to A by which they promise A that all of B's debts for labor and materials on the house will be paid. B later employs C as a carpenter and buys lumber from D. C and D are intended

beneficiaries of S's promise to A, whether or not they have power to create liens on the house.

15.   A buys food from B, a grocer, for household use, relying on B's express warranty. C, A's minor child, is injured in person by breach of the warranty. Under Uniform Commercial Code § 2–318, without regard to the intention of A or B, the warranty extends to C.

e.   Incidental beneficiaries. Performance of a contract will often benefit a third person. But unless the third person is an intended beneficiary as here defined, no duty to him is created. See § 315.

Illustrations:

16.   B contracts with A to erect an expensive building on A's land. C's adjoining land would be enhanced in value by the performance of the contract. C is an incidental beneficiary.

19.   A contracts to erect a building for C. B then contracts with A to supply lumber needed for the building. C is an incidental beneficiary of B's promise, and B is an incidental beneficiary of C's promise to pay A for the building.

§ 313.   *Government Contracts.*

(1)   The rules stated in this Chapter apply to contracts with a government or governmental agency except to the extent that application would contravene the policy of the law authorizing the contract or prescribing remedies for its breach.

(2)   In particular, a promisor who contracts with a government or governmental agency to do an act for or render a service to the public is not subject to contractual liability to a member of the public for consequential damages resulting from performance or failure to perform unless

(a)   the terms of the promise provide for such liability; or

(b)   the promisee is subject to liability to the member of the public for the damages and a direct action against the promisor is consistent with the terms of the contract and with the policy of the law authorizing the contract and prescribing remedies for its breach.

DOE v. WAL-MART STORES, INC.
572 F.3d 677 (9th Cir. 2009)

GOULD, J.

The appellants were among the plaintiffs in the district court and are employees of foreign companies that sell goods to Wal-Mart Stores, Inc. ("Wal-Mart"). They brought claims against Wal-Mart based on the working conditions in each of their employers' factories.[1] These claims relied primarily on a code of conduct included in Wal-Mart's supply contracts, specifying basic labor standards that suppliers must meet. . . .

Plaintiffs are employees of Wal-Mart's foreign suppliers in countries including China, Bangladesh, Indonesia, Swaziland, and Nicaragua. . . . In 1992, Wal-Mart developed a code of conduct for its suppliers, entitled "Standards for Suppliers" ("Standards"). These Standards were incorporated into its supply contracts with foreign suppliers. The Standards require foreign suppliers to adhere to local laws and local industry standards regarding working conditions like pay, hours, forced labor, child labor, and discrimination. The Standards also include a paragraph entitled "RIGHT OF INSPECTION":

> To further assure proper implementation of and compliance with the standards set forth herein, Wal-Mart or a third party designated by Wal-Mart will undertake affirmative measures, such as on-site inspection of production facilities, to implement and monitor said standards. Any supplier which fails or refuses to comply with these standards or does not allow inspection of production facilities is subject to immediate cancellation of any and all outstanding orders, refuse [sic] or return [sic] any shipment, and otherwise cease doing business [sic] with Wal-Mart.

Thus, each supplier must acknowledge that its failure to comply with the Standards could result in cancellation of orders and termination of its business relationship with Wal-Mart.

Wal-Mart represents to the public that it improves the lives of its suppliers' employees and that it does not condone any violation of the Standards. However, Plaintiffs allege that Wal-Mart does not adequately monitor its suppliers and that Wal-Mart knows its suppliers often violate the Standards. Specifically, Plaintiffs claim that in 2004, only eight percent of audits were unannounced, and that workers are often coached on how to respond to auditors. Additionally, Plaintiffs allege that Wal-Mart's inspectors were pressured to produce positive reports of factories that were not in compliance with the Standards. Finally, Plaintiffs allege that the short deadlines and low prices in Wal-Mart's supply contracts force suppliers to violate the Standards in order to satisfy the terms of the contracts. . . .

Plaintiffs [claim they] are third-party beneficiaries of the Standards contained in Wal-Mart's supply contracts . . . The common law in California and elsewhere establishes that, as recited in the applicable Restatement (Second) of Contracts: "A promise in a contract creates a duty in the

---

[1] The complaint also included claims by California plaintiffs, who were employees of Wal-Mart's competitors. However, this appeal is brought only by the foreign plaintiffs.

promisor to any intended beneficiary to perform the promise, and the intended beneficiary may enforce the duty." Restatement (Second) of Contracts § 304 (1981). However, the Restatement also explains that a beneficiary is only "an intended beneficiary if recognition of a right to performance in the beneficiary is appropriate to effectuate the intention of the parties. . . ." Restatement (Second) of Contracts § 302(1). . . .

Plaintiffs argue that Wal-Mart promised the suppliers that it would monitor the suppliers' compliance with the Standards, and that Plaintiffs are third-party beneficiaries of that promise to monitor. Plaintiffs rely on this language in the Standards: "Wal-Mart will undertake affirmative measures, such as on-site inspection of production facilities, to implement and monitor said standards." . . . [T]his language does not create a duty on the part of Wal-Mart to monitor the suppliers, and does not provide Plaintiffs a right of action against Wal-Mart as third-party beneficiaries.

The language and structure of the agreement show that Wal-Mart reserved the right to inspect the suppliers, but did not adopt a duty to inspect them. The language on which Plaintiffs rely is found in a paragraph entitled "Right of Inspection," contained in a two-page section entitled "Standards for Suppliers." And after stating Wal-Mart's intention to enforce the Standards through monitoring, the paragraph elaborates the potential consequences of a supplier's failure to comply with the Standards- Wal-Mart may cancel orders and cease doing business with that supplier- but contains no comparable adverse consequences for Wal-Mart if Wal-Mart does not monitor that supplier. Because, as we view the supply contracts, Wal-Mart made no promise to monitor the suppliers, no such promise flows to Plaintiffs as third-party beneficiaries.

Plaintiffs alternatively argue that they are third-party beneficiaries of the suppliers' promises to maintain certain working conditions, and that Plaintiffs may therefore sue Wal-Mart. This theory fails because Wal-Mart was the promisee vis-a-vis the suppliers' promises to follow the Standards, and Plaintiffs have not plausibly alleged a contractual duty on the part of Wal-Mart that would extend to Plaintiffs.[4]

Plaintiffs' allegations are insufficient to support the conclusion that Wal-Mart and the suppliers intended for Plaintiffs to have a right of performance against Wal-Mart under the supply contracts. See Restatement (Second) of Contracts § 302(1). We therefore conclude that Plaintiffs have not stated a claim against Wal-Mart as third-party

---

[4]   The Restatement does suggest that a promisee may be liable to a third-party beneficiary when "the performance of the promise will satisfy an obligation of the promisee to pay money to the beneficiary." Restatement (Second) of Contracts § 302(1)(a). The third-party creditor in such a case is commonly known as a "creditor beneficiary." Restatement (Second) of Contracts § 302, cmt. d. However, Plaintiffs have alleged no prior obligation by Wal-Mart that could support finding a contractual duty owed to Plaintiffs by Wal-Mart, and so the suppliers' employees cannot be considered to be creditor beneficiaries.

beneficiaries of any contractual duty owed by Wal-Mart, and we affirm the district court's dismissal of the third-party beneficiary contract claim. . . .

NOTES AND QUESTIONS

1.   What is a "corporate code of conduct," and what is the purpose of such a code? Aside from safety and treatment of workers, what other matters might a corporate social responsibility code include?

2.   Why would a corporation such as Wal-Mart decide to adopt such a code?

3.   Were the workers in *Doe v. Wal-Mart* stores "intended beneficiaries" or "incidental beneficiaries" of the contract? What is the difference between these two categories, and what is their legal import?

4.   Is the workers' status as foreign nationals relevant to the outcome of the case? Is there an element of work in global supply chains that is "out of sight, out of mind?" For more on this topic, see INVISIBLE LABOR HIDDEN WORK IN THE CONTEMPORARY WORLD (eds. Marion Crain, Winifred R. Poster & Miriam A. Cherry) (2016).

CHEN V. STREET BEAT SPORTSWEAR, INC.

226 F.Supp. 2d 355 (E.D.N.Y. 2002)

GLASSER, J.

. . . Plaintiffs Fen X. Chen, Qui Chen, Yu Zheng, Chai Chen, Dang Zheng, Hua Chen, Yong Chen, Kun Huang, and Qi Liu ("plaintiffs") bring this action against two garment factories, 1A Fashions Inc. and Red Arrow Inc. ("factory defendants"), three individuals who allegedly own and operate said garment factories, a manufacturer of women's sportswear, Street Beat Sportswear, Inc. ("Street Beat") . . . (collectively "manufacturer defendants"). The manufacturer defendants now move [to dismiss a] third-party beneficiary claim, for breach of contract. For the reasons that follow, the motion is denied. . . .

The factory defendants and the manufacturer defendants are the plaintiffs' "employers or joint employers within the meaning of the [federal Fair Labor Standards Act (FLSA)]." The manufacturer defendants "hired, retained or contracted with the [f]actory [d]efendants" to produce their sportswear providing them with garment designs, sewing instructions, textiles, trimmings and other materials. The factory defendants are a "fully integrated element of Street Beat's manufacturing operation," and approximately 90% of the garments made by the factory defendants are produced for the manufacturer defendants.

The plaintiffs worked for the "defendants" from 1996 until 2000 as garment inspectors, hangers, button sewers, iron pressers, or general helpers. The plaintiffs worked seven days a week with only one or two days off a year, and often worked from early in the morning until past midnight and into the next morning. The plaintiffs were paid either by the piece or by the hour, and were never paid overtime wages for the hours worked past forty hours a week. The factory workers were threatened with the loss of their jobs if they did not comply with this work schedule. The [defendants] maintained false employment records, including false time records, in an effort to conceal their employment practices.

The plaintiffs allege that the manufacturer defendants knew or should reasonably have known that the plaintiffs were not paid minimum wage and overtime pay. Street Beat had a representative present in the factories on an average of three times a week who monitored the production and quality of the plaintiffs' work. In addition, Street Beat was put on notice of prior violations because it had been previously sued by other factory workers, and the United States Department of Labor ("DOL") had found that Street Beat had violated the FLSA in the past. According to the plaintiffs, the manufacturer defendants contracted with the factory defendants at prices too low and at delivery conditions too onerous to allow for payment of minimum wage and overtime pay.

On February 26, 1997, the manufacturer defendants signed a Memorandum of Agreement ("MOA") with the DOL by which the manufacturer defendants entered into an ongoing Augmented Compliance Program Agreement ("ACPA") to ensure factory compliance with the FLSA. According to the plaintiffs, the ACPA imposed several duties on the manufacturer defendants, including but not limited to (1) the pre-contract evaluation of the economic feasibility, based on the price terms involved, of a contractor's compliance with the FLSA; (2) the ongoing monitoring of contractor compliance with the FLSA; and (3) in the event that FLSA violations by a contractor were detected by the manufacturer defendants, a suspension of shipment of all goods affected by said violations and payment of all unpaid back wages.

The plaintiffs allege that the manufacturer defendants "completely controlled and dominated" the factory defendants, and "each defendant aided and abetted the wrongful acts of the others." In addition, "each of the defendants was the agent, employee and/or joint venture partner of, or was working in concert with the co-defendants and was acting within the course and scope of such agency, employment and/or joint venture or concerted activity."

[The plaintiffs stated various negligence and statutory causes of action as well as a] third-party beneficiary claim for breach of contract alleging that they are the "third-party beneficiaries" to the [DOL's] contract with Street Beat, and that Street Beat "materially beached" the terms of that agreement. . . . The plaintiffs seek unpaid wages, including minimum wage, overtime pay and spread hours pay, and liquidated damages and/or interest. . . .

In New York, a third-party may enforce a contract if that third-party is an intended beneficiary of the contract. . . . The applicable law provides that a non-party to a contract may recover "by establishing (1) the existence of a valid and binding contract between other parties, (2) that the contract was intended for his benefit, and (3) that the benefit to him is sufficiently immediate, rather than incidental, to indicate the assumption by the contracting parties to compensate him if the benefit is lost." Cabrera v. DeGuerin, No. 96–CV–4411, 1999 WL 438473, at *4 (E.D.N.Y. May 18, 1999) . . . . A contract is intended for the benefit of a third-party if (1) "no one other than the third party can recover if the promisor breaches the contract or (2) the language of the contract otherwise evidences an intent to permit enforcement by third parties." MBL Contracting Corp. v. King World Prod., Inc., 98 F.Supp.2d 492, 496 (S.D.N.Y.2000) . . . . An intention to benefit a third-party may be gleaned from the contract as a whole and the party need not be named specifically as a beneficiary. . . .

Here, the first element with respect to enforcement by third-parties is satisfied because the agreement between the DOL and Street Beat is a valid and binding contract between parties other than the plaintiffs. As for the second element, the plaintiffs argue that the intent to benefit and permit enforcement of the contract by the plaintiffs as intended third-parties is clear from the language of the ACPA. . . . Specifically, the plaintiffs argue that the ACPA evidences an intent to benefit the plaintiffs because the focus of the ACPA, and every provision therein, is on ensuring through pre-evaluation and monitoring by Street Beat, that factories like those in which plaintiffs worked, pay minimum wage and overtime. They argue that, had Street Beat complied with its obligations under the agreement, the plaintiffs would have been paid what they were legally entitled to, and that the ACPA provides for recovery by the plaintiffs in the event of a breach. Street Beat argues that the plaintiffs were only incidental beneficiaries to the agreement because the ACPA expressly provides for the DOL's enforcement and recovery in the event of a breach, and that any payment to employees is simply to effectuate compliance with the FLSA. Moreover, Street Beat argues that, assuming that the ACPA did in fact contemplate enforcement by third-parties, only employees of the factories listed in the MOA, Excel Fashions Inc. ("Excel Fashions") and Monami Fashions Inc. ("Monami Fashions"), would be entitled to enforce the agreement, and not the plaintiffs in this case.

Based on the language of the agreement itself, it is strikingly obvious that the entire purpose of the ACPA is to ensure that employees of factories which contract with Street Beat are paid minimum wage and overtime, and that it was they who were directly intended to be benefitted. As described in the preamble of the ACPA, Street Beat entered into the agreement with the DOL to "promot[e] compliance . . . with Section 15(a)(1) of the [FLSA]." Section 15(a) states in pertinent part: "it shall be unlawful for any person . . . to transport, offer for transportation, ship, deliver, or sell in commerce . . . any goods in the production of which any employee was employed in violation of section 206 or section 207 of this title." 29 U.S.C. § 215(a). Section 206 of the FLSA provides for minimum wage payments, and Section 207 provides for overtime compensation. . . . Thus, the ACPA explains . . . that its purpose is to ensure that factories hired by Street Beat for the production of its garments pay their employees minimum wage and overtime.

The intent to benefit factory employees such as plaintiffs here is further evidenced in the body of the ACPA . . . . Section 3 describes the procedures by which Street Beat agreed to evaluate a potential factory in determining whether to engage in business with that factory for the production of its garments. Before contracting with any factory, Street Beat must review with the owner of the factory the terms and purposes of the Employer Compliance Program ("ECP")[8] . . . and the ACPA; the economic feasibility of the price terms that are involved, in light of compliance with the FLSA; the factory's willingness and ability to fully understand and fully comply with the FLSA; and the obligation of the factory to advise the manufacturer when and if it is unable to meet the requirements of the FLSA. . . .

Section 4 states that Street Beat will monitor and enforce full compliance with the FLSA and the ECP "by all contractors in all activities connected with any purchase by the [manufacturer]," and Section 5 describes Street Beat's record keeping obligations of all of its purchases. Section 6 outlines the duties and steps Street Beat must take when it discovers that a factory has failed to comply with the FLSA. Once a violation has been detected, Street Beat must notify the DOL, and may be required to provide the DOL with a report, including copies of payroll records for each week the violations occurred, a certification from the factory that the records are accurate, copies of employee paystubs, and copies of payroll checks.

Most significantly, Section 8 outlines the procedures for payment of back wages to the employees of contracting factories. Section 8 states that Street Beat

> will make payments to the DOL in an amount sufficient to enable the DOL to allocate and disburse monies to the employees of [c]ontractors (or, at the option of the [manufacturer] if authorized by the DOL, to enable the [manufacturer] to do so directly to the employees of the [c]ontractors) in amounts sufficient to

---

[8]   The ECP is a contract between the factory and the manufacturer, and obligates the factory to comply with, inter alia, the minimum wage and overtime provisions of the FLSA.

compensate the employees for back wages due to them under the [FLSA] from the [c]ontractor.

Id. . . . Section 8(a)(ii) provides the payment schedule for compensation to employees of any contractor who violates the FLSA during the term of the ACPA and Section 8(a)(i) provides for a special payment schedule to certain factories . . . where violations had been detected prior to Street Beat's entering into the ACPA. . . . Notwithstanding Section 8(a)(i), the ACPA specifically provides that Street Beat will pay back wages to employees of contractors who engage in business with Street Beat and who violate the FLSA. Thus, recognizing "a right to performance in the beneficiary," the ACPA evidences an intent to benefit employees such as plaintiffs in this case. . . .

Section 9 describes the remedial process for contractor violations, and states, in pertinent part, that the DOL and Street Beat will attempt to reach an agreement on the total amount to be paid to the affected employees, but, in the absence of a prompt agreement, the DOL will decide the proper amount on its own.

Section 10 describes the potential of litigation in the event of a breach of the ACPA. That section states that the DOL will not initiate litigation against Street Beat without first providing written notice to allow Street Beat an opportunity to respond to the allegations. However, such notice will not be required if the DOL determines, inter alia, that Street Beat willfully violated the FLSA and/or the ACPA or that such violation was imminent. Section 10(c) states that "the activities that [Street Beat] undertakes by this ACPA to engage in are subject to enforcement by specific performance during the term of the ACPA at the instance of the DOL." . . . Because the ACPA's remedial scheme does not expressly provide for third-party beneficiary suits to enforce the ACPA, the defendants argue that the parties to the contract never intended to permit enforcement by persons other than the DOL.

However, the ACPA's silence on this issue is not fatal to the plaintiffs' claim because, as noted supra, an intent to benefit the plaintiffs may otherwise be gleaned from the contract as a whole. . . . Moreover, while Section 10 provides that Street Beat's compliance with the ACPA are subject to specific performance at the instance of the DOL, this statement does not necessarily preclude enforcement by persons other than the DOL. The manifest purpose of the ACPA is to benefit employees of factories who contract with Street Beat by ensuring that factory workers are paid minimum wage and overtime as required by the FLSA. The plaintiffs in this case are exactly those persons whom the ACPA was intended to benefit. Thus, the plaintiffs may sue on the contract for an alleged breach committed by Street Beat. . . .

Neither party explicitly addresses the third element necessary to show enforcement of a contract by third-parties-whether the benefit to the factory workers would be sufficiently immediate to indicate the assumption by the contracting parties of an obligation to compensate them if the benefit is lost. . . . The Court's own review of the agreement evidences an intent in the ACPA to immediately compensate employees for violations of the FLSA. Specifically, the ACPA requires that once violations are detected by Street Beat, it must report its findings to the DOL, and include in such report, copies of payroll records, a certification from the factory that the records are accurate, employee paystubs, and payroll checks. Employees are then paid as provided in Section 8(a)(ii): "to the extent that an employing [c]ontracter fails to do so no later than 30 days after demand by the [manufacturer] or the DOL, the [manufacturer] will (no later than 60 days after such demand) pay an amount equal to the back wages due to the employees of the [c]ontractor." Such payment will be made either to the DOL for disbursement to the employees of contractors, or, if requested by the manufacturer and authorized by the DOL, directly to the employees. This payment scheme provides for an immediate benefit to factory workers in the event of a breach of the ACPA.

Thus, having concluded that the agreement between the DOL and Street Beat evidences a specific intent to benefit employees such as the plaintiffs in this action, and that such compensation is immediate, the Court concludes that the plaintiffs may enforce the terms of the ACPA. Accordingly, the motion to dismiss the plaintiffs' third-party beneficiary claim is denied. . . .

NOTES AND QUESTIONS

1.   In New York, what is the test for a third party to enforce a contract? Under New York law, how is the element of "intent to benefit" shown? Must the contract itself explicitly name a third party for it to be enforceable by that third party?

2.   Why did the workers in the *Doe v. Wal-Mart* case have their case dismissed for failure to state a claim upon which relief could be granted, while the workers in *Chen v. Beat Street* were able to continue litigating their case?

PROBLEM: CORPORATE CODES OF CONDUCT

Using the Internet, go online and do a search for corporate codes of conduct. Find the corporate code of conduct from a business that you either routinely buy from or that you think well of as a socially responsible company. Once you have selected a company and its code, read the code and determine what practices it covers, whether those practices cover worker safety, environmental concerns, or involvement in local communities. Read the code closely to determine if there is any monitoring of the corporate code of conduct. Do any constituencies (internal or external to the corporation, including workers, investors, and community members) have the ability to enforce the corporate code of conduct? If you thought the company was violating its code of conduct, what options might you have for enforcement as a consumer or community member? An investor? An advocate on behalf of workers?

B. ASSIGNMENT

Common law through the nineteenth century was suspicious of transfers of contract rights, but modern contract law is much more supportive. There is value in freely transferable contract rights, because people sometimes need to relieve themselves of contractual obligations and others find it valuable to be in on a deal. One way to enable that is a transfer, formally called "assignment." If the identity of the performer is important—so-called "personal service" contracts—assignment is typically not permitted without the other party's consent. But so long as performance quality under a contract does not vary with a performing party's identity, the other party should not care. What happens, though, when the assignment involves a business competitor? The next two cases examine this scenario.

BERLINER FOODS CORP. v. PILLSBURY CO.
633 F.Supp. 557 (D. Md. 1986)

MOTZ, J.

This action arises from defendants' termination of Berliner Foods Corporation as a distributor of Haagen-Dazs Ice Cream after the Berliner family sold Berliner Foods to Dreyer's Grand Ice Cream, Inc. Plaintiffs seek injunctive relief as well as monetary damages. . . .

In or about 1974 Berliner Foods first became a distributor for Haagen-Dazs Ice Cream. . . . It is undisputed that the agreement was oral. According to plaintiffs, Reuben Mattus, then the owner of the Haagen-Dazs Company, promised that they would remain as Haagen-Dazs distributors as long as they met Haagen-Dazs' performance standards. Plaintiffs concede that the subject of a transfer of the ownership of the distributorship was not discussed between Mattus and themselves. Over the next decade both parties flourished through their relationship. The concept of manufacturing and marketing high quality and high priced ice cream took hold (despite initial resistance to it) and the Berliners successfully promoted the sale of Haagen-Dazs to supermarket chains and other retailers in the Baltimore-Washington area.

In 1983 the Pillsbury Company acquired Haagen-Dazs. Although the Berliners (as well as other Haagen-Dazs distributors throughout the country) were concerned as to whether Pillsbury would adhere to the oral distribution agreements which they had made with Reuben Mattus,

Berliner Foods remained as a distributor for Haagen-Dazs. It was notably successful, and Pillsbury indicated interest in buying the Berliners out. However, in December 1985 the Berliners entered into a contract to sell Berliner Foods not to Pillsbury but to Dreyers, the manufacturer of a premium ice cream which has heretofore been sold primarily in the western part of the United States. Dreyers is attempting to expand its market to the east and chose to purchase Berliner Foods as the means to effect distribution in the mid-Atlantic region.[2]

The Berliners did not advise Pillsbury of the sale of Berliner Foods to Dreyers until after the sale was final. When Pillsbury learned of the sale, it advised Berliner Foods that its distributorship for Haagen-Dazs would be terminated. Pillsbury indicated to Berliner Foods, as it contends in this suit, that it did not want the distribution of Haagen-Dazs to be in the control of a distributor owned by one of its competitors.

Plaintiffs, drawing a distinction between "premium" ice cream and "super premium" ice cream, contend that Dreyers and Haagen-Dazs are not competitors. They point to the fact that Dreyers and Haagen-Dazs, with Pillsbury's knowledge and consent, have shared distributors in other areas. Pillsbury responds that while it did agree to share a distributor with Breyers in northern California, it did so only on an experimental basis and that it has decided—and has so advised Dreyers—that this relationship is to be discontinued. Dreyers and Haagen-Dazs are very much in competition, asserts Pillsbury, not only in the ultimate consumer market but also in the interim market for display and storage of their products in retailers' freezers.

The Fourth Circuit has ruled that in deciding whether or not to issue a preliminary injunction in a case where "serious issues" are presented, a court should "balance the 'likelihood' of irreparable harm to the plaintiff against the 'likelihood' of harm to the defendant; . . . the importance of probability of success increases as the probability of irreparable injury diminishes, . . . and where the latter may be characterized as simply 'possible,' the former can be decisive. Even so, it remains merely one 'strong factor' to be weighed along side both the likely harm to the defendant and the public interest." Blackwelder Furniture Co. v. Seilig Mfg. Co., 550 F.2d 189, 194–95 (4th Cir.1977). . . . In a case such as this, where the stakes are high and plaintiffs are represented by able counsel, it is difficult to say that the issues presented are not "serious" ones. However, it seems clear that plaintiffs will not prevail on the merits.

It is one thing to say, as plaintiffs allege and as can be presumed for present purposes, that Reuben Mattus told the Berliners that they could remain as distributors as long as they met performance standards. It is

---

[2]   Because of the similarity of the name "Dreyers" with the name "Breyers," Dreyers' chief competitor in the east, Dreyers has decided to sell its ice cream under the name "Edy's" there.

quite another thing to say, as plaintiffs further argue, that by virtue of such a representation the Berliners were free to sell their distributorship to anyone whom they chose without the prior approval of Haagen-Dazs. It is hornbook law that contracts calling for the performance of personal services, including distributorship agreements, which are silent regarding assignments, cannot be assigned without the prior consent of the other contracting party. See Crane Ice Cream Co. v. Terminal Freezing & Heating Co., 147 Md. 588, 128 A. 280 (1925) . . . Further, it defies common sense to require a manufacturer to leave the distribution of its products to a distributor under the control of a competitor or potential competitor. . . .[4]

The balancing of the respective irreparable harms to the parties by the issuance or non-issuance of the preliminary injunction also argues in favor of denial of the injunction. If the injunction is not issued, there will be no legal obstacle to Berliner Foods distributing ice cream for Dreyers. Plaintiffs argue that the effectiveness of Berliner Foods distribution efforts might be hampered by the fact that it will not also be distributing Haagen-Dazs. However, Berliner Foods and Dreyers both knew when they entered into their contract that this was a distinct possibility—the contract expressly contemplates that the right to distribute Haagen-Dazs might not survive the sale of the distributorship.

Defendants, on the other hand, would be substantially injured by requiring them to continue Berliner Foods as a distributor. Dreyers is aggressively entering the Mid-Atlantic market and this will be a time of intense competition among ice cream manufacturers for the freezer space of the retailers. During this period, defendants need a distributor of whose loyalty they can be assured, both for maintaining short term sales and establishing long term ties with retailers. Moreover, the Good Humor Company, the defendants' new distributor, is new to the Haagen-Dazs product and the confusion caused by a dual distribution system just as Good Humor is coming on board might well have detrimental effects in the marketing of Haagen-Dazs.

The final factor to be taken into account is, to the extent that it exists independently of other considerations, the public interest. Plaintiffs seek to invoke that interest on their behalf by arguing that they are the champions of other Haagen-Dazs distributors throughout the United States whose rights Pillsbury is attempting to violate by imposing as a

---

[4]   Plaintiffs also argue a theory of promissory estoppel. Assuming that under Maryland law promissory estoppel can be applied to make enforceable an agreement which is unenforceable under the law of contracts, there is no promissory estoppel here. First, on the facts as they have thus far been developed, the Court does not find that the Berliners were promised that they could sell their distributorship to a Haagen-Dazs competitor. Second, the Berliners have been handsomely paid by Dreyers for the reliance damages which they claim—capital investment in their business—and Dreyers has obtained an active distributorship in exchange. Third, Berliner Foods' most recent investment in the expansion of storage space—which plaintiffs heavily stressed in first advancing their promissory estoppel argument—was made in contemplation of the sale of the distributorship to Dreyers.

condition to the transfer of a distributorship prior approval by Pillsbury. Of course, it is really Dreyers' own interest which Dreyers is seeking to further. It wants to be free to take over Haagen-Dazs distributors in order to capitalize upon the relationships which those distributors have built up (on behalf of Haagen-Dazs) with retailers over the years. Furthermore, while Dreyers alleges that Pillsbury is following a cynical strategy to exploit Haagen-Dazs distributors, specifically to deprive them of the value of the goodwill which they have been able to generate in their businesses, plaintiffs have produced no substantial evidence of that fact. Given the history of the relationship between Haagen-Dazs and its distributors, it may well be that the distributors have rights greater than those which inhere in a simple at will arrangement. However, on the state of this record there is no reason to believe that at the inception of their relationship, Reuben Mattus and the distributors contemplated, discussed or intended that the distributors would have the right to undermine the Haagen-Dazs operation by selling their distributorship to a Haagen-Dazs competitor. Indeed, this would have been contrary to the very relationship of mutual trust which plaintiffs allege to have existed between Mattus and the distributors.

NOTES AND QUESTIONS

1.   Could Berliner have effectively "served two masters"? Could it have distributed Haagen-Dazs and Dryers equally well? If the interests of Haagen-Dazs and Dryers conflicted, how would Berliner resolve the conflict? If Berliner faced an inherent conflict, why sue to compel Haagen-Dazs to stay in the relationship?

2.   What, if anything, could Haagen-Dazs have done differently to avoid these problems? In particular, think about the alleged oral statement by the Haagen-Dazs president that Berliner could remain as a distributor as long as it met performance standards. As a practical matter, that may have been the typical outcome. But if the legal arrangement could be terminated at will, should such a commitment be reduced to writing?

SALLY BEAUTY CO. V. NEXXUS PRODUCTS CO.
801 F.2d 1001 (7th Cir. 1986)

CUDAHY, J.

Nexxus Products Company ("Nexxus") entered into a contract with Best Barber & Beauty Supply Company, Inc. ("Best"), under which Best would be the exclusive distributor of Nexxus hair care products to barbers and hair stylists throughout most of Texas. When Best was acquired by and merged into Sally Beauty Company, Inc. ("Sally Beauty"), Nexxus cancelled the agreement. Sally Beauty is a wholly-owned subsidiary of Alberto-Culver Company ("Alberto-Culver"), a major manufacturer of hair care products and a competitor of Nexxus'. Sally Beauty claims that Nexxus breached the contract by cancelling; Nexxus asserts by way of defense that the contract was not assignable or, in the alternative, not assignable to Sally Beauty. The district court granted Nexxus' motion for summary judgment, ruling that the contract was one for personal services and therefore not assignable. We affirm on a different theory—that this contract could not be assigned to the wholly-owned subsidiary of a direct competitor under section 2–210 of the Uniform Commercial Code.

[The court first found that the sales aspects of the distributorship dominated the transaction such that it was governed by Article 2 of the UCC as that statute had been adopted and interpreted under Texas law, the law applicable to the contract.]

. . . The fact that this contract is considered a contract for the sale of goods and not for the provision of a service does not, as Sally Beauty suggests, mean that it is freely assignable in all circumstances. The delegation of performance under a sales contract (whether in conjunction with an assignment of rights, as here, or not) is governed by UCC section 2–210(1) . . . The UCC recognizes that in many cases an obligor will find it convenient or even necessary to relieve himself of the duty of performance under a contract, see Official Comment 1, UCC § 2–210 ("[T]his section recognizes both delegation of performance and assignability as normal and permissible incidents of a contract for the sale of goods."). The Code therefore sanctions delegation except where the delegated performance would be unsatisfactory to the obligee: "A party may perform his duty through a delegate unless otherwise agreed to or unless the other party has a substantial interest in having his original promisor perform or control the acts required by the contract." UCC § 2–210(1) . . . . Consideration is given to balancing the policies of free alienability of commercial contracts and protecting the obligee from having to accept a bargain he did not contract for.

We are concerned here with the delegation of Best's duty of performance under the distribution agreement, as Nexxus terminated the agreement because it did not wish to accept Sally Beauty's substituted performance. . . . Only one Texas case has construed section 2–210 in the context of a party's delegation of performance under an executory contract. In McKinnie v. Milford, 597 S.W.2d 953 (Tex.Civ.App.1980, writ ref'd, n.r.e.), the court held that nothing in the Texas Business and Commercial Code prevented the seller of a horse from delegating to the buyer a pre-existing contractual duty to make the horse available to a third party for breeding. "[I]t is clear that Milford [the third party] had no particular interest in not allowing Stewart [the seller] to delegate the duties required by the contract. Milford was only interested in getting his two breedings per year, and such performance could only be obtained from McKinnie [the buyer] after he bought the horse from Stewart." Id. at 957. In McKinnie, the Texas court recognized and applied the UCC rule that bars delegation of duties if there is some reason why the non-assigning party would find performance by a delegate a substantially different thing than what he had bargained for.

In the exclusive distribution agreement before us, Nexxus had contracted for Best's "best efforts" in promoting the sale of Nexxus products in Texas. UCC § 2–306(2) . . . states that "[a] lawful agreement by either buyer or seller for exclusive dealing in the kind of goods concerned imposes unless otherwise agreed an obligation by the seller to use best efforts to supply the goods and by the buyer to use best efforts to promote their sale." This implied promise on Best's part was the consideration for Nexxus' promise to refrain from supplying any other distributors within Best's exclusive area. . . . It was this contractual undertaking which Nexxus refused to see performed by Sally.

In ruling on Nexxus' motion for summary judgment, the district court noted: "Unlike Best, Sally Beauty is a subsidiary of one of Nexxus' direct competitors. This is a significant distinction and in the court's view, it raises serious questions regarding Sally Beauty's ability to perform the distribution agreement in the same manner as Best." . . . In *Berliner Foods Corp. v. Pillsbury Co.*, 633 F.Supp. 557 (D.Md.1986), the court stated the same reservation more strongly on similar facts. Berliner was an exclusive distributor of Haagen-Dazs ice cream when it was sold to Breyer's, manufacturer of a competing ice cream line. Pillsbury Co., manufacturer of Haagen-Dazs, terminated the distributorship and Berliner sued. The court noted, while weighing the factors for and against a preliminary injunction, that "it defies common sense to require a manufacturer to leave the distribution of its products to a distributor under the control of a competitor or potential competitor." Id. at 559–60.[7] We agree with these assessments and hold that Sally Beauty's position as a wholly-owned subsidiary of Alberto-Culver is sufficient to bar the delegation of Best's duties under the agreement.

We do not believe that our holding will work the mischief with our national economy that the appellants predict. We hold merely that the duty of performance under an exclusive distributorship may not be delegated to a competitor in the market place-or the wholly-owned subsidiary of a competitor-without the obligee's consent. We believe that such a rule is consonant with the policies behind section 2–210, which is concerned with preserving the bargain the obligee has struck. Nexxus should not be required to accept the "best efforts" of Sally Beauty when those efforts are subject to the control of Alberto-Culver. It is entirely reasonable that

---

[7]   The effort by the dissent to distinguish Berliner merely because the court there apparently assumed in passing that distributorship agreements were a species of personal service contracts must fail. The Berliner court emphasizes that the sale of a distributorship to a competitor of the supplier is by itself a wholly sufficient reason to terminate the distributorship.

Nexxus should conclude that this performance would be a different thing than what it had bargained for.

At oral argument, Sally Beauty argued that the case should go to trial to allow it to demonstrate that it could and would perform the contract as impartially as Best. It stressed that Sally Beauty is a "multi-line" distributor, which means that it distributes many brands and is not just a conduit for Alberto-Culver products. But we do not think that this creates a material question of fact in this case. When performance of personal services is delegated, the trier merely determines that it is a personal services contract. If so, the duty is per se nondelegable. There is no inquiry into whether the delegate is as skilled or worthy of trust and confidence as the original obligor: the delegate was not bargained for and the obligee need not consent to the substitution.[9] And so here: it is undisputed that Sally Beauty is wholly owned by Alberto-Culver, which means that Sally Beauty's "impartial" sales policy is at least acquiesced in by Alberto-Culver-but could change whenever Alberto-Culver's needs changed. Sally Beauty may be totally sincere in its belief that it can operate "impartially" as a distributor, but who can guarantee the outcome when there is a clear choice between the demands of the parent-manufacturer, Alberto-Culver, and the competing needs of Nexxus? The risk of an unfavorable outcome is not one which the law can force Nexxus to take. Nexxus has a substantial interest in not seeing this contract performed by Sally Beauty, which is sufficient to bar the delegation under section 2–210 . . . . Because Nexxus should not be forced to accept performance of the distributorship agreement by Sally, we hold that the contract was not assignable without Nexxus' consent. . . .

Nor is distrust of one's competitors a trait unique to lawyers (as opposed to ordinary businessmen), as the dissent may be understood to suggest. [Affirmed.]

POSNER, J. (dissenting).

My brethren have decided, with no better foundation than judicial intuition about what businessmen consider reasonable, that the Uniform Commercial Code gives a supplier an absolute right to cancel an exclusive-dealing contract if the dealer is acquired, directly or indirectly, by a competitor of the supplier. I interpret the Code differently. . . . [Judge Posner first explained how he could find not support in the text of the UCC

---

[9]   Of course, the obligee makes such an assessment of the prospective delegate. If it thinks the delegated performance will be as satisfactory, it is of course free to consent to the delegation. Thus, the dissent is mistaken in its suggestion that we find it improper-a "conflict of interest"—for one competitor to distribute another competitor's products. Rather, we believe only that it is commercially reasonable that the supplier in those circumstances have consented to such a state of affairs. To borrow the dissent's example, Isuzu allows General Motors to distribute its cars because it considers this arrangement attractive.

or judicial interpretations of it to support "the per se rule that my brethren announce."]

My brethren find this a simple case—as simple (it seems) as if a lawyer had undertaken to represent the party opposing his client. But notions of conflict of interest are not the same in law and in business, and judges can go astray by assuming that the legal-services industry is the pattern for the entire economy. The lawyerization of America has not reached that point. Sally Beauty, though a wholly owned subsidiary of Alberto-Culver, distributes "hair care" supplies made by many different companies, which so far as appears compete with Alberto-Culver as vigorously as Nexxus does. Steel companies both make fabricated steel and sell raw steel to competing fabricators. General Motors sells cars manufactured by a competitor, Isuzu. What in law would be considered a fatal conflict of interest is in business a commonplace and legitimate practice. The lawyer is a fiduciary of his client; Best was not a fiduciary of Nexxus.

Selling your competitor's products, or supplying inputs to your competitor, sometimes creates problems under antitrust or regulatory law—but only when the supplier or distributor has monopoly or market power and uses it to restrict a competitor's access to an essential input or to the market for the competitor's output . . . . There is no suggestion that Alberto-Culver has a monopoly of "hair care" products or Sally Beauty a monopoly of distributing such products, or that Alberto-Culver would ever have ordered Sally Beauty to stop carrying Nexxus products. Far from complaining about being squeezed out of the market by the acquisition, Nexxus is complaining in effect about Sally Beauty's refusal to boycott it!

How likely is it that the acquisition of Best could hurt Nexxus? Not very. Suppose Alberto-Culver had ordered Sally Beauty to go slow in pushing Nexxus products, in the hope that sales of Alberto-Culver "hair care" products would rise. Even if they did, since the market is competitive Alberto-Culver would not reap monopoly profits. Moreover, what guarantee has Alberto-Culver that consumers would be diverted from Nexxus to it, rather than to products closer in price and quality to Nexxus products? In any event, any trivial gain in profits to Alberto-Culver would be offset by the loss of goodwill to Sally Beauty; and a cost to Sally Beauty is a cost to Alberto-Culver, its parent. Remember that Sally Beauty carries beauty supplies made by other competitors of Alberto-Culver; Best alone carries "hair care" products manufactured by Revlon, Clairol, Bristol-Myers, and L'Oreal, as well as Alberto-Culver. Will these powerful competitors continue to distribute their products through Sally Beauty if Sally Beauty displays favoritism for Alberto-Culver products? Would not such a display be a commercial disaster for Sally Beauty, and hence for its parent, Alberto-Culver? . . .

Another relevant consideration is that the contract between Nexxus and Best was for a short term. Could Alberto-Culver destroy Nexxus by failing to push its products with maximum vigor in Texas for a year? In the unlikely event that it could and did, it would be liable in damages to Nexxus for breach of the implied best-efforts term of the distribution contract. Finally, it is obvious that Sally Beauty does not have a bottleneck position in the distribution of "hair care" products, such that by refusing to promote Nexxus products vigorously it could stifle the distribution of those products in Texas; for Nexxus has found alternative distribution that it prefers-otherwise it wouldn't have repudiated the contract with Best when Best was acquired by Sally Beauty.

Not all businessmen are consistent and successful profit maximizers, so the probability that Alberto-Culver would instruct Sally Beauty to cease to push Nexxus products vigorously in Texas cannot be reckoned at zero. On this record, however, it is slight. And there is no principle of law that if something happens that trivially reduces the probability that a dealer will use his best efforts, the supplier can cancel the contract. . . . At most, so far as the record shows, Nexxus may have had grounds for "insecurity" regarding the performance by Sally Beauty of its obligation to use its best efforts to promote Nexxus products, but if so its remedy was not to cancel the contract but to demand assurances of due performance. See UCC § 2–609; Official Comment 5 to § 2–306. No such demand was made. . . .

NOTES AND QUESTIONS

1. Whether the transaction was for goods under the UCC or personal services appears to be a difficult determination. What parts of the contract make that determination a difficult one?

2. To what degree is *Sally Beauty* about third parties as compared to good faith? What role does good faith play in the majority's determination?

3. What is the economic argument that Judge Posner states in dissent? Does his view account adequately for anti-competitive behavior and the possibility of conflict of interest?

4. A few words on the legal vocabulary surrounding contract transfers. "Assignment" typically refers to a transfer of rights and duties (or perhaps just rights). In an assignment, the party transferring rights (or rights and duties) is called an *assignor*, and the party that receives the rights (or rights and duties) is the *assignee*. The other party to the contract is known as the *obligor*. A "delegation," on the other hand, refers to a transfer of just the duties under a contract. The *delegator* transfers duties to a *delegatee*, and the other party to the contract, who is owed the duty, is the *obligor*. Contractual obligations requiring distinctive personal performance cannot be delegated (and are often referred to as non-delegable duties). Examples: the artistic performance of an opera singer, the sports performance of a professional athlete, or the

professional expertise of a physician or attorney that inspires personal trust and confidence.

PROBLEM: UNAUTHORIZED OUTSOURCING

Bill is a computer programmer hired as an independent contractor with a five-year contract to provide software development services at a U.S. company. He is paid a six-figure annual salary, and he typically can work from home, but finds his work tedious and repetitive.

Bill discovers a solution, though. He can hire computer programmers in China to do his work for about one-fifth of his pay. Bill reviews their work and supervises them as necessary, but is largely free to enjoy himself during the workday while pocketing four-fifths of his salary. His employment contract is silent on delegation, assignment, and outsourcing.

For several months, there are no problems with the submitted work, and some is considered among the company's best. Within one year, however, a security audit reveals unexpected access to the company network from China using Bill's account, and the company discovers Bill's outsourcing activities.

Bill's manager is vexed and sends the matter to you, in the company's legal department. Would the company be entitled to declare breach and terminate Bill's contract? Or would such an action itself constitute a breach entitling Bill to damages? How could the company prevent this scenario from happening again in the future with other workers?

EXAMPLE: ANTI-ASSIGNMENT CLAUSES

JP Morgan, a large bank based in New York, made $225 million loan to Cablevision, a Mexican telecom company. Typically, borrowers of larger sums share confidential information with their lender, and in turn, the lender promises to keep the information confidential. The loan between JP Morgan and Cablevision involved an exchange of confidential information. In addition, in exchange for the loan, Cablevision granted JP Morgan some oversight rights, including veto power over business expansion, another common concession in large commercial loan agreements to reduce lender risk of borrower default.

When commercial loan agreements grant such powers to a lender, they also often limit the lender's power to transfer the loan or interests in the loan to other banks. Agreements usually let banks hive off small parts of loans to other banks, such as 2–3 percent, called participations, but the other lenders are passive, having no control over the borrower. Contractual provisions, however, normally require the borrower's permission before the entire loan (an "assignment") is transferred, because all lender rights and duties (including access to the borrower's confidential information) are also transferred. The JP Morgan-Cablevision loan followed the typical pattern: JP Morgan could sell small participations in its loan to other lenders without Cablevision's consent, but was forbidden to assign the loan without Cablevision's permission.

The financial crisis of 2009 dried up interest among most lenders to share participations or to take assignments, but JP Morgan found interest with Banco Inbursa, a Mexican bank controlled by billionaire Carlos Slim Helu, owner of Telmex, Cablevision's arch-rival. JP Morgan sought out Cablevision's management to agree to an assignment, but Cablevision refused. JP Morgan then began threatening to let Inbursa in on the deal as a participation, rather than an assignment, to avoid needing Cablevision's consent. Despite Cablevision's repeated refusal, JP Morgan went forward anyway with what it labeled a "participation," transferring 90 percent of the loan to Inbursa.

If Cablevision brought a lawsuit to stop the transfer to Inbursa, what result? Consult *Empresas Cablevisión v. JP Morgan Chase Bank*, 680 F. Supp. 625 (S.D.N.Y. 2010), *aff'd* 381 Fed. Appx. 117 (2d Cir. 2010).

C. TORTIOUS INTERFERENCE

Third parties also play a role when they create interference in a deal between two parties. Such actions sit at the intersection of contract and tort law, and they are known as *tortious interference with contractual relations*. The following is an illustrative sampling of three opinions under Massachusetts law, the first two by the state's high court more than a century apart—the first seen as seminal and the second a sturdy general statement—and the third by a lower state court, on a very close call with which other courts have disagreed.

WALKER V. CRONIN
107 Mass. 555 (Mass. 1871)

[T]he plaintiff was a manufacturer of shoes, and for the prosecution of his business it was necessary for him to employ many shoemakers; that the defendant, well knowing this, did unlawfully and without justifiable cause molest him in carrying on said business, with the unlawful purpose of preventing him from carrying it on, and wilfully induced many shoemakers who were in his employment, and others who were about to enter into it, to abandon it without his consent and against his will; and that thereby the plaintiff lost their services, and profits and advantages which he would have derived therefrom, and was put to great expense to procure other suitable workmen, and compelled to pay larger prices for work than he would have had to pay but for the said doings of the defendant, and otherwise injured in his business.

[T]he plaintiff entered into contracts with certain shoemakers for them severally to make stock, which he delivered to them, into shoes, and return the shoes to his factory; that the defendant, well knowing this, with the unlawful purpose of preventing him from carrying on his business, inducing them to return the stock unfinished to the factory, and to neglect and refuse to make it into shoes as they had agreed to do; and that the stock was thereby damaged, and the plaintiff put to trouble and expense in reassorting it and procuring it to be finished, and compelled to pay larger prices for the finishing of it than he would have done under said contracts, and by reason of the said unlawful doings of the defendant was hindered and put to expense and otherwise injured in his business. . . .

WELLS, J.

The declaration, in its first count, alleges that the defendant did, "unlawfully and without justifiable cause, molest, obstruct and hinder the plaintiffs from carrying on" their business of manufacture and sale of boots and shoes, "with the unlawful purpose of preventing the plaintiffs from carrying on their said business, and wilfully persuaded and induced a large number of persons who were in the employment of the plaintiffs," and others "who were about to enter into" their employment, "to leave and abandon the employment of the plaintiffs, without their consent and against their will;" whereby the plaintiffs lost the services of said persons, and the profits and advantages they would otherwise have made and received therefrom, and were put to large expenses to procure other suitable workmen, and suffered losses in their said business.

This sets forth sufficiently (1) intentional and wilful acts (2) calculated to cause damage to the plaintiffs in their lawful business, (3) done with the unlawful purpose to cause such damage and loss, without right or justifiable cause on the part of the defendant, (which constitutes malice,) and (4) actual damage and loss resulting.

The general principle is announced in Com. Dig. Action on the Case, A.: "In all cases where a man has a temporal loss or damage by the wrong of another, he may have an action upon the case to be repaired in damages." The intentional causing of such loss to another, without justifiable cause, and with the malicious purpose to inflict it, is of itself a wrong. This proposition seems to be fully sustained by the references in the case of *Carew v. Rutherford*, 106 Mass. 1, 10, 11.

In the case of *Keeble v. Hickeringill,* as contained in a note to *Carrington v. Taylor,* 11 East, 571, 574, both actions being for damages by reason of frightening wild fowl from the plaintiff's decoy, Chief Justice Holt alludes to actions maintained for scandalous words which are actionable only by reason of being injurious to a man in his profession or trade, and adds: "How much more, when the defendant doth an actual and real damage to another when he is in the very act of receiving profit in his employment. Now there are two sorts of acts for doing damage to a man's employment, for which an action lies; the one is in respect of a man's privilege, the other is in respect of his property." After considering injuries to a man's franchise or privilege, he proceeds: "The other is where a violent or malicious act is done to a man's occupation, profession, or way of getting a livelihood; there an action lies in all cases."

From the several reports of this case it is not clear whether the action was maintained on the ground that the wild ducks were frightened out of the plaintiff's decoy, as would appear from 3 Salk. 9, and Holt, 14, 17, 18; or upon the broader one, that they were driven away and prevented from resorting there, as the case is stated in 11 Mod. 74, 130. But the doctrine thus enunciated by Lord Holt covers both aspects of the case; as does his illustration of frightening boys from going to school, whereby loss was occasioned to the master. Of like import is the case of *Tarleton v. McGawley,* Peake, 205, in which Lord Kenyon held that an action would lie for frightening the natives upon the coast of Africa, and thus preventing them from coming to the plaintiff's vessel to trade, whereby he lost the profits of such trade.

There are indeed many authorities which appear to hold that to constitute an actionable wrong there must be a violation of some definite legal right of the plaintiff. But those are cases, for the most part at least, where the defendants were themselves acting in the lawful exercise of some distinct right, which furnished the defence of a justifiable cause for their acts, except so far as they were in violation of a superior right in another.

Thus everyone has an equal right to employ workmen in his business or service; and if, by the exercise of this right in such manner as he may see fit, persons are induced to leave their employment elsewhere, no wrong is done to him whose employment they leave, unless a contract exists by which such other person has a legal right to the further continuance of their services. If such a contract exists, one who knowingly and intentionally procures it to be violated may be held liable for the wrong, although he did it for the purpose of promoting his own business. . . .

Everyone has a right to enjoy the fruits and advantages of his own enterprise, industry, skill and credit. He has no right to be protected against competition; but he has a right to be free from malicious and wanton interference, disturbance or annoyance. If disturbance or loss come as a result of competition, or the exercise of like rights by others, it is *damnum absque injuriâ,* unless some superior right by contract or otherwise is interfered with. But if it come from the merely wanton or malicious acts of others, without the justification of competition or the service of any interest or lawful purpose, it then stands upon a different footing, and falls within the principle of the authorities first referred to.

It is a well settled principle, that words, not actionable in themselves as defamatory, will nevertheless subject the party to an action for any special damages that may occur to another thereby. Bac. Ab. Slander, C. The same is true of words spoken in relation to property, or the title thereto, whereby the party is defeated of a sale, or suffers damage in any way. Bac. Ab. Action on the Case, I. Com. Dig. Action on the Case, C. So also, if, by a wrongful claim of title or lien, the owner is prevented from perfecting a sale, or a purchaser from obtaining delivery to himself of goods, an action will lie. *Green v. Button,* 2 Cr., M. & R. 707.

In all these cases, the damage for which the recovery is had is not the loss of the value of actual contracts by reason of their non-fulfilment, but the loss of advantages, either of property or of personal benefit, which, but for such interference, the plaintiff would have been able to attain or enjoy. Indeed, it has been held that loss by the breach of contract, or the wrongful conduct of another than the defendant, would not be recoverable as damages under a *per quod. Vicars v. Wilcocks,* 8 East, 1. *Morris v. Langdale,* 2 B. & P. 284. Bac. Ab. Slander, C.

This doctrine has been doubted, especially in *Lumley v. Gye,* 2 El. & Bl. 216, 239, where the case of *Newman v. Zachary,* Aleyn, 3, is cited to the contrary. That was an action on the case, maintained for wrongfully representing to the bailiff of a manor that a sheep was an estray, in consequence of which it was wrongfully seized; the reason for the decision being, "because the defendant, by his false practice, hath created a trouble, disgrace and damage to the plaintiff." But the distinction is unimportant in a case like the present, where the damage to the plaintiffs is alleged to have been the direct result of the wrongful conduct of the defendant, and so intended by him; except that it is significant of the point that the existence and defeat of rights by contract are not essential to the maintenance of an action for malicious wrong, when the defendant has no pretext of justifiable cause.

The case of *Green v. Button,* 2 Cr., M. & R. 707, is especially on point in this connection. The defendant, by means of a false claim of a lien, and of words discrediting the plaintiff, induced one who had sold goods to the plaintiff to refuse to deliver them, whereby he was injured in his business. The court, alluding to the doubts that had been expressed as to *Vicars v. Wilcocks* and *Morris v. Langdale,* and without deciding that question, distinguished the case under consideration, on the ground that, the goods not having been paid for, there was no absolute contract to deliver, upon which the plaintiff could have his remedy against the seller; that is, as the delivery was prevented by the wrongful conduct of the defendant, and there was no binding contract broken by the seller, therefore the plaintiff was entitled to recover in his action on the case *per quod.*

In *Gunter v. Astor,* 4 J. B. Moore, 12, an action was maintained for enticing away workmen from their employment for a piano manufacturer. They were not hired for a limited time, but worked by the piece. The discussion indicates that damages were considered to be recoverable for the breaking up or disturbance of the business of the plaintiff, whereby he suffered the loss of his usual profits for a long period. The grounds of damage were apparently regarded as altogether independent of the mere loss of any contracts with the workmen.

In *Benton v. Pratt*, 2 Wend. 385, it is held that proof of loss by the plaintiff of what he would otherwise have obtained, though there was no contract for it which he could enforce, will sustain an action for the wrongful conduct by which the loss was occasioned.

The difficulty in such cases is to make certain, by proof, that there has been in fact such loss as entitles the party to reparation, but that difficulty is not encountered in the present stage of this case, where all the facts alleged are admitted by the demurrer. The demurrer also admits the absence of any justifiable cause whatever. This decision is made upon the case thus presented, and does not apply to a case of interference by way of friendly advice, honestly given; nor is it in denial of the right of free expression of opinion. We have no occasion now to consider what would constitute justifiable cause.

The second and third counts recite contracts of the plaintiffs with their workmen for the performance of certain work in the manufacture of boots and shoes; and allege that the defendant, well knowing thereof, with the unlawful purpose of hindering and preventing the plaintiffs from carrying on their business, induced said persons to refuse and neglect to perform their contracts, whereby the plaintiffs suffered great damage in their business.

It is a familiar and well-established doctrine of the law upon the relation of master and servant, that one who entices away a servant, or induces him to leave his master, may be held liable in damages therefor, provided there exists a valid contract for continued service, known to the defendant. It has sometimes been supposed that this doctrine sprang from the English statute of laborers, and was confined to menial service. But we are satisfied that it is founded upon the legal right derived from the contract, and not merely upon the relation of master and servant; and that it applies to all contracts of employment, if not to contracts of every description. . . .

In *Lumley v. Gye,* 2 El. & Bl. 216, the plaintiff had engaged Miss Wagner to sing in his opera, and the defendant knowingly induced her to break her contract and refuse to sing. It was objected that the action would not lie, because her contract was merely executory, and she had never actually entered into the service of the plaintiff; and Coleridge, J., dissented, insisting that the only foundation for such an action was the statute of laborers, which did not apply to service of that character; but after full discussion and deliberation it was held that the action would lie for the damages thus caused by the defendant. . . .

Upon careful consideration of the authorities, as well as of the principles involved, we are of opinion that a legal cause of action is sufficiently stated in each of the three counts of the declaration.

NOTES AND QUESTIONS

1.   *Lumley v. Gye*, cited in the penultimate paragraph of *Walker*, arose from the same facts as *Lumley v. Wagner*, the prominent case enjoining breach of a personal services contracts rather than decreeing its specific performance. See Chapter Seven.

2.   *Walker* is generally viewed as the seminal U.S. case on tortious interference law. The case and its progeny led to the articulation of several different formulations of this tort within Section 766 of the Restatement (Second) of Torts. These variations address different ways a tortfeasor can interfere with a contract, including by inducing one party to breach or preventing another party from performing. The following more modern case explores this terrain in an opinion with the promise of achieving a level of influence akin to that of *Walker*.

SHAFIR V. STEELE
727 N.E.2d 1140 (Mass. 2000)

LYNCH, J.

The defendant appeals from the denial of his motion for a directed verdict and motion for judgment notwithstanding the verdict (judgment n.o.v.) after a jury found him liable for defamation and intentional interference with contractual relations. The evidence warranted finding the defendant liable for intentional interference with another's performance of his own contract, a tort not heretofore expressly recognized in Massachusetts. Restatement (Second) of Torts § 766A (1979).

The defendant argues that this variation of the tort of intentional interference of a contract is not and should not be part of the law in Massachusetts. Based on that assertion, the defendant claims (1) it was error to deny his motion for a directed verdict on the intentional interference with contractual relations claim because the plaintiff did not prove that the defendant induced a *third* party to breach the contract; and (2) the jury instructions and special verdict regarding the intentional interference with contractual relations count were flawed because they incorporated the elements of § 766A. . . .

We summarize the pertinent evidence in the light most favorable to the plaintiff. The defendant owns The Provincetown Advocate News Corporation, which publishes a newspaper called The Advocate in Provincetown. In 1993, the defendant and his business entities were in default on loans from Shawmut Bank (Shawmut), secured by a mortgage on the property at issue in this case, at 100 Bradford Street in Provincetown (property).

A loan restructuring agreement was worked out between Shawmut and the defendant, the only relevant details of which are that Shawmut would foreclose on the property, and that the defendant's children, through a trust, would bid at least $175,000 at the foreclosure sale. However, under the terms of the agreement, if a third party outbid the trust, the restructuring agreement would be null and void. Shawmut had valued the property at $275,000.

The foreclosure sale was held on July 6, 1993, and there were three or four bidders including the plaintiff, who was accompanied by a real estate agent, Patricia Shultz. The plaintiff's bid of $240,000 was $5,000 higher than the highest bid made by the defendant's children. She paid a $10,000 deposit and signed a purchase and sale agreement with Shawmut.

That evening, the defendant went to the plaintiff's movie theater. He stood "a little too close" to the plaintiff and, conveying "a sense of menace," told her that he was "not very well." On July 8, 1993, the defendant's newspaper published an editorial which essentially accused the plaintiff of bidding at the sale as retribution for The Advocate's refusing to drop its "Screen Scene" column which had once been critical of the plaintiff's movie theater. It concluded with a statement implying that the plaintiff intended to muzzle the newspaper.

The defendant then requested that the plaintiff and Shultz meet with him without attorneys present; he stated that he was going to bring papers to show the two "what [they] were in for." The meeting took place on July 11, 1993, during which the defendant was "quite distraught" and told the women that they did not understand and kept insisting that the building "was his." Near the end of the meeting, the plaintiff offered to have the defendant buy out her position for $15,000, which the defendant rejected.

Although the papers the defendant promised to the women did not arrive in time for the meeting, the next day the defendant had them hand delivered to Shultz's office and the plaintiff picked up a copy. The "papers" were an unsigned legal complaint prepared by the defendant's attorney for filing in the United States Bankruptcy Court. Naming both the plaintiff and Shultz, the complaint charged them with fraud, extortion, and malicious interference with an advantageous contract (between the defendant and Shawmut). The complaint was never filed but, when the plaintiff read it, she knew the charges were crimes, and she felt "terror," "bludgeoned," "stun[ned]," "totally numb," and, later, "outrage," and "anger." The defendant testified that he had read the complaint before he had it delivered to Shultz, and admitted that he, essentially, had no factual basis for any of the charges in the complaint.

Shortly thereafter, the plaintiff decided that the defendant's harassment was not going to stop. On July 26, 1993, the plaintiff's attorney sent a letter to Shawmut declaring her intention not to close the sale and requesting the return of her $10,000. Shawmut refused to return the deposit and maintained its right to seek recovery of additional expenses.

The plaintiff, herself, wrote a letter to Shawmut seeking the return of her deposit. Shawmut again refused, stating that it was "ready, willing and able" to close the sale.

We have previously recognized that §§ 766 and 766B reflect the law of Massachusetts. See United Truck Leasing Corp. v. Geltman, 406 Mass. 811, 816, 551 N.E.2d 20 (1990); Restatement (Second) of Torts § 766 comment c & § 766B comment b (1979) (historical development of the torts). [These provide, respectively, as follows:

> § 766   *Intentional Interference with Performance of Contract by Third Person.* One who intentionally and improperly interferes with the performance of a contract (except a contract to marry) between another and a third person by inducing or otherwise causing the third person not to perform the contract, is subject to liability to the other for the pecuniary loss resulting to the other from the failure of the third person to perform the contract.

> § 766B   *Intentional Interference with Prospective Contractual Relation.* One who intentionally and improperly interferes with another's prospective contractual relation (except a contract to marry) is subject to liability to the other for the pecuniary harm resulting from loss of the benefits of the relation, whether the interference consists of (a) inducing or otherwise causing a third person not to enter into or continue the prospective relation or (b) preventing the other from acquiring or continuing the prospective relation.]

[Section 766A provides:]

> § 766A   *Intentional Interference with Another's Performance of His Own Contract.* One who intentionally and improperly interferes with the performance of a contract (except a contract to marry) between another and a third person, by preventing the other from performing the contract or causing his performance to be more expensive or burdensome, is subject to liability to the other for the pecuniary loss resulting to him.]

Thus, the only difference between the torts described in § 766 . . . and § 766A is that, under § 766, the tortious conduct causes the third person not to perform, whereas § 766A involves interference preventing the plaintiff from performing his own part of the contract.

We see no compelling reason not to recognize such conduct as being tortious. We have never specifically disavowed it. Several other jurisdictions have adopted it. See also Restatement (Second) of Torts, supra at § 766A comment b (this tort is "now consistently recognized").

In addition, as discussed in Boyle v. Boston Found., Inc., 788 F.Supp. 627, 630 (D.Mass.1992), we closely approached recognizing § 766A-type liability in Anzalone v. Massachusetts Bay Transp. Auth., 403 Mass. 119, 123, 526 N.E.2d 246 (1988), where the plaintiff alleged that his supervisor interfered with his employment. Although we affirmed the dismissal of the complaint, we did not reject the principle of interference with the plaintiff's own performance of his employment contract, but focused instead on the fact that the plaintiff was still employed and did not allege loss of any advantage. *Id.* Furthermore, we are not persuaded by the defendant's essentially public policy arguments in view of the indorsement of this theory of liability by the Restatement and the majority of States that have considered it.

NOTES AND QUESTIONS

1.   *Shafir* recognized a new tort. New theories of liability invariably attract lawsuits and induce different behavior among those covered. What kinds of claims would be expected to multiply following *Shafir*?

2.   Section 766A has been criticized as too broad and a threat to business competition. Do you perceive a risk that it would frustrate good old fashioned competition for fear of liability?

NEW ENGLAND PATRIOTS V. STUBHUB

2009 WL 995483 (Mass. Super. Jan. 26, 2009)

GANTS, J.

The New England Patriots ("the Patriots") . . . brought this action seeking, among other things, permanent injunctive relief barring defendant StubHub, Inc. ("StubHub") from participating in the resale of Patriots tickets on its internet website. . . . [The Patriots allege] intentional interference with advantageous relations [and other claims]. . . . StubHub has moved for partial summary judgment on Count I. For the reasons detailed below, the motion is DENIED. . . .

The following facts are undisputed unless otherwise noted. Each season, the Patriots make available tickets to home football games. Over 95% are season tickets issued by NEP; the balance are premium seating tickets issued by NPS. Until 2007, the following warning was printed on the back of each ticket in large block letters:

> ANY NON-LICENSED INDIVIDUAL RESELLING THIS TICKET BY ANY METHOD INCLUDING WITHOUT LIMITATION, IN PERSON, ON AN AUCTION WEB SITE, OR OTHERWISE OVER THE INTERNET AND ANY LICENSED INDIVIDUAL OR ENTITY RESELLING THIS TICKET IN VIOLATION OF APPLICABLE LAW, IS SUBJECT TO ARREST,

LEGAL ACTION AND LOSS OF SEASON TICKET PRIVILEGES.[5]

In addition, each ticket stated that it was a revocable license, that the Patriots reserved the right to revoke the ticket at any time and for any reason, and that the Patriots may refuse admission to, or eject, any ticket holder who fails to comply with any applicable rules or terms.

In an effort to maintain what the Patriots describe as a safe, secure, and family-friendly environment for home games, they have exercised their right to revoke season tickets when ticket holders, either the ticket owners themselves or their guests, have engaged in what the Patriots consider to be unsafe or unacceptable conduct. . . . Thus, for example, should a season ticket holder give his or her tickets to another person for any single home game, and should the Patriots eject that person for unacceptable conduct, the Patriots may revoke the season tickets, regardless of the fact that the original holder was not present at the game. Upon learning that a ticket holder has impermissibly transferred a ticket or tickets, the Patriots have revoked that holder's season tickets and refunded the full face value. In this way, all season ticket holders are responsible for the behavior of their guests. In order to effectuate this policy, each ticket bears a unique bar code that is electronically scanned upon entrance. Should the Patriots cancel a ticket, the bar code is voided, and the ticket is useless.

The Patriots are blessed with many loyal fans who wish to buy season tickets but are unable to do so. The Patriots have therefore established a wait list where, for a $100 deposit per seat, fans may join the list and await the opportunity to buy season tickets as they become available. The deposit is credited toward the purchase of season tickets when they do become available, and is refundable if no seats are available when the fan removes his or her name from the wait list.

The Patriots also recognize that season ticket holders may not be able to attend all the pre-season and home games. For this reason, the Patriots provide an online forum through TicketMaster, called TicketExchange, whereby holders may post their tickets on a secure website accessible only to other season ticket holders and wait list members. . . . Once a match is made on TicketExchange between the season ticket holder who has posted the seats, and the person seeking them, the Patriots cancel the original tickets, void the bar code, and issue to the recipient new tickets with a different and valid bar code. The Patriots sell the tickets at face value, and reimburse the original holder of the unused tickets. Since the tickets sold

---

[5] The Patriots revised this language for the 2007 NFL season to read: "This ticket is a non-transferable revocable license. . . . ANY PERSON NOT LICENSED PURSUANT TO M.G.L. c. 140, § 185A RESELLING THIS TICKET BY ANY METHOD INCLUDING WITHOUT LIMITATION IN PERSON, ON AN AUCTION WEB SITE, OR OTHERWISE OVER THE INTERNET, AND ANY PERSON OR ENTITY SO LICENSED RESELLING THIS TICKET ON AN AUCTION WEB SITE OR IN VIOLATION OF APPLICABLE LAW, IS SUBJECT TO ARREST, LEGAL ACTION AND LOSS OF SEASON TICKET PRIVILEGES."

through TicketExchange are cancelled, not transferred, the original holder is not responsible for the behavior of persons sitting in those seats. Neither the selling ticket holder, the purchasing ticket holder, nor the Patriots profit in any way from any TicketExchange transaction. . . .

StubHub operates a website (www.stubhub.com) that allows people to buy and sell tickets to sporting, concert, theater, and other live entertainment events. In order to use the website, an individual must register as a StubHub member, and agree, among other things, to comply with "all applicable local, state, federal and international laws, statutes and regulations regarding the use of the Site and the selling of tickets." On its seller "Q & A" page, StubHub [accurately] states that Massachusetts [statutory] law prohibits the reselling of tickets at more than $2.00 above face value, except that a licensed broker may charge additional expenses "related to acquiring and selling the ticket." . . .

Sellers list their available tickets on the website and assign a price to each ticket in one of three formats: (1) auction, where the seller lists a minimum price and an auction length, up to seven days, and buyers may bid accordingly; (2) fixed price, where the seller lists a definite price at which the ticket will sell immediately when the buyer clicks "Buy Now;" and (3) declining price, whereby the seller sets a maximum price which will decrease linearly each day until the seller's minimum price has been reached. Pursuant to the user agreements, StubHub receives a 25% commission from each sale: 15% of the selling price from the seller, and 10% added to the total sales price due from the buyer. It is undisputed that the majority of Patriots tickets sell on StubHub for prices greatly in excess of face value.

StubHub offers buyers its "FanProtect Guarantee" in the event that tickets are invalid, or are not honored by the venue. To invoke this Guarantee, the buyer must first obtain independent confirmation from the venue, in this case the Patriots, that the tickets are invalid. Upon receipt of this confirmation, StubHub will refund the full purchase price to the buyer, including all service fees and handling charges. This guarantee is limited to two claims, or a lifetime maximum of $1,000.

In addition to the above services, in 2005 StubHub created a category of sellers it has identified as "LargeSellers." As defined by StubHub, LargeSellers are those who "take a large interest in tickets spanning over multiple events and genres" for whom StubHub provides extended privileges and incentives above those provided to its regular users. The 2005 "LargeSeller's Handbook" states that "StubHub strongly urges our LargeSellers to check the website from time to time for underpriced tickets or exclusive listings that may not be seen elsewhere." . . . As an incentive to LargeSellers, StubHub offers "the additional benefit of purchasing tickets with no 'buy-side' fee. In other words, the standard fee of 10% that is added to the listing price at the END of the transaction is removed for LargeSellers." LargeSeller's Handbook, April 2005. . . .

Beginning in 2007, StubHub started allowing LargeSellers to "mask" ticket locations by listing a different row, up to five rows away, than that printed on the original ticket. If the tickets offered are further than five rows from the original ones, or are in a different section, the LargeSeller must provide StubHub with the actual location and obtain approval before confirming the order. That exact location, however, is not passed on to the buyer until he or she receives the tickets.

According to the Patriots, starting in 2005 they noticed a larger number of patrons seeking admission through cancelled tickets; the majority of those fans reported that they had purchased those tickets through StubHub.[10] The Patriots assert that the increase in invalid tickets presented for admission required them to devote personnel to manage not only the confirmation that StubHub requires for a buyer to qualify for a refund, but also inquiries and complaints from fans who had driven some distance and paid for parking, only to be turned away at the gate. In a letter dated November 21, 2006, the Patriots requested that StubHub immediately stop facilitating the resale of Patriots tickets. When StubHub refused to comply, the Patriots initiated the instant action. . . .

. . . The tort of intentional interference with advantageous relations "protects a plaintiff's present and future economic interests from wrongful interference." Blackstone v. Cashman, 448 Mass. 255, 259 (2007). The Patriots' Amended Complaint essentially incorporates into a single claim two related torts: tortious interference with contract and tortious interference with a prospective contractual relationship. In short, the Patriots allege both that StubHub has intentionally interfered with its existing contractual relationships with season ticket holders and with its prospective contractual relationships with those same season ticket holders and with wait list members. The melding of these torts into a single claim has little practical consequence, since the substantive elements are substantially similar and Massachusetts courts have not consistently distinguished between the two. . . .

The Patriots' tortious interference claim centers around the relationship they have with their fans, both season ticket holders and those on the wait list, and their commitment to maintain a safe and family friendly environment for home games. In a nutshell, the Patriots argue:

- "The purchase of a ticket to a sports or entertainment event typically creates nothing more than a revocable license."

---

[10] Presumably this occurs in large part when a season ticket holder, whose tickets have been cancelled for any reason, then decides to sell them on StubHub in the expectation of making a profit, rather than obtaining a refund for face value from the Patriots. Because the Patriots void the bar code on any cancelled tickets, those tickets subsequently sold on StubHub are not honored at the gate.

Yarde Metals, Inc. v. New England Patriots Ltd. Partnership, 64 Mass.App.Ct. at 658. The Patriots have expressly declared that their tickets to home games are not transferable, and that anyone who chooses to transfer them except through TicketExchange may have their season tickets revoked.

- The Patriots' commitment to nontransferability is intended to permit them to determine who is responsible for inappropriate behavior and hold the ticket holder responsible for such behavior, which allows them to maintain control over the entire venue. Since buyers on StubHub are likely one time anonymous buyers, they do not have the same incentive to behave appropriately as do season ticket holders who know that their tickets may be revoked at any time.

- In addition, when tickets are sold on StubHub, they are not offered on TicketExchange to other season ticket holders and wait list members, which interferes with the goodwill the Patriots have fostered with their most loyal fans.

To prevail on their tortious interference claim, the Patriots must prove that "(1) [they] had an advantageous relationship with a third party (e.g., a present or prospective contract or employment relationship; (2) [StubHub] knowingly induced a breaking of the relationship; (3) [StubHub's] interference with the relationship, in addition to being intentional, was improper in motive or means; and (4) the [Patriots were] harmed by [StubHub's] actions." Blackstone v. Cashman, 448 Mass. at 260, citing Weber v. Community Teamwork, Inc., 434 Mass. 761, 781 (2001). Harm has been described as a loss of advantage or damage to an economic relationship that resulted directly from the defendant's conduct. . . . The harm must result in economic loss; where the plaintiff does not suffer any pecuniary loss as a result of the defendant's actions, there can be no recovery on a tortious interference claim. . . .

1.   Did the Patriots have an Advantageous Relationship with Season Ticket Holders or Wait List Members? StubHub first argues that the Patriots cannot satisfy the first element of their claim-that they had a financially advantageous relationship with their season ticket holders or wait list members. "It is well settled that an existing or even a probable future business relationship from which there is a reasonable expectancy of financial benefit is enough" to satisfy this element. Owen v. Williams, 322 Mass. 356, 361–362 (1948). The Patriots certainly have an existing relationship with their season ticket holders for each football season, and a probable future business relationship with both their season ticket holders (who are not contractually promised a right to renew but generally do so) and their wait list members (who join the wait list to become eligible for season tickets as they become available).

StubHub, however, contends that there is no "reasonable expectancy of financial benefit" from the Patriots' relationship with existing season ticket holders because that reasonable expectancy is extinguished once the season ticket holders purchase their tickets. According to StubHub, even if the Patriots were to revoke the season ticket holder's "license" for the season (because the ticket holder had sold tickets online through StubHub) and refund the face value of the remaining tickets, the Patriots still would suffer no economic loss because the remaining tickets would quickly be scooped up by wait list members at the face value price. . . . StubHub also contends that there is no "reasonable expectancy of financial benefit" from the Patriots' relationship with wait list members because the Patriots admit that they receive no financial benefit from the ticket sales arranged through TicketExchange.

StubHub's analysis of this first element of tortious interference is far too narrow and is conflated with the third element-that the plaintiff suffer some financial harm from the third party's interference with contract. It cannot reasonably be disputed that the Patriots have both an existing and a probable future business relationship with both season ticket holders and wait list members-who are would-be season ticket holders-and that they have a reasonable expectancy of financial benefit from the ticket prices they would pay for these season tickets. This is enough to satisfy this first element. Massachusetts courts have repeatedly stated that a plaintiff may prevail on a tortious interference claim by proving either "a business relationship or contemplated contract of economic benefit. . . ." Powers v. Leno, 24 Mass.App.Ct. 381, 384 (1987). . . .

2.   Was StubHub's alleged interference improper in motive or means? . . . [T]he Patriots' tortious interference claim alleges improper means, perhaps recognizing that StubHub's motive to make money and benefit its customers does not constitute an improper motive under the law. . . . Improper means must consist of conduct that violates a statute or constitutes a common law tort. . . . The issue, then, is whether the Patriots have presented evidence of improper means.

The Patriots essentially argue that StubHub is engaged in three types of illegal conduct: common law misrepresentation, trespass, and contributing to violation of the "anti-scalping" [statutes]. As to common law misrepresentation, the Patriots argue that StubHub affirmatively sought to prevent the Patriots from learning which of its season ticket holders were selling tickets online with StubHub by allowing LargeSellers to "mask" ticket locations by listing a different row, up to five rows away, than that printed on the original ticket and by not informing the buyer of the exact location of the tickets until the buyer receives them. This Court, however, can find nothing in the record to support the contention that StubHub was misrepresenting the location of the tickets to the buyer of the tickets. . . .

The Patriots also allege that a non-season ticket holder commits a trespass when he uses a transferred ticket to enter Gillette Stadium to watch a Patriots game, and that StubHub facilitates such a trespass. This argument may have been persuasive if the Patriots, like an airline, had placed a name on a ticket and permitted only that person, verified by photographic identification, to enter the stadium with that ticket, but they did not. The Patriots' counsel candidly admitted that, if a season ticket holder gives or sells a ticket to a family member, friend, or business associate, the Patriots would not consider that transfer to justify a loss of season ticket privileges. Consequently, the Patriots do not deem transfer alone to warrant revocation of their revocable season ticket "license;" it is only transfer by sale to strangers that warrants revocation. Since it does not consider all those with transferred tickets to be trespassers, it cannot prevail in proving that anyone with a transferred ticket should be deemed a trespasser.

As to the "anti-scalping laws," [the state statute] provides that "[n]o person shall engage in the business of reselling any ticket or tickets of admission . . . to any theatrical exhibition, public show or public amusement or exhibition . . . without being licensed therefor by the Commissioner of Public Safety. . . ." The precise meaning of "engag[ing] in the business of reselling any ticket or tickets" has yet to be articulated by our appellate courts. The Supreme Judicial Court declared in 1929 "that the offence denounced by [the statute] is engaging in the business 'of reselling' tickets; and it is the occupation and not an isolated act which is forbidden." Commonwealth v. Sovrensky, 269 Mass. 460, 462 (1929). . . . Even licensed ticket brokers engaged in the business of reselling tickets are limited in the price they may charge-the price of a resold ticket may not exceed the price printed on the face of the ticket, plus $2, plus service charges. . . . The service charges may not include the purchase price of the ticket above face value, since that "would add as an allowable cost one which emasculates the basic provision limiting the price to be charged." Commonwealth v. Santangelo, 25 Mass.App.Ct. 583, 584 (1988). Consequently, if a ticket reseller purchases a $30 ticket for $80, he may not charge more than $30, plus $2, plus service charges, and may not include the $50 paid above face value as a service charge. See id. . . . StubHub's definition of LargeSellers may not match precisely the definition under Massachusetts law of those engaged in the business of reselling tickets under [the statute], but it is close enough to suggest that most, perhaps all, LargeSellers are so engaged.

There is abundant evidence in the record that the resale prices of Patriots tickets on StubHub generally far exceed the price threshold permitted [by law]. StubHub correctly observes that it does not sell tickets itself, but simply provides an online forum for others to sell tickets. That alone, however, is not enough to establish that it does not engage in improper means. The Patriots may prove that StubHub induced a breach of contract by improper means if they can show that StubHub intentionally induced or encouraged others to violate [the law], or profited from such violations while declining to stop or limit it. See Metro-Goldwyn-Mayer Studios, Inc. v. Grokster, Ltd., 545 U.S. 913, 930 (2005) ("Grokster") (applying this standard to claim of copyright infringement against software company that facilitated download of copyrighted music and video). . . .

StubHub argues that it should be treated no differently from the newspaper "want-ads," where a seller of any property, including football tickets, invites others to purchase the property, often at a set price. There are, however, at least two fundamental differences between StubHub's website and the "want-ads" in the classified pages of a newspaper or comparable website. First, the newspaper generally charges a fixed price for the advertisement; its price is not dependent on the amount of the sale. See Chicago Lawyers' Comm. for Civil Rights Under Law, Inc. v. Craigslist, 519 F.3d 666, 671–672 (7th Cir.2008). Second, newspapers do not affirmatively seek to increase the price charged in the classified ad, especially when doing so may constitute a violation of law. In Craigslist, the Seventh Circuit, rejecting a claim that craigslist helped to violate the anti-discrimination laws in the Fair Housing Act, noted that nothing in the service provided by craigslist encouraged those posting listings for rental or sale properties to add discriminatory preferences in violation of the Act. Id. at 671. "For example, craigslist does not offer a lower price to people who include discriminatory statements in their postings." Id. at 671–672.

3.   Did the Patriots suffer any pecuniary loss as a result of StubHub's alleged tortious interference? StubHub argues that the Patriots cannot show any pecuniary loss and that, even if they could do so, any financial loss would not be a result of StubHub's actions. The gist of StubHub's argument in this regard is that the Patriots receive payment from season ticket holders regardless of any alleged interference, since the tickets are bought before they are listed on the website and, in any event, any revocation of season tickets cannot result in pecuniary loss where those tickets may be sold immediately to wait list members.

The Patriots allege two types of pecuniary loss: the loss of goodwill arising from damage to their relationship with their season ticket holders and wait list members, and direct costs arising from the sale of invalid tickets through StubHub. The alleged loss of goodwill arises from the Patriots' commitment to provide a safe and family-friendly environment for home football games. The Patriots contend that, since those who purchase Patriots tickets on StubHub are likely one-time anonymous buyers, and do not have the same incentive to behave appropriately as do those season ticket holders who know that their tickets may be revoked at any time for bad behavior, StubHub interferes with the goodwill the Patriots have built with their fans by creating a civil venue to watch a football game. . . .

The alleged direct costs are sustained because (1) Patriots staff at ticket windows must respond to inquiries and complaints from those fans who, having purchased invalid tickets through StubHub, are then turned away at the gate and ask for the written confirmation needed to obtain a refund of the ticket price through StubHub, (2) Patriots staff must investigate ticket resale and revoke season tickets from holders who have been encouraged by StubHub to sell their tickets on its website, and (3) the increased likelihood of improper conduct by anonymous StubHub buyers necessitates increased security measures.

The element of economic loss required to establish tortious interference cannot be established by "speculative or conjectural losses." Chemawa Country Golf, Inc. v. Wnuk, 9 Mass.App.Ct. 506, 510 (1980). It is not enough that the conduct was "intensely irritating." Id. at 511. "Chemawa is a corporation which has no heart to ache or ulcer to bleed and, in any event, it is not vexation but interference with beneficial relations with third parties which must be established." Id. Without more, it is not enough that the Patriots allege damage to the somewhat vague and not easily quantifiable concept of "goodwill" that they claim they assiduously cultivated with their fans. There is no evidence that fans who obtained their tickets from StubHub were more unruly than other fans, or that instances of unruly conduct have increased as a result of StubHub's ticket sales. Nor is there any evidence that more individuals would seek to be season ticket holders if more tickets were made available through TicketExchange rather than StubHub. Nor is there any evidence that any such increased interest in season tickets would have any financial impact on the Patriots, who already have a waiting list of at least 19,000 fans. Nor is there any expert testimony that, if the team were placed on the market to be sold, the fair market value of the team's goodwill would be greater if StubHub stopped selling Patriots' tickets. . . .

A far closer call, however, is whether the Patriots incur increased administrative costs as a result of the sale of invalid tickets through StubHub. There is evidence, albeit scant, that the Patriots' personnel at ticket windows must deal with complaints and inquiries from fans with tickets purchased through StubHub who are turned away at the gate, and must provide them with the confirmation necessary for StubHub to refund the ticket price. There is also evidence, again scant, that the sale of Patriots' tickets through StubHub increases the cost to the Patriots of investigating and addressing ticket resale activity. While it is not clear from the record before the Court whether, as a result of these additional administrative burdens, the Patriots must hire additional personnel, add to the hours worked by existing personnel, divert current staff from other duties, or pay the same employees more to perform additional work, this Court is satisfied that, viewing the evidence in the light most favorable to the Patriots, there is a genuine issue of material fact as to whether the

Patriots have incurred or will incur additional administrative costs as a result of StubHub's conduct. These administrative costs are, at best, a toehold to establish pecuniary loss, but a toehold is sufficient to survive a motion for summary judgment. . . .

NOTES AND QUESTIONS

1.   For a contrary view, see *Hill v. StubHub, Inc.*, 727 S.E.2d 550 (N.C. App. 2012) ("we simply do not find the reasoning employed by [the trial judge in the *New England Patriots* case] persuasive . . . and decline to follow it in deciding the present case").

2.   What are the elements of a case for tortious interference with contractual relations? Why is this such a close case for the *New England Patriots* court?

3.   Describe StubHub's business model. Is it any better or worse than the way ticket reselling used to be done in the old days, when re-sellers would stand outside the venue, hawking their wares (which might or might not have been legitimate tickets)? What problem did StubHub pose for the New England Patriots?

4.   Today, Stubhub (or as it has been re-branded, "Stubhub!") continues to operate, re-selling tickets. Stubhub was purchased by online retail giant eBay in 2007 for some $300 million. To clear the way for its operations, Stubhub has been partnering with sports teams and concert venues, to work as part of their distribution network rather than be viewed by teams as "ticket scalpers."

5.   In some areas of regulatory law, like antitrust law, a key consideration can be whether consumers will ultimately benefit from corporate activities. To what degree, if any, did the trial court in the *New England Patriots* case consider the interests of Patriots' fans? Would this have been its job, considering it is examining a commercial dispute between two different parties, neither of whom were the ultimate consumers? Do Stubhub's activities help or harm fans? Is that relevant? Should it be relevant? Might this information be developed at trial (recall the opinion is on a motion for summary judgment)?

D. EXCULPATORY CLAUSES

Our last section on third parties focuses on the externalities or third-party effects of contracts that contain exculpatory clauses. If you have ever visited a gym to take a yoga class, accompanied a small child to a trampoline park, or ridden in a helicopter, you're likely familiar with such clauses. Some might argue that exculpatory clauses (also called "hold harmless" or waivers of liability) actually create negative third-party effects by shifting the cost of injury from someone's negligence to the injured individual, or if the injured individual can't pay, then to the public or society. Note that this section picks up on themes in our earlier chapter on defenses to contracts that are against public policy. The public policy implicated by exculpatory clauses is the social harm that radiates from using contracts to shift the cost of injury from tortfeasors onto those who have been injured by gross negligence.

TUNKL V. REGENTS OF UNIVERSITY OF CALIFORNIA
383 P.2d 441 (Cal. 1963)

TOBRINER, J.

This case concerns the validity of a release from liability for future negligence imposed as a condition for admission to a charitable research hospital. For the reasons we hereinafter specify, we have concluded that an agreement between a hospital and an entering patient affects the public interest and that, in consequence, the exculpatory provision included within it must be invalid under Civil Code section 1668.

Hugo Tunkl brought this action to recover damages for personal injuries alleged to have resulted from the negligence of two physicians in the employ of the University of California Los Angeles Medical Center, a hospital operated and maintained by the Regents of the University of California as a nonprofit charitable institution. Mr. Tunkl died after suit was brought, and his surviving wife, as executrix, was substituted as plaintiff.

The University of California at Los Angeles Medical Center admitted Tunkl as a patient on June 11, 1956. . . . Upon his entry to the hospital, Tunkl signed a document setting forth certain 'Conditions of Admission.' The crucial condition number six reads as follows: 'RELEASE: The hospital is a nonprofit, charitable institution. In consideration of the hospital and allied services to be rendered and the rates charged therefor, the patient or his legal representative agrees to and hereby releases The Regents of the University of California, and the hospital from any and all liability for the negligent or wrongful acts or omissions of its employees, if the hospital has used due care in selecting its employees.' [Plaintiff at the time of signing the release was in great pain, under sedation. and probably unable to read.—Eds.]

. . . The trial court ordered that the issue of the validity of the exculpatory clause be first submitted to the jury and that, if the jury found that the provision did not bind plaintiff, a second jury try the issue of alleged malpractice. When, on the preliminary issue, the jury returned a verdict sustaining the validity of the executed release, the court entered judgment in favor of the Regents. Plaintiff appeals from the judgment.

We shall first set out the basis for our prime ruling that the exculpatory provision of the hospital's contract fell under the proscription of Civil Code section 1668; we then dispose of two answering arguments of defendant.

We begin with the dictate of the relevant Civil Code section 1668. The section states: 'All contracts which have for their object, directly or indirectly, to exempt anyone from responsibility for his own fraud, or willful injury to the person or property of another, or violation of law, whether willful or negligent, are against the policy of the law.'

The course of section 1668, however, has been a troubled one. Although, as we shall explain, the decisions uniformly uphold its prohibitory impact in one circumstance, the courts' interpretations of it have been diverse. Some of the cases have applied the statute strictly, invalidating any contract for exemption from liability for negligence. The court in England v. Lyon Fireproof Storage Co. (1928) 94 Cal.App.562, 271 P. 532, categorically states, 'The court correctly instructed the jury that the defendant cannot limit its liability against its own negligence by contract, and any contract to that effect would be void." (94 Cal.App. p. 575, 271 P. p. 537.) (To the same effect: Union Constr. Co. v. Western Union Tel. Co. (1912) 163 Cal. 298, 314–315, 125 P. 242.) . . . Other cases hold that the statute prohibits the exculpation of gross negligence only; still another case states that the section forbids exemption from active as contrasted with passive negligence.

In one respect, as we have said, the decisions are uniform. The cases have consistently held that the exculpatory provision may stand only if it does not involve 'the public interest.' . . . Thus in Nichols v. Hitchcock Motor Co. (1937) 22 Cal.App.2d 151, 159, 70 P.2d 654, 658, the court enforced an exculpatory clause on the ground that 'the public neither had nor could have any interest whatsoever in the subject-matter of the contract, considered either as a whole or as to the incidental covenant in question. The agreement between the parties concerned 'their private affairs' only.' . . .

In Barkett v. Brucato (1953) 122 Cal.App.2d 264, 276, 264 P.2d 978, 987, which involved a waiver clause in a private lease, Justice Peters summarizes the previous decisions in this language: "These cases hold that the matter is simply one of interpreting a contract; that both parties are free to contract; that the relationship of landlord and tenant does not affect the public interest; that such a provision affects only the private affairs of the parties." . . . On the other hand, courts struck down exculpatory clauses as contrary to public policy in the case of a contract to transmit a telegraph message (Union Constr. Co. v. Western Union Tel. Co. (1912) 163 Cal. 298, 125 P. 242) and in the instance of a contract of bailment (England v. Lyon Fireproof Storage Co. (1928) 94 Cal.App. 562, 271 P. 532). . . .

If, then, the exculpatory clause which affects the public interest cannot stand, we must ascertain those factors or characteristics which constitute the public interest. The social forces that have led to such characterization are volatile and dynamic. No definition of the concept of public interest can be contained within the four corners of a formula. The concept, always the subject of great debate, has ranged over the whole course of the common law; rather than attempt to prescribe its nature, we can only designate the situations in which it has been applied. We can determine whether the instant contract does or does not manifest the characteristics which have been held to stamp a contract as one affected with a public interest.

In placing particular contracts within or without the category of those affected with a public interest, the courts have revealed a rough outline of that type of transaction in which exculpatory provisions will be held invalid. Thus the attempted but invalid exemption involves a transaction which exhibits some or all of the following characteristics. It concerns a business of a type generally thought suitable for public regulation. The party seeking exculpation is engaged in performing a service of great importance to the public, which is often a matter of practical necessity for some members of the public. The party holds himself out as willing to perform this service for any member of the public who seeks it, or at least for any member coming within certain established standards. As a result of the essential nature of the service, in the economic setting of the transaction, the party invoking exculpation possesses a decisive advantage of bargaining strength against any member of the public who seeks his services. In exercising a superior bargaining power the party confronts the public with a standardized adhesion contract of exculpation, and makes no provision whereby a purchaser may pay additional reasonable fees and obtain protection against negligence. Finally, as a result of the transaction, the person or property of the purchaser is placed under the control of the seller, subject to the risk of carelessness by the seller or his agents.

While obviously no public policy opposes private, voluntary transactions in which one party, for a consideration, agrees to shoulder a risk which the law would otherwise have placed upon the other party, the above circumstances pose a different situation. In this situation the releasing party does not really acquiesce voluntarily in the contractual shifting of the risk, nor can we be reasonably certain that he receives an adequate consideration for the transfer. Since the service is one which each member of the public, presently or potentially, may find essential to him, he faces, despite his economic inability to do so, the prospect of a compulsory assumption of the risk of another's negligence. The public policy of this state has been, in substance, to posit the risk of negligence upon the actor; in instances in which this policy has been abandoned, it has generally been to allow or require that the risk shift to another party better or equally able to bear it, not to shift the risk to the weak bargainer.

In the light of the decisions, we think that the hospital-patient contract clearly falls within the category of agreements affecting the public interest.

To meet that test, the agreement need only fulfill some of the characteristics above outlined; here, the relationship fulfills all of them. Thus the contract of exculpation involves an institution suitable for, and a subject of, public regulation. . . . That the services of the hospital to those members of the public who are in special need of the particular skill of its staff and facilities constitute a practical and crucial necessity is hardly open to question. . . The hospital, likewise, holds itself out as willing to perform its services for those members of the public who qualify for its research and training facilities. . .

In insisting that the patient accept the provision of waiver in the contract, the hospital certainly exercises a decisive advantage in bargaining. The would-be patient is in no position to reject the proffered agreement, to bargain with the hospital, or in lieu of agreement to find another hospital. The admission room of a hospital contains no bargaining table where, as in a private business transaction, the parties can debate the terms of their contract. As a result, we cannot but conclude that the instant agreement manifested the characteristics of the so-called adhesion contract. Finally, when the patient signed the contract, he completely placed himself in the control of the hospital; he subjected himself to the risk of its carelessness.

In brief, the patient here sought the services which the hospital offered to a selective portion of the public; the patient, as the price of admission and as a result of his inferior bargaining position, accepted a clause in a contract of adhesion waiving the hospital's negligence; the patient thereby subjected himself to control of the hospital and the possible infliction of the negligence which he had thus been compelled to waive. The hospital, under such circumstances, occupied a status different than a mere private party; its contract with the patient affected the public interest. We see no cogent current reason for according to the patron of the inn a greater protection than the patient of the hospital; we cannot hold the innkeeper's performance affords a greater public service than that of the hospital.

CITY OF SANTA BARBARA V. SUPERIOR COURT
41 Cal.4th 747 (Cal. 2007)

GEORGE, C.J.

The mother of Katie Janeway, a developmentally disabled 14 year old, signed an application form releasing the City of Santa Barbara and its employees (hereafter the City or defendants) from liability for "any negligent act" related to Katie's participation in the City's summer camp for developmentally disabled children. Katie drowned while attending the camp, and her parents (plaintiffs, real parties in interest in the present proceedings) commenced this suit. The Court of Appeal below (1) held unanimously that the agreement embodied in the application form was effective and enforceable insofar as it concerned defendants' liability for future *ordinary* negligence, but (2) concluded, by a two-to-one vote, that a release of liability for future *gross* negligence generally is unenforceable, and that the agreement in this case did not release such liability.

In granting review, we limited the issue to be briefed and argued to the second issue—whether a release of liability relating to recreational activities generally is effective as to *gross* negligence. As explained below, we answer that question in the negative, and affirm the judgment rendered by the Court of Appeal. We conclude, consistent with dicta in California cases and with the vast majority of out-of-state cases and other authority, that an agreement made in the context of sports or recreational programs or services, purporting to release liability for future gross negligence, generally is unenforceable as a matter of public policy. Applying that general rule in the case now before us, we hold that the agreement, to the extent it purports to release liability for future gross negligence, violates public policy and is unenforceable.

. . . The City has provided extensive summer recreational facilities and activities for children, including a camp for children with developmental disabilities—Adventure Camp. Katie Janeway, who suffered from cerebral palsy, epilepsy, and other similar developmental disabilities, participated in Adventure Camp in 1999, 2000, 2001, and 2002. Adventure Camp was conducted from noon until 5:00 p.m. on weekdays for approximately three weeks in July and August. Camp activities included swimming, arts and crafts, group games, sports, and field trips. In 2002, as in prior years, swimming activities were held on two of five camp days each week in a City swimming pool.

In 2002, the application form for Adventure Camp included a release of all claims against the City and its employees from liability, including liability based upon negligence, arising from camp activities. Katie's mother, Maureen Janeway, signed the release. She had signed similar releases covering Katie's participation in the camp in prior years. Maureen Janeway disclosed Katie's developmental disabilities and medical problems to the City, specifically informing the City that Katie was prone to epileptic seizures, often occurring in water, and that Katie needed supervision while swimming. In addition, the City was aware that Katie had suffered seizures while attending Adventure Camp events in 2001. She had a seizure when sitting on the pool deck and another seizure at the skating rink. Paramedics were called after her seizure on the pool deck. Nevertheless, Maureen Janeway indicated that Katie was a good swimmer, and she never sought to prevent or restrict Katie's participation in the swimming portion of Adventure Camp.

Based upon the information provided by Maureen Janeway and Katie's history of seizures, the City took special precautions during the

Adventure Camp swimming activities in 2002. The City assigned Veronica Malong to act as a "counselor." Malong's responsibility was to keep Katie under close observation during the camp's swimming sessions. Previously, Malong, a college student, had worked for one year as a special education aide at the middle school attended by Katie. Malong had observed Katie experience seizures at the school, and she received instruction from the school nurse regarding the handling of those seizures. Malong also attended training sessions conducted by the City concerning how to respond to seizures and other first aid matters.

Katie participated in the first swimming day at the 2002 Adventure Camp without incident. On the second swimming day she drowned.

Approximately one hour before drowning, while waiting to enter the locker room at the pool, Katie suffered a mild seizure that lasted a few seconds. Malong observed the seizure and sent another counselor to report the incident to a supervisor. According to the pleadings, the supervisor stated that the report never was received. Malong watched Katie for approximately 45 minutes following the mild seizure. Then, receiving no word from her supervisor, Malong concluded that the seizure had run its course and that it was safe for Katie to swim.

Malong sat on the side of the pool near the lifeguard, watching the deep end of the pool. In addition to the Adventure Camp participants, there were as many as 300 other children in the pool area. Malong watched Katie jump off a diving board and swim back to the edge of the pool. At Malong's insistence, Katie got out of the pool and rested for a few minutes. Malong then asked Katie whether she wished to dive again, and Katie said she did. Katie dove into the water, bobbed to the surface, and began to swim toward the edge of the pool. As Katie did so, Malong momentarily turned her attention away from Katie. When Malong looked back no more than 15 seconds later, Katie had disappeared from her sight. After Malong and others looked for Katie somewhere between two and five minutes, an air horn blew and the pool was evacuated. Lifeguards pulled Katie from the bottom of the pool, and she died the next day.

Katie's parents, Terral and Maureen Janeway, filed a wrongful death action alleging the accident was caused by the negligence of the City and Malong.

We begin by defining the terms that underlie the issue presented. "Ordinary negligence"—an unintentional tort—consists of a failure to exercise the degree of care in a given situation that a reasonable person under similar circumstances would employ to protect others from harm." "Gross negligence" long has been defined in California and other jurisdictions as either a "want of even scant care" or "an extreme departure from the ordinary standard of conduct." (*Eastburn v. Regional Fire*

Protection Authority (2003) 31 Cal.4th 1175, 1185–1186, 7 Cal.Rptr.3d 552, 80 P.3d 656 (*Eastburn*), and cases cited. . .)

As observed in *Gardner v. Downtown Porsche Audi* (1986) 180 Cal.App.3d 713, 716, 225 Cal.Rptr. 757 (*Gardner*), "[t]raditionally the law has looked carefully and with some skepticism at those who attempt to contract away their legal liability for the commission of torts." Courts and commentators have observed that such releases pose a conflict between contract and tort law. On the one hand is the freedom of individuals to agree to limit their future liability; balanced against that are public policies underlying our tort system: as a general matter, we seek to maintain or reinforce a reasonable standard of care in community life and require wrongdoers—not the community at large—to provide appropriate recompense to injured parties.

The traditional skepticism concerning agreements designed to release liability for future torts, reflected in *Gardner, supra,* 180 Cal.App.3d 713, 225 Cal.Rptr. 757, and many other cases, long has been expressed in Civil Code section 1668 (hereafter cited as section 1668), which (unchanged since its adoption in 1872) provides: "All contracts which have for their object, directly or indirectly, to exempt any one from responsibility for his [or her] own fraud, or willful injury to the person or property of another, or violation of law, whether willful or negligent, are against the policy of the law."

In *Tunkl v. Regents of University of California* (1963) 60 Cal.2d 92, 32 Cal.Rptr. 33, 383 P.2d 441 (*Tunkl*), we applied section 1668 in the context of a release required by a nonprofit research hospital as a condition of providing medical treatment. In that case, the plaintiff had signed a contract releasing the operators of the hospital—the Regents of the University of California—" 'from any and all liability' " for " 'negligent . . . acts or omissions of its employees' " so long as the hospital used due care in selecting those employees. (*Id.,* at p. 94, 32 Cal.Rptr. 33, 383 P.2d 441.) Thereafter, the plaintiff sued for ordinary negligence based on the treatment received from two of the hospital's doctors.

Turning to section 1668, Justice Tobriner's unanimous opinion for the court noted that past decisions had differed concerning the reach of that statute (*Tunkl, supra,* 60 Cal.2d 92, 96–97, 32 Cal.Rptr. 33, 383 P.2d 441), but that those decisions agreed in one significant respect: they consistently "held that [an agreement's] exculpatory provision may stand only if it does not "involve [and impair] 'the public interest.' " (*Id.,* at p. 96, 32 Cal.Rptr. 33, 383 P.2d 441.) Exploring the meaning and characteristics of the concept of "public interest" as illuminated by the prior cases (*id.,* at pp. 96–98, 32 Cal.Rptr. 33, 383 P.2d 441), we read those precedents as recognizing a general rule that an *"exculpatory clause which affects the public interest cannot stand."* (*Id.,* at p. 98, 32 Cal.Rptr. 33, 383 P.2d 441, italics added.)

[The court reviewed *Tunkl* paragraph-by-paragraph, including its "factors or characteristics" paragraph and "rough outline" paragraph.]

As the parties observe, no published California case has upheld, or voided, an agreement purporting to release liability for future *gross* negligence. Some decisions have stated, in dictum, that such a release is unenforceable. (*Farnham v. Superior Court* (1997) 60 Cal.App.4th 69, 74, 70 Cal.Rptr.2d 85 ["exemptions from *all* liability for . . . gross negligence . . . have been consistently invalidated"]; *Health Net, supra,* 113 Cal.App.4th 224, 234, 6 Cal.Rptr.3d 235 [liability for future gross negligence cannot be released].) Others carefully have specified that liability for "ordinary" or "simple" negligence generally may be released (that is, so long as doing so is consistent with *Tunkl, supra,* 60 Cal.2d 92, 32 Cal.Rptr. 33, 383 P.2d 441)—thereby implicitly differentiating gross negligence from the class of conduct as to which liability generally may be released. Indeed, for more than three decades, [a leading treatise on California contract law] has asserted that California law categorically bars the prior release of liability for future gross negligence: "The present view is that a contract exempting from liability for ordinary negligence is valid where no public interest is involved. . . . [¶] *But there can be no exemption from liability for* intentional wrong [or] *gross negligence* . . . ." (1 Witkin, Contracts, § 660, pp. 737–738, italics added) . . . As defendants observe, however, Witkin does not cite any relevant California decision in support of that proposition.

On the other hand, as defendants and their amici curiae also observe, a number of cases have upheld agreements insofar as they release liability for future *ordinary* negligence in the context of sports and recreation programs, on the basis that such agreements do not concern necessary services, and hence do not transcend the realm of purely private matters and implicate the "public interest" under *Tunkl, supra,* 60 Cal.2d 92, 32 Cal.Rptr. 33, 383 P.2d 441. Our lower courts have upheld releases of liability concerning ordinary negligence related to gymnasiums and fitness clubs, auto and motorcycle racing events, ski resorts and ski equipment, bicycle races, skydiving or flying in "ultra light" aircraft, and various other recreational activities and programs such as horseback riding, white-water rafting, hypnotism, and scuba diving. Most, but not all, other jurisdictions have held similarly. In light of these decisions, some more recent appellate decisions have concluded categorically that private agreements made "in the recreational sports context" releasing liability for future ordinary negligence "do not implicate the public interest and therefore are not void as against public policy." (E.g., *Benedek, supra,* 104 Cal.App.4th at pp. 1356–1357, 129 Cal.Rptr.2d 197.)

In the absence of an authoritative discussion in any California opinion concerning the enforceability of an agreement releasing liability for future *gross* negligence, we consider the law of other jurisdictions. We find that the vast majority of decisions state or hold that such agreements generally are void on the ground that public policy precludes enforcement of a release that would shelter *aggravated misconduct*. . . .

. . . The reasoning of the foregoing out-of-state decisions holding that liability for future gross negligence never can, or generally cannot, be released, is based upon a public policy analysis that is different from the "public interest" factors considered under *Tunkl, supra,* 60 Cal.2d 92, 32 Cal.Rptr. 33, 383 P.2d 441. *Tunkl's* public interest analysis focuses upon the overall transaction—with special emphasis upon the importance of the underlying service or program, and the relative bargaining relationship of the parties—in order to determine whether an agreement releasing future liability for *ordinary* negligence is unenforceable. By contrast, the out-of-state cases cited and alluded to above, declining to enforce an agreement to release liability for future gross negligence, focus instead upon the degree or extent of the misconduct at issue, as well as the "public policy to discourage" (or at least not facilitate) "aggravated wrongs." (Prosser & Keeton, *supra,* § 68, p. 484.) Those cases hold, in essence, that an agreement that would remove a party's obligation to adhere to even a minimal standard of care, thereby sheltering aggravated misconduct, is unenforceable as against public policy.

. . . Ultimately, defendants and their amici curiae argue that rejection of the majority rule described above, and adoption of the opposite rule proposed by them, is mandated by public policy, as they perceive it. They stress the asserted uncertainty of the gross negligence standard and argue that unless providers of recreational services and related programs can be assured that agreements purporting to release liability for future gross negligence will be enforced, (1) subsequent suits against recreational service providers—private, public, for-profit, or nonprofit—will not be readily resolvable in favor of defendants on summary judgment, with the result that unwarranted liability will be threatened or imposed, and (2) service providers will react by greatly restricting, or simply declining to afford, such services or programs in California. . .

The various amici curiae in support of defendants echo and amplify these predictions. For example, amici curiae NASCAR and the California Speedway Association assert that limiting agreements releasing liability for future ordinary negligence, while not permitting the release of liability for future gross negligence, ultimately will "deprive [the public] of the . . . opportunity to participate and recreate in many . . . cherished [pastimes]," including being spectators at NASCAR and similar motor vehicle racing events. Likewise, amici curiae Bally Total Fitness Corporation and 24 Hour Fitness USA, Inc., claim the appellate decision below, enforcing the release as to negligence but not as to gross negligence, "[wreaks] havoc on recreational providers," leading them to a "precipice from which there will be no return." . . .

We are sensitive to the policy arguments advanced by defendants and their amici curiae that caution against rules triggering wholesale elimination of beneficial recreational programs and services—and we are especially sensitive to the concerns relating to the continued availability of programs such as the one here at issue, serving the recreational needs of developmentally disabled children. But we find no support for such broad predictions in the present setting. . . .

Indeed, if the premise of defendants and their amici curiae were correct—that is, if failing to enforce agreements releasing liability for future *gross* negligence would imperil the very existence of sports and recreational industries—we at least would expect to see some analogous evidence in the experience of those states that prohibit even agreements releasing liability for future *ordinary* negligence. Ordinary negligence, after all, occurs much more commonly than gross negligence, and hence judicial decisions holding unenforceable any release of liability for ordinary negligence would, under the theory of defendants and their amici curiae, pose a much greater threat to the continued availability of recreational sports programs than would a rule holding unenforceable releases of liability for gross negligence generally. And yet, as explained below, in numerous contexts concerning recreational sports and related programs, courts categorically have voided agreements releasing liability for future ordinary negligence without (so far as we can discern) triggering in any substantial degree the dramatically negative effects predicted by defendants and their amici curiae.

. . . We observe that Vermont has voided agreements releasing liability for future ordinary negligence in the context of recreational skiing and racing; Connecticut has acted similarly concerning "snow tubing" and horseback riding lessons; West Virginia has voided a release of liability for ordinary negligence executed by a university student who was injured while playing "club" rugby; and Washington has voided agreements releasing public school districts from liability for future ordinary negligence related to interscholastic athletics. Virginia long has categorically and broadly voided *all* preinjury releases, even in the recreational sports context. Perhaps most significantly, the New York Legislature, for three decades, has barred enforcement of agreements between operators of "gymnasium[s]" and places of "amusement or recreation, or similar establishment[s]," and their paying members or customers, purporting to release liability for future negligence by the operator. (See N.Y. Gen. Oblig. Law, § 5–326.) . . .

We brought the cases from these six states (Connecticut, Utah, Vermont, Virginia, Washington, and West Virginia) and the New York statute to the parties' attention and solicited supplemental briefing concerning defendants' policy argument that enforcing releases of liability for future ordinary negligence, but not for future gross negligence, would lead to the demise or substantially diminished availability of recreational services and programs. Thereafter, pursuant to a request by defendants, we allowed additional supplemental briefing. The ensuing briefing, however, disclosed no empirical study suggesting that holdings such as those described above, . . . have triggered the predicted elimination or even widespread substantial reduction of the affected services or programs. Indeed, defendants forthrightly concede in their supplemental briefs that they found no empirical support for such assertions.

We find defendants' arguments unpersuasive. Of course legal, economic, social, and other differences can make interjurisdictional comparisons inexact. But that does not mean we should ignore what might be gleaned from the legal laboratory that is the product of our federal system, under which states may, and do, undertake different solutions to common problems. The circumstance that neither defendants nor their supporting amici curiae have found from the experience of our sister states any substantial empirical evidence supporting their dire predictions is, we believe, both relevant and telling.

. . . Nor are we aware of any empirical evidence to suggest, as defendants postulate, that a holding declining to enforce an agreement purporting to release liability for future gross negligence would jeopardize programs, such as the one here at issue, that provide recreational opportunities for developmentally disabled children—and indeed, initial research casts doubt upon such predictions.

We reject the arguments of defendants and their amici curiae that considerations of public policy mandate the adoption of a rule under which agreements releasing liability for future gross negligence always, or even generally, would be enforced.

NOTES AND QUESTIONS

1.   What was the reasoning behind the decision in *Tunkl*? What are the factors that Justice Tobriner addresses as being important to determining whether an exculpatory clause impairs the public interest?

2.   How are the *Tunkl* factors close to, or different from, the factors for invalidating a contract under the defenses of unconscionability or public policy?

3.   What is the difference between ordinary negligence and gross negligence? Why does this distinction matter to the defendants in *Janeway*? Why does the court find their arguments unconvincing?

4.   Why does the *Janeway* court discuss the decisions in other jurisdictions? Why does the court ask about empirical studies of recreational activities available in these other jurisdictions?

PROBLEM: CONTRACTS VERSUS TORTS

Using reliable online legal research tools, find out whether an exculpatory clause is valid in your state of residence, both for ordinary and gross negligence. (If your jurisdiction is California, pick a different state, say one you would like to visit on your next vacation or eventually work in).

Having studied both contracts and torts, can you articulate firm distinctions between these two sources of civil obligation? Do you see overlaps in any respects? Consult GRANT GILMORE, THE DEATH OF CONTRACT (1974), coining the term *contorts* to describe, lamentably, a blurring of the boundaries, an infiltration of the status-based impositions of tort law into the freedom of volition associated with contracts. Can you think of any doctrinal developments to support or refute this lament? Promissory estoppel? Third party beneficiary doctrine?

INDEX

References are to Pages